CRITICAL COMPANION TO

J. D. Salinger

CRITICAL COMPANION TO

J. D. Salinger

A Literary Reference to His Life and Work

BRUCE F. MUELLER

WILL HOCHMAN

Facts On File

An imprint of Infobase Publishing

Critical Companion to J. D. Salinger

Facts On File, Inc.
An imprint of Infobase Publishing
132 West 31st Street
New York NY 10001

Library of Congress Cataloging-in-Publication Data

Mueller, Bruce F. (Bruce Frederick), 1950–
Critical companion to J. D. Salinger / Bruce F. Mueller, Will Hochman.
p. cm.
Includes bibliographical references and index.
ISBN 978-0-8160-6597-4 (hc : alk. paper) 1. Salinger, J. D. (Jerome David),
1919–2010—Handbooks, manuals, etc. I. Hochman, Will. II. Title.
PS3537.A426Z76 2010
813'.54—dc22   2009051278

Facts On File books are available at special discounts when purchased in bulk quantities for businesses, associations, institutions, or sales promotions. Please call our Special Sales Department in New York at (212) 967-8800 or (800) 322-8755.

You can find Facts On File on the World Wide Web at http://www.factsonfile.com

Text design by Erika K. Arroyo
Composition by Hermitage Publishing Services
Cover printed by Sheridan Books, Ann Arbor, Mich.
Book printed and bound by Sheridan Books, Ann Arbor, Mich.
Date printed: November 2010

Printed in the United States of America

10 9 8 7 6 5 4 3 2 1

This book is printed on acid-free paper.

For my parents, Walt and Charlotte Mueller,
in appreciation of their loving support, and for my wife, Joan E. Borrelli,
in appreciation of our shared San Francisco years.
—Bruce F. Mueller

For Bruce F. Mueller and Tim O'Connor, my "Glass Brothers,"
and with respect for Salinger's readers and their polysemantic conspiracy
to keep his families of characters alive.
—Will Hochman

CONTENTS

ACKNOWLEDGMENTS

Joint acknowledgment of the authors: We wish to thank Joan E. Borrelli, who contributed the critical analyses of the following stories: "Blue Melody," "De Daumier-Smith's Blue Period," "A Girl I Knew," "Just Before the War with the Eskimos," "The Laughing Man," "Once a Week Won't Kill You," "Pretty Mouth and Green My Eyes," "Soft-Boiled Sergeant," and "A Young Girl in 1941 with No Waist at All." We also thank her for stylistic suggestions throughout the manuscript. We thank Jeff Soloway, our editor, for his patience and work in shepherding the book to completion.

For their courtesy and permission to reproduce photographs, we thank Greg Herriges, the Library of Congress, the Ramakrishna-Vivekananda Center of New York, and the Lotte Jacobi Collection, University of New Hampshire. For her technical assistance, we thank Lisa Nugent of Photographic Services, University of New Hampshire. For her photographic work, we thank Laura Fairbanks.

Bruce F. Mueller acknowledgment: My grateful thanks, for reasons on the heart's compass, to Joan E. Borrelli; Eric Brody; Will Hochman; Indu Ranchan; Som P. Ranchan; Stan Rice; Louis M. Vuksinick; my sisters, Betsy and Cindy; my sister-in-law, Elaine; and members of the Busic, Mack, Mueller, Rios, and Schmitz families. I offer a special thanks to my mother, who, in 1966, gave me a copy of *The Catcher in the Rye*.

Will Hochman acknowledgment: Thanks to Bruce F. Mueller, who made the project worthwhile. I would also like to acknowledge the support I received from Southern Connecticut State University. My critical achievements have been guided by my New York University teachers (Carl Schmidt, John Mayer, and Joy Boyum) and by Warren French. Finally, as with all of my work, I am most grateful for the support from my wife, Jan Ellen Spiegel.

INTRODUCTION

J. D. Salinger (1919–2010) is the author of one of America's best-known, influential, and enduring novels, *The Catcher in the Rye* (1951). The novel's enormous impact has unjustly overshadowed his other fiction. Salinger's *Nine Stories* (1953) shows the author as a consummate craftsman at work on constructing complex and experimental narratives. His innovative novellas (1955–65) frame a window onto the extraordinary and unforgettable Glass family. Beyond that, Salinger's reclusive temperament, together with his decision to stop publishing at the age of 46, adds an intriguing dimension to his life and work.

The popularity of Holden Caulfield, the larger-than-life, 17-year-old narrator of *The Catcher in the Rye,* has created the misperception of Salinger as a "young-adult" writer. The critic Morris Dickstein, in *Leopards in the Temple: The Transformation of American Fiction, 1945–1970,* however, places Salinger's fiction among that of his great peers: James Baldwin, John Barth, Saul Bellow, William Burroughs, Truman Capote, John Cheever, Ralph Ellison, Joseph Heller, Jack Kerouac, Norman Mailer, Bernard Malamud, Flannery O'Connor, Philip Roth, and John Updike. Other critics agree that Salinger is one of the most important American writers of his time.

In summer 2009, when Salinger initiated legal action against an unauthorized sequel to *The Catcher in the Rye,* court documents revealed that the author had established the J. D. Salinger Literary Trust in 2008. Readers worldwide may therefore hope that Salinger authorized new works to be released eventually. Salinger's death on January 27, 2010, ignited speculation regarding the possibility of posthumous publications. (As of June 2010, no information has been divulged by the trust.) Inasmuch as Salinger's most recently published story, "Hapworth 16, 1924," dates from 1965, and his last published book, *Raise High the Roof Beam, Carpenters and Seymour: An Introduction,* dates from 1963, it is quite possible that more of his work will be forthcoming and, therefore, that the complete story of this singular writer and his contribution to American literature and culture remains unfinished.

How to Use This Book

Part I of this volume provides an extensive biographical essay on Salinger's life. The essay, in conjunction with the detailed Salinger chronology of Part IV, offers an overview of Salinger's life, work, and literary times. Part II includes entries on all of Salinger's published fiction as well as many of his miscellaneous nonfiction pieces, published and unpublished, and many unpublished stories. Each entry on a published work of fiction, including all those works Salinger chose to gather in his four books, contains subsections titled "synopsis," "critical analysis," "publication history," "characters," and "further reading." Part III is made up of entries on people, places, and topics related to Salinger's life and works. Cross-references to entries in Part III are indicated by SMALL CAPITAL LETTERS the first time the term appears in an individual entry. Part IV, in addition to the

Salinger chronology, contains a bibliography of Salinger's published works and a bibliography of secondary sources.

Note on Editions

Page references for *The Catcher in the Rye* and the 13 stories collected in Salinger's three other books are keyed to the Little, Brown and Company first editions, reprinted many times in hardback. These page references also match the trade paperback editions published by Little, Brown and Company. Both hardback and trade paperback editions remain in print. For Salinger's 22 uncollected stories, page references are keyed to the original magazine publications. (See the bibliography of Salinger's published works in Part IV for further details.) Page references to secondary materials are keyed to items in the further reading sections after individual entries or to the bibliography of secondary sources.

PART I

Biography

J. D. Salinger
(1919–2010)

J. D. Salinger abhorred literary biography. He would have preferred that his publicly known life consist solely of the straightforward information that he wrote and published four books: *The Catcher in the Rye* (1951), *Nine Stories* (1953), *Franny and Zooey* (1961), and *Raise High the Roof Beam, Carpenters and Seymour: An Introduction* (1963). Unfortunately for the author, he did not find it possible to stem the natural curiosity of the readers of his books to know more about the man. (Entries on all Salinger works are included in Part II of the *Critical Companion*.)

In 1986, Salinger sought to stop the publication of the first book-length biography of him, IAN HAMILTON's *J. D. Salinger: A Writing Life*. Salinger based his lawsuit on the grounds that the book's use of quotations from the author's unpublished letters constituted an infringement of copyright. Salinger won his case, and the court blocked the book's release.

Although an in-depth authorized biography has yet to appear, two short unauthorized biographies have been published. (A third unauthorized biography, *J. D. Salinger: A Life Raised High*, by Kenneth Slawenski, was published in Britain on March 15, 2010. Unfortunately, the book appeared too late to incorporate any of its findings into the *Critical Companion*.) In addition, two memoirs by women very close to the author have shed light on his life. After the court battle, Hamilton substantially rewrote *J. D. Salinger: A Writing Life*, which was published in 1988 as *In Search of J. D. Salinger*. In 1999, Paul Alexander, utilizing the newly available NEW YORKER archives, published *Salinger: A Biography*. JOYCE MAYNARD's 1998 memoir, *At Home in the World*, devoted a substantial section to her affair with Salinger. In 2000, MARGARET ANN SALINGER, the author's daughter, published a revealing memoir about the Salinger family, titled *Dream Catcher*. Prior to the publication of these four books, the most substantial depiction of Salinger's known life could be found in a 15-page chapter in Warren French's monograph of literary criticism, *J. D. Salinger* (1963; 1976).

J. D. Salinger in October 1950. One of several photos taken by Lotte Jacobi in a sitting for the first-edition dust jacket of *The Catcher in the Rye* (© *The Lotte Jacobi Collection, University of New Hampshire*)

These existing accounts of Salinger's life, unfortunately, do not, even together, produce a fully documented picture and do, on the other hand, contribute conflicting, unsubstantiated, or erroneous facts to the portrait. Salinger's biography still awaits a complete and definitive treatment. Nonetheless, from these publications and ancillary materials an attentive reader may clearly discern the outline and important events in the life of J. D. Salinger.

1919–1939

Childhood and Education

Jerome David Salinger, the second child, and only son, of SOLOMON SALINGER ("Sol") and MIRIAM SALINGER (née Marie Jillich), was born on January 1, 1919, in NEW YORK CITY. Jerome was immediately nicknamed Sonny. Unlike his large fictional families—the Caulfields and the Glasses—Salinger's actual family counted only one sibling, a sister, DORIS SALINGER, born on December 17, 1912. Miriam evidently favored her son, as Doris is quoted, "It was always Sonny and Mother, Mother and Sonny" (Margaret A. Salinger 19). Salinger's first book, *The Catcher in the Rye*, is dedicated to his mother.

Salinger's father, born in Cleveland, Ohio, on March 16, 1887, was Jewish, and his mother, born in Atlantic, Iowa, on August 26, 1893, was Catholic. Sol and Marie had been married by a justice of the peace and had kept the fact from their families. After living apart for approximately two years, the couple made the marriage known. Marie converted to Judaism and changed her name to Miriam for the formal Jewish wedding ceremony. The young couple initially ran a movie theater in Chicago. Later, Sol worked for J. S. Hoffman and Company, an importer of meats and cheeses, and by the time of Salinger's birth, he had become the head executive of the company's New York office.

From 1919 to 1932, the Salinger family lived at various addresses on the Upper West Side of MANHATTAN. Salinger attended public schools through eighth grade. The first sign of Salinger's recurrent interest in acting occurred in 1930, when he was voted the most popular actor at Camp Wigwam, a summer camp in Harrison, Maine, that was run by Abraham Mandelstam for well-to-do Jewish children. Though the family celebrated Christmas, and Sonny and Doris were sent to a nondenominational Sunday school called the Ethical Culture School, the Salinger children identified themselves as Jewish. When the children were told, shortly after Salinger's bar mitzvah, that their mother had been born a Christian, they were shocked to realize that they were not fully Jewish.

The family moved to prestigious Park Avenue on the Upper East Side of Manhattan in the fall of 1932. Salinger attended the private preparatory school McBurney, on West 63rd Street, for two years. At his initial interview, he claimed an interest in dramatics and tropical fish. Although Salinger earned poor grades, he did participate in school activities, acting in three school plays and also managing the fencing team. (In *The Catcher in the Rye*, Holden Caulfield manages Pencey Prep's fencing team and loses the equipment before their scheduled match with McBurney.)

In September 1934, for his junior year, Salinger was sent to VALLEY FORGE MILITARY ACADEMY, an all-male college preparatory boarding school, located in Wayne, Pennsylvania. How and why Valley Forge was chosen is not known. (One may extrapolate from a statement by Holden Caulfield

Portion of the 1930 U.S. Census page recording information about the Salinger family (Sol, Miriam, Doris, and Jerome) and their servant, Jennie Burnett. In 1930, the Salingers lived on West 82nd Street in Manhattan. *(Courtesy of the Bruce F. Mueller Collection; photo by Laura Fairbanks)*

after flunking out of Pencey Prep: "He'll [Holden's father] give me hell again, and then he'll send me to that goddam military school" [216]. Perhaps Sol Salinger had threatened his son with that possibility if Salinger did not improve his grades at McBurney. Likewise, Salinger's reaction to being sent to Valley Forge may also be mirrored in Holden's comment. However, according to Margaret Ann Salinger, the decision was "not something that was forced on him against his will" [Margaret A. Salinger 32].) The two years at Valley Forge, on the other hand, are the most documented period of Salinger's pre-adult life and are exceedingly important on several fronts: The school provided a model for Holden Caulfield's Pencey Prep; this initial exposure to a military regime prepared Salinger for his World War II service; and while at Valley Forge, Salinger began to write creatively. At Valley Forge, Salinger's grades improved. Unlike Holden Caulfield, the author did not flunk out of this or any prep school. While at Valley Forge, Salinger continued acting in school plays. During his senior year, he became the literary editor of the class yearbook, *Crossed Sabres,* and composed a substantial, though unsigned, portion of the yearbook. Salinger's first "publication" is the signed "Class Poem," which describes the cadets' June 1936 graduation day at Valley Forge. The poem begins, "Hide not thy tears on this last day." The graduating cadets "march ahead / Success we go to find / . . . [though] Our hearts are left behind" (Hamilton 1988, 27). Salinger's poem has since become established as Valley Forge's graduation song.

Salinger's unsuccessful college career began with his enrollment in New York University's Washington Square College in the fall of 1936. While it cannot be determined whether Salinger "flunked out," the author would not return for a second year. Instead, in mid-August 1937, Salinger sailed for Europe, as his father had arranged for him to learn more about the meat and cheese importing business. Salinger remained in Europe for approximately eight months, with much of his visit spent in Vienna, where he wrote English advertising copy. While in Vienna, he lodged with a Jewish family, and his short story, "A Girl I Knew," draws on his time in that city. Salinger also spent a couple

of months in Bydgoszcz, Poland, where, in his own words, he "slaughtered pigs, wagoned through the snow with the big slaughter-master, who was determined to entertain [him] by firing his shotgun at sparrows, light bulbs, fellow employees" ("Contributors" 1944, 1). During this overseas sojourn, the author submitted short stories to American magazines, only to have them all rejected.

Salinger returned to the United States in early 1938. Sol's plans to bring his son into the meat and cheese importing business were not to succeed, for Salinger enrolled in URSINUS COLLEGE, in Collegeville, Pennsylvania, that September. Before leaving New York, he was introduced to Elizabeth Murray, the older sister of a Valley Forge friend. Murray encouraged Salinger's efforts at writing and also suggested writers to read. Although Salinger did not stay beyond his first semester, the Ursinus period is important because it was there that Salinger wrote a weekly column, prophetically titled, "J. D. S.'s The Skipped Diploma," for the student paper, *Ursinus Weekly.* (Salinger additionally wrote a couple of reviews of college plays, but he did not act in any school productions.) In his very first column (titled, "Musings of a Social Soph: The Skipped Diploma"), Salinger explains his return to school: "Once there was a young man [. . . who] did not want to go to work for his Daddykins—or any other unreasonable man. So the young man went back to college" (Fiene 1961, appendix). Each column consists of a variety of items commenting on college life, recent movies and plays, actors, and general observations. In a number of instances, Salinger includes rhyming poems and snatches of dialogue. A Holden Caulfield-like remark appears in one short poem, "Children floor me; / Society stinks" (Fiene 1961, appendix). Sprinkled within the total of nine columns that Salinger wrote for the paper are literary references to Ernest Hemingway, Margaret Mitchell, Shakespeare, and Oscar Wilde. The last column to appear is dated December 12, 1938.

Salinger left Ursinus abruptly and returned to his parents' apartment in New York City. In an effort to concentrate on his writing, he enrolled in two classes at Columbia University's Extension Division for spring 1939: WHIT BURNETT's short-story class and Charles Hanson Towne's poetry-writing class. Burnett was a well-known short-story writer, teacher and, moreover, the editor of STORY magazine. *Story*, at the time, had been in existence for eight years. Salinger took Burnett's class for two semesters. Burnett said in an interview, "He was a silent fellow. Almost never a question. Never a comment. I thought he was nothing" (Bryan 26). A student in the class, Hallie Burnett (she later married Whit Burnett), described Salinger as a "grave, charming young man with an almost Egyptian quality of reserve" (Bryan 28). At the end of the second class, Salinger submitted several stories that impressed Whit Burnett. (Nothing is known about the Towne class apart from the fact that some of Salinger's poems are included in Towne's papers held by the New York Public Library.)

1940–1947

First Publications, World War II, and Aftermath

Burnett's name would become intertwined with Salinger's early writing career. In January 1940, Burnett decided to publish in *Story* magazine one of Salinger's class assignments. Salinger was understandably jubilant. He confided to the editor that since the age of 17 writing had been important to him, and that he was currently working on a play. The story Burnett chose is aptly titled "The Young Folks," now considered the first official publication of Salinger's career, though the author decided never to include the piece in any of his books. The five-page story, which consists mainly of dialogue, concerns a gathering of college students at a party. The contributors' note for the issue (March–April 1940) states that the 21-year-old writer "is particularly interested in playwriting" ("Contributors" 1940, 2). Though surprising to today's reader, Salinger's early interest in writing for the theater and also acting in his own plays is a recurrent theme throughout his early years.

In January 1940, Salinger told Burnett that he would not return to Columbia. (Salinger's formal college education thus comprises only short enrollment periods at three colleges, and no progression beyond the freshman year. Nonetheless, Salinger stayed in close contact with Burnett for the next four years. Burnett would publish three more Salin-

J. D. Salinger in October 1950. One of several photos taken by Lotte Jacobi in a sitting for the first-edition dust jacket of *The Catcher in the Rye* (© *The Lotte Jacobi Collection, University of New Hampshire*)

ger stories in *Story* magazine, and moreover almost published Salinger's first book. During this period, he and Salinger exchanged more than 50 letters.) Salinger redoubled his efforts in writing and continued to send out his stories. On September 4, he wrote Burnett that he was thinking of an autobiographical novel. This is the first intimation of what later would become *The Catcher in the Rye*. Also in 1940, Salinger informed the editor of the UNIVERSITY OF KANSAS CITY REVIEW that he wrote verse and may submit some later. Instead, he sent the editor his story "Go See Eddie" after ESQUIRE had rejected it. "Go See Eddie" was accepted and published in December 1940, thus allowing Salinger to end the year with two publications. Both, however, were in small magazines, and their remuneration would not support him financially. At the time, the notable magazines that paid a living wage for short stories were the SATURDAY EVENING POST, COLLIER'S, *Esquire,* and the *New Yorker.* The latter two were for the sophisticated reader, the first two were for the masses. The *New Yorker,* founded and edited by Harold Ross, was Salinger's ideal target from the beginning of his career. In 1940, the magazine had published its first anthology of short stories; among the chosen authors were John Cheever, WILLIAM MAXWELL, John O'Hara, Dorothy Parker, James Thurber, and E. B. White.

On February 15, 1941, Salinger sailed from New York on the *Kungsholm* for a 19-day cruise to the West Indies as a member of the social staff. Though it has been speculated that he was a performer on the ship, most likely he was a dancing partner who organized social activities. The experience did provide Salinger with the setting for his story, "A Young Girl in 1941 with No Waist at All." A friend from Salinger's Valley Forge days was also on the voyage as an employee. This friend, Herbert Kauffman, later attested that he and Salinger unsuccessfully attempted to break into acting on Broadway. In an unpublished interview given to a Columbia student shortly after his first publication in *Story,* Salinger is quoted as saying he had "tried acting for a while . . . but I stopped because my writing is more important" (Bryan 33).

The year 1941 was a breakthrough one for Salinger's writing. He signed with the Harold Ober Agency and began his decades-long relationship with his agent, DOROTHY OLDING. Salinger's third published story, "The Hang of It," appeared in *Collier's* on July 12th. In 1941, although the United States had not as yet entered World War II, the country was mobilizing toward war. The short story light-heartedly deals with the basic training of a recruit and contains a surprise ending. (The story would be reprinted in 1942 for America's servicemen—*The Kitbook for Soldiers, Sailors, and Marines*—and would constitute the first time Salinger's work appeared in a book.) Salinger continued his success that year with his first publication in *Esquire,* "The Heart of a Broken Story." The story, which is about writing a story, pokes fun at *Collier's* and its readers. In October, Salinger hit the jackpot: The *New Yorker* accepted one of his stories. Called "Slight Rebellion Off Madi-

son," the story featured a confused prep school boy named Holden Caulfield. Not only did the magazine accept the story, but it also asked Salinger to write more stories about Holden. "Slight Rebellion Off Madison," with its Christmastime setting, was scheduled to appear in December 1941. (During that year, the *New Yorker* had rejected seven Salinger stories, including two with the intriguing titles of "Monologue for a Watery Highball" and "I Went to School with Adolf Hitler" [Yagoda 233].) In just the second year of his publishing career, Salinger had sold stories to *Collier's, Esquire* and the *New Yorker.* On a personal front, in the summer of 1941, Elizabeth Murray had introduced the 22-year-old Salinger to the 16-year-old Oona, daughter of the American playwright Eugene O'Neill. Salinger fell in love, and the two began dating. Everything seemed perfect just as, on December 7, 1941, Japan bombed Pearl Harbor. The *New Yorker* informed Salinger that it had decided to put off publishing "Slight Rebellion Off Madison" because the story clashed with the recent war developments. The author, who earlier in the year had tried to enlist in the army but was rejected owing to a slight cardiac condition, wrote the head of Valley Forge Military Academy, Colonel Milton Baker, asking him to recommend something he could do to assist the war effort.

In a 1955 story, "Raise High the Roof Beam, Carpenters," a Salinger character states, "I think I'll hate 1942 till I die, just on general principles" (11). In that year commenced Salinger's experience of World War II, a war that would be life-changing for the author. In April, Salinger was reclassified and drafted into the army. On April 27, he reported to Fort Dix, New Jersey, and was transferred to Fort Monmouth, New Jersey, for an instructor's course with the Signal Corps. Salinger wanted to attend Officer Candidate School but was not accepted. Instead, he was assigned an instructor's job with the Army Aviation Cadets in Bainbridge, Georgia. In the fall, Salinger's next published story, "The Long Debut of Lois Taggett," appeared in *Story.* And in the December 12 issue of *Collier's,* "Personal Notes on an Infantryman" saw print. Oona O'Neill had moved to Hollywood to try acting, and she and Salinger corresponded.

Salinger was shuttled around the United States, and in the summer of 1943, he was transferred from Nashville, Tennessee, to Patterson Field in Fairfield, Ohio, where he wrote publicity releases. His relationship with Oona O'Neill had cooled, but upon learning of her wedding to Charlie Chaplin on June 16, he nonetheless was distraught. Salinger finally made his first sale to the *Saturday Evening Post* with "The Varioni Brothers," published on July 17, 1943. He had hoped Hollywood would be interested in the story; he wanted to make a big sale to set himself up after the war to do some serious writing. The serious writing was the novel Salinger had told Burnett about in September 1940. Salinger had first thought he would write a series of linked short stories about Holden Caulfield. In 1943, he realized he would make it a full-length novel. The other momentous occurrence that year was that Salinger was again transferred, this time to Fort Holabird, Maryland, to train for the Counter Intelligence Corps (CIC). This training would eventually lead Salinger into combat in Europe. Two CIC agents would be assigned to an overseas regiment; as towns were captured, the agents would "cut off the telephones and impound the mails. They would then begin interrogating the hundreds of prisoners who were rounded up in the so-called Civilian Cage: on the look-out for collaborators and for German army deserters in civilian clothing" (Hamilton 1988, 85).

Before embarking for England on January 18, 1944, for more training with the CIC, Salinger sold three stories to the *Saturday Evening Post*. This was a huge financial bonanza, and an emphatic confirmation of mainstream success. Soon, however, the success turned bitter as the magazine changed two of his titles: "Wake Me When It Thunders" appeared under "Both Parties Concerned"; "Death of a Dogface" saw print as "Soft-Boiled Sergeant." In April, Whit Burnett wrote Salinger that he would be interested in publishing a volume of Salinger's short stories. He even suggested a title— *The Young Folks*—and a theme. All of the stories would be about young people: before the war, during the war, and a few after its eventual conclusion. Salinger was unsure if he wanted to publish a book yet, but in a May 2, 1944, letter he listed his

best stories to date: "The Young Folks," "The Long Debut of Lois Taggett," "Elaine," "Last Day of the Last Furlough," "Death of a Dogface," "Wake Me When It Thunders," "Once a Week Won't Kill You," and "Bitsey." He also told Burnett that he had six stories about Holden Caulfield, but he wanted to save them for the novel. He realized the novel needed to be put off until after the war and that it needed to be written in first person. Salinger then generously donated $200 to *Story's* short-story contest for college students.

On June 6, 1944—D-day—Salinger, with the 12th Infantry Regiment, 4th Division, landed on Utah Beach, Normandy. Thus began his 11-months' experience of the fighting inferno of World War II. These 11 months would alter Salinger forever: He was either engaged in, or witnessed the results of, many major battles; he was also among the first to arrive at a liberated concentration camp. On July 15, the *Saturday Evening Post* printed "Last Day of the Last Furlough." This is the first published story that presents a character named Caulfield. Vincent Caulfield, elder brother to Holden, visits the story's protagonist, Babe Gladwaller. In the story, Vincent alludes to Holden as missing in action in World War II.

After heavy fighting at Utah Beach, Cherbourg, St-Lô, and Mortain, Salinger's regiment took part in the liberation of Paris on August 25. While in Paris, Salinger sought out ERNEST HEMINGWAY. He brought along a copy of "Last Day of the Last Furlough" for Hemingway to read. The older author reportedly liked it quite a bit. Salinger's regiment was involved in the notoriously bloody and unnecessary battle of the Hürtgen Forest in November and December. Sometime in the spring of 1945, Salinger was among the first to arrive at an unidentified concentration camp (Salinger scholar Eberhard Alsen suggests Kaufering Lager IV, near Hurlach, Bavaria). Margaret Ann Salinger revealed that her father told her in the 1960s, "You never really get the smell of burning flesh out of your nose entirely, no matter how long you live" (Margaret A. Salinger 55). On May 7, the Allies achieved victory in Europe, and Salinger's 11 months of fighting ended. Sometime that summer, Staff Sergeant Salinger admitted himself into an army hospital in Nuremberg, Germany, because of battle fatigue and depression. (In "For Esmé—with Love and Squalor," collected in *Nine Stories,* Staff Sergeant X has been released from a two-week stay in a hospital; his mental condition is described, "Then, abruptly, familiarly, and, as usual, with no warning, he thought he felt his mind dislodge itself and teeter, like insecure luggage on an overhead rack" [158].) It is not known how long Salinger remained hospitalized. Shortly before leaving the hospital, he wrote an important letter to Hemingway on July 27, 1945. Since last seeing Hemingway in Paris, Salinger told Hemingway, he had written a couple of stories, several poems, and part of a play about Holden Caulfield. He yearned to leave the army, but not on a psychiatric discharge. Salinger inferred that he did not want to provide future reviewers with a basis to attack an emotional novel he planned to publish circa 1950. Salinger also mentioned, without rancor, that his proposed book of short stories had fallen through. He thinks, in fact, that this turn of events would prove beneficial to his writing. (Whit Burnett's publication of *The Young Folks* was vetoed by the parent publisher of Story Press. The table of contents would have been chosen from "The Daughter of the Late, Great Man," "Elaine,"* "The Last and Best of the Peter Pans," "Both Parties Concerned,"* "The Long Debut of Lois Taggett,"* "Bitsey," "The Young Folks,"* "I'm Crazy,"* "Boy Standing in Tennessee," "Once a Week Won't Kill You,"* "Last Day of the Last Furlough,"* "Soft-Boiled Sergeant,"* "The Children's Echelon," "Two Lonely Men," "A Boy in France,"* "A Young Man in a Stuffed Shirt," "The Magic Foxhole," "Slight Rebellion Off Madison,"* "What Got into Curtis in the Woodshed," and "The Ocean Full of Bowling Balls" [Alexander 119]. Salinger never collected any of these 20 stories in his books; the stories followed by an asterisk were published in magazines.)

In November 1945, Salinger was honorably discharged from the army. In an impetuous decision, he also married. This chapter of Salinger's life is especially shrouded in mystery. His first wife, named Sylvia, was a German-born, naturalized French citizen, an ophthalmologist by profession.

Salinger's daughter, Margaret Ann, asserts that SYLVIA SALINGER was a low-level Nazi and was arrested by Salinger himself (mirroring the events in Salinger's 1950 story, "For Esmé—with Love and Squalor"); and that Salinger found Sylvia to be "accomplished" but "a terrible, dark woman of passion, an evil woman who bewitched him"; and that "their relationship was extremely intense, both physically and emotionally" (Margaret A. Salinger 71). The couple lived in Germany for six months, as Salinger had signed a contract with the U.S. Department of Defense for undisclosed civilian work. The final months of 1945 saw the publication of three important Salinger stories: "This Sandwich Has No Mayonnaise," which featured Vincent Caulfield and his anguish over his brother

J. D. Salinger in October 1950. One of several photos taken by Lotte Jacobi in a sitting for the first-edition dust jacket of *The Catcher in the Rye* (© The Lotte Jacobi Collection, University of New Hampshire)

Holden being classified as missing-in-action; "The Stranger," which depicted Babe Gladwaller's difficult readjustment to civilian life after the death of his friend, Vincent Caulfield, in the war; and "I'm Crazy," a story about a young man who gets expelled from prep school and returns home to New York City, told by Holden Caulfield.

Salinger and Sylvia arrived in New York City on May 10, 1946, and lived with his parents. Sometime in July, Sylvia returned to Europe and filed for divorce. By Salinger's own account, he had not written one story during the marriage.

To Salinger's great joy, the *New Yorker* finally decided to publish "Slight Rebellion Off Madison." After a few minor changes from the 1941 version, the story appeared in the December 21, 1946, issue. By the end of 1946, Salinger had completed a 90-page version of *The Catcher in the Rye* that had interested a publisher. Salinger, however, decided to redo the book and declined the publisher's offer.

In January 1947, Salinger moved out of his parents' apartment to rent an apartment over a garage in Tarrytown, New York. Later that year, he would move to a barn studio in Stamford, Connecticut. During 1947, Salinger published a short story based on his *Kungsholm* experience, "A Young Girl in 1941 with No Waist at All," in MADEMOISELLE. A short novella, "The Inverted Forest," which dealt with the conflicted psyche of a poet, appeared in COSMOPOLITAN (at one point, the novella was to be published as a separate book by Harcourt, Brace, but the publication did not go forward).

1948–1954

**New Yorker *Success*, The Catcher in the Rye,
Move to Cornish, New Hampshire, and
Nine Stories**

On January 1, 1948, J. D. Salinger turned 29. To date, he had published 19 stories but no books. A handful of his stories had been reprinted in anthologies. Once Salinger began to collect his stories in his own books, he chose not to print any of these 19 stories or the numerous unpublished works dating from 1940 through 1947.

The year 1948 was significant for Salinger. On January 31, the *New Yorker* published "A Perfect Day for Bananafish," the story that inaugurated the Seymour Glass saga, albeit with the protagonist's suicide. ("A Perfect Day for Bananafish" would be the earliest magazine publication Salinger eventually collected in *Nine Stories*.) The week "A Perfect Day for Bananafish" appeared, the noted author John Cheever wrote, "I thought the Salinger piece was one hell of a story" (Yagoda 234). On the strength of "A Perfect Day for Bananafish," Salinger was offered a "first reading agreement" with the *New Yorker*. Henceforth, the magazine would have the first shot to publish any future story. Salinger had been invited to join the *New Yorker* family; he had finally reached the pinnacle he had desired since his early days as a writer. Two more classic Salinger stories soon followed "A Perfect Day for Bananafish" in the *New Yorker*: "Uncle Wiggily in Connecticut," on March 20, and on June 5, "Just Before the War with the Eskimos," both of which would also be collected in *Nine Stories*. (In 1948, Salinger also published two stories elsewhere—"A Girl I Knew" in GOOD HOUSEKEEPING and "Blue Melody" in *Cosmopolitan*—but he never collected either story in a book.)

The March 19, 1949, issue of the *New Yorker* featured Salinger's 25th published story, "The Laughing Man" (later collected in *Nine Stories*). After the *New Yorker* declined "Down at the Dinghy," the story was sold to HARPER'S and appeared in the April issue. During 1949, the *New Yorker* rejected an additional six Salinger stories. On the bright side, the magazine selected "A Perfect Day for Bananafish" to be included in an anthology of the best *New Yorker* stories published during the 1940s.

In the fall, Salinger moved once again, this time to a rented house in Westport, Connecticut. At the invitation of Hortense Flexner King, a faculty member at Sarah Lawrence College, Salinger spoke to an all-girl writing class in November. (Salinger's alter ego, Buddy Glass, teaches writing at a girls' college.) As Salinger later told William Maxwell, he "got very oracular and literary. I found myself labeling all the writers I respect. . . . A writer, when he's asked to discuss his craft, ought to get up and call out in a loud voice just the *names* of the writers he *loves*. I love Kafka, Flaubert, Tolstoy, Chekhov, Dostoyevsky, Proust, O'Casey, Rilke, Lorca, Keats,

Rimbaud, Burns, E. Bronte, Jane Austen, Henry James, Blake, Coleridge. I won't name any living writers. I don't think it's right" (Maxwell 6). During the year, Robert Giroux, an editor at the publishing house of Harcourt, Brace, contacted Salinger and asked him if he would be interested in publishing a volume of short stories. Salinger told him not yet—the novel he was working on should come out first.

Salinger's 1948 story "Uncle Wiggily in Connecticut" about the reunion of two former college girlfriends, was purchased by Hollywood and made into a movie, *My Foolish Heart*. Released on January 21, 1950, the movie embarrassed Salinger, and he vowed never to allow another story of his to be made into a film. (With the passage of each decade, the movie rights for *The Catcher in the Rye* would undoubtedly have made him very rich.) In its April 8, 1950, issue, the *New Yorker* printed Salinger's World War II story, "For Esmé—with Love and Squalor." The story has since achieved classic stature. By the fall, Salinger had finalized *The Catcher in the Rye*. As he had promised, Salinger showed the manuscript to Robert Giroux. Giroux wanted to publish it but was overruled by his boss, Eugene Reynal of Harcourt, Brace. Reynal wondered if Holden Caulfield was crazy. Later that fall, Salinger signed a contract with LITTLE, BROWN AND COMPANY. In October, the publishers sent Salinger to the photographer LOTTE JACOBI to have his picture taken for the dust jacket. (Salinger initially resisted the need for a photo on the book's jacket and had to be convinced by the editor in chief, Angus Cameron.) About the same time, Salinger attended a party given by the Flaubert scholar and translator, Francis Steegmuller, where he became entranced by a 16-year-old schoolgirl named CLAIRE DOUGLAS, with whom he began to correspond.

Salinger had invested an incredible amount of himself in *The Catcher in the Rye*. By his own admission, he had worked on it sporadically for 10 years. (In 1953, when asked if the book could be considered autobiographical, he told an interviewer, "Sort of. I was much relieved when I finished it. My boyhood was very much the same as that of the boy in the book, and it was a great relief telling people about it" [Blaney ed. pg.].) He looked forward to the *New Yorker* printing substantial excerpts from

the novel in one of its issues. To his great dismay, the magazine declined to publish any; the editors said the Caulfield children were not believable.

At Little, Brown and Company's request, Salinger wrote an autobiographical statement—four paragraphs long—to be used in the upcoming promotion of *The Catcher in the Rye*. In this statement, Salinger reveals that he has been writing since the age of "fifteen or so" (Kunitz 859). He highlights his years in the army and says that his stories have appeared in a variety of magazines, but "mostly—and most happily—in *The New Yorker*" (Kunitz 859). Salinger continues, "I'd like to say who my favorite fiction writers are, but I don't see how I can do it without saying why they are. So I won't" (Kunitz 859). A portion of this "press release" was used on the dust jacket of the book. The most interesting paragraph, however, was omitted, in which Salinger wrote, "I'm aware that a number of my friends will be saddened, or shocked, or shocked-saddened, over some of the chapters of *The Catcher in the Rye*. Some of my best friends are children. In fact, all of my best friends are children. It's almost unbearable to me to realize that my book will be kept on a shelf out of their reach" (Kunitz 859). To generate orders, Little, Brown and Company created a prepublication publicity broadside, consisting of the first three pages of the book and the eventual dust jacket author photo, mailed out to 861 booksellers.

On July 14, 1951, the *New Yorker* published Salinger's "Pretty Mouth and Green My Eyes," an austerely crafted story about adultery told in the third person. *The Catcher in the Rye*, Holden Caulfield's loquacious first-person narrative, was published by Little, Brown and Company on July 16, 1951, in Boston, Massachusetts. The book included a large photograph of Salinger filling the back cover.

Little, Brown and Company had highly publicized *The Catcher in the Rye*. The book was extensively reviewed, and critical opinion ran the gamut from laudatory to damning. The very first review (May 15, 1951), by *Virginia Kirkus' Bookshop Service*, was, as its name implies, for the benefit of booksellers preordering new books. Termed "a dark horse" ("Dark Horse" 247), *The*

Catcher in the Rye is described as "the dream world of Holden Caulfield and his first person story is down to the basic, drab English of the pre-collegiate" ("Dark Horse" 247). The book portrays "the old hells of young boys, the lonesomeness and tentative attempts to be mature and secure, the awful block between youth being grown-up, the fright and sickness that humans and their behavior cause the changeling," and is "tender and true" and "worthy of respect" ("Dark Horse" 247). Harrison Smith's assessment in the *Saturday Review,* appearing two days before the novel's publication date of July 16, says "what was wrong with Holden was his moral revulsion against anything that was ugly, evil, cruel, or what he called 'phony' and his acute responsiveness to beauty and innocence, especially the innocence of the very young" (Harrison Smith 12). The *New York Times* ran reviews on July 15 (James Stern's "Aw, the World's a Crumby Place") and July 16 (Nash K. Burger's untitled review). Stern's review, ineptly written in Holden's vernacular, contrasts Salinger's success as a short-story writer who "knows how to write about kids" with "this book though, it's too long. Gets kind of monotonous" (Stern 5). Burger believes "Salinger's rendering of teen-age speech is wonderful: the unconscious humor, the repetitions, the slang and profanity, the emphasis, all are just right" (Burger 19). Also on July 16, reviews in *Time* and the *New Republic* appeared. The anonymous reviewer at *Time* declares "the prize catch in *The Catcher in the Rye* may well be Novelist Salinger himself. He can understand an adolescent mind without displaying one" ("With Love" 97). Ann L. Goodman, writing for the *New Republic,* concludes, "*The Catcher in the Rye* is a brilliant tour-de-force, but in a writer of Salinger's undeniable talent one expects something more" (Goodman 21). On July 19, T. Morris Longstreth, in the *Christian Science Monitor,* sounds the alarm over Salinger's language: "Holden's dead-pan narrative is quick-moving, absurd, and wholly repellent in its mingled vulgarity, naivete, and sly perversion" (Longstreth 11). Longstreth worries that the book "may multiply [Holden's] kind—as too easily happens when immorality and perversion are recounted by writers of talent whose work is countenanced in the name of art or good intention" (Longstreth 11). The *New Yorker* finally reviewed the book in its August 11, 1951, issue, with S. N. Behrman's long and laudatory "The Vision of the Innocent." Behrman finds the book to be "brilliant, funny, meaningful . . . [told by Holden] in his own strange idiom" (Behrman 71).

The Catcher in the Rye sold briskly, which necessitated several reprints in July 1951. For the third printing, Salinger insisted that his photograph be removed from the dust jacket, and the publisher complied.

Little, Brown and Company had sold *The Catcher in the Rye* to the Book-of-the-Month Club as one of the membership's summer main selections. Salinger agreed to give an interview to William Maxwell for a short biographical sketch to accompany that edition. This interview was, to date, the most extensive personal portrait of Salinger available to his readership. Maxwell ended the essay quoting Salinger, "I think writing is a hard life. But it's brought me enough happiness that I don't think I'd ever deliberately dissuade anybody (if he had talent) from taking it up. The compensations are few, but when they come, if they come, they're very beautiful" (Maxwell 6).

The Catcher in the Rye was reprinted 11 times in 1951 and remained on the best-seller list of *Publishers Weekly* for five months. The novel proved an initial success, but not to the degree one would imagine from today's perspective. *The Catcher in the Rye* failed to make *Publishers Weekly's* list of the 10 top-selling novels of the year. James Jones's *From Here to Eternity* was the number one best seller, followed by Herman Wouk's *The Caine Mutiny,* Sholem Asch's *Moses,* Henry Morton Robinson's *The Cardinal,* Frank Yerby's *A Woman Called Fancy,* Nicholas Monsarrat's *The Cruel Sea,* J. P. Marquand's *Melville Goodwin, U.S.A.,* James Michener's *Return to Paradise,* Cardinal Spellman's *The Foundling,* and Mike Waltari's *The Wanderer.* Notable books contemporaneously published with *The Catcher in the Rye* included James Agee's *The Morning Watch,* Truman Capote's *The Grass Harp,* WILLIAM FAULKNER's *Requiem for a Nun,* Norman Mailer's *Barbary Shore,* Carson McCullers's *The Ballad of the Sad Cafe,* Wright Morris's *Man and*

Boy, William Saroyan's *Rock Wagram*, and William Styron's *Lie Down in Darkness*.

As the year ended, Harold Ross, founder and editor in chief of the *New Yorker*, died. Salinger attended the memorial service. Speculation about Ross's successor ran high among all associated with the magazine. The choice would be WILLIAM SHAWN.

As a first-time book author, Salinger had to comply with standard publication and marketing practices, such as an author photo and bio on the dust jacket, and the giving of interviews. Salinger even replied to the *New York Times's* Christmas 1951 query about books he planned to give as presents. The author is quoted as saying, "I may give it [*The Catcher in the Rye*] away this Christmas, but not till I'm sure that boys really talk that way" (Dempsey 244). In February 1952, in responding to a journalist's question, he revealed, "I feel tremendously relieved that the season of success for *The Catcher in the Rye* is nearly over. I enjoyed a small part of it, but most of it I found hectic and professionally and personally demoralizing. . . . Many of the letters from readers have been very nice" (Hazard 16). One of the immediate aftereffects of the book's success was that Salinger was selected for a distinguished alumnus award at Valley Forge Military Academy. He was in Mexico at the time of the awards presentation and was unable to attend the ceremony.

The Catcher in the Rye was a watershed event in Salinger's life. Salinger had finally put to rest the autobiographical novel he had spoken of to Whit Burnett in September 1940. On the other hand, he discovered he was uncomfortable with the practices of book publishing and the resulting notoriety.

All of Salinger's post–*The Catcher in the Rye* stories reflect his growing interest in religion. This interest in especially Eastern religions and philosophy cannot be pinpointed to a specific year. However, after Salinger's return from Germany in 1946, he socialized in Greenwich Village with some young writers who "remember his avid interest in grammar, Japan and Zen, and the fond way he talked about his mother and sister" (Bryan 50). When Salinger's future wife, Claire, first knew him in 1950, he was "seriously considering becoming a monk. He had become friends with Daisetz Suzuki and meditated . . . at a Zen center" (Margaret A. Salinger 11). The first allusion to the East in Salinger's work occurs in *The Catcher in the Rye*, when a character tells Holden Caulfield, "I simply happen to find Eastern philosophy more satisfactory than Western" (190). Additionally, Holden sees his sister Phoebe sitting on her bed "with her legs folded like one of those Yogi guys" (227). This religious interest would finally become apparent in Salinger's next story, "De Daumier-Smith's Blue Period," whose Western protagonist is a Buddhist and who has a self-proclaimed mystical experience. The author worked on the story for five months and was profoundly disappointed with a rejection by the *New Yorker* at the end of 1951. He did not submit this story to another American magazine, but the piece appeared later in the London-based WORLD REVIEW in May 1952. (Salinger would also include "De Daumier-Smith's Blue Period" in his next book, *Nine Stories*, in 1953.) In July 1952, Salinger suggested to the English publisher of *The Catcher in the Rye*, Hamish Hamilton, a possible publication of a British edition of *The Gospel of Sri Ramakrishna*. Salinger had read the original edition published by the RAMAKRISHNA-VIVEKANANDA CENTER OF NEW YORK. Salinger took classes from its founder and spiritual leader, SWAMI NIKHILANANDA, and became his friend.

In the fall of 1952, Salinger decided to leave the Greater New York Area. Initially drawn to the north shore of Massachusetts, he found the real estate too expensive. He and his sister, Doris, drove north along the Connecticut River and ended up in Windsor, Vermont. Across the river, Salinger was shown a modest cottage, which lacked plumbing and a furnace, located on 90 wooded acres in CORNISH, NEW HAMPSHIRE, a small town with a population of circa 1,000. On February 16, 1953, the deed to the property became Salinger's. (Salinger, as it were, had achieved Holden Caulfield's dream in *The Catcher in the Rye*: "I'd build me a little cabin somewhere with the dough I made and live there for the rest of my life. I'd build it right near the woods, but not right *in* them, because I'd want it to be sunny as hell all the time" [258].) He moved in as early as January 1, 1953, his 34th birthday. On January 31, the *New Yorker* published "Teddy," Salinger's controversial story about a young religious genius who believes in the Vedantic theory of reincarnation. Henceforth, all of Salinger's future stories would appear in the *New Yorker*.

The Catcher in the Rye began to attract international attention. In 1952, translations of the novel were published in Italy, Japan, and Norway. In February 1953, the first paperback edition of the novel was published in America; the huge first printing consisted of 350,000 copies, priced at 25 cents. After requesting there be no illustration, Salinger was highly displeased that the publisher went ahead and commissioned an artist to design a cover depicting Holden Caulfield.

On April 6, 1953, Salinger's second book, *Nine Stories,* was published by Little, Brown and Company in Boston, Massachusetts. (*Nine Stories* appeared the same year in England under the title *For Esmé—with Love and Squalor, and Other Stories.*) Of his 30 stories that had already been published in magazines—dating from 1940 to January 1953—Salinger chose to reprint only nine: "A Perfect Day for Bananafish," "Uncle Wiggily in Connecticut," "Just Before the War with the Eskimos," "The Laughing Man," "Down at the Dinghy," "For Esmé—with Love and Squalor," "Pretty Mouth and Green My Eyes," "De Daumier-Smith's Blue Period," and "Teddy." All but two had appeared in the *New Yorker* from January 1948 through January 1953 (the exceptions were "Down at the Dinghy" in *Harper's,* in April 1949, and "De Daumier-Smith's Blue Period," in *World Review,* in May 1952). The severity of Salinger's choices effectively consigned 21 stories, published from 1940 through 1948, to obscurity (until they were illegally reprinted in bootleg paperbacks in 1974). Salinger had appended an epigraph to *Nine Stories.* His choice of a ZEN koan—"We know the sound of two hands clapping. But what is the sound of one hand clapping?"—would lead critics to overvalue the influence of Zen Buddhism on his work. (This overvaluation would irritate Salinger to such an extent that he has Buddy Glass, his alter ego, in the 1959 story, "Seymour: An Introduction," declare Buddy isn't a Zen Buddhist.)

The reviews for *Nine Stories* were mixed. Eudora Welty, in the *New York Times Book Review,* writes, "J. D. Salinger's writing is original, first rate, serious and beautiful" (Welty 4). She values the stories even more than *The Catcher in the Rye* and believes Salinger "will find many forms as time goes by—interesting forms" (Welty 4). Welty praises "his sensitive eye, his incredibly good ear, and something I can think of no word for but grace" (Welty 4). Gene Baro, in the *New York Herald Tribune Book Review,* though acknowledging "the special quality of Mr. Salinger's stories is humaneness," finds "the scope of these stories is strictly limited . . . more concerned with a slice of life . . . than with life itself" (Baro 6). Baro asserts that Salinger's "vision tempers an all-embracing sentimentality with a personal sophistication, so that these stories run to a kind of intellectual and emotional chic" (Baro 6). The anonymous reviewer of the *Nation* acknowledges Salinger's "great brilliance; the danger is that he will become [a writer] of definite and ultimately disappointing limitations" ("Youthful Horrors" 332). The book sold well for a volume of short stories, remaining on the *New York Times* best-seller list for 15 weeks, though it did not make the *Publishers Weekly* list of the 10 best-selling fiction volumes for the year. Salinger was outsold by Thomas B. Costain, A. J. Cronin, Lloyd C. Douglas, Ernest K. Gann, James Hilton, James Jones, Annemaire Selinko, Samuel Shellabarger, Leon Uris, and Ben Ames Williams. Notable books contemporaneously published with *Nine Stories* included James Baldwin's *Go Tell It on the Mountain,* Saul Bellow's *The Adventures of Augie March,* William Burroughs's *Junkie,* John Cheever's *The Enormous Radio, and Other Stories,* Wright Morris's *The Deep Sleep,* and Richard Wright's *The Outsider.*

Nine Stories was dedicated to Dorothy Olding, Salinger's literary agent, and GUS LOBRANO, his editor at the *New Yorker.* (Salinger initially had been edited by William Maxwell, who became a friend.) At least by late 1947, Lobrano had become Salinger's editor. He would remain so until his death in 1956.

After moving to New Hampshire, Salinger befriended some teenagers who lived in Windsor, Vermont, inviting them to his house, playing favor-

J. D. Salinger in October 1950. One of several photos taken by Lotte Jacobi in a sitting for the first-edition dust jacket of *The Catcher in the Rye* (© The Lotte Jacobi Collection, University of New Hampshire)

ite records, serving snacks and drinks. Salinger also attended their school's sporting events. One of the teens, Shirlie Blaney, had the idea of interviewing Salinger for the high school page of a local New Hampshire newspaper. But the short interview appeared on the editorial page of the *Daily Eagle* on November 13, 1953. Blaney explains that Salinger is "a very good friend of all the high school students" and that he has moved to Cornish "wanting only to be left alone to write" (Blaney ed. pg.). In her interview, Blaney asks if *The Catcher in the Rye* is autobiographical and reports Salinger's reply: "Sort of. I was much relieved when I finished it. My boyhood was very much the same as that of the boy in the book" (Blaney ed. pg.). Blaney also mentions that Salinger had plans to go to Europe

and Indonesia, and possibly to London to make a movie. Shortly after the interview appeared, Salinger stopped socializing with the teenagers. Salinger would not consent to another interview until 1974.

In 1953, Salinger had asked Claire Douglas, now 19 and attending Radcliffe, to drop out of college and move in with him. She refused, and the relationship faltered. (Claire would shortly thereafter marry a man from the Harvard Business School, only to have the marriage annulled.) By the summer of 1954, Salinger and Claire had resumed their relationship. In the fall, the two divided their time between Cornish and Cambridge, Massachusetts, so that Claire could continue her classes at Radcliffe. Salinger found this arrangement disruptive to his writing schedule. During this time, the couple began to read and study a religious book, *The Autobiography of a Yogi*, by Paramahansa Yogananda. Yogananda did not espouse strict monasticism but stressed that a married couple could also be God-seeking. Salinger and Claire wrote to the Self-Realization Fellowship seeking a guru and initiation for themselves and learned that the nearest teacher lived outside Washington, D.C. Swami Premananda informed Salinger and Claire that "he would receive them, after their marriage, and initiate them as householder devotees" (Margaret A. Salinger 90).

1955–1959

The Glass Family, and Salinger's Own Family

In 1955, Salinger got married, his first child was born, and two major stories were published. In January, he persuaded Claire Douglas to drop out of Radcliffe, one semester shy of graduating. During 1954, Salinger had been working on a long short story about a collegiate girl named Franny. The character was given several of Claire's attributes. (Franny carries a navy blue suitcase, like the one owned by Claire at the time. Most notably, however, is Franny's interest in the Jesus Prayer, as was Claire herself.) On January 29, 1955, the *New Yorker* published "Franny." The story, with its ambiguous ending, caused a sensation, especially since the story's end left the reader wondering whether Franny's actions signaled a nervous breakdown or a pregnancy. The story generated a mountain of letters from its readers and became the talk on campuses throughout the nation. On February 17, Salinger married Claire Douglas in Barnard, Vermont. (His best man was E. Michael Mitchell, who had designed the first-edition dust jacket of *The Catcher in the Rye*.) Salinger was 36 years old, Claire was 21. Their wedding certificate stated a first marriage for both. "Franny" has been called an early wedding gift of Salinger's to Claire. Shortly after the marriage, the author and CLAIRE SALINGER traveled to outside Washington, D.C., to meet Swami Premananda. The couple were initiated, given a mantra, and instructed in the breathing exercises of Kriya yoga.

During the spring of 1955, something momentous and significant occurred within Salinger's imagination: The author decided to create a full-blown family, one even more complex than the Caulfield family. With this in mind, Salinger raided his earlier stories to help create the nine-member Glass family. He resurrected Seymour Glass from the 1948 story "A Perfect Day for Bananafish"; retrieved Boo Boo Glass from the 1949 story "Down at the Dinghy"; turned a reference to a Webb Glass in the same story into the character Buddy; and incorporated Walt, who lacked a surname, from the 1948 story "Uncle Wiggily in Connecticut" and the also first-name-only Franny from the January 1955 story "Franny." To these five brothers and sisters Salinger invented Zooey and Waker as the sixth and seventh children. He also created Bessie and Les as the parents. The complete Glass family was introduced in the November 19, 1955, issue of the *New Yorker* with "Raise High the Roof Beam, Carpenters," a story about Seymour's wedding day, as recounted by Buddy Glass. Little did anyone suspect at the time that the Glass family would dominate the remainder of Salinger's published work, nor that he would publish only three more stories before lapsing into silence after 1965.

In 1955, Salinger also was included in a standard literary reference work. *Twentieth Century Authors*, edited by Stanley J. Kunitz and Vineta Colby, allotted one and one-half columns of text to the entry on Salinger, plus the reproduction of the Lotte Jacobi portrait. Nearly half of the text comprises Salinger's autobiographical statement written for Little, Brown and Company's prepublication publicity of *The Catcher in the Rye*. Salinger is described as a "modest and conscientious young man who shuns publicity," while Holden Caulfield is termed a "semi-sophisticated and startlingly articulate young hero" (Kunitz 859). William Maxwell is quoted from his Book-of-the-Month Club essay, describing Salinger as working "with infinite labor, infinite patience, and infinite thought for the technical aspects of what he is writing" (Kunitz 859). Short extracts from the reviews of *Nine Stories* by Eudora Welty and William Peden describe Salinger's writing as "original, first rate, serious and beautiful" and Salinger as "an extreme individualist" with "a saving grace of humor" (Kunitz 860).

On December 10, 1955, Salinger's first child, Margaret Ann Salinger, known as Peggy, was born. Salinger wanted to name her Phoebe, after Holden Caulfield's sister, but Claire's choice prevailed. The crying child exasperated Salinger, and he soon built for himself a one-room writing cabin in the woods to which he would retreat for days at a time.

In 1956, the academic world began to take some notice of Salinger's work. Before this time, only a few references to *The Catcher in the Rye* had appeared in scholarly journals. An article fully devoted to Salinger now appeared in the Spring 1956 issue of *Western Humanities Review*, Arthur Heiserman's and James E. Miller, Jr.'s "J. D. Salinger: Some Crazy Cliff." In this article, the authors link Holden Caulfield to MARK TWAIN's immortal character Huckleberry Finn and claim that *The Catcher in the Rye* may "belong to an ancient and honorable narrative tradition, perhaps the most profound in western fiction: . . . the tradition of the Quest" (Heiserman 129). The authors also single out three stories of *Nine Stories* as holding special significance in Salinger's works: "A Perfect Day for Bananafish," "Uncle Wiggily in Connecticut," and "For Esmé—with Love and Squalor." In 1956, Salinger was likewise included in the definitive reference work on American literature, the *Oxford Companion to American Literature*, 3rd edition, albeit with a one-sentence entry.

On May 4, 1957, the story "Zooey" appeared in the *New Yorker*. The story was a long sequel to the 1955 "Franny" and was originally rejected by the fiction editors at the *New Yorker*. William Shawn, the editor in chief, intervened, editing the story himself for eventual publication in the magazine. Henceforth, Shawn would be Salinger's sole editor. "Zooey" continues the Glass saga, and the use of Buddy Glass as its narrator. The story also evidences Salinger's awareness of adverse reaction to his most recent work. Salinger has Buddy Glass, his self-acknowledged alter ego, write, "People are already shaking their heads over me, and any immediate further professional use on my part of the word 'God,' except as a familiar, healthy American expletive, will be taken—or, rather, confirmed—as the very worst kind of name-dropping and a sure sign that I'm going straight to the dogs" (48).

"Zooey," though, was welcomingly received by the august American critic Edmund Wilson, who, in a May 10, 1957, letter, six days after the story's publication, writes, "I think they [Salinger's Glass stories] are very remarkable, quite unlike anything else" (Wilson 545). Another critic, Ihab Hassan, published in *Western Review* an in-depth article on Salinger's career to date, titled "Rare Quixotic Gesture: The Fiction of J. D. Salinger." In it, Hassan notes, "We like to think that in the talent which he undoubtedly possesses we have found something winning and unexpected, a quality as refreshing as it is unique, though, to be sure, rather acute and eccentric" (Hassan 1957, 261). The young writer Truman Capote remarked in the same year, "He [Salinger] makes an immediate electrical contact. I like his stories very much" (Walter 2). And the popular press weighed in with the assessment that Salinger's work was generating an unusual readership response: *Time* magazine, in a November 18, 1957, article on America's college students, states, "The one new American author who has something approaching universal appeal is J. D. Salinger" ("No-Nonsense Kids" 52).

In 1958, perhaps the most eminent man of American literature, William Faulkner, declared in a lecture at the University of Virginia, that of the novels written by the new generation, "I rate the best one: Salinger's *Catcher in the Rye*" (Faulkner 244). Salinger's star had risen, by 1958,

to such a height that a short monograph devoted to his work was published, Frederick L. Gwynn's and Joseph L. Blotner's *The Fiction of J. D. Salinger*. Gwynn and Blotner give a sense of the time when they note, " . . . the only Post-War fiction unanimously approved by contemporary literate American youth consists of about five hundred pages by Jerome David Salinger" (Gwynn 1). These authors anoint the story "For Esmé—with Love and Squalor" as "the high point of Salinger's art" (Gwynn 4) and predict "it is not inconceivable that some day Holden Caulfield may be as well known an American boy as Huck Finn" (Gwynn 29). But the Glass family stories—with "Zooey" the most recent at the time of the monograph's publication—caused Gwynn's and Blotner's foretelling concern: "Admirers of this writer are, of course, entitled to worry a little. . . . Whatever is going on right now with the Glass Family evidences a curious esthetic amnesia . . . and the sympathetic reader can only hope that all is not lost" (Gwynn 54). The statement glimmers with the type of criticism that would engulf Salinger's final two books when they were eventually published in 1961 and 1963.

"Seymour: An Introduction"—a story of novella-length, as are "Zooey" and "Raise High the Roof Beam, Carpenters"—appeared in the June 6, 1959, issue of the *New Yorker*. The story indicates Salinger's determination to further explore the Glass family, again noting possible reader disapproval. At the story's outset, its narrator, Buddy Glass, admits to being "no longer in a position to look after the reader's most immediate want; namely to . . . get the hell on with [the] story" (115), and if that's bothersome such readers should "leave now, while . . . the leaving's good and easy" (116). In "Seymour: An Introduction," Salinger also conflates his and Buddy's life when he assigns authorship of "A Perfect Day for Bananafish," "Raise High the Roof Beam, Carpenters," "Teddy" and *The Catcher in the Rye* to Buddy Glass. Buddy/Salinger teasingly speaks of "poignant Get-Well-Soon notes from old readers . . . who have somewhere picked up the bogus information that I spend six months of the year in a Buddhist monastery and the other six in a mental institution" (153).

At least two great American poets, contemporaries of Salinger, are on record concerning this story about Seymour Glass, whom Buddy terms as one of the "three or four *very* nearly nonexpendable poets" (157) in the history of American literature. Sylvia Plath, in a June 1959 entry in her journal, notes that after being "put off at first by the rant at the beginning . . . [she became] increasingly enchanted" (Kukil 492) as she read the story. On the other hand, Elizabeth Bishop, in a September 9, 1959, letter, states, "I *hated* [emphasis added] the Salinger story. . . . It took me days to go through it, gingerly, a page at a time, blushing with embarrassment for him every ridiculous sentence of the way" (Bishop 375).

Salinger also published in 1959 a letter to the editor of the *New York Post Magazine,* appearing on December 9, in which the author protests the practice in New York State of sentencing men to life imprisonment without the possibility of parole. This unusual civic display on Salinger's part has been attributed to an outgrowth of his friendship with Judge Learned Hand, the famous judge of the Second U.S. Court of Appeals. Salinger had developed a close friendship with the judge, who was a summer resident of Cornish, New Hampshire. The depth of the friendship is evidenced by Learned Hand's role of godfather to Salinger's daughter.

The critical reaction in highbrow circles regarding Salinger's work is articulated by George Steiner's essay, "The Salinger Industry," published in the November 14, 1959, issue of the *Nation.* Terming Salinger "a good minor writer with an audience which is, by any traditional tokens, largely illiterate," Steiner castigates Salinger for "flatter[ing] the very ignorance and moral shallowness of his young readers" (Steiner 360). The attack constitutes the first instance of a prominent critic's refutation of Salinger, in part, because of the author's readership. The oft-repeated knock would resound for decades and stems from the misperception of Salinger as merely an author for young adults. Steiner also chides critics before him for having unleashed a welter of essays on Salinger's work, thus elevating the author to the immortal pantheon of writers. Norman Mailer that year wrote the damning quip that, well recognized five decades later, is still much

J. D. Salinger in October 1950. One of several photos taken by Lotte Jacobi in a sitting for the first-edition dust jacket of *The Catcher in the Rye* (© The Lotte Jacobi Collection, University of New Hampshire)

invoked in any negative discussion of Salinger: "Salinger is everyone's favorite. I seem to be alone in finding him no more than the greatest mind ever to stay in prep school" (Mailer 1959, 467).

So ended the 1950s, which more than one critic has, however, since termed "The Age of Salinger." During this decade, Salinger published *The Catcher in the Rye* and the stories "For Esmé—with Love and Squalor," "Pretty Mouth and Green My Eyes," "De Daumier-Smith's Blue Period," and "Teddy," which were gathered together with five stories from the late 1940s to compose the 1953 book *Nine Stories.* Salinger also published "Franny" and three novella-length works, "Raise High the Roof Beam, Carpenters," "Zooey," and "Seymour: An Introduction." (These four works would be gathered together in the early 1960s to become Salinger's last two books published during his lifetime.)

1960–1965

The Two Glass Family Books and "Hapworth 16, 1924"

With the advent of 1960 and the beginning of a new decade, seven years had elapsed since Salinger's last book publication. The author, however, had struck a nerve with *The Catcher in the Rye*. A January 15, 1961, article in the *New York Times*, "Everybody's Caught 'The Catcher in the Rye,'" states that the book had been on the newspaper's best-seller list for paperbacks for the past two years. *The Catcher in the Rye* was selling approximately 250,000 copies a year. Already required reading at 275 universities and colleges throughout America, the novel was also finding its way into the hands of high school students, to the consternation of certain parents and secondary school systems.

Salinger turned 41 on January 1, 1960. The next month saw the birth of his second, and last, child, Matthew Robert Salinger, known as Matt. On May 30, the first article focusing on Salinger's private life was published in *Newsweek*, "The Mysterious J. D. Salinger . . . His Woodsy, Secluded Life." This article set into motion the now-codified public perception of Salinger, with declarations that "Salinger has built an iron curtain of secrecy which extends not only to his family, but to the characters of his fiction as well" (Elfin 92); "Salinger can be irascible and even ill-mannered with adults" (Elfin 93); and "he refuses to allow anyone or anything ever to interfere with his work" (Elfin 93). The article praises Holden Caulfield, "who has universal appeal," while the "Glass menagerie actually bores many readers" and "strike[s] some readers as metaphysical soap opera" (Elfin 93). No photo of Salinger accompanies the article; there are only pictures of his mailbox and his house amid the birch trees. This same year, Salinger's mythic stature as an American author reached into a lecture given at Stanford University by Philip Roth, who called Salinger "the man who, by reputation at least, is *the* writer of the age" (Roth 125). The year ended with Salinger's 1955 story, "Raise High the Roof Beam, Carpenters," being picked by the editors of the New

Yorker as one of the best stories published in the magazine during the previous decade. The story was included in a *New Yorker* anthology, along with work by Roger Angell, Saul Bellow, Maeve Brennan, Harold Brodkey, John Cheever, Mavis Gallant, Nadine Gordimer, Elizabeth Hardwick, R. Prawer Jhabvala, William Maxwell, Mary McCarthy, Vladimir Nabokov, Dorothy Parker, V. S. Pritchett, Philip Roth, Jean Stafford, John Updike, and Eudora Welty. The year 1960 would be the final year in which Salinger allowed his stories to be anthologized. Henceforth, a noticeable gap would exist in compilations of short stories and American literature. Salinger's work could be found only in his own four books.

Despite Salinger's acclaim, however, a lengthy Salinger piece was turned down by the *Saturday Review* in 1960. In response to James Thurber's 1959 critical memoir, *The Years with Ross*, Salinger wrote a 25-to-30-page open-letter essay about Harold Ross, William Shawn, and the *New Yorker* and submitted it to the *Saturday Review*. Donald M. Fiene, Salinger's first bibliographer, was told by Hallowell Bowser, general editor of *Saturday Review*, that the Salinger piece was "rejected because of its length and unusual style" (Fiene 1963, 116). As James Bryan remarks, "One can scarcely imagine a literary magazine passing up anything of Salinger's then, at the height of his popularity. The piece must have been, as I heard, embarrassingly fulsome" (Bryan 56–57).

Speculation had abounded since the late 1950s that Salinger would refashion his *New Yorker* Glass stories into a novel, or a trilogy. Nothing had come of it, however. But in 1961, readers would see the release of Salinger's third book, *Franny and Zooey*. For this publication, Salinger chose to reprint the 1955 story "Franny" and its sequel, the 1957 "Zooey" as they had appeared in the magazine printings. The two stories, as they were originally published in the *New Yorker* would not, however, form a seamless novel. The first-person prologue to "Zooey" invalidated such a possibility. Moreover, the subsequent third-person narration of "Zooey" did not match the tone of the third-person narration used in "Franny." To accompany *Franny and Zooey*'s release, Salinger was asked for a thousand-word introduction. The circa 250 words that he delivered easily fit on the two inside flaps of the dust jacket. Short as it was, this author contribution is the first public statement made by Salinger on his Glass series. Salinger terms the two stories "early, critical entries in a narrative series . . . about a family of settlers in twentieth-century New York." The series was to be a "long-term project," and the author was hopeful he would finish it. Salinger confesses, "I love working on these Glass stories, I've been waiting for them most of my life." He refers to two other stories already published in the *New Yorker* ("Raise High the Roof Beam, Carpenters" and "Seymour: An Introduction") and promises that "some new material is scheduled to appear there soon or Soon." Additionally, he has "a great deal of thoroughly unscheduled material on paper" and blames the infrequent rate of publication on his "alter-ego and collaborator, Buddy Glass, [who] is insufferably slow." Salinger ends his dust jacket remarks saying that he believes "a writer's feelings of anonymity-obscurity are the second-most valuable property on loan to him during his working years." He would however reveal, at his wife's suggestion, that he lived in Westport, Connecticut (contrary to the truth, as the couple resided in Cornish, New Hampshire). The remainder of the dust jacket consists simply of the book's title and Salinger's name on the front and rear covers. The dust-jacket presentation was, for the period and still to this day, a highly unusual approach in that it lacked advertising blurbs and a photo of the author. The dust jacket of *Nine Stories* had eliminated an author's photo but still retained six blurbs about *The Catcher in the Rye*. The front cover had also prominently identified Salinger as "author of *The Catcher in the Rye.*"

Salinger dedicated *Franny and Zooey* to William Shawn, in part, no doubt, for the latter's having overruled the fiction editors of the *New Yorker* in seeing the story "Zooey" into print. This dedication has since achieved renown in its own right, as, with it, Salinger brings attention to Shawn by referring to him as "my editor, mentor and (heaven help him) closest friend, . . . *genius domus* of The *New Yorker,* lover of the long shot, protector of the unprolific, defender of the hopelessly flamboy-

ant, most unreasonably modest of born great artist-editors." Salinger ruled out all book club offers for *Franny and Zooey,* explaining to Little, Brown and Company that he thought the book would do fine without them. He was proved right when the book, immediately after release, sold 125,000 copies in two weeks, an astounding number of sales for the 1960s. Part of the reason for success was the buildup that preceded the publication. Once it became known that a Salinger book was in the offing, both *Time* and *Life* magazines began preparations for major articles on Salinger to coincide with the book's fall release. *Time* had decided to place Salinger on its cover the same week as the book's release. As this would mean an extensive cover story, *Time* sent a team of reporters into the field to ferret out everything they could discover about the reclusive author. The usual approach of interviewing old schoolmates, army buddies, and fellow authors was employed, but at the same time, the editors believed that Salinger's reclusive life signaled that the author had something to hide. They therefore focused on Salinger's mysterious first marriage and attempted to identify the real-life counterpart to Sybil in "A Perfect Day for Bananafish." *Time* was successful in locating Claire Salinger's brother, Gavin Douglas, who was quite willing to talk and who provided a great deal of personal background information. Doris, Salinger's sister, was approached at her job at Bloomingdale's, but she stated, "I wouldn't do anything in the world my brother didn't approve of. . . . Why don't you leave us alone. *Hundreds* of people want to write stories about him" (Hamilton 1988, 173). Neither did the author Peter de Vries cooperate: "No, I don't want to hear your questions. If you asked me how to spell his name, I wouldn't feel free to tell you. If there are gaps in your story, they're gaps Salinger *wants* in the story" (Hamilton 1988, 173). Though *Time* did track down a girl who had met Salinger in Florida, her age didn't correspond correctly with Sybil's. After all of the research into Salinger's life, which pained him no end, the magazine produced a very laudatory cover story. Nonetheless, Salinger felt his privacy had been invaded, and this invasion extended to the inclusion of three photos of himself, one of Claire, one of their house, and artist renderings of Holden Caulfield, and Franny, Zooey, and Bessie Glass. Not to mention that his portrait on the cover of the magazine was shown against a field of rye and a child near a cliff's edge in the background. The horror of the *Time* experience obviously stayed with Salinger. Twenty-five years later, he alluded to it when trying to dissuade Ian Hamilton from commencing research for his biography.

Franny and Zooey was heavily reviewed. Though there was praise—for example, Charles Poore in the *New York Times* calls the book "better than anything Mr. Salinger has done before" (Poore 29); Granville Hicks in the *Saturday Review* declares *Franny and Zooey* "has something to say about the human predicament, and it makes its point with humor and the shrewdness that are Salinger's great assets" (Hicks 18)— negative assessments were in the majority. The most important review was John Updike's in the *New York Times Book Review*, three days after the book's release. The criticism Updike voiced that year still informs criticism of the Glass family to this day. Updike warns, "Salinger loves the Glasses more than God loves them. He loves them too exclusively. Their invention has become a hermitage for him. He loves them to the detriment of artistic moderation" (Updike 52). Another criticism of the book, which still holds currency today, found expression in the August 1961 issue of the *Atlantic*, where Alfred Kazin writes, "I am sorry to have to use the word 'cute' in respect to Salinger, but there is absolutely no other word that for me so accurately typifies the self-conscious charm and prankishness of his own writing and his extraordinary cherishing of his favorite Glass characters" (Kazin 49). Nonetheless, *Franny and Zooey* quickly topped the best-seller lists, and it would remain number one on the *New York Times* list for 26 consecutive weeks. Published as late in the year as mid-September, *Franny and Zooey* would nonetheless achieve the status in *Publishers Weekly* of the second best-selling work of fiction in 1961, beaten only by Irving Stone's *The Agony and the Ecstasy*. The book would outsell other best sellers such as Harper Lee's *To Kill a Mockingbird*, Henry Miller's *Tropic of Cancer*, Harold Robbins's

The Carpetbaggers, John Steinbeck's *The Winter of Our Discontent*, and Leon Uris's *Mila 18*. Notable books contemporaneously published with *Franny and Zooey* included William Burroughs's *The Soft Machine*, John Cheever's *Some People, Places and Things That Will Not Appear in My Next Novel*, John Dos Passos's *Midcentury*, John Hawkes's *The Lime Twig*, Joseph Heller's *Catch-22*, Bernard Malamud's *A New Life*, Larry McMurtry's *Horseman Pass By*, Walker Percy's *The Moviegoer*, Isaac Bashevis Singer's *The Spinoza of Market Street and Other Stories*, and Kurt Vonnegut's *Mother Night*.

Though published in September of the previous year, *Franny and Zooey* continued to sell at such a rate in 1962 that the book placed as the year's fifth best-selling work of fiction. Publishers of literary criticism realized Salinger had become a desirable subject. Two collections of previously published articles in newspapers, magazines, and journals were assembled: *Salinger: A Critical and Personal Portrait*, edited by Henry Anatole Grunwald, and *J. D. Salinger and the Critics*, edited by William F. Belcher and James W. Lee. Thus, a substantial amount of ephemeral and disparate material had been gathered on Salinger's life and work, material that would fuel future criticism.

On January 28, 1963, Salinger published his fourth and final book during his lifetime: *Raise High the Roof Beam, Carpenters and Seymour: An Introduction*. In design, the volume visually was produced as a matching companion to 1961's *Franny and Zooey*, except for the use of yellow instead of green on the spine of the dust jacket. Salinger again wrote some comments on the inside dust-jacket flaps. In these, he acknowledges that the two stories, again reprints from their original *New Yorker* appearances, are both about Seymour Glass, "the main character in [his] still-uncompleted series about the Glass family." Salinger states the reason for the stories now appearing in book form is to "avoid unduly or undesirably close contact with new material in the series," which he then terms "several new Glass stories coming along—waxing, dilating—each in its own way." He admits that "the joys and satisfactions of working on the Glass family peculiarly increase and deepen for [him] with the years."

Raise High the Roof Beam, Carpenters and Seymour: An Introduction, like *Franny and Zooey*, was poorly received. The author still had his backers, most notably Ihab Hassan, who writes in the *Saturday Review*: "The new Salinger book is a confounding and holy joy. . . . The comic battle Salinger wages against language is also the tragic battle man fights with eternity. No one in recent fiction has accepted more difficult terms for that battle than Salinger. It is to our honor that he persists in it with love and grace" (Hassan 1963, 38). But Salinger's critical reputation, already damaged by influential negative reviews of *Franny and Zooey* by Joan Didion, Leslie Fiedler, Alfred Kazin, Frank Kermode, Mary McCarthy, and John Updike, now was further assaulted by attacks from Irving Howe and Norman Mailer. Though Howe acknowledges Salinger's manifold gifts as a writer, he calls Salinger a "priest of an underground cult" (Howe 4) and finds the book "hopelessly prolix . . . marred by self-indulgence . . . [the stories] betray a loss of creative discipline, a surrender to cherished mannerisms" (Howe 34). Norman Mailer, in the July 1963 issue of *Esquire*, terms the story "Seymour: An Introduction" "the most slovenly portion of prose ever put out by an important American writer" (Mailer 1963, 68). Mailer then assesses the four Glass stories reprinted in the past two books and declares, "*The Catcher in the Rye* was able to change people's lives. The new books are not even likely to improve the conversation of college dormitories. It is time Salinger came back to the city and got his hands dirty with a rough corruption or two, because the very items which composed the honor of his reputation, his resolute avoidance of the mass media and society, have now begun to back up on him" (Mailer 1963, 68).

Despite the critics turning on Salinger, the public remained constant in its affections. *Raise High the Roof Beam, Carpenters and Seymour: An Introduction* was propelled to the top of the *New York Times* best-seller list for 10 weeks and achieved the status in *Publishers Weekly* of the third best-selling work of fiction in 1963. The book would sell fewer copies than only Morris L. West's *The Shoes of the Fisherman* and Mary McCarthy's *The Group*. *Raise High the Roof Beam, Carpenters and Seymour:*

An Introduction would outsell other bestsellers such as Taylor Caldwell's *Grandmother and the Priests*, James Michener's *Caravans*, John O'Hara's *Elizabeth Appleton*, and John Rechy's *City of Night*. Notable books contemporaneously published with *Raise High the Roof Beam, Carpenters and Seymour: An Introduction* included Joan Didion's *Run River*, Jack Kerouac's *Visions of Gerard*, Joyce Carol Oates's *By the North Gate*, Sylvia Plath's *The Bell Jar*, Thomas Pynchon's *V.*, Susan Sontag's *The Benefactor*, John Updike's *The Centaur*, and Kurt Vonnegut's *Cat's Cradle*.

In 1963, the floodgates of books and special issues on Salinger and his work opened. The esteemed academic journal *Wisconsin Studies in Contemporary Literature* devoted an entire issue to a gathering of essays on Salinger and included a revised and condensed bibliography drawn from Fiene's thesis, thus providing access to the first extensive bibliography on Salinger and his work. Three casebooks of collected Salinger criticism—mostly centered on *The Catcher in the Rye*—were also published: *If You Really Want to Know: A 'Catcher' Casebook* edited by Malcolm Marsden; *Salinger's 'Catcher in the Rye': Clamor vs. Criticism*, edited by Harold P. Simonson and Philip E. Hagar; and *Studies in J. D. Salinger: Reviews, Essays, Critiques of 'The Catcher in the Rye' and Other Fiction*, edited by Marvin Laser and Norman Fruman. The most important volume released in 1963 on Salinger was a first book-length monograph, Warren French's *J. D. Salinger*, in the prestigious series Twayne's United States Authors. French remarks that his book is "not written for Salinger's fans, who don't need to be told why they admire him and who, indeed, would be affronted by any effort to tell them. It is rather for those parents, teachers, and other representatives of a beleaguered older generation who are puzzled by the enthusiasm aroused by [Salinger's fiction]" (French 1963, preface).

The American Book Publishers Council stated in 1963 that *The Catcher in the Rye* had become the most objectionable book in America's public school systems. The first recorded cases of *The Catcher in the Rye* being censored as objectionable reading occurred during 1954 in Los Angeles and Marin counties, in California. Efforts to ban the book took place in high schools and colleges alike. For the period of 1966 to 1975, *The Catcher in the Rye* was banned in schools more often than any other book. To this day, *The Catcher in the Rye* continues to appear on the American Library Association's tabulation of the most frequently challenged books taught in schools. Salinger was aware of the controversy caused by his book. Quoted in a newspaper article about a 1961 incident in Texas, Salinger acknowledges *The Catcher in the Rye* "doesn't invariably make a big hit with school boards" (Matis sec. 7, p. 6). He realizes some teachers have lost their jobs and this "distresses [him] very much" (Matis sec. 7, p. 6). Salinger "values" the teachers' "goodwill," but concludes there is nothing he can do about the situation (Matis sec. 7, p. 6).

Salinger had been upset by the covers of his two paperback books as published by New American Library. When the contract ended, the author switched his paperback reprint rights to Bantam Books in 1964. He exercised great control over Bantam's covers and would allow no illustrations or biographical material. In fact, Salinger himself designed all aspects of the cover for *The Catcher in the Rye. Franny and Zooey,* Salinger's third book, had been so successful in its original hardback publication that not until 1964 was a paperback finally released. In 1965, Bantam would publish *Raise High the Roof Beam, Carpenters and Seymour: An Introduction* in paperback, thus finally making all four Salinger titles cheaply available to the American reading public.

In 1964, Salinger was at work on a piece of nonfiction. Whit Burnett, his former teacher and publisher of his first story, had asked Salinger to write a foreword for an anthology of stories Burnett planned to assemble from the back files of *Story* magazine. Surprisingly, Salinger agreed. The 570-word piece recalls his experience of taking Burnett's class at Columbia University in 1939. Salinger terms it "a good and instructive and profitable year" and praises Burnett for having had "no particular pets, no fashionable prejudices. He was there . . . in the service of the Short Story" (Burnett 187). He distinctly remembers Burnett's reading aloud to the class William Faulkner's story

"That Evening Sun Go Down." Salinger explains that Burnett "very deliberately forbore to perform [and instead] turned himself into a reading lamp, and his voice into paper and print," which created no intrusion between Faulkner "and his beloved silent reader" (Burnett 188). The piece ends with "Salutes to Whit Burnett, to Hallie Burnett, and to all *story* readers and contributors" (Burnett 188). When *Story Jubilee: 33 Years of Story* was published, Salinger's foreword was not included. Burnett told Salinger he had felt embarrassed to use the piece because it had focused on Burnett himself and not on the magazine. (A decade later, Hallie Burnett assembled Burnett's notes for a handbook on writing fiction. *Fiction Writer's Handbook,* by Hallie and Whit Burnett, was published in 1975, with a preface by Norman Mailer. Without Salinger's consent, his remembrance of Whit Burnett's Columbia class was used as the book's epilogue. This "fugitive" Salinger piece was unknown in Salinger scholarship until Craig Stoltz published his essay, "J. D. Salinger's Tribute to Whit Burnett," in the Winter 1981 issue of the academic journal *Twentieth Century Literature.*)

The *New Yorker* magazine celebrated its 40th anniversary in February 1965. Tom Wolfe, then a young journalist, had the idea of doing a profile of the magazine and its editor in chief, William Shawn. Shawn was nearly unknown to the general reading public. Wolfe, with the intention of exposing Shawn and the moribund state of the magazine, wrote a two-part inflammatory essay in an effort to attract attention to the new Sunday supplement of the *New York Herald Tribune* for which he worked. He succeeded beyond his wildest dreams. The first part, titled "Tiny Mummies! The True Story of the Ruler of 43rd Street's Land of the Walking Dead!" portrays Shawn as a highly neurotic but manipulative embalmer of Harold Ross's original magazine; the second part, "Lost in the Whichy Thickets: *The New Yorker,*" reduced the *New Yorker* to one of the glossy magazines created for the educated suburban woman to display on her coffee table. The *New Yorker* had become, in Wolfe's opinion, merely an excuse to print ads that would guide and substantiate the targeted woman's taste in life's finer things. Wolfe's articles provoked outrage among

New Yorker editors and contributors, who sent letters of protest to the *New York Herald Tribune*. Salinger's telegram, addressed to Jock Whitney, the blue-blood owner of the newspaper, said, "With the printing of that inaccurate and sub-collegiate and gleeful and unrelievedly poisonous article on William Shawn, the name of the *Herald Tribune* and certainly your own will very likely never again stand for anything either respect-worthy or honorable" (Wolfe 288–289).

Whether coincidence or not, Salinger, just two months after the attack on Shawn and the *New Yorker*, published his first new story in six years in the June 19, 1965, issue of the magazine. The story was "Hapworth 16, 1924." "Hapworth 16, 1924" begins with a four-paragraph introduction by Buddy Glass. Next follows a letter, written from summer camp by a seven-year-old Seymour Glass, which nearly fills the entire issue of the magazine, as it runs from page 32 through page 113. The immediate assessment of "Hapworth 16, 1924" was summed up in a June 26, 1965, letter written by Louise Bogan, the *New Yorker* poetry editor and an esteemed poet in her own right: "The Salinger is a disaster. Maxwell [William Maxwell] came to call, and rather deplored its total cessation of talent" (Limmer 364).

Salinger's work was still commanding critical attention in 1965, though the pace of scholarly articles had plummeted from the highs of the early 1960s. Nonetheless, the new edition of the *Oxford Companion to American Literature* accorded him two entries, a biographical one filling half a page, and a second entry devoted exclusively to *The Catcher in the Rye*. The University of Minnesota published James E. Miller, Jr.'s *J. D. Salinger* in its well-respected Pamphlets on American Writers series. Miller's 40-page essay devotes a third of its pagination to *The Catcher in the Rye*. He praises Holden Caulfield: "There can be no doubt that for today's American youth, Holden is an embodiment of their secret terrors and their accumulated hostilities, their slender joys and their magnified agonies" (Miller 5). After a handful of pages on *Nine Stories*, the remainder of the essay focuses on the Glass saga. Miller's volume appeared shortly after the printing of "Hapworth 16, 1924," and apart from a terse notice in *Time* magazine and a Canadian newspaper, his essay contains the first published response to the story: "Hapworth 16, 1924" "tended to accentuate those characteristics of the later work which most readers found disturbing— a tedious length, a humor often self-consciously cute, a muting of narrative in favor of philosophical asides. But in spite of its apparent defects, the story was an important addition to the life of the Glasses, particularly as it shed new light on the remarkable character of Seymour" (Miller 42–43). Miller's essay ends on a high point and, in retrospect, constitutes the last critical hurrah for Salinger's work for quite a while: "Although Salinger's total creative production, to date, has been relatively small, his impact and influence—and his artistic achievement—have been enormous. No serious history of post-World War II American fiction can be written without awarding him a place in the first rank, and even, perhaps, the pre-eminent position" (Miller 45).

Salinger's creative production, at least what the public has been allowed to see, completely stopped with his 35th published story, "Hapworth 16, 1924," in 1965. With each passing year, and now, four-and-one-half decades later, the author's work has receded from most critics' "first rank"; the "pre-eminent position" may exist only in the minds of his committed amateur readers. This turn of events, as such, ironically fulfills Salinger's hope, "his untellable affection and gratitude," that his works reach directly to the "amateur reader—or anybody who just reads and runs," as he states in the dedication of his final book published during his lifetime, the 1963 *Raise High the Roof Beam, Carpenters and Seymour: An Introduction*.

At the time of "Hapworth 16, 1924"'s publication, no one realized this was to be the final published story of the 46-year-old author. Buddy Glass's introduction to "Hapworth 16, 1924" hints at a companion story; it was "reportedly set in type at the same time only to be withdrawn because Salinger wasn't satisfied with it" (Bryan 75).

In retrospect, Salinger is indelibly linked with the *New Yorker*, and rightly so. Of his 35 stories published in magazines, Salinger chose to reprint only 13 of them in his books, and of these 13 stories, all but two had appeared in the *New Yorker*.

His three books of stories contain "A Perfect Day for Bananafish" (1948), "Uncle Wiggily in Connecticut" (1948), "Just Before the War with the Eskimos" (1948), "The Laughing Man" (1949), "Down at the Dinghy" (*Harper's*, 1949), "For Esmé—with Love and Squalor" (1950), "Pretty Mouth and Green My Eyes" (1951), "De Daumier-Smith's Blue Period" (*World Review*, 1952), "Teddy" (1953), "Franny" (1955), "Raise High the Roof Beam, Carpenters" (1955), "Zooey" (1957), and "Seymour: An Introduction" (1959). Salinger's sole novel is *The Catcher in the Rye* (1951). For the vast majority of his readers, the works contained in these four books constitute the author's entire known output. All of these works were originally published from 1948 to 1959, though his publishing career spanned 1940 to 1965.

In 1965, the year that saw the publication of "Hapworth 16, 1924," the following notable authors published either stories or books: Thomas Berger, Gina Berriault, Stanley Elkin, Mavis Gallant, Herbert Gold, Shirley Jackson, Jerzy Kosinski, Norman Mailer, William Maxwell, Cormac McCarthy, Joyce Carol Oates, John O'Hara, William Saroyan, May Sarton, Anne Tyler, John Updike, Kurt Vonnegut, Richard Yates, and Marguerite Young.

During that same year, Princeton University's FIRESTONE LIBRARY acquired the archives of Whit Burnett and *Story* magazine. Included were five unpublished Salinger stories—"The Last and Best of the Peter Pans," "The Ocean Full of Bowling Balls," "The Magic Foxhole," "Two Lonely Men," and "The Children's Echelon"—all written between 1942 to 1945, 36 Salinger letters addressed to Burnett or the magazine (most dating from 1940 to 1944), and copies of 21 Burnett letters to Salinger. The Princeton archive is considered the premier Salinger archive in the world.

1966–1973

Divorce and Disappearance

On September 9, 1966, Claire Salinger filed for divorce. Though Salinger was enamored of his children, Margaret Ann and Matthew, the relationship with Claire had badly faltered. According to the divorce papers on file, Salinger, "for a long period of time . . . has treated [Claire] with indifference,

has for long periods of time refused to communicate with her, has declared that he does not love her and has no desire to have their marriage continue" (Alexander 236).

Salinger's daughter, Margaret Ann, in her memoir, *Dream Catcher*, provides the only inside details of what family life had been like in Cornish, New Hampshire. Margaret Ann turned to her mother, Claire, and Salinger's sole sibling, Doris, as her sources, in addition to her own memories. According to the memoir, Salinger's devotion to his writing took precedence over all human relationships. Nothing was to come between him and his work. But the writing process was agonizing for the author, and "when he reached the point of almost finishing up a piece, the 'home stretch,' he'd leave for weeks at a time . . . only to return with the piece he was supposed to be finishing all undone or destroyed and some new 'ism' [he and Claire] had to follow" (Margaret A. Salinger 94–95). Claire would be forced to follow, or indulge, Salinger's next new interest, or "ism" as she termed it, whether it was Kriya yoga, Zen, VEDANTA, Christian Science, Dianetics, homeopathy, macrobiotics, or acupuncture. Claire felt Salinger's enthusiastic jumping from "ism" to "ism" was to distract himself from dwelling on the fact he "had just destroyed or junked or couldn't face the quality of, or couldn't face publishing, what he had created" (Margaret A. Salinger 95).

Cornish, New Hampshire, was a very isolated town during the period of the Salingers' marriage. In winter, the family would see no one at home, and even during the other seasons, Salinger discouraged visitors. Yet Salinger was a good father to his children, especially when they were younger. Rather than read to Margaret Ann and Matthew, he would make up stories to tell the children, continuing narratives whose characters and adventures would populate their everyday world of Cornish. Salinger's books were never mentioned in the household, though he would tell his children "things his characters said . . . quoting them as though he were talking about old friends" (Margaret A. Salinger 146). Salinger distrusted doctors and would practice homeopathy and acupuncture on the two children.

In spring 1963, the Salingers were invited to the White House for a celebration of writers and artists. When Salinger delayed his response, Jacqueline Kennedy personally telephoned in an attempt to solicit a commitment. But Salinger's sense of privacy won out. Margaret Ann believed her father had always remained a soldier in bearing; the only time she saw him cry was during the funeral procession of John F. Kennedy.

The original house Salinger had purchased in 1953 was remodeled, but this still didn't give the author enough privacy. As the marriage slowly unraveled, Salinger built in the early 1960s a second house for himself, one "perched on the side of a steep hill . . . a modest, chalet-style, one-level ranch . . . [with a] view of Mt. Ascutney" (Margaret A. Salinger 204). On October 3, 1967, Salinger and Claire were finally divorced. Claire got the original house and custody of the children, and Salinger retained an adjacent property and the house he had built for himself.

In 1969, the HARRY RANSOM CENTER, at the University of Texas at Austin, purchased the Salinger archive of Elizabeth Murray, the first person to encourage the author's writing. Over a period of 22 years, Salinger had written Murray 37 letters and postcards and had additionally given her two unpublished stories—"Birthday Boy," dating from circa 1946, and a draft of an untitled story, undoubtedly the "Mrs. Hincher" story referenced in an October 31, 1941, letter to Murray (most likely reworked and retitled "Paula," which was sold to *Stag* magazine but never printed)—as well as an early corrected draft of the Holden Caulfield story "I'm Crazy." This archive is second in importance only to Firestone Library's at Princeton.

During 1970, Salinger repaid Little, Brown and Company a $75,000 advance he had received in the mid-1960s for the book publication of "Hapworth 16, 1924" and a companion story. He was now no longer under contract to any publisher for another book. By 1971, the author's six-year publishing silence had been noticed by at least one scholar, Ihab Hassan. In his book, *The Dismemberment of Orpheus,* Hassan speaks of "the sacramental language of silence" (Hassan 1971, 251) for certain modernist writers, including Salinger. "The writer

behind Buddy, Salinger himself, gradually becomes as silent as an ideal reader. At first, the silence is metaphoric. . . . In the end, Salinger ceases to publish. Is this some form of holy refusal?" (Hassan 1971, 251). Salinger's silence, which had deepened from decade to decade, has become almost as well known and emblematic as the popularity of *The Catcher in the Rye.*

On April 23, 1972, the *New York Times Sunday Magazine* published a long article titled "An Eighteen-Year-Old Looks Back on Life," written by a Yale freshman named Joyce Maynard. The magazine cover features a photo of the younger-than-her-years-looking Maynard, who prominently wears an oversized man's watch (this is reminiscent of the character Esmé in "For Esmé—with Love and Squalor"). Two days later, a 53-year-old J. D. Salinger wrote his first letter to the young writer. (In Maynard's memoir, *At Home in the World,* published 26 years later, she tells her side of the one-year affair, *summarizes* Salinger's letters written to her, and reconstructs conversations.) Salinger's first letter to Maynard, "speaking from an unfortunate wealth of personal experience," warns her that the offers she's about to receive in response to her article "are not likely to demonstrate even the smallest measure of true concern" about her or her writing (Maynard 71). He himself "has experienced the dangers as well as the appeal of youthful success" (Maynard 72). Salinger's second letter "offers a kind of regretful apology about his compulsion for privacy" and "cautions that a glimpse of fame can distract a writer" (Maynard 74). As Maynard completed her freshman year, Salinger and she also exchanged phone calls. "Jerry assures me he isn't any kind of guru. He's fairly intuitive, he tells me, and an inveterate reader" (Maynard 83). They talked about films, actors, and acting (Maynard, at that time, also held acting aspirations), and television shows, especially *The Andy Griffith Show.* Maynard asks Salinger if he has been writing, and he replies that "he writes every day. Always has" (Maynard 87). One night she asks him why he has not published since 1965, and Salinger explains, "All those loutish, cocktail-party-going opinion-givers, so ready to pass judgment. Bad enough when they do that to a writer. But when they start

Salinger's four books in the current three editions published by Little, Brown and Company *(Courtesy of the Bruce F. Mueller Collection; photo by Laura Fairbanks)*

in on your characters—and they do—it's murder. It's just more of a damned interruption than I can tolerate" (Maynard 97).

In early summer, Maynard and Salinger finally met, and Maynard then returned to New York City for a summer job. In September 1972, she dropped out of Yale, at Salinger's pleading, to live full time with him. Every morning Salinger would go into his study, meditate, and then write. He would not reappear until the afternoon. Maynard states that Salinger never showed her any of his writings, though he did share with her the archives he was keeping on each member of the Glass family. She thought the author had two unpublished novels hidden in his safe. The couple would often take a walk in the afternoon and in the evenings watched old movies and television. Maynard adopted Salinger's diet of mostly raw and uncooked foods, and when they did eat something unhealthy, he taught her how to regurgitate the meal. Though the two were unable to consummate the relationship due to Maynard's vaginismus, they did talk about a future together and having a baby.

While she lived with Salinger that fall and winter, Maynard was working on a book. Maynard gave Salinger's phone number to her editor as the place she could be reached; rumors about the affair began to swirl around New York's publishing world. As the year ended, discord had entered into the relationship, with Maynard wanting to be involved in the world with her aspirations of becoming a noticed success in her career. In spring 1973, Salinger and Maynard, along with his two children, traveled to Daytona Beach, Florida, for a vacation, and to consult (unsuccessfully) with a naturopathic practitioner for Maynard's vaginismus. Later, on the beach, Salinger is quoted as saying, "I can never have any more children. I'm finished with all this" (Maynard 206). He abruptly told Maynard to return to Cornish and clear her belongings out of the house before he and the children would return. Maynard was devastated and vowed to herself never to speak or write about the affair.

Salinger had remained out of the public's eye since 1965 and had effectively disappeared into his reclusion. At this point, the most substantial biographical information about the author could be found in a 15-page chapter of Warren French's 1963 monograph of literary criticism, *J. D. Salinger.* Interest in Eastern religions in the late 1960s had sparked a renewed readership for Salinger's post–*Catcher in the Rye* stories. In fact, all four Bantam paperbacks were selling briskly. Additionally, both of Salinger's parents had died in the early 1970s, and this would have left Salinger and his sister, Doris, as the probable sole inheritors of the family's estate. With a substantial inheritance, along with sizable royalties from *The Catcher in the Rye* and steady royalties from his other three books, Salinger may have found that his financial situation did not force him to publish.

1974–1987

Bootlegged Stories Appear, Salinger Speaks, and Biography Blocked

In 1974, a handful of unidentified Berkeley, California, Salinger fans decided to publish, without Salinger's consent, all of the 22 magazine stories he had chosen not to collect in one of his books. By late summer, the group had completed an initial run of an illegal two-volume set of paperbacks, poorly produced, titled, *The Complete Uncollected Short Stories of J. D. Salinger.* The books were sold to San Francisco Bay Area bookstores that, in turn, sold them openly, although pirated editions. Salinger readers, without having to consult libraries with extensive back files, could now, for $3 to

$5 a volume, read 21 stories: "The Young Folks," "Go See Eddie," "The Hang of It," "The Heart of a Broken Story," "The Long Debut of Lois Taggett," "Personal Notes on an Infantryman," "The Varioni Brothers," "Both Parties Concerned," "Soft-Boiled Sergeant," "Last Day of the Last Furlough," "Once a Week Won't Kill You," "A Boy in France," "Elaine," "This Sandwich Has No Mayonnaise," "The Stranger," "I'm Crazy," "Slight Rebellion Off Madison," "A Young Girl in 1941 with No Waist at All," "The Inverted Forest," "A Girl I Knew," "Blue Melody"—all published between 1940 to 1948—in addition to Salinger's most recent work, the June 19, 1965, story, "Hapworth 16, 1924." Selling at a good rate, the volumes were then reprinted in a more attractive manner and were hawked to bookstores in other major American cities. By the time Salinger got wind of the enterprise, approximately 25,000 copies had been sold. Salinger filed a lawsuit against certain bookstores for selling the bootleg books. Two detectives were hired by Salinger's lawyers in an effort to locate the elusive publisher. The search for a "John Greenberg" was joined by the FBI, but to no avail.

On November 2, 1974, Salinger granted his first interview in 21 years. Lacey Fosburgh, the San Francisco–based correspondent for the *New York Times,* had left a request for an interview with Salinger's agent. To the reporter's surprise, Salinger phoned and spoke for a half hour. He condemned the theft of his stories but asserted he wasn't "trying to hide the gaucheries of my youth. I just don't think they're worthy of publishing . . . I wanted them to die a perfectly natural death" (Fosburgh 69). In answer to Fosburgh's question of whether he intended to publish soon, Salinger said, "Publishing is a terrible invasion of my privacy. I like to write. I love to write. But I write just for myself and my own pleasure" (Fosburgh 1). He also revealed that he didn't "necessarily intend to publish posthumously" (Fosburgh 69). Salinger, who had for all intents and purposes dropped out of the limelight with the 1963 publication of his last book, *Raise High the Roof Beam, Carpenters and Seymour: An Introduction,* awoke the next morning to his interview on the front page of the *New York Times.* The piece of journalism reverberated across literary America.

In hindsight, Salinger's November 1974 interview ended his nine-year disappearance from the American scene. Though Salinger concluded the interview with the statement, "I just want all this to stop. It's intrusive. I've survived a lot of things . . . and I'll probably survive this" (Fosburgh 69), he and his work would be in the news for the next 35 years.

Salinger myths, rumors, sightings, and "meetings" began to proliferate. In April 1976, the *Soho Weekly News* ran a story by John Calvin Batchelor, asserting that Salinger had stopped publishing under his own name. Batchelor proposed the farfetched thesis that the equally reclusive Thomas Pynchon could be identified as J. D. Salinger. February 1977 brought the publication of an unsigned story, "For Rupert—with No Promises," in *Esquire*. The media mistakenly leapt to the false conclusion that Salinger was its author. Gordon Lish, an *Esquire* editor, later revealed that he himself had written the story. In June 1978, Salinger's attendance at a testimonial dinner for John L. Keenan, a friend from World War II, was considered newsworthy by newspapers and weeklies alike. On January 1, 1979, Salinger turned 60 years old. Dorothy Olding, his trusted, longtime agent, was quoted in the *New York Times* as saying that the author was "working right ahead. He just writes and keeps it there" ("Notes on People" 22). Concurrently, Salinger was being actively sought out by his readers. Greg Herriges, a high school English teacher, had traveled to Cornish in the summer of 1978. The January 1979 issue of *Oui* magazine ran Herriges's article, "Ten Minutes with J. D. Salinger," in which Salinger explains, "Contact with the public hinders my work. . . . Everything I have to say is in my fiction" (Herriges 1979, 129). *Newsweek*, in its July 30, 1979, issue, quoted a college-age couple who had been seen talking with Salinger: "He told us not to take anybody's advice, including his, and that it's very important to read" (Keerdoja 13).

In November 1979, Michael Clarkson, a young reporter and struggling writer, traveled to Cornish to seek Salinger's advice. Afterward, he wrote an article about his visit for the *Niagara Falls Review*. During the meeting, Clarkson identifies himself as a reporter. Salinger replies, "I've made my stand clear. I'm a private person. Why can't my life be

my own? I never asked for this and I have done absolutely nothing to deserve it. . . . When I started in this business I had no idea this was going to happen. In ways, I regret ever having been published; it's the insanest profession" (Clarkson 52–53). After Clarkson explains that he wants to be a fiction writer, Salinger remarks, "You can't teach somebody how to write. It's the blind leading the blind" (Clarkson 53). The Clarkson interview was given increased exposure when *People* magazine ran an article in its February 25, 1980, issue, titled "A Young Writer Brings the World a Message from J. D. Salinger: 'Go Away.'"

A year later, Clarkson returned to Cornish. During that encounter, Clarkson remarks that Salinger's writing forms "attachments in its readers"; Salinger replies, "I can't be held responsible. There are no legal obligations. I have nothing to answer for" (Clarkson 61). When asked why he abandoned his fans by stopping publishing, Salinger explains, "Being a public writer interferes with my right to a private life. I write for myself" (Clarkson 61).

In the summer of 1980, Salinger gave an extended interview to Betty Eppes. Eppes left a note for Salinger at his post office explaining she had traveled from Baton Rouge, Louisiana, to talk with him. She added the detail that she was "tall with green eyes and red-gold hair" (Eppes 228) and would wait for him the next day. If he didn't show up, she would leave and not bother him. Salinger appeared at the appointed hour. Eppes proceeded to ask the author questions, scribbling down his replies while surreptitiously tape recording the conversation. In answer to Eppes's question of whether there would be a sequel to *The Catcher in the Rye*, Salinger said, "It's all in the book. Read the book again, it's all in there. Holden Caulfield is only a frozen moment in time" (Eppes 232). When asked if he had consciously chosen writing as a career, Salinger confessed, "I don't know. (A long pause.) I truly don't. I just don't know" (Eppes 233). Eppes also asked the author if he intended to publish again, and relates that "Salinger said he had *no* plans to publish. *Writing* was what was important to him—and to be left alone so that he could write. To be left in peace. He couldn't tell me *why* he felt he wanted to be left in peace . . . but that he felt that way in grade school, at the academy, and before and after military service. And he felt it now, too" (Eppes 233). The conversation ranged over multiple topics: Salinger didn't believe an author should give autographs; he did believe in organic foods. Though he wasn't interested in politics, he had his own idea of the American Dream and that men and women should pursue their own version of it. When Eppes asked if she could take a close-up photo of the author, Salinger firmly declined. Eppes initially published a short newspaper article about her meeting with Salinger; in 1981, a greatly expanded version appeared in the summer issue of the *Paris Review*, gaining widespread notice.

The tragic intersection of Salinger's work with an obsessed fan took place in New York City on December 8, 1980. Mark David Chapman, imagining himself to be Holden Caulfield, murdered the former Beatle John Lennon. After shooting Lennon four times in the back, Chapman calmly sat down on the curb and began to read his copy of *The Catcher in the Rye*. The delusional Chapman later claimed that the novel explained why he had killed Lennon and exonerated him from murder. "To prove it, during his sentencing hearing, Chapman read out loud in the courtroom the famous 'catcher in the rye' speech from Salinger's book" (Alexander 271). Chapman was sentenced to 20 years to life in prison. He remains incarcerated in Attica State Prison in New York State.

Rumors of Salinger publishing under a different name continued to surface. In February 1981, one such claim identified the author as writing under the pseudonym of William Wharton. Both Wharton's and Salinger's agents issued denials.

In 1982, Salinger, now 63, began to date the 37-year-old actress Elaine Joyce. Salinger traveled to Jacksonville, Florida, to see Joyce perform in a dinner theatre production. Later that year, Elaine Joyce was quoted as saying, "Salinger has accumulated enough manuscripts to fill two safes and will permit at least one to be published in 1983" (Sloan A-1).

W. P. Kinsella's novel *Shoeless Joe*, which features a character named "J. D. Salinger" being kidnapped and taken to a baseball game, was published in 1982. While the book was being made into a movie, Salinger's lawyers successfully pressured the producers to change the name of the Salinger character. In 1983, Gordon Lish published a prize-winning story, "For Jeromé—with Love and Kisses," ostensibly a long letter from Sol Salinger to his son, pleading with him to revert back to his given name, Jerome David, instead of using the initials J. D. In the story, Sol believes that the initials stand in the way of his son's receiving the Nobel Prize in literature.

An effort to identify unknown and pseudonymous Salinger works occurred in the November–December 1985 issue of the *Saturday Review*, in which an article suggests that Salinger had published two long autobiographical pieces in 1970 and 1971 in a small literary journal, the *Phoenix*, under the name of Giles Weaver.

Though the number of academic articles on Salinger were few from 1975 to 1985, several critical books were published: Gerald Rosen's *Zen in the Art of J. D. Salinger* (1977), James Lundquist's *J. D. Salinger* (1979) in Ungar's Modern Literature Monographs series, Eberhard Alsen's *Salinger's Glass Stories as a Composite Novel* (1983), the first book devoted solely to the Glass family, and Jack R. Sublette's definitive bibliography, *J. D. Salinger: An Annotated Bibliography, 1938–1981* (1984).

Ian Hamilton, a respected English poet, editor, and biographer, began work on the first biography of J. D. Salinger in 1983. Hamilton informed Salinger of his project and asked for his cooperation. After receiving Salinger's adamant refusal, the biographer decided to restrict his book to Salinger's life through 1965, the year in which the author ceased publishing. Hamilton acknowledged that Salinger's decision to cease publication of his work signaled a withdrawal into a private life, and the biographer felt it unfair, a breach of privacy, to proceed beyond that year. Hamilton contacted Salinger's old classmates at Valley Forge Military Academy and Ursinus College and received numerous responses. He also solicited cooperation from Salinger's friends and colleagues, but he was for the most part unsuccessful. While conducting his research in university and publisher archives, Hamilton discovered several caches of unpublished Salinger letters. The majority were addressed to Whit Burnett, Elizabeth

Murray, Hamish Hamilton, and Judge Learned Hand. The biographer pieced together the existing known facts of Salinger's life and incorporated a substantial number of direct quotations from the Salinger letters. The 207-page biography, titled *J. D. Salinger: A Writing Life,* did not pursue any controversial aspect of Salinger's private life. In May 1986, 150 bound galleys of the biography were sent to reviewers. One of the bound galleys, which was subsequently sold to a book dealer, made its way into Salinger's hands. Later that month, Hamilton and his publisher, Random House, were informed that Salinger requested that the quotations from his unpublished letters be excised from the book or he would sue to stop publication. That summer, Hamilton complied with Salinger's request by closely paraphrasing nearly all of the quotations. In the meantime, Salinger moved to copyright all of the letters in question. When the revised version of the book was sent to Salinger and his lawyers, Hamilton and Random House believed the author would be placated. To their surprise, on October 3, 1986, the author sued to stop publication of the biography, citing copyright infringement. On October 10, Salinger traveled to New York City to be deposed for the lawsuit, where he answered questions for six hours. Most of Salinger's deposition was put under seal. However, the author's answer to the lawyer's question of how would he describe the nature of his writing over the past 20 years became public. Salinger replied, "Just a work of fiction. That's all. That's the only description I can really give it. . . . It's almost impossible to define. I work with characters, and as they develop, I just go from there" (Hamilton 1988, 202). The court's initial ruling upheld Hamilton, though the judge allowed Salinger's lawyers to appeal. On January 29, 1987, the Federal Appeals Court in Manhattan ruled in Salinger's favor and blocked publication of the biography. The ruling shocked many biographers and publishers alike, since it was seen to overturn the accepted practice of "fair use" of unpublished materials, and especially since the biographer had deleted the direct quotations and had substituted paraphrases. Hamilton and his publisher were left with only the U.S. Supreme Court as a last resort. On October 5, 1987, the

Supreme Court declined to hear the case and the decision stood: *J. D. Salinger: A Writing Life* could not be published. During the months of litigation, the case had attracted extensive ongoing coverage in the news media. Salinger had not received such a degree of media attention since September 1961, when he had published *Franny and Zooey* and appeared on the cover of *Time* magazine. The 150 review copies of Hamilton's thwarted book instantaneously became very expensive collectors' items.

1988–PRESENT

Biographies and Memoirs Published, Renewed Academic Interest, a Cultural Icon

Ian Hamilton substantially revised his biography to comply with the court's decision and revamped it to reflect his quest to write about Salinger. In 1988, *In Search of J. D. Salinger* appeared in bookstores. Though it contained useful testimonies of Salinger's Valley Forge and Ursinus classmates, descriptions of some early Salinger writings at the two schools, Hamilton's inside explication of the lawsuit, and a gathering of already-known but disparate information on Salinger, the biography did not create a full picture of him.

In the late 1980s and early 1990s, several lesser events occurred in Salinger's life that received media attention. William Shawn's dismissal from the editorship of the *New Yorker* in 1987 was followed by Salinger's assenting to have his name added as a signer to the letter of protest. Salinger's agent, Dorothy Olding, suffered a stroke in 1990, and her assistant, Phyllis Westberg, took her place as Salinger's agent. Brandeis University withdrew an award to Salinger at his request, and one of the judges, the author Harold Brodkey, commented, "His [Salinger's] is the most influential body of work in English prose by anyone since Hemingway" (Brozan 26). On October 23, 1992, a fire damaged half of Salinger's house. The fire was reported by a woman identifying herself as his wife, COLLEEN SALINGER. The fate of Salinger's manuscripts in the fire was not made known to the public.

The controversy over the Hamilton biography had sparked renewed interest in Salinger's works. In 1987, Harold Bloom edited the first of his numerous collections of essays on Salinger. In

1988, Warren French published his second book on the author, *J. D. Salinger, Revisited. An Adventure in Vedanta: J. D. Salinger's The Glass Family,* by Som P. Ranchan, was published in India in 1989. A compendium of essays covering four decades of criticism on *The Catcher in the Rye* was edited by Joel Salzberg in 1990. In 1991, to celebrate the 40th anniversary of the publication of *The Catcher in the Rye,* a new collection of essays was commissioned and published. Also in 1991, the Twayne series, Studies in Short Fiction, published John Wenke's *J. D. Salinger: A Study of the Short Fiction.* In 1992, Elizabeth N. Kurian's *A Religious Response to the Existential Dilemma in the Fiction of J. D. Salinger* was published in India. And in 1993, Sanford Pinsker's *The Catcher in the Rye: Innocence under Pressure* was published in the series Twayne's Masterwork Studies.

Salinger and his work have been welcomed by the age of the Internet. In November 1995, the Holden Server appeared on the World Wide Web. Created by Luke Seemann, the Web site offered random quotes from *The Catcher in the Rye* when the viewer clicked on the icon of a red hunting hat. In late 1995, a listserv named bananafish became home to a lively discussion of all things Salingerian. On June 27, 1996, however, Seemann received notification from Harold Ober and Associates (Salinger's literary agency) informing that he was in violation of Salinger's copyright in posting the quotes. Seemann complied by removing the material, though he posted his e-mail exchanges with Ober on his Web site. Sites on the World Wide Web have been periodically policed by Salinger's representatives for copyright infraction, especially for the appearance of his uncollected stories.

The next flare-up between Salinger and the media also originated on the Web. Amazon.com, in late 1996, began to take orders for a forthcoming book, titled *Hapworth 16, 1924.* The book, simply a reprint of the 1965 *New Yorker* story, was to be published by a small press, Orchises, run by Roger Lathbury, an English professor. On November 15, an article appeared in the print media about the release of *Hapworth 16, 1924.* Soon articles proliferated, and orders for the book steadily increased at Amazon.com. By early February 1997, prepub-

lication orders for the book had made it the third-largest seller at Amazon.com, with its release due in March. The question of why the author would publish the piece in book form, 32 years after its initial publication in a magazine, began to be asked. Was Salinger testing the waters for the possible release of a new work, or simply tidying up his past publications, wanting to assure that his final Glass story would remain accessible? On February 20, 1997, Michiko Kakutani published a major review of the story and, by extension, of the Glass works, in the *New York Times.* Kakutani criticized the story, and the Glasses, and, like the majority of literary critics before her, lamented that the author had not remained in these pieces "the infinitely engaging author of *The Catcher in the Rye*" (Kakutani C-19). The March 1997 publication date for *Hapworth 16, 1924* passed without the book's release. Without explanation by Lathbury, the book seemingly entered into limbo. In 2002, Amazon.com rescinded all prepublication orders. (After Salinger's death in 2010, Lathbury finally revealed how he almost published *Hapworth 16, 1924,* and how the deal fell through after he "foolishly gave an interview" [Shapira C-1].)

As the possibility of a Salinger book faded, the publication of Joyce Maynard's memoir, *At Home in the World* (1998), captured the media's attention. The personal memoir offered a firsthand glimpse into Salinger's private post-divorce life in Cornish. Maynard devoted a substantial section of her book to her 1972–73 affair with Salinger, who had begun courting her when he was 53 and she 18. Maynard's account began the tarnishing of Salinger's reputation as a gurulike figure with a portion of the reading public. The question of whether Maynard's publishing the book during Salinger's lifetime constituted an invasion of his privacy became an issue in the literary and media worlds.

During the next year, 1999, Salinger was increasingly discussed in the news. The second biography of the author appeared: Paul Alexander's *Salinger: A Biography.* Alexander had utilized the recently available *New Yorker* Archives and the Ian Hamilton Working Papers now located at Princeton University (which Hamilton had gathered for his biography). While Hamilton for the most part did not dwell on Salinger's private life, Alexander did so and moreover presented a jaundiced view of aspects of Salinger's behavior. Alexander argued that Salinger had consciously manipulated his public. "By cutting himself off from the public . . . he made sure the public would remain fascinated with him. By refusing to publish any new work, by letting the public know he had new work but was not publishing, he ensured a continued fascination in the four books that were in print. . . . To guarantee that there was no way the public could forget him, he periodically surfaced in the press" (Alexander 301–302). Alexander flatly refused to believe that Salinger had continued writing after the publication of "Hapworth 16, 1924." He also asserted, "In his life and in his fiction, one obsession of Salinger's was becoming clear. As Salinger aged . . . he remained attracted to young women . . ." (Alexander 180). The biography had been released by a small West Coast publisher, after the large established publishing houses passed on it possibly for fear of litigation on Salinger's part. Alexander's publisher did not issue any reviewers' copies, and the book was largely overlooked in the wake of Maynard's memoir.

Also in 1999, Maynard offered for auction the 14 letters she had received from Salinger over the period of their relationship. Her action reignited the controversy over whether Salinger had exploited her when she was a very young woman, or whether Maynard was now exploiting Salinger. The letters were purchased by Peter Norton, a software entrepreneur, for $156,500. Norton then offered to return the letters to Salinger or to destroy them. Their final resting place is not known. The paperback edition of Maynard's memoir was issued in 1999. In its afterword, Maynard defends her publication of *At Home in the World.*

Another media incursion on Salinger's privacy occurred when the BBC broadcast, in March 1999, an unauthorized documentary on Salinger's life, titled *J. D. Salinger Doesn't Want to Talk.* A film crew caught Salinger on tape while he was walking in town. Footage of his house and surrounding land, as well as interviews with townspeople and assorted people associated with Salinger, were likewise included. One of Salinger's former neigh-

bors, Jerry Burt, was quoted as saying that the author told him he had "15 or 16 books finished but that he didn't know if they would be published" (Brooks 3).

The final and deepest breach of Salinger's privacy, during the period of 1997 to 2000, occurred when his daughter, Margaret Ann, published her memoir, *Dream Catcher,* about the Salinger family. Using her mother, Claire, and Salinger's sole sibling, Doris, as sources, in addition to her own memories and research, Margaret Ann provides the most intimate version of Salinger's life to date. Salinger's childhood, his war experiences, his first wife, Sylvia, the courtship of Claire, and his religious and writing struggles—all events before Margaret Ann's birth—are covered in the book as well. Margaret Ann describes her parents' child-rearing techniques, the two Salinger homes, the unraveling of the Salingers' marriage, and the depiction of Salinger later as a single father. The memoir confirms that Salinger continued to write and devised a color-coded system for his unpublished stories: "a red mark [means], if I die before I finish my work, publish this 'as is,' blue [means] publish but edit first, and so on" (Margaret A. Salinger 307). After *Dream Catcher*'s publication, Salinger's son, Matthew, wrote a letter to the *New York Observer* in which he protested Margaret Ann's depiction of their childhood in Cornish: "I can't say with any authority that she is consciously making anything up. I just know that I grew up in a very different house, with two very different parents from those my sister describes" (Malcolm 22).

The media attention given to the ghost book, *Hapworth 16, 1924;* Maynard's memoir, *At Home in the World;* Maynard's auctioning of Salinger's love letters, and her subsequent defense of her actions in the paperback edition of the book; and Margaret Ann Salinger's memoir about the Salinger family all helped stimulate renewed attention in Salinger's work between the years 1998 and 2002. Books on Salinger, to an unprecedented amount, were published during this period: *Readings on The Catcher in the Rye,* edited by Steven Engel (1998); a pirated edition of Salinger's uncollected stories, *Twenty-two Stories,* by Train Bridge Recluse (1998); *Understanding The Catcher in the*

Rye: A Student Casebook to Issues, Sources and Historical Documents, by Sanford and Ann Pinsker (1999); *J. D. Salinger,* edited and with an introduction by Harold Bloom, in Chelsea House's Bloom's Major Short Story Writers series (1999); *In Cold Fear: The Catcher in the Rye Censorship Controversies and Postwar American Character,* by Pamela Hunt Steinle (2000); *J. D. Salinger's The Catcher in the Rye,* edited and with an introduction by Harold Bloom, in Chelsea House's Modern Critical Interpretations series (2000); *The Fiction of J. D. Salinger: A Study in the Concept of Man,* by Subhash Chandra (2000); *The Catcher in the Rye,* by John C. Unrue, in Gale Group's Literary Masterpieces series (2001); *With Love and Squalor: 14 Writers Respond to the Work of J. D. Salinger,* edited by Kip Kotzen and Thomas Beller (2001); *A Reader's Guide to J. D. Salinger,* by Eberhard Alsen (2002); *The Catcher in the Rye: New Essays,* edited by J. P. Steed (2002); *An Annotated Bibliography, 1982–2002, of J. D. Salinger,* by Brett E. Weaver (2002); *J. D. Salinger,* edited and with an introduction by Harold Bloom, in Chelsea House's Bloom's BioCritiques series (2002); *Letters to J. D. Salinger,* edited by Chris Kubica and Will Hochman (2002); and *J. D. Salinger,* by John C. Unrue, in Gale Group's Literary Masters series (2002).

The year 2001 marked the 50th anniversary of the publication of *The Catcher in the Rye.* At Salinger's request, the date passed unmarked by the book's publisher, Little, Brown and Company. The 50th anniversary of the publication of *Nine Stories* was marked in 2003. Dominic Smith notes in a critical essay discussing the volume, "Not since Hemingway's *In Our Time* had a collection of stories so raised the bar on the form, creating characters and scenes that were hypnotic, mysterious, and unusually powerful" (Dominic Smith 639). In 2005, Salinger's publishing silence reached 40 years since "Hapworth 16, 1924"'s appearance in the June 19, 1965, issue of the *New Yorker.* In the same year, Myles Weber's *Consuming Silences: How We Read Authors Who Don't Publish* was released, with a long chapter on Salinger. A few years earlier, a journalist, Ron Rosenbaum, had suggested, "the Wall of Silence [Salinger had] built around himself, around his work—was in a way his most

powerful, most eloquent, perhaps his most lasting work of art" (Rosenbaum 65).

On January 1, 2009, Salinger turned 90 years old. His birthday was noted in the press worldwide. Five months later, Salinger was back in the spotlight: An unauthorized sequel to *The Catcher in the Rye* was published by a small press in London. *60 Years Later: Coming through the Rye,* by the pseudonymous author John David California, featured a 76-year-old narrator named "Mr. C." "Mr. C" leaves his nursing home in upstate New York to return to New York City to revisit people, including his sister, Phoebe, and places from his past. On June 1, 2009, Salinger's lawyers filed a complaint seeking an injunction against the sale and distribution of the sequel in America. Salinger's lawyers asserted his copyright of the character, Holden

J. D. Salinger in October 1950. One of several photos taken by Lotte Jacobi in a sitting for the first-edition dust jacket of *The Catcher in the Rye* (© The Lotte Jacobi Collection, University of New Hampshire)

Caulfield, and his right to *not* write a sequel. Phyllis Westberg, Salinger's agent, revealed in an affidavit that Salinger, though in ill health, was aware of the legal action. Westberg estimated that were Salinger to write a sequel to *The Catcher in the Rye*, the novel would command a $5 million advance. With the matter before Judge Deborah Batts, the author of *60 Years Later: Coming through the Rye* identified himself as Fredrik Colting, a 33-year-old Swede, the cofounder of a small Swedish publishing house. Colting, the author of several books of humor, said *60 Years Later* was his first novel. Colting's lawyers tried to defend his book by describing it as parody and denying that it was a sequel to *The Catcher in the Rye*. The lawyers asserted that Colting's book critiqued Salinger's relationship with Holden Caulfield—noting Colting's use of a character named Salinger—and they sought protection to publish in America under the doctrine of fair use. On July 1, 2009, Judge Batts ruled in Salinger's favor and issued a temporary order against the publication and distribution of *60 Years Later: Coming through the Rye* in America. (The ruling did not affect sales outside of the United States.) In September 2009, Colting's appeal was heard by the U.S. Second Circuit Court of Appeals. On April 30, 2010, that court, in general agreement with Judge Batts's ruling in Salinger's favor, returned the case to her for additional consideration. (As of June 2010, no decision has been announced.)

Significantly, Salinger's original complaint revealed that the author, in July 2008, had created the J. D. Salinger Literary Trust, of which he was sole trustee during his lifetime. Apart from signing over his copyrights to the trust, no other information was divulged. The existence of the trust strongly suggests that Salinger took legal steps to ensure that his wishes regarding posthumous publication are followed.

On January 27, 2010, Jerome David Salinger, one of America's greatest writers of the 20th century, died of natural causes at his home in Cornish, New Hampshire, at the age of 91. The author's death commanded worldwide notice, and a flurry of Salinger-related events followed in its wake. (See the Salinger chronology in Part IV for a full accounting.) Intense speculation about the existence of unpublished manuscripts and their possible publication proliferated. Salinger's representatives, however, steadfastly refused comment. (As of mid-April 2010, no official announcements have been made concerning the author's literary estate.) Nonetheless, any unpublished writings by Salinger that may be published in the future—if, in fact, he actually authorized the future release of new works through the J. D. Salinger Literary Trust—will possibly reshape the assessment of his work and perhaps further illuminate aspects of his life.

FURTHER READING

Alexander, Paul. *Salinger: A Biography*. Los Angeles: Renaissance Books, 1999.

Baro, Gene. "Some Suave and Impressive Slices of Life." *New York Herald Tribune Book Review*, 12 April 1953, p. 6.

Behrman, S. N. "The Vision of the Innocent." *New Yorker*, 11 August 1951, 71–76.

Bishop, Elizabeth. *One Art: Letters*. New York: Farrar, Straus & Giroux, 1994.

Blaney, Shirlie. "Twin State Telescope: Interview with an Author." *Daily Eagle*, 13 November 1953, editorial page.

Brooks, Richard. "J. D. Salinger 'Has 15 New Books in Safe.'" *Sunday Times*, 21 March 1999, p. 3.

Brozan, Nadine. "J. D. Salinger Receives an Apology for an Award." *New York Times*, 27 April 1991, p. 26.

Bryan, James. "Salinger and His Short Fiction." Ph.D. diss., University of Virginia, 1968.

Burger, Nash K. "Books of The Times." *New York Times*, 16 July 1951, p. 19.

Burnett, Hallie, and Whit Burnett. *Fiction Writer's Handbook*. New York: Harper & Row, 1975.

California, John David [Fredrik Colting]. *60 Years Later: Coming through the Rye*. London: Windupbird Publishing, 2009.

Clarkson, Michael. "Catching the 'Catcher in the Rye,' J. D. Salinger" [originally published in *Niagara Falls Review*, November 1979]. In *If You Really Want to Hear about It: Writers on J. D. Salinger and His Work*, edited by Catherine Crawford, 49–62. New York: Thunder's Mouth Press, 2006.

"Contributors." *Story* 16 (March–April 1940): 2.

———. *Story* 25 (November–December 1944): 1.

"A Dark Horse." *Virginia Kirkus' Bookshop Service*, 15 May 1951, 247.

Dempsey, David. "Ten Best-Selling Authors Make Their Holiday Choices." *New York Times Book Review,* 2 December 1951, p. 244.

Elfin, Mel. "The Mysterious J. D. Salinger . . . His Woodsy, Secluded Life." *Newsweek,* 30 May 1960, 92–94.

Eppes, Betty. "What I Did Last Summer." *Paris Review* 23 (Summer 1981): 221–239.

Faulkner, William. "A Word to Young Writers." In *Faulkner in the University: Class Conferences at the University of Virginia 1957–1958,* edited by Frederick L. Gwynn and Joseph L. Blotner, 244–248. Charlottesville: University of Virginia Press, 1959.

Fiene, Donald M. "A Bibliographical Study of J. D. Salinger: Life, Work and Reputation." Master's thesis, University of Louisville, 1961.

———. "J. D. Salinger: A Bibliography." *Wisconsin Studies in Contemporary Literature* 4, no. 1 (Winter 1963): 109–149.

Fosburgh, Lacey. "J. D. Salinger Speaks about His Silence." *New York Times,* 3 November 1974, pp. 1, 69.

French, Warren. *J. D. Salinger.* New York: Twayne Publishers, 1963.

———. *J. D. Salinger, Revisited.* New York: Twayne Publishers, 1988.

Goodman, Anne L. "Mad about Children." *New Republic,* 16 July 1951, 20–21.

Gwynn, Frederick L., and Joseph L. Blotner. *The Fiction of J. D. Salinger.* Pittsburgh: University of Pittsburgh Press, 1958.

Hamilton, Ian. *In Search of J. D. Salinger.* New York: Random House, 1988.

———. *J. D. Salinger: A Writing Life.* New York: Random House, 1986 [bound galleys; book publication blocked by Salinger].

Hassan, Ihab. "The Casino of Silence." *Saturday Review,* 26 January 1963, 38.

———. *The Dismemberment of Orpheus: Toward a Postmodern Literature.* New York: Oxford University Press, 1971.

———. "Rare Quixotic Gesture: The Fiction of J. D. Salinger." *Western Review* 21 (Summer 1957): 261–280.

Hazard, Eloise P. "Eight Fiction Finds." *Saturday Review,* 16 February 1952, 16–18.

Heiserman, Arthur, and James E. Miller, Jr. "J. D. Salinger: Some Crazy Cliff." *Western Humanities Review* 10 (Spring 1956): 129–137.

Herriges, Greg. *JD: A Memoir of a Time and a Journey.* La Grande, Oreg.: Wordcraft of Oregon, 2006.

———. "Ten Minutes with J. D. Salinger." *Oui,* January 1979, 86–88, 126–130.

Hicks, Granville. "Another Look at the Deserving." *Saturday Review,* 23 December 1961, 18.

Howe, Irving. "More Reflections in the Glass Mirror." *New York Times Book Review,* 7 April 1963, pp. 4–5, 34.

Kakutani, Michiko. "From Salinger, A New Dash of Mystery." *New York Times,* 20 February 1997, pp. C-15, C-19.

Kazin, Alfred. "J. D. Salinger: 'Everybody's Favorite'" [originally published in *The Atlantic,* August 1961]. In *If You Really Want to Hear about It: Writers on J. D. Salinger and His Work,* edited by Catherine Crawford, 109–119. New York: Thunder's Mouth Press, 2006.

Keerdoja, E., and P. E. Simons. "The Dodger in the Rye." *Newsweek,* 30 July 1979, 11, 13.

Kukil, Karen V., ed. *The Unabridged Journals of Sylvia Plath.* New York: Anchor Books, 2000.

Kunitz, Stanley J., and Vineta Colby, eds. *Twentieth Century Authors.* New York: H. W. Wilson, 1955.

Limmer, Ruth, ed. *What the Woman Lived: Selected Letters of Louise Bogan, 1920–1970.* New York: Harcourt, Brace, Jovanovich, 1973.

Longstreth, T. Morris. "New Novels in the News." *Christian Science Monitor,* 19 July 1951, p. 11.

Mailer, Norman. *Advertisements for Myself.* New York: G. P. Putnam's Sons, 1959.

———. "Some Children of the Goddess." *Esquire,* July 1963, 64–69, 105.

Malcolm, Janet. "Justice to J. D. Salinger." *New York Review of Books,* 21 June 2001, pp. 16, 18–22.

Matis, Jim. "'The Catcher in the Rye': Controversy on Novel in Texas Is Just One in Long List of Episodes." *Houston Post,* 4 May 1961, sec. 7, p. 6.

Maxwell, William. "J. D. Salinger." *Book-of-the-Month Club News,* July 1951, 5–6.

Maynard, Joyce. *At Home in the World: A Memoir.* New York: Picador, 1998.

McGrath, Charles. "J. D. Salinger, Author Who Fled Fame, Dies at 91." *New York Times,* 29 January 2010, pp. A-1, A-16, A-17.

Miller, James E., Jr. *J. D. Salinger.* Minneapolis: University of Minnesota Press, 1965.

"The No-Nonsense Kids." *Time,* 18 November 1957, 51–52, 54.

"Notes on People: J. D. Salinger Privately Passes a Milestone." *New York Times,* 1 January 1979, p. 22.

Pillsbury, Frederick. "Mysterious J. D. Salinger: The Untold Chapter of the Famous Writer's Years as a Valley Forge Cadet." *Sunday Bulletin Magazine,* 29 October 1961, 23–24.

Poore, Charles. "Books of The Times." *New York Times,* 9 April 1953, p. 25.

Rosenbaum, Ron. "The Catcher in the Driveway" [originally published as "The Man in the Glass House" in *Esquire,* June 1997]. In *If You Really Want to Hear about It: Writers on J. D. Salinger and His Work,* edited by Catherine Crawford, 63–87. New York: Thunder's Mouth Press, 2006.

Roth, Philip. "Writing American Fiction." In *Reading Myself and Others,* 117–135. New York: Farrar, Straus & Giroux, 1975.

Salinger, Margaret A. *Dream Catcher: A Memoir.* New York: Washington Square Press, 2000.

Shapira, Ian. "For a Very Brief While, J. D. Salinger Returned His Calls." *Washington Post,* 29 January 2010, p. C-1.

Skow, Jack. "Sonny: An Introduction." *Time,* 15 September 1961, 84–90.

Slawenski, Kenneth. *J. D. Salinger: A Life Raised High.* Hebden Bridge, England: Pomona Books, 2010.

Sloan, Robin Adams. "The Gossip Column." *Washington Post,* 17 October 1982, p. A-1.

Smith, Dominic. "Salinger's *Nine Stories:* Fifty Years Later." *Antioch Review* 61, no. 4 (Fall 2003): 639–649.

Smith, Harrison. "Manhattan Ulysses, Junior." *Saturday Review,* 14 July 1951, 12–13.

Steiner, George. "The Salinger Industry." *Nation,* 14 November 1959, 360–363.

Stern, James. "Aw, the World's a Crumby Place." *New York Times Book Review,* 15 July 1951, p. 5.

Updike, John. "Anxious Days for the Glass Family." *New York Times Book Review,* 17 September 1961, pp. 1, 52.

Walter, Eugene. "A Rainy Afternoon with Truman Capote." *Intro Bulletin* 2 (December 1957): 1–2.

Welty, Eudora. "Threads of Innocence." *New York Times Book Review,* 5 April 1953, p. 4.

Wilson, Edmund. *Letters on Literature and Politics.* New York: Farrar, Straus & Giroux, 1977.

"With Love & 20-20 Vision." *Time,* 16 July 1951, 97.

Wolfe, Tom. "The *New Yorker* Affair." In *Hooking Up,* 247–293. New York: Farrar, Straus & Giroux, 2000.

Yagoda, Ben. *About Town: The New Yorker and the World It Made.* n.p.: Da Capo Press, 2000.

"Youthful Horrors." *Nation,* 18 April 1953, 332.

Part II

Works A–Z

"Are You Banging Your Head Against the Wall?"

"Are You Banging Your Head Against the Wall?" is one of Salinger's "lost" stories, neither published nor to be found in a library archive. According to the bibliographer Jack R. Sublette, Salinger mentions a story with this title in a 1943 letter to WHIT BURNETT. The author adds that the story is under consideration for publication at the NEW YORKER, and that it is about Holden Caulfield. Unless the manuscript can be located among Salinger's literary estate, the story's whereabouts are unknown.

"Birthday Boy"

"Birthday Boy" is an unpublished story, whose nine-page, undated (circa 1946) typescript can be found at the HARRY RANSOM CENTER, at the University of Texas at Austin. "Birthday Boy" is available for on-site reading only. According to the premier Salinger Web site, www.deadcaulfields.com, the story consists of Ethel's tense visit with her boyfriend, Ray, hospitalized for alcoholism.

"Bitsey"

"Bitsey" (sometimes spelled "Bitsy") is one of Salinger's "lost" stories, neither published nor to be found in a library archive. According to the bibliographer Jack R. Sublette, Salinger mentions a story with this title in a 1943 letter to WHIT BURNETT. "Bitsey" was included on the proposed table of contents for Salinger's unpublished book, The YOUNG FOLKS. Unless the manuscript can be located among Salinger's literary estate, the story's whereabouts are unknown.

"Blue Melody"

Appearing in the September 1948 issue of COS-MOPOLITAN, "Blue Melody" portrays the friendship between two white Tennessee children and an African-American blues singer, Lida Louise Jones, as well as the tragic events of her death due to racial discrimination. The story draws loosely on the legendary events surrounding the death of the blues singer Bessie Smith in 1937. "Blue Melody" is Salinger's 24th published story. The author, however, chose not to include the story in his three books of collected stories.

SYNOPSIS

The unnamed narrator, addressing the reader in a first-person voice from the vantage point of 1948, explains the circumstances in which he finds himself in 1944 during wartime, aboard a GI truck en route from Luxembourg City to Halzhoffen, Germany. Jammed into the overcrowded truck with 40 men who have recently been released from hospitals in England (and who are now, although not yet fully recovered, en route to the front again as infantry), he realizes that the soldiers are to serve under a certain general known mostly for his bravado. The general, who "seldom stepped into his command car without wearing a Luger and a photographer, one on each side" (51), is concerned only with keeping his image intact and thus is hesitant to surrender to the enemy, even when outnumbered. The narrator, understanding that most of these men may lose their lives in battle as a consequence, rides for hours "without looking anybody in the truck very straight in the eye" (51).

The soldiers sing "spirited war songs" (51) during the day to boost their morale, but as night falls and the truck attaches its blackout curtains, the men fall silent, asleep and huddled against the cold. The narrator finds that only one other man besides himself remains vigilant—he is Rudford (the original narrator of the tale about to be told).

The narrator explains to the reader that Rudford (whose surname is never revealed) has a "very slight Southern accent and a chronic foxhole cough" (51) and is wearing a helmet with the "red cross of a captain in the medics" (51). Claiming not to know anything else about Rudford except what "comes naturally out of his story" (51), the narrator also requests that readers not write to the magazine to ask for more information, particularly if those readers believe that the story to be told reflects "a slam against one section of this country" (112). Emphasizing that the story is not "a slam against anybody or anything" (112), the narrator next recounts the story of Rudford (who had recounted to the narrator, in 1944, his story and that of Lida Louise).

At 11 years old, Rudford, from Agersburg, Tennessee (one hour's drive from Memphis), is a precocious boy. His father, a Bostonian typewriter salesman, met a wealthy Agersburg girl during a business trip before World War I, and the two married. When Rudford's mother died in childbirth, his father invested in a local publishing house and became successful as a self-published writer of high school textbooks that enjoyed a wide circulation in the States (the narrator himself had studied from the science textbook in the series while attending high school in Philadelphia in 1932). Quizzed daily by his father—on topics ranging from chromosomes to lima beans to astronomy—Rudford possesses, at age 11, the academic knowledge of a high school freshman. Because of his father's heavy-handed discipline, Rudford is also emotionally isolated. The two most important "footnotes" (112) in Rudford's life, however, are Black Charles and Peggy Moore.

Impressed that Peggy can hide her gum in the hollow of her neck, Rudford steals a moment in the classroom to invite her to meet Black Charles. She accepts, and Rudford takes her to the café (a hamburger joint) that Black Charles runs by day. No one patronizes the café for its food (delicious, nonetheless). They go there because Black Charles plays piano "like somebody from Memphis—maybe even better" (112). The children moreover love Black Charles because he is something that "few white piano players are . . . kind and interested" (112) in them. Charles respects the children's wishes for songs; he listens to them and pays attention to their needs.

Rudford, and now Peggy, are the youngest patrons at the café, going there two to three times a week to hear Black Charles play. (Although he must sleep during daylight hours, the musician does not mind being woken up by the two young admirers.) Rudford grows to admire Peggy, as well, for her tomboyish courage and her camaraderie. The

only problem Rudford finds with Peggy is her tendency to become "lovey-dovey" (112). During the upcoming summer vacation, Rudford and Peggy visit Black Charles every day. The two children grow emotionally close and exchange ambitions: Peggy wants to be a "war nurse. Also a movie actress. Also a piano player. Also a crook" (114); Rudford wants to be "a piano player" (114), but also an auto racer in his spare time. One afternoon at the café (which doubles as a residence), they meet Black Charles's "sister's chile" (114), Lida Louise Jones, a singer.

Lida Louise, a "grown-up girl," wears a "yellow dress and a yellow ribbon in her hair," and smokes a cigarette held between "long, elegant fingers" (114). She is not "a pretty girl" (114) but impresses both Rudford and Peggy with her friendly and forthright manner. Lida Louise guesses that Peggy is sweet on Rudford; Peggy confirms but Rudford denies the attachment. When Lida Louise asks Peggy why she likes Rudford, Peggy responds that she likes "the way he stands at the blackboard" (114). Lida Louise then sings a song that stuns both children.

The narrator interrupts the story at this point to again address the reader, explaining that Rudford, in telling his story of Lida Louise, insisted that her voice could not be described. The narrator had disagreed, telling Rudford that he himself owned most of Lida Louise's recordings and that an attempt to describe her voice could be made: "She had a powerful, soft voice. Every note she sang was detonated individually. She blasted you tenderly to pieces. In saying her voice can't be described, Rudford probably meant that it can't be classified. And that's true" (114).

Rudford's story now continues, recounting that, during Christmas 1926, both he and Peggy attend Lida Louise's opening night at Black Charles's café. Wearing her yellow dress, Lida Louise, accompanied on the piano by her uncle, is an extraordinary success. Peggy cries so hard at Lida Louise's singing that Rudford must take her home. That evening, Rudford tells Peggy that he loves her.

Lida Louise sings at Black Charles's café for the next six months and is eventually discovered by a big record producer from Memphis. Unimpressed by the opportunity, Lida Louise goes to Memphis (Rudford believes) not from ambition but because she hopes to find someone there or to be found by someone. Rudford makes this assumption of Lida Louise's motives based on the events of one evening in the Agersburg café, when a young man from Yale had requested that Lida Louise sing the tune "Slow Train to Jacksonville." Lida Louise, cautiously, questioned where the college man had heard the song. Learning that a fellow in New York had played the tune, Lida Louise asked whether the fellow was a "colored man" (116) named Endicott Wilson and whether the Yale student knew of Endicott's current whereabouts. The young man replied only that the piano player was a small man with a mustache. Lida Louise then played the tune herself and sang the song about "an unfortunate man with the wrong shade of lipstick on his collar" (116).

In Memphis from May to September 1927, Lida Louise gains rapid fame and is quickly picked up by record companies. She attracts attention from the jazz greats of the period, including Louis Armstrong, who comes to Memphis to hear her sing. (Likewise, Joe and Sonny Varioni from Chicago—the fictional jazz duo of Salinger's short story "The VARIONI BROTHERS"—stay two nights in Memphis and write a song for Lida Louise to sing, titled "Soupy Peggy," about "a sentimental little girl who falls in love with a little boy standing at the blackboard in school" [116].) Despite her success, Lida Louise leaves Memphis abruptly after an incident in which, outside the Beale Street studio, she hits a "short well-dressed colored man" (116) in the face with her purse. An hour after the incident, Lida Louise packs to return to Agersburg. Once there, she immediately writes a note to Peggy and Rudford (the note is reproduced in the text) inviting them to visit her and hear her new songs.

Rudford's story comes to a climax with the tragic circumstances surrounding the death of Lida Louise. As Rudford would be leaving for boarding school that same month, September 1927, a farewell picnic is arranged for him by Black Charles, Peggy, Lida Louise, and her mother. As the five friends relax after eating, Lida Louise is suddenly stricken by a pain in her abdomen and screams, writhing in agony. Rudford recognizes that Lida Louise's appendix has burst, and he directs Black Charles to drive quickly to the nearby Samaritan hospital. Black Charles questions Rudford's choice of Samaritan, a private hospital (and therefore for whites only), but Rudford insists and responds: "What's the difference?" (117).

Arriving at the hospital's "great white entrance" (118), Rudford tells the nurse at reception that Lida Louise is dying and must be admitted immediately. The nurse recognizes Lida Louise's name and perfunctorily responds that the hospital does not allow "Negro patients" (118). Rudford returns to the car and orders Charles to drive to another local hospital, Jefferson Memorial. Once there, both children tell the male reception attendant that a lady has burst her appendix. The attendant goes at once to the car but does not initiate any procedure to admit Lida Louise, instead stalling by insisting that the resident surgeon must first be contacted. Rudford realizes that this hospital will likewise refuse to admit Lida Louise because of her race. Rudford directs Charles to drive to Memphis. On the road there, Lida Louise, who is lying with her head on Rudford's lap, opens her eyes as the car stops at a red light. Looking up at Rudford, she asks for Endicott, and Rudford responds, "I'm right here, Honey!" (118). She smiles, closes her eyes, and dies. The unnamed narrator now interrupts to address the reader: "A story never ends. The narrator is usually provided with a nice, artistic spot for his voice to stop, but that's about all" (118).

After Lida Louise's funeral, Rudford departs for boarding school. He does not see Peggy again for 15 years and never returns to Agersburg. In 1942, before entering the army, Rudford sits waiting for a date in the Biltmore Hotel in MANHATTAN (having recently completed a medical residency in the city). He hears a girl's voice with a Tennessee accent and turns to see that the girl is Peggy, who is telling the plot of a Taylor Caldwell novel to her husband, Richard. Peggy spots Rudford and gives him a "warm, if glancing kiss" (119). She introduces Rudford to Richard, a navy flier. The reader then learns of Rudford's perspective on Richard, that he is "eight feet tall, and he had some theater tickets or flying goggles or a lance in one of his hands. Had

Rudford brought a gun along, he would have shot Richard dead on the spot" (119). Peggy reminisces with Rudford about Agersburg and childhood friends, then asks him about Lida Louise, whom she thinks of all the time. Peggy played Lida Louise's records through college, but her copy of "Soupy Peggy" was broken, stepped on by a drunken boy. She has tried, but has not been able, to get another copy. Rudford responds that he has one and asks Peggy if she would like to hear it. She jumps at the chance, but Richard interrupts, reminding her about their appointment. Peggy apologizes to Rudford, imploring him to phone her in the morning, which he promises to do. The reader learns (through the story's narrator) that Rudford does not phone and that he never sees Peggy again: "In the first place, he almost never played the record for *anybody* in 1942. It was terribly scratchy now. It didn't even sound like Lida Louise any more" (119).

CRITICAL ANALYSIS

The narrative structure of "Blue Melody" is one of the most experimental of Salinger's uncollected fiction. An unnamed narrator, from the perspective of 1948, frames the story's events to the reader as he tells the story of Rudford (the original narrator of the story told in 1944), which comprises the story of Lida Louise Jones—the consummate blues singer—and that of her death in 1927. Salinger employs his expertise with a tale-within-the-tale technique—that of the events surrounding the death of Lida Louise—and utilizes the tale to shed light, in turn, on comments made by the unnamed narrator of the story's frame. (Salinger had effectively used the tale-within-the-tale in such uncollected stories as "SOFT-BOILED SERGEANT," "The HEART OF A BROKEN STORY," and "The Varioni Brothers," and would later employ the technique to great effect in "The LAUGHING MAN" of his NINE STORIES collection.)

The kernel story within "Blue Melody"— that of Lida Louise Jones, the blues singer, and of her uncle, Black Charles, a consummate piano player—emphasizes the overwhelming prejudice facing African Americans of the 1920s and 1930s in America's Deep South. The story of Lida Lou-

ise's death, due to the refusal of the whites-only hospitals to admit a nonwhite, even under emergency circumstances, is based on events surrounding the tragic death of Bessie Smith, the Empress of the Blues. (Warren French, in his 1988 study of Salinger's fiction, points out that Lida Louise's death parallels the death of Bessie Smith regarding a whites-only hospital's refusal to admit her after she had suffered a burst appendix [French 1988, 26].) This scenario draws from popular legend arising after Bessie Smith's death in 1937 following her involvement in a car accident while en route to a singing engagement. Although the exact circumstances regarding Bessie Smith's ordeal in facing prejudice at the time of hospital admittance can never be clearly known, the fact that hospitals for whites only did, indeed, exist at the time of the accident is indisputable.

One of the imbedded themes within "Blue Melody" is, moreover, the struggle of the artist to survive in a hostile world. Lida Louise is not only an African American, but she is also a musical artist and a woman. As such, she must overcome racial prejudice, gender bias, and economic obstacles to her success. Salinger, in his story "The Varioni Brothers," had previously sketched a similar portrayal of the artist who faces insurmountable obstacles in the character of Joe Varioni, who, although considered by his mentor to be a true poet, must, because of his brother's ambitions for wealth, agree to write song lyrics for the great financial success of their musical team, but at the expense of his higher literary gift. Joe meets a tragic death (as does Lida Louise) and is prevented (as is she) from reaching his true potential as an artist. A Salinger reader will find "Blue Melody" remarkable, as well, in that the story contains an appearance by the Varioni brothers, Joe and Sonny, who write the song, "Soupy Peggy," for Lida Louise to sing. The meeting of characters from different stories underlines Salinger's interest in meta narration early in his career. "The Varioni Brothers" likewise attempts a narrative structure equally as complex as that of "Blue Melody" by being told from three different narrative perspectives—with the tale-within-the-tale comprising the story of Joe Varioni's death and Sonny's attempt to reassemble Joe's lost novel.

While "Blue Melody" represents Salinger's attack on racial discrimination and an attempt, as well, to raise social consciousness on the issue, the story simultaneously addresses another social injustice—that of the tragic loss of life in World War II. When the unnamed narrator emphasizes that the story about to be told is not a "slam" (51) against any one part of the country (with Salinger's implicit inference that it may be a "slam" against the whole country in its prevailing attitude towards people of color), the narrator, then, follows up his statement by saying that the story is about "Mom's apple pie, ice-cold beer, the Brooklyn Dodgers, and the Lux Theater of the Air—the things we fought for, in short" (112). Warren French points out in his 1963 study of Salinger's fiction: "These were indeed the things that the more sentimental propagandists of the period said that Americans were fighting for, and this story comes close . . . to criticizing the 'phony' heroic pose of a country that fights for freedom abroad and still practices fatal discrimination at home" (French 1963, 90). Most explicitly, in fact, Salinger imbeds in the story his attack on wartime conditions and judgments made by those in authority in the unnamed narrator's comments about the group of soldiers en route to the German front. The narrator points out to the reader that the soldiers have "just got out of hospitals in England, where they had been treated for wounds received in action somewhat earlier in the war. Ostensibly rehabilitated . . ." (51). In other words, these infantry replacements, "ostensibly" (and, therefore, not fully) recovered from their wounds, are nonetheless being sent prematurely into combat at the front. Not only is the unfairness of the military decision observed, but the narrator likewise comments on the bad judgment of the commander-in-charge, who will sacrifice his men to preserve the appearance of victory and to appease his own vanity: "a brigadier general who seldom stepped into his command car without wearing a Luger and a photographer, one on each side" (51). The general, more interested in projecting his heroic image, is prone to refuse defeat "even when outnumbered or surrounded" (51) by the enemy, thus caring little for the loss of life among his troops, but interested only in enhancing his reputation as unvanquished. For this reason, the narrator, who knows of the commander's posturings, cannot look anybody in the eye. The figure of the brigadier general parallels that of Corporal Clay in Salinger's "FOR ESMÉ—WITH LOVE AND SQUALOR" of the *Nine Stories* collection—Clay also is successful at projecting a "phony" heroic image as he is photographed by a national magazine holding two Thanksgiving turkeys after a bloody battle in Hürtgen Forest.

Further antiwar sentiment within "Blue Melody" resides with the narrator's comments about the type of songs being sung by the soldiers to boost their morale. Describing the tunes as "spirited war songs, chiefly, composed by patriotic Broadway song writers" (51), the narrator implies that the sentiments therein are conjured by men who hold very little knowledge of the real circumstances of war, especially having "through some melancholy, perhaps permanently embittering turn of the wheel of fortune . . . been disqualified from taking their places at the front" (51). Salinger's voice cannot be more cynical. (Salinger had previously criticized those who concoct false representations of war in the story "Soft-Boiled Sergeant," in which the protagonist, Philly Burns, condemns the American movies for creating deceptively pretty pictures of heroism and for not representing the harsh realities and true look of sacrifice by genuine heroes like that of his staff sergeant, Burke.) The soldier-singers en route to the front raise their voices, as does the blues singer, Lida Louise, against overwhelming obstacles and inevitable death. Like Lida Louise, the soldiers are victimized by social prejudice—as infantry, they are the most underprivileged rank of the militia, their lives valued as disposable by those in authority. Thus does Salinger portray these singers as the unsung heroes who, in spirit, rise above social iniquity.

"Blue Melody" contains a secondary, yet important, protagonist in the figure of Rudford. In structuring the story with an unnamed narrator who relates its events, Salinger makes visible a dual perspective of Rudford who, although described as the "original narrator" (51) of the story of Lida Louise, may also be viewed as a character within the greater narrative frame. Rudford's story along with that of Lida Louise—told simultaneously by the unnamed narrator of 1948—thus turns "Blue Melody" into a story as much about Rudford as about Lida Louise Jones. The critic Eberhard Alsen, in his study of Salinger's fiction, sees Rudford as a nonconformist: "His non-conformity has to do with the issue of race because Rudford swims against the stream of racism in Southern society when he befriends the piano player Black Charles and his niece, the blues singer Lida Louise" (Alsen 27). Rudford may also be viewed as a prototype Holden Caulfield figure in that he is seen throughout the story as possessing a great need to save or rescue others. For example, during a day spent together, the 11-year-olds, Peggy and Rudford, linger on Miss Packer's Street, where they exchange youthful ambitions. Distracted, Peggy falls from the rafters of a house being newly constructed where the children have perched, and she hits the ground with a thud. Rudford climbs down to inspect her head, pushing back "a hank or two of the patient's lovely black-Irish hair" (114). Rudford is later seen, when the narrator meets him in 1944, in a more classifiable role as a savior of "patients": "The bars and red cross of a captain in the medics were painted . . . on his helmet" (51). Moreover, within the tale of Lida Louise's death, it is Rudford who recognizes the signs of a burst appendix and who attempts in vain to get urgent medical attention for her. The symbolism at story's end extends the portrayal of Rudford as savior. The reader learns that Rudford, in 1942, was still in possession of a copy of Lida Louise's record, "Soupy Peggy." The reader also learns, however, that the record has become "terribly scratchy" (119) and no longer sounds like Lida Louise. Perhaps Rudford's decision not to phone Peggy the next morning after their meeting lies in an acceptance that he has not been able to save that which he has loved. He was not successful in saving Lida Louise from her destiny and likewise has not been able to save the essence of the singer's voice on the record. The reader likewise knows no more of the fate of Rudford, whether he himself has been saved, as the story's unnamed narrator states: "I don't even know if the man is alive today" (51). Rudford is as lost to the narrator as Lida Louise is lost to Rudford.

The theme of loss in "Blue Melody" extends further to that of lost love. For example, Rudford has related to the narrator his suspicions that Lida Louise went to Memphis not to bolster her career but because "she was looking for somebody, or because she wanted somebody to find her" (115)—that "somebody" being her beau, Endicott Wilson, the musician who had played the song "Slow Train to Jacksonville" for the Yale student in New York. The song concerns "an unfortunate man with the wrong shade of lipstick on his collar" (116)—that is, a man discovered by his girlfriend (presumably Lida Louise) in an affair with another woman. Lida Louise, just before she dies, asks for Endicott. She is thus still suffering from her unrequited love for him. Similarly, Rudford suffers from the loss of his childhood love, Peggy Moore. In the NEW YORK CITY meeting of 1942 between Rudford and Peggy and Richard, Rudford's emotional attachment for Peggy makes itself clear: "Had Rudford brought a gun along, he would have shot Richard dead on the spot" (119). Richard proves himself uninterested in Peggy's past as she reminisces about her childhood memories and about Lida Louise: "he listened with an iron smile" (119)—the author implying that Rudford could not save Peggy from her own destiny, perhaps, in marrying a man that will not appreciate her emotional depth.

At story's end, the reader is left with multiple and resonant meanings within "Blue Melody"—a melancholy leitmotif of unrequited love, a subtle lament for lost childhood innocence, and the recurrent notes of the tragic loss of life through racial prejudice and through war. The unnamed narrator confides: "A story never ends. The narrator is usually provided with a nice, artistic spot for his voice to stop, but that's about all" (118). To our chagrin, many "blue" refrains of the inhumanity of our human race continue to play out—both recorded and not on record.

Salinger titled the story "SCRATCHY NEEDLE ON A PHONOGRAPH RECORD." He was overruled by the editors of *Cosmopolitan*, who substituted the title "Blue Melody."

Cosmopolitan illustrated the story with one double-spread drawing—Rudford and Peggy sitting on the café floor, listening to Black Charles play the piano.

PUBLICATION HISTORY

"Blue Melody" was published in the September 1948 issue of *Cosmopolitan*. Salinger never reprinted the story in his three books of collected stories. "Blue Melody" later appeared in the bootleg editions *The COMPLETE UNCOLLECTED SHORT STORIES OF J. D. SALINGER* (1974) and *TWENTY-TWO STORIES* (1998).

CHARACTERS

Black Charles   A consummate piano player who plays the piano "like somebody from Memphis— maybe even better" (112), Black Charles runs a café-hamburger joint in Agersburg, Tennessee. The African-American musician is beloved by his 11-year-old admirers, Rudford and Peggy, who not only recognize his musical talents but also love him for his "kind and interested" (112) respect for them. Sleeping by day, Black Charles plays piano by night for a crowd at his café. When Lida Louise Jones visits Black Charles, her uncle, she meets Rudford and Peggy. Charles introduces Lida Louise as his "sister's chile" (114) and a singer. In late 1926, Lida Louise begins to sing every evening at the café. Six months later, she is discovered there by a well-known producer who takes her to Memphis to record her songs. Black Charles, at the picnic when Lida Louise suffers a burst appendix, drives from hospital to hospital in vain seeking medical attention for his niece.

Jones, Lida Louise   An African-American blues singer with an unclassifiable talent and voice, Lida Louise Jones meets Rudford and Peggy at Black Charles's café in Agersburg, Tennessee. Lida Louise and her mother, who is Charles's sister, live in "gator country" (114). A "grown-up" (114) girl, Lida Louise wears a yellow dress and yellow ribbon in her hair, and smokes cigarettes held between her "long, elegant fingers" (114). Not pretty but generous and forthright, Lida Louise befriends the children and stuns them with her singing. When she begins to perform nightly at her uncle's café, she is discovered by Lewis Harold Meadows, a well-

known music producer, who takes her to his Beale Street studio in Memphis to record her songs. Lida Louise goes to the city, not from ambition, but because she hopes to find, or to be found by, a former boyfriend, Endicott Wilson, from New York. Gaining swift popularity and recognition from the jazz greats, Lida Louise leaves Memphis abruptly, however, after an altercation on the street corner where she hits a small African-American man (presumably Endicott) in the face with her handbag. In 1927, soon after returning to Agersburg, she suffers a burst appendix at the farewell picnic for Rudford. When two local hospitals refuse her admittance due to her race, she dies in the car en route to Memphis. Lida Louise's death haunts both Rudford and Peggy through adulthood, and for Rudford, signals the day his world came to an end.

Moore, Marguerite ("Peggy")   The 11-year-old Peggy Moore, who impresses her classmate Rudford with her ability to hold gum in the hollow of her neck, is invited by him to meet Black Charles, an African-American piano player who runs a café in Agersburg, Tennessee. Rudford takes Peggy after school to the hole-in-the-wall hamburger joint on Willard Street (where Peggy has been instructed by her parents not to go). Peggy loves Black Charles and his music and likewise reacts to Lida Louise's singing with deep emotion. She also develops and admits to having a crush on Rudford. Rudford, in turn, falls in love with her. The two children exchange ambitions: hers to become "a war nurse. Also a movie actress. Also a piano player. Also a crook—one that swiped a lot of diamonds and stuff, but gave some of it to poor people; *very* poor people" (114). When Lida Louise asks why Peggy likes Rudford, Peggy replies that she likes "the way he stands at the blackboard" (114). Lida Louise enjoys the comment so much that, after meeting Joe and Sonny Varioni (the fictional jazz musicians from Salinger's story "The Varioni Brothers"), she has them write a song based on "a sentimental little girl who falls in love with a little boy standing at the blackboard in school" (116). The song, titled "Soupy Peggy," becomes a rare item, with only a few copies produced. When Lida Louise, with a burst appendix, is barred from the second whites-only hospital in Agersburg, Peggy screams out at those in charge: "Damn you! Damn you all!" (118). The tragic death of the blues singer haunts Peggy through her young adulthood, up to the day in 1942 when she sees Rudford after a separation of 15 years. She is now married to Richard, a navy flier, whom she introduces to Rudford. After Peggy reminisces about childhood schoolmates, she asks Rudford about Lida Louise, confessing that she thinks of the singer all the time. She also tells Rudford that she played "Soupy Peggy" all through college until the record was broken by a drunken boy. She has tried without success to find or buy another copy. Rudford promises to phone Peggy the next day so that she can hear the song again, as he still owns a copy. In 1944, Rudford explains to the story's narrator why he did not phone Peggy again, saying that his record was "terribly scratchy" (119) and no longer sounded like Lida Louise.

Narrator   The unnamed narrator of "Blue Melody," addressing the reader in a first-person voice (from the vantage point of 1948, the date of the story's publication), relates the events of wartime 1944 when, on the back of a GI truck heading for combat, he meets Rudford, the original narrator of the story of Lida Louise. The unnamed narrator, in turn, thus simultaneously relates both the story of Rudford and of Lida Louise (the tale-within-the-tale) to the reader.

Richard   A navy flier in 1942, Richard, now married to Peggy (née Moore), is, in Rudford's description, "eight feet tall" (119). Richard and Peggy are staying at the Biltmore Hotel in New York City when Peggy spots Rudford at another table. Richard listens "with an iron smile" (119) to Peggy reminisce about her childhood and interrupts when she excitedly exclaims to Rudford that she would like to hear "Soupy Peggy" right away. Richard reminds Peggy again of their appointment to meet Eddie and cuts off her conversation with Rudford.

Rudford   One of the protagonists of "Blue Melody," Rudford (whose surname is never revealed), from Agersburg, Tennessee, is described by the unnamed narrator of the story as having a "slight Southern accent and a chronic foxhole cough" (51). A captain in the medics in 1944, Rudford meets the story's narrator (unnamed) on a GI truck en route from Luxembourg City to the German front. As the other men sleep, Rudford tells the unnamed narrator of his friendship with Lida Louise Jones, the African-American blues singer, and of her tragic death. The narrator, in turn, narrates the story of Rudford and of Lida Louise to the reader.

FURTHER READING

Alsen, Eberhard. *A Reader's Guide to J. D. Salinger.* Westport, Conn.: Greenwood Press, 2002.
French, Warren. *J. D. Salinger.* New York: Twayne Publishers, 1963.
———. *J. D. Salinger, Revisited.* New York: Twayne Publishers, 1988.

"Both Parties Concerned"

Appearing in the February 26, 1944, issue of the SATURDAY EVENING POST, "Both Parties Concerned" treats, from a young husband's perspective, a crisis point in a marriage. "Both Parties Concerned" is Salinger's eighth published story. The author, however, chose not to include the story in his three books of collected stories.

SYNOPSIS

Billy Vullmer, the story's narrator, tells about a recent problem in his marriage. Even though Ruthie, his wife, was 17 years old and he was not quite 20 when they married, and even though everyone they knew thought they were too young, the narrator believes that as long as he and his wife understand each other, everything will be fine. But the couple are mismatched: Ruthie completed high school at 15 and wanted to become a doctor; Billy works at a factory building airplane fuselages. He claims to know Ruthie "like a book" (14).

The story Billy wants to tell begins with a night out at Jake's Place, a nightclub. Ruthie is unhappy they are there—she wants to stay home with their baby—but Billy insisted they go. Billy argues that he is entitled to a night out once in a while, but it becomes apparent that the couple goes out often (including the night before—though in Billy's view they just had a beer that night and went right home). At Jake's, after waiting for a table, Ruthie refuses to drink. Instead, she lights matches while they argue about Mrs. Widger, their babysitter, whom Ruthie intensely dislikes. Ruthie wants Billy to accept his role as a husband and father. She doesn't think Billy loves their child (never once referred to by name by either character), and when Billy insists he does, she then asks rhetorically why they are not at home. All Billy can respond is that he works hard. Finally, Ruthie leads Billy onto the dance floor as the band plays "Moonlight Becomes You." Although the old song is one she used to sing to him, they dance stiffly. By the time the couple returns to their table, Ruthie is crying. She leaves Jake's abruptly and goes to the car. They make it home, but not without more crying and their differences spreading the gulf between them.

The next day, with Billy at work, Ruthie leaves him a short note saying they should not stay together, and tells him that she and the baby have gone to her parents' house. When Billy returns home, he is stunned. He gets drunk and then memorizes the note backward and forward. He imagines himself to be exactly like Humphrey Bogart in the film *Casablanca,* and he also imagines himself as Sam, the pianist character in the film, listening to his imaginary Bogart-self who asks that "Moonlight Becomes You" be played. He grows tired of what he calls this "crazy stuff" (48) and phones a friend who is out. Billy finally dials Ruthie's parents' home and, although her mother says she is asleep, Ruthie comes to the phone and agrees to return home.

Once there, Ruthie cannot explain why she has returned beyond the feeling that she didn't belong in her parents' home (she offers the explanation that seeing her mother wearing a hairnet while talking on the phone to Billy made her realize that she could no longer live at home with her parents). Later that night, during a thunderstorm, Billy wakes up and finds Ruthie in the kitchen. When he tells her that he memorized her note backward and recites the last line about seeing the baby, she begins to cry. Ruthie tells Billy: "I don't care about anything now" (48). Billy thinks she is crying from the thunder and tells her to wake him when it thunders. His concern makes Ruthie cry even harder. Billy concludes the story by saying that Ruthie "wakes [him] now" (48) when it thunders, and that he wouldn't care if she woke him up every night.

CRITICAL ANALYSIS

Billy, the first-person narrator, tells his story as though in an offhanded manner. The story, however, relates a serious crisis in his marriage. As a narrator, he is thus unreliable—that is, the reader must intuit the underlying reality of the events described. For example, Billy will distort or ignore his wife's feelings by explaining her as a "funny kid" (48). Readers can comprehend Ruthie's actual feelings more clearly than can Billy. This discrepancy between what the events portray and the way in which Billy frames them shows how little Billy is actually tuned in to what "both parties concerned" (14) really think and heightens the contrast between Ruthie's intelligence and his lack of understanding. Billy, an immature father, prefers that he and Ruthie go out almost every night, while Ruthie would rather stay at home with their baby. Ruthie, emotionally more developed than Billy, tries to explain to him in her good-bye note that they "are supposed to grow out of certain things" and create "a new kind of fun" (48). (In the note, reproduced in the text and thus representing an early use of Salinger's text-within-text technique, Ruthie signs her name as "Ruth" [48], echoing the way in which Franny Glass, in the 1955 story "FRANNY," when writing to her boyfriend, Lane Coutell, will sign her letter including her given name, "Frances.") When Ruthie leaves Billy and returns to her parents' home, however, she realizes she cannot stay there. She thus decides to make the best of her marriage even though her husband can only misunderstand her unhappiness as a fear of thunder.

The story pre-echoes some of Holden Caulfield's speech patterns (his tendency, for example, to generalize carelessly, with phrases like "and all" [48]). This stylistic similarity in the narrative voice is the only reason most critics ascribe any significance to "Both Parties Concerned" (since Billy, as a character, lacks Holden's intelligence, soulfulness, and sensitivity). William F. Purcell, in a 1996 article, examines the speech patterns used by Billy and compares and contrasts them to Holden's speech patterns in the 1945 story "I'M CRAZY" and in *The CATCHER IN THE RYE*. Purcell suggests that "Both Parties Concerned" is an example and forerunner of the spontaneous speech patterns that Salinger would develop further in the novel, and likewise identifies this type of narrative as "*skaz* . . . which leaves the reader with the impression of listening to an unrehearsed, rambling monologue" (Purcell 278). Moreover, Billy imagining himself as a character in the film *Casablanca* is very similar to Holden's self-aggrandizement in imagining himself dramatically getting shot when he has actually been punched by a pimp.

The thematic content of "Both Parties Concerned" may also be viewed as an early experiment that will be played out in several of Salinger's future works. The intellectual differences between Ruthie and Billy parallel those between Ray Ford and Bunny Croft in the 1947 story "The INVERTED FOREST" and also the differences between Seymour and Muriel Glass. Each of these couples has a "both parties concerned" type of love that is incomprehensible to others outside the relationship. In "Both Parties Concerned," the dramatic tension between husband and wife concentrates the action. Salinger's resolution to the story, metaphorically drawn as fear of thunder, is well enough accomplished to make believable the couple's ability to stay together. Salinger leaves just enough ambiguity in the couple's interactions for readers to feel the disjunction of love without necessarily having to understand it completely.

Salinger titled the story "WAKE ME WHEN IT THUNDERS." He was overruled by the editors of the *Saturday Evening Post*, who created the published title by using a phrase in the first paragraph of the story.

The *Saturday Evening Post* illustrated the story with one drawing—Billy in his chair imagining himself drinking alone like Humphrey Bogart, and also playing the piano like Sam, in *Casablanca*.

PUBLICATION HISTORY

"Both Parties Concerned" was published in the February 26, 1944, issue of the *Saturday Evening Post*. Salinger never reprinted the story in his three books of collected stories. "Both Parties Concerned" later appeared in the bootleg editions *The COMPLETE UNCOLLECTED SHORT STORIES OF J. D. SALINGER* (1974) and *TWENTY-TWO STORIES* (1998).

CHARACTERS

Baby, the   Billy and Ruth Vullmer's baby is sleeping when the couple returns home from their night out at Jake's Place. Billy holds the baby's foot tenderly and observes how the baby sucks his thumb, even when sleeping—thus showing paternal caring for the child. Ruthie, however, reprimands Billy for ignoring the baby most of the time.

Cropper, Mrs.   The mother of Ruthie Vullmer, Mrs. Cropper had opposed Ruthie's marriage at the young age of 17, preferring to see her daughter attend college. Mrs. Cropper does not want Ruthie to return home to Billy Vullmer on the night that Ruthie and her baby leave their house to shelter with Mr. and Mrs. Cropper. When Mrs. Cropper answers the phone call from Billy, she tries to dissuade Ruthie from talking to her husband. Ruthie takes notice of her mother's hairnet. The way her mother looks in the hairnet, Ruthie explains to Billy later that night, made her realize that she could no longer live at her parents' home.

Vullmer, Billy   Billy Vullmer, the story's narrator, is the husband of Ruthie Vullmer and a young father to their baby boy. In a halting style, in which Billy struggles to tell of a crisis in his marriage, he shows himself as both a stubborn and, at the same time, willing partner in trying to resolve the causes of his wife's unhappiness. Billy has respect for Ruthie and claims to love his baby (he likes to hold the baby's feet and watch him as he sleeps; he considers his baby "smart" and "healthy" [48]). However, from Ruthie's conversation, the reader learns that Billy does not spend much time with the baby and prefers that they go out every night. These contradictions in what Billy says and how the other characters react to him inform the reader that Billy is an unreliable narrator. (For example, when Ruthie and Billy argue at Jake's Place, Billy tells the reader: "I asked her, very quiet like, what she wanted me to do" [14], whereupon Ruthie responds: "Please don't shout" [14].) Although Ruthie, at the story's end, decides to stay in their marriage, she is extremely unhappy. In the last scene of the story, the reader is left with Ruthie weeping during a thunder and lightning storm. Billy has memorized her good-bye note backward and forward, and when he tells her this fact during the storm, she understands how deeply he has been affected by her attempt to leave the marriage. She thus feels the great chasm between them and knows that he may never understand the causes. Billy believes only that Ruthie is weeping because of her fear of thunder.

Vullmer, Ruth ("Ruthie") Ruthie Vullmer, a young mother, married Billy Vullmer when she was 17 years old. A precocious student, Ruthie graduated from high school at the age of 15 and aspired to become a doctor. No college would admit her until she reached 18. She thus, in the interim, chooses marriage and motherhood. Intelligent and serious, Ruthie finds herself in an unhappy marriage to a man who does not take her seriously and who does not understand her reasons for the marital crisis: her growing dissatisfaction with the lack of attention her husband gives to their baby and his insistence that she and he continue their social nights out at the same pace as they had before the baby was born. Billy hires a babysitter, Mrs. Widger, whom Ruthie dislikes intensely. She no longer wants to go out drinking and tells Billy that they should stay home with the baby. Billy, however, has the upper hand. At Jake's (the nightclub of Billy's choosing), Ruthie starts lighting matches, begins to cry, and walks out after arguing with Billy. She later leaves Billy a note in which she tells him that, as parents, he and she need to "grow out of certain things" (48) and "get a new kind of fun" (48). She then takes the baby to her parents' home. Realizing that she cannot live there successfully any longer, she returns to Billy and they reconcile. Nonetheless, Ruthie, who often wakes during the night,

remains unhappy in the final scene of the story. Billy believes the cause of her sleeplessness is a fear of thunder. Ruthie, however, sobs because she realizes that Billy may never understand the reasons for the emotional chasm between them.

Widger, Mrs. The babysitter hired by Billy Vullmer, Mrs. Widger is paid what Billy considers a large sum for just a couple of hours' work each night. Ruthie Vullmer dislikes Mrs. Widger and disapproves of her reading magazines in the living room rather than tending to the baby. Billy disagrees, saying that Mrs. Widger has had quite a few babies of her own and thus must know how to hold and care for one. When the couple arrives home from the nightclub, Mrs. Widger leaves quickly, without saying good-bye.

FURTHER READING

Purcell, William F. "Narrative Voice in J. D. Salinger's 'Both Parties Concerned' and 'I'm Crazy.'" *Studies in Short Fiction* 33 (Spring 1996): 278–280.

Wenke, John. *J. D. Salinger: A Study of the Short Fiction.* Boston: Twayne Publishers, 1991.

"Boy in France, A"

Appearing in the March 31, 1945, issue of the SATURDAY EVENING POST, "A Boy in France," a sequel to "LAST DAY OF THE LAST FURLOUGH," portrays Babe Gladwaller on a battlefield in France. "A Boy in France" is Salinger's 13th published story. The author, however, chose not to include the story in his three books of collected stories.

SYNOPSIS

An American soldier, referred to as "the boy" throughout the narrative (identifiable as Babe from a letter), eats some canned food and falls "almost instantly asleep" (21) on a French battlefield. Babe wakes to the sky darkening and, realizing where he is, knows he must find somewhere safe to sleep. He sees Hurkin and Eeves digging their foxholes. Babe tells Eeves to wake him "if anything gets hot" (21); once he has his own foxhole, he will yell his location to Eeves. Babe hopes to find an existing foxhole so he doesn't have to dig one.

Babe finds an abandoned foxhole, with "a terrible blanket on which some German had recently lain and bled and probably died" (21). He throws away the "unlamented Kraut blanket" (21). The foxhole's dirt floor, "messy with what had permeated" the blanket, forces Babe to mechanically dig "out the bad places" (21). He lowers his own blankets into the foxhole and steps "with his muddy shoes into his bed" (21). The foxhole, too short for his legs, causes him to bend them "sharply at the knees" (21) so he can stretch out. Babe rests his "filthy head . . . on his filthier field jacket" (21). As an ant bites him on the leg, he attempts to kill it but reels in pain when he reinjures his finger that "had lost a whole fingernail" (21) that morning. Babe places his hand under the blanket and "let himself work the kind of abracadabra familiar to and special for G.I.'s in combat" (21). His incantation takes him back home. He is clean and well-dressed; there is coffee, music, and his books; "a nice quiet girl—not Frances, not anyone" (21) he knows, will visit him, and he will "bolt the door" (21). He will ask her to read to him, in her "American voice" (21), poems by Emily Dickinson and William Blake.

Babe takes his hand out, and "expecting and getting no change, no magic" (21), he extracts some news clippings from his pocket. He reads an arch entertainment column about a young movie star's first visit to New York. The starlet, quoted as wanting to get a "date with a real, honest-to-goodness G.I.," succeeds: At the Waldorf Hotel, she runs into another star, now "a major in public relations" (92) whose assignment keeps him in NEW YORK CITY. Disgusted, Babe stops reading and speaks to himself aloud, "half snickering, half weeping, 'Oo la-la!'" (92).

Babe extracts a letter, dated July 5, 1944, from a "soiled, unrecent envelope" and reads it for "the thirty-oddth time" (92). The letter, addressed to "Babe," begins, "Mama thinks you are still in England, but I think you are in France" (92). The letter writer (Babe's sister, Mattie, who signs the letter "Matilda") fills him in on events at the beach. Jackie Benson has borrowed one of Babe's books. She likes Babe "a lot" and isn't conceited like "Frances" (92). Older couples, kids, girls populate the beach—"you never see any boys" (92). A neighbor's son was killed in the Pacific; one girl has married a soldier, honeymooned, and now "lays on the beach by herself" (92). Mattie has found a comb in his car's backseat and guesses the comb belongs to Frances. The letter ends with a P.S.: "I miss you. Please come home soon. Love and kisses, Matilda" (92).

Babe returns the letter safely to its envelope, raises himself in the foxhole, and shouts his location to Eeves. Babe slumps back, speaks "aloud to nobody, 'Please come home soon,'" and falls "crumbily, bent-leggedly, asleep" (92).

CRITICAL ANALYSIS

"A Boy in France" continues Babe Gladwaller's life after "Last Day of the Last Furlough." Both stories were published in the *Saturday Evening Post*; only readers of the earlier story would recognize "Babe" and "Matilda" as Babe and Mattie Gladwaller. Although "Last Day of the Last Furlough" is a much more complex and accomplished story, "A Boy in France" stands out as Salinger's only published story whose events unfold on a battlefield. American soldiers have fought with German soldiers "during the long, rotten afternoon" (21). The Americans have advanced, overtaking the German position, evidenced by Babe seeing the German blanket in the foxhole he will occupy.

The story, basically a vignette, lacks Salinger's usual finesse with language and technique. Through a profusion of adjectives and some explicit ironies, Salinger, however, encapsulates "that moment of total physical, mental and emotional exhaustion that completely deadens the sensibilities of even a sensitive character like Babe" (Purcell 88). The story, additionally, continues a theme from the earlier story "Last Day of the Last Furlough." There, Babe declares he is going to war to protect the people he loves. This protection especially extends to his 10-year-old sister, Mattie, who embodies the innocence of childhood.

The conclusion of "A Boy in France," and its underlying meaning, hinge on the letter from Mattie. (The letter's date, July 5, 1944, allows the reader to locate the "prequel" story, "Last Day of the Last Furlough," to November 1943.) As the critic William Purcell notes, the letter embodies Mattie and serves as "an anchor that Babe can hold on to and weather the storms of despair that the war situation threatens him with" (Purcell 88). Babe reads the letter to reconnect with his past life. The letter invokes his parents, Jackie Benson, Frances, and a number of people the Gladwallers know from the beach they stay at each summer. Additionally, through the letter, Salinger evokes the uncertainty of war for those left behind: "Daddy tells mama that he thinks you are in England still, but I think he thinks you are in France" (92). Mattie fears that Babe is in France too; her letter is dated a month after D-day. Salinger also indicates the changed life "back home." Mattie reports the death of a soldier and his parents' grief; a girl's quick marriage and her husband-soldier's return to duty; the absence of young men at the beach. Last, and perhaps most important, the letter serves as a talisman for survival (Babe has read the letter, since receipt, more than 30 times). He is desperate to read the letter before the light dies away. This newest rereading is undertaken to protect him through (yet another) night, for the situation could get "hot" (21).

After Babe repeats Mattie's closing line, "Please come home soon," "aloud to nobody," he falls "crumbily, bent-leggedly, asleep" (92). Although this scene resembles the famous conclusion of a later story, "FOR ESMÉ—WITH LOVE AND SQUALOR," significant differences are discernible. In "For Esmé—with Love and Squalor," the war is over; Sergeant X is safe in a house; he has received and read Esmé's letter for the first time. Sergeant X has suffered a nervous breakdown and hasn't been able to sleep. Esmé's letter induces a healing sleep, as the story's narrator explicitly indicates. In contrast, the war is emphatically not over in "A Boy in France." Babe has no trouble sleeping; he has already fallen asleep that afternoon. Babe's "bed" is a too-small foxhole, where

a German soldier "had recently lain and bled and probably died" (21). Babe falls asleep again, but this sleep is an uncomfortable (hardly healing) sleep, as Salinger signals with "crumbily, bent-leggedly, asleep" (92). This sleep, in the gravelike foxhole, brings oblivion. It could be sleep that grants another morning or, symbolically, sleep as Babe's imminent death. Babe has no guarantee he will ever get home alive, let alone soon. The story abandons the soldier in a precariously dangerous situation, his future unknown. Salinger reveals Babe's fate in the last of the three Gladwaller stories, "The STRANGER."

The *Saturday Evening Post* illustrated the story with one drawing—Babe in his foxhole as he reads Mattie's letter.

PUBLICATION HISTORY

"A Boy in France" was published in the March 31, 1945, issue of the *Saturday Evening Post*. The story was chosen by Ben Hibbs for inclusion in the anthology *The Saturday Evening Post Stories, 1942–1945*, published in 1945. Salinger never reprinted the story in his three books of collected stories. "A Boy in France" later appeared in the bootleg editions *The COMPLETE UNCOLLECTED SHORT STORIES OF J. D. SALINGER* (1974) and *TWENTY-TWO STORIES* (1998).

CHARACTERS

Babe (Gladwaller) Babe, the story's protagonist, is referred to as "the boy." He finds a foxhole formerly occupied by a wounded German soldier (who later probably died). Babe reads some news clippings and a letter from his sister, Matilda (Mattie).

Babe is the protagonist of "Last Day of the Last Furlough" and "The Stranger."

Benson, Jackie Matilda's letter mentions that Jackie Benson has borrowed one of Babe's books; Jackie, Babe's former girlfriend, remains infatuated with him.

Jackie is referenced in "Last Day of the Last Furlough."

Daddy (Professor Gladwaller) Matilda's letter mentions that Babe's father tries to reassure his wife that their son is still safe in England, although he suspects Babe now to be fighting in France.

Professor Gladwaller appears in "Last Day of the Last Furlough."

Eeves Eeves, Babe's fellow soldier, has watch duty that evening. Babe tells Eeves to wake him if anything should develop.

Frances Matilda's letter mentions that she saw Frances, but the young woman ignored Mattie. Mattie finds a woman's comb in Babe's car's backseat and believes it is Frances'.

Frances is referenced in "Last Day of the Last Furlough."

Hurkin Babe walks past Hurkin digging his foxhole, and the two soldiers ignore each other.

Mama (Mrs. Gladwaller) Matilda's letter mentions that her mother believes Babe is still in England and expects him to be home later this summer. In her expectation, she has brought some of Babe's books to the beach.

Mrs. Gladwaller appears in "Last Day of the Last Furlough" and is referenced in "The Stranger."

Matilda (Mattie Gladwaller) Babe reads a letter from his sister, Matilda (better known as Mattie). Her letter, which informs him about the happenings that summer at the beach, ends with her hope that he will return home soon.

Mattie appears in "Last Day of the Last Furlough" and "The Stranger."

FURTHER READING

French, Warren. *J. D. Salinger.* New York: Twayne Publishers, 1963.

Lundquist, James. *J. D. Salinger.* New York: Ungar, 1979.

Purcell, William F. "World War II and the Early Fiction of J. D. Salinger." *Studies in American Literature* 28 (1991): 77–93.

Wenke, John. *J. D. Salinger: A Study of the Short Fiction.* Boston: Twayne Publishers, 1991.

"Boy in the People Shooting Hat, The"

"The Boy in the People Shooting Hat" is one of Salinger's "lost" stories, neither published nor to be found in a library archive. Ben Yagoda photographically reproduces the NEW YORKER's rejection letter of a story with this title in *About Town: The New Yorker and the World It Made* (Yagoda 236). The undated letter, written by GUS LOBRANO (most likely in 1948), reveals that "The Boy in the People Shooting Hat" concerns a fight between characters named Bobby and Stradlater over a June Gallagher. One can surmise that portions of the story were incorporated into *The CATCHER IN THE RYE.* Holden Caulfield says that his red hunting hat is "a people shooting hat" (30). Additionally, Holden has a fight with Stradlater over Jane Gallagher. Unless the manuscript of "The Boy in the People Shooting Hat" can be located among Salinger's literary estate, the story's whereabouts are unknown.

"Boy Standing in Tennessee"

"Boy Standing in Tennessee" is one of Salinger's "lost" stories, neither published nor to be found in a library archive. According to the bibliographer Jack R. Sublette, Salinger mentions a story with this title in a 1944 letter to WHIT BURNETT. "Boy Standing in Tennessee" was included on the proposed table of contents for Salinger's unpublished book, *The YOUNG FOLKS.* Unless the manuscript can be located among Salinger's literary estate, the story's whereabouts are unknown.

"Broken Children, The"

"The Broken Children" is one of Salinger's "lost" stories, neither published nor to be found in a library archive. According to the bibliographer Jack R. Sublette, Salinger mentions a story with this title in a 1943 letter to WHIT BURNETT. Unless the manuscript can be located among Salinger's literary estate, the story's whereabouts are unknown.

Catcher in the Rye, The

The Catcher in the Rye, Salinger's first book and only novel, was published on July 16, 1951, by LITTLE, BROWN AND COMPANY in Boston, Massachusetts. The book features and is narrated by one of the best-known and most-beloved characters in literature, the teenager Holden Caulfield. *The Catcher in the Rye* is considered Salinger's masterpiece, as well as one of the major American novels.

INTRODUCTION

The Catcher in the Rye has become the classic coming-of-age tale. Generations of readers have responded passionately to Holden Caulfield's adolescent story, and almost all important coming-of-age novels published since Salinger's have been compared to *The Catcher in the Rye*. Even today, the novel continues to attract new readers, who experience, through Holden, the process of maturing from childhood to adulthood. Salinger's keen sense of human observation and ear for the way young people talk are evident throughout the book.

Salinger worked on a number of stories about Holden Caulfield (and other Caulfield family members) during the 1940s. Most notably, a character named "Holden Caulfield" narrated the 1945 story "I'M CRAZY" in COLLIER'S. Readers encountered another "Holden Caulfield" character when NEW YORKER editors chose to print Salinger's "SLIGHT REBELLION OFF MADISON" in 1946. According to WILLIAM MAXWELL, Salinger had submitted and withdrawn a 90-page novella of *The Catcher in the Rye* in 1946 as well. There are unpublished stories by Salinger in which Holden appears as a minor character. In some of Salinger's published stories during the 1940s, the author uses other Caulfield family members along with references to Holden. (For an overview, *see* CAULFIELD STORIES.) Clearly, Salinger had been experimenting with his central character and narrator long before Holden Caulfield appeared in the 275-page novel, *The Catcher in the Rye*.

It is unlikely that Salinger himself imagined that his novel would become such a classic. The paperback edition continues to be bought by more than 20,000 readers a month and has been part of the American educational curricula since the mid-1950s. The novel has been translated into more than 30 languages and reprinted innumerable times. Despite ongoing attempts to censor the work

Facsimile of the rare first-edition dust jacket of *The Catcher in the Rye*, published by Little, Brown and Company on July 16, 1951 *(Courtesy of the Bruce F. Mueller Collection; photo by Laura Fairbanks)*

since its publication, it continues to be an important text for young readers.

The first edition of *The Catcher in the Rye* has been, since the late 1950s, a collectors' item. In the beginning, the book's value was augmented by the fact that the dust jacket carried a picture of Salinger that the author insisted be removed after the second printing. The photo, taken by LOTTE JACOBI, is a fairly standard black-and-white head shot of Salinger. At the time of *The Catcher in the Rye*'s publication, Salinger seemed eager to pursue respect for his status as a writer. But as the author's desire to shun publicity became more and more of an issue in his writing life, the book's value continued to climb. At the close of the first decade of the

J. D. Salinger in October 1950. This photograph by Lotte Jacobi was chosen for the first-edition dust jacket of *The Catcher in the Rye*. The photograph appears here in its original state—neither reversed nor cropped. (© *The Lotte Jacobi Collection, University of New Hampshire*)

21st century, the first edition of *The Catcher in the Rye* enjoys the status of an exclusive cultural artifact. A rare copy in very fine condition will fetch up to $25,000 on the antiquarian market, signed first-edition copies bring twice as much, while inscribed copies command a premium. Moreover, *The Catcher in the Rye* shares with Harper Lee's *To Kill a Mockingbird* the distinction of being the most expensive collectible post–World War II American novel.

Salinger's retreat to CORNISH, NEW HAMPSHIRE, and his eventual decision to cease publication of new works raises various questions: Did publication of *The Catcher in the Rye* make Salinger too well known? Did the author fear he would be pigeonholed as a coming-of-age novelist? Did the excessive attention that *The Catcher in the Rye* earned from the reading public become too distracting to the writer? Although the answers to these questions may be resolved only if future documentation reveals that Salinger explicitly explained his reasons for withdrawing from the public eye, it is fair to conclude that *The Catcher in the Rye* changed Salinger's writing life in addition to changing our literary culture and affecting the lives of millions of readers.

OVERVIEW

The Catcher in the Rye is built on Salinger's strength in telling a very good story about a boy on the verge of manhood. Holden Caulfield is a teenager who is lost and who must find himself. He is not necessarily a completely reliable narrator. As Holden tells his own story, he even admits to being a liar. Even while he describes the experiences that add up to a young man's soulful and honest search for himself, Holden struggles with the fact of flunking out of Pencey Preparatory School in Agerstown, Pennsylvania. He decides to return to his home in NEW YORK CITY several days before the end of the school term and the beginning of Christmas break without telling the school or his parents where he is going.

Readers learn that this is not the first time Holden has failed to stay in school. They also learn to listen to the voice of an adolescent coping with some of life's tougher lessons. Holden's early departure was precipitated by a fight with his roommate, Ward Stradlater. However, it is likely that most of his difficulties in and out of school began when his younger brother, Allie, died of leukemia on July 18, 1946, three years before the events in the novel begin (December 1949). Allie's death causes Holden to feel a sense of angst and conflict that goes beyond doing poorly in school. Indeed, from the moment readers "meet" the narrator and main character of *The Catcher in the Rye,* they become aware that beyond his problems Holden seems to be an intelligent, sensitive, honest, and caring person, or at least has the possibility of showing those qualities as he matures.

Much of the book's earliest critical praise focused on Salinger's use of language and skill with dialogue. Although only the first quarter of the book takes place in the Pencey Prep of nearly 60 years ago, *The Catcher in the Rye* is still considered today to be one of the finest portrayals of prep school life. Most modern-day readers have little difficulty believing in the fictional school and its denizens, perhaps because the way students talk to one another changes less over time than one might imagine.

When Holden arrives in New York City on a Saturday night, he experiences a weekend in the city that depresses him as he attempts to enjoy the city in adult ways. Holden's depression is best expressed when he criticizes "phonies" and analyzes the ways people (even himself, though rarely) are hypocritical. He seeks compassion, which he gives to strangers but cannot find for himself (in ways he can believe) from anyone except his younger sister, Phoebe. In the city, Holden looks up old friends, his girlfriend, and a former teacher while encountering a cast of New York characters, including a pimp, a prostitute, taxi drivers, nuns, tourists, and children. By Sunday, he has already paid a short, secret visit to his family's apartment, but he does not stay for the sheltering and nurturing he really needs. As Holden describes his problems with each encounter, readers sense how desperately he needs understanding from others. The child in Holden wishes, as he describes it, to stand by a cliff to stop children from falling or to catch them if they do fall. The adult in Holden wishes that the world

could see the values in love, art, religion, and childhood. Later in the story, as people continue to disappoint Holden, there are moments (as he stops to tighten a young girl's skates, helps nuns, receives Mr. Antolini's wisdom) when Holden's values are displayed in ways that deepen our experience of how maturation changes certain values.

After spending his Saturday night in a sleazy hotel, Holden spends Sunday night with his former English teacher from one of the prep schools he flunked out of before the events in *The Catcher in the Rye* begin. The teacher, Mr. Antolini, is fond of Holden in ambiguous ways that frighten the boy, who then leaves the Antolini apartment to spend the rest of the night in Grand Central Station. Part of Holden's search during the three days of the narrative is propelled by his adolescent attempts to find himself sexually. Almost everyone he talks with has sexual potential. Holden even perceives his old teacher as a homosexual and then doubts his own perception. His sexual questions add to his confusion as he tries too hard to find his balance.

Holden's dreams, especially his plans to escape New York and to live on his own, finally cease when his younger sister, Phoebe, insists on joining him. He has been unable to convince his girlfriend, Sally Hayes, to view his plan as anything but childish. Not until Phoebe tries to tag along does Holden see he is not ready to support himself or anyone else. Perhaps it takes the younger sibling to expose the child in the older brother, but in any case, Holden abandons his idea of running away. Instead, brother and sister go to CENTRAL PARK and eventually arrive at the carousel. While watching his younger sister ride the carousel and attempt to reach for a gold ring, Holden experiences an epiphany. He understands that he cannot rescue falling children, possibly not even himself. He then begins to cry. In the final chapter of the novel, the reader returns to present time and rejoins Holden in a sanatorium in California. A psychoanalyst employed there has asked whether Holden will apply himself when he returns to school in September. Holden is uncertain but says he thinks he will. Salinger concludes the book by letting Holden reflect with some irony on his narration, telling readers not to "tell anybody anything," while paradoxically admitting to "missing everybody" (277) he has described.

SYNOPSIS

Chapter 1

Salinger begins *The Catcher in the Rye* with his adolescent narrator and central character Holden Caulfield claiming his intention to avoid talking about his childhood and family in order to resist "all that David Copperfield kind of crap" (3). The allusion to Charles Dickens's autobiographical novel about a young man making his way in the world, without much of the parental guidance that most children experience, alerts readers to Holden's difficulties with his family and with his own maturation process. Holden will be a narrator who is capable of contradicting himself without being a character who is dishonest. As Holden claims to avoid becoming personal, his tone and the description of his older brother, D. B., for example, seem to be the kind of unfiltered expression of truth typical of young people.

This first chapter is important, not only for providing readers with a sense of the narrator's unreliability and his desire to be honest about selected events, but also for introducing a character who is believable and who seems to be striving toward an honest understanding of how he will fit into society. Readers learn that Holden distrusts his brother because D. B. now writes for the movies instead of writing stories for books. Although Holden claims to hate movies, readers can glean some of the younger brother's admiration for his older brother's success. In later chapters, readers will find plenty of evidence that Holden is knowledgeable about movies and sees them too often to support his statement of hating them.

The first chapter frames the events and the "madman stuff" (3) that had taken place in Agerstown, Pennsylvania, and New York City, landing Holden in a sanatorium near Hollywood, California. (Salinger, it should be noted, does not specifically identify the kind of facility where Holden is residing as he tells his story. Holden's statements that he "got pretty run-down and had to come out here and take it easy" (3); he "practically got t.b. and came out here for all these goddam checkups"

(8); and that they made him quit smoking, leave the reader in ambiguity. Nonetheless, some critics believe Holden tells his story from a mental hospital or a psychiatric ward.)

Holden begins by describing what led up to his departure from Pencey Prep, located in Agerstown, Pennsylvania. Pencey is a private preparatory school that claims to mold boys into "splendid, clear-thinking young men" (4). Holden criticizes the claim, because he believes that the only clear-thinking students he knew there probably came to the school that way; he also says that Pencey seems to him no different from other schools in its "molding" processes of education. Holden's initial criticism of the school is framed by the fact that he has been expelled, yet his intelligence and insights about education have continued to interest generations of students assigned to read *The Catcher in the Rye*. Salinger's narrator is both an insider and outsider when it comes to fitting in and failing out of several prep schools. This dual perspective allows readers to experience Holden's failures on a number of interpretive levels, often colored by the reader's own experiences in school.

The novel's initial chapter, moreover, informs readers that Holden grew six-and-one-half inches in the last year, which illustrates that the boy's physical growth has bounded ahead of his psychological growth. Holden's height remains an ongoing issue throughout the novel; his physical descriptions of himself, likewise, may consistently be connected to his need for social maturation and acceptance. Holden not only has failed four of his five classes, but he also has proven unsuccessful as manager of the fencing team. To bring the reader into his world, Holden begins to narrate the events of the day of the football game with Saxon Hall. That morning, he has lost the team's fencing equipment on a New York subway before a match. Though the whole team ostracizes Holden for losing the equipment, he thinks it "pretty funny, in a way" (6). Holden tells the reader he has been kicked out of the school, and at the moment he is hanging around the campus, "trying to feel some kind of good-by" (7). From the outset, readers see that Holden's career at Pencey is not noteworthy, yet he does not respond in bitter ways to those who point out his failures. At the end of the first chapter, Holden goes to visit Mr. Spencer, one of the teachers who failed him. When Mrs. Spencer opens the door, the reader finally learns the narrator's name as she greets him as "Holden."

Chapter 2

The second chapter takes place in the home of Holden Caulfield's history teacher at Pencey Prep. Mr. Spencer is sick with a flulike illness called "the grippe." After Mrs. Spencer welcomes Holden and directs him into his teacher's bedroom, Holden thinks to himself, "The minute I went in, I was sort of sorry I'd come" (11). He reflects that he is "not too crazy about sick people" (11). The physical age of the Spencers and the discomfort of sitting on the hard bed of his ill teacher create a scene that quickly deepens to reveal central issues and themes in the novel. Mr. Spencer stresses the importance of following rules in the game of life, while Holden realizes that life is a game only for those on the winning side. While discussing parental notification of his failure at Pencey with Spencer, Holden begins to criticize his own vocabulary skill in using the word "boy" too often. He describes himself as sometimes acting like he was 13. Holden is a tall, partially gray-haired 16-year-old during the events of the novel that take place in Pennsylvania and New York. He is 17 while he narrates the story during his recovery in California. Though Holden admits to acting childish sometimes, he also claims to act older than his age "but people never notice it" (13). This point seems to challenge the reader to see what others do not see in the character, and it certainly frames many of the issues of behavior and maturation that arise in the following chapters.

In addition to setting up themes of class consciousness, education versus learning, language awareness, and maturation, this second chapter reveals some of the "David Copperfield . . . crap" (3) that Holden in the first chapter said he would avoid. As Mr. Spencer reviews Holden's history exam essay, Holden feels tortured to be revisiting the failure in detail. The only part of the essay offered to readers describes the embalming enigma of the Egyptian dead. The word *mummy* may not be used in Holden's essay, but its absence doesn't obscure the pun on *mother*, a pun that may be seen to espouse the idea that Holden needs nurturing. (Noteworthy here is the fact that Salinger dedicates the book to his own mother.) Holden has appended a note to his essay addressed to Spencer. The teacher reads Holden's note aloud, and the reader now learns the full name of the narrator, "Holden Caulfield." Spencer, unaware of the discomfort he is causing Holden to feel, even seeks the boy's forgiveness for having given him a failing grade. However, even while Holden assuages the teacher's guilt and admits to being "a real moron" (17), he also wishes Spencer would stop calling him "boy" (17). Frustrated, Holden retreats mentally and wonders to himself where the ducks go when the lagoon in Central Park freezes over. Salinger's use of Holden's concern about the ducks suggests that Holden really is concerned about flunking out, but that he is trying not to face his worry so much as to express concern for others.

Chapter 2 provides a foundation for much of the novel's construction. How and why Holden sees people as phony is one of the keys to understanding the novel. Holden's problem with the idea that life is a game for winners but pretty hard on the rest of the people is linked to his claims that he left his earlier preparatory schools—Whooten and Elkton Hills—because of all the phonies there. Holden describes the headmaster at Elkton Hills, Mr. Haas, as the quintessential phony, charming to some of his classmates' parents and inattentive to others who were less attractive. Holden thinks words like "grand" are phony because that is how life's winners are described by other winners. Holden even objects to the simple phrase "good luck." The character's attention to language shows that he is hardly the moron he considers himself to be and demonstrates a deep thought process about communication. Holden is a proficient critical thinker despite his low opinion of himself.

Chapter 3

Chapter 3 begins with Holden declaring, "I'm the most terrific liar" (22). Even as he confesses to his dishonesty, however, he gains credibility. Holden is both an adolescent who tells lies and a narrator who must be believed. His confession shows him to be a typical teenager who will use lies in awkward social situations. At the same time, the statement presents him as a narrator who is seeking adult truth by trying to face his own shortcomings honestly. Holden's problems with his sense of integrity actually display his maturation despite many of his childish actions. The novel achieves its paradoxical edge by pitting Holden's adolescent insecurities against his own enduring sense of truth, a conflict played out often in the book as Holden seeks to overcome hypocritical or phony aspects of life while also being able to see his own and others' phoniness quite clearly and insightfully.

To further the theme of phoniness in others, Holden describes where he lives by recounting the dedication of the Ossenburger Memorial Wing. Holden understands that the building's name was the result of a large donation to the school by an undertaker. When Mr. Ossenburger makes a speech in the school chapel, he tells the students that they shouldn't hesitate to pray to Jesus and consider him a friend to whom they can talk at all times. Holden regards the speaker as phony and imagines a perfectly hypocritical scene where Mr. Ossenburger asks his "buddy" Jesus "to send him a few more stiffs" (23). The hypocrisy is punctuated with a loud fart from Edgar Marsalla, a boy in a row in front of Holden.

The third chapter gives readers their first image of Holden in a red hunter's hat, which he likes to wear "catcher" style, with the long brim turned around to the back. He bought the hat after losing the fencing equipment, and it seems as though wearing it makes Holden feel better. He even puts it on to read *Out of Africa* in his dorm room during his last day at Pencey. As readers see Holden reading, they realize that he is not resistant to literature and culture the way many are who flunk out of school and that his sensitivity as a reader is more intelligent than Holden himself might admit. He is mature enough to know about the pleasures of rereading books, yet he claims to be illiterate. Nevertheless, Holden cannot hide his ability.

This chapter presents Holden offering paradoxical insights about his telling lies and reading. Out of this confusion comes the impression that Holden is trying to be honest and literate. Holden may be

awkward and may make self-defeating claims, but evidence to the contrary arises from his actions. For example, to further the sense of paradox and truth in this chapter, Holden describes his desire to phone an author whenever he is inspired by what he reads. This part of the novel has become famous because Salinger clearly believes that authors should not have to communicate personally with readers at all. Beyond the irony of Salinger's best-known character wanting something his author is noted for refusing, readers can see that Holden seeks contact with authors. That desire proves the point that Holden is literate for a 16-year-old reader. At least in and through books, Holden seeks further communication with intellectually successful adults.

This chapter continues with Holden reading *Out of Africa* by Isak Dinesen. Holden explains that his favorite author is his brother, D. B., and then Ring Lardner. The highest compliment about an author's work, according to Holden, is that after finishing a book "you wish the author that wrote it was a terrific friend of yours and you could call him up on the phone whenever you felt like it" (25). Holden's reading is interrupted by a visit from Robert Ackley, his next-door neighbor in the prep school dorm. Ackley is ugly and obnoxious, and Holden admits to not being too crazy about him. However, even after dropping broad hints that Ackley should leave, Holden lets him stay and continue to be a bother. Holden then dramatically pulls his cap bill forward, hiding his eyes, and starts acting blind, saying, "Mother darling . . . why won't you give me your *hand*" (29). Although he asks that question as a way of "horsing around" (29), Holden is also signaling his own need for parental guidance. Ackley nags Holden, asking him where he got his hat, and comments that, where he comes from, Holden's hat is a hunting hat worn while shooting deer. Holden cryptically counters, "This is a people shooting hat. I shoot people in this hat" (30).

The appearance of Ward Stradlater, Holden's roommate, creates a reason for Ackley to return to his own room. Stradlater, while preparing for a quick shave, asks to borrow Holden's sport coat. Though equal in height, Holden admits that Stradlater "had a damn good build" (34). Stradlater, a senior, is a year ahead of Holden and has matured more than Holden in build and facial hair. In this chapter, Salinger deftly gives his three prep school students the realistic voices of adolescents in different stages of the spectrum of maturation; Holden is more mature than Ackley and less mature than Stradlater. For example, Ackley has no sexual experience; Holden has a girlfriend but is still a virgin; and Stradlater is able to make his date wait for him in the school annex while he cleans up for his probable seduction of her. Salinger likewise convincingly creates a typical and interesting impression of dorm life while also managing to give Holden credibility as a narrator despite his admitted and often awkward problems with maturation.

Chapter 4

Just as Ackley wants attention from Holden in Chapter 3, Holden similarly tags along with Stradlater in Chapter 4. As the older boy shaves, Holden wears his red hunting hat and sits on the sink next to Stradlater while playing with the faucets. Holden is thinking about how poorly Stradlater whistles and how he is a "secret slob" (35) who manages to look like a "Year Book kind of handsome guy" (36). Stradlater asks Holden to write a composition about anything descriptive for his English class on Monday. Though Holden notes the irony of completing an assignment after he has flunked out, he agrees to write the composition. The irony is furthered by the fact that Holden both admires Stradlater and criticizes him because the older boy is a "winner" in life's game while those who don't look as good lose out.

As part of his request, Stradlater asks Holden to use commas incorrectly in the essay (in order to hide the fact that Holden is Stradlater's ghost writer for the assignment). Holden rightly sees through the ploy because he understands that compositions are much more about ideas than about punctuation. The example furthers the theme of winners and losers in the game of life: Holden believes that the substance of a person matters more than his appearance; Stradlater exemplifies the value of appearances—looking good and being stronger. As Holden horses around annoying Stradlater, he learns that Stradlater's Saturday night

blind date is Jane Gallagher, a girl Holden lived next door to the summer before last.

As the roommates continue their dialogue, Stradlater focuses on finishing grooming and dressing himself, neither concerned about Jane Gallagher nor curious about what Holden knows of her. Holden suggests he might go down to say hello to Jane, and Stradlater encourages him to do so, but Holden does not move and finally admits he isn't in the mood. Instead, he explains to Stradlater how Jane played checkers and liked to keep her kings in the back row because they looked pretty. Although Holden understands "that kind of stuff doesn't interest most people" (41), he also shows how well he knows her. After mentioning that he used to caddy for her mother at the country club to which both of their families belonged, he describes how Jane's mother divorced her husband to marry a "booze hound" who walked "around the goddam house naked" (42). Holden understands that Stradlater is interested in "very sexy stuff," but he does not seem willing to empathize with Jane's "lousy childhood" (42). The one thing that unites the roommates at that moment is a mutual understanding: that Stradlater will probably honor Holden's request not to tell Jane about Holden flunking out, and that Holden will probably write Stradlater's composition.

When Stradlater leaves, Holden sits in the room for half an hour, during which time he admits to feeling "so nervous [he] nearly went crazy" (45). Holden fears for Jane because Stradlater is "a very sexy bastard" (42) and perhaps for himself because he hasn't matured in his ability to relate to women as easily as Stradlater does. When Ackley intrudes again, Holden admits, "For once in my stupid life, I was really glad to see him" (45). The sudden reappearance of the less sexually experienced Ackley at the end of the chapter helps balance Holden in his interaction with the more sexually advanced Stradlater.

Chapter 5

At the beginning of Chapter 5, Salinger returns readers to the facts of Saturday night at Pencey Prep. Steak is served, seemingly to impress parents who most often visit on Sunday, but the meal is not very good. Three inches of snow provide the fun of a spontaneous, postdinner snowball fight that Holden describes as "very childish, but everybody was really enjoying themselves" (46). Holden, not yet ready for a more adultlike Saturday night date, is still able to enjoy himself when he can "horse around" and playact without real consequence.

Holden and his friend Mel Brossard agree to a bus trip into Agerstown for a burger and maybe "a lousy movie" (47). Holden purports to disliking movies while, at the same time, remaining knowledgeable about current actors and films. Brossard agrees to let Ackley come along, though he is not thrilled about his inclusion. Since only Holden had not yet seen the picture, the boys decide instead to have some burgers, play pinball, and return to Pencey before 9 P.M. Brossard leaves to find a bridge game, and Ackley makes himself at home in Holden's room on Holden's bed. Ackley's pimple popping and his monotone descriptions of his supposed sex life make Holden think that Ackley is "a virgin if ever [he] saw one" (49). Holden finally persuades Ackley to leave so he can write Stradlater's composition.

Dressed in his pajamas, robe, and red hunting hat, Holden decides to write about his younger brother Allie's baseball mitt. Allie's mitt is covered with poems he had copied in green ink "so he'd have something to read when he was in the field and nobody was up at bat" (49). As Holden remembers Allie in the composition, readers see a bright, red-haired, smarter, humorous sibling of Holden's whom teachers enjoy so much that they send letters to Holden's parents saying what "a pleasure it was having a boy like Allie in their class" (50). The night that Allie died, three years ago, Holden, age 13, slept in the garage and broke his hand punching out the windows. Holden's parents "were going to have [him] psychoanalyzed" (50). The phrase, in the conditional, implies that Holden did not receive counseling right after his brother's death even though losing Allie disturbed Holden deeply. Holden next retrieves the glove from his suitcase in order to copy its poems into the composition. Holden then naively imagines he can change Allie's name in the essay and hide his own authorship, reasoning that not using Allie's name

is mediated by the fact that writing about Allie is something Holden says he likes doing. The chapter ends when Holden, hearing Ackley snoring, feels a little sorry for him.

Chapter 6

Holden begins the narration of Chapter 6 by saying, "Some things are hard to remember" (52). Where Chapter 3 began with Holden calling himself a liar, in Chapter 6 he now admits that his memory is a bit foggy. Holden's perceptions certainly seem heightened and his mood agitated as he listens for Stradlater's returning footsteps. Some critics believe Holden's statements make him an unreliable narrator. His self-doubt also shows, however, that Holden is a narrator who questions his own perceptions, especially when he feels troubled. Holden is troubled in a number of ways, and this chapter dramatizes his frustrations with school, sexuality, and himself.

Although Holden is very bothered by Stradlater's date with Jane Gallagher, he doesn't ask about the date when Stradlater returns. The first element of drama is set up by Holden's anticipation of Stradlater's return. The second element is the conflict over the composition. As the two roommates discuss the composition Holden has left on Stradlater's bed, their misunderstandings and frustrations begin to heat up. Stradlater wanted a composition about a room or a house, while Holden thought the essay just had to be descriptive. Stradlater does not question how he "gave" Holden the assignment, and he has no sympathy for Holden still struggling with his brother's death. Instead, Stradlater connects Holden's misdirected writing with the reason for his flunking out. Stradlater accuses the younger boy of not doing things "the way you're supposed to" (53). Holden responds by taking the composition from Stradlater and ripping up the only copy of writing he had enjoyed composing. This second element of drama shows that Holden's path to healing from his brother's death is partially blocked by the adolescent, self-centered, and shallow actions of Stradlater.

The final, third element of drama in this chapter is escalated by the roommates' conflict becoming an actual fight. After Holden destroys the composition, the boys remain silent for a while. Holden lies down in bed, smoking, because he knows it drives Stradlater "crazy when you broke any rules" (54). Then Holden breaks the silence and interrogates Stradlater about his date. Holden wants to know if Jane received his regards, and if she still keeps her kings in the back row. Stradlater responds, "What the hell do ya think we did all night—play checkers, for Chrissake?" (55). Holden continues to ask about the date but can't conceal his nervousness. Instead of feeling any pity for Holden for being less advanced in his relations with females, or just because Holden did not have a Saturday night date, Stradlater finishes cutting his toenails and playfully shadow socks Holden on the shoulder. In between brushing his teeth, Stradlater tells Holden that he did not go to New York with Jane and that they just sat in his basketball coach's car.

Holden's fears about Stradlater seducing Jane continue to escalate. He asks whether Stradlater had sex with Jane, and the shadow-boxing, toothbrushing Stradlater simply says, "That's a professional secret, buddy" (56). Holden can't hold himself back and tries to sucker punch Stradlater. The swing misses its mark and only glances Stradlater on the side of the head. Holden explains that he did not land the punch well because he used his right hand and he has not made a good fist with it since Allie died. Stradlater quickly pins Holden to make him stop his insults and be quiet. Holden agrees to shut up, but as soon as Stradlater releases him, Holden insists that Stradlater is "a dirty stupid sonuvabitch of a moron" (58).

The conflict becomes a crisis when Stradlater punches Holden in the nose. The fight's only real punch stuns them both. Holden sees that Stradlater is worried and nervous that he may have hurt the younger boy. After some time, Stradlater leaves the room, and Holden searches for his red hunting hat and looks at his bloody face. Holden imagines that the blood makes him look tough as he also realizes he has lost the only two fights of his life. Holden declares himself to be "a pacifist, if you want to know the truth" (59). The pain of this assertion of truth is that Holden knows he is unable to fight well for Jane or even for himself. He retreats to Ackley's room. Holden does not

clearly see the war of sanity and maturation that is going on inside him. The need to know more about Holden's social and psychological problems is nicely set up by the dramatic conflicts within this short chapter.

Chapter 7

Holden's conflict with Ackley does not involve fists. Instead, in Chapter 7, Holden enters Ackley's room seeking comfort and refuge. Ackley is almost asleep and isn't interested in paying much attention to Holden beyond finding out about his fight with Stradlater. Despite Holden's having allowed Ackley to tag along on the Saturday night trip to Agerstown, Ackley does not return any good feeling or show any care for Holden despite seeing his bloody face. Holden finally lies down on Ackley's absent roommate's bed and thinks about how some kids talk about sex (like Ackley) while others, like Stradlater, experience it. After some time worrying about Jane and Stradlater together, Holden wakes Ackley to ask him about joining a monastery. Holden offhandedly wonders if one has to be Catholic to become a monk. Ackley misunderstands Holden and thinks he is offending the Catholic religion. Holden rises and takes Ackley's hand in "a big, phony handshake" (65). Ackley, confused, pulls his hand away. As Holden leaves, he pays Ackley phony compliments. Ackley responds, "somebody's gonna bash your—" (66) while Holden closes the door on a boy who is less mature (and possibly even more troubled) than himself.

As Holden walks the lonely hall of his Pencey Prep dorm, he thinks about seeing what Mal Brossard is up to. But he then decides to leave Pencey immediately, instead of waiting to leave at the end of term on Wednesday. He plans to stay in an inexpensive hotel in New York City and get some rest until his parents have digested the news of his flunking out. Holden calculates when his parents will receive the expulsion letter from Pencey. He is afraid of his mother's initial outburst and reasons that he needs "a little vacation" (67) because his nervous condition is not good.

Although Holden turns on the light in his room, smokes a cigarette, and packs two suitcases,

Stradlater remains asleep. Holden counts his money, then sells his typewriter to Frederick Woodruff, and stands in the dormitory hall "sort of crying" (68). He puts on his red hunting hat, with the brim to the rear, and yells out, "*Sleep tight, ya morons!*" (68). In the last sentence of the chapter, Holden notices peanut shells on the stairs as he almost breaks his "crazy" (68) neck leaving.

Chapter 8

During the cold walk to the train, Holden notices his face stinging from Stradlater's punch, but he is comforted by the warmth his new hunting hat provides and by his enjoyment of the fresh air. Holden does not care that the hunting hat makes him look silly. He reaches the train station about 10 minutes before the next departure for New York and cleans his face with some snow. Sitting down in the train, he thinks about reading magazine stories while riding trains at night. But he does not read this time and simply removes his hat. When an attractive, middle-aged woman boards at the next stop and enters Holden's almost-empty car, he immediately wonders why she sits next to him.

The woman who sits next to Holden is Mrs. Morrow. She notices Holden's Pencey Prep sticker and asks if he knows her son, Ernest. Holden thinks her son is "doubtless the biggest bastard that ever went to Pencey" (71). He hides his identity from Mrs. Morrow by giving his name as Rudolph Schmidt (actually the name of the dorm janitor). Holden's lying doesn't stop there. He tells Mrs. Morrow that her son adapts well. The mother believes her son is sensitive and not a "terribly good mixer" (72), while Holden remembers Ernest as someone who snaps people's asses with wet towels. Despite disliking his classmate, Holden is attracted to Mrs. Morrow. He appreciates her sincere smile and almost seems aware that she is insightful about her troubled son in ways that Holden wishes his own mother would be about himself.

Nonetheless, Holden continues to lie about Ernest. Holden and Mrs. Morrow light up cigarettes as he suggests they have a cocktail. At first, Mrs. Morrow questions Holden's age, but he believes that he does not usually have trouble being served because he is tall and has gray hair on one side of his head. Mrs. Morrow reminds Holden that the club car is probably closed. Holden's social approach to Mrs. Morrow is muffled not only by the facts she points out but also by her next question about the start of Christmas vacation for Pencey. Holden explains his early departure by lying about having "a tiny little tumor on the brain" (75). Even in his lie the reader gains a seed of truth—clearly Holden's head or state of consciousness is troubled and confused. After all, he is experiencing the psychological trauma of flunking out, while still struggling with ways to reconcile the death of his brother and to mature into a man. Mrs. Morrow politely invites Holden to join her family during the summer. The Morrows have a house in Gloucester, Massachusetts, right on the beach, complete with a private tennis court. Holden rejects the offer, knowing no amount of money could make him like a fellow such as Ernest.

Chapter 9

Salinger sketches Holden's closest contacts by starting Chapter 9 with Holden thinking about whom he can call from Penn Station. Holden considers calling his older brother, D. B., his younger sister, Phoebe, Jane Gallagher's mother (to find out when Jane would be home for the holidays), his girlfriend, Sally Hayes, and Carl Luce, an older friend from his time at Whooten. Holden, however, calls no one and instead catches a cab.

By mistake, Holden gives the cab driver his home address in MANHATTAN and, realizing this, then directs the driver to turn around in the middle of a one-way street cutting through Central Park. He next asks the driver where the ducks go when the lagoon near Central Park South freezes over. The driver thinks Holden is kidding him. Holden offers to buy the cabbie a drink, but the driver refuses. Clearly, Holden's attempts to phone people or even just talk to a cab driver are not working. When he arrives at the Edmont Hotel, he removes his hat before checking in so that he doesn't look like a "screwball" (79). At the same time, he observes that the hotel is "full of perverts and morons" (79).

From his hotel room, Holden can see into the room of a man dressing up as a woman and into a room of a couple spitting water (or alcohol) onto each other. Holden supposes that he himself is a sex maniac in his mind and thinks about possible sexual behaviors. He reasons that one should not have sexual fun with a girl if one does not like her, and if one does like her, he should not do "crumby" (sexual or sexually belittling) things. Holden doesn't understand the mysteries of sexual attraction. He feels left out because he is beginning to sense that "crumby stuff is a lot of fun sometimes" (79) and that he is somewhat sexually aroused.

Holden admits and swears to God that sex is something he does not understand. Then he thinks about calling Jane Gallagher at school or calling her mother to find out when Jane will be home. But Holden doesn't confront his fear and confusion about Jane. He decides not to call her because he is not "in the mood" (82) and instead calls up Faith Cavendish, a girl whose phone number he got from a friend at Princeton. Holden does not know Faith, but she is a girl who "did not mind doing it once in a while" (83). It takes Holden some time to connect with her through his friend, Eddie Birdsell. She does not remember anyone by that name until Holden finally adds that his friend is from Princeton. That seems to open the door on the phone conversation because Faith then remembers Eddie Birdsell as "a grand person" (84). She sounds a bit phony to Holden. When she asks how Eddie is doing, Holden equivocates. He is being just as phony as Faith because he only met Eddie Birdsell once at a party. Nonetheless, she actually entertains the idea of meeting Holden for a cocktail. After she begs off for this evening and suggests tomorrow, he insists he cannot make it except now. After he hangs up, he realizes that he "*really* fouled . . . up" (86) a chance to get together with Faith. In this chapter, Holden's frustration with his own lack of maturation is clearly illustrated through the discourse difficulties he experiences. His attempts to better understand his place in the world and to deepen his experience with sex and love are hindered by his inability to talk with Jane or talk honestly with Faith Cavendish.

Chapter 10

Chapter 10 begins with Holden thinking about calling his younger sister, Phoebe. He does not call her, though, because he is afraid that his parents might answer the phone. He believes his mother is "psychic" (87) about him and would know it is Holden calling even if he were to say nothing and hang up. As Holden ponders calling Phoebe, readers learn more about Holden's family. They learn that Holden's siblings are very bright and close to each other. Despite Holden's expressed dislike of movies, he takes Phoebe to them often and claims he took her to see her favorite movie (*The 39 Steps,* directed by Alfred Hitchcock) 10 times. Phoebe writes detective stories, and Holden sees humor in her thinking someone in his twenties is an old man. He then refers to her as "Old Phoebe" (89). She is 10 years old in the current happenings of the novel, but even as Holden remembers her at an earlier age, readers begin to see Phoebe as a character more mature than her age would indicate.

Once again, Holden decides not to make a phone call. Instead, he cleans himself up, puts on a fresh shirt, and decides to visit a nightclub in his hotel. He notices some "pimpy-looking guys, and a few whory-looking blondes" (90) in the lobby, and hears the Buddy Singer band playing in the Lavender Room. Holden follows the music into the nightclub and reflects that there are not any people his age there and that the music is not very good. He tries to order an alcoholic drink, but after the waiter asks to see his driver's license, Holden has a Coke instead. Holden remarks he should have tried to bribe the waiter because "in New York, boy, money really talks" (90). Throughout the novel he struggles with questions of age and maturity, but at least at this moment he realizes he's still "a goddam minor" (91).

Shortly after ordering his Coke, Holden starts to eye three women at the next table. He finally asks them to dance. Though they giggle, one of the girls, Bernice, agrees. Although she dances very well, she ignores Holden's conversation. Just as Holden is settling into enjoying dancing and not talking, Bernice mentions that she and her friends saw the movie star Peter Lorre as he was buying a newspaper. Because of her remark, Holden thinks she is not too smart. Nevertheless, he feels that she is such a good dancer that he suddenly kisses her where she parts her blond hair. Bernice questions this action, and Holden tries to explain why he kissed her, but uses the word "goddam." She seems to object to his language even more than to the forwardness of the kiss and asks him his age. He sarcastically replies that he's 12. Then they dance some more, even doing some jitterbugging. Though Holden knows he cannot really talk to her, he is "half in love" (95) and admits that girls drive him crazy.

Holden sits down with the three girls and tells them his name is Jim Steele. One of them, Marty, keeps asking Holden if his father is around for a date. Holden wants to engage in intelligent conversation, but the ladies would rather enjoy the music and talk about movie stars. Holden realizes that the girls, being tourists, mistakenly imagine that movie stars would frequent a place like the Lavender Room. He then tells Marty that he just saw Gary Cooper across the way (in order to get her to stop dancing), and when she turns around, he says that the star has left and that she just missed him. Marty rushes back to the table and lies to the other two girls about catching a glimpse of the movie star. The girls tell Holden that they must leave in order to get up early and catch the first show, a mix of film and live entertainment, at Radio City Music Hall. Holden protests, but the girls depart. As if to further his own attack on the movies, Holden says he is depressed because they are going to Radio City Music Hall, and not because they left him alone. At the end of the evening, Holden is stuck with the bill for all their drinks.

Chapter 11

Holden leaves the Lavender Room and sits in a chair in the lobby where he thinks about Jane and Stradlater in the back seat of a car. He tries to convince himself that he knows Jane "like a book" (99) while admitting his intimate relationship with her isn't "*physical*" (99). Salinger's use of italics in "physical" emphasizes the underlying potential sexuality of the physically close adolescents. During one summer, they lived next door to each other, they were members of the same country club, they often played tennis and golf together, and they held hands in the movies.

In the same way Holden knows movies too well to believe he really hates them, he shows conflict about Jane Gallagher. He remembers helping her improve her golf game. Holden says he was so good at golf that he was asked to be in a short golf movie. He decided not to be in the movie because he would prove himself to be a phony about hating movies. His mother is not fond of Jane or her mother and does not think Jane is very pretty, but Holden likes her. In fact, as he is feeling depressed and alone in the run-down hotel lobby, he seems determined to remember every possibly sexual touch they have had. Holden then decides to go to a jazz club in Greenwich Village. He knows about Ernie's because his brother D. B. was a regular there and used to take Holden along before D. B. "went out to Hollywood and prostituted himself" (104).

Chapter 12

In this chapter, Holden continues to feel lonesome and depressed. On his way to Ernie's, he asks another cab driver where the ducks in the Central Park lagoon go in the winter. This time, his cabbie, named Horwitz, is a talkative person who curses like Holden. At first, Horwitz appears so grouchy that Holden stops talking. Then suddenly, Horwitz seems willing to reason out the duck question. Horwitz asserts his claim that the ducks do not go anywhere by thinking about how the fish do not go anywhere. Holden questions the difference between ducks and fish and wonders where fish go when the whole lagoon freezes. In the end, Horwitz prevails by arguing that it is in their nature. Holden says he has no pleasure discussing this further with Horwitz but invites the cabbie to join him for a drink. Once again an adult questions the boy's age and wonders why he isn't home. After they arrive at Ernie's and Holden pays his fare, Horwitz perhaps realizes that Holden may be saying "ducks" and "fish" but is actually talking about himself. Horwitz's final comment to Holden begins, "If you were a fish, Mother Nature'd take care of *you*, wouldn't she?" (109).

Holden scans the audience at Ernie's, a thick crowd of mostly "prep school jerks and college jerks" who make Ernie's piano seem almost "*holy*" (109). Holden does not appreciate the fact that a mirror is set up to show the piano player's face instead of his hands. Holden is also critical about the way he hears Ernie overplaying a song and reflects that the morons who applaud the song are like people who laugh loudly at movies even when the scenes aren't very funny. As he waits for a table, he decides that, if he had Ernie's talent, he would be more humble. Holden blames the adoring audience for blinding Ernie to his ego and claims, "People always clap for the wrong things" (110). In some ways, Holden's comments about Ernie may point to some explanation of why Salinger himself became a recluse. Salinger's adoring fans and voluminous critical response probably overwhelmed him with applause that was often "wrong."

Holden is so upset with Ernie and depressed by the people in the club that he considers leaving. Instead of going, though, he is finally seated at a table and served an alcoholic drink. He settles into people-watching, eavesdropping, and criticizing particular people in the audience. One couple he notices is not very attractive, and Holden empathizes with ugly girls. Then he spots another couple: The girl is attractive, and the boy is probably from an Ivy League school. Holden comments, "All those Ivy League bastards look alike. My father wants me to go to Yale, or maybe Princeton, but I swear, I wouldn't go to one of those Ivy League colleges if I was *dying*" (112). The fellow Holden focuses on is trying to give his pretty date "a feel under the table" (112) while telling her about a guy in his dorm who attempted suicide. Holden is not only depressed by the people he is watching but sad sitting in the club alone. He requests the waiter to ask Ernie if he would join him for a drink.

The paradoxes of Holden liking and disliking people, and of being lonely and feeling uncomfortable with people, continue when Lillian Simmons arrives at his table with her date in tow. She once dated Holden's older brother, D. B., and her conversation ("Don't you have a date, baby?" [113]) and the crowded tables make Holden uncomfortable. Although Lillian invites Holden to join them, he lies and says he has to meet someone. Reluctantly leaving before he hears Ernie play something good, Holden asserts at the very end of the chapter that "People are always ruining things" (114). The completion of this chapter not only echoes an earlier observation about people clapping for the wrong things but states a basic claim about humanity. Readers may sense that this claim is more skeptical than Holden really feels. People may ruin things, but Holden's need for people is clearly dramatized despite his continuing awkwardness with most people he describes in the novel.

Chapter 13

Holden walks the cold two miles back to his hotel because he is tired of getting in and out of cabs. Though his new hat provides warmth, he misses his stolen gloves and imagines himself confronting the student at Pencey who stole them. Holden admits to himself that he's too "yellow" to confront anyone and sock him, and hopes that he is not "*all* yellow" (117). He might insult his imagined adversary, but he believes that he would avoid a fistfight despite just having had one with Stradlater. He rationalizes his fear by thinking that he does not have much he would care about losing and that he could not stand looking at a face he was hitting. However, Holden finally admits "it's yellowness, all right. I'm not kidding myself" (117) and realizes on his walk that the more aware he is of his own cowardice, the more depressed he gets.

As Holden returns to his hotel room, he is approached by the elevator operator, named Maurice, and asked if he would be interested in sex with a girl for $5. For $15 she would stay the whole night. Holden accepts the pimp's offer and decides on a "throw" (119) for $5. Maurice says he will send a girl up in 15 minutes, and Holden asks if she is attractive because he does not want "any old bag" (119). Although Holden sounds experienced with prostitutes, he admits to being a virgin as he gets ready for his visitor. He explains his virginity by saying that when girls tell him to stop just before having intercourse, he does stop. Holden thinks a prostitute will be good "practice" if he ever gets married. He remembers once reading about how a woman's body is like a violin and "it takes a terrific musician to play it right" (121).

Holden needs plenty of practice because when he hears the prostitute's knock, he trips over his suitcase on his way to answer the door. His inexperience continues from physical to verbal tripping.

Sunny, the prostitute, is a skinny young woman with a "wheeny-whiny voice" (123), but she is certainly not an "old bag." Holden claims to be "Jim Steele" and 22 years old. Sunny remains skeptical, and when Holden asks how old she is, she responds, "Old enough to know better" (123). The prostitute tries to rush him into sex by pulling her dress over her head. Holden supposes this should produce a sexy feeling in him, but instead he feels "much more depressed than sexy" (123). Stalling, Holden asks Sunny if she wants to chat. Although he wonders how she became a prostitute, he instead asks if she comes from New York. Sunny tells Holden she is from Hollywood and asks him to hang up her dress. Holden decides he could not have sex with someone who spends most of her day in the movies. He tells her he does not feel like himself but that he will still pay her. When she asks what the problem is, Holden lies about a recent operation on his "clavichord" (126). (A clavichord is actually a musical instrument.) Sunny says he is cute and looks like someone in the movies. She tries to seduce him by sitting on his lap and "getting funny" (126) with him, but she is upset when he does not want to continue and complains that Maurice woke her up to go to Holden's room. Holden admits he was "a little premature in [his] calculations" (127) that he was ready for sex after his operation. He pays her the agreed-upon $5 only to have her say it costs $10. Holden does not give Sunny the extra money but thinks that her little voice sounds pretty scary as she gets dressed and leaves.

Chapter 14

Mathematically, the 14th chapter should mark the beginning of the second half of the 26-chapter book. Although the chapter opens as the sun begins to rise on Sunday, Chapter 14 conversely represents the low point of the first part of *The Catcher in the Rye*. Holden is so upset that he starts talking to his dead brother, Allie, about an incident from their boyhood in Maine years ago. Holden planned to ride bikes and shoot a BB gun with his friend Bobby Fallon. Instead of including Allie, Holden told his younger brother that he could not go along with them since he was still a child. Holden finally stops talking out loud to the imaginary Allie and tries to pray.

Although this chapter contains depressing events for Holden, the reader gets a sense of Holden's spirituality, despite his inability to pray. Holden reveals that he possesses a critical sense of the Bible by the way he questions the roles of the disciples in supporting Jesus. He likewise shows compassion and depth in imagining that Jesus could forgive Judas and allow his own betrayer to enter heaven. Evidently, Holden has read the Bible closely and has given serious thought about issues that are key for him. Nonetheless, he displays little interest in organized religion (his parents came into the marriage from different religions) and says that the ministers at the schools he has attended have "Holy Joe voices" (131) that sound much too phony.

Holden's reverie about religion and spiritual matters is interrupted by Sunny and Maurice at his door. The prostitute and pimp have returned to collect $5 more from Holden. Although Holden tries to stand up to them, Maurice shoves his way in. Holden, now afraid, attempts with his voice cracking to argue the original prices Maurice stated, but Sunny grabs Holden's wallet and takes $5. Holden begins to cry. Sunny suggests that Maurice leave the boy alone, but Maurice snaps his finger on Holden's pajamas near his genitals. When Holden throws some insults at Maurice, the pimp punches the boy in the stomach and the couple leaves. Only the wind has been knocked out of Holden, but he is afraid he is dying.

On his way to the bathroom, Holden pretends the punch was a bullet. He imagines himself in a Hollywood shootout fantasy where he, in turn, shoots Maurice. He then imagines that Jane Gallagher comes over to "bandage up [his] guts" (136). Holden's faulty guts would likely be "bandaged" by a relationship with Jane, but he probably realizes the relationship in reality is out of reach as he ends the fantasy by cursing the movies, which he claims ruin people. Holden gets in bed but does not feel tired. He admits that what he "felt like, though, was committing suicide" (136). He considers jumping out of the window and thinks he would if he could be sure someone would cover him up from passersby gawking at his gory body.

Chapter 15

When Holden awakes at around 10 o'clock, he considers giving Jane a call (but, as always, "isn't in the mood" [137]). Instead, he phones Sally Hayes. He thinks about how Sally seems intelligent because she is cultured, but that she really is not intelligent. Holden reflects on the fact that anyone he is kissing seems intelligent at the time. In a typically paradoxical way, Holden believes that intelligence and sexual attraction are not connected; however, he also cannot stop thinking about the problem. After Sally agrees to meet him later for a matinee of a play, Holden feels irritated because she uses phony words like "grand" (138). He reasons that Sally is "a pain in the ass, but she was very good looking" (139). Although still confused about relating to women, Holden realizes his depression from the night before has decreased. Instead of considering suicide, he decides he is hungry and leaves the hotel.

In this chapter, Holden discusses money and class issues by focusing on luggage. After storing his own luggage in a locker in Grand Central Station, he goes to get breakfast. While he is eating his eggs at the counter, two nuns awkwardly sit down beside him and do not seem to know where to put their luggage. Holden notices the nuns' cheap suitcases, which cause him to remember an incident with Dick Slagle, a new roommate of his at Elkton Hills. Where Slagle's luggage was shoddy, Holden's was very fine. When Slagle removed his own luggage from the rack in their dorm room and hid it under his bed, Holden did the same to spare his roommate's feelings. However, Slagle then put Holden's luggage back on the rack to give the illusion that Holden's finer bags might be his own. Slagle accused Holden of being "bourgeois" (141), at first in a humorous way. Soon the differences in the two boys' economic backgrounds provided too much friction, and they stopped rooming together. But Holden remarks that he "missed" (142) Slagle afterwards. (Holden's use of the word "miss" will echo in his statement at the novel's conclusion of "missing everybody" [277].)

After Holden notices the nuns' luggage, he also sees their collection basket and offers to contribute. He donates $10 (the same amount Sunny and Maurice had extracted from him) and discusses *Romeo and Juliet* with the nun who said she teaches English. Holden is less interested in the romance between the main characters than empathizing with Mercutio. He is upset that Mercutio is killed because of Romeo. Holden feels Mercutio (perhaps like Allie) is too intelligent and entertaining to get killed by mistake.

Holden, sensitive about discussing religious affiliation, is glad the nuns do not ask if he is Catholic. He remembers the first boy he met at the Whooten School, Louis Shaney. The two were becoming friendly discussing tennis when, at one point, Louis asked Holden if he had noticed the whereabouts of the Catholic church. Holden feels upset with the way people connect to other people through religion. He is trying to figure out his frustration with religious labels and economic difficulties. If readers follow Holden's observations about cheap and expensive luggage, they are given hints of his struggles to bridge human differences.

Holden's problems continue. His confusion between sex and love is ongoing; his sense of morality is insightful but needs more development; and he is troubled about the economic disparity among the people he knows. The chapter concludes with Holden expressing his regrets about not giving the nuns more money.

Chapter 16

This chapter begins with Holden imagining his mother, one of his aunts, and Sally Hayes's mother collecting money for people on the street. He can picture his mother participating in such a charitable activity but not his aunt or Sally Hayes's mother because their superficial concerns would never allow them to humble themselves to help others.

Not only does Holden feel uncomfortable with differences in class, but he also addresses race in this chapter. He decides to buy a record of "Little Shirley Beans" for his younger sister, Phoebe, because he loved the recording the first time he heard it. However, Holden is not talking here about a quick infatuation with some popular music. He explains that he likes the recording of "Little Shirley Beans" because it was done in the 1920s by an African-American singer, Estelle Fletcher. Holden admires Fletcher's style (even though he calls it "very Dixieland and whorehouse" [149]) and insightfully praises her ability to avoid making the song sound cute. Though it is quite natural today to appreciate entertainers regardless of race, in the l950s, white Americans were only beginning to give equal admiration to black performers.

Chapter 16 begins to deepen the meaning of the novel's title. As Holden walks toward his date with Sally and his hopes of finding a recording of "Little Shirley Beans" for sale, he notices a poor family walking directly ahead of him. The parents are not paying any attention to their young son, who is walking in the street, though next to the curb. The child's life is somewhat endangered as the traffic zooms close to him and "brakes screeched all over the place" (150). The boy is singing, "If a body catch a body coming through the rye" (150). The correct lyric to the song is "If a body *meet* a body coming through the rye" (224), based on the poem, "Comin Thro' the Rye" by Robert Burns. (Burns [1759–96] is the national poet of Scotland and one of Salinger's self-acknowledged beloved writers. Burns is also referred to in "SEYMOUR: AN INTRODUCTION" [162].) The substitution of "catch" for "meet" and the fact that the child is endangered emphasize the need for children to be "caught" and saved. Holden, however, at this time does not consciously acknowledge the significance of the lyric or the danger. The kid's "singing for the hell of it" simply makes Holden "feel not so depressed any more" (150).

Further along on his walk to the theater, Holden starts to become depressed by seeing all of the people attired in their Sunday clothes and lined up at the movie houses. He quickly leaves Broadway and finds a copy of "Little Shirley Beans" in a record store. Holden remarks that it cost him $5 (the reader will recall this is the same price Maurice quoted him for a "throw" with the prostitute), but this high (at the time) price does not bother him. He is happy to find a copy of the difficult-to-locate record that he can now give to Phoebe.

Holden is finally in the mood to call Jane Gallagher and goes into a drugstore to phone. When her mother answers, however, he hangs up because he does not feel like talking to Jane's mother. He then buys theater tickets on Broadway for a benefit performance of a play titled (and the reader will recognize the irony) *I Know My Love*. Holden says he does not like the theater much but admits it is better than the movies. *I Know My Love* stars the Lunts, an acting duo with a sophisticated style, and Holden thinks the play will impress Sally. Holden implies that Sally likes phony sophistication by explaining that the play is not so good but that the Lunts will appeal to Sally because of their status. He then remembers his older brother D. B. taking him to see *Hamlet* starring Sir Laurence Olivier. Although Olivier was considered one of the greatest Shakespearean actors of all time, Holden thinks he was not well cast as Hamlet, being more suited to play a general than "a sad, screwed-up type guy" (152).

Holden goes to the bandstand in Central Park because he used to skate there and knows Phoebe does too. When he does not see her there, he asks a young girl if she knows Phoebe Caulfield, a fourth grader who lives on Seventy-first Street. It turns out that the girl does know Phoebe. When Holden asks where his sister is, the girl replies that Phoebe may be at the museum because her own class went there last Saturday. Holden learns "the museum" (154) is the Museum of Natural History. Holden helps the girl with her skates, remarking, "God, I love it when a kid's nice and polite when you tighten their skate for them" (155). The girl then skates off to be with her friends, and Holden walks to the Museum of Natural History even though he has realized it is actually Sunday and Phoebe wouldn't be there with her class. He reflects that he likes the museum because nothing ever changed even if you went there repeatedly. Holden laments that "the only thing that would be different would be *you*" (158). A central part of Holden's psychology is revealed in this chapter when he tells the reader, "Certain things they should stay the way they are. You ought to be able to stick them in one of those big glass cases and just leave them alone. I know that's impossible, but it's too bad anyway" (158). When he finally arrives at the museum, he does not want to go in.

Chapter 17

Holden catches a cab to the Biltmore Hotel to meet Sally. As he waits for her, he watches girls in the lobby. This chapter really begins to focus on how Holden views girls and misunderstands them a great deal. One of the reasons students continue to read and enjoy *The Catcher in the Rye* is most certainly the fact that they can identify with Holden's awkwardness. At the same time, young readers may learn from Holden's social, cultural, and psychological insights as he describes the way he works through his problems. Holden's descriptions, however, are more poetical than logical, and he somehow leaps in his mind from watching the girls to wondering what will eventually happen to them. Holden imagines the girls ending up with men who are not like himself. (It is interesting to note that in this list, which includes men obsessed with their car's mileage, with winning sports contests, and with being mean, or who are just bores, is that Holden includes "Guys that never read books" [160].) When Holden says "bores," he then remembers Harris Macklin, another former roommate at Elkton Hills. Holden calls Harris a bore but cautions himself. He admits that he does not understand boring people but he does remember Harris as a great whistler. In other words, Holden is starting to question his judgments about people, as he concedes that boring people may be "terrific whistlers" (161).

Chapter 17 presents the adolescent problem of young folks simply trying to be comfortable and enjoy a date. Holden's first sighting of Sally Hayes sends him into a whirl of emotion. He admits he is crazy about her even though he does not like her. The moment he sees Sally in her black coat and beret, he feels love and wants to marry her. As he predicted, Sally is thrilled about seeing a play starring the Lunts. In the cab ride to the theater, Holden makes out with Sally and even tells her he loves her. Sally says she loves him too, but "in the same damn breath" (163) she asks him to let his hair grow because she thinks crew cuts look corny. She assuages him by saying his hair is "lovely," and Holden responds, "Lovely my ass" (163). Holden careens between foolishly trying to love Sally and seeing right through her.

He almost comically falls off the seat in the cab several times.

The play gives Holden a chance to continue observing phoniness and to fumble with his date. He experiences the Lunts more as celebrities than as actors and views the rest of the actors as just actors who don't create enough of their characters for him to see them as anything but actors. Holden remains very critical during the intermission. He claims to see all of the "jerks" and "phonies" (164) in the lobby. Sally notices an acquaintance across the lobby, and "George something" (165) comes to join them between acts. Holden feels left out as George (in a "very phony, Ivy league voice" [166]) and Sally praise the Lunts and talk about people they know. Holden thinks it "the phoniest conversation you ever heard in your life" (166) and admits to hating Sally a little after the other boy has left. However, she changes his mood by suggesting they go skating at Radio City. Sally is interested in renting a short skating skirt, and Holden admits that he enjoys watching her in it, even while he thinks he and Sally are the worst skaters on the ice.

After struggling on the ice, they stop for drinks. Holden is once again refused alcohol and responds in a stranger manner, by lighting matches uselessly. When Sally asks Holden whether he intends to spend Christmas Eve at her house, he rants about hating school. Sally agrees school is boring but will not agree to hate it. Holden starts telling Sally that he hates many things until she responds that she doesn't know what he's talking about. Holden's shouting and jumping from point to point escalates into his suggesting that they escape to New England and eventually marry and live near a brook. Sally tries to have him see reason and explains the impossibility of his scheme by correctly saying "we're both practically *child*ren" (172). Soon their discussion becomes an argument. When Holden finally tells Sally that she gives him "a royal pain in the ass" (173), she refuses to accept his apologies or let him take her home. The date ends with Holden leaving without saying good-bye. He admits to himself that he must be crazy because, though he realizes Sally is not someone he would want to run away with, he was sincere when he asked her to join him.

Chapter 18

Hungry, Holden goes to a drugstore lunch counter and has "a Swiss cheese sandwich and a malted" (175), the exact lunch he has told the reader, in Chapter 15, that he usually gets when out. Going into a phone booth there, he considers calling Jane and reflects on his trouble with girls. Holden meditates on a series of impressions. He concludes that if a girl likes someone and if that boy talks about himself, the girl decides he has an inferiority complex. On the other hand, when a girl is not attracted to the boy, and the boy talks about himself, he is perceived as conceited. Holden then tries to call Jane and "take her dancing or something somewhere" (175), but he gets no answer. He then decides to phone a young man he knew from the Whooten School. Carl Luce is three years older than Holden, has an exceptionally high IQ, and attends Columbia University. Although Holden once called Carl a phony, Carl seems to be one of Holden's only acquaintances. The young man declines Holden's invitation to dinner and some "slightly intellectual conversation" (177), but agrees to meet Holden at the Wicker Bar at 10 P.M. for a drink.

As if his failed date with Sally Hayes were not enough, Holden, in order to kill some time, subjects himself to more punishment by seeing the Christmas show and a movie at Radio City Music Hall (where he had gone to the Christmas show with Sally the year before). Holden's criticism of this year's performance is nonstop. Everything but the man playing the kettle drum displeases Holden. He explains that Jesus himself wouldn't be very pleased with anything in the Christmas performance either, except for the drummer because he drums "so nice and sweet" (179). Holden is just as annoyed with the plot of the war movie he then watches; he is angry at a mother sitting near him who cries at the sentimental parts while ignoring her son's need to be taken to the bathroom.

When Holden leaves, he continues to think about war. He mentions that his brother D. B. was in World War II, landing in France on D-day, and was in the army for a total of four years. At one point, Holden declares that D. B. "hated the Army worse than the war" (181) and that his brother said "the Army was practically as full of bastards as the Nazis" (182). Holden emphasizes that he himself would have nothing to do with either war or the army. He then questions D. B.'s ability to hate war but yet enjoy ERNEST HEMINGWAY's war novel, *A Farewell to Arms*. Holden prefers books by Ring Lardner, as well as F. SCOTT FITZGERALD's *The Great Gatsby*. Holden claims he is "sort of glad they've got the atomic bomb invented. If there's another war, I'm going to sit right the hell on top of it. I'll volunteer for it, I swear to God I will" (183). One example of the novel's impact on filmmakers can be found in this image by Salinger made famous by Stanley Kubrick as the conclusion to his 1964 cinematic masterpiece, *Dr. Strangelove or: How I Learned to Stop Worrying and Love the Bomb*.

Chapter 19

Holden displays a fairly sophisticated social history for a 16-year-old boy. In this chapter he thinks about homosexuality, spiritual sexuality, and his own loneliness. Holden arrives early at the Wicker Bar to meet Carl Luce, an older boy who was Holden's student adviser while at Whooten. (Luce would "give these sex talks and all, late at night when there was a bunch of guys in his room" [185].) Holden realizes he has been at the bar before and remembers two women who sang in French accents and played piano there. Holden passes the time drinking a couple of Scotch and sodas while he watches "phonies," especially one guy telling his date that "she had aristocratic hands" (185). He thinks that "the other end of the bar was full of flits" (185) ("flit" is a derogatory term for homosexual). Holden greets Carl Luce by suggesting Luce may have an interest in a flit. Luce calmly asks Holden when he is going to grow up. Holden persists and asks Luce if he is majoring in perverts at Columbia University. Luce finally asks if this is going to be "a typical Caulfield conversation" (188). Holden continues to pry into the older boy's sex life. Luce admits to having a relationship in Greenwich Village with a Chinese sculptress in her thirties. He also tells Holden that he finds "Eastern philosophy more satisfactory than Western" (190). This is the first mention in Salinger's works of his abiding interest in the East, as Salinger makes evident that Holden admires Luce's experience and intelligence.

Luce orders a second, drier martini, and explains that those in the East approach sex as both a physical and spiritual experience. Holden instantly and too emphatically identifies with the idea. He then confesses that he has to like a girl a lot before he can have sex with her, and that his sex life is not good. Luce responds to Holden without hesitation. He claims to know the problem already and has the solution—psychoanalysis. Luce, whose father is a psychoanalyst, explains to Holden that psychoanalysis helps people see the patterns that their minds make in life, and that his father helps people make adjustments. He suggests that Holden see his father, but then says he does not care one way or the other. Holden touches Luce on the shoulder and calls him "a real friendly bastard" (192). Luce informs Holden that he is leaving. Even though Holden admits he is lonely, he cannot convince Luce to stay for another drink.

Chapter 20

Holden remains in the Wicker Bar after Luce has left. He drinks more, listens to music, and asks the headwaiter to invite the singer to his table for a drink. However, Holden guesses his invitation will not be delivered because people in general don't forward messages. His attempts to reach out to Luce and the singer at the Wicker Bar have failed. Holden realizes he is drunk and mimes that he is concealing bleeding guts from an imaginary gunshot. He imagines himself, with irony, hiding "the fact that [he] was a wounded sonuvabitch" (195) in this fantasy that reflects the opposite of his reality. Holden decides to call Jane, loses the mood, and calls Sally Hayes instead. Though clearly drunk, he gets through to "old Sally" (196) and tells her that he will come over to trim her tree on Christmas Eve. She asks if he is drunk and whom he is with. Holden admits to being drunk and alone. He then brings Sally into his fantasy world by sarcastically claiming to have been shot and that he is actually holding his guts. Finally, he repeats his intention to trim her Christmas tree, though this time with possible sexual overtones. After Sally agrees to his coming over on Christmas Eve, he hangs up. Holden remains in the phone booth doubting the wisdom of his call and

thinking that when he gets drunk he is "a madman" (197).

Holden staggers out of the phone booth and into the men's room, where he douses his head in a washbowl of water. He then sits on the radiator for warmth while the water from his head drips down and makes him cold. When the piano player enters the men's room, Holden inquires about the singer and asks the piano player to give her his compliments. The older man suggests that Holden go home. Holden persists, first admiring the man's talent and hair, then offering to be the musician's manager, and, finally, claiming that he has no home. The musician finishes combing his hair and leaves. Holden decides the piano player is shallow like Stradlater and other handsome guys because after their hair is combed they always leave. Having failed to gain help, Holden begins to cry. At the hatcheck room, he realizes he is missing his ticket, but the hatcheck girl gives him his coat nonetheless. She declines his tip and his request for a date but maternally makes Holden put his hat on as he leaves.

Holden emerges into the night air not feeling drunk so much as cold. He drops "Little Shirley Beans" and breaks the record, but keeps the pieces in his coat pocket. Shattered himself, and still a bit drunk, Holden goes into Central Park and decides to see about the ducks in the lagoon. He has great difficulty finding the lagoon even though he says he knows "Central Park like the back of [his] hand" (200). When he does finally find the lagoon, he discovers it is only partly frozen. He does not see any ducks around, even though he walks completely around the lagoon and nearly falls into the water searching. Holden sits on a bench, shivering, with ice forming on the back of his head although he has kept his hunting hat on. He fears he may be getting pneumonia and that he will die. The thought causes Holden to visualize "millions of jerks" (200) coming to his funeral. He says he feels sorry for his parents, especially because his mother has not recovered from Allie's death. Holden is relieved to think that, should he die, his parents will not allow Phoebe to attend his funeral. Readers learn that Holden did not attend his younger brother's funeral because he was still in the hospital after hurting his hand by smashing the windows of the garage upon Allie's death. Holden hates the idea of cemeteries and declares, "I hope to hell when I do die somebody has sense enough to just dump me in the river" (201). Holden explains he has gone to Allie's grave, and that is okay if the sun is out. But one day, when it started to rain hard, he realized that the cemetery visitors "could get in their cars and turn on their radios and all and then go someplace nice for dinner—everybody except Allie. [He] couldn't stand it" (202). To change his line of thought, Holden decides to count his money. Although he was "pretty loaded" (67) when he left Pencey, he now has left only three dollar bills, five quarters and a nickel. As another illustration of the way Holden's reasoning sometimes hurts him, he decides that skipping the coins into the lagoon will take his mind off pneumonia. He finally leaves the park and decides to sneak home to see Phoebe.

Chapter 21

Holden maneuvers his way past the new night elevator operator by claiming to be visiting the Dicksteins, who share the other half of the floor of the building with the Caulfields. He successfully sneaks into the apartment and finds Phoebe sleeping in D. B.'s room. Holden watches his younger sister sleep for a while and thinks that adults "look lousy" (207) when they sleep but kids do not. After reading through her school notebooks and smoking his last cigarette, Holden wakes Phoebe. At first they talk about Phoebe playing Benedict Arnold in her play, "A Christmas Pageant for Americans," and about D. B.'s latest work in Hollywood. Holden asks her about a bandage on her arm and learns that Curtis Weintraub, a young boy, pushed her and hurt her. The push may have been in response to a prank when Phoebe and her friend put ink on Weintraub's windbreaker. Holden then asks if she is "a child for God's sake?" (213).

Holden's ploy to distract Phoebe from his unexpected appearance quickly deteriorates as she begins to realize the reason he is home early: He got kicked out again. She hits him and warns, "Daddy'll kill you!" (214). Phoebe's disappointment with her brother for flunking out of yet another school is not assuaged when he tells her that he may get a job on a ranch in Colorado. She hides her head under her pillow, and Holden leaves to get more cigarettes from the living room cigarette box. This brief pause ends the chapter but not this first scene between the two siblings.

Chapter 22

Chapter 22 is central to understanding the title of the novel. Holden may be able to talk his way in and out of trouble with many of the book's characters, but when he talks with Phoebe, he is faced with the truth of his own youth. Although Phoebe is only a 10-year-old child in the fourth grade, she is shown in the chapter as a character who is precociously wise. Holden tries to minimize his recent failure at Pencey by saying it does not matter because he is going to a ranch in Colorado. Phoebe replies, "Don't make me laugh. You can't even ride a horse" (216). Although Holden is six years older than his sister, he can't manipulate her thinking.

Holden's failure to mature as a student means that he will probably be sent to a military academy instead of another prep school. Phoebe and Holden both know this, but she probes further. When she asks why he is flunking out, she already is aware of Holden's intelligence and knows that he has chosen to fail. He says that Pencey was filled with phonies and mean guys. In this sense, however, Holden's sensitivity is deepened beyond his usual accusations of phoniness. He admits he is too much of a coward *not* to join a secret fraternity. The values of social fairness and human sensitivity that Holden uses to criticize Pencey are turned around and used by Phoebe to challenge her brother. She wisely corners him into talking about what he likes, for a change. Holden stalls, trying to think of a reply, and says it is because he cannot concentrate too well.

When Holden finally tries to tell Phoebe about something he likes, he instead tells the sad story of James Castle, a fellow student at Elkton Hills. Castle killed himself by jumping out of a window because a group of boys had tried to make him take back something he had said about one of them. When Castle jumped, he was wearing a turtleneck sweater Holden had lent him. Phoebe again claims Holden cannot think of anything he likes. Holden responds that he likes Allie and talking with Phoebe. He does not convince his younger sister that he likes something, though; she then pushes further by asking what he would like to be. Holden responds by explaining that he does not want to be a lawyer like their father because he would become unaware of his own phoniness.

Holden finally reveals what he would like to do by quoting from the song he heard the little boy singing: "If a body catch a body comin' through the rye" (224). Phoebe corrects Holden and says the lyric is "if a body *meet* a body coming through the rye" (224). Holden's use of "catch" instead of "meet" is incorrect, but it does not stop him from telling Phoebe he is imagining kids playing in a field of rye where he is the only big person around. Holden says, "I'm standing on the edge of some crazy cliff. . . . I have to catch everybody if they start to go over the cliff—I mean if they're running and they don't look where they're going I have to come out from somewhere and *catch* them. . . . I'd just be the catcher in the rye and all. I know it's crazy, but that's the only thing I'd really like to be" (224–225). Phoebe listens to his fantasy; her only comment is that their father is going to kill Holden. Holden finally says he does not care and decides to call Mr. Antolini, a teacher whom he knew and liked from Elkton Hills. Mr. Antolini is now an English professor at New York University.

Chapter 23

Holden tells Mr. Antolini that he has flunked out of Pencey and agrees to come right over when his concerned former teacher invites him. Holden remembers that Mr. Antolini was the person who found James Castle; he recalls, too, that the teacher did not care that the dead boy bloodied his sport coat as he carried the body to the infirmary. Mr. Antolini is young, not much older than Holden's older brother, D. B., and Holden considers Mr. Antolini the best teacher he has ever had.

When Holden returns from calling Mr. Antolini, he finds Phoebe listening to music on the radio. The two siblings dance for several songs. Just after they stop, their parents come home. Holden hides in the closet. Mrs. Caulfield has seen the light on and comes into the room. When she says she

smells cigarette smoke, Phoebe covers for Holden by saying she only had one puff and threw the cigarette away. After the mother expresses her dislike of Phoebe's smoking, she inquires about the rest of the child's evening before leaving the room to take aspirins for her headache. Holden decides to slip out of the apartment while his parents are getting ready for bed. He has to borrow the money Phoebe was saving for Christmas presents. Holden accepts her money but cries as he takes it. After calming down, Holden gives Phoebe his red hunting hat, because he believes his sister "likes those kind of crazy hats" (223) and also because he wants to show her that she is helping him understand some of his own craziness, or at least sharing it with him.

Chapter 24

Chapter 24 may be one of the novel's most challenging chapters to read because it artfully employs ambiguity regarding Mr. Antolini's character and Holden's perceptions. Since their days at Elkton Hills, Mr. Antolini has married a wealthy older woman and has become close to Holden and the Caulfields. Mr. Antolini intellectually understands D. B.'s story-writing talent and echoed Holden in advising D. B. not to go to Hollywood. Holden remembers that his teacher is a heavy drinker when the latter opens the door while holding a highball. Mr. Antolini directly asks what the trouble was at Pencey and wonders how Holden did in English. Holden replies that he did all right in English but that he flunked Oral Expression because the students were instructed to say "Digression!" whenever a student speaker digressed from the point of a speech. Holden felt very sensitive about the way the class interrupted "nice" (239) things when a fellow student digressed and seemed to care about what he was telling the class. Mr. Antolini suggests that there is a time and a place for everything and that maybe it isn't always so bad to avoid digressing.

Mrs. Antolini serves coffee and cake. After asking after Holden's mother, she ignores the boy's response and inquires if "you boys" (241) can make the couch up. The Antolinis kiss goodnight and she leaves. Mr. Antolini then tells Holden he has been in touch with Holden's father. Not only is Mr. Antolini a caring teacher long after his student has left his class, but he is also honest enough to tell Holden that he realizes the boy is heading for some type of horrible fall. Mr. Antolini is worried that Holden will end up hating everybody, but Holden says he hates people only for a little while. He realizes that when he hasn't seen them, he "sort of missed them" (243). (This is another fore-echo of the novel's conclusion of "missing everybody" [277].) Antolini goes on to predict the fall Holden will have: "The man falling isn't permitted to feel or hear himself hit bottom. He just keeps falling and falling" (243). He explains the fall is the result of Holden's looking for something in his environment that is not there. The real problem that Mr. Antolini diagnoses is that Holden's unwarranted expectations will cause the boy to stop trying to mature and learning to improve his life. "I can very clearly see you dying nobly . . . for some highly unworthy cause" (244), Mr. Antolini predicts. He then writes down a quote from William Stekel, a psychoanalyst, for Holden, asking him to keep the paper. Here, Holden tells the reader he still has the paper and that the quote reads, "The mark of the immature man is that he wants to die nobly for a cause, while the mark of the mature man is that he wants to live humbly for one" (244). The teacher continues by saying that once Holden learns where he really wants to go, he will have to apply himself in school. Mr. Antolini is passionate in his belief about Holden's need for academic learning: "You're a student—whether the idea appeals to you or not. You're in love with knowledge" (245). He wants Holden to understand that his troubles are not dissimilar from the troubles that others face. The teacher also argues that an academic education can teach Holden to measure the size of his mind and better understand what belongs in it and what does not.

Although Mr. Antolini is passionately trying to teach the boy about life as an educated man, Holden yawns and they make up the couch for his bed. Mr. Antolini asks Holden about Sally and Jane, asks if the light in the kitchen will bother him, and then says, "Good night, handsome" (248). Holden tries to think about what he has been told but quickly falls asleep on the couch. He is awakened by Mr. Antolini patting his head. Holden thinks the teacher's act of stroking his head is "perverty" (249). Panicked, he abruptly leaves the apartment.

Chapter 25

This penultimate chapter of the book begins with Holden reconsidering the meaning of Mr. Antolini's head patting, and he gives the teacher the benefit of the doubt. Holden retrieves his bags at Grand Central Station and sleeps on a bench in the waiting room until he is awakened by Monday morning commuters. As he leaves Grand Central Station to find some breakfast, he hears two workmen taking a large Christmas tree off a truck and cursing, "Hold the sonuvabitch *up*! Hold it *up*, for Chrissake!" (255). He laughs, but then it makes him nauseous. After attempting to eat breakfast, but not being able to swallow a doughnut, Holden enjoys the Christmas spirit on Fifth Avenue. He walks and walks until he develops a panic attack as he steps off the curb at the end of the block. This leads Holden to start talking to Allie, begging his dead brother not to let him disappear as he crosses each street. Once Holden gets safely across the street, he thanks Allie. Finally, Holden decides to run away, but he wants to first say good-bye to Phoebe and to return her Christmas money. Holden imagines that he will hitchhike out west and become a gas station attendant. He will pretend to be a deaf-mute person to avoid stupid conversations. He even imagines finding a beautiful deaf-mute girl to marry and decides that if they were to have any children, they would hide them.

Holden dashes into a stationery store to buy a pad and pencil. He walks to Phoebe's school and, while sitting on the school stairs, writes her a note. Holden tells his sister that he plans to hitchhike out west that afternoon, but he wants to meet her at the Museum of Art near her school at 12:15. As he is walking to the principal's office to have them deliver his note, he sees "Fuck you" (260) written on the wall. The graffiti drives Holden crazy, and he musters the courage to rub it off the wall so that it will not hurt young children. After giving the note to the school secretary, and lying about their sick mother not being able to prepare lunch, Holden sees a second "Fuck you" (262). This time, he cannot remove it because the words are scratched into the wall. Holden realizes the futility of his actions: "If you had a million years to do it in, you couldn't rub out even *half* the 'Fuck you' signs in the world. It's impossible" (262).

While Holden waits for Phoebe inside the front doors of the museum, he meets two young brothers searching for "*mummies*—them dead guys" (263). He guides them to a reconstructed Egyptian tomb, explaining the mystery of Egyptian mummification, which recalls to the reader Holden's poor test paper for Mr. Spencer's class. However, the mummy frightens the two younger boys, and they leave. Holden feels peaceful in the tomb until he sees another "Fuck you." He comments, "You can't ever find a place that's nice and peaceful, because there isn't any" (264). Holden even imagines someone writing "Fuck you" on his own tombstone. He leaves the exhibit, goes into the bathroom, and passes out. When he revives, he emerges from the bathroom feeling better.

Phoebe arrives at the museum wearing Holden's red hunting hat and carrying his old suitcase full of her clothes. He almost faints when she tells him that she is going to accompany him out west. Holden refuses to entertain any possibility of this. When Phoebe cries, he reminds her that she is supposed to be in a play. He checks her suitcase at the museum and tells her that he is not going anywhere. Phoebe throws his red hunting hat at him and uses reverse psychology when she declares *she* isn't going back to school. Holden accuses Phoebe of being crazy. He suggests they go to the zoo, but she runs across the street. They walk downtown but on opposite sides of the street. She finally joins her older brother when he heads into the Central Park Zoo, although she continues to maintain a careful distance.

After visiting some of the animals, they walk toward the carousel in Central Park. They are surprised to hear the carousel music in winter. Holden explains that the carousel is probably open for Christmas, and though Phoebe says she is too old to ride the carousel, Holden buys her a ticket and persuades her to ride. As he watches his sister, he fears she might fall from her horse while she tries to grab for the gold ring. But Holden shows maturity as he comments that if kids try for that ring, "you have to let them do it, and not say anything. If they fall off, they fall off, but it's bad if you say anything to them" (273–274). The epiphany helps Holden stop wanting to be "a catcher in the rye," as he begins to understand that he must pick himself up from his own fall. Phoebe gets off the carousel and says she isn't mad at Holden anymore. When it starts to rain, Phoebe takes Holden's hat from her pocket and puts it on his head. She confirms the fact that Holden has decided not to run away. Phoebe returns to the carousel for another ride as it starts to downpour. Everyone not on the carousel seeks cover, but Holden remains sitting there and gets soaked as he watches Phoebe go round and round. Holden is "damn near bawling" but feels "so damn happy" because Phoebe "looked so damn *nice*" (275) on the carousel. He wishes the reader "could've been there" (275).

Chapter 26

In the short final chapter of *The Catcher in the Rye*, readers are fast-forwarded to present time, with Holden in a California sanatorium (where he is located in the first page of the novel). Holden concludes his story of the three-day Christmas adventure by saying, "That's all I'm going to tell about" (276). He could tell the reader about what he did when he got home, and how he "got sick" (276) and what school he will be attending in the fall, but he says he isn't interested in that right now. A psychoanalyst has asked Holden whether he will apply himself in school, and though Holden believes he will, he does not know, because "how do you know what you're going to do till you *do* it?" (276). D. B. visited last Saturday and wanted to know what Holden thought about the events of the three days he has just finished telling about. Holden comments, "I don't *know* what I think about it. . . . About all I know is, I sort of *miss* everybody I told about" (277), including Stradlater, Ackley, and Maurice. The novel ends with Holden cautioning the reader not to "ever tell anybody anything. If you do, you start missing everybody" (277).

CRITICAL ANALYSIS

The Catcher in the Rye prompts young readers to respond to it more powerfully than almost any other book they encounter. Just as it is logical to think about how Holden's adolescent struggle reflects Salinger's own maturation processes, *The Catcher in the Rye* enables readers to live transactionally between the fiction and their own maturation processes. (When Shirlie Blaney interviewed Salinger in 1953, she asked if the book was autobiographical. He replied, "Sort of. My boyhood was very much the same as that of the boy in the book, and it was a great relief telling people about it" [Blaney ed. pg.]) The key element of fiction is conflict. Conflict is also elemental to maturation. One way to view the novel is to consider its concentrated three-day period of events as a series of conflicts illustrating how young people attempt to find themselves when they are no longer girls and boys but have not yet become women and men. Reading *The Catcher in the Rye* with this perspective certainly explains why the novel has found a place in the curriculum of required reading in most educational systems. Unfortunately, this fact is also cited by those critics who doubt elements of "greatness" in the novel precisely because it is literature that is easily lived with and well understood by readers in their teens.

Just as fiction is driven by conflict, so, too, is criticism. However, the best way to approach critical perspectives of *The Catcher in the Rye* is not to worry about which critic's viewpoint may be wrong or right. There are many ways to understand and live with any novel, and often novels that many consider to be very good are novels that validly help readers generate a good variety of interpretations. In other words, readers may conclude that a work may be "good literature," but at the same time they may be basing their opinion on entirely different things. Sometimes reading is an escape that brings us face-to-face with our inner selves while at other times it takes us further from ourselves than we have ever been. Sometimes we hear language and phrases more clearly than we see the characters in a novel, and sometimes we become those characters. The core idea of *living with* a book is that readers transact with its ideas and feelings in ways that enhance their lives while emerging from the "stuff" of their own lives. The more possibilities of meaning that readers consider valid and interest-

ing in a literary work, the more likely that a book will become a living thing and a positive force in readers' lives. This does not mean that whatever one thinks or believes or imagines about a book may be right, but it does mean that there are many powerful ways to experience a book, and the more we remain open to each, the deeper the reading experience. We may know or feel a book to say one thing on one reading, but at another time it may say something entirely different to us, depending on our situations. A reading of an author at one time creates the possibility, on the next reading, of feeling as if we are in conversation with an old friend—the history of the readings and our varying perspectives are in flux and broaden our understanding.

Great literature requires close reading, because authors who write books that endure beyond their own generation create ideas and feelings that may not be as simple as they seem. Adolescence, like literature, reveals many of the complex ways we mature from child to adult. One way to focus closely on *The Catcher in the Rye* is to analyze the ways in which Holden is being childish and the ways in which he is being an adult. Holden's sometimes tentative and pathetic voice throughout the novel remains in conflict with an inner voice that seems more mature and knowing. As he ranges from simply being childish to making awkward and childish attempts at appearing to be an adult, Holden frequently bounces almost uncontrollably between wanting to stay young and needing to mature. His maturation process is complex and contradictory. Holden's parents remain ambiguous characters in the story, and many of the adults he encounters are not appropriate role models. Nevertheless, he shows a conscious understanding of his conflicts that readers frequently recognize and that they identify with parts of their own maturation processes.

One of Salinger's most important critics, Warren French, wrote an essay titled "The Phony World and the Nice World" as a way to explain how a close analysis of Salinger's use of the words "phony" and "nice" helps readers gain key understandings of the fiction. Holden's use of the word "nice" not only displays a comfort with teenage ambiguity but also is linked to moments in the novel when he encounters innocence and happiness with children younger than himself. When Holden tightens a child's skates, he thinks that she is "a very nice, polite little kid" (155). The repeated use of "nice" creates a motif of acceptable meaning throughout Salinger's work. Holden's use of "phony" is more complex, as he calls most of the people in the novel phonies at one time or another. His critical ability to sense hypocrisy (especially in himself), moreover, is insightful and true. However, Holden is honest about liking and eventually even missing most of the phonies in his life. These words come alive on the page and engage the reader in what seems like a conversation in which an opinion is formed about someone based on the words he or she uses repeatedly. Close reading of how Holden uses words like "nice" and "phony" shows readers that these general and commonly understood terms gain new, more complex meanings in the context of the novel.

As French points out, Holden sees young, innocent children as nice, and he sees most other people as phony. However, just as the maturation process in adolescence creates ambiguity as one moves between the states of childhood and adulthood, Holden's use of "nice" and "phony" shift and mature as the novel progresses. One of the ways readers can live the novel is to understand Holden even as contexts and character developments change his understandings of his own repeatedly used words. Salinger convinces his readers to share a gentle understanding and fondness for Holden's ambiguity that actually matures in the reading and likewise promotes deeper analysis of the novel's main character and narrator.

Brian Way, a British critic for the *New Left Review*, perceives Holden as possessing "the blend of penetration and immaturity in judgment which is the mark of the intelligent adolescent" (Way 75). Way asserts that the balance of Holden's smart perceptions and "school-boyish crudities of overstatement" (Way 75) make the narrator's tone successful. This point remains valid from a technical perspective, and Way has approached Salinger's writing craft carefully in his essay "'Franny and Zooey' and J. D. Salinger." However, as both

character and narrator, Holden is certainly not balanced. The structure of the novel, moreover, seems to depend on Holden's loss of direction, which affects its characters and, in turn, its readers through Salinger's insightful blending of pathos, humor, and perceptive social criticism. Critic Wayne C. Booth, on the other hand, cites Holden as a classic example for his explication of "unreliable narrators" in his book *The Rhetoric of Fiction*. Booth analyzes the different narrative voices that authors employ to tell their stories and explains Salinger's use of Holden Caulfield as an unreliable character (early in the novel's narration, Holden confesses to being "the most terrific liar you ever saw in your life" [22]). Holden may indeed be a liar, but he is an honest liar as well. As critics continue to unpack the art of *The Catcher in the Rye* and as readers continue to find new meanings therein, the novel takes on an enduring, treelike quality, alive with meaning and with many branches for people to climb upon more than once. The novel's youngest readers tend to see in it an honesty and the truth in very black-and-white terms because that is how one first learns right from wrong; mature teen readers sense that they would not get the whole story from a troubled youth in most cases; and adult readers report that Holden tells his story with more candor and honesty than their own children might at times employ.

Language and literature are living things in our effort to connect with one another, and through its language, *The Catcher in the Rye* attracted some of its initial interpretations. In an early piece of criticism, Donald Costello closely examined Salinger's use of words to show how the author succeeded in making Holden a believable, adolescent character. Salinger created a language typical of how young folks speak and think. Costello analyzed Holden's language for such rhetorical, teenage characteristics as talking loosely or generally, cursing profusely, cursing meaninglessly, and needing to reinforce one's sincerity (often at one's most insincere moments). The sensitivity of Salinger's ear in creating dialogue that is truly adolescent beyond the trappings of the time and place cannot be disputed. Salinger's mastery with dialogue in his short stories has been widely praised, but the author has accomplished even more with the speech patterns and word choice employed in *The Catcher in the Rye*. Costello calls Salinger's dialogue "an accurate rendering of the informal speech of an intelligent, educated, Northeastern American adolescent" (Costello 173). However, language issues have deepened since Costello first explored the novel. For example, female adolescents today respond deeply to Holden, as have young people around the world, so there must be more to Holden's language than making an illusion seem real in fiction. Costello does fine work in his focus on rhetorical patterns as indicators of Holden's character and situation, but the question of how language becomes alive in readers today must move beyond the obvious contexts. Perhaps readers see how Holden creates his own spin on adolescent dialects and, like today's rappers, how he tells his story without kowtowing to societal conventions. In this way, Holden is a truth seeker similar to music artists who struggle to find new language and compose art in order to make sense of a confusing and paradoxical world. By the end of Holden's "song," readers understand what Holden means when he advises them not to tell anything to anyone. They are glad for Holden's telling despite his advice to the contrary and, like Holden, are probably also missing the characters in his story in some of the bittersweet ways one often experiences upon the completion of a good book.

In *The Critical Path,* Northrop Frye observes that "criticism will always have two aspects, one turned toward the structure of literature and one turned toward the other cultural phenomena that form the social environment of literature" (Frye 25). Early and important Salinger critics Arthur Heiserman and James E. Miller, Jr., use Frye's "critical path" to understand *The Catcher in the Rye*. Heiserman and Miller employ one of literature's oldest archetypes—the quest—and frame their understanding of the novel in terms of Holden's quest for love. The search for love in life is ongoing, and in Holden's case, his desire to seek love is so complex and daunting that he is often unable to understand his and others' emotions as he experiences them. Sex is particularly confusing for Holden because he has not learned how to find love with (or without)

sex, so much as only just beginning to address his adolescent sex drive and his changing role in his family.

Holden is confronted with a variety of sexual questions and opportunities in *The Catcher in the Rye*. When he learns that his roommate, Ward Stradlater, is on a blind date with an old friend of his, Jane Gallagher, Holden attempts to deal with several sexual issues. He is jealous of Stradlater in general as someone more attractive and mature, and he is specifically jealous of what he believes to be Stradlater's sexual intentions towards Jane Gallagher. For Holden, Jane Gallagher is "the girl next door," and not simply because they were neighbors during a summer vacation. Holden was 14 years old when he met Jane, and the two teenagers spent most of their time at a country club where they golfed, played tennis, swam, and played checkers. Although there was no actual dating or a sexually charged rendezvous between them, Holden was deeply attracted to Jane, and he recalls the few times he kissed her and held her hand. He desired to comfort Jane, who was living in a home with an alcoholic stepfather. Holden has, moreover, stayed abreast of Jane's whereabouts long after their summer together. Nonetheless, when offered an easy opportunity to chat with her as she waits downstairs while Stradlater gets ready for the date, Holden defers. His true fondness for her makes him too clumsy to really reach out to her. Although he thinks of calling "old Jane" (99) quite often throughout the three days of the novel's main events, he repeatedly retreats from doing so.

Jane Gallagher is someone Holden cares deeply about and is strongly attracted to, and yet he is so confused about sex that he is unable to realize his own loving feelings and desire to even approach having a romantic relationship with her. Carl F. Strauch structured his reading of the novel through the lens of what sex with Holden means to Jane Gallagher when she refuses to move her kings from the back row. Strauch claims that Jane's reluctance to put her kings into play is not merely an expression of her desire to remain sexually innocent but also symbolizes "the impotence of Holden's secret world, for the kings should range freely over the checkerboard" (Strauch 24). This interpretation brings into focus the fact that Holden does not understand his own feelings or Jane clearly enough to advance their relationship. Holden's lack of experience and his awkward attraction to "the girl next door" make it unlikely that he could hope to date Jane or that she could help him work through his crisis.

Holden's story begins on his last day at Pencey Prep. He has flunked out, and he experiences his last weekend at the school without enough companionship to soften his depression. Holden most likely needs to fuel his sexual fantasies with thoughts of Sally Hayes and Jane Gallagher and also imagines he can leave his education behind to work at a menial job while settling in with a wife in Colorado or Vermont. Holden may or may not be deeply bothered by flunking out of Pencey Prep, but Stradlater's unexpected blind date with Jane Gallagher extends Holden's feeling of failure beyond his failure at school. Perhaps the failures are felt more deeply because Holden's adolescent ideas about his sex appeal are likewise in flux.

After Holden leaves Pencey, he boards the train to New York and sits alone in an empty car, until an attractive older woman boards at Trenton and sits next to him. Holden is sexually attracted to her although she is in her forties. He admits that "I don't mean I'm oversexed or anything like that—although I'm quite sexy" (70). The attractive woman turns out to be Mrs. Morrow, the mother of another Pencey Prep student. She is interested in Holden because of the Pencey sticker on his luggage. Despite Holden's adultlike offers of cigarettes and drinks, Mrs. Morrow deflects any sexual attraction and makes her motherly status quite clear. The encounter with Mrs. Morrow could represent another failed attempt by Holden to reach out to the opposite sex, but there is more to the significance of the scene than mistaken attraction. When Holden says, "Mothers are all slightly insane" (72), he evidences a typical adolescent claim. However, Holden's mother seems somewhat strangely removed from the care of her children, at least since the tragic death of Holden's younger brother, Allie. When Holden lies about Ernest Morrow to make Mrs. Morrow feel good about her son, he knows that most mothers love their children and

see them favorably despite character flaws. Holden believes the false stories he tells Mrs. Morrow about her son's supposed goodness will succeed in hiding Morrow's bad qualities. Holden believes mothers "aren't too sharp about that stuff" (74). Certainly, Holden's own mother is not shown to be particularly perceptive about her children's problems. One critic, Edwin Haviland Miller, believes that, from Holden's perspective, Mrs. Caulfield seems to be "so preoccupied with Allie that she continues to neglect Holden, as presumably she did when Allie was dying" (Edwin Haviland Miller 130). Though the Caulfield mother does not ignore her living children, she remains somewhat out of touch with their realities. After all, what mother would take light notice of a young girl of 10 (Phoebe) smoking in bed late at night? Part of Holden's quest for love is a quest to find the nurturing and understanding of his parents that he so needs.

In addition to searching for romantic and parental love, Holden, because he is confused about how love and sex work in relationships, and because he is troubled about life in general, also searches for love from strangers. Holden attempts to make a date with Faith Cavendish, a loose woman he has not met but who is an acquaintance of an acquaintance. He then attempts to charm three female tourists from Seattle with drinks and dancing, but the women show more interest in seeing film stars and going to Radio City Music Hall. Holden even purchases a prostitute, but his attempts to simply talk to her, as well as her attempts to simply have sex with him, end in failure. Dan Wakefield, in his essay "Salinger and the Search for Love," claims that Salinger "speaks, surely, for all who have not lost hope—or even if they have lost hope, have not lost interest—in the search for love and morality" (Wakefield 178). Holden Caulfield's confusion about sex and love runs throughout the novel, but his desire for love and his moral sensibilities remain constant. While Sally Hayes, for example, displays many of the traits that Holden understands as phony, he still feels love for her. Is his feeling of love an illusion created by sexual potential and adolescent stimulation? Is sex a natural outcome of his attraction for women? Is sex an outcome of his fear of men and their attraction? Holden, unable to untangle his own feelings about love and sex, forms some ideas about how sex can be dirty or unloving, but he remains almost clueless in understanding how sex can be an act of love.

Nowhere in the novel is this ambiguity and confusion about sex better dramatized than in the scene where Holden arrives at Mr. and Mrs. Antolini's apartment seeking shelter and comfort from flunking out of Pencey Prep. Holden knows Mr. Antolini to be a fine teacher, family friend, and trusted mentor, but he comes to doubt his former teacher's intentions. After Mrs. Antolini has left Holden and Mr. Antolini to talk, the teacher offers key insight into the boy's crisis. Mr. Antolini is quite possibly the most clear and prescient advisor Holden finds on his journey. His attempt to guide and mentor the troubled teenager seem to reach to the very core of Holden's conflicts. Nonetheless, Holden is spooked a little later in the scene by the possible homosexual act as Salinger has Mr. Antolini stroke the sleeping boy's head. Salinger is very careful here and does not let readers know with any provable certainty whether Mr. Antolini is gay or simply acting as a caring teacher who strokes his student's head to further show how well he empathizes and understands Holden's troubles.

Holden's conversation with Carl Luce (his former student adviser at the Whooten School) shows that Holden understands homosexuality as part of a range of possibilities that prep school life and city life present. Holden himself, it may even be possibly argued, acts gay in the ways he talks about people at the Wicker Bar. Holden remembers Luce leading "sex talks" (185) late at night with other guys in the dorm and recalls that Luce was especially knowledgeable about perversion and homosexuality. However, when the two visit several years later at the Wicker Bar, it is Holden who initiates and promotes a discussion of homosexuality. After testing Luce's limits on the topic, Holden wants to discuss Luce's current sex life with an older Chinese woman. Holden seems to be encouraging Luce to continue the sexual instruction he once offered, and Holden received, at Whooten. Instead, Luce suggests psychoanalysis as the instruction Holden needs. Despite some very direct and candid advice from Mr. Antolini and Carl Luce, Holden cannot

understand that his breakdown is linked to his confused search for love and his confusion about sex. Harold Bloom introduces his 1990 critical collection on the character Holden Caulfield by claiming that "Holden evades the adolescent obsession with the sexual drive only to yield himself to the shadows of the Death Drive" (Bloom 1990, 1). Whether Holden is vulnerable from his brother's death or learning to move on, the critical point remains that Holden's sexual confusion is complex and too troubling to become untangled in the novel.

Holden senses he needs love. Ultimately, he can only trust love when he finds it in children. Whether dancing innocently with his sister, Phoebe, in her pajamas, or helping a small child with a skate, Holden feels as though the only true love he understands is embedded in children. As long as he believes in love and innocence, he can avoid the complexities of love, sex, and death. Not only is Holden reduced to loving only children, but his search for family love has been thwarted by the loss of his younger brother. In this regard, Salinger, influenced by William Blake, may have wished to build on the latter's *Songs of Innocence and Experience*. Blake believed innocence to be a state of unfallen man and experience to be a state of consciousness after the fall. Like Holden's thoughts, Blake's poems of innocence involve ecstatic visions of humanity as shown through the eyes of children. Through the child's innocent vision, both Blake and Salinger express direct criticism and despair for the "experienced" world of adults.

As the reader considers the Caulfield family from Holden's point of view, Phoebe and Allie illustrate the innocence and wisdom of youth in conflict with death. Holden continually questions the belief systems of adults and views his older brother, D. B., as a writer who has turned adult by selling out his talent to the movies. Holden's parents have long since crossed over into adult worlds. Holden takes a negative stance towards his father's success as a lawyer. He also believes that his mother has not been as effective a mother as she might have been. Allie's death continues to cast a shadow of grief over the entire family, and only Phoebe seems well-adjusted enough to cope with and accept the loss. This may be why Phoebe ultimately becomes the character whose love helps put Holden back on track. One perspective on *The Catcher in the Rye* may be to consider the Caulfield family and the way that Holden's living siblings give him the support system necessary to recover from his inability to distinguish maturity from death. Phoebe's child-like innocence and D. B.'s *recent* maturation and experience offer Holden two fixed points on a confusing continuum of maturation. Salinger shows clearly, through these characters, how the wisdom of youth is necessary to orient Holden's conflicts with the maturation process.

The power of the Caulfield family and the help it lends begs the question of why Holden was sent away in the first place. Holden may have been deeply disturbed by Allie's death, but he is also an adroit city dweller, and there are plenty of prep schools in Manhattan. Perhaps there may be more to Holden's parents that Holden simply is not telling? After completing *The Catcher in the Rye*, Salinger wrote an extended set of stories based on the Glass family. In these stories, the author again makes the seven Glass siblings (as he did the Caulfield siblings) the main focus of the storytelling, while delegating parents to minor roles. When readers look to their own experiences to understand Holden and the Caulfield family, a sense of living with the novel may be created by identifying their own family experiences with those of the fiction.

In a 1990 essay, the literary critic Mary Suzanne Schriber concluded that reader identification with Holden is the reason why *The Catcher in the Rye* has achieved such financial success. Her statement invited an avalanche of critical response. Schriber, however, makes an important and crucial point in her analysis that readers of both genders identify strongly with Holden's male adolescent experience. She further asserts that literary critics have been overlooking the interpretive transitions between genders. Moreover, Schriber questions the quality and validity, although abundant, of most of the literary criticism generated by *The Catcher in the Rye*. She concludes her essay by finding the body of Salinger criticism "guilty of androcentricity as charged because it fails to be self-reflexive. It remains oblivious to the possibility of a female

perspective . . ." (Schriber 236). Schriber's essay, written specifically for *Critical Essays on Salinger's The Catcher in the Rye*, edited by Joel Salzberg, appears as the final essay in the collection. Henceforward, the body of ongoing *Catcher* criticism has accepted Schriber's challenge and displays a flowering of gender perspectives more appropriate to the ways readers of both sexes experience the novel. Although very few early reviews of *The Catcher in the Rye* were written by women, the chorus of female voices in literary criticism has progressively grown stronger since readers first responded to the novel.

When analyzed closely, Holden's sense of religion is not only deep but indicates Salinger's understanding and respect for a number of the world's religions. In ways that are similar to being multilingual, Salinger fluently uses ideas from a variety of belief systems. Jonathan Baumbach, Jr., in his essay "The Saint as a Young Man: A Reappraisal of *The Catcher in the Rye*" in *Modern Language Quarterly*, sees in Holden a desire to become a saint and a search for a spiritual father. Baumbach equivocates on the novel's place in the literary canon, however, claiming "Salinger's small book is an extraordinary achievement; it is, if such a distinction is meaningful, an important minor novel" (Baumbach 461). Nonetheless, Baumbach aptly builds a reading of *The Catcher in the Rye* that shows that Holden searches for redemption and spiritual understanding "by praying to his saint-brother [Allie], who in his goodness has God in him" (Baumbach 470). Harold Bloom, espousing an "American Religion," believes that "Holden possesses neither a saving doctrine nor spiritual authorities to whom he can turn, yet his sensibility is wholly religious" (Bloom 1990, 2). The critics Bernice and Sanford Goldstein see *The Catcher in the Rye* as "the germ of the enlightened or to-be-partially enlightened Glass children" (Goldstein 322), and find that Salinger's work employs "a verbal, highly speeded-up version of the Zen enlightenment" (Goldstein 316). Following "the Zen trail," Gerald Rosen, with his 1977 publication of *Zen in the Art of J. D. Salinger*, claims that "in rough outline, and without the Buddha's final conscious mature understanding, this is the form of the story of Holden Caulfield"

(Rosen 5). The Salinger critics John Howell and Tom Davis see Holden as a Buddhist bodhisattva (holy person) because he is, at times, attempting to save others regardless of himself. Salinger's interest in religions would flourish in his later fiction. The critic Eberhard Alsen in his two books—*Salinger's Glass Stories as a Composite Novel* and *A Reader's Guide to J. D. Salinger*—tracks the more than 20 religious texts mentioned in Salinger's later writings. Alsen especially focuses on the influence of ADVAITA VEDANTA upon the author. Perhaps the most plausible and useful approach to Salinger's spiritualism was composed by Elizabeth N. Kurian in her book *A Religious Response to the Existential Dilemma in the Fiction of J. D. Salinger*. Kurian identifies and analyzes Hebrew, Christian, Buddhist, and Hindu spiritualism in Salinger's fiction. She uses the more secular context of existentialism to show how some of Salinger's deepest ideas are drawn from or linked to major religious concepts. Kurian's multi-religion approach to reading *The Catcher in the Rye* parallels Salinger's approach to religion. Instead of getting caught up in religious practices involved in particular organized religions, both critic and author prefer to focus on religious principles practiced outside of organized houses of worship and derived from a variety of texts.

Although many readers and critics of *The Catcher in the Rye* focus on the interior aspects of the novel, the 1970s critics Carol and Richard Ohmann read Holden's story as a negative commentary on capitalism and class differences in America. The Ohmanns have examined *The Catcher in the Rye* from textual, Marxist, and educational perspectives and assert that previous critics had focused too much on maturation, morality, and religious ideas in *The Catcher in the Rye* to the exclusion of class consciousness. Possibly as a result of this critical insight or as part of a trend in the 1970s, James Lundquist connected social criticism from John Kenneth Galbraith (*The Affluent Society*), C. Wright Mills (*The Power Elite*), Vance Packard (*The Hidden Persuaders*), and David Riesman (*The Lonely Crowd*) to deepen our understanding of Salinger's criticism of society.

New Essays on The Catcher in the Rye, edited by Jack Salzman and published in 1991, continues the study of how Holden confronts society. One critic in this collection, Christopher Brookeman, believes that Salinger does not confront so much a "generalized concept of American culture or society, but the codes and practices of a particular instrument of social control—the American prep school" (Brookeman 58). However, Brookeman at the same time asserts that "Holden Caulfield is clearly well on his way toward being entirely formed by a postindustrial, other-directed culture" (Brookeman 69) and that "Salinger shows through Holden . . . someone cracking up and breaking down under the pressure of a society" (Brookeman 69). Whether Holden's sense of society and culture comes from rebelling against prep school, family, friends, teachers, maturation, and even death, his character continuously scrapes against the grain of societal pressures and expectations.

In 1986, Sanford Pinsker, through both a personal narrative and a cultural analysis, offered his ideas about the ways *The Catcher in the Rye* is (but may not continue to be) a "formative novel." Pinsker believes his generation may have been among the last to be so affected by a book and by characters like Holden Caulfield. Instead of a "formative process" in which imagination is triggered by texts like *The Catcher in the Rye*, Pinsker believes that culture today does not possess the patience for "formative experiences;" instead, contemporary culture "demands *new* ones—slicker, trendier, and (most important of all) disposable" (Pinsker 1986, 967) experiences that do not linger as the story and voice of Holden Caulfield have stayed with him. Pinsker understands that "formative books survive not only subsequent readings but also *ourselves*" (Pinsker 1986, 957) and explains how, as a current reader, he loves Holden less than he did as a younger reader. He now identifies more with Mr. Antolini. This thoughtful critic humorously predicts that he will not only age like Mr. Spencer, but that as a reader, he will find the old teacher "more sympathetically drawn than I did when I first encountered him reeking of Vicks Nose Drops" (Pinsker 1986, 958). Despite Pinsker's opinion that formative novels may not have the effect on young people that they once did, he may be underestimating the roles of readers. Technology and multimedia draw our attention away from the printed page, but for those who enjoy narrative and honest language (off screen or on), *The Catcher in the Rye* still offers universal adolescent ideas and fine writing that attract readers of all ages and with a variety of media interests.

Perhaps Pinsker did not see the ability of *The Catcher in the Rye* and Salinger's reclusive aura to reach far beyond literature's scope. A quick Google check or scan of the *New York Times* archives will yield more than enough evidence to claim that Salinger and his formative novel continue to influence both literature and our culture. For example, a variety of musicians have used Salinger allusions, titles, and even "J. D. Salinger" as an album cover. Salinger did authorize one story, "UNCLE WIGGILY IN CONNECTICUT," to be filmed, but his battles over copyrights were formidable. Nonetheless, unauthorized films such as *Pari,* an Iranian version of FRANNY AND ZOOEY by Darush Mehrjooee, and shorter YouTube videos of scenes from *The Catcher in the Rye* and other Salinger short stories demonstrate the visual literacy and ongoing creative and critical response to the author. Although Salinger was well known for protecting his copyrights as well as for limiting the marketing and design of his books, he did not anticipate how enduring cultural needs (like guidance through adolescence) would appropriate his literature. Emerging media and Internet connectivity have proven to be fertile spaces for readers to live with the novel. On the Internet, for example, where 21st-century copyrights and reproduction processes are not as clearly and legally controlled as those governing works in print format, one finds an incredible flowering of Salinger-created inspiration. From visual art to music and back to print, *The Catcher in the Rye* on the Internet is alive with alternative endings, access to uncollected stories, and online discussion. New writing about *The Catcher in the Rye* in news, blogs, Web pages, and e-mail lists shows up in daily Google alerts. Moreover, since Google employed its alert software feature, not one day has passed without one or more mentions of J. D. Salinger in our media as "studied" by Google's search engines.

"The reasonable man adapts himself to the world; the unreasonable one persists in trying to adapt the world to himself." The aphorism by George Bernard Shaw (*Man and Superman* [1903]) goes straight to the point of understanding Holden Caulfield and the tension that drives *The Catcher in the Rye.* The critic Bruce Bawer believed that this tension makes Salinger a very overrated writer. In 1986, Bawer wrote about "Salinger's Arrested Development" and, in 14 pages, presents a fairly comprehensive overview of Salinger and his fiction. Bawer bases his negative assessment of Salinger on two major assumptions. First, the critic asserts that Salinger's withdrawal from public view fueled more interest and curiosity about Salinger than the stories and novel deserve. Second, due to the scarcity of biographical information about Salinger, Bawer believes that what can be understood about the author might be understood in Salinger's relationships to his own characters. Bawer, asserting that Salinger admires the arrested development of his characters and that the author remains naive about childhood innocence, harshly concludes that Salinger is "less interested in creating a credible fictional universe than in sequestering himself within a private, privileged nursery with his child-heroes and childish heroes, a place from which he can look down upon those numberless masses who are not only less sensitive and intelligent, but less beautiful, sophisticated, and wealthy, than his protagonists" (Bawer 47). Although Bawer expresses a minority opinion, he does bring into focus Salinger's emphasis on character development and childhood values. Additionally, Bawer's negative assessment of Salinger's view of youth and innocence provides a good way of negotiating claims from other critics like Pinsker who see the novel in overwhelmingly positive ways.

Critics are taught to write persuasively, and as criticism approached the end of the 20th century, no critic was more persuasive or more highly regarded than Harold Bloom. Bloom edited a collection of Salinger criticism in 1987 and then, in 1990, edited a collection of criticism on Holden Caulfield as part of a series about major literary characters. Bloom achieved his reputation as a critic through his reading of the canon of English literature. Bloom's subsequent, numerous collections of essays on Salinger and his works, as well as his introductory comments, place the author within the American canon of literature. Bloom ranks *The Catcher in the Rye* as a "younger, weaker brother" (Bloom 1990, 3) of *The Sun Also Rises* by Ernest Hemingway and *The Great Gatsby* by F. Scott Fitzgerald. Bloom does understand Holden to be a durable character in American fiction and states: "Forty years of readership have not dimmed his [Holden's] poignance, his ability to represent the idealism and the refusal to be deceived that have marked the American tradition of representing adolescence" (Bloom 1990, 1). However, Bloom believes that "wrong" readers' interpretations may "dim" a character's validity and fails to see how *The Catcher in the Rye* can be both a classic work of American fiction while also making itself and its author cultural icons woven more deeply into the fabric of American life than present-day critics may be able to appreciate.

When *The Catcher in the Rye* was published, New Criticism (a form of critical response that presumed that texts possess organic unity and that they require highly educated readers with "valid" interpretations) reigned as the literary trend. Response to *The Catcher in the Rye* soon spread, however, from New York critical circles to college campuses. By the time the book had been in print for as many years as Holden's age (17), the protests, rebellion, and love ethos of the 1960s were gaining mainstream attention. Somewhere in that American gaze at its youth was a lens sharpened by *The Catcher in the Rye*. Holden's odyssey as both a literary character and a cultural icon may have been sustained and increased by the confluence of large numbers of young people questioning society's values and practices. Holden's questions and struggles with school, family, class, war, race, sexuality, and even sanity were likewise echoed by the young folks of the '60s and '70s in their protests and stories.

Within our literary tradition and culture, the use of an adolescent protagonist to dramatize the confusion, isolation, and even desperation one may experience in our modern society is by no means original. However, when Salinger added the self-conscious narrative voice of Holden Caulfield, the author may have given voice, in turn, to young readers in truly original ways. From the first pub-

lication of the novel, adults would express fear over, and condemnation of, Holden's voice, and attempts to censor the book (reaching their highest frequency from 1965 to 1976) continue today. The correlation between censorship and rebellion against adult values provides yet more support for the idea that *The Catcher in the Rye* reaches powerfully beyond the literary page in its effect on our culture. Whichever way the pendulum of the literary and cultural continuum of *The Catcher in the Rye* might swing, the questions of how the book affects culture and how culture currently brings *The Catcher in the Rye* to life are inextricably bound together.

PUBLICATION HISTORY

The Catcher in the Rye was published on July 16, 1951, by Little, Brown and Company. The first printing comprised a hardback edition of an unspecified run (perhaps about 3,000 copies), priced at $3. The book's dust jacket, designed by E. Michael Mitchell, features a sketch of a carousel horse, with a photo of Salinger by Lotte Jacobi filling the rear cover. (The author photo would be eliminated at Salinger's request later that July, after the second printing.) The novel was reprinted 11 times during 1951 and remained on the *Publishers Weekly* best-seller list for five months, although failing to make the year's list of the 10 top-selling fiction titles. *The Catcher in the Rye* reached a high of number four on the *New York Times* best-seller list. The novel was also issued by the Book-of-the-Month Club as the 1951 midsummer selection, an edition that included the Jacobi photograph of Salinger.

On February 26, 1953, the first paperback "pocketbook" edition of *The Catcher in the Rye* was published by New American Library, featuring a cover depicting Holden Caulfield. The first printing consisted of 350,000 copies, priced at 25 cents. By May 1961, more than 1,675,000 copies of the paperback had been printed. After Salinger's contract with New American Library expired, Bantam Books took over the paperback edition. Salinger himself designed its distinctive, nonillustrated maroon cover with yellow lettering. In 1958, a new hardcover edition was published in the prestigious Modern Library series while Little, Brown and Company continued to reprint its own hardback edition. By 1975, nearly 6 million copies of *The Catcher in the Rye* had been sold in America; of these, more than 400,000 were in hardback. In May 1991, Little, Brown and Company took over from Bantam Books the mass-market paperback edition and released it in the austere matching set of Salinger's four books, each bound in white covers with the author's name and the title in black. In January 2001, Little, Brown and Company published the first trade paperback edition, reproducing the front cover and spine of the original dust jacket. The mass-market paperback edition would soon adopt the same cover. *The Catcher in the Rye* continues to sell an estimated 20,000 copies a month. Although total worldwide sales are usually reported to have topped 65 million copies, a more realistic figure (as stated by Salinger's lawyers in a June 2009 court document) is 35 million.

The Catcher in the Rye has never gone out of print. The novel is available in three editions from Little, Brown and Company: an exact reproduction of the hardback first edition from 1951 (albeit excluding the author photo on the back cover of the dust jacket); a trade paperback that mimics the production of this hardback (although featuring only the front cover and spine of the dust jacket, while lacking the flap material); and a mass-market paperback with its pagination differing from the above editions.

CHARACTERS

As the protagonist and narrator of *The Catcher in the Rye,* Holden Caulfield "filters" the following characters through his perceptions. The novel, moreover, has become a kind of lens through which to observe adolescent maturation. However artful Salinger's crafting of this lens, it includes only part of the subjectivity and imagination that bring characters to life. As Mary B. Wiseman observes in her essay "Identifying with Characters in Literature," readers themselves, through a confluence of their own imagination and empathetic feeling, bring fictional characters to life, yet the same characters will vary from reader to reader depending upon interpretative context and self-identification.

Ackley, Robert This character is often simplified and stereotyped as "a loser." Robert Ackley lives in the room next to Holden Caulfield's in a dorm at Pencey Prep. He is often addressed by others as "Ackley" and seems to have few friends and not much of a social life. Ackley has problems with facial acne and cleanliness in general. His slovenly character traits not only show a reality of prep school life but also serve as a counterbalance to Ward Stradlater's obsession with his personal appearance. Even though Ackley is two years older than Holden, he is more immature. Both boys are less mature than Stradlater. Holden pities Ackley enough to include him on a Saturday night visit to town even though he knows Ackley is not anyone's preferred company. Ackley's character provides evidence that some of Holden's fellow students at Pencey are working through their adolescence as awkwardly as Holden. For example, Ackley is less sexually experienced than Holden and obviously tries to lie about it. He is both phony and ungenerous in some of the small-minded ways that are typical of prep school dorm life. Ackley is not very intelligent and seems unconcerned with the critical sarcasm Holden directs toward him. Ackley is also unaware of, or harshly unsympathetic with, Holden's real problems. He prefers to sleep through Holden's crisis at Pencey rather than offer any real assistance or comfort. In more negative ways, Ackley illustrates how prep school kids can be tough on each other. He is both an easy target for other boys and pretty hard on Holden when the younger boy is going through his most difficult time at Pencey. Holden admits to hating Ackley sometimes, but not for long, and even misses Ackley when he is not around.

Ackley's babe While lying on Holden Caulfield's bed, Robert Ackley once again tells Holden a story about having sexual intercourse with a girl the previous summer. Each time Ackley tells the story, the intercourse occurs in a different place. Holden believes Ackley is actually a virgin.

Aigletinger, Miss Although this character doesn't actually make an appearance in the events of the novel, Holden Caulfield remembers her because she was the teacher (in the same unnamed elementary school that his sister Phoebe attends) who used to take Holden and his classmates to the Museum of Natural History on Saturdays. Holden's memories of the museum are distinct and revolve around the theme of niceness. The teacher was nice to students who were not always well-behaved, and the guards nicely told students not to touch the exhibits. Miss Aigletinger's care and the museum visits become a memory for Holden where the nice smells of rain, the weekly visits, and the museum artifacts mix in his mind to form an image of security. Holden reveals this innocent feeling of being safe in his impressionistic description of the museum, which "always smelled like it was raining outside, even if it wasn't, and you were in the only nice, dry, cozy place in the world" (156). Miss Aigletinger's significance lies in that she provides Holden with memories he uses to form a comfortable sense of his fitting in at school. Through her, he learns about a place (symbolized by the museum) that protects young children from the problems of the world at large. In general, readers share common memories of nurturing and kind elementary schoolteachers. Salinger links Miss Aigletinger to the Museum of Natural History to dramatize how Holden, in his most immature moments, must still cling to the teacher's manner of elementary school nurturing.

Antolini, Mr. This character may be the most sexually ambiguous character in the novel; at the same time, Mr. Antolini understands Holden Caulfield more deeply than do his parents or other teachers. Mr. Antolini got to know Holden at Elkton Hills, where he taught English, and has remained friendly with his former student and the Caulfield family. When we meet him in *The Catcher in the Rye*, Mr. Antolini has progressed from teaching middle-school English at a prep school to teaching English at New York University. He lives with his wealthy, older wife in a posh Sutton Place apartment. Through Holden's recounting, the reader may guess that the teacher has successfully climbed into the social ranks of those he once served at Elkton Hills. Nonetheless, Mr. Antolini remains the most compassionate teacher

in Holden's educational experience. Mr. Antolini's goodness is etched into Holden's memory as the teacher who cared for James Castle, a classmate who was bullied to the point of suicide. When Holden phones to seek asylum late on a Sunday night, his former teacher does not hesitate to offer his home as a place to stay. Mr. Antolini is the kind of teacher that students feel comfortable "horsing around" with, and Holden trusts him because of his honesty. Mr. Antolini is acutely aware of Holden's intelligence and confusion. Unfortunately, the chance that Mr. Antolini is a homosexual man hoping to seduce his former student clouds the possibility that Holden will take his teacher's advice. Nevertheless, Mr. Antolini does predict Holden's fall and even says it is caused by Holden's search for something his environment will not supply. Mr. Antolini is the only adult in the novel who really understands that Holden is breaking down and in danger of killing himself. Just before Holden drifts off to sleep and awakens to Mr. Antolini's stroking his head, the teacher quotes the psychoanalyst Wilhelm Stekel as if to offer evidence that he understands what Holden is going through. Stekel is best remembered for saying, "People who do not understand themselves have a craving for understanding." This observation expresses, in a very succinct way, the central notion of the novel. Mr. Antolini quotes the once-famous analyst even more carefully for Holden and shows much empathy as he further writes down the quote for Holden: "The mark of the immature man is that he wants to die nobly for a cause, while the mark of the mature man is that he wants to live humbly for one" (244). Although Mr. Antolini has tapped into Holden's problems almost perfectly, the boy's doubts about sexuality overcome his ability to receive his teacher's advice in a timely manner.

Antolini, Mrs. Lillian This character is the wife of Holden Caulfield's former teacher Mr. Antolini. She is a rich woman, considerably older than her husband. Holden describes her as a serious intellectual with asthma. When Holden seeks refuge at Mr. Antolini's apartment late Sunday night, Mrs. Antolini enters the room to serve coffee and cake, and she then retires to bed. The fact of her wealth and age relative to her husband's (in addition to his ambiguous sexual orientation) suggests that Holden's teacher may have made a marriage of convenience.

Atterbury, Selma A classmate of Phoebe Caulfield, Selma Atterbury helps Phoebe put ink on a coat belonging to another classmate, Curtis Weintraub. Selma is mentioned only once in the novel by Phoebe. Holden Caulfield calls Phoebe a child for putting ink on Curtis's windbreaker and suggests that Curtis follows her because he likes her. The childish but hurtful prank serves to point out that Phoebe and Selma (and other children of their age) are not old enough to understand or yet experience sexual attraction.

Banky, Ed The Pencey basketball coach is referred to but does not actually appear in the novel. On occasion, he lends his car to Ward Stradlater despite the school rule against students using faculty cars. This character supports the idea that athletes get special treatment in school, as he provides a place for Stradlater to make his sexual overtures, the thought of which sickens Holden Caulfield with jealousy. The coach's preferential treatment of his athletes also provides a concrete example of Holden's problem with "Life being a game" (12). Adolescent life in the '50s, and today, is more socially comfortable for the "winners" who have access to a car.

Bernice "Crabs or Krebs", Marty, and Laverne These three ladies in their twenties are visitors from Seattle. They enjoy the Edmont Hotel nightclub because they don't know about better nightclubs. Holden Caulfield is seated next to them when he goes to the club for a drink and "gives them the eye." He asks each of them to dance but is attracted most to Bernice, a blonde. Although the bar is located in an inexpensive hotel, the three visitors expect to see movie stars there, and Holden tricks them into believing they just missed Gary Cooper. Holden admires Bernice's dancing but feels she lacks the intelligence and sophistication to understand him well. Bernice and Holden dance without talking, and much of the interaction between

Holden and the three women is full of misunderstanding. Holden does not even use his real name when he introduces himself to them as "Jim Steele." He describes Laverne as "the ugly one" (96) but notes that she can at least dance. He finds Marty neither attractive nor a good dancer. After they dance and drink, the girls leave Holden. They want to go to sleep so they can wake up early and see the first show at Radio City Music Hall. Their shallow desire to visit New York in order to see movies bothers Holden more than the fact that the girls leave him to pay the bill for all of their drinks.

Birdsell, Eddie This boy is a Princeton student whom Holden Caulfield meets once at a party the summer before the events in the novel take place. At the party, he writes down the name of a promiscuous girl, Faith Cavendish, on a scrap of paper that Holden has carried with him ever since. When Holden phones Faith to invite her for a drink, she defers. During the conversation, both Holden and Faith try to remember Eddie Birdsell, though neither appears to know him well enough to say very much about him. The character thus provides an opportunity for Salinger to show how people can be phony in their pretense about relationships. Eddie Birdsell never appears in the novel but is referenced in the phone conversation only.

Blop, Commander Holden Caulfield calls this character "Commander Blop or something" (113) after he is introduced to him by Lillian Simmons in Ernie's. The naval commander epitomizes false masculinity; Holden describes him as "one of those guys that think they're being a pansy if they don't break around forty of your fingers when they shake hands with you" (113).

Brossard, Mal This character makes a brief appearance as a Pencey schoolmate of Holden Caulfield. Readers learn that Mal Brossard is on the wrestling team, that he is a bridge player, and that he is friendly with Holden but not so much with Robert Ackley. Nonetheless, the three boys board a bus to Agerstown, where they eat some hamburgers and play pinball. Brossard leaves Ackley and Holden to play bridge after the three boys return from their Saturday night visit to town. Later in the evening, Holden, troubled after his fight with Ward Stradlater and uncomfortable staying in Ackley's room, thinks about stopping in on Brossard but decides instead to leave Pencey. Mal Brossard is one of the few characters in the book whom Holden doesn't dislike and whom Holden does not describe as being phony.

Buddy Singer's clarinet player   At the Lavender Room, Marty, one of the Seattle women, thinks Buddy Singer's clarinet player is a great musician and refers to his instrument as a "licorice stick" (97).

Bus driver   The bus driver makes Holden Caulfield toss away his snowball before boarding the bus into Agerstown, where Holden, Mal Brossard, and Robert Ackley plan to have a hamburger and see a movie. Holden tells the driver he will not throw the snowball at anyone, but the driver will not relent. Holden comments, "People never believe you" (48).

Cab driver, first   After Holden Caulfield's arrival at Penn Station in New York City, he mistakenly gives the unnamed cab driver the Caulfields' home address and must correct himself later during the ride. The cabbie is not helpful regarding which bands are playing at the Taft and New Yorker hotels, so Holden tells the driver to take him to the Edmont Hotel. This first cab ride allows Salinger to reintroduce Holden's important question about where the ducks in the lagoon near Central Park South go during winter. Holden asks the cab driver about the ducks and the cabbie, in turn, thinks Holden is kidding him with this question.

Cab driver, second   *See* Horwitz.

Cab driver, third   This cab driver takes Holden Caulfield from the Edmont Hotel to Grand Central Station. On the way, Holden counts what is left of his money.

Cab driver, fourth   This cab driver takes Holden Caulfield and Sally Hayes from the Biltmore Hotel to the theater. On the way, the two adolescents

neck. Holden complains that the driver does not pay attention to his driving as he twice jams on his brakes, nearly throwing Holden from the backseat.

Cab driver, fifth   This cab driver takes Holden Caulfield from his family's building to the Antolini apartment. Although Holden did not want to spend any of his sister Phoebe's money on a fare, he decides to take a cab because he feels dizzy.

Cabel, R. and W.   The two Pencey Prep students (without first names provided) are mentioned by Holden Caulfield when he remembers his math class and the roll call that put James Castle's name directly before his own. Salinger may be suggesting, with the roll call, that Holden will be next in line to commit suicide, after James Castle.

California psychoanalyst   Holden Caulfield tells his story while in residence at a California sanatorium. The psychoanalyst there keeps asking whether Holden plans to apply himself when he goes back to school in September. Holden considers this "a stupid question" (276).

Callon, Miss   This character is Phoebe Caulfield's fourth grade teacher and is referred to by the little girl skating in the park.

Campbell, Paul   Holden recalls tossing a football around with Paul Campbell and Robert Tichener, fellow students at Pencey Prep. When evening falls, a teacher, Mr. Zambesi, tells the boys to get ready for dinner. The boys enjoy tossing a football even as it becomes increasingly dark that October evening. Darkness does not stop them from feeling good, but a teacher does. Holden's bittersweet memory of the evening allows him "to feel some kind of a good-by" (7) for Pencey Prep.

Castle, James   James Castle is a young boy who went to school with Holden Caulfield at Elkton Hills. He provides some of the novel's reality for Holden's fantasy of catching kids before they fall. Castle also epitomizes the boy who tragically becomes the target of group bullying. He is skinny and small-boned, but too stubborn to recant his claim that Phil Stabile, another Elkton Hills schoolmate, is conceited. Stabile and several other boys gang up on Castle, who refuses to take anything back. Instead, James Castle jumps out of his dorm window and kills himself. When he dies, he is wearing Holden's turtleneck sweater.

Caulfield, Allie   Allie Caulfield, Holden Caulfield's younger brother, died of leukemia in Maine on July 18, 1946, three years before the events of Christmas 1949 as related by Holden. Although Allie appears only in Holden's reminiscences, he remains a very key character of the novel. Holden remembers Allie as one of the few things in life he likes. Holden, who was 13 when his 11-year-old brother died, has not yet recovered from the loss. Holden names Allie as the nicest and most intelligent member of the Caulfield family. The deep appreciation of Allie by his teachers contrasts with the estimation of Holden by his own teachers. Allie had bright red hair but never got mad at people. He copied poems in green ink onto his baseball mitt so he could read them when play was slow. Allie's baseball mitt is the subject of the essay that Holden writes when he does Ward Stradlater's assignment. Throughout *The Catcher in the Rye*, Holden consistently tries to deal with the anger of losing his brother. As Holden remembers Allie, he is also mistakenly seeing a version of himself that he considers much less worthy of life than Allie had been. Some readers perceive Allie as a better version of Holden, and some assert that Holden's unresolved grief for Allie is the driving psychological force in the novel. Regardless of the ways Allie appears to readers, his effects on Holden cannot be minimized. Allie is one of several child characters who embody the holy wisdom and beauty of innocent childhood.

Caulfield, D. B.   At the very beginning of the novel, readers learn that Holden Caulfield's older brother, D. B., has achieved success as a writer of short stories and Hollywood films. Holden deeply values his brother's short stories, particularly one called "The Secret Goldfish." D. B. drives an expensive sports car and has clearly succeeded as a Hollywood writer. Nonetheless, Holden calls D. B.

"a prostitute" (4), because instead of writing more short stories, D. B. now sells his narrative talents to make movies. Beneath Holden's anger and unreliable "hatred" of the movies may lay a jealousy of his older brother's success. Overwhelmingly obvious to readers, however, is Holden's opinion that movies are not as valuable as other forms of art.

After seeing a movie at Radio City Music Hall, Holden considers D. B.'s four years of service in the army. D. B. landed on D-day and drove a general's jeep. At home on furloughs, D. B. did little but lie in bed, saying "the Army was practically as full of bastards as the Nazis were" (182). Despite his long service record, D. B. seems to have been an ambivalent soldier. Holden has difficulty resolving the contradiction of D. B.'s loving Hemingway's *A Farewell to Arms* while, at the same time, hating war.

By the end of the novel, Holden shows fondness for his older brother ("D. B. isn't as bad as the rest of them, but he keeps asking me a lot of questions, too" [276]). The novel concludes with Holden trying to answer D. B.'s question of what Holden thinks about the events following his flunking out of Pencey. D. B.'s importance in framing the novel cannot be understated. In some ways, he is the Caulfield sibling who has matured and succeeded in the real world. In a continuum of living Caulfield siblings, D. B. is the experienced young adult, Phoebe is the innocent child, and Holden is caught in between. D. B. Caulfield provides the adult "pull" for his adolescent brother, but Holden is not sure he is ready to give up his rebellion against the insensitive and morally lacking adult world. D. B.'s character allows readers to hypothesize that Holden may become a writer because his older brother is talented.

Caulfield, Holden   Holden Caulfield may be said to be one of the best-remembered characters in all of literature. In *The Catcher in the Rye*, Holden takes a dual role as both the main character and the novel's narrator. Readers quickly learn that he is a tall, skinny 17-year-old boy from a well-to-do New York family. More than a half year later, he recalls the events leading up to the breakdown from which he is recovering. (These events take place during a three-day period shortly before Christmas when Holden was still 16 years old.) Despite the character's tenuous psychological state (he is still in the sanatorium at the novel's end), readers easily learn to enjoy and follow Holden's narration. Despite the fact that he has flunked out of several schools, Holden displays an intelligent innocence in his ideas and in his insightful observations that make him very credible as a narrator. Not only is his older brother a published short-story author (and his younger sister an aspiring writer of mysteries), but Holden himself possesses that potential. One of his former English teachers, Mr. Antolini, calls Holden an "ace composition writer" (237).

Although believable, Holden is not completely straightforward, as he bundles together a number of contradictions. For example, although Holden is mentally precarious, a great number of readers identify with his sensitivity, share many of his moral beliefs, and perhaps, most powerfully, sense the truth in Holden's social and psychological observations despite his personal troubles understanding those truths. Holden manages to become part of young readers' lives because he serves as a signpost in the confusing process of maturation.

Just as adolescence itself presents many paradoxes, a great deal of truth may be found in the paradoxes that surround Holden. Holden claims to be a liar, but he admits when he is lying. Throughout the novel, he acutely detects dishonesty and hypocrisy, and to do so well, one must be a truth seeker. Despite his David Copperfield denial, Holden remains sincere and accessible about his most personal concerns. He sounds truthful about what he observes, confesses, and questions, as though trying his best to be honest and meaningful. Like those of any young person, Holden's feelings and opinions are malleable. Perhaps the character's desperate need to grow and to mature encourages readers to be sympathetic toward him. Holden makes immature mistakes as a character in a novel but displays a very mature intelligence as a 17-year-old narrator.

One of the first outstanding qualities of the novel to be deeply praised and studied is Salinger's use of language. Most readers hold the opinion that Holden's way of talking in the novel is both authentic and universal to adolescence. Holden's language blends the intelligence of maturity and the innocence of childhood into a perfect middle spot that resonates with readers, who may have used similar discourse patterns to evade adult scrutiny and to question their own identities and roles. Although Holden may at times sound immature, he likewise sounds like someone who will eventually understand how to mature. For example, as Holden recounts advice he receives from Mr. Antolini, he shows he can learn and absorb key ideas that will help him outgrow his rebellion against adult life. In this sense, Salinger artfully combines in Holden a character's ability to tell his own story and at the same time create active roles for readers and that character to learn and mature. Holden has fulfilled Mr. Antolini's comment that ". . . someday, if you have something to offer [a record of his 'troubles'], someone will learn something from you. It's a beautiful reciprocal arrangement. And it isn't education. It's history. It's poetry" (246).

The exact origin of Holden Caulfield's name remains unknown. Some speculate that Salinger saw the last names of movie stars William Holden and Joan Caulfield on a movie marquee and created a fusion. The two actors, however, did not appear together until 1947, and Salinger had already given the name Holden Caulfield to a character in his 1941 story "Slight Rebellion Off Madison" (which was not published, however, until 1946). Some critics suggest "Holden" signifies the character's holding on to the past; attempting to hold on to innocence; or holding on to the endangered children playing in the field of rye. "Caulfield" possibly combines "caul" (a protective fetal membrane covering a baby's head) with part of the name of Charles Dickens's character David Copperfield, whom Holden invokes on the novel's first page. David Copperfield was born with a caul. Holden's caul might be seen in his red hunting hat.

As a fictional character, Holden Caulfield gained popularity on college campuses in the 1950s. By the rebellious '60s and '70s, Holden Caulfield and his author had become popular cultural characters as well. One might see the seeds of the tumultuous social changes of those decades planted and nurtured in *The Catcher in the Rye*, in the way Holden talks about rebelling against his father's way of life and as he criticizes religion, education, sexism, and materialism. Literature quite possibly had not heard a young narrator speak to so many so wisely about social conditions since MARK TWAIN's Huck Finn led readers to understand racism and the process of maturation in the century before Holden's. *The Catcher in the Rye*, moreover, has transcended its own era because Holden Caulfield's telling of his troubled times so powerfully addresses the conflicts and struggles most young folks have faced or will encounter in any era. Indeed, Holden's ability to loom large on the literary scene ironically counterbalances, or may even relate to, Salinger's public withdrawal and legendary status as America's best-known recluse.

Caulfield, Mr. and Mrs. Though the Caulfield parents appear infrequently in the novel, they remain important as characters. A close understanding of Holden's parents becomes essential to understanding the dynamics of the Caulfield family. Holden Caulfield says little about his father and mother. Rather, he attempts to maintain his vow to avoid biographical facts, since his parents "would have about two hemorrhages apiece" (3) if he revealed anything personal about them. In bits and pieces throughout the novel, readers observe Holden rebelling against his father's way of making money—as a very successful corporate lawyer—and against the unfairness of having the money. Like Holden, Mrs. Caulfield may not have recovered from her son Allie's death and seems unable to care for Holden and his sister, Phoebe, although she dresses them well. In her one appearance in the novel, Mrs. Caulfield smells smoke in her 10-year-old daughter's bedroom late at night but hardly pauses to worry. Both parents are unable to help Holden; instead, they send him away to prep schools rather than deal with him directly. Nonetheless, the reader may discern parental concern in the fact that Mr. Caulfield having contacted Mr. Antolini about Holden (before Holden's return to New York) and that the parents have sent Holden to recover in a sanatorium located near D. B., his brother.

Caulfield, Phoebe Josephine Phoebe Caulfield, the youngest Caulfield sibling, is 10 years old and in fourth grade but seems more intelligent and sophisticated than most people her age. Second to Holden Caulfield, Phoebe is the most important character seen in the novel. Holden views his sister as the most perfect female in his world, and he loves her unreservedly. Holden wants to protect Phoebe's innocence, while at the same time, he is trying hard to understand how to lose his own innocence. Phoebe acts adult and nurturing when necessary. However, when Holden sees her acting too childishly, he finally learns how to mature himself. Phoebe teaches Holden to mature by using her own immaturity to inspire his growth.

Holden tells the reader that Phoebe, like Allie Caulfield, is smart and has red hair. She's "roller-skate skinny" (88), emotional, affectionate, and perceptive. Perhaps in attempting to emulate her older brother, D. B., Phoebe writes stories, and hers are about a girl detective.

The reader first encounters Phoebe shown with Holden as he arrives home early. She realizes at once that he has been kicked out of yet another school. After Holden lists everything he disliked about the school, Phoebe challenges him to name something in life that he likes. When she discounts his answer, her query of what he would want to do in life elicits Holden's response of wanting to be "the catcher in the rye" (225). After phoning Mr. Antolini, Holden returns to Phoebe (she is sleeping in D. B.'s room), who is sitting on the bed with "her legs folded like one of those Yogi guys" (227). They then dance for four songs. The reader, through this scene, understands that, while Holden dances with Phoebe, he feels completely at peace.

The second scene with Holden and Phoebe brings the novel to a climax. After Phoebe meets Holden with a suitcase in preparation to accompany her brother out west, Holden snaps out of his escapist mentality. He suggests that they go to the zoo, and they finally arrive at the carousel. While Holden fears that Phoebe might fall from the carousel horse as she reaches for the gold ring, he experiences his epiphany: He must let children mature and experience life irregardless of its dangers; he cannot be their catcher in the rye.

Cavendish, Faith   Faith Cavendish is the young woman whose name was given to Holden Caulfield by a casual acquaintance at a party. Holden knows that Faith was almost kicked out of a dance at Princeton and that she currently works as a burlesque dancer. Holden has kept the slip of paper with her name and number for months because he was led to believe Faith did not mind "doing it once in a while" (83). Although Holden is right in his supposition, he is wrong in his timing. He wakes Faith up when he phones her and learns that, though ordinarily it would be "grand" (85) for him to stop in for a cocktail, her roommate is sick. When Faith suggests meeting tomorrow, Holden insists on that night and she demurs. Her voice is friendly and willing, though Holden senses her phoniness even while she remains unusually polite to him, a complete stranger. For a variety of adolescent reasons, Holden tends not to like girls with whom he shares a sexual interaction. Nevertheless, he puts aside the thought of calling Jane Gallagher, a girl he might love, and instead calls Faith Cavendish, a girl he has never met.

Cemetery visitors   When Holden Caulfield talks about his brother Allie's grave, he damns the cemetery visitors who run their cars when it begins to rain. Holden moreover comments on the unfairness of life in that Allie is dead and these people can listen to the radio and go out to dinner while the rain continues to drench Allie's grave.

Charlene   Charlene is the Caulfields' live-in, partially deaf maid. Thus, when Holden Caulfield sneaks into his parents' apartment, he is not afraid of being found out by Charlene. Phoebe Caulfield complains that the maid breathes on the food as she serves it.

Childs, Arthur   Holden Caulfield finds Arthur Childs, a Quaker, to be memorable because of a religious discussion the two once had as classmates at the Whooton School. The recollection occurs at a low point in the novel, just after Holden's troubling visit from a prostitute. Holden, disturbed, gets in bed alone and feels like praying but doesn't because he is "sort of an atheist" (130). Instead,

thinking about Jesus, he decides he does not like the disciples, and at this point in his thoughts, he remembers Childs. The Quaker student, a serious reader of the Bible, believes that in loving the disciples, one loves Jesus himself. The two boys will never see eye-to-eye because Childs believes Holden's religious problems stem from the latter's not attending church. The brief characterization of Arthur Childs defines an important religious standard held by Holden. Despite seeking answers and focusing on spiritual and moral issues, Holden has too many problems with organized religion to find any solace there. Instead of praying in a moment of desperation, Holden describes the ministers' voices he heard in prep schools as phony, "Holy Joe" (131) voices. Arthur Childs represents another religious dead end for Holden, but the discourse the two classmates have about events in the Bible shows both students to be serious young religious thinkers.

Chinese sculptress   The nameless Chinese sculptress is the much older girlfriend of Carl Luce. A recent arrival to America from Shanghai, she provides Luce with a good sex life, as she embodies sex as a physical and spiritual experience.

Coyle, Howie   This character is the best basketball player at Pencey Prep. Holden Caulfield admires Coyle's shooting ability, but Robert Ackley admires his "perfect *build* for basketball" (38). Howie Coyle does not appear in the novel, but he serves as a reference to the overvaluing of attractive appearance that Holden sees operating for both Ackley and Ward Stradlater.

Cuban-looking guy and pal   As Holden Caulfield is about to enter a run-down bar, he encounters two drunken men, a Cuban-looking guy with his pal. The two ask directions to the subway. As Holden gives directions, the Cuban-looking guy keeps breathing in Holden's face.

Cudahy, Mr.   Mr. Cudahy, a next-door neighbor of the Caulfields at their summer home in Maine, is Jane Gallagher's alcoholic stepfather and a shadowy character. The possible abuse that Cudahy perpetrates on Jane cannot be soothed by Holden

Caulfield's kisses. Holden's tenderness, however, at least softens Jane's distress. Mr. Cudahy walks around the house in his underwear and also naked. Although not definitely abusive to Jane, he poses a possible threat to her innocence. Holden senses strongly the discomfort the stepfather creates for Jane at home. In one of Holden's memories of Jane, Mr. Cudahy makes a brief appearance when he asks Jane the whereabouts of the cigarettes. She ignores him, and he leaves the room. Jane then starts to cry and finds comfort in Holden's arms. Mr. Cudahy's importance as a character lies in his representing one of those people who "are always ruining things" (114). He also illustrates a dark side of maturity that Holden knows instinctively to avoid.

Cultz, Jeanette Jeanette Cultz inspires Sally Hayes to appear sexy in a skating outfit even though Sally cannot skate at all. Jeanette, presumably a friend or classmate of Sally's, has recently ice-skated at Radio City. On their date, when Sally suggests skating to Holden Caulfield, she mentions Jeanette Cultz skating there recently. Jeanette had rented one of those "darling little skating skirts" (167). Neither Holden nor Sally skates well, but Holden is indeed charmed by the "butt-twitcher" (167) Sally wears. Holden's admiration of Sally's rear end captures one of the few times in the novel when Holden does not feel confused by his sexuality. Moreover, he seems direct about his emotions, but that time is brief. The date falls apart soon thereafter when the two stop skating to have a drink.

D. B. Caulfield's desk-seller The desk-seller is an alcoholic woman in Philadelphia who sold D. B. Caulfield his large desk, which Phoebe Caulfield loves to use.

Dicksteins, the The Dickstein family shares the 12th floor of the apartment building with the Caulfields. Holden Caulfield lies to the night elevator boy, identifying himself as the Dicksteins' nephew.

Edmont Hotel bellboy The nameless bellboy is about 65 years old. Holden Caulfield criticizes the comb-over the man uses to hide his baldness.

Edmont Hotel couple Across the way, Holden notices the couple who are enjoying squirting water or alcohol onto each other. He terms them "perverts." In a further comment, Holden considers himself to be "the only normal bastard in the whole place—and that isn't saying much" (81).

Edmont Hotel cross-dresser Holden notices the nameless cross-dresser across the way. The man is putting on women's undergarments and an evening dress and acting like a woman. Holden terms him a "pervert."

Elevator boy, Antolini building The nameless elevator boy gives Holden Caulfield a hard time before he lets him ride up to the Antolini apartment late at night.

Elevator boy, Caulfield building The nameless new night elevator boy is unknown to Holden Caulfield at the Caulfield's apartment building, a fact that Holden terms as a break. When Holden asks to be taken up to the same floor as his family's apartment so he can visit the Dicksteins (the other family on the 12th floor), the elevator boy replies that the Dicksteins are at a party on the 14th floor and that Holden had better wait in the lobby. Holden considers the elevator boy stupid because he has been outwitted by Holden's posing as the Dicksteins' nephew and moreover by Holden's pretending to suffer from a bad leg that thus necessitates that he rest on the chair outside the Dicksteins' apartment.

Ely Ely, Robert Ackley's roommate, spends most of his weekends at home. This character does not actually appear in the novel. After Holden Caulfield fights with his own roommate, Ward Stradlater, he wants to sleep in Ely's unused bed in Ackley's room. When Holden wakes Ackley up at 11:30 P.M., Ackley is not willing to give Holden permission to use Ely's bed, but he does not stop Holden from lying down there. Ely's bed is the first of several temporary beds Holden uses in the novel. Holden decides to leave Pencey after resting in Ely's bed for a little while.

English babe The unnamed woman was D. B. Caulfield's date when D. B. visited his brother,

Holden, in the California sanatorium the previous Saturday. She is "pretty affected, but very good-looking" (276), a description that gives the reader a sense of D. B.'s taste in women.

Ernie Ernie, an African-American jazz pianist, performs songs and plays piano in his own nightclub in Greenwich Village. Ernie obviously enjoys his image, as he has positioned a mirror to reflect his face, and not his hands, to the audience. Holden Caulfield knows Ernie through his older brother, D. B. Caulfield, and also from having been at the club previously. By the time Holden hears Ernie perform, he has come to see the talented artist as egotistical. Without being racist, Holden believes Ernie does not deserve the respect and awe his applauding audiences offer. Holden likewise holds the hypercritical opinion that the performer is being phony about being humble when he bows. Nevertheless, Holden does have some appreciation for this character and instantly regrets deciding to leave before hearing Ernie play something "halfway decent" (114).

Fallon, Bobby Bobby Fallon is Holden Caulfield's friend in Maine. The two boys rode bikes together to Lake Sedebego so they could shoot their BB guns. Holden had refused to take his brother Allie along on this excursion and now regrets his decision.

Fencer, Harry Holden Caulfield tells Ernest Morrow's mother that Harry Fencer was elected class president because her son refused to run for the office. The name "Harry Fencer" may have been composed by Holden as part of the lies he told Mrs. Morrow on the train to New York.

Fitzgerald Fitzgerald is a young lady who used to date Ward Stradlater. When Stradlater admits being "through with that pig" (39), Holden Caulfield attempts to persuade Stradlater to give the girl to him. With no hesitation, Stradlater wryly replies to Holden by saying, "Take her . . . She's too old for you" (39). Any character named "Fitzgerald" by Salinger is likely to reflect some of the author's known appreciation for his predecessor, F. Scott Fitzgerald. This character, however, is a very minor one who appears in the novel only as part of other characters' memories.

Fletcher, Estelle Estelle Fletcher is an African-American Dixieland-jazz singer on a record titled "Little Shirley Beans." This character avoids sounding mushy or cute, even though she performs a song about a little girl who does not want to leave her house because her front teeth are missing. Fletcher recorded the song in the 1920s. Holden Caulfield hears "Little Shirley Beans" in a Pencey dorm room and immediately thinks it one of the best records he has heard.

Funny-looking couple at Ernie's Holden Caulfield notices the couple sitting near him in the nightclub and comments on their unattractive appearance. He then ponders the unfortunate circumstances of "real ugly girls" (111) trying to date.

Gale, Herb This character is a past roommate of Robert Ackley's. Holden Caulfield briefly mentions Herb Gale as someone who never called Robert Ackley anything but "Ackley."

Gallagher, Jane Although one of the most important characters in *The Catcher in the Rye*, Jane Gallagher never actually makes an appearance in the novel. Everything readers can glean of her is told through Holden Caulfield as he knew her at 14 years of age, and through Ward Stradlater (when she is 16 years old). For Holden, Jane Gallagher embodies the cliché of the girl next door. Jane is a constant friend who seems virtuous and who is attractive to Holden. The two are 14 years old during the summer they meet. They become tennis and golf buddies at a country club where their families have a membership, and they often play checkers together. Holden makes a point of remembering that Jane Gallagher always kept her kings in the back row. With the allusion, Salinger may be suggesting that Jane has kept her innocence and virginity. Although presented as a typical prep school student, Jane differs in that her parents are divorced and her stepfather is an alcoholic. Holden becomes very nervous at the thought of Ward

Stradlater getting fixed up and taking Jane out on a date. Stradlater seems more focused on himself than on Jane (he calls her "Jean"). One of the most important things readers learn about Jane is that she is a dancer. Throughout the novel, Holden dances with a number of partners, but never the one he really wants. He and Jane were probably too young (for the era) to initiate sexual contact when they spent their adolescent summer together, but Holden thinks of calling her at almost every sexual juncture in the novel. She is one of the few characters Holden does not accuse of being phony.

George Holden Caulfield and Sally Hayes run into George "something" (165) (a boy Sally barely knows) during intermission after the first act of the Lunts' play. George, who seems older than Holden, attends Andover. Holden finds George irritating. Not only does George interrupt Holden's date with Sally, but he also tends to amplify her social phoniness. Sally and George attempt to keep the conversation going by talking about people each barely knows. They even talk again after the next act. Holden thinks George has a "very phony, Ivy League" (166) voice.

Goldfarb, Raymond A past schoolmate at the Whooten School, Raymond Goldfarb drinks a pint of scotch with Holden Caulfield in the chapel. The boy's only distinguishing characteristic is that he gets drunk more easily than Holden.

Guys unloading Christmas tree While walking in New York looking for a place to eat breakfast, Holden Caulfield sees two guys struggling to unload a Christmas tree from a truck. He finds it funny when one of the men tells the other, "Hold the sonuvabitch *up*! Hold it *up*, for Chrissake!" (255).

Guy with car Holden Caulfield tells Sally Hayes that he knows a guy in Greenwich Village who would lend them his car so the two can escape New York permanently and drive to Massachusetts or Vermont.

Guy with Colorado grandfather When Holden Caulfield tells his sister, Phoebe, that he is plan-

ning to move out west, he claims to know a guy whose grandfather owns a ranch in Colorado where Holden may possibly find work.

Haas, Mr. While talking with Mr. Spencer at Pencey, Holden Caulfield remembers his former headmaster, Mr. Haas, at Elkton Hills. Mr. Spencer asks why Holden did not stay at Elkton. Holden refuses to explain but believes he left Elkton because there were too many phonies there. Holden remembers Mr. Haas as more phony than his current headmaster because Mr. Haas would pay deference to attractive, wealthy parents and all but ignore others. Although he does not appear in the novel, Mr. Haas is important as a character because he illustrates how adults discriminate among one another. Holden possibly sees far too much phoniness in his world, but many times he is a good social and educational critic. With the example of Mr. Haas, the reader understands how Holden senses truth even as he is blinded by seeing nearly everyone as phony. Holden's opinion of Mr. Haas shows how the administration of education is phony when fairness is not consistently practiced.

Hartzell Although this character is Ward Stradlater's English teacher at Pencey, he is also aware of Holden Caulfield. According to Stradlater, Hartzell knows Holden writes well. This English teacher has challenged Stradlater's class to write a descriptive essay for their assignment due on Monday. Because Stradlater thinks that good writing is only a matter of proper punctuation, he believes that Hartzell will not know Holden is ghostwriting the assignment if Holden makes certain not to write everything correctly.

Harvard guy When Holden Caulfield makes a date with Sally Hayes over the phone, she tells him about an unnamed Harvard guy who is crazy about her. Holden thinks the guy must be a freshman, although Sally does not volunteer that information.

Hayes, Mr. When Holden Caulfield phones Sally Hayes for a date, the maid hands the phone to Sally's father. Holden identifies himself to Mr. Hayes and asks to speak with his daughter. At the end of his date with Sally, Holden calls her "a pain in the ass" (173) and fears that Sally will tell her father, whom Holden characterizes as "one of those big silent bastards" (173).

Hayes, Mrs.   Mrs. Hayes is Sally Hayes's wealthy mother. Holden Caulfield has a low opinion of her. Mrs. Hayes once (sensibly) told Sally that she considered Holden to be "wild" and that he "had no direction in life" (78).

Hayes, Sally   Sally Hayes is Holden Caulfield's girlfriend. The two know each other from living in familiar circles in Manhattan. Sally, an attractive prep school student at the Mary A. Woodruff School, is an important character for several reasons. Sally attracts Holden sexually and shares his social status, although Holden remains very sensitive and insecure about his status with her. During their date, Holden and Sally display much of the adolescent awkwardness to dating. Their feelings about each other fluctuate while they are learning to live in their social worlds. Sally seems fond enough of Holden to want him to decorate her Christmas tree, and Holden wants to run away with Sally, but both are smart enough to question differences between phony and real love. When Holden tells Sally he loves her, she responds in kind but adds that he should let his hair grow. (Young folks often struggle between the appearances of love and the realities that love engenders.) During their single date together, Sally Hayes effectively helps Holden sense the spectrum of love-hate emotions. More importantly, Sally understands Holden's need for patience in his maturation process. Sally Hayes has fewer adolescent doubts about being an adult than Holden does. Though Holden believes Sally is being phony when she acts like an adult, Sally has a more realistic understanding about their need for further maturation.

Hayes's maid   When Holden Caulfield phones Sally Hayes for a date, the maid answers and gives the call to Mr. Hayes. The fact that the Hayes family, like the Caulfields, employs a maid shows both families to be financially privileged.

Holden Caulfield's aunt at Allie Caulfield's funeral   According to D. B. Caulfield, this aunt kept saying how peaceful Allie Caulfield looked. Holden Caulfield describes her as stupid and as having bad breath.

Holden Caulfield's "charity" aunt   After Holden Caulfield meets the two nuns, he thinks of his aunt who does charity work for the Red Cross. Holden could easily imagine her collecting for the poor, unlike Sally Hayes's mother.

Holden Caulfield's grandfather   When Holden Caulfield imagines his own funeral, he tells the reader his grandfather from Detroit would attend. Holden complains that this grandfather, when he rides a bus, calls out each street number.

Holden Caulfield's grandmother   Holden Caulfield explains he has lots of money with him to stay a while in New York because his grandmother keeps forgetting she has already sent him his birthday money and sends gifts to him four times a year.

Holmborg, Alice   This young child is Phoebe Caulfield's classmate. Alice's mother has just taken the children to see a movie (*The Doctor*). Phoebe tries to explain about the movie and about Alice, but Holden Caulfield (for once!) wants to avoid digressions and cuts Phoebe off after she declares Alice to be her best friend. Nothing more is said about the character.

Holmborg, Mrs.   Mrs. Holmborg is the mother of Phoebe Caulfield's friend, Alice. She has taken her daughter and Phoebe to see a movie (*The Doctor*) and bothers Phoebe by repeatedly leaning over her to ask Alice whether she feels okay.

Horwitz   This character is the most important cabbie in the novel, and Holden Caulfield describes him as a "much better guy" (106) than the Penn Station cab driver. Holden flags down Horwitz for his trip downtown to Ernie's. Horwitz drives an old and smelly Checker cab, and he is rude, aggressive, and quite clever. Holden asks this late-night, probably pretty tired driver if he knows where the ducks go when the ice freezes on the Central Park Lagoon. Horwitz gets angry and silences Holden by saying, "How the hell should I know?" (107). The cabbie later resumes the conversation by reasoning that fish do not freeze and further reasons that fish have it tougher than ducks because they do not go anywhere and have to live off themselves under (and in) the ice. "That's their *nature*, for Chrissake," (108) he adds. (In other words, survival is a natural thing for most creatures, including fish.) At the end of the cab ride, after Horwitz has declined Holden's invitation to join him at Ernie's, the cabbie offers several aggressive "if-you-were-a-fish" questions. Horwitz seems to hit the mark or at least stun Holden by shooting two questions at the boy with the obvious answer that Mother Nature always takes care of things. Horwitz leaves in the split second after Holden agrees with the cabbie's reasoning and before Holden gets further than saying "but—." Horwitz might be seen as just another chatty cabbie anxious to get rid of a passenger who does not seem quite sane. On the other hand, Horwitz may be viewed as wise and Zenlike in his response to Holden's odd question about the ducks. Despite his harsh tone, Horwitz understands that Holden is worried about himself, not ducks or fish. The cabbie attempts to give the boy some momentary, reasonable shelter from adolescent confusion and growing depression.

Jane Gallagher's mother On several occasions, Holden Caulfield thinks of phoning Jane Gallagher's mother to find out when Jane will be home for the Christmas holidays. Holden's mother felt Jane's mother believed herself to be above the Caulfields because she would avoid Mrs. Caulfield in the village near the beach. Jane's mother is remarried to the alcoholic Mr. Cudahy.

Joe Yale-looking guy and date At Ernie's nightclub, Holden Caulfield notices this couple at a nearby table. The guy, while telling his date about his dorm mate who tried to commit suicide, is trying simultaneously to touch the girl sexually beneath the table. Holden expresses his condemnation of this character by adding that he himself would never attend an Ivy League school (as his father wishes).

Kid at Phoebe Caulfield's school While writing a note to his sister Phoebe at her school, Holden Caulfield sees this "colored" (259) boy. The child, on his way to the bathroom, is carrying a wooden pass, just as Holden had done as a school child.

Kid at Radio City Music Hall Holden Caulfield sees a child being neglected by his mother during the movie. Instead of taking her little boy to the bathroom, the mother is crying over the movie's plot.

Kid at zoo Holden Caulfield gets a kick out of this child who wants his father to make a bear come out of its cave.

Kid brothers at Museum of Art As Holden Caulfield waits for Phoebe Caulfield, the unnamed brothers ask Holden where the mummies are located. Holden shows consideration by walking the kids to the mummies' cases. He recalls his history essay for Mr. Spencer and explains to the kids about how the Egyptians buried their dead.

Kids downtown When Holden Caulfield sees "a million little kids" (256) downtown shopping with their mothers, he suddenly gets the feeling of Christmas.

Kid singing in the street This child sings the lyric, "If a body catch a body coming through the rye" (150). The phrase lays the foundation for Holden Caulfield eventually telling his sister, Phoebe, that he wants to be "the catcher in the rye." Although the singing boy is accompanied by his parents, they remain unaware of him as he walks in the street near the curb, endangered by the speeding traffic.

Kids on seesaw Holden Caulfield sees two kids of unequal weight on a playground seesaw. When Holden tries to even the seesaw, he feels that the kids don't want him to help and he leaves.

Kid with skates   This child tells Holden Caulfield that Phoebe Caulfield's class might be at the museum with the Indians. Holden helps her tighten her skates. After she thanks him, he remarks that "she was a very nice, polite little kid" (155).

Kinsella, Richard   When Holden Caulfield tries to answer Mr. Antolini's questions about why he flunked out of Pencey, he tells his former teacher about another student named Richard Kinsella in his Oral Expression class. Holden describes Richard Kinsella's experience in the class as one reason he (Holden) flunked. In that class, students are encouraged to yell out "Digression!" when a speaker does not stick to his topic. Richard Kinsella is a nervous boy who speaks too softly and with trembling lips. Holden tells Mr. Antolini about the time Kinsella spoke about his father's farm in Vermont. Instead of developing details about the farm in his speech, Kinsella digressed and talked about his 42-year-old uncle who had polio and would not see anyone in the hospital. Holden argues to Mr. Antolini that the digression was nice and that Kinsella was too excited about what he was saying to be interrupted by students shouting at him. Perhaps inspired by his strong sense of compassion, Holden tells Mr. Antolini that he likes Kinsella's speeches best. Holden's appreciation for his classmate's approach to public speaking emphasizes Holden's own problems with digression and shows, as well, that Holden is sensitive and empathetic toward others. Richard Kinsella is an object of Holden's compassion and "proof" of why he flunked out of Pencey. The immature speaking qualities of Richard Kinsella illustrate similar traits in Holden that Mr. Antolini knows he must grow beyond.

Leahy and Hoffman   Leahy and Hoffman are Pencey Prep roommates and live in the same dorm as Holden Caulfield. After Holden takes his final leave of Robert Ackley, he sees a box of toothpaste outside the door of these two students.

Levine, Gertrude   Holden Caulfield remembers holding hands with Gertrude Levine when they were elementary school classmates. Gertrude has sticky or sweaty hands that Holden holds when the two visit the Museum of Natural History.

Luce, Carl   Carl Luce meets Holden Caulfield for a drink at the Wicker Bar inside of the "swanky" (184) Seton Hotel. Luce was Holden's student adviser at the Whooton School, and in the present tense of the novel, he is a student at Columbia University. On his way to the Wicker Bar to see Luce, Holden thinks about his older brother, D. B. In some ways, Carl Luce is Holden's older prep school brother. Holden remembers the "sex talks" (185) Luce gave in his room and also remembers Luce as extremely intelligent. Holden wonders how Luce came to know quite a bit about "perverts" (185) and also wonders if Luce is "flitty" (186) (homosexual).

When the two meet at the bar, Holden is almost overtly homosexual in his conversation, wildly tossing out sexual hints. Luce does not want to talk with Holden in such a charged manner. After Holden calms down, he learns that Luce is dating an older Chinese woman. Holden questions Luce about this relationship, and Luce explains that Eastern philosophy views sex as a physical and spiritual convergence.

Not only does Luce serve as a guide to ease some of Holden's awkwardness and share with him insights about sex, but he also attempts to guide Holden towards psychoanalysis. Luce's father is a psychoanalyst who helped Luce. Luce sees Holden's problems with immaturity and "adjusting" to society more clearly than do most of the characters in the novel. Just before he leaves Holden alone and depressed, Luce repeats a previous suggestion about getting psychological help.

Luce, Dr.   Dr. Luce, the father of Carl Luce, is a psychoanalyst. He has helped his son "ad*just*" and would, according to Carl, help Holden Caulfield "recognize the patterns of [his] mind" (192).

Macklin, Harris   Harris Macklin and Holden Caulfield were roommates for a term at Elkton Hills. Holden remembers his classmate as someone who had few good qualities except for the ability to whistle quite well. Macklin embodies hope for Holden, who believes that, if you have one redeeming quality, you may be okay.

Marco and Miranda These two characters are mentioned by Holden Caulfield when he dances with Bernice in the Lavender Room of the Edmont Hotel. Holden, focusing on how well people dance, explains to Bernice that she is a better dancer than Miranda of the dance team "Marco and Miranda."

Margulies, Phyllis Phyllis, a friend of Phoebe Caulfield's, has taught Phoebe how to belch.

Marsalla, Edgar Holden Caulfield remembers this character who farts during a pretentious speech by Mr. Ossenburger. Mr. Ossenburger, a graduate of Pencey Prep, went on to make a lot of money as an undertaker. Although Edgar Marsalla incites the wrath of Dr. Thurmer, the headmaster, Holden appreciates the way Marsalla's fart in a chapel makes fun of Mr. Ossenburger's speech.

Maurice Maurice is the elevator operator at the Edmont Hotel and also operates as a pimp. In his low-class, New York accent, Maurice calls Holden Caulfield "Chief." He bullies Holden in an attempt to get more money when he returns to Holden's room with the prostitute, Sunny. Although the agreed-upon price for "a throw" had been decided at $5, Sunny and Maurice ask for $10. When Sunny takes another $5 from Holden's wallet, Maurice finger-flicks Holden's genitals. Holden, who begins to cry, will not stop calling Maurice names, and the pimp punches Holden in the stomach. Maurice leaves but becomes an actor in Holden's fantasy in which Holden imagines that Maurice has shot him instead of hitting him. Holden then imagines shooting Maurice six times and that Jane Gallagher appears to bandage Holden's wound. Although Maurice plays the role of a villain in the novel, Holden ends up missing everybody he has told about, even "that goddam Maurice" (277).

Morrow, Ernest This Pencey Prep student is the son of Mrs. Morrow, a woman Holden Caulfield meets on his train ride to New York. Although Holden thinks Ernest Morrow is not very nice at all (Morrow likes to snap wet towels at other students' asses in the dormitory hall), he lies about Ernest to the boy's mother. Holden tries to convince Mrs. Morrow that her son is very popular at school but that he was too modest to become class president (despite the fact that Holden describes Ernest, in an aside to the reader, as the "biggest bastard" [71] at Pencey).

Morrow, Mrs. This character is an attractive woman who talks with Holden Caulfield on a train from Agerstown to New York. She wears an orchid, and Holden thinks she has a terrific smile, charm, and sex appeal. Though she is old enough to be his mother, Holden is attracted to Mrs. Morrow and believes that she likes him in return. In actuality, she is attracted to the Pencey sticker on Holden's suitcase because her son attends Pencey. Holden and Mrs. Morrow try to find nice ways to discuss her son, but it is clear that she doesn't know the meaner prep school side of her son Ernest. This disjunction is explained by Holden's thinking, "Mothers are all slightly insane" (72). Holden lies to Mrs. Morrow about her son and about why he himself has left school early. When she gets off the train at Newark, she invites Holden to visit Ernest and the Morrow family at their summer home in Gloucester, Massachusetts, but it is an invitation Holden knows he will never accept.

Mother at Radio City Music Hall This parent of a young son cries at a maudlin movie and does not want to interrupt her viewing to take her boy to the bathroom. She personifies for Holden Caulfield a human hypocrisy: "You take somebody that cries their goddam eyes out over phony stuff in the movies, and nine times out of ten they're mean bastards at heart" (181).

Movie actor and date Holden Caulfield sees a movie actor, along with his beautiful date, during an intermission of the play he attends with Sally Hayes. Holden comments on the actor's feigned unawareness that people are staring at him.

Museum of Natural History guard The guard is one of the few adults in the novel of whom Holden Caulfield approves. If a child touched something in a display, the guard would warn them "in a nice voice, not like a goddam cop" (157).

Nuns   Holden Caulfield meets two nuns from Chicago during his breakfast at a sandwich bar near Grand Central Station. The nuns are on their way to teach at an uptown convent school, and Holden helps them stow their inexpensive suitcases. Holden feels uncomfortable eating his large breakfast of bacon and eggs while they order only coffee and toast, and he convinces them to accept a $10 donation. The nun sitting next to Holden has "a helluva kind face" (143) and teaches English. Her smile reminds him of Ernest Morrow's mother's smile. As they discuss reading, Holden has trouble imagining how the nun can teach literature when stories involve sex, but he does discuss *Romeo and Juliet* with her because she asks his opinion. The contradiction (for Holden) expands, and he is relieved when the nuns do not ask him if he is Catholic. Holden's brief interaction with the nuns illustrates that the appearance of differences can help or hurt "nice conversation" (147).

Ossenburger, Mr.   This character is a wealthy undertaker who has given enough money to Pencey Prep to have a wing in the new dorm named after him. Holden Caulfield lives in the Ossenburger Memorial Wing of the dorm and imagines that Ossenburger grew rich by deceiving people about the burial of the dead. Holden's assumption is probably due to his not attending Allie Caulfield's funeral or to dorm hearsay. But Holden probably perceives Ossenburger correctly as an overly self-important, Cadillac-driving hypocrite. During the undertaker's speech in the school chapel, the wealthy alumnus tells the boys at Pencey to think of Jesus as their buddy and remarks that he himself talks to Jesus constantly, even when driving his car. Holden sees through the trappings of the speaker's wealth by imagining Ossenburger shifting gears and "asking Jesus to send him a few more stiffs" (23). This character is important because he shows Holden how a good education and success at Pencey may not necessarily make him a better person.

Parents of kid singing in street   The parents, who have just exited from church, are unaware of their child's endangerment by passing traffic as he walks in the street near the curb.

Pete   Pete is the elevator operator in the apartment building where the Caulfields live. Pete is normally on duty in the evenings but is not on duty the night Holden Caulfield sneaks in to visit his sister, Phoebe.

Pike, Al   Al Pike is an athletic and muscular Choate student who dated Jane Gallagher. It is likely that Holden Caulfield felt quite jealous of Al Pike during the summer Holden lived next door to Jane. Holden watched Al diving in a tight white "Lastex" bathing suit at the country club and assumed the boy to be a show-off and not very intelligent. Holden admits, however, that he does not know Pike well. Later, Jane tries to make Holden understand that Pike shows off because of an inferiority complex.

Radio City Music Hall audience couple   Holden Caulfield overhears the man telling his wife that the dancing, kicking Rockettes embody precision.

Radio City Music Hall kettle drummer   Of the entire Christmas pageant show, Holden Caulfield is convinced Jesus would like only the kettle drummer because he bangs the drums "so nice and sweet" (179).

Radio City Music Hall roller skater   Holden Caulfield can't enjoy the tuxedoed man who skates under tables while telling jokes because he imagines the absurdity of the man practicing his act.

Roberta Walsh's roommate   The roommate of Roberta Walsh doesn't like Holden Caulfield's friend, Bob Robinson. She finds Robinson conceited because he tells her he is the captain of the debating team.

Robinson, Bob   After Holden Caulfield tries to understand how girls equate poor character traits in guys with inferiority complexes, he recalls his friend Bob Robinson. Holden thinks Robinson really did have a problem with an inferiority complex but also recalls that Roberta Walsh's roommate did not like Robinson and thought he was conceited. Robinson's character is part of a psychological equation that Holden is working on to calculate how women's perceptions of men are based on affection, factoring in opinions about conceit and inferiority complexes.

Sally Hayes's grandmother When Holden Caulfield drunkenly phones Sally Hayes's number late at night, Sally's grandmother answers the call. She tells Holden that Sally is asleep and asks the sensible question of why Holden is calling so late.

Salvation Army girls Holden Caulfield, downtown on Monday, sees women, who wear no lipstick, ringing the Salvation Army bells for donations.

Santa Clauses Holden Caulfield, downtown on Monday, sees "scraggy-looking" (255) Santa Clauses ringing bells on street corners.

Schmidt, Mrs. An older woman, possibly in her sixties, Mrs. Schmidt is married to one of Pencey's janitors. Holden suggests satirically that Stradlater have sex with Mrs. Schmidt on his way to the bathroom.

Schmidt, Rudolf Rudolf Schmidt is the janitor in Holden Caulfield's dorm. Holden uses the janitor's name when he meets Mrs. Morrow, the mother of a Pencey student Holden dislikes. Lying about his real name and introducing himself as "Rudolf Schmidt" is the first of the lies Holden tells Mrs. Morrow.

School secretary The elderly secretary at Phoebe Caulfield's school gives Holden Caulfield's note for his sister to another lady to deliver. The secretary asks Holden where he goes to school, and he lies by replying Pencey Prep. The secretary considers Pencey to be a good school, but Holden refrains from disabusing her of the opinion. Holden feels depressed when she wishes him "good luck."

Shaney, Louis Louis Shaney, a Catholic boy, is the first student Holden Caulfield meets at the Whooton School. Although the two are enjoying a conversation about tennis, Shaney interrupts to ask if Holden knows of a Catholic church nearby,

a subtle attempt to learn if Holden is Catholic. The intrusion of religion into relationships bothers Holden, and he remarks that he is glad the two nuns didn't ask him if he was Catholic.

Sherman, Anne Louise When Holden Caulfield settles into his room at the Edmont Hotel, he observes some sexual scenes from his window and considers how confused he is about sex. Holden remembers Anne Louise Sherman because one night he promised himself that he would quit going out with girls that gave him "a pain in the ass" (82), and he broke his own rule with Anne Louise that same night. Even though Holden thinks she is a "terrible phony" (82), he necked with her all night long. Reflecting on this contradiction, Holden swears sex "is something I just don't understand" (82).

Shoe salesman, Bloomingdale's Holden Caulfield recalls the Christmas before last when he took his sister, Phoebe, shopping. The Bloomingdale's salesman good-naturedly allowed Phoebe to try on 20 pairs of shoes before she decided to buy some moccasins.

Simmons, Lillian Lillian Simmons is a large-breasted girl who used to go out with Holden Caulfield's brother, D. B. Lillian runs into Holden at Ernie's, where she is accompanied by a naval officer whom Holden calls "Commander Blop or something" (113). Even though he feels a little sorry for Lillian Simmons, Holden believes nobody likes her very much. Not only is she oblivious to the human traffic jam she has created in the middle of a crowded club, but she also makes Holden want to leave Ernie's to avoid her. He regrets leaving before he can hear some good music, though, and has Lillian Simmons in mind when he declares that "People are always ruining things for you" (114).

Singer, Buddy This character is the leader of the band playing the Lavender Room at the Edmont Hotel. Holden Caulfield thinks the band and its leader are "putrid" (90). However, even they can't ruin "Just One of Those Things" by Cole Porter. Holden dances quite a bit to the band's music with three women from Seattle, even though Buddy Singer and his band are too brassy and sentimental for Holden's taste.

Slagle, Dick   Once a roommate of Holden Caulfield at Elkton Hills, Dick Slagle comes from a less wealthy background than Holden's. Slagle teases Holden for being bourgeois, and the economic differences between the two boys seem to cause too much misunderstanding for them to remain roommates for more than a couple of months. The disparity in their luggage objectifies their class differences. Holden has Mark Cross leather suitcases, and Slagle's luggage is inexpensive and looks cheap. Holden tries to cover up the difference by placing his bags out of sight under his bed, but Slagle returns the better luggage to the racks the next day. Holden does not immediately realize that Slagle may want people to think that Holden's suitcases are his own. Later, at Pencey Prep, Holden misses Dick Slagle, but he concludes that it might be better to room with someone like Ward Stradlater, remembering that "his suitcases were as good as mine" (142).

Smith, Phyllis   Phyllis Smith's reason for cancelling a date with Ward Stradlater is not made clear. Although Phyllis had agreed to go out with Stradlater on the Saturday night date, Jane Gallagher replaces her.

Spencer, Mr.   A history teacher at Pencey Prep, Mr. Spencer is old and has back problems. When he appears in the novel, he is sick with the grippe as well. Holden Caulfield is depressed by Mr. Spencer's age and sickness but is otherwise respectful of his teacher. Mr. Spencer has invited Holden to come by and attempts to express concern for Holden's troubles. Despite wanting to help the boy, Mr. Spencer finds it necessary to rake over why Holden failed, perhaps to justify in his mind that he was not responsible for Holden's failure. Mr. Spencer is dressed in a worn-out bathrobe and smells of Vick's nasal drops, but he does have a sense of humor and laughs at his own jokes. He remains a caring, dedicated teacher who enjoys students but probably misunderstands them. Mr. Spencer is still interested in history and is still amused by historical artifacts ("You take somebody old as hell, like old Spencer, and they can get a big bang out of buying a blanket" [10]). Despite his efforts, Mr. Spencer is not very good at reaching Holden and fails to offer timely compassion when Holden attempts to explain his problems. Mr. Spencer illustrates an irony in Holden's dilemma: Holden will learn he needs to understand his own family history, not the kind of history he can learn in a school.

Spencer, Mrs.   Mrs. Spencer, the wife of Holden's history teacher, Mr. Spencer, answers the door when Holden Caulfield rings the bell. Only when Mrs. Spencer exclaims Holden's first name does the reader learn the name of the story's narrator. She pointedly asks Holden if he is "frozen to death" (9).

Stabile, Phil   Holden Caulfield recalls Phil Stabile, a student at Elkton Hills, when Phoebe Caulfield asks her brother to name one thing that he likes, and he cannot. Instead, Holden remembers how Phil Stabile led a group of six prep school students against James Castle because Castle had said Stabile was conceited and would not recant his opinion. Stabile and his six friends locked Castle's door and did such repulsive things to the frail boy that Castle killed himself by jumping out of his window. Stabile and his friends were subsequently expelled from Elkton Hills.

Steele, Jim   "Jim Steele" is the second alias Holden Caulfield uses to introduce himself to several female characters in the novel. The pseudonym does not create for Holden his hoped-for sense of manliness either time he uses the name.

Stradlater, Ward   Ward Stradlater, a year older than Holden Caulfield, is Holden's roommate at Pencey Prep. Stradlater comes from a wealthy background similar to Holden's, and both boys are tall and socially attuned. However, Stradlater's maturity is more advanced. Holden believes that his roommate is no longer a virgin, and he considers Stradlater "a sexy bastard" (45), able to attract a lot of girls because of his manly appearance.

Holden and Robert Ackley, much less physically attractive as men, believe that Stradlater is conceited and has an attitude of superiority. Nonetheless, Holden defends his roommate from Ackley's hatred by claiming that Stradlater is "very generous in some things" (32). Holden's defense, however, lacks convincing evidence. Stradlater shows himself to be self-absorbed (when he whistles, he is loud but not in tune). Stradlater, moreover, is always in a self-important rush. Though Stradlater is usually friendly, Holden knows that his roommate is often phony and just acting polite. Stradlater embodies the stereotypical student athlete, more advanced in sports and girls than in studies, and willing to cheat when academically necessary. Stradlater, moreover, is an ungrateful cheater who does not recognize the gift of Holden's essay (about Holden's brother Allie's baseball glove). Stradlater does not possess the ability to understand that Holden's essay represents a cry for help. Stradlater, however, is not altogether a shallow prep school student. Even though he stops his fight with Holden by delivering a hard punch, he also shows restraint with Holden's inept attempts to fight his way into Stradlater's private life. On some levels, Stradlater lives comfortably with Holden as his roommate. However, Holden's friendship with Stradlater comes to an end not because Holden has flunked out of Pencey but because Stradlater may have had sex with Jane Gallagher. Stradlater is a successful prep school student. Holden's final fight with his roommate dramatizes that Holden is ineptly rebelling against some of the things that make Stradlater a winner in the game of life.

Sunny Sunny is a dyed-blond prostitute from Hollywood whom Maurice, her pimp, sends to Holden Caulfield late at night in the Edmont Hotel. She is young, possibly Holden's age, though neither she nor Holden will reveal to each other their exact ages. Sunny is not fooled when Holden lies about being 22 years old. She has a nervous habit of jiggling her foot and prefers to rush Holden into sex even though he would prefer conversation. Holden thinks that, even with her little voice, Sunny can be "spooky" (127). As Sunny removes her green dress, Holden does not react to her physi-

cally (except to notice that she is skinny) but imagines the scene of Sunny buying the dress, with no one in the store knowing it is a dress for a prostitute. Instead of being sexy and arousing Holden, Sunny seems pathetic to him. When she reveals that all she does during the day is watch movies, he realizes he is not at all attracted to her. The two do not have sex, but Sunny sits on Holden's lap for a little while to entice him. Sunny is a brazen and tough street criminal, and she returns later with Maurice to take another $5 from Holden.

Superintendent, Caulfield building When Holden Caulfield plans to sneak into his parents' apartment to see his sister, Phoebe, he remembers that the front door squeaks because the superintendent is too lazy to fix it.

Thaw, Bud Bud Thaw is a student at Pencey Prep. His Saturday night date's roommate is Holden Caulfield's friend, Jane Gallagher.

Thurmer, Dr. As the headmaster of Pencey Prep, Dr. Thurmer expels Holden Caulfield from Pencey and lectures the boy for two hours about how life is a game, advising Holden to follow the rules of the game. Although not portrayed as hypocritical as Mr. Haas, Holden's former headmaster at Elkton Hills, Dr. Thurmer is devious enough to serve steak every Saturday night before parental visits on Sunday.

Thurmer, Selma Selma is the unattractive daughter of the headmaster of Pencey Prep, Dr. Thurmer. Holden Caulfield sits next to Selma on a bus ride from Agerstown and appreciates that she does not try to convince him that her father is a wonderful person.

Tichener, Robert Holden Caulfield recalls tossing a football around with Robert Tichener and Paul Campbell, fellow students at Pencey Prep. Holden remembers Tichener as particularly nice. When evening falls, a teacher, Mr. Zambesi, tells the boys to get ready for dinner. The boys enjoyed tossing the football even as it became increasingly dark. Darkness does not stop them from feeling good, but a teacher does. Holden's bittersweet memory of that October evening allows him "to feel some kind of a good-by" (7) for Pencey Prep.

Tina and Janine   These two characters do not appear but are mentioned as French musicians who used to play at the Wicker Bar. Tina plays piano, and Janine, a bilingual singer, sings sexy songs.

Valencia   Valencia is the singer who replaced the French musicians, Tina and Janine, at the Wicker Bar. Holden Caulfield thinks Valencia isn't very good but that she sings better than Tina and Janine and chooses better songs to sing. Holden, attracted to Valencia, gives her "the old eye" (194), but she ignores him.

Veteran's Day visitor at Pencey Prep   Holden Caulfield tells his sister Phoebe about the 50-year-old Pencey alumnus who wanted to see whether his initials, which he had carved in the bathroom door, were still visible. He advises Holden and Ward Stradlater to take advantage of their time at Pencey.

Vinson, Mr.   Mr. Vinson, an Oral Expression (Speech) teacher at Pencey Prep, encourages students to shout "Digression!" at a speaker who doesn't stay on track during a speech. Vinson tries to teach his students to "*unify* and *simplify*" (240). Holden Caulfield believes Mr. Vinson to be intelligent but lacking brains. In other words, Holden recognizes the need to communicate coherently but also perceives that Vinson does not have the brains to understand human digression as something that may be emotionally important.

Waiter, cheap restaurant   The waiter, whom Holden Caulfield characterizes as nice, does not charge for the doughnuts Holden was unable to eat.

Waiter, Lavender Room   The waiter will not take Holden Caulfield's order of a scotch and soda without first seeing some identification. Holden becomes upset, as the encounter reminds him of being "a goddam minor" (91).

Waiter, Radio City   Like the waiter at the Lavender Room, this unnamed waiter will not serve Holden Caulfield a scotch and soda, and instead Holden must settle for a Coke.

Walsh, Roberta   Holden Caulfield knows Roberta Walsh, who sets up a date for her roommate with Holden's friend, Bob Robinson.

Weintraub, Curtis   This character is a classmate of Phoebe Caulfield. The reader learns that there is tension between Curtis and Phoebe, because Phoebe and Selma Attenbury decide to put ink on Curtis's coat. Curtis, moreover, had pushed Phoebe down the park stairs and caused her to cut her arm. Curtis follows Phoebe around. When Holden Caulfield suggests to Phoebe that Curtis follows her because he may like her, she replies, "I don't want him to like me" (213). Phoebe's reaction to Curtis shows that she remains innocent with regard to sexual attraction. Curtis Weintraub also illustrates how presexual children use conflict to learn about each other.

West Point cadet   When Holden Caulfield makes a date with Sally Hayes over the phone, Sally tells him about an unnamed West Point cadet, in addition to a Harvard guy, who is crazy about her.

Wicker Bar bartender   Holden Caulfield calls the bartender a snob, but the man serves Holden some alcoholic drinks.

Wicker Bar couple   Holden remarks that the man was "snowing hell" out of his date in telling her that "she had aristocratic hands" (185).

Wicker Bar flits   Holden Caulfield terms some men at the end of the bar "flits" (185) (a derogatory term for homosexual). The observation begins the motif of Holden's possible confusion about his own sexuality.

Wicker Bar hatcheck girl   Before Holden Caulfield can leave the Wicker Bar in the Seton Hotel, he needs to retrieve his coat. Although Holden cannot find his ticket, the hatcheck girl, a middle-aged woman, nonetheless gives him his coat. She also makes Holden put on his hat and advises him to go home and go to bed.

Wicker Bar headwaiter Holden Caulfield asks the headwaiter to invite the singer, Valencia, over to Holden's table for a drink. He doubts, however, that the headwaiter has delivered his invitation.

Wicker Bar piano player The wavy-haired piano player accompanies the singer, Valencia. After a very drunk Holden Caulfield goes into the bathroom to dunk his head in water, the piano player, who enters to comb his hair, tries to give Holden some good advice by telling him to go home.

Woodruff, Frederick Frederick Woodruff, a student in the same dorm as Holden Caulfield, is asleep and not pleased when Holden wakes him up, even though Holden has lent Woodruff his typewriter. When Holden offers to sell the type-writer, Woodruff answers that he just wants to borrow it. He finally agrees to buy the typewriter for $20, even though it cost close to $90. Woodruff is the last character Holden sees before shouting, "*Sleep tight, ya morons*" (68), as he leaves Pencey for good.

Zambesi, Mr. The biology teacher at Pencey Prep, Mr. Zambesi tells Holden Caulfield and two other boys, Paul Campbell and Robert Tichener, to stop throwing a football and prepare for din-ner one October evening. In the context of the scene, Holden thinks of the teacher as someone who spoiled a simple pleasure too early and need-lessly. Remembering the incident and Mr. Zambesi helps Holden "to feel some kind of a good-by" (7) for Pencey Prep.

FURTHER READING
Books Exclusively on The Catcher in the Rye

Beidler, Peter G. *A Reader's Companion to J. D. Salin-ger's The Catcher in the Rye.* Seattle: Coffeetown Press, 2009.

Bloom, Harold, ed. and intro. *Holden Caulfield.* Major Literary Characters. New York: Chelsea House, 1990.

———. *Holden Caulfield.* New ed. Bloom's Major Literary Characters. Philadelphia: Chelsea House, 2005.

———. *J. D. Salinger's The Catcher in the Rye.* Mod-ern Critical Interpretations. Philadelphia: Chelsea House, 2000.

———. *J. D. Salinger's The Catcher in the Rye.* New ed. Bloom's Modern Critical Interpretations. New York: Chelsea House, 2009.

———. *J. D. Salinger's The Catcher in the Rye.* Bloom's Notes. New York: Chelsea House, 1996.

———. *J. D. Salinger's The Catcher in the Rye.* Bloom's Guides. New York: Chelsea House, 2007.

Bryfonski, Dedria, ed. *Depression in J. D. Salinger's The Catcher in the Rye.* Detroit: Greenhaven Press, 2009.

Creeger, George R. *'Treacherous Desertion': Salinger's The Catcher in the Rye.* Middletown, Conn.: Wes-leyan University, 1961.

Engel, Steven, ed. *Readings on The Catcher in the Rye.* San Diego: Greenhaven Press, 1998.

Graham, Sarah. *J. D. Salinger's The Catcher in the Rye.* London: Routledge, 2007.

———. *Salinger's The Catcher in the Rye.* London: Continuum, 2007.

Laser, Marvin, and Norman Fruman, eds. *Studies in J. D. Salinger: Reviews, Essays, Critiques of "The Catcher in the Rye" and Other Fiction.* New York: Odyssey Press, 1963.

Marsden, Malcolm, ed. *If You Really Want to Know: A "Catcher" Casebook.* Chicago: Scott, Foresman, 1963.

McDaniel, Sean. *A Catcher's Companion: The World of Holden Caulfield.* Santa Monica, Calif.: Lit. Hap-pens Publishing, 2009.

Pinsker, Sanford. *The Catcher in the Rye: Innocence Under Pressure.* New York: Twayne Publishers, 1993.

Pinsker, Sanford, and Ann Pinsker. *Understand-ing The Catcher in the Rye: A Student Casebook to Issues, Sources, and Historical Documents.* Westport, Conn.: Greenwood Press, 1999.

Salzberg, Joel, ed. *Critical Essays on Salinger's The Catcher in the Rye.* Boston: G. K. Hall, 1990.

Salzman, Jack, ed. *New Essays on The Catcher in the Rye.* Cambridge: Cambridge University Press, 1991.

Simonson, Harold P., and Philip E. Hager, eds. *Salinger's "Catcher in the Rye": Clamor vs. Criticism.* Lexington, Mass.: D. C. Heath, 1963.

Steed, J. P., ed. *The Catcher in the Rye: New Essays.* New York: Peter Lang, 2002.

Steinle, Pamela Hunt. *In Cold Fear: The Catcher in the Rye Censorship Controversies and Postwar American Character.* Columbus: Ohio State University Press, 2002.

Unrue, John C. *The Catcher in the Rye.* Detroit: Gale Group, 2001.

Chapters of Books, Individual Essays, Reviews, and Miscellaneous Material on **The Catcher in the Rye**

Alsen, Eberhard. *"The Catcher in the Rye."* In *A Reader's Guide to J. D. Salinger,* 53–77. Westport, Conn.: Greenwood Press, 2002.

Amur, G. S. "Theme, Structure, and Symbol in *The Catcher in the Rye." Indian Journal of American Studies* 1 (1969): 11–24.

Baumbach, Jonathan, Jr. "The Saint as a Young Man: A Reappraisal of *The Catcher in the Rye." Modern Language Quarterly* 25 (December 1964): 461–472.

Bawer, Bruce. "Salinger's Arrested Development." *New Criterion* 5, no. 1 (September 1986): 34–47.

Behrman, S. N. "The Vision of the Innocent." *New Yorker,* 11 August 1951, 71–76.

Beidler, Peter G. "What Holden Looks Like and Who 'Whosis' Is: A Newly Identified Movie Allusion in *The Catcher in the Rye." ANQ: A Quarterly Journal of Short Articles, Notes, and Reviews* 20, no. 1 (Winter 2007): 52–57.

Bhaerman, Robert D. "Rebuttal: Holden in the Rye." *College English* 23, no. 6 (March 1962): 508.

Blaney, Shirlie. "Twin State Telescope: Interview with an Author." *Daily Eagle,* 13 November 1953, editorial page.

Blythe, Hal, and Charlie Sweet. "The Caulfield Family of Writers in The Catcher in the Rye." *Notes on Contemporary Literature* 32, no. 5 (November 2002): 6–7.

———. "Falling in Salinger's Catcher in the Rye." *Notes on Contemporary Literature* 32, no. 4 (September 2002): 5–7.

———. "Holden, the Bomb, and Dr. Strangelove." *Notes on Contemporary Literature* 34, no. 3 (May 2004): 11–12.

———. "Holden's Mysterious Hat." *Notes on Contemporary Literature* 32, no. 4 (September 2002): 7–8.

Booth, Wayne C. "Censorship and the Values of Fiction." *English Journal* 53 (March 1964): 155–164.

———. *The Rhetoric of Fiction.* Chicago: University of Chicago Press, 1961.

Bowen, Elizabeth. "Books of 1951: Some Personal Choices." *Observer,* 30 December 1951, p. 71.

Branch, Edgar. "Mark Twain and J. D. Salinger: A Study in Literary Continuity." *American Quarterly* 9 (Summer 1958): 144–158.

Bratman, Fred. "Holden, 50, Still Catches." *New York Times,* 21 December 1979, p. A-35.

Breit, Harvey. "Reader's Choice." *Atlantic,* August 1951, 82–85.

Brookeman, Christopher. "Pencey Preppy: Cultural Codes in *The Catcher in the Rye.*" In *New Essays on The Catcher in the Rye,* edited by Jack Salzman, 57–76. Cambridge: Cambridge University Press, 1991.

Bryan, James. "The Psychological Structure of *The Catcher in the Rye." PMLA* 89, no. 5 (October 1974): 1,065–1,074.

———. "Sherwood Anderson and *The Catcher in the Rye:* A Possible Influence." *Notes on Contemporary Literature* 1, no. 5 (November 1971): 2–6.

Bufithis, Philip. "J. D. Salinger and the Psychiatrist." *West Virginia University Bulletin: Philological Papers* 21 (December 1974): 67–77.

Burger, Nash K. "Books of The Times." *New York Times,* 16 July 1951, p. 19.

Burrows, David J. "Allie and Phoebe: Death and Love in J. D. Salinger's 'The Catcher in the Rye.'" In *Private Dealings: Modern American Writers in Search of Integrity,* edited by David J. Burrows, et al., 106–114. Rockville, Md.: New Perspectives, 1974.

Cagle, Charles. *"The Catcher in the Rye* Revisited." *Midwest Quarterly* 4 (Summer 1963): 343–351.

Cahill, Robert. "J. D. Salinger's Tin Bell." *Cadence* 14 (Autumn 1959): 20–22.

Carpenter, Frederic L. "The Adolescent in American Fiction." *English Journal* 46 (September 1957): 313–319.

Castronovo, David. "Holden Caulfield's Legacy." *New England Review* 22, no. 2 (Spring 2001): 180–186.

Cohen, Hubert I. "'A Woeful Agony Which Forced Me to Begin My Tale': *The Catcher in the Rye*." *Modern Fiction Studies* 12, no. 3 (Autumn 1966): 355–366.

Coles, Robert. "Anna Freud and J. D. Salinger's Holden Caulfield." *Virginia Quarterly Review* 76, no. 2 (Spring 2000): 214–224.

Corbett, Edward P. "Raise High the Barriers, Censors." *America,* 7 January 1961, 441–443.

Costello, Donald P. "The Language of 'The Catcher in the Rye.'" *American Speech* 34, no. 3 (October 1959): 172–181.

Cowan, Michael. "Holden's Museum Pieces: Narrator and Nominal Audience in *The Catcher in the Rye*." In *New Essays on The Catcher in the Rye,* edited by Jack Salzman, 35–55. Cambridge: Cambridge University Press, 1991.

Cox, James M. "Toward Vernacular Humor." *Virginia Quarterly Review* 46 (Spring 1970): 311–330.

Curry, Renee R. "Holden Caulfield Is Not a Person of Colour." In *J. D. Salinger's The Catcher in the Rye,* by Sarah Graham, 78–88. London: Routledge, 2007.

Cutchins, Dennis. "*Catcher* in the Corn: J. D. Salinger and *Shoeless Joe.*" In *The Catcher in the Rye: New Essays,* edited by J. P. Steed, 53–77. New York: Peter Lang, 2002.

Dahl, James. "What *about* Antolini?" *Notes on Contemporary Literature* 13, no. 2 (March 1983): 9–10.

"A Dark Horse." Virginia *Kirkus' Bookshop Service,* 15 May 1951, 247.

Daughtry, Vivian F. "A Novel Worth Teaching: Salinger's The Catcher in the Rye." *Virginia English Bulletin* 36, no. 2 (Winter 1986): 88–94.

Davis, Tom. "J. D. Salinger: 'Some Crazy Cliff' Indeed." *Western Humanities Review* 14 (Winter 1960): 97–99.

Drake, Robert Y. "Two Old Juveniles." *Georgia Review* 13 (Winter 1959): 443–453.

Ducharme, Edward R. "J. D., D. B., Sonny, Sunny, and Holden." *English Record* 19, no. 2 (December 1968): 54–58.

Dudley, Robin. "J. D. Salinger's Uncollected Stories and the Development of Aesthetic and Moral Themes in *The Catcher in the Rye*." Master's thesis, Idaho State University, 2004.

Dugan, Lawrence. "Holden and the Lunts." *Notes and Queries* 52, no. 4 (2005): 510–511.

Edwards, Duane. "Holden Caulfield: 'Don't Ever Tell Anybody Anything.'" *Journal of English Literary History* 44, no. 3 (Fall 1977): 554–565.

Eppes, Betty. "What I Did Last Summer." *Paris Review* 23 (Summer 1981): 221–239.

Evertson, Matt. "Love, Loss, and Growing Up in J. D. Salinger and Cormac McCarthy." In *The Catcher in the Rye: New Essays,* edited by J. P. Steed, 101–142. New York: Peter Lang, 2002.

Fadiman, Clifton. *Book-of-the-Month Club News,* July 1951: 1–4.

Faulkner, William. "A Word to Young Writers." In *Faulkner in the University: Class Conferences at the University of Virginia 1957–1958,* edited by Frederick L. Gwynn and Joseph L. Blotner, 244–248. Charlottesville: University of Virginia Press, 1959.

Fiedler, Leslie. "The Eye of Innocence." In *Salinger: A Critical and Personal Portrait,* edited by Henry Anatole Grunwald, 218–245. New York: Harper & Row, 1962.

Fleissner, Robert F. "Salinger's Caulfield: A Refraction of Copperfield and His Caul." *Notes on Contemporary Literature* 3, no. 3 (May 1973): 5–7.

Fogel, Amy. "Where the Ducks Go: *The Catcher in the Rye*." *Ball State Teachers College Forum* 3 (Spring 1962): 75–79.

Foran, Donald J. "A Doubletake on Holden Caulfield." *English Journal* 57 (October 1968): 977–979.

Fowler, Albert. "Alien in the Rye." *Modern Age* 1 (Fall 1957): 193–197.

Freedman, Carl. "Memories of Holden Caulfield and of Miss Greenwood." *Southern Review* 39, no. 2 (Spring 2003): 401–417.

French, Warren. "The Artist as a Very Nervous Young Man." In *J. D. Salinger,* 102–129. New York: Twayne Publishers, 1963.

————. "The Holden Caulfield Story." In *J. D. Salinger, Revisited*, 33–62. New York: Twayne Publishers, 1988.

————. "Holden's Fall." *Modern Fiction Studies* 10 (Winter 1964–1965): 389.

————. "The Phony World and the Nice World." *Wisconsin Studies in Contemporary Literature* 4, no. 1 (Winter 1963): 21–30.

————. "Steinbeck and J. D. Salinger: Messiah-Moulders for a Sick Society." In *Steinbeck's Literary Dimension: A Guide to Comparative Studies*, edited by Tetsumaro Hayashi, 105–115. Metuchen, N.J.: Scarecrow Press, 1973.

Frye, Northrop. *The Critical Path*. Bloomington: Indiana University Press, 1971.

Furst, Lilian R. "Dostoyevsky's *Notes from the Underground* and Salinger's *The Catcher in the Rye*." *Canadian Review of Comparative Literature* 5 (Winter 1978): 72–85.

Glasser, William. "The Catcher in the Rye." *Michigan Quarterly Review* 15 (Fall 1976): 432–457.

Goldstein, Bernice, and Sanford Goldstein. "Zen and Salinger." *Modern Fiction Studies* 12, no. 3 (Autumn 1966): 313–324.

Goodman, Anne L. "Mad about Children." *New Republic*, 16 July 1951, 20–21.

Gutwillig, Robert. "Everybody's Caught 'The Catcher in the Rye.'" *New York Times Book Review*, 15 January 1961, pp. 38–39.

Hainsworth, J. D. "Maturity in J. D. Salinger's 'The Catcher in the Rye.'" *English Studies* 48 (October 1967): 426–431.

Hale, John K. "Salinger's The Catcher in the Rye." *Explicator* 60, no. 4 (Summer 2002): 220–221.

Hassan, Ihab. "The Idea of Adolescence in American Fiction." *American Quarterly* 10 (Fall 1958): 312–324.

Heiserman, Arthur, and James E. Miller, Jr. "J. D. Salinger: Some Crazy Cliff." *Western Humanities Review* 10 (Spring 1956): 129–137.

Hekanaho, Pia Livia. "Queering *Catcher*: Flits, Straights, and Other Morons." In *J. D. Salinger's The Catcher in the Rye*, by Sarah Graham, 90–97. London: Routledge, 2007.

Howell, John M. "Salinger in the Waste Land." *Modern Fiction Studies* 12, no. 3 (Autumn 1966): 367–375.

Hughes, Riley. "New Novels: *The Catcher in the Rye*." *Catholic World* 174 (November 1951): 154.

Jacobs, Robert G. "J. D. Salinger's *The Catcher in the Rye*: Holden Caulfield's 'Goddam Autobiography.'" *Iowa English Yearbook* 4 (Fall 1959): 9–14.

Johnson, James W. "The Adolescent Hero: A Trend in Modern Fiction." *Twentieth Century Literature* 5 (April 1959): 3–11.

Jones, Ernest. "Case History of All of Us." *Nation*, 1 September 1951, 176.

Jonnes, Denis. "Trauma, Mourning and Self-(Re)fashioning in *The Catcher in the Rye*." In *J. D. Salinger's The Catcher in the Rye*, by Sarah Graham, 99–108. London: Routledge, 2007.

Kaplan, Charles. "Holden and Huck: The Odysseys of Youth." *College English* 18, no. 2 (November 1956): 76–80.

Kearns, Francis E. "Salinger and Golding: Conflict on Campus." *America*, 26 January 1963, 135–139.

Kegel, Charles H. "Incommunicability in Salinger's *The Catcher in the Rye*." *Western Humanities Review* 11 (Spring 1957): 188–190.

Kinney, Arthur F. "The Theme of Charity in *The Catcher in the Rye*." *Papers of the Michigan Academy of Science, Arts, and Letters* 48 (1963): 691–702.

Kinnick, Bernard C. "Holden Caulfield: Adolescents' Enduring Model." *High School Journal* 53 (May 1970): 440–443.

Kurian, Elizabeth N. *A Religious Response to the Existential Dilemma in the Fiction of J. D. Salinger*. New Delhi: Intellectual Publishing House, 1992.

Laser, Marvin. "Character Names in *The Catcher in the Rye*." *California English Journal* 1 (Winter 1965): 29–40.

Lee, Robert A. "'Flunking Everything Else Except English Anyway': Holden Caulfield, Author." In *Critical Essays on Salinger's The Catcher in the Rye*, edited by Joel Salzberg, 185–197. Boston: G. K. Hall, 1990.

Lettis, Richard. "Holden Caulfield: Salinger's 'Ironic Amalgam.'" *American Notes & Queries* 15 (November 1976): 43–45.

Levine, Paul. "J. D. Salinger: The Development of the Misfit Hero." *Twentieth Century Literature* 4, no. 3 (October 1958): 92–99.

Lewis, Jonathan P. "'All That David Copperfield Kind of Crap': Holden Caulfield's Rejection of Grand

Narratives." *Notes on Contemporary Literature* 32, no. 4 (September 2002): 3–5.

Light, James F. "Salinger's *The Catcher in the Rye*." *Explicator* 18 (June 1960): item 59.

Longstreth, T. Morris. "New Novels in the News." *Christian Science Monitor,* 19 July 1951, p. 11.

Luedtke, Luther S. "J. D. Salinger and Robert Burns: *The Catcher in the Rye*." *Modern Fiction Studies* 16, no. 2 (Summer 1970): 198–201.

Lundquist, James. "Against Obscenity: *The Catcher in the Rye*." In *J. D. Salinger,* 37–68. New York: Ungar, 1979.

Marcus, Fred H. "*The Catcher in the Rye*: A Live Circuit." *English Journal* 52 (January 1963): 1–8.

Margolis, John D. "Salinger's *The Catcher in the Rye*." *Explicator* 22 (November 1963): item 23.

Martin, Hansford. "The American Problem of Direct Address." *Western Review* 16 (Winter 1952): 101–114.

Martin, John S. "Copperfield and Caulfield: Dickens in the Rye." *Notes on Modern American Literature* 4 (1980): item 29.

Martin, Robert A. "Remembering Jane in *The Catcher in the Rye*." *Notes on Contemporary Literature* 28, no. 4 (September 1998): 2–3.

Matis, Jim. "'The Catcher in the Rye': Controversy on Novel in Texas Is Just One in Long List of Episodes." *Houston Post,* 4 May 1961, sec. 7, p. 6.

McNamara, Eugene. "Holden as Novelist." *English Journal* 54, no. 3 (March 1965): 166–170.

Mellard, James M. "The Disappearing Subject: A Lacanian Reading of *The Catcher in the Rye*." In *Critical Essays on Salinger's The Catcher in the Rye,* edited by Joel Salzberg, 197–214. Boston: G. K. Hall, 1990.

Menand, Louis. "Holden at Fifty: 'The Catcher in the Rye' and What It Spawned." *New Yorker,* 1 October 2001, 82–87.

Meral, Jean. "The Ambiguous Mr. Antolini in Salinger's *The Catcher in the Rye*." *Caliban* 7 (1970): 55–58.

Miller, Edwin Haviland. "In Memoriam: Allie Caulfield in *The Catcher in the Rye*." *Mosaic: A Journal for the Interdisciplinary Study of Literature* 15, no. 1 (Winter 1982): 129–140.

Miller, James E., Jr. "*Catcher* In and Out of History." *Critical Inquiry* 3, no. 3 (Spring 1977): 599–603.

Miltner, Robert. "Mentor Mori; or, Sibling Society and the Catcher in the Bly." In *The Catcher in the Rye: New Essays,* edited by J. P. Steed, 33–52. New York: Peter Lang, 2002.

Moore, Robert P. "The World of Holden." *English Journal* 54 (March 1965): 159–165.

Moss, Adam. "Catcher Comes of Age." *Esquire,* December 1981, 56–58, 60.

Nadel, Alan. "Rhetoric, Sanity, and the Cold War: The Significance of Holden Caulfield's Testimony." *Centennial Review* 32, no. 4 (Fall 1988): 351–371.

O'Hara, J. D. "No Catcher in the Rye." *Modern Fiction Studies* 9 (Winter 1963–1964): 370–376.

Ohmann, Carol, and Richard Ohmann. "Reviewers, Critics, and *The Catcher in the Rye*." *Critical Inquiry* 3, no. 1 (Autumn 1976): 15–37.

———. "Universals and the Historically Particular." *Critical Inquiry* 3, no. 4 (Summer 1977): 773–777.

Olan, Levi A. "The Voice of the Lonesome: Alienation from Huck Finn to Holden Caulfield." *Southwest Review* 48 (Spring 1963): 143–150.

Oldsey, Bernard S. "The Movies in the Rye." *College English* 23, no. 3 (December 1961): 209–215.

Panova, Vera. "On J. D. Salinger's Novel." In *Soviet Criticism of American Literature in the Sixties,* edited and translated by Carl R. Proffer, 4–10. Ann Arbor, Mich.: Ardis, 1972.

Parker, Christopher. "'Why the Hell *Not* Smash All the Windows?'" In *Salinger: A Critical and Personal Portrait,* edited by Henry Anatole Grunwald, 254–258. New York: Harper & Row, 1962.

Peavy, Charles D. "'Did You Ever Have a Sister?' Holden, Quentin, and Sexual Innocence." *Florida Quarterly* 1, no. 3 (Winter 1968): 82–95.

Pilkington, John. "About This Madman Stuff." *University of Mississippi Studies in English* 7 (1966): 67–75.

Pinsker, Sanford. "*The Catcher in the Rye* and All: Is the Age of Formative Books Over?" *Georgia Review* 40, no. 4 (Winter 1986): 953–967.

Poster, William. "Tomorrow's Child." *Commentary* 13 (January 1952): 90–92.

Purcell, William F. "From Half-Shot to Half-Assed: J. D. Salinger and the Evolution of a *Skaz*." *Studies in American Literature* 35 (February 1999): 109–123.

————. "Narrative Voice in J. D. Salinger's 'Both Parties Concerned' and 'I'm Crazy.'" *Studies in Short Fiction* 33 (Spring 1996): 278–280.

Rachels, David. "Holden Caulfield: A Hero for All the Ages." *Chronicle of Higher Education,* 30 March 2001, p. B-5.

Ralston, Nancy C. "Holden Caulfield: Super-Adolescent." *Adolescence* 6 (Winter 1971): 429–432.

Reiman, Donald H. "Salinger's *The Catcher in the Rye,* Chapters 22–26." *Explicator* 21 (March 1963): item 58.

Roberts, Preston Thomas, Jr. "*The Catcher in the Rye* Revisited." *Cresset* 40 (November–December 1976): 6–10.

Robinson, Sally. "Masculine Protest in *The Catcher in the Rye.*" In *J. D. Salinger's The Catcher in the Rye,* by Sarah Graham, 70–76. London: Routledge, 2007.

Roemer, Danielle M. "The Personal Narrative and Salinger's Catcher in the Rye." *Western Folklore* 51, no. 1 (January 1992): 5–10.

Rogers, Lydia. "The Psychoanalyst and the Fetishist: Wilhelm Stekel and Mr. Antolini in *The Catcher in the Rye.*" *Notes on Contemporary Literature* 32, no. 4 (September 2002): 2–3.

Roper, Pamela E. "Holden's Hat." *Notes on Contemporary Literature* 7, no. 3 (May 1977): 8–9.

Rosen, Gerald. "A Retrospective Look at *The Catcher in the Rye.*" *American Quarterly* 29 (Winter 1977): 547–562.

————. *Zen in the Art of J. D. Salinger.* Berkeley, Calif.: Creative Arts Book Company, 1977.

Rowe, Joyce. "Holden Caulfield and American Protest." In *New Essays on The Catcher in the Rye,* edited by Jack Salzman, 77–95. Cambridge: Cambridge University Press, 1991.

Schriber, Mary Suzanne. "Holden Caulfield, C'est Moi." In *Critical Essays on Salinger's The Catcher in the Rye,* edited by Joel Salzberg, 226–238. Boston: G. K. Hall, 1990.

Seelye, John. "Holden in the Museum." In *New Essays on The Catcher in the Rye,* edited by Jack Salzman, 23–33. Cambridge: Cambridge University Press, 1991.

Seng, Peter J. "The Fallen Idol: The Immature World of Holden Caulfield." *College English* 23, no. 3 (December 1961): 203–209.

Shaw, Peter. "Love and Death in *The Catcher in the Rye.*" In *New Essays on The Catcher in the Rye,* edited by Jack Salzman, 97–114. Cambridge: Cambridge University Press, 1991.

Sherr, Paul C. "'The Catcher in the Rye' and the Boarding School." *Independent School Bulletin* 26 (December 1966): 42–44.

Silverberg, Mark. "'You Must Change Your Life': Formative Responses to *The Catcher in the Rye.*" In *The Catcher in the Rye: New Essays,* edited by J. P. Steed, 7–32. New York: Peter Lang, 2002.

Slabey, Robert M. "*The Catcher in the Rye*: Christian Theme and Symbol." *College Language Association Journal* 6 (March 1963): 170–183.

Smith, Harrison. "Manhattan Ulysses, Junior." *Saturday Review,* 14 July 1951, 12–13.

Spanier, Sandra Whipple. "Hemingway's 'The Last Good Country' and *The Catcher in the Rye*: More Than a Family Resemblance." *Studies in Short Fiction* 19 (1982): 35–43.

Stern, James. "Aw, the World's a Crumby Place." *New York Times Book Review,* 15 July 1951, p. 5.

Stone, Edward. "Salinger's Carrousel." *Modern Fiction Studies* 13, no. 4 (Winter 1967–1968): 520–523.

Strauch, Carl F. "Kings in the Back Row: Meaning through Structure—A Reading of Salinger's *The Catcher in the Rye.*" *Wisconsin Studies in Contemporary Literature* 2, no. 1 (Winter 1961): 5–30.

Symula, James Francis. "Censorship of High School Literature: A Study of the Incidents of Censorship Involving J. D. Salinger's 'The Catcher in the Rye.'" Ph.D. diss., State University of New York at Buffalo, 1969.

Takeuchi, Yasuhiro. "The Burning Carousel and the Carnivalesque: Subversion and Transcendence at the Close of *The Catcher in the Rye.*" *Studies in the Novel* 34, no. 3 (Fall 2002): 320–336.

————. "Salinger's *The Catcher in the Rye.*" *Explicator* 60, no. 3 (Spring 2002): 164–166.

————. "The Zen Archery of Holden Caulfield." *English Language Notes* 42, no. 1 (September 2004): 55–63.

Travis, Mildred K. "Salinger's *The Catcher in the Rye.*" *Explicator* 21 (December 1962): item 36.

Trowbridge, Clinton W. "Hamlet and Holden." *English Journal* 57 (January 1968): 26–29.

————. "Salinger's Symbolic Use of Character and Detail in *The Catcher in the Rye.*" *Cimarron Review* 4 (June 1968): 5–11.

————. "The Symbolic Structure of *The Catcher in the Rye.*" *Sewanee Review* 74 (July–September 1966): 681–693.

Vail, Dennis. "Holden and Psychoanalysis." *PMLA* 91, no. 1 (January 1976): 120–121.

Vanderbilt, Kermit. "Symbolic Resolution in *The Catcher in the Rye*: The Cap, the Carrousel, and the American West." *Western Humanities Review* 17 (Summer 1963): 271–277.

Vogel, Albert W. "J. D. Salinger on Education." *School and Society* 91 (Summer 1963): 240–242.

Wakefield, Dan. "Salinger and the Search for Love" [originally published in *New World Writing*, No. 14, 1958]. In *Salinger: A Critical and Personal Portrait*, edited by Henry Anatole Grunwald, 176–191. New York: Harper & Row, 1962.

Walker, Joseph S. "The Catcher Takes the Field: Holden, Hollywood, and the Making of a Mann." In *The Catcher in the Rye: New Essays*, edited by J. P. Steed, 79–99. New York: Peter Lang, 2002.

Way, Brian. "'Franny and Zooey' and J. D. Salinger." *New Left Review* 15 (May–June 1962): 72–82.

Weinberg, Helen. "J. D. Salinger's Holden and Seymour and the Spiritual Activist Hero." In *The New Novel in America: The Kafkan Mode in Contemporary Fiction*, 141–164. Ithaca, N.Y.: Cornell University Press, 1970.

Wells, Arvin R. "Huck Finn and Holden Caulfield: The Situation of the Hero." *Ohio University Review* 2 (1960): 31–42.

Whitfield, Stephen J. "Cherished and Cursed: Toward a Social History of *The Catcher in the Rye.*" *New England Quarterly* 70, no. 4 (December 1997): 567–600.

Wiseman, Mary B. "Identifying with Characters in Literature." *Journal of Comparative Literature and Aesthetics* 4, nos. 1–2 (1981): 47–57.

"With Love & 20–20 Vision." *Time*, 16 July 1951, 97.

Caulfield stories

The seven extant Caulfield stories—stories featuring or referencing members of the Caulfield family—consist of five stories that appeared in magazines and two unpublished stories located in a library archive. The five published stories are: "Last Day of the Last Furlough" (*Saturday Evening Post*, July 15, 1944), "This Sandwich Has No Mayonnaise" (*Esquire*, October 1945), "The Stranger" (*Collier's*, December 1, 1945), "I'm Crazy" (*Collier's*, December 22, 1945), "Slight Rebellion Off Madison" (*New Yorker*, December 21, 1946). The two unpublished stories, in typescript, are housed at Princeton University's Firestone Library: "The Last and Best of the Peter Pans" and "The Ocean Full of Bowling Balls."

Salinger's writing of Caulfield stories dates back at least to the autumn of 1941, when "Slight Rebellion Off Madison" was sold to the *New Yorker*. (To the author's great dismay, the magazine pulled the story from a pre-Christmas 1941 publication date due to the bombing of Pearl Harbor. A revised version of the work was published five years later.) "Slight Rebellion Off Madison" features Holden and alludes to his parents, but to no siblings. Holden's father owns a business where his son does not want to work.

The earliest published Caulfield stories—"Last Day of the Last Furlough," "This Sandwich Has No Mayonnaise," and "The Stranger"—focus on Vincent Caulfield. The Caulfield family, as referenced in these three stories, and the two unpublished stories, "The Last and Best of the Peter Pans" and "The Ocean Full of Bowling Balls," consists of parents who are actors; the eldest son, Vincent, originally a writer of short stories, then a director of radio shows, before being drafted into the army; the middle son, Holden, who has flunked out of several schools, before serving in the army and eventually declared missing-in-action in World War II; the youngest son, Kenneth, who dies as a young boy; and the sole daughter, and last-born child, Phoebe.

After the publication of "The Stranger," which reports Vincent Caulfield's death in World War II, Salinger published "I'm Crazy." "I'm Crazy" holds the distinction of being the sole Caulfield story narrated by Holden. The Caulfield family now consists of parents who seem similar to those in The CATCHER IN THE RYE; Holden, apparently, has just two siblings, his sisters Phoebe and Viola.

Whether the "missing link" between these stories and The Catcher in the Rye is the 90-page novella Salinger submitted for publication in 1946, and subsequently withdrew, remains debatable; the novella is unavailable for consultation. The critic John Wenke suggests that "the attempt to make the various Holden Caulfield stories a consistent body of work would be not only futile but wrongheaded: such an attempt would belie the *process* of Salinger's discovery, disposal, and recovery of a character too significant to let go" (Wenke 24). This process, which started 10 years before the publication of the novel, remained known solely by Salinger.

The seven extant Caulfield stories provide today's readers with two jarring realizations concerning The Catcher in the Rye. First, Salinger's original plans for Holden Caulfield situated the character in a World War II time period, and apparently, the character would become a casualty of that war. Second, the Caulfield family existed in an earlier, albeit similar, incarnation to that presented in The Catcher in the Rye. Given the discrepancies between the stories and the novel, Salinger's decision not to collect his Caulfield stories becomes understandable. Nonetheless, reader fascination with the Caulfields extends to these stories, where Salinger constellated his first great fictive family.

"Children's Echelon, The"

"The Children's Echelon" is an unpublished story whose 26-page, undated (circa 1944) typescript can be found at Princeton University's FIRESTONE LIBRARY, as part of the WHIT BURNETT–STORY magazine archive. "The Children's Echelon" is available for onsite reading only. According to the bibliographer Jack R. Sublette, the story consists of diary entries written by an 18-year-old girl named Bernice Herndon. In one of the entries, she observes children riding a carousel. "The Children's Echelon" was included on the proposed table of contents for Salinger's unpublished book, The YOUNG FOLKS.

"Class Poem"

See CROSSED SABRES WRITINGS.

The first volume of the unauthorized publication *The Complete Uncollected Short Stories of J. D. Salinger* (2nd ed., 1974) *(Courtesy of the Bruce F. Mueller Collection; photo by Laura Fairbanks)*

Complete Uncollected Short Stories of J. D. Salinger, The

The Complete Uncollected Short Stories of J. D. Salinger is an illegal, 1974 reprinting of 22 stories that were originally published individually in magazines between 1940 and 1965. Salinger chose not to include any of these works in his three book collections of stories. The two-volume bootleg paperback set comprises: "THE YOUNG FOLKS" (*STORY*, March–April 1940), "GO SEE EDDIE" (*UNIVERSITY OF KANSAS CITY REVIEW*, December 1940), "THE HANG OF IT" (*COLLIER'S*, July 12, 1941), "THE HEART OF A BROKEN STORY" (*ESQUIRE*, September 1941), "THE LONG DEBUT OF LOIS TAGGETT" (*Story*, September–October 1942), "PERSONAL NOTES ON AN INFANTRYMAN" (*Collier's*, December 12, 1942), "THE VARIONI BROTHERS" (*SATURDAY EVENING POST*, July 17, 1943), "BOTH PARTIES CONCERNED" (*Saturday Evening Post*, February 26, 1944), "SOFT-BOILED SERGEANT" (*Saturday Evening Post*, April 15, 1944), "LAST DAY OF THE LAST FURLOUGH" (*Saturday Evening Post*, July 15, 1944), "ONCE A WEEK WON'T KILL YOU" (*Story*, November–December 1944), "ELAINE" (*Story*, March–April 1945), "A BOY IN FRANCE" (*Saturday Evening Post*, March 31, 1945), "THIS SANDWICH HAS NO MAYONNAISE" (*Esquire*, October 1945), "THE STRANGER," (*Collier's*, December 1, 1945), "I'M CRAZY" (*Collier's*, December 22, 1945), "SLIGHT REBELLION OFF MADISON" (*NEW YORKER*, December 21, 1946), "A YOUNG GIRL IN 1941 WITH NO WAIST AT ALL" (*MADEMOISELLE*, May 1947), "THE INVERTED FOREST" (*COSMOPOLITAN*, December 1947), "A GIRL I KNEW" (*GOOD HOUSEKEEPING*, February 1948), "BLUE MELODY" (*Cosmopolitan*, September 1948), and "HAPWORTH 16, 1924" (*New Yorker*, June 19, 1965). *The Complete Uncollected Short Stories of J. D. Salinger* constitutes the first book publication of each of these stories, except for "Go See Eddie," "The Hang of It," "The Long Debut of Lois Taggett," "A Boy in France," "This Sandwich Has No Mayonnaise," and "A Girl I Knew" (each of these latter stories had previously been included in anthologies).

Volume two of the unauthorized publication *The Complete Uncollected Short Stories of J. D. Salinger* (2nd ed., 1974) *(Courtesy of the Bruce F. Mueller Collection; photo by Laura Fairbanks)*

In 1974, a handful of unidentified Berkeley, California, Salinger fans decided to publish, without Salinger's consent, all of the magazine stories he had never collected in book form. By late summer, the group had produced an initial run of poorly produced paperbacks. The books were wholesaled to San Francisco Bay Area bookstores that in turn openly sold them. Readers, without having to consult libraries with extensive back files, could now, for $3 to $5 a volume, access 22 stories not available in Salinger's own authorized book publications. After selling at a good rate, the volumes were reprinted in a more attractive manner. Soon the volumes were made available in bookstores in other major American cities. By the time Salinger successfully sued to stop their sale, approximately 25,000 copies had been sold. Two detectives were hired by Salinger's lawyers to locate the elusive publisher, allegedly named "John Greenberg." Although the search for the suspect was joined by the FBI, no one was ever caught and charged with the crime.

The sale of *The Complete Uncollected Short Stories of J. D. Salinger* elicited Salinger's first interview in 21 years. Lacey Fosburgh, the San Francisco–based correspondent for the *New York Times,* had left a request for an interview with Salinger's agent. To the reporter's surprise, Salinger phoned and spoke for a half hour. He condemned the theft of his stories but asserted he was not "trying to hide the gaucheries of my youth. I just don't think they're worthy of publishing . . . I wanted them to die a perfectly natural death" (Fosburgh November 3, 1974, 69).

Copies of both editions of *The Complete Uncollected Short Stories of J. D. Salinger* are often offered for sale by rare book dealers, with the first edition scarcer and more valuable. This first edition, offset from a typescript, lists story titles on the plain covers; volume one is bound with a stapled spine, while volume two is perfect bound. The two volumes of the second edition are perfect bound, set by type, with matching illustrated covers that reproduce the *Collier's* illustration accompanying the 1945 story "The Stranger." The second edition includes story titles beneath the illustration. Both editions have neither publication date nor publisher listed and contain printing errors.

contributors' notes

Contributors' notes (biographical notes about the contributors to a magazine issue) accompany a number of Salinger's stories published from 1940 to 1949. Though usually written by the editors and often based on information the contributor has supplied, contributors' notes may also be written by the author. In Salinger's case, five of the contributors' notes provide the first biographical information about him, two photographs that predate his photograph on the dust jacket of *The* CATCHER

IN THE RYE, and the early instances of the author speaking directly to the reading public.

Salinger's first published story, "The YOUNG FOLKS," appeared in the March–April 1940 issue of STORY, and its three-sentence contributor's note introduces Salinger: "J. D. Salinger, who is twenty-one years old, was born in New York. He attended public grammar schools, one military academy, and three colleges, and has spent one year in Europe. He is particularly interested in playwriting" (2). The source of this information surely was Salinger. The note intimates a checkered schooling and, surprising to today's readers, speaks of the possibility of Salinger as a playwright.

The publication of "The HEART OF A BROKEN STORY" in the September 1941 issue of ESQUIRE supplies additional biographical information and, though written in third person, undoubtedly reflects Salinger's own phrasings. Salinger's academic career is now almost flauntingly described as "three colleges, never advancing beyond the freshman year" (24). While visiting Vienna, he is "winning high honors in beer hoisting" (24). The reader learns of Salinger's first writings, "a smug little column" ("J. D. S.'s The SKIPPED DIPLOMA," for URSINUS COLLEGE's student paper) (24). The contributor's note concludes with the first mention of the author's studying with WHIT BURNETT at Columbia University and is accompanied by the first photograph of Salinger, the writer.

The contributor's note for "The LONG DEBUT OF LOIS TAGGETT," published in the September–October 1942 issue of *Story*, contains the first text undeniably written by Salinger: "I'm in the Officers, First Sergeants and Instructors Prep School of the Signal Corps, determined to get that ole message through. . . . The men in my tent—though a damn nice bunch—are always eating oranges or listening to quiz programs, and I haven't written a line since my re-classification and induction" (2). The United States has been at war for nearly a year, and Salinger is still in the United States.

The November–December 1944 issue of *Story* printed "ONCE A WEEK WON'T KILL YOU." By this time, Salinger is overseas, and the entire note, written in the first person, is nostalgic: "I used to go pretty steady with the big city, but I find that my memory is slipping since I've been in the Army. Have forgotten bars and streets and buses and faces; am more inclined, in retrospect, to get my New York out of the American Indian Room of the Museum of Natural History, where I used to drop my marbles all over the floor" (1). This fore-echoes a scene from Chapter 16 of *The Catcher in the Rye*. On Sunday, Holden Caulfield walks through CEN-TRAL PARK in MANHATTAN over to the Museum of Natural History. He tells the reader that he loves the museum and recalls the Indian Room. "The floor was all stone, and if you had some marbles in your hand and you dropped them, they bounced like madmen all over the floor and made a helluva racket . . ." (156).

Esquire published "THIS SANDWICH HAS NO MAYONNAISE" in its October 1945 issue with an expansive contributor's note. Written in the first person, and accompanied by a photograph of Salinger in uniform, the reader hears Salinger's unguarded voice speaking about his writing: "I have trouble writing simply and naturally. . . . I am a dash man and not a miler, and it is probable that I will never write a novel" (34). A revealing passage ends the note with an assessment of the just-concluded war, its combatants, and the artist's obligation: "So far the novels of this war have had too much of the strength, maturity and craftsman-ship critics are looking for, and too little of the glorious imperfections which teeter and fall off the best minds. The men who have been in this war deserve some sort of trembling melody rendered without embarrassment or regret" (34).

The publication of "DOWN AT THE DINGHY" in the April 1949 issue of *HARPER'S* is the final Salinger story to have a contributor's note. (The magazine's editors wrote the short note.) After this, Salinger exclusively published in the *NEW YORKER*, which did not have contributors' notes during the time his stories appeared there.

Crossed Sabres writings

During Salinger's senior year at VALLEY FORGE MIL-ITARY ACADEMY (1935–36), the author became the literary editor of the class yearbook, *Crossed Sabres*. Salinger composed a substantial, though unsigned, portion of the yearbook. Most importantly, the last page of the yearbook is titled "Class Poem" and is signed "Jerome D. Salinger, '36." This work is Salinger's first attributable publication of his writ-ing career: a 24-line rhyming poem describing the cadets' June 1936 graduation day at Valley Forge. The poem begins, "Hide not thy tears on this last day / Your sorrow has no shame." The graduating cadets "march ahead, / Success we go to find. / Our forms are gone from Valley Forge: / Our hearts are left behind" (Ian Hamilton 1988, 27). Salin-ger's poem has since become established as Val-ley Forge's graduation song. The poem's existence was made known and reprinted in *Time* magazine's September 15, 1961, cover story. The entire text of "Class Poem," and other extracts from the 1936 yearbook, can now be most easily found in IAN HAMILTON's *In Search of J. D. Salinger* (Ian Hamil-ton 1988, 26–30).

"Daughter of the Late, Great Man, The"

"The Daughter of the Late, Great Man" is one of Salinger's "lost" stories, neither published nor to be found in a library archive. According to the bibliographer Jack R. Sublette, WHIT BURNETT, in a 1959 letter to Salinger, offered to buy the much-earlier-submitted story, which Burnett had found in the files of STORY magazine. (He was prepar-ing to revive the magazine.) Burnett likened "The Daughter of the Late, Great Man" to Salinger's earlier *Story* publications, "The LONG DEBUT OF LOIS TAGGETT" and "ELAINE." Salinger, however, refused to sell the story, and it was returned to the author. "The Daughter of the Late, Great Man" was included on the proposed table of contents for Salinger's unpublished book, *The YOUNG FOLKS*. Given that this "lost" story surfaced as late as 1959, "The Daughter of the Late, Great Man" probably can be located among Salinger's literary estate.

"Death of a Dogface"

"Death of a Dogface" was retitled by the editors at the SATURDAY EVENING POST and published as "Soft-Boiled Sergeant." *See* "SOFT-BOILED SERGEANT."

"De Daumier-Smith's Blue Period"

"De Daumier-Smith's Blue Period" is the eighth story in Salinger's second book, NINE STORIES (1953). With a first-person narrative, the main events of the story are told in the adolescent and comically self-conscious voice of a pseudonymous Jean de Daumier-Smith. "De Daumier-Smith's Blue Period" is the first time Salinger's religious interests surface in his fiction. Rejected for publication by the NEW YORKER, the story is the only Salinger work initially published abroad (in the London-based WORLD REVIEW). "De Daumier-Smith's Blue Period" is Salinger's 29th published story.

SYNOPSIS

The first-person narrator, who identifies himself only by a pseudonym, Jean de Daumier-Smith, begins by dedicating the story to the memory of his stepfather, Robert "Bobby" Agadganian, Jr., who died in 1947. The narrator's parents had divorced when he was eight years old, and his mother had soon remarried Agadganian, a stockbroker. After the Wall Street crash, the family moved to Paris, where Agadganian reinvented himself as an art agent and appraiser. After his mother's death in 1939, the narrator, at age 19, returned to America with his stepfather.

The return to NEW YORK CITY unnerves de Daumier-Smith. He explains, the change "threw [him], and threw [him] terribly" (199). He and his stepfather take a single suite at the Ritz. The lonely narrator recalls an embarrassing incident on a crowded bus where the driver tells him, "All right, buddy . . . let's move that ass" (200). He tells of having half-heartedly enrolled in an art school,

though in Europe he had won three first-place prizes in junior exhibitions. By day, de Daumier-Smith undergoes extensive dental work; by night, he reads his set of the *Harvard Classics* or paints in the suite. The awkwardness of his living situation with his stepfather increases when both discover they are "in love with the same deceased woman" (203).

After some months, the narrator sees an ad for a bilingual—French and English—art instructor at a Montreal correspondence art school, Les Amis Des Vieux Maîtres. In a long letter to the school's head, M. Yoshoto, he applies for the position (this letter is not reproduced in the text; the narrator informs the reader of its contents). In the letter, de Daumier-Smith fabricates a number of lies regarding himself: that he is 29 and a great-nephew of Honoré Daumier, and that Pablo Picasso is a family friend. He claims that he has painted since childhood, though never exhibited, and after the death of his wife he has had to leave his estate in the south of France. After deliberating, he finally signs the letter with the pseudonym Jean de Daumier-Smith.

De Daumier-Smith quickly makes a dozen samples of American commercial art and sends them, along with a half-dozen of his paintings, to M. Yoshoto. He is offered the job for the school's upcoming summer session and telegrams his acceptance. De Daumier-Smith wants to tell his stepfather the news at dinner, but the older man has brought a young woman along. When the narrator imparts the news, the stepfather expresses reservation, saying he had expected his stepson to move with him to Rhode Island.

De Daumier-Smith arrives in Montreal on a Sunday and is met by a small Japanese man, M. Yoshoto. To fill up the silence of the bus ride, the narrator repeats his earlier lies and concocts a story about his conversation with Picasso, whom he defines as a friend of the family. The two arrive at the school, which is housed in a three-story tenement building. On the ground floor is an orthopedic appliances shop. Above the shop, on the second floor, is the school's large instructors' room and a bathroom, with a staircase leading to the third floor, which consists of two bedrooms and a kitchen. The walls of the instructors' room are lined with watercolors done by M. Yoshoto. One wonderful picture of a flying goose, with "the blueness of the sky, or an ethos of the blueness of the sky, reflected in the bird's feathers" (213), still haunts the narrator. De Daumier-Smith meets the only other instructor at the school, the wife of M. Yoshoto. He is shown to his room—formerly occupied by the Yoshotos' son, who is away at college. The room lacks any chairs. The narrator insists this does not matter, since he is a student of Buddhism. He later learns that the Yoshotos are Presbyterians. Upon retiring to bed that night, and each subsequent night, de Daumier-Smith hears through the wall one of the Yoshotos give out "a high, thin, broken moan, and it seemed to come less from an adult than from either a tragic, subnormal infant or a small malformed animal" (215).

On the following Monday morning, having taken an unappetizing breakfast with the Yoshotos, the narrator and his employers walk down to the instructors' room. The narrator is shown to his distant desk across the room. The Yoshotos then open and review the students' Manila envelopes filled with their applications and sample artwork and start to correct the samples. At first, de Daumier-Smith is assigned only the task of translating from French to English M. Yoshoto's comments on the students' work. Though de Daumier-Smith judges M. Yoshoto to be "a really good artist [he] taught drawing not a whit better than it's taught by a so-so artist who has a nice flair for teaching" (219). When lunchtime arrives, the narrator makes his excuses and rushes out to find something edible. Upon returning, he worries whether M. Yoshoto may harbor suspicions about his credentials and artistic ability. Later that afternoon, de Daumier-Smith is brought the work of three students to correct.

The first student is Bambi Kramer, a young housewife. Attached to her sample drawings, she encloses a photo of herself in a provocative bathing suit. One crudely executed drawing, which she has titled "Forgive Them Their Trespasses," shows three boys fishing in a pond, and a "No Fishing" sign half-covered by one of the boy's jackets. The second student is R. Howard Ridgefield, a self-proclaimed society photographer, who indulges in satiric art. One of his paintings is of a young blond woman with large breasts being sexually assaulted by her minister next to an altar. Ridgefield's art talent is as poor as Bambi Kramer's.

In near despair, de Daumier-Smith opens the final envelope and finds the work of a nun, Sister Irma. Instead of a photo of herself, she encloses one of her convent. Sister Irma has had no formal art training and teaches cooking and drawing to children at the convent school near Toronto. She wants to improve her artistic skills because of her teaching responsibilities. Six samples of her work are enclosed, four of which, the narrator declares, he can still recall 13 years later. Sister Irma's best picture portrays Christ being carried to his sepulchre. De Daumier-Smith assesses the watercolor, even with its certain understandable limitations, as a near-masterpiece, "an artist's picture, steeped in high, high, organized talent and God knows how many hours of hard work" (229).

De Daumier-Smith's first impulse is to let the Yoshotos know about this miracle pupil. Fearing, however, that they might take Sister Irma's instruction away from him, he says nothing. Instead, he commences to do overlay corrections to Ridgefield's male and female nudes. Shortly before dinnertime, de Daumier-Smith hides Sister Irma's envelope inside his shirt. After dinner, he works in secret in his room on instructional drawings for Sister Irma and writes her a long, accompanying letter. In the letter, de Daumier-Smith goes beyond his initial and appropriate comments and calls her "greatly talented," further telling her he would not be even slightly startled if she were to develop into "a genius before many years have gone by" (234). The narrator believes Sister Irma is "too passionate to paint just in watercolors and never in oils" (236), and he wants to know the visiting hours of the convent in case he may find himself in her neighborhood "some Saturday by chance" (236). De Daumier-Smith finishes the letter and the drawings, and goes out at 3:30 A.M. to mail them. Upon returning to his room, he hears the moaning from the Yoshotos' bedroom. The narrator fantasizes that at breakfast they will ask him to help them with their problem, and he would "reach down into Mme. Yoshoto's throat, take up her heart in [his] hand and warm it as [he] would a bird" (237). He would then joyfully show Sister Irma's work to the Yoshotos.

De Daumier-Smith dutifully works on Bambi Kramer's and R. Howard Ridgefield's drawings for several days, while wondering to himself how he will hold out until Sister Irma's next envelope arrives. On Thursday evening, the narrator returns to his building late and looks into the orthopedic appliances lit shop window. He realizes that "no matter how coolly or sensibly or gracefully [he] might one day learn to live [his] life, [he] would always at best be a visitor in a garden of enamel urinals and bedpans, with a sightless, wooden dummy-deity standing by in a marked-down rupture truss" (241). While lying awake in bed, he again hears the moaning through the wall. The narrator imagines himself going to the convent and meeting Sister Irma, "a shy, beautiful girl of eighteen who had not yet taken her final vows and was still free to go out into the world" (241).

On Friday afternoon, M. Yoshoto delivers to de Daumier-Smith a letter written by Sister Irma's Mother Superior. At the behest of Father Zimmermann, the letter withdraws Sister Irma from participating in the art instruction program. Stunned, the narrator decides to write letters, in French, to his remaining students, informing them that they have no talent and are wasting everyone's time. Later that night, de Daumier-Smith writes a letter to Sister Irma that he does not mail but which he reproduces in the story. In his letter, he worries that he has said something wrong in his previous letter to her. He goes on to warn Sister Irma that she needs more instruction, or otherwise she "will be only a very, very interesting artist the rest of your life instead of a great one" (244). He writes that "the worst that being an artist could do to you would be that it would make you slightly unhappy constantly" (245). Fearing that Father Zimmermann might be forcing her to leave due to financial reasons, he offers to teach her for free. Finally, de Daumier-Smith pleads with Sister Irma that he be allowed to visit her the next Saturday afternoon.

De Daumier-Smith goes out for a late dinner, bringing the letter to Sister Irma with him to reread. He decides, however, to rewrite parts of the let-ter and returns to his room. As he approaches the orthopedic appliances shop window, he sees a shop girl changing the truss on the wooden dummy and stops to watch. She senses that someone is watching her and turns to see the narrator, at which point de Daumier-Smith smiles, trying to defuse the situation. The shop girl blushes and falls. Reaching out for her on impulse, his fingers hit the glass window. Unhurt, she returns to her feet, and without looking at him, resumes lacing the truss on the dummy. At this moment, de Daumier-Smith has what he terms his "extraordinary experience, one that still strikes [him] as being quite transcendent" (249): "the sun came up and sped toward the bridge of [his] nose at the rate of ninety-three million miles a second" (250). Blinded for a moment, he steadies himself and tries to keep his balance by putting his hand on the window. When he regains his vision, he realizes that the shop girl "had gone from the window, leaving behind her a shimmering field of exquisite, twice-blessed, enamel flowers" (250).

Returning to his room, de Daumier-Smith records, in French, in his diary, "I am giving Sister Irma her freedom to follow her own destiny. Everybody is a nun" (251). He then writes letters (not reproduced in the text) to his other students reinstating them under his instruction, blaming their expulsion on an administrative mistake.

In a coda, the narrator informs the reader that shortly after his experience before the orthopedic appliances window, the correspondence school was closed down for lacking a license to operate. De Daumier-Smith subsequently returned to America and joined his stepfather in Rhode Island. He spent the weeks until he could resume art school "investigating that most interesting of all summer-active animals, the American Girl in Shorts" (252). He never got in touch again with Sister Irma, though he does occasionally hear from Bambi Kramer. He closes his story declaring that Bambi Kramer is now designing her own Christmas cards, and "they'll be something to see, if she hasn't lost her touch" (252).

CRITICAL ANALYSIS

One of the most ambitious of the *Nine Stories*, "De Daumier-Smith's Blue Period" displays the use of narrative devices with which Salinger had been experimenting throughout his earlier fiction. In this long work—the longest of the *Nine Stories* collection—the author makes use of text-within-text, already employed in, for example, "The VARIONI BROTHERS," "BOTH PARTIES CONCERNED," "The HEART OF A BROKEN STORY," and "The INVERTED FOREST." Most importantly, however, is Salinger's use of a narrative frame, in which the first-person voice of the protagonist at an older and more mature time of life addresses the reader to introduce his younger and immature self, who will narrate the middle of the tale. (Salinger utilizes a frame technique to great advantage in "The LAUGHING MAN," "FOR ESMÉ—WITH LOVE AND SQUALOR," and within the Glass family saga.) The story likewise incorporates verisimilitude (that is, the use of references to historical figures, geography) as well as use of text in the French language that the author chooses not to translate into English. Although the plot of "De Daumier-Smith's Blue Period" remains straightforward in its telling of how the young protagonist comes to understand, through the experience of a "transcendent" (249) moment, how he must change his perspective on life, the interpretation of Salinger's message is far from simple—leading some critics to see the intention of the piece in entirely opposite ways. Some of the problem of interpretation regarding Salinger's message and symbolism lies in the narrative devices that, paradoxically, contribute to the story's meaning.

In one of the earliest, in-depth explications of "De Daumier-Smith's Blue Period," the critics Frederick L. Gwynn and Joseph L. Blotner, in their 1958 study of Salinger's work, see, in the young protagonist's struggle toward psychological and sexual maturity, the Oedipal dilemma. These scholars find many narrative clues to support their reading—particularly in de Daumier-Smith's job application to the correspondence art school in Montreal, Les Amis Des Vieux Maîtres. The young painter explains to M. Yoshoto that he has left the South of France after the death of his "wife" (204), when, in actuality, it is the protagonist's mother who had died. Likewise, Gwynn and Blotner suggest that de Daumier-Smith's strong feelings for his mother are equal in strength to his hostility

toward and rivalry with his stepfather: "he finally articulates the nature of the situation with his stepfather ('we gradually discovered that we were in love with the same deceased woman')" (Gwynn 34). In this Freudian reading, the "repressed sexual component" (Gwynn 34) in the narrator's love for his mother is transferred to several other women who represent the mother image: Madame Yoshoto (who cooks for de Daumier-Smith and who shows him concern; Sister Irma, with whom the narrator fantasizes a romantic yet chaste union). The young protagonist is finally released from "the pure image he has subconsciously tried to preserve of his mother" (Gwynn 37), through his "Experience" (250) of transcendence while standing before the orthopedic appliances shop's "wooden dummy-deity" (241). Gwynn and Blotner summarize their analysis of the story, considering the narrator's experience to be a "redirection of love to a conventional object . . . by means of a religious impulse" (Gwynn 33–34). That is, the protagonist, at story's end, is released from his emotional dilemma and achieves a successful transfer into sexual and psychological maturity with his ability to appreciate the "American Girl in Shorts" (252).

The intensity of the young narrator's experience and its focal place in the story command from the reader a sincere acceptance of the profound change in the protagonist's understanding of life. However, because the story has been framed at the outset by the voice of a psychologically well-adjusted narrator who, in his attempt, *à la recherche du temps perdu*, to recount from a happier vantage point his earlier suffering—punctuated by comments and observations made in a jocular and witty tone—some critics have been led to divergent readings of the story's imagery and message.

The critic John Wenke, in his 1991 study of Salinger's fiction, for example, reads "De Daumier-Smith's Blue Period" as a tongue-in-cheek "parody" (Wenke 59) of a spiritual experience. In the young protagonist's obsessive love for Sister Irma, Wenke sees "a mixed-up young man who so craves a relationship that he fabricates one; on another level, the story offers a Salinger riddle: how do we read and take seriously the perceptions of a narrator who mistakes the origin of the 'moaning sound' coming through the wall?" (Wenke 58). Wenke defines the story as "a trap" (Wenke 58), believing the narrator to be an unreliable one, misinterpreting with his runaway imagination much that he experiences. Subsequently, the reader "must entertain some doubts about the story's peak moments" (Wenke 58). "One must consider the possibility that Salinger's narrator is involved in self-parody" (Wenke 58), Wenke suggests, and he therefore considers de Daumier-Smith's "Experience" (250) to be "a parody of transcendence" (Wenke 59).

Taking the opposite interpretive assessment regarding the story's epiphany, the critic Warren French, in his 1988 study of Salinger's fiction, defines de Daumier-Smith's moment of vision before the shop window as "a mystical experience" (French 81).

Edward Stone, in his 1969 reading of the story, attempts to integrate the serious nature of the protagonist's experience with the jocular narrative tone. Stone believes that the emotion underlying the narrator's plight is "mocked good-naturedly—perhaps in an attempt to avoid mawkishness" (Stone 121). Stone further defines "De Daumier-Smith's Blue Period" as "an intimate confession of the irrational conduct that grief at his mother's death caused in a young man of nineteen" (Stone 121).

The contrasting critical valuations of "De Daumier-Smith's Blue Period" may be seen to arise from the story's narrative structure. The voice of the first-person narrator at the story's beginning creates confusion for the reader who must make a number of adjustments to the first-person voice of the young protagonist as he experiences a deepening despair and alienation. However, Salinger's intention is, paradoxically, to use the narrative frame as a springboard for understanding the story's underlying message.

Commencing to tell the tale of his youthful "blue period," the narrator addresses the reader from a psychologically happier time. From a mature vantage point, he proclaims the love he holds for his lately deceased stepfather. He also laments having, for so many years, begrudged his stepfather the recognition of his positive attributes. Descriptive terms like "magnetic" and "generous" (198),

applied to the late art dealer, render the mature narrator as a comfortably well-adjusted personality. The narrator must now, however, take the reader into the depths of the state of mind of his younger self for whom the entire world is rendered in blue. To do so, Salinger is confronted, as an author, with making the interpretation of events and the psychological insight of the young protagonist realistic to the reader, especially since these present a jarring contrast to the outlook of the previous teller of the tale from the narrative frame. The successful suspension of disbelief (that is, the ability of the reader to believe that the happy narrator just encountered is now a most unhappy and alienated person) must be accomplished in order to understand the spiritual struggle of the young protagonist and the message at the story's center. Salinger must make the descriptions of place and time and the psychological state of mind of the young protagonist quickly believable so that the reader may participate in the "Experience" (250) as it unfolds.

To effect reader participation, Salinger employs a number of narrative tactics—for example, dislocations of place for the young protagonist (Paris to New York; New York to Montreal); emotional alienation from others (the New York bus fiasco replete with the protagonist's response to the driver in French); socioeconomic dislocations (posh New York hotel to the working-class Verdun district, with its bedraggled shops and inhabitants). As the reader follows the young painter's depictions of both his exterior and interior worlds, and his interpretation of events, the story's creation of what Gwynn and Blotner describe as Kafkaesque cul-de-sacs (Gwynn 39) leaves both the protagonist and reader at dead ends. This leveling of perception between reader and narrator works to bring the reader into the state of mind in which the "Experience" (250) might be understood simultaneously with its occurrence in the text. In this way, Salinger, as he does with many of his stories, invites maximum reader participation in the epiphany of the central character.

To make all this so, Salinger chooses to inject humor and self-mockery in the narrator's tone at the beginning of the story to allow the reader to make the transitions necessary for suspension of disbelief. Salinger paints with surreal imagery the setting of the Montreal neighborhood and the squalid surroundings of the art school and orthopedic shop to add to the color and feeling of alienation that inhabit the psychological state of the young protagonist. The fact that the school's proprietors, the Yoshotos, speak very little English also serves to instill a feeling of isolation and lack of information about the other characters with whom the narrator communicates. The letters from the narrator to Sister Irma, reproduced verbatim, on the other hand—in Salinger's use of the text-within-text technique—render the young narrator's consciousness and his interpretation of his surroundings more and more realistic, as the letters act like visual signposts of something tangible in this journey of loss and of tangled emotions. By the time the narrator reaches the point from which he will relate his transcendent experience, the suspension-of-disbelief in the reader must be accomplished. The reader may thus share the epiphany that comprises the story's raison d'être. The "Experience" (250), then, acts as would the vanishing point of a canvas, from which, once realized, all perspective is determined. However, from the sharing of the epiphany and what it means to be "twice blessed" (250), Salinger asks the reader to turn a somersault—back out to the narrative frame he had constructed at the story's beginning. In this way, the narrative technique in "De Daumier-Smith's Blue Period" acts as an integral part of the comprehension of the imagery.

One clue to the story's message lies in the painting that the young protagonist names in his imaginary conversation with Pablo Picasso. "Les Saltimbanques," an important work of Picasso's Blue Period, is conjured as representing the great master's "glory, long forfeited" (213). Although the narrator uses this anecdote to denounce Picasso's later veer into painting for financial gain (at the expense of his truer and more spiritual quest), the mention of "Les Saltimbanques" (or "The Acrobats") also lends direction to the reader's interpretation of the "Experience" (250) that comprises the young man's transcendent understanding. In other words, Salinger asks his reader to attempt, as would an acrobat, to turn a somersault from the

platform of singularly spiritual pursuit (that is, the narrator's "blue" life preceding the "Experience" at the orthopedic shop window) and to right himself, regaining balance, in the "sunnier" life of the physical world (that is, back into the psychologically balanced perspective at the story's beginning and end). Language that the author has imbedded within the text now lends a hand in the exercise. At the beginning of the story, for example, the young de Daumier-Smith says, of his move to New York after his mother's death, that it "threw me, and threw me terribly" (199). Later, as he gazes into the window of the orthopedic shop, just before the "Experience" (250), the shopgirl's tumble into the urinal basins renders visually the about-face that the narrator is to undergo in his understanding: "her feet [go] out from under her" (250) in what might be seen as the acrobatic tumble, and what Gwynn and Blotner term a "pratfall" (Gwynn 37). In the gathering night, the impact of a miraculously rising sun, which catalyzes the narrator's experience, is then summarized: "I had to put my hand on the glass to keep my balance" (250). Just as in performing a physical somersault—where much is dependent on the kinesthetic and mental coordination during its execution—the realization of having done so successfully is comprehended only upon coming upright in its aftermath. So, too, Salinger implies, much is left to trusting the miracle, which cannot be fully comprehended until one finds "balance." From the story's frame, then, at the beginning of the narrative—a time of happiness and psychological adjustment—the author requires the reader to be "thrown" into spiritual and emotional crisis and, in the end, through the "Experience" (250), to come out, "in balance" once again into that "sunnier" frame of mind. In interpreting the "Experience" (250), the author also requires the reader to somersault into another way of thinking; that is, to "balance" within his being two mutually exclusive realms—the spiritual and the physical—in order to be "twice blessed" (250). Perhaps, Salinger implies, the ability to live successfully requires the simultaneous acceptance of the dualities inherent in our human nature. The young narrator, who has attempted in his "blue period" to adhere to a singularly spiritual and nonmaterialistic life, has been unsuccessful and unhappy because he has not allowed himself to experience the joys of his physical nature. The knowledge of God—or true transcendent experience—requires balancing our natural duality lest we would worship only a "wooden dummy-deity" (241). The young protagonist, after his epiphany, realizes that "Everybody is a nun" (251)—that is, perhaps to say, all beings are spiritual; that every "body" is sacred. Thus, Salinger may be implying, we may see God in all people; Jesus in the Fat Lady (as the author postulates in the 1957 story "ZOOEY"). The young protagonist follows this statement with another in French: "*Tout le monde est une nonne*" (251) (which Salinger does not translate but which may be rendered into English as "All the world is a nun" or "Everything is a nun"). Salinger may be implying here that every "thing in the world" is sacred. Thus, we may see God in a thing like the wooden dummy of the orthopedic shop—now understood through epiphany as a deity. The reader comes to realize that elements that the human mind may perceive as polarities—spiritual/physical, blue/sunny, nun/American Girl in Shorts, death/life—really exist as equals on the same continuum. We, as human beings, must integrate our notions of duality in order to achieve a state of enlightenment—that of being "twice blessed" (250). In renouncing his pursuit of Sister Irma—who represents for him the pursuit of the "spiritual" via the effacement of the "physical" self (in her art school application she had submitted a photo of her convent in place of a photo of herself), the narrator realizes that he cannot achieve transcendence along that path. After his epiphany, he finds himself in a "sunnier" place both physically and psychologically, contemplating those "summer active animals" (252)—enjoying the physical side of his human nature. He also notes that he will soon return to art school (he has not, therefore, completely renounced his "spiritual" side). He can now, however, appreciate that his student Bambi Kramer (who had submitted in her art school application a photo of herself in a strapless bathing suit and who thus represents to him the carnal side of life) may also ironically represent an example of "balance" or enlighten-

ment (her favorite painters are Walt Disney and Rembrandt). The mature narrator likewise points out at the end of the tale that Bambi has begun to paint Christmas cards.

Gwynn and Blotner define "De Daumier-Smith's Blue Period" as an attempt on Salinger's part to introduce "transcendental mysticism in satiric fiction" (Gwynn 33), observing that: "De Daumier-Smith reveals himself as at once 'a student of Buddhism,' 'an agnostic,' 'an admirer of St. Francis of Assisi,' a man 'especially delighted with Martin Luther,' who falls in love with a painting of Christ's burial by a Roman Catholic nun, and who has a 'transcendent' mystical experience" (Gwynn 33). The leveling of differences between the religions would, in fact, serve the story's intention to equalize the playing field in defining spiritual awareness.

Other critics contribute various perspectives on "De Daumier-Smith's Blue Period." Edward Stone, in his 1969 study of the story, finds a striking parallelism between the imagery of a poem by RAINER MARIA RILKE and that utilized by Salinger in describing de Daumier-Smith's vision. In his explication, Stone relates the actions surrounding the "wooden dummy-deity" (241) of the orthopedic shop to the imagery of Rilke's epiphany as the poet stands before the archaic torso of Apollo in a Paris museum (Stone 124, 125). Just as Rilke feels that the torso speaks to him—"You must change your life" (Rilke 181)—so, too, does the young protagonist of Salinger's story reach the same conclusion, immediately giving Sister Irma her freedom and accepting his changed perspective.

The critic John Russell, in his 1963 explication of the story, sees Salinger taking de Daumier-Smith through two of the three "stages of readjustment" that the sensitive person must pass to achieve self-realization as "artist" (Russell 73).

Critics seem to agree, however, that "De Daumier-Smith's Blue Period" represents "one of the most spiritual selections in *Nine Stories*" (Unrue 133). If one takes into consideration the ZEN koan that serves as an epigraph to *Nine Stories*—"We know the sound of two hands clapping. But what is the sound of one hand clapping?"—then this story, in its narrative technique and in its message, represents Salinger's attempt, perhaps, to lead the reader to that state of ineffable understanding of how a human being might integrate the polarities composing human experience. Certainly, Salinger wishes the reader, at the end of the tale, to hear the voice of the mature and the immature protagonist as one integrated voice—one balanced personality. The reader must do the somersault and balance on the equation. Like a koan, which John Wenke defines as an "epigrammatic form designed to eclipse the pursuit of solutions through logic and rationality" (Wenke 33), and which "opens one's being to the impress of intuition, which achieves its most conscious expression through the experience of epiphany" (Wenke 34), the story invites participation toward that end. As John Unrue, in his 2002 study of Salinger's fiction observes: "'De Daumier-Smith's Blue Period' [is] most informed by Salinger's increasingly mature awareness of transcendental mysticism and Zen Buddhism during his own personal search for enlightenment and [is one of the] truest examples of his spiritual life in his art" (Unrue 133).

PUBLICATION HISTORY

"De Daumier-Smith's Blue Period" was first published in London, England, in the May 1952 issue of the journal *World Review*. The story appeared in *Nine Stories,* published by LITTLE, BROWN AND COMPANY in 1953. *Nine Stories,* Salinger's second book, has never gone out of print.

Nine Stories is available in three editions from Little, Brown and Company: an exact reproduction of the hardback first edition from 1953; a trade paperback that mimics the production of the hardback; and a mass-market paperback, with its pagination differing from the above editions.

CHARACTERS

Agadganian, Robert "Bobby" Jr.   Robert "Bobby" Agadganian, Jr., is Jean de Daumier-Smith's (the narrator's) stepfather. Having lost everything in the Wall Street crash of 1929, he remade himself from a stockbroker into an art appraiser. Bobby marries the narrator's mother shortly after her divorce, when de Daumier-Smith is eight years old. The family moves to Paris to benefit Bobby's new profession. After the death of de Daumier-Smith's mother, the narrator and Bobby relocate to New York City and live together in a suite at the Ritz. Bobby is described as "adventurous, extremely magnetic, and generous" (198). The narrator dedicates the story to the memory of his stepfather, who died in 1947.

Bunting, Douglas   Douglas Bunting is Sister Irma's self-proclaimed favorite painter. Puzzled by the name, Jean de Daumier-Smith unsuccessfully seeks to discover information about Bunting.

Bus driver   The New York City bus driver insultingly commands the narrator to move to the back of the bus. Jean de Daumier-Smith responds to him disparagingly, in French, with a tirade of epithets and then steps to the rear, elated.

De Daumier-Smith, Jean   Jean de Daumier-Smith is a pseudonym that the narrator creates in applying for a teaching position at the Montreal correspondence art school, Les Amis Des Vieux Maîtres (Friends of the Old Masters). The narrator (never revealing his real name) is a 19-year-old American who has returned to New York City with his stepfather, Bobby Agadganian, Jr., after the death of his mother in Paris. Lonely and at loose ends in New York City, the narrator, who is also a budding artist, sees an ad for an art instructor at the art school. He applies for the position and includes a letter full of fabrications about himself: that he is 29 years old and a great-nephew of Honoré Daumier, that Pablo Picasso is a family friend, and that he has left his South of France estate after the death of his wife.

The bulk of "De Daumier-Smith's Blue Period" chronicles Jean de Daumier-Smith's misadventures at the art school, owned and staffed solely by a middle-aged Japanese couple, the Yoshotos. Throughout the story, de Daumier-Smith projects a facade of sophistication, although he is quite naive. At night, he hears moans through the common wall he shares with the Yoshotos and is puzzled by the sounds. De Daumier-Smith falls in love with one of his students, a nun named Sister Irma, whom he romanticizes and believes to be a potentially great artist. He encourages her art and writes a letter in which he asks whether she finds being a nun "very satisfactory, in a spiritual way" (236). After Sister Irma's superiors withdraw her from the school, de Daumier-Smith composes a second letter that he intends to mail the next day. That evening, while looking into the lit window of the orthopedic appliances shop housed below the school, he has a transcendent "Experience" (250). De Daumier-Smith, returning at twilight from a meal out, notices a shopgirl in the window of the store. The window, full of "enamel urinals and bedpans, with a sightless wooden dummy-deity standing by in a marked-down rupture truss" (241), is transfigured after the girl, who becomes embarrassed by the narrator's presence, stumbles and falls while changing the truss. As de Daumier-Smith gazes at the girl, the sun miraculously rises and blinds him. When he regains his vision, the girl has disappeared, "leaving behind her a shimmering field of exquisite, twice-blessed, enamel flowers" (250). De Daumier-Smith realizes he must allow Sister Irma "her freedom to follow her own destiny" (251). He realizes, as well, that "Everybody is a nun" (251). He does not mail the letter nor does he attempt again to get in touch with Sister Irma.

Father Zimmermann Father Zimmermann decides to withdraw Sister Irma from the art correspondence school and instructs the Mother Superior to inform the Yoshotos by letter.

Kramer, Bambi Bambi Kramer is one of the original three students assigned to Jean de Daumier-Smith. Her questionnaire form includes a photograph of herself in a bathing suit. Her favorite artists, she states on her form, are Rembrandt and Walt Disney. Bambi submits an unforgettable watercolor titled "Forgive Them Their Trespasses," in which she has painted three boys fishing in front of a "No Fishing" sign. De Daumier-Smith believes her to be without talent and a hopeless pupil.

Mother Superior At the behest of Father Zimmermann, the Mother Superior writes to the art school informing the Yoshotos that the convent is withdrawing Sister Irma as a pupil.

Mrs. X Mrs. X, an attractive, young divorcée, dines with Bobby Agadganian, Jr., on the evening the narrator informs Bobby, his stepfather, that he will leave New York City to teach in Montreal. Unlike Bobby, Mrs. X thinks it is a wonderful opportunity.

Narrator, the *See* De Daumier-Smith, Jean.

Narrator's mother The narrator's mother divorced his father when Jean de Daumier-Smith was eight years old and, shortly thereafter, married Bobby Agadganian, Jr. Upon her death 11 years later in Paris, the narrator and Agadganian return to live in New York City.

Ridgefield, R. Howard R. Howard Ridgefield is one of the three correspondence art students assigned to Jean de Daumier-Smith. He is a middle-aged "society photographer." His major picture accompanying his submission depicts a minister assaulting a large-breasted, young blonde parishioner near the altar. The narrator believes that, like Bambi Kramer, Ridgefield is without talent and a hopeless pupil.

Sister Irma Sister Irma is one of the three students assigned to Jean de Daumier-Smith. She has been enrolled in the correspondence art course to improve her drawing ability because she teaches drawing to children at the convent's school. De Daumier-Smith believes that one of her watercolors is "an artist's picture, steeped in high, high, organized talent and God knows how many hours of hard work" (229). De Daumier-Smith becomes infatuated with Sister Irma. Although he has no personal information about her, he imagines her to be "a shy, beautiful girl of eighteen who had not yet taken her final vows" (241), free to leave the convent and return to the world. De Daumier-Smith writes Sister Irma a letter and expresses the desire to meet her, but he never receives a reply. Instead, she is withdrawn from the art school by her superiors.

Shopgirl During twilight, Jean de Daumier-Smith notices the shopgirl in the display window of the orthopedic appliances shop as she changes the truss on the wooden dummy. She becomes embarrassed by his watching her and stumbles and falls. At the moment she falls, the sun miraculously rises and blinds de Daumier-Smith, who has what he terms a transcendent experience.

Yoshoto, M. M. Yoshoto, a Japanese artist, along with his wife, Mme. Yoshoto, runs the art school that employs Jean de Daumier-Smith. M. Yoshoto's watercolors adorn the instructors' room. One painting, of a goose in flight, which de Daumier-Smith describes as "one of the most daring and accomplished feats of craftsmanship" (213) he has ever seen, still haunts the narrator.

Yoshoto, Mme. Mme. Yoshoto, wife of M. Yoshoto, assists her husband in running the art school that employs Jean de Daumier-Smith. The narrator fantasizes that, by warming Mme. Yoshoto's heart in his hands, as he would a bird, he will solve the secret problem of the Yoshotos and put an end to the moaning he hears each night through the bedroom wall.

Yoshotos' son The Yoshotos' son is away at college. Jean de Daumier-Smith, while he teaches at the art school, sleeps in the son's chairless room.

Zimmermann Zimmermann is the New York City dentist who pulls out eight of de Daumier-Smith's teeth after the narrator's return from Paris.

FURTHER READING

Alsen, Eberhard. *A Reader's Guide to J. D. Salinger.* Westport, Conn.: Greenwood Press, 2002.

French, Warren. *J. D. Salinger, Revisited.* New York: Twayne Publishers, 1988.

Gwynn, Frederick L., and Joseph L. Blotner. *The Fiction of J. D. Salinger.* Pittsburgh: University of Pittsburgh, 1958.

Lundquist, James. *J. D. Salinger.* New York: Ungar, 1979.

Piwinski, David J. "Salinger's 'De Daumier-Smith's Blue Period': Pseudonym as Cryptogram." *Notes on Contemporary Literature* 15, no. 5 (November 1985): 3–4.

Rilke, Rainer Maria. *Translations from the Poetry of Rainer Maria Rilke.* New York: W. W. Norton, 1938.

Russell, John. "Salinger, From Daumier to Smith." *Wisconsin Studies in Contemporary Literature* 4, no. 1 (Winter 1963): 70–87.

Stone, Edward. "De Daumier-Smith's Blue Period." In *A Certain Morbidness: A View of American Literature,* 121–139. Carbondale: Southern Illinois University Press, 1969.

Tierce, Mike. "Salinger's 'De Daumier-Smith's Blue Period.'" *Explicator* 42, no. 1 (Fall 1983): 56–58.

Unrue, John C. *J. D. Salinger.* Detroit: Gale Group, 2002.

Wenke, John. *J. D. Salinger: A Study of the Short Fiction.* Boston: Twayne Publishers, 1991.

dedications

Perhaps the most personal of all pages in a book is the dedication page. The dedication, which no author decides lightly, may reflect love, respect, gratitude, or friendship. All four of Salinger's books bear dedications. The reader's attention to these dedications offers insight into Salinger's affections, his sense of indebtedness, and his views regarding his preferred readership.

The dedication of Salinger's first book, *The* Catcher in the Rye (1951), reads, "To My Mother" (Miriam Salinger). This dedication is a straightforward example of familial love and debt. (It might easily have said, "To My Parents," but Solomon Salinger and, for that matter, the other member of the Salinger family, the author's sister, Doris Salinger, never received public acknowledgment.) Salinger's mother always supported her son's ambitions, while his father wanted him to enter the family business.

The dedication of Salinger's second book, *Nine* Stories (1953), reads, "To Dorothy Olding and Gus Lobrano." This dedication is an example of professional gratitude and friendship. Dorothy Olding of the Harold Ober Agency was Salinger's literary agent for 50 years. At the time of this dedication, her future role as main privacy-protector and gatekeeper wasn't as yet needed. The dedication perhaps helped ensure her lifelong constancy to Salinger's cause. The other dedicatee, GUS LOBRANO, was his editor, following the author's initial working with WILLIAM MAXWELL. Lobrano, who became a very close friend, edited Salinger until his death at the age of 53, in 1956.

The dedication of Salinger's third book, FRANNY AND ZOOEY (1961), published at the height of the author's fame, spotlighted the name of WILLIAM SHAWN, editor in chief of the NEW YORKER, for the reading public. The dedication, which has achieved renown, reads in entirety: "As nearly as possible in the spirit of Matthew Salinger, age one, urging a luncheon companion to accept a cool lima bean, I urge my editor, mentor, and (heaven help him) closest friend, William Shawn, *genius domus* of *The New Yorker,* lover of the long shot, protector of the unprolific, defender of the hopelessly flamboyant, most unreasonably modest of born great artist-editors, to accept this pretty skimpy-looking book." Each phrase, each word, even each pause in the dedication bears testimony to the remarkable relationship between writer and editor. The circumstances that led to the dedication were that after Salinger published "FRANNY" in the *New Yorker* in 1955, he later submitted "ZOOEY," only to have the story unanimously rejected by *New Yorker* fiction editors. Shawn intervened, overruling the editors, and decided to edit it himself. Utilizing his legendary editing skills, Shawn "trimmed" "Zooey" to its *New Yorker*–record length for a work of fiction. From this point on, Shawn was Salinger's sole editor.

The dedication of Salinger's fourth and final book published during his lifetime, RAISE HIGH THE ROOF BEAM, CARPENTERS AND SEYMOUR: AN INTRODUCTION (1963), reflects familial love and Salinger's statement about his preferred readership. The dedication reads in entirety: "If there is an amateur reader still left in the world—or anybody who just reads and runs—I ask him or her, with untellable affection and gratitude, to split the dedication of this book four ways with my wife and children." The people referred to are Salinger's second wife, CLAIRE SALINGER, and his two children from the marriage, MARGARET ANN SALINGER and MAT-THEW SALINGER. The "amateur reader" is Salinger's response to academic reading and a refusal to accept literary critics' dismissal of his Glass stories. The often-overlooked phrase in this dedication is "or anybody who just reads and runs." This is an allusion to a more informal manner of reading and reinforces Salinger's preference for circumventing the critical establishment. Notably, the phrase echoes F. SCOTT FITZGERALD's words to his own readers in his 1922 book, *Tales of the Jazz Age.* Fitzgerald wrote: ". . . I tender these tales of the Jazz Age into the hands of those who read as they run and run as they read" (Fitzgerald 2000, 802).

Salinger's dedications provide some of the best evidence of his personal desire to connect with readers and people in his life through his work.

"Down at the Dinghy"

"Down at the Dinghy" is the fifth story in Salinger's second book, *NINE STORIES* (1953). Originally published in the April 1949 issue of *HARPER'S,* the story introduces the character, Boo Boo Glass, the eldest daughter of the Glass family. Boo Boo must overcome the emotional trauma suffered by her son, Lionel, after the boy hears an ethnic slur against his father. "Down at the Dinghy" is Salinger's 26th published story.

SYNOPSIS

Sandra, the maid, grimly looks out the kitchen window toward the lake on "an Indian Summer afternoon" (111) in October. For the past four hours, she has done this repeatedly. Sandra now joins Mrs. Snell, the cleaning woman, at the kitchen table for tea. Nearly a half dozen times the maid has said that she is not going to worry about the situation, and Mrs. Snell agrees that she should not. Sandra tells Mrs. Snell that she is being driven crazy because of the four-year-old child, Lionel. She has to watch every word she says, and she never knows when he is around because he is so quiet.

When Mrs. Snell remarks that Lionel is good-looking, Sandra contradicts her by stating that the child will inherit his father's nose. Sandra does not know why the family stays at the lake this late into the season; she looks forward to their return to NEW YORK CITY. The maid asks Mrs. Snell what she would do in her situation. As Mrs. Snell begins to tell Sandra that she would look for another job, the dining room door opens and their employer, Boo Boo Tannenbaum, enters the kitchen.

Boo Boo is a plain-looking woman of 25 but "in terms of permanently memorable, immoderately perceptive, small-area faces—a stunning and final girl" (115). Boo Boo opens the refrigerator hoping to find some pickles for her son, only to discover that he has already eaten all of them. She goes to the kitchen window and looks out at the lake. Mrs. Snell remarks to Boo Boo that she has heard that Lionel is supposed to be running away from home. Boo Boo admits as much, and adds that Lionel has been running away since the age of two. She explains that usually he does not get far, but once he made it into CENTRAL PARK at night. He left home because a kid told him, "you stink" (118). Boo Boo tells the two women she will "have another go at it" (118) and leaves.

Boo Boo stands at the water's edge looking at Lionel, two hundred yards away, sitting in a dinghy tied to the far end of the pier. She walks onto the pier and squats within an oar's length of her son. Lionel does not respond as Boo Boo addresses him as "Friend. Pirate. Dirty dog" (120). She identifies herself as "Vice-Admiral Tannenbaum. Née Glass" (121). Lionel contests that his mother is an admiral; he says she is a lady. He moves the boat's tiller and changes its drift. Boo Boo tries to convince him that she is indeed an admiral by making a bugle-like call that "only admirals are allowed to hear" (123). When Lionel wants her to make the call again, she tries to bargain with him: If he tells her why he is running away, she will do all of her secret bugle calls. This fails to persuade Lionel.

Boo Boo tries to reason with her son that he had promised to stop running away. As she starts to step into the dinghy, he tells her to stay out. Lionel, with his foot, then flips a pair of goggles into the lake, whereupon they sink. Boo Boo tells him that the goggles "belong to [his] Uncle Webb . . . they once belonged to [his] Uncle Seymour" (127). Lionel does not care about this fact. The mother takes

out a small, wrapped package and tells her son that it is a key chain like his father's. Lionel wants her to throw it to him. Boo Boo says to her son that she should throw the package in the lake. When Lionel replies to Boo Boo that the package belongs to him, she tells her son that she does not care. Lionel watches her, and "his eyes reflected pure perception, as his mother had known they would" (128). Boo Boo throws the package, which lands on Lionel's lap. He picks it up, tosses it into the lake, and starts to cry. Boo Boo steps into the dinghy and places him on her lap and kisses him. As she rocks him and tells him sailors do not cry, Lionel interrupts, "Sandra—told Mrs. Smell—that Daddy's a big—sloppy—kike" (129). (The child mispronounces Mrs. Snell's name, but not the racial slur.) Boo Boo flinches slightly and then tells Lionel that what he heard Sandra say is not horrible. She asks him if he knows the meaning of "kike." The child answers, "It's one of those things that go up in the *air*, . . . with *string* you hold" (129). Boo Boo tucks in Lionel's shirt and tells him they will go buy some pickles, pick up his father, and the three of them will go sailing in the dinghy. Mother and son then race back to the house. Lionel is the winner.

CRITICAL ANALYSIS

"Down at the Dinghy," the shortest of the *Nine Stories,* "clearly belongs to the Glass family history through its introduction of Seymour and Buddy's sister Boo Boo and her young son Lionel, the only third-generation Glass that readers ever meet" (French 1988, 74). Readers are alerted to Boo Boo's identity when she refers to herself as "née Glass" (121), followed by a minor reference to two of Lionel's uncles: "Uncle Webb" (Buddy Glass's given name) and "Uncle Seymour" (127). "Down at the Dinghy," which appeared in the April 1949 issue of *Harper's,* is the only Glass story not published in the NEW YORKER. The story makes evident that Salinger had at least an embryonic Glass family in mind as early as 1949, since, in this narrative, the author names three of the nine Glass members. (Salinger did not assemble and introduce the entire Glass family until the 1955 story "RAISE HIGH THE ROOF BEAM, CARPENTERS." For more information regarding the eight published Glass stories, *see* GLASS STORIES. "Down at the Dinghy"'s significance, in relation to the author's body of work, primarily resides in its introduction of Boo Boo and the fact that it is the only direct focus on her within the Glass saga.

The theme of "Down at the Dinghy" is "social hate in the form of anti-Semitism" (Gwynn 26). Boo Boo, introduced as "Boo Boo Tannenbaum" (115), has married a Jewish man, Mr. Tannenbaum, who is not seen in the story's events. Boo Boo's four-year-old son, Lionel, has overheard an ethnic slur spoken by their maid, Sandra. The child has thus "run away" and has sought refuge in the family's dinghy on the lake. As the critics Frederick L. Gwynn and Joseph L. Blotner insightfully suggest, "one anticipates the woundings to come later in childhood, adolescence, and adulthood, [and] it seems that the time of the story, Indian Summer, may be symbolic—the last of the kind of innocence which makes possible for [Lionel] the semantic confusion at the end of the story" (Gwynn 26). The confusion to which the critics refer is that the four-year-old Lionel—overhearing the ethnic slur "kike"—mistakenly interprets the word's meaning to be the same as that of "kite."

"Down at the Dinghy," set at an idyllic lake in October, consists of three short scenes. In the first scene, Sandra, the Tannenbaums' year-round maid (she lives with the family in MANHATTAN and accompanies them to their summer home at the lake) and Mrs. Snell (the Tannenbaums' summer cleaning lady, who lives within a bus ride of the lake) converse in the Tannenbaums' kitchen. Salinger portrays Sandra as the story's antagonist. She complains to Mrs. Snell that although it is already October, the family has delayed returning to Manhattan. Sandra has said something that Lionel has overheard, but Salinger does not divulge what that may be. The reader infers that whatever Lionel overheard was significant, for Mrs. Snell recommends to Sandra that she look for another job. Sandra has no remorse about what she has said; instead, she blames Lionel for being so quiet that she never knows when he is nearby. Sandra worries aloud whether Lionel will tell his mother of her indiscretion; over a four-hour period, she has repeatedly looked out the kitchen's lakeside window. The text, however, withholds information about the object of her search. In contrast to Sandra, Mrs. Snell is portrayed sympathetically and comically: She wears an old but expensive hat and owns an equally expensive handbag, albeit very worn; the reader infers these are hand-me-downs from her wealthy summer lakeside employers. (Her matches, with their Stork Club insignia, confirm the economic status of her employers.) Mrs. Snell's comments about Lionel's good looks are countered by Sandra's retort that Lionel will inherit his father's nose.

The first scene ends with Boo Boo Tannenbaum's entrance into the kitchen. Boo Boo is a plain-looking 25-year-old, but her spirit animates her being: "she was—in terms of permanently memorable, immoderately perceptive, small-area faces—a stunning and final girl" (115). The critic James Bryan observes, "For all the ostensible demerits Boo Boo's appearance might carry to the undiscerning eye," her face "reflects an inner grace which is in full display as she sees her child through his crisis" (Bryan 176). That Boo Boo lacks vanity is also evidenced by a hairstyle that emphasizes her large ears. Boo Boo's conversation with Sandra and Mrs. Snell reveals that Lionel has "run away" to the dinghy, which he refuses to leave. (Boo Boo has returned to the kitchen to—unsuccessfully—procure a pickle to lure Lionel out of the boat.) Boo Boo recounts two earlier episodes of Lionel having "run away" after conversations that upset him—indicating him to be an emotionally sensitive child.

The next and climactic scene of the story showcases the delicate interaction between mother and child. Boo Boo stands on the pier, while Lionel (seated in the dinghy securely tied to the pier's end) obstinately forbids his mother entrance onto the boat. Boo Boo wants to understand why Lionel has run away again, especially since he promised he would stop doing so. Boo Boo identifies herself as "Vice-Admiral Tannenbaum. Née Glass" (121), but the child denies her military status, informing his mother that she is "a *lady*" (121). When Boo Boo reasserts her admiralship, the precocious Lionel queries, "where's your *fleet?*" (125). Salinger nuances the emotional bond between mother and child in descriptive phrases, such as: "Boo Boo not only listened to his voice, she seemed to watch it" (125). Salinger's ability to fuse dramatic events with dialogue in order for the characters to reach and resolve a crisis is underscored by this interaction between Lionel and his mother.

Salinger likewise uses this scene to invoke the existence of other Glass family members. When Lionel, in a pique of spite, flips a pair of underwater goggles into the lake (whereupon they sink out of sight), Boo Boo observes that the goggles belong to Lionel's "Uncle Webb . . . [and] once belonged to [his] Uncle Seymour" (127). (The use of past tense in referencing Seymour reminds the reader of Salinger's earlier story, and that Seymour is no longer living. "Down at the Dinghy" was published one year after "A PERFECT DAY FOR BANANAFISH," the story of Seymour's suicide.) When Boo Boo tells Lionel that the wrapped present contains a key chain, he eagerly asks her to toss it to him. She instructs Lionel that she should toss the present into the lake. The child senses his error regarding the goggles; he claims the key chain belongs to him, but "on a diminishing note of justice" (128). When Boo Boo echoes Lionel's earlier comment about having sunk the goggles—"I don't care" (127: Lionel; 128: Boo Boo)—her repetition precipitates the story's highpoint: Lionel's "eyes reflected pure perception, as his mother had known they would" (128). After Boo Boo tosses Lionel the key chain, he flings it into the water, "punishing himself for spitefully throwing away his uncle's goggles" (French 1963, 95). The critics Gwynn and Blotner view the goggles and key chain as symbolic "objects from the adult world associated with [Lionel's] uncle and father . . . a world of facts [Lionel] unconsciously does not want to see, whose doors he does not want to open" (Gwynn 26).

Salinger finally lets the reader in on what had transpired four hours earlier at the house. Lionel, now in tears, blurts out to Boo Boo: "Sandra—told Mrs. Smell—that Daddy's a big—sloppy—kike" (129). Lionel mispronounces Mrs. Snell's name, but not the ethnic slur. After Boo Boo responds that the slur "isn't the *worst* that could happen" (129), she asks Lionel whether he knows "what a kike is" (129). Lionel's answer, "It's one of those things that go up in the *air* . . . with *string* you hold"

(129), provides a surprise. Boo Boo does not disabuse Lionel of his error. The critic John Wenke insightfully observes that Lionel "does not need to know the meaning of words. While he does not understand ethnic prejudice, he does understand the universal language of hate. He translates the tone of Sandra's ethnic slur into the closest literal equivalent. He is horrified, therefore, to think of a 'big, sloppy' father floating in the sky" (Wenke 48).

Warren French, in his 1963 monograph, argues that the interpretation of "Down at the Dinghy" should focus on the significance of Lionel's attachment to his father. French reasons that, since the child does not know the meaning of "kike," the story needs to be analyzed by taking into account a child who worries that his father might literally be like a kite. French finds Lionel "immensely *attached* to his father" and would be frightened by the prospect that his father, a *kite,* "would 'fly away'" (French 1963, 96) if the string should break or be let slip. French further suggests that Lionel "probably suffers terrifying fears of being unwanted. To such a child the thought that his father was a 'kite' would be as disturbing as would the term 'kike' if he knew what it meant" (French 1963, 96).

In the story's denouement, Boo Boo, after hearing Lionel's definition of "kike," puts her "wild hand inside the seat of [Lionel's] trousers," and her action startles him. James Bryan suggests the action to be emblematic of Boo Boo's "own clutching after the baby Lionel has been—and his surprise indicates that the gesture is now foreign to a growing little 'boy'" (Bryan 177–178). Boo Boo ensures that the race back to the house—after her promise of purchasing pickles, picking up Mr. Tannenbaum at the station, and a boat ride—will be won by Lionel, who will later help his father "carry the sails" (130).

Critics remain divided over the success of Boo Boo's resolution of her son's psychological distress. French argues that the story relies on "cute sentimentality" (French 1988, 74); Boo Boo has "only deferred a crisis, and not confronted it" (French 1988, 75). Gwynn and Blotner suspect that Boo Boo "is only a little better equipped to meet the Sandras of this world than her son is" (Gwynn 27) and believe that the "efficacy of the kind of palliative [Boo Boo] offers . . . may not retain its potency much beyond Indian Summer" (Gwynn 27). On the other hand, James Bryan, in his essay "The Admiral and Her Sailor in Salinger's 'Down at the Dinghy,'" concludes that Salinger shows Lionel to be "on his way to greater maturity, that he will be firmer when the next shock comes" (Bryan 178). The reader, Bryan believes, "finishes the story with the conviction that—piloted by Boo Boo—[Lionel] will surely manage" (Bryan 178).

PUBLICATION HISTORY

"Down at the Dinghy" was first published in the April 1949 issue of *Harper's* magazine. The story appeared in book form in *Nine Stories,* published by LITTLE, BROWN AND COMPANY, 1953. *Nine Stories,* Salinger's second book, has never gone out of print.

Nine Stories is available in three editions from Little, Brown and Company: an exact reproduction of the hardback first edition from 1953; a trade paperback that mimics the production of the hardback; and a mass-market paperback, with its pagination differing from the above editions.

CHARACTERS

Naomi   Naomi, a small child and Lionel Tannenbaum's friend, told him that she had a worm in her thermos. This information catalyzed one of Lionel's runaway episodes when he hid in the apartment building's basement.

Sandra   Sandra is the Tannenbaums' year-round maid. Lionel Tannenbaum has overheard her comment to Mrs. Snell that his father is "a big, sloppy kike" (129). Sandra worries that Lionel will tell his mother what she said.

Snell, Mrs. Mildred   Mrs. Snell is the Tannenbaums' cleaning woman when they reside at the lake. She suggests to Sandra that the maid look for a new job after Sandra's ethnic slur about Mr. Tannenbaum.

Tannenbaum, Boo Boo (Glass)   Boo Boo Tannenbaum, née Glass, is Lionel Tannenbaum's 25-year-old mother and wife to Mr. Tannenbaum. She employs Sandra and Mrs. Snell. Boo Boo faces the problem of finding out why her four-year-old

son, Lionel, has "run away" and taken refuge in the family's dinghy on the lake. Boo Boo employs astute child psychology to help her son overcome this trauma, as she slowly eases herself into her son's confidence so she can find out what is wrong and comfort him.

Boo Boo Tannenbaum is Boo Boo Glass, the third-oldest child of the Glass family. She figures in all of the Glass family stories. In "Raise High the Roof Beam, Carpenters," her saucy, opinionated letter to Buddy Glass imploring him to get to their brother Seymour's wedding is reproduced; her message to Seymour—quoting the Sappho poem that supplies the title of the story—is written with a sliver of soap on the bathroom mirror. Although Boo Boo is vacationing in Europe during the events portrayed in "ZOOEY," she is mentioned several times. Boo Boo believes that Mr. Ashe of Kilvert's *Diary,* rather than God, created the world. She has a quirky sense of humor as evidenced when describing a look on her mother's face as meaning either that Mrs. Glass has just talked with one of her sons on the phone or that everyone's bowels in the world will be flawlessly working for a week. In "SEYMOUR: AN INTRODUCTION," Boo Boo chooses Seymour's John Keats poem for inclusion by Buddy in that story. Boo Boo is one of the five addressees of Seymour's letter, "HAPWORTH 16, 1924." Seymour tells Boo Boo to work on her manners; he also devises a nonoffensive prayer specifically for her. By 1959, Boo Boo has three children and lives in Tuckahoe, New York.

Tannenbaum, Lionel   Lionel Tannenbaum is Boo Boo (Glass) Tannenbaum's four-year-old son. When Lionel overhears the family's maid, Sandra, refer to his father as a "big, sloppy kike" (129), he "runs away" and seeks refuge in the family's dinghy on the lake. Though the child misunderstands the word "kike" as "kite," he nonetheless knows that the comment is an attack on his father. Since the age of two, Lionel, sensitive to what people say, has run away several times.

Tannenbaum, Mr.   Mr. Tannenbaum is husband to Boo Boo and father to Lionel. During the story's events, he is at work. Mr. Tannenbaum is the object of Sandra's ethnic slur.

It is unclear whether Mr. Tannenbaum is the young man in the framed photograph that Boo Boo has brought with her in "Raise High the Roof Beam, Carpenters."

Uncle Seymour (Glass)   The goggles that Lionel Tannenbaum tosses overboard once belonged to his Uncle Seymour. At the time of the story, Seymour is dead. The reader knows that this Seymour is Seymour Glass because Boo Boo Tannenbaum identifies herself as née Glass.

Prior to the publication of "Down at the Dinghy," Seymour appears in one story, "A Perfect Day for Bananafish," where he is seen on a beach, meets a very young girl, goes for a swim, tells her a parable about bananafish, and later shoots himself on the hotel bed next to his sleeping wife. "Raise High the Roof Beam, Carpenters," the first Glass family story, introduces the family and reveals that Seymour is the eldest of seven children. The story describes Seymour's wedding day (although he fails to show up for the ceremony). Seymour's diary entries, which serve as a stand-in for him, dominate the story's close. At the time "Zooey," the longest of the Glass family stories, takes place, Seymour has been dead for more than seven-and-one-half years. Nonetheless, Seymour plays a significant role as "Zooey" ends with Seymour's parable of the Fat Lady that brings Franny Glass to joy and understanding of her life's purpose. The next Glass family story, "Seymour: An Introduction," is an extensive effort, by Buddy, to convey the life and identity of his brother. The final Glass family story, "Hapworth 16, 1924," contains the most extended presentation of Seymour's own words, albeit written at the age of seven.

Uncle Webb (Glass, Buddy)   The goggles that Lionel Tannenbaum tosses overboard belong to his Uncle Webb. The reader knows that Webb is a Glass family member because Boo Boo identifies herself as née Glass, and Webb has "inherited" the goggles after Seymour's death. Since Buddy Glass is referred to as W. G. Glass at the end of the 1965 story "Hapworth 16, 1924," it is gener-ally assumed that his first name is Webb. ("Buddy" is a nickname, derived from his years on *It's a Wise Child,* as is disclosed in "Raise High the Roof Beam, Carpenters.") The first mention of Webb/Buddy Glass in Salinger's work appears in "Down at the Dinghy."

Webb/Buddy, the second-eldest child, appears in all of the Glass family stories. He narrates the story "Raise High the Roof Beam, Carpenters," in which his 13-year-younger self is the protagonist trying to attend his brother Seymour's wedding. Webb/Buddy also writes the story "Zooey." Although Webb/Buddy is in Upstate New York when the action of "Zooey" takes place, nonetheless he figures prominently via his first-person author's introduction, in addition to his 14-page letter that Zooey Glass reads in the bathtub. Webb/Buddy writes "Seymour: An Introduction," in which he and Seymour are the main characters. There, the reader is offered a most intense experience of the middle-aged Webb/Buddy as chronicler of the Glass family saga. Many anecdotes from Webb/Buddy's youth are, in addition, related in that story. In "Hapworth 16, 1924," Webb/Buddy receives from his mother, Bessie, Seymour's 41-year-old letter and types a copy for publication. In Seymour's letter, the five-year-old Webb/Buddy is at summer camp with Seymour and is referred to often.

FURTHER READING

Alsen, Eberhard. *A Reader's Guide to J. D. Salinger.* Westport, Conn.: Greenwood Press, 2002.

Bryan, James. "The Admiral and Her Sailor in Salinger's 'Down at the Dinghy.'" *Studies in Short Fiction* 17 (Spring 1980): 174–178.

French, Warren. *J. D. Salinger.* New York: Twayne Publishers, 1963.

———. *J. D. Salinger, Revisited.* New York: Twayne Publishers, 1988.

Gwynn, Frederick L., and Joseph L. Blotner. *The Fiction of J. D. Salinger.* Pittsburgh: University of Pittsburgh Press, 1958.

Lundquist, James. *J. D. Salinger.* New York: Ungar, 1979.

Wenke, John. *J. D. Salinger: A Study of the Short Fiction.* Boston: Twayne Publishers, 1991.

dust-jacket comments

Salinger wrote dust-jacket comments (copy) for three of his four published books, all except NINE STORIES.

Though most of the dust-jacket copy for the 1951 The CATCHER IN THE RYE was anonymously penned, the biographical note was extracted from the publicity release Salinger wrote for LITTLE, BROWN AND COMPANY (see "IN J. D. SALINGER'S OWN WORDS"). The biographical note begins, "J. D. Salinger was born in New York City in 1919 and attended Manhattan public schools, a military academy in Pennsylvania and three colleges (no degrees)," and then Salinger is directly quoted: "A happy tourist's year in Europe when I was eighteen and nineteen. In the Army from '42 to '46, most of the time with the Fourth Division. I'm now living in Westport, Connecticut, some fifty miles out of New York. [new paragraph] I've been writing since I was fifteen or so. My short stories have appeared in a number of magazines over the last ten years, mostly—and most happily—in The New Yorker. I worked on The Catcher in the Rye, on and off, for ten years." Salinger's words used on the dust-jacket copy for The Catcher in the Rye are in keeping with the publishing practices of the time.

For the 1961 publication of FRANNY AND ZOOEY (eight years after Nine Stories), Salinger promised to write a substantial introduction. Instead, a 250-word text filled the two inside flaps of the dust jacket. This text remains important, however, as it represents the first time Salinger had publicly commented on his Glass stories. The author explains that the two stories, "FRANNY" and "ZOOEY," are part of "a narrative series [he's] doing about a family of settlers in twentieth-century New York, the Glasses." He calls the work "a long-term project" and admits that there is a danger he might "bog down, perhaps disappear entirely." Salinger states, "I love working on these Glass stories, I've been waiting for them most of my life, and I think I have fairly decent, monomaniacal plans to finish them with due care and all-available skill." He informs the reader that

"some new material is scheduled to appear [in the New Yorker] soon" and that he has a "great deal of thoroughly unscheduled material on paper, too." (As it turned out, the only new story to be published after Franny and Zooey was "HAPWORTH 16, 1924" in the June 19, 1965, issue.) Salinger identifies Buddy Glass as his "alter-ego and collaborator" and expresses the belief that "a writer's feelings of anonymity-obscurity are the second-most valuable property on loan to him in his working years" (the most valuable is the "all-available skill" Salinger refers to earlier). He concludes the text with the misinformation that he lives with his dog in Westport (by the time of this writing, he had been living in CORNISH, NEW HAMPSHIRE, for eight years).

The dust jacket for the final book Salinger published during his lifetime, the 1963 RAISE HIGH THE ROOF BEAM, CARPENTERS AND SEYMOUR: AN INTRODUCTION, includes a 165-word text filling its two inside flaps. Salinger explicitly states that Seymour "is the main character in my still-uncompleted series about the Glass family." The author explains that he is publishing the two stories "in something of a hurry" to prevent "unduly or undesirably close contact with new material in the series" and alludes to "several new stories coming along—waxing, dilating—each in its own way." The text concludes, "Oddly, the joys and satisfactions of working on the Glass family peculiarly increase and deepen for me with the years. I can't say why, though. Not, at least, outside the casino proper of my fiction." This was Salinger's last public statement about the Glass stories.

The Catcher in the Rye, Franny and Zooey, and Raise High the Roof Beam, Carpenters and Seymour: An Introduction are still published in hardback editions by Little, Brown and Company with their original dust-jacket copy. (The dust jacket of The Catcher in the Rye excises the sentence, "I'm now living in Westport, Connecticut, some fifty miles out of New York.") Additionally, Eberhard Alsen's A Reader's Guide to J. D. Salinger reproduces the entire texts of the dust jackets of Franny and Zooey (Alsen 2002, 206) and Raise High the Roof Beam, Carpenters and Seymour: An Introduction (Alsen 2002, 207).

"Elaine"

Appearing in the March–April 1945 issue of STORY, "Elaine" portrays a beautiful but naive adolescent girl's unfortunate destiny in the harsh, working-class reality of a Bronx upbringing. "Elaine" is Salinger's 12th published story. The author, however, chose not to include the story in his three books of collected stories.

SYNOPSIS

Dennis Cooney, an assistant watch repairman, has dropped dead while attending a circus performance. He leaves behind his wife, Evelyn Cooney, and six-year-old daughter, Elaine Cooney. Elaine has already won two beauty contests: one at the age three and one at age five. With the little insurance money from her husband's death, Mrs. Cooney moves to the Bronx and sends for her mother, a Mrs. Hoover, from Michigan. Pooling their meager resources, the two women are able to live comfortably in the Bronx. However, Mrs. Cooney must accept the sexual advances of the superintendent or "super" (38) of the apartment building, Mort Freedlander.

At seven years old, Elaine enters Public School 332; she is tested and placed with the slow learners. Either her mother or her grandmother deposits her at school every day. As Mrs. Cooney attends the movies most afternoons (or is otherwise busy with Mr. Freedlander), she relies on her mother, Mrs. Hoover, to pick Elaine up after school. Mrs. Hoover, however, often leaves her granddaughter waiting alone at the school exit after closing time, sometimes for as long as an hour. Despite this seemingly negligent and ineffectual mothering, Elaine is a "happy" (39) and smiling child who does not "seem to live in the unhappy child's world" (39). However, when Elaine reaches the fourth grade, her inability to keep pace with the class work forces her schoolteacher to discuss the problem with the principal. Elaine is thus dropped to a lower grade level. The schoolteacher remains hesitant about the decision and somewhat remorseful, especially since Elaine is, as the teacher describes her, "the most *exquisite* thing [she has] ever seen in [her] life.

She looks like Rapunzel" (39). Elaine continues to be a slow learner and does not graduate from the eighth grade until the age of 16 (the average child would be age 12 or 13). At the graduation pageant, Elaine is given the part of the Statue of Liberty—"the only nonspeaking part" (40)—and does not complain, even though she must hold a solid-lead torch above her head for nearly an hour (and despite two other girls' trampling her foot). After the ceremony, Elaine, her mother and grandmother, and Mr. Freedlander attend a film to celebrate. The Mickey Mouse cartoon being shown with the movie causes Elaine a fit of hysterical laughter. Mrs. Hoover is forced to slap and punch her granddaughter, reminding her that the film is only a "*picture*" (41). Throughout the film, Mr. Freedlander has been pressing his leg against Elaine, who does not recognize the intended sexual advance. Salinger gives the reader a direct insight into Elaine's incomprehension of Freedlander's motives: "She was sixteen years old and mature enough physically to like or dislike leg pressure from a man in the dark, but she was totally unqualified to accommodate sex and Mickey Mouse simultaneously. There was room for Mickey; no more" (41).

During the summer before Elaine's entrance into high school, she attends the movies with her mother almost daily. She has no girlfriends and knows no boys. Whenever a boy invites her for a date, she lies to quell her confusion about "unfamiliar, evadable issues" (41) and responds that she is not allowed to go. Elaine thus spends all of her summer safe within the fantasy world of the Hollywood movies, which are populated by their beautifully coifed leading men, who pose neither threat nor instruction about real-life sexual intimacy. September arrives, and as she waits alone in the lobby for her mother, Elaine meets Teddy Schmidt, an usher at one of the much-frequented movie houses. Teddy invites her to the beach on a double date. Elaine likes Teddy's "wavy, effeminate hair" (42) and replies that she will ask her mother for permission.

Mrs. Cooney buys a cheap bathing suit for her daughter, and the following Sunday, Elaine is picked up by Teddy and his party, who are late by one and one-half hours. During her wait outside at the curb, Elaine has been propositioned by a "masher" (43) without realizing the man's sexual intentions and has been honked at by men in passing cars. Although he apologizes, Teddy feels no guilt about the late arrival. Teddy introduces Elaine to his friend Frank Vitrelli and to Monny Monahan, Frank's date.

At the beach, after having spent hours in the sun, Frank and Monny decide (upon Frank's insistence) to play paddle tennis. Monny suggests a doubles match, but Teddy declines. During the match, Monny expresses reservations about leaving "that kid" (45) unchaperoned with Teddy, but Frank ignores her, saying that Teddy is "a good guy" (45). Once alone with his date, Teddy suggests that they move out of the sun and into the shade under the boardwalk. Elaine for the first time notices that the beach has become deserted. As they stand up, Elaine experiences a "private, terrible panic" (44). She has enjoyed the beach, and although she had never been out to a beach before, "she had seen hordes of Coney Islanders in newsreel shots" so that "the occasion had not estranged her violently from the dimensions of her own world" (44). Elaine's heart beats violently as she believes the beach to be a monster that will "swallow her up" (44). Teddy, likewise, takes on "a new meaning for her. He was no longer Teddy Schmidt, pretty, wavy-haired, male; he was Teddy Schmidt, not her mother, not her grandmother, not a movie star" (44). Once under the boardwalk, however, Elaine's panic subsides in the cool and dark place, and her heart beats more calmly. Teddy, "with the eternal rake's despicable but seldom faulty intuition" (45), however, realizes and takes advantage of Elaine's vulnerable emotional state and her sexual naïveté.

When Elaine arrives home, her mother questions her about whether she has had a good time and whether her bathing suit has shrunk. Mrs. Cooney then asks: "Anybody get wise with you?" (45), and Elaine responds in the negative. One month later, however, Elaine is married to Teddy Schmidt in a ceremony at his family home. Elaine, wearing a cheap suit and "a dreary gladioli corsage" (46), appears happier than she has ever seemed, even at the movies. Teddy, however, is nervous and irritable, especially with his new bride. When Elaine cannot cut the wedding cake appropriately, Teddy must do so, "thoroughly disgusted with her incompetence" (46). Mrs. Schmidt and Mrs. Cooney begin to argue about "the virility of a certain popular male movie star" (46), whereupon Mrs. Cooney slaps Mrs. Schmidt hard across the mouth. Frank Vitrelli and Mr. Freedlander break up the scrabble, while Teddy draws back "frightened . . . pretending to comfort his bride" (46). Monny Monahan tells Teddy to get Elaine away from the fracas. Teddy panics, and Elaine runs from his grasp toward her mother, begging to say good-bye. Suddenly, Mrs. Cooney, with "a great tenderness" (46) in her face, cradles her daughter's "beautiful face" (46) in her hands and kisses Elaine on the mouth, with a parting of, "Good-by, dolly" (46). Mrs. Hoover sobs and embraces her granddaughter. Abruptly, Mrs. Cooney takes control of the situation and calls out to her daughter: "You come back, you beautiful" (47). She then orders Elaine and Mrs. Hoover to exit the house. Teddy, insisting that Elaine is now his wife, threatens to have the marriage annulled. Seemingly unaware of the import of the drama, Elaine says good-bye to Teddy "in a friendly way" (47) as Teddy's mother exclaims: "Let the riffraff go!" (47).

Once outside, Mrs. Cooney rebuffs the company of Mr. Freedlander. The three women—Elaine, Mrs. Cooney, and Mrs. Hoover—move slowly up the street. Mrs. Cooney suggests that they go see "a nice movie" (47). When Mrs. Hoover prefers a movie house nearby, Mrs. Cooney insists on giving Elaine the choice of destination. Elaine, "looking down at her gladioli corsage" (47), remarks: "They're all dying. They were so *beautiful*" (47). She then asks what movie is showing at the theater her grandmother favors and, hearing that the actor is Henry Fonda, begins to skip "ecstatically" (47).

CRITICAL ANALYSIS

Although "Elaine" does not demonstrate, as do many of Salinger's stories, an innovative or experimental narrative technique, the story is remarkable for its attempt to penetrate the childlike mind and emotional life of a very naive adolescent girl. The narrative also attempts, from a sociological vantage point, a glimpse into the gritty reality of a Bronx upbringing and the narrow choices offered the disadvantaged working-class woman. "Elaine" moreover explores Salinger's growing concern with the inadequacy of the public education system and the subsequent detrimental effects of that system upon children with special needs.

With the character of Elaine, the "beautiful child" among her classmates and at the same time the least intellectually gifted, Salinger champions the intrinsic value of beauty in and of itself as a quality to be honored—viewing its uniqueness aside from any other positive attributes a child might possess. In showing the reaction of her family, teachers, and acquaintances to Elaine's beauty, Salinger attempts to instruct the reader about the inappropriate ways to regard this special gift. Elaine's beauty, rather than affording her any special attention or assistance, becomes, in the end, a burden and a disadvantage to her, especially since its extraordinary depth is disproportionate to her shallow intelligence. At a very early age, Elaine is named as the winner of two "Beautiful Child" (38) contests. For the quality of her beauty alone, she should thus, in the system of ethics being formed in Salinger's fiction, command protection. This beauty, coupled with Salinger's defining her simultaneously as a "child" (in Elaine's case, the eternal child due to an inability to comprehend the adult world), makes Elaine the possessor of two attributes often combined with vulnerability in Salinger's characters. However, with other characters who have the quality of beauty, the quality of intelligence has not otherwise been lacking, and, moreover, in those characters, the transition to adulthood has already been accomplished. For example, the theme of beauty—its advantages and disadvantages—had been explored by the author in the 1944 story, "ONCE A WEEK WON'T KILL YOU," in which Virginia Camson, wife of the protagonist, has used her beauty to marry into wealth. Despite his wife's ambition to climb the social ladder, her husband honors her for the quality of her beauty. In the 1940 story, "GO SEE EDDIE," the beautiful Helen also takes advantage of her good looks in order to play the field of available (and not so available) men, becoming the "kept" woman of a married man and thus able to support herself in some

luxury. In Helen's situation, however, her beauty becomes a disadvantage, as her brother views her glamour as a factor in the undermining of her virtue. As possessors of beauty, Virginia and Helen differ greatly from the naive Elaine in that they are well aware of how to use their gift as a tool in their economic survival. Elaine, on the other hand, seems unaware of her beauty and even less aware of how she might use her good looks to practical advantage. Rather, Elaine's beauty, combined with her innocence and lack of protection, leads to her unintended pregnancy and adds to her economic hardship.

With "Elaine," Salinger moreover explores the theme of the educational system and its ineffectual handling of children with learning disabilities. The ill-equipped teachers and administrators that Elaine relies upon lack the means, and skill, to properly assess the unique gifts and individual learning styles of their pupils. Despite her docile, sweet nature and cooperative behavior, Elaine is harmed by the one-size-fits-all regimen that the public school program enforces. Had she been allowed to continue with her same-age classmates, she may have learned from her peers the social cues necessary to keep her from becoming prey to unwanted sexual advances. Instead, Elaine's understanding is guided by the fantasy-romance of the movies and is confined to a "Mickey Mouse" cartoon reality—leaving her defenseless against the adult male attention that her physical maturity and extraordinary beauty invite.

Salinger uses the story of Elaine to capture, as well, the economic reality facing women who lack a male breadwinner in the household. In the portrait of the three women—Mrs. Hoover, Mrs. Cooney, and Elaine—the reader is reminded that the economic plight of the working-class woman without a male earner's paycheck to support her is a hard one. Mrs. Cooney and Mrs. Hoover have pooled their resources in order to rent what is most probably a tenement apartment in a disadvantaged neighborhood. Moreover, Mrs. Cooney (as Salinger deftly implies by what is not said in her conversation with Mort Freedlander) must acquiesce to the sexual advances of the building superintendent and, in doing so, hopes (the reader may infer) to get a break on her rent. Salinger likewise creates, in the character of Monny Monahan, the practical-minded girl who feels she must capitulate to the demands of her boorish boyfriend (Frank Vitrelli) because he holds the promise of an economically secure future. For example, when Frank refuses to return to Teddy and Elaine (knowing that Teddy intends to seduce his date), Monny hates him but hesitates to contradict him, "aware that he made sixty-five dollars a week, aware of the great potential security of him" (45). Salinger had previously created, in the character of Sarah Daley Smith in the 1943 story "The VARIONI BROTHERS," a similarly practical-minded young woman (albeit from a different sociological and educational background) with regard to her understanding of the economic requirements in raising children and maintaining a household. Sarah reflects upon the type of man (a Douglas Smith and not a Joe Varioni) who would be capable of offering the needed security.

Aside from attempting a realistic portrayal of working-class Bronx—its hard-luck life and its ethnic mix of Irish, Italian, Jewish, and German inhabitants—"Elaine" offers a closely rendered insight into the experience of psychological panic. In the scene between Elaine and Teddy at the beach, the author captures both the physically overwhelming sensations of a panic (or agoraphobic) attack and the subsequent emotional vulnerability of the victim.

Finally, the feeling of comfort that the American movie theater can provide—the opportunity to escape, however briefly, from the dilemmas of life—dominates the heart of Elaine's family of lost women. Notwithstanding Salinger's later noted distrust of Hollywood, with other narratives, and for other characters, as well, the author creates respite and relief by way of movie-going, most specifically for Franklin Graff in the 1948 story "JUST BEFORE THE WAR WITH THE ESKIMOS," for Aunt Rena in the 1944 story "Once a Week Won't Kill You," and for Lois Taggett in the 1942 story "The LONG DEBUT OF LOIS TAGGETT." As long as Elaine and her mother can take in a picture, the movies provide them "a sudden lurch of romance" in the "familiar darkness" (45) and screen them from the harsh light of their unfortunate and only-too-real plight.

PUBLICATION HISTORY

"Elaine" was published in the March–April 1945 issue of *Story*. Salinger never reprinted the story in his three books of collected stories. "Elaine" later appeared in the bootleg editions *The COMPLETE UNCOLLECTED SHORT STORIES OF J. D. SALINGER* (1974) and *TWENTY-TWO STORIES* (1998).

CHARACTERS

Cooney, Dennis   Dennis Cooney, a watch repairman, drops dead while attending a flea circus. He is the husband of Evelyn Cooney and father of the six-year-old Elaine Cooney.

Cooney, Elaine   At six years of age, Elaine Cooney is a beautiful girl who has already won two "Beautiful Child" (38) contests. When her father dies suddenly, Elaine moves with her mother and her grandmother, Mrs. Hoover, to an apartment in the Bronx. Elaine attends public school where she is classified as a slow learner and is thus kept from graduating from eighth grade at an appropriate age. She is 16 years old when she is finally allowed to graduate. Despite her physical maturity, Elaine remains intellectually and emotionally childlike. As she lacks any contact with girls or boys her own age, her world revolves around attending the movies with her mother. Elaine's ingenuous grasp of reality with regard to sex makes her easy prey to the advances of mature men (like Mr. Freedlander, the superintendent of the apartment building and boyfriend of Mrs. Cooney). Teddy Schmidt, a movie-house usher, succeeds in getting a date with Elaine and consequently seduces her. Elaine becomes pregnant, and one month after their date, she is married to Teddy. Just after the wedding ceremony, however, Mrs. Cooney insists that her daughter return to live at the apartment. Elaine bids goodbye to her new husband and skips off to the movies.

Cooney, Evelyn (Mrs.)   Mrs. Evelyn Cooney is the mother of Elaine Cooney and the wife of Dennis Cooney, who has died suddenly, leaving little behind but an insurance policy. Because Mrs. Cooney cannot fully provide for herself and Elaine, she brings her mother, Mrs. Hoover (previously a cashier in Michigan), to live with them. The three women take up residence in a Bronx apartment where Mr. Mort Freedlander is "the super" (38). Mrs. Cooney enjoys the movies and attends the matinee shows on an almost daily basis. She therefore cannot find time to take her daughter to school and back everyday. Instead, she relies on Mrs. Hoover to do so. Mrs. Hoover, likewise, is unavailable most afternoons so, on many occasions, Elaine is left to wait at the school exit for an hour until her grandmother arrives "irritably" (39) to collect her. While Mrs. Hoover and Elaine are out of the apartment, Mrs. Cooney acquiesces to the advances of Mr. Freedlander (a liaison of convenience that may presumably give her a break on the rent). Mrs. Cooney neglects Elaine in other ways, clothing her daughter in uncomplimentary "horrid" (40) dresses, but she appreciates Elaine's beauty. She also perceives Elaine's emotional vulnerability. She understands that her child survives in a fantasy world, and she calls Elaine her "dolly" (45, 46) throughout their conversations. At the story's close, Mrs. Cooney displays a strong motherly protectiveness when she insists that the pregnant (and now married) Elaine return to live with her and Mrs. Hoover at the apartment.

Freedlander, Mort (Mr.) Mr. Mort Freedlander is the superintendent or "super" (38) at the Bronx apartment building where Evelyn Cooney, Mrs. Hoover, and Elaine Cooney take up residence after the death of Elaine's father. Mort brags to Mrs. Cooney that he had been on a first-name basis with Bloomy Bloomberg, a gangster who was shot dead at the previous building where Mr. Freedlander was the "super." Mr. Freedlander forces his sexual advances on Elaine's mother. He also makes sexual advances toward the 16-year-old Elaine at the movies, pressing his leg up against hers during a Mickey Mouse cartoon. At the story's close, he assists in breaking up the fight between Mrs. Cooney and Mrs. Schmidt at the wedding reception. Nonetheless, Mrs. Cooney rebuffs him as she, Elaine, and Mrs. Hoover depart for the movies.

Hoover, Mrs. Mrs. Hoover is Elaine's grandmother and mother to Evelyn Cooney, who asks her to come from Grand Rapids, Michigan, to live in the Bronx. Previously a cashier, she contributes a small savings account to the household. Mrs. Hoover "irritably" (39) collects her granddaughter after school, as Mrs. Cooney neglects to do so on most days. She often leaves Elaine waiting alone for an hour after school has closed.

Monahan, Monny Monny Monahan, the girlfriend of Frank Vitrelli, goes to the beach on the double date with Teddy Schmidt and Elaine Cooney. Monny feels uncomfortable leaving Elaine unchaperoned with Teddy while she and Frank play paddle tennis (ping-pong). She asks to rejoin the other couple, but Frank assures her that Teddy is "a good guy" (45). Monny remains unconvinced and hates Frank for allowing Teddy to take advantage of the ingenuous Elaine. She hesitates to contradict him, however, being aware of his potential as a candidate for marriage and his prodigious earning power. At the wedding reception, Monny tells Teddy to take Elaine out of the room and away from the fight. She thus shows concern for Elaine's situation a second time, as she had the day at the beach.

Vitrelli, Frank Frank Vitrelli, who owns a Pontiac convertible, drives his girlfriend, Monny Monahan, on the double date to the beach with his friend, Teddy Schmidt, and Elaine Cooney. The "muscle bound" (44) Frank cavorts with Monny to show off his physique. As he catapults Monny atop his shoulders, she endures the painful posture and feigns admiration. When Frank suggests a game of paddle tennis, Monny hesitates about leaving Elaine alone with Teddy. Frank ignores her concerns. Monny believes that Frank knows Teddy's sexual intentions towards Elaine. She fears losing favor with Frank, however, if she does not go along with his pretence. She considers Frank, with his high salary of $65 a week, a good candidate for marriage and a chance at economic security. At the wedding reception, Frank helps to break up the fight between Mrs. Schmidt and Mrs. Cooney.

FURTHER READING

French, Warren. *J. D. Salinger*. New York: Twayne Publishers, 1963.

Wenke, John. *J. D. Salinger: A Study of the Short Fiction*. Boston: Twayne Publishers, 1991.

"For Esmé—with Love and Squalor"

"For Esmé—with Love and Squalor" is the sixth story in Salinger's second book, NINE STORIES (1953). Originally published in the April 8, 1950, issue of the NEW YORKER, this famous story features the young girl, Esmé, and the part she plays in the healing process of the war-stricken Sergeant X. "For Esmé—with Love and Squalor" ranks as a masterpiece of the American short story. "For Esmé—with Love and Squalor" is Salinger's 27th published story.

SYNOPSIS

A first-person narrator, who never reveals his name, announces that he has recently been invited to a wedding soon to take place in England. He very much would like to attend and acknowledges that he had thought of flying there. But after conferring with his wife, "a breathtakingly levelheaded girl" (131), he has decided not to go. The narrator had forgotten that his mother-in-law would be visiting during the time of the wedding. He tells the reader that he has written down some notes about the bride, Esmé, whom he knew six years ago. The narrator's purpose is "to edify, to instruct" (132).

The narrator then tells the story of how he met Esmé. In April 1944, he was one of 60 American enlisted soldiers taking a preinvasion course conducted by British Intelligence in Devon, England. After the last session, and several hours before he would leave for London to assemble for D-day, he goes into town. It is raining hard with flashes of lightning, to which he pays no attention. The narrator stops before a church bulletin board. He reads an announcement for a children's choir practice and the accompanying list of the singers' names. He enters the church and takes a seat, just in time for the final hymn. The choir coach instructs the 20 children to "absorb the *meaning* of the words they sang, not just *mouth* them . . ." (135). They sing without accompaniment, and "their voices were melodious and unsentimental, almost to the point where a somewhat more denominational man than myself might, without straining, have experi-

enced levitation" (135). He intently watches one child: a girl of about 13 years old, blond, attractive, and whom he judges as having the best voice.

After the rehearsal, the narrator leaves the church and takes refuge from the rain in a tearoom. He gives his order to a waitress and then rereads two perfunctory letters he finds in his pocket, one from his wife and one from his mother-in-law.

The young girl from the choir (Esmé), her five-year-old brother (Charles), and their governess (Miss Megley) enter the tearoom. Charles acts up, but the trio finally seat themselves a few tables from the narrator. Esmé notices him staring, and she stares back. She then gives a "small, qualified smile . . . oddly radiant" (139). Soon, she is standing at his table, and he invites her to join him. The two begin to converse, and he notices that she is wearing a large, military wristwatch. When she asks him if he attends the supposedly secret military school, he denies it, to which she replies, "I wasn't born yesterday" (142). Esmé says he seems intelligent, unlike most Americans she has met. She then abruptly asks if he is in love with his wife, a question to which he does not respond. Esmé explains she has come over to talk because he looks lonely and sensitive; her aunt, with whom she has been living since her parents' death, judges Esmé to be "cold" (144), and she is trying to become more compassionate. The narrator tells her his name, but Esmé only tells him her first name, because she has "a title and you may just be impressed by titles. Americans are, you know" (145).

Charles appears at the table and tells Esmé that the governess wants her to return. He immediately sits down with Esmé and the narrator, and she introduces her brother. Charles wants to know why film actors kiss sideways. Esmé tells the narrator that her brother misses his father, who was slain in North Africa, spelling the word out letter by letter as s-l-a-i-n. Esmé talks about her parents, describing her mother as passionate, an extrovert, and, although intelligent, not possessed of an intellect equal to her father's. Esmé idolizes her father, describing him in superlatives: handsome, lovable, a genius.

Charles taps the narrator and asks him a riddle: "What did one wall say to the other wall?" (149).

After the narrator gives up, the boy supplies the answer at full volume: "Meet you at the corner!" (149). This puts Charles into convulsions of laughter. Esmé explains that Charles tells the same riddle to everyone and always has the same reaction.

Esmé asks the narrator what he did before the war. He explains that he has been out of college for a year but thinks of himself as "a professional short-story writer" (150). Asked if he has published, the narrator defensively starts to "explain how most editors in America were a bunch of" (150), at which point Esmé interrupts, interjecting that her father "wrote beautifully . . . [and she was] saving a number of his letters for posterity" (150–151). The narrator again takes notice of the watch and asks if it belonged to her father. She explains that he gave it to her shortly before the two children were evacuated. Esmé asks if the narrator will "write a story exclusively for [her] sometime" (151). When the narrator tells her that he isn't "terribly prolific," Esmé, as she has done on several occasions in the conversation, reveals she does not know as much as she pretends, for she replies, "It doesn't have to be terribly prolific!" (151). Esmé says that she prefers "stories about squalor" (151). After she reiterates her interest in squalor, Charles pinches the narrator and again asks the riddle. The narrator makes the mistake of supplying the correct answer, and Charles huffily returns to the governess's table. Esmé soon wraps up her visit with the narrator. In leaving, she asks if he would like her to write him. The narrator says he would love it and gives Esmé his "name, rank, serial number, and A.P.O. number" (154). She tells him she'll write him first so he doesn't "feel *comp*romised" (154). Esmé returns to her table, and she, Charles, and Miss Megley leave.

A minute later, Esmé returns with Charles and tells the narrator that her brother wants to kiss him good-bye. After Charles kisses him and starts to leave, the narrator grabs him and asks, "What did one wall say to the other wall?" (155). The child shrieks the answer and races out of the tearoom. Esmé reminds the narrator about writing a story for her. He says he will not forget and adds that he has never written a story for anyone, but that it was time he tried. Esmé requests him to "make it extremely squalid and moving" (156) and asks

if he is familiar with squalor. The narrator replies that he is "getting better acquainted with it, in one form or another, all the time" (156). Esmé finds it unfortunate that they have met under these circumstances, and he agrees. Her final words to the narrator are: "I hope you return from the war with all your faculties intact" (156).

In the second half of the story, the narrator begins by explaining that "this is the squalid, or moving, part of the story, and the scene changes. The people change, too" (156). The narrator, however, is still in the story, and directly addresses the reader: "For reasons I'm not at liberty to disclose, I've disguised myself so cunningly that even the cleverest reader will fail to recognize me" (156–157). The story is now told in the third person.

The time is late May 1945, several weeks after victory has been declared in Europe. On this particular morning, Sergeant X has been released from a two-week stay in a hospital. He has been picked up by his old jeep-mate, Corporal Z, and, after a long, dusty ride, they reach an American-occupied house in Gaufurt, Bavaria. The time is now 10:30 in the evening, and Sergeant X is seated on a flimsy chair at a small crowded writing table, trying to read a novel. He has "not come through the war with all his faculties intact" (157). Sergeant X can't concentrate. He is chain smoking. His gums bleed at the touch of his tongue. "Then, abruptly, familiarly, and, as usual, with no warning," he feels "his mind dislodge itself and teeter, like insecure luggage on an overhead rack" (158). To counteract the episode, he presses his temples.

Sergeant X stares at the two-week accumulation of packages and letters on the writing table. He reaches for a book—Goebbels's *Die Zeit Ohne Beispiel*—owned by a former occupant of the house, a 38-year-old unmarried woman. The woman, a low-level official in the Nazi Party, had fallen within the arrest mandate, and Sergeant X had arrested her himself. For the third time since his return from the hospital, he opens her book and reads an inscription, in German, on the flyleaf, which he translates as, "Dear God, life is hell." He picks up a pencil and inscribes in English beneath the inscription, "Fathers and teachers, I ponder 'What is hell?' I maintain that it is the suffering of being unable to love" (159–160). Sergeant X begins to write Dostoevski's name under the inscription, but sees "with fright that ran through his whole body—that what he had written was almost entirely illegible" (160). He then picks up a letter from his older brother. Reading that his brother wants him to send home some bayonets or swastikas for the kids, Sergeant X tears up the letter. He notices that he has unintentionally torn up a photo and sees only a person's feet standing on a lawn. "He ached from head to foot, all zones of pain seemingly interdependent" (161).

Corporal Z opens the door, without knocking, and remarks that the room is spooky as the only light on is a naked bulb over the writing table. Sergeant X invites Corporal Z, calling him by his name, Clay, to come in, but to avoid stepping on the imaginary dog. Clay is good-looking, self-centered, and insensitive. He is the "photogenic" soldier, having posed for an American magazine in the Hürtgen Forest, holding a "Thanksgiving turkey in each hand" (161). Sergeant X tells Clay to turn on the overhead light. The small room becomes illuminated, and Clay sits on the bed facing Sergeant X. Clay lights a cigarette and, without anything to really say, mentions that Bob Hope will be on the radio in a few minutes. Sergeant X lies and says he had just turned off the radio. He tries to light a cigarette. Clay, "with spectator's enthusiasm" (163), comments on Sergeant X's hands shaking. He asks Sergeant X how many pounds he lost while in the hospital and remarks that when he had picked him up this morning, he "looked like a goddam *corpse*" (163). Sergeant X changes the subject by asking Clay if he has received any mail from his girlfriend, Loretta. Loretta wrote Clay "from a paradise of triple exclamation points and inaccurate observations" (163). It was Clay's custom to read her letters aloud to Sergeant X and ask him for his help in answering. Clay mentions that he recently wrote Loretta, who is majoring in psychology, telling her that Sergeant X had suffered a nervous breakdown. Loretta wrote back responding that "nobody gets a nervous breakdown just from the war" (165–166). She suspects that Sergeant X was always unbalanced. Sergeant X replies that "Loretta's insight into things was always a joy" (166). After Clay

tells him that Loretta knows more about psychology than he does, Sergeant X reproaches Clay, saying "take your stinking feet off my bed" (166). Clay delays a moment and then complies. Clay then relates the story of the time he shot a cat during combat. Sergeant X doesn't want to hear about the incident yet again. Clay explains that he told Loretta about the incident, which her psychology class then discussed. The class diagnosed Clay as "temporarily insane . . . from the shelling and all" (167). Sergeant X replies facetiously that Clay was not insane; he was doing his duty because the cat "was a spy . . . a very clever German midget dressed up in a cheap fur coat" (167). Clay wants to know why Sergeant X can't ever be sincere, upon which Sergeant X immediately vomits into the wastebasket. Clay, "keeping his distance but trying to be friendly over it" (168), again asks Sergeant X to come downstairs to listen to Bob Hope. Sergeant X declines, saying he will look at his stamp collection instead. When Clay invites him to a dance scheduled for late that evening, Sergeant X says he might practice some steps in his room. As Clay begins to leave, he asks Sergeant X if he'll look over a letter to Loretta and fix the German. Clay's mother is glad her son has been with Sergeant X during the war because, since then, she has found his letters to be more intelligent. Sergeant X tells Clay to thank his mother for him.

Alone in the room, Sergeant X decides to type a short letter to a friend in New York, hoping it will do him some good. But because his fingers are "shaking so violently now" (170), he cannot insert the paper. He tries again, fails, and crumples the paper. Too tired to remove the wastebasket, he rests his head on the typewriter and closes his eyes. When he reopens them, he is looking at a small package, which has been readdressed several times, and notices at least three of his old A.P.O. numbers. Without interest, he burns the string tied around the package and finds inside a note and a small item wrapped in paper. Sergeant X reads the note: a letter written by Esmé 11 months earlier, dated one day after D-day. Esmé apologizes for waiting "38 days to begin our correspondence" (171), due to circumstances beyond her control. She admits to thinking of him often and reminds him of their afternoon on April 30, 1944. Esmé and Charles are worried about him and hope that he was not among the first to land on D-day. She asks him to reply posthaste. In her postscript, she explains that she is enclosing her father's watch to "keep in your possession for the duration of the conflict" (172). After listing its virtues, Esmé remarks that Sergeant X would "use it to greater advantage in these difficult days . . . and will accept it as a lucky talisman" (172). She has been teaching her brother to read and write. Charles closes the letter with 10 hello's and signs off with "love and kisses," although he misspells his name.

Sergeant X, after holding onto the note for a long time, unwraps the watch and notices that the crystal is broken. He wonders if the watch still works, but he doesn't have "the courage to wind it and find out" (173). After he holds the watch in his hand for a long period, he notices that "suddenly, almost ecstatically, he felt sleepy" (173).

In a direct address, the narrator tells Esmé that a "really sleepy man . . . *always* stands a chance of again becoming a man with all of his fac—with all his f-a-c-u-l-t-i-e-s intact" (173).

CRITICAL ANALYSIS

Salinger published "For Esmé—with Love and Squalor" in the April 8, 1950, issue of the *New Yorker*. By 1958, the critics Frederick L. Gwynn and Joseph L. Blotner had declared that "the high point of [Salinger's] art . . . comes in his most famous story, 'For Esmé—with Love and Squalor'" (Gwynn 4). In 1981, John Wenke assessed "For Esmé—with Love and Squalor" as Salinger's "best short story" (Wenke 251). Readers frequently point to the story as one of their favorites, and they often mention Esmé, a 13-year-old British war orphan who has arrived at the crossroads of her childhood and adulthood, as one of Salinger's most endearing characters. After Holden Caulfield, she is Salinger's best-known adolescent character. "For Esmé—with Love and Squalor" dramatically illustrates love's redemptive healing of the wounds of war.

The complex narrative structure that Salinger utilizes in "For Esmé—with Love and Squalor" lends drama to the story, which consists of two distinct sections, each with a short prologue. The narrative encompasses three different time periods, in which Salinger likewise employs both a first-person and a third-person voice. The story ends with a final coda.

A two-paragraph prologue at the story's beginning, written in the first person, takes place in present time. An unnamed American narrator, a World War II veteran approximately 32 years old, regrets his inability to attend Esmé's wedding in England, soon to take place in April 1950. Instead, he offers as a wedding gift the story he had promised to write for Esmé, six years earlier, when they had met in Devon, England. For this reason, Ihab Hassan terms "For Esmé—with Love and Squalor" a "modern epithalamium" (Hassan 270). (An epithalamium is a poem or song written in honor of the bride, the groom, or the couple.)

It is important to focus for a moment upon the tone that dominates the prologue and carries through the first section of the story that concludes with the narrator's tearoom meeting with Esmé and her five-year-old brother, Charles. In the prologue, the narrator's jocular tone is evident as he explains that he would like to attend Esmé's wedding, "expenses be hanged" (131), but that his wife, "a breathtakingly levelheaded girl" (131), has convinced him otherwise. His wife reminds him that her mother is due to visit during the time of the wedding. The narrator informs the reader that he's "jotted down a few revealing notes" (132) about Esmé and adds that he doesn't care if the notes might give the groom "an uneasy moment" (132). The prologue evidences a well-adjusted man with a bemused sense of humor.

In the initial section of the story, the narrator explains why he is stationed in England and describes his chance meeting with Esmé and Charles in April 1944 in a Devon tearoom. As the narrator looks back on his younger self as an American soldier in Devon and his meeting with Esmé shortly before D-day, he speaks with "ironic, detached, but not intolerant humor" (Burke 346). This tone masks the seriousness of the situation in which the narrator finds himself. (The story, the reader should remember, is being written from the safety of 1950, with the war over.)

British Intelligence has trained the narrator, one of 60 Americans, for the invasion of Europe. The afternoon on which he meets Esmé is the same day he will leave for London, "to be assigned to infantry and airborne divisions mustered for the D Day landings" (133). He has already packed for his departure. To undercut his apprehensiveness, he notes that instead of having the requisite gas mask in its container, he has filled the container with books. To kill time, he walks into town in the midst of a raging storm. Of the lightning flashes, he says with feigned bravado, "They either had your number on them or they didn't" (134). The narrator, alienated from his fellow soldiers, has not spoken to anyone all day.

The narrator and the reader first see the title character, Esmé, at the church-choir practice: "She was about thirteen, with straight ash-blond hair of ear-lobe length, an exquisite forehead, and blasé eyes . . ." (136). Esmé's singing voice had "the best upper register, the sweetest-sounding, the surest, and it automatically led the way" (136). The narrator doesn't speak to Esmé; he leaves immediately after the practice. His avoidance of more soldiers in the Red Cross recreation room in town further indicates his sense of aloneness. He chooses to enter a tearoom to pass the time.

The narrator's lack of connection with his wife and mother-in-law is conveyed by the reference to his rereading their "stale letters" (137) that show no comprehension of his situation. By chance, Esmé and her younger brother Charles (accompanied by their governess) now enter the tearoom. The two children, of British nobility, are war orphans being raised by an aunt.

This scene, "delicately wrought by the author and charged with meaning" (Bryan 280), creates the bond that transforms the conclusion of "For Esmé—with Love and Squalor." The narrator, it should be recalled, is at his own crossroads: He is about to leave the safety of England, headed toward the perilous invasion of Europe. Esmé observes the narrator staring at her (her party has been seated at a table near his), and she takes the initiative to approach, which pleases the narrator; he needs real human contact before embarking toward D-day. The narrator and Esmé are in each

other's company for only 30 minutes. She is poised but retains the awkwardness of early adolescence, self-conscious about her wet hair. Esmé pretends to have a larger vocabulary than she really does, as evidenced when she comically misunderstands the word *prolific*. She displays an adolescent's refreshing naïveté with her future plans to "sing jazz on the radio and make heaps of money . . ." and, after she turns 30, to "retire and live on a ranch in Ohio" (141).

At this point in the story, the soldier's vulnerability is overshadowed by the fact that Esmé and Charles have already been wounded deeply by the war (the narrator has yet to experience the war's devastating effects firsthand). The children's father was killed in North Africa, and their mother has subsequently died of undisclosed causes. When Esmé tells the narrator about her father's death, she spells out the word *slain* so that her five-year-old brother, Charles, will not understand. (Much to the governess's chagrin, Charles has joined Esmé at the narrator's table.) Esmé's deep connection to her dead father is evident throughout the scene: She praises him in superlatives—calling him handsome, lovable, a genius—and proudly wears his watch that he gave her before they were separated by the war. Esmé has approached the narrator because she senses attributes of her father in him. The reader learns that she noticed the soldier at the church, and she now comments on his "extremely sensitive face" (144).

Esmé is easy to love and, as a war orphan, is in need of love in return. Just as she may be seeking love from a father figure, the narrator, on his part—lonely and scared—may likewise be seeking solace without being able to openly express his need. After Esmé learns that the narrator is a writer, she requests that he write a story about squalor especially for her. She also offers to initiate a correspondence with him, and he willingly obliges by giving her his Army Post Office number. When, at the scene's close, Charles kisses the narrator-soldier affectionately, the reader realizes how much the two children miss their parents and how much the soldier needs human love. Esmé concludes with the hope that the narrator "will return from the war with all [his] faculties intact" (156), and her statement tellingly sets up the second half of the story.

The one-paragraph prologue to the second section of the story continues in the first person, and in the same tone. The narrator explains to the reader that what follows is "the squalid, or moving, part of the story" and, though "the scene changes" and "the people change, too," he is still present (156). However, he adds that he has "disguised [himself] so cunningly that even the cleverest reader will fail to recognize [him]" (156–157).

The second half of "For Esmé—with Love and Squalor" takes place in a civilian home in Gaufurt, Bavaria, in May 1945, several weeks after victory has been declared in Europe. The narrative voice reverts to third person in this second section of the story as the narrator fulfills Esmé's request from April 1944 for a story about "squalor" (151). It is important to note that, here, the jocular tone that has infused the story up to this point abruptly ends.

In this section, despite the prologue's claim to the contrary, the narrator is disguised transparently as Sergeant X. Salinger's decision not to name the narrator—but to identify him as an "X"—makes the figure of the Sergeant representative of every sensitive war veteran. (Tom Davis mistakenly attempts to identify Sergeant X as Seymour Glass; subsequent critics refute his article.) The narrator portrays the culmination of his post-D-day experiences in Sergeant X's breakdown of May 1945. The switch to a third-person narrative voice "reduces the sentimental possibilities of a narrator reporting his own breakdown" (Burke 346). More importantly, from a psychological standpoint, the use of a third-person voice creates a distancing effect and shields the narrator from the immediacy of re-experiencing his debilitating breakdown. In the story's second section, the war is won, but Sergeant X is lost. Salinger portrays the soldier in stark and emotional terms. Released that day, after a two-week stay in a hospital, Sergeant X's state of mind is described: "Then, abruptly, familiarly, and, as usual, with no warning, he thought he felt his mind dislodge itself and teeter, like insecure luggage on an overhead rack" (158).

As the scene opens, Sergeant X sits alone at a table in a small room, unable to concentrate on a novel. After "triple-reading paragraphs" (157) and then sentences, he picks up another book, by the Nazi Goebbels. The book's inscription, written by its previous owner, reads: "Dear God, life is hell" (159). (Sergeant X had arrested a female low-level Nazi official, the book's owner, who had been living in the house.) Sergeant X finds the words to possess "the stature of an uncontestable, even classic indictment" (160). He can only manage to respond to the inscription by inserting below it a quote from *The Brothers Karamazov*: "'What is hell?' I maintain that it is the suffering of being unable to love" (160). The critic James Bryan postulates that the war has caused Sergeant X to lose "the faculty of love" (Bryan 284). Salinger graphically demonstrates Sergeant X's awareness of his deterioration when the psychologically wounded soldier starts to write Dostoevski's name under the quote, only to notice, "with fright that ran through his whole body—that what he had written was almost entirely illegible" (160).

Sergeant X and his jeep mate, Corporal Z, "Clay," have been together through D-day and five campaigns. Salinger utilizes Clay, the only person shown in the second half of the story in addition to Sergeant X, to contrast the effects of war on two different types of soldiers. Clay is celebrating the end of the war: He is looking forward to listening to Bob Hope on the radio and then plans to take in a dance later that night. Clay has been unscathed by the 11 months of horrific fighting, which included the infamous battle of the Hürtgen Forest. "The battle for the Hürtgen Forest has been widely chronicled, and all the histories agree that it was one of the toughest and bloodiest episodes of America's European war. . . . casualties were on a scale that 'appalled even D-Day soldiers'" (Hamilton 87). Salinger includes a satiric indictment of the obscene presentation of war by the media when he notes that a national magazine photographed the handsome Clay standing in the Hürtgen Forest, holding two turkeys for Thanksgiving. The insensitive Clay blithely talks to Sergeant X of the latter soldier's nervous breakdown shortly after V-E Day (the declaration of victory in Europe). According to Clay, Sergeant X "looked like a goddam *corpse*" (163) when he picked him up at the hospital. Clay observes Sergeant X's facial tics and hands uncontrollably shaking.

Clay, however, has been psychologically untouched by the war due to his ability to dissociate himself from his actions. (The reader learns that, while under attack, Clay gunned down a cat.) Salinger employs bitter irony when Clay's girlfriend, a psychology major named Loretta, writes Clay about his recent description of Sergeant X's breakdown. Her response, "from a paradise of triple exclamation points and inaccurate observations" (163), is that "nobody gets a nervous breakdown just from the war" (165–166). According to Loretta's diagnosis, Sergeant X must always have been unstable. Loretta and her psychology class, along with the professor, have diagnosed Clay's cat shooting as a moment of temporary insanity. The cat episode that Clay has introduced especially upsets Sergeant X, who unsuccessfully, however, tries to prevent Clay from regurgitating its details. Sergeant X attempts to defuse the memory by facetiously replying that the cat was "a very clever German midget dressed up in a cheap fur coat. So there was absolutely nothing brutal, or cruel, or dirty . . ." (167) in Clay shooting the cat. But as the critic Warren French notes, Sergeant X "makes it clear that he thinks Clay has been 'brutal,' 'cruel,' and 'dirty'" (French 77). Immediately after this exchange, Sergeant X vomits in front of Clay, which affords Clay an excuse to retreat from the room. In short, Sergeant X is not the same person he was when he first met Esmé a year ago; he is suffering from post-traumatic stress disorder. He has not come through "the war with all [his] faculties intact" (156).

Once alone, Sergeant X attempts twice to insert paper into his typewriter, but he can't steady his hands enough to do so. In despair, he lays his head on the machine. He then notices a green package (like the remarkable green eyes of Charles) on his table. Sergeant X opens the package and first reads an enclosed letter from Esmé, with a postscript from Charles. As the critic Fidelian Burke notes, "the letter is a vivid re-introduction of Esmé, capturing all of her mannerisms with statistics, her charming dislocations of vocabulary, her competence in managing a situation" (Burke 346). The words of Esmé's and Charles's letter, unlike other forms of

written communication shown in the story, "have meaning and propagate love" (Wenke 252). Esmé expresses her own and Charles's concern for Sergeant X's safety: she has written the letter one day after D-day and hopes for his reply. But due to the war and troop movements, Sergeant X has only now received the package, nearly a year after it was mailed. Esmé has enclosed her father's watch as "a lucky talisman" (172) for Sergeant X to keep for the duration of the war, "a gift far out of proportion to their half-hour's acquaintanceship" (Bryan 284). Esmé's unspoken love—dramatized by the gift of her father's watch to Sergeant X—allows the soldier to feel "almost ecstatically" (173) sleepy, with the kind of sleep that will help begin his healing. (Salinger will again introduce a healing sleep at the close of the story "ZOOEY" [1957].)

The story's one-sentence-long coda returns the reader to present time, with the narrator directly addressing Esmé: "You take a really sleepy man, Esmé, and he *always* stands a chance of again becoming a man with all his fac—with all his f-a-c-u-l-t-i-e-s intact" (173). Critics view the spelling out of the word *faculties* letter-by-letter, together with the earlier instance when Esmé spells out the word *slain* (to protect Charles from remembering anew their father's death), to symbolize the narrator's and Esmé's "earlier communing" (Burke 346). In addition, Salinger mirrors Esmé's earlier attempt to protect Charles with his own attempt to protect himself; that is, the narrator, now in recovery and in present time, wishes to protect himself from fully re-experiencing what he suffered in the past (through avoiding to pronounce the word that would reawaken his vulnerability). He thus spells out the word in single letters to keep himself "intact."

In "For Esmé—with Love and Squalor," readers learn that the unspoken bond between Esmé and the soldier is a rare type of love between people who can deeply understand and help each other. The healing powers of Salinger's narrative of injury and recovery continue to be needed and felt 60 years after the story's publication.

PUBLICATION HISTORY

"For Esmé—with Love and Squalor" was first published in the *New Yorker* magazine on April 8,

1950. The story was subsequently chosen to appear in the anthology *Prize Stories of 1950: The O. Henry Awards,* edited by Herschel Brickell (Doubleday, 1950). "For Esmé—with Love and Squalors"'s first publication in a book consisting exclusively of Salinger's work was in *Nine Stories* (LITTLE, BROWN AND COMPANY, 1953). *Nine Stories,* Salinger's second book, has never gone out of print.

Nine Stories is available in three editions from Little, Brown and Company: an exact reproduction of the hardback first edition from 1953; a trade paperback that mimics the production of the hardback; and a mass-market paperback, with its pagination differing from the above editions.

CHARACTERS

Alvin   Alvin is the imaginary dog in Sergeant X's room. Sergeant X warns Clay, when he enters the darkened room, not to step on Alvin.

American soldiers in Devon, England   Sixty American soldiers attend the preinvasion course conducted by British Intelligence. The story's narrator is one of them.

American soldiers in Gaufurt house   Ten American soldiers live in a requisitioned house in Gaufurt, Bavaria. Among the 10 are Sergeant X, Clay, Walker, and Bernstein.

Bernstein   Clay tells the newly arrived soldier, Bernstein, the story of his shooting a cat while under attack.

Bulling   Bulling's bureaucratic refusal to open some forms that evening will force Clay and Sergeant X to get up the next morning at 5:00 to drive to Hamburg.

Charles   Charles, a five-year-old British war orphan, along with his sister, Esmé, meets the narrator in the Devon, England, tearoom. Charles is rambunctious and can be controlled only by his sister. When Charles first approaches the narrator's table, he asks him, "Why do people in films kiss sideways?" (145). Later, the boy twice asks the narrator a riddle, "What did one wall say to the other

wall?" (149, 152). When the narrator says he gives up, Charles supplies the answer, "Meet you at the corner!" (149). This convulses Charles with laughter. The second time he is asked the riddle, the narrator makes the mistake of supplying the correct punch line and Charles stomps off in anger. Yet, after Charles, Esmé, and their governess leave the tearoom, Charles returns and goes to the narrator's table for the purpose of kissing the narrator goodbye. Charles closes Esmé's letter to Sergeant X by adding 10 hellos and signs off with love and kisses, although he misspells his own name.

Choir   The narrator listens to a church choir that consists of 20 children, mostly girls, from seven to 13 years of age.

Choir coach   The choir coach is a very large woman dressed in tweeds. She tells the children "to absorb the *meaning* of the words they sang, not just *mouth* them . . ." (135).

Church adults   The narrator walks past a dozen adults in church pews who are listening to the choir practice.

Clay   Clay is initially referred to as Corporal Z. He is Sergeant X's handsome jeep mate and insensitive companion through five campaigns in World War II. Clay has picked up Sergeant X from the hospital and driven him back to the American-occupied house in Gaufurt, Bavaria. In addition to Sergeant X, Clay is the only character seen in the second part of the story.

Clay's mother   Clay's mother is grateful that Clay has been assigned with Sergeant X because she believes her son's letters, since that time, have become much more intelligent. In truth, Sergeant X has rewritten or dictated parts of Clay's letters to his mother and girlfriend.

Corporal Z   *See* Clay.

Esmé   Esmé, a 13-year-old war orphan who is titled in the British nobility, meets the narrator on his last day in Devon, England, April 30, 1944. Her impending marriage, in April 1950, presents the impetus for the narrator to write a story for her, as he had promised, six years previously. In the first section of the story, Esmé is initially seen singing in the children's church choir. The narrator is drawn to her face: she has "straight ash-blond hair of earlobe length, an exquisite forehead, and blasé eyes" (136). Esmé's voice is by far the best in the choir. When the narrator later meets Esmé by chance in a tearoom, the girl is self-possessed but tries to act older than her age. Esmé speaks openly about her deceased parents and her brother, Charles. She wears her father's oversized watch, which the narrator notices. Esmé tells the narrator how her father gave her the watch before he went into battle. After Esmé learns that the narrator is an author, she asks if he would write a story especially for her, one that is "extremely squalid and moving" (156). Esmé suggests that she and the narrator correspond, and that she will write the first letter. At the end of their conversation, Esmé says to the narrator, "I hope you return from the war with all your faculties intact" (156). In the second section of the story (which takes places 13 months later), Esmé is not physically present. After Sergeant X opens a package, he discovers Esmé's letter, along with her gift of her father's watch. This reawakens the memory of their meeting a year earlier in Devon and will help commence Sergeant X's healing from a breakdown suffered after V-E Day.

Esmé's aunt   Esmé's aunt has taken care of Esmé and Charles since the death of their parents. Esmé tells the narrator that her aunt feels Esmé is a cold person.

Esmé's father   Esmé's father, whom Esmé adores, has been killed in battle in World War II. Esmé describes him in superlatives: intelligent, handsome, lovable, a genius. Before separating from his children, Esmé's father gave his military watch to his daughter, and it is this watch that Sergeant X receives in a parcel at the story's close.

Esmé's groom   At the beginning of the story, the narrator says that he has never met Esmé's husband-to-be. If the narrator's "notes should cause

the groom . . . an uneasy moment or two, so much the better" (132).

Esmé's mother   Esmé's mother has died during the war from an undisclosed cause, predeceased by her husband. Esmé describes her as a sensuous extrovert and intelligent, though not intelligent enough for her husband.

Loretta   Loretta is Clay's girlfriend, majoring in psychology. According to Sergeant X, she writes to Clay "from a paradise of triple exclamation points and inaccurate observations" (163). Loretta believes that the war could not, by itself, cause Sergeant X to have a nervous breakdown. In her view, he must have been unstable already. Loretta has also discussed with her psychology class her boyfriend's "temporary insanity" in shooting a cat while under attack.

Loretta's brother   Clay tells Sergeant X that Loretta's brother is being discharged from the navy due to a faulty hip.

Megley, Miss   Miss Megley is the governess of Esmé and Charles. She has trouble getting the children to do her bidding in the tearoom.

Mother Grencher   Mother Grencher is the mother of the narrator's wife. Mother Grencher's imminent visit contributes to the decision that the narrator will not attend Esmé's wedding.

Narrator, the   The unnamed American narrator explains how he has recently received an invitation for an April 18, 1950, wedding in England. Instead of attending the wedding, he writes a two-part story for Esmé, the bride-to-be. In the first part, he tells how he met Esmé in April 1944. At that time, the narrator is about to leave Devon, England, to make his way toward the events of D-day. On his last day in Devon, he listens to a church choir comprised of children. Afterward, he takes refuge in a tearoom and meets up with one of the girls in the choir, Esmé. The narrator's promise to write, at her request, a story for her that is "extremely squalid and moving" (156) is revealed. Esmé concludes the meeting by telling the narrator that she hopes that he will "return from the war with all [his] faculties intact" (156). This promised story composes the second part of "For Esmé—with Love and Squalor." The narrator no longer speaks in the first person, though he is still present in the story, transparently disguised as Sergeant X. The third-person narrator directly addresses Esmé in the last sentence of the story.

Narrator's wife The narrator describes his wife at the story's outset as "a breathtakingly levelheaded girl" (131). Her letter, which he reads in England, talks about the service at a MANHATTAN restaurant. When Esmé asks the narrator if he deeply loves his wife, he doesn't answer her question.

Nazi official Sergeant X has arrested the low-level Nazi official, a 38-year-old unmarried woman, whose family's house the 10 American soldiers now occupy. She wrote the book inscription—"Dear God, life is hell."—that Sergeant X reads for the third time that day.

Sergeant X Sergeant X is the protagonist of the second half of "For Esmé—with Love and Squalor," which takes place in Gaufurt, Bavaria. He is the thinly veiled narrator from the first half of the story, seen after having gone through D-day and five major battles. Sergeant X has not come through these experiences with all of his "faculties intact" (156). On the day of his release from a two-week stay in a hospital for a nervous breakdown, he is chain smoking, his hands shake, he suffers from a facial tic, and he experiences "his mind dislodge itself and teeter, like insecure luggage on an overhead rack" (158). Sergeant X's receipt of Esmé's letter and the gift of her father's watch begin his healing process, allowing him to feel sleepy.

Sergeant X's brother Sergeant X's brother, in America, wants the soldier to send back some bayonets or swastikas for his kids. Sergeant X tears up the partially read letter. An enclosed photograph is also torn unintentionally.

Waitress A middle-aged waitress is alone in the tearoom when the narrator escapes from the rain. She casts a disapproving look at the narrator's wet raincoat.

Walker Walker has the radio on in his room, where the soldiers are gathering to hear an anticipated show by Bob Hope. Sergeant X declines to go downstairs to listen.

FURTHER READING

Alsen, Eberhard. "New Light on the Nervous Breakdowns of Salinger's Sergeant X and Seymour Glass." *C.L.A. Journal* 45, no. 3 (March 2002): 379–387.

———. *A Reader's Guide to J. D. Salinger.* Westport, Conn.: Greenwood Press, 2002.

Antico, John. "The Parody of J. D. Salinger: Esmé and the Fat Lady Exposed." *Modern Fiction Studies* 12, no. 3 (Autumn 1966): 325–340.

Browne, Robert M. "In Defense of Esmé." *College English* 22, no. 8 (May 1961): 584–585.

Bryan, James. "A Reading of Salinger's 'For Esmé—with Love and Squalor.'" *Criticism* 9 (Summer 1967): 275–288.

Burke, Brother Fidelian. "Salinger's 'Esmé': Some Matters of Balance." *Modern Fiction Studies* 12, no. 3 (Autumn 1966): 341–347.

Davis, Tom. "J. D. Salinger: The Identity of Sergeant X." *Western Humanities Review* 16 (Spring 1962): 181–183.

Freeman, Fred B., Jr. "Who Was Salinger's Sergeant X?" *American Notes and Queries* 11 (September 1972): 6.

French, Warren. *J. D. Salinger, Revisited.* New York: Twayne Publishers, 1988.

Gwynn, Frederick L., and Joseph L. Blotner. *The Fiction of J. D. Salinger.* Pittsburgh: University of Pittsburgh Press, 1958.

Hamilton, Ian. *In Search of J. D. Salinger.* New York: Random House, 1988.

Hassan, Ihab. "Rare Quixotic Gesture: The Fiction of J. D. Salinger." *Western Review* 21 (Summer 1957): 261–280.

Hermann, John. "J. D. Salinger: Hello Hello Hello." *College English* 22, no. 4 (January 1961): 262–264.

Lundquist, James. *J. D. Salinger.* New York: Ungar, 1979.

Slabey, Robert M. "Sergeant X and Seymour Glass." *Western Humanities Review* 16 (Autumn 1962): 376–377.

Tierce, Mike. "Salinger's 'For Esmé—with Love and Squalor.'" *Explicator* 42, no. 3 (Spring 1984): 56–57.

Tosta, Michael R. "'Will the Real Sergeant X Please Stand Up?'" *Western Humanities Review* 16 (Autumn 1962): 376.

Wenke, John. "Sergeant X, Esmé, and the Meaning of Words." *Studies in Short Fiction* 18 (Summer 1981): 251–259.

"Franny"

Though only 41 pages in length, "Franny," with its memorable depiction of its two collegiate protagonists—Franny and Lane—is considered one of Salinger's major works. Originally published in the January 29, 1955, issue of the NEW YORKER, "Franny" represents Salinger's last short story before the author began work on his four novellas about the Glass family. In 1961, Salinger paired "Franny" with "ZOOEY"—a 1957 sequel to "Franny"—to compose his third published book, FRANNY AND ZOOEY. "Franny" is Salinger's 31st published story.

SYNOPSIS

Lane Coutell, a senior at an unnamed Ivy League college, is expectantly waiting for the Saturday morning train that carries his date for the weekend of the Yale football game and subsequent dance. More than 20 college men are at the station. Lane is one of a half-dozen on the platform braving the cold. The others are in the waiting room, talking in "collegiately dogmatic" (3) voices. Standing apart on the platform, Lane, from an inside pocket of his Burberry raincoat, takes out a letter he has reread on other occasions. Though he is interrupted halfway through this particular reading, the entire letter, written by Franny, his girlfriend of 11 months, is reproduced in the story.

Franny's typed letter, replete with typographical and grammatical errors, is in response to one

of Lane's. Written from her dorm room, the letter conveys her excitement about the upcoming weekend now at hand. She praises the part of his letter in which Lane wrote about T. S. ELIOT, while she, in turn, writes about Sappho, whose poem she quotes. She complains he does not once say "I love you" in his letter. Concluding with three "I love you's," she hopes the dance will not be too formal and signs off as "Franny" (5) followed by 16 Xs. In a PS, she tells him of family matters and that he doesn't have to worry about that night when they sneaked into her parents' home. In a PPS, she expresses her fear that her letters sound unsophisticated; she says that he can analyze why, but she hopes he won't analyze everything, especially her. She signs this postscript as "Frances (her mark)" (6).

Lane's reading is interrupted by Ray Sorenson, a classmate in Modern European Literature 251. Sorenson asks if Lane understands their current assignment, the fourth "Duino Elegy" by the poet RAINER MARIA RILKE. Lane, who does not like Sorenson, answers yes, that he understands the poem pretty well. Sorenson responds that Lane is lucky. Their interaction ends with the arrival of the train. Lane tries "to empty his face of all expression that might quite simply, perhaps even beautifully, reveal how he felt about the arriving person" (7). But upon seeing Franny debark, he waves his arm enthusiastically to catch her attention and, in that gesture, reveals his true feeling and excitement. She waves back. Noticing Franny's coat, Lane affectionately recalls one time kissing it as though it were a part of Franny herself. Franny spontaneously exclaims his name and they kiss. Franny immediately asks him if he has received her letter. Lane dissembles and asks which one. When Franny thinks the letter has not arrived in time, he finally admits that he received it. Lane picks up her blue-and-white suitcase, glimpses a "small pea-green cloth-bound book" (8) in her hand, and asks about the volume. Franny immediately puts the book into her handbag and changes the subject to her dress and a description of other coeds on the train. Like herself, they attend elite colleges: Vassar, Bennington, Sarah Lawrence, and Smith. She knew several of the girls by sight. Lane admits he could not get Franny a room in Croft House for the weekend, and she silently registers this failure. He then announces he is starved and says they should go to lunch after depositing her suitcase. As soon as Franny says she has missed him, she guiltily realizes it is not true.

The remainder of the story takes place in a French restaurant, Sickler's, a popular gathering spot for the intellectual crowd at Lane's college. With martini in hand and the very attractive Franny across the table, Lane exudes male pride. Franny notices but feels guilty about perceiving Lane's posturing. Lane, pontificating critically on Flaubert, judges the French writer to be effete and proudly states that he has recently received an A for his paper on Flaubert's work. Lane continues to dominate the conversation, indulging in literary ranking, confidently comparing Flaubert to Tolstoy, Dostoevski, and Shakespeare. Saving the big news for last, he boasts that his professor, Brughman, thinks he should try to publish the paper. Franny, ending her dutiful listening, accuses Lane of speaking just like a "section man" (14). She explains that a section man is a graduate student who substitutes for the professor and tears down the writer under discussion. Lane cuts her off and asks what's wrong. Franny admits to feeling destructive; he counters that her letter did not reflect that. Looking intently at a small circle of sunlight on the tablecloth, Franny says she forced herself to write the letter. The waiter arrives and asks if they would like another martini. Distracted, Franny gazes at the sunlight "as if she were considering lying down in it" (15). Lane calls her back to the waiter's question, and she finally says yes. Lane begins to think that Franny's behavior might endanger the weekend. Anxious to clear up the situation, he is about to speak when Franny apologizes out of guilt. Unable to remain quiet, however, she then makes a blanket attack on college professors, declaring to Lane that if she had had the courage, she would not have returned to college for her senior year. Lane replies sarcastically about her generalization and points out that her college is lucky to have Manlius and Esposito—nationally known poets—on its English faculty. Franny retorts that the two professors are not authentic poets. She begins to turn pale. Combatively, Lane demands

to know her definition of a real poet. Franny, with perspiration on her forehead, desires to end the discussion but, after a pause, answers that a real poet is "supposed to *leave* something beautiful" (19) on the page. She believes Manlius and his kind leave "fascinating, syntaxy *droppings*" (19), not poems. Lane reminds her that a month ago she had said she liked Manlius. Franny admits as much, but she now wants to "meet somebody [she] could respect" (20). By this time very pale, she rises abruptly from her chair, grabs her handbag, and heads toward the restroom. Lane, alone at the table, smokes and nurses his martini. He notices Franny's coat on her chair and is annoyed. Lane's expression reflects his worry that the weekend may be off to a bad start. When he sees a classmate with a date at another table, he pulls himself together and feigns boredom while awaiting Franny's return.

In the large ladies' room, Franny, ever-paler and perspiring, enters the farthest stall and struggles to lock the door. She sits, draws herself together, presses her hands over her eyes, then breaks down completely and cries for five minutes. Stopping suddenly, and feeling as though a shift has occurred inside her mind, she retrieves the book from her handbag and places it on her knees, gazing. In the next instant, she embraces the book, stands, and exits the stall. She cleans up at the washbasin and leaves the ladies' room.

Upon returning to the table, Franny, now smiling, looks her stunning self and apologizes for her absence. Lane asks if something is wrong with her stomach, but Franny is noncommittal. When the waiter approaches to take their order, Franny wants only a chicken sandwich and milk. Lane is exasperated by her choice. She, however, urges him to order a full meal, and he does: the house specialty—snails—plus frogs' legs along with a salad laced with garlic. Lane then mentions they will be stopping at Wally Campbell's for a pregame drink and will go to the game all together in Wally's car. When Franny cannot remember Wally, Lane responds that she has met him many times. She erupts in defense with an indictment of the Wally Campbells of the world, people who "look like everybody else, and talk and dress and act like everybody else" (24). Franny says she knows when the Wally Campbells will be charming and gossipy, and when they will begin bragging ". . . or *name*-dropping in a terribly quiet, *casual* voice" (25), or boasting that they have spent the summer break in Italy. Lane corrects her that Wally was in France last summer, realizes that he has reinforced her point, and then tries to agree with her. Franny says Wally himself is not the problem; she could just as well have used a girl as an example. The girl would have spent her summer working backstage in a theater or on a magazine or in an advertising firm in New York. Franny goes on to explain that she finds what people do "so tiny and meaningless and—sad-making" (26). On the other hand, going bohemian is not an option, as she believes that choice to be just as conforming, or in the same way, conforming differently. Perspiring and pale again, Franny wonders whether she might be going crazy. Lane observes her "with genuine concern" (26).

The waiter brings their food. Franny encourages Lane to eat, while she experiences a touch of nausea. As they chat over the meal—Franny smokes nonstop and takes a sip of milk—it is revealed that she has quit a play and her college's theater department (acting is Franny's true passion). She has decided that acting is an expression of mere vanity, and all of her previous summer-stock roles, though they were important ones, were embarrassing. She would not have wanted anyone she "respected—[her] brothers, for example" (28)—to attend. She then exempts one role, Pegeen in *The Playboy of the Western World*. But the male lead opposite her ruined it; he was lyrical. Lane calls her on this, saying the man got rave reviews that Franny herself had sent him. Franny then counters that the man was fine given he had talent, but the role calls for a genius to play it right. As she says this, she feels physically odd. Lane replies, "You think you're a genius?" (29). Franny begs him not to say that. She thinks she is losing her mind, but sums up, "I'm just sick of ego, ego, ego. My own and everybody else's" (29). Lane suggests she is afraid to compete. She retorts that, on the contrary, her fear is that she *will* compete. Her teeth begin to chatter; her forehead is sweating. The waiter returns to ask if she wishes to change her order and notices her pallor. Lane

offers her his handkerchief, but Franny does not want to get it soiled.

In searching for some Kleenex in her overcrowded handbag, Franny begins to place objects on the table, including a gold-plated swizzle stick given to her by "a very corny boy" (32) and finally the small green book. When Lane asks again about the book, a startled Franny immediately returns it to her handbag. She plays down the book as just something to read on the train. Lane wants to see it and for the third time in the story asks, "What is it?" (31). Seemingly oblivious to his question, Franny glances into her compact mirror and blurts out, "God" (31). Lane commences to eat his frogs' legs and sarcastically asks why she is so secretive. Franny finally acknowledges, but in a deliberately offhanded manner, that the book is *The Way of a Pilgrim*, which the teacher of her religion survey had mentioned. She had borrowed it from the library but keeps forgetting to return it. Lane then asks who wrote the book, and Franny begins a casual description. As Lane digs into his frogs' legs, Franny tells him that the author is an anonymous 19th-century Russian peasant. He is 33, his wife is dead, and he has a withered arm. The peasant, or "pilgrim," wants to learn what the Bible means, in Thessalonians, when "it says you should pray incessantly" (33). As Lane continues to eat, Franny explains how the pilgrim wanders over Russia seeking spiritual counsel on how to achieve unceasing prayer and what the prayer would be. She tells of the pilgrim meeting a starets (a profound religious person) and the book the starets recommends, *The Philokalia*. After the pilgrim perfects the method of praying, he continues on his travels teaching the prayer to people he meets along the journey. Lane interjects that he is going to smell of garlic. Franny then recounts a scene in the book she loves more than any she has ever read. In the scene, the pilgrim meets two children who mistake him for a beggar. The children insist that he come home with them because their mother likes beggars. The pilgrim then joins the entire family, along with their servants, for dinner. After the meal, the pilgrim stays up talking with the father about the way to achieve incessant prayer.

Lane interjects that he hopes Franny will have time to look at his Flaubert paper. She says yes, adding he might like the book, though she cannot lend her copy to him as it is overdue. Lane asks if she wants her butter. He also notices Franny has not eaten any of her sandwich. Saying she will, she asks if he would like to hear about the special manner of praying. Lane, continuing to eat, absently nods an assent. Franny then becomes completely absorbed in explaining how to say the Jesus Prayer: "Lord Jesus Christ, have mercy on me." She recounts how one just needs to keep repeating the phrase, even without faith. "You only have to just do it with your *lips*" (36) and miraculously the prayer becomes "synchronized with the person's heartbeats" (36) and thus one is praying without ceasing. Franny tells Lane that the practice purifies your perception, and that you "get an absolutely new conception of what everything's about" (37). Lane has finished eating, and he now becomes aware of her enraptured soliloquy. Franny continues to explain how the prayer's method resembles a Buddhist practice. Lane warns her that she is about to burn herself with her untended cigarette. Still entranced, Franny recalls a like approach to prayer in another mystical Christian book, *The Cloud of Unknowing,* in which one simply repeats the word "God." She exclaims over the similarity of the methods of prayer and feels that the resemblance can't be coincidental. Franny suddenly becomes aware of Lane's censure and stops speaking. Asked if she believes all this, she skirts the question of belief and defensively replies, "I didn't say I believed it or I didn't believe it . . . I said it was fascinating" (38). She then relates another like example: the practice, in India, of repeatedly saying "Om." Lane asks what the intended result of "all this synchronization business and mumbo-jumbo" (39) might be. Franny responds, "You get to see God" (39), but quickly deflects any possible question from Lane about God. Yet just as Franny starts to tell Lane what she thought about God as a child, the waiter arrives to clear the table and hand them the dessert menu. Lane asks if she wants dessert or coffee. Franny wants only her milk, and the waiter takes away her untouched chicken sandwich. Lane, who now realizes they are too late for the planned

drinks at Wally's, orders a coffee. Satiated, he attempts to placate Franny by admitting that the similarities between the different religions are of interest. However, he cannot help but condescend, expressing his opinion that all religious experiences stem from psychological needs. Lane finally tells Franny that he loves her. Franny rises abruptly. Lane asks if she is again feeling sick. Franny replies, "Just funny" (39), and heads toward the restroom. She stops suddenly at the cocktail bar, where the bartender looks at her. She reaches out with her right hand to try and support herself at the bar, and she bows her head. The fingertips of her left hand touch her forehead, and she faints to the floor.

Five minutes later, Franny regains consciousness while lying on a couch in the manager's office. She asks the time, and Lane replies not to worry about that. She recalls the cocktail party, which Lane dismisses along with the game. He declares the important thing for her to do is to simply rest. Lane then tells Franny he will find out if there are some back stairs to her room in Blue Shutters. She remains silent. He remarks about the previous time he and Franny had sex: "When was that Friday night? Way the hell early last month . . . Too goddamn long between drinks. To put it crassly" (42). Lane observes Franny intently and asks if she feels better. Nodding yes, she asks for some water. He says he will get it brought to her and then wrap up things at the restaurant and secure a taxi. Telling her not to move, Lane leaves the office. Now alone, Franny remains motionless, eyes on the ceiling. Her lips begin "to move, forming soundless words, and they continue[] to move" (43).

CRITICAL ANALYSIS

Though often perceived merely as "the prequel to 'Zooey'" (Alsen 2002, 117), "Franny," in and of itself, is important for multiple reasons. "Franny" is Salinger's last published work in the short-story form. The story is, moreover, his last unqualified success, a success that derives from "Franny's" strength of characterization, dramatic tension, and tightly written dialogue. Featuring students in a college milieu, the story depicts Salinger's condemnation of 1950s Ivy League education and its social pressure to conform, while mirroring the corruption of character such an education may cause. Salinger also uses "Franny" to incorporate his views on poetry, poets, and reading. In "Franny," Salinger's burgeoning religious influences, separately evident in his prior two stories, are combined for the first time, as he charts the spiritual awakening of the heroine. Most important, the writing of "Franny" catalyzed Salinger's realization and subsequent creation of the entire Glass family, with the character of Franny becoming its youngest member. This fact cannot be overemphasized, for the Glass stories are the work that would occupy the author during the last 10 years of his publishing career. (For more information regarding the eight published Glass stories, *see* GLASS STORIES.) As Salinger wrote in the dust jacket comments of his fourth and final book published during his lifetime, RAISE HIGH THE ROOF BEAM, CARPENTERS AND SEYMOUR: AN INTRODUCTION: "Oddly, the joys and satisfactions of working on the Glass family peculiarly increase and deepen for me with the years. I can't say why, though. Not, at least, outside the casino proper of my fiction." It is conjectured that in the ensuing 45 years of silence (since the final published Glass story, "HAPWORTH 16, 1924" in 1965) Salinger continued to write other Glass stories that might be posthumously released.

The perception of "Franny" as a prequel stems logically from the fact that Salinger returned to Franny and her situation with his 1957 story "Zooey," picking up the story line two days later in MANHATTAN and resolving the ambiguities and tensions of "Franny." Salinger's decision in 1961 to pair the two stories together into their own book creates the scenario of the reader first encountering Franny and her boyfriend, Lane, with the story ending midpage, a distraught Franny perceptibly repeating the Jesus Prayer. Turning the page, the reader then comes to another story, titled "Zooey." That the plot of "Zooey" continues the plot of "Franny" is not initially apparent. To begin with, the narration of the new story is confusingly and jarringly begun in the first person, contrasting sharply with the third person narrative in "Franny." Though "Zooey's" narrator—soon to be identified as Buddy Glass—on the very first page refers to a "leading lady . . . a languid, sophisticated type"

(47–48), the reader doesn't connect this person with Franny. The name Franny itself doesn't appear in "Zooey" until the 14th page—and this in a four-year-old letter that Zooey is reading. The first quarter of "Zooey" is dominated by Buddy, Zooey, and Bessie Glass. The reader doesn't know until nearly 40 pages into the story that this story is going to continue the plotline of the previous story. Not until one reads references to Franny coming home Saturday night, having a nervous breakdown, and "reading too many religious books" (86) does the reader realize that this situation is to be the subject of "Zooey." Thus, the longer story, it could be said, turns the shorter "Franny" into a prequel.

"Franny" is a story about a coed who is experiencing an internal conflict between the social conformity and materialism that her education and background have instilled and the awakening of her own spiritual life. Salinger, through the actions of the characters and their conversation, dramatizes Franny's conflict. At the same time, the author likewise casts Lane as a young man undergoing conflict and in the last stage of changing from a caring lover and student of literature into a self-centered man who believes that conforming to academic and social demands leads one to a successful career. In this tour-de-force short story, Salinger renders both college students with lifelike accuracy, bringing the reader into the French restaurant and seating him at the next table, as the interaction between Franny and Lane clarifies their polarity. Franny and Lane, each separately and together, are at a crossroads.

The story opens with Lane, his presence and personality dominating the action until Franny breaks her silence during lunch. On the train platform, Lane is portrayed as a young man who is experiencing his very last moments of being in touch with his feelings. At the outset, he looks forward to seeing Franny. He has braved the cold to wait on the train platform. He reads Franny's letter with his mouth slightly open (an unsophisticated pose), a letter he has read carefully on several other occasions. And though he tries to empty his face of all emotion when he sees Franny arrive, his hand tellingly shoots up, betraying his happiness. The former depth of his feeling is suggested when

Lane sees Franny's coat and remembers the time he kissed the coat lapel as an extension of Franny herself. But upon asked by Franny if he has received her letter, he begins to build a detached facade and pretends at first not to remember the letter, as if receiving it was of no consequence. A buried reference to what is happening to Lane before the reader's very eyes lies in the line from the Sappho poem Franny quotes in her letter: "delicate Adonis is dying" (5).

Franny's conflict is foreshadowed in her letter where her excitement about attending the big social weekend and her affection for Lane are contrasted with her fear of the possible formality of the dance and her not wanting Lane to analyze her. (". . . I've only danced with you *twice* in eleven months. . . . I'll kill you if there's a receiving line at this thing" [5].) Lane's behavior at the restaurant shows he has unquestioningly internalized the values of the privileged class. He has chosen the elite restaurant Sickler's, as opposed to a more common steakhouse like Mory's or Cronin's. He upholds the prescribed analytical approach to literature he is being taught in college. He is turning into a "section man" (a graduate student who substitutes for the professor and tears down a writer under discussion). As the story progresses, Lane is seen striving to conform to the actions and opinions of the abiding academic and social culture in an effort to achieve status and success. He wants to be in the right place with the right girl. He views works of literature and their authors as things to be analyzed intellectually and not something to relate to himself. He believes Manlius and Esposito to be great poets because they are acknowledged by the establishment as such. Most of all, Lane wants Franny to reflect back his inflated sense of self; she is to be his trophy.

Franny, on the other hand, has begun to rebel against the role intended for her: a coed now nearly graduated and thus in search of a husband to whom she will act as an audience. Salinger, in subtle asides, alludes to Franny's fear that, in rebelling, she may be perceived as moving outside the norm. For example, when referring to her enthusiasm for the lesbian poet Sappho, Franny writes, "and no vulgar remarks, please" (5). Fran-

ny's concern is also reflected in her thoughts about the boarding house, where she imagines that the first girl to arrive would naturally choose to take the single daybed for herself, while the other two girls would then have to share the double bed. On the other hand, Franny has become completely disenchanted by all actions and values of her privileged class. Moreover, she sees everything people do to be the result of ego, and she craves to transcend her own ego.

Franny finds herself in the throes of a spiritual crisis and losing all sense of who she is. She feels trapped and has begun to explore religion in a serious manner. Her involvement with *The Way of a Pilgrim* has focused her internal conflict, and she believes the Jesus Prayer might be the way out of her dilemma. Franny desires the selflessness of the pilgrim, and the social and spiritual equality that is portrayed in the scene she loves most in all of literature: when the pilgrim dines with a family where the servants also eat with the master and mistress of the house. Franny's physical and nervous breakdown is her body's mirroring the fact that the social situation she has put herself into is literally making her sick.

Lane's last vestiges of real concern for Franny occur in the early part of the lunch. He twice recognizes her physical symptoms and shows concern for her well-being. But once the meal is served, he completes the tragic transformation into a totally self-centered, manipulative person without compassion or humanity. When Lane tells the frogs' legs to "hold still" (33), Salinger can be seen to hint to the reader that Lane would like to control Franny, to keep her from moving in the direction she is starting to take. At the very end of the story, Salinger has Lane state in his last directive to her, "Don't move" (43). Lane's overriding concern, wanting to have sex with Franny even though she is ill and has fainted, is the final indictment of his character. Franny's fate remains unclear at the story's close, when the reader is ultimately shown that Franny has not been lightly interested in the Jesus Prayer but is literally repeating it.

"Franny's" initial publication in 1955 caused a sensation. News of the story spread by word of mouth, and eventually all back-issue copies of the

New Yorker were sold. Franny (identified throughout the story by only her first name) and her plight divided readers' reactions as to what was wrong with her. The repeated references to her physical symptoms led many readers to the then-shocking conclusion that Franny might be pregnant. As Ben Yagoda reported in his excellent book about the *New Yorker*, titled *About Town: The New Yorker and the World It Made*, editors at the magazine, prior to publication of "Franny," had pointed out this possible interpretation to Salinger. The author hoped to forestall the misreading by adding Lane's remark about the last time Lane and Franny had sex: "When was that Friday night? Way the hell early last month . . . Too goddam long between drinks" (42). Salinger mistakenly thought he had indicated that enough time had elapsed for Franny to have had her period. Ironically, readers and some critics cited this passage as evidence of her pregnancy, with the direct reference to sex providing a context for her physical symptoms. Since the reader isn't informed of the time of month in which the story takes place, Lane's reference to "early last month" (42) does not completely rule out the possibility of pregnancy. Thus, as a stand-alone story, and for any reader coming to "Franny" without the benefit of having read "Zooey," Franny's dilemma could well be twofold: possible pregnancy plus her spiritual tribulations. With the publication of "Zooey," the pregnancy inference was laid to rest. As Warren French observed, Franny "was not pregnant . . . but was, as sympathetic readers had thought all along, suffering a nervous breakdown resulting from a spiritual crisis" (French 1988, 90).

Another reason for "Franny's" success was the story's convincing depiction of a college milieu. Although Lane's Ivy League college is never specified, John Updike, in his influential review of *Franny and Zooey*, wrote, "She arrives by train from a Smith-like college to spend the week-end of the Yale game at what must be Princeton" (Updike 1). Salinger's artistry allows the reader to observe the pretentious young men waiting for their dates, cigarettes in hand, solving the world's problems in their "collegiately dogmatic" (3) voices. Until Franny begins to expound on *The Way of a Pilgrim* and the Jesus Prayer, the story is a literature major's

delight, dominated by references to Rilke, Eliot, Sappho, Flaubert, Tolstoy, Dostoevski, Shakespeare, Turgenev, Stendahl, and Synge. At the time of its original publication in the *New Yorker*, the story "did more to establish Salinger's reputation in universities than had *The Catcher in the Rye*, because the 'section man' mentality abounds, and many students and even professors—egotistically identifying with Franny—reveled to see it at last get its comeuppance" (French 1963, 142).

"Franny" also provides an opportunity for Salinger to express his views on poetry, poets, and the proper way to read literature. Lane's invocation of the professor-poets, Manlius and Esposito, allows the author, through Franny's comment, to contrast their academic, sterile poetry with "real" poetry. For Franny, "If you're a poet, you do something beautiful. . . . you're supposed to *leave* something beautiful after you get off the page" (19). The Manlius/Esposito school takes for its model the poet T. S. Eliot (alluded to in the text of Franny's letter and aligned with Lane). Examples of "real" poets, on the other hand, are also named in the story proper: Sappho and Rilke. Theirs is a poetry of the heart as opposed to the more formalistic, intellectual poetry of Eliot's followers, which was dominant during the 1950s. (The Greek poetess Sappho is likewise named in "RAISE HIGH THE ROOF BEAM, CARPENTERS," which takes as its title a direct quotation from Sappho's poetry. In that work, Buddy Glass also speaks of Sappho as a family favorite. The Austrian Rainer Maria Rilke is considered by Seymour Glass as the "*only great poet of the* [20th] *century*" [7], in "A PERFECT DAY FOR BANANAFISH.") The formalistic, cerebral poems of the Eliot school necessitated explications from literary critics in order to have their meanings disclosed. Franny terms this type of poetry "some kind of terribly fascinating, syntax *droppings*" (19). Real poetry, on the other hand, is not manufactured by the intellect. In "The INVERTED FOREST," published in 1947, Raymond Ford (Salinger's only other poet character apart from Seymour Glass) explains that poetry is found by the poet and not created from his imagination. Ford then likens this finding to the discovery of a sacred river. It is known that Salinger himself wrote poetry. One can surmise that his poems would be unlike those of Manlius and Esposito and more in line with the double haikus written by Seymour, whose poetry Buddy Glass describes in detail in "SEYMOUR: AN INTRODUCTION." Salinger, as is apparent in his depiction of Lane (a section man in the making), abhors the practice of dissecting literature and analyzing authors. In contrast, Salinger would prefer the more natural reader response, like Franny's reaction to the quoted Sappho poem, a heartfelt, "Isn't that *marvellous?*" (5). Salinger's dedication of his final book, *Raise High the Roof Beam, Carpenters and Seymour: An Introduction,* in part to the "amateur reader . . . or anybody who just reads and runs," would represent the hoped-for audience response: a more immediate appreciation lacking the intrusion of analysis.

The Way of a Pilgrim, originally published in Russian in 1881, plays a central role in the understanding of "Franny." The other two books mentioned by Franny, the *Philokalia* and *The Cloud of Unknowing,* in addition to the references to Buddhist and Hindu prayer, are authentic works and practices from the world's religions. These references by Salinger serve to create a realistic context for his characters and at the same time allow the writer to point out and emphasize teachings that Salinger himself values. The references also assist in explicating the feelings and actions of the characters. The first English translation of *The Way of a Pilgrim* appeared in 1930. ". . . I went to church to say my prayers there during the Liturgy. The first Epistle of St. Paul to the Thessalonians was being read, and among other words I heard these—'Pray without ceasing'" (*Pilgrim* 11). While *The Way of a Pilgrim* plays a decisive part in Franny's spiritual quest, the book may also be seen as the third major character in the story, centered as it is in the dialogue and action. The book is introduced immediately as Lane meets Franny. Lane, an inveterate reader, notices the little green volume in her hand. Soon, it becomes obvious that Franny does not want Lane to see or handle the book. Her embrace of the book in the restroom allows her to return to face Lane and the lunch. The depth of meaning of the book for Franny is highlighted when Lane, for the third time, asks what it is. Though Franny is actually commenting to herself about her appearance in her compact mirror, the next word she speaks aloud in response to Lane's question is "God" (31). Franny believes the book's message to be the solution to all of her problems; she has begun her own pilgrimage. By story's end, *The Way of a Pilgrim* has seemingly replaced Lane as her beloved.

In "Franny," Salinger combines, for the first time in his work, references to aspects of both Eastern and Western religions. The author's two short stories immediately preceding "Franny"—"DE DAUMIER-SMITH'S BLUE PERIOD" and "TEDDY"— introduced some of Salinger's religious interests to his readership, with each story predominately imbued with a single religion (Christianity and VEDANTA, respectively). In "Franny," Salinger references Christian in addition to Buddhist and Hindu practices. "Franny" therefore suggests the *spectrum* of spiritual sources in Salinger's work. That interest will be brought to the forefront in the remaining stories that follow "Franny": "Raise High the Roof Beam, Carpenters," "Zooey," "Seymour: An Introduction," and "Hapworth 16, 1924." A significant difference in focus, however, must be recognized in that "De Daumier-Smith's Blue Period," "Teddy," and "Franny" are all short stories still adhering to classic short-story conventions, each with the religious element seemingly secondary to the telling of the story. The post-"Franny" stories, on the other hand, foreground Salinger's spiritual themes, and their forms follow their own inner logic as they organically grow beyond the short-story genre into unique novella-length works.

"Franny" occupies a pivotal place in Salinger's oeuvre. Critics nearly without exception praise it as an example of the classic short story. "Franny" marks the end of a period of astounding critical success for its author: January 1948 to January 1955. In this short time span, Salinger published the work that secured his reputation then and continues to do so to this day: all of the NINE STORIES, The CATCHER IN THE RYE, and "Franny." With Salinger's next story, "Raise High the Roof Beam, Carpenters," the mythic world of the controversial Glass family is formally introduced. Here, the reader learns the names of the entire Glass family. Salinger's next three (and final) published works will remain within the Glass family circle, until the author stopped publishing entirely. These four Glass novellas have divided critics and readers into two camps, but with a vociferous negative in the vast majority.

Though the story "Franny" is now considered a Glass story, at the time of its release there was no way of knowing that the young coed was supposed to be Franny Glass. At no point in the story is Franny's last name mentioned. (Textually, Franny is linked with the word "glass" six times [on pages 12, 23, 24, twice on 30, and 35], yet each time with the word denoting a container for holding either her martini or milk. Lane Coutell is linked with the word "glass" four times via his martini.) All other characters in the story have surnames; Franny's lack of one makes her, in a sense, anonymous like the Russian pilgrim. Many critics, notably Eberhard Alsen, Warren French and John Updike, believe the Franny of "Franny" was not *at the time of composition* a Glass sibling.

As Salinger's Glass manuscripts are unavailable for consultation, one can only surmise that, after completing "Franny," Salinger hit upon the idea of a full-fledged successor family to the Caulfields of *The Catcher in the Rye.* Up through the time of the publication of "Franny," the only certifiable Glass family members consisted of Seymour, the protagonist of the 1948 "A Perfect Day for Bananafish," and his sister Boo Boo, who is featured in the 1949 "DOWN AT THE DINGHY." In addition, the latter story contains a reference to Seymour and a Webb Glass ("Hapworth 16, 1924," published in 1965, reveals Buddy's given name begins with a "W"). To this embryonic family, Salinger then added Walt from the 1948 "UNCLE WIGGILY IN CONNECTICUT," who lacked a surname. Salinger also added to the family his most recent creation, Franny, who, like Walt, lacked a surname in her first story appearance. That left Salinger to invent only two more children, Zooey and Waker, plus the parents, Les and Bessie. The entire family was assembled and introduced in the 1955 story "Raise High the Roof Beam, Carpenters," published 10 months after "Franny." Thus, "Franny" represented a turning point for Salinger; its writing led to a decisive fork in the road, which brought him

to the Glass family hermitage, where he remained the rest of his publishing career.

Sadly, the Glass stories, the work that Salinger held dearest to his heart—in the dust jacket comments of *Franny and Zooey* he writes, "I love working on these Glass stories, I've been waiting for them most of my life. . ."—has caused his critical reputation to suffer. With the publication of "Zooey" in book format, along with the last volume of Glass stories—*Raise High the Roof Beam, Carpenters and Seymour: An Introduction*—Salinger, once anointed ERNEST HEMINGWAY's successor in popularity and influence, experienced an ever-increasing critical disdain. The almost unanimous condemnation of "Hapworth 16, 1924," originally printed in the June 19, 1965, issue of the *New Yorker,* has been cited as the culminating reason Salinger decided to stop publishing. "Franny" therefore remains Salinger's last acknowledged success with nearly all literary critics who assess his work. Eberhard Alsen and Som P. Ranchan are notable exceptions; each has contributed a laudatory book devoted entirely to the Glass stories (*Salinger's Glass Stories as a Composite Novel* and *An Adventure in Vedanta: J. D. Salinger's The Glass Family,* respectively).

Assessments of the Glass stories by some writers contemporary to Salinger, however, seem to indicate a different perspective from that of the critics. John Updike finds Salinger's artistry still in full flourish in "Raise High the Roof Beam, Carpenters" and calls the work "a magic and hilarious prose-poem with an enchanting end effect of mysterious clarity" (Updike 52). Vladimir Nabokov was said to be "particularly smitten" (Schiff 275) with the same story. As late as 1965—the year of "Hapworth 16, 1924's" publication—Nabokov unreservedly stated, "Salinger and Updike are by far the finest artists in recent years" (Nabokov 57). Even though Updike's overall review of the book *Franny and Zooey* (as opposed to just the story "Franny") was harsh, his final sentence is an affirmative summing up of Salinger's Glass stories: "When all reservations have been entered, in the correctly unctuous and apprehensive tone, about the direction he has taken, it remains to acknowledge that it is a direction, and that the refusal to rest content, the willingness to risk excess on behalf of one's obsessions, is what distinguishes artists from entertainers, and what makes some artists adventurers on behalf of us all" (Updike 52).

A close reading of "Franny" will also yield biographical touches from Salinger's personal life. MARGARET ANN SALINGER, the author's daughter, reveals in her memoir, *Dream Catcher,* that the 31-year-old Salinger had met a stunning English-born girl of 16, Claire Douglas (who would later became Margaret Ann's mother). A stormy five-year courtship ensued. Claire, who had just completed the fall semester of her senior year at Radcliffe as an English major, dropped out to marry Salinger. ". . . If I'd had any guts at all, I wouldn't have gone back to college at all this [senior] year," Franny remarks (17). Claire had been given an ultimatum: Choose between college and Salinger. Two weeks after the publication of "Franny," Salinger and Claire Douglas wed. Some critics, calling the story Salinger's early wedding present to his bride, cite *Time* magazine's research that revealed that Franny's suitcase was a direct description of Claire's. More importantly, Claire's brother let it be known that Claire, while dating Salinger, was interested in the Jesus Prayer. Margaret Ann Salinger quotes CLAIRE SALINGER as saying, "it wasn't even 'Franny's' story, it was mine, and that's *not* how it happened" (Margaret A. Salinger 84).

Another footnote to the story "Franny" is the "recycling" of its characters, Franny and Lane, by the American writer Philip Roth in his 1974 novel, *My Life as a Man.* In Roth's work, Franny and Lane make a cameo appearance as an "ill-matched couple" (Searles 1986, 7) running a literary magazine. A character who has them over for dinner observes, "if you want to see unhappiness, you should see this marriage in action" (Roth 2006, 485). Franny is described as "bristling with spiritual needs" (Roth 2006, 485); Lane as "arrogant and, in a way, brilliant" (Roth 2006, 485). Roth has each of them provide written comments about creative works by the novel's narrator. This allows Roth to have Lane refer to a book "very much a relic of the fifties [influenced by] the upper reaches of the Himalayas" (Roth 2006, 486). By extension, this is a sly jab at Salinger's Glass stories. At one point Roth's Franny writes, "and I pray (actually) . . ."

(Roth 2006, 487), a humorous statement when knowingly applied to the Franny of "Franny." The Roth-Salinger connection reveals Roth, in a 1960 lecture, calling Salinger "*the* writer of the age" though immediately qualified "by reputation at least" (Roth 1975, 125). Roth does state that Salinger "has managed to put his finger on whatever struggle of significance is going on today between self and culture" (Roth 1975, 125). As late as 1987, Roth again spoke highly of Salinger, acknowledging that *The Catcher in the Rye* (along with MARK TWAIN's *Adventures of Huckleberry Finn*) taught him narrative voice and "what the power of a voice was" (Searles 1992, 213). Roth's repeated use of the Zuckerman family—especially Nathan—might possibly have been influenced by Salinger's earlier example of Seymour and the Glass family.

PUBLICATION HISTORY

"Franny" was first published in the *New Yorker* magazine on January 29, 1955. The story was published in book form in *Franny and Zooey* (LITTLE, BROWN AND COMPANY, 1961). *Franny and Zooey,* Salinger's third book, has never gone out of print.

Franny and Zooey is available in three editions from Little, Brown and Company: an exact reproduction of the hardback first edition from 1961, which includes the dust-jacket comments written by Salinger; a trade paperback that mimics the production of the hardback, though Salinger's dust-jacket comments are not retained; and a mass-market paperback, also lacking Salinger's dust-jacket comments, with its pagination differing from the above editions.

CHARACTERS

Bartender, the   The unnamed bartender at the cocktail bar in the restaurant helps Lane Coutell carry Franny, after she faints, into the manager's office. He has made the martinis (which Franny praised) that Lane and Franny enjoy at lunch.

Brughman   Brughman is Lane Coutell's professor who gave him an A on the Flaubert paper that Lane wants Franny to read. In all probability, the paper was written for the Modern European Literature class that has moved on to Rilke by the time of the story. Brughman is a scholar sympathetic to Flaubert, or at least Lane thinks so. Thus, Lane is puzzled that his paper, which attacked Flaubert on a personal level, would still receive an A. The reader may thus surmise that Lane wouldn't be able to impartially judge a paper if it did not agree with his own assessment of the writer under consideration. The character of Brughman, who is only referred to by Lane, provides a contrast to this bias in Lane's literary judgment.

Campbell, Wally　Wally is Lane Coutell's friend who is hosting the pregame cocktail party that Franny and Lane will miss. The couple would have gone in Wally's car to the game. When Lane mentions Wally, Franny says she does not know him. Lane's rebuke that she has met him many times triggers Franny's tirade against the Wally Campbells of the world: the phony conformists, especially of the privileged class. When Franny says she is not attacking Wally personally, she invents a hypothetical girl who is close to her very self (the girl does scenery in a summer stock company; later, it is revealed Franny acted in summer stock). Franny fears she might become one of the Wally Campbells of the world.

Coutell, Lane　Lane, a senior majoring in literature at an unnamed Ivy League college, is Franny's boyfriend. While he is waiting at the train station for her arrival, he is the first person the reader meets. At the very outset, his character is treated sympathetically by the narrator. Only at the restaurant does Lane's true nature become fully revealed. The choice of the French restaurant Sickler's, a favorite of the college intellectuals, shows Lane's pretense to sophistication. Lane's opening speech, with martini in hand as he skewers the writer Flaubert, reflects the pompous pseudo-intellectual posturing that he is learning to imitate in his literature classes. His egotism and sense of self-importance suffuse his initial speech, with Franny as a captive listener. When Franny interrupts and accuses him of sounding like a section man (a graduate student who substitutes for the professor and tears down the writer under discussion), Lane begins to combat her in conversation.

Wanting to counter her negative depiction of college professors, he proclaims Manlius and Esposito as examples of eminent faculty. Franny's view of them contrasts with Lane's, which again points out the differences between the couple. The polarity between Franny and Lane is even reflected in their use of their favorite adjective: Lane's "goddam" versus Franny's "marvellous." When Franny tells Lane she has withdrawn from the play and the theater department, Lane analyzes her motive (that she is afraid to compete) in a condescending manner. On the train platform, and twice in the first half of the restaurant scene, Lane does show feeling and concern for Franny. Thus, he is more than a cardboard character, more than the mere object of Salinger's total disdain. But as the story progresses, Lane's complete self-centeredness comes to the fore. Lane is totally engrossed in eating his meal, oblivious to Franny's narration of *The Way of a Pilgrim* and the Jesus Prayer. When he finally becomes aware of what she is saying, he attacks her nascent belief. He becomes progressively more self-serving by placating her about the prayer and manipulatively declaring that he loves her. Most damning, however, is the short coda scene at the very end of the story, immediately after Franny has fainted. Lane's telling Franny to forget about the party and game and instead rest up is not out of true concern for her own well being, but because he wants to have sex with her later. Lane's character provides vivid contrast to Franny's spiritual awakening. He embodies the Ivy League education that Salinger rails against and the mentality of the section man. Lane's last name is close to the French word *coutelier*, which means cutler. Lane is seen dissecting literature, frogs' legs, and Franny. By story's end, he embodies the epitome of a phony, a person devoid of a spiritual self.

Lane is referred to in only one other story, "Zooey," the sequel to "Franny," though he does not physically appear in the story. Mrs. Bessie Glass, Franny's mother, reports that Lane has telephoned several times, expressing great concern for Franny. Lane tells Mrs. Glass that the source of Franny's problem is her involvement with the book *The Way of a Pilgrim*. The reader learns that Lane has met both Mrs. Glass and Zooey, Franny's brother. On one occasion, Lane has told Zooey he formerly listened to Zooey and Franny on the radio show *It's a Wise Child.* According to Zooey, Lane conveyed this only to ingratiate himself. Though Mrs. Glass is taken in by Lane, Zooey, on the other hand, pegs him as "a charm boy and a fake" (96). From a reference by Zooey, the reader may infer that Lane is the editor of the campus literary magazine. The inclusion of Lane in the subsequent story allows Salinger to try to create a seamless continuation between "Franny" and "Zooey."

Eleanor somebody   Eleanor is one of three girls whom Franny knows on the train to Lane Coutell's college. Franny met her while at boarding school.

Esposito   Esposito is a nationally known poet who teaches at Franny's college. Lane Coutell approvingly invokes him, along with Manlius, to counter Franny's characterization of English departments populated with professors who are "pedants and . . . tearer-downers" (17). Franny, however, thinks the two professors are examples of poets who don't write real poems. The professor-poets provide contrast to what a real poet does: creates and leaves beauty on the page.

Farrar, Martha   Martha is one of three girls whom Franny knows on the train to Lane Coutell's college.

Franny [Glass]   Franny, a senior interested in theater, poetry, and religion, attends an unspecified prestigious girls' college. She is on the verge of a nervous collapse due to a spiritual crisis. In the story, Salinger never mentions her last name. (From a historical perspective, it was only when "Raise High the Roof Beam, Carpenters" was published 10 months after "Franny" that the reader learned of a Franny *Glass.*) The subsequent creation of "Zooey," a sequel to "Franny," has affected assessments of the character Franny in the earlier short story. As a character, Franny is now viewed through the prism of Franny Glass.

Franny has been Lane Coutell's girlfriend for 11 months. She travels by train to Lane's college to attend a football game and later a dance that she

hopes will not be too formal. The reader first meets her through her letter that Lane is reading. The letter, at initial glance, is a fairly typical love letter. But on closer inspection it shows the contrasting parts of Franny's nature. On the one hand, the letter expresses her love for Lane, but on the other, it states her reservations about his being silent about his feelings for her and being critical of her. The split in Franny's character and her feelings for Lane are reflected typographically, as well, by the letter proper being signed as "Franny" (5), followed by a profusion of Xs (kisses). The PPS is signed "Frances," followed by "(her mark)" (6) (signifying her true self). Salinger, in naming her Frances, is aligning her with attributes of St. Francis; as Zooey Glass remarks in "Zooey," "St. Francis, with enough time to knock out a few canticles, or preach to the *birds,* or to do any of the other endearing things so close to Franny Glass's heart" (170).

Since last seeing Lane about a month ago (when they slept together at Franny's parents' home), Franny has been undergoing a change in character. Once satisfied to be acting in plays, she has now quit the theater department and is becoming absorbed in religious matters, exemplified by her interest in the Jesus Prayer. The phony conformists and achievers of the world are driving her, like Holden Caulfield in *The Catcher in the Rye,* nearly crazy. She wants to meet people she can respect, like her unnamed brothers. She hopes that repeating the Jesus Prayer, as instructed by *The Way of a Pilgrim* (the book she carries with her and jealously guards), will free her from her own ego and allow her peace of mind. The fact of the matter is that she is descending into a nervous breakdown, unable to reconcile her desire to act—her true passion—and her belief that acting is sheer vanity.

Franny accuses Lane of speaking like a section man (a graduate student who substitutes for the professor and tears down the writer under discussion). She advocates a poetry of the heart, as opposed to Lane's adherence to the dominant intellectual-formalistic poetry of the time period, the 1950s. She is not aloof, disdainful, or intellectual, though she is well read in literature and religion. She is a person of feeling and sentiment. Her inability to throw away the gold-plated swizzle stick given to her by "a very corny boy" (32) is emblematic of her subconsciously recognizing that gift as an authentic expression of love. The unguarded giving with genuine feeling ("he thought it was such a beautiful and inspired gift, and he kept watching my face while I opened the package" [32]) contrasts with Lane's lack of attention and feeling for Franny.

Franny's collapse is caught in stages, almost cinematically, throughout the scene at Sickler's. The war between her body and spirit is chronicled in precise visual detail. At the end of the scene, her spirit has won out, but at the cost of a complete physical breakdown. The story finishes with a vivid image of Franny silently moving her lips repeating the words of the Jesus Prayer.

Franny, the youngest member of the Glass family, appears in all of the Glass family stories except "Hapworth 16, 1924" (which is set in 1924 and predates her birth in 1935). She is first introduced in the initial Glass family story, "Raise High the Roof Beam, Carpenters," as a 10-month-old baby. Her crying awakens the teenagers Seymour and Buddy. To quiet her back to sleep, Seymour reads her a Taoist tale. Much later in life, Franny says she remembers him reading that story to her. Like all of the Glass siblings, Franny appeared on the radio show, *It's a Wise Child*, where at eight years old she recounted how at the age of four she flew around the empty apartment. When the announcer stated that she must have had a dream, Franny countered that she knew she had flown because she had dust from the light bulbs on her hands. This anecdote is another example of Salinger's biographical connection of Franny with Claire Douglas, his wife. Claire's daughter, Margaret Ann, tells that, "Mamma said that when she was a little girl . . . she would fly up and down the passageway. She knew she hadn't been dreaming because when she awoke on mornings after flight, there would be dust on her fingertips where she touched the ceiling" (Margaret A. Salinger 3).

In "Zooey," nearly four times the length of "Franny," the reader encounters Franny's personal life story for the longest duration. Her story, where Salinger left off in "Franny," is picked up just two days after her collapse in Sickler's restaurant. The dramatic action of "Zooey," set in the Glass family apartment in Manhattan, centers around Zooey's effort to rescue Franny from her nervous breakdown. Zooey struggles to free his sister from her self-delusion in thinking that the Jesus Prayer is an answer to her spiritual plight. He must also set Franny on her proper path in life, for she possesses a true desire to become an actress. Zooey leads her to the realization that acting can be a spiritual practice. He recounts to her Seymour's parable of the Fat Lady. In that parable, the Fat Lady, who is the symbolic audience of the radio program, comes to represent all of humanity. Zooey then reveals to Franny that the Fat Lady, in truth, is Jesus Christ. "Zooey" ends with Franny, as in "Franny," looking at the ceiling. But this time, instead of repeating the Jesus Prayer, she is simply smiling in gratitude for the wisdom she has received, and falls into a healing sleep. (For a complete account, *see* "ZOOEY.")

In the story "Seymour: An Introduction," which was published next after "Zooey," one learns that Franny has become a professional actress. This information confirms Franny's successful transformation at the end of "Zooey," as she is now on her true path in life. (Moreover, in this story, there is no mention of Lane Coutell in connection with Franny. The reader infers that Franny has finally seen what the reader knew all along: that she and Lane would not succeed as a couple.)

Franny's brothers   The unnamed and unspecified number of brothers are mentioned by Franny as examples of people she respects. She wouldn't have wanted them to see her in the plays in which she performed. (Some critics cite this allusion to these brothers as support for the supposition that Salinger had already made Franny, at the time of this story, a member of the fledgling Glass family.)

Franny's parents   The unnamed parents are mentioned in the postscript of Franny's letter. The father has had good news regarding the results of his X-rays; Franny conveys her mother's regards to Lane. (There is no indication that these parents represent Les and Bessie Glass.)

Manlius Manlius is a nationally known poet who teaches at Franny's college. Lane Coutell invokes him, along with Esposito, to counter Franny's characterization of English departments populated with professors who are "pedants and . . . tearer-downers" (17). Franny, however, thinks the two men are examples of poets who don't write real poems. Manlius, like Esposito, provides contrast to what a real poet does: creates and leaves beauty on the page. Franny admits, though, that she likes Manlius, but she can't respect him. Later in the story, she invokes her unnamed brothers as people she respects. Manlius's name also appears in "Zooey," helping Salinger to weave together the two stories.

Sorenson, Ray Sorenson is Lane Coutell's classmate in Modern European Literature 251. While waiting on the train platform, he complains to Lane about the class assignment, Rainer Maria Rilke's "Fourth Dunio Elegy," and asks if Lane understands the poem. Sorenson's honesty about his own lack of comprehension of the difficult poem contrasts to Lane's facade of understanding.

Tibbett, Tippie Tippie Tibbett is one of three girls whom Franny knows on the train to Lane Coutell's college.

Waiter, the The waiter is the only person in the restaurant who interacts with Lane Coutell and Franny. After seeing that she hasn't touched her chicken sandwich, he asks Franny whether she wishes to change her order and notices Franny's pallor. The waiter provides a second witness to Franny's apparent physical distress. He possesses an understated element of concern beyond his role as waiter.

FURTHER READING

Alsen, Eberhard. *A Reader's Guide to J. D. Salinger.* Westport, Conn.: Greenwood Press, 2002.

———. *Salinger's Glass Stories as a Composite Novel.* Troy, N.Y.: Whitston Publishing Company, 1983.

[Anonymous]. *The Way of a Pilgrim.* London: Society for Promoting Christian Knowledge, 1941.

Baskett, Sam S. "The Splendid/Squalid World of J. D. Salinger." *Wisconsin Studies in Contemporary Literature* 4, no. 1 (Winter 1963): 48–61.

Dev, Jai. "Franny and Flaubert." *Journal of American Studies* 25, no. 1 (April 1991): 81–85.

———. "Strategies of Self-Defence: Self-Reflexivity in *Franny and Zooey.*" *Panjab University Research Bulletin* 21, no. 1 (April 1990): 17–41.

French, Warren. *J. D. Salinger.* New York: Twayne Publishers, 1963.

———. *J. D. Salinger, Revisited.* New York: Twayne Publishers, 1988.

Kurian, Elizabeth N. *A Religious Response to the Existential Dilemma in the Fiction of J. D. Salinger.* New Delhi: Intellectual Publishing House, 1992.

Mizener, Arthur. "The Love Song of J. D. Salinger." *Harper's,* February 1959, 83–90.

Nabokov, Vladimir. *Strong Opinions.* New York: McGraw-Hill Book Company, 1973.

Panichas, George A. "J. D. Salinger and the Russian Pilgrim." In *The Reverent Discipline: Essays in Literary Criticism and Culture,* 292–305. Knoxville: University of Tennessee Press, 1974.

Ranchan, Som P. *An Adventure in Vedanta: J. D. Salinger's The Glass Family.* Delhi: Ajanta Publications, 1989.

Razdan, Brij M. "From Unreality to Reality: *Franny and Zooey*—A Reinterpretation." *Panjab University Research Bulletin* 9, nos. 1–2 (April–October 1978): 3–15.

Roth, Philip. *Novels 1973–1977.* n.p.: Library of America, 2006.

———. "Writing American Fiction." In *Reading Myself and Others,* 117–135. New York: Farrar, Straus and Giroux, 1975.

Salinger, Margaret A. *Dream Catcher: A Memoir.* New York: Washington Square Press, 2000.

Schiff, Stacy. *Vera: Mrs. Vladimir Nabokov.* New York: Random House, 1999.

Searles, George J., ed. *Conversations with Philip Roth.* Jackson: University Press of Mississippi, 1992.

———. "Salinger Redux via Roth: An Echo of *Franny and Zooey* in *My Life as a Man.*" *Notes on Contemporary Literature* 16, no. 2 (March 1986): 7.

Updike, John. "Anxious Days for the Glass Family." *New York Times Book Review,* 17 September 1961, pp. 1, 52.

Wenke, John. *J. D. Salinger: A Study of the Short Fiction.* Boston: Twayne Publishers, 1991.

Yagoda, Ben. *About Town: The New Yorker and the World It Made.* n.p.: Da Capo Press, 2001.

Franny and Zooey

Franny and Zooey, published on September 14, 1961, by LITTLE, BROWN AND COMPANY, is Salinger's third book. The volume is not a novel but reprints two NEW YORKER stories: "FRANNY," originally published in the January 29, 1955, issue, and "ZOOEY," originally published in the May 4, 1957, issue. The two stories, however, when taken together, narrate a crisis and its resolution in the life of the coed Franny Glass. In "Franny," the reader follows her on a weekend date while she undergoes a nervous breakdown fraught with spiritual questions. In "Zooey," Franny has returned to her family home and is given guidance by her brother Zooey Glass. The book culminates in Salinger's parable of the Fat Lady: that everyone is Jesus Christ.

INTRODUCTION

Franny and Zooey is the first of Salinger's two books dealing with the Glass family (RAISE HIGH THE ROOF BEAM, CARPENTERS AND SEYMOUR: AN INTRODUCTION, published in 1963, is the second). On the volume's dust jacket, the author introduces and publicly comments on his Glass stories, explaining that the stories "Franny" and "Zooey" form part of "a narrative series . . . about a family of settlers in twentieth-century New York, the Glasses." He calls the series "a long-term project" and admits to a danger that he might "bog down, perhaps disappear entirely." Salinger states, "I love working on these Glass stories, I've been waiting for them most of my life, and I think I have fairly decent, monomaniacal plans to finish them with due care and all-available skill."

Salinger dedicates *Franny and Zooey* to WILLIAM SHAWN, editor in chief of the *New Yorker,* in part, no doubt, for the latter's having overruled the *New Yorker* fiction editors' initial rejection of "Zooey."

This dedication has since achieved renown in its own right (*see* DEDICATIONS).

Franny and Zooey's publication was impatiently awaited by the reading public. Little, Brown and Company forbade stores to sell any copies before the official publication date. Salinger ruled out all book club offers for *Franny and Zooey,* explaining to Little, Brown and Company his belief that the book would do fine without them. He was proved right when, immediately after its release, the book sold 125,000 copies in two weeks, an astounding number of sales for the 1960s. Part of the reason for this immediate success may be attributed to the buildup preceding publication. Once it became known that a Salinger book was in the offing, *Time* and *Life* magazines began preparing major articles on Salinger to coincide with the book's fall release. Salinger's publishers ran ads showing the following text superimposed over a sketch of a book: "Little, Brown and Company is proud to present the first appearance in book form of FRANNY and ZOOEY, members of a now famous family named Glass created by J. D. Salinger, author of The Catcher in the Rye." No blurbs appeared in the publication ad; just a statement: "At all bookstores $4.00."

At the time of its release, *Franny and Zooey* received more than 50 reviews, the most positive perhaps that of James G. Murray: "Salinger has genuinely come of age in only his third book . . . we find acute perceptions, sympathy, insight" (Murray 72). Murray notes that the book is made up mainly of dialogue, "but what talk it is. Here it is mood and idea and character and movement all in one" (Murray 72). Murray concludes that Salinger's characters "are interesting . . . his craftsmanship is impeccable" (Murray 73). Though the book received praise from other critics—for example, Charles Poore calls *Franny and Zooey* "better than anything Mr. Salinger has done before" (Poore 29) and Granville Hicks declares that the book "has something to say about the human predicament, and it makes its point with humor and the shrewdness that are Salinger's great assets" (Hicks December 23, 1961, 18)—most assessments were negative. In hindsight, the most important review was that of John Updike, as the opinions he expressed in 1961 continue to inform criticism of the Glass family to this day. Updike warns, "Salinger loves the Glasses more than God loves them. He loves them too exclusively. Their invention has become a hermitage for him. He loves them to the detriment of artistic moderation" (Updike 52). Updike's voice joins a chorus of criticism: Joan Didion terms the book "spurious" because of "Salinger's tendency to flatter the essential triviality within each of his readers, his predilection for giving instructions for the living . . . it is self-help copy" (Didion 79); Norman Mailer finds "nothing in *Franny and Zooey* [that] would hinder it from becoming first-rate television" (Mailer 68); Mary McCarthy scathingly attacks Salinger and his characters alike; Alfred Kazin writes, "I am sorry to have to use the word 'cute' in respect to Salinger, but there is absolutely no other word that for me so accurately typifies the self-conscious charm and prankishness of his own writing and his extraordinary cherishing of his favorite Glass characters" (Kazin 115). Nonetheless, *Franny and Zooey* quickly topped the bestseller lists and would remain number one on the *New York Times* list for 26 consecutive weeks. Published as late in the year as mid-September, *Franny and Zooey* would nonetheless achieve the status in *Publishers Weekly* of the second best-selling work of fiction in 1961.

SYNOPSIS

For a synopsis of *Franny and Zooey*, see "FRANNY" and "ZOOEY."

CRITICAL ANALYSIS

For a critical analysis of *Franny and Zooey*, see "FRANNY" and "ZOOEY."

PUBLICATION HISTORY

Franny and Zooey was published on September 14, 1961, by Little, Brown and Company. The first printing was a hardback edition of an unspecified run (undoubtedly a substantially large one given Salinger's increasing popularity at the time), priced at $4. The book's dust jacket, front and back (without illustration or blurbs), conveyed the title and author's name in a black calligraphic font against a white background. Salinger wrote the dust-jacket comments that easily fitted on the two flaps.

In 1964, the paperback "pocketbook" edition of *Franny and Zooey* was published by Bantam Books. In May 1991, Little, Brown and Company took over from Bantam Books the mass-market paperback edition and released it in the austere matching set of Salinger's four books, each bound in white covers with the author's name and the title in black. In January 2001, Little, Brown and Company published the first trade edition, reproducing the front and rear covers of the original dust jacket. The mass-market paperback edition would eventually adopt the same look.

Franny and Zooey, Salinger's third book, has never gone out of print and is available in three editions from Little, Brown and Company: an exact reproduction of the hardback first edition from 1961, which includes the dust-jacket comments written by Salinger; a trade paperback that mimics the production of the hardback, though Salinger's dust-jacket comments are not retained; and a mass-market paperback, also lacking Salinger's dust-jacket comments, with its pagination differing from the above editions.

CHARACTERS

For the characters in *Franny and Zooey*, see "FRANNY" and "ZOOEY."

FURTHER READING

Bradbury, Malcolm. "Other New Novels: Franny and Zooey." *Punch*, 27 June 1962, 989–990.

Bryden, Ronald. "Living Dolls." *Spectator*, 8 June 1962, 755–756.

Didion, Joan. "Finally (Fashionably) Spurious" [originally published in *National Review*, November 18, 1961]. In *Salinger: A Critical and Personal Portrait*, edited by Henry Anatole Grunwald, 77–79. New York: Harper & Row, 1962.

Dolbier, Maurice. "Franny and Zooey." *New York Herald Tribune*, 14 September 1961, p. 19.

Engle, Paul. "Brilliantly Detailed Glimpses of the Glass Family." *Chicago Tribune*, 24 September 1961, p. 3.

Fiedler, Leslie. "Up from Adolescence." *Partisan Review* 29 (Winter 1962): 127–131.

Fremont-Smith, Eliot. "Franny and Zooey." *Village Voice*, 8 March 1962: pp. 5–6.

Gilman, Richard. "Salinger Considered." *Jubilee* 9 (October 1961): 38–41.

Green, Martin Burgess. "Franny and Zooey." In *Re-Appraisals: Some Common-Sense Readings in American Literature*, 197–210. New York: Norton, 1965.

Hicks, Granville. "Another Look at the Deserving." *Saturday Review*, 23 December 1961, 18.

———. "Sisters, Sons and Lovers." *Saturday Review*, 16 September 1961, 26.

Hugh-Jones, Siriol. "The Salinger Puzzle." *Tatler and Bystander*, 20 June 1962, 748.

Kapp, Isa. "Salinger's Easy Victory." *New Leader*, 8 January 1962, 27–28.

Kazin, Alfred. "J. D. Salinger: 'Everybody's Favorite'" [originally published in *Atlantic*, August 1961]. In *If You Really Want to Hear about It: Writers on J. D. Salinger and His Work*, edited by Catherine Crawford, 109–119. New York: Thunder's Mouth Press, 2006.

Kermode, Frank. "J. D. Salinger: One Hand Clapping." *New Statesman*, 8 June 1962, 831.

Lerman, Leo. "It Takes 4." *Mademoiselle*, October 1961, 108–111.

Mailer, Norman. "Some Children of the Goddess." *Esquire*, July 1963, 64–69, 105.

Maple, Anne. "Salinger's Oasis of Innocence." *New Republic*, 18 September 1961, 22–23.

Mayhew, Alice Ellen. "Salinger's Fabulous Glass Family." *Commonweal*, 6 October 1961, 48–50.

McCarthy, Mary. "J. D. Salinger's Closed Circuit" [originally published in *Harper's*, October 1962]. In *If You Really Want to Hear about It: Writers on J. D. Salinger and His Work*, edited by Catherine Crawford, 127–133. New York: Thunder's Mouth Press, 2006.

McIntyre, John P. "A Preface for 'Franny and Zooey'" *Critic* 20 (February–March 1962): 25–28.

Murray, James G. "Franny and Zooey." *Critic* 20 (October–November 1961): 72–73.

Nordell, Rod. "The Salinger Phenomenon." *Christian Science Monitor*, 14 September 1961, p. 7.

Phelps, Robert. "A Writer Who Talks to and of the Young." *New York Herald Tribune Books*, 17 September 1961, pp. 3, 14.

Poore, Charles. "Books of The Times." *New York Times*, 14 September 1961, p. 29.

Raymond, John. "The Salinger Situation." *Sunday Times*, 3 June 1962, p. 33.

Rowland, Stanley J. "Love Parable." *Christian Century*, 6 December 1961, 1,464–1,465.

Updike, John. "Anxious Days for the Glass Family." *New York Times Book Review*, 17 September 1961, pp. 1, 52.

Walker, Gerald. "Salinger and the Purity of Spirit." *Cosmopolitan*, September 1961, 36.

Way, Brian. "'Franny and Zooey' and J. D. Salinger." *New Left Review* 15 (May–June 1962): 72–82.

For further reading on *Franny and Zooey*, see "FRANNY" and "ZOOEY" under the "Further Reading" sections.

"Girl I Knew, A"

Appearing in the February 1948 issue of GOOD HOUSEKEEPING, "A Girl I Knew" portrays the fledgling love relationship between a Jewish girl and a young American prior to the Nazi occupation of Vienna. The story draws on the author's personal experiences in pre–World War II Europe. "A Girl I Knew" is Salinger's 21st published story. The author, however, chose not to include the story in his three books of collected stories.

SYNOPSIS

The story's narrator, from the vantage point of 1948, addresses the reader in a first-person voice to recall the events leading up to his voyage to Europe in 1936. After he flunks out of his freshman year of college (having shown more interest in pursuing "big dates in New York" [37] than in pursuing his grades), his parents realize that their son is not cut out for a formal education. His father therefore suggests that, before entering the family business, the narrator travel to Paris and Vienna in order to learn some languages that would be useful to the firm. In July 1936, the narrator, then an 18-year-old, very tall (six feet two) and slim (119 pounds) chain-smoker, sails sorrowfully (having just broken up with "a girl on Seventy-Fourth Street" [37] on the *S.S. Rex*. After the ship docks at Naples, he travels by train to Vienna.

During the five months that he spends in Vienna, the narrator enjoys himself dancing, ice-skating, skiing, and socializing. He arranges to take German lessons from a young lady he meets in the "lounge of the Grand Hotel" (37); he undergoes psychoanalysis "by a young Hungarian woman who smoked cigars" (188). He also finds less-expensive lodging in one of the outlying districts of the city (presumably so that he can spend more money on leisure pursuits). In the apartment building where he boards with a family, he meets Leah.

A shy, Jewish girl, Leah lives with her family in the apartment (the only one with a balcony) below the narrator's. Sixteen years old and "beautiful in an immediate yet perfectly slow way" (188), Leah has dark hair, lovely features, and very large eyes that seem "in danger of capsizing in their own innocence" (188). To the narrator, Leah's beauty is "wholly legitimate" (188). The two young people begin to see each other, but only within the apartment house; Leah joins the narrator for coffee and conversation a few times a week in his sitting room.

The narrator next informs the reader of how he came to meet Leah. In possession of a phonograph in his room, he has been given two American records by his landlady. On one, Dorothy Lamour sings "Moonlight and Shadows." On the other, Connee Boswell sings "Where Are You?" As his landlady expects to hear him enjoying her gift, the narrator plays the records often. One evening, he overhears someone singing snatches of "Where Are You?" From his window, he sees Leah standing on her balcony, singing and "holding the universe together" (191). He invites himself to join her, but she, a little flustered by the suggestion, instead arranges to visit him in his apartment. During the next few months, Leah and the narrator meet often in his sitting room over coffee, where the two struggle to get acquainted across their language barriers. (He speaks "murderous German" (191), and she speaks very limited English.) For the most part, they exchange formal pleasantries, with the narrator choosing topics ranging widely from her family's health and the daily weather to American football (explained to her in his sparse German). In one meeting, he names all the presidents of the United States for her edification. In another, he

draws (inaccurately) a map of New York City. He also reads his own play-in-progress to her. These conversations (throughout which Leah blushes frequently) also reveal that she works with her father at his cosmetics factory.

After one month, the narrator learns accidentally (the topic never having come up in their meetings) that Leah is engaged to be married. As he waits in the lobby of a Viennese movie house for the film to begin, he sees Leah "neither alone nor with a girl friend or someone old enough to be her father" (192). She, very flustered, introduces the narrator to her young escort, who is "wearing his hat down over one of his ears" (192) and whom the narrator sizes up as not much competition.

During their next conversation at the apartment, Leah tells the narrator that the young man, a Pole, is her fiancé, and that her father has arranged for her to be married when she reaches the age of 17. Consulting his German dictionary, the narrator manages to ask Leah: "Do you love marriage?" (193). She responds that she doesn't know. The narrator then declares to her (in German, not translated in the text) how beautiful she is and asks her whether she realizes it. At the close of this evening together, Leah, suddenly noticing the lateness of the hour, rushes toward the door, and the two young people experience the only physical contact they would have (aside from their formal handshake) when, both arriving at the narrow doorway, they squeeze together "facing each other" (193) which, the narrator says, "nearly killed us" (193).

A short time later, the narrator leaves Vienna for Paris in order to learn some French. Leah happens to be away visiting her fiancé's family in Warsaw, so a formal good-bye does not take place. The narrator leaves Leah a note in German (the note is reproduced in the text) in which he expresses his hope that her marriage will go well, and in which he promises to write to her from Paris and to send her the novel *Gone with the Wind*. The narrator also translates the note into English for the reader and signs it as "John." He then admits to the reader that he never wrote to Leah from Paris and that he never sent her the novel.

A year later, in late 1937, the narrator, back in the States and also back in college, receives a letter and package from Leah (the letter is reproduced in the text). Leah tells John that she, now married, is living in Vienna with her husband. She also mentions that her parents are still living in their apartment building, and that his landlady, Mrs. Schlosser, has passed away. Mrs. Schlosser had asked Leah to be certain to send John the two phonograph records that he "forgot" (194) when he departed Vienna. Leah invites John to write frequently but does not give him her new name or her address. The narrator carries Leah's letter around for months, reading and rereading it, until the letter becomes so fragile that he must put it away.

As Hitler advances into Vienna, the narrator continues his college classes, aware, however, of the oppression of the Jewish people there and thinking often of Leah. He examines newspaper articles with "photographs of Viennese Jewesses on their hands and knees scrubbing sidewalks" (194), after which, in his imagination, he takes an automatic weapon from his dormitory desk drawer and climbs into a monoplane with a silent engine to seek revenge. In 1940, at a party in New York City, the narrator meets a Viennese girl who had gone through school with Leah. The girl states matter-of-factly that "Leah had either got out of Vienna or hadn't got out of Vienna" (194).

The narrator now describes to the reader his wartime military duty in Europe. As part of an Intelligence unit, he comes in contact with both civilians and former Nazis, now prisoners, some of whom are Austrians. Questioning the military prisoners, he learns of the atrocities committed against the Jewish people in Vienna, but he does not succeed in finding out anything about Leah. Then, a few months after the war ends, in 1945, the narrator is ordered to deliver some papers to Vienna. He takes the opportunity to enter the American Zone, the location of his old street and apartment building. He questions the tobacconist, the pharmacist, and several neighbors about Leah and her family. Two people inform him that Leah is dead. The pharmacist suggests that he visit a Dr. Weinstein, who had been held prisoner in the Buchenwald concentration camp. That afternoon, the narrator visits Dr. Weinstein (their meeting is not described in the story).

As evening falls, the narrator drives back to his old building, which is being used as the army officers' living quarters. He enters and encounters a redheaded staff sergeant stationed at a desk. The narrator asks whether he might be allowed to take a quick look at his old apartment on the second floor, explaining that he lived there before the war. The sergeant refuses him permission. Again, the narrator asks, but the sergeant refuses with the excuse that he has orders not to let anyone upstairs "unless they belong there" (195). The phone rings, and the sergeant reassures his colonel of having completed a list of preparations for an upcoming party: The drinks are being put on ice; the orchestra will play from the balcony; the ladies' coats will be placed in the major's room. The sergeant ends by telling the colonel to hurry so as not to "miss any of that moonlight" (195). When the sergeant hangs up the phone, the narrator again asks whether he can go up to the second floor for a minute, just to take a look at the balcony, and explains that a girl he used to know lived in the balcony apartment. The sergeant asks where the girl is now. When the narrator states that she is dead, the sergeant asks why. Learning that "she and her family were burned to death in an incinerator" (196), the sergeant responds: "Yeah? What was she, a Jew or something?" (196). When the narrator confirms, the sergeant loses interest and finally allows him access upstairs.

In his old sitting room, the narrator encounters army bunks and officers' belongings strewn around, and he notes: "Nothing in the room had been there in 1936" (196). He looks down "at the balcony where Leah had once stood" (196). He then exits quickly, thanking the sergeant, whose last words are to ask about the right way to store champagne on ice. The narrator claims not to know and takes his leave.

CRITICAL ANALYSIS

With the portrait of Leah, Salinger captures the tragic loss of an individual who, through religious persecution, is destroyed just as she crosses the threshold from girlhood to maturity. The author weaves into his remembrance of Leah, however, elements that remain indestructible—human love, youth, beauty, and innocence—values that will continue to live at least as long as his own memory will endure.

The story, told in a first-person voice, immediately seeks to establish rapport between the narrator and the reader, as Salinger employs a good-natured self-mockery in his look back to his immature attitudes of 1936. (The story spans an extended range of chronological time, with a first-person narrator in current time speaking to the reader of 1948 and the first-person narrator as a youth, speaking through his consciousness of 12 years past and prior to World War II.) The young man of 1936, who has flunked out of college and remains cavalier about future prospects, is portrayed as girl-happy, happy-go-lucky, uninformed, and untried as yet by mature concerns. In casting the backward look and in developing the youthful self in this way, Salinger is able to render more poignant the budding love between the 18-year-old American college student and the 16-year-old Leah by creating an emotional parity between the two young people. The fledgling relationship is enriched by Salinger's skill with dialogue and setting (and with humor, especially appreciated in the comical range of conversation topics—including the listing of all U.S. presidents—and the aborted attempts to communicate by way of "murderous German" [191] on his part, and sparse English vocabulary on hers). Yet, despite these obstacles, the two overcome the barriers of language and of custom to form a loving (and perhaps romantic) bond.

That Salinger intends for Leah to represent more than her individual beauty and innocence is evidenced in the author's descriptions of her: "she was probably the first appreciable thing of beauty I had seen that struck me as wholly legitimate" (188); "standing there leaning on the balcony railing, holding the universe together" (191). The existence of Leah—that is, of true and "legitimate" beauty—somehow makes the universe cohere. With her murder, therefore, at the hands of the Nazis, the just and beautiful "universe" has fallen apart. Salinger moreover bestows upon the figure of Leah one of his highest accolades, in that she symbolizes poetry itself: "Leah's knock on my door was always poetry—high, beautifully wavering,

absolutely perpendicular poetry. Her knock started out speaking of her own innocence and beauty, and accidentally ended speaking of the innocence and beauty of all very young girls" (191).

Not only, then, is the legitimate beauty of the world lost with Leah's death, but other cultural justices are trampled as well in the wake of World War II. In "A Girl I Knew," Salinger raises the issue of the respect for personal property that had been violated by the Nazi regime. The author observes that the American army likewise seemed not to remember or to respect the belongings of the victims at the close of the war. Salinger plants this theme subtly, for example, when the young narrator discloses his landlady's insistence that Leah be sure to send him the two phonograph records he "forgot" (194) to take when departing for Paris. Although the young narrator had "forgotten" the records and although the records had been a gift to him by Mrs. Schlosser (his landlady), the landlady still considers them his rightful property. This consciousness of and respect for personal belongings was completely disregarded by the Nazi regime in seizing the property of Jewish victims during the prewar and wartime takeover of European countries. Only now, more than 60 years past the close of World War II, are the victims of the Holocaust and their survivors reclaiming lost property from that illegal seizure. In the story's final scene, the contrast that Salinger makes between the narrator's memory of his sitting room and the usurpation of the apartment as an officers' living quarters, with "Officers blouses . . . suspended on hangers everywhere" (196), underscores the fact that the apartment's owners, now destroyed by the war, can never again claim legitimate restoration, either of their lives or of their possessions. "Nothing in the room had been there in 1936" (196).

The isolation that the narrator feels as he says his last farewell to Leah's place, along with his alienation from his fellow soldiers, are evident in the story's final scene. The narrator is shabbily treated by the staff sergeant, who, along with comrades and officers, is busy celebrating the fruits of victory in the carefree, postwar atmosphere. The reluctance of the sergeant to allow anyone up to the apartment "unless they belong there"

(195) delivers the bitter twist of irony—in that the narrator more legitimately belongs to the apartment (by virtue of his loving memory of its prior inhabitants) than do the sergeant or the officers presently installed there. With the sergeant's party preoccupations, Salinger captures the callous attitude of the American troops, who, without personal memory or emotional connection with those whose lives had been destroyed by the war, carry on with victory parties in the very premises once belonging to the victims. Warren French, in his 1963 study of Salinger's fiction, suggests that one purpose of "A Girl I Knew" is to "arouse antipathy for those Americans who are unmoved by [Leah's] destruction" (French 85). The sergeant's attitude, upon learning that Leah was Jewish, may infer, as well, a presiding anti-Semitism. Salinger's view of this callousness extends also to non-Americans, represented by the girl whom the young narrator meets at the party in New York City and who had grown up with Leah in Vienna. When the narrator inquires about Leah's fate after the Nazi occupation, she responds dispassionately that "Leah either had got out of Vienna or hadn't got out of Vienna" (194) and remains more interested in discussing American movie stars.

Finally, in his refusal to inform the sergeant of the correct way to store champagne on ice, the narrator draws the line between himself and his peers, underscoring his sense of emotional separation from them. His emotions are more attuned to a prior and more legitimately beautiful Vienna, a time when Leah (and not the army orchestra) stood singing on her own balcony.

"A Girl I Knew," written just after Salinger's wartime experience, draws on elements of the author's personal history. Like the story's young narrator, who has flunked out of his first year of college (prior to the American involvement in World War II), Salinger had decided to drop out of New York University after being enrolled for less than one year. Just as the narrator is sent by his father to Europe to learn some languages that may prove useful to the business, Salinger was sent by his father, SOLOMON SALINGER, albeit in the summer of 1937, for the same reason. Like the narrator, Salinger also returned to college after his

European trip. As Eberhard Alsen observes in his study of Salinger's fiction, the story "reflects some of Salinger's experiences in Vienna . . . The narrator's unrequited love for a pretty Jewish girl named Leah may also be autobiographical, for in a letter that Salinger wrote to Ernest Hemingway from Germany in 1945, he says that now that the war is over, he hopes to have a chance to get to Vienna 'to put ice skates on the feet of a Viennese girl again'" (Alsen 3). Alsen likewise notes that, before World War II, Salinger lived with a Jewish family in Vienna, and that Salinger's daughter, MARGARET ANN SALINGER, reports in her memoir, *Dream Catcher,* that her father "loved this family [who] were all killed in concentration camps" (Alsen 3). Salinger's biographer, IAN HAMILTON, contributes information pertaining to the autobiographical elements of "A Girl I Knew," noting that "Salinger, it seems certain, was in Vienna during the first two months of 1938 and very likely saw, firsthand, Nazi street mobs on the rampage" (Hamilton 41). Like the story's narrator, who, during his wartime experience in Europe, held an "Intelligence job with a regiment of an infantry division" (194), Salinger (as Alsen notes) had been "trained by the Counter Intelligence Corp. His CIC section was attached to the 12th Infantry regiment . . . Toward the end of the war, Salinger's regiment participated in the occupation of Southern Germany, and during the last days of the war, Salinger saw with his own eyes what the concentration camps were all about" (Alsen 5).

Salinger titled the story "Wien, Wien." He was overruled by the editors of *Good Housekeeping,* who supplied the title.

Good Housekeeping illustrated "A Girl I Knew" with one drawing—depicting Leah as she stands on her balcony.

PUBLICATION HISTORY

"A Girl I Knew" was published in the February 1948 issue of *Good Housekeeping.* The story was chosen by Martha Foley for inclusion in the anthology *The Best American Short Stories of 1949; and the Yearbook of the American Short Story,* published in 1949. Salinger never reprinted the story in his three books of collected stories. "A Girl I Knew" later appeared in the bootleg editions *The Com-PLETE UNCOLLECTED SHORT STORIES OF J. D. SALIN-GER* (1974) and *Twenty-two Stories* (1998).

CHARACTERS

John The narrator of the story, John is not named until midpoint within the text, when he signs the good-bye note he leaves Leah before departing Vienna for Paris. The mature narrator begins the story from the vantage point of 1948 and recounts, with self-mockery, his immature state of mind during his European trip of 1936. He then relates the events surrounding his stay in Vienna, where he meets Leah. At 18 years old, he is a tall (six feet two), slim young man who has flunked out of his first year of college. His father, proposing that his son enter the family business, sends him first to Vienna (to learn some German) and then on to Paris (to learn some French)—languages that will prove useful to the firm. John returns to college the next year. During World War II, he is enlisted as part of an Intelligence unit in Europe. After the war, and stationed in Germany, he returns to Vienna and seeks information about Leah's destiny. Learning she is dead, he makes a final visit to the apartment building where he had lived in 1936 and where he first saw Leah, singing on her balcony.

Leah Leah, a beautiful, shy, and innocent girl of Jewish heritage, is 16 years old when she meets the 18-year-old narrator in 1936. With very limited English, she visits the young man several afternoons a week in his sitting room to have coffee and conversation. During their talks, Leah and John come to know each other—despite the narrator's "Jack-the-Ripper German" (193) and Leah's sparse English vocabulary—and they form an emotional (and perhaps a romantic) bond. Leah's father, however, has arranged for her to be married when she reaches the age of 17 to a young Polish man, who, according to the narrator, possesses a "violently long name" (193) and who may therefore hail from Polish nobility. When John departs Vienna, Leah is absent from the city, visiting with her future in-laws. He is thus unable to say good-bye in person and leaves her a note. She writes to him once in New York and tells him of her marriage, inviting

him to write back to her. During the occupation of Vienna in the early 1940s, the narrator (now back in the States and attending college again) meets a girl who attended school with Leah in Vienna, but who does not know anything of Leah's fate. After World War II, the narrator, who is still stationed in Europe as part of an Intelligence unit, returns to Vienna and learns from Dr. Weinstein, who had been held prisoner at Buchenwald concentration camp, that Leah was killed there, along with her family.

Schlosser, Mrs. The landlady of the apartment in Vienna, Mrs. Schlosser makes a gift of two American phonograph records to the young narrator, her boarder of 1936. Mrs. Schlosser expects to hear the records played and enjoyed often. When the narrator departs Vienna, he leaves the records behind. Mrs. Schlosser thus, before her death in 1937, requests that Leah send both records to him in a package, which he receives in late 1937. Leah reminds him, in her letter accompanying the package, that he "forgot" (194) to take the records when he departed Vienna.

FURTHER READING

Alsen, Eberhard. *A Reader's Guide to J. D. Salinger.* Westport, Conn.: Greenwood Press, 2002.

French, Warren. *J. D. Salinger.* New York: Twayne Publishers, 1963.

Hamilton, Ian. *In Search of J. D. Salinger.* New York: Random House, 1988.

Salinger, Margaret A. *Dream Catcher: A Memoir.* New York: Washington Square Press, 2000.

Gladwaller stories

The three Gladwaller stories, featuring the World War II soldier Babe Gladwaller, his sister, Mattie, and their parents, are: "LAST DAY OF THE LAST FURLOUGH," published in the July 15, 1944, issue of the *SATURDAY EVENING POST*; "A BOY IN FRANCE," published in the March 31, 1945, issue of the *Saturday Evening Post*; and "The STRANGER," published in the December 1, 1945, issue of *COLLIER'S*.

Glass stories

The eight published stories that compose the Glass saga are: "A PERFECT DAY FOR BANANAFISH," published January 31, 1948; "UNCLE WIGGILY IN CONNECTICUT," published March 20, 1948; "DOWN AT THE DINGHY," published April 1949; "FRANNY," published January 29, 1955; "RAISE HIGH THE ROOF BEAM, CARPENTERS," published November 19, 1955; "ZOOEY," published May 4, 1957; "SEYMOUR: AN INTRODUCTION," published June 6, 1959; and "HAPWORTH 16, 1924," published June 19, 1965. In length, the stories run the gamut from succinct short stories to novellas.

All of the Glass stories originally appeared in the NEW YORKER magazine, with the exception of "Down at the Dinghy" in HARPER'S. "A Perfect Day for Bananafish," "Uncle Wiggily in Connecticut," and "Down at the Dinghy" are collected in NINE STORIES (1953); "Franny" and "Zooey" compose the book FRANNY AND ZOOEY (1961); "Raise High the Roof Beam, Carpenters" and "Seymour: An Introduction" compose the book RAISE HIGH THE ROOF BEAM, CARPENTERS AND SEYMOUR: AN INTRODUCTION (1963). Salinger did not reprint "Hapworth 16, 1924" in book format.

The Glass stories portray members of the Glass family. The parents, Les and Bessie, are vaudevillians, a song-and-dance team that retired in 1925. Les is a Jew from Australia; Bessie, a Catholic from Dublin. At an unknown date they become New Yorkers, first residing on the Upper West Side of MANHATTAN, then later on the Upper East Side. The marriage produces seven children. The eldest, Seymour, a child prodigy born in 1917, a God-seeker and poet, later an English professor and an emotionally disturbed war veteran, is the family's guru, but his suicide in 1948 shatters the Glasses. Buddy (Webb), born in 1919, is a part-time writing instructor and writer who chronicles the life of the Glasses. Boo Boo (Beatrice), the first daughter, most likely born in 1921, is a mother of three, living in suburbia. The male twins, Walt (Walter) and Waker, were most likely born in 1923. Walt, a dancer, dies a noncombatant death after the end of World War II; Waker is a Roman Catholic priest.

Zooey (Zachary), the youngest male, born in 1930, is a successful television actor. Franny (Frances), the youngest child, born in 1935, survives a spiritual crisis and becomes an actress. All of the children are gifted to a degree; each appeared on a radio quiz program called It's a Wise Child. (Salinger's erratic arithmetic, as evidenced in "Hapworth 16, 1924" in the stated ages of Boo Boo, Walt, and Waker when contrasted to references in the earlier stories, blurs their exact years of birth, but the chronological order remains unvarying.)

The first four published stories, each of short-story length, feature individual Glass members: "A Perfect Day for Bananafish" (Seymour); "Uncle Wiggily in Connecticut" (Walt, albeit, without his surname); "Down at the Dinghy" (Boo Boo; the story glancingly alludes to Seymour and Webb); and "Franny" (Franny, albeit, without her surname). These four stories are often termed "Glass member stories." The entire Glass family is featured in the final four published stories (each of novella length): "Raise High the Roof Beam, Carpenters"; "Zooey"; "Seymour: An Introduction"; and "Hapworth 16, 1924" (which, albeit, omits Zooey and Franny, who were not yet born). These latter four stories are often termed "Glass family stories." The events portrayed in the various stories span from 1922 through 1965.

Salinger commented only very rarely on his work, at least in a public forum. But on the dust jackets of his final two books—the 1961 Franny and Zooey and the 1963 Raise High the Roof Beam, Carpenters and Seymour: An Introduction—he speaks about the Glass stories. On the Franny and Zooey dust jacket, Salinger states that he is at work on "a narrative series . . . about a family of settlers in twentieth-century New York, the Glasses." He calls it "a long-term project" and admits that there is a danger he might "bog down, perhaps disappear entirely." Salinger confides, "I love working on these Glass stories, I've been waiting for them most of my life, and I think I have fairly decent, monomaniacal plans to finish them with due care and all-available skill." He terms Buddy Glass to be his "alter-ego and collaborator." On the dust jacket of Raise High the Roof Beam, Carpenters and Seymour: An Introduction, Salinger writes that the two stories "are both very much concerned with Seymour Glass, who is the main character in my still-uncompleted series about the Glass family." He reveals that he has "several new Glass stories coming along—waxing, dilating—each in its only way." Salinger concludes, "Oddly, the joys and satisfactions of working on the Glass family peculiarly increase and deepen for me with the years. I can't say why, though. Not, at least, outside the casino proper of my fiction." Since writing the dust-jacket comments, Salinger published only one more Glass story, "Hapworth 16, 1924."

A number of critics suspect that Salinger continued to write additional Glass stories after he ceased publishing in 1965. Readers will have to wait to see whether this was indeed true.

"Go See Eddie"

Published in the December 1940 issue of the UNIVERSITY OF KANSAS CITY REVIEW, "Go See Eddie" represents the first sibling relationship in Salinger's fiction. "Go See Eddie" is Salinger's second published story. The author, however, chose not to include the story in his three books of collected stories.

SYNOPSIS

Helen Mason's well-appointed bedroom is the scene in which the entire action of "Go See Eddie" unfolds. Elsie, Helen's maid, announces a visit from Bobby, Helen's brother, who has just returned from a trip to Chicago. Elsie hands Helen a robe and then shows Bobby into the room. Bobby expresses concern about his sister wasting her life and tells her to see Eddie Jackson about a possible job in a new theatrical production. Bobby asks Elsie to bring him a cup of coffee. Helen files her nails while her brother tries unsuccessfully to persuade her to go see Eddie. Frustrated, Bobby knocks the emery board from her hand, upon which Helen walks to her dressing table, where she begins to brush her hair.

Tensions increase between brother and sister with Helen's repeated refusals to go see Eddie.

Bobby threatens his sister that he will tell Phil Stone's wife that Helen is having an affair with her husband. Helen informs her brother that the wife already knows. Bobby contrasts the wife's "nice face" (122) with his sister's glamorous one. When Helen declares that she will not stop seeing Phil Stone, Bobby jabs his fingers into the hollow in her shoulder. Helen screams with pain and in turn wallops Bobby's hand with her hairbrush. He backs away, his hand throbbing, just as Elsie arrives with coffee on a tray. The sister and brother sit in silence while Helen fixes her hair and Bobby drinks his coffee and smokes. Helen then sits at Bobby's feet in an effort to make up with him. Bobby again urges her to see Eddie, and she continues to defend her affair. Helen calls Phil "a grand person" (123), and Bobby retorts, "You and your god damn grand persons" (123).

Bobby tells Helen about hearing in Chicago that she is dating Hanson Carpenter. She denies that she is seeing Hanson. Bobby worries about her reputation and doesn't want to believe what other men say, telling Helen that she "used to be such a swell kid" (123). Bobby then informs her that he has had lunch with Phil Stone's wife, who he describes as "a swell kid. Class"(124). Bobby repeats his plea for Helen to see Eddie about the possible job he has lined up for her, and then takes his leave. Helen immediately phones Phil Stone to complain that his wife has told Bobby about their relationship. Helen refuses Phil's request to see her that day, and she tells him he can contact her tomorrow. She next phones Hanson Carpenter. The story ends on her opening line of the phone conversation, in which she calls Hanson "you dog" (124).

CRITICAL ANALYSIS

At the time of writing "Go See Eddie," Salinger was very interested in the theater. This interest may be seen to inform the story's structure—its plot and conflict—which resemble the elements and pacing of a one-act play. The entire scene, its dialogue and action, takes place in Helen Mason's bedroom. In addition to Helen, only two other characters appear—her brother, Bobby, and her maid, Elsie—who enter and exit the bedroom. The conflict between the brother and sister focuses on one theme—Helen's virtue—a serious moral question during the time "Go See Eddie" was published. Bobby wants to help Helen become a working showgirl instead of a girl men talk about when they talk about loose women. Helen, as the story reveals, is in fact a "kept woman." The story's title and the repeating phrase, "see Eddie" (122, 124), are meant to indicate a conflict between Helen's wanting to have affairs and Bobby's wanting her to work.

"Go See Eddie" represents Salinger's first "family" story, and one in which readers see Salinger's characters seemingly driven to focus on their sibling relationships with intimate concern and commitment.

The language and characters, in addition to the narrative's ambiguous ending, portend later developments in Salinger's fiction. For example, the author's use of "swell" makes a contrast between Helen's loose ways (Bobby tells Helen she "used to be such a swell kid" [123]) and a married woman's virtue (Bobby describes Stone's wife as "a swell kid" [124]). A similar contrast may be seen in Salinger's later story "UNCLE WIGGILY IN CONNECTICUT." In that 1948 story (collected in NINE STORIES), the now-hardened Eloise wants her former college friend to acknowledge that she, Eloise, was once "a nice girl" (56). Bobby Mason describes Stone's wife as having "just a nice face" (122). Bobby's description represents Salinger's first use of the word "nice," the same word that Holden Caulfield in The CATCHER IN THE RYE repeatedly invokes whenever he likes something. And, like Holden, Bobby Mason shows himself to detest the word "grand" and what it represents (when he admonishes Helen for calling everyone a "grand" person).

Helen Mason may be seen, moreover, as a prototypical Muriel Glass (Seymour's wife in "A PERFECT DAY FOR BANANAFISH"). In that later story by Salinger, Muriel is described as a girl who dropped nothing for a ringing phone (she is polishing her nails) even though she has been waiting for two and one-half hours for the phone call. In "Go See Eddie," Salinger depicts Helen filing her nails with an emery board that may be taken as her defensive weapon, one that shields her from her brother's insistence that she get a job. Helen continues to file while Bobby continues to urge her to see Eddie for a job until he slaps the emery board out of her hands. She ignores her brother's aggression, picks up her brush, and begins brushing her red hair. When Bobby once again becomes too aggressive, Helen uses her brush to slam his hand. With Helen's actions, Salinger dramatizes Helen's real sword and shield to be her beauty (thus connecting her first name, Helen, with Homer's Helen of Troy and, likewise, showing Helen Mason, like Helen of Troy, to be dependent upon her beauty for her power and her survival. Her beauty—although an asset—however also leads her to become a pawn in the game of men's sexual conquest).

The apparent ambiguity presented by the conclusion of "Go See Eddie" forces the reader to decipher the meaning of Helen's final actions. After Helen phones Phil Stone to complain that his wife has told Bobby about their affair, she rebuffs Stone's desire to see her that evening. However, she also informs him that he can phone her tomorrow. The telling detail in the story happens next: Helen bites her cuticle "thoughtfully" (124) and then commands the maid to remove Bobby's coffee tray. These two actions indicate Helen's refusal to acquiesce to Bobby's pleas to "go see Eddie" (i.e., to get a job to support herself) and, moreover, to release Phil Stone from the relationship. Helen then phones Hanson Carpenter, and her opening line (which ends the story) concludes with the playful phrase "you dog" (124); the endearment is Helen's ploy to solidify her relationship with Hanson. Helen has no intention to release the married Phil Stone from her clutches (he can call her tomorrow). The reader deduces that Helen will not be going to see Eddie about a job.

"Go See Eddie" was not known to Salinger scholars until February 1965. Warren French's article, "An Unnoticed Salinger Story," revealed that J. C. Cederstrom had discovered the unknown-to-date story in the back files of the *University of Kansas City Review*. No other undocumented Salinger stories have been discovered.

PUBLICATION HISTORY

"Go See Eddie" was published in the December 1940 issue of the *University of Kansas City Review*.

Salinger chose not to include the story in his three books of collected stories. "Go See Eddie" was reprinted without the author's knowledge in *Fiction: Form and Experience*, edited by William M. Jones in 1969, and in the illegal, bootleg edition *The COMPLETE UNCOLLECTED SHORT STORIES OF J. D. SALINGER* in 1974. The successor publication of the *University of Kansas City Review—New Letters*—reprinted the story in its fall 1978 issue. "Go See Eddie" also appeared in the 1998 unauthorized volume *TWENTY-TWO STORIES*.

CHARACTERS

Carpenter, Hanson   Hanson Carpenter, a rich man in Chicago, is one of Helen Mason's boyfriends. He has evidently been boasting about his affair with her. The story ends with Helen phoning Hanson and calling him "you dog" (124).

Elsie   Elsie, Helen Mason's maid, announces Bobby Mason's arrival and later brings him coffee.

Jackson, Eddie   Eddie Jackson, the "Eddie" of the story's title, is producing a new show that Bobby Mason wants his sister Helen to try out for. Helen says that Eddie always makes passes at her and that he keeps her in the back of the chorus line.

Mason, Bobby   Bobby Mason, Helen's brother, attempts to persuade Helen to change the direction of her life.

Mason, Helen   Helen Mason, Bobby's sister and the protagonist of the story, is carrying on affairs with at least two men, Phil Stone and Hanson Carpenter. Helen forcefully resists her brother's suggestion to go see Eddie Jackson about a job in his new show.

Phil Stone's wife   Phil Stone's wife is aware of the affair between her husband and Helen Mason. Bobby Mason contrasts the wife's "nice face" (122) with his sister Helen's glamorous one.

Stone, Phil   Phil Stone, a married man, is having an affair with Helen Mason. When Helen phones him, he insists on seeing her that day to no avail. Helen, however, tells Phil she will see him tomorrow.

FURTHER READING

French, Warren. "An Unnoticed Salinger Story." *College English* 26, no. 5 (February 1965): 394–395.
Wenke, John. *J. D. Salinger: A Study of the Short Fiction.* Boston: Twayne Publishers, 1991.

"Hang of It, The"

Published in the July 12, 1941, issue of *COLLIER'S*, "The Hang of It" is Salinger's first story with a war-related theme. A year later, the story was reprinted in an anthology, *The KITBOOK FOR SOLDIERS, SAILORS, AND MARINES*, and thus represents Salinger's first publication in a book. "The Hang of It" is Salinger's third published story. The author, however, chose not to include the story in his three books of collected stories.

SYNOPSIS

The narrator, whose name is not revealed until the end, begins by stating that his son, Harry, has been recently drafted into the army. His son reminds the narrator of a man he himself served with in 1917, a "Bobby Pettit." Pettit was an inept recruit; his repeated failures to learn and perform the activities of army life drove his drill sergeant, Grogan, to distraction. Each time Grogan criticized or made fun of "Bobby Pettit," Pettit's response would be, "I'll get the hang of it" (22). The narrator then recounts Pettit's final failure, after which the recruit tells Grogan that he likes being in the army and goes on to predict that one day he'll "be a colonel" (22).

The narrator has not told his wife that their son, Harry, reminds him of "Bobby Pettit." He adds that Harry is having trouble with his sergeant, just as Pettit had done. The narrator believes that his son likes the army and that Harry's problems with his first sergeant will be resolved when his son learns "the hang of it" (22). The narrator's wife complains about the behavior of the sergeant and about the fact that the colonel of the regiment won't intervene on Harry's behalf.

Finally, the narrator recalls the events of a few Sundays ago. He and his wife are together in a reviewing stand for a parade. They observe their son marching out of step and even dropping his rifle. When the parade ends, Harry's sergeant, whose name is revealed to be Grogan, approaches the narrator and his wife to pay his respects. Grogan addresses the wife as "Mrs. Pettit." When the narrator asks whether there is a chance his son will succeed in the army, the sergeant grinningly replies, "No," addressing the narrator as "Colonel Pettit." This surprise ending reveals to the reader that Grogan had been sergeant to Bobby Pettit and is currently sergeant to Harry Pettit. The "Bobby Pettit" of 1917 has indeed become Colonel Bobby Pettit of 1941.

CRITICAL ANALYSIS

"The Hang of It," Salinger's first publication in a "slick" magazine, marks the point where the author aims his nascent writing career at a larger readership. (The term "slick" not only refers to paper stock but to the types of widely distributed publications that would use photographs and illustrations to attract more readers and better advertising revenues.)

To introduce the story, *Collier's* offers the tag line, "A SHORT SHORT STORY COMPLETE ON THIS PAGE [emphasis added]" (22), with half of the page given over to an illustration depicting a sergeant glaring at a soldier shooting a rifle. The two figures display comic-book expressions, the sergeant scowling and the prone soldier shooting with his eyes wide open and mouth agape. (This type of illustration accompanying a story was common to "slick" magazines of the period.)

Although not a complex or seemingly important story, "The Hang of It" is a patriotic tale that depends on a surprise twist at its end. Yet, both Bobby Pettit's and his son Harry's difficulties with getting "the hang" of army life might possibly be viewed as germinal seeds for elements of Holden Caulfield's difficulties at Pencey Prep in *The CATCHER IN THE RYE*. In 1941, Salinger continued to make "young folks" a growing part of his fiction, and to sharpen his foci on maturation and adjustment issues. In this story, the difficulties of adjusting to military life are shown to be heredi-

tary—both Pettits share traits that the same drill sergeant detests, and both father and son use the same trial-and-error persistence to remain positive about being in the army. The narrative moreover experiments with the use of family relationships to enable unreliable narration and plot twists. At the time "The Hang of It" was published, the United States was beginning to see the configuration of the elements of war. Salinger, however, had already lived and worked overseas in Europe, had been educated at a military prep school, and more than likely sensed more keenly than most the eventual entry of the United States into World War II.

Salinger began his collaboration with DOROTHY OLDING, a literary agent in the Harold Ober Agency, in 1941, and the year marks a pivotal one for the young author. Not only was the *Collier's* publication followed up by *ESQUIRE'S* acceptance of "THE HEART OF A BROKEN STORY," but the *NEW YORKER* also accepted "SLIGHT REBELLION OFF MADISON" for publication in 1941. (To Salinger's dismay, the *New Yorker* delayed publication of "Slight Rebellion Off Madison" due to the bombing of Pearl Harbor and America's entry into the war.) Salinger's growth as a writer may be attributed not only to the development of his talent but also to his ability to attune his work to "slick" publications' styles and reader expectations. This combination of skills marks a clear starting point for an emerging writer who will eventually move beyond the writing of fiction geared only to the literary expectations of his time.

PUBLICATION HISTORY

"The Hang of It" was published in the July 12, 1941, issue of *Collier's*. The story was chosen by R. M. Barrows for inclusion in an anthology, *The Kitbook for Soldiers, Sailors, and Marines*, published in 1942. Salinger never reprinted the story in his three books of collected stories. "The Hang of It" later appeared in the bootleg editions *The COMPLETE UNCOLLECTED SHORT STORIES OF J. D. SALINGER* (1974) and *TWENTY-TWO STORIES* (1998).

CHARACTERS

Grogan, Sergeant Grogan is a career sergeant who drilled both Bobby Pettit in 1917 and Harry Pettit in 1941.

Narrator   See Pettit, Colonel.

Pettit, Bobby   Bobby Pettit, the inept recruit of 1917, reminds the narrator of his son, Harry. Bobby's standard reply to Sergeant Grogan's criticisms is the phrase, "I'll get the hang of it" (22). Bobby predicts that he will master army life to one day become a colonel.

Pettit, Colonel   Colonel Pettit is the story's narrator, although this fact is not revealed until the final sentence. The narrator, at an earlier age, is actually the "Bobby Pettit" of whom he speaks in the third person.

Pettit, Harry   Harry Pettit, the son of Colonel and Mrs. Pettit, is having problems getting the hang of army life in 1941.

Pettit, Mrs.   Mrs. Pettit, married to Colonel Pettit, believes that Sergeant Grogan is too rough on the young men in the army, one of whom is her son, Harry.

FURTHER READING

Lundquist, James. *J. D. Salinger.* New York: Ungar, 1979.
Purcell, William F. "World War II and the Early Fiction of J. D. Salinger." *Studies in American Literature* 28 (1991): 77–93.

"Hapworth 16, 1924"

"Hapworth 16, 1924," published in the June 19, 1965, issue of the NEW YORKER, was Salinger's last story to appear during his lifetime. Apart from a short prologue by Buddy Glass, the novella-length story consists entirely of a letter written by Seymour Glass, age seven, addressed to his family from summer camp. "Hapworth 16, 1924" is Salinger's 35th published story. The author, however, never reprinted the story in a book.

SYNOPSIS

"Hapworth 16, 1924" begins with a succinct, four-paragraph prologue written by Buddy Glass. Buddy tells the reader his name and age (46). He states his belief that his life's purpose is to illuminate the life of his eldest brother, Seymour, who committed suicide in 1948 at the age of 31. Buddy informs the reader that he plans to reproduce "an exact copy" (32) of one of Seymour's letters. He adds that he had not seen the letter until today, but that his mother, Bessie, recently mailed it to him. He had spoken with her on the telephone concerning a story he was in the process of writing. The story's subject is an important party that Bessie, her husband Les, Seymour, and Buddy had attended in 1926. Buddy remarks that this "fact has some small but . . . marvellous relevance to the letter" (32). Buddy reiterates that he is about to start typing the letter exactly as Seymour wrote it and concludes with the present date: May 28, 1965.

After a "bullet" mark, the reader encounters the return address of the letter: "Camp Simon Hapworth / Hapworth Lake / Hapworth, Maine / Hapworth 16, 1924, or quite / in the lap of the gods!!" (32). The salutation is addressed to Seymour's parents, Bessie and Les, and his three siblings—Beatrice (Boo Boo), Walter (Walt), and Waker—as Buddy is with Seymour at Camp Simon Hapworth.

Seymour tells his family that Buddy, at the moment, is elsewhere and, while his younger brother can withstand separations from family, he cannot. Seymour believes that the letter will afford him an opportunity to practice his "new and entirely trivial mastery of written construction and decent sentence formation" (32). He requests that a portion of the letter be shown to Miss Overman, a librarian, for possible writing errors, though he fears she will instead focus on his penmanship. Although his penmanship should improve with age, he acknowledges that it now reflects his "personal instability and too much emotion" (33).

After a short digression about the inadequacies of the food at camp, as prepared by Mr. and Mrs. Nelson, Seymour returns to the subject of Miss Overman. He laments that Miss Overman draws the wrong conclusions from the fact that he is "an omnivorous reader" (33) and states: "ninety-eight per cent of [his] life, thank God, has nothing to do with the dubious pursuit of knowledge" (33).

Turning to camp life, Seymour remarks about the campers' tendency to join cliques. He is relieved that most of the children are down to earth when spoken with one-on-one. The camp counselors, however, are harshly assessed. Seymour muses about the mistakes parents make in naming their children and calls his own name "quite a gigantic, innocent mistake" (34). Seymour likens his name problem to that of another child, Griffith Hammersmith, and remarks that he, Seymour, is seven years old, as is Griffith. Griffith, who suffers from a pronounced speech impediment (and who is also a bed-wetter), follows the Glass brothers around camp and has become their friend. When Griffith's mother visits camp, she is dismayed to see that her son is consorting with Seymour and Buddy. Initially, Buddy and Seymour were assigned to sleep in different bungalows, but Buddy convinced Mrs. Happy, the wife of the camp director, to allow them to bunk together.

Seymour segues into a description of Mrs. Happy, a very attractive, 22-year-old woman in her second or third month of pregnancy. She is a big fan of Bessie and Les Glass's vaudeville act and confides in Seymour about the state of her marriage. Seymour freely admits that Mrs. Happy arouses his "unlimited sensuality" (35). He next addresses his father directly, asking Les to share his own childhood fantasies about sensuality with Seymour (who again remarks that he is seven years old) and with Buddy (who, at age five, is beginning to become aware of his own sensuality). Seymour hopes that Les's disclosure might help him combat the lure of the flesh later in life, because "there is monumental work to be done in this appearance" and his "time is too limited" (36). Seymour comments on Mr. Happy's previous incarnation as a ropemaker; he adds that he is trying to reduce these "glimpses" (38) into other people's past lives.

Seymour warns Les that "this is going to be a very long letter" (38) and gives his father permission not to read the entire communication. He praises the originality of the vaudevillian, Mr. Fay, who, Seymour has learned, recently performed with Les and Bessie in Chicago. Seymour feels that after the trait of kindness, "originality is one of the most thrilling things in the world, also the most rare!"

(39). He then criticizes his parents for believing that Buddy never misses anyone but himself. Seymour believes that Buddy hides his emotions and that his brother's main goal in life is to write. He lavishes praise on the five-year-old Buddy, calling him the "most resourceful creation of God" (39) he has met. Seymour predicts that Buddy, in the future, will be offering guidance to all of the siblings after Seymour himself is "quite burned out and useless or out of the picture" (39).

A United States congressman, a friend of Mr. Happy's from World War I, visits the camp. Seymour is appalled by the two men but consents to the request that he and Buddy perform for the congressman. Mrs. Happy accompanies the boys on her accordion. Although Mrs. Happy, "a gorgeous, untalented creature" (40), plays the accordion badly, the two brothers do a superb soft-shoe because they are vulnerable to the attractions of beautiful girls.

The identity of the Glass boys' parents is known throughout the camp, in addition to the fact that Seymour and Buddy have "certain abilities, prowesses, knacks, and facilities" (40). Seymour describes how Buddy made the mistake of betting Mr. Nelson that he (Buddy) could memorize an entire book in half an hour so that Buddy and Seymour could use the mess hall as a study room in off hours. Buddy won the bet, and the incident became camp gossip. The head counselor, Whitey Pittman, made a cutting remark to Buddy in Seymour's presence. Seymour says it is lucky that he did not have a weapon to use against Pittman and tells his parents that he warned the counselor not to abuse Buddy again or he would face Seymour's wrath. Seymour comments that in his previous two incarnations he has failed to deal with "a vein of . . . troublesome instability" (44).

Seymour tells his family that Buddy is embracing country life, while he, Seymour, feels at home only in large cities. He requests that his parents send more paper for Buddy to write his stories; Buddy has already composed six new stories since the boys' arrival at camp several weeks ago. Seymour has written 51 poems, though none please him. The poem that he holds high hopes for is the one he has not yet written; its subject will be a pair of honeymooners splashing each other joyfully in a lake.

Les is again given the opportunity to stop reading the letter, as Seymour fears his father might be "tired or frankly bored" (52). Seymour admits that he and Buddy are not popular with other campers in their bungalow. One child, however, John Kolb, socializes with the Glass brothers, and Seymour praises the boy's traits. He warns John, though, to avoid hard alcohol later in life. Seymour and Buddy are partaking of camp sports, and Seymour admits to their proficiency in all games with a ball. He credits this ability to their previous incarnations. Seymour warns Bessie that her sons, in the future, will engender active dislike from strangers. He hopes that he and Buddy can reduce this dislike by improving their personalities.

Seymour reminds Bessie of the time he told her about "the magnificent light" (58) that the mind, once quieted, can play in. He acknowledges that he and Buddy have brought their "creative genius" (58) with them from their previous incarnations. The two boys are, however, perfectly normal, he reassures his mother. Seymour tells his parents that whichever brother should die first, the other will be present. He predicts that he himself "will live at least as long as a well-preserved telephone pole, a generous matter of thirty (30) years or more" (60).

Seymour next recounts a recent vision. He foresees himself, his parents, and Buddy attending an important party, either during the forthcoming or the following winter. There, they will meet a man who will make them a business offer based upon the boys' dancing and singing abilities, in addition to other unnamed attributes. The offer will affect the boys' future childhood. Additionally, Seymour foresees Buddy (long after Seymour's own death many years hence) writing about this particular party he has envisioned. Seymour provides vivid details of Buddy's middle-age appearance, his typewriter, and his writing room. The room has a ceiling window, wonderful shelves for Buddy's books, along with paper and pencils: the exact room Buddy now fantasizes about as a young boy. Seymour enjoins the middle-age Buddy to start his story about the party by describing "the beautiful positions of the bodies in the living room" (62)

before the four Glasses leave the apartment. Seymour finds "the entire glimpse of the evening quite a sober joy to behold, from start to finish" (62) and stipulates that God himself ties together the loose ends of the world; "one cannot even light a casual cigarette unless the artistic permission of the universe is freely given!" (62).

Seymour next confesses that he is shedding tears. He apologizes for writing such "a very long, boring letter" (62), but now explains the reason for its length. Yesterday, the campers set out for a destination miles from the camp in order to pick strawberries. The cart they rode in became stuck in the mud. When the children were forced to help push it, Seymour's leg was deeply gouged by a protruding piece of metal. Bleeding profusely, Seymour was driven back to camp by Mr. Happy on his motorcycle. Seymour openly acknowledges that he dislikes Mr. Happy and tells his parents that he threatened Mr. Happy with a possible lawsuit. The camp nurse, Miss Culgerry, cleaned and bandaged Seymour's wound ineptly. As stitches were needed, the doctor from the town of Hapworth was summoned. Seymour declined anesthesia; he had already "snapped the communication of pain between the leg and the brain" (73), and he thus demonstrated to the doctor and Mr. Happy that he did not need the drug. (Seymour says that he avoided the anesthesia because "the human state of consciousness is dubiously precious" [73] to him.) He is now recovering in an empty bungalow because there is no more room in the infirmary. In bed and alone, he is writing the letter. The other campers are engaged elsewhere.

Seymour now turns to address each of his five family members individually. He reminds Bessie about her cyst needing attention and also about the way to breathe properly. Seymour also forewarns Bessie not to retire from performing at too soon an age (she is 28), even though she has been performing for many years. As Bessie and Les are about to make a recording of a song, Seymour offers tips on how to sing and cautions Les to minimize his native Australian accent. Addressing Boo Boo, Seymour tells his four-year-old sister to practice writing entire words and to improve her manners, especially when she is alone. Addressing the three-year-old Walt, Seymour instructs him to practice his tap dancing, or at least to wear his tap shoes if it is too hot to practice. Addressing Walt's twin, Waker, Seymour instructs him to practice his juggling, or at least to carry his juggling objects with him. Returning to Boo Boo, Seymour says that he feels badly about his earlier critical remarks and then compliments her on her good manners. He explains that he knows, however, that she is enamored of excellent manners. Finally, Seymour closes the letter, saying that he will "tyrannize no one any further" (85). He sends his and Buddy's "naked hearts" (85) to the family.

But to Seymour's "relief and utter amusement" (85), he has discovered more paper and has determined that the clock shows the incorrect time. He will therefore continue writing the letter.

He consults his parents' road schedule and notes their return date to MANHATTAN. Once back, he asks them to see Miss Overman (the branch librarian) and have her contact Mr. Fraser, who sits on the city's library council. Before Seymour departed for summer camp, Mr. Fraser said that he would authorize the shipment of library books to the camp, although without specifying the number of books he would send. Seymour instructs his parents that if he has "taken too many liberties with the quantity" (88) of books requested, they may have Miss Overman reduce the size of the list that follows. (The Glass boys still have a month left at camp.)

Seymour's reading list commences with a request for a book on conversational Italian, followed by "any unbigoted or bigoted books on God or merely religion" (88) written by authors whose last names begin with the letter "H" or by any authors whose names fall alphabetically after that. Seymour believes he has already read all books of this type by authors whose last names precede that letter. Seymour also wants any poems with which he is unfamiliar; at home, there exists a list of already-known poems in a drawer mistakenly marked "athletic equipment." The complete works of Leo Tolstoy can be borrowed from Miss Overman's younger sister; Seymour remarks that he and Buddy take exceptional care of borrowed books. The boys particularly want to reread *Anna Karenina*. Requesting a volume of the Gayatri Prayer

in Sanskrit accompanied by its English translation, Seymour next addresses his sister, Boo Boo. He tells her that since she has a problem with the word "God," he has devised a prayer she can use to circumvent the word. Seymour then asks for *Don Quixote* and hopes Miss Overman will send the volume herself because Mr. Fraser cannot refrain from commenting on masterpieces.

Raja-Yoga and *Bhakti-Yoga*, by SWAMI VIVEKANANDA, are the next books to appear on the list. Seymour lauds Vivekananda as "one of the most exciting, original, and best equipped giants of this century" (92). Seymour says he would trade 10 years of his life to have been able to greet Vivekananda and remarks that the swami is fully conversant with "the lights" (92) that he (Seymour) has already mentioned to Bessie. Seymour wishes for a true understanding between sensual and nonsensual people; the lack of this understanding upsets him. He terms his reaction as "another looming sign of instability" (92).

The book-request list continues: any or all books by Charles Dickens, whom Seymour greatly respects; a selection of volumes by George Eliot and William Makepeace Thackeray, as chosen by Miss Overman and Mr. Fraser; and any or all books by Jane Austen (except *Pride and Prejudice*, which he already has with him at camp). Seymour notes that he cannot discuss Austen with Miss Overman; the author means too much to him. In requesting the work of John Bunyan, Seymour takes Bunyan to task for not making an allowance for human weaknesses. Seymour praises the loyalty of "slothful, delightful Herb Cowley" (93). Seymour does not believe that God expects humans to be "flawless" (94); even God's own perfection "allows for a touching amount of maddening leeway, such as famines, untimely deaths, on the surface, of young children, lovely women and ladies, valiant, stubborn men" (94). The list continues with Warwick Deeping, a recommendation from a stranger at the library, and with Charlotte and Emily Brontë.

Requesting *Chinese Materia Medica* because he thinks the book would help Buddy with his newfound interest in plants, Seymour praises the Chinese and the Hindus for their openness concerning the human body.

A batch of French authors is next listed: Victor Hugo, Gustave Flaubert, Honoré Balzac, Guy de Maupassant, Anatole France, Martin Leppert, and Eugene Sue. Seymour requests that Miss Overman dissuade Mr. Fraser from including any biographies about Maupassant. (Seymour has already read three.) Seymour and Buddy are "sensualists," but neither has "the slightest intention of dying by the phallus"; they plan "to come to grips with the subject of sensuality" (96). Seymour rejects Maupassant as an example of a doomed sensualist and also turns his back on Anatole France because of the author's use of irony. He asks that Miss Overman herself send the entire works of Marcel Proust. Seymour believes that Buddy is ready to read Proust and that his brother wouldn't be adversely affected by the homosexuality in the books. Seymour doesn't want Mr. Fraser to know about this particular request since he suspects that Fraser will misuse the information in social conversation at Buddy's expense. Seymour wants to ensure that his brother be able to "keep his precious shares in the divinely human state of nobodyness!" (98).

The next author to appear on the book list is Sir Arthur Conan Doyle, his works in full, apart from anything not concerning Sherlock Holmes. Seymour recalls that Miss Constable at the main library loves Goethe, but remarks that he does not. He has recently realized the difference between loving and respecting an author. This insight leads him to suggest that no one over the age of 21 should undertake any important action or decision in his life without prior consultation with "a list of persons in the world, living or dead, whom he loves" (98). Seymour reveals that the only singer on his own list is Mr. Bubbles, of the vaudevillian team Buck & Bubbles.

Seymour requests "any unflinching book on the World War, in its shameful, exploitive entirety, preferably unwritten by vainglorious or nostalgic veterans or enterprising journalists" (100). He wants volumes on Alexander the Great written by two particular "distinguished, false scholars, men of condescension, exploitation, and quiet, personal ambition" (102). He will pass these books to Buddy so that his brother can realize "the feculent curse of intellectuality and smooth education running

rampant without talent or penetrating humanity" (102). Seymour critiques the first volume on Alexander, written by Alfred Erdonna. Seymour writes several paragraphs and then realizes that he doesn't have time to point out the pitfalls of the second book by Theo Acton Baum.

Next up are any books on the custom of whirling or spinning when done by people in an effort to make important decisions. Seymour announces that he soon plans to stop this activity himself. Seymour also wants any books in English by the Cheng brothers or by others who wrote after the "towering, incomparable geniuses of Lao-tse and Chuang-tse, not to mention Gautuma Buddha!" (104–105). He admits that Mr. Fraser and Miss Overman do not understand his interest in religion. Edgar Semple has told Mr. Fraser that Seymour could become a great poet. Mr. Fraser and Miss Overman worry that Seymour's involvement in spiritual matters might prevent him from developing his poetry. Seymour is not sure what his duty might be in this life, but he does not want God to tell him. Were God to "raise one human being up over another, lavishing handsome favors upon him" (105), Seymour would "leave His charming service forever, and quite good riddance!" (105). Seymour then addresses God directly and demands no favors; he insists he does not want to "join any elite organization of mortals that is not widely open to all and sundry" (106). Seymour admits to loving God's son, Jesus Christ, but only because he believes that God did not play favorites where Jesus was concerned. Seymour has doubts, though, about the use of miracles by Jesus, and worries that the miracles preclude some people, such as Leon Sundheim and Mickey Waters, from being believers. Seymour is now crying. He thanks God for allowing him to follow his "own dubious methods, such as industrious absorption with the human heart and brain" (106). He then professes his love of God and offers him his services.

After pausing to note that either the sun is shining or his mind is shining, Seymour recommences his list-making, asking for books on the Medicis and the Transcendentalists, and also for the essays of Montaigne. Additionally, he desires books on any human civilization that occurred before the

Greeks' but after other civilizations that he has already listed; the list can be found in his old raincoat. Also wanted are any volumes on "the structure of the human heart" (107) that are not on the list in his top drawer. He calls the heart "this incomparable organ, the finest of the body" (107), but one that cannot adequately be shown pictorially. Drawings fail to convey the heart's "best parts [which] can only be viewed at very odd, thrilling, unexpected seconds when one's lights are quite definitely turned on" (107).

Seymour requests a book on how callus is formed, especially with regard to a broken bone. He wishes for a book by the Czech poet Otakar Brezina. The author was recommended to him by a woman from Czechoslovakia whom he met at the library. Seymour concludes his list by requesting that his parents contact Miss Overman. He wants them to ask her to phone Mrs. Hunter, presumably a librarian at the main library, to find specific issues of three 19th-century journals that contain articles about Sir William Rowan Hamilton. Hamilton was a friend in Seymour's previous appearance (incarnation), but Seymour does not want his parents to explain to the librarian why he wants the magazines. He suggests that they ask Miss Overman to also include any books she has read recently and liked.

Seymour hopes that Bessie will quickly post the cartoon strips *Mr. and Mrs.* and *Moon Mullins*, along with some copies of *Variety*. He suggests to Bessie that she warn Miss Overman that Mr. Fraser might be upset and "quite floored at the number of books requested" (111). Seymour concludes by noting that Mr. Fraser might send only "two or three books on the entire list! . . . there is a maddening, comical thought!" (112).

Seymour then announces that Buddy has arrived in the bungalow (after an absence of seven and one-half hours) and dubs his younger brother "W. G. Glass, the superb author" (112). Seymour signs off, "Your loving sons and brothers, Seymour and W. G. Glass; united forever by spirit and blood and uncharted depths and chambers of the heart" (112).

Seymour then adds two more paragraphs below their names. In regard to the lengthy book-request list, he asks Miss Overman to impress upon Mr. Fraser that the Glass brothers won't be coming to the library for the next six months. They will be studying the dictionary and thus forgoing even the reading of poetry. Seymour hopes that "layers of unnatural, affected, stilted fustian and rotten, disagreeable words" (113) will leave him during that time. He again reminds Bessie not to retire too soon and to send more tablets of paper for Buddy to write on, in addition to "middle bunny" (113), as the larger bunny was lost during the train ride. He returns to the subject of Buddy's writing tablets, specifying the exact type and noting that Buddy's "leonine devotion to his literary implements . . . will be the eventual cause of his utter release, with honor and happiness, from this enchanting vale of tears, laughter, redeeming human love, affection, and courtesy" (113). Seymour ends the letter to his family "with 50,000 kisses from the two looming pests of Bungalow 7 who love you" (113).

CRITICAL ANALYSIS

"Hapworth 16, 1924," published in the June 19, 1965, issue of the *New Yorker*, holds the distinction of being Salinger's last new story to see print during his lifetime. The author never reprinted "Hapworth 16, 1924" in a book. At the time of publication, no one could have imagined that Salinger, who had published one novel and 35 stories over the course of a 25-year writing career—or, put another way, who had published four books between 1951 and 1963—would not, after June 1965, publish another story or book. Salinger stopped publishing at the age of 46; he was 91 when he died.

Although Salinger chose not to reprint "Hapworth 16, 1924" in a book, the story may be regarded, due to its length, as a novella. At the outset of the narrative, the length of Seymour's letter is not apparent to the reader. The *New Yorker* did not utilize a table of contents during the years Salinger published in the magazine; thus, the reader, upon turning to page 32 of the magazine, discovers "Hapworth 16, 1924." The story will not end until the byline "—J. D. Salinger" appears on page 113.

"Hapworth 16, 1924," the fourth of the Glass family novellas, appeared six years after Salinger's previous story, "SEYMOUR: AN INTRODUCTION."

The unusual title derives from the return address of Seymour's letter: "Camp Simon Hapworth / Hapworth Lake / Hapworth, Maine / Hapworth 16, 1924" (32), in which Seymour substitutes the word "Hapworth" for the month. The critic Eberhard Alsen suggests that the story title represents 16 days at Camp Simon Hapworth during the summer of 1924. Seymour's letter—written to his parents, Bessie and Les, and his three younger siblings, Boo Boo, Walt, and Waker (Buddy has accompanied Seymour to camp)—composes almost the entire narrative.

"Hapworth 16, 1924" commences with a four-paragraph prologue written by Buddy Glass. The year is 1965. Where Buddy's prose (in his authorship of Salinger's previous story, "Seymour: An Introduction") was both ornate and loquacious, Buddy now writes that he will be "as plain and bare" (32) as possible as he provides a context for presenting Seymour's letter. Buddy had recently spoken with his mother, Bessie, and told her about his story in progress, which describes the 1926 party that he attended with his parents and Seymour. Bessie consequently mailed Seymour's letter to Buddy, a letter that Buddy had never seen. After reading the letter, Buddy commences to type up "an exact copy" (32). He alludes to a "marvellous relevance" (32) between his party story and Seymour's letter. Although Buddy, in the prologue, provides Seymour's age and the year of his death (this information would allow the calculation of Seymour's age in 1924), most readers start the letter without giving a thought to how old Seymour might be at the time of its composition. In actuality, Seymour is seven years old. The critic John Wenke rightly states that Salinger's "intentions seem to demand that Seymour be unlike any imaginable child, that he be unique" (Wenke 108). Salinger assigns the tender age of seven to Seymour at the time of his letter writing to ensure that Seymour appear even more extraordinary than the author's 10-year-old religious genius, Teddy McArdle (of the 1953 story "TEDDY").

The ideas expressed, and the sheer precociousness, exhibited in the letter may be said to stretch credulity. Twice, early in the story (34, 38), Salinger has Seymour state that he is seven years old, a jolt to the reader who is obliged either to accept Seymour's age and to willingly suspend disbelief, or to reject the story's plausibility. Seymour speaks of his "unlimited sensuality" (35) towards Mrs. Happy, the pretty 22-year-old wife of the camp director. He adds that he hopes to see her nude. Seymour also writes about the "monumental work to be done in this appearance" (i.e., incarnation) (36). He refers to past lives, his own and those of other characters. He is preoccupied with God and religious matters. Seymour predicts the length of his life and has a vision of Buddy composing the very story Buddy refers to in the prologue. (Buddy's story relates how, in 1926, the Glass parents, along with Seymour and Buddy, attend the important party where they meet a man who makes the boys an offer to perform. The meeting presumably led to the children's appearance, in 1927, on the radio program *It's a Wise Child*.) Seymour lectures his parents and siblings on sundry matters. He advises his mother, Bessie, about the most propitious time for her and Les to retire from vaudeville. Although Seymour has been at camp for only several weeks, he has already written 51 poems, in addition to studying Spanish. The five-year-old Buddy, like Seymour, has brought his creativity with him from past incarnations and has written six new stories. Both boys are voracious readers. Buddy's sensuality is already beginning to flourish, as was the case with Seymour at the age of five. The two boys have paranormal powers: Buddy has a photographic memory and memorizes an entire book in half an hour, while Seymour does not need anesthesia when a deep gash in his leg requires stitches. The list of books that Seymour requests for himself and Buddy fills the last quarter of the letter and simply staggers the reader's imagination. (Warren French terms the inclusion of the book-request list "one of those monstrous mischances in the secret history of creativity" [French 110]. French expresses the opinion that the letter should have stopped before Seymour found that last pad of paper to commence "a pompous display of erudition [which is] simply unreadable" [French 110].)

The narrative seeds for "Hapworth 16, 1924" are evident in Salinger's previously published story, and, in fact, "Seymour: An Introduction" displays relevant comparables: Buddy visualizes Seymour "wearing a summer camper's red-striped shorts" (199); Seymour can revisit his past lives (183); Seymour wrote poetry as early as age eight (144); Buddy alludes to his own belief, before the age of five, that he would be a great writer (210); Buddy refers to his "powers of recall" and worries "how ugly will it look in print" (198); Buddy claims to have read "no fewer than two hundred thousand words a day . . . from early childhood" (153); the date of the Glass parents' retirement from vaudeville is established as the spring of 1925 (169). Moreover, as IAN HAMILTON observes, Salinger's unpublished story "The OCEAN FULL OF BOWLING BALLS" includes a letter home written by Holden Caulfield from summer camp. On a biographical note, Salinger himself attended summer camp on at least one occasion during childhood at the age of 11.

Warren French, who believes that the invention of Buddy Glass as chronicler of the Glass family was as important to Salinger's fiction as the author's decision that The CATCHER IN THE RYE be written from Holden Caulfield's perspective, terms Seymour's authorship of "Hapworth 16, 1924" a "disastrous shift" (French 109). French conjectures that "Salinger may have become impatient with working through the medium of Buddy" (French 109). The critic acknowledges, however, that Salinger had already written some small pieces of the Glass saga in Seymour's voice: the dialogue in "A PERFECT DAY FOR BANANAFISH," Seymour's diary entries in "RAISE HIGH THE ROOF BEAM, CARPENTERS," Seymour's 21st birthday notation in "ZOOEY," and Seymour's notes to Buddy in "Seymour: An Introduction." Thus, a letter composed by a young Seymour would not have seemed a bad idea. French believes, however, that "in the course of this bold experiment something went wrong" (French 110).

John Wenke remarks of the story: "Possibly the least structured and most tedious piece of fiction ever produced by an important writer, 'Hapworth' seems *designed* to bore, to tax patience, as if Salinger might be trying to torment his readers away from ever wanting the next new thing from him" (Wenke 67). Wenke wonders whether the story is meant as "a joke, a hoax," but considers Salinger's

effort to be a serious one (Wenke 108). However, he calls "Hapworth 16, 1924" "virtually unreadable" and "an enigma" (Wenke 108). WILLIAM MAXWELL, Salinger's former editor at the *New Yorker,* deplores the story's "total cessation of talent" (Limmer 364). Michiko Kakutani calls "Hapworth 16, 1924" "a sour, implausible and, sad to say, completely charmless story" (Kakutani C-19). Max F. Schulz comments that "the child as saint grows somewhat stale in repetition—and quite suspicious when, as in this case, he is merely a ventriloquistic device for the voice and thoughts of an author" (Schulz 138). Ian Hamilton writes, "in 'Hapworth,' the reader is blithely disregarded: 'Take it or leave it' is Salinger's unmistakable retort to any grumbles from the nonamateurs [i.e., literary critics, book reviewers, professors of literature] among his audience and he seems fairly certain (indeed *makes* certain) that most of them will leave it" (Hamilton 188). James Lundquist notes that "the character [Seymour] that emerges is monstrous . . . a grotesque, but then so are the lives of most saints" (Lundquist 149). James E. Miller, Jr., writes that "in spite of its apparent defects . . . a tedious length, a humor often self-consciously cute, a muting of narrative in favor of philosophical asides . . . the story was an important addition to the life of the Glasses, particularly as it shed new light on the remarkable character of Seymour" (Miller 42–43).

Eberhard Alsen, however, may be regarded as the Salinger critic who has presented the most detailed analysis of "Hapworth 16, 1924." Alsen elucidates his first impression upon reading the story: "Seymour was an even more astonishing child prodigy and passionate God-seeker" than the reader had realized from "Seymour: An Introduction" (Alsen 2002, 185). Alsen's main thesis holds that the letter reveals Seymour's three character flaws: "his sensuality, his emotional instability, and the malice he felt toward unspiritual people" (Alsen 2002, 185). The critic, moreover, believes that these perceived flaws illuminate Seymour's eventual suicide at the age of 31. Thus, Alsen calls "Hapworth 16, 1924" a companion story to "A Perfect Day for Bananafish" and interprets the events portrayed in "Hapworth 16, 1924" as a turning point in Seymour's life. Seymour's "major fights" with the camp director, Mr. Happy, and the head counselor, Whitey Pittman, cause Seymour to "decide to withdraw from the world of normal, unspiritual people" (Alsen 2002, 185) and "to withdraw even more into the spiritual world, to concentrate even more on his studies than he did before coming to Camp Hapworth" (Alsen 2002, 191). Alsen interprets the Glass brothers' breaking their promise to themselves not to utilize their unusual gifts (Buddy's photographic memory in memorizing a book to secure use of the mess hall; Seymour demonstrating how he could forgo anesthesia when his leg is sewn up) as an indication that "from now on, Seymour and Buddy will no longer try to make themselves and others believe that they are average, regular boys" (Alsen 2002, 199). According to Alsen, this refusal to maintain the pretense of normalcy is what Seymour means by the statement that his parents "are paying a very exorbitant price for our frivolous summer's enjoyments and recreations" (112).

Alsen also asserts "the possibility" (Alsen 2002, 193) that the seven-year-old Seymour is not the author of the letter, but that its composer is, in truth, the 46-year-old Buddy. To support his controversial interpretation, Alsen finds suspect Buddy's repetition of his statement that he intends to type up "an exact copy of the letter" (32). Alsen reasons that, if Buddy had made this declaration "only once, there would be no reason to doubt him" (Alsen 2002, 193). He believes that "the positively lurid style of the letter, and its structural resemblance to 'Seymour—an Introduction' suggest that we ought to interpret it not as a letter written by Seymour but as an attempt by Buddy to re-create what might have been going on in Seymour's mind at a crucial time of his life" (Alsen 1983, 78). In this question of authorship and to bolster his novel idea, Alsen could likewise have interpreted Seymour's statement at the very end of the letter— when Seymour sees the five-year-old Buddy return to the bungalow—as a sly clue planted by Salinger. In his remark, Seymour dubs Buddy "the superb author" (112) who "has obviously had a productive day's work!" (112). Alsen offers the opinion that Buddy might have forged the letter, because "Hapworth 16, 1924" presents "more negative informa-

tion about Seymour's personality" (Alsen 2002, 193) than all Glass stories except "A Perfect Day for Bananafish." That is, because Buddy "worships" (Alsen 2002, 193) Seymour, he cannot openly or easily admit to authoring a story that reveals his brother's flaws. Instead, Seymour must be seen to incriminate himself before the reader. Alsen considers Seymour a failed God-seeker. He thus imagines Buddy, in authoring the story, to be "pondering the failure of Seymour's spiritual quest" (Alsen 2002, 193) and suspecting the source of the problem to lie at Camp Simon Hapworth. To discover that source, Alsen believes that Buddy "decided to find out what these problems were by writing the kind of letter that Seymour would have written back then, at the age of seven" (Alsen 2002, 193). Thus Buddy, by writing Seymour's letter himself, would actually be following Seymour's advice to write the piece of writing he, Buddy, would most want to read. (This advice is conveyed to Buddy in "Seymour: An Introduction," whereupon Buddy writes his answer to the question: What did Seymour look like?) Alsen states: "And a letter from Seymour that would explain the reasons for the failure of his spiritual quest is what Buddy would most want to read. Thus Buddy wrote 'Hapworth' for an audience of one, for himself" (Alsen 1983, 95).

Other readings and other critical approaches to "Hapworth 16, 1924" have been offered throughout the years. Although Donald Newlove memorably quips, "You have to suspend disbelief on the same scale as if raising Atlantis from the seabottoms by sheer mind-power," he also confesses to "finding the whole [letter] full-voiced, inspired, and commanding rapt devotion to every word" (Newlove 27). Seymour's letter exhibits, for Newlove, "the redeeming power of love and that power's eternal reappearance," as embodied in the character's "heart, that marvelous lump of radium and spiritual light which Salinger has given us forever" (Newlove 27). Robert Fulford calls Seymour "a touching figure. His anxiety to remain alive to the world around him, while not allowing that world to destroy him, can hardly fail to arouse sympathy" (Fulford 16). Fulford finds Salinger's "major achievement of the story [to be] Seymour's seven-year-old writing style . . . a mixture of sincerity and affectation, of slang and 19th-century novelist's prose" (Fulford 16). Seymour's delight in the act of writing, and his earnestness to communicate with his distant loved ones, are apparent throughout the story. Bernice and Sanford Goldstein find the letter the product of a "state of mind [which] seems to be a state of total involvement with all of one's being in each moment of experience" (Goldstein 160). They suspect that Salinger's repeated insistence upon Seymour's past lives and allusions to karma indicate the author's desire "to take the suicide out of the realm of personal action analyzable in psychoanalytic terms . . . and to put the suicide into a larger context, including that of weaknesses unsolved in previous existences and the general notion of the imperfectability of all human beings" (Goldstein 161). Nonetheless, other critics view Seymour's suicide as a spiritual act and find "Hapworth 16, 1924" supportive of that interpretation. For example, G. E. Slethaug postulates that because Seymour possesses the ability to foresee "the time of his own death, he acts in accordance with the divine dictate" (Slethaug 127). Slethaug calls "Seymour's suicide . . . the utmost in his commitment to God; he acts according to God's wishes . . . Seymour is not negative and irresponsible; within the Glass world created by Salinger, Seymour's particular sort of spiritual insight and suicide form the most dedicated commitment to a divinely ordained pattern of life" (Slethaug 127–128).

One could argue that whatever flaws the seven-year-old Seymour might seemingly exhibit, "Hapworth 16, 1924" stands as a benchmark to which the later Seymour may be compared. The seven-year-old Seymour admits to his sensuality and to the necessity of overcoming carnal temptations. Seymour was apparently successful in this discipline, as Mrs. Fedder, in "Raise High the Roof Beam, Carpenters," admits that he did not seduce her daughter during the couple's courtship. The excesses in the Hapworth letter's writing style provide marked contrast to the restraint of the older Seymour's prose and his double haikus. The idea that Seymour intends, at age seven, to withdraw from people for the exclusive development of his spiritual quest is contradicted by the personality of Seymour as presented in "Seymour: An Introduction." In the latter story, Buddy remarks that his older brother "was wild about everybody in the family and most people outside it" (210). Seymour likewise exhibits sensitivity toward others in his concern that his barber, Victor, might be exposed to his (Seymour's) unwashed neck. Upon completing a poem, Seymour would always think of Miss Overman and worry whether she would like it. The older Seymour does not come off as aloof. Rather, he is engaged in life at all levels: participating on *It's a Wise Child* for more than six years and dynamically changing the nature of the show, playing sports, teaching, and finally serving in World War II. The adult Seymour moreover does not exhibit malice except for the manner in which, as portrayed by Buddy Glass, he commits suicide in "A Perfect Day for Bananafish." Worth noting in this regard is Buddy's statement in "Seymour: An Introduction" that he does not plan to write about "the details of [Seymour's] suicide . . . for several more years" (196). Therefore, the reader might well reserve final judgment on Seymour's nature. Until Buddy further discounts or elaborates the particulars of the suicide as he has portrayed it in "A Perfect Day for Bananafish"—he undercuts the story's veracity in "Seymour: An Introduction" when he admits that the "'Seymour' who did the walking and talking . . . not to mention the shooting, was not Seymour at all but, oddly, someone with a striking resemblance to . . . [him]self" (131)—the verdict on whether Seymour is, or is not, a failed God-seeker cannot be conclusively reached. Finally, one cannot help but wonder whether the fact that "Hapworth 16, 1924" has accidentally become Salinger's last story published during his lifetime has magnified its import. For, if Salinger continued to write additional Glass stories over the past 45 years, and if a number of those stories eventually see print, these further developments of the Glass family saga will, in all likelihood, affect the critical perspective of "Hapworth 16, 1924." (For more information regarding the eight published Glass stories, *see* GLASS STORIES.) However, the chronology of Salinger's publications during his lifetime provides us with an apt symbolism. Because "Hapworth 16, 1924" (apart from Buddy's short prologue) represents one Glass member writing to his family, the story demonstrates (as Ian Hamilton notes) that "the Glass family has . . . become both Salinger's subject and his readership, his creatures and his companions. His life is finally made one with art" (Hamilton 188).

PUBLICATION HISTORY

"Hapworth 16, 1924" was published in the June 19, 1965, issue of the *New Yorker*. Although Salinger had intended to reprint the story as a book in 1997, that publication did not appear. (For more information, *see* HAPWORTH 16, 1924.) "Hapworth 16, 1924" was subsequently included in two bootleg books, *The* COMPLETE UNCOLLECTED SHORT STORIES OF J. D. SALINGER (1974) and TWENTY-TWO STORIES (1998).

CHARACTERS

Abraham, R. J.   R. J. Abraham, the fictitious author of *Conversational Italian*, heads Seymour Glass's book-request list.

Baum, Theo Acton   Theo Acton Baum, a fictitious author of a book about Alexander the Great, is named in Seymour Glass's book-request list. Baum, along with Alfred Erdonna, exemplifies false scholarship.

Benford, Honorable Louis   Louis Benford, in response to a January 1924 letter from Seymour Glass, granted Seymour borrowing privileges in the main library.

Brady, Martine   Martine Brady, like her friend, Boo Boo Glass, is four years old.

Constable, Miss   Miss Constable, a librarian at the main library, admires the author Goethe.

Cowley, Herb   Herb Cowley, a lazy, but cheerful man, works menial jobs at theaters.

Culgerry, Miss   Miss Culgerry, the nurse at Camp Simon Hapworth, bandages Seymour Glass's leg after his accident.

Davilla, Lotta   Lotta Davilla, age four, is a friend of Boo Boo Glass. Supposedly religious, Lotta is, in actuality, a mean little girl.

Doctor of the town of Hapworth   The unnamed doctor of the town of Hapworth is summoned to sew up the gash in Seymour Glass's leg. He believes that Seymour, who declines the anesthesia, is only showing off.

Erdonna, Alfred   Alfred Erdonna, a fictitious author of a book about Alexander the Great, is named in Seymour Glass's book-request list. Erdonna, along with Theo Acton Baum, exemplifies false scholarship.

Foley and Chamberlin   Foley and Chamberlin are the fictitious authors of the book *Hardwoods of North America* that Buddy Glass memorizes.

Folsom, Douglas   Douglas Folsom, a fellow camper with Seymour and Buddy Glass, resides in the same bungalow.

Fraser, Mr. Wilfred G. L.   Mr. Fraser, a member of the library council of NEW YORK CITY, told Seymour Glass that the library would send Seymour any books he might want at camp. Seymour's very substantial book-request list is intended for Mr. Fraser.

Glass, Bessie   Bessie Glass, wife of Les Glass, mother of the five Glass children (Zooey and Franny Glass, at the time of the story, have not yet been born), and the first of the letter's addressees, has saved Seymour Glass's 1924 letter. Buddy Glass explains in his prologue that Bessie, after hearing of Buddy's newest story, mailed him the letter in late May 1965. In the letter, Seymour directly addresses the 28-year-old Bessie a number of times. Seymour tells Bessie to have a cyst removed; he instructs her on how to breathe like a yogi; he coaches her in how to approach singing for the upcoming recording with Les. Bessie wants to retire from vaudeville, and Seymour twice addresses this issue with her. Bessie and the attractive Mrs. Happy (the object of the seven-year-old Seymour's lust) share the same physical attributes.

Bessie appears in all of the other Glass family stories. In "Raise High the Roof Beam, Carpenters," she is living temporarily in Los Angeles with her husband and her two youngest children, while Les Glass is employed at a motion-picture studio. Bessie is given her largest role in the story "Zooey," where she is described in detail as she attempts to persuade her youngest son, Zooey, to help her youngest daughter, Franny, recover from a nervous breakdown. "Seymour: An Introduction" contains several references to Bessie. The reader learns that she had a twin sister who died young, backstage. She thus comes from a family of entertainers, and it was Bessie who decided when she and Les would retire from vaudeville.

Glass, Boo Boo   Boo Boo (Beatrice) Glass, third-eldest Glass child and, at the time of the story, the sole daughter (Franny Glass has not yet been born), is one of the five addressees of Seymour Glass's letter. Seymour wants his four-year-old sister to practice her writing of words and to work on her manners, both in public and private. Boo Boo has experienced trouble with the word *God,* so Seymour devises a prayer for her use.

Boo Boo first appears in the story "DOWN AT THE DINGHY" (1949), in which she is the protagonist and mother of Lionel Tannenbaum. With astute child psychology, Boo Boo solves her son's emotional crisis. Boo Boo likewise figures in all the Glass family stories. In "Raise High the Roof Beam, Carpenters," her saucy, opinionated letter to Buddy Glass imploring him to get to the wedding is reproduced (as a secretary in the Waves, she, on the other hand, must accompany her boss, an admiral, on an out-of-state trip and is therefore unable to attend); her message to her brother Seymour—quoting the Sappho poem that supplies the title of the story—is written with a sliver of soap on the bathroom mirror. In "Zooey," Boo Boo, vacationing in Europe, is invoked several times. She, along with her sister, Franny, would like to dispose of their mother's tattered house coat, an old kimono, and Boo Boo recommends giving the kimono a ritual stabbing before tossing. Boo Boo possesses a quirky sense of humor, as shown when she describes a look on her mother's face as indicating either that Mrs.

Glass has just talked with one of her sons on the phone or that everyone's bowels in the world will be flawlessly working for a week. In "Seymour: An Introduction," she chooses Seymour's John Keats poem, written when he was eight, for inclusion by Buddy Glass.

Glass, Buddy   Buddy Glass, the second eldest of the Glass children, writes a short prologue to accompany his brother Seymour's 1924 letter. Buddy, age 46, has been at work on a story about an important party the Glasses attended in 1926, when he receives Seymour's letter from his mother, Bessie. In the letter, the five-year-old Buddy has joined Seymour at summer camp. The young Buddy exhibits attributes nearly as precocious as Seymour's. For example, Buddy's own sensuality is awakening; he uses his photographic memory to memorize an entire book in half an hour; a budding writer, he has written six stories since arriving at camp. Buddy, passionately responding to country life, causes Seymour to predict that his brother will one day abandon living in New York. Seymour lauds Buddy's devotion to his literary implements and describes the writing room Buddy will have in middle age.

Buddy appears in all of the other Glass family stories. He narrates the story "Raise High the Roof Beam, Carpenters," in which his 13-year-younger self is the protagonist trying to attend Seymour's wedding. Buddy also narrates "Zooey"; the reader learns a great deal about him via his first-person author's introduction, in addition to his 14-page letter that Zooey Glass reads in the bathtub. Buddy writes "Seymour: An Introduction" and is, along with Seymour Glass, one of its two main characters.

Glass, Les   Les Glass, husband to Bessie and father of the five Glass children (Zooey and Franny Glass, at the time of the story, have not yet been born), is one of the five addressees of Seymour Glass's letter. Several times, Seymour gives Les permission to stop reading the letter. Seymour coaches Les to mute his Australian accent for an upcoming record in order to help his father make a hit recording. Seymour suspects that Les had the same early experience of sensuality (that Seymour and his brother Buddy are recognizing in themselves) and asks his father to confide his sexual fantasies from when he, too, was seven. The reader learns that Seymour and Buddy Glass had a discordant relationship with Les in their previous incarnation. Les believes that his two sons are not normal; Seymour tries to reassure him that they are.

Les appears in all of the other Glass family stories. In "Raise High the Roof Beam, Carpenters," Les is referred to as a "retired Pantages Circuit vaudevillian" (6) and currently employed by a motion-picture studio as a talent scout. During "Zooey," he is absent from the apartment. However, Les's sentimental personality is attested to by Bessie Glass and confirmed by Franny Glass. In "Seymour: An Introduction," Les asks Seymour the important question of whether Seymour remembers riding on Joe Jackson's bicycle in Australia in 1922.

Glass, Seymour   Seymour Glass, the eldest child of the Glass family, is the seven-year-old author of the letter that composes nearly all of "Hapworth 16, 1924." The letter evidences Seymour's precocious and extraordinary character. Seymour reports that he experiences glimpses into his own and other characters' past lives; he also foresees the future. The letter shows Seymour to be a God-seeker, voracious reader, and prolific poet. He can control himself from feeling physical pain when his leg is gashed and stitches are necessary. Seymour has written 51 poems since arriving at summer camp. He creates an enormous book-request list that composes the final quarter of the letter. He touches upon his emotional nature and his instability, and predicts a life span of 30 years for himself. Nonetheless, Seymour stresses his normalcy.

The character of Seymour was initially introduced in the 1948 story "A Perfect Day for Bananafish." In that story, Seymour is seen on a beach where he meets a very young girl, goes for a swim, and tells her a parable about bananafish. Later, he shoots himself on the hotel bed next to his sleeping wife. A minor reference to Seymour appears in the 1949 "Down at the Dinghy." Salinger resurrects Seymour in 1955 in the first Glass family story, "Raise High the Roof Beam, Carpenters." The story is a description of Seymour's wedding day, although

Seymour fails to show up for the ceremony. However, Seymour's physical absence informs the story's action and dialogue. Seymour's revealing diary entries, moreover, serve as a stand-in for him, dominate the story's close, and afford the reader an opportunity to assess this remarkably complex character. Though Seymour has been dead for more than seven-and-one-half years at the time "Zooey" takes place, he nonetheless plays a notable role in a number of ways in that story, where important information about him is divulged. Significantly, Seymour's parable of the Fat Lady will bring Franny Glass to the understanding of her life's purpose. In "Seymour: An Introduction," Seymour is the title character and one of the story's two protagonists. The latter story is Buddy Glass's most extensive effort to convey the life and identity of his brother.

Glass, Waker   Waker Glass, the younger twin of Walt Glass, is the youngest Glass child (Zooey and Franny Glass have not yet been born). Waker, one of the five addressees of Seymour Glass's letter, is three years old. Seymour lauds Waker's ability to pray. Waker, like Griffith Hammersmith, is a bed wetter. He wants to be a juggler when he grows up.

Waker appears in the other Glass family stories, but without much attention being paid him. In "Raise High the Roof Beam, Carpenters," he is interned in a conscientious objectors' camp in Maryland. In "Zooey," he is away at a Jesuit conference in Ecuador. In "Seymour: An Introduction," the narrative reveals that an older Waker canonized W. C. Fields and juggled cigar boxes.

Glass, Walt   Walt Glass, the older twin of Waker Glass, is the fourth-oldest child in the Glass family. One of the five addressees of Seymour Glass's letter, Walt is three years old. Seymour believes Walt will share his and Buddy's early experience of sensuality. The reader learns that Walt's name is Walter F. Glass and that Walt wants to be a dancer when he grows up.

Walt first appears in the 1948 story "UNCLE WIGGILY IN CONNECTICUT," though without his surname. In that story, Walt is the former boyfriend, with a unique sense of humor, of the protagonist, Eloise Wengler. Walt once called her twisted ankle

"Uncle Wiggily." During the time of "Raise High the Roof Beam, Carpenters," Walt is in the army and, stationed in the Pacific, is unable to attend his brother Seymour's wedding. Walt will be killed three years later in Japan in a noncombat accident shortly after the end of World War II. In "Zooey," Walt is described as Bessie Glass's "only truly light-hearted son" (90). In "Seymour: An Introduction," the narrative reveals that the mature Walt was a dancer in civilian life.

Green, Désirée The eight-year-old Désirée Green, Seymour Glass's friend, is not in attendance at Camp Simon Hapworth. If Désirée were a camper, she and Seymour could demonstrate to Mr. and Mrs. Happy a successful method of lovemaking.

Hammersmith, Griffith Griffith Hammersmith, a fellow camper with Seymour and Buddy Glass, is seven years old, though physically smaller than the five-year-old Buddy. The unpopular Griffith, burdened with a speech impediment and a bed wetter, becomes the Glass brothers' friend.

Hammersmith, Mrs. Mrs. Hammersmith, mother of Griffith Hammersmith and an attractive, rich divorcée, visits Camp Simon Hapworth. Upon seeing that Seymour and Buddy Glass are Griffith's best friends, she experiences disappointment.

Happy, Mr. Mr. Happy, 30 years old, is the director of Camp Simon Hapworth and husband to Mrs. Happy. When he instructs the campers to push a cart stuck in the mud, Seymour Glass injures himself on a protruding piece of metal. As Mr. Happy drives Seymour back to the camp on his motorcycle, Seymour threatens him that Les Glass might sue him.

Happy, Mrs. Mrs. Happy, the 22-year-old attractive wife of Mr. Happy, has told Seymour Glass of her pregnancy. Mrs. Happy gives attention to the Glass brothers because she idolizes their parents.

Herzberg, Marjorie Marjorie Herzberg, a friend of Boo Boo Glass, is supposedly religious. In actuality, she is mean.

Hunter, Mrs. Mrs. Hunter, a librarian at (presumably) the main library, presides over the periodicals collection. Seymour Glass wants Miss Overman to phone her to request several 19th-century periodicals that include articles on a friend of Seymour's from Seymour's previous incarnation.

Immington, Midge Midge Immington, a fellow camper with Seymour and Buddy Glass, resides in the same bungalow.

Kolb, John John Kolb, a slightly older camper, has become friends with Seymour and Buddy Glass. Seymour lavishes compliments on the boy's personality. Because Seymour worries that the adult Kolb will seek refuge in alcohol, he warns Kolb against alcohol consumption.

Kurz, Robert Robert Kurz, a fictitious author of a biography about Guy de Maupassant, appears in Seymour Glass's book-request list.

Lantern, Tom Tom Lantern, a fellow camper with Seymour and Buddy Glass, resides in the same bungalow. Seymour is fascinated by the boy's name.

Mace, Richard Richard Mace, a fellow camper with Seymour and Buddy Glass, is one of Mrs. Hammersmith's preferences as a friend for her son, Griffith.

Miss Overman's sister Miss Overman's younger sister, also unmarried, owns the complete works of Leo Tolstoy. Seymour wants Miss Overman to borrow most of them for him to read.

Nelson, Mr. and Mrs. Mr. and Mrs. Nelson are the cooks at Camp Simon Hapworth. Seymour Glass holds a low opinion of them. Buddy Glass bets Mr. Nelson that he (Buddy) can memorize an entire book in half an hour.

Overman, Miss Miss Overman is the librarian at the New York public-library branch that Seymour and Buddy Glass frequent. Seymour asks his parents to show Miss Overman a part of his letter so that she can critique his grammar and punctuation. Seymour also informs his parents that they will need to contact Miss Overman to get Mr. Fraser's address so they can forward the list of desired books. Seymour realizes that the list might be too long and Miss Overman should reduce it.

In "Seymour: An Introduction," Miss Overman is introduced as the librarian of the first library Seymour and Buddy used as children. She loved the poets Robert Browning and William Wordsworth. Seymour felt he needed to discover a form for his poetry that would engage Miss Overman's attention, despite her taste in poets.

Pittman, Roger "Whitey" Whitey Pittman, the head counselor at Camp Simon Hapworth, makes fun of Buddy Glass. Seymour Glass threatens Pittman with violence if Pittman repeats his indiscretion.

Semple, Edgar Edgar Semple, in all likelihood a poet, has told Mr. Fraser that Seymour Glass could become a fine poet.

Sharfman, Barry Barry Sharfman, a fellow camper with Seymour and Buddy Glass, resides in the same bungalow.

Silverman, Red Red Silverman, a fellow camper with Seymour and Buddy Glass, resides in the same bungalow.

Smith, Derek, Jr. Derek Smith, Jr., a fellow camper with Seymour and Buddy Glass, resides in the same bungalow.

Suchard, Elise Elise Suchard, a fictitious author of a biography about Guy de Maupassant, appears in Seymour Glass's book-request list.

Sundheim, Leon Leon Sundheim, an elevator operator at the Hotel Alamac, where the Glass family resides, is an atheist, his belief due in part to his doubt that Jesus Christ performed miracles.

United States congressman The unnamed United States congressman, a friend of Mr. Happy's

from World War I, visits the camp. Appalled by him, Seymour Glass nonetheless consents to Mr. Happy's request that he and his brother Buddy sing and dance for the congressman.

Virginia Virginia, whose opinions on childbearing have influenced the pregnant Mrs. Happy, was a college friend of hers.

Walker, Leonard Beland Leonard Beland Walker, a fictitious author of a biography about Guy de Maupassant, appears in Seymour Glass's book-request list.

Waters, Mickey Mickey Waters, a drifter whom Seymour Glass knows, is an atheist, his belief due in part to his doubt that Jesus Christ performed miracles.

Wiegmuller, Donald Donald Wiegmuller, a fellow camper with Seymour and Buddy Glass, is one of Mrs. Hammersmith's preferences as a friend for her son, Griffith.

Woman from Czechoslovakia In February 1924, Seymour met a woman from Czechoslovakia in the main library, where she recommended her favorite poet to him. Seymour now includes the poet, Otakar Brezina, on his book-request list.

FURTHER READING

Alsen, Eberhard. *A Reader's Guide to J. D. Salinger.* Westport, Conn.: Greenwood Press, 2002.

———. *Salinger's Glass Stories as a Composite Novel.* Troy, N.Y.: Whitston Publishing Company, 1983.

Bellman, Samuel Irving. "New Light on Seymour's Suicide: Salinger's 'Hapworth 16, 1924.'" *Studies in Short Fiction* 3 (Spring 1966): 348–351.

French, Warren. *J. D. Salinger, Revisited.* New York: Twayne Publishers, 1988.

Fulford, Robert. "Newsstand: Seymour Glass at 7." *Toronto Star,* 21 June 1965, p. 16.

Goldstein, Bernice, and Sanford Goldstein. "Ego and 'Hapworth 16, 1924.'" *Renascence* 24 (Spring 1972): 159–167.

Hamilton, Ian. *In Search of J. D. Salinger.* New York: Random House, 1988.

Kakutani, Michiko. "From Salinger: A New Dash of Mystery." *New York Times*, 20 February 1997, pp. C-15, C-19.

Kurian, Elizabeth N. *A Religious Response to the Existential Dilemma in the Fiction of J. D. Salinger.* New Delhi: Intellectual Publishing House, 1992.

Limmer, Ruth, ed. *What the Woman Lived: Selected Letters of Louise Bogan, 1920–1970.* New York: Harcourt, Brace, Jovanovich, 1973.

Lundquist, James. *J. D. Salinger.* New York: Ungar, 1979.

Miller, James E., Jr. *J. D. Salinger.* Minneapolis: University of Minnesota Press, 1965.

Newlove, Donald. "'Hapworth 16, 1924.'" *Village Voice*, 22 August 1974, p. 27.

"People." *Time*, 25 June 1965, 52.

Quagliano, Anthony. "Hapworth 16, 1924: A Problem in Hagiography." *University of Dayton Review* 8, no. 2 (Fall 1971): 35–43.

Ranchan, Som P. *An Adventure in Vedanta: J. D. Salinger's The Glass Family.* Delhi: Ajanta Publications, 1989.

Schulz, Max F. "Epilogue to 'Seymour: An Introduction': Salinger and the Crisis of Consciousness." *Studies in Short Fiction* 5 (Winter 1968): 128–138.

Slethaug, G. E. "Seymour: A Clarification." *Renascence* 23 (Spring 1971): 115–128.

Wenke, John. *J. D. Salinger: A Study of the Short Fiction.* Boston: Twayne Publishers, 1991.

Hapworth 16, 1924

Hapworth 16, 1924 was to be the title of Salinger's fifth book, composed solely of the author's last published story, "HAPWORTH 16, 1924" (June 19, 1965, issue of the NEW YORKER). Salinger bypassed his usual publisher, LITTLE, BROWN AND COMPANY. Instead, to the shock of the publishing world, Salinger chose Orchises, a small press owned by Roger Lathbury, a professor of English at George Mason University. After Salinger's death in 2010, Lathbury revealed the full story of how he almost published *Hapworth 16, 1924,* and how the deal fell through after he "foolishly gave an interview" (Shapira C-1).

In 1988, Lathbury wrote to Salinger, care of the CORNISH, NEW HAMPSHIRE, post office. He asked Salinger, who had not published a book since 1963, whether he would consent to the novella-length story, "Hapworth 16, 1924," being reprinted by Orchises Press. (The press specializes in publishing contemporary poetry and reprints of classic literature and is run out of Lathbury's home in Alexandria, Virginia.) When Salinger replied that he would think about it, Lathbury was stunned. Eight years of silence followed.

In 1996, Salinger's literary agency requested a catalog and a few sample books from Orchises. Shortly thereafter, Phyllis Westberg, Salinger's agent, informed the publisher that Salinger would contact him. A meeting at the National Gallery of Art in Washington, D.C., was set up. In anticipation, Lathbury created a prototype of the book. In early summer, Salinger and Lathbury met over lunch. Salinger stipulated that the text exactly replicate the *New Yorker's*. The slim volume, its lines generously spaced, would be bound in blue buckram. The title and Salinger's name would also be on the front cover; there would be no dust jacket. (Later, Salinger changed his mind and requested that his name be removed.)

Lathbury engaged in a warm exchange of letters with the author, while Westberg handled the contractual aspects. Lathbury had until June 1, 1997, to publish the volume; no discounts to vendors or stores would be allowed. The publisher priced the volume at $15.95 and set the publication date at January 1, 1997, Salinger's 78th birthday.

In fall 1996, Lathbury filled out the Library of Congress Cataloging-in-Publication Data form. (By this time, the book had fallen behind schedule.) Unknown to Lathbury, the action automatically triggered the book's listing on Amazon.com as forthcoming. Lathbury was contacted by a reporter for a small business paper and consented to a short interview. David Streitfeld, a *Washington Post* reporter, noticed the article and telephoned Lathbury. Lathbury, now circumspect, did not speak of meeting Salinger, nor did he confirm the print run. He voiced a completely noncommercial attitude toward the book's publication and a nonacademic approach toward reading, which, seemingly, resonated with Salinger's philosophy. Streitfeld's article ended, "Barring last-minute troubles, the book will be on sale by early March at the latest" (Streitfeld D-1).

After the appearance of Streitfeld's article, a media firestorm erupted. Lathbury still needed Salinger's answers to a number of details before he could proceed to press, but according to Westberg, the author was now unavailable. As Lathbury held to the contract's stipulation of no discounts, vendors and online bookstores unilaterally, however, raised their list price to $22.95. By February 1997, prepublication orders for *Hapworth 16, 1924* made it the third-largest seller at Amazon.com.

The question as to why Salinger would publish "Hapworth 16, 1924" in book form 32 years after its initial publication in a magazine began to be raised. Was Salinger testing the waters for the possible release of a new work or simply tidying up his past publications, wanting to assure that his final Glass story would remain accessible? On February 20, 1997, Michiko Kakutani published a major review of the story and, by extension, of the Glass works, in the *New York Times*. Kakutani caustically criticized the story and the Glasses and, like the majority of literary critics before her, lamented that the author had not remained in these pieces "the infinitely engaging author of *The Catcher in the Rye*" (C-19).

In retrospect, Lathbury believed that the timing of Kakutani's review, coupled perhaps by suspicions within the Salinger camp that Lathbury had raised the book's price, had ended the book's last chance for publication. Lathbury felt unable to contact Salinger directly, as he felt he had betrayed the author's trust. To Lathbury's credit, he did not simply proceed and publish the book without Salinger's further input. On June 1, 1997, the contract was terminated; any future negotiation was incumbent upon Salinger's initiation. The book's publication fell into limbo, as Amazon.com continued to list it as forthcoming. (Evidently, Lathbury had failed to inform Amazon.com of the book's true status.) In 2002, Amazon.com rescinded all prepublication orders.

A rumor arose that *Hapworth 16, 1924* would be published to coincide with Salinger's 90th birthday,

January 1, 2009. At the end of December 2008, Lathbury acknowledged that he had lost the contract to publish *Hapworth 16, 1924* but declined to discuss the matter. (After Salinger's death, Lathbury's full account of the events appeared on the Web site of *New York* magazine on April 4, 2010 [http://nymag.com/arts/books/features/65210].) Whether Salinger, when he created the J. D. Salinger Literary trust in July 2008, authorized the future publication of "Hapworth 16, 1924" in book form remains to be seen.

"Heart of a Broken Story, The"

Appearing in the September 1941 issue of *Esquire*, "The Heart of a Broken Story" displays Salinger's sophistication with narrative experimentation early in his career. The story incorporates such techniques as text-within-text and meta-narration (story-within-a-story) to sketch several possible, but improbable, scenarios of a boy-meets-girl tale as told from the fiction-writer's perspective. "The Heart of a Broken Story" is Salinger's fourth published story. The author, however, chose not to include the story in his three books of collected stories.

SYNOPSIS

Between the story's title and the author's name, the editors at *Esquire* insert the phrase, "The only real difficulty in concocting a boy-meets-girl story, is that, somehow, he must" (32). Just below J. D. Salinger's name, the story is labeled as "SATIRE." The text then commences with four paragraphs, in a third-person narrative voice, of how Justin Horgenschlag, a printer's assistant, experiences falling in love at first sight with Shirley Lester, a stenographer, while the two commute to work on a MANHATTAN bus.

In the fifth paragraph, the unnamed author of the story breaks in with a first-person address to the reader and confesses that the four previous paragraphs were the beginning of a boy-meets-girl story that he was in the process of writing for the magazine COLLIER'S. (The reader is thus led to assume that the author's voice is Salinger's.) The author explains that he did not continue the story because he couldn't figure out how the two characters could meet and "have it make sense" (32). The author then postulates different scenarios for a possible meeting but negates each one. Horgenschlag couldn't simply lean over and tell Shirley he was in love with her and ask whether they could go out that night. Horgenschlag might be, as the author explains, "a goof, but not *that* big a goof" (32). Besides, *Collier's* readers wouldn't believe that scenario. The author then reasons that he likewise couldn't turn Horgenschlag into a debonair magazine illustrator and have him express his desire to sketch Shirley; nor would there be an opening line in which Horgenschlag pretends to recognize her as someone from his hometown of Seattle work to win her favor; nor would Horgenschlag faint to the floor of the bus and, in his fall, tear Shirley's stocking (as he grabs her ankle for support) so as to have an excuse for asking for her address, which he would need (he would explain to her) in order to send her the money for a new pair of stockings.

Another scenario, which the author considers "more logical" (131), takes the next and substantial portion of the story. Horgenschlag, now desperate, would steal Shirley's handbag. He would be apprehended and tried in court. Since Shirley would be required to attend the hearing, Horgenschlag would finally learn her address. He would then be sent to prison. From there he would write Shirley a letter (the letter is reproduced in the text) telling her that he loves her. In the letter, he would ask her to write back and to visit him in jail. Shirley would reply with a perfunctory letter (again reproduced in the text), but there would be no chance of her visiting him. Horgenschlag would write a second letter to Shirley, in which he would admit to his loneliness living in New York and would again ask her to visit. Shirley would never answer this second letter (feeling that she had done enough already for the man). In the meantime, Horgenschlag's time in prison would become more difficult and more dangerous. His gangster cellmates, who mistake him for the man that ratted on them in Chicago, would threaten Horgenschlag. Made desperate from not receiving a reply to his second

letter, he would therefore try, along with a group of inmates, to break out of prison and would be the only one killed in the attempt.

The author again breaks into the narrative at this point and, in a first-person voice, explains that the death of the hero could have been avoided had Shirley replied to Horgenschlag's second letter. The author then laments that Horgenschlag did not write the following letter (which is reproduced in the text)—one that would have elicited a reply of understanding and acceptance by Shirley (her letter is also reproduced). The author, however, calls the possibility of these last two letters "unlikely" (132). In these last two letters, both Horgenschlag and Shirley express the truth to each other of their loneliness and their emotional vulnerability.

Breaking the skein of conjectured scenarios, the author next admits that the two characters did not meet and did not get to know each other. Instead, Shirley Lester and Justin Horgenschlag disembark at different bus stops. That night, Shirley goes to a movie with a man she is in love with, but who thinks of her only as "a darn good sport" (133). Horgenschlag soon meets a woman "who was beginning to be afraid that she wasn't going to get a husband" (133), and the memory of Shirley fades from his mind.

The story concludes with the author explaining the reason why he has never written "a boy-meets-girl story for *Collier's*" (133)—in that type of story, "the boy should always meet the girl" (133).

CRITICAL ANALYSIS

"The Heart of a Broken Story" creates a myth of a writer claiming more writing experience than J. D. Salinger had at the time of its publication (although Salinger does not make the claim of experience for himself, but for his story's author-narrator). The young Salinger and his agent, DOROTHY OLDING, seem to have possessed a clear sense of their market and potential success.

The story is narrated by a seasoned author who reflects on the problems he is facing in the process of writing a love story for *Collier's*. The narrator sounds like someone with a good deal of story-writing prowess. Salinger, in creating this very urbane and charming piece, utilizes the illusion of the plot problems confronting the author in order to create other playful illusions as a subtext. He likewise places two interesting characters in several possible romantic alternatives in the context of the author's consciousness about what he might write. Salinger's author offers witty and amusing ways that would allow a simple bus ride to turn into a love story between two strangers. Each scenario, however, is left unresolved, defeated by its own particular twists of fate. Salinger compounds the story-within-the-story technique by reproducing the texts of the hypothetical letters between Justin Horgenschlag and Shirley Lester to further the outlined story imagined from their possible love. However, the love story of Justin Horgenschlag and Shirley Lester is, in fact, never resolved successfully. The narrative ends with the author's dismissal of the two main characters. The two do not get to know each other on the bus, and simply get off at different stops. The author finally states that he doesn't write the boy-meets-girl story for *Collier's* because the characters didn't meet. He also implies that most boy-meets-girl stories are a lot more complex than they tend to be in slicks like *Collier's*.

One of the more notable moments in "The Heart of a Broken Story" occurs during the "unlikely" (132) letter exchange. In Horgenschlag's letter (which he would not have written), the young man would have shown himself at his most vulnerable and would have told Shirley of his love and of "the truth" (132) about himself. Shirley, in her response (again not likely to have been written), would have asked her young suitor for a second chance for him to see her, this time without makeup, so that she would be sure he hadn't caught her "at a phony best" (132). In the text of Shirley's "unlikely" (132) letter, the first use of the word "phony" appears in Salinger's work. At this point in the story, the narrator concludes that the boy doesn't meet the girl, a clever and satirical way to imply that, if two people do not see deeply into each other, there can be no love story. These two final letters, in which the two young people expose their vulnerabilities to each other and their true feelings, would, the reader now understands, have been the letters that would have made possible the love between them. These are the letters that reside at the "heart" of

love. Without their exchange, the love story will remain "broken."

Although a very early story by Salinger, "The Heart of a Broken Story" exhibits the developed narrative technique of which the author was already capable. The literary critic John Wenke, in his 1991 study of Salinger's fiction, perceives the story as a harbinger of the kind of meta-narration that would develop later in the works of such "postmodern practitioners as John Barth, Kurt Vonnegut, Thomas Pynchon, and Philip Roth" (Wenke 12). Wenke also observes Salinger's ability, even at an early stage of his writing career, to construct and then deconstruct his own tale to comment on the type of popular love story (fashionable in the slicks) that is not a truthful story of love.

PUBLICATION HISTORY

"The Heart of a Broken Story" was published in the September 1941 issue of *Esquire*. Salinger never reprinted the story in his three books of collected stories. "The Heart of a Broken Story" later appeared in the bootleg editions *The* COMPLETE UNCOLLECTED SHORT STORIES OF *J. D.* SALINGER (1974) and TWENTY-TWO STORIES (1998).

CHARACTERS

Author   The author of the story within Salinger's "The Heart of a Broken Story" speaks directly to the reader in the first-person voice. He explains that the four paragraphs the reader has just read at the story's beginning represent the start of a story he was going to write for the magazine *Collier's*. He could not write the story, he explains, because he was not able to have the boy character meet the girl character. The author then creates several possible scenarios for the two to get together but proceeds, after each one, to explain to the reader why each possibility would not work or be believable. In these scenarios, the author also presents the texts of letters that would have been written between the two characters. At the conclusion of the would-be scenarios, each of which is thrown out as implausible, the author tells the reader what really happens to his boy character, Justin Horgenschlag, and his girl character, Shirley Lester—they do not meet. He then states the reason why he has never written a boy-meets-girl story: it's because "the boy should always meet the girl" (133).

Horgenschlag, Justin The "boy" character of the author's would-be "boy-meets-girl" story, Justin Horgenschlag, 31 years old and from Seattle, is a printer's assistant earning a small salary in NEW YORK CITY, where he has resided for four years. On the Third Avenue bus, he experiences love at first sight for the very pretty Shirley Lester. Horgenschlag may, the author explains, be "a goof" (32), but not enough to think he could approach Shirley. Being neither well dressed nor good-looking nor suave nor financially successful, he does not have the necessary attributes to attract such a girl. Horgenschlag is definitely lonely and definitely in love with Shirley, but he does not approach her. He simply gets off the bus at a different stop from hers. He thinks about Shirley often during the following month, but suddenly meets another girl and forgets about Shirley entirely.

Lester, Shirley The "girl" character of the author's would-be "boy-meets-girl" story, Shirley Lester, 20 years old and from Manhattan, is riding the Third Avenue bus when Justin Horgenschlag sees her and falls in love at first sight. Shirley, the author explains, is not a *"femme fatale* in every sense of the word" (32) but is "as pretty as a picture" (32). A stenographer, she lives with her mother, whom she supports. Shirley is reading an ad for cosmetics. Whenever Shirley reads, her jaw relaxes and her lips part. At the moment her lips part, Horgenschlag falls head-over-heels for her. Despite all the possible scenarios concocted by the author—in which Horgenschlag might approach and win Shirley's love—each is found implausible in getting this girl together with that boy. Shirley, who would have answered Horgenschlag's first letter—in which she would say she feels "abominable" (131) about having been the cause for his imprisonment (the letter is reproduced in the text)— would never "in a hundred years" (132) respond to a second letter from him. Instead, she would consider him "a goof" (132). Furthermore, even if Horgenschlag had been able to write the letter (reproduced in the text) in which he would

confess the truth of himself to Shirley, it would be very "unlikely" (132) that she would reply with the kind of letter (reproduced in the text) in which she would confess her true feelings to him. Shirley does not meet Horgenschlag and gets off the bus at a different stop from his. She is in love with the man who takes her to the movies that night, but who does not reciprocate her love.

FURTHER READING

Alsen, Eberhard. A *Reader's Guide to J. D. Salinger.* Westport, Conn.: Greenwood Press, 2002.

Wenke, John. *J. D. Salinger: A Study of the Short Fiction.* Boston: Twayne Publishers, 1991.

"I'm Crazy"

Appearing in the December 22, 1945, issue of COL-LIER'S, "I'm Crazy" is Salinger's sole published short story that features the first-person narrative voice of Holden Caulfield. Holden describes a visit with his history teacher, Mr. Spencer, before he leaves a prep school named "Pentey" (36); he goes immediately home and talks with his sisters, Phoebe and Viola; and when his parents return that evening, he breaks the news that he has flunked out. "I'm Crazy" is Salinger's 16th published story. The author, however, chose not to include the story in his three books of collected stories.

SYNOPSIS

Holden Caulfield stands by the cannon on Thomsen Hill, staring at the windows of his school's gym, during a freezing rainstorm. He acknowledges that "only a crazy guy" would be outside in such weather (36). Holden hears the loud home-team cheers for Pentey's successful basketball shots as compared to those for Saxon Charter's. He is waiting "to feel the goodby" (36). Holden remembers tossing a football with "Buhler and Jackson" (36), but the memory of that evening has died, "and no one was at the funeral" except Holden (36). On a roar from the gym, Holden experiences the awaited goodby "like a real knife" (36) and starts to run down the hill with his suitcases.

Central Park in Manhattan. Photographed by Lotte Jacobi in 1936. Note the ice skaters in the foreground. In "I'm Crazy," Holden Caulfield wonders if he will see skaters on the duck lagoon when he returns to New York. *(© The Lotte Jacobi Collection, University of New Hampshire)*

Holden arrives at the doorstep of the Spencers. Mrs. Spencer opens the door and greets him, "Holden . . . are you frozen to death?" (36). Holden visits with old Mr. Spencer, his history teacher, who has the grippe. He informs Mr. Spencer that after their talk, he is leaving Pentey; Dr. Thurmer gave him permission. Holden tells Mr. Spencer that Dr. Thurmer told him "about life being a game" (48). Holden admits this is the third school he has flunked out of; he failed all four of his classes.

Mr. Spencer reads from Holden's exam paper on the Egyptians, and Holden agrees he deserved to flunk. Holden tunes out Mr. Spencer and wonders to himself: would the "lagoon in CENTRAL PARK . . . be frozen over," and, if so, would people be ice skat-ing on it when he "looked out the window in the morning"; and, if so, "where did the ducks go" (48).

Mr. Spencer tells Holden he will miss the school. Holden says he will "miss the Pentey stickers" (48) on his suitcases. He tells his teacher about the time "Mrs. Warbach" saw the Pentey stickers and asked him if he "knew Andrew Warbach" (48). Holden thinks Warbach's "a louse" (48), but nonetheless, he praised her son. His teacher asks Holden if he wants to attend college. When Holden tells Mr. Spencer that he lives "one day to the next," Holden thinks to himself that his answer "sounded phony, but [he] was beginning to feel phony" (48). This feeling causes Holden to wrap up the visit with his teacher.

Holden arrives home "after one that night" (48). He lost his key so the maid, Jeannette, has to open the door. She informs Holden that his parents are out playing bridge. When Jeannette asks Holden why he is home, he tells the maid that he "came home for the race . . . the human race" (48). Holden walks into the room his two sisters, Phoebe and Viola, share. He wakes up the 10-year-old Phoebe, who immediately wants to know why he is home. Holden tells Phoebe that he flunked out; she exclaims, "Daddy'll *kill* you" (48). After Holden says he didn't like the school, his sister accuses him of not liking "*anything*" (51). Holden disagrees, and Phoebe challenges him to identify something he likes. Holden likes "girls that you can just see the backs of their heads, a few seats ahead of you on the train" (51), and he likes being with Phoebe.

Viola wakes, and Phoebe comments that Viola "squeezes right out through the bars" (51) of her crib. Holden places Viola on his lap. She addresses her brother, "Holdie . . . make Jeannette give me Donald Duck" (51). Phoebe explains that the maid, mad at Viola for saying she had bad breath, took away her toy. Phoebe assures Viola that Holden will retrieve Donald Duck. After Holden returns Viola to her crib, she asks him for "ovvels" (51). Phoebe explains to her brother that Viola is crazy about olives. Holden hears his parents come home. Phoebe quickly coaches him on what to say to his parents and tells him to return to her afterward.

After "they were all done with [him]" (51), Holden returns to the girls' room, but Phoebe has fallen asleep. He places Donald Duck under Viola's blankets and some olives on the edge of her crib. Holden goes into his room and can't sleep. He "knew everybody was right and [he] was wrong" (51). He knew he wouldn't be going back to school because his father would force him "to work in that man's office" (51). Holden's thoughts turn to the question of "where the ducks in Central Park went when the lagoon was frozen over" (51), and he falls asleep.

CRITICAL ANALYSIS

"I'm Crazy," published in the December 22, 1945, issue of *Collier's*, is Salinger's only short story narrated by Holden Caulfield. (For more information

regarding the seven extant Caulfield stories, *see* CAULFIELD STORIES.) In May 1944, Salinger changed his mind regarding his novel about Holden. Up to this time, the author wrote chapters, or stories, in the third person. Salinger realized the novel would need to be written wholly in Holden's voice. "I'm Crazy" is important because the story marks the first known instance of Salinger utilizing Holden Caulfield as a narrator; additionally, the story has pre-echoes of parts of *The* CATCHER IN THE RYE.

"I'm Crazy" is one of Salinger's two published stories (the other, "SLIGHT REBELLION OFF MADISON") from which incidents are incorporated into *The Catcher in the Rye*. Of the two, the significance of "I'm Crazy" outweighs "Slight Rebellion Off Madison." "Slight Rebellion Off Madison," narrated in the third person, offers a glimpse of Holden Caulfield, home on his Christmas vacation from prep school, and focuses on his interactions with Sally Hayes. The story contains no mention of his sister, Phoebe, or other siblings. On the other hand, "I'm Crazy" serves as an outline, albeit it in a very sketchy form, of aspects of the novel and, crucially, is narrated by Holden himself. (The sections of *The Catcher in the Rye* fore-echoed by "I'm Crazy" are noted in parentheses.) Holden relates his flunking out, and taking leave, of prep school (chap. 1, pp. 4–9); his visit with his teacher, Mr. Spencer, the story's strongest scene (chap. 2); his encounter with a classmate's mother on a train (chap. 8, pp. 70–74); his arrival at his family's home in MANHATTAN (chap. 21, p. 204); waking up Phoebe and talking with her (chap. 21, pp. 209–215; chap. 22, pp. 216–222); and his parents' arrival home (chap. 23, p. 229).

As Peter G. Beidler indicates in his indispensable book, *A Reader's Companion to J. D. Salinger's The Catcher in the Rye*, numerable minor differences between story and novel are readily apparent, such as the names of Holden's school and his classmates. More important, "I'm Crazy" does not foretell major aspects of the novel's story arc; additionally, the Caulfield siblings in the story do not match the novel's. Most notably, Holden doesn't return to his dorm after his visit with Mr. Spencer, thus the story lacks Ackley, Stradlater, and Jane Gallagher. None of Holden's adventures in Manhattan—neither those that occur before he sneaks into his family's apartment nor those that take place after he sneaks out—appear in the story. In "I'm Crazy," Holden returns directly home from the school, and the story ends with him going to bed in his room. Even the story's scene with Phoebe is but a ghost of that in the novel. Although Phoebe recognizes the seriousness of Holden's flunking out, half of the very short scene centers on their younger sister, Viola, who doesn't exist in *The Catcher in the Rye*. For that matter, "I'm Crazy" omits any mention of either Allie or D. B. The most notable moment of the Phoebe-Holden conversation from the novel does not appear in the story. Phoebe does challenge Holden to "name one thing" (51) he likes. But, since Allie doesn't exist, Holden's answer can't be, as in the novel, Allie. Instead, Holden replies, "I like girls I haven't met yet; girls that you can just see the backs of their heads, a few seats ahead of you on the train" (51). Holden does, however, say, as in *The Catcher in the Rye*, that he likes being there with Phoebe. In "I'm Crazy," Phoebe doesn't ask Holden what he would want to do in life; thus, there is no catcher-in-the-rye speech by Holden. In short, huge chunks of the novel are not suggested by the story. "I'm Crazy" was, possibly, the basis for a 90-page novella about Holden Caulfield that Salinger had completed in 1946. This must remain a guess, however, since the novella remains unavailable for consultation.

Warren French, in his comparison of "I'm Crazy" with *The Catcher in the Rye* in his 1963 monograph, suggests that Salinger's dropping of Viola from the Caulfield family was unfortunate; the critic calls her "one of his most delightful creations" (French 1963, 67). Twenty-five years later, French notes that "becoming acquainted with her is the principal reason readers may still enjoy going back to the short story" (French 1988, 37). Viola unquestionably steals the scene in "I'm Crazy," and one suspects that Salinger realized this when he was writing the novel. With Viola's absence, all attention is focused on Holden's only sister, Phoebe. French finds "I'm Crazy" "more realistic than the novel" and its Holden "a vastly different boy from the narrator of *The Catcher in the Rye*" (French 1963, 67). The Holden of "I'm Crazy" is "a much less complex and more familiar type . . .

whose intellectual capacities simply do not measure up to his ambitious parents' expectations" (French 1963, 67). The Holden of *The Catcher in the Rye* "is a more complex and touching figure than his callow prototype, he is also more pretentious and unrepresentative—he is youth as it would like to fancy itself rather than as it is" (French 1963, 67).

The critic William F. Purcell, in two informative essays, addresses the important issue of Holden Caulfield's "voice" in "I'm Crazy" as compared with *The Catcher in the Rye*. Purcell, following the lead of the English novelist and critic David Lodge, utilizes a Russian term, *skaz*, which denotes a narrative that achieves the semblance of spontaneous speech. Purcell believes *The Catcher in the Rye* to be a successful *skaz*, "a carefully prepared and highly polished text . . . [but] leaves the reader with the impression of listening to an unrehearsed, rambling monologue" (Purcell 1996, 278). The critic assesses Holden's voice in "I'm Crazy" to be a "simple first-person colloquial narration" (Purcell 1999, 109). Purcell postulates differences between the two types of narratives and then applies them to "I'm Crazy" and *The Catcher in the Rye*, and concludes that the voices are not identical.

To compare Holden's voice in "I'm Crazy" and *The Catcher in the Rye*, listen to two versions of a pivotal scene. As Holden stands on Thomsen Hill, he waits for his "goodbye," the intrinsic moment of leave-taking. In "I'm Crazy," Salinger begins with a ghastly worded opening sentence: "But I had to stand there to feel the goodby to the youngness of the place, as though I were an old man" ("Crazy" 36). In an elaborate metaphor, Holden constructs the death of a memory of an evening when he tossed a football with two classmates: "It was as though Buhler and Jackson and I had done something that had died and been buried, and only I knew about it, and no one was at the funeral but me" (36). The sentence, and its immediate successor, suffer from literate artificiality and belie spontaneous speech: On one of the cheers from the basketball game, Holden "felt the goodby like a real knife, [he] was strictly at the funeral" (36). Now, compare Salinger's handling of the scene in *The Catcher in the Rye*: "What I was really hanging around for, I was trying to feel some kind of a good-by. . . . I don't care if it's a sad good-by or a bad good-by, but when I leave a place I like to *know* I'm leaving it. If you don't, you feel even worse" (*Catcher* 7). The difference is astoundingly breathtaking. The unstrained naturalness, the unimpeded spontaneity of Holden's voice, as it articulates his thoughts and sensibility, incarnates the character into living flesh-and-blood. In contrast to the belabored funeral metaphor in "I'm Crazy," Holden continues in the novel, "I was lucky" (7). He remembers a fall evening tossing a football with two classmates, ". . . it was getting pretty dark out, but we kept chucking the ball around anyway. It kept getting darker and darker, and we could hardly *see* the ball any more, but we didn't want to stop doing what we were doing" (7). A teacher intervenes and tells the boys to get ready for dinner. Holden concludes, matter-of-factly, "If I get a chance to remember that kind of stuff, I can get a good-by when I need one—at least, most of the time I can" (8). In both narratives, Holden then immediately runs down Thomsen Hill, commencing his "journey." In "I'm Crazy," his journey will end as he falls asleep in bed at home, not "going back to school again ever . . . [but] to work in that man's office" ("Crazy" 51)—a journey that has disappeared in the back files of *Collier's*. In *The Catcher in the Rye*, his journey will end as he watches Phoebe ride the carousel, with an eventual return to school that fall, "missing everybody" (*Catcher* 277)—a journey immortalized.

Collier's illustrated the story with one drawing—Holden running with his suitcases as he leaves his prep school's grounds.

PUBLICATION HISTORY

"I'm Crazy" was published in the December 22, 1945, issue of *Collier's*. Salinger never reprinted the story in his three books of stories. "I'm Crazy" later appeared in the bootleg editions *The COMPLETE UNCOLLECTED SHORT STORIES OF J. D. SALINGER* (1974) and *TWENTY-TWO STORIES* (1998).

CHARACTERS

Buhler and Jackson   Buhler and Jackson are two Pentey classmates who tossed a football with Holden Caulfield one September evening. This memory allows Holden to "feel the goodby" (36).

In *The Catcher in the Rye*, these characters are named Robert Tichener and Paul Campbell.

Caulfield, Holden   Holden Caulfield narrates his story of leaving school, a visit to Mr. Spencer, a conversation with his sisters, Phoebe and Viola, and informing his parents of his expulsion and the consequences.

Holden appears in or is referenced in additional Caulfield stories: "LAST DAY OF THE LAST FURLOUGH," "THIS SANDWICH HAS NO MAYONNAISE," "Slight Rebellion Off Madison," and the unpublished "The LAST AND BEST OF THE PETER PANS" and "The OCEAN FULL OF BOWLING BALLS."

Caulfield, Mr. and Mrs.   Mr. and Mrs. Caulfield are out playing bridge when their son Holden comes home. After they arrive, he leaves his sisters' room to inform them that he has flunked out again. Holden's father informs him that his schooling is over; he will have to "work in that man's office" (51).

The Caulfield parents, either singly or together, appear in or are referenced in additional Caulfield stories: "Last Day of the Last Furlough," "This Sandwich Has No Mayonnaise," "The STRANGER," "Slight Rebellion Off Madison," and the unpublished "The Last and Best of the Peter Pans" and "The Ocean Full of Bowling Balls."

Caulfield, Phoebe   Phoebe Caulfield is Holden Caulfield's 10-year-old sister. Upon being woken by Holden, she immediately asks him why he is home. She exclaims that their father will punish him. Phoebe challenges Holden to tell her something that he actually likes.

Phoebe appears in or is referenced in additional Caulfield stories: "Last Day of the Last Furlough," "This Sandwich Has No Mayonnaise," and the unpublished "The Last and Best of the Peter Pans" and "The Ocean Full of Bowling Balls."

Caulfield, Viola   Viola Caulfield is Holden's youngest sister (her age isn't specified). Around three years old, she sleeps in a crib. Viola loves olives and is mad at Jeannette.

Viola neither appears in nor is referenced in any of the six other extant Caulfield stories or in *The Catcher in the Rye*.

Gonzales, Edward; Theodore Fisher; Lawrence Meyer   Holden Caulfield names the three as examples of "successful guys" (51).

In *The Catcher in the Rye*, none of these characters is referenced.

Jeannette   Jeannette, the Caulfields' black maid, asks Holden why he has arrived home early and tells him that his parents are out playing bridge. The maid, mad at Viola Caulfield, has taken away the child's toy.

In *The Catcher in the Rye*, the Caulfields' maid is named Charlene, of undetermined race.

Keefe, Miss   Miss Keefe, Phoebe Caulfield's teacher, assigns Phoebe the job of coat monitor.

In *The Catcher in the Rye*, Phoebe's teacher's name is Miss Callon.

Pete   Pete, the elevator boy at the Caulfield building, tells Holden Caulfield about domestic problems his sister is experiencing with her husband, a policeman.

In *The Catcher in the Rye*, Pete, the elevator boy at the Caulfield building, isn't on duty when Holden arrives home.

Schutz, Kinsella, Tuttle   The three boys are the best shooters on the Pentey prep basketball team.

In *The Catcher in the Rye*, Holden Caulfield has a classmate named Richard Kinsella, who digresses in Oral Expression class. Schutz and Tuttle aren't mentioned in the novel.

Spencer, Mr.   Mr. Spencer, Holden Caulfield's history teacher, has flunked his student. Mr. Spencer reads aloud Holden's essay on the Egyptians. The teacher tells the boy that he will miss Pentey.

Spencer, Mrs.   Mrs. Spencer answers the door, greets Holden Caulfield, and asks him if he is "frozen to death" (36).

Thurmer, Dr.   Dr. Thurmer, the headmaster at Pentey, advises Holden Caulfield that "life is a game" (48). He allows Holden to leave that night to return home.

Warbach, Andrew   Holden Caulfield tells Mr. Spencer about meeting the mother of his classmate, Andrew Warbach, whom he calls "a louse" (48).

In *The Catcher in the Rye*, this character is renamed Ernest Morrow.

Warbach, Mrs.   Holden Caulfield tells Mr. Spencer that he once met Mrs. Warbach on a train. When she noticed the Pentey stickers on his suitcase, she asked him if he knew her son, Andrew.

In *The Catcher in the Rye*, this character is renamed Mrs. Morrow.

FURTHER READING

Beidler, Peter G. *A Reader's Companion to J. D. Salinger's The Catcher in the Rye*. Seattle: Coffeetown Press, 2009.

French, Warren. *J. D. Salinger*. New York: Twayne Publishers, 1963.

———. *J. D. Salinger, Revisited*. New York: Twayne Publishers, 1988.

Purcell, William F. "From Half-Shot to Half-Assed: J. D. Salinger and the Evolution of a *Skaz*." *Studies in American Fiction* 35 (1999): 109–123.

———. "Narrative Voice in J. D. Salinger's 'Both Parties Concerned' and 'I'm Crazy.'" *Studies in Short Fiction* 33 (1996): 278–280.

Wenke, John. *J. D. Salinger: A Study of the Short Fiction*. Boston: Twayne Publishers, 1991.

"In J. D. Salinger's Own Words"

At LITTLE, BROWN AND COMPANY's request, Salinger wrote an autobiographical statement— four paragraphs' long—to be used as a publicity release in the upcoming promotion for the 1951 publication of *The CATCHER IN THE RYE*. In this statement, titled by the publisher, Salinger reveals where and when he was born; his education, including "three colleges (no degrees)" (Kunitz 859); his military service, specifically mentioning D-day; and that he now lives in Westport, Connecticut. He says that he has been writing since the age of "fifteen or so" (Kunitz 859) and that his stories have appeared in a variety of magazines, but "mostly—and most happily—in the *New Yorker*" (Kunitz 859). Salinger continues, "I'd like to say who my favorite fiction writers are, but I don't see how I can do it without saying why they are. So I won't" (Kunitz 859). A portion of this "publicity release" was excerpted on the dust jacket of *The Catcher in the Rye*. The most interesting paragraph, however, was omitted, in which Salinger wrote, "I'm aware that a number of my friends will be saddened, or shocked, or shocked-saddened, over some of the chapters of *The Catcher in the Rye*. Some of my best friends are children. In fact, all of my best friends are children. It's almost unbearable to me to realize that my book will be kept on a shelf out of their reach" (Kunitz 859).

The one-page release has since become a very rare and valuable collectors' item. Salinger's text can be found, in full, in *Twentieth Century Authors*, edited by Stanley J. Kunitz and Vineta Colby (Kunitz 859). The text is often mistakenly referred to as a "letter to the editor," but Donald M. Fiene, Salinger's first bibliographer, reveals that Kunitz and Colby had no contact with Salinger and had simply reproduced the publicity release without identifying it as such.

"Inverted Forest, The"

Appearing in the December 1947 issue of Cosmo-politan, "The Inverted Forest" is Salinger's longest work prior to *The Catcher in the Rye*. The novella features the strange, tragic tale of Raymond Ford, a self-made poet of genius. "The Inverted Forest" is Salinger's 19th published story. The author, however, chose not to include the story in his three books of collected stories.

SYNOPSIS

A third-person narrator begins the novella by explaining that a diary excerpt to follow was written by Corinne von Nordhoffen on December 31, 1917, the eve of her 11th birthday. Corinne, daughter of a German baron and an American heiress who committed suicide, lives in Shoreview, Long Island. In the charming diary extract, Corinne muses about the invitees for the birthday party, and she focuses on Raymond Ford, whom she calls the nicest person and whom she intends to marry.

The narrative resumes on the evening of the birthday. Everyone is in attendance, except Raymond Ford. The conversation reveals that he is a "very strange child [and] not a good mixer" (74) and that his mother beats him. Mr. Miller, the baron's secretary, convinces Corinne that they should drive to Raymond's home to get him. Corinne and Miller arrive in front of an apartment situated above the Lobster Palace, where Mrs. Ford waitresses. As Corinne and Miller stand near the door, Mrs. Ford pushes past them. She and her son are in the process of leaving town. Mrs. Ford has been fired and has lost her domicile as well. She pounds on the closed restaurant's window and curses the owner's underling. The man insinuates that she is an alcoholic. Raymond sees Corinne and apologizes that he couldn't attend her birthday party. Miller offers to drive mother and son to the station, and the belligerent woman agrees. Before exiting the car, she threatens Raymond with bodily harm if he drops the suitcases. Raymond struggles with the two suitcases, which "were huge and looked dead-weight" (78). Corinne asks him where they are moving, but he doesn't know.

The narrative fast-forwards and alludes to the baron's death, the estate being sold, and Corinne in college at Wellesley. She grows to nearly six feet tall; she is uncommonly direct with male dates; and she "did not like to be touched unnecessarily" (79). Corinne graduates and moves to Europe for three years, buying numerous cars. Her one confidante, a boy named Pat, dies after falling off the running board of her car. Corinne returns to America and takes an expensive apartment on the Upper East Side of Manhattan. She phones a college friend,

Robert ("Bobby") Waner, to ask if he can secure her a job on the newsmagazine at which he works. The narrator breaks into the story, revealing himself to be Robert Waner. He states he will continue to refer to himself in the third person.

Waner dated Corinne during her college years. He was, and still is, in love with her. Corinne becomes employed at the magazine and steadily advances until she is the drama critic. For Corinne's 30th birthday, Waner buys her an engagement ring (which she refuses) and a volume of poems, titled *The Cowardly Morning.* He includes a note with the book stating that the poet is "Coleridge and Blake and Rilke all in one, and more" (80). That night, Corinne begins to half-heartedly read the poems. She feels guilty by her lack of attention and returns to the opening poem. When she comes to the lines, "Not wasteland, but a great inverted forest / with all foliage underground" (80), Corinne is overwhelmed by "the deluge of truth and beauty" (80). She looks closely at the book's cover and phones Waner. She tells him that she knew someone named Raymond Ford, although the poet's name is Ray Ford. When Waner tells her he doesn't know anything about the poet apart from the biographical blurb, she quickly reads it. The poet is 30 years old (the right age for Raymond Ford) and teaches at Columbia University.

The next day, Corinne phones Columbia and reaches Ford. He remembers her as soon as she identifies herself. Corinne expresses admiration for his poems. During their conversation, she learns that Ford's mother died a number of years ago. Ford invites Corinne to lunch. At a Chinese restaurant, the two former acquaintances catch up on the intervening 19 years. Ford explains how he became a poet. Not until the age of 19 did he begin high school; he worked evenings for a bookmaker at the dog races. One night, during his senior year, he helped a Mrs. Rizzio save a substantial amount of money from impetuous wagers. After Ford declined Mrs. Rizzio's offer of much-needed dental work, she brought him a poem, written by a famous poet, each time she came to the track. The first poem was by W. B. Yeats. Ford, for the fun of it, memorized the poem: "suddenly part of the beauty of it caught on" (86). He never

told Mrs. Rizzio what the poems meant to him; he "was afraid of breaking the spell—the whole thing seemed magic" (86). After Ford graduated from high school, Mrs. Rizzio allowed him use of her library during that summer. The young man read poetry for 18 hours a day for two months until he nearly went blind. Ford entered college at age 23, and poetry became his entire life. He never fell in love, never drank or smoked, and hardly dated. Ford confesses to Corinne, "I can't get past half my childhood dogmas" (88). As they talk that lunch, Ford realizes Corinne has fallen in love with him. He tries to warn her with a glance; he knows he has lost the ability to reciprocate. Corinne invites him to a small gathering of friends, and he reluctantly accepts.

Ford fails to show up for the party. He calls and apologizes, saying he was working all night. The couple see each other for the next four months, mostly at the same Chinese restaurant. Corinne does a great deal of the talking. One day, Ford nonchalantly kisses her for the first time as he sits down in the restaurant. Corinne again asks him to meet some of her friends. The poet admits he doesn't socialize. Corinne explains how much his poetry means to these people, and Ford relents and agrees to come.

Ford arrives an hour late for the gathering. He charms and impresses everyone. He is eloquent about poetry and a variety of poets. The next day, Waner, who talked with Ford about the poetry of Hopkins, calls Corinne. He bluntly tells her that Ford doesn't love her. He explains that Ford "writes under pressure of dead-weight beauty" (90); that the poet is unfit for normal relations between men and women; that "he's standing up to his eyes in psychosis" (90). Waner warns her not to marry Ford. When Corinne protests Waner's assessment, he simply says Ford will propose marriage, though the poet is "cold as ice" (90).

Shortly thereafter, Ford and Corinne marry. The narrator breaks into the story, stating, "I know nothing at all about their honeymoon" (90). Returning to the third person, Waner explains that a few days after the honeymooners' return to New York, Corinne received a letter from Mary Gates Croft. The letter is reproduced in the text and reveals Miss Croft to be a junior in college. She encloses some of her own poems in hopes that Corinne will intercede with her husband to solicit his opinion about her work. Miss Croft alludes to her upcoming visit to NEW YORK CITY with her aunt.

Ford agrees to look at the poems. Corinne sets a date for Miss Croft's visit to their apartment. When the girl rings the bell, Corinne realizes Ford hasn't read the poems yet. She stalls for time. Miss Croft tells Corinne to call her Bunny. She regales Corinne with tales about her Aunt Cornelia and their servants. Ford finally enters the room and brutally assesses the poems. He explains that she isn't a poet. The most damning reason is because she is "inventive" (95). "A poet doesn't invent his poetry—he finds it. The place . . . where Alph the sacred river ran—was found out, not invented" (95). Ford abruptly leaves.

The next day Bunny calls Corinne at work. (Corinne had forgotten she suggested that the girl call so they could lunch together.) To Corinne's surprise, she greatly enjoys the lunch with Bunny. At one point she tells the girl, "you seem to be able to hold your liquor like an old trooper" (95–96). Corinne invites Bunny to attend the theater that evening with herself and Ford.

The narrative halts; a letter from Corinne, addressed to Waner, is reproduced. The letter reveals that all of the events of the foregoing novella have been told to Waner by Corinne. She doesn't want to talk about what happened next and instead will relate "the Big Business . . . in the form of a private detective's log" (96).

Corinne, Ford, and Bunny go to the theater. Ford invites Bunny to his next-day lecture. At dinner, he tells his wife that he and Bunny had lunch at a Chinese restaurant, although he is evasive about the details. That night, while Corinne is up late in the living room, she hears Ford screaming in his sleep. When she wakes him, he doesn't recognize her initially. He finally speaks "her name; but with great difficulty, like a man physically and emotionally exhausted" (96). When she returns to his room, he has fallen asleep. Later in the night, Ford weeps for nearly an hour, "but there seemed to be no way of relieving him of his sorrow or even

of reaching it" (96). At breakfast, when Corinne attempts to find out what is wrong, Ford is again evasive. She asks him if he loves her. That night, Ford phones her and says he must work late. The next morning Corinne asks if he has seen Bunny; he denies this. Corinne is stood up by Bunny that evening at the theater. When Corinne returns home and finds Ford hasn't returned, she goes to an all-night movie. At four in the morning, she runs into her husband outside their apartment building. He asks her if she thinks he is drunk. Corinne answers in the affirmative. Ford tells her that he's eaten "an olive from 'her' Martini" (98), but won't identify whose.

The next day, while at the office, Corinne receives a phone call from Ford informing her that he and Bunny are at the train station; they are leaving New York together. Upon hearing this, Corinne faints. Corinne returns home to discover all of Ford's effects gone from the apartment, whereupon she faints again.

Approximately 10 days later, a caller arrives for Corinne. The maid lets him in, and he hands Corinne his card: "I'M HOWIE CROFT [emphasis added] / Who the Hell / are you, Bud?" (100). When Corinne learns that Howie is Bunny's husband, she faints. Revived, she is told that Bunny is not a 20-year-old junior in college, but a 31-year-old wife with an 11-year-old child. Bunny doesn't have an Aunt Cornelia. Howie tells Corinne that he allowed his wife to come to New York so that Ford could help Bunny become a successful writer (she writes unsuccessfully for the movies). After returning home from a sales trip, Howie received a letter from Bunny explaining that she had run off with Ray Ford. Howie tells Corinne he is relieved that his wife has run away; "she's nuts . . . she was always nuts" (100). He makes an unsuccessful pass at Corinne. She screams that she wants her husband back, and Howie leaves.

Corinne, Ford's publishers, and his employer, Columbia University, have tried, without success, to locate the vanished poet for 18 months. One day, Waner phones Corinne to let her know that he has located Ford in a Midwest city. She travels to the unnamed city. Arriving late at night, she telephones and Bunny answers. Upon hearing that

Corinne is in town, Bunny speaks in "a voice full of rich, creamy delight" (107). Bunny tells Corinne that she and Ford had intended to get in touch with her; Bunny even half apologizes for "what's happened and stuff" (107). Thinking nothing is amiss, Bunny exuberantly invites Corinne over for a drink.

Corinne arrives at a squalid apartment. While Bunny goes to fix drinks, Corinne enters another room and sees Ford. He sits at a card table with "papers strewn messily" (107) over its surface. She "already knew that everything was wrong with him" (107). Corinne asks Ford why he is not wearing his glasses (he is nearly blind without them). He tells her that Bunny forbids it; Bunny thinks he looks like a movie star without his glasses. Her cousin, profession unknown, has given him some eye exercises. Corinne realizes Ford is drunk. She asks him to come home with her. Ford says he "can't get away"; he's "with the Brain again" (107). When Corinne doesn't understand, he explains, "The Brain, the Brain . . . *You* saw the original . . . Think of somebody pounding on the window of a restaurant on a dark street. *You* know the one I mean" (107). Bunny returns with highballs. She castigates Ford for their financial state: if only he "would stoop to writing for money" (107). Bunny asks Corinne to look at her novel while she's in town. Corinne explains that she is leaving tomorrow morning. Ford, who has gulped down his drink, leaves the room and returns with straight whiskey. Corinne abruptly gets up to depart. She asks her husband to return to New York with her. Ford shakes his head. Bunny says she hopes that the three of them can keep in touch. Bunny upbraids Ford to turn on the staircase light for Corinne's departure. When Corinne reaches the street, she breaks into a run.

CRITICAL ANALYSIS

"The Inverted Forest" is Salinger's most extended work prior to the publication of *The Catcher in the Rye* in 1951. The flawed novella retains importance due to its presentation of the first authentic poet in Salinger's work, Ray Ford. Additionally, the author's early views on creativity, poetry, and poets are showcased in the novella.

Given the importance Salinger accords poetry and poets throughout his body of work, "The Inverted Forest" is fascinating. There are numerous references to different poets: Blake (80), Byron (85, 86), Coleridge (80, 86), T. S. ELIOT (80, 86, 88), Hopkins (90), Keats (86), Milton (86), Marianne Moore (80), RAINER MARIA RILKE (80, 88), Shakespeare (86), Shelley (86), Whitman (86 twice, 90), Wordsworth (86, 90), and Yeats (86 twice). This profusion of references to poets is, by far, the most in any single Salinger text.

Waner's taste in poetry is exhibited when he terms Ford to be a combination of Coleridge, Blake, and Rilke. Waner's two favorite lines of poetry are Whitman's "I am the man, I suffered, I was there" (from "Song of Myself") and one of Ford's, paraphrased as, "the one about the man on the island inside the other island" (86). Ford's reference to "Alph the sacred river ran" (95) is a direct quotation from Coleridge's poem "Kubla Khan." Ford's taste in poetry obviously runs to Coleridge and is perhaps further indicated by his choice of poets when "he talked whole essays away. One on Rilke, one on Eliot" (88). Ford seems especially interested in Rilke, as the only time he came to Corinne's apartment before they were married was to see her Rodin, "which had once belonged to Clara Rilke" (88). Clara, a sculptress who married Rainer Maria Rilke, studied with the great sculptor Auguste Rodin. Waner's and Ford's tastes in poetry are indicative of Salinger's own.

Salinger presents poetry in laudatory terms. When Corinne reads Ford's opening poem in *The Cowardly Morning,* she experiences "the deluge of truth and beauty" (80). Ford indicates the magnitude of poetry's importance when he states that he "nearly died looking for it" (86). Salinger differentiates between verse and poetry when Waner notes that poetry results from writing "under pressure of dead-weight beauty" (90). Verse is merely inventive; Ford declares, "A poet doesn't invent his poetry—he finds it" (95). The sacral nature of poetry is inferred when Ford notes that "where Alph the sacred river ran—was found out, not invented" (95).

In the story, Salinger suggests that the source of creativity is almost brutal. He links writing "under pressure of dead-weight beauty" (95) (writing that produces real poetry) to the pain of child-hood through the use of the phrase "dead-weight." When the 11-year-old Ford struggles with the suit-cases under threat of bodily harm by his mother not to drop them, the suitcases are described as "huge and looked dead-weight" (78).

A negative aspect of creativity resides in Waner's assessment of Ford's character and the novella's depiction of the poet's nearly pathological disintegration. Waner tells Corinne that Ford can't love her because the poet writes "under pressure of dead-weight beauty" (90). In a cryptic statement, Waner states that this "pressure" must mean that Ford is "standing up to his eyes in psychosis" (90). Waner calls Ford "cold as ice" (90) and implies that the poet "either lost or forfeited some natural interior dimension of mysterious importance" (88). This "dimension" is almost certainly the ability to reciprocate love. Salinger paints a portrait of the poet's painful regression after his lunch with Bunny Croft. That same night, Ford screams in his sleep, doesn't recognize his wife, clenches his hands, and weeps uncontrollably. Three days later, he absconds with Bunny. Bunny is a double for Ford's mother: She, too, is alcoholic, a fabricator of lies, and abusive toward him. Ford sinks into desti-tution with Bunny, becoming an alcoholic, nearly blind without the use of his glasses (which Bunny denies him).

Given the proximity in publication between "The Inverted Forest" (December 1947) and "A PERFECT DAY FOR BANANAFISH" (January 31, 1948), one notes that Salinger, for the first time in his fiction, uses the name, Seymour: "Seymour and Frances Hertz, Corinne's intellectual friends" (90). Hertz is subsequently referred to as "Sy" (90); he is at work on a book about the Wordsworths (presumably William and his sister, Dorothy). The linkage between the two stories is further strength-ened in that the two essays Ford composed orally concern Eliot and Rilke. The sole lines of Ford's poetry quoted in "The Inverted Forest" are a rebut-tal to T. S. Eliot's poem "The Waste Land." In "A Perfect Day for Bananafish," Seymour quotes from Eliot's "The Waste Land" and alludes to Rilke as the only great poet of the century (though Salin-

ger does not directly name either the poem or the poets). It should be stressed, however, that "A Per-fect Day for Bananafish" does not specify that Sey-mour writes poetry.

"The Inverted Forest" has not generated the amount of critical response one might expect; Salinger's decision not to collect the work has con-tributed to this situation. In 1957, the critic Ihab Hassan terms the novella "at best terrifying and at worst awkward. The style vacillates between glamour and doom; the story unfolds ponder-ously" (Hassan 267). The critic finds, however, that it "strikes with impact" (Hassan 267). In 1958, Frederick L. Gwynn and Joseph L. Blotner are befuddled by the novella's "irredeemably fan-tastic plot" (Gwynn 12) and its "improbable note from Corinne stating that she will tell the rest of the story in the form of a private detective's log" (Gwynn 13) and they wonder, "what *is* significant about what *has* happened?" (Gwynn 14). Warren French, in his 1963 monograph on Salinger, offers the most extensive reading of the novella. French views the work not as a realistic piece of fiction but as "an allegory of the plight of the imaginative artist in the modern, mechanistic, success-oriented world" (French 1963, 74). French cites the title of Ford's second book of poetry, *Man on a Carousel,* as "further indication of the poet's rejection of the busy world of news magazines and cocktail parties where people are constantly preoccupied with 'getting somewhere'" (French 1963, 72). This rejection allows French to conclude that the artist wants to "live entirely within his imagina-tion" (French 1963, 72). The artist's sole concern, according to French, is "to remain a child and to have his mother—or the figure who replaces her—shield him from *all* responsibilities" (French 1963, 74). French notes that it makes no difference whether Mrs. Ford or Bunny Croft torments Ray Ford; he can retreat into his imagination. (The two women are linked through Ford's reference to each of them as "the Brain" [107].) The ques-tion arises, however, whether Ford continues to be able to write poetry now that he has become an alcoholic and lives with Bunny. (The name "Ford" next to their doorbell is written in green ink, symbolic of poetry. The poems that Mrs. Rizzio gave Ford were written in green ink; similarly, in *The Catcher in the Rye* the poems Allie Caulfield copied onto his baseball glove were also written in green ink. It is almost as if Salinger suggests it is immaterial whether Ford writes poems or not; he remains a poet as long as he dwells within his imagination.) French further interprets the story as a rebuttal of T. S. Eliot and his poem "The Waste Land." The only two lines of Ford's poetry Salinger includes, and excerpts as the title of the novella ("Not wasteland, but a great inverted forest / with all foliage underground" [80]), "answers Eliot by asserting that the world is not really all wasteland . . . but that the 'nice' world exists beneath the surface (in the mind) where beautiful, green things grow that cannot be observed externally" (French 1963, 71). Additionally, Salinger specifies that a real poet "doesn't invent his poetry—he finds it. The place . . . where Alph the sacred river ran—was found out, not invented" (95). French terms Eliot's poetry as "largely based upon traditional learning . . . 'invented' rather than 'found'" (French 1963, 75). Twenty-five years later, French reassesses "The Inverted Forest" and now thinks that the story had "few redeeming features" (French 1988, 29). He notes that "none of the characters is plausible as the allegorical demigods they seem to be (the wounded poet, the benevolent patron, the destructive witch)" (French 1988, 29). The story's residual importance lies in the fact that Ray Ford can be viewed as "a false start toward the creation of Seymour Glass" (French 1988, 30). (Seymour would be introduced one month after the publication of "The Inverted Forest" in "A Perfect Day for Bananafish.") French concludes that Ford is "as hopelessly frozen in his childhood as the Indians in the Museum of Natural History in *The Catcher in the Rye* are frozen in their diorama—a condition that Salinger seems to suppose necessary for the cultivation of poetic genius" (French 1988, 31).

Eberhard Alsen devotes an entire chapter to "The Inverted Forest" in his 2002 *Reader's Guide to J. D. Salinger*. Alsen notes that the novella "prefigures [Salinger's] later tendency to give equal emphasis to two major characters so that we can't tell who the central character is suppose to be" (Alsen 41). Although Alsen refers here to Corinne

von Nordhoffen and Raymond Ford (and is correct apropos the story itself), Ford is an exponentially more important character in regard to Salinger's body of work. Alsen notes the experimental narrative structure and the author's use of multiple points of view. The changes of point of view create a tripartite structure. Part one, told (almost always) in the third person by Robert Waner, covers the initial 60 percent of the work, up to Corinne's letter addressed to Waner. Her "private detective's log" (96), in which she refers to herself as "Mrs. Ford," covers the ensuing 10 percent (starting with the theater night with Ford and Bunny, continuing through Ford and Bunny's departure from New York, and Corinne's fainting at home upon realizing all of Ford's effects are gone from the apartment). The final 30 percent of the novella, starting with Howie Croft's arrival at Corinne's apartment, reverts to the third-person narrative reflective of the work's first part: "Mrs. Ford" becomes "Corinne," and the prose resumes the characteristics of that part. The narrator of the final 30 percent of the novella twice refers to "we." "We know now that the itinerary of Ford and Bunny Croft once they left New York together . . . We know that they turned back North . . ." (102). This narrator, in all likelihood, is Robert Waner. The "we" could mean Waner and Corinne (or, possibly, include the reader). Alsen notes Salinger's unusual method of Waner intruding into the third-person narrative with an occasional first-person comment. This "anticipates the post-modernist fashion of self-reflexive fiction . . . a story told by a narrator who comments on the progress of his own narrative" (Alsen 44). The critic expresses ambivalence regarding the success of the work but stresses Salinger's innovative techniques. Alsen also notes that "as character types, Robert Waner and Raymond Ford anticipate the characters of Buddy and Seymour Glass" (Alsen 45). The critic terms Bunny Croft "the most despicable female character in all of Salinger's fiction" (Alsen 45) due to her alcoholism, compulsive lying, and violent character.

Cosmopolitan illustrated "The Inverted Forest" with two drawings—Corinne shaking Ford awake from his nightmare; and Corinne in an armchair, unconscious, as her maid and Howie Croft look on.

PUBLICATION HISTORY

"The Inverted Forest" was published in the December 1947 issue of *Cosmopolitan*. Salinger never reprinted the novella in his three books of collected stories. Despite Salinger's objections, *Cosmopolitan* included "The Inverted Forest" in its Diamond Jubilee issue of March 1961. "The Inverted Forest" later appeared in the bootleg editions *The Complete Uncollected Short Stories of J. D. Salinger* (1974) and *Twenty-Two Stories* (1998).

CHARACTERS

Croft, Howie   Howie Croft, husband of Bunny Croft, visits Corinne von Nordhoffen at her apartment. He reveals Bunny's true identity. In the process, the crude salesman makes a pass at Corinne.

Croft, Mary Gates "Bunny"   Mary Gates Croft, better known as Bunny, enters the story through a letter she addresses to Corinne von Nordhoffen. Pretending to pass herself off as a junior in college, a fledgling poet, and an admirer of Raymond Ford, the letter persuades Corinne to ask her husband to critique Bunny's enclosed verses. Bunny arrives in New York City and meets Corinne and Ford. Bunny, an alcoholic, lures Ford away from Corinne, and they leave New York together. They eventually end up living in a Midwest tenement. Bunny thinks Ford looks like a movie star without his glasses and forbids him to wear them. She is an unsuccessful writer who wants to sell her work to the movies.

Ford, Mrs.   At the story's outset, Mrs. Ford, the alcoholic mother of Raymond Ford, has lost her waitress job. She pretends to have married beneath her station, but her diction indicates she is from the lower working class. A single parent, Mrs. Ford beats her son. By the time Raymond has become a highly successful poet, Mrs. Ford has been dead a number of years.

Ford, Raymond "Ray"   Raymond Ford, son of Mrs. Ford, grows up from a disadvantaged childhood to become a renowned poet at the age of 30. Ford's first book of poetry, *The Cowardly Morning*, causes Robert Waner to describe him as a combination of the poets Coleridge, Blake, and Rilke. Ford, an instructor at Columbia University, meets Corinne von Nordhoffen after a hiatus of 19 years. They marry shortly after Ford's second book of poems, *Man on a Carousel*, is published. Ford has trouble adjusting to Corinne's Upper East Side Manhattan life. Mary Gates "Bunny" Croft ensnares Ford, and they leave New York together. Ford becomes an alcoholic, like Bunny, and, at her command, stops wearing his glasses. He tells Corinne he can't leave Bunny because he is "with the Brain again" (107).

Rizzio, Mrs.   Raymond Ford tells Corinne von Nordhoffen about Mrs. Rizzio, who introduced him to poetry. The older woman copied poems by famous poets on slips of paper and gave Raymond a slip each time she came to the racetrack where he worked. After he graduated from high school, Mrs. Rizzio allowed him use of her library all summer. Ford dedicates his first book of poems to the memory of Mrs. Rizzio.

von Nordhoffen, Corinne   Corinne von Nordhoffen's diary extract and 11th birthday open the novella. She is in love with a classmate, Raymond Ford, whom she plans to marry one day. Corinne, daughter of a German baron and an American heiress, becomes quite wealthy when the baron, her remaining parent, dies. Robert Waner gives her Ford's book of poems as a 30th birthday present. She engineers a meeting with Ford after a hiatus of 19 years. Corinne falls in love with Ford over lunch, and they eventually marry. Corinne makes the mistake of allowing Mary Gates "Bunny" Croft access to her husband. Corinne, devastated after Bunny and Ford flee New York, travels to a Midwest city in an unsuccessful attempt to persuade Ford to return with her to their home on the Upper East Side of Manhattan.

Waner, Robert ("Bobby")   Robert Waner, who narrates most of the story, met Corinne von Nordhoffen when they were in college. Waner has been in love with Corinne since that time; on her 30th birthday he asks her to marry him. Waner gives Corinne a copy of Ford's first book of poems. When

Waner realizes that Corinne has fallen in love with Ford, he warns her not to marry him.

FURTHER READING

Alsen, Eberhard. *A Reader's Guide to J. D. Salinger.* Westport, Conn.: Greenwood Press, 2002.

French, Warren. *J. D. Salinger.* New York: Twayne Publishers, 1963.

———. *J. D. Salinger, Revisited.* New York: Twayne Publishers, 1988.

Gwynn, Frederick L., and Joseph L. Blotner. *The Fiction of J. D. Salinger.* Pittsburgh: University of Pittsburgh Press, 1958.

Hassan, Ihab. "Rare Quixotic Gesture: The Fiction of J. D. Salinger." *Western Review* 21 (Summer 1957): 261–280.

"I Went to School with Adolf Hitler"

"I Went to School with Adolf Hitler" is one of Salinger's "lost" stories, neither published nor to be found in a library archive. According to Ben Yagoda, the NEW YORKER rejected a story with this title in 1941. Unless the manuscript can be located among Salinger's literary estate, the story's whereabouts are unknown.

"J. D. Salinger—Biographical"

This is the title HARPER'S gave to a contributors' note Salinger wrote for the magazine to accompany its April 1949 printing of "DOWN AT THE DINGHY." The magazine did not print the text, however, until its February 1959 issue to accompany an essay about Salinger, Arthur Mizener's "The Love Song of J. D. Salinger."

The belatedly published 1949 contributors' note starts with Salinger telling *Harper's* that if he were a magazine owner, he would never include biographical notes about the contributors. Salinger admits he has written such notes in the past but states, "I

doubt I ever said anything honest in them" (87). This time, however, Salinger asserts that he will be truthful. He reveals that he has "been writing seriously for over ten years" (87). Though he does not claim to be "a born writer," he is "certainly a born professional" (87). He is not sure if he "*selected* writing as a career"(87); all he knows is once he started to write, he never stopped. Salinger ends by stating, "I almost always write about very young people" (87).

The contributors' note is mostly readily found in Henry Anatole Grunwald's *Salinger: A Critical and Personal Portrait* (Grunwald 21).

"J. D. S.'s The Skipped Diploma"

See URSINUS WEEKLY WRITINGS.

"Just Before the War with the Eskimos"

"Just Before the War with the Eskimos" is the third story in Salinger's second book, NINE STORIES (1953). Originally published in the June 5, 1948, issue of the NEW YORKER, the story marked Salinger's third appearance in five months in that magazine, thus consolidating his association with the publication. Set shortly after World War II, "Just Before the War with the Eskimos" features two young men, Franklin and Eric (neither of whom served active duty in the war), in conversations with Ginnie, a 15-year-old girl. "Just Before the War with the Eskimos" is Salinger's 23rd published story.

SYNOPSIS

On a Saturday morning in May, two prep school classmates, Ginnie Mannox and Selena Graff, are returning from the East Side tennis courts in a taxi. Ginnie considers Selena to be "the biggest drip at Miss Basehoar's" (57), but Selena always provides the tennis balls—new ones that her father manufactures. Ginnie has gotten stuck with cab fare the past four weeks and is determined that this time she will collect what Selena owes her. Ginnie tells Selena she can't afford to keep footing the tab for the cab fare. Selena pretends that she's been paying half all along. When Ginnie confronts her with the truth, Selena protests that she always brings the tennis balls.

Ginnie insists that she be reimbursed for the past cab rides that same day, as she needs the money to go to the movies in the evening. Selena says she will have to go upstairs and ask her mother for the money. The girls finish their ride in silence until they reach Selena's apartment building. The ungainly Ginnie—she's 15, stands five feet nine inches, and wears size 9-B shoes—once again pays the fare and follows Selena into the lobby. Selena tells Ginnie that her mother is very ill—"she virtually has pneumonia" (60)—but the information doesn't deter Ginnie's insistence on being paid.

After ringing the bell and being admitted to the apartment by a maid, Selena disappears, ostensibly to ask for the money, while Ginnie waits in the living room. From elsewhere in the apartment, a male voice asks loudly whether Eric has arrived. Ginnie guesses that the speaker is Selena's brother (whose name, Franklin, she does not learn until later in the story). Franklin soon appears in pajamas, unshaven, and wearing glasses. "He was the funniest-looking boy, or man—it was hard to tell which he was—she had ever seen" (63). Franklin, holding his hand to his chest, exclaims that he has just cut his finger to the bone and asks whether Ginnie had ever done so. Ginnie responds in the negative and inquires about the circumstances. Franklin explains that he was rummaging in the wastebasket and it was filled with razor blades. He then remarks sardonically to Ginnie that he's bleeding to death and that he may need a transfusion. In answer to Ginnie's question as to whether he has put any medicine on the cut, Franklin replies, "just some goddam toilet paper" (64).

Franklin asks Ginnie who she is. After being told her name, he informs her that he knows her sister, a "goddam snob" (64). Ginnie hotly disputes this characterization and asserts that Franklin

doesn't know her sister. When Franklin correctly tells Ginnie her sister's name—Joan—Ginnie asks him to describe her. His reply that Joan isn't as good-looking as she believes she is interests Ginnie. Ginnie tells Franklin that she has never heard her sister mention him, and informs him that Joan is getting married next month. When Franklin asks to whom, Ginnie holds back the information. Franklin then says he pities the man, and this quip causes Ginnie to laugh.

Franklin's finger is still bleeding, and he asks Ginnie what he should put on it. She recommends iodine, which he fears will sting. Franklin asks if she's eaten and offers her a chicken sandwich that he has in his room. Ginnie refuses the offer, saying that her mother will have her lunch ready when she gets home. Franklin then offers her a glass of milk. She refuses, but thanks him. Franklin asks Ginnie the name of Joan's fiancé. When she replies that he is Dick Heffner, a lieutenant commander in the navy, Franklin comments, "Big deal" (68). When Ginnie asks Franklin how he knows her sister, he explains that he met Joan at a Christmas party in 1942. Ginnie inquires why he thinks her sister is a snob and learns that Franklin wrote eight letters from Ohio to Joan, who never answered a single one. Franklin at that time had been assigned work at an Ohio airplane factory for 37 months during the war. He had been turned down from active military service due to a heart problem.

Franklin walks to the window and looks out, commenting, "They're all goin' over to the goddam draft board. We're gonna fight the Eskimos next" (72). When Ginnie asks him why we would fight the Eskimos, Franklin doesn't know. He muses that the next war will have only men around 60 years old fighting it, but to accommodate their age, they'll have shorter hours. Ginnie replies that Franklin would not have to go to that war and realizes she has said the wrong thing. Franklin acknowledges that he wouldn't have to serve and leaves the window. He then asks Ginnie to tell Eric, who is expected, that he will be ready in a minute. Franklin next inquires if Selena knows that Ginnie is waiting. After declining Ginnie's suggestion that he put a bandage on his cut finger, Franklin leaves the room. He soon returns with half a chicken sandwich he had bought at a deli the previous night. Franklin tells Ginnie to eat the sandwich. When she refuses politely, he insists that he hasn't poisoned the sandwich, whereupon she accepts, remarking that it looks good. Franklin prods her to eat, and Ginnie takes a bite, swallowing uneasily. The apartment bell rings, and Franklin leaves to shave.

Eric, a well-dressed man in his early thirties, enters the apartment. Ginnie looks for a place to put down the sandwich and quickly stashes it in her coat pocket. Eric asks Ginnie if she has seen Franklin, at which point the reader learns Franklin's name. After hearing that Franklin is shaving, Eric takes a seat and remarks histrionically, "This has been the most horrible morning of my entire life" (75). Claiming that he doesn't bore people he doesn't know, Eric nonetheless launches into a long story, flamboyantly emphasizing his words, as he tells Ginnie of how he let a writer live with him at his apartment. During his stay, the writer filled the apartment with his belongings. After Eric introduced him to "every theatrical producer in New York" (77), the writer ungratefully moved out of the apartment that very morning, taking everything he could grab. Eric interjects how much he loves Ginnie's coat, gushing over its quality, and rises from his chair to feel the material, declaring it to be "the first really *good* camel's hair [he's] seen since the war" (77). Eric asks where Ginnie got the coat, and upon hearing that her mother bought the coat in Nassau, Eric comments that his own mother was recently there, but that he couldn't join her for the trip this year.

After learning that Ginnie is not "the famous *Maxine* that Selena talks about," Eric fusses, "I am dog hairs from head to foot" (78), explaining that he is keeping his mother's dog over the weekend. Still waiting for Franklin, Eric comments, "I have never known that boy to be on time" (79) and explains that he and Franklin are going to Cocteau's film *Beauty and the Beast*. When Eric learns Ginnie has never seen the film, he proudly admits having seen the movie eight times and calls it "absolutely pure genius" (79). He then laments Franklin's terrible taste in films. During the war, on Franklin's insistence, they would go to Westerns, gangster mov-

ies, and musicals. Ginnie then asks Eric if he, too, worked in the airplane factory, and upon learning that he had, she asks if Eric, too, suffers from a heart problem, to which Eric replies no.

Selena enters the living room. She has changed from her tennis outfit into a dress and apologizes for keeping Ginnie waiting. Selena explains that she has woken her mother, whereupon Ginnie quietly tells her friend she no longer wants the cab money, offering as an explanation that she and Selena are even because Selena brings the tennis balls. Ginnie asks Selena to walk her to the door. When Selena protests that Ginnie needed the money to go to the movies that evening, Ginnie counters that she is tired. Ginnie then asks whether Selena is busy later. When Selena says no, Ginnie asks whether she can come over and the stunned Selena agrees. Ginnie tells Selena about meeting her brother, Franklin, and asks what he does and how old he is. Selena relates that Franklin, who is 24, has just quit his job and won't go back to college as his father suggests.

Now out on the sidewalk, Ginnie puts her hand into her coat pocket for her purse and encounters the sandwich half. She is about to drop the sandwich into the street, but she stops and returns it to her pocket. The story ends with the information to the reader that, several years earlier, Ginnie took "three days to dispose of the Easter chick she had found dead on the sawdust in the bottom of her wastebasket" (82).

CRITICAL ANALYSIS

"Just Before the War with the Eskimos" invites interpretation on several levels. The title of the story, with its bitterly ironic allusion to an imaginary future war with a group of minority people, strengthens one reading of the narrative as a caustic antiwar statement on Salinger's part (at the time of publication, the Eskimos—or Inuit—would have been considered by most Americans as a geographically remote people. Alaska had not yet become part of the United States). Simultaneously, however, Salinger infuses the narrative action with a portrayal of the development of a young girl's emotional life. Moreover, the author's apparent condemnation of the "conforming" society in which Americans found themselves during the post–World War II period is reflected in the characters of Eric, a homosexual, and Franklin, whom some critics of Salinger's work have identified as a symbolic Christ.

The story initially focuses attention on the dynamics between two adolescent friends, Ginnie Mannox and Selena Graff, who are returning to their homes in Upper East Side MANHATTAN after playing tennis. The reader enters the relationship in the middle of a spat between the girls, with Ginnie, resentful of Selena's failure to keep up her share of the cab expenses, now determined to get back the money due her. Upon Ginnie's insistence that she be paid immediately for past cab fare owed, the reader learns several facts about the Graff family: that Selena's mother, who is ill with pneumonia, will have to be awakened for the money; that Selena's father manufactures tennis balls; and that the Graffs employ a "colored maid" (61). That Selena has always supplied the tennis balls does not count, in Ginnie's estimation, of what Selena owes in terms of their tennis date expenses, as Selena does not have to pay for the balls. When Ginnie further bolsters her reasoning of why she must be paid back immediately, explaining that she "needs" (60) the money "to go to the movies" (60) that evening, the reader understands that both girls are affluent and do not suffer from any economic need.

Although Salinger utilizes a third-person narrative voice throughout the story, it is Ginnie whom the reader shadows most closely as the events of the story unfold. At 15 years old, she is a tall girl, with large feet, whose "self-conscious . . . awkwardness lent her a dangerous amateur quality" (60). She holds a poor opinion of her friend, whom she "openly" considers "the biggest drip" (57) in her class. Ginnie has likewise entertained the Mannox family at dinner with a humorous anecdote of what she imagines dinner at Selena's home would be like, with "a perfect servant coming around to everyone's left with, instead of a glass of tomato juice, a can of tennis balls" (57). Upon entering the Graff apartment, Ginnie is asked to wait in the living room, which she sums up as "expensive but cheesy" (62). From these initial descriptions of Ginnie and from her observations, the reader

forms an impression of a girl who, although from a wealthy and privileged background, is in danger of becoming a bit mean-spirited, opinionated, and insensitive.

When Franklin Graff, Selena's older brother, enters the room, dramatically holding his cut and bleeding finger to his chest, Ginnie's curiosity is piqued, and her focus on what were, essentially, external clues of the Graffs begins to shift to a more personal and interdependent engagement. In the give-and-take conversation between Franklin and Ginnie, Salinger deftly creates the tentative exchange of a nascent romantic involvement. At first sight, Ginnie finds Franklin "the funniest-looking boy, or man—it was hard to tell which he was—she had ever seen" (63). The impression may be interpreted in a number of ways, with one perception of Franklin—that he is between boyhood and manhood—matching Ginnie's own "awkward" growth stage. The critic John Wenke, in his 1991 study of Salinger's fiction, comments on the dynamic between Franklin and Ginnie, observing that "through his conversational posturing—his tough-guy bravado, his swearing, his slang, his smoking, his caustic, though playful, assertions—Franklin is obliquely soliciting Ginnie's friendship . . . In Ginnie's case the question of Franklin's 'appeal' focuses her growing interest in him" (Wenke 41–42).

As the two converse, Ginnie's changing perception of Franklin becomes evident. At first standoffish, she gradually gives in to Franklin's demand for her empathy. For example, in their exchange concerning what medicine Franklin should use on his cut finger, Ginnie initially dismisses the wound as something that she agrees "stings" (66) but "won't kill you or anything" (66). She finally delivers, however, the motherly advice (or command) that Franklin seems to need: "Stop touching it" (66), at which Franklin sits up "a trifle straighter—or rather, slumped a trifle less" (66), with his face assuming a "dreamy expression" (67). Immediately after this exchange, Franklin offers Ginnie the chicken sandwich.

Franklin's need for motherly attention is emphasized in contrast to the consistent mothering that Ginnie enjoys. Likewise, Franklin's obvious mothering of Ginnie, whom he assumes must be "hungry" (67) after tennis, is answered by her emphatic insistence that her mother "always has lunch ready" (67). She responds, moreover, that her mother would go "insane" if she were "not hungry" (67). Later, the reader will learn that Ginnie's mother has gifted her with a "really *good* camel's hair" (77) coat from Nassau. In contrast to Ginnie's always-attentive mother, Selena and Franklin's mother remains absent and ill.

Aside from establishing a dynamic between Ginnie and Franklin, the dialogue between them introduces the antiwar message of the story. Franklin, upon asking Ginnie her name, learns that she is the younger sister of Joan Mannox, a former love interest of his and a disappointment, as Joan did not respond to any of the eight letters that he wrote her from Ohio. When Franklin asks whom Joan will be marrying, Ginnie responds, "Nobody *you* know" (65). Ginnie later informs him that Joan is engaged to a "lieutenant commander in the Navy" (68), whereupon Franklin's immediate response is "Big deal" (68). Upon further questions from Ginnie as to why he was in Ohio, Franklin makes a trenchant indictment of the military-industrial economy that the United States quickly adopted after the Second World War. Calling all the people he sees from the window "Goddam fools" (71), Franklin says: "They're all goin' over to the goddam draft board . . . We're gonna fight the Eskimos next" (72). Salinger further underlines the point in the follow-up statement: "This time all the old guys're gonna go. Guys around sixty . . . Just give 'em shorter hours is all" (72).

Although some critics have found in Franklin's condemnation a personal defensiveness for his inability to serve active duty (because he has been classified as 4-F due to a heart problem), the strength of the antiwar statement is made more poignant when one considers how American culture during the postwar period defined the individual by the sole criterion of his relationship to past military service. Franklin, who through no fault of his own, has been barred from active duty, is not considered by Joan Mannox as an appropriate candidate for marriage. Instead, Joan has chosen a man who served successfully as a naval officer. Gin-

nie's statement that the lieutenant fiancé is nobody Franklin knows may be interpreted in the first, and stinging, sense that Franklin does not know the man because he did not serve actively, and that Franklin is therefore less of a man than the successful suitor. In Ginnie's statement lies a second inference, however, that Franklin does not know the fiancé because the two men did not travel in the same social circles before the war. In this second reading of the statement, therefore, the lieutenant, by the sole virtue of having served in the military, is now acceptable as a match for Joan, a wealthy New York girl. Thus, military duty counts more in a bachelor's eligibility score than social status. And, of course, Franklin's alternative service for the war effort through his work at the airplane factory does not count at all. Moreover, Franklin's disdainful claim that only old men will be sent to the next war also infers that the war with the Eskimos will be a production-line type of affair—that is, the old men can work at it as if it were an hourly (and salaried) occupation. That Franklin has pinpointed the Eskimos as the next enemy underscores the bitter truth that postwar America would prosper through an economy dependent on the continuation and production of the war machine and the tools of war. Any target, no matter how remote or absurd, will suffice for the maintenance of American prosperity.

Another aspect of Salinger's condemnation of American postwar society may be seen in the author's creation of Eric, Franklin's friend. After her conversation with Franklin, Ginnie next meets Eric, who has arrived at the Graff apartment to take his friend to the movies. Ginnie, who watches Eric for some minutes before they speak, attempts to place the young man into a category according to the way he is dressed. He "might have been on the staff of a news magazine. He might have just been in a play . . . He might have been with a law firm" (74–75), but his looks give "no really final information" (74) about him. (Salinger has already planted clues within the narrative about the importance of dress in defining social status when both Ginnie and Selena are described as "wearing topcoats over their shorts" [58] and doing so "despite the warm May weather" [58]. The necessity to dress appropriately for social acceptance and not according to what nature dictates forces everyone into conforming to artificial rules.) Through Eric's exaggerated expressiveness—his use of dramatic overstatements such as "I never bore people I haven't known for at least a thousand years" (75); and "I am *dog hairs* from head to foot" (78)—but especially through his divulging to Ginnie the circumstances concerning the young male writer whom he has helped, like a "Good Samaritan" (76), to introduce into the art/theater crowd of NEW YORK CITY, the reader is keyed to the fact that Eric is homosexual. Naively, Ginnie questions Eric whether he was placed with Franklin—who has a bad "ticker" (70)—at the airplane factory for the same reason. "Heavens, no. Knock wood." (80) Eric responds. "I have the constitution of—" (80). This statement confirms Eric's sexual preference, as the reader (and perhaps Ginnie) realizes that Eric has been kept from active military duty because of his sexual orientation.

The fact that Ginnie cannot confirm from Eric's appearance and dress where he might be employed likewise infers that Eric (as a homosexual) does not fit the accepted or usual categories by which American masculinity is defined. Rather, Eric seems more closely allied to the feminine-defining social categories (for example, his excited interest over Ginnie's camel hair coat and his knowledge of "really *good*" [77] camel's hair). Eric and Ginnie also compete over how many times his mother visits Nassau as opposed to the number of her mother's annual visits. Overall, Eric's friendly demeanor, his mannerisms, and his open approach to others make him a most likable and charming character. Nonetheless, when Selena appears with the money, Ginnie quickly rises without a parting statement to Eric. Her action could suggest her dismissal of a young man whom she has recognized as homosexual (thus demonstrating the shunning of Eric by society in general). On the other hand, Ginnie may suspect Eric of entertaining a sexual interest towards Franklin and may therefore resent the competition. As Wenke observes: "The story's implied drama suggests that Franklin's inability to participate in conventionally masculine domains are leading him toward homosexuality" (Wenke 42). Ginnie's determination to return to the Graff apartment that evening may then be seen as her

desire to influence Franklin toward a heterosexual relationship with her and perhaps save him, as well, from Eric's fate.

Despite the possibility that Eric might cause Franklin to change his sexual preference, it seems more likely that the character of Eric has been introduced to mirror the harsh condemnation that both young men face because of their inability to serve active duty during the war. Through no fault of Eric's, he has been deemed unfit (4-F) for duty. Likewise Franklin, through no fault of his own, has suffered (and will continue to suffer) the same labeling as a misfit because of his military status (4-F because of his heart condition). While Eric seems quite at home and well-adjusted to society—connected to a group of theater folks and to his mother (he watches her dogs while she is away; he travels regularly with her)—Franklin, on the other hand, seems more likely to be shunned by others. Of the two men, Franklin is the more isolated individual. This quality of isolation and its consequent emotional suffering is apparent in the narrative's descriptive clues of Franklin—his "bed-disheveled" (63) appearance while he remains in his pajamas (thus not allowing Ginnie to fit him into any recognizable social definition through the way he is dressed); his vulnerable, barefoot status (he is without slippers when Ginnie meets him); his "goofy" (63) manner; his refusal to return to college and his inability to stay in his job. The critic Warren French, in his 1963 study of the story, makes this observation of Franklin's situation: "His bitter assertion that this time only 'the old guys' will go denounces the older generation both because it starts wars that younger men must fight and because it has borne him with a defective heart that has cut him off from the company of his normal contemporaries in the armed forces. His refusal to return to college could be prompted by the knowledge that he would be asked embarrassing questions by the war veterans who in 1948 comprised the majority of student bodies" (French 88).

Among the possible perceptions of the character of Franklin, the Christian imagery that Salinger associates with him lifts the story's interpretation to another symbolic level and has led some critics, especially James Bryan—in his 1961 article comparing "Just Before the War with the Eskimos" with "Zooey"—to see in Franklin a representation of Jesus Christ.

The strongest evidence for the association of Franklin with Jesus resides in the story's "wastebasket" imagery. In his conversation with Ginnie, Franklin explains how he cut his finger: "I was lookin' for something in the goddam wastebasket" (63), which he says was full of razor blades. He then exclaims, "Christ, I'm bleedin' to death" (63). At the story's conclusion, the reader learns that Ginnie had once found a dead Easter chick at "the bottom of her wastebasket" (82) and that she could not discard the chick for three days. In the Christian faiths, the body and spirit of Christ rise into heaven on Easter Sunday, on the third day after the Crucifixion. The allusion to Easter therefore directly ties the "chick" to this miracle and lends symbolic spiritual meaning to the "chicken sandwich" that Ginnie protects in her pocket. Bryan likewise suggests that the story hides other clues to define Franklin as the Christ figure. For instance, when Franklin insists that Ginnie accept the sandwich, he states: "*Take* it, for Chrissake" (73). Bryan observes: "Franklin *means* for Christ's sake. Again through the use of a banal echo Salinger has transfigured a mundane situation into the Holy Sacrament. The chicken sandwich is the Eucharist" (Bryan 228). (In the Roman Catholic faith, the Eucharist becomes, through the sacrament of the Mass and the miracle of transubstantiation, the actual body of Christ.) Bryan further believes that, in taking a bite of the sandwich, "Ginnie has accepted the repulsive Franklin and thus Christ" (Bryan 228) as a spiritual sustenance. With this perspective in mind, the story now resonates with the understanding that Ginnie has undergone, in meeting Franklin, a spiritual and Christian growth experience. Other dynamics in the narrative would support this reading, such as Franklin's emotional sensitivity towards Ginnie (he insists that she must be "hungry" after playing tennis and he offers her the sandwich to eat). If Franklin is accepted as a Christ figure, the "hunger" he wishes to assuage in Ginnie is a spiritual as well as physical need. Moreover, Franklin, in the role of "savior," may therefore be saving Ginnie from

becoming a "snob" like her sister, Joan. Ginnie is in real danger of becoming so if she persists in defining other people according to the conforming codes of social acceptance. Indeed, the critics Frederick L. Gwynn and Joseph L. Blotner see, in their 1958 study of Salinger's fiction, that "the chicken sandwich . . . which Franklin offers and which Ginnie finally accepts [is] a gesture of charitable love" (Gwynn 48). The spiritual imagery cannot be disputed, and the story carries this dimension in its reading. However, in viewing the narrative from a broader perspective, what Ginnie may feel towards Franklin and what Franklin may offer Ginnie can also be read as the opportunity for a physical and a romantic love.

Franklin lacks female attention. Joan Mannox has spurned him as a suitor. He does not get along with his sister, Selena, whom he terms "the jerk" (64). His mother is ill and unavailable. As Wenke observes: "Franklin's need for female companionship emerges through his insistence that Ginnie take his leftover chicken sandwich" (Wenke 42). When Franklin hands Ginnie the chicken sandwich, the other "half" of which he had consumed the night before, Salinger may be inferring that the sandwich stands in for Franklin's "other half." In accepting it and taking a bite, Ginnie may be seen as Franklin's "match" or his "other half" who accepts the role. Furthermore, Ginnie's questioning of Selena about Franklin's age and her eagerness to return to the Graff home that evening (to Selena's stunned surprise) seem to support a budding romantic, rather than a spiritual, interest. If Franklin, on the one hand, is seen as a spiritual "savior" in offering Ginnie a glimpse past the material world together with the possibility of emotional growth, Ginnie, on the other hand, may be seen as Franklin's possible "savior" in that she offers him the opportunity for a romantic bond and a link back to the realm of social acceptance (in the role of boyfriend, fiancé, and husband). In Ginnie's explanation that her mother, when offering food, would go "insane" if Ginnie were not "hungry" (67), the reader comes to realize that Franklin, likewise, may go "insane" if Ginnie, whom he insists must be "hungry," does not accept his offering. Franklin, in danger of losing his emotional health, must find someone to love and to nurture in order to mature fully and to participate in life.

As in much of Salinger's fiction, many questions are left for the reader to ponder at the story's conclusion. Gwynn and Blotner characterize "Just Before the War with the Eskimos" as a dramatization of "the growth of an adolescent's human sympathy" (Gwynn 23). The story likewise poses, with its Christian imagery, a question of broader concern. Will the "chick" and the "chicken sandwich"—representative of human compassion and Christian moral values—rise again to guide American social consciousness? Or will these values be discarded into the "wastebasket" (82) or dropped into the "street" (82) by the dependence of post–World War II America upon a war-based economy? In the latter scenario, the only thing rising to the heavens may be airplanes (like those manufactured in the Ohio factory) to "drop" (82) death and destruction on the enemy "Eskimos" or on any other defenseless target, however remote. The resolution lies, evidently, in whatever action Ginnie might take, and the narrative, as John Wenke observes of the *Nine Stories* narratives in general, ends "with open-ended suggestion" (Wenke 33). Wenke sees in Ginnie a girl who "has been touched emotionally and alerted to the possibility of a new friendship. She will supposedly come back to try to find what she feels, but Salinger does not take us back with her" (Wenke 43).

PUBLICATION HISTORY

"Just Before the War with the Eskimos" was first published in the *New Yorker* magazine on June 5, 1948. The story was subsequently chosen to appear in the anthology *Prize Stories of 1949*, edited by Herschel Brickell (Doubleday, 1949). "Just Before the War with the Eskimoss"'s first book publication in a volume consisting exclusively of Salinger's work was in *Nine Stories* (LITTLE, BROWN AND COMPANY, 1953). *Nine Stories*, Salinger's second book, has never gone out of print.

Nine Stories is available in three editions from Little, Brown and Company: an exact reproduction of the hardback first edition from 1953; a trade paperback that mimics the production of the hard-

back; and a mass-market paperback, with its pagination differing from the above editions.

CHARACTERS

Eric   Eric, a man in his early thirties, calls on Franklin at the Graffs' apartment. He was assigned, as was Franklin, to the same airplane factory in Ohio during World War II to perform alternative service for the war effort. Eric now lives in New York City. By his speech mannerisms, interests, and the inference that the reason for his not serving in the army was not medically related, the reader comes to realize Eric's sexual orientation as homosexual.

Eric's mother   Eric explains to Ginnie Mannox that he and his mother usually vacation together in Nassau, though she went without him this past winter. Eric is keeping her dog at his apartment this weekend and complains about dog hair being all over his clothes, as he fussily brushes off his trousers.

Graff, Franklin   Franklin Graff, Selena's brother and Eric's friend, encounters Ginnie Mannox in his family's apartment in Manhattan. Franklin has spent World War II working in an airplane factory because of a bad heart. With the war over, he is now 24 and at loose ends. Franklin is about to go out to a movie, but he is still in his pajamas. Hearing the door, he thinks Eric has arrived, only to find Ginnie waiting for his sister, Selena. Franklin has badly cut his finger while fishing in the wastebasket, which he describes as being full of razor blades, and seeks Ginnie's commiseration. Though he looks "goofy" (63), he attracts Ginnie's interest. Franklin was once interested in Ginnie's sister, Joan, whom he now calls a snob. He insists that Ginnie eat his leftover half of a chicken sandwich. Franklin is unimpressed by the military and declares that in the next war "we're gonna fight the Eskimos" (72).

Graff, Mr.   Ginnie Mannox thinks Mr. Graff, Selena's father, manufactures tennis balls.

Graff, Mrs.   Mrs. Graff is Selena's mother; she is ill and possibly asleep in the apartment. Selena tells

Ginnie Mannox she will have to ask her mother for the money to cover her share of the cab fares she has avoided paying to Ginnie.

Graff, Selena Selena Graff is Franklin's sister and an acquaintance of Ginnie Mannox. She and Ginnie have just finished playing tennis and are sharing a taxicab home. Selena has avoided paying half of their previous cab fares, and Ginnie insists on getting her money today. The two girls ride the elevator up to Selena's family's apartment so that Selena can ask her mother for the money. During the time that Selena keeps her schoolmate waiting, Ginnie will encounter and have conversations with Franklin and Eric.

Graff maid The black maid opens the front door for Selena Graff and Ginnie Mannox. The maid and Selena are not on speaking terms with each other.

Heffner, Dick Dick Heffner is engaged to Joan Mannox. Upon learning that Heffner is a lieutenant commander in the navy, Franklin Graff comments, "Big deal" (68).

Mannox, Ginnie Ginnie Mannox is a 15-year-old girl who meets and becomes romantically interested in the 24-year-old Franklin Graff. Ginnie's insistence upon being reimbursed for cab fare from Franklin's sister, Selena, brings her to the Graff apartment. While she waits for her money, she meets Franklin. Franklin gives her half of a leftover chicken sandwich. After Franklin leaves the living room to get ready for his appointment with his friend, Eric, Ginnie converses with Eric as they wait in the Graffs' living room. When Selena appears with the cab money, Ginnie does not take it. Instead, she asks about Franklin and invites herself over for that evening. After leaving the apartment, Ginnie starts to throw the sandwich into the street, but she instead chooses to return it to her coat pocket.

Mannox, Joan Joan Mannox is Ginnie's older sister. She met Franklin Graff at a Christmas party in 1942. Franklin calls her "Joan the Snob" because she never answered any of the eight letters he wrote her while he was working in Ohio at the airplane factory.

Mannox, Mrs. Mrs. Mannox purchased the camel's hair polo coat that her daughter Ginnie is wearing. She brought the coat back from Nassau during the past winter.

Maxine Eric asks Ginnie Mannox if she is the "famous Maxine," a classmate of Selena Graff.

Writer The unnamed writer, who hails from Altoona, Pennsylvania, has been staying in Eric's apartment. Eric has helped the young man break into the theater crowd by introducing him to producers in New York City. On the morning of the story, the writer has left the apartment taking everything he could, his own as well as Eric's belongings.

FURTHER READING

Bryan, James. "J. D. Salinger: The Fat Lady and the Chicken Sandwich." *College English* 23, no. 3 (December 1961): 226–229.

French, Warren. *J. D. Salinger.* New York: Twayne Publishers, 1963.

Gwynn, Frederick L., and Joseph L. Blotner. *The Fiction of J. D. Salinger.* Pittsburgh: University of Pittsburgh Press, 1958.

Lundquist, James. *J. D. Salinger.* New York: Ungar, 1979.

Wenke, John. *J. D. Salinger: A Study of the Short Fiction.* Boston: Twayne Publishers, 1991.

"Kissless Life of Reilly, The"

"The Kissless Life of Reilly" is one of Salinger's "lost" stories, neither published nor to be found in a library archive. According to the bibliographer Jack R. Sublette, Salinger mentions a story with this title in a 1942 letter to WHIT BURNETT. Unless the manuscript can be located among Salinger's literary estate, the story's whereabouts are unknown.

Kitbook for Soldiers, Sailors, and Marines, The

Salinger's first publication in a book occurred when his 1941 COLLIER'S story, "The Hang of It," was chosen by R. M. Barrows to appear in *The Kitbook for Soldiers, Sailors, and Marines*. Published by Consolidated Book Publishers in 1942, the small (approximately five by six inches) hardback is a collection of "Favorite stories, verse, and cartoons for the entertainment of servicemen everywhere" (as described on its title page, where it is spelled "Kitbook"). The book's cover depicts a soldier, a sailor, and a marine each reading a book, with the title (spelled "Kit Book") blazoned across the red, white, blue, and black cover. The jacketless book was issued with a corrugated mailing carton, mim-

Table of contents of *The Kitbook for Soldiers, Sailors, and Marines* (Salinger's first publication in a book), a 1942 anthology that includes "The Hang of It" *(Courtesy of the Bruce F. Mueller Collection; photo by Laura Fairbanks)*

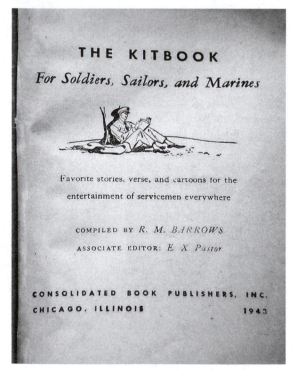

Title page of *The Kitbook for Soldiers, Sailors, and Marines* (Salinger's first publication in a book), a 1942 anthology that includes "The Hang of It" (2nd ed., 1943, pictured) *(Courtesy of the Bruce F. Mueller Collection; photo by Laura Fairbanks)*

icking its cover, to facilitate shipping to servicemen. The intention of the book—dedicated "To Our Fighting Yanks All Over the World"—was for it to be part of a serviceman's kit (a collection of personal items he would carry with him throughout his service).

Salinger, who at the time had published only a handful of stories, appears in this publication alongside well-known authors, such as Richard Armour, O. Henry, Rudyard Kipling, Ellery Queen, and Damon Runyon, as well as unknowns such as Hurd Barrett, Bertram B. Fowler, and W. E. Johns. The anonymous "Abdullah Bulbul Amirs"'s lyrics are also included; this is the song sung by Franny Glass for her brother Seymour's birthday in "Zooey."

The Kitbook for Soldiers, Sailors, and Marines is currently out of print. The 1942 volume was reprinted in 1943. Both editions are offered for sale by rare book dealers, with the 1942 edition significantly scarcer and more expensive.

"Last and Best of the Peter Pans, The"

"The Last and Best of the Peter Pans" is an unpublished Caulfield story whose 12-page, undated (circa 1942) typescript can be found at Princeton University's FIRESTONE LIBRARY, as part of the WHIT BURNETT–STORY magazine archive. "The Last and Best of the Peter Pans" is available for onsite reading only. According to the bibliographer Jack R. Sublette, the story, "written from the point of view of Vincent (Caulfield) . . . focuses on a conversation between Vincent and his mother—Mary Moriarity, an actress" (Sublette 21). The conversation takes place after Vincent has "found his questionnaire from the draft board that his mother has hidden" (Sublette 21). "The Last and Best of the Peter Pans" contains references to Holden, Phoebe, and Kenneth Caulfield, in addition to an image of a very young child near the edge of a cliff. (For more information regarding the seven extant Caulfield stories, *see* CAULFIELD STORIES.) The story was included on the proposed table of contents for Salinger's unpublished book, *The* YOUNG FOLKS.

"Last Day of the Last Furlough"

Appearing in the July 15, 1944, issue of the SATUR-DAY EVENING POST, "Last Day of the Last Furlough" introduces the Gladwaller family, in addition to the original Caulfield family. The story focuses on two soldiers, Babe Gladwaller and his friend, Vincent Caulfield, on their last day of freedom before departing overseas to fight in the war. "Last Day of the Last Furlough" is Salinger's 10th published story. The author, however, chose not to include the story in his three books of collected stories.

SYNOPSIS

As Valdosta, New York, lies covered in snow, Technical Sergeant John F. Gladwaller, Jr. (Babe), 24 years old, rereads favorite passages from favorite books in his book-strewn room, knowing that his furlough is almost finished. He hasn't told his family that he is being shipped overseas. Mrs. Gladwaller brings him cake and milk. She wants to know when "the Corfield boy" (26) will be arriving and what he did before the war. Babe corrects her: "Caulfield . . . he's twenty-nine . . . directed three radio programs" and "he's a writer too. . . . He has a kid brother in the Army who flunked out of a lot of schools" (26). Babe's friend is due to arrive on the six-o'clock train. Mrs. Gladwaller asks Babe to pick up his 10-year-old sister, Mattie, at school. Instead of driving, Babe decides he will take the sled. Before leaving his room, he glances into his closet, admires his suits, and wonders "if he would ever wear them again" (26).

Babe waits outside Mattie's school; she has stayed late to listen to the teacher read *Wuthering Heights*. Though Babe thinks to himself, "I don't have much time" (26), he is proud of Mattie's interest in books. Brother and sister see each other "at the same instant . . . her face lit up like nothing he ever saw before . . . it was worth fifty wars" (26). Babe wants to sled down a dangerous street, but when he realizes Mattie is frightened, they take a safer route home.

"Corp. Vincent Caulfield in uniform . . . a pale young man with large ears" (61) opens the door for Babe and Mattie. Babe, surprised by his friend's early arrival, introduces his sister. Vincent tells Mattie that he has a sister about her age and charms her with witty comments. After the two soldiers retire to Babe's room, Vincent confides that a letter arrived while he was in NEW YORK CITY, informing the family that his brother Holden "is missing" (61). Vincent reminisces about finding Holden, during Holden's school vacations, at "a beer joint for college kids and prep-school kids" (61). He would be "the noisiest, tightest kid in the place . . . drinking Scotch" (61). Holden has gone missing in action one month shy of his 20th birthday; Vincent wants "to kill so badly" (61) he can't wait. Vincent tells Babe that he didn't see his former girlfriend, Helen, now married and expecting a child. He thanks Babe for inviting him to the Gladwallers, commenting that soldier friends "belong together these days" (62).

At dinner, Babe's father, Professor Gladwaller, regales the table with stories from the previous war. Babe protests that war is being made into a game, which helps perpetuate war from generation to generation. He believes this is a just war but declares "it's the moral duty of all the men who have fought and will fight in this war to keep our mouths shut, once it's over, never again to mention it in any way" (62).

The soldiers return to the house after a double date—Vincent's date is Babe's former girlfriend, Jackie Benson; Babe's date is Frances. Vincent tells Babe that he is a fool not to be with Jackie; "she's twice the girl Frances is . . . better-looking . . . warmer . . . smarter . . . she'll give you ten times the understanding" (62). Babe knows this, but he is hopelessly in love, though unrequitedly, with Frances. After Vincent and Babe retire to their separate rooms to sleep, Babe thinks about Mattie growing up. He muses all sorts of advice to her, concluding, "try to live up to the best that's in you" (62). Babe then wakes up Mattie to simply say, "be a good girl" (64). Mattie tells him she knows that he is going to war; she saw him kick Vincent when she was under the table, tying together Vincent's shoelaces. Babe tells his sister not to let their mother know. Mattie pleads with her brother not to get hurt. He returns to his room, smokes, and looks out the window at the freshly falling snow. Babe thinks to himself that he is willing to die to protect those he loves here in Valdosta, but he would "like to come back too" (64).

Babe, surprised by a knock on his door, sees his mother enter. He tries to make a joke, but she cuts him off: "You're going over, aren't you?" (64). She calmly tells her son that she knows he will do his duty and "come back" (64). Mrs. Gladwaller then suggests that he wake Vincent, and the two should eat some chicken. The story ends: "'Maybe I will,' Babe said happily" (64).

CRITICAL ANALYSIS

"Last Day of the Last Furlough," published July 15, 1944, marks a major milestone in Salinger's early writing career. The story introduces two of his fictive families: the Gladwallers and the original Caulfield family. By virtue of this fact, "Last Day of

the Last Furlough" is known as both a Gladwaller and a Caulfield story. "Last Day of the Last Furlough" is Salinger's first story that shows the author beginning "to write of characters who moved from one adventure to another in a fictional world that seemed increasingly more real and that excited and perplexed readers" (French 60). With this story, Salinger "began publishing stories that would endear him to readers above all other authors to emerge from World War II" (French 60).

In "Last Day of the Last Furlough," readers meet the Gladwallers, who live outside of New York City in Valdosta, New York. Professor Gladwaller teaches biology; Mrs. Gladwaller is a homemaker. They have two children: John Jr., a 24-year-old son, known as Babe, and Matilda, a 10-year-old daughter, known as Mattie. The story features Babe during his last day home on his army furlough. Members of the Gladwaller family will appear in two later stories: "A Boy in France" (March 31, 1945) and "The Stranger" (December 1, 1945).

"Last Day of the Last Furlough" also introduces the original Caulfield family (distinguished from the Caulfields in the 1951 *The Catcher in the Rye*). In this story, readers learn the following facts about the Caulfields. The family home is in New York City. Vincent, who before the war directed three radio programs, is a 29-year-old corporal in the army and a writer. He has a brother, Holden (who flunked out of schools), also in the army. Holden has recently been declared missing in action, one month short of his 20th birthday. Vincent has a 10-year-old sister (her name, Phoebe, is not revealed until "This Sandwich Has No Mayonnaise" [October 1945]). ("Last Day of the Last Furlough" does not reference the youngest brother, Kenneth, also known as Red, who dies as a boy. Kenneth, alluded to in the later published stories, "This Sandwich Has No Mayonnaise" and "The Stranger," prefigures Allie Caulfield of *The Catcher in the Rye*; Vincent prefigures D. B. Caulfield in the novel.) The only information in the story regarding the parents is that Vincent is "the son of an actor" (62).

"Last Day of the Last Furlough" chronicles the final hours of Babe's and Vincent's furlough before being shipped overseas. Babe, a bookish young man, "can be seen as Salinger's re-creation of himself" (Lundquist 15). As IAN HAMILTON points out, the Army Service Number assigned to Babe is Salinger's. The story, written when Salinger was 24 years old (Babe's age), was sold to the *Saturday Evening Post* on the eve of Salinger's departure overseas. The text subtly suggests that Babe is a young writer. Babe's comment about Vincent, "He's a writer too" (26), coupled with Mrs. Gladwaller's response—"Oh, a writer! That's nice for you" (26)—would indicate that Babe, too, is an aspiring writer. Babe's passionate attachment to his books (Salinger favorites *Anna Karenina, The Brothers Karamozov,* and *The Great Gatsby*) and the author's emphasis on Babe's desk also are evidence that the character is a writer.

The story's idyllic setting—a snowbound Valdosta; Babe, surrounded by his books, eating cake and drinking milk; his sled ride with Mattie—contrasts with the upcoming departure for war. The reality of war obtrudes when Vincent tells Babe that his brother, Holden, is missing in action. Before Vincent's arrival at the Gladwaller house, Babe has mused on war, but not in realistic terms. Salinger indicates Babe's naive nature when the character looks at his closet full of clothes and, though he wonders "if he would ever wear them again" (26), Babe focuses on how a new white coat would wow all the girls, especially his unrequited love, Frances. When Babe, alongside Mattie, feels "happier than [he's] ever been in [his] life" (26), he welcomes death from Japanese snipers he has seen only in newsreels. He is willing to go to war to protect the people he loves; this protection especially extends to his young sister who, for Babe, embodies innocence.

Babe Gladwaller's youthful idealism and sentiment is contrasted with the depiction of Vincent Caulfield, who is five years older. Vincent's sophisticated wit and quick humor, evident in his verbal interactions, makes Babe seem even younger than he is. Indicative of Vincent's true feeling and state of mind, however, is his comment when he pretends that Babe and Mattie have arrived at the Gladwaller house to read the gas meter: "We don't use gas. We burn the children for heat" (61). As the critic John Wenke points out, Vincent's "dark

joke implies his obsessed comprehension of how war normalizes the slaughter of children," specifically Holden (Wenke 19). Vincent illustrates his own change of character when he confesses to Babe that, though he has avoided violence all of his life, he now wants to "kill so badly" (61) he can't wait to get overseas. The critic William F. Purcell suggests that the story can be read as a contrast of "two possible responses to the circumstances of the times . . . Babe's is an affirming, if somewhat desperate, faith in the basic decency of mankind . . . Vincent's more mature 'realistic' outlook is a capitulation to cynical pessimism which leads ultimately to lonely isolation and alienation" (Purcell 87).

"Last Day of the Last Furlough" seemingly embodies Salinger's personal stance on World War II and war in general. Babe states, "I believe in this war. If I didn't, I would have gone to a conscientious objectors' camp . . . I believe in killing Nazis and Fascists and Japs, because there's no other way" (62). But he objects to his father's war stories because they reduce war to "some kind of rugged, sordid game" (62) played to separate the men from the boys. Babe argues that this attitude, passed down from generation to generation, perpetuates war. He believes there is one way to break the chain: "it's the moral duty of all the men who have fought and will fight in this war to keep our mouths shut, once it's over, never again to mention it in any way" (62). Otherwise, if the returning soldiers of all nations are "talking, writing, painting, making movies of heroism and cockroaches and foxholes and blood, then future generations will always be doomed to future Hitlers" (62).

"Last Day of the Last Furlough" provides today's reader with two jarring realizations concerning *The Catcher in the Rye.* First, Salinger's original plans for Holden Caulfield situated the character in a World War II time period, and apparently, the character would be a casualty of that war. Second, the Caulfield family existed in an earlier, albeit similar, incarnation. Given these discrepancies, Salinger's decision not to collect this story, along with other stories that feature Caulfield characters, in his books of stories, is understandable. (For more information regarding the seven extant Caulfield stories, *see* CAULFIELD STORIES.

The publication of "Last Day of the Last Furlough" in the *Saturday Evening Post* was accompanied by two illustrations—Babe seated on a chair, as his mother, on a footstool, watches him eat cake; and Babe bending over the sleeping Mattie before he wakes her.

PUBLICATION HISTORY

"Last Day of the Last Furlough" was published in the July 15, 1944, issue of the *Saturday Evening Post*. Salinger never reprinted the story in his three books of stories. "Last Day of the Last Furlough" later appeared in the bootleg editions *The Complete Uncollected Short Stories of J. D. Salinger* (1974) and *Twenty-two Stories* (1998).

CHARACTERS

Benson, Jackie   Jackie Benson, Babe Gladwaller's former girlfriend, is Vincent Caulfield's date when Babe and Vincent double date. Afterward, Vincent, unimpressed with Babe's date, Frances, tells Babe that he is a fool not to still be with Jackie.

Jackie is referenced in "A Boy in France."

Caulfield, Holden   Holden Caulfield, one month shy of his 20th birthday, has been declared missing in action by the army. His older brother, Vincent, tells Babe Gladwaller that the family received the notification letter while he was home on furlough. Holden has "flunked out of a lot of schools" (26).

Holden appears in or is referenced in additional Caulfield stories: "This Sandwich Has No Mayonnaise," "I'm Crazy," "Slight Rebellion Off Madison," and the unpublished "The Last and Best of the Peter Pans" and "The Ocean Full of Bowling Balls."

Caulfield, Mr. and Mrs.   One of Vincent Caulfield's parents is referred to as an actor; the story, however, doesn't specify which parent.

The Caulfield parents, either singly or together, appear in or are referenced in additional Caulfield stories: "This Sandwich Has No Mayonnaise," "The Stranger," "I'm Crazy," "Slight Rebellion Off Madison," and the unpublished "The Last and Best of the Peter Pans" and "The Ocean Full of Bowling Balls."

Caulfield, Vincent   Vincent Caulfield, a 29-year-old corporal in the army, visits his friend, Babe Gladwaller, at Babe's family home. Before the war, Vincent directed three radio programs. Vincent is a writer, although it is unclear whether for radio. Upset by the news that his younger brother, Holden, has been declared missing in action, he relishes his assignment to go overseas so that he can kill.

Vincent appears in or is referenced in additional Caulfield stories: "This Sandwich Has No Mayonnaise," "The Stranger," and the unpublished "The Last and Best of the Peter Pans" and "The Ocean Full of Bowling Balls."

Frances   Babe Gladwaller brings Frances on a double date with Vincent Caulfield and Jackie Benson. Frances, whom Babe's parents disapprove of (they adore Jackie), has had Babe in thrall for seven years. The story implies that Frances is not of Babe's sociological class, unlike Jackie. There is a suggestive hint that Frances will indulge in sexual activity, unlike Jackie, who embodies a "nice" girl.

Frances is referenced in "A Boy in France."

Gladwaller, Babe   Babe Gladwaller, the 24-year-old protagonist, is home on furlough from the army. He is departing the next morning to go overseas, a fact he has withheld from his family. The bookish Babe, in all likelihood a young writer, has invited his older friend, Vincent Caulfield, to visit on the last day of their furloughs. Babe is idealistic, sentimental, and somewhat naive. He is very attached to his family and has been in love with Frances since he turned 17.

Babe is the protagonist of "A Boy in France" and "The Stranger."

Gladwaller, Mattie   Mattie Gladwaller, Babe's 10-year-old sister, inspires him with her innocence to want to go to war to protect her. Mattie knows that Babe is going overseas because she saw him warningly kick Vincent Caulfield under the table while she was tying Vincent's shoelaces together.

Mattie's letter figures prominently in "A Boy in France," and she appears in "The Stranger."

Gladwaller, Mrs. Mrs. Gladwaller brings her son, Babe, milk and cake. She lovingly watches him eat. Although Babe has hid from his mother the fact that he is going overseas, she guesses the truth.

Mrs. Gladwaller is referenced in "A Boy in France" and "The Stranger."

Gladwaller, Professor Professor Gladwaller teaches biology in college. His tales about World War I upset his son, Babe, and provoke Babe's statements on war and soldiers' duty.

Professor Gladwaller is referenced in "A Boy in France."

Helen (Beebers) Helen, Vincent Caulfield's former girlfriend, has married and is expecting a child.

Helen is referenced in "This Sandwich Has No Mayonnaise" and appears in "The Stranger" as Mrs. Helen Polk.

Vincent Caulfield's sister [Phoebe] Vincent Caulfield refers to an unnamed sister, who is the same age as Mattie Gladwaller (10 years old). She is smart but not as good-looking as Mattie.

Phoebe appears in or is referenced in additional Caulfield stories: "This Sandwich Has No Mayonnaise," "I'm Crazy," and the unpublished "The Last and Best of the Peter Pans" and "The Ocean Full of Bowling Balls."

FURTHER READING

French, Warren. *J. D. Salinger*. New York: Twayne Publishers, 1963.

Lundquist, James. *J. D. Salinger*. New York: Ungar, 1979.

Purcell, William F. "World War II and the Early Fiction of J. D. Salinger." *Studies in American Literature* 28 (1991): 77–93.

Wenke, John. *J. D. Salinger: A Study of the Short Fiction*. Boston: Twayne Publishers, 1991.

"Laughing Man, The"

"The Laughing Man" is the fourth story in Salinger's second book, NINE STORIES (1953). Originally published in the March 19, 1949, issue of the NEW YORKER, the first-person narrative evokes the childhood of a nine-year-old boy and his adulation of a "big brother" figure. The story features a tale-within-a-tale, also titled "The Laughing Man." "The Laughing Man" is Salinger's 25th published story.

SYNOPSIS

A first-person narrator, who never reveals his name, relates the story of the time, when, at age nine in 1928, he belonged to the Comanche Club in NEW YORK CITY. The club was the invention of a young man nicknamed the Chief, who was paid by their parents to pick up 25 boys after school and on Saturdays in his large bus and involve them in sports or take them to a museum. The Chief's name was John Gedsudski, and he was a law student at New York University. Although short and stocky, the Chief was an outstanding sports player in college and, although unattractive, was the idol of each of the Comanches: "every one of [them], from the smallest hoodlum to the biggest, loved and respected him" (85).

Each afternoon, when the boys had finished playing sports, they would reassemble in the bus to listen to the Chief tell the next installment of a tale of his own creation called "The Laughing Man" (which the narrator summarizes for the reader).

Born to a missionary couple in China, the Laughing Man had been kidnapped by bandits as an infant. When the Laughing Man's parents refused to pay the ransom, the bandits placed the child's head in a vise and gave it a couple of turns. The boy "grew into manhood" with "a hairless, pecan-shaped head and a face that featured, instead of a mouth, an enormous oval cavity below the nose. The nose itself consisted of two flesh-sealed nostrils . . . Strangers fainted dead away at the sight of the Laughing Man's horrible face" (87). The bandits adopted the boy and did not mind his deformity as long as he kept his face covered with "a pale-red gossamer mask made out of poppy petals" (88). This mask caused the Laughing Man to smell of opium. The Laughing Man communed with the animals in the forest, learning to speak their languages. Only with the animals would he remove his mask. Soon the Laughing Man became a more successful bandit than his stepfamily. "His ingenious criminal methods, coupled with his singular love of fair play, found him a warm place in the nation's heart" (89). The popularity and adulation infuriated the bandits, and they unsuccessfully tried to kill the Laughing Man. The Laughing Man would cross "the Chinese border into Paris, France" (90), where he would confound the famous detective Marcel Dufarge and his daughter. Consequently, the Dufarges grew to hate him. The Laughing Man became the wealthiest person in the world and contributed money anonymously to local monks. "He subsisted exclusively on rice and eagles' blood, in a tiny cottage with an underground gymnasium and shooting range, on the stormy coast of Tibet" (91). The Laughing Man lived with four companions: Black Wing, a timber wolf; Omba, a dwarf; Hong, a giant Mongolian; and a beautiful Eurasian girl who was unrequitedly in love with him. None of the Laughing Man's companions, however, was allowed to see his face.

The narrator reveals that at present he considers "the Laughing Man as some kind of super-distinguished ancestor" (91). He then comments that all of the boys in the Comanche Club felt the same way.

On a fateful day in February 1928, the narrator notices a framed photograph of a girl, which he feels "clashed with the general men-only décor of the bus" (93). He asks the Chief her identity, and the Chief reluctantly admits that she is Mary Hudson, a recent graduate of Wellesley College. The narrator wonders why the picture is in the bus. He accepts the Chief's answer of a shrug, and soon he and the Comanches no longer notice the picture. A couple of weeks later, however, the Chief pulls the bus over to the curb, and a young woman climbs aboard, possessing "unclassifiably great beauty at first sight" (94). Mary Hudson sits between the narrator and a boy named Edgar, while she tells the Chief about her difficulties getting there from Long Island, where she lives. Her presence shocks the boys, and even more so when she insists on joining them in their game of baseball. The Chief tries to dissuade Mary but to no avail. To the chagrin of the narrator, she is assigned as center fielder of the team he captains.

Mary Hudson incongruously wears a catcher's mitt in the outfield. Each time the narrator glances at her from his position at first base, she waves excitedly to him. After instructions from the Chief on how to bat, Mary hits a triple on her at-bat. The narrator experiences feelings of astonishment, awe, and delight at her prowess. From third base, she again waves to him. He returns her wave, noting that "she happened to be a girl who knew how to wave to somebody from third base" (98). Mary continues to make hits each time, and although she cannot catch the ball because of the mitt she refuses to change, the team easily wins. Mary continues to play baseball with the Comanches a couple of times a week. The narrator comments that "when you sat next to her in the bus, she smelled of a wonderful perfume" (99).

One day in April, the Chief stops the bus at the spot where he would normally pick up Mary Hudson. To kill time, he tells another installment of "The Laughing Man." The Laughing Man's best friend, the timber wolf, Black Wing, has been captured by the Dufarges. Because of his loyalty, the Laughing Man will trade his own freedom for that of Black Wing's, and his enemies know this. The Dufarges, though, plan to trick the Laughing Man. In the forest where the exchange is to be made, they substitute another wolf made to resemble Black Wing. The Laughing Man allows himself to be tied with barbed wire to a tree. When the Dufarges liberate the imposter wolf, the Laughing Man recites a lengthy farewell speech. As he continues, the imposter wolf tells the Laughing Man that he is not Black Wing; that his name is, in fact, Armand. Realizing he has been tricked, the Laughing Man angrily removes his mask with his tongue, and the sight of his face causes Mlle. Dufarge to faint. Her father, looking away at the time, is not affected by the Laughing Man's face. Instead, M. Dufarge sees his daughter on the ground and surmises what has happened. M. Dufarge then fires "the full clip in his automatic toward the sound of the Laughing Man's heavy sibilant breathing" (102). At this point in the story, the Chief abruptly ends the installment and starts the bus. The narrator asks whether he is going to wait for Mary Hudson, and the Chief replies, "Let's have a little quiet in this damn bus" (102–103). The remark is gratuitous, as the busload of boys, thinking about the just-concluded Laughing Man episode, had already fallen into silence.

The bus arrives at the park, and the boys begin to play ball. During the game, the narrator notices Mary Hudson sitting on a bench in the distance, "sandwiched between two nurse-maids with baby carriages" (103). He points her out to the Chief. The Chief slowly goes over to her and talks. They return together to the ball field, but Mary does not want to play. When the narrator tells her he needs an outfielder, she puts him off. He is persistent, and she finally replies, "Just please leave me alone" (105). He senses that "Mary Hudson had permanently dropped out of the Comanche lineup" (105). After the game has ended, the narrator sees the Chief with Mary. He notices that she is crying. She breaks away from the Chief and runs off as he watches her disappear. When the narrator asks the Chief if he and Mary have fought, the Chief tells him to tuck in his shirt.

After the boys reassemble on the bus, the Chief tells them the next, and final, installment of "The Laughing Man." The Laughing Man had been struck by four bullets fired by Dufarge, two of them in the heart. Hearing "a queer exhalation of agony from the direction of the target" (108), Dufarge goes to his daughter and revives her. They approach the tree-bound Laughing Man, whose head, slumped to his chest, makes them believe that he is dead. The Laughing Man, however, has been "contracting his stomach muscles in a secret manner" (108). When the Dufarges draw near, he raises his head, gives "a terrible laugh, and neatly, even fastidiously, regurgitate[s] all four bullets" (108). The Dufarges' hearts explode, and they fall dead at the Laughing Man's feet. Bleeding to death and in need of eagles' blood, the Laughing Man asks the animals in the forest to find and bring Omba to him. By the time the dwarf arrives with fresh eagles' blood and a medical kit, he finds the Laughing Man in a coma. Omba retrieves the mask, covers his friend's face, and treats his wounds. As Omba raises a vial of eagles' blood to the Laughing Man's lips, the latter asks about the fate of Black Wing, the timber wolf.

Omba responds that Black Wing was killed by the Dufarges. Upon hearing this news, the Laughing Man takes the vial and, instead of drinking its contents, crushes the glass. He then tells Omba to look away, and when the latter does so, "the Laughing Man's last act, before turning his face to the bloodstained ground, [is] to pull off his mask" (110). The story of the Laughing Man ends, never to be resumed by the Chief.

The narrator remembers that this last installment of the story caused his knees to shake. When he steps from the bus, he sees "a piece of red tissue paper flapping in the wind against the base of a lamppost," which looks to him like "someone's poppy-red mask" (110). When the narrator arrives home, his teeth are chattering, and he is sent directly off to bed.

CRITICAL ANALYSIS

Resembling "DE DAUMIER-SMITH'S BLUE PERIOD" in narrative structure, "The Laughing Man" is one of the most ambitious of the *Nine Stories* collection. Salinger has set both stories within a frame, that of a mature narrator who, in the first-person voice, tells the story of a youthful experience that has left its mark in his memory. The framed story in "The Laughing Man," however, also contains a fable that composes the tale-within-the-tale: The allegory of the Laughing Man as told to the group of young boys, the Comanches, by their hero-figure, John Gedsudski. Within this fable, Gedsudski creates an alter ego whose circumstances, as Gedsudski tells the tale, begin to parallel the events in Gedsudski's own life. Finally, Salinger leaves the reader of "The Laughing Man" to discern, or to intuit, by way of the symbols imbedded in the fable, the meaning of the experience to both the storyteller, Gedsudski, and to the unnamed narrator of Gedsudski's story. Like "De Daumier-Smith's Blue Period," "The Laughing Man" moves dramatically toward a moment of epiphany for the narrator's younger self. However, the realization (or intuitive understanding) that the narrator-as-youth experiences is not one of resolution (as in Jean de Daumier-Smith's "transcendent" experience), but is the unmasking of a "terrible" emotional truth about the reality of the adult world.

That Salinger intends to present John Gedsudski, the "Chief," as a hero to the boys of 1928 is underlined by the author's stressing the young man's prowess in sports and the skills acquired as a scout. The narrator unabashedly states, "Every one of [the Comanches], from the smallest hoodlum to the biggest, loved and respected him" (85). That Gedsudski, as well as his alter ego, the Laughing Man, remains a hero to the mature narrator of 1949 is likewise evident in declarations by him, such as: "I happen to regard the Laughing Man as some kind of super-distinguished ancestor of mine . . . And this illusion is only a moderate one compared to the one I had in 1928, when I regarded myself not only as the Laughing Man's direct descendant but as his only legitimate living one" (91–92).

In forming the hero-figure of Gedsudski, Salinger may have returned to another undeniable hero-figure, that of Sergeant Burke, in his 1944 story "SOFT-BOILED SERGEANT." The narrative structure of the earlier story parallels that of "The Laughing Man." "Soft-Boiled Sergeant" is told within a frame as well, of the mature narrator, Philly Burns, recounting his relationship to his hero, Sergeant Burke, who had befriended him as a young army private. The early story likewise utilizes the tale-within-the-tale: The letter from a fellow soldier to the story's narrator, in which are recounted the events of the sergeant's heroic self-sacrifice to save some young privates from death during the bombing of Pearl Harbor. Salinger's descriptions of the physical attributes of Sergeant Burke and of John Gedsudski parallel each other. Sergeant Burke, described as "a real ugly guy" with "bushy black hair . . . slopy-like, peewee shoulders" (82), is also short. Gedsudski is similarly described: "a stocky five three or four—no more than that. His hair was blue-black . . . his shoulders were powerful, but narrow and sloping" (85). In "Soft-Boiled Sergeant," the tale-within-the-tale ends with the death of Burke, who does not die a Hollywood-movie kind of death but a horrible and lonely one, facially disfigured by gunfire. Similarly, the Laughing Man, or fabled hero of Gedsudski's imagination and projection for his spiritual/emotional self, likewise dies a lonely death of self-sacrifice in the story's

tale-within-the-tale and simultaneously unmasks his face to reveal a disfigurement. Specifically, in "Soft-Boiled Sergeant," Burke is hit by four bullets to his torso, and his face becomes disfigured: "Burke had four holes between his shoulders, close together, like group shots, and . . . half of Burke's jaw was shot off. He died all by himself" (85). In "The Laughing Man": "Four of Dufarge's bullets struck the Laughing Man, two of them through the heart" (108). Just before he dies, the Laughing Man's last act is "to pull off his mask" (110) from his disfigured face. The bullets in the fable, however, do not cause the hero's death. Rather, the Laughing Man chooses suicide in refusing to drink the life-sustaining eagles' blood. Similarly, Sergeant Burke chooses to risk his life, and he dies in a self-sacrificial act to save his men. As the letter (the tale-within-the-tale) informs the narrator of "Soft-Boiled Sergeant": "Burke put his own number up" (85). Although both heroes die a lonely death, each death is witnessed and comes to be narrated by the mature storyteller of each of these stories. In "Soft-Boiled Sergeant," the soldier who has written the letter, Frankie Miklos, has witnessed Burke's death and writes to (narrator) Philly Burns, who subsequently tells about the tragedy. In "The Laughing Man," the witnessing is more complicated. The boys bear witness, along with Gedsudski, to the death of the Laughing Man. Moreover, within the tale, Omba, the dwarf friend of the fabled Laughing Man, is also an imbedded witness to the symbolic death. (The dwarf within the fable most likely stands in for the narrator's younger self, which would make him an active participant in Gedsudski's world of imagination.) The mature narrator, then, telling about the death of the Laughing Man, and thus about the death of some part of his real-life hero, Gedsudski, also participates in the mythic death. The narrators of "Soft-Boiled Sergeant" and "The Laughing Man" are once removed, through the frame, from the hero's true sacrifice. But the imagination of the narrator of "The Laughing Man" has felt the death, through myth, in a more universal way. In both stories, Salinger has managed to make the tale-within-the-tale bear the experience, or truth, of the heroism.

The intent of the narrator in Salinger's 1944 "Soft-Boiled Sergeant," originally titled by the author as "DEATH OF A DOGFACE," is to portray to his wife, Juanita, the phoniness of Hollywood-movie depictions of war by giving her a true picture of what it is like to be a hero. Likewise, one may interpret a similar intent on the part of Gedsudski. The Chief had employed the story of his hero, the Laughing Man, to give the boys courage and to boost their morale after a hard day of sports: "Every afternoon, when it got dark enough for a losing team to have an excuse for missing a number of infield popups or end-zone passes, we Comanches relied heavily and selfishly on the Chief's talent for storytelling" (86). In killing off the hero at fable's end, and depriving the boys of that illusion, Gedsudski essentially unmasks the illusion of a world in which the hero always wins. The narrator-as-youth intuits, in a profoundly emotional way, this loss of a sense of justice and is left to face the world as Gedsudski does (or, put differently, in revealing his true face, Gedsudski's Laughing Man unmasks the world's phoniness).

Another parallel element contained in both "Soft-Boiled Sergeant" and "The Laughing Man" is the hero's loss of the beloved girl of his dreams. In Sergeant Burke's case, she is a redheaded girl who does not return his love. Although the two had been in a relationship, she instead chooses to marry a civilian. Likewise, Mary Hudson chooses to walk away from the ball field, never to return to Gedsudski. In "Soft-Boiled Sergeant," when Sergeant Burke tells the young Philly Burns (the narrator) why he does not like watching a Charlie Chaplin movie, he says: "I don't like no funny-looking little guys always getting chased by big guys. Never getting no girl, like. For keeps, like" (85). The narrator of Sergeant Burke's story believes that the red-headed girl may have been put off by his sergeant's ugliness, unable to see past the physical tissue to the hero's spiritual strength and valor. The reasons for the breakup of Mary Hudson and John Gedsudski, however, may be more difficult to unmask.

As the critics Frederick L. Gwynn and Joseph L. Blotner observe, the reason for the breakup may lie more in the separation of the social classes between the hero and the girl, the ugly truth being

that, in real life, these gaps cannot be easily bridged (Gwynn 25–26). Gedsudski, who by his surname might be identified as of Eastern European heritage, and who hails from a working-class background (Staten Island), is a New York University law student who must work every afternoon and on Saturdays and holidays to make ends meet. The girl he falls in love with, Mary Hudson, hails from a WASP background (surmised by evidence of her surname) and has been educated at Wellesley, "a very high class college" (93). She lives with her parents in a wealthy community on Long Island. Nonetheless, Mary falls in love with John Gedsudski and makes every effort to enter his world on his terms. (Salinger represents her acceptance into the Comanche world symbolically, as Paul Strong notes [Strong 94], with the fact that she wears a "beaver coat" [94, 104, 106]. Within the imagery of the fable, the coat would make her a trustworthy kin to the hero's circle, comprised of furry friends like Black Wing, the wolf. These friends, however, do not see the Laughing Man's face but follow him blindly. With other followers, however, the Laughing Man need not wear his mask. Unmasked, he speaks with them in their own languages and thus shows them his true nature; they do not "think him ugly" [88].) Mary is drawn to the "shy" and aspiring law student, perhaps for his sense of ethics and fair play. Perhaps she does not see his "disfigurement," which Salinger may intend to imply as his humble economic origins, his ethnic background, and perhaps, too, his physical characteristics. Salinger does not inform the reader of any aspect of the couple's mutual attraction. However, at the crisis point in their relationship, it is Mary who runs from Gedsudski.

Richard Allan Davison, in his 1981 explication of "The Laughing Man," suggests the possibility that Mary Hudson may be pregnant (Davison 9). Salinger in fact employs, and underscores, imagery to support this reading, with Mary "sandwiched between two nursemaids with baby carriages" (103) in the final meeting between the couple. As the young narrator puzzles over why Mary is crying, he walks backwards and "bumps smack into a baby carriage" (105). Another clue suggestive of Mary's pregnancy is the author's attribution to her of physical beauty. The mature narrator describes Mary as an "unclassifiably great beauty at first sight" (94). Only a few women in Salinger's fiction have been granted this definition. One is the protagonist of the story "ELAINE," who becomes pregnant out of wedlock. Another is Mrs. Happy (of Salinger's last published story, "HAPWORTH 16, 1924"), whose initials—M. H.—match those of Mary Hudson. Mrs. Happy happens also to be pregnant.

The reader may look for some reason for Mary and John's breakup in the symbolism Salinger employs within the fable of the Laughing Man. In the fable, the Laughing Man calls for his trusty dwarf, Omba, who tries to save the hero by bandaging his wounds. (The Laughing Man is bleeding to death, held by barbed wire to a tree trunk, after being shot by Marcel Dufarge's bullets. Like Omba, the youthful narrator attempts to bandage Gedsudski's "wounds" by inviting Mary to come to his family's apartment, where Gedsudski often goes to have dinner.) Omba offers the life-sustaining eagles' blood to the Laughing Man, who, before taking a drink, asks the question: What has happened to Black Wing (whom the Dufarges have kidnapped)? Learning that the Dufarges have killed the wolf, the Laughing Man refuses the drink, thus choosing death by suicide. If Salinger has meant for the boys (and the reader) to understand that the Dufarges—a father-and-daughter team from Paris—represent, within the fable, Mary and her father, then the death of the Laughing Man may be seen as a death chosen because something beloved had already died. Perhaps it is the death of hope, or innocence, or justice, or love, or truth. Perhaps the death has something to do with the pregnancy and its subsequent consequences.

Davison views the possible pregnancy of Mary and the subsequent breakup of the couple as hinging on Gedsudski's inability to accept adult responsibilities as a father/provider (Davison 9). Strong argues, however, in his 1986 explication of the story, that it is Mary who has betrayed Gedsudski. Taking the betrayal as signifying something deeper than the end of romance, and with a reading of a pregnant Mary, Mary's last visit to the ball field may have been made to inform Gedsudski of her decision either to carry the pregnancy to term and to

place the baby up for adoption or to terminate the pregnancy. In 1928, the year of the story's events, abortion was illegal in the United States. Mary, however, coming from an economically privileged background, would likely have had access to a safe abortion procedure, perhaps by crossing borders (as the characters do so easily within the fable) or by some illicit but privately arranged means within the States. She would certainly have been able, with support from her parents, to be sent away for a time until the birth of the child.

Some critics give weight to the socioeconomic difference between the young couple as the overriding factor in their breakup, and see the rupture of the relationship hinging on the disapproval of Mary's father (who, as M. Dufarge in the fable, will shoot four bullets, two through the heart, of the Laughing Man). Perhaps, then, to unmask the Laughing Man is to reveal the injustice of social-class realities. Women of lower social classes who became pregnant in 1928 would not have had an easy time ending their pregnancies. Perhaps, too, Gedsudski's adherence to the law, or his moral or religious convictions, would have opposed Mary's choice. The symbolism of baby carriages that Salinger plants earlier in the story, when the young narrator states that the Comanches would seek out places to play "where the opposing team didn't include a baby carriage or an irate old lady with a cane" (84), may perhaps be interpreted as the undeniable fact of women's biological reality.

Mary, however, who tearfully runs from Gedsudski at the couple's last meeting, may be driven (against her own wishes) by her father's disapproval of the young man's economic prospects (in the fable, the daughter has fainted when M. Dufarge shoots the Laughing Man). Despite Gedsudski's (or the Laughing Man's) "singular love of fair play" (89) and his self-made success thus far, the young man will never realistically fit, with his Staten Island upbringing, into Long Island society. The "terrible" (108) laugh of the Laughing Man as he regurgitates M. Dufarge's bullets, therefore, may represent Gedsudski's own intuitive understanding that, although he has done what he could to conform to the acceptable standards of achievement (Eagle Scout, almost–All America football star, almost New York Giants baseball player, self-made law student), he does not measure up to Mary's world. Even if Gedsudski had proposed to Mary that they marry and that he support the family on his income, her parents' expectations for her would more than likely have barred the way. As Sergeant Burke, in Salinger's earlier story, explains in communicating his own disappointment and emotional pain to the young narrator, Philly Burns, the little guys never get the girl, "For keeps, like" (85).

Strong observes in his very insightful analysis of "The Laughing Man" that the story's central concern is "with John's agony after Mary's betrayal, with his need for love and understanding. Unlike his creation, however, John gets no comfort from his animals of the forest, the Comanches, for the nine-year-olds are simply unable to fathom the nature of his pain. If there is to be sympathy it must come from the understanding reader, and I believe Salinger intends us to extend our compassion to the 'extremely shy, gentle young man' whose story demonstrates how the denial of love can twist, even destroy a life" (Strong 95).

In the fable of the Laughing Man, Gedsudski tells the boys that the hero, after being shot by the bullets from Dufarge's gun, does not die. Instead, when both father and daughter Dufarge approach to inspect his body, the Laughing Man with "a terrible laugh" (108) regurgitates the bullets, which causes the Dufarges' hearts to burst, and the two drop dead at the hero's feet. Perhaps the "terrible laugh" is Gedsudski's hopeless and sardonic laugh at himself as he realizes that, while he played fair, the world will never play fair with him. The Laughing Man as hero and as what Warren French describes as a Robin Hood figure (French 1988, 72) must die—both for Gedsudski as well as for the boys. In fact, Salinger has planted a clue earlier in the story about how to interpret the laughter of the Laughing Man. As the narrator speaks through the prism of his younger self, he explains: "I was not even my parents' son in 1928 but a devilishly smooth imposter, awaiting their slightest blunder as an excuse to move in ... to assert my true identity. . . . But the *main* thing I had to do in 1928 was watch my step. Play along with the farce. Brush my teeth. Comb my hair. At all costs,

stifle my natural hideous laughter" (92). French, in his 1963 assessment of the story, suggests that Gedsudski is "a man who will sacrifice children's feelings in order to salve his own wounds" (French 1963, 93). However, a different interpretation may be considered for Gedsudski's killing-off of the hero figure for the boys. Salinger has used the word "hideous" in another story, "De Daumier-Smith's Blue Period," to describe the alienation of the young de Daumier-Smith. In that story, the protagonist, standing before the orthopedic appliance shop window one evening, says: "something altogether hideous happened. The thought was forced on me that no matter how coolly or sensibly or gracefully I might one day learn to live my life, I would always at best be a visitor in a garden of enamel urinals and bedpans, with a sightless, wooden dummy-deity standing by in a marked-down rupture truss" (214). No matter, perhaps, how conformingly, or gracefully, or fair-mindedly the young Gedsudski might learn to live his life, he must not unmask his true nature (or true hope to commune) with the Hudsons, who, seeing this "hideous" truth, would burst their black hearts. The death of the Laughing Man, then, may be read as the death of hope for the young law student, who has tried to bridge the gap between the social classes with honest initiative. His may be a "hideous" laugh at the illusion of social equality and justice.

In the figure of John Gedsudski, some critics have found a similarity to that of Holden Caulfield of The CATCHER IN THE RYE, in that both characters strive to be a "catcher" to the young—wishing to keep them from the harsh and hurtful experience of adult realities. Both characters make the realization that the young must tough it through the transformation from childhood to adulthood. Both struggle with this transformation within themselves as well; and both realize themselves powerless to stop that growth, however painful. Sergeant Burke of "Soft-Boiled Sergeant" sacrifices his mortal life to save the lives of his charges but retains his hero status in their memories. Gedsudski, in sacrificing his alter ego, the Laughing Man, kills the boys' emotional dependence on the illusion that heroism might overcome all obstacles, but gives them (as Philly Burns gives Juanita, his wife, the Hollywood war-movie buff of the earlier story) a truer picture of what it is like to be a hero. The critics Irving Deer and John H. Randall III observe: "By the use of myth, the Chief has conveyed to the boys the essential inner meaning of his adult experience" (Deer 19).

"The Laughing Man" commands additional interest in its possible depiction of an experience in Salinger's own life. As a youth, Salinger would have belonged to the class of "Comanches" to be collected at MANHATTAN apartment houses and kept active by a watchful "hero" such as a Gedsudski. Likewise, the age of the young narrator, nine years old, would match Salinger's biological age in 1928. That year marks, moreover, the adaptation of Victor Hugo's 1869 novel *L'homme qui rit* into a popular movie, *The Man Who Laughs*. Salinger may well have chosen 1928 in which to set the events of this story as a salute to a personal memory and hero.

The critics Gwynn and Blotner gave early and high praise to "The Laughing Man" in their 1958 analysis of Salinger's work and summarize the story in this way: "Salinger . . . has seemed to present from the point of view of sardonic recollection an experience of childhood fantasy in which adult concerns intruded without being recognized by the child, at the same time that he has presented an experience of adulthood symbolized in fantasy without being recognized by either child or adult" (Gwynn 26–27). French similarly assesses the story, in his 1988 study of Salinger's work, and considers, in the character of Gedsudski, a man who "illustrates the . . . painful achievement of transcending his own defeat in order to force others towards enlightenment" (French 1988, 72). Davison argues for a different interpretation, one of "arrested development" (Davison 1) in a Gedsudski unable to accept adult responsibility. French, on the other hand, who in 1963 interpreted the story as a "bitter fable of the disillusionment of misplaced hero-worship" (French 1963, 93) leaves room, in his reconsideration of the tale in 1988, for the possibility that Salinger's intent is to exemplify Gedsudski as a bona fide hero. Strong argues for a reading of betrayal on the part of Mary and her father (Strong 92–94) but also leaves open the question of Mary's complicity in the betrayal. As with so many of Salinger's highly crafted stories, meanings remain elusive. "The Laughing Man" invites and supports multiple and diverse readings. Perhaps Strong's final assessment comes closest to an understanding in appraising the story as "a cautionary tale, a warning to the young about the dangers of entrapment in a deceptive world" (Strong 95).

PUBLICATION HISTORY

"The Laughing Man" was first published in the *New Yorker* magazine on March 19, 1949. The story appeared in a book publication in *Nine Stories* (LITTLE, BROWN AND COMPANY, 1953). *Nine Stories*, Salinger's second book, has never gone out of print.

Nine Stories is available in three editions from Little, Brown and Company: an exact reproduction of the hardback first edition from 1953; a trade paperback that mimics the production of the hardback; and a mass-market paperback, with its pagination differing from the above editions.

CHARACTERS

Armand Armand is the wolf that the Dufarges disguise to impersonate the Laughing Man's wolf, Black Wing. When Armand tires of the Laughing Man's long farewell, he reveals his true identity.

Black Wing Black Wing, a timber wolf, is one of the Laughing Man's four close associates who live with him. After the Dufarges capture Black Wing, the Laughing Man offers himself if they will free his best friend. Unknown to the Laughing Man, the Dufarges kill the wolf.

Chief, the The Chief of the Comanche Club is a law student named John Gedsudski. He picks up the boys after school and on Saturdays to take them to play sports or to visit museums. He also tells the boys the saga of the Laughing Man, whom the reader comes to realize is his alter ego. The Chief, and his creation the Laughing Man, are heroes to the boys. The story soon parallels events in the Chief's relationship with his girlfriend, Mary Hudson. Unlike Mary, the Chief does not come from a privileged family. The relationship falters, and when she leaves him, the Chief kills off the Laughing Man in the last episode of the narrative.

Chinese bandits   The Chinese bandits have kidnapped the Laughing Man, while an infant, from his wealthy missionary parents. After the parents refuse to pay the ransom, the bandits deform the baby's head by screwing it in a vise. The bandits then raise the child as their own but require him to wear a mask of poppy petals. When the Laughing Man eventually becomes more successful as a bandit, the Chinese bandits attempt to kill him.

Comanche Club   The Comanche Club, led by the Chief, consists of the 25 boys whose parents pay him to pick up their sons and take them to play sports or to visit museums. When he was nine years old, the narrator belonged to the club.

Dufarge, Marcel   Marcel Dufarge, a French detective, considers the Laughing Man his archenemy. He shoots the Laughing Man four times, twice through the heart.

Dufarge, Mlle.   Mlle. Dufarge is Marcel Dufarge's daughter. She faints from the sight of the Laughing Man's face shortly before her father shoots him.

Edgar   When Mary Hudson first rides in the bus, she takes a seat between Edgar and the narrator. The narrator doesn't know Edgar's last name but is aware that the boy's uncle's best friend was a bootlegger.

Eurasian girl   The unnamed beautiful Eurasian girl is one of the Laughing Man's four close associates who live with him. She is unrequitedly in love with the Laughing Man.

Gedsudski, John   *See* the Chief.

Hong   Hong, a Mongolian giant, is one of the Laughing Man's four close associates who live with him.

Hudson, Mary   Mary Hudson is the Chief's girlfriend. She lives on Long Island and comes from a well-to-do family. The narrator and the other Comanches notice that the Chief has hung her photograph in the bus. Mary travels to New York City to see the Chief and play baseball with the boys. She impresses the narrator with her "unclassifiably great beauty at first sight" (94). The reader never learns how the Chief and Mary met. Their breakup, for unspecified reasons, causes the Chief to kill off the Laughing Man.

Laughing Man, the   The Laughing Man is the hero of the Chief's ongoing narrative that he tells, in episodes, to the Comanches. The Laughing Man's exploits as a benevolent bandit thrill the children. He lives with four close associates: Black Wing, Omba, Hong, and a Eurasian girl. Due to his facial disfigurement, caused in infancy by the Chinese bandits who had placed his head in a vise, he wears "a pale-red gossamer mask made out of poppy petals" (88). The Laughing Man is shot by Marcel Dufarge. He does not die of the bullet wounds but finally chooses death by refusing to drink life-giving eagles' blood. His last act before dying is to remove his mask.

Narrator   The narrator, who never reveals his name, relates the events of the story, which took place when he was a nine-year-old member of the Comanche Club in 1928. He idolizes the club's Chief, John Gedsudski, and considers Gedsudski's fictive creation, the Laughing Man, to be an ancestor to himself. The adult narrator chronicles his nine-year-old self's first awareness of the emotional complexities in love relationships between young men and women.

Omba   Omba, a dwarf, is one of the Laughing Man's four close associates who live with him. Omba attends to the dying Laughing Man and must tell him of Black Wing's death.

Walsh, Billy   Billy Walsh is the youngest boy in the Comanche Club. At the end of the Chief's last installment about the Laughing Man's death, he bursts into tears.

FURTHER READING

Alsen, Eberhard. *A Reader's Guide to J. D. Salinger.* Westport, Conn.: Greenwood Press, 2002.

Davison, Richard Allan. "Salinger Criticism and 'The Laughing Man': A Case of Arrested Development." *Studies in Short Fiction* 18 (Winter 1981): 1–15.

Deer, Irving, and John H. Randall III. "J. D. Salinger and the Reality Beyond Words." *Lock Haven Review* 6 (1964): 14–29.

French, Warren. *J. D. Salinger.* New York: Twayne Publishers, 1963.

———. *J. D. Salinger, Revisited.* New York: Twayne Publishers, 1988.

Gwynn, Frederick L., and Joseph L. Blotner. *The Fiction of J. D. Salinger.* Pittsburgh: University of Pittsburgh Press, 1958.

Lundquist, James. *J. D. Salinger.* New York: Ungar, 1979.

Strong, Paul. "Black Wing, Black Heart—Betrayal in J. D. Salinger's 'The Laughing Man.'" *West Virginia University Philological Papers* 31 (1986): 91–96.

Wenke, John. *J. D. Salinger: A Study of the Short Fiction.* Boston: Twayne Publishers, 1991.

letter to the editor, *Twentieth Century Authors*

See "In J. D. Salinger's Own Words."

"library archive" stories

"Library archive" stories are stories that Salinger never published but whose typescripts reside in a library archive. To date, there are six known stories, plus one untitled work-in-progress.

Five stories are housed at Princeton University's Firestone Library as part of the Whit Burnett–Story magazine archive. Each of these five stories can be found individually listed in this volume: "The Children's Echelon," "The Last and Best of the Peter Pans," "The Magic Foxhole," "The Ocean Full of Bowling Balls," and "Two Lonely Men."

Two stories are housed at the Harry Ransom Center, at the University of Texas at Austin. Both stories were originally from Elizabeth Murray's collection of Salinger materials. "Birthday Boy" is a complete, titled story. The other story, an untitled work-in-progress, is undoubtedly a draft of "Mrs. Hincher," which became the story "Paula." (No complete, titled typescripts for either "Mrs. Hincher" or "Paula" have been located; thus, these two stories are termed "lost.")

All "library archive" stories are available for onsite reading only.

"Long Debut of Lois Taggett, The"

Appearing in the September–October 1942 issue of Story, "The Long Debut of Lois Taggett" relates the emotional transformation of a Manhattan socialite—through her experiences of trauma and grief—from a shallow to a deeper understanding of love. "The Long Debut of Lois Taggett" is Salinger's fifth published story. The author, however, chose not to include the story in his three books of collected stories.

SYNOPSIS

The story begins by noting Lois Taggett's middle standing in the graduating class of Miss Hanscomb's School. The following fall, her parents throw a posh debutante's ball for her at the Hotel Pierre. Lois's party is a success, although the male guests find the liquor more attractive than they do the debutante. Nonetheless, Lois does not do too badly with finding dates with the elite young men at the Stork Club during the winter. By spring of "the first big year for debutantes to Do Something" (28), Lois accepts a job as a receptionist at her uncle's downtown office. Within two weeks, and while applying nail polish to her toenails, she decides to join some of her friends on a cruise to

Rio de Janeiro, reasoning that the men she meets at her workplace are "a bunch of *dopes*" (28).

Returning to Manhattan the following fall, Lois takes a few classes at Columbia University, but by spring, she has fallen in love with Bill Tedderton, a press agent. Salinger paints their love relationship in a one-sentence brushstroke: "She fell hard, and Bill, who had been around plenty since he'd left Kansas City, trained himself to look deep enough into Lois' eyes to see the door to the family vault" (29). Tedderton, who is tall and broad-shouldered, also dresses extremely well.

To Bill's surprise, he finds himself falling deeply in love with Lois. The reader is also surprised to learn that "She never looked worse in her life—and at that instant Bill fell in love with her" (29). For 15 days, they experience the exhilaration of marital bliss, but after the 16th day, in a lover's embrace, Bill teases Lois with his lit cigarette with which he is drawing circles just above her hand. Inexplicably, he suddenly burns her hand until she screams and runs into the bathroom. In desperation, Bill apologizes, claiming that he didn't know what he was doing. The two reconcile, but a week later during a playful golf lesson in the apartment and while still in their pajamas and barefoot, Bill smashes Lois's foot with a metal club.

Lois leaves Bill and returns to live at her parents' apartment. She adopts a three-month-old Scottish terrier but gives the dog away a few days later because it refuses to be housebroken. Instead of waiting until spring as she had originally planned, Lois departs abruptly for Reno to file for divorce.

Back in Manhattan, Lois runs into Bill at the Stork Club. He explains that he has been "at this psychoanalyst's place" (31). The doctor believes Bill will recover. When Bill suggests that he and Lois get together, she refuses. She then proceeds to get drunk with her friends. When she sobers up and returns to her parents' apartment that evening, Carl Curfman phones. Lois considers Carl a "dope" (31) as he is an unattractive, short, stocky man who wears white socks because of allergic reactions to colored socks. Lois's mother contradicts her daughter's assessment of Carl.

Lois and Carl date for a few months. Returning from a charity ball at the Waldorf Astoria Hotel, Carl proposes to Lois "in the negative" (32), saying: "You wouldn't wanna marry me, would you, Lois?" (32). She defers, replying that she doesn't want to think about marriage for a while. During lunch at the Stork Club the following week, Lois tells her friend Middie Weaver about Carl, describing him in a very positive manner as "terribly sweet. And terribly intelligent" (32). Middie concurs, remarking that Carl is a "grand person" (32). On the way home, Lois thinks about Middie and assesses her friend as "*really* intelligent" and "swell" (32). Since Middie thinks Carl "grand" (32), Lois decides to accept his proposal.

After they marry, Lois tries to change Carl: She no longer permits him to wear white socks; she dresses him in more stylish clothes; she criticizes him for trying too hard to be helpful; she complains that he doesn't inhale when he smokes. Lois goes to movies at 11:00 A.M. and now has only one friend, Cookie Benson. The two women meet often at the Stork Club to drink and to criticize people. When Lois learns that she is pregnant, she stops going to early movies and on drinking dates.

Motherhood changes Lois. She loves her baby, Tommy, and in doing so finds that people in her life now take her more seriously. However, this success is threatened when Tommy's blanket suffocates him. About six months after the baby's death, the reader learns of Lois that "finally she made it" (34). Other people, not only from her own social set but also from all walks of life—cab drivers, butchers, and her own maid—begin to notice Lois, to assist her, and to confide in her. In the story's final scene, "the man Lois didn't love" (34)—her husband, Carl—has "never looked . . . more stupid and gross" (34) to his wife. Lois, however, must tell him something. "Put on your white socks" (34), she suggests quietly to him. "Put them on, dear" (34).

CRITICAL ANALYSIS

"The Long Debut of Lois Taggett" represents the longest story that Salinger published during the first three years of his writing career. The story shows an advance in how the author experiments with short fiction in increasingly complex and artistic ways. At the same time, the narrative tone, with its mimetic quality, captures Salinger's sophistication of style when writing about upper-class Manhattanites. The author moreover employs his familiarity with the Upper East Side of Manhattan to create an interesting character, both urbane and shallow, and follows her passage until she settles into less stylistic, and more humanly realistic, expectations. Lois Taggett does not give up on wanting to be stylish, but she does realize that she can accept others for who they are, stylish or not, and in that acceptance grows to love them and perhaps herself more honestly.

"The Long Debut of Lois Taggett" is unusual regarding Salinger's fictional motifs because of the spousal abuse issues that arise suddenly in Lois's first marriage. Although marriages that harbor violence rarely dissolve as simply as does Lois and Bill's, Salinger nonetheless succeeds in bringing Lois's story beyond a one-act scene. At the beginning of her emotional journey, Lois's ability to learn about acceptance and love is not very strong. At the end of her "long debut," however, she displays a depth of understanding toward her husband, a change the reader may glean in her loving suggestion that her husband may again wear the unstylish, but more comfortable, socks. Her signal in letting Carl wear his white socks is simultaneously about defeat and acceptance. Lois may be defeated in her pursuit of style and high society, but she has gained a deeper understanding of love. This knowledge has been won through the trauma to Lois of the psychosis of her first husband and its resultant abuse together with her subsequent grief over losing her beloved child. People with whom Lois now comes in contact also note the deeper love of others that she possesses. As the narrator describes Lois's transformation: "Then finally she made it" (34). Lois has become someone who is no longer shallow. She has finally made her debut into adulthood.

Not only is "The Long Debut of Lois Taggett" a longer story for the young Salinger to attempt, but the narrative also indicates the author's developing skill with dramatic dialogue as well as with character realization and plot. The third-person voice utilizes the raising of questions from various points of view that serve to turn the reader's focus more closely on Lois. (Salinger will utilize the technique with great mastery in his 1951 story,

"PRETTY MOUTH AND GREEN MY EYES.") The series of questions about Lois posed by others deftly situate readers as attendees of her debutante ball and confirm that it is her parents' money that makes Lois a debutante. She is not a stunning woman, nor does she possess much personality and intelligence. Some clues about Lois's potential character development, however, also may be gleaned from the first descriptions of her: She is considered a "*very* sweet child" (28) by the elderly ladies at her coming-out party, and she wears a "rather lovely, awkward smile" (28). After her party, however, Lois is focused on living her life as a successful debutante who would be noticed at the Stork Club. At this phase, Lois, instead of being able to think intelligently on her own, lets others influence her career and love life (for example, she passively takes a job at her uncle's firm; she seeks out the advice of other debutantes and their assessment of Carl before she will agree to marry him). Lois's lack of discrimination concerning the character of others is also pointed out in Salinger's use of repetition in the way the protagonist describes and thinks about each of her friends. For example, in assessing Cookie Benson, Lois determines that Cookie is "sweet," "*really* intelligent," and "swell" (33). Lois summarizes Cookie as "perfect" (33). On the other hand, the reader later comes to learn that Cookie drinks heavily and phones Lois from the Stork Club in fits of crying. Lois likewise deduces the same characteristics in her friend Middie Weaver, whom she assesses with the exact adjectives that she has used in determining Cookie's character. The narrative informs the reader, on the other hand, that Middie functions only as a "nodder and cigarette-ash tipper" (32) in the friendship, and that Lois describes Carl Curfman as "grand" (32)—a word Salinger reserves to pinpoint the person who makes use of it as a "phony."

Although the narrative does not explicitly state the changes within Lois's understanding as she undergoes her emotional growth, her actions give some subtle clues. For example, after marrying Carl and before becoming pregnant, Lois goes to the movies on a daily basis, beginning with the morning shows. (Characters of future Salinger stories will seek comfort via moviegoing: Franklin Graff in the 1948 story "JUST BEFORE THE WAR WITH THE ESKIMOS"; Elaine Cooney and her family in the 1945 story "ELAINE.") However, as the narrative explains: "when Lois discovered she was going to have a baby, she stopped going to the movies so much" (33). That is, something of import happens within Lois, and she no longer needs the comfort or romance of the movies to escape from her marriage to Carl. (A similar change is seen in Ginnie Mannox, the protagonist of "Just Before the War with the Eskimos," when, after meeting Franklin Graff, she no longer needs to attend the movies that evening but is more interested in returning to the Graff apartment in hopes of seeing Franklin again and perhaps finding love.) Another example of how the narrative divulges that Lois goes from not loving Carl upon their marriage to loving him and caring about him by story's end lies in the parallelism of Salinger's description of falling in love. When Bill realizes he is in love with Lois (after having married her without being in love), the reader learns that Lois "never looked worse in her life—and in that instant Bill fell in love with her" (29). The narrative leaves no reason to doubt the depth of Bill's love and moreover points out that his love is not based on a superficial attraction. Likewise, in Lois's perception of her second husband at the story's end, the reader learns of Carl that "never in his life had he looked more stupid and gross" (34) to Lois. Nonetheless, right after this thought, Lois speaks her loving words to Carl, allowing him to wear his white socks. Lois has gained the maturity needed to accept Carl as he is and now sees beyond the superficiality of looks and style to a deeper view of love. Moreover, the use of the past tense throughout the story may echo in the reader's ear a little differently, perhaps, as a truth about Lois's past rather than current, feelings towards Carl—"the man Lois didn't love" (34); that is, she did not love him *before* her emotional trials but may now actively love him. Lois ends her long debut with a change of heart and comes of age in the presence of love.

"The Long Debut of Lois Taggett" contains a parallel—in the portrayal of the protagonist's emotional reactions—to the intensity that the character Elaine (of the 1945 story "Elaine") will feel when confronted with a situation that threatens to overwhelm her coping ability. In his 1991 study of Salinger's fiction, the critic John Wenke observes in these two early stories a similarity of approach regarding how the author "explores, respectively, the incursions of psychosis and sexual seduction" (Wenke 8). Specifically, when Lois travels to Reno, a tall, good-looking cowboy named Red approaches her. Even though the ranch hand makes advances to Lois "in a nice way" (31), Lois suddenly screams at him to get away. This sudden gesture mirrors Elaine's reaction when, becoming panicked at the advances of Teddy Schmidt at the beach, she snatches her hand away from him suddenly and rebuffs him with an emphatic "No!" (45). Salinger shows, through the actions of these characters more so than through the use of interior monologue, the violence of their emotional turmoil. This narrative device shocks the reader into paying great attention to how Salinger's characters move and what their dialogue reveals, and likewise infuses the stories with dramatic force. Therefore, in Lois's quiet suggestion that Carl return to wearing white socks, the reader must infer that she has finally accepted her husband as he is and that she cares about his well being. However, as in many of Salinger's stories, the reader must make the leap of understanding (as the narrative does not explicitly confirm) that Lois has given up on love as a romantic and exhilarating feeling, and she has found love in the acceptance of others and of herself.

PUBLICATION HISTORY

"The Long Debut of Lois Taggett" was published in the September–October 1942 issue of *Story* magazine. The story was chosen by Whit and Hallie Burnett for inclusion in the anthology *Story: The Fiction of the Forties*. Salinger never reprinted the story in his three books of collected stories. "The Long Debut of Lois Taggett" later appeared in the bootleg editions *The COMPLETE UNCOLLECTED SHORT STORIES OF J. D. SALINGER* (1974) and *TWENTY-TWO STORIES* (1998).

CHARACTERS

Benson, Cookie Cookie Benson, a friend of Lois's, is among the group of debutantes who travel on a cruise to Rio in the year that debutantes are expected to "Do Something" (28). After Lois marries Carl Curfman, she often spends hours at the Stork Club with Cookie, where the two girls pass the time criticizing friends and exchanging "dirty jokes" (33). Lois considers Cookie "*really* intelligent" and "swell" and "perfect" (33) and concludes that Cookie is "a grand, intelligent person" (33). After the death of Lois's baby, Cookie, still lunching at the Stork Club, begins to phone Lois at home and cries through their conversations.

Bertha As maid at the Curfman home, Bertha is chastised about the overly hot temperature of the baby's bathwater by Lois Taggett. After the baby dies, Bertha begins to make an effort to please Lois by using a wet, rather than a dry, cleaning cloth.

Curfman, Carl Several months after Lois Taggett's divorce, Carl Curfman proposes marriage while he and Lois decide what to do about the dead battery in Carl's car. The young man—unattractive, shy, and overly eager to please others (shown by his helpfulness in providing information to everyone about the most efficient driving routes)—is considered a "dope" (31) by Lois but not by Lois's mother. A successful businessman, Carl manages his father's company. With good-natured amusement, he tolerates Lois's desire to change him and even begins to wear colored socks (one of Lois's demands to make him more stylish) despite the allergic reactions he suffers from itching. Carl is hardworking and a good provider, and therefore a heavy sleeper who does not hear Lois's nighttime crying after she learns of her pregnancy. As Carl arrives home late from work most nights, the baby does not readily recognize him.

Curfman, Thomas Taggett ("Tommy") Tommy Curfman, the first child of Lois Taggett and Carl Curfman, is a much-beloved infant—healthy, blond, sweet—"in short, a most successful production" (33). At the age of six months, Tommy dies in his sleep, suffocating on his blanket. Tommy's death catalyzes his mother's emotional growth—through her grief upon losing him—and lends her

a deeper understanding and tolerance for other human beings.

Gus A three-month-old Scottish terrier, Gus is purchased by Lois Taggett after her divorce from Bill Tedderton. Several days later, the dog is given away because of his refusal to be housebroken.

Red Red, the good-looking ranch hand, is invited to a party at the Reno bar where Lois and two other women are celebrating their recently granted divorces. Red makes a pass at Lois, "but in a nice way" (31), upon which Lois screams for him to get away from her. The other partygoers don't understand Lois's action and disapprove. The reader learns, however, that Lois is "afraid of tall, good-looking men" (31) (which implies that she is reacting emotionally to her experience of physical abuse from her first husband, Bill Tedderton, who is also a tall, good-looking man). Lois has thus not yet learned to judge people beyond their superficial attributes, such as "looks."

Taggett, Lois A young woman from a wealthy Manhattan family, Lois Taggett makes her social debut after graduating from a private school for girls. Despite her "rather lovely, awkward smile" (28) and her sweet disposition, Lois is overlooked by the young men at her coming-out party. She dresses well, is considered intelligent, and makes the social rounds at the Stork Club. During the year when debutantes are expected to "Do Something" (28), Lois is offered a job as a receptionist at her uncle's downtown office, presumably to expose her to future candidates for marriage. Lois considers all the young men she meets to be "*dopes*" (28) and decides impulsively to quit her job and take a cruise to Rio. Returning, she falls in love with a social climber and gold digger, Bill Tedderton, who marries her for her family's money. Early in the marriage, however, Bill falls deeply in love with his wife. The two enjoy a brief time of marital bliss. Suddenly and inexplicably, however, Bill begins to abuse Lois physically—he burns her hand with a cigarette and smashes her foot with a metal golf club. Lois leaves Bill and files for divorce. Soon afterward, upon the advice of her mother, she begins to date Carl Curfman, an unattractive man whom she does not love. However, since her friends endorse Carl as an acceptable marriage candidate, Lois accepts Carl's proposal. Unhappy in this marriage, Lois escapes to a daily regimen of moviegoing and drinking. Learning she is pregnant, she weeps at night. Gradually, however, as her maternity progresses, she enjoys the solicitous behavior of others and her outlook changes. Once she gives birth to a baby boy, Tommy, she displays love and happiness in being a mother to her child. When Tommy dies suddenly from SIDS (sudden infant death syndrome), Lois's emotional life comes into maturity. About six months after her baby's death, Lois speaks words of loving kindness to her husband: "Put on your white socks . . . dear" (34). The narrative informs the reader that "finally she made it" (34)—that Lois has learned, through her own experience of trauma and grief, to understand and to empathize with the plight of others. She thus finally makes her "debut" into adulthood.

Tedderton, Bill   Lois Taggett meets Bill Tedderton, a press agent, at the Stork Club and falls in love with him. Bill, a good-looking, tall, and very well-dressed young man from Kansas City, marries Lois for her family's money. Soon after the wedding, Bill discovers, to his own surprise, that he is deeply in love with his wife after gazing at her one morning while she sleeps. The couple enjoys 15 days of marital bliss when, on the 16th day, Bill—inexplicably but deliberately—burns Lois's hand with a lit cigarette. One week later, he just as inexplicably smashes her bare foot with a metal golf club. Lois leaves Bill and files for divorce. Bill later runs into Lois at the Stork Club and tells her of his psychiatrist's prognosis for his recovery. He suggests that they see each other again, but Lois rebuffs him. The narrative does not offer any clue to the reason behind Bill's unprovoked violence toward Lois. Neither does Bill himself understand his illness, declaring to Lois that he didn't know what he was doing when he burned her hand. The reader learns only that Bill "did what he had to do" (30).

Weaver, Middie   Middie Weaver, a friend of Lois Taggett's, serves the relationship as a "nodder and cigarette-ash tipper" (32)—that is, as a listener. Lois explains to Middie her changing opinions toward Carl Curfman, who has recently proposed marriage. After Middie pronounces Carl "a grand person" (32), Lois perceives Middie as "*really* intelligent" and "swell" and "perfect" (32). After her talk with Middie, Lois decides to marry Carl.

FURTHER READING

French, Warren. *J. D. Salinger.* New York: Twayne Publishers, 1963.

Wenke, John. *J. D. Salinger: A Study of the Short Fiction.* Boston: Twayne Publishers, 1991.

"lost" stories

"Lost" stories are stories that have neither been published nor been found in a library archive. Titles of such stories derive from references in Salinger's letters, letters of various editors, and early compiled lists of the author's works. Some of the following "lost" stories possibly have had their title changed to another "lost" story title or have been published under a new title: "ARE YOU BANGING YOUR HEAD AGAINST THE WALL?"; "BITSEY," "The BOY IN THE PEOPLE SHOOTING HAT," "BOY STANDING IN TENNESSEE," "The BROKEN CHILDREN," "The DAUGHTER OF THE LATE, GREAT MAN," "I WENT TO SCHOOL WITH ADOLF HITLER," "The KISSLESS LIFE OF REILLY," "The LOVELY DEAD GIRL AT TABLE SIX," "LUNCH FOR THREE," "The MALE GOODBYE," "MEN WITHOUT HEMINGWAY," "MONOLOGUE FOR A WATERY HIGHBALL," "MRS. HINCHER," "OVER THE SEAS LET'S GO, TWENTIETH CENTURY FOX," "PARIS," "PAULA," "REQUIEM FOR THE PHANTOM OF THE OPERA," "REX PASSARD ON THE PLANET MARS," "A SUMMER ACCIDENT," "The SURVIVORS," "TOTAL WAR DIARY," "WHAT BABE SAW, OR OOH-LA-LA!" "WHAT GOT INTO CURTIS IN THE WOODSHED," and "A YOUNG MAN IN A STUFFED SHIRT."

"Lovely Dead Girl at Table Six, The"

"The Lovely Dead Girl at Table Six" is one of Salinger's "lost" stories, neither published nor to be found in a library archive. According to IAN HAMILTON, Salinger wrote a story with this title in August 1941. Unless the manuscript can be located among Salinger's literary estate, the story's whereabouts are unknown.

"Lunch for Three"

"Lunch for Three" is one of Salinger's "lost" stories, neither published nor to be found in a library archive. According to Ben Yagoda, Salinger submitted a story with this title to the NEW YORKER in 1941. Unless the manuscript can be located among Salinger's literary estate, the story's whereabouts are unknown.

"Magic Foxhole, The"

"The Magic Foxhole" is an unpublished story, whose 21-page, undated (circa 1944) typescript can be found at Princeton University's FIRESTONE LIBRARY, as part of the WHIT BURNETT–STORY magazine archive. "The Magic Foxhole" is available for onsite reading only. According to the bibliographer Jack R. Sublette, the story, set shortly after D-day, is told in the first person by a soldier named Garrity and "recounts Garrity's association with a soldier named Lewis Gardner, who suffers severe battle fatigue" (Sublette 22). "The Magic Foxhole" was included on the proposed table of contents for Salinger's unpublished book, The YOUNG FOLKS.

"Male Goodbye, The"

"The Male Goodbye" is one of Salinger's "lost" stories, neither published nor to be found in a library

archive. According to IAN HAMILTON, Salinger mentions a story with this title in a 1946 letter to Elizabeth Murray. This work is the first story Salinger wrote after his separation from his first wife, SYLVIA SALINGER, in 1946. Unless the manuscript can be located among Salinger's literary estate, the story's whereabouts are unknown.

"Man-Forsaken Men"

This title was assigned by the *New York Post Magazine* to Salinger's letter to the editor concerning men sentenced to life in prison without the possibility of parole. In his letter, Salinger employs irony to castigate New York State for such a practice and closes with the statement: "the New York State lifer is one of the most crossed-off, man-forsaken men on earth" (December 9, 1959, p. 49). Critics have assumed the letter might have arisen from discussions with Salinger's friend, Judge Learned Hand. (Jack R. Sublette, Salinger's bibliographer, mistakenly attributes the letter to 1955.) The entire letter is reproduced in Donald M. Fiene's thesis, "A Bibliographical Study of J. D. Salinger: Life, Work and Reputation."

manuscript about Ross, Shawn, and the *New Yorker*

In response to James Thurber's 1959 critical memoir, *The Years with Ross*, Salinger wrote an open-letter essay of approximately 25 pages in length about Harold Ross, WILLIAM SHAWN and the NEW YORKER, which he then submitted to the *Saturday Review*. Donald M. Fiene, Salinger's first bibliographer, reports he was told by Hallowell Bowser, general editor of the *Saturday Review*, in an October 8, 1962, letter, that the Salinger piece was "rejected because of its length and unusual style" (Fiene 1963, 116). As James Bryan remarks in his 1968 dissertation, "Salinger and His Short Fiction," "One can scarcely imagine a literary magazine passing up anything of Salinger's then, at the height of his popularity. The piece must have been, as I heard, embarrassingly fulsome" (Bryan 1968, 56–57). The manuscript is considered "lost," although, in all likelihood, Salinger retained a copy. It probably can be located among Salinger's literary estate.

"Men without Hemingway"

"Men without Hemingway" is one of Salinger's "lost" stories, neither published nor to be found in a library archive. According to IAN HAMILTON, Salinger mentions a story with this title in a 1942 letter to Elizabeth Murray. "Men without Hemingway" was rejected by the NEW YORKER. Unless the manuscript can be located among Salinger's literary estate, the story's whereabouts are unknown.

"Monologue for a Watery Highball"

"Monologue for a Watery Highball" is one of Salinger's "lost" stories, neither published nor to be found in a library archive. According to Ben Yagoda, the NEW YORKER rejected a story with this title in 1941. Unless the manuscript can be located among Salinger's literary estate, the story's whereabouts are unknown.

"Mrs. Hincher"

"Mrs. Hincher" is one of Salinger's "lost" stories, neither published nor to be found in a library archive. Salinger refers to an almost-finished story with this title in an October 31, 1941, letter to Elizabeth Murray. (The letter is photographically reproduced in John C. Unrue's *J. D. Salinger* [Unrue 2002, 43].) The HARRY RANSOM CENTER, at the University of Texas at Austin, purchased Murray's archive of Salinger material. The archive includes an untitled work-in-progress whose protagonist is

named Paula Hincher. (The story was eventually retitled "PAULA.") Unless the manuscript can be located among Salinger's literary estate, the completed story's whereabouts are unknown.

Nine Stories

Nine Stories, published on April 6, 1953, by LITTLE, BROWN AND COMPANY, is Salinger's second book. The table of contents consists of: "A PERFECT DAY FOR BANANAFISH," "UNCLE WIGGILY IN CONNECTICUT," "JUST BEFORE THE WAR WITH THE ESKIMOS," "THE LAUGHING MAN," "DOWN AT THE DINGHY," "FOR ESMÉ—WITH LOVE AND SQUALOR," "PRETTY MOUTH AND GREEN MY EYES," "DE DAUMIER-SMITH'S BLUE PERIOD," and "TEDDY."

INTRODUCTION

For his first story collection, Salinger selected only nine of his 30 stories that had already appeared in magazines from 1940 to 1953. (The severity of Salinger's choices effectively consigned 21 stories, published from 1940 through 1948, to obscurity, until they were illegally reprinted in 1974 in two bootleg paperback volumes.) The order of the nine stories mimics the chronology of their publication dates, which spans exactly five years: January 31, 1948, to January 31, 1953. Seven stories had originally appeared in the NEW YORKER: "A Perfect Day for Bananafish," January 31, 1948; "Uncle Wiggily in Connecticut," March 20, 1948; "Just Before the War with the Eskimos," June 5, 1948; "The Laughing Man," March 19, 1949; "For Esmé—with Love and Squalor," April 8, 1950; "Pretty Mouth and Green My Eyes," July 14, 1951; and "Teddy," January 31, 1953. "Down at the Dinghy" appeared in the April 1949 issue of HARPER'S, while "De Daumier-Smith's Blue Period" appeared in the May 1952 issue of WORLD REVIEW. All of the stories range in length from 20 to 30 pages, except for "For Esmé—with Love and Squalor" (43 pages), "Teddy" (50 pages), and "De Daumier-Smith's Blue Period" (55 pages). Three of the stories, "A Perfect Day for Bananafish," "Uncle Wiggily in Connecticut," and "Down at the Dinghy" feature Glass family members. *Nine Stories* is generally considered one of the most notable collections of short stories by an American author in the 20th century. "A Perfect Day for Bananafish" and "For Esmé—with Love and Squalor" are considered masterpieces of American literature.

The publication of *Nine Stories* was widely noted in the press, garnering at least 30 reviews, the most positive being that of Eudora Welty: "J. D. Salinger's writing is original, first rate, serious and beautiful" (Welty 4). Welty praises Salinger's "sensitive eye, his incredibly good ear, and something I can think of no word for but grace" (Welty 4). Seymour Krim lauds Salinger's "feeling for textures, and situations, and the freshness of his irony," and deems him "a unique talent . . . a born writer" (Krim 78). Krim, however, believes that the author "is not quite clear about the meaning of his material . . . one suspects a dodging of issues" (Krim 78). Hansford Martin detects "a sense of desperate slyness, warily disguised by the simulation of surface honesty" (Martin 172). Gene Baro stresses that "the special quality of Mr. Salinger's stories is humaneness," while noting Salinger's "vision tempers an all-embracing sentimentality with a personal sophistication, so that these stories run to a kind of intellectual and emotional chic" (Baro 6). Sidney Monas observes that the stories exhibit "a peculiar conceptual separation of the child from the adult, as though they were of different species, not merely different ages" (Monas 467). The anonymous reviewer of the *Nation* acknowledges Salinger's "great brilliance; the danger is that he will become [a writer] of definite and ultimately disappointing limitations" ("Youthful Horrors" 332). Stories that merited praise from reviewers included "A Perfect Day for Bananafish," "For Esmé—with Love and Squalor," and "De Daumier-Smith's Blue Period."

Later critics sought to discover hidden connections among the stories. Paul Kirschner, in 1969, suggests that the stories "reveal more in sequence than they do separately: an artist's search for spiritual meaning in a society where relationships seem invariably superficial and materialistic" (Kirschner 34). Kirschner discerns within the stories "a pattern: a despairing flight from glossy, greedy society, through provisional rescue by intelligence suffused

with intuition and love, and finally to transcendence of individual personality" (Kirschner 53). Bernice and Sanford Goldstein took the epigraph of *Nine Stories*, a ZEN koan ("We know the sound of two hands clapping. But what is the sound of one hand clapping?"), to be the key to the collection. The Goldsteins argue that Zen provides an "integrating principle" to "these disturbing stories in which the real and unreal, youth and age, love and squalor . . . either merge or remain separate" (Goldstein 182). Warren French concludes that the reader should not look for a "narrative progression" but instead "a progression based upon the slow and painful achievement of spiritual enlightenment . . . successive stages that a soul would pass through according to Vedantic teachings in at last escaping fleshly reincarnations" (French 63–64). Ruth Prigozy, in her 1995 essay, sensibly stresses that "to search for a unifying principle in *Nine Stories* is to admit that the individual stories must be bent and shaped to conform to a preconceived pattern" (Prigozy 114). She believes the Zen koan epigraph "instructs the reader to forgo the effort to devise a too logical scheme linking the individual works that follow" (Prigozy 114). Prigozy concludes that "the mysteries in *Nine Stories* account for its continuing appeal as much as does its enormous readability" (Prigozy 114). In 2003, 50 years after the publication of *Nine Stories,* Dominic Smith declares, "Not since Hemingway's *In Our Time* had a collection of stories so raised the bar on the form, creating characters and scenes that were hypnotic, mysterious, and unusually powerful," and concludes that the book is "arguably the highpoint of [Salinger's] foreshortened publishing career" (Smith 639).

Nine Stories is dedicated to DOROTHY OLDING, Salinger's literary agent, and to GUS LOBRANO, his *New Yorker* editor at the time of publication. Salinger's use of a Zen koan as the book's epigraph would lead literary critics to overvalue the influence of Zen Buddhism on the author's work. (Perhaps as a private joke, Salinger imitates the "one hand clapping" twice in the stories: Muriel Glass, in "A Perfect Day for Bananafish" waves "her left—the wet—hand back and forth through the air" [4]; and Teddy McArdle, in "Teddy," who has some water in his ear, "gave his right ear a light clap with his hand" [283].) Published just two years after *The CATCHER IN THE RYE, Nine Stories* sold extremely well for a volume of short stories, remaining on the *New York Times* best-seller list for 15 weeks (though not achieving a place on the *Publishers Weekly* list of the 10 best-selling volumes for the year).

SYNOPSIS

For a synopsis of the stories in *Nine Stories, see* "A PERFECT DAY FOR BANANAFISH," "UNCLE WIGGILY IN CONNECTICUT," "JUST BEFORE THE WAR WITH THE ESKIMOS," "THE LAUGHING MAN," "DOWN AT THE DINGHY," "FOR ESMÉ—WITH LOVE AND SQUALOR," "PRETTY MOUTH AND GREEN MY EYES," "DE DAUMIER-SMITH'S BLUE PERIOD," and "TEDDY."

CRITICAL ANALYSIS

For a critical analysis of the stories in *Nine Stories, see* "A PERFECT DAY FOR BANANAFISH," "UNCLE WIGGILY IN CONNECTICUT," "JUST BEFORE THE WAR WITH THE ESKIMOS," "THE LAUGHING MAN," "DOWN AT THE DINGHY," "FOR ESMÉ—WITH LOVE AND SQUALOR," "PRETTY MOUTH AND GREEN MY EYES," "DE DAUMIER-SMITH'S BLUE PERIOD," and "TEDDY."

PUBLICATION HISTORY

Nine Stories was published on April 6, 1953, by Little, Brown and Company. The first printing was a hardback of an unspecified run (certainly a larger-than-usual one for a volume of short stories, given the notable success of *The Catcher in the Rye*), priced at $3. The front and rear covers of the dust jacket consisted solely of the title and Salinger's name, with a line of text under his name identifying him as the author of *The Catcher in the Rye*. (*Nine Stories* was published in England in 1953 under the title *For Esmé—with Love and Squalor, and Other Stories*.)

In 1954, the paperback "pocketbook" edition of *Nine Stories* was published by New American Library. In 1959, a new hardcover edition was published in the prestigious Modern Library series while Little, Brown and Company continued to reprint its own hardback edition. When the contract with New American Library expired, Bantam Books issued the paperback "pocketbook" edition in 1964.

In May 1991, Little, Brown and Company took over the mass-market paperback from Bantam Books and released it in the austere matching set of Salinger's four books, each bound in white covers with the author's name and the title in black. In January 2001, Little, Brown and Company published the first trade paperback edition, reproducing the front and rear covers of the original dust jacket (albeit eliminating the line of text under Salinger's name that had identified him as the author of *The Catcher in the Rye*). The mass-market paperback edition would eventually adopt the same look.

Nine Stories, Salinger's second book, has never gone out of print and is available in three editions from Little, Brown and Company: an exact reproduction of the hardback first edition from 1953; a trade paperback that mimics the production of the hardback; and a mass-market paperback, with its pagination differing from the above editions.

CHARACTERS

For the characters in the stories in *Nine Stories, see* "A PERFECT DAY FOR BANANAFISH," "UNCLE WIGGILY IN CONNECTICUT," "JUST BEFORE THE WAR WITH THE ESKIMOS," "THE LAUGHING MAN," "DOWN AT THE DINGHY," "FOR ESMÉ—WITH LOVE AND SQUALOR," "PRETTY MOUTH AND GREEN MY EYES," "DE DAUMIER-SMITH'S BLUE PERIOD," and "TEDDY."

FURTHER READING

Baro, Gene. "Some Suave and Impressive Slices of Life." *New York Herald Tribune Book Review*, 12 April 1953, p. 6.

French, Warren. *J. D. Salinger, Revisited.* New York: Twayne Publishers, 1988.

Goldstein, Bernice, and Sanford Goldstein. "Zen and *Nine Stories*." *Renascence* 22 (Spring 1970): 171–182.

Highet, Gilbert. "New Books: Always Roaming with a Hungry Heart." *Harper's*, June 1953, 100–109.

Kirschner, Paul. "Salinger and His Society: The Pattern of *Nine Stories*." *London Review* 6 (Winter 1969–70): 34–54.

Krim, Seymour. "Surface and Substance in a Major Talent." *Commonweal*, 24 April 1953, 78.

Larrabee, C. X. "Nine Short Stories by a Writer with an Extraordinary Talent." *San Francisco Chronicle,* 3 May 1953, p. 13.

Martin, Hansford. "Four Volumes of Short Stories: An Irreverent Review." *Western Review* 18 (Winter 1954): 172–174.

Mizener, Arthur. "In Genteel Traditions." *New Republic,* 25 May 1953, 19–20.

Monas, Sidney. "Fiction Chronicle: 'No Mommy and No Daddy.'" *Hudson Review* 6 (Autumn 1953): 466–470.

Peden, William. "Esthetics of the Story." *Saturday Review,* 11 April 1953, 43–44.

Pickrel, Paul. "Outstanding Novels." *Yale Review* 42 (Summer 1953): vi–xvi.

Poore, Charles. "Books of The Times." *New York Times,* 9 April 1953, p. 25.

Prigozy, Ruth. "*Nine Stories*: J. D. Salinger's Linked Mysteries." In *Modern American Short Story Sequences: Composite Fictions and Fictive Communities,* edited by J. Gerald Kennedy, 114–132. Cambridge: Cambridge University Press, 1995.

Smith, Dominic. "Salinger's *Nine Stories*: Fifty Years Later." *Antioch Review* 61, no. 4 (Fall 2003): 639–649.

Toynbee, Philip. "Voice of America." *Observer,* 14 June 1953, p. 9.

Welty, Eudora. "Threads of Innocence." *New York Times Book Review,* 5 April 1953, p. 4.

"Youthful Horrors." *Nation,* 18 April 1953, 332.

For further reading on the stories in *Nine Stories,* see "A PERFECT DAY FOR BANANAFISH," "UNCLE WIGGILY IN CONNECTICUT," "JUST BEFORE THE WAR WITH THE ESKIMOS," "THE LAUGHING MAN," "DOWN AT THE DINGHY," "FOR ESMÉ—WITH LOVE AND SQUALOR," "PRETTY MOUTH AND GREEN MY EYES," "DE DAUMIER-SMITH'S BLUE PERIOD," and "Teddy."

"Ocean Full of Bowling Balls, The"

"The Ocean Full of Bowling Balls" is an unpublished Caulfield story, whose 18-page, undated (circa 1945) typescript can be found at Princeton University's FIRESTONE LIBRARY, as part of the WHIT BURNETT–STORY magazine archive. "The Ocean Full of Bowling Balls" is available for onsite reading only. According to the bibliographer Jack R. Sublette, "Vincent Caulfield writes of his relationship with one of his younger brothers, Kenneth, and of Kenneth's death" (Sublette 21) after Kenneth's swim in a turbulent ocean off Cape Cod. The story contains references to a very young Phoebe Caulfield and reproduces a letter written by Holden Caulfield from summer camp. (For more information regarding the seven extant Caulfield stories, *see* CAULFIELD STORIES.) "The Ocean Full of Bowling Balls" was included in the proposed table of contents for Salinger's unpublished book, *The* YOUNG FOLKS.

"Once a Week Won't Kill You"

"Once a Week Won't Kill You" was published in the November–December 1944 issue of STORY. The narrative focuses on the relationship of a recently drafted soldier in the last hours before he must report to overseas duty, two months before D-day. "Once a Week Won't Kill You" is Salinger's 11th published story. The author, however, chose not to include the story in his three books of collected stories.

SYNOPSIS

The dialogue between a young man, smoking while he packs a suitcase, and a young woman, seated in an oversize chair, immerses the reader in the story's central action—that of a soldier preparing for departure overseas.

As he packs, the man considers the woman's good looks and her youth, unspoiled and undiminished even by the morning sunlight. The woman puts a series of rhetorical questions and statements to him: She asks why he does not allow Billy to do the packing; she remarks that he is leaving at a "*horrible*" and "*crazy*" time (23); and she expresses how much she will miss him. Her actions, however, contradict the concern she declares, as she yawns nonchalantly.

The man asks the woman to find some music on the radio. As the conversation continues, the reader learns that the two are husband and wife, and that the man, who decides to lie down on the bed for a stretch, especially enjoys jazz. As they discuss his departure, he considers her manner of speaking—always "in italics" (24)—and corrects her mispronunciation of the word *cavalry* which she has pronounced as "Calvary" (24), where she hopes he will be assigned (since he enjoys riding horseback). He also corrects her confusion in the use of the verb form "to lie" when she comments on his decision to "lay" down, to which he responds "lie" down. She wishes that he, whom she addresses as "Sweetie" throughout, would telephone an acquaintance, the Colonel, to try for a commission in intelligence so as to avoid the infantry, reminding him that he speaks both French and German, and that he would probably prefer intelligence since he doesn't like talking or socializing with other people. Irritated, he reacts negatively to her suggestion about the commission. She hopes he will be stationed in London and remarks suddenly, as an aside, that she would love to have some tweed fabric sent back home to her. She then asks her husband whether he has said good-bye to his aunt.

The young man, who has been relaxing while he listens to his wife's banter, abruptly sits up and addresses her in a serious tone, and by her first name, Virginia. He replies that he had intended last night to ask if she would take his aunt to the movies while he is away and states, "once a week won't kill you" (24). He repeats the phrase several more times to her protestations as she attempts to come up with excuses for not being able to do so. She finally agrees to his request, while expressing her belief that his aunt is "*worse . . . so batty*" (24). The young man asks her to have the cook prepare breakfast, kisses her "wonderful mouth" (24), and leaves the room.

After ascending a set of stairs, he knocks at a door that displays a do-not-disturb sign from the Waldorf Astoria Hotel. In the sign's margin, he reads a note (which he has read many times

throughout the years) written in a script now become very faded. The note (the reader will later learn) initially had been written to the young man's mother several decades earlier, during the time of the First World War.

When a voice directs him to enter, he opens the door and sees a woman in her fifties who is seated at a card table. She exclaims his name: Dickie Camson. He kisses her and asks about her progress of the morning (she has been busily arranging her collection of canceled two-cent American stamps into large leather-bound albums). He notices the radio tuned to the same station he had been enjoying. Addressing her as "Aunt Rena," he observes that she is wearing dirty gym shoes and admonishes her for having done the exercises to the morning program. She objects, reassuring him that she is strong enough to exercise and that she enjoys the activity because she likes the music, the "old tunes" (25). While he struggles with his remorse in having to tell her of his departure, because "He had wanted her to be the one woman in 1944 who did not have someone's hourglass to watch . . ." (25), she remarks how much he resembles his mother (her sister) and asks whether he remembers her at all. He replies yes and says that his mother always seemed to move quickly and happily, and often whistled a particular tune that he could not recall until, in college, his roommate happened to play it on the phonograph. He does not, however, remember his mother's looks.

The aunt explains that her sister was "quite a package" (26) and that his father could not take his eyes off her, even in company. The aunt considered her brother-in-law a rude person, and one that knew nothing except how to make money. He would insist on taking her sister out in his sailboat and, on those excursions, would wear his "funny little English sailor hat" (26), which his wife would try to hide. The young man then asks whether the hat had been all that was found, but his aunt's attention has suddenly fallen to her album.

The young man approaches her, explaining that there is a war on, and questions whether she is aware of it, to which she responds, almost insulted, that certainly she is aware. He then tells her that he must depart that morning for duty and reassures her that Virginia will take her to the movies often.

The aunt, nonplussed by his information, rises and moves "briskly" (26) across the room to her desk, telling her nephew that she has written something for him to present, a "letter of introduction" to "a friend" of hers (26). She extracts an envelope, returns to her nephew, and hands the envelope to him, letting him know that he may read the contents as she has not sealed the flap. The letter is addressed to Lieutenant Thomas E. Cleve, Jr. She explains that "Tommy" is "a wonderful young man" (26) who will be able to help him get settled. Now, hesitating from uncertainty, she returns "less briskly" (26) to the desk to retrieve a photograph of a young man in a 1917 lieutenant's uniform. Faltering in her steps, she walks back to her nephew at the card table to show him the photo and explains that it is of Tom Cleve. She reiterates that Tom will be able to help. The two, aunt and nephew, then say their good-byes.

As soon as the young man reaches the downstairs landing—having "stumbled down the stairs" (27)—he rips the envelope into pieces and shoves the remains into his pocket. When his wife announces that "*Everything's* cold" (27), meaning his breakfast, he responds: "You can take her to the movies once a week . . . It won't kill you" (27).

CRITICAL ANALYSIS

Although an early Salinger story, "Once a Week Won't Kill You" already displays many elements characteristic of Salinger's mature style. The dialogue, in particular, allows the reader to infer, through subtle hints in conversation, the underlying reality of the drama as well as the nature of the characters involved.

The story begins with a description of a young woman, the protagonist's wife, who possesses a beautiful face and whose "marvelous" (23) arms, which are "brown and round and good" (23), are much appreciated by her husband. The narrative suggests her apparent lack of education (shown in her substitution of the word *Calvary* for cavalry) and in her other grammatical mistakes (the common error in substituting the phrase "lay down" for "lie down") and underscores her physical supe-

riority, indicating her to be an athletic person (her arms are brown, perhaps from playing an outdoor sport). She likewise displays a keen sense of social status, remarking that her husband should let Billy do the packing (the reader later understands Billy to be a domestic servant). She moreover exhorts her husband to phone an acquaintance, "the Colonel . . . in Intelligence" (24), who may be able to pull some strings to keep him out of the infantry. The reader also understands, from the description of her hand with "the gold-band wedding ring and on the little finger beside it the incredible emerald" (23), that the emerald has not been fitted specifically for her and represents, more than likely, an heirloom from her husband's family (the ring's former, or original, owner having possessed smaller, more delicate fingers than those of the wife). This detail, so characteristic of Salinger's narrative technique, speaks volumes in providing a deeper insight into the couple: That he is born to wealth and has given his wife a family treasure for which she is not exactly suited. Moreover, nuance in their dialogue makes it clear that the couple's relationship is based on sexual attraction. For example, when he attempts for the second time to request that she take his aunt to the movies once a week, he states that "before he could finish last night" (24), he wanted to ask her something important. His first attempt to ask her, however, had evidently been interrupted, and the reader is subtly encouraged to infer, from what is not said, that the interruption would most likely have been their lovemaking.

Salinger's masterful use of and emphasis on dialogue over description not only pulls the reader into the action but also highlights personality differences between the characters. The protagonist is sentimental (he worries about his aunt's well-being during his absence) and considerate (he will not allow Billy to pack, as the servant is elderly). He is nervous (he chain-smokes), where his wife is relaxed (yawns as they converse) and casual, almost offhanded in her concern about his military assignment (she hints about the tweed fabric he might ship her from London). She is not so considerate of the household help (she wonders why he does not have Billy do the packing). She is practical, with a strong instinct for survival, encouraging him to make use of their social contacts to obtain a better assignment in intelligence. He, on the other hand, is idealistic and eschews the privilege of his social class to obtain favors, even if it means facing more danger and less chance of survival.

In contrast to the portrait of the young, resilient wife, the narrative next paints that of the aunt who resides in a second-floor room in what may be understood as a posh MANHATTAN townhouse (the family's wealth is represented in their employment of two servants, Billy and "Cook"). The reader is introduced to the aunt not physically but by way of a "white formal" (24) card, a do-not-disturb sign from the old Waldorf Astoria. The faded script in the card's margin suggests the passing of the years but more importantly brings into focus a key element of the drama—the existence of a "Tom" mentioned in the note with its instruction to meet Tom in the lobby after the Liberty Bond rally. The reader may also guess, from the content of the note, that Tom was to be introduced to the protagonist's mother (the intended recipient) because Aunt Rena must describe his appearance—"His left shoulder is higher than his right and he smokes a darling little pipe" (25)—so that her sister can identify him in the lobby.

When the protagonist opens the door to his Aunt Rena, the reader quickly gleans salient information that the dialogue will come to bear out: that the aunt (represented by the note card) is living in a past from which she should not be disturbed (the "do-not-disturb" sign); that she is delicate and sophisticated (her nephew notices her "thin, elegant hands" [26], which provide contrast to his wife's "round" arms and brown skin); that she is frail (she is "faded" like the script on the card, and her nephew, worried for her health, admonishes her for having done gymnastics to the radio program); that she is no longer able to venture outside (her gym shoes are dirty—suggesting that she had, at one time, exercised outdoors and that she must currently exercise inside); that the two, aunt and nephew, share the same taste (they listen to the same radio program and are thus on the same wavelength). During this second conversation of the story, that between aunt and nephew, much more is revealed about the protagonist's nature:

that he is emotionally sensitive and feels remorse in having to tell his aunt of his departure, thus intruding upon her reality and causing her concern. His actions also convey his attentiveness and love as he kisses her gently. The scene moreover builds to the story's dramatic conclusion. The reader learns that the letter of introduction is addressed to the same Tom mentioned in the note on the do-not-disturb sign. He is now identified more explicitly as Tom Cleve, whose photo shockingly reveals to the reader that Cleve had been a soldier in World War I. The aunt's state of mind is crystallized. She has chosen to stop time several decades earlier, before the death of her beloved Tom in World War I. She believes him to be yet alive and able to protect her nephew during his military duty in Europe, failing to realize that the current time is 1944 and that the present conflict is World War II. Most poignant is Salinger's touch by way of the protagonist's observation that his aunt is "the sanest woman in the world" (26). Her confusion about, or confluence of, the two world wars comments on the reality of those decades, with war remaining ever-present to the American experience. Although the war may change its name and era, the nature and outcome of war remains constant. The aunt, who confuses the two wars, nonetheless clarifies the reality of war's destruction. Her nephew's remorse in giving her his "hourglass" (25) to watch has been unfounded. Her mind, already affected by loss (the death of Tom in World War I), is now lost to real time. The current war, therefore, will not inflict a larger measure of pain, nor will the possible loss of her nephew.

The letter, now in the hands of the young man, ties his fate symbolically to that of Tom Cleve: He has been given an introduction from the living to the dead. (Salinger's technique in utilizing the letter as artifact and its importance as a vehicle of communication will come to prominence in later stories, such as "FOR ESMÉ—WITH LOVE AND SQUALOR," "ZOOEY," "SEYMOUR: AN INTRODUCTION," and "HAPWORTH 16, 1924.") The protagonist will most likely meet the same end as that of Tom Cleve (in handing him the letter, the aunt instructs her nephew to "find Tom Cleve" [27]). His aunt, however, will forever believe him to be among the living. Tom will not be able to help him get settled in Europe but may help him, by way of inference, get settled after death. The letter further conveys bitter irony in that, despite the aunt's hopes for special treatment from a social connection, the protagonist will go to his assignment without the privilege of social class to protect him against his fate. His destiny is suggested by his wife's use of the word *Calvary*, where she hopes he will be placed, an allusion that identifies him with the crucified Christ.

The story's end brings into relief the solitary and vulnerable figure of the chivalric young man as soldier: one without a mother to anxiously await his return, without a family (represented by his aunt, now in dementia) to remember him and to mark his death. His wife, the reader surmises, will survive whether or not her husband returns from battle.

PUBLICATION HISTORY

"Once a Week Won't Kill You" was published in the November–December 1944 issue of *Story*. Salinger never reprinted the story in his three books of collected stories. "Once a Week Won't Kill You" later appeared in the bootleg editions *The COMPLETE UNCOLLECTED SHORT STORIES OF J. D. SALINGER* (1974) and *TWENTY-TWO STORIES* (1998).

CHARACTERS

Aunt Rena   Aunt Rena, in her fifties and suffering from dementia, can no longer distinguish past from present time. Her nephew, the protagonist of the story, is a young soldier, who must tell his aunt (his mother's sister) that he is about to embark for military duty in Europe. The time is 1944, and the conflict is World War II. Aunt Rena has written a letter of introduction for her nephew to present to Tom Cleve (her beau), whose photograph she shows to him. The dialogue between aunt and nephew reveals her belief that Tom is still alive and stationed overseas when, in fact, his photograph shockingly reveals him to have been a lieutenant in World War I.

Billy   An elderly domestic servant of the household, Billy is spared the task of preparing the suit-

cases. He has most likely been in the service of the family for many decades.

Camson, Richard "Dickie"   Dickie Camson, the story's protagonist, is a young soldier who must depart for military duty within a few hours' time. The reader learns much about his nature through his conversations, first with his wife and then with his Aunt Rena. He shows sensitivity and affection toward both women, worries about his aunt's well-being during his absence, and appreciates his wife's beauty, her youth, and her banter even though she speaks in banalities. He has been born into wealth and in his wife, Virginia, has married below his social station. His mother and father, drowned in a boating accident in the distant past, have left him without family, save his aunt. He enjoys jazz, speaks both French and German, and rides horseback. He is not talkative or gregarious. He will not take advantage of his social network to gain a privileged commission in intelligence but will accept, with resignation, an assignment in the infantry.

Camson, Virginia   Virginia, wife of the protagonist, Dickie Camson, displays a casual attitude toward her husband's imminent departure for military duty. She seems to understand war from a child's perspective (for example, she hopes her husband will be assigned to the "Calvary" [she means the cavalry], because she loves the "little sword-do-hickies" [24] that the soldiers wear on their uniforms). Contradicting her innocent, almost naive, conversation, she shows herself very astute regarding how he might avoid a dangerous assignment in the infantry and coaxes him to use his social connections to obtain a "commission" in intelligence. In conversing with her husband, she makes a number of grammatical mistakes that he patiently corrects. Her husband appreciates her for her beauty and kisses her "wonderful mouth" (24), despite the trite phrases she utters concerning his departure. The couple's relationship is based on sexual attraction and not on mutual interests or intellectual equality. She, although not as well-educated as her husband, has been successful in climbing the social ladder and has married into wealth. She is healthy, resourceful, and outgoing. She lacks, however, any true affection for Aunt Rena, whom she considers a burden. She therefore does not readily agree to her husband's repeated request that she take his aunt to the movies once a week in his absence. The reader may conclude Virginia to be emotionally shallow and thus not likely to suffer much should her husband perish in war.

Cleve, Thomas "Tom" E., Jr., Lieutenant Through the protagonist Dickie Camson's rereading of a note, written in the margin of a do-not-disturb sign on his Aunt Rena's door, the reader learns of a "Tom" who will be in the lobby of the old Waldorf Astoria Hotel in Manhattan after the Liberty Bond rally. The note describes Tom's physical appearance and was written by Aunt Rena during the time of World War I. As Dickie talks with his aunt in preparing to tell her of his departure for duty, the reader understands that the "Tom" of the note had been Aunt Rena's beau whom she believes is still alive and thus able to help her nephew get settled in Europe during World War II. Though now in dementia, she portends—with the letter of introduction and her instruction to her nephew to "find Tom Cleve" (27)—that Dickie will meet his death, as her Tom had done.

FURTHER READING

French, Warren. *J. D. Salinger.* New York: Twayne Publishers, 1963.

Purcell, William F. "World War II and the Early Fiction of J. D. Salinger." *Studies in American Literature* 28 (1991): 77–93.

"Over the Seas Let's Go, Twentieth Century Fox"

"Over the Seas Let's Go, Twentieth Century Fox" is one of Salinger's "lost" stories, neither published nor to be found in a library archive. According to IAN HAMILTON, Salinger mentions a story with this title in a 1942 letter to Elizabeth Murray. "Over the Seas Let's Go, Twentieth Century Fox" was rejected by the NEW YORKER. Unless the manuscript

can be located among Salinger's literary estate, the story's whereabouts are unknown.

"Paris"

"Paris" is one of Salinger's "lost" stories, neither published nor to be found in a library archive. According to the premier Salinger Web site, www.deadcaulfields.com, Salinger mentions a story with this title in a 1943 letter to Elizabeth Murray. Unless the manuscript can be located among Salinger's literary estate, the story's whereabouts are unknown.

"Paula"

"Paula" is one of Salinger's "lost" stories, neither published nor to be found in a library archive. According to Donald M. Fiene, Salinger's first bibliographer, "Paula" was sold to *Stag* magazine in 1942; the story was never printed. In 1961, the magazine informed Fiene that the story was no longer in its possession. "Paula" became the new title for "Mrs. Hincher.") (For more information, *see* "MRS. HINCHER." Unless the completed manuscript of "Paula" can be located among Salinger's literary estate, the story's whereabouts are unknown.

"Perfect Day for Bananafish, A"

"A Perfect Day for Bananafish" is the opening story in Salinger's second book, NINE STORIES (1953). Originally published in the January 31, 1948, issue of the NEW YORKER, "A Perfect Day for Bananafish" is the first story to feature a member of the Glass family. This famous tale of suicide introduces Seymour Glass, the character who will dominate the final decade—1955 to 1965—of Salinger's published work. "A Perfect Day for Bananafish" is Salinger's 20th published story.

SYNOPSIS

In the first of the story's three sections, Mrs. Muriel Glass is in a Florida hotel room, waiting to place a long-distance phone call to New York. The hotel's phone lines have been tied up for two and one-half hours by 97 New York advertising men. During her wait, Muriel has read a magazine article titled "Sex Is Fun—or Hell," cleaned her comb and brush, altered two articles of clothing, and removed two hairs from a mole. She is applying nail polish to her left hand in the window seat when the operator rings her room's number. "She was a girl who for a ringing phone dropped exactly nothing. She looked as if her phone had been ringing continually ever since she had reached puberty" (3–4). To dry her nails, Muriel waves her left hand back and forth, and then picks up the phone on the nightstand between two twin beds.

The phone operator informs Muriel that her phone call to New York has gone through. She begins to converse with her mother. Muriel's mother is concerned about Muriel's safety due to the unbalanced mental condition of her husband, Seymour. Seymour has recently damaged his in-laws' car, apparently by driving it into a tree. Muriel responds to her mother's question about who drove down to Florida, explaining that Seymour had driven without problems; "he was even trying not to look at the trees" (6). Muriel admits to her mother that Seymour has created a new nickname for her: Miss Spiritual Tramp of 1948. She then asks whether her mother knows the whereabouts of the book Seymour had sent her from Germany. Seymour had asked Muriel, on the drive to Florida, whether she had read the unnamed volume of poems. Muriel's mother exclaims in surprise, as her daughter does not read German. Seymour had told Muriel that "the poems happen to be written by the *only great poet of the century*" (7–8) and expected her to have gotten a translation or learned the language.

Muriel's mother tells Muriel that her father recently spoke with a psychiatrist about Seymour. He told Dr. Sivetski about "the trees. That business with the window. Those horrible things he said to Granny about her plans for passing away. What he did with all those lovely pictures from Bermuda" (8). Dr. Sivetski had responded that "it was a perfect *crime* the Army released him from the hospital" (8) and that "Seymour may com*pletely* lose control of himself" (9). According to Muriel, there is a good psychiatrist staying at the hotel, a Dr. Rieser, though her mother has never heard of him. Muriel's mother wants her daughter to come home immediately, but she refuses. Muriel explains that this is her first vacation in years and that she couldn't return anyway because she is painfully sunburned. Muriel tells her mother that she has spoken with Dr. Rieser and his wife in the hotel bar while Seymour was playing the piano in the Ocean Room. The doctor's wife asked if Seymour was a relative of Suzanne Glass, who runs a millinery shop in NEW YORK CITY. Muriel's mother wants to know Dr. Rieser's assessment of Seymour, but Muriel explains that it was too noisy in the bar and that the psychiatrist would need to know about Seymour's childhood. Mother and daughter then talk about the fashions in Florida. Muriel, in answer to her mother's question about the room, explains that she and Seymour "couldn't get the room [they] had before the war" (12). Muriel's mother repeats her request that Muriel come home and that her father would pay for her to "go away someplace by [herself] and think things over" (12–13). Muriel turns the offer down. Muriel's mother laments that her daughter waited for Seymour through the war. Muriel tries to end the call by saying Seymour may return from the beach at any minute. When her mother asks whether Seymour should be alone by himself on the beach, Muriel replies, "you talk about him as though he were a raving *maniac*" (13). She explains to her mother that Seymour just lies on the beach with his bathrobe on because he does not want people looking at his (nonexistent) tattoo. Muriel's mother gets Muriel to promise to phone her "the instant [Seymour] does, or *says*, anything at all funny" (14). Muriel states, "I'm not afraid of Seymour" (14).

The second section of the story begins with words spoken by a very young child named Sybil Carpenter, who sits on a beach ball while facing the ocean: "See more glass. Did you see more glass?" (14). Mrs. Carpenter, spreading suntan oil on Sybil's shoulders, asks her to stop repeating that phrase. Mrs. Carpenter is engaged in a conversation with a Mrs. Hubbel. She then tells Sybil that she and Mrs. Hubbel are going to the hotel to have a martini and she will bring her daughter the olive. Left alone, Sybil, dressed in a two-piece yellow bathing suit, "one piece of which she would not actually be needing for another nine or ten years," walks along the shore for a quarter of a mile until she finds a young man alone, lying on his back in his terry-cloth robe, beyond "the area reserved for guests of the hotel" (15). Sybil immediately asks, "Are you going in the water, see more glass?" (16). (From here to the story's end, "see more glass" is never referred to as "Seymour" by Salinger, but only as "the young man.")

Startled, Seymour grabs the lapels of his robe and then sees that the speaker is Sybil. When she repeats her question about going in the water, he explains he has been waiting for her. Sybil kicks sand into Seymour's face and tells him that her father is arriving tomorrow in an airplane. Seymour holds onto her ankle and replies that he has been "expecting him hourly. Hourly" (16). When asked where Muriel is, Seymour says, "At the hairdresser's. Having her hair dyed mink. Or making dolls for poor children, in her room" (17). He compliments Sybil on her blue bathing suit, only to be corrected by her that it is yellow. Seymour admits his error. He then tells her that his astrological sign is Capricorn and wonders what hers is. Sybil's non sequitur is that Seymour has let another child, Sharon Lipschutz, sit on the piano bench with him. Seymour explains to Sybil that she was nowhere in sight, and what could he do but let Sharon join him. Besides, he pretended that the other little girl was Sybil.

Sybil tells Seymour that they should go in the water and adds that next time Seymour should push Sharon off the piano bench. Seymour replies, "How that name comes up. Mixing memory and desire" (19). Seymour looks at the ocean and tells Sybil they will see if they can "catch a bananafish" (19). Seymour takes Sybil's hand, and they walk toward the ocean. He is carrying a rubber float. Ignoring her reply of "a what?" Seymour remarks that she must have already seen many bananafish in her life. When she shakes her head, Seymour

asks her where she lives. At first she denies that she knows. When Seymour tells her that Sharon, who is only three and a half years old, knows where she lives, Sybil pipes up with her own hometown of Whirly Wood, Connecticut. Sybil asks Seymour if he has read *Little Black Sambo*. He tells the child that he just happened to finish it last night. Sybil wants to know if the tigers ran around the tree, and Seymour replies that he thought the tigers would never stop. He exclaims about how many tigers there were, but Sybil counters there were only six. After asking Seymour if he likes wax and olives, Sybil asks if he likes Sharon. Seymour firmly says yes, and he lauds Sharon's refusal to be mean to dogs in the hotel's lobby, unlike other little girls who he pointedly says poke sticks at a particular dog. This silences Sybil until she admits she likes to chew candles, and Seymour joins in, "Who doesn't?" (22).

Upon entering the water Seymour remarks how cold it is. Once they have waded out till the water reaches Sybil's waist, he picks her up and lays her on her stomach on the float. Sybil commands him not to let go of her. Seymour tells her to look out for bananafish because "this is a *perfect* day for bananafish" (22). The child does not see any, and Seymour says it is understandable. He explains that bananafish "lead a very tragic life" (23) because they are "very ordinary-looking fish when they swim *in* [to a banana hole]. But once they get in, they behave like pigs" (23). The bananafish eat so many bananas that they "can't get out of the hole again. Can't fit through the door" (23). Sybil cautions Seymour not to go too far out in the water. She asks him what happens next to the bananafish. He explains that they die because "they get banana fever. It's a terrible disease" (23). A wave approaches, and Seymour holds Sybil's ankles and maneuvers the float over the wave while "the water soaked Sybil's blond hair, but her scream was full of pleasure" (24). She wipes her hair from her eyes and then tells Seymour she has seen a bananafish. Upon asking her if the fish had any bananas in his mouth, she says six. Seymour "suddenly picked up one of Sybil's wet feet . . . and kissed the arch" (24). She protests against being kissed. Seymour immediately says it is time to go back. He asks the child if she has had enough, and, though she says no, he apologizes and pushes the float toward the shore. After Sybil gets off, she runs "without regret in the direction of the hotel" (25).

The short, third section of the story commences as Seymour puts on his robe, closes it tightly, and slowly returns to the hotel, carrying the rubber float. When Seymour reaches the elevator, a woman enters with him. As they begin to ascend, Seymour remarks that he sees she is looking at his feet. The woman begs his pardon. Seymour insists that she is looking at his feet. When she exclaims to the contrary, that she is looking at the floor, Seymour replies, "If you want to look at my feet, say so . . . don't be a God-damned sneak about it" (25). The woman quickly asks the girl who is operating the elevator to let her out and exits. Seymour says to the elevator girl, "I have two normal feet and I can't see the slightest God-damned reason why anyone should stare at them" (26). He exits on the fifth floor and goes into Room 507.

Seymour sees Muriel asleep on one of the twin beds. He goes to a piece of luggage, takes out a handgun, and makes sure it is loaded. In the story's final sentence, Seymour sits on the other twin bed, looks at his wife, aims the handgun, and fires "a bullet through his right temple" (26).

CRITICAL ANALYSIS

"A Perfect Day for Bananafish," originally published in the January 31, 1948, issue of the *New Yorker,* is a landmark in Salinger's career. The story introduces, for the first time in Salinger's work, a member of the Glass family, Seymour Glass. The character fascinated Salinger, as the author would later create a host of other family members to encircle him. (For more information regarding the eight published Glass stories, *see* GLASS STORIES.)

Although Salinger had already published once in the *New Yorker* ("SLIGHT REBELLION OFF MADISON," in the back pages of the December 21, 1946, issue), "A Perfect Day for Bananafish" caused a sensation with *New Yorker* readers and heralded a new author. Upon its publication, *New Yorker* contributor and eminent short-story writer John Cheever called "A Perfect Day for Bananafish" "one hell of a story" (Yagoda 234). Then as now,

readers wanted to know why Seymour commits suicide.

To answer that question, "A Perfect Day for Bananafish" should be approached in two ways: first, as a stand-alone story; and, second, in conjunction with Salinger's later presentation of Seymour Glass.

Reading "A Perfect Day for Bananafish" as a separate entity, a salient consideration is the story's publication date, only two and a half years after the end of World War II. Difficulties experienced by returning soldiers were being reflected in literature and in the movies. In the story, a veteran named Seymour Glass, recently released from an army hospital (possibly located in Germany), has rejoined his wife, Muriel, and her family in New York City. The couple has traveled to an unspecified Florida beach and, as the scene opens, are now at the same hotel they visited before the war. Some critics locate the story in Miami Beach and categorize this vacation as the couple's second honeymoon. The true nature of Seymour's mental state and what he may or may not do propel the narrative.

The reader initially views Seymour's state of mind through the prism of a long-distance phone call between Muriel and her mother, a conversation that likewise allows for the assessment of the two women. While Muriel waits for her phone call to be put through to New York, she attends to her physical appearance and reads a magazine article, "Sex Is Fun—or Hell." The reader is thus presented with one clue as to what may be troubling the relationship. Muriel is an extremely attractive, self-possessed woman. Her attributes are not conveyed by direct statement but inferred, in subtle touches and within the dialogue. When the operator rings, Muriel is described as "a girl who for a ringing phone dropped exactly nothing. She looked as if her phone had been ringing continually ever since she had reached puberty" (3–4). Muriel's mother, a disembodied voice on the other end of the phone call, is a loud, controlling busybody who begins by exhibiting concern for her daughter, wanting to know if Muriel is safe, as she has not had a phone call from her daughter in two days. Seymour had recently damaged his in-laws' car by running into some trees, possibly in a suicide attempt, and Muriel's mother insists on knowing who had driven from New York to Florida. In her responses, Muriel displays that she does not easily bow to her parents' wishes, as she did not keep her promise that she would be the driver. Muriel informs her mother that Seymour had driven very safely, "even trying not to look at the trees" (6). Thus, Salinger paints Muriel as a wife who trusts her husband and who perhaps thinks what he needs is a vacation to help regain his balance. However, on the drive down, Seymour has displayed further irrational behavior, and he now calls his wife Miss Spiritual Tramp of 1948. Likewise, although Muriel does not read German, Seymour had mailed her a volume of German poems in the original language. He expresses disappointment that she has not read the volume, expecting her to have purchased a translation or "*learned the language*" because the poems are "written by the *only great poet of the century*" (7–8). Seymour's precarious emotional state is further signaled when Muriel's mother reveals that Dr. Sivetski, a psychiatrist—after being told by Muriel's father about Seymour's tree episode and "that business with the window. Those horrible things [Seymour] said to Granny about her plans for passing away. What he did with all those lovely pictures from Bermuda" (8)—has assessed the situation and declared "it was a perfect *crime* the Army released [Seymour] from the hospital" (8), and that "Seymour may com*plete*ly lose control of himself" (9). The reader has now been primed that something is seriously wrong. Yet, when Muriel's mother suggests that her daughter return home at once, Muriel again exhibits independence by refusing. Motherly concern subsequently evaporates as the conversation turns to Muriel's sunburn, her clothes, and the seasonal Florida fashions, with the two women snobbishly commenting on other guests at the hotel. Near the end of the phone call, Muriel's independence from her parents' perception of Seymour is again underscored when she refuses to leave her husband to go, as her mother suggests, on a cruise paid for by her father. Muriel tells her mother that she is "not afraid of Seymour" (14).

In the second section of the story, the reader directly encounters Seymour, portrayed in a more sympathetic light. Sybil Carpenter, a child near four years of age, has found Seymour far from the hotel. Wrapped tightly in a robe, he is lying on the sand, alone. Sybil tellingly addresses him as "see more glass," glossed by the critics Frederick L. Gwynn and Joseph L. Blotner as "he sees more than others and he shatters like glass" (Gwynn 20). (In the third-person narrative, however, Salinger refers to Seymour in this and the final scenes only as "the young man.") Entering into the child's world, Seymour engages in a sensitive, imaginative, give-and-take conversation with Sybil. So far, the Seymour portrayed does not seem to be the same person whom Muriel and her mother have just been discussing.

As the two prepare to go into the ocean, Seymour tells Sybil, "We'll see if we can catch a bananafish" (19), declaring, "this is a *perfect* day for bananafish" (22). Sybil has never heard of a bananafish, and Seymour imparts his parable to her. The parable, however, darkens the scene between Seymour and Sybil, as he explains that bananafish are "very ordinary-looking fish when they swim . . . into a banana hole" (23), but they become gluttons. Bananafish grow "so fat they can't get out of the hole again"; they develop "banana fever, . . . a terrible disease" (23), which causes their death. As Seymour takes Sybil out into the water on his float, a latent concern for her safety is triggered in the reader by her comments "Don't let go" (22) and "Not too far" (23). After a wave soaks her blond hair, Sybil declares she has seen a bananafish with six bananas in his mouth. Seymour immediately seizes her foot and kisses the arch, then terminates their time in the water. Back on the beach, Sybil and Seymour part company on her prophetic last word, "goodbye."

The short, third section of the story begins with Seymour carrying the "slimy wet, cumbersome float" (25) back to the hotel, to rejoin the adult world. When Seymour accuses a woman of staring at his feet, and declares, "If you want to look at my feet, say so . . . don't be a God-damned sneak about it" (25), the reader is stunned by his sudden profanity and paranoia. Back in his hotel room, Seymour sits on one of the twin beds, looks at his wife asleep on the other, and aims a cocked gun.

The reader quickly grows anxious that Muriel has been misguided in not fearing her husband, but the final words of the last sentence reveal Seymour's intention: "and [he] fired a bullet through his right temple" (26). The shocking conclusion sends the reader back to the beginning of the story, searching for clues that might reveal the reason why Seymour has killed himself.

Seymour and Muriel seem to be an unlikely couple. Seymour is presented as a refined sensibility—he reads the poetry of RAINER MARIA RILKE in German (critics agree that Rilke is the intended reference in Seymour's "the *only great poet of the century*" [7–8]); he quotes from T. S. ELIOT's poem "The Waste Land" ("Mixing memory and desire" [19]); he plays the piano—while Muriel, pragmatic and down-to-earth, reads about sex in a women's magazine and focuses on her appearance, fashion, and class differences. Seymour is not comfortable with the adult world of the hotel, filled with advertising conventioners, its bingo, and the bar. When he goes on the beach, he leaves the area reserved for the hotel's guests. Muriel, on the other hand, is completely comfortable and in her element at the hotel. That Seymour and Muriel are not compatible has led to an interpretation such as Gwynn and Blotner's: They believe that the story's imagery suggests "an underlying motif: Seymour's sexual inadequacy" (Gwynn 20). These critics employ Freudian theory in their analysis, perceiving phallic symbols in Seymour's "obsession with trees, his story of the engorged bananafish trapped in the banana hole, his paranoiac suspicion that a woman is staring critically at his bare feet, and his choice of the pistol as the suicide weapon" (Gwynn 20). A sexual disfunctionality may then be inferred as stemming from post-traumatic stress disorder, a psychiatric condition suffered by many returning soldiers.

Seymour, cognizant that Sybil's name is a homonym for "sibyl," a prophetess, declares her swimming suit is blue, the color associated in Western literature with a deity and spirituality. Sybil corrects him, stating that her suit is, in fact, yellow. (Seymour himself wears royal blue swim trunks.) When Sybil tells Seymour that she has seen a bananafish with six bananas in his mouth, he interprets her sighting in reference to him-self, his own fate and, perhaps, his wish. As John Wenke points out, the epigraph of Eliot's "The Waste Land," attributed to the Sibyl of Cumae, reads, "What do you want? I want to die" (Wenke 36). The tradition of the Sibyl of Cumae also records that she burned six of a total of nine books of prophecy after King Tarquinius refused to meet her selling price. She then charged Tarquinius the same price for the remaining three books. One meaning of the word *sibylline*, or *exorbitant*, derives from this historical occasion. Thus Salinger may be inferring that Seymour will pay the ultimate and exorbitant price: his life.

James Bryan suggests that "the bananafish this sibyl has seen is Seymour, and it is probably at this instant that he decides to shoot himself. In what may be taken as a final tribute to the yet unsullied hopes of the world he is leaving, Seymour suddenly kisses the instep of Sybil's foot" (Bryan 229). The kiss may also be interpreted as Seymour's grateful-ness to Sybil for her perception, one that sanctions his final escape from a world that has no place for him. As James E. Miller, Jr., explains, Seymour is "a bananafish, not because he has indulged his senses to the point of grossness, but rather because of his keen sensitivity to the overwhelming physi-cality of existence—his senses have been ravaged by the physical world, and he has found himself entrapped and must die" (Miller 28–29). Though Seymour has packed his war-memento gun—an Ortgies caliber 7.65 automatic—for the trip, this does not necessitate a premeditated use of it. Seymour's unplanned encounter with a little girl named Sybil, and her response to his bananafish parable, is the trigger he has needed to commit sui-cide. Salinger often employs a young, female char-acter to rescue an endangered male (for example, Esmé and Sergeant X in "FOR ESMÉ—WITH LOVE AND SQUALOR"; Phoebe Caulfield and Holden Caulfield in The CATCHER IN THE RYE; Mattie Gladwaller and Babe Gladwaller in the GLAD-WALLER STORIES). In this story, however, the young girl, Sybil, does not save Seymour but triggers his demise. If read differently, though, the prophecy, by allowing Seymour to leave a world that he can-not withstand or to which he cannot adjust, may be seen as a spiritual rescue.

Identifying Seymour as a bananafish is one way to interpret the story. If, on the other hand, bananafish are identified with the greedy material world of Muriel, her mother, and even Sybil, as Eberhard Alsen believes, they are the ones who die in the banana hole, because "banana fever is the effect of materialism on their spirit, and the death they die is a spiritual death" (Alsen 1983, 15). Alsen, citing the references to T. S. Eliot's "The Waste Land," concludes that Seymour "realizes that there is no hope for a spiritual regeneration of the wasteland, since even children like Sybil are already greedy bananafish" (Alsen 1983, 15). (Alsen assesses Sybil to be "a miniature Muriel . . . a small adult," noting Sybil's two-piece yellow bathing suit, her mother's endearment of "pussy," her possessiveness of Seymour in relation to Sharon Lipschutz, and her cruelty to the dog in the hotel [Alsen 1983, 13–14].) Seen through this perspective, the story shows the events to occur on a perfect day for bananafish—bananafish in the plural. With Seymour dead, his presence, his mere being, will no longer contradict the bananafish's world of material pursuit. The phrase, it's a "perfect *crime*" (8) (the only other time the word "perfect" is employed in the story, apart from "a *perfect* day for bananafish" [22]) may thus be read in the sense that, because Seymour did the deed himself, society will now be able to judge itself guiltless.

Other critics uphold an entirely different perspective regarding Seymour's interaction with Sybil, stating that the sequence exhibits heterosexual pedophilia. Frank Metcalf argues that one should identify Sybil, with her yellow bathing suit and blond hair, as a banana, and thus Seymour's "nearly conscious desires expressed in his bananafish story and in his erotic pretense with the girl are made fully conscious to him by Sybil's innocent responses to his story and to the kiss on her foot" (Metcalf 246). The horror of this self-recognition, in Metcalf's view, drives Seymour to suicide. Though Metcalf does not allude to Seymour's float, the narrative suggestively offers that after Sybil leaves him, Seymour is alone with his "slimy wet, cumbersome float" (25). Leslie Fiedler agrees that Seymour "trifles erotically with the child Sybil, playing with her fingers, kissing her feet in an appalling demonstration" but acknowledges that Salinger intends Seymour's actions not be taken as "pathological" (Fiedler 241). Fiedler contends that the author "demands that [the reader] accept this ambiguous love-making as a moment of sanity before suicide" and Sybil as "the embodiment of all that is clean and life-giving as opposed to the vulgar, destructive (i.e., fully sexual) wife" (Fiedler 241).

Dallas E. Wiebe, in a different reading, explains the suicide by interpreting Sybil's seeing a bananafish with six bananas in his mouth as "a description of a foot in the sand with the toes protruding" (Wiebe item 3). Wiebe contends that Seymour, "despite the fact that he says he has two normal feet . . . , has, or thinks he has, or thinks that other people think he has, six toes on one of his feet" (Wiebe item 3). In Wiebe's view, when Sybil announces that she has seen six bananas, "Seymour realizes his abnormality and he shoots himself" (Wiebe item 3).

The number six's repeated occurrence in "A Perfect Day for Bananafish" caused Charles V. Genthe to note that Sybil's assertion, in her conversation with Seymour on the number of tigers in the children's tale of *Little Black Sambo,* is incorrect. Sybil insists on six, when there are actually only four tigers. Genthe believes Salinger consciously changed the number, linking the tigers in "A Perfect Day for Bananafish" with the story's symbolism. Genthe also notes that the word *sex* in the magazine article Muriel reads is Latin for six. This critic also sees significance in Seymour and Muriel's room number, 507: "the middle, missing integer in the room number series, is synonymous with zero, a total void" (Genthe 171).

Other critics, specifically Gary Lane and James Finn Cotter, attempt to unlock the story's mystery by focusing on identifying the book of poems Seymour mailed to Muriel. No Salinger critic disputes that the author of the book is the Austrian poet Rainer Maria Rilke, a Salinger favorite mentioned by name in "The STRANGER" and "FRANNY." Lane claims the book to be Rilke's 1923 *Duineser Elegien (Duino Elegies),* the poet's culminating masterwork, and asserts that the poems, "informed by a basic thematic lamentation over the insufficiency of man and pervaded by a symbolic Angel [who is] the reminder, in his transcendence of human limitation, at once of man's aspiration and necessary failure," are thus "reflections about precisely the problems that . . . oppress Seymour" (Lane 28). Cotter's choice for the book Seymour posted to Muriel is Rilke's 1906 *Das Buch der Bilder (The Book of Pictures)*, which contains the poem "The Song of the Suicide." The speaker in this lyric poem is sickened by the food of life and wants to diet for a thousand years. Cotter finds an analogy to Salinger's character: "like the Suicide of Rilke's poem, Seymour doesn't 'want any more' of this nauseating existence" (Cotter 88).

In a short essay, the critic Samuel Irving Bellman cites Salinger's last-published story, "HAPWORTH 16, 1924," as the key to understanding Seymour's suicide. Bellman believes that Seymour's ability to recall his past lives and, additionally, to see into the future explains why Seymour's present life "was *fated to end* on that perfect bananafish day" (Bellman 351).

Despite multiple and contradicting perspectives on its meaning and symbolism, "A Perfect Day for Bananafish," if read as a stand-alone story—and without knowledge of the later Glass family stories—portrays the enigmatic final hours of a disturbed war veteran. As John Wenke summarizes: "The narrator of 'A Perfect Day for Bananafish' is detached, retentive, cryptic, relaying surface action but rarely explaining or judging events. The reason for Seymour's suicide offers, consequently, an open field for speculation" (Wenke 37). In 1972, Vladimir Nabokov, the celebrated author and former professor, compiled his list of a handful of American short stories that deserved to be graded A plus. "A Perfect Day for Bananafish" is included, with his comment, "this is a great story, too famous and fragile to be measured here by a casual conchometrist" (Nabokov 313) (a conchometrist is one who measures shells and the angles of their spires). Salinger's 24-page story invites multiple rereadings but tantalizingly withholds its secret (as would, in antiquity, the sibyl's utterance and prophesy—ambiguous, mysterious, and always open to interpretation).

A second approach to "A Perfect Day for Bananafish" is to read the story in conjunction with Salinger's final four published stories: "RAISE HIGH THE ROOF BEAM, CARPENTERS" (1955), "ZOOEY" (1957), "SEYMOUR: AN INTRODUCTION" (1959), and "Hapworth 16, 1924" (1965). These four novella-length stories portray, in the author's own words, "a family of settlers in twentieth-century New York, the Glasses" (see DUST-JACKET COMMENTS), of whom Seymour Glass is "the main character" (see DUST-JACKET COMMENTS). ("Franny," published 10 months prior to "Raise High the Roof Beam, Carpenters," must be omitted in this analysis, as Seymour is not mentioned in that story.)

Before turning to the presentation of Seymour in the Glass family stories, and then to its resulting impact on the interpretations of "A Perfect Day for Bananafish," one must recall that the 1948 story reveals only a limited number of facts about Seymour. He was in the army and has been recently released from an army hospital (it is not clear whether the hospital was in Germany). He is exhibiting strange behavior, as noticed by his wife and her family: He has driven into a tree (possibly a suicide attempt, though it is unclear); there has been an incident concerning a window ("presuming that Seymour shattered the glass, [it] foreshadows his suicide with verbal irony" [Bryan 228]); he has insulted his wife's grandmother, saying "horrible things" concerning "her plans for passing away" (8) and doing something odd with her chair; he has done something inappropriate with the pictures from Bermuda (in all likelihood, honeymoon photos that he has defaced, torn up, or thrown away); he has invented nicknames for his wife and now calls her Miss Spiritual Tramp of 1948. The narrative also provides the information that Seymour reads poetry of the highest order (though nowhere does the story indicate that Seymour himself writes poems). Seymour stayed in this same hotel with Muriel before the war, and the reader may safely assume that the two were a married couple at the time, deduced from Muriel's statement to her mother that they couldn't get the same room they had had previously (an unmarried daughter in 1948 would not likely admit to sharing a room with her beau). Seymour is pale and obviously sick, as noted by a hotel guest, a psychiatrist. He plays the piano and associates more comfortably with children than with adults; his astrological sign is Capricorn; and he enjoys speaking in parables (though the narrative does not specify that Seymour takes an interest in any specific religion). Together, these pieces of information construct the biography of a character that critics reference as "the bananafish Seymour" (for ease of distinguishing him from the Seymour appearing in the four later Glass family novellas, referenced as "the Glass family [or Glass Saga] Seymour").

Seymour Glass does not reappear in Salinger's fiction until "Raise High the Roof Beam, Carpenters," published in the November 19, 1955, issue of the *New Yorker* (apart from an offhand mention of an Uncle Seymour in the 1949 story "DOWN AT THE DINGHY"). Written by Buddy Glass, "Raise High the Roof Beam, Carpenters" introduces the entire Glass family and centers around the events of Seymour and Muriel's wedding day, June 4, 1942. This date creates the first discrepancy in the Seymour character's biography, as "A Perfect Day for Bananafish" indicates the couple had married before the war. "Raise High the Roof Beam, Carpenters" fleshes out much of Seymour's background: He was a child prodigy; he appeared on a children's radio show, *It's a Wise Child,* where he spoke like a poet; at the age of 12, he threw a rock at a girl friend "because she looked so beautiful" (104), a girl to whom Muriel, as a child, had an uncanny resemblance; his passion for poetry influenced his six brothers' and sisters' taste in poetry (though there is no specific mention of Seymour writing poems himself); he entered college at the age of 15 and became a full professor of English at Columbia University before his induction into the army; at some point in the past, he attempted suicide by slitting his wrists (no date is specified), before he met Muriel in 1941; in his diary, he writes that he "love[s] and need[s] her undiscriminating heart" (77); his future mother-in-law and her psychoanalyst believe Seymour to be a schizoid personality; his future mother-in-law suspects Seymour might be a homosexual because he hasn't tried previously to seduce her daughter; he calls himself "a paranoiac in reverse" because he believes people are "plotting to make [him] happy" (88); before the wedding, he feels "too keyed up

to be with people" and as if he were "about to be born" (106), so he has begged Muriel to forgo a wedding and to elope instead (and after he stands her up at the ceremony, they do elope); before they marry, he promises to undergo psychoanalysis; he is interested in religion, specifically, TAOISM, ZEN, and VEDANTA. Seymour's demise is explained in "Raise High the Roof Beam, Carpenters" simply as "the bridegroom is now, in 1955, no longer living. He committed suicide in 1948, while he was on vacation in Florida with his wife" (6).

In "Zooey" (published in 1957), the reader learns an additional fact about the afternoon of the suicide: Seymour wrote a poem on the hotel's desk blotter: "The little girl on the plane / Who turned her doll's head around / To look at me" (64) (there is no poem mentioned in "A Perfect Day for Bananafish"). This is the first concrete indication of Seymour writing poetry. Up until now, the character has evinced interest in poetry and spoke like a poet while on *It's a Wise Child.* "Zooey" also specifies that Seymour committed suicide on March 18, 1948 (in "A Perfect Day for Bananafish" no date is specified; ironically, the story was published in the January 31, 1948, issue); that he was born in the month of February (another discrepancy with the Seymour of "A Perfect Day for Bananafish," who in that story refers to himself as a Capricorn, thus with a late December/January birthday); and that he, along with his brother Buddy, instructed the other siblings in world religions.

In 1959, Salinger published "Seymour: An Introduction," ready to stand behind the true (and fully revised) Seymour. Acknowledging the problem of squaring his depiction of Seymour in "Raise High the Roof Beam, Carpenters" and "Zooey" with that of "A Perfect Day for Bananafish," Salinger, in this story, now attributes the writing of "A Perfect Day for Bananafish" to his narrator, Buddy Glass. Buddy explains that the Glass family members have criticized the previous story because "the 'Seymour' who did the walking and talking in that early story, not to mention the shooting, was not Seymour at all but, oddly, someone with a striking resemblance to—alley oops, I'm afraid—myself" (131). In a further attempt to mitigate the impact of Seymour's suicide on a reader's assessment of his brother's character, Buddy contends that despite the coroner's ruling, "the true artist-seer, the heavenly fool who can and does produce beauty, is mainly dazzled to death by his own scruples, the blinding shapes and colors of his own sacred human conscience" (123). The "real" Seymour is the Seymour that Buddy proclaims in his following litany: "He was a great many things to a great many people while he lived, and virtually all things to his brothers and sisters in our somewhat outsized family. Surely he was all *real* things to us: our blue-striped unicorn, our double-lensed burning glass, our consultant genius, our portable conscience, our supercargo, and our one full poet" (123–124). Buddy continues with another effort at lessening the negative ethical implications of suicide in the opening clause, "with or without a suicide plot in his head, he was the only person" who "tallied with the classical conception, as I saw it, of a *mukta*, a ringding enlightened man, a God-knower" (124). Buddy reveals that Seymour, since the age of eight, wrote poetry. During the last three years of his life, Seymour wrote 184 "double-haikus," which, Buddy believes, will eventually rank his brother as one of the three or four greatest American poets of all time. Seymour is also presented as a master of meditation, who can recall his past lives. In "Seymour: An Introduction," Salinger alters one detail he had added in "Zooey" regarding Seymour's suicide: The poem Seymour wrote on the blotter about the little girl on the plane is now said to have been written in Japanese, in the form of a classical-style haiku. As for revisiting the suicide, Buddy, the narrator, remarks, "I don't expect to be ready to do that, at the rate I'm going, for several more years" (196). Salinger has called Buddy Glass his "alter-ego and collaborator" (*see* DUST-JACKET COMMENTS); "Seymour: An Introduction" creates the distinct impression of Buddy as the author's mouthpiece.

Six years after the publication date of "Seymour: An Introduction," Salinger published his final story during his lifetime, "Hapworth 16, 1924," in the June 19, 1965, issue of the *New Yorker*. Apart from a short introduction by Buddy, the story is a long (perhaps implausible) letter written by the seven-year-old Seymour to his family. The letter reveals Seymour to be even more of a child prodigy than previously indicated: He writes reams of poetry; he reads numberless books; he is obsessed with God; he can interrupt the sensation of pain from a deep gash in his leg; via meditation, he knows his past lives and glimpses the future (and foretells a short story that Buddy will write years hence); he predicts he will live to be about 30 years old (though he doesn't specify how he will die).

The four Glass family stories appreciably expand and deepen the character of Seymour, but in altering his biography, they create an obvious problem of interpretation: How can the Seymour as reflected in these four stories be the same character portrayed in "A Perfect Day for Bananafish," who commits suicide in such a cruel manner?

Critics generally align into three camps regarding this question. The first camp, with the quickest and perhaps cleanest interpretative stance, holds that when Salinger wrote the 1948 short story, he had no intention of delving further into the character. When, seven years later, he resurrects the Seymour persona, the character has understandably grown and changed in the author's vision. Warren French believes that "rather than explaining anything about the enigmatic 'A Perfect Day for Bananafish,' the later stories shed doubt upon its authenticity" (French 1988, 100–101) as part of the narrative on the Glass family. French concludes that the best approach to "A Perfect Day for Bananafish" is as a stand-alone story.

The second camp includes "A Perfect Day for Bananafish" as part of the Glass family saga but interprets the narrative events in a positive light, with the suicide viewed through the prism of the later stories. William Wiegand writes, "Without 'Carpenters' the suicide which closes 'Bananafish' appears motivated chiefly by Seymour's inability to put up with his bourgeois wife. With 'Carpenters,' however, we see Seymour as a man not deprived of, but rather surfeited with, the joy of life" (Wiegand 5). Wiegand interprets banana fever as a "curious surfeit of sensation" (Wiegand 5) and that "Seymour, a bananafish himself, has become so glutted with sensation that he cannot swim out into society again" (Wiegand 6). Elizabeth N. Kurian's reading of the four Glass family stories concludes that "Seymour Glass is Salinger's idealized version of the most perfectly realized human being" (Kurian 117). Kurian remarks that "it is important to bear in mind that suicide does not have the negative connotations in Buddhism that it has in Christianity" and interprets Seymour's suicide as "a positive act, a transcendent declaration of faith" signifying "his release from the wheel of life or the round of incarnations" (Kurian 132). Som P. Ranchan, citing Vedantic terminology, believes Salinger intends Seymour to be considered a Buddha-like Ishtam, explaining, "Ishtams are incarnations of Godhead who impinge upon the historical scene . . . from time to time with a view to reminding man of his true, hidden divine nature and to help him realize it and manifest it in his thinking, feeling and doing" (Ranchan 4). Ranchan terms "A Perfect Day for Bananafish" "a koan on Mahaparinirvana" (Ranchan 55) about "an explosive entry of the God-knower, the *mukta*, the ringding enlightened man into the mystery of . . . the non-residual Nirvana from which there is no return" (Ranchan 63).

The third camp of interpretation, like the second, includes "A Perfect Day for Bananafish" as part of the Glass family saga. However, in a reversal, these critics read the stories as Seymour's failure to attain enlightenment, citing the suicide as the final strike against him in that search. Eberhard Alsen, who has focused more closely than any other Salinger scholar on the Glass family, approaches the Glass stories, taken together, as a composite novel. Alsen constructs a narrative of Seymour's life and its meaning "radically different from those of previous commentaries. . . . Seymour should not be seen as a saint . . . but a God-seeker whose quest failed . . . because he pursued it in such a self-directed and single-minded fashion that he estranged himself from common humanity" (Alsen 1983, xiii). Alsen locates the source of Seymour's problems in the seven-year-old Seymour's letter from Camp Simon Hapworth; the critic identifies "three negative character traits . . . Seymour's sensuality, his emotional instability, and his latent malice" (Alsen 2002, 193–194). Seymour's experience of World War II and his relationship with Muriel constitute significant and fateful blows. In "Raise High the Roof Beam, Carpenters," Alsen interprets Seymour's diary remark about the scars

on his wrists (which undoubtedly mean Seymour had, at some point, attempted suicide) to mean a suicide attempt took place in 1941. A further remark, about not wanting to discuss the Charlotte stone-throwing incident over just one drink, Alsen feels, indicates that Seymour "now drinks quite a bit" (Alsen 2002, 238). Alsen believes that "Seymour's war experiences brought about the change in his personality" (Alsen 2002, 132) and reads Dr. Sivetski's comment in "A Perfect Day for Bananafish"—"it was a perfect *crime* the Army released him from the hospital" (8)—to mean that "Seymour was in the psychiatric ward of an Army hospital" (Alsen 2002, 132). Since in "A Perfect Day for Bananafish" Seymour is not released from the army hospital until, apparently, early 1948, Alsen argues that "his case was so severe that the Army kept him locked up for three years" (Alsen 2002, 132). (Alsen seems to arrive at this conclusion in the following manner. Alsen takes Buddy Glass's comment in "Seymour: An Introduction"—Seymour's "last three years of his life, both in and out of the Army, but mostly in, well in" [133]—and combines it with Dr. Sivetski's comment above, to extrapolate a chronology: "1945: Seymour, 28, has a nervous breakdown and is treated in an Army hospital in Germany. 1945–1948: Seymour remains in psychiatric wards of Army hospitals for most of the last three years of his life" [Alsen 2002, 238].) Alsen surmises that the psychiatric treatment Seymour received "increased his instability rather than curing it, probably because he resented the concept of 'normalcy' with which the Army psychiatrists were operating, and these feelings of resentment may have accelerated his spiritual deterioration" (Alsen 1983, 206). Alsen contends that the cruelty Seymour exhibited as a boy of 12, when he threw the stone that injured Charlotte, was reawakened by the war and was later evidenced by "cruelty in his decision to blow his brains out . . . sitting near the sleeping Muriel" (Alsen 2002, 132). Alsen dates the suicide to March 19, 1948 (Alsen 2002, 239), instead of the usually accepted March 18. He bases that on indirect information derived from "A Perfect Day for Bananafish," plus the use of a perpetual calendar, over clear-cut information in "Zooey," which states that Seymour's suicide took place exactly "three years, to the day" (62) prior to the date of Buddy's letter (3/18/51) to Zooey. The date of the 18th apparently holds special significance for Salinger; the author has his other cherished character, Allie Caulfield in *The Catcher in the Rye,* also die on the 18th (July 18, 1946).

The existence of these conflicting camps of interpretation indicates the richness and complexity of Salinger's four beautifully enigmatic and mythic novella-length narratives: "Raise High the Roof Beam, Carpenters," "Zooey," "Seymour: An Introduction," and "Hapworth 16, 1924." Though Salinger's last published work, "Hapworth 16, 1924," appeared in 1965, there is strong evidence he continued to work on more Glass family stories. Should these unseen stories ever reach the reading public, they will no doubt alter and amplify the interpretation of the existing stories already in print.

The reader of Salinger's work cannot know whether the author intended to gloss over the harsher aspects of Seymour's personality by envisioning the character as a God-seeker in the later Glass stories. What can be acknowledged, however, is that the Seymour figure reflects many of the spiritual concerns of Salinger. Likewise, a parallel can further be drawn between the life events of the two: DORIS SALINGER, the author's sister, related to Salinger's daughter that when Doris and the author were children, their father would hold brother and sister in the waves and instruct them to look for the bananafish; some time after the declaration of victory in Europe (V-E Day, May 7, 1945), Salinger hospitalized himself in Germany for battle fatigue, a condition now recognized as post-traumatic stress disorder; Salinger's wartime marriage to Sylvia took place in November 1945; in June 1946, the author was vacationing alone in Florida, as SYLVIA SALINGER had returned to Europe to file for an annulment.

Following closely on the heels of his own postwar life events, Salinger, during the second half of 1946, composed the draft of "A Perfect Day for Bananafish." The initial submission to the *New Yorker* was titled "The Bananafish." On January 22, 1947, the *New Yorker* editor WILLIAM MAXWELL wrote Salinger's agent that the magazine liked parts

of the piece "very much but it seems to lack any discoverable story or point. If Mr. Salinger is around town, perhaps he'd like to come in and talk to me about *New Yorker* stories" (Yagoda 234). Salinger talked with Maxwell and added the phone-call scene, which the original draft had lacked. The magazine sent the story back for a rewrite, and after Salinger resubmitted the work, now titled, "A Fine Day for Bananafish," the story was finally accepted. The *New Yorker* queried whether "bananafish" should be printed as one or two words; Salinger decided one word would make it more nonsensical. The title was tweaked once again, and "A Perfect Day for Bananafish," Salinger's 20th magazine publication, hit the newsstands in the January 31, 1948, issue of the *New Yorker.*

In 1953, Salinger chose the contents for his first collection of short stories. "A Perfect Day for Bananafish" is the earliest of his story publications the author wished to preserve in book form. In 1963, Warren French, in the initial full-length monograph devoted to Salinger's work, comments that this story "enabled Salinger at last to attract the attention of the public and to break into the ranks of the regular contributors to one of the nation's most influential magazines. The 'perfect day' was the death of Seymour Glass, but the making of J. D. Salinger, who, ironically, was within a few years to find himself trapped by his own fame" (French 1963, 85).

PUBLICATION HISTORY

"A Perfect Day for Bananafish" was first published in the *New Yorker* magazine on January 31, 1948. The story was subsequently chosen to appear in an anthology selected by *New Yorker* editors, titled *55 Short Stories from The New Yorker, 1940–1950,* released in 1949. "A Perfect Day for Bananafish's" first book publication in a volume consisting exclusively of Salinger's work was in *Nine Stories* (LITTLE, BROWN AND COMPANY, 1953). *Nine Stories,* Salinger's second book, has never gone out of print.

Nine Stories is available in three editions from Little, Brown and Company: an exact reproduction of the hardback first edition from 1953; a trade paperback that mimics the production of the hardback; and a mass-market paperback, with its pagination differing from the above editions.

CHARACTERS

Carpenter, Mr.   Mr. Carpenter is Sybil's father and husband to Mrs. Carpenter. According to Sybil, he will be flying in the next day. Seymour Glass cryptically remarks, "it's about time he got here . . . I've been expecting him hourly. Hourly" (16).

Carpenter, Mrs.   Mrs. Carpenter is Sybil's mother and wife to Mr. Carpenter. She complains that Sybil's repeating the phrase, "Did you see more glass?" (14, 15) is driving her crazy. Mrs. Carpenter rubs suntan oil on Sybil and talks with Mrs. Hubbel. Abandoning Sybil to her own devices, Mrs. Carpenter goes with Mrs. Hubbel into the hotel bar for a martini.

Carpenter, Sybil   Sybil Carpenter, the young child of Mr. and Mrs. Carpenter, encounters Seymour Glass on a Florida beach. Wearing a "canary-yellow two-piece bathing suit, one piece of which she would not actually be needing for another nine or ten years" (15), Sybil converses with Seymour. He compliments her on her blue bathing suit, upon which she corrects him that her suit is yellow. She is jealous of Seymour's allowing another child, Sharon Lipschutz, to sit with him at the piano. She asks Seymour whether he has read *Little Black Sambo*. Seymour tells Sybil about bananafish, concluding "this is a *perfect* day for bananafish" (22). The two go into the water. After she claims to have seen a bananafish with six bananas in its mouth, Seymour kisses the arch of her foot. Though Sybil wants to remain in the water, Seymour makes them return to shore, whereupon she runs off "without regret in the direction of the hotel" (25).

Elevator operator girl   The unnamed elevator operator girl witnesses the exchange between Seymour Glass and the woman in the elevator and hears their remarks concerning his feet. When the woman exits, the elevator operator is alone with Seymour when he remarks that he has "two normal feet and . . . can't see the slightest God-damned reason why anybody should stare at them" (26).

Freddy   Muriel Glass's mother refers to Freddy during her phone call with Muriel. The mother tells her daughter that the book of German poems Seymour Glass gave Muriel is in Freddy's room. In all likelihood, Freddy is Muriel's brother.

Glass, Muriel (Fedder)   Muriel Glass is Seymour Glass's wife. She is in a room at a Florida hotel waiting for her call to go through to her parents in New York. Her independence from them is exhibited when she stands up to her parents' insistence that she leave her husband. Muriel tells her mother that she's "not afraid of Seymour" (14). Though Muriel seems somewhat shallow, with her emphasis on her appearance, she defends Seymour's behavior and refuses to accept her mother's characterization of him as "a raving *maniac*" (13). Muriel is asleep on one of the twin beds when Seymour, seated on the other bed, shoots himself through the temple.

Muriel briefly appears in "Raise High the Roof Beam, Carpenters," where she is seen being escorted by her parents down the steps after the wedding fails to take place. In that story, Seymour frequently speaks about Muriel in his diary, and the reader also learns that her maiden name is Fedder. Muriel is also mentioned in "Zooey" and "Seymour: An Introduction."

Glass, Seymour   Seymour Glass is a war veteran who recently has been released from an army hospital. Though Seymour recently damaged his in-laws' car in an accident (which may have been a deliberate suicide attempt) by running the car into some trees, he has driven his wife, Muriel, and himself safely from New York to Florida. The couple is staying at the hotel where they had stayed before the war, but they are not successful in getting the same room. Seymour is interested in poetry, shown by his sending Muriel a book of poems "written by the *only great poet of the century*" (7–8). Unfortunately, the poems are written in German, and his wife doesn't read the language. Seymour does not socialize with the adults at the hotel; he plays the piano while Muriel, the Riesers, and others play bingo. Muriel describes Seymour as pale and laments to her mother that he nonetheless refuses to remove his robe, even when alone on the beach far from the hotel, so that he could get some sun.

Sybil Carpenter finds Seymour on the beach, far past the area for hotel guests, and asks if he is going in the water. She addresses him as "see more glass" (16). A light, bantering conversation ensues. When Seymour and Sybil get ready to go into the ocean, he tells her his parable of the bananafish, remarking that today "is a *perfect* day for banana-fish" (22). While in the water, Sybil explains, after the two have "nosed over the top of the wave" (24) on Seymour's float, that she has seen a bananafish with six bananas in his mouth. Seymour imme-diately kisses the arch of Sybil's foot, and though she wants to remain longer in the water, he makes them return to shore. Sybil runs off toward the hotel. Seymour wraps himself in his robe and car-ries "the slimy wet, cumbersome float" (25) as he returns to the hotel.

While in the hotel's elevator, Seymour accuses a female passenger of looking at his feet. When she denies this, he responds, "I have two normal feet and I can't see the slightest God-damned reason why anybody should stare at them" (26). Upon entering the hotel room, he sees Muriel asleep on one of the twin beds. He takes his gun and, seated on the other bed, shoots himself through the temple.

Seymour is resurrected in "Raise High the Roof Beam, Carpenters" (1955), the first of the Glass family stories. "Raise High the Roof Beam, Car-penters" reveals that Seymour is the eldest child of the nine-member Glass family. The story, a descrip-tion of Seymour's wedding day and his failure to show up for the ceremony, features his revealing diary entries. In "Zooey" (1957), the longest of the Glass family stories, Seymour has been dead for more than seven and one-half years. Nonethe-less, Seymour plays a significant role as "Zooey" ends with Seymour's parable of the Fat Lady that brings Franny to joy and understanding of her life's purpose. The next Glass family story, "Sey-mour: An Introduction" (1959) is an extensive effort, by Buddy, to convey the life and identity of his brother. The final Glass family story to date, "Hapworth 16, 1924" (1965) contains the most extended presentation of Seymour's own words, albeit written at the age of seven.

Glass, Suzanne   Suzanne Glass owns a millinery shop on Madison Avenue in MANHATTAN. Mrs. Rieser asks Muriel Glass if her husband Seymour is related to Suzanne and learns that he is not.

Granny   Muriel Glass's mother refers twice to Granny in her phone call with her daughter. She reports that her husband told Dr. Sivetski about the time Seymour Glass said "those horrible things to Granny about her passing away" (8). The mother asks Muriel if she mentioned to Dr. Rieser what Seymour did to Granny's chair. It remains unclear whether the character is Muriel's maternal or paternal grandmother.

Hubbel, Mrs.   Mrs. Hubbel exclaims to Mrs. Carpenter about a silk handkerchief some woman has ingeniously used as a fashion item. She will accompany Mrs. Carpenter to the hotel bar for a martini.

Lady from Canada   Seymour Glass refers to an unnamed lady from Canada at the hotel whose dog is poked by Sybil Carpenter.

Lipschutz, Sharon   Sharon Lipschutz, three and a half years old, is a younger rival of Sybil Carpen-ter for Seymour Glass's attention. Seymour allows Sharon to sit on the piano bench with him while he plays the piano. This upsets Sybil, who wants him to push Sharon off. Seymour lauds Sharon's char-acter by contrasting her kindness to dogs with Syb-il's meanness. At one point in the story, when Sybil again mentions Sharon's name, Seymour remarks, "How that name comes up. Mixing memory and desire" (19).

Muriel Glass's father (Mr. Fedder)   Muriel Glass's father is frequently referenced in the phone call between Muriel and her mother. He has spo-ken with Dr. Sivetski about the multiple incidents of Seymour Glass's strange behavior. The father wants to rescue his daughter from the marriage by offering to pay for Muriel's immediate return from Florida and a cruise.

Muriel's father also appears in the story "Raise High the Roof Beam, Carpenters." Along with his wife, he is seen escorting Muriel down the steps after the wedding fails to take place. He is mentioned in Seymour's diary. In "Raise High the Roof Beam, Carpenters," the reader learns his last name is Fedder.

Muriel Glass's mother (Mrs. Rhea Fedder) Muriel Glass's mother lives with her husband in New York, where she receives her daughter's phone call from Florida. She worries about Muriel's well-being because of what she perceives to be Seymour Glass's instability. She wants Muriel to leave instantly and return to New York. Yet the mother seems almost equally interested in Muriel's vacation outfits, her sunburn, and this season's fashion trends in Florida.

Muriel's mother also appears in "Raise High the Roof Beam, Carpenters." Along with her husband, she is seen escorting Muriel down the steps after the wedding fails to take place. She is referred to often by the Matron of Honor and in Seymour's diary. In "Raise High the Roof Beam, Carpenters," the reader learns her name is Rhea Fedder.

New York advertising men Ninety-seven New York advertising men in the hotel are keeping the telephone lines tied up, delaying Muriel Glass's phone call to her mother.

Phone operator The voice of an unnamed operator tells Muriel Glass that her call to New York is finally ready.

Rieser, Dr. Muriel Glass tells her mother that Dr. Rieser is a psychiatrist staying at the hotel. She says she met Rieser and his wife at bingo. Rieser asked Muriel if the man playing the piano was her husband and whether he had been sick. After bingo, Rieser and his wife have a drink with Muriel in the bar. Muriel talks with him a bit about her husband, Seymour, but the din of the bar prevents any meaningful exchange. Rieser stays in the bar all day, according to Muriel.

Rieser, Mrs. Mrs. Rieser is the wife of Dr. Rieser and meets Muriel Glass one night at bingo. Muriel tells her mother that Mrs. Rieser is wear-

ing an awful dinner dress. Mrs. Rieser asks Muriel if her husband, Seymour, is related to Suzanne Glass, who owns the millinery shop on Madison Avenue.

Sivetski, Dr. Muriel Glass's mother tells her daughter that her husband has spoken with Dr. Sivetski about Seymour Glass. Sivetski said that it was "a perfect *crime*" (8) Seymour was released from the Army hospital, and that Seymour "may com*pletely* lose control of himself" (9).

Woman in elevator The unnamed woman rides up in the hotel elevator with Seymour Glass. Seymour accuses her of looking at his feet. When she denies doing so, he remarks, "If you want to look at my feet, say so . . . don't be a God-damned sneak about it" (25).

FURTHER READING

Alsen, Eberhard. *A Reader's Guide to J. D. Salinger.* Westport, Conn.: Greenwood Press, 2002.
———. *Salinger's Glass Stories as a Composite Novel.* Troy, N.Y.: Whitston Publishing Company, 1983.
Bellman, Samuel Irving. "New Light on Seymour's Suicide: Salinger's 'Hapworth 16, 1924.'" *Studies in Short Fiction* 3 (Spring 1966): 348–351.
Bryan, James. "Salinger's Seymour's Suicide." *College English* 24, no. 3 (December 1962): 226–229.
Cotter, James Finn. "A Source for Seymour's Suicide: Rilke's 'Voices' and Salinger's *Nine Stories.*" *Papers on Language and Literature* 25, no. 1 (Winter 1989): 83–98.
Fiedler, Leslie. "The Eye of Innocence." In *Salinger: A Critical and Personal Portrait,* edited by Henry Anatole Grunwald, 218–245. New York: Harper & Row, 1962.
French, Warren. *J. D. Salinger.* New York: Twayne Publishers, 1963.
———. *J. D. Salinger, Revisited.* New York: Twayne Publishers, 1988.
Genthe, Charles V. "Six, Sex, Sick: Seymour, Some Comments." *Twentieth Century Literature* 10, no. 4 (January 1965): 170–171.
Gwynn, Frederick L., and Joseph L. Blotner. *The Fiction of J. D. Salinger.* Pittsburgh: University of Pittsburgh Press, 1958.

Kurian, Elizabeth N. *A Religious Response to the Existential Dilemma in the Fiction of J. D. Salinger.* New Delhi: Intellectual Publishing House, 1992.

Lane, Gary. "Seymour's Suicide Again: A New Reading of J. D. Salinger's 'A Perfect Day for Bananafish.'" *Studies in Short Fiction* 10 (Winter 1973): 27–33.

Metcalf, Frank. "The Suicide of Salinger's Seymour." *Studies in Short Fiction* 9 (Summer 1972): 243–246.

Miller, James E., Jr. *J. D. Salinger.* Minneapolis: University of Minnesota Press, 1965.

Nabokov, Vladimir. *Strong Opinions.* New York: McGraw-Hill Book Company, 1973.

Ranchan, Som P. *An Adventure in Vedanta: J. D. Salinger's The Glass Family.* Delhi: Ajanta Publications, 1989.

Wenke, John. *J. D. Salinger: A Study of the Short Fiction.* Boston: Twayne Publishers, 1991.

Wiebe, Dallas E. "Salinger's 'A Perfect Day for Bananafish.'" *Explicator* 23 (September 1964): item 3.

Wiegand, William. "J. D. Salinger's Seventy-eight Bananas." *Chicago Review* 11, no. 4 (Winter 1958): 3–19.

Yagoda, Ben. *About Town: The New Yorker and the World It Made.* n.p.: Da Capo Press, 2001.

"Personal Notes on an Infantryman"

Appearing in the December 12, 1942, issue of COLLIER'S, "Personal Notes on an Infantryman" is Salinger's first war-related story to be published after his induction into the army. "Personal Notes on an Infantryman" is Salinger's sixth published story. The author, however, chose not to include the story in his three books of collected stories.

SYNOPSIS

Lawlor, a man in his early forties, dressed in a suit, asks the unnamed narrator at the Orderly Room to look over his enlistment papers. The narrator demurs, saying he is not the recruiting officer and adds that Lawlor is not in an induction center. Lawlor insists on enlisting. The narrator comments to Lawlor that his current job as a foreman may be more important to the war effort than his service in the infantry. During the narrator's questions, the reader learns that Lawlor is married and that he has two sons who have served in the war—one currently in the army and one, until he lost an arm at Pearl Harbor, in the navy. The narrator warns Lawlor that he would have to take basic training at the base and then asks how Lawlor's wife feels about his enlisting. Lawlor exclaims, "She's delighted. . . . All wives are anxious to see their husbands go to war" (96). He then gets huffy, asks for directions to the recruitment office, and steps out.

Soon after Lawlor leaves the Orderly Room, his wife phones the narrator, who tells her there is nothing he can do to stop her husband from enlisting. The narrator can't resist the sweetness of Mrs. Lawlor's voice. Salinger hints at the relationship between Mrs. Lawlor and the narrator, who remarks that he "couldn't be unkind to [her] voice" and "never could" (96).

The narrator observes that Lawlor, after his enlistment, is successful in basic training. However, when the time comes for his company to be shipped overseas to fight, Captain Eddy doesn't include Lawlor. The new soldier is furious and accuses the narrator of influencing Captain Eddy's decision. The narrator denies the charge. Lawlor declares to the narrator that he wants action in the war. He also asks whether his wife has been calling the narrator again. The narrator says no, whereupon Lawlor salutes and leaves.

The narrator notes that Lawlor, in his new company, later became a corporal, then a buck sergeant. Lawlor's commanding officer thought Lawlor the best man in Company L. Lawlor is then "shipped across" (96). After Lawlor's company has landed, the narrator calls Mrs. Lawlor to tell her the news. He can't get her voice to sound normal, but he says he made her happy. He accomplished this by telling her that his brother, Pete (formerly in the navy), joined him in seeing off "Dad" (96). Their father saluted and kissed his two sons goodbye before departing for overseas combat.

CRITICAL ANALYSIS

This one-page, very short story echoes Salinger's "The HANG OF IT." Both stories appeared in *Col-*

lier's with the tag line, "A SHORT SHORT STORY COMPLETE ON THIS PAGE [emphasis added]," and each was illustrated. The illustration for "Personal Notes on an Infantryman" shows a soldier with his fist clenched and stating, "I want action," while three soldiers sit at desks. One of the soldiers wears a funny smirk. Another, who faces the standing soldier, is profiled and looks right into the eye of the speaker. In the background, behind the standing soldier, two more people look on. The illustration is not quite a war poster but very close to one.

Salinger's work in *Collier's* at the time of these publications already seems formulaic. Both stories depend on the narrator revealing a surprise relationship to the character he has been describing. In "The Hang of It," the narrator refers to his younger self in the third person. In "Personal Notes on an Infantryman," the surprise is created in that the narrator, an officer, relates the story of his own father's desire to join the army, and that the officer the father has been talking to is also the father's son (who outranks his father). The title of the story is often incorrectly cited as "Personal Notes *of* [emphasis added] an Infantryman." The actual title, "Personal Notes *on* [emphasis added] an Infantryman" correctly captures the meaning of the story, that the notes are personal because a son (an officer) is writing the notes about, i.e., "on," his own father, who is the infantryman referenced in the title.

Literary scholars are correct to argue that the story is a failure because its twist is not created artistically so much as deceptively. The reader may guess that the narrator is related to Lawlor, but the story presents obfuscations that stymie such guessing. Primarily, the son is obscured as an officer and the father as an infantryman. The son's phone conversations with his own mother provide the attentive reader with a hint of the relationship between these three people, although Salinger masks the clues by having the narrator refer to his mother throughout as "Mrs. Lawlor." Not until the story's end, when "Dad," "Ma," and "my brother" (96) are explicitly stated, does Salinger fully reveal the trick.

"Personal Notes on an Infantryman" befits its appearance in a mainstream popular magazine such as *Collier's* for a number of reasons. In 1942, most American families were beginning to be affected by the war, with the drama of enlistment or draft played out in thousands of families every day. The story dramatizes how families turn themselves upside down to serve their country. The visual literacy of the story's illustration and caption serves as a recruiting poster. The notes on this infantryman (Lawlor) are personal because a son is writing them about his own father. The story captures the sociological impact of full family support for military service during wartime.

PUBLICATION HISTORY

"Personal Notes on an Infantryman" was published in the December 12, 1942, issue of *Collier's*. Salinger never reprinted the story in his three books of collected stories. "Personal Notes on an Infantryman" later appeared in the bootleg editions *The* COMPLETE UNCOLLECTED SHORT STORIES OF J. D. SALINGER (1974) and TWENTY-TWO STORIES (1998).

CHARACTERS

Lawlor Lawlor, a married man and the middle-aged father enlisting in the army, is the infantryman referred to in the story's title. He has two sons: Pete and the unnamed narrator.

Lawlor, Mrs. Mrs. Lawlor has phoned the Orderly Room in an attempt to have the narrator (later revealed as her son) try to stop his father from enlisting in the army.

Lawlor, Pete While in the navy, Pete Lawlor lost his arm at Pearl Harbor. He joins his brother (the story's narrator) to send off their father, who is being shipped out for active duty overseas.

Narrator The narrator, who never directly reveals his name, is the officer at the Orderly Room where his father tries to enlist.

FURTHER READING

French, Warren. *J. D. Salinger*. New York: Twayne Publishers, 1963.

Lundquist, James. *J. D. Salinger*. New York: Ungar, 1979.

Purcell, William F. "World War II and the Early Fiction of J. D. Salinger." *Studies in American Literature* 28 (1991): 77–93.

Wenke, John. *J. D. Salinger: A Study of the Short Fiction.* Boston: Twayne Publishers, 1991.

"Pretty Mouth and Green My Eyes"

"Pretty Mouth and Green My Eyes" is the seventh story in Salinger's second book, NINE STORIES (1953). This terse third-person tale of adultery originally appeared in the July 14, 1951, issue of the NEW YORKER, two days before the release of *The* CATCHER IN THE RYE. The story features a phone call that reveals the love triangle of Arthur, Joanie, and Lee. "Pretty Mouth and Green My Eyes" is Salinger's 28th published story.

SYNOPSIS

A young, blue-eyed woman and a gray-haired man are in bed when his phone rings. He asks her if she would prefer that he did not answer. She is undecided and asks his opinion. He declares that it doesn't make any difference now and answers the phone while she observes him. On the line, a "man's voice—stone dead, yet somehow rudely, almost obscenely quickened for the occasion" (175) asks if he is speaking with Lee. The older man glances at the young woman (who, throughout the story, is never directly named), as he recognizes the voice on the phone as Arthur's.

Arthur worries that he has woken Lee with the phone call, which Lee denies, saying that he is "in bed, reading" (176). Arthur then asks Lee if he had seen Joanie, Arthur's wife, leave the party they had all attended earlier in the evening. Glancing again in the direction of the woman, but not directly at her, Lee replies in the negative, then asks Arthur, "Didn't she leave with you?" (176). Arthur says that he does not know where Joanie is, whereupon Lee suggests that Arthur phone the Ellenbogens, who were also at the party. Arthur replies that he has already phoned them and has learned from their babysitter that the couple is not yet

home. Arthur tells Lee, "I'm through beating my brains out. I mean it. I really mean it this time. I'm through. Five years. Christ" (177). Lee tries to calm Arthur by suggesting that Joanie and the Ellenbogens may have taken a cab to Greenwich Village to continue partying and would probably return shortly. Arthur suspects, however, that his wife has left the party with another man. His statement causes Lee to ask where Arthur is calling from at the moment. Learning that Arthur is at home, Lee reiterates that the Ellenbogens and Joanie would no doubt show up soon. He advises Arthur to get into bed and have a last drink. Arthur exclaims that he is already very drunk and that he can't trust his wife. Whenever he comes home, he tells Lee, he "half expect[s] to find a bunch of bastards hiding all over the place. *Elevator* boys. *Delivery* boys. *Cops*" (181). Lee defends Joanie, reproaching Arthur for not giving his wife credit for any taste or intelligence. Arthur explodes, declaring Joanie to be an animal, whereupon Lee replies, "Basically, we're all animals" (182). Arthur retorts, "Like hell we are. I'm no goddam animal. I may be a stupid, fouled-up twentieth-century son of a bitch, but I'm no animal" (182).

Arthur relates, with sarcasm, how his wife considers herself an intellectual because she reads about plays in the newspaper and watches television all day. Lee motions to the woman to light him a cigarette. According to Arthur, Joanie "describes every man she sees as 'terribly attractive.' It can be the oldest, crummiest, greasiest—" (183), at which point Lee interrupts, asking Arthur how the case went that day. The question signals that the two men are lawyers in the same law firm. Arthur admits losing the hotel case but blames circumstances beyond his control, explaining how the plaintiff's lawyer surprised him by bringing in a chambermaid and sheets with bedbug stains to prove the prosecution's case. Anxious, he asks whether Lee thinks the head of the law firm—nicknamed Junior—will be upset. At this point, the woman places an ashtray on the bed between herself and Lee. When Lee responds that Junior will most likely be upset, Arthur says that he might return to the army. Lee turns toward the woman "to show her how forbearing, even stoic, his countenance" is (186), but she has overturned the ash-tray and is tending to the mess. Arthur exclaims that he should have left his wife last summer, but he didn't because he felt sorry for her. He believes, however, that he and Joanie are "mismated" (188) and tells Lee that he suspected as much even before they were married. Unfortunately, he says, he ignored his own "flashes" (188) of realization. Arthur claims that his failure to confront Joanie about her philandering is due to his being "weak" (188). When Lee objects, Arthur heatedly under-scores his self-opinion, reiterating several times over, "Certainly I'm weak!" (189).

In a state of despair, Arthur now apologizes repeatedly to Lee for keeping him up all night and insists that Lee hang up on him. Lee responds that he wants to help and says that Arthur is his own worst enemy. Arthur interrupts and, in a long solil-oquy, relates his belief that Joanie doesn't "respect" (189) him and that she doesn't love him. He also says that he no longer loves her but quickly quali-fies his statement by explaining: "I don't know. I do and I don't. It varies. It fluctuates" (189). Arthur tells Lee how, many times, he would be just about to confront Joanie regarding her cheating, but she would then appear wearing "these goddam white *gloves*" (189), upon which he could not go through with his accusations. He recalls small, mundane moments that reaffirm, in his mind, the existence of their love: Once she bought him a suit as a sur-prise gift; another time, when helping him change a flat tire, she "held the flashlight" (190). Arthur remembers a poem he sent Joanie when they first started going together and quotes, "Rose my color is and white, / Pretty mouth and green my eyes" (190). Arthur tells Lee that the poem reminds him of Joanie, despite the fact, he explains, that his wife does not have green eyes, but that her eyes are "like goddam *sea* shells" (190).

Lee, turning to the woman, suggests to Arthur, once again, that he get into bed. He reiterates that Joanie will probably be there soon. Arthur asks impulsively if he can come over to Lee's place, given that he is keeping him up anyway with the phone call. The request takes Lee aback. He replies that Arthur is welcome to come over, but he thinks it best, instead, that Arthur stay at home so as to

"be right there on the spot when she waltzes in" (192). Arthur isn't convinced, but Lee coaxes him again to get into bed and wait for his wife, telling him to phone later if he feels like talking.

Lee returns the phone to the receiver and picks up a cigarette. The young woman promptly asks, "What did he say?" (193). Lee explains that Arthur wanted to come over for a drink. When she repeats the question, Lee counters with, "You could hear me. Couldn't you?" (193). She responds immedi-ately with, "You were wonderful. Absolutely mar-vellous. God, I feel like a dog!" (193). Lee then states, "it's a very, very tough situation. The guy's obviously going through absolute—" (194), when the phone rings to interrupt his sentence. The caller, again, is Arthur. After asking whether Lee had been asleep, Arthur says, "I just thought you'd want to know. Joanie just barged in" (194). Lee utters a surprised "What?" and places his hand above his eyes. Arthur thanks Lee for his help and explains that Joanie was indeed with the Ellenbo-gens. He then condemns NEW YORK CITY as a rat race and as a possible cause for Joanie's behavior. He muses that he and Joanie might leave the city and move to Connecticut, where they could lead a "normal goddam life" (195), and where Joanie would "go mad" (195) with "her own goddam gar-den" (195). Arthur counts Lee as their only normal friend. Lee remains silent and keeps his eyes closed, shielded beneath his hand. Arthur states that he wants to try and save his marriage. He also wants to clean up the "lousy bedbug mess" (196). Finally, Arthur asks whether Lee thinks that he might be exonerated if he goes directly to Junior to explain how he lost the hotel case. Lee interrupts, saying that he has just gotten a terrible headache and would like to end the call. He reassures Arthur that they can talk in the morning at work and hangs up the phone.

The young woman immediately speaks to Lee, but he does not answer. Instead, he mistakenly takes her lit cigarette from the ashtray, and as he brings it to his mouth, it slips from his fingers. She tries to help him retrieve the cigarette before any-thing is burned, but he commands her to "just *sit still,* for Chrissake" (197), at which she pulls back her hand.

CRITICAL ANALYSIS

In "Pretty Mouth and Green My Eyes," Salinger brings to the fore his technical virtuosity to create what is, in essence, a compact morality play. With a quick-moving, truncated, back-and-forth dialogue between characters and a minimal, yet highly charged, use of description, the story invites, and actually requires, maximum reader participation in order to make sense of the enigma of its climax. Unfortunately, "Pretty Mouth and Green My Eyes" has not enjoyed the critical attention given to a number of other stories in Salinger's collection *Nine Stories*. The story warrants, however, further study and explication for the mastery of its narrative technique, cleverly conceived and precisely executed.

The poetic syntax of the title, with its erotic suggestiveness, initially teases the reader into wondering to whom these attributes might be assigned. Almost immediately, though, the reader is involved in a situation that is anything but poetry.

The phone has rung and the scene describes a gray-haired man and a girl interrupted in their lovemaking. The girl has opened one eye, "so blue as to appear almost violet" (174), and to the man's question of whether he should answer the call, her response, and the first sentence of dialogue uttered by a character, is: "God. I don't know. I mean what do you think?" (174). The reader has thus already gleaned that the eyes of the girl do not match the green eyes introduced in the title. Salinger has created, within the story's opening lines, the atmosphere of ambiguity that will shadow the action. (In the girl's response, the author may also be directly challenging the reader to unlock the ensuing enigma.)

Because the story's introductory paragraph contains the longest descriptive stretch that Salinger will offer, the reader must pay close attention to the imagery selected. The girl opens one "disingenuously" (174) large eye to her lover, whose hair is "gray, mostly white" (175) and who is summed up as "rather 'distinguished-looking'" (175). The tryst between the older man and the younger girl with the calculating eye is given a biblical overtone with the first word that she declares: "God." That the relationship may be judged in the moral sense

is underscored by the introduction of the scene's third character, a voice "stone dead, yet somehow rudely, almost obscenely quickened for the occasion" (175), the voice of the cuckolded husband, Arthur. Salinger's description, therefore, even in these initial paragraphs, guides the interpretation of the remaining action as it would be judged morally, by God, and defined as obscene.

As the critic Kenneth Hamilton notes in his 1967 essay devoted to "Pretty Mouth and Green My Eyes," the identification of the voice on the phone as Arthur's likewise points the reader to the Arthurian legends and to the story of Lancelot and Guinevere (Hamilton 399). The Arthurian tale, Hamilton observes, introduces the "heroic" (Hamilton 399) conception of the character of Arthur (and likewise, Arthur's possible image of himself as a King Arthur betrayed by his wife's infidelity). Salinger's description of Arthur's voice, moreover, as "dead" adds yet another element to the overall approach to the story: that the characters are to be understood as they would be judged after death. The reader, therefore, must look for a definitive spiritual meaning within the text's elusive clues.

That all three players of the story already inhabit a hellish environment is portrayed through the combined effect of dialogue, imagery, and dramatic technique. In one of the few critical appraisals of the text, John V. Hagopian, in his 1966 essay, suggests that "Salinger has rendered in an American idiom Dante's Paolo and Francesca in Manhattan" (Hagopian 353). The observation aptly indicates the story's point of reference. In fact, a quick look at Dante's *Inferno*, and specifically at Canto V, provides a springboard to the interpretation of the Salinger work.

Dante Alighieri (1265–1321), one of the most renowned poets of the Western literary canon, is considered the consummate Italian poet. His masterpiece, *The Divine Comedy*, comprised three books—*Inferno, Purgatorio*, and *Paradiso*—and is a narrative allegory of Christian moral standards. *The Divine Comedy* is, moreover, regarded to be the highest literary expression of the Middle Ages. In the poem, Dante, the protagonist and poet-pilgrim, is lost in a dark forest. He has strayed from the "true way." He can see, at a distance, the rays of

Paradise, where his beloved Beatrice (who acts as a shining light on his path to spiritual salvation) resides. Unfortunately, Dante is barred from a direct ascent by several beasts, one of which is the "She-wolf of Incontinence" (the word "incontinence" in this context represents an inability to "contain" the physical and sensual appetites). Dante learns that the she-wolf kills all men and still is not sated. Furthermore, she mates with any "animal." Dante must take an indirect path around her.

In the Inferno, Dante meets and questions various historical personages, one of whom is Francesca da Rimini. In 1275, Francesca (of Ravenna) had been given in an arranged marriage to Gianciotto Malatesta (of Rimini), a man much older than herself. The two were not a suitable match. Francesca thus carried on an extramarital affair with her husband's younger brother, Paolo. When, by surprise, Gianciotto discovered the two in bed together, he murdered both in a single act of rage, running them through with a sword. In the Inferno, the souls of the dead are punished in a way that reflects the nature of their sin. That is, Divine Justice metes out a torture precisely fitted to the seriousness of the transgression. Dante encounters Francesca and Paolo, who are condemned to the second circle, where those guilty of carnal excess, or sins of the flesh, and specifically the sin of lust are punished. These spirits, the "*incontinenti*" or "incontinent" ones, have been unable to "contain" their passions, and, above all, their sexual passion. Lust, during Dante's time, was considered one of the most "deadly" of the sins.

As Dante enters the second circle, he experiences a great whirlwind (symbol of the great lust that had overwhelmed the sinners in their lifetime). Thus those who, in life, had allowed their reason, or good judgment, to be overwhelmed by the carnal appetite of lust must consequently be tossed and driven eternally by that same passion in death. The whirlwind is an unceasing one from which the sinners will never find rest or peace. Among the souls Dante sees whirling through the space are Helen of Troy and Cleopatra. The poet also reports seeing many of the "ladies and knights of old" and remarks that he hears all around him the sounds of the damned, whose voices rise in curses against

God. (This auditory element is a strong link to the emphasis on dialogue in the Salinger story, where the reader—in the same position as that of Dante from a narrative perspective—first sees the couple in bed together and shortly thereafter hears the voice of Arthur, cursing heavily throughout his phone call with Lee. Lee, moreover, enforces his own conversation with curses and blasphemies, as does Joanie, who has uttered the story's first word: "God" [174].) Dante sees Francesca and Paolo tossed upon the wind and asks to speak to them. In the name of love, the two are allowed to pause. Francesca addresses Dante, calling him "*animal grazioso*"—a phrase that has been translated into English in various ways, usually as "living creature" or "gracious creature." However, the phrase may well be translated as "pretty creature" ("pretty" being a secondary, but precise, translation of the adjective "*grazioso*"). The use of the term "animal" is a strong one in Italian as well as in English, and Salinger makes good use of it when Arthur accuses Joanie: "She's an animal!" (182). Salinger moreover repeats the word in Lee's defense of Joanie: "We're all animals" (182). Arthur repeats the word three more times in his own defense: "I'm no goddam animal. I may be a stupid, fouled-up twentieth-century son of a bitch, but I'm no animal. Don't gimme that. I'm no animal" (182). (Salinger, one is very tempted to imagine, may have enjoyed planting the noun as a subtle homage to the language of Dante. With the use of the descriptor "animal" applied to each character in his story, Salinger also underlines the moral interpretation of his narrative.) Dante-as-author, moreover, in the dialogue he creates for Francesca, presents her as flirtatious toward the living man, Dante-as-pilgrim. The poet-pilgrim is the only one "in the flesh" allowed into the underworld (that is, Dante's is the only body still alive or "animal"—the other inhabitants of the Inferno being spirits of the afterlife and thus deprived of their physical selves). Francesca, in addressing Dante, shows that she is very aware of the physical man, and she reveals her attraction to him by describing him as "*grazioso*" or "pretty." In this interpretation and translation of Dante's phrase "*animal grazioso*," the reader glimpses a Francesca still lustful after death. Her words reveal her to be guilty of the sin for which she is most fittingly punished. She is unable to "contain" her lust even in a disembodied state.

Francesca goes on to reveal her tragic tale to Dante, telling him that the turning point, or catalyst, for hers and Paolo's spiritual fall from grace and into lust was the book that they happened to be reading together that fatal afternoon, "the rhyme of Lancelot." Coming upon the passage in which Lancelot kisses Guinevere's "*disiato riso*" or "desired smile" (like the "pretty mouth" of the Salinger story?), their passion overcomes them, and Paolo "all trembling" kisses Francesca's "mouth." Francesca ends her story, with Paolo weeping at her side, by saying: "That day, we read no further" (Alighieri 62). (Francesca's double meaning is cleverly mirrored in Salinger's text, when Lee, in bed with Joanie and having engaged in the act of lovemaking, tells Arthur that he is "in bed, reading" [176].)

Other elements of Dante's Canto V may also be superimposed on those of the Salinger story. Poetry's involvement with the sin of lust (which Francesca indicates in her identification of the "rhyme of Lancelot" and its author, and which she, moreover, blames as the cause of her fall) is subtly hinted within the syntactical structure of Salinger's story title. Likewise, during the first phone call, when Arthur quotes to Lee the entire poem he had sent Joanie during their courtship, the reader realizes that this poem has been truncated to form the title of the story. Arthur explains that, although he knows Joanie's eyes are not green, he had sent the poem to her because it reminded him of her. Given this information, the reader may surmise that Arthur once held or created a vision of his ideal mate, perhaps before he even met Joanie. Furthermore, if Arthur were actually the writer of the poem (not explicitly stated by Salinger), he logically would not have written the poem specifically for Joanie, as her eyes are very blue. The critic Warren French, in his 1963 discussion of "Pretty Mouth and Green My Eyes," observes that Salinger attributes green eyes to only two other characters in his fiction, both of whom are children (French 131). One of these children, Jimmy Jimmereeno, is a make-believe playmate to Ramona in "Uncle

Wiggily in Connecticut." Perhaps Arthur, like Ramona, has created a make-believe, ideal mate, whom, as he comes to learn, Joanie fails to resemble in every sense. Joanie's eyes are not green like those of the other Salinger child characters but are "like goddam *sea* shells" (190). Although the meaning of the description will remain forever unclear, one sees in the interior cavern of many seashells a smoky blue-violet color. Perhaps the true color of Joanie's eyes hint at a symbolic shadowy interior, a color most aptly suited for these souls or "shades" of Salinger's depiction of Hell. (In fact, the color Salinger paints for Joanie's eyes mirrors Francesca's description to Dante of the color of the space in which she and Paolo are tossed, "l'aere perso" or "air [the color] perse.")

Arthur, who expresses hope that his vision of Joanie will come true, nostalgically recalls incidents in his marriage when he felt that she embodied that ideal. He tells Lee of the time when she had been so thoughtful as to purchase a suit for him. On another occasion, she helped when he changed a flat tire. In this latter memory, Arthur remarks that Joanie "held the flashlight while I fixed the goddam thing—You know what I mean" (190). Perhaps Arthur envisions Joanie as his guiding light, just as Dante envisions Beatrice (with Salinger giving the suggestion a playful 20th-century twist). The action of changing a tire is not heroic, but Arthur's imagination is, as Hamilton observes (Hamilton 396).

In a superficial reading of the story, Arthur, who portrays himself as the betrayed husband, may be seen as the victim of betrayal through no fault of his own, although he "ignored [his own] flashes" (188) about how it would truly be for him to be married to Joanie. However, a second and closer reading of the text may reveal Arthur to be a man not as innocent as first supposed.

Arthur has made a mistake, he believes, in marrying Joanie. The problem, as he states to Lee, is that the two are "mis*mated*" (188). (The lesson to be learned, perhaps, is that one must look realistically at the beloved before taking the sacred vows.) Arthur blames Joanie for his unhappiness and desperation. He accuses her of being "an animal" (182) while he is "no goddam animal" (182). In a first gloss of the story, Joanie's promiscuous actions and adulterous love affairs may well be interpreted as the cause of all the spiritual and emotional suffering. Arthur presents himself, in the first phone call, as having been victimized throughout five years of marriage by his wife's bestial or "animal" appetites, during which he has remained in suffering silence and presumably innocent of blame. In this reading of the character of Arthur, Hamilton suggests, Salinger has created a poetic and chivalric figure. Hamilton states that Salinger usually "makes his heroes poets, either in intention or in performance. The present story runs true to form, since it takes its title from a poem that Arthur wrote out of his early love for Joanie" (Hamilton 396). However, by examining the story under a different kind of microscope, further clues can be discovered about the dynamics of Arthur and Joanie's relationship.

In the Western poetic tradition, the troubadour poets, who invented the concept of "courtly love," as well as the poets who continued in that tradition, including Dante, believed love to be engendered through the eyes, which represent the windows to the soul. These poets, and especially Dante, redefined love as being inspired by the gaze of the beloved woman who was understood as a guide to the lover's spiritual salvation. Dante perceives Beatrice in this manner throughout *The Divine Comedy*. For Dante, both as man and as poet-pilgrim on his journey to salvation, Beatrice symbolizes the spiritual force that guides him towards a Divine Love. The love of the woman, in the "courtly love" tradition, must produce a moral effect in the lover. This love, engendered by a glance into the eyes of the beloved "lady," enters the poet's heart (again through his eyes) and motivates him to strive for moral perfection. The "passion" he feels is not a physical but a spiritual one.

In superimposing this poetic tradition from Dante on the imagery of the Salinger story, the reader may perceive, at the beginning of Salinger's narrative, that Joanie's eyes, "more just open than alert or speculative, *reflected* [emphasis added] chiefly their own size and color" (175). Her eyes are what they are and reflect only themselves. That they "reflect" suggests that they possess a mirror-like quality, capable of reflecting back or substan-

tiating how the lover will see himself therein. In blaming Joanie for his own unhappiness, Arthur contradicts the stance of the "courtly love" poet toward his "lady." It is incumbent upon the courtly lover, and not upon the beloved, to find in her gaze a "true way" to his own spiritual salvation. If anything, the courtly lover, rather than denigrate the source of his inspiration, would sing her praises to the skies. Arthur compares Joanie's eyes to "goddam *sea* shells" (190). A shell is an empty cavity. In the context of the Salinger story, Joanie's eyes might therefore represent a spiritual emptiness attributable to her own character—or, in other words, through Arthur's eyes, she represents a narcissistic love and not a transcendental or transformational one. In blaming Joanie for the demise of their marriage, Arthur refuses to take any share of the responsibility for his own obligation of self-transformation. In this reading, Salinger may intend to infer that Arthur's mistake is to have projected his own desires for the ideal mate onto Joanie, instead of having found in her an inspiration and a challenge to transform his love into his quest for spiritual love and enlightenment. Arthur thus becomes disillusioned when Joanie cannot fulfill his requirements. If one understands Arthur's situation, therefore, to be somewhat of his own making, Arthur may also be culpable in having encouraged Joanie's promiscuity. Lee accuses Arthur of this outcome in his statement during the first phone call when he says: "You actually *inspire* Joanie—" (181). Thus Joanie, realizing that she is not able to please Arthur and feeling herself inferior to him intellectually (although she attempts to improve her mind with courses that her husband scorns, cynically dubbing her a "Madame Bovary [who] takes a course in Television Appreciation" [182]), has been driven to find companionship in the arms of other men. Arthur's ideal vision, which he expands upon in his second phone call to Lee—"we'll get ourselves a little place in Connecticut" (195)—may be the very element that has damned the relationship to failure, in that his "if only" vision of life entraps both partners in a vicious cycle of disillusionment.

The reader might also take this interpretation a step further, examining Arthur's culpability through the perspective of feminist literary theory. Arthur, as a "courtly lover," is obliged to idolize his "lady" and is moreover forbidden to touch her sexually. The love is enacted on a platonic, not physical, plane. In a feminist reading, the tradition of "courtly love," in idealizing the woman, is seen as preventing her from becoming man's equal. She is placed "on a pedestal" and therefore is not allowed to enter the arenas of power. A feminist reading of "Pretty Mouth and Green My Eyes" would therefore see, in Arthur's idealized love, his role in Joanie's inability to "find her way" in life. The Salinger narrative leaves room for this interpretation in that it would explain Arthur's complaint that Joanie is "the *greatest living undeveloped, undiscovered actress, novelist*, psychoanalyst, and all-around unappreciated celebrity-genius in New York" (182).

What else does the story's dialogue suggest about Arthur's character? For one thing, he admits to being "weak" (188) in feeling sorry for his wife and thus not able to confront her infidelity. Perhaps, however, Arthur's weakness may be understood to be a moral one. He, too, at the beginning of his love for Joanie, had been guided by lust, attracted by her physical beauty (as the couple share no intellectual interests). Interesting to note in this context is that Canto I of the *Inferno* presents Dante as driven from the "true way" by the she-wolf of lust. Literary criticism throughout the centuries has interpreted Dante's reference to mean that the poet recognizes himself guilty of that particular sin, which hinders his progress towards spiritual enlightenment. Arthur may likewise be guilty of the sin for which he condemns his wife, and of which Lee is apparently guilty. The reader may now come to realize that the sin of lust has been committed by all three of the characters in the Salinger narrative.

During Arthur's first phone call to Lee, the reader may well fall into sympathizing with the duped husband, whom Salinger has engendered with poetic and sensitive attributes. On the other hand, the coarse nature of Arthur's character, developed throughout his "obscenely quickened" (175) dialogue with his colleague, precludes an unconditional sympathy for him. This aspect of Arthur's character casts doubt, as well, on his

reliability as the teller of the tale of his marriage. Arthur begins his phone call with a tirade of suspicion about Joanie. He is drunk and enraged, letting loose with a barrage of expletives and blasphemies, calling down Christ in almost every sentence he utters. He is filled with jealousy. At no time, however, does Salinger confirm to the reader that Joanie is assuredly guilty of all the philandering of which her husband accuses her. Another look may now be taken at the story's title, which consists of the truncated version of the poem that Arthur had sent to Joanie. The full poem reads: "Rose my color is and white, / Pretty mouth and green my eyes" (190). Taking only the poem's second line (which is the title of the drama at hand), an alternate reading of Arthur's character may be revealed. Throughout his first phone call, Arthur does not hold back in expressing his insane jealousy. Perhaps Arthur himself may be viewed as the one who possesses "green" eyes. In most folklore traditions, green is associated with the character flaw of envy (as in the saying "green with envy"). Arthur may therefore be guilty of another "deadly sin" of Christian hagiology. In marrying a beautiful woman, a "pretty mouth," he has condemned himself to remain forever jealous and suspicious. The story's title therefore takes a different twist: the "pretty mouth" still describing Joanie, but the "green" attributed to Arthur. (Moreover, if Arthur is the poem's author and has actually penned the lines, Salinger may be slyly inserting the alternative reading, with the pronominal possessive adjective "my" now assigned to Arthur's description of his own eyes, which, forever jealous, can see nothing but a betraying, "pretty" wife.) Arthur, therefore, will never find peace unless Joanie becomes the white-gloved lady, who would love a garden in Connecticut. It would also help matters if she were no longer "pretty."

If the first phone call raises so many questions about Arthur's character, the reader is obliged to focus on the character of Lee for some interpretive assistance. Perhaps Lee, on the other hand, may be seen as the chivalric lover? At the story's outset, Salinger turns the spotlight on Lee, who grazes his head on the lamp shade while reaching for the ringing phone. The description initially suggests that Lee might be taken as a "knight in shining armor" with the "light . . . particularly, if rather vividly, flattering to his gray, mostly white, hair" (175). Lee has asked Joanie "with quite some little deference" (174) whether he should interrupt their lovemaking to answer the first phone call. He defends Joanie from Arthur's accusations that she is "an animal" (182), and comes to her defense again, accusing Arthur of not giving his wife a chance. Lee, in fact, attributes some intelligence to Joanie: "You give that kid absolutely no credit for having any good taste—or brains, for Chrissake, for that matter—" (181). Lee, moreover, exhibits remorse during Arthur's heartrending account of his romantic love and courtship of Joanie. As Hagopian observes, Lee's "own suffering from compassion and guilt, his sense of shame, is presented with such discipline and restraint that most readers fail to see it: 'Well, it's a very, very tough situation. The guy's obviously going through absolute—'" (Hagopian 352).

As opposed to Arthur, however, Lee possesses no perceptible intellectual prowess. For example, where Arthur displays his literary repertoire, with references to Madame Bovary, Lee cannot follow the allusions and must ask, "Who?" (183). The reader is thus led to perceive Lee as being more akin to Joanie, especially when he states to Arthur: "We're all animals" (182). Would Lee, rather than Arthur, be more appropriately "mated" to Joanie? Like Joanie, he seems able to take on the world and other people as they are in a physical and practical way. Unlike the "courtly" lover, Lee does not place Joanie on a pedestal. (On the contrary, he regards her in a somewhat paternalistic way: "She's a wonderful kid" [181].)

Lee's bits of dialogue, aimed at controlling the situation, at first smack of dishonesty, as he repeatedly offers patronizing advice to Arthur, who, the reader believes, is unaware of Joanie's presence in his colleague's bed. As the action unfolds, however, Lee's apparent vanity (his mannered and deliberate poses to show Joanie how "forbearing, even stoic" [186] he is holding up under Arthur's tirade and whimpering) gives way to the view of an older man, at first thinking himself the victor, now realizing himself in bed with the spoils of a girl for whom he

is only one in a string of lovers. Although Salinger does not make clear Lee's internal changes of heart, the reader is firmly led to perceive, through the character's actions (his shielding of his eyes and his sudden headache at the story's close), Lee's process of assimilating the fact that he has been duped and burned. Salinger playfully expresses the imminent denouement through Joanie's comment to Lee at the story's close: "I think you're on fire" (194). Moreover, the imagery of smoke and ash is most closely associated with Salinger's description of Lee, who takes a "drag on his cigarette" (184), "taps the ash of his cigarette on the rim of the ashtray" (184), takes "a freshly lighted cigarette from the girl" (189), and finally picks up a "burning cigarette—the girl's—out of the ashtray" (197). Lee's psychological state of mind is clearly indicated by Salinger's stage directions in the story's final paragraph. As the character picks up a "burning cigarette—the girl's—out of the ashtray . . . [he starts] to bring it to his mouth, but it [slips] out of his fingers" (197). Lee has finally lost his composure. Whether Lee is burned by lust and his consequent adultery, by conscience and remorse, or simply by rage at having been duped remains open to interpretation. Although Salinger handles the imagery with a touch of sardonic humor, Hagopian champions the story's moral conclusion: "The fire and ashes symbolism suggests that Lee and Joanie are in a Dantean inferno" (Hagopian 353).

And what is the reader to believe of Joanie's character? "Joanie lost?" (177), Lee asks Arthur in the early lines of dialogue. She is lost to Arthur physically (after the party) and, perhaps, lost in a moral sense. Her eyes are not reflective of anything but themselves. Perhaps she has not pretended at being anything but herself, but does not yet know who that self may be? The allusive descriptions of Joanie that Salinger provides have led some to interpret Joanie's character as guileless—that of a "grown child" (187), as Arthur describes her to Lee. She exists on the physical plane and "describes every man she sees as 'terribly attractive'" (183). Perhaps, as Arthur suggests in his second phone call to Lee, it is an outside force that has caused Joanie to become promiscuous: "I think it's this goddam New York" (195). In this reading, Salinger mirrors the excuse for lustful behavior given by Dante's Francesca da Rimini. Francesca blames her moral downfall on her and Paolo's reading of the "book" in which the love of Lancelot for Guinevere is described, and she blames the book's author as well. The salacious influence of what, in Dante's time, was considered pornographic reading is the outside force or catalyst, according to Francesca's statement, that sent the lovers into each other's arms. In the last analysis, however, Francesca is (like Joanie) most definitely guilty of the sin of lust and condemned to be eternally battered by the force of the wind of her uncontained passion. That Joanie, like Francesca, will never find peace or rest from her desires is intimated in Lee's last frustrated command, or his futile prayer, to her: ". . . just *sit still,* for Chrissake" (197). Salinger has made explicit that Joanie and Lee have consummated their affair when Lee, at the first rings of the telephone, says that it doesn't make "a helluva lot of difference one way or the other" (174–175) whether he answers, meaning it will not matter whether Arthur discovers that the two are in bed together. The act cannot be undone. And God, not Arthur, will be the final judge.

The true genius of Salinger's narrative is evident in the wrap-up of the action. When Arthur phones Lee a second time, he asks whether Lee thinks that he would get back in good standing if he explained to Junior why he lost the case that morning. He also adds that he wants to "straighten out this lousy bedbug mess" (196). Salinger, with the rather comical legal case concerning bedbugs, seems to wink to the reader by indicating that the bedbugs also refer to Arthur's problem of Lee and Joanie's affair (they are his personal bedbugs). Arthur's reference also slyly hints at another interpretation of the story. Arthur, *knowing* Lee and Joanie are in bed together, may be implying that he will go to Junior to let him know of the affair, thus exposing Lee to slander and professional injury. Has Arthur found a way to climb the ladder to success by manipulating his older colleague? Arthur's question may thus be read as a veiled threat to Lee, or perhaps even an attempt to blackmail the older man into helping him return to Junior's good graces. Hamilton suggests the possibility of this interpretation through Lee's perspective: "Knowing that Joanie is in bed with him, he can interpret Arthur's message that she has come home solely as a cunning lie to put him at a disadvantage. Is Arthur reserving his knowledge of the adultery to force him to make things right with 'Junior'?" (Hamilton 397). This darkest reading of the text cannot be ruled out completely, as Salinger, even in introducing Arthur, describes the character's voice (and Arthur exists in the story only as a "mouth" and not a pretty one) as "obscenely quickened for the occasion" (175). Perhaps even before placing his first phone call, Arthur well knew that Joanie had left the party with Lee, and he will now use the knowledge to his advantage. Did Arthur, from the beginning, intend to use Joanie as a means to gain help from Lee, a senior partner in the firm, in the face of the lost "bedbug" case?

At the story's conclusion, Salinger leaves the reader with as many questions as have been posed by the dialogue. The intentional ambiguity forces an immediate second reading of the text. Should Arthur be viewed as the chivalric, duped, and idealistic husband to be pitied? Or is he nothing more than a manipulative, controlling pimp looking to gain favors and promotions in blackmailing his older colleague? Is Lee the remorseful adulterer or simply burning with anger at having learned that he is just one in a string of Joanie's trysts? "God! I feel like a dog!" (193), Joanie concludes several times. Is she, then, to be read as the promiscuous, adulterous she-wolf predator of anything in trousers (as is, perhaps, Dante's Francesca)? Or, has she, on the other hand, been driven into a single affair due to Arthur's growing discontent with her?

The first question put forth in the story's dialogue, which the reader will encounter on a second go-round, affords the only firm ground for interpretation: "God. I don't know. What do you think?" (174). Likewise, Lee's last reassurance to Arthur that the conversation will continue the next morning sums up the unending nature of this entangled predicament. Salinger's Arthur, Joanie, and Lee (as Dante's Francesca and Paolo, along with all those "ladies and knights of old" revolving in the second circle of the Inferno) will forever be battered by the wind of lust, condemned to a vicious cycle of blame, regret, and distrust. Salinger has caught, both in the content and in the form of this story, the feeling of betrayal and its consequent spinning of lies. The story's structure, now realized as circular and therefore eternal, reflects the punishing Hell in which the characters turn and toss, and may be seen as Salinger's nod to the Italian bard.

PUBLICATION HISTORY

"Pretty Mouth and Green My Eyes" was first published in the *New Yorker* magazine on July 14, 1951. The story appeared in book form in *Nine Stories* (LITTLE, BROWN AND COMPANY, 1953). *Nine Stories*, Salinger's second book, has never gone out of print.

Nine Stories is available in three editions from Little, Brown and Company: an exact reproduction of the hardback first edition from 1953; a trade paperback that mimics the production of the hardback; and a mass-market paperback, with its pagination differing from the above editions.

CHARACTERS

Arthur The voice of Arthur (who is never seen) is heard on the phone talking to Lee. Arthur has phoned in an effort to locate his wife, Joanie, after a party attended earlier that evening by the three of them. He suspects that Joanie has left the party with another man. Arthur is a young lawyer in the same firm as his older colleague, Lee, a senior partner. Arthur pours his heart out to Lee concerning his failed marriage with Joanie. At the end of the story, Arthur lies to Lee when he tells him that Joanie has just arrived home, and that she was late because she had been with Bob and Leona Ellenbogen. Arthur stuns Lee with his statement because Joanie, at that very moment, happens to be in bed with Lee.

Ellenbogen, Bob and Leona Arthur asks Lee if he had noticed whether his wife, Joanie, left the party with the Ellenbogens. To pacify Arthur, Lee suggests that Joanie must have left with the Ellenbogens and they probably all went to Greenwich Village to continue partying.

Girl in bed, the *See* Joanie.

Joanie Joanie is Arthur's wife and, crucially, the young, blue-eyed woman in bed with Lee. The story's narrative experimentation hinges on the young woman's name never being mentioned. During the phone conversation between Lee and Arthur, the gestures and glances between the older man and the young woman clue the reader that the woman in Lee's bed is Joanie, Arthur's wife. After Lee gets off the phone with Arthur the first time, Salinger makes Joanie's identity explicit when the young woman says to Lee, "You were wonderful . . . God, I feel like a dog!" (193).

Junior Junior is the nickname of the head lawyer of the firm. Junior has succeeded his father, Shanley, the law firm's founding partner. Arthur wonders whether he might retain his job if he were to discuss with Junior the reasons why he lost the hotel case.

Lee Lee is the gray-haired man in bed with Arthur's wife, Joanie. A "distinguished-looking" (175) senior partner in the same law firm as the much-younger Arthur, Lee seemingly controls the phone conversation. Arthur's honesty about his wife's philandering nature causes Lee to realize slowly that he may not be the only man in Joanie's string of lovers. At the story's close, Lee is stunned by Arthur's statement that his wife has just arrived home because Joanie, at that very moment, is in bed with Lee.

Lissberg Lissberg is the attorney to whom Arthur lost the hotel case in court that morning.

Shanley Shanley was the former head of the law firm and father of Junior. He originally brought the hotel accounts to the firm.

Vittorio, Judge Judge Vittorio presided over the hotel case Arthur lost. Arthur offers the excuse that the judge holds a grudge against him.

FURTHER READING

Alighieri, Dante. *The Inferno*, translated by John Ciardi. New York: New American Library, 1954.

Alsen, Eberhard. *A Reader's Guide to J. D. Salinger.* Westport, Conn.: Greenwood Press, 2002.

French, Warren. *J. D. Salinger*. New York: Twayne Publishers, 1963.

Gwynn, Frederick L., and Joseph L. Blotner. *The Fiction of J. D. Salinger*. Pittsburgh: University of Pittsburgh Press, 1958.

Hagopian, John V. "'Pretty Mouth and Green My Eyes': Salinger's Paolo and Francesca in New York." *Modern Fiction Studies* 12, no. 3 (Autumn 1966): 349–354.

Hamilton, Kenneth. "Hell in New York: J. D. Salinger's 'Pretty Mouth and Green My Eyes.'" *Dalhousie Review* 47 (Autumn 1967): 394–399.

Lundquist, James. *J. D. Salinger*. New York: Ungar, 1979.

Wenke, John. *J. D. Salinger: A Study of the Short Fiction*. Boston: Twayne Publishers, 1991.

"Raise High the Roof Beam, Carpenters"

"Raise High the Roof Beam, Carpenters" introduces the entire Glass family. The novella-length story begins Salinger's 10-year focus on the nine-member family over the course of his final four publications and resurrects Seymour Glass, a suicide in the 1948 story "A PERFECT DAY FOR BANANAFISH." Seymour becomes the central character within the family and the most complex in Salinger's work. "Raise High the Roof Beam, Carpenters" is the first of Salinger's stories narrated by Buddy Glass, the author's self-acknowledged collaborator and alter ego. Originally published in the November 19, 1955, issue of the NEW YORKER, the story was later paired with the June 6, 1959, *New Yorker* story "SEYMOUR: AN INTRODUCTION" to form Salinger's fourth and final book published during his lifetime, the 1963 volume, RAISE HIGH THE ROOF BEAM, CARPENTERS AND SEYMOUR: AN INTRODUCTION. "Raise High the Roof Beam, Carpenters" is Salinger's 32nd published story.

SYNOPSIS

In a short prologue set in current time—1955—Buddy Glass tells the reader of an incident that took place 20 years previously when his youngest sister, Franny, age ten months, is moved into the room Buddy shares with his brother Seymour to avoid exposure to mumps. One night she awakens and cries. To lull Franny to sleep, Seymour reads her an old Taoist tale. The tale is about Po Lo, a finder of superlative horses (horses that raise no dust and leave no tracks), who works for Duke Mu. Po Lo is retiring and, at the request of the Duke, recommends someone to take his place. Po Lo suggests Chiu-fang Kao, a seller of fuel and vegetables. Kao, however, does not know either the sex or the color of the first horse he discovers for the Duke. When the Duke relates the problem to Po Lo, Po Lo expresses admiration for Kao; he realizes Kao's abilities exceed his own. Po Lo explains that Kao sees only the spiritual attributes that compose a superlative horse and disregards the inessentials that are mere material aspects. Kao has the ability "to judge something better than horses" (5). The horse, when finally brought to the Duke, is superlative. Buddy goes on to state that Seymour is now dead—having committed suicide in 1948. Since that time, Buddy hasn't found anyone he would "care to send out to look for horses" (6) instead of Seymour.

After this prologue, Buddy commences "Raise High the Roof Beam, Carpenters" by enumerating the whereabouts of his entire family, the Glasses, in May 1942. He is a private with pleurisy in a Fort Benning, Georgia, hospital; Waker, one of his twin brothers, is in Maryland in a conscientious objectors' camp; Walt, the other twin, is in the Pacific, a member of a field-artillery unit; Boo Boo, his sister, is an ensign in Brooklyn; Seymour, his eldest brother, is a corporal in California; and Zooey, his youngest brother, and Franny, his youngest sister, both still children, are in Los Angeles with his parents, Les and Bessie, retired vaudevillians. (The Glasses have left MANHATTAN because Les has gotten a job with a motion-picture company.) Zooey and Franny are currently appearing on a kids' radio quiz program, *It's a Wise Child*, on which all of the Glass children have been participants. Buddy and Seymour were the first, starting in 1927. All seven Glass children used pseudonyms on the show.

Buddy receives a letter from Boo Boo telling him Seymour is getting married on June 4 on Manhattan's Upper East Side. She cannot attend the wedding as she will be traveling out of town with her boss. Boo Boo implores Buddy to attend; no one else from the family can be there due to extenuating circumstances. She has met the bride, and "she's a zero in [her] opinion, but terrific-looking" (9). She has also met the mother, who is into analysis. Boo Boo tells Buddy that Seymour "weighs about as much as a cat and he has that ecstatic look on his face that you can't talk to" (11).

Buddy gets permission to attend the wedding, but only after ingratiating himself with his commander by pretending that his favorite author is also the commander's: L. Manning Vines. With his ribs wrapped in tape to treat his pleurisy, Buddy is discharged from the hospital and takes a train to a hot, humid NEW YORK CITY, arriving only an hour before the wedding. A cab drops him at the bride's grandmother's home, where the wedding is to take place. After Buddy is seated, a woman introduces herself as Helen Silsburn. As Buddy is about to disclose who he is, she indicates three o'clock has arrived, the stated start of the wedding. While waiting for the wedding music to commence, Buddy tries to control his coughing spells. At 4:20, the distraught bride and her parents leave the building, as the guests "pour out . . . however decorously, in alert, not to say goggle-eyed, droves" (15). Although the wedding does not take place, it is announced that the assembled rental cars are to be used by the guests to attend the still-on reception at the parents' apartment. Buddy is drafted to assist people into the cars. Finally, and as he admits, inexplicably, he jumps into one, cracking his head as he enters. The occupants are Helen Silsburn (a fiftyish, fashionably dressed widow), the Matron of Honor (a sizable, athletic woman around 25, dressed in pink satin), her husband (a Lieutenant in the Signal Corps), and a very short, "tiny elderly man" (19). The old man is holding an unlit Havana cigar and is formally dressed in a top hat. Crammed into the car, Buddy takes the jump seat next to Mrs. Silsburn, while the Matron of Honor is wedged between her husband and the old man on the back seat.

The car proves very hot and uncomfortable. Mrs. Silsburn asks Buddy if he is Dickie Briganza.

After learning that he is not, she then asks if he is a friend of the bride or the groom. About to identify himself, Buddy is interrupted by the Matron of Honor, who warns him that he had better not be a friend of the groom, whom she would like to strangle. She says that no one has met the groom as he did not attend the wedding rehearsals. The Matron of Honor tells the captive audience that the groom flew in, arriving at one in the morning. He then called Muriel—his bride-to-be—asking her to meet him to talk. She did so, and till a quarter-to-five in a hotel lobby, they talked. The Matron of Honor heatedly condemns the groom for not showing up and for not ending the engagement considerately. She asks Buddy, since he is a friend of the groom, if he knows where the groom is; Buddy replies that he just got to New York two hours ago.

Buddy interrupts his story to address a couple of questions he thinks his reader might have at this point. Why did he continue to stay in the car, since it was headed to the parents' apartment, and why did he get in it to start with? He explains there were many reasons, but he settles on the fact he was very young and lonely and "one simply jumped into loaded cars . . . and stayed seated in them" (29).

Continuing to cough throughout the ride, Buddy glances at the tiny old man and notices that his feet do not touch the floor: "they looked like old and valued friends of [Buddy's]" (29). The Matron of Honor then asks Buddy if he knows what the groom does for a living. Buddy asks her if she means Seymour; this is the first time Seymour's name has been used by the riders in the car. Buddy suspects that the Matron of Honor knows quite a bit about Seymour: that he had been "a national radio 'celebrity' for some six years of his boyhood" (30); had entered college at age 15; and had been a professor of English before his induction into the army. Buddy even suspects she might know that Buddy is Seymour's brother. Buddy lies and responds that Seymour is a chiropodist.

The car's progress to the bride's parents' apartment is abruptly stopped by a parade. After a bit, the Lieutenant orders the driver to ask a nearby cop how long will it be until they can continue. The laconic answer is till the parade passes. Buddy notices the delay doesn't bother the tiny old man. He "stared ferociously ahead at the windshield . . . and if Death stepped miraculously through the glass and came in after you, in all probability you just got up and went along with him, ferociously but quietly" (36).

The husband of the Matron of Honor lights a cigarette for her, and in doing so the match folder catches Mrs. Silsburn's eye. Imprinted upon the cover is: "These Matches Were Stolen from Bob and Edie Burwick's House." Mrs. Silsburn thinks it is an innovative idea; the Matron of Honor tells her she got the idea from Muriel's mother, Mrs. Fedder. This leads to the Matron of Honor's praising Mrs. Fedder as a Renaissance woman: a voracious reader, former teacher, and newspaper employee; her own clothes maker, housekeeper, and excellent cook. Mrs. Silsburn takes this opportunity to ask if Mrs. Fedder approved of the marriage. The Matron of Honor tells her Mrs. Fedder discreetly had not spoken of it until today. She then reveals that Mrs. Fedder said Seymour was "a latent homosexual and . . . was basically afraid of marriage" (42) and "was a really schizoid personality" (43). Buddy speaks up, asking why Mrs. Fedder thought this.

The Matron of Honor's reply is to ask whether Buddy thought what happened today was normal. She then tells Buddy that Seymour told Muriel the night before the wedding that "he's too *happy* to get married and that she'll have to post*pone* the wedding till he feels *steadier* or he won't be able to come to it" (45). She says that Muriel then explained about the planning and her father's expense and people traveling to attend. Yet Seymour replied he was "terribly sorry but he can't get married till he feels less *happy*" (45). The Matron of Honor rhetorically asks, "Does that sound like a normal person—a normal *man*—to you?" (46). She then mentions the name of a famous actress-singer and asks Mrs. Silsburn if she has ever noticed the actress's odd smile. The Matron of Honor then reveals that the crooked smile was caused by Seymour hitting the actress, necessitating nine stitches. Buddy asks where the Matron of Honor heard about this incident, and she replies from Muriel's mother. She then says she thinks he is Seymour's brother; they look alike, and she was told he

was going to attend the wedding. Buddy admits his identity. She tells him she knows Seymour is not a chiropodist, and that he was Billy Black on the kids' radio quiz show *It's a Wise Child*. The Glass children appeared under pseudonyms. The Matron of Honor then asks Buddy if he was Georgie Black. Buddy tells her that was Walt. Mrs. Silsburn asks Buddy (still not knowing his first name) if he was "Buddy Black" (50). Before he can answer, the Matron of Honor interrupts, declaring she hated that program and the type of kids who appeared on it. As she says she "loathe[s] precocious children" (51), the car is inundated with incredibly loud, cacophonous music from a drum-and-bugle corps passing in the parade.

The Matron of Honor declares they should abandon the car; additionally, she needs to seek out a place to phone Muriel. Mrs. Silsburn informs everyone that a restaurant, Schrafft's, is nearby. The Matron of Honor commands Buddy to come along. He shouts back, "fine." But the tiny old man seems unaware of the noisy music and that all are abandoning ship. The Matron of Honor, yelling to be heard over the band, attempts to tell him of the plan, but he is unresponsive. Then Mrs. Silsburn explains he is Muriel's father's uncle, who is deaf and dumb. Buddy, on a pad of paper, writes that they are delayed by the parade and are leaving the car to seek out a phone and a cold drink, and asks if he wants to join them. The old man writes his one-word reply, "Delighted." Buddy attempts to convey with his facial expression that everyone in the car recognized "a poem when [they] saw one, and were grateful" (57).

As the Matron of Honor, her husband, and Mrs. Silsburn head toward the restaurant, Buddy and the old man bring up the rear, grinning at each other. When the two of them finally catch up with the others, it is revealed that the restaurant is closed for repairs. Buddy lets it be known that he and Seymour have an apartment close by, and that they all could rest and have a drink, and the Matron of Honor could use the phone there. The Matron of Honor seeks confirmation that there is a phone and, more to the point, wonders if Seymour might be at the apartment. Buddy tells her the phone should work unless Boo Boo, who has been using the apartment in Buddy's and Seymour's absence, has had it shut off before her long trip. He doubts Seymour will be there, but there is a possibility. The Matron of Honor decides they should go the apartment but lets it be known that if Seymour is there, she will kill him. Buddy and the little old man then lead the way.

When they arrive, Buddy first enters alone to see if Seymour is on the premises. He is not. The apartment is incredibly hot, with the Matron of Honor declaring it hotter than outside. While Buddy struggles with the air-conditioners, the guests spread out. The Lieutenant is looking at period pictures of Buddy's and Seymour's co-panelists from *It's a Wise Child* that are tacked to the wall. Buddy says he will make some drinks. Before he can leave, the Lieutenant asks him where all the pictures come from. Buddy explains their source. The Lieutenant admits he never listened to the program and asks if it was a kids' quiz show. Buddy says that Seymour changed the program into "a kind of children's round-table discussion" (67). The Matron of Honor interjects that being on a show like that warps a child for life; that that is probably what is wrong with Seymour. Such a childhood, she declares, precluded Seymour from being normal, from relating to people, and instead he went around causing people to need stitches in their faces. Or so Mrs. Fedder, Muriel's mother, said that very day. Buddy interrupts and curses at what Mrs. Fedder has said about Seymour. Buddy explains Seymour wasn't a "high-I.Q. showoff" or an "exhibitionist" (69) but a poet. Even "if he never wrote a line of poetry, he could still flash what he had at you with the back of his ear if he wanted to" (69).

After this outburst, Buddy says he will start making some Tom Collinses. The Matron of Honor asks to use the phone. The phone is in the bedroom, where Buddy spots Seymour's diary in a valise. He grabs the diary and hides it in a laundry hamper in the bathroom. There, on the mirror, is a message written in soap. In keeping with an old family custom among the children, Boo Boo has left a long and loving message addressed to Seymour, in which she quotes Sappho, "Raise high the roof beam, carpenters. Like Ares comes the bride-groom, taller far than a tall man" (76). She tells Seymour to be happy with Muriel. Without explanation, Buddy then sits on the side of the bathtub and starts to read part of the diary. The entries he reads are reproduced verbatim; Buddy says they all date from the time Seymour met Muriel, up to a few months prior to their deciding to get married.

In the first entry, Seymour tells of standing at attention with a rifle, but it does not bother him as he has "no circulation, no pulse" (77). Afterward, he and Muriel go to a movie. Commenting on how she is wrapped up in the sentimental tragedy on the screen, Seymour writes, "how I love and need her undiscriminating heart" (77). He later explains to Muriel R. H. Blyth's definition of sentimentality: giving "to a thing more tenderness than God gives to it" (78). He acknowledges that her love for him is not constant. The first entry ends: "The human voice conspires to desecrate everything on earth" (78).

The second entry describes one evening at the Fedders'. The meal ends with an unusual dessert made by Muriel, which causes Seymour in his diary to quote the haiku poet Saigyo. Mrs. Fedder suggests they all listen to *It's a Wise Child*, where they hear a 13-year-old Zooey say that he likes houses that look alike and that, in fact, he wishes "everybody in the world looked exactly alike" (80) so you would think everyone you met was a member of your family. Seymour recognizes how close Muriel and her mother are to each other.

The third entry is about meeting Muriel for a Chinese dinner. Muriel is upset because her mother, after talking with her psychoanalyst, thinks Seymour is "a schizoid personality" (81) and wonders if insanity runs in the family. Seymour has told Muriel how he "got the scars on [his] wrists" (81), and Muriel has evidently informed her mother. What disturbs Mrs. Fedder is not the suicide attempt, but that Seymour does not relate to people and that he has not seduced her daughter. She is also disturbed by his comment about wanting to be a dead cat. Seymour writes that Mrs. Fedder had wondered what he wanted to be after the war was over and that he had answered a dead cat. He acknowledges that he did not explain this to be an answer by a ZEN master as to the most valuable thing in the world because no price could be put on a dead cat. Seymour goes on to write about how Muriel is trying to teach him to smile. He is happy with her; he doubts he makes her as happy. He acknowledges she wants to get married, but for all the usual reasons. Seymour surmises that Buddy will not like Muriel's reasons for marriage or her mother. Yet Seymour loves Mrs. Fedder; he finds her brave as she still goes on living, though lacking "any understanding or taste for the main current of poetry that flows through things, all things" (84).

Seymour's fourth entry relates how he was unable to get to town that day to see Muriel, but that this did not bother her. He suggests most fiancées would lie and say that they were bothered. He then writes, "How I worship her simplicity, her terrible honesty" (85).

In the fifth entry, Buddy reads Seymour's description of dinner at the Fedders' attended by Mrs. Fedder's analyst, Dr. Sims. The analyst grills Seymour. He also tells Seymour that he had heard the latter's comment about the Gettysburg Address that had gotten him expelled from It's a Wise Child when he was 16. Seymour explains to the analyst that he felt it was an inappropriate speech for children to commit to memory, and that a completely honest speaker would "have come forward and shaken his fist at his audience and then walked off" (86). Dr. Sims decides Seymour has a perfection complex. The analyst recommends that Seymour learn to live with the frailties and contradictions of being human. Seymour acknowledges that indiscrimination is a worthwhile goal; that it is, in essence, the pathway of the Tao. "But for a discriminating man to achieve this, it would mean that he would have to dispossess himself of poetry, go *beyond* poetry" (86), for there is no way one could learn to like bad poetry or claim it was the same as good poetry. Seymour infers that Mrs. Fedder must have told Dr. Sims about the Charlotte rock-throwing incident ("that old finished business" [87]), but Seymour "had no intention of discussing Charlotte's stitches with Sims. Not over just one drink" (87). Seymour admits he promised Muriel he would undergo psychoanalysis one day. He remarks, "M. loves me, but she'll never feel really close to me, *familiar* with me, *frivolous* with

me, till I'm slightly overhauled" (87). Seymour says a dermatologist also will need to attend the sessions, because he has "scars on [his] hands from touching certain people" (88), including Zooey's head and one of Charlotte's dresses he loved. He opines, "if I'm anything by a clinical name, I'm a kind of paranoiac in reverse. I suspect people of plotting to make me happy" (88).

After reading this last word, Buddy slams Seymour's diary shut. He finds he is sweating profusely. Buddy throws the diary into the laundry hamper. He then looks at Boo Boo's message to Seymour on the medicine-cabinet mirror. He goes into the kitchen and makes the Tom Collinses he had earlier promised his guests, but before leaving the kitchen, Buddy swallows a substantial amount of Scotch in one gulp, while admitting he is not a true drinker. He enters the living room with the Tom Collinses. Mrs. Silsburn has been looking at one of the pictures of the cast of It's a Wise Child tacked to the wall. She remarks how beautiful one of the girls is and asks her name. Buddy replies, "Charlotte Mayhew" (the real name of the actress-singer with the crooked smile). Mrs. Silsburn asks him if he knew who she looked like. Buddy does not, but then tells her how Charlotte would stomp on Seymour's feet whenever he said something on the show that she especially liked. Seymour wanted her on the show, not because she was bright, but because he liked her accent. They had met when he and Buddy were playing stoopball, and Charlotte, from a 12th-story window, was bombarding them with marbles. Mrs. Silsburn asks the Lieutenant whom the child looks like; he finally says, Muriel. Mrs. Silsburn confirms that Charlotte "could double for Muriel at that age. But to a T" (97). Buddy admits he had never seen Muriel until the wedding. Mrs. Silsburn asks Buddy how Charlotte got the stitches—if it was an accident. Buddy, who is now feeling the effects of his drink, responds with an explicative. At that moment, the Matron of Honor enters the room, informing them she has spoken with everyone at Muriel's parents' apartment. After swilling a drink, she explains everything has worked out: She drops the bombshell that Muriel and Seymour have eloped. Seymour was at the Fedders' apartment when everyone returned there after the aborted ceremony. Also, she says he has "promised to start going to an analyst and get himself straightened out" (101). The Matron of Honor, her husband, and Mrs. Silsburn leave for the Fedders' apartment.

Now quite drunk, Buddy realizes that the old man is still in his apartment. The old man raises his glass and grins at Buddy, who pours himself a Tom Collins, spilling some. Buddy asks the old deaf-mute man if he wants to know the circumstances of Charlotte's stitches and explains that Charlotte was visiting the Glasses at the lake. While she was petting Boo Boo's cat, Seymour, age 12, threw a stone "at her because she looked so beautiful sitting there in the middle of the driveway with Boo Boo's cat" (104). He says everyone understood that was the reason. But then Buddy immediately admits Charlotte never understood why Seymour threw the rock. The old man grins at Buddy, as though he believes every word. Buddy then gets up and leaves the room, goes to the bathroom, and retrieves Seymour's diary from the hamper. He goes through the pages until he finds the very last entry and reads it.

In the entry, Seymour is at his army base, waiting to see if the weather will clear up to permit a plane flight to the wedding. Seymour phones Muriel to inform her of the situation. He then asks her to elope with him because he is "too keyed up to be with people" (106). He feels he is "about to be born" (106). Seymour has been reading a book of VEDANTA concerning marriage. The ideal is to serve each other and to raise any children knowing they cannot be thought of as possessions since they are God's. Seymour acknowledges he should go to bed, but "someone must sit up with the happy man" (106).

Buddy brings the diary back to the bedroom where he had originally found it. He falls on the nearest bed and passes out. A couple of hours later, he awakens hung over and thirsty. He goes into the living room and finds that the old man has let himself out, leaving behind an empty glass and a smoked cigar end. Buddy, to this day, believes "the cigar end should have been forwarded on to Seymour . . . in a small, nice box . . . possibly with a blank sheet of paper enclosed, by way of explanation" (107).

CRITICAL ANALYSIS

The importance of "Raise High the Roof Beam, Carpenters" within Salinger's body of work cannot be overstated. This 1955 story—105 pages in its original book publication—assembles and introduces the Glass family in its entirety and may be considered a watershed event in Salinger's publication history. Salinger continued to focus exclusively upon the Glass family during the final 10 years of his publishing career. Additionally, it is generally believed that during his 45 years of publishing silence, Salinger continued to write more Glass family stories.

Before turning to an analysis of "Raise High the Roof Beam, Carpenters," one would be prudent to consider the evolution and scope of the Glass family within Salinger's oeuvre. Prior to the November 19, 1955, publication of "Raise High the Roof Beam, Carpenters," the first story to portray a Glass family member is "A Perfect Day for Bananafish" (January 31, 1948; featuring Seymour's final hours and suicide). The second story is "DOWN AT THE DINGHY" (April 1949; featuring Boo Boo's interaction with her son, Lionel). "Down at the Dinghy," in an aside, also mentions Seymour by name, and another character, "Webb" Glass. This reference cannot be overlooked and definitively shows that Salinger had at least an embryonic Glass family in mind as early as 1949. (Webb has been surmised to be Buddy's real name, given the use of the initial "W" at the close of the 1965 story, "HAPWORTH 16, 1924.") Thus, by 1949, Salinger's fiction contained three Glass siblings. However, after the April 1949 publication of "Down at the Dinghy," no story was published with a character whose last name was Glass up to and *including* the January 29, 1955, publication of "FRANNY." Early in that year, something momentous and significant occurred within Salinger's imagination: The author decided to create a full-blown family, one even more complex than the Caulfield family of *The CATCHER IN THE RYE*.

With this in mind, Salinger raided his earlier stories to help create the nine-member Glass family. This was done by resurrecting Seymour Glass; retrieving Boo Boo Glass; turning Webb Glass into Buddy; and incorporating two characters who lacked surnames: Walt, from "UNCLE WIGGILY IN CONNECTICUT," and the also first-name-only Franny from "Franny." Salinger invented Zooey and Waker as two more siblings and created Bessie and Les as the parents.

A concise family synopsis yields the following facts: The parents, Les and Bessie, are vaudevillians, a song-and-dance team that retired in 1925. Les is a Jew from Australia; Bessie, a Catholic from Dublin. At an unknown date they become New Yorkers, first residing on the Upper West Side of Manhattan, then later on the Upper East Side. The marriage produces seven children. The eldest, Seymour, a child prodigy born in 1917, a God-seeker and poet, later an English professor and an emotionally disturbed war veteran, is the family's guru, but his suicide in 1948 shatters the Glasses. Buddy (Webb), born in 1919, is a part-time writing instructor and writer who chronicles the life of the Glasses. Boo Boo (Beatrice), the first daughter, born in (most likely) 1921, is a mother of three, living in suburbia. The male twins, Walt (Walter) and Waker, were born in (most likely) 1923. Walt, a dancer, dies a noncombatant death after the end of World War II; Waker is a Roman Catholic priest. Zooey (Zachary), the youngest male, born in 1930, is a successful television actor. Franny (Frances), the youngest child, born in 1935, survives a spiritual crisis and becomes an actress. All of the children are gifted to a degree; each appeared on a radio quiz program called *It's a Wise Child.* (Salinger's erratic arithmetic, as evidenced in "Hapworth 16, 1924" in the stated ages of Boo Boo, Walt and Waker when contrasted to references in the earlier stories, blurs their exact years of birth, but the chronological order remains unvarying.) The eight stories that compose the Glass saga are: "A Perfect Day for Bananafish," published January 31, 1948; "Uncle Wiggily in Connecticut," published March 20, 1948; "Down at the Dinghy," published April 1949; "Franny," published January 29, 1955; "Raise High the Roof Beam, Carpenters," published November 19, 1955; "ZOOEY," published May 4, 1957; "Seymour: An Introduction," published June 6, 1959; and "Hapworth 16, 1924," published June 19, 1965. All of the stories, with the exception of "Down at the Dinghy," originally

appeared in the *New Yorker* magazine; in length they run the gamut from succinct short stories to novellas. Eberhard Alsen, the Salinger scholar who has devoted the most attention to the Glasses, tabulates the word counts of the major Glass stories as follows: "Zooey," 41,130; "Seymour: An Introduction," 31,000; "Hapworth 16, 1924," 28,000; "Raise High the Roof Beam, Carpenters," 23,350; and "Franny," 10,700. "A Perfect Day for Bananafish" and "Down at the Dinghy" are substantially shorter than "Franny," while the section of "Uncle Wiggily in Connecticut" that deals with Walt Glass amounts to but one-fifth of that story. The events portrayed in the various stories span from 1922 through 1965.

Salinger commented only very rarely on his work, at least in a public forum. But on the dust jackets of his final two books—the 1961 FRANNY AND ZOOEY, and the 1963 *Raise High the Roof Beam, Carpenters and Seymour: An Introduction*—he speaks about the Glass family. On the *Franny and Zooey* dust jacket, Salinger states that he is at work on "a narrative series . . . about a family of settlers in twentieth-century New York, the Glasses." He calls it "a long-term project" and admits that there is a danger he might "bog down, perhaps disappear entirely." Salinger confides, "I love working on these Glass stories, I've been waiting for them most of my life, and I think I have fairly decent, monomaniacal plans to finish them with due care and all-available skill." He terms Buddy Glass to be his "alter-ego and collaborator." On the dust jacket of *Raise High the Roof Beam, Carpenters and Seymour: An Introduction,* Salinger writes that the two stories "are both very much concerned with Seymour Glass, who is the main character in my still-uncompleted series about the Glass family." He reveals that he has "several new Glass stories coming along—waxing, dilating—each in its own way." Salinger concludes, "Oddly, the joys and satisfactions of working on the Glass family peculiarly increase and deepen for me with the years. I can't say why, though. Not, at least, outside the casino proper of my fiction." And an inside glimpse into Salinger's involvement within the Glass realm was provided by Joyce Maynard, Salinger's girlfriend in 1972–73. "One thing he [Salinger] does show me are his archives of the Glass family. . . . He has compiled stacks of notes and notebooks concerning the habits and backgrounds of the Glasses—music they like, places they go, episodes in their history. Even the parts of their lives that he may not write about, he needs to know" (Maynard 159).

Readers unsuspectingly meet Salinger's preoccupation with the nine-member Glass family in the first sentence of "Raise High the Roof Beam, Carpenters": "One night some twenty years ago, during a siege of mumps in our enormous family, my youngest sister, Franny, was moved, crib and all, into the ostensibly germ-free room I shared with my eldest brother, Seymour" (3). Attentive *New Yorker* readers would be reading this sentence a mere 10 months after publication of the controversial "Franny." A veteran *New Yorker* reader would also recall a Seymour Glass from seven years earlier in the unforgettable "A Perfect Day for Bananafish." Moreover, that story led off Salinger's second book, NINE STORIES, published two years before "Raise High the Roof Beam, Carpenters." The name of the narrator—the "I" of the opening sentence—is not revealed until the seventh page of the story, when a letter is addressed to him as "Buddy." But the reader has been forewarned that the family is "enormous" (3). Buddy will list the family on the fourth and fifth pages of the story. Boo Boo's and Walt's names would be familiar as their stories both appeared in *Nine Stories*. This leaves Les, Bessie, Buddy, Waker, and Zooey as the only names that a dedicated Salinger reader had not yet encountered prior to reading "Raise High the Roof Beam, Carpenters." Perhaps Salinger himself at the time of writing did not fully realize the story would not be his last dealing with the Glass family. It remains to be seen whether Salinger's preoccupation with the Glass family may be revealed to span 55 years' duration if unpublished works eventually see the light of day.

Significantly, a major focus of "Raise High the Roof Beam, Carpenters" is the resurrection of a character Salinger had previously killed off, that of Seymour Glass. Seven years earlier, Salinger had crafted a compressed, third-person narrative of Seymour's final hours before his suicide by

gunshot, an act committed next to his sleeping wife, Muriel. Now, in a humorous, garrulous first-person narrative of short-novella length, written by Seymour's brother Buddy, Salinger tells the story of Seymour's wedding day. Why Salinger chose to resurrect this character has remained unclear to critical opinion. The Seymour of the 1948 "A Perfect Day for Bananafish" was a maladjusted war veteran, evidently interested in poetry, and more comfortable with young children than with adult society, especially his wife. There was no pronounced spiritual element to the character. Nor was he identified as a poet. Earlier in his career, Salinger had been concerned with a poet, the psychologically scarred Raymond Ford of the 1947 story, "The INVERTED FOREST." And in the 1953 story "TEDDY," he had created an extraordinary genius, a young boy who was a confirmed God-seeker. One is tempted to say that Salinger grafted together the Seymour of "A Perfect Day for Bananafish" with Raymond Ford of "The Inverted Forest" along with the 10-year-old Teddy of "Teddy" to create the "new" Seymour Glass of the Glass family. Yet, to create a consistent narrative body, Salinger could not simply leave out the suicide; thus, this overwhelming fact must accompany the revisionist Seymour. As Salinger continued the Glass series, the fact of the suicide would prove difficult to reconcile with the religious dimensions of the Glass-family Seymour.

The Seymour of "Raise High the Roof Beam, Carpenters" is now described by Buddy Glass as a child prodigy who participated on a kids' radio quiz program called *It's a Wise Child*. Seymour turns the program into a roundtable discussion among the children, where he speaks like "a *poet*. If he never wrote a line of poetry, he could still flash what he had at you with the back of his ear if he wanted to" (69). The reader learns the disquieting fact that a preadolescent Seymour threw a stone at his close friend and program co-panelist Charlotte Mayhew "because she looked so beautiful" (104), slightly disfiguring her face. Buddy further reveals that Seymour entered college at the age of 15 and became a full professor of English at Columbia University before being inducted into the army. Through Seymour's diary entries that dominate the final quarter of the story, the reader meets a hypersensitive, articulate young man of 24 and 25 who is immersed in poetry and spirituality.

But in addition to the rock-throwing episode, the reader learns of a previous suicide attempt when Seymour mentions in his diary "the scars on [his] wrists" (81). No specific date is given for this suicide attempt, which is not mentioned in the other Glass stories. However, this information certainly gives the reader pause and undercuts other positive impressions of the character while reading the diary entries.

"Raise High the Roof Beam, Carpenters" is not only an effort at a rehabilitation of Seymour. Importantly, the story introduces the figure of Buddy Glass. A 36-year-old Buddy begins the story, only to recede to write about an incident from when he was 23 years old and a private in the army. Buddy is charming, in part due to the perspective of middle age poking fun at a much-younger self. Alfred Kazin aptly stresses Salinger's use of comedy in his depiction of Buddy as a "fumbling, theatrically awkward observer and narrator . . . confessedly a failure and somehow ridiculous in his excessive feelings of alienation" (Kazin 116). Buddy's presence at the reader's side will continue through the remainder of the Glass stories (though there will be only a short introduction penned by him in "Hapworth 16, 1924"). Buddy is narrator, guide, and participant in the stories, though to a different degree in each. At one point in "Seymour: An Introduction," Buddy refers to himself as "a narrator, but one with extremely pressing personal needs. I want to introduce, I want to describe, I want to distribute mementos, amulets, I want to break out my wallet and pass around snapshots, I want to follow my nose" (125). Buddy serves within the Glass family stories as the constant referential point. Much of a reader's liking or disliking of the Glass stories will hinge on a personal reaction to Buddy's character. Buddy is grating and off-putting to some readers but thoroughly captivating to others.

Buddy begins the story by reproducing the old Taoist tale (found in *Taoist Teachings from the Book of Lieh Tzu*) read by Seymour to Franny about a man who can identify a superlative horse, but who, at the same time, disregards the mundane outer attributes of the animal. Such a man concerns himself with the spiritual nature of things in the world. Buddy believes his brother Seymour to be such a person. The parable introduces the "new" Seymour as a God-seeker. In addition to Seymour's familiarity with TAOISM, the story contains references to Seymour's interest in Zen and Vedanta. Unlike Salinger's previous story, the 1955 "Franny," with its emphasis on Christianity, "Raise High the Roof Beam, Carpenters" continues the Eastern religious influence that also permeated the 1953 "Teddy." In the story, the figure of the old deaf-mute is decidedly a religious figure and produces a playful echo to Holden Caulfield in *The Catcher in the Rye*, who was going to pretend to be a deaf-mute. The old deaf-mute is detached, nonjudgmental, and unafraid of death. Buddy remarks how the deaf-mute might react: "if Death . . . came in after you, in all probability you just got up and went along with him, ferociously but quietly. Chances were, you could take your cigar with you . . ." (36). The Indian Salinger scholar Som P. Ranchan believes that yogic aspects of the old deaf-mute derive from Salinger's teacher and friend, SWAMI NIKHILANANDA, who headed the RAMAKRISHNA-VIVEKANANDA CENTER OF NEW YORK, which Salinger frequented. The deaf-mute's cigar end and the possible accompanying blank piece of paper that Buddy thinks of including in the gift—apart from the humorous jab at the usefulness of wedding presents in general—end the story with the air of a quixotic koan.

"Raise High the Roof Beam, Carpenters," in and of itself, is a delightfully inventive rendering of a wedding day gone awry, replete with a plethora of memorable incidents and characters. One critic describes the story as "written with a dazzling, almost showy, technical brilliance. Its dialogue is expert, its satirical comedy amusing, its style fluid and graceful" (Prescott 9). Even without the subsequent Glass stories, "Raise High the Roof Beam, Carpenters" can stand securely on its own. The editors of the *New Yorker*, when deciding upon which Salinger story to include in their anthology of the best stories published by the magazine in the 1950s, overlooked the more popular and critically lauded "For Esmé—with Love and Squalor" and instead selected "Raise High the Roof Beam, Carpenters." Perhaps the best summation of the story can be found in John Updike's assessment of it as "a magic and hilarious prose-poem with an enchanting end effect of mysterious clarity" (Updike 52).

PUBLICATION HISTORY

"Raise High the Roof Beam, Carpenters" was first published in the *New Yorker* magazine on November 19, 1955. The story was subsequently chosen to appear in an anthology selected by *New Yorker* editors, titled *Stories from The New Yorker, 1950–1960*, released in 1960. "Raise High the Roof Beam, Carpenters"'s first book publication in a volume consisting exclusively of Salinger's work was in *Raise High the Roof Beam, Carpenters and Seymour: An Introduction* (Little, Brown and Company, 1963). *Raise High the Roof Beam, Carpenters and Seymour: An Introduction*, Salinger's fourth book, has never gone out of print.

Raise High the Roof Beam, Carpenters and Seymour: An Introduction is available in three editions from Little, Brown and Company: an exact reproduction of the hardback first edition from 1963, which includes the dust-jacket comments written by Salinger; a trade paperback that mimics the production of the hardback, though Salinger's dust-jacket comments are not retained; and a mass-market paperback, also lacking Salinger's dust-jacket comments, with its pagination differing from the above editions.

CHARACTERS

Admiral Behind-pincher Nicknamed by Boo Boo Glass in her letter to her brother Buddy, the Admiral is her boss and wants Boo Boo, his secretary, to accompany him on a long trip. The trip will cause her to miss Seymour Glass's wedding.

Aspesi, Al Mentioned by Seymour Glass in his diary, Al Aspesi allows Seymour to sit in the Orderly Room at the B-17 base in California, provided that Seymour will answer the phone. Instead of doing his job, Al goes to sleep on the floor.

Boy and father While waiting for the parade, a small boy runs into the cleared street. His father grabs him and then strikes the child, to the boos of the assembled crowd.

Briganza, Dickie Mrs. Helen Silsburn, when she meets Buddy Glass, thinks he is Dickie Briganza. Dickie's mother, Celia, is a friend of Mrs. Silsburn.

Buddy Glass's company commander Buddy tries to ingratiate himself with his company commander to get permission to attend his brother Seymour's wedding. Buddy claims that he and the company commander share the same favorite author, L. Manning Vines. Vines is also the name of the favorite writer of Eloise Wengler's husband in "Uncle Wiggily in Connecticut." This fact would lead a reader to believe that Lew Wengler was Buddy's company commander.

Burke girl, the The unnamed girl is a participant on *It's a Wise Child* with Franny and Zooey Glass in 1942. Seymour Glass mentions her in his diary as having participated in the program that takes place one night when Mrs. Fedder suggests they listen in. Unlike Zooey, the girl doesn't like identical houses.

Burwick, Bob *See* the Lieutenant.

Burwick, Edie *See* the Matron of Honor.

Carl and Amy Carl and Amy, referred to in Boo Boo Glass's letter to her brother Buddy, are a couple who formerly lived on (East) 63rd Street in Manhattan, two doors up from Muriel Fedder's grandmother's home. Boo Boo uses them to explain to Buddy where the wedding is being held.

Carl and Amy are also mentioned in "Seymour: An Introduction." In 1939, they arranged a blind date for Seymour Glass with "that very strange girl" (183) and accompanied the two to a performance of *Die Zauberflöte*. However, since Seymour does not meet Muriel Fedder until 1941, the girl of the date must not be confused with Muriel.

Deaf-mute, the *See* Muriel Fedder's father's uncle.

Driver, the   The anonymous driver of the car carrying Buddy Glass, Mrs. Silsburn, the Matron of Honor, the Lieutenant, and Muriel Fedder's father's uncle to the reception is seated directly in front of Buddy. When the parade causes the car to stop, the driver is ordered by the Lieutenant to ask a policeman when the car will be able to recommence its journey. Instead of acquiring the much-sought-after information, the driver seems to be sharing dirty jokes with the cop.

Drum-and-bugle corps   The deafening corps forces Buddy Glass, the Matron of Honor, the Lieutenant, Mrs. Silsburn, and Muriel Fedder's father's uncle to abandon their hot, parade-stopped car and seek a restaurant for refreshments and a phone.

Fedder, Mr.   He is Muriel's father and husband to Rhea Fedder. Along with his wife, he is seen escorting his daughter Muriel down the steps after the wedding fails to take place. Seymour Glass states in his diary that he wishes Mr. Fedder would take a more active part in the conversations when Seymour is present in the Fedder household.

Muriel's father is also referred to in "A Perfect Day for Bananafish" during the phone call between Muriel and her mother.

Fedder, Mrs. Rhea   Mrs. Fedder is Muriel's mother and wife to Mr. Fedder. Additionally, it is revealed that she is Mrs. Silsburn's late husband's baby sister. She is seen in the story, along with her husband, escorting Muriel down the stairs after the wedding fails to take place. Mrs. Fedder, a firm believer in psychoanalysis (she sees a Jungian, Dr. Sims, twice a week), believes that Seymour Glass has a schizoid personality and is latently homosexual. Seymour recognizes that Mrs. Fedder and her daughter Muriel are extremely close. He says he loves Mrs. Fedder because she goes on living even though she is dead to life's inherent poetry. The Matron of Honor thinks Mrs. Fedder is a brilliant woman because of her past careers as a teacher and a newspaper worker, and because she now makes her own clothes, does her own housework, and is an excellent cook. Mrs. Fedder tells the Matron of

Honor that Seymour, before he and Muriel eloped, had promised to see a psychoanalyst.

Muriel's mother is also in "A Perfect Day for Bananafish." Muriel phones her; they discuss Seymour and various matters.

Fedder, Muriel   Muriel is Seymour Glass's bride-to-be and later his widow. In the story "Raise High the Roof Beam, Carpenters," the ostensible subject of which is her wedding day, June 4, 1942, Muriel appears only briefly. After Seymour's failure to show up for the wedding, she is led dejectedly down the steps of her grandmother's house into a waiting car. Muriel's character and personality are conveyed in this story, however, through many references in Seymour's diary and by several comments made by the Matron of Honor. In "Raise High the Roof Beam, Carpenters," Muriel is a beautiful, young, uncomplicated woman who still lives with her parents. Seymour senses that Muriel, although still emotionally close to her mother, wants to break away. She and Seymour meet in late 1941. The rapid courtship takes place while Seymour is stationed at Fort Monmouth, New Jersey, and later at a B-17 base in California. In his diary, Seymour portrays Muriel as a sentimentalist who responds to Hollywood movies and wants to be a wife living a typically normal life. Seymour acknowledges that he needs "her undiscriminating heart" (77) and "her simplicity, her terrible honesty" (85). Her solicitude is evident when Seymour meets Muriel the night before the wedding; he wants to postpone the wedding or to simply go away alone to get married. Muriel stays up talking with him in a hotel lobby until 4:45 A.M. on the morning of the wedding, trying to explain why that change would be impossible at this point. (The wedding is to take place at 3:00 P.M., though in two instances Salinger mistakenly refers to the event happening in the morning [41, 42].) Yet, when Seymour fails to show up for the ceremony, Muriel does elope with him. An arresting comment in Seymour's diary notes, "she [Muriel] was trying to teach [him] to smile" (83). By contrast, in "Zooey" the reader learns the younger Seymour was almost always smiling. Given that Muriel has met Seymour during World War II, Salinger infers here that the worldwide cataclysm of the war has immeasurably changed Seymour's personality. In one sense, Seymour's choice of the innocent Muriel counterbalances his traumatic wartime experience.

Muriel Fedder Glass appears in or is mentioned in several other Glass stories. She appears as one of the three protagonists of "A Perfect Day for Bananafish." Her character there, though, contrasts vividly with that reflected in "Raise High the Roof Beam, Carpenters." In "A Perfect Day for Bananafish," she is six years older, now a wife, who has waited through the war for her husband. Apparently, Seymour and Muriel have had no children, though in "Raise High the Roof Beam, Carpenters" Seymour acknowledges that Muriel wants them. At the outset of "A Perfect Day for Bananafish," she is presented in an unflattering egocentric manner, reading a magazine article, "Sex Is Fun—or Hell." While talking on the phone with her mother, Muriel shows some independence when she tells Mrs. Fedder that she will not leave Seymour and come back home. The reader is given the impression, however, that Muriel is hardened and self-centered, a far cry from the character of the Muriel portrayed in Seymour's 1941–42 diary, which the reader sees in "Raise High the Roof Beam, Carpenters." In "Zooey," she is mentioned in Buddy Glass's letter. When Buddy travels to Florida to retrieve Seymour's body after the suicide, he deplores Muriel's appearing in "Bergdorf Goodman Black" (62), as though she is trying to play the part of "the Bereaved Widow" (62). In "Seymour: An Introduction," Muriel has agreed to Buddy's finding a publisher for Seymour's poems, though she will not allow him to directly quote any in his story.

Glass, Bessie   Bessie is the mother of the Glass family and wife to Les Glass. A former performer in vaudeville—a dancer and singer with her husband—she has seven children (in birth order): Seymour, Buddy, Boo Boo, Walt, Waker, Zooey, and Franny. During the time of "Raise High the Roof Beam, Carpenters," Bessie is living temporarily in Los Angeles with her husband and their two youngest children, as Les Glass is working at a motion-picture studio.

Bessie appears in all of the other Glass family stories. She is given her largest role in "Zooey,"

where she is described in detail as she attempts to persuade her youngest son, Zooey, to help her youngest daughter, Franny, recover from a nervous breakdown. In "Seymour: An Introduction," Bessie is given several small cameos in Buddy's recollections of incidents from his and Seymour's childhood. In the 1965 prologue to "Hapworth 16, 1924," Buddy Glass explains that his mother has just sent him Seymour's letter (written in 1924). Bessie is the first of the five addressees of the letter, and many passages are directed solely to her.

Glass, Boo Boo   Boo Boo is the eldest daughter of the Glass family and the third-oldest child. Though she is not seen directly in "Raise High the Roof Beam, Carpenters," she plays a decisive role as her letter to her brother Buddy informs him of their brother Seymour's forthcoming wedding. Boo Boo exhorts Buddy to attend the ceremony and provides the reader with the first estimation of Seymour's bride, Muriel Fedder ("she's a zero . . . but terrific looking" [9]), and of Muriel's mother, Mrs. Fedder. Boo Boo has taken over Seymour and Buddy's old apartment in New York City while they are in the army. She is an ensign in the Waves, secretary to an admiral. She cannot attend the wedding because her boss wants her to accompany him on an extended trip. When Buddy goes into the apartment's bathroom, he sees Boo Boo's message addressed to Seymour on the bathroom mirror. In the message, she quotes a Sappho poem about a groom, a line of which provides the title of the story.

Boo Boo first appears in the story "Down at the Dinghy" (1949), where she is the protagonist and mother of Lionel. In this story, she is hauntingly described, "her joke of a name aside, her general unprettiness aside, she was—in terms of permanently memorable, immoderately perceptive, small-area faces—a stunning and final girl" (115). With astute child psychology, she solves her son's emotional crisis. Boo Boo figures in all of the other Glass family stories. In "Zooey," Boo Boo, vacationing in Europe, is invoked several times. She, along with her sister, Franny, would like to dispose of their mother's tattered housecoat, an old kimono, and recommends giving the kimono a ritual stabbing before tossing it. Boo Boo possesses a quirky sense of humor, as shown when describing a look on her mother's face as meaning either Mrs. Glass has just talked with one of her sons on the phone or that everyone's bowels in the world will be flawlessly working for a week. She humorously describes her brother Zooey (quoted by Buddy) as "the blue-eyed Jewish-Irish Mohican scout who died in your arms at the roulette table at Monte Carlo" (51). In "Seymour: An Introduction," she chooses Seymour's John Keats poem, written when he was eight, for inclusion by Buddy in that story. Boo Boo is one of the five addressees of Seymour's letter in "Hapworth 16, 1924." Seymour tells Boo Boo to work on her manners; he also devises a non-offensive prayer specifically for her.

Glass, Buddy   Buddy, the second-eldest son and second child of the Glass family, is the narrator and main character of "Raise High the Roof Beam, Carpenters." At the time of the events that compose the story, Buddy is a 23-year-old private in the army, stationed at Fort Benning, Georgia. (However, in the story's prologue, Buddy is a 36-year-old self-appointed chronicler of his family, who opens the story with a flashback of 20 years before, then settles in to recount the events of 1942.) Through a first-person narrative voice, the reader experiences the events from Buddy's controlling perspective (excepting the extensively quoted sections from Seymour Glass's diary).

Buddy does not appear in a Glass story until "Raise High the Roof Beam, Carpenters." (However, a Webb Glass is mentioned in "Down at the Dinghy," and most critics equate Webb Glass with the Buddy Glass character.) Although Buddy narrates "Zooey," he does not physically appear in the story. Nonetheless, in "Zooey," the reader learns a great deal about Buddy via his first-person author's introduction, in addition to his 14-page letter that Zooey Glass reads in the bathtub. Buddy pens "Seymour: An Introduction," in which he and Seymour are the main characters. In that story, the reader is given an intense experience of the middle-aged Buddy as chronicler of the Glass family stories and, in addition, many anecdotes from Buddy's youth. In "Hapworth 16, 1924," Buddy receives Seymour's 41-year-old letter from his mother and types a copy for publication. In the letter, the five-year-old Buddy is at summer camp with Seymour and is referenced often.

Glass, Franny   Franny is the younger of the two Glass daughters and the seventh and last-born child in the family. Franny appears in the prologue of "Raise High the Roof Beam, Carpenters" as a ten-month-old baby to whom Seymour Glass reads the Taoist tale about the superlative horse. Franny swears she still remembers Seymour reading her the tale. At the time of the events of "Raise High the Roof Beam, Carpenters" (1942), the eight-year-old Franny is living in Los Angeles with her parents and her brother Zooey. She is memorably referred to in Boo Boo Glass's letter to Buddy Glass at the outset when Boo Boo tells her brother that she has recently heard Franny on It's a Wise Child recounting how she would fly around the apartment at night. When the announcer suggested that she must have been dreaming, Franny replied that she knew she flew because she then found dust from the light bulbs on her fingers. (Margaret Ann Salinger, the author's daughter, reveals in her memoir that the source for Franny's experience is her mother's own childhood recollection.) At the time of the wedding, Franny has come down with a case of the measles, which precludes the family from attending.

Franny first appears in the story "Franny" (1955), though without her surname. The reader meets her during a weekend at her boyfriend's college while she undergoes a religious crisis. Franny's crisis is dealt with more extensively in "Zooey" and is resolved at the story's close. In "Seymour: An Introduction," Franny makes several cameo appearances. Most importantly, Franny is described there as, in 1959 (four years after the events of "Zooey"), a "budding young actress" (135). This confirms that the transformation of her character at the close of "Zooey" has indeed taken permanent effect. At the time of "Hapworth 16, 1924," Franny has not yet been born.

Glass, Les   Les Glass is husband to Bessie and father to the seven Glass children. Like Bessie, he is a former vaudeville performer, a singer, and a dancer. During the time of "Raise High the Roof Beam, Carpenters," Les is employed by a motion-picture company in Los Angeles. He lives there with his wife and their two youngest children and is not seen in the story.

Les plays a role—though a decidedly minor one—in all of the other Glass family stories. During "Zooey" he is absent from the apartment. However, his sentimental personality is attested to by Bessie and confirmed by Franny Glass. In "Seymour: An Introduction," Les asks his eldest son, Seymour, the important question of whether Seymour remembers riding on Joe Jackson's bicycle in Australia in 1922. Les is one of the five addressees of Seymour's "Hapworth 16, 1924" letter. A few passages are directly addressed to Les, though Seymour, more than once, excuses Les from reading the entire letter due to its length. In that story, the reader finally learns that Les was born in Australia.

Glass, Seymour   Seymour is the eldest son and first Glass child. Ostensibly the story "Raise High the Roof Beam, Carpenters" recounts Seymour's wedding day in June 1942, though Seymour himself does not physically appear during the events. (That is, excluding the opening vignette of the story, where the 17-year-old Seymour at two in the morning decides to read a Taoist tale to quiet a crying ten-month-old Franny Glass. In that cameo, Buddy Glass scoffs at the idea, and Seymour replies that babies "have ears. They can hear" [4]. Seymour has already gotten up once and fed Franny her bottle.) As Buddy later describes the events of "Raise High the Roof Beam, Carpenters" in "Seymour: An Introduction," "The details [of Seymour's wedding day] were served up with a fullness possibly just short of presenting the reader with a sherbet mold of each and every wedding guest's footprint to take home as a souvenir, but Seymour himself—the main course—didn't actually put in a physical appearance anywhere" (131). Seymour's physical absence informs the action and dialogue of the story. His revealing diary entries, moreover, serve as a stand-in for him, dominate the story's close, and afford the reader an opportunity to assess this remarkably complex character. Addi-

tionally, Buddy and the Matron of Honor relate further information about Seymour and offer diametrically opposing perspectives.

Seymour is in the Air Corps, stationed in California, and has arrived in New York City the night before the wedding. In the past, Seymour has requested Muriel Fedder to forgo a large wedding ceremony and simply go away with him to get married. He meets her at a hotel lobby in the very early morning hours of the day of the wedding and again makes this request. When Seymour fails to show up for the wedding, the reader is led to believe he has jilted Muriel.

Seymour Glass was introduced in the 1948 story "A Perfect Day for Bananafish," where he lies on a beach, meets a very young girl, goes for a swim, tells the girl a parable about bananafish, and later shoots himself on the hotel bed next to his sleeping wife. (A minor reference to Seymour appears in the 1949 story "Down at the Dinghy.") Though Seymour has been dead for more than seven and a half years at the time "Zooey" takes place, he nonetheless plays a notable role in that story in a number of ways, and important information about him is divulged. Significantly, Seymour's parable of the Fat Lady will bring Franny Glass to the understanding of her life's purpose. The story that follows "Zooey"—"Seymour: An Introduction"—is Buddy's most extensive effort to convey the life and identity of his brother. Here, Seymour, the beloved eldest brother, poet, and God-seeker, is portrayed in detail. The final Glass family story, "Hapworth 16, 1924" furnishes the most extended example of Seymour's own words, albeit written at the age of seven.

Glass, Waker   Waker is the fourth-oldest son and fifth-oldest child in the Glass family. He is 12 minutes younger than his twin brother, Walt. During the time (1942) of the events of "Raise High the Roof Beam, Carpenters," Waker is interned in a conscientious objectors' camp in Maryland. Later in life, he becomes a Roman Catholic priest.

Of the seven Glass children, Waker is the least known. He appears in the other Glass family stories but without much attention being paid him. In "Zooey," he is away at a Jesuit conference in Ecuador. His mother sketches his temperament with,

"If you tell Waker it looks like *rain*, his eyes all fill up" (94). In "Seymour: An Introduction," in one of the most important scenes of the story, Waker gives away his ninth-birthday present—a Davega bicycle—to a stranger who asks for it; the memory of this action triggers Buddy Glass's illuminated realization that his brother Seymour is *his* (Buddy's) Davega bicycle. Waker is one of the five addressees of Seymour's "Hapworth 16, 1924" letter; Seymour admonishes him to practice his juggling. In "Seymour: An Introduction" it is revealed that an older Waker canonized W. C. Fields and juggled cigar boxes.

Glass, Walt Walt is the third-oldest son and fourth-oldest child in the Glass family. He is 12 minutes older than his twin brother, Waker. During the time of "Raise High the Roof Beam, Carpenters," Walt is in the army and cannot attend his brother Seymour's wedding as he is stationed in the Pacific or en route there (Buddy Glass is not certain), as a member of a field-artillery unit. He will be killed in Japan in a noncombat accident shortly after the end of World War II.

Walt first appears in the 1948 story "Uncle Wiggily in Connecticut," though without his surname. In that story, Walt is the former boyfriend, with a unique sense of humor, of the protagonist, Eloise Wengler. Walt once called her twisted ankle "Uncle Wiggily." Walt is mentioned in all of the Glass family stories. In "Zooey," he is memorably described as Bessie Glass's "only truly lighthearted son" (90). In "Seymour: An Introduction," Walt receives a poem by Seymour Glass about a boy who catches a fish; he terms Seymour's facial expression of excited discovery as "his Eureka Look" (158). Walt is one of the five addressees of Seymour's "Hapworth 16, 1924" letter; Seymour admonishes him to practice his tap dancing. In "Seymour: An Introduction," the narrative reveals that the mature Walt was a dancer in civilian life.

Glass, Zooey Zooey is the youngest son and sixth-youngest child in the Glass family. During "Raise High the Roof Beam, Carpenters," Zooey is 13 years old, living in Los Angeles with his parents and younger sister, Franny. He and Franny are both appearing on *It's a Wise Child*. Though Zooey is not seen directly in the story, he is mentioned by name in his eldest brother Seymour's diary. At Mrs. Fedder's suggestion, the Fedders and Seymour listen to a broadcast of *It's a Wise Child*. Seymour records in his diary that Zooey was in excellent form when he answered the question about identical houses: Zooey likes them because they allow people to live beyond the confines of their own homes; he further wishes that everyone looked alike and thus the world would be an extended family.

Zooey's most prominent appearance is in "Zooey." Here the reader experiences an extended encounter with his character. In this story, Zooey rescues Franny from her nervous breakdown and puts her on her life's path. (Zooey does not appear in the story "Franny.") In "Seymour: An Introduction," Zooey is referenced only a couple of times. However, Seymour remarks that he, Buddy, and Zooey have been brothers for at least four incarnations. At the time of "Hapworth 16, 1924," Zooey has not yet been born.

Grant Grant is the name of one of the earlier announcers on *It's a Wise Child*. Boo Boo Glass refers to him in her letter to Buddy Glass.

Lavender-haired woman After the woman asks Buddy Glass whether he is a friend of the bride or the groom, she seats him to await the ceremony.

Lieutenant, the The Lieutenant (his name is Bob Burwick, though he is simply referred to by his rank in the story) is married to the Matron of Honor. He is one of the four wedding guests in the car with Buddy Glass and later at Buddy and Seymour Glass's apartment. He is the least developed of the four characters. The Lieutenant outranks Buddy, a fact that defines the relationship between the two men. In a good-natured way, the Lieutenant attempts to tone down some of his wife's more strident assessments of Seymour's character. At one point in the apartment, he is seen earnestly browsing among the bookshelves, an indication that he is an educated man. He asks Buddy about the photographs on the wall, and the question leads to a brief discussion of Seymour's influence in changing the format of *It's a Wise Child*. It is not stated if the Lieutenant has been drafted (like Buddy) or has become a career military man by choice.

Matron of Honor, the   Muriel Fedder's matron of honor for the wedding is married to the Lieutenant. She is one of the four wedding guests in the car with Buddy Glass and later at Buddy and Seymour Glass's apartment. (Her name is Edie Burwick, nickname Bunny, though she is almost always called the Matron of Honor.) She is an overweight, spunky young woman of about 25 who proves to be Buddy's nemesis. During the car ride, she slanders Seymour, saying that she wants to kill him. She pretends to know less about Seymour than she does. Early in the story, while Buddy is still unnamed, the Matron of Honor suspects that he is Seymour's brother, though she feigns otherwise. The Matron of Honor conveys what immediately happened after the aborted wedding, notably Mrs. Fedder's appraisal of Seymour as a schizoid personality and latent homosexual. She raises the consequential childhood incident of Seymour throwing a stone that disfigures Charlotte Mayhew's face. The Matron of Honor needs to phone the Fedders' household; this causes the party of five to abandon the car. She announces to Buddy, to the Lieutenant, to Mrs. Silsburn, and to the elderly deaf-mute that Seymour and Muriel have eloped and provides them with the information that Seymour has promised to see a psychoanalyst.

Mayhew, Charlotte   Charlotte is a childhood friend of Seymour and Buddy Glass's; at the time of the story, she is a famous motion-picture actress. Although she does not appear physically, she does play a prominent role in the story. Charlotte was on *It's a Wise Child*, thanks to Seymour's insistence. Near the end of the story, Buddy is astounded to learn that Muriel as a child looked exactly like Charlotte does in a 1929 *It's a Wise Child* group photograph on the wall of Buddy and Seymour's apartment. Additionally, the childhood incident of Seymour throwing a stone at Charlotte (the stone hits her in the face and causes a barely-perceptible partial paralysis) is used by the Matron of Honor to bolster her condemnation of Seymour's character.

Charlotte is also mentioned in "Seymour: An Introduction" as being smitten with Seymour and Buddy and is called "Charlotte the Harlot, who was a trifle mad" (209).

Muriel Fedder's father's uncle   Better known as the elderly deaf-mute, he is one of the four wedding guests in the car with Buddy Glass and later at Buddy and Seymour Glass's apartment. Mrs. Silsburn identifies him as Muriel Fedder's father's uncle, a deaf-mute. Buddy describes him as "tininess itself . . . without being either a midget or a dwarf" (19). He is formally dressed in a top hat and holds an unlit cigar. His enigmatic presence provides Buddy with a sense of companionship during the ride. Outnumbered by the bride's supporters, Buddy periodically glances at the old man and appreciates his detachment from the conversation. (It is only later that he, along with everyone else, realizes the old man can't hear what is being said.) When the group decides to abandon the car, Buddy prints a note to inform the old man of this plan. As the group walks toward a restaurant, the old man walks with Buddy as they trail the others. Only after the others have left the apartment does Buddy explain to the old man why Seymour threw the stone at Charlotte Mayhew. Buddy muses on sending the old man's cigar end to Seymour as a wedding gift.

Oppenheim   Mentioned in Seymour Glass's diary, Oppenheim is stationed at the B-17 base in California. He is not hopeful that the weather will allow Seymour's plane to take off so that Seymour can fly back East for the wedding.

Policeman   A policeman has halted traffic for the upcoming parade. The Lieutenant orders the car's driver to ask the policeman when the car will be able to recommence its journey. Instead of acquiring the much-sought-after information, the driver seems to be sharing dirty jokes with the cop.

Ranker, Judge   Ranker is the judge who is to marry Muriel Fedder and Seymour Glass. According to Mrs. Silsburn, he has the face of a saint.

Second lieutenant While Buddy Glass searches for a cab to take him to the wedding, he fails to salute a second lieutenant. The officer takes down Buddy's name, serial number, and address, as witnessed by a group of civilians.

Silsburn, Mrs. Helen Mrs. Silsburn is one of the four wedding guests in the car with Buddy Glass and later at Buddy and Seymour Glass's apartment. Buddy initially meets her at the wedding. Mrs. Silsburn is distantly related to Muriel Fedder's mother, which is why she is in attendance. She is a proper, older woman and a widow. When Buddy jumps into the departing car, he ends up sitting next to her. She mistakes him for a child of one of her friends. Mrs. Silsburn later asks Buddy if he is the Buddy Black on *It's a Wise Child*. Since the Glass children had participated on the show under assumed names—at their mother's insistence—the reader infers that Buddy, unlike the other children, retained his pseudonym as his nickname. It is Mrs. Silsburn who supplies the identity of the mysterious elderly deaf-mute as Muriel Fedder's father's uncle. She offers the startling information that the picture of the young Charlotte Mayhew could double for Muriel at that age. Mrs. Silsburn asks Buddy to explain how Charlotte's face was injured by Seymour.

Sims, Dr. Sims is Mrs. Fedder's Jungian analyst who sees her twice a week. Mrs. Fedder tells Sims about Seymour Glass; he agrees with her that Seymour has a schizoid personality. Seymour records in his diary that one evening Sims is a guest at the Fedders' for dinner when Seymour is also invited. No doubt Mrs. Fedder has invited Sims to assess Seymour firsthand. Sims seems to think Seymour has a perfection complex and recommends a healthy acceptance of the imperfections of life.

Sullivan Sullivan is the name of one of the earlier announcers on *It's a Wise Child*. Boo Boo Glass refers to him in her letter to Buddy Glass. According to Boo Boo, Sullivan is worse than an earlier announcer named Grant. The current unnamed announcer is even worse than Sullivan.

Uncle Al He is an uncle of Muriel Fedder. Reportedly, he allows the wedding guests to use the cars after the aborted ceremony.

Vines, L. Manning This fictitious author is the favorite writer of Buddy Glass's company commander. Buddy claims Vines is his favorite writer, too, just to get permission to attend his brother Seymour's wedding.

Vines is also the name of the favorite writer of Eloise Wengler's husband in "Uncle Wiggily in Connecticut." This fact would lead a reader to believe that Lew Wengler had been Buddy's company commander.

FURTHER READING

Alsen, Eberhard. "'Raise High the Roof Beam, Carpenters' and the Amateur Reader." *Studies in Short Fiction* 17 (Winter 1980): 39–47.

———. *A Reader's Guide to J. D. Salinger.* Westport, Conn.: Greenwood Press, 2002.

———. *Salinger's Glass Stories as a Composite Novel.* Troy, N.Y.: Whitston Publishing Company, 1983.

Baskett, Sam S. "The Splendid/Squalid World of J. D. Salinger." *Wisconsin Studies in Contemporary Literature* 4, no. 1 (Winter 1963): 48–61.

Cotter, James Finn. "Religious Symbols in Salinger's Shorter Fiction." *Studies in Short Fiction* 15 (Spring 1978): 121–132.

French, Warren. *J. D. Salinger.* New York: Twayne Publishers, 1963.

Hassan, Ihab. "Almost the Voice of Silence: The Later Novelettes of J. D. Salinger." *Wisconsin Studies in Contemporary Literature* 4, no. 1 (Winter 1963): 5–20.

Hyman, Stanley Edgar. "J. D. Salinger's House of Glass." In *Standards: A Chronicle of Books of Our Time,* 123–127. New York: Horizon Press, 1966.

Kazin, Alfred. *Bright Book of Life: American Novelists and Storytellers from Hemingway to Mailer.* Boston: Little, Brown and Company, 1973.

Kurian, Elizabeth N. *A Religious Response to the Existential Dilemma in the Fiction of J. D. Salinger.* New Delhi: Intellectual Publishing House, 1992.

Lunquist, James. *J. D. Salinger.* New York: Ungar, 1979.

Maynard, Joyce. *At Home in the World: A Memoir.* New York: Picador, 1998.

Mizener, Arthur. "The American Hero as Poet: Seymour Glass." In *The Sense of Life in the Modern Novel*, 227–246. Boston: Houghton Mifflin, 1964.

O'Connor, Dennis L. "J. D. Salinger's Religious Pluralism: The Example of 'Raise High the Roof Beam, Carpenters.'" *The Southern Review* 20, no. 2 (Spring 1984): 316–332.

Prescott, Orville. "Books of The Times." *New York Times*, 28 January 1963, p. 9.

Purcell, William F. "Waker Glass: Salinger's Carthusian Doppelganger." *Literature and Belief* 20 (2000): 153–168.

Ranchan, Som P. *An Adventure in Vedanta: J. D. Salinger's The Glass Family.* Delhi: Ajanta Publications, 1989.

Salinger, Margaret A. *Dream Catcher: A Memoir.* New York: Washington Square Press, 2000.

Updike, John. "Anxious Days for the Glass Family." *New York Times Book Review,* 17 September 1961, pp. 1, 52.

Wenke, John. *J. D. Salinger: A Study of the Short Fiction.* Boston: Twayne Publishers, 1991.

Raise High the Roof Beam, Carpenters and Seymour: An Introduction

Raise High the Roof Beam, Carpenters and Seymour: An Introduction, published on January 28, 1963, by LITTLE, BROWN AND COMPANY, is Salinger's fourth and final book published during his lifetime. The volume is not a novel but reprints two NEW YORKER stories: "RAISE HIGH THE ROOF BEAM, CARPENTERS," originally published in the November 19, 1955, issue, and "SEYMOUR: AN INTRODUCTION," originally published in the June 6, 1959, issue. Both stories, as Salinger explains on the dust jacket, are about Seymour Glass, "the main character in [his] still-uncompleted series about the Glass family." "Raise High the Roof Beam, Carpenters" concerns Seymour's wedding day, while "Seymour: An Introduction" is Buddy Glass's meditation on his brother as a God-knower and quintessential poet, in which he recalls incidents from their childhood.

INTRODUCTION

Raise High the Roof Beam, Carpenters and Seymour: An Introduction is Salinger's second Glass family book (*FRANNY AND ZOOEY*, published in 1961, is the first). The volume is dedicated to Salinger's second wife, CLAIRE SALINGER, his two children from the marriage, MARGARET ANN SALINGER and MATTHEW SALINGER, and any "amateur reader still left in the world—or anybody who just reads and runs." (The dedication page was inadvertently omitted in production and had to be tipped in.)

Raise High the Roof Beam, Carpenters and Seymour: An Introduction, at the time of its release, received about 25 reviews, the majority of which were critical. Ihab Hassan remained Salinger's staunchest supporter: "The new Salinger book is a confounding and holy joy . . . . The comic battle Salinger wages against language is also the tragic battle man fights with eternity. No one in recent fiction has accepted more difficult terms for that battle than Salinger. It is to our honor that he persists in it with love and grace" (Hassan 38). A number of reviewers, such as Frank Kermode and Orville Prescott, praised the story "Raise High the Roof Beam, Carpenters" while lambasting "Seymour: An Introduction." But Salinger's critical reputation, already damaged by influential negative reviews of *Franny and Zooey* by Joan Didion, Leslie Fiedler, Alfred Kazin, Mary McCarthy, and John Updike, was now further assaulted by strong attacks from Irving Howe and Norman Mailer. Though Howe acknowledges Salinger's manifold gifts as a writer, he calls Salinger a "priest of an underground cult" (Howe 4) and finds the book "hopelessly prolix . . . marred by self-indulgence . . . [the stories] betray a loss of creative discipline, a surrender to cherished mannerisms" (Howe 34). Norman Mailer terms the story "Seymour: An Introduction" "the most slovenly portion of prose ever put out by an important American writer" (Mailer 68). Mailer concludes, "It is time Salinger came back to the city and got his hands dirty with a rough corruption or two, because the very items which composed the honor of his reputation, his resolute avoidance of the mass media and society, have now begun to back up on him. There is a taste of something self-absorptive, narcissistic, even putrefactive in his long contemplation of a lintless navel" (Mailer 68).

Despite the dismissal of the book by a majority of critics, the public remained constant in its affections. *Raise High the Roof Beam, Carpenters and Seymour: An Introduction* was at the top of the *New York Times* best-seller list for 10 weeks and became the third best-selling work of fiction in *Publishers Weekly* in 1963.

SYNOPSIS

For a synopsis of *Raise High the Roof Beam, Carpenters and Seymour: An Introduction, see* "Raise High the Roof Beam, Carpenters" and "Seymour: An Introduction."

CRITICAL ANALYSIS

For a critical analysis of *Raise High the Roof Beam, Carpenters and Seymour: An Introduction, see* "Raise High the Roof Beam, Carpenters" and "Seymour: An Introduction."

PUBLICATION HISTORY

Raise High the Roof Beam, Carpenters and Seymour: An Introduction was published on January 28, 1963, by Little, Brown and Company. The first printing was a hardback edition of an unspecified run (undoubtedly a substantially large one given Salinger's popularity at the time), priced at $4. The book's dust jacket, front and back (without illustration or blurbs), conveyed the title and author's name in black calligraphic font against a white background. Salinger wrote the dust-jacket comments that easily fit on the two flaps.

In 1965, the first paperback "pocketbook" edition of *Raise High the Roof Beam, Carpenters and Seymour: An Introduction* was published by Bantam Books. In May 1991, Little, Brown and Company took over from Bantam Books the mass-market paperback edition and released it in the austere matching set of Salinger's four books, each bound in white covers with the author's name and the title in black. In January 2001, Little, Brown and Company published the first trade paperback edition, reproducing the front and rear covers of the original dust jacket. The mass-market paperback edition would eventually adopt the same look.

Raise High the Roof Beam, Carpenters and Seymour: An Introduction, Salinger's fourth book, has never gone out of print and is available in three editions from Little, Brown and Company: an exact reproduction of the hardback first edition from 1963, which includes the dust-jacket comments written by Salinger; a trade paperback that mimics the production of the hardback, though Salinger's dust-jacket comments are not retained; and a mass-market paperback, also lacking Salinger's dust-jacket comments, with its pagination differing from the above editions.

CHARACTERS

For the characters in *Raise High the Roof Beam, Carpenters and Seymour: An Introduction, see* "Raise High the Roof Beam, Carpenters" and "Seymour: An Introduction."

FURTHER READING

Bruccoli, Matthew. "States of Salinger Book." *American Notes & Queries* 2 (October 1963): 21–22.

Fry, John R. "Skill Is the Word." *Christian Century*, 6 February 1963, 175–176.

"The Glass House Gang." *Time*, 8 February 1963, 86.

Gold, Arthur R. "J. D. Salinger: Through a Glass Darkly." *New York Herald Tribune Books*, 7 April 1963, p. 8.

Hassan, Ihab. "The Casino of Silence." *Saturday Review*, 26 January 1963, 38.

Howe, Irving. "More Reflections in the Glass Mirror." *New York Times Book Review*, 7 April 1963, pp. 4–5, 34.

"In Place of the New, A Reissue of the Old." *Newsweek*, 28 January 1963, 90, 92.

Kermode, Frank. "The Glass Menagerie." *New Statesman*, 15 March 1963, 388.

Mailer, Norman. "Some Children of the Goddess." *Esquire*, July 1963, 64–69, 105.

Prescott, Orville. "Books of The Times." *New York Times*, 28 January 1963, p. 9.

"Saint or Slob?" *Times Literary Supplement*, 8 March 1963, p. 165.

Sheed, Wilfred. "Raise High the Roof Beam, Carpenters and Seymour: An Introduction." *Jubilee* 10 (April 1963): 51, 53–54.

Wain, John. "Go Home, Buddy Glass." *New Republic*, 16 February 1963, 21–22.

For further reading on *Raise High the Roof Beam, Carpenters and Seymour: An Introduction*, see "Raise High the Roof Beam, Carpenters" and "Seymour: An Introduction" under the "Further Reading" sections.

"Requiem for the Phantom of the Opera"

"Requiem for the Phantom of the Opera" is one of Salinger's "lost" stories, neither published nor to be found in a library archive. According to the premier Salinger Web site, www.deadcaulfields.com, Salinger mentions a story with this title in a 1951 letter to Gus Lobrano. Unless the manuscript can be located among Salinger's literary estate, the story's whereabouts are unknown.

"Rex Passard on the Planet Mars"

"Rex Passard on the Planet Mars" is one of Salinger's "lost" stories, neither published nor to be found in a library archive. According to the bibliographer Jack R. Sublette, Salinger mentions a story with this title in a 1943 letter to Whit Burnett. Unless the manuscript can be located among Salinger's literary estate, the story's whereabouts are unknown.

"Salute to Whit Burnett 1899–1972, A"

This 570-word homage to Whit Burnett, Salinger's writing teacher at Columbia University as well as publisher of his first story ("The Young Folks" in the March–April 1940 issue of Story), was writ-

ten in 1964. The important nonfiction piece eventually appeared as an epilogue to *Fiction Writer's Handbook*, by Hallie and Whit Burnett, published in 1975.

In the tribute, Salinger recalls his experience of taking Burnett's class at Columbia University in 1939. Salinger terms it "a good and instructive and profitable year" (Burnett 1975, 187). He praises Burnett for having had "a passion for good short fiction, strong short fiction," without "particular pets" or "fashionable prejudices" (Burnett 1975, 187). The second half of the homage is devoted to Salinger's remembrance of Burnett reading aloud to the class William Faulkner's 1931 story, "That Evening Sun Go Down." Salinger explains that Burnett chose not to make the reading a performance but instead "turned himself into a reading lamp, and his voice into paper and print" (Burnett 1975, 188). Burnett caused no intrusion between Faulkner "and his beloved silent reader" so that the listener experienced the story "without any middlemen between" (Burnett 1975, 188). Salinger's emphasis on noninterference in this tribute seems to parallel the point of the conclusion to "Raise High the Roof Beam, Carpenters" when a blank piece of paper is offered "by way of explanation" (107). In other words, the story itself tells readers all they need to know. The autobiographical essay is one of the rare times that Salinger's readers can connect published, nonfiction proof of the author's academic and aesthetic thinking with their interpretations of it in his fiction.

Salinger mentions that he never met Faulkner but had thought of writing him a letter telling him about Burnett's memorable reading. The piece ends with "Salutes to Whit Burnett, Hallie Burnett, and to all *Story* readers and contributors" (Burnett 1975, 188). Burnett's reading of the Faulkner story truly impressed Salinger. In a March 1, 1940, letter to Burnett, he told his teacher how much it had affected him. Then, nearly 25 years later, in the 1964 homage, Salinger again recalls the same reading.

The work was originally composed at the request of Whit Burnett to serve as a foreword to the 1965 celebratory volume for *Story* magazine, *Story Jubilee: 33 Years of Story*. Burnett, however, embarrassed by the fact that the text focused on himself rather than on the magazine, decided not to use Salinger's foreword (as he later informed the author in an April 17, 1965, letter that accompanied a gift copy of the book). Hallie Burnett found the unused preface in the *Story* archives at Princeton University's FIRESTONE LIBRARY and subsequently published the piece in 1975 without Salinger's knowledge or consent. Given that the piece was written for a volume published in 1965, and that the title includes Burnett's death year (1972: albeit that is an error; Burnett died in 1973), one must conclude that the title as it now stands is the creation of someone other than Salinger.

This "fugitive" Salinger work was unknown in Salinger scholarship until Craig Stoltz published his essay, "J. D. Salinger's Tribute to Whit Burnett," in the Winter 1981 issue of the academic journal *Twentieth Century Literature*. The existence of the homage was made more widely known when the piece was notated in Jack R. Sublette's definitive Salinger bibliography in 1984. Sublette reveals that the piece, referred to as "foreword," contains an introductory paragraph not included by Hallie Burnett. *Fiction Writer's Handbook* is still in print in a paperback edition; Salinger's name is prominently featured on the cover.

"Scratchy Needle on a Phonograph Record"

"Scratchy Needle on a Phonograph Record" was retitled by the editors at COSMOPOLITAN and published as "Blue Melody." *See* "BLUE MELODY."

"Seymour: An Introduction"

"Seymour: An Introduction" is the longest and most important story about Seymour Glass, the central character of the Glass family. Salinger's experimental technique allows the reader to witness Buddy Glass writing the novella-length work. In doing so, Buddy becomes as much a protagonist of the story as Seymour. Originally published in

the June 6, 1959, issue of the NEW YORKER, "Seymour: An Introduction" was later paired with the November 19, 1955, *New Yorker* story "RAISE HIGH THE ROOF BEAM, CARPENTERS," to form Salinger's fourth and final book published during his lifetime, the 1963 volume, RAISE HIGH THE ROOF BEAM, CARPENTERS AND SEYMOUR: AN INTRODUCTION. "Seymour: An Introduction" is Salinger's 34th published story.

SYNOPSIS

Two unattributed quotations preface the story. The first deals with an author's realization that what he has written about his characters is false. This falsity derives from an author's "steadfast love . . . but varying ability" (111). The varying ability fails to fully and correctly portray the characters. The author's love for his characters wants him not to write. The second quotation concerns an author's making a mistake in his writing, "a clerical error" (111). Yet the error perhaps wasn't a mistake but "an essential part of the whole exposition" (111). Nonetheless, the error rises up against the author as a witness to his failure as a writer.

The story opens with its author, Buddy Glass, remarking that "the general reader" is his "last deeply contemporary confidant" (112). Buddy directly addresses the reader, saying he knows *his* general reader loves birds, because, as he quotes from a short story by John Buchan—"Skule Skerry"—they seem "of all created beings the nearest to pure spirit" (112). Buddy also quotes another Buchan sentence about the remarkable curlew sandpiper, whose nest has been seen by only three people. Though Buddy acknowledges he cannot expect his reader to have seen the nest, he nonetheless presents him with a "bouquet of very early blooming parentheses" (114) before they (Buddy and the reader) join "the grounded" (113) who aren't interested in birds (i.e., spiritual matters). Buddy tells the reader that he is "ecstatically happy" (114) and realizes that a writer in this condition is difficult to read. Such a writer cannot indulge in short paragraphs, be detached from the story, or be concerned about the plot. He is prone to digressions (hence the gift of parentheses at the outset). Buddy acknowledges this is not the usual method of writing a story and suggests to readers who want or need a normal story that they should quit reading now.

Buddy then identifies the authors of the two quotations prefacing "Seymour: An Introduction." The first quote is by FRANZ KAFKA, the second is by Søren Kierkegaard. Buddy acknowledges they are writers he loves and that the two quotations are representative of the four men he seeks counsel from when he needs "perfectly credible information about modern artistic processes" (118). (The other two men are Vincent van Gogh and the as-yet-unnamed Seymour.) Buddy admits the two quotations reflect his relationship with the particulars of the story-to-come, and he also hopes they will serve notice to literary critics being trained in "neo-Freudian Arts and Letters clinics" (118). He mentions the rumors about the nature of the true artist. The oldest, and the one that pleases him the most, is that the artist dismisses his critics as not worth considering. A newer rumor is that the artist is a neurotic, but one that does not want to become well. Buddy calls the true artist "a Sick Man" (120) who "gives out terrible cries of pain" (120), as if seeking help to become well. Yet, when confronted with his condition, the artist decides to abide with it, for he realizes everyone dies, but the reason for his (the true artist's) death is special. Buddy admits he had such a person in his family, though he does not name him. His relative emitted "not only cries of pain but cries for help" (121). Buddy believes, however, that scholars, biographers, and intellectuals who base insights on psychological reasoning do not know how to listen to the cries, for "they're a peerage of tin ears" (121). They mistakenly think the source of the problem can be located in childhood or in the libido. Buddy postulates that the "true poet or painter [is] a seer" (122) (and denies this attribute to the scientist or the psychiatrist). Buddy then asks which part of a seer's body would be most affected, and answers, the eyes. Though the death of such a person might be attributed to consumption, loneliness, or suicide, the "true artist-seer, the heavenly fool who can and does produce beauty, is mainly dazzled to death by his own scruples, the blinding shapes and colors of his own sacred human conscience" (123). Buddy believes

the truth of what follows is predicated on his "being at least *nearly* right" (123).

Buddy goes on to explain his subtitle, "An Introduction." He states that his brother "Seymour Glass" (123) is the central character of the story (and now, for the first time in the story, names him). In "one obituary-like sentence" (123), Buddy records that Seymour, 31 years old, committed suicide in 1948 while on vacation in Florida with his wife. To counterbalance that sentence, Buddy then writes that while Seymour lived, "he was all *real* things to [his brothers and sisters]: our blue-striped unicorn, our double-lensed burning glass, our consultant genius, our portable conscience, our supercargo, and our one full poet" (123–124). Though Seymour became known, via a kids' radio quiz program, as the family's "notorious 'mystic' and 'unbalanced type,'" Buddy emphatically states that "with or without a suicide plot in his head," Seymour was "a ringding enlightened man, a God-knower" (124). The vastness of Seymour's character precludes Buddy from encapsulating him in either one story or a series of stories. Buddy decides that he himself is "a thesaurus of undetached *prefatory* [emphasis added] remarks" (125) (hence the story is termed an introduction) about his brother. He is not a short-story writer in this case. Buddy realizes that so far he has painted a saint's picture of Seymour and hastens to admit that his brother had faults, most noticeably that he often behaved like a fool, in addition to the fact that he could, at times, be a nonstop talker. Seymour was the champion talker of the family, though Buddy knows Seymour wanted the others to best him. But the title remained Seymour's until the suicide. Buddy admits he will not be able to write about the suicide "for another few years" (129).

Buddy then talks about his own earlier writings. He has published one novel (he omits the title), whose protagonist was most assuredly not influenced by Seymour. He has, however, published two stories about Seymour, the more recent about his wedding ("Raise High the Roof Beam, Carpenters"); the earlier about his suicide ("A PERFECT DAY FOR BANANAFISH"). (Buddy does not mention these titles either.) Buddy admits some members of his family have told him that the "Seymour" in the suicide story reminded them of Buddy, rather than resembling the real Seymour. As an excuse, Buddy explains that he wrote the story on a German typewriter, shortly after the suicide.

In a long section of narrative, Buddy focuses on Seymour as poet and includes a description of his poetry. Buddy surmises that this topic must be something his reader is yearning to know because, after birds, poets are next in the reader's affections. Buddy has been holding on to a notebook that is filled with 184 poems Seymour wrote during the last three years of his life. Buddy is willing to see about 150 of them published. His four living siblings—Boo Boo, Waker, Zooey, and Franny—have been pressuring him to find a publisher for the poems. He remarks that Boo Boo is now 38, married, and living in Westchester County; Waker is 36, a former Carthusian monk-reporter, now at a parish; Zooey is 29, an actor; and Franny is 25, "a budding young actress" (135). The other reason Buddy would like to have the poems published is that he feels "extensively burned" (137) by his overexposure to them.

Buddy explains that Seymour loved Chinese and Japanese poetry most of all, and even provides a footnote on good translators, recommending Witter Bynner, Lionel Giles, and R. H. Blyth. He launches into a discussion of the essence of Chinese and Japanese poetry, saying he believes this poetry to be written by poets who know "a good persimmon or a good crab or a good mosquito bite on a good arm" (138), as opposed to emphasizing intellectual concerns in their work. Buddy relates an anecdote about Seymour that he feels demonstrates that his brother possessed the requisite ability to be a poet. In 1925, when their parents, Les and Bessie Glass, retired from vaudeville, they threw a party for 60 people. Seymour and Buddy were already in bed when the guests arrived, but later they were allowed to come down and mingle with the partygoers. As the guests were leaving, Seymour asked his parents if he could bring each of the guests his or her coat and hat. Although Seymour had not seen the guests arrive, he accomplished this task almost perfectly (Buddy notes that his brother had some problems with the women's hats).

Seymour discovered Eastern poetry when he was 11 years old. He was fishing for new authors in the library and came across some translated Chinese poems by P'ang. Regarding the perils of "fishing," Buddy paraphrases a poem written by Seymour, given to his younger brother, Walt, as a birthday gift. The poem describes a boy fishing, who, as he reels in the fish, feels a pain in his own lip. When the boy gets home, he discovers the fish in the bathtub, wearing the boy's own school cap.

Buddy phones his sister Boo Boo in Tuckahoe, New York, to ask if there is a poem written by Seymour during his childhood that she would like Buddy to include in the story. She chooses "John Keats/John Keats/John/Please put your scarf on" (144), written when Seymour was eight.

At the age of 22, Seymour had gathered together a group of poems that Buddy urged him to publish. Seymour thought not, because the poems seemed "too un-Western, too lotusy . . . the poems read as though they'd been written by an ingrate" (145). Whenever Seymour finished a poem, he thought of Miss Overman, the librarian of the first branch library he frequented as a child. Seymour worried that he needed to find a form of poetry that would be acceptable to Miss Overman, but that he also would like. Seymour loved classical haiku more than any other poetry and created for himself a double-haiku form: a six-line verse with a total of 34 syllables. Buddy attempts to explain to the reader that the poems are like nothing else but Seymour. Buddy realizes that the best way to illustrate this quality would be to quote several poems, but he will not be allowed to do this, as Seymour's widow has refused her consent. Buddy writes about the "acoustics" of Seymour's poems: ". . . unsonorous . . . quiet . . . [but with] intermittent short blasts of euphony" (148–149). Buddy terms most of the poems "high-hearted" but "wouldn't unreservedly recommend the last thirty or thirty-five poems to any living soul who hasn't died twice in his lifetime, preferably slowly" (149).

The final two poems of Seymour's collection are Buddy's favorites. The next-to-last poem concerns a young married woman engaged in an adulterous affair. She returns from a tryst to discover a green balloon on her bedspread. The last poem depicts a young widower, wearing pajamas and a robe, as he sits on his lawn looking at the moon. A cat, "a former kingpin of his household" (150), bites the widower's left hand.

Buddy tells the reader of his ability to differentiate actual experience from feigned experience in an author's writings—he claims he use to read 200,000 to 400,000 words a *day*—and he could not help but wonder if Seymour had not buried a wife, if not now, then in a past reincarnation. Buddy thinks that the more personal Seymour's poems read, the more they stray from representing his current life, instead recalling past "memorable existences in exurban Benares, feudal Japan, and metropolitan Atlantis" (155). Buddy then paraphrases the poem Seymour wrote, in Japanese, on a desk blotter the day of his suicide. The poem is about a little girl on a plane turning her doll's head around to look at Seymour. Seymour, the week before, had been on a plane. Boo Boo once suggested to Buddy that such an incident had actually occurred; Buddy does not concur with his sister. Buddy believes that writing the "Introduction" may be his last chance to advocate for Seymour's poetry; he suspects that the poems, upon publication, will not be acknowledged for their true worth. He believes, however, that, over time, Seymour will be recognized as one of the "three or four *very* nearly non-expendable poets" (157) in the history of American literature.

Eventually, Buddy believes, people will seek him out to ask about Seymour's poems. Buddy once had a young man seek him out concerning a piece Buddy had written several years ago that was influenced by Sherwood Anderson's style. It is Buddy's opinion that many readers are wrongly attracted to the work of a writer because of something in the writer's lifestyle. He thinks "our gusto for the lurid or the partly lurid (which, of course, includes both low and superior gossip) is probably the last of our fleshly appetites to be sated or effectively curbed" (163). Buddy believes there to be an undeniably human interest in creative people with flaws in their personalities. He then paraphrases one of Seymour's poems to illustrate this proclivity. Buddy accuses Percy Shelley of living too glamorous a life and not investing enough effort in his poetry. He contrasts Robert Burns to Shelley,

though acknowledging Burns had his own excesses. He then wonders whether perhaps Shelley was not insane *enough*. Buddy believes that he has the most intimate and extensive knowledge of Seymour, and he wholeheartedly, enthusiastically welcomes people's interest.

In the next section, Buddy narrates the vaudeville heritage of the Glass family. Les and Bessie were a song-and-dance team on the Pantages and Orpheum circuits in America, and they reached almost top billing in Australia, where Buddy and Seymour spent nearly two years while very young. Bessie decided when it was time for her and Les to retire; she foresaw the end of the two-shows-a-day era. She therefore asked an influential admirer to get Les a job in radio administration. All seven of the children inherited some theatrical ability. Buddy relates that Zooey and Franny are now professional actors. Boo Boo "at all supremely joyful moments" will "dance for her life" (170). Walt was a professional dancer until his early death. Waker, as a boy, adored W. C. Fields, in whose honor he would juggle cigar boxes. It is rumored that Waker, a Roman Catholic priest, tosses the wafer over his shoulder into the mouths of his parishioners. Buddy dances a bit, too, and feels his Great-Grandfather Zozo watches over him. Buddy observes that Seymour indulged in "highly literate vaudeville" (172) in that he did not drop an autobiographical reference in his poems.

Buddy next relates an incident from the past, when he and Seymour had just rented their own apartment. Their father, Les Glass, visits them. He asks Seymour if he remembers being ridden around the stage in 1922 in Australia on the handlebars of Joe Jackson's shining trick bicycle. Seymour says, "he wasn't sure he had ever got off Joe Jackson's beautiful bicycle" (173).

Buddy then tells the reader that he has not been able to work on the story because he has been sick for the past 10 weeks. He tries to restart but cannot because Seymour had "*grown too much while I was away*" (176). Seymour is "the one person who was always much, much too large to fit on ordinary typewriter paper—any typewriter paper of mine, anyway" (176). About to despair, Buddy rereads an old letter from Seymour and realizes that he will be able to continue writing about him after all. Buddy relates Seymour's custom of responding with short notes about Buddy's new stories after hearing them read aloud to him by the author. Buddy has saved these notes and reproduces seven in the text.

Buddy then reproduces, in full, Seymour's lengthiest response and explains that it references some writing Buddy had been working on in 1940. The letter-memo consists of six pages, with the salutation reading, "Dear Old Tyger That Sleeps" (182). Seymour begins by noting that he is looking at Buddy's manuscript pages as Buddy snores in the same room (in the Glass family's Upper East Side MANHATTAN apartment). Seymour tells Buddy that he recently wrote a letter to his English department chairman, and that the letter sounded like Buddy. This pleased Seymour, although he knows that Buddy took offense when one of the other children thought something Buddy said sounded like Seymour. Seymour believes Buddy's attitude is wrong because "the membrane is so thin between us" (183). Seymour explains that, during deep meditation two years ago, he realized Buddy, Zooey, and himself have been brothers for four incarnations. Seymour tells Buddy he is trying to gather his thoughts about the story, but he says that the story makes huge jumps. Seymour dreams of Buddy jumping beyond his (Seymour's) vision. Seymour then asks Buddy not to keep him up out of pride but to "Keep me up till five only because all your stars are out, and for no other reason" (185). Seymour thinks any other literary advice besides this is like Flaubert's literary friends urging him to write Madame Bovary. Seymour acknowledges that Flaubert wrote a masterpiece, but after reading the author's letters, he judges that Flaubert never wrote the books he should have, that the Frenchman never wrote "his heart out" (185). Seymour tells Buddy to follow his heart in regard to his writing. He reminds his brother about the time when they registered for the draft. Seymour smiled when he saw that Buddy wrote down on the form that his profession was "writer." He now tells Buddy that writing has always been Buddy's religion. Seymour believes that the real questions a writer will be asked when he dies are: "Were most of your stars out? Were you busy writing your heart out?" (187).

He tells Buddy to remember that he was first a reader, then a writer. The way to answer the two questions is to keep that fact in mind and then ask yourself what you would want to read more than anything else. "You just sit down shamelessly and write the thing yourself" (187). That is what Seymour would most want to read.

Buddy promises the reader that tomorrow night he will start on that piece of writing. He wants the piece to provide a reply to the question, "What did your brother Look Like?" (188).

Buddy's first sentence the next night is "His [Seymour's] hair jumping in the barbershop" (189). Buddy explains that when he and Seymour would go for haircuts, they would sit side by side while the barbers cut their hair. By the end of the haircuts, Buddy would have more of Seymour's hair covering him than his own. Buddy once asked whether Seymour could not keep his hair from jumping on him. The situation worried Seymour, who tried to find a way to stop his hair from bothering his brother. Buddy pauses to comment that he has done enough for one night's work, but he wonders what he might want from the description he is planning to write. He acknowledges wanting to publish it—"I always want to publish" (191)—but what concerns him is how he would prefer the piece to get to the magazine. Instead of using the usual envelope and stamps, Buddy would like the piece of writing to travel by train. He wants the writing—and Seymour—to emerge from this "a trifle high" (191).

The next night Buddy returns to the subject of hair and describes Seymour as having had "very wiry black hair" (192) until it started to fall out at age 19. The younger children were "fascinated by his wrists and hands" (192). Franny, age four, once complimented Seymour on his nice yellow teeth; Seymour loved this. Seymour enjoyed the ragging from the other children, whereas Buddy did not. Buddy acknowledges the special position Seymour held in the family and comments that he, Buddy, was not bothered by the fact. He knows Seymour did not hide any of his faults. Buddy says the reader should not jump to any conclusions about Seymour's suicide being a selfish act (in relation to the family). Buddy will not be able to write about that question now, because in order to explain the situation, he would "have to touch on . . . the details of [Seymour's] suicide" and Buddy does not "expect to be ready to do that . . . for several more years" (196).

Buddy informs the reader that Seymour will not appear in these pages as a very young child, but he wishes the reader would hint at which Seymour to describe. Buddy admits to having perfect recall, yet keeps picturing a cubist portrait of Seymour at the ages of eight, 18, and 28.

Not knowing where to begin again, Buddy remembers that his mother, Bessie, thought of Seymour as very tall; in fact, he was five feet, ten and one-half inches. Seymour was against excessive height; he lamented when the twins, Walt and Waker, grew to over six feet. Zooey is short, and Buddy thinks Seymour would approve, since Seymour believed in short actors. Mentioning that Seymour would be "all smiles" (200) about Zooey's height, Buddy then talks about Seymour's smile. He terms it a very good smile, given that Seymour had poor teeth. Buddy acknowledges, though, that Seymour's smile did not appear or disappear as one would expect. "His smile often went backward or forward when all the other facial traffic in the room was either not moving at all or moving in the opposite direction. His distributor wasn't standard, even in the family" (201). Buddy believes Seymour to have had "the last absolutely unguarded adult face in the Greater New York Area" (202).

Buddy next writes about Seymour's ears. He recalls when his sister Boo Boo, at about age 11, put the rings from a notebook on Seymour's ears, which made him look like a pirate. Buddy, however, would describe Seymour's ears as those of a cabalist or a Buddha. Buddy tells the reader this is enough for one night and says he will probably do the eyes and maybe the nose, but that is it. He wants to leave something to the reader's imagination.

When Buddy returns the following night to his narrative, he describes Seymour's eyes as being the same color as his own, Les's, and Boo Boo's: "Plaintive Jewish Brown" (204). The best pairs of eyes in the family, in Buddy's opinion, would be Seymour's and Zooey's. In a short story Buddy had earlier published about a young boy on a transatlantic ship, he described the boy's eyes. (Buddy then quotes the description, which is taken from Salinger's 1953 story, "TEDDY.") Buddy explains that this was not an accurate description of Seymour's eyes, though a couple of family members suggested that Buddy had intended to transplant Seymour's eyes to the boy. Buddy attempts to describe the unusual aspect of Seymour's eyes: "There was something like a here-again, gone-again, super-gossamer cast over his eyes—except that it wasn't a cast at all. . . ." (206). This fugitive quality created a problem in trying to describe such an exceptional pair of eyes, Buddy believes, noting that Schopenhauer once faced a similar problem.

Buddy decides to do the nose and writes that the one surefire way to tell that he and Seymour were brothers was by their noses and chins. They didn't have any chins to speak of; each had "great, fleshy, drooping, trompe-like [noses]" (206), much like Great-Grandfather Zozo's. The only appreciable difference between Buddy's and Seymour's noses was that Seymour's had a slight bend due to being hit by a baseball bat. Buddy exalts that the nose is done and announces that he is going to bed.

Buddy confesses that he is afraid to reread his description. He realizes his description would lead the reader to think Buddy and Seymour were homely children, which was true, though their appearances improved with age. However, as kids, they stood out due to their bad looks, which were noticed by adults and children alike. Only their friend Charlotte Mayhew found their looks desirable. Buddy knows that he has not conveyed the "life" (211) of Seymour's face. He firmly believes that Seymour's qualities "cannot be got at with understatement" (212). Buddy tells the reader that he has written and destroyed at least a dozen stories about Seymour because they failed to render his remarkable nature, even though some of the stories were artistic successes.

Seymour's hands were extraordinarily fine and long, even longer than their mother Bessie's. He had broad palms with a developed muscle between the thumb and forefinger. Buddy describes this muscle as "strong" and then upbraids himself for putting the word in quotes. He wonders whether his use of quotation marks would signal a hint of homosexuality on his part and fears that his love of Seymour might be incorrectly construed as a homosexual one by the reader. Buddy then claims for himself an active heterosexual life in his college days, but he concludes that all good prose writers are androgynous.

Seymour's skin was dark and without pimples, even though he ate the same fast food as Buddy. And Seymour didn't bathe enough; he was more concerned that the other kids got their baths. On the days he went for a haircut, Seymour would often worry that his neck might be too dirty, and he would ask Buddy to check.

As children, Buddy and Seymour were well dressed. Their brother Walt thinks their mother asked an Irish traffic cop for a recommendation on where to buy boys' clothing, and that he had recommended De Pinna's. Once Buddy reached his teen years, though, he dropped the sedate look and became a snappy dresser. Although Seymour showed some interest in his clothes, they never fit him properly. "Once an article of clothing was actually on his body, he lost all earthly consciousness of it" (219).

Buddy, in the next day's narrative, turns to the question of sports. He is enamored of them, but says, "I'm forty and I think it's high time all the elderly boy writers were asked to move along from the ballparks and the bull rings" (225). Buddy has been hesitant to discuss sports because he remembers an incident from childhood when he laughed (to Seymour's consternation) at Curtis Caulfield for the way Curtis threw a ball. Seymour loved sports as a boy and teenager. Franny recalls watching Seymour play table tennis when she was very little; Seymour would enthusiastically bang away, inadvertently causing his opponent, most likely Buddy, to chase after the errant balls.

At cards, Seymour would throw the game if he were playing against the younger children; when playing against adults, he would telegraph a good hand "like an Easter Bunny with a whole basketful of eggs" (228). Seymour was poor at most outdoor sports, but he excelled at stoopball and marbles, using his own method of "Formlessness" (231). In stoopball, he would score a home run nearly every time. Whenever someone else tried to emulate Seymour's method of throwing, it would backfire.

In curb marbles, Seymour would use an unusual flick of the wrist with great success. In describing Seymour's unorthodox method of marble aiming, Buddy recalls an incident from their youth. While playing with a boy named Ira one dusky evening in 1927, Buddy was trying to use Seymour's wrist method but kept losing. Seymour, from across the street, told Buddy not to aim so much. Seymour said that if Buddy aimed and succeeded, that would be just luck. Buddy questioned how it could be luck if he aimed. Seymour explained it this way: "You'll be *glad* if you hit his marble . . . won't you? And if you're *glad* . . . then you sort of secretly didn't expect too much to do it. So, there'd have to be some luck in it . . . quite a lot of *accident* in it" (236). Seymour started to come across the street to join Buddy and Ira, but Buddy broke up the game. Buddy then reveals this last anecdote has him sweating, and remarks, "A place has been prepared for each of us in his own mind" (237). Buddy has seen his place four times, this is the fifth. He then goes to lie down.

Buddy wakes up three hours later and apologizes to the reader, admitting that his total recall of the marble incident was not what incapacitated him. The real reason was his "sudden realization that Seymour is [his] Davega bicycle" (238). Buddy explains his meaning by telling an anecdote. Years ago, his twin brothers, Walt and Waker, were given expensive matching bicycles from Davega's Sports Store for their ninth birthdays. That evening, when Les Glass checked to see if the two bikes were secured, he discovered one of them gone. It turned out that Waker had given his bike away to an unknown boy in CENTRAL PARK. The boy had never owned a bike, and he had asked Waker for his. As the discussion between the Glass parents and Waker grew tense, Seymour and Buddy appeared on the scene. Les and Bessie were aware of the generosity of Waker's action but told Waker that he should have instead just given the boy a ride on the bike. Les recapped the situation to Seymour. The 15-year-old Seymour, according to Buddy, blundered his way to effecting a loving reconciliation between the parents and Waker.

Buddy returns to the narrative of the marble incident of 1927. He remarks that Seymour's coaching him not to aim his marble seems to him similar to a Japanese master instructing his student not to aim his arrows at the target: the "archery master permits, as it were, Aiming but no aiming" (242). Buddy says he would prefer to leave ZEN out of this discussion because Zen is becoming "a rather smutty, cultish word to the discriminating ear" (242). He parenthetically remarks that true Zen will outlast all fads. Buddy says he is not, in fact, a Zen Buddhist or an adept, but that "both Seymour's and [his] roots in Eastern philosophy . . . were, are, planted in the New and Old Testaments, Advaita Vedanta, and classical Taoism" (242). Buddy follows his "own rather natural path of extreme Zenlessness" (243) because that is what Seymour begged him to do. Buddy thinks he can explain Seymour's marble-coaching advice about not aiming by referring to the example of a smoker successfully propelling a cigarette butt into a wastebasket across the room only when there are no other observers, including the smoker himself. Buddy notes that whenever Seymour successfully tossed his marble, he would hear "a responsive click of glass striking glass" (244), but without being aware of who had won.

Buddy announces he will tell one more anecdote and then go to bed. At age nine, he explains, he believed himself to be the world's fastest runner. One day, Bessie asked him to get some ice cream from a store several blocks away. Buddy went out of the apartment building and started to sprint toward the store; he increased speed, but after a bit, he heard footsteps behind him in pursuit. Finally, a hand grabbed him, and Seymour brought him to a halt. Seymour asked him what was wrong, what had happened. Buddy profanely told him nothing was wrong. A relieved Seymour said he could not believe how fast Buddy was running; Seymour could barely catch up. The two brothers then walked the rest of the way to the store. Buddy remarks, "the morale of the now Second-Fastest Boy Runner in the World had not been very perceptibly lowered" (246) because it was Seymour who had bested him.

Buddy announces that he has finally finished and that his "mind has always balked at any kind of ending" (247). He has written through the night; he will just have time for a quick nap and then will get ready for a nine o'clock class. Buddy is tempted to say something caustic about the young women returning from their weekends but will not, because he is Seymour's brother. Buddy then realizes that he is supposed to go into Room 307 and teach, and that all of the female students are as much his sister as Boo Boo or Franny. He declares there is nowhere else he would rather go this moment than Room 307. "Seymour once said that all we do our whole lives is go from one little piece of Holy Ground to the next" (248).

Buddy ends the story by speaking to himself: "Just go to bed, now. Quickly. Quickly and slowly" (248).

CRITICAL ANALYSIS

"Seymour: An Introduction," at 138 pages in its original book publication, is Salinger's longest story about Seymour Glass. The author set himself multiple tasks for the novella: to mitigate the negative impression that Seymour's suicide engenders and to supplant that impression with Seymour's identity as a poet and God-knower; to fully develop Buddy Glass as his "alter-ego and collaborator" (as Salinger refers to Buddy in the author's dust-jacket comments of FRANNY AND ZOOEY); and to have the reader intimately experience Buddy's composition of the story. The title, "Seymour: An Introduction," is ironic inasmuch as the story does not constitute Salinger's introduction of Seymour; the character had played a role in three earlier stories: "A Perfect Day for Bananafish" (1948), "Raise High the Roof Beam, Carpenters" (1955), and "ZOOEY" (1957). Published in the June 6, 1959, issue of the New Yorker, "Seymour: An Introduction" holds the distinction of being Salinger's most experimental Glass story. (For more information regarding the eight published Glass stories, see GLASS STORIES.)

The critics Bernice and Sanford Goldstein interpret "Seymour: An Introduction" as a "fictional treatise on the artistic process" (Goldstein 249). Contradicting Norman Mailer's highly dismissive comment ("the most slovenly portion of prose ever put out by an important American writer" [Mailer 68]), the Goldsteins stress that through "Salinger's *controlled verbosity*, we watch the artistic process as it seems to be happening in Buddy at that very moment" (Goldstein 249). The Goldsteins suggest that Salinger's intent is to "focus on the *process* of creation" without concern for "the final product, the story itself" (Goldstein 249). In fact, Salinger both mirrors the artistic process and produces a highly polished story. The author creates the illusion of an "improvisational unfolding of [Buddy's] thoughts" by utilizing "present tense [for] the turns of Buddy's mind as he thinks, while the past tense is reserved for anecdotal excursions on Seymour's life" (Wenke 102). Salinger, a consummate craftsman, undoubtedly revised the story. "Seymour: An Introduction" employs an intricate sentence structure that reflects the influence of Henry James, one of Salinger's favorite authors. Additionally, the seemingly digressive story possesses a clear structure. Eberhard Alsen discerns that the typographical layout of the text of "Seymour: An Introduction" indicates "six major sections: I. Seymour as a Sick Man/Buddy's Artistic Credo; II. Seymour as God-knower; III. Seymour's Poetry; IV. Seymour's Vaudeville Background; V. Seymour as Buddy's Artistic Mentor; VI. Physical Description of Seymour" (Alsen 2002, 167). The sixth section, Buddy's "answer" to Seymour's "Dear Old Tyger That Sleeps" (182) letter in the fifth section, is subdivided into eight parts: "1. Seymour's Hair Jumping in the Barber Shop; 2. Seymour's Hair and Teeth; 3. Seymour's Height, Smile, and Ears; 4. Seymour's Eyes, Nose, and Chin; 5. Seymour's Hands, Voice, and Skin; 6. Seymour's Clothes; 7. Seymour as Athlete and Gamesman; 8. Seymour as Buddy's Gift to the Reader" (Alsen 2002, 168).

As Salinger further committed himself to the Glass stories, he faced the dilemma of reconciling Seymour's suicide with developing the portrait of Seymour as the idealized human being. At the outset of "Seymour: An Introduction," Seymour's suicide is uppermost in Salinger's mind. The author posts two quotations that serve as epigraphs: The first speaks of the writer's realization that he may misrepresent his characters because of his "varying ability" (111) (taken from the diary of Franz Kafka); the second speaks of a writer's "slip of the pen" that creates a "clerical error" that nonetheless is "an essential part of the whole exposition" (111) (taken from *Sickness Unto Death*, by Søren Kierkeg-

aard). This "clerical error," as it relates to Salinger's writings, is Seymour's suicide in the story "A Perfect Day for Bananafish." Nonetheless, the suicide is "an essential part" of the Seymour character as the suicide creates complexity and drama. Without the suicide, the character of Seymour would lose his intriguing mystery.

In a daring but strategic move, Salinger conflates Buddy Glass with himself. Salinger assigns to Buddy the authorship of his own (Salinger's) 1948 story, "A Perfect Day for Bananafish," his one novel (the title is not specified, though unmistakably *The Catcher in the Rye*), and his 1953 story, "Teddy." ("Raise High the Roof Beam, Carpenters" and "Zooey" are written with Buddy Glass openly declared as the narrator/author.) In an effort to undercut negative aspects of the characterization of Seymour in "A Perfect Day for Bananafish," Salinger has Buddy confess that "the young man, the 'Seymour,' who did the walking and talking . . . not to mention the shooting, was not Seymour at all but, oddly, someone with a striking resemblance to . . . myself" (131). This narrative ploy allows Salinger to ascribe responsibility to Buddy for aspects in "A Perfect Day for Bananafish" that clash with the Seymour character as subsequently developed in "Raise High the Roof Beam, Carpenters" (1955) and "Zooey" (1957). Additionally, Salinger strives to create a distinction between a "fictional" Seymour and a "real" Seymour, when Buddy remarks of "A Perfect Day for Bananafish": ". . . that particular story was written just a couple of months after Seymour's death, and not too very long after I myself, like both the 'Seymour' in the story and the Seymour in Real Life, had returned from the European Theater of Operations" (132). The stratagem aims to create the impression of flesh-and-blood Glass family members. (Salinger employs the same stratagem in "Zooey": Buddy Glass, in a prologue, explains that Franny, Bessie, and Zooey have told him "what happened"; Buddy writes their story and shows the work to his three relatives; Zooey then tries to dissuade him from publishing "Zooey.")

"Seymour: An Introduction" purports to be the authentic accounting of Seymour Glass as exemplary poet and God-knower. Buddy, at the story's outset, buttonholes the reader in direct address as "you." Buddy wants to convince the reader of his credo: A true poet (or painter), one who experiences life to the fullest, including "the whole ambulance load of pain" (122), is, in actuality, "a seer" (122). Buddy calls the unnamed poet-painter a "heavenly fool who can and does produce beauty" (123). He warns the reader not to believe the coroner's verdict as to how a seer dies. (One example of an incorrect cause of death, according to Buddy, is "suicide.") Instead, Buddy contends that a seer "is mainly dazzled to death by his own scruples, the blinding shapes and colors of his own sacred human conscience" (123). Buddy identifies Seymour as a true seer, calling him his family's "one full poet" (124) and, "with or without a suicide plot in his head . . . a ringding enlightened man, a God-knower" (124).

The suicide nonetheless forces the question as to what happened during the last years of Seymour's life to cause the self-destructive act. "Raise High the Roof Beam, Carpenters" presents Seymour from late 1941 through June 4, 1942, the period of his early army service. "A Perfect Day for Bananafish" conveys information about Seymour's release from an army hospital and his (apparently) recent behavior leading up to and including the afternoon of his suicide in 1948. This nearly six-year interval has remained a blank until the little that "Seymour: An Introduction" reveals. Buddy says that the suicide occurred "not too very long after" (132) Seymour and he both returned from the European Theater of Operations. Since the war in Europe ended in May 1945, and the suicide took place on March 18, 1948, the reader is left to wonder what happened during those intervening years in Europe. The only definite fact that Salinger has so far provided about these years is that Seymour wrote his 184 double-haiku poems "during the last three years of his life, both in and out of the Army, but mostly in, well in" (133). As the story opens, Buddy is in the process of editing Seymour's manuscript to about 150 poems, after which he will seek a publisher.

Alsen, the only critic to have speculated on Seymour's final years, contends that Seymour suffered a nervous breakdown in 1945 and received treatment in an army hospital in Germany (which

mirrors Salinger's own biography). According to Alsen, Seymour was confined to "psychiatric wards of Army hospitals for most of the last three years of his life" (Alsen 2002, 238). In Alsen's reading, this would mean that Seymour wrote his 184 poems—poems of such caliber that they will immortalize the poet (according to Buddy)—mostly while institutionalized in psychiatric wards. Alsen's interpretation, perhaps, invites doubts. At the very least, one could question whether the poems would be termed, by Buddy, as "high-hearted" (149). However, Buddy does not recommend Seymour's final 30 or 35 poems to any reader who "hasn't died at least twice in his lifetime, preferably slowly" (149), which seems an indication of an extreme darkening of Seymour's vision of life. The fact of the matter is that Salinger has touched on nearly all of Seymour's life except for the period from June 4, 1942 (Seymour and Muriel's wedding day) through 1947. This lacuna forces the reader to acknowledge that Seymour's life resists conclusive interpretation.

"Seymour: An Introduction" provides flashbacks to incidents from 1922 through 1940. In addition, the story adds a small number of facts regarding Seymour's post-1940 life. The 184 poems were written during the last three years of his life. Most of that time, Seymour was in the army. Seymour (and Buddy) returned from Europe "not too very long" (132) before Seymour's suicide. The Glass brothers did not see each other while stationed in Europe (deduced from Buddy's statement that he can visually render Seymour at all times of Seymour's life "barring the overseas years" [198]). Seymour read Buddy the final poem of his collection shortly after it was written. Seymour rode on a commercial airplane a week before his suicide. "Seymour: An Introduction" nowhere alludes to Seymour being released from a hospital, but that fact probably would be covered in Buddy's statement directly below.

Salinger skirts the details of the suicide in "Seymour: An Introduction" by having Buddy state, "I don't expect to be ready to do that [i.e., speak of the details of the suicide] . . . for several more years" (196). Salinger has already added a detail to the suicide as presented in "A Perfect Day for Bananafish." In "Zooey," he reveals that Seymour wrote a haiku-style poem in English on the hotel room's desk blotter and quotes the poem: "The little girl on the plane / Who turned her doll's head around / To look at me." (64). In "Seymour: An Introduction," Salinger has even altered the added detail. He says that Seymour's poem was written in Japanese and now gives a "literal translation" (155). Salinger makes Seymour even more of a genius poet when Buddy tells the reader that his brother wrote his double-haikus in English, Japanese, German, and Italian. (Seymour's double-haikus mirror the haiku format of three lines (which consist of five syllables/seven syllables/five syllables) repeated once, thus creating a six-line poem with a total of thirty-four syllables.) The fact that Seymour chose to write some of his double-haikus in Japanese makes sense, given the haiku was created by Japanese poets. Seymour choosing to write his suicide poem as a haiku in Japanese shows him emulating a tradition among Zen masters and haiku poets to write a poem on their deathbeds. The additional languages of German and Italian are noteworthy. German would allude to the book of German poems Seymour sent Muriel in "A Perfect Day for Bananafish," with Seymour's insistence that the poems were written by the only great poet of the 20th century, RAINER MARIA RILKE. Italian would allude to the first book on Seymour's book-request list in "HAPWORTH 16, 1924": *Conversational Italian*. Seymour's interest in Italian (and, by extension, Salinger's) would seemingly stem from critical consensus that the West's greatest poet of the past thousand years, Dante Alighieri (1265–1321), wrote in Italian. It is understandable that Seymour would want to write some of his own poems in the languages of these two poets as an act of homage. (It is worth noting that Salinger has given the eldest girl in the Glass family the name Beatrice, the renowned name of Dante's poetic and spiritual inspiration. Salinger's 1951 story, "PRETTY MOUTH AND GREEN MY EYES," has a heavy indebtedness to Dante's *The Divine Comedy*, specifically Canto V of the *Inferno*.)

A substantial portion of "Seymour: An Introduction" is devoted to a discussion of Seymour's poetry. Buddy makes the claim that Seymour will eventually be recognized as one of the three or four greatest American poets, but he does not quote any poems that would buttress this assertion. Buddy blames this omission on Seymour's widow, Muriel, who owns the rights to the poems. Muriel will not allow him to directly quote the work, which also gives Salinger an "out." Since Buddy claims that Seymour will eventually be regarded as a great American poet, Salinger would be presented with the Herculean task of creating poems of such merit. Even so, when Buddy paraphrases a few of the poems, some readers are less than overwhelmed. The most extended, and sympathetic, treatment of Seymour's poetry can be found in Bernice and Sanford Goldstein's essay, "Seymour's Poems." The Goldsteins perceive biographical elements of Seymour's life deriving from the immortal Japanese haiku poet, Basho. The critics provide a close reading of the final two poems of Seymour's 184-poem collection and the suicide poem.

In addition to Seymour's being a true poet-seer, Buddy calls him "a ringding enlightened man, a God-knower" (124). There is no doubt that Buddy worships his eldest brother. Som P. Ranchan, citing Vedantic terminology, believes that Salinger intends Seymour to be considered a Buddha-like Ishtam, explaining, "Ishtams are incarnations of Godhead who impinge upon the historical scene . . . from time to time with a view of reminding man of his true, divine nature and to help him realize it" (Ranchan 4). Ranchan reads "Seymour: An Introduction" as Buddy's meditation on his chosen Ishtam, Seymour. As the story progresses and Buddy becomes further and further involved with his memories of Seymour, he is eventually suffused with an illumination that Seymour is his "Davega bicycle" (238).

Salinger prepares the groundwork for Buddy's Davega-bicycle epiphany with an earlier recollection in "Seymour: An Introduction" concerning a bicycle. Buddy remembers his father, Les, in 1940, asking Seymour if he recalled Joe Jackson giving Seymour a ride on the handlebars of his trick bicycle "that shone like something better than platinum" (172). This ride took place during 1922 in Australia on a vaudeville stage, "around and around" (173), when Seymour was five years old. Seymour replied to Les that "he wasn't sure he had ever got off Joe Jackson's beautiful bicycle" (173). Seymour's answer conveys his experience of being alive from age 5 to 23: an elation and thrilling joy equivalent to that which a child would undergo while perched on the handlebars of a shining bike cycled by an internationally famous vaudevillian. Salinger, through the use of the phrase "better than platinum" (172), describes the ineffable state of being that Seymour has attained.

The Davega bicycle epiphany occurs during Buddy's recollection of the marble-shooting incident from 1927. After he recalls Seymour's advice about a better method to toss his marble—"try not aiming so much" (236)—Buddy comments, "Oh, God, what a noble profession this is" (237). Buddy experiences a deep insight into his own life for the "fifth time" (237): Seymour is his own "Davega bicycle" (238). (Buddy explains: In 1932, Waker Glass, on his ninth birthday, gave away his new bicycle purchased from Davega Sports Store to an unknown boy who asked for the bike. Waker's parents, though cognizant of his generosity, were upset. Seymour, age 15, effected a family reconciliation.) But because Buddy's insight occurs immediately after relating Seymour's Zen-like marble-shooting method, some critics mistake the marble-throwing advice as the story's epiphany. For example, Alsen writes, "like his little brother, Waker, Buddy has just received a valuable gift, and he is now giving it away to his readers. The valuable gift is Seymour's belief in 'Aiming but no aiming,' in aiming to make perfect shots and not to win marbles, or, to put it differently, to do things not for a tangible reward but for spiritual satisfaction" (Alsen 2002, 170). The "valuable gift" is, in fact, Seymour himself, who (in Buddy's "sudden realization" [238]) is Buddy's "Davega bicycle" (238). Salinger underscores the hierarchy of importance between the (lesser) marble-throwing advice and the Seymour-as-Davega-bicycle realization: Buddy alludes to the significance of the marble-throwing advice as "contributive and important" (241), but he declares, ". . . almost nothing seems more contributive and important . . . than the fact of [Buddy] at long last being presented with a Davega bicycle of his own to give away" (241). Buddy (and by extension, Salinger) is giving away, to his readers, Seymour, who

was "all *real* things to us: our blue-striped unicorn, our double-lensed burning glass, our consultant genius, our portable conscience, our supercargo, and our one full poet" (123–124).

Buddy concludes "Seymour: An Introduction" with another insight: that the girls in his writing class, where he is due in a few hours, are, in actuality, his sisters. And he is stunned to realize that he wants to go into that room more than anywhere else. He recalls, "Seymour once said that all we do our whole lives is go from one little piece of Holy Ground to the next" (248). The critic John Wenke aptly comments, "The cessation of 'Seymour' finds Buddy opening himself to the world. This moment is as moving as Holden Caulfield's realization at the end of *Catcher* that he misses everybody" (Wenke 106).

"Seymour: An Introduction" reflects an effort by Salinger to link the story with his earlier novella-length work about Seymour, "Raise High the Roof Beam, Carpenters." A reading of the two stories reveals, among others, the following echoes: Buddy's pleurisy while in the army ("Raise High the Roof Beam, Carpenters" 6; "Seymour: An Introduction" 136); Seymour as English professor ("Raise High" 30; "Seymour" 182); Buddy and Seymour's apartment ("Raise High" 7, 60, passim; "Seymour" 172, 173); the corduroy armchair in their apartment ("Raise High" 65, 91; "Seymour" 173); Taoism ("Raise High" 4, 86; "Seymour" 242); VEDANTA ("Raise High" 106; "Seymour" 242); Zen ("Raise High" 53, 82; "Seymour" 114, 242, 243); the Pantages vaudeville circuit ("Raise High" 6; "Seymour" 168); Louis Sherry candies ("Raise High" 63), Louis Sherry ice cream ("Seymour" 245); the Biltmore Hotel ("Raise High" 77; "Seymour" 220); Carl and Amy ("Raise High" 10–12; "Seymour" 182); Charlotte ("Raise High" 87, passim; "Seymour" 209); R. H. Blyth ("Raise High" 78; "Seymour" 137); Emily Post ("Raise High" 62; "Seymour" 158); and the Glass family residence on Riverside Drive ("Raise High" 95; "Seymour" 190, 208, 245). Given the prominence of Buddy's recollection of the 1927 marble-shooting incident in "Seymour: An Introduction," it is worth noting that in Salinger's previous story, "Zooey," one of the items housed in the Glass medicine cabinet is "an unclouded blue marble (known to marble shooters, at least in the twenties, as a 'purey')" (75).

"Seymour: An Introduction" also references a Curtis Caulfield. Curtis, "an exceptionally intelligent and likable boy" (225), was on *It's a Wise Child* with Seymour and Buddy Glass. Curtis was killed during World War II in the Pacific. (Similarly, the original Holden Caulfield was reported missing in action in the Pacific, as the reader learns from Holden's older brother, Vincent, in the 1945 story "THIS SANDWICH HAS NO MAYONNAISE.") The critic Robert M. Slabey believes this reference to be a conscious linkage by Salinger between his two major fictive families. (Slabey also observes that the character Jane Gallagher, in *The Catcher in the Rye*, shares the same surname with Bessie Glass's maiden name and muses whether Jane may be identified as a distant relative of Bessie.) On the other hand, the critic Warren French dismisses any connection between Holden Caulfield and Curtis Caulfield, calling Curtis "just the kind of red herring that Salinger would employ to tease those who insisted upon working out too literal interrelations between all details in his fiction" (French 178).

"Seymour: An Introduction," published in June 1959, constitutes an ambitious, challenging story, as it "anticipated by a decade the self-reflexive trend in American postmodernist fiction, a trend that became fashionable in the late sixties and early seventies" (Alsen 2002, 182). Salinger, in eight short years since the publication of *The Catcher in the Rye*, progressed from the narrative voice of Holden Caulfield to his quintessential rendering of the voice, in the author's own words, of his "alter-ego and collaborator," Buddy Glass. Additionally, "Seymour: An Introduction" articulates Salinger's philosophy of writing. Alsen's excellent essay in *A Reader's Guide to J. D. Salinger*, "Salinger's Philosophy of Composition," explicates Salinger's belief in an art based on "inspiration and the divine origin of the artist's ideas, the personality of the artist as seer, spontaneous creation and organic form, and the religious and secular purpose of literary art" (Alsen 2002, 243). The nuanced complexity of "Seymour: An Introduction" invites multiple readings for a full experience of Salinger's tour-de-force achievement.

PUBLICATION HISTORY

"Seymour: An Introduction" was first published in the *New Yorker* magazine on June 6, 1959. The story appeared in a book publication in *Raise High the Roof Beam, Carpenters and Seymour: An Introduction* (LITTLE, BROWN AND COMPANY, 1963). *Raise High the Roof Beam, Carpenters and Seymour: An Introduction*, Salinger's fourth book, has never gone out of print.

Raise High the Roof Beam, Carpenters and Seymour: An Introduction is available in three editions from Little, Brown and Company: an exact reproduction of the hardback first edition from 1963, which includes the dust-jacket comments written by Salinger; a trade paperback that mimics the production of the hardback, though Salinger's dust-jacket comments are not retained; and a mass-market paperback, also lacking Salinger's dust-jacket comments, with its pagination differing from the above editions.

CHARACTERS

Bessie Glass's sister   The unnamed sister, Bessie's twin, died of malnutrition in childhood, backstage in Dublin.

Bob B.   Seymour Glass calls Bob B. the "archenemy" (179) of his brother Buddy. Seymour critiques one of Buddy's short stories by suggesting that Bob B. would like it.

Boy in Central Park   The unnamed boy asks the nine-year-old Waker Glass for his new Davega bicycle.

Carl and Amy   Carl and Amy are referenced in Seymour Glass's "Dear Old Tyger That Sleeps" letter. In 1939, the couple arranged a blind date for Seymour and accompanied them to a performance of *Die Zauberflöte*.

Carl and Amy are also referred to in "Raise High the Roof Beam, Carpenters." Boo Boo Glass, in a letter to her brother Buddy, uses Carl and Amy's former address to explain where Seymour Glass's wedding is to be held.

Caulfield, Curtis   Curtis Caulfield is a co-panelist with Seymour and Buddy Glass on *It's a Wise Child*.

Buddy relates that one day, while the three boys were playing catch, Buddy laughed at Curtis, accusing him of throwing like a girl. Curtis is killed in the Pacific during World War II. Despite his surname, Curtis is not a member of Salinger's original Caulfield family, which makes appearances in various published and unpublished stories of the 1940s, nor is he a member of the Caulfield family portrayed in *The Catcher in the Rye.*

Charlotte   *See* Mayhew, Charlotte.

Freudians, group of   A group of Freudians examined Seymour Glass for nearly seven hours when he was 13 years old.

Glass, Bessie   Bessie Glass is the wife of Les Glass and mother of the seven Glass children. Bessie, along with Les, performs in vaudeville. The reader learns that she decided the duo would retire in 1925. Bessie is also mentioned in a number of small cameos.

Bessie appears in all of the other Glass family stories. In "Raise High the Roof Beam, Carpenters," she is living temporarily in Los Angeles with her husband and two youngest children, as Les Glass is working at a motion-picture studio. She is given her largest role in the story "Zooey," where she is described in detail as she attempts to persuade her youngest son, Zooey, to help her youngest daughter, Franny, recover from a nervous breakdown. In the 1965 prologue to "Hapworth 16, 1924," Buddy Glass explains that his mother has just sent him Seymour's letter (written in 1924). Bessie is the first of the five addressees of the letter, and many passages are directly solely to her.

Glass, Boo Boo   Boo Boo (Beatrice) is the older of the two Glass daughters, and the third-eldest child in the family. In the story, Boo Boo chooses Seymour Glass's John Keats poem, written when he was eight, for inclusion by Buddy Glass. The reader learns that Boo Boo (as of 1959) has three children and lives in Tuckahoe, New York.

Boo Boo first appears in the story "Down at the Dinghy" (1949), in which she is the protagonist and mother of Lionel Tannenbaum. With astute child psychology, Boo Boo solves her son's emotional crisis. Boo Boo figures in all the Glass family stories. In "Raise High the Roof Beam, Carpenters," her saucy, opinionated letter to Buddy imploring him to get to the wedding is reproduced (as a secretary in the Waves, she, on the other hand, must accompany her boss, an admiral, on an out-of-state trip and is therefore unable to attend); her message to her brother Seymour—quoting the Sappho poem that supplies the title of the story—is written with a sliver of soap on the bathroom mirror. In "Zooey," Boo Boo, vacationing in Europe, is invoked several times. She, along with her sister, Franny, would like to dispose of their mother's tattered house coat, an old kimono, and she recommends giving the kimono a ritual stabbing before tossing. Boo Boo possesses a quirky sense of humor, as shown when describing a look on her mother's face as meaning either Bessie Glass has just talked with one of her sons on the phone or that everyone's bowels in the world will be flawlessly working for a week. She humorously describes her brother Zooey (quoted by Buddy) as "the blue-eyed Jewish-Irish Mohican scout who died in your arms at the roulette table at Monte Carlo" (51). Boo Boo is one of the five addressees of Seymour's letter, "Hapworth 16, 1924." Seymour tells Boo Boo to work on her manners; he also devises a nonoffensive prayer specifically for her.

Glass, Buddy   Buddy, the second eldest of the Glass children, writes "Seymour: An Introduction" and is, along with Seymour Glass, one of its two main characters. The reader witnesses the 40-year-old Buddy writing the story in 1959. During this time, Buddy is single, employed as a part-time writing teacher at a girls' college in Upstate New York, and a successful author. In a number of anecdotes about Seymour's childhood, Buddy figures prominently.

Buddy appears in all of the other Glass family stories. He narrates the story "Raise High the Roof Beam, Carpenters," in which his 13-year-younger self is the protagonist trying to attend Seymour's wedding. Buddy also narrates "Zooey"; the reader learns a great deal about him via his first-person author's introduction, in addition to his 14-page letter that

Zooey Glass reads in the bathtub. In "Hapworth 16, 1924," Buddy receives Seymour's 41-year-old letter from his mother and types a copy for publication. In the letter, the five-year-old Buddy is at summer camp with Seymour, and is referenced often.

Glass, Franny   Franny is the youngest of the Glass children and makes several cameo appearances in the story. Most importantly, she is described, in 1959 (four years after the events of "Zooey), as a "budding young actress" (135). This confirms that the transformation of her character at the close of "Zooey" has indeed taken permanent effect. The reader learns that Franny's birth year is 1935.

Franny first appears in the story "Franny" (1955), though without her surname. The reader meets her during a weekend at her boyfriend's college while she undergoes a religious crisis. Franny is introduced as a member of the Glass family in the prologue of "Raise High the Roof Beam, Carpenters." Later in the story, her performance on *It's a Wise Child* is praised in Boo Boo Glass's letter to Buddy Glass. On that radio program, Franny will memorably reply to the announcer that she knows she flew around the Glass apartment because, afterward, she would always find dust on her hands from the light bulbs. At the time of "Raise High the Roof Beam, Carpenters," she is living in Los Angeles with her parents. Franny's religious crisis from the earlier story, "Franny," is continued and dealt with more extensively in "Zooey" and is resolved at the story's close. At the time of "Hapworth 16, 1924," Franny has not yet been born.

Glass, Les   Les Glass is husband to Bessie and father of the seven Glass children. In "Seymour: An Introduction," Les asks his eldest son, Seymour, the important question of whether Seymour remembers riding on Joe Jackson's bicycle in Australia in 1922.

In "Raise High the Roof Beam, Carpenters," Les is referred to as a "retired Pantages Circuit vaudevillian" (6) who is currently employed by a motion-picture studio as a talent scout. During "Zooey" he is absent from the apartment. However, his sentimental personality is attested to by Bessie Glass and confirmed by Franny Glass. Les

is one of the five addressees of Seymour's "Hapworth 16, 1924" letter. A few passages of the letter are directly addressed to Les, though Seymour, more than once, excuses his father from reading the entire letter due to its length. In that story, the reader finally learns that Les was born in Australia.

Glass, Muriel Fedder   During the time of "Seymour: An Introduction" (1959), Muriel is Seymour Glass's widow. She will not allow Buddy Glass to quote any of Seymour's final 184 poems in the story (though he has been given power to seek a publisher for them). This prohibition by Muriel allows Salinger an out; he does not have to create the text of the poems, poems which would have to support the fact that they were written by one of the greatest American poets (as per Buddy's assertion). Buddy does, however, paraphrase several poems from Seymour's collection.

Muriel takes part in other Glass stories. She is one of the three major characters (along with Seymour Glass and Sybil Carpenter) in "A Perfect Day for Bananafish." She is seen talking with her mother on the phone about Seymour, and she becomes a widow in the story's final paragraph. Her wedding day is the subject matter of "Raise High the Roof Beam, Carpenters." She is briefly seen being led dejectedly to a car after Seymour fails to show up for the ceremony. However, she appears in many of Seymour's diary entries reflecting their courtship period. In these, the reader is given the clearest sense of her pre–"A Perfect Day for Bananafish" character. Though she is not directly named in "Zooey," Buddy Glass refers to her in his letter to Zooey Glass as the "Bereaved Widow" (62). Buddy is recounting the time he went to Florida to collect Seymour's body after the suicide. Muriel meets him at the airport decked out in "Bergdorf Goodman black" (62), a remark that indicates that Buddy suspected Muriel of enjoying the role of widow. (Buddy has never held a high opinion of Muriel; Seymour surmised that Buddy would not respect her and notes as much in his diary in "Raise High the Roof Beam, Carpenters.")

Glass, Seymour   Seymour, the eldest Glass child, is the title character of the story and one of its two protagonists. At the time of the story's composition (1959), Seymour has been dead for 11 years. "Seymour: An Introduction" emphasizes Seymour as poet and describes his poetry; his quest to know God; and his position within the family as its guru figure. A number of anecdotes from his childhood are recalled by Buddy Glass.

Seymour was introduced in the 1948 story "A Perfect Day for Bananafish," where he is seen on a beach, meets a very young girl, goes for a swim, tells her a parable about bananafish, and later shoots himself on the hotel bed next to his sleeping wife. (A minor reference to Seymour appears in the 1949 story "Down at the Dinghy.") The character is resurrected in the first Glass family story, the 1955 "Raise High the Roof Beam, Carpenters." This story is a description of Seymour's wedding day, although Seymour fails to show up for the ceremony. However, Seymour's physical absence informs the action and dialogue of the story. Seymour's revealing diary entries, moreover, serve as a stand-in for him, dominate the story's close, and afford the reader an opportunity to assess this remarkably complex character. Though Seymour has been dead for more than seven and a half years at the time "Zooey" takes place, he nonetheless plays a notable role in a number of ways in that story, and important information about him is divulged. Significantly, Seymour's parable of the Fat Lady will bring Franny Glass to the understanding of her life's purpose. The final Glass family story to date, "Hapworth 16, 1924," contains the most extended example of Seymour's own words, albeit written at the age of seven.

Glass, Waker   Waker is the fourth-oldest son and fifth-oldest child in the Glass family. In "Seymour: An Introduction," in one of the most important scenes of the story, Waker gives away his ninth-birthday present—a Davega bicycle—to a stranger who asks for it; the memory of this action triggers Buddy Glass's illuminated realization that his brother Seymour is *his* (Buddy's) Davega bicycle. Waker, when an adult, tells Buddy that he thinks Seymour's poems draw upon his previous lives in Benares, feudal Japan, and Atlantis. The reader learns that Waker canonized W. C. Fields and juggled cigar boxes.

Waker appears in the other Glass family stories, but without much attention being paid him. In "Raise High the Roof Beam, Carpenters," he is interned in a conscientious objectors' camp in Maryland. In "Zooey," he is away at a Jesuit conference in Ecuador. Waker is one of the five addressees of Seymour's "Hapworth 16, 1924" letter; Seymour admonishes him to practice his juggling.

Glass, Walt   Walt is the third-oldest son and fourth-oldest child of the Glass family. In "Seymour: An Introduction," Walt receives, as a birthday gift, a poem by Seymour Glass about a boy who catches a fish. Walt calls Seymour's facial expression of excited discovery "his Eureka Look" (158). The reader learns that Walt was a debonair dresser and a dancer before his death in postwar Japan.

Walt first appears in the 1948 story "Uncle Wiggily in Connecticut," though without his surname. In that story, Walt is the former boyfriend, with a unique sense of humor, of the protagonist, Eloise Wengler. Walt once called her twisted ankle "Uncle Wiggily." Walt is mentioned in all of the Glass family stories. During the time of "Raise High the Roof Beam, Carpenters," Walt is in the army and cannot attend his brother Seymour's wedding because he is in the Pacific. He will be killed three years later in Japan in a noncombat accident shortly after the end of World War II. In "Zooey," Walt is described as Bessie Glass's "only truly lighthearted son" (90). Walt is one of the five addressees of Seymour's "Hapworth 16, 1924" letter; Seymour admonishes him to practice his tap dancing.

Glass, Zooey   Zooey is the youngest son and sixth-youngest child in the Glass family. In "Seymour: An Introduction," Zooey is referenced only a couple of times. However, Seymour Glass importantly remarks that he, Buddy, and Zooey have been brothers for at least four incarnations. (Of the five brothers, these three brothers interest Salinger the most; the other two brothers, Walt and Waker, are given exponentially fewer words and description in Salinger's work.) The reader learns that Zooey's birth year is 1930.

Zooey is introduced in the first Glass family story, "Raise High the Roof Beam, Carpenters."

Seymour and the Fedder family listen to Zooey and Franny Glass on the kids' radio program *It's a Wise Child.* Seymour notes his youngest brother's comments in his diary. Zooey's most prominent appearance is in "Zooey." Here the reader experiences an extended encounter with his character. In the story, Zooey rescues Franny from her nervous breakdown and puts her on her life's path. At the time of "Hapworth 16, 1924," Zooey has not yet been born.

Glass, Zozo Zozo Glass, the Glass children's paternal great-grandfather, was a Polish Jewish clown. Buddy and Seymour have inherited Zozo's large nose. Buddy feels that Zozo is his guardian angel.

MacMahon MacMahon is the Glass children's maternal great-grandfather who made his living by dancing on the sides of empty whiskey bottles.

Mario and Victor Mario and Victor are barbers to Buddy and Seymour Glass, respectively, in childhood. When Buddy sits down to write the piece of writing that in all the world he wants to read, he begins with a scene set in their barbershop.

Mayhew, Charlotte Charlotte Mayhew, a childhood friend of Seymour and Buddy Glass's, goes on to become a famous motion-picture actress. She is mentioned as the only girl who was ever smitten by the two brothers. Buddy calls her "Charlotte the Harlot, who was a trifle mad" (209).

Charlotte appears in one other story, "Raise High the Roof Beam, Carpenters," where she plays an important role, being the girl whom Seymour hit with the stone when they were 12 years old. The incident is used by the Matron of Honor to bolster her condemnation of Seymour's character. Charlotte Mayhew and Muriel Fedder, as children, could be taken for twins.

Monahan, Ferris L. Ferris L. Monahan is a fictitious writer, beloved by his readers, to whom Buddy Glass compares himself.

Overman, Miss Miss Overman is the librarian at the first NEW YORK CITY public-library branch that Seymour and Buddy Glass frequented as children. Miss Overman loved the poets Robert Browning and William Wordsworth. Seymour felt he needed to discover a form for his poetry that would engage Miss Overman's attention, despite her taste in poets.

Miss Overman plays an important role in "Hapworth 16, 1924"; her name crops up repeatedly as Seymour discusses the books he wants sent to him and Buddy.

Prof. B. Prof. B., referenced in one of Seymour Glass's notes to his brother Buddy, apparently is Buddy's writing instructor. Seymour cautions Buddy not to follow the professor's advice.

Reader, Buddy Glass's general Buddy Glass directly addresses the reader throughout the story. He believes his general reader is interested in birds and poets.

Seymour Glass's date The unnamed woman, a friend of Carl and Amy's, is Seymour's blind date to attend a 1939 performance of *Die Zauberflöte.* Seymour calls her "that very strange girl" (183). The girl was not Muriel Fedder, whom Seymour eventually marries, as Seymour and Muriel do not meet until 1941.

Sugarman, Arnold L., Jr. One day during study hall, Arnold Sugarman told Buddy Glass to read John Buchan's short story "Skule Skerry." Several sentences from the story, which are influential to the narrative of Buddy's "introduction," are quoted at the outset of "Seymour: An Introduction."

Valdemar, Miss Miss Valdemar is one of Buddy Glass's students at the girls' college where he is teaching at the time he writes "Seymour: An Introduction."

Yankauer, Ira Ira Yankauer is the child with whom Buddy Glass is playing marbles when Seymour Glass instructs Buddy not to intentionally aim.

Young man who visits Buddy Glass Buddy Glass recounts an anecdote about a young man who is interested in the influence of Sherwood Anderson on one of Buddy's stories. The young man is an example, in Buddy's mind, of someone who physically seeks out authors.

Zabel, Miss Miss Zabel is one of Buddy Glass's students at the girls' college during his composition of "Seymour: An Introduction" and is named as seated in Room 307. Though Buddy refers to her as "Terrible" (248), he realizes at the end of the story that she (and all the young women in the class) is "as much [his] sister as Boo Boo or Franny" (248).

FURTHER READING

Alsen, Eberhard. *A Reader's Guide to J. D. Salinger.* Westport, Conn.: Greenwood Press, 2002.

———. "The Role of Vedanta Hinduism in Salinger's Seymour Novel." *Renascence* 33, no. 2 (Winter 1981): 99–116.

———. *Salinger's Glass Stories as a Composite Novel.* Troy, N.Y.: Whitston Publishing Company, 1983.

Baskett, Sam S. "The Splendid/Squalid World of J. D. Salinger." *Wisconsin Studies in Contemporary Literature* 4, no. 1 (Winter 1963): 48–61.

Cullen, Frank. *Vaudeville, Old and New.* New York: Routledge, 2007.

French, Warren. *J. D. Salinger.* New York: Twayne Publishers, 1963.

Goldstein, Bernice, and Sanford Goldstein. "'Seymour: An Introduction'—Writing as Discovery." *Studies in Short Fiction* 7 (Spring 1970): 248–256.

———. "Seymour's Poems." *Literature East and West* 17 (June–December 1973): 335–348.

Hassan, Ihab. "Almost the Voice of Silence: The Later Novelettes of J. D. Salinger." *Wisconsin Studies in Contemporary Literature* 4, no. 1 (Winter 1963): 5–20.

Hyman, Stanley Edgar. "J. D. Salinger's House of Glass." In *Standards: A Chronicle of Books of Our Time,* 123–127. New York: Horizon Press, 1966.

Johannson, Ernest J. "Salinger's Seymour." *Carolina Quarterly* 12 (Winter 1959): 51–54.

Kurian, Elizabeth N. *A Religious Response to the Existential Dilemma in the Fiction of J. D. Salinger.* New Delhi: Intellectual Publishing House, 1992.

Lyons, John O. "The Romantic Style of Salinger's 'Seymour: An Introduction.'" *Wisconsin Studies in Contemporary Literature* 4, no. 1 (Winter 1963): 62–69.

Mailer, Norman. "Some Children of the Goddess." *Esquire,* July 1963, 64–69, 105.

Mizener, Arthur. "The American Hero as Poet: Seymour Glass." In *The Sense of Life in the Modern Novel,* 227–246. Boston: Houghton Mifflin, 1964.

Ranchan, Som P. *An Adventure in Vedanta: J. D. Salinger's The Glass Family.* Delhi: Ajanta Publications, 1989.

Schulz, Max F. "Epilogue to 'Seymour: An Introduction': Salinger and the Crisis of Consciousness." *Studies in Short Fiction* 5 (Winter 1968): 128–138.

Schwartz, Arthur. "For Seymour—with Love and Judgment." *Wisconsin Studies in Contemporary Literature* 4, no. 1 (Winter 1963): 88–99.

Slabey, Robert M. "Salinger's 'Casino': Wayfarers and Spiritual Acrobats." *English Record* 14 (February 1964): 16–20.

Slethaug, Gordon E. "Seymour: A Clarification." *Renascence* 23 (Spring 1971): 115–128.

Weinberg, Helen. "J. D. Salinger's Holden and Seymour and the Spiritual Activist Hero." In *The New Novel in America: The Kafkan Mode in Contemporary Fiction,* 141–164. Ithaca, N.Y.: Cornell University Press, 1970.

Wenke, John. *J. D. Salinger: A Study of the Short Fiction.* Boston: Twayne Publishers, 1991.

Wiegand, William. "Salinger and Kierkegaard." *Minnesota Review* 5 (May–July 1965): 137–156.

"Skipped Diploma, The"

See URSINUS WEEKLY WRITINGS.

"Slight Rebellion Off Madison"

Appearing in the December 21, 1946, issue of the NEW YORKER, "Slight Rebellion Off Madison" portrays, in a third-person narrative, Holden Caulfield home from prep school on his Christmas vacation.

The story, Salinger's first about Holden, was scheduled for a pre-Christmas 1941 publication by the *New Yorker* but was pulled due to the bombing of Pearl Harbor. Five years later, a revised version saw publication and became Salinger's initial appearance in the magazine with which he is indelibly identified. "Slight Rebellion Off Madison" is Salinger's 17th published story. The author, however, chose not to include the story in his three books of collected stories.

SYNOPSIS

"Holden Morrisey Caulfield" (82), a student at "Pencey Preparatory School for Boys" (82), has returned home to MANHATTAN for his Christmas vacation. He favors wearing his "hat with a cutting edge at the 'V' in the crown" (82). Holden drops his bag in the hall of the family's apartment, kisses his mother, and immediately calls Sally Hayes for a date. Sally agrees to go dancing that night. The two prep schoolers "made a wonderful thing out of the taxi ride home" (82).

The next day, Holden takes Sally to see a matinee of *O Mistress Mine*. During intermission, "George Harrison" (82) recognizes Sally. George calls the stars of the play, the Lunts, "absolute angels" (82). After the show, Sally suggests to Holden that they go ice skating at Radio City later that evening.

Neither Holden nor Sally can ice skate; they soon stop and have a drink. Sally wants to know whether Holden intends to come to her house on Christmas Eve to "trim the tree" (82). Holden launches into a harangue, attacking school, in addition to life in NEW YORK CITY. He tries to persuade Sally to run away to New England. They will live in "cabin camps" until "the money runs out" (83). Holden says he will find work and they will eventually "get married or something" (83).

Sally resists the idea and tries to reason with Holden that there is plenty of time to do such things after he completes college. Holden disagrees "so quietly" (84). Waiting until after college would change everything, he reasons. They would have to lead a conventional life. Holden does not want to "have to work at [his] father's" (84). When he claims Sally does not understand what he is talking about, she counters that he does not either. This retort causes Holden to tell Sally that she gives him "a royal pain" (84) and leave.

After midnight of the same evening, Holden sits at "the Wadsworth Bar" (84) with another Pencey Prep student, Carl Luce. Luce, "a fat unattractive boy . . . led his class" (84). The two have a drink. When Holden tells Luce he is thinking of quitting school, Luce replies, "You've always got a bug" (84). Luce finishes his drink and leaves. Holden continues drinking until two in the morning. He drunkenly calls Sally Hayes, but her mother answers. When Sally comes on the line, Holden incoherently tells her he will show up on Christmas Eve to trim the tree. She terminates the call. Holden redials, and after asking for Sally, the answerer hangs up.

Holden goes into the men's room, dunks his head into cold water, and, with water dripping, sits on the radiator. When the piano player from the bar comes in, Holden tells him, "I'm on the hot seat. They pulled the switch . . . I'm getting fried" (85). The piano player grins; Holden compliments him on his playing. The man suggests that Holden use a towel and go home. Holden declines both ideas, and the piano player leaves.

Holden gets off the radiator and lets "the tears out of his eyes" (86). After he retrieves his coat and hat, he stands on the corner, waiting for "a Madison Avenue bus" (86). The story ends: "It was a long wait" (86).

CRITICAL ANALYSIS

"Slight Rebellion Off Madison" provokes more interest than its few pages would seemingly warrant. There are multiple reasons: the story's status as the "original" conception of Holden Caulfield; Salinger's use of nearly all of the story's incidents in his novel, *The* CATCHER IN THE RYE; and a close comparison between passages in the story with those in the novel allows readers to witness the author's artistry.

The publication history of "Slight Rebellion Off Madison" influences the assessment of its significance. On October 31, 1941, Salinger, age 22, wrote a close friend announcing he had sold his first story to the *New Yorker*: "Slight Rebellion Off

Madison." (The letter is photographically reproduced in John C. Unrue's *J. D. Salinger* [Unrue 2002, 43].) Not only did the magazine want this particular story about Holden Caulfield, but the editors also desired additional stories featuring the same character. The young author had aspired to publish in the *New Yorker* above all other magazines. Understandably, he was elated at this turn of events. As befits the story's subject matter, publication of "Slight Rebellion Off Madison" was set for pre-Christmas 1941. However, after Pearl Harbor was bombed on December 7, the *New Yorker*, to Salinger's consternation, decided to pull the story. Five years and numerable *New Yorker* rejections later, J. D. Salinger and Holden Caulfield both appeared for the first time in the *New Yorker*, when the magazine ran "Slight Rebellion Off Madison" in the back pages of the December 21, 1946, issue. Ironically, the story constitutes Holden's sole appearance in the *New Yorker*, and his last in any magazine. Nearly another five years would elapse until Holden Caulfield would reappear, fully realized—immortalized—in *The Catcher in the Rye*.

As best can be determined, "Slight Rebellion Off Madison" is the first story Salinger wrote about Holden Caulfield (albeit the story published is the revised version). Holden debuts with his full name, as Salinger includes the character's middle name of Morrisey (the sole time in the author's published work). Holden does not wear a red hunting hat as he does in *The Catcher in the Rye*; he is an elegant young man-about-town in his "chesterfield and a hat with a cutting edge at the 'V' in the crown" (82). Holden arrives home for Christmas vacation; he has not flunked out of prep school (as he has in the novel). However, in the story, Holden says he hates school four times. He hates life in New York City too and wants "to quit school . . . and get the hell out of New York" (84). In "Slight Rebellion Off Madison," there is no mention of Holden's siblings, unlike all other stories that include the character. The lack of siblings would perhaps indicate that Salinger had not yet developed the idea of a fully-fledged Caulfield family. (For more information regarding the seven extant Caulfield stories, *see* CAULFIELD STORIES .)

Salinger utilizes, and amplifies, almost all of "Slight Rebellion Off Madison" in *The Catcher in the Rye*. Although the author does not incorporate the story's opening two paragraphs, Holden's phone call to Sally Hayes appears in Chapter 15 of the novel (the story lacks Sally's use of "grand" and Holden's classic line, "If there's one word I hate, it's grand" [*Catcher* 138]). Salinger recycles Holden and Sally's making out in the cab ride home after dancing at the Wedgwood Room ("Rebellion" 82) in Chapter 17's cab ride to the matinee (*Catcher* 162–163). The story devotes only a couple of paragraphs to the intermission at the matinee, which Salinger expands in Chapter 17 (*Catcher* 164–166). Although "Slight Rebellion Off Madison" includes Sally's suggestion to go ice skating, the story lacks reference to Sally's "darling little skating skirts" (*Catcher* 167) or Holden's characterization, "this little blue butt-twitcher of a dress" (*Catcher* 167). Much of "Slight Rebellion Off Madison" centers on the teenagers' conversation after ice skating at Radio City, and it becomes the part of the story most recognizable in the novel (*Catcher* 168–174). "Slight Rebellion Off Madison" includes a quick scene with Carl Luce, but it in no way resembles the character and conversation in Chapter 19 of the novel. The story portrays Holden drunkenly phoning Sally and then being in the men's room of a bar, which is amplified in Chapter 20 (*Catcher* 195–199).

In May 1944, Salinger changed his mind regarding his novel about Holden Caulfield. Up to this time, the author wrote chapters or stories in the third person. Salinger realized the novel would need to be written wholly in Holden's voice. The shift from third to first person "makes our identification with Holden more immediate and lets us hear his famously judgmental voice more consistently" (Beidler 22).

A comparison of one small moment of a scene in "Slight Rebellion Off Madison" and the same scene in the novel demonstrates Salinger's transformation of his material. The scene is the intermission at the Lunts' play when Holden, Sally, and George interact. After Sally and George see each other and "connect," the story's third-person narrator states: "Sally asked George if he didn't think the show was marvellous. George gave himself a little room for his reply, bearing down on the foot of the woman behind him" ("Rebellion" 82). In the novel, these two sentences become: "You should've seen him when old Sally asked him how he liked the play. He was the kind of a phony that have to give themselves *room* when they answer somebody's question. He stepped back, and stepped right on the lady's foot behind him. He probably broke every toe in her body" (*Catcher* 165–166). The story's presentation is pedestrian; the novel's flies. The next sentence in the story reads: "He said that the play itself certainly was no masterpiece, but that the Lunts, of course, were absolute angels" ("Rebellion" 82). In the novel, Salinger gives the sentence verbal punch by emphasizing "itself" and omitting the first "that" and "certainly": "He said the play *itself* was no masterpiece, but that the Lunts, of course, were absolute angels" (*Catcher* 166). The story then continues with: "'Angels,' Holden thought. 'Angels. For Chrissake. *Angels*'" ("Rebellion" 82). This line ends the story's depiction of the matinee intermission. The novel's equivalent reads: "Angels. For Chrissake. *Angels*. That killed me" (*Catcher* 166). The novel can drop the intrusive phrase "Holden thought," because Holden is the narrator. Salinger reduces Holden's three instances of saying "angels" in the story's version to the novel's perfect two, topped by a Holdenesque "That killed me" (*Catcher* 166). "Slight Rebellion Off Madison" continues with Sally's suggestion of going ice skating. *The Catcher in the Rye,* however, stays with Sally, George, and Holden. This threesome remains together for another two-thirds of a page. Holden imparts more of the conversation between Sally and George during intermission and, with a comedian's punch line, "when the next act was over, they *continued* their goddam boring conversation" (*Catcher* 166). Salinger keeps the "joke" running by having George, once the show is over, accompany Sally and Holden for two blocks as the couple seeks a cab. Holden comments, George "didn't *hesitate* to horn in on my date, the bastard. I even thought for a minute that he was going to get in the goddam cab with us" (*Catcher* 166).

A comparison of each part of "Slight Rebellion Off Madison" that is absorbed into *The Catcher in the Rye* provides a laboratory for witnessing the alchemy of Salinger's artistry.

PUBLICATION HISTORY

"Slight Rebellion Off Madison" was published in the December 21, 1946, issue of the *New Yorker*. Salinger never reprinted the story in his three books of stories. "Slight Rebellion Off Madison" later appeared in the bootleg editions *The COMPLETE UNCOLLECTED SHORT STORIES OF J. D. SALINGER* (1974) and *TWENTY-TWO STORIES* (1998). In 2000, the story was reprinted in an anthology edited by David Remnick, *Wonderful Town: New York Stories from The New Yorker*.

CHARACTERS

Caulfield, Holden Holden Morrisey Caulfield, home on his Christmas vacation from Pencey Preparatory School for Boys, has two dates with Sally Hayes, a quick drink with a classmate named Carl Luce, drunkenly phones Sally to promise he will come over for Christmas Eve, dunks his head in a men's room's washbowl, and, as the story ends, waits for a Madison Avenue bus.

Holden appears in or is referenced in additional Caulfield stories: "LAST DAY OF THE LAST FURLOUGH," "THIS SANDWICH HAS NO MAYONNAISE," "I'M CRAZY," and the unpublished "The LAST AND BEST OF THE PETER PANS" and "The OCEAN FULL OF BOWLING BALLS."

Caulfield, Mr. and Mrs. When Mrs. Caulfield's son, Holden, arrives home for the beginning of his Christmas vacation, she receives a kiss. Holden refers to his father when he tells Sally Hayes that he does not want to work at his father's place of business.

The Caulfield parents, either singly or together, appear in or are referenced in additional Caulfield stories: "Last Day of the Last Furlough," "This Sandwich Has No Mayonnaise," "The STRANGER," "I'm Crazy," and the unpublished "The Last and Best of the Peter Pans" and "The Ocean Full of Bowling Balls."

Halsey, Fred Holden Caulfield tells Sally Hayes that he could borrow Fred Halsey's car to drive them to New England.

In *The Catcher in the Rye,* Holden does not name the owner of the car; he refers to a guy in Greenwich Village.

Harrison, George George Harrison, who met Sally Hayes once at a party, recognizes her in the lobby during the intermission of *O Mistress Mine.* George criticizes the play but thinks the Lunts' performance angelic.

In *The Catcher in the Rye,* Holden gives only the first name of Sally's acquaintance, calling him "George something" (165). Holden, Sally, and George attend a performance of *I Know My Love.*

Hayes, Mrs. When Holden Caulfield drunkenly telephones Sally Hayes at two in the morning, Mrs. Hayes answers.

Hayes, Sally Sally Hayes, whose Christmas vacation coincides with Holden Caulfield's, has two dates with him. After making out during a cab ride, she tells Holden to let his crew cut grow out. Sally rejects Holden's idea of running away to New England and questions whether he knows what he is saying.

Luce, Carl Carl Luce, the brightest boy in his class at Pencey, has a drink with Holden Caulfield at the Wadsworth Bar. When Holden talks about dropping out of school, Carl ends the conversation by finishing his drink and leaving.

Salinger retains the name of Carl Luce in *The Catcher in the Rye,* but the two characters (and scenes) are unalike.

Wadsworth Bar piano player The piano player enters the men's room and finds Holden Caulfield sitting on a radiator, his hair soaked, water dripping down his shirt. He suggests that Holden use a towel and go home.

In *The Catcher in the Rye,* the piano player works at the Wicker Bar.

FURTHER READING

Beidler, Peter G. *A Reader's Companion to J. D. Salinger's The Catcher in the Rye.* Seattle: Coffeetown Press, 2009.

French, Warren. *J. D. Salinger.* New York: Twayne Publishers, 1963.

———. *J. D. Salinger, Revisited.* New York: Twayne Publishers, 1988.

"Soft-Boiled Sergeant"

"Soft-Boiled Sergeant," published in the April 15, 1944, issue of the SATURDAY EVENING POST, is Salinger's last wartime story to appear before his involvement in the D-day invasion of Europe. The story depicts the heroic death of a staff sergeant as told in hindsight by a soldier who, as a young private, had been befriended by the seasoned veteran. "Soft-Boiled Sergeant" is Salinger's ninth published story. The author, however, chose not to include the story in his three books of collected stories.

SYNOPSIS

The narrator, an enlisted man during the time of the Second World War, informs the reader that his wife, Juanita, is a war-movie buff who insists on "dragging" (18) him "to a million movies" (18). He complains about the false picture the movies give of the reality of war: leading men who have "plenty of time, before they croak" (18) to send messages to their girls back home; heroes able to pass on enemy secrets before dying; handsome comrades who have time to "watch the handsomest guy croak" (18); and finally the bugle taps and the fancy funeral back in the hero's hometown, with the guy's girlfriend and everyone including the mayor or even the president all dressed up and in attendance.

To counteract his wife's penchant for this kind of Hollywood war, the narrator has told her the story of Burke. He is then sorry that he told her and says that she is "no ordinary dame" (18). If Juanita, he says, sees even a dead rat in the road, she starts hitting him with her fists, as if he is to blame for its death. The narrator then offers the reader his first piece of advice about women: "Don't never marry no ordinary dame . . . Wait for the kind that starts smacking you with their fists when they see a dead rat laying in the road" (18). Addressing the reader as "*you*" (18), he then explains that he will start from the beginning and tell the story of Burke.

The narrator, in the army, has no regrets about having enlisted four years after the end of World War I, even though he entered at the young age of 16. The army has allowed him to see "big things" (82). He often tells Juanita about these events, which give her goose pimples every time. The narrator, whom the reader now knows as Philly (Juanita's response to his last story has included his first name), then offers his second piece of advice about women: "Don't marry no dame that don't get goose pimples when you tell her about something big you seen" (82).

Philly recommences the tale. On his first day in the army, Philly meets Staff Sergeant Burke. Although Burke is only 25 or so at the time, he does not look young. He is physically ugly, with his "bushy black hair that stood up like steel wool," his "slopy-like, peewee shoulders," his large head and "goo-goo-googly eyes," and he has a "two-toned" (82) voice. Burke's ugliness, however, does not prevent him from doing big things (where handsome soldiers, on the other hand, fall apart if they do not have a letter from their girl or will not do what is expected if no one is watching). Burke reminds Philly of another man, a hobo, who—although almost dead from tuberculosis—prevented two thugs from beating Philly up on a freight car long ago.

Philly goes on to tell of his first day in the service. At 16 years old, he spends the early evening in his bunk, afraid of the other soldiers—tough guys who had been part of the toughest company in the war (World War I) and who had fought in France. Philly cries for hours until Burke, the company's staff sergeant, notices his despair and gives him a handkerchief, in which are tied up all of the sergeant's own war medals. With the gift, Philly introduces himself to Burke as Philly Burns and stops crying. Philly recognizes among the medals and ribbons some of the best—including the "Crah de Gairry" (84) (La Croix de Guerre). Burke tells the boy to pin the medals to his long underwear. (Philly again remarks that Burke "knowed how to do big things" [84].) Burke next tells Philly to get dressed, and to Philly's surprise, Burke eas-

ily gets a pass. Burke takes the boy into town to a restaurant, where Philly eats heartily. Burke, however, eats very little and confides that he keeps thinking about a certain redheaded girl who "Don't wiggle much when she walks. Just kind of walks straight like" (84). The girl has just been married, but Burke had known her before that. Burke then takes Philly to a Charlie Chaplin movie where the two encounter a redheaded girl with her civilian husband. She and Burke exchange hellos, and Philly learns that she is the girl Burke had been thinking about. Philly enjoys the movie, but Burke waits outside during the showing, explaining that he doesn't like the "funny-looking little guys always getting chased by the big guys. Never getting no girl, like. For keeps, like" (85). Philly then remarks that he feels remorse for not having been able to tell his hero how he felt—that Burke was better off without the redheaded girl. He regrets that a man like Burke could go his whole life as a great man, but only a few people at most would ever know about him. And no women would ever know. Only maybe "a coupla ordinary dames, but never the kind that don't wiggle when they walk, the kind that sort of walks straight like. Them kind of girls, the kind Burke really liked, was stopped by his face and that rotten joke of a voice of his" (85).

Several weeks pass, and Philly wears Burke's medals day and night. The medals keep the other soldiers, who deeply respect Burke, from razzing the young private. Philly grows emotionally closer to the sergeant. One evening, he sees Burke sketching and remarks how good the drawing is—a picture of a redheaded girl. He also learns that Burke shares the same background as his own, the hard-luck life of a hobo.

Burke arranges for Philly Burns to be transferred to the Army Air Corps, where Philly will see "big stuff" (85). Years pass without Philly ever again encountering the sergeant, although Burke, too, had transferred to the Air Corps. Receiving a letter from Frankie Miklos, who had been at Pearl Harbor, Philly finally learns of Burke's fate. Frankie wants to tell Philly about a man named Burke, "a master, with nine hash marks" (85).

Philly ends his story by telling about Burke's death. "His number come up there at Pearl Harbor. Only it didn't exactly come up like other guys' numbers do. Burke put his own up. Frankie seen Burke put his own number up" (85). Philly then describes what Frankie's letter says about how Burke, in a barracks under heavy attack from Japanese bombers, learned of three young privates who had locked themselves in a mess-hall refrigerator to shelter from danger. Burke reacted violently to the news, knowing that the vibration from the bombs would surely kill the men. Running toward the mess hall, Burke was hit by gunfire. Frankie had specified that the hit, Philly relates, was "four holes between his shoulders . . . and half of Burke's jaw was shot off" (85). Although mortally wounded, Burke successfully released the men and directed them to safety. However, "he died all by himself, and he didn't have no messages to give to no girl or nobody" (85). Philly laments that Burke would not have been honored with a fancy funeral and that he would not have had any bugle taps. He remarks that "the only funeral Burke got was when Juanita cried for him . . . Juanita she ain't no ordinary dame" (85). Philly then imparts his final piece of advice: "Don't never marry no ordinary dame, bud. Get one that'll cry for a Burke" (85).

CRITICAL ANALYSIS

"Soft-Boiled Sergeant" is primarily a portrait of a heroic army sergeant and his selfless act of courage in saving his men at the expense of his own life. To shape the story, however, Salinger utilizes a complex device, and one that he will develop more fully in many of his later works—that of the narrative frame, with a first-person narrator, in current time, telling of past events (in this case, the story of his relationship to someone once very close to him, now deceased). "The LAUGHING MAN," a later, more significant work in Salinger's NINE STORIES collection, shows evidence of both the content and structure of "Soft-Boiled Sergeant" and echoes the frame of the mature narrator telling of his relationship to a hero figure of his youth. These stories also contain a tale-within-a-tale, or meta-narration. The tale-within-the-tale in "Soft-Boiled Sergeant" comprises the information in the letter that Frankie Miklos writes about the events surrounding Sergeant Burke's heroism. In "The Laughing Man,"

the tale-within-the-tale comprises the fable that its creator, John Gedsudski, contrives for the entertainment of the boys. (Other examples of Salinger's use of meta-narration in his uncollected stories can be found in "The VARIONI BROTHERS" and "The HEART OF A BROKEN STORY".)

Along with the solemn tale of Burke, "Soft-Boiled Sergeant" injects some serious advice from its narrator about the kind of girl the reader/listener must marry. The critic Warren French, in his 1963 study of Salinger's fiction, in fact sees the primary purpose of "Soft-Boiled Sergeant" as a vehicle "to offer advice to prospective husbands. The narrator's point is that one should shy away from the kind of girl who avoids Burke and marry only the kind that cries when she hears his story" (French 59).

With the use of colloquial speech and colorful phrases, Salinger creates a believable character in the narrator, Philly Burns, and in his impoverished childhood and hard-luck life. Philly displays, as does the sergeant he admires, an emotional sensitivity beneath his seemingly rough exterior. Salinger had previously experimented at length with a working-class vernacular in the voice of Billy Vullmer, the first-person narrator of "BOTH PARTIES CONCERNED," also published earlier the same year in the *Saturday Evening Post*. However, the speech pattern Salinger creates for Billy Vullmer, with its halting repetitions and use of generalizations, makes Billy, as William Purcell observes in his 1996 article on the speech patterns of Salinger's characters, seem uncertain about what he is saying. Billy's speech signals him to be an unreliable narrator (Purcell 278), leaving the reader on his own to interpret the events of the narrative and to question the veracity of Billy's interpretation of events. Philly Burns, on the other hand, does not exhibit any unreliability about what he intends to convey. On the contrary, he delivers each statement as if no doubt could exist about the veracity of the tale.

Salinger likewise incorporates in this story (as in other works, including "ELAINE," "ONCE A WEEK WON'T KILL YOU," "The LONG DEBUT OF LOIS TAGGETT," and "JUST BEFORE THE WAR WITH THE ESKIMOS") the protagonist's search for solace via moviegoing. For example, when young Philly Burns is discovered crying in his bunk by Sergeant Burke, the sergeant takes him to see a Charlie Chaplin film to cheer him up. Salinger likewise uses this story, however, to skewer the type of Hollywood movie that falsifies the actualities of war. (The story begins with the narrator's outright disapproval of the kind of war movies his wife, Juanita, drags him to see.) The critic John Wenke observes that the story "debunks the sentimentalized popularization of war, especially the way in which the movies present cosmetically-serene surfaces" (Wenke 16). Wenke also notes that "the true story of the ugly, unphotogenic Burke . . . provides a sobering antidote to Hollywood's fantasy portrayals" (Wenke 17).

"DEATH OF A DOGFACE," the story's original title, was changed to "Soft-Boiled Sergeant" by the editors at the *Saturday Evening Post*. Neither phrase appears within the text of the work.

The *Saturday Evening Post* illustrated the story with one drawing—Philly Burns sitting on his bunk, wearing Sergeant Burke's medals on his long underwear. Another soldier stares at the medals; Burke is off to the side.

PUBLICATION HISTORY

"Soft-Boiled Sergeant" was published in the April 15, 1944, issue of the *Saturday Evening Post*. Salinger never reprinted the story in his three books of collected stories. "Soft-Boiled Sergeant" later appeared in the bootleg editions *The COMPLETE UNCOLLECTED SHORT STORIES OF J. D. SALINGER* (1974) and *TWENTY-TWO STORIES* (1998).

CHARACTERS

Burke, Sergeant Staff Sergeant Burke, a veteran of World War I, befriends the very young private Philly Burns, whom he finds crying in his bunk on his first day as an enlisted soldier. Burke, a well-respected army man, saw the worst of the fighting in the previous war and was decorated as a war hero many times over. Burke gives his medals—including the Croix de Guerre—to the young Burns to protect him from the other soldiers' harassment and to cheer him up. Burke confides in Burns of his unrequited love for a redheaded girl who has recently married a civilian. A physically ugly man, Burke cannot hope to attract the woman of his dreams. Although a hardened soldier on the exterior, he is emotionally sensitive (or "soft-boiled"). Burke is also seen to be good at drawing and sketching, and so carries with him an artistic sensibility. Burke's sensitivity is displayed in his kindness toward Burns, a boy soldier, and is finally blended with his war-hardened ability to give his life to save three young privates from certain death during the attack on Pearl Harbor.

Burns, Juanita Juanita Burns, wife of Philly Burns, drags her husband to the movies to see war pictures. Philly disapproves of these Hollywood wars, with their false depictions of the realities of war. When Philly tells Juanita the story of Burke, a true war hero, she cries for the fallen sergeant. In her act of grief, she gives Burke "the only funeral" (85) he would receive. Juanita, described by her husband as "no ordinary dame" (18), is the marrying type of woman (according to Philly)—the type who will "cry for a Burke" (85).

Burns, Philly The narrator of the tale of Sergeant Burke, Philly Burns enlisted in the army at the very young age of 16. The frightened Burns, befriended by his staff sergeant, Burke, comes to know the older soldier perhaps more intimately than most of his comrades. The two men share the same kind of hard-luck, impoverished childhood as hobos. Like Burke, Philly shows a sensitive and emotional side. He understands his hero's vulnerability, and he appreciates his wife's sympathy and grief for the fallen war hero. A happily married man, Philly offers sound advice throughout the narrative about the kind of woman to marry—one like his wife, Juanita (and not, presumably, like the redheaded girl who did not reciprocate Sergeant Burke's love).

Miklos, Frankie Frankie Miklos, who was with Sergeant Burke during the attack on Pearl Harbor, witnessed Burke's heroism in sacrificing his own life to save three young privates. Frankie writes the letter (which represents the tale-within-the-tale) that informs Philly Burns about the details surrounding Burke's death. The letter is not reproduced in the text, but its contents are conveyed by Philly Burns.

FURTHER READING

French, Warren. *J. D. Salinger.* New York: Twayne Publishers, 1963.

Purcell, William F. "Narrative Voice in J. D. Salinger's 'Both Parties Concerned' and 'I'm Crazy.'" *Studies in Short Fiction* 33 (Spring 1996): 278–280.

Wenke, John. *J. D. Salinger: A Study of the Short Fiction.* Boston: Twayne Publishers, 1991.

"Stranger, The"

Appearing in the December 1, 1945, issue of COL-LIER'S, "The Stranger" features Babe Gladwaller's visit to the former girlfriend of a deceased soldier, Vincent Caulfield. "The Stranger" is Salinger's 15th published story. The author, however, chose not to include the story in his three books of collected stories.

SYNOPSIS

In late August 1945, Babe Gladwaller, recently released from army service, has gone into NEW YORK CITY with his sister Mattie to eat Chinese food and see a show. They first visit Vincent Caulfield's former girlfriend, Helen Beebers, now married to Bob Polk. The maid lets Babe and Mattie into the apartment; Helen is delayed in another room. Babe notices "some fine books" and wonders "who owned and cared about Rainer Maria Rilke, and *The Beautiful and Damned* and *A High Wind in Jamaica*" (18). He picks up a prewar record and notices Helen's maiden name as its owner. The record brings him back to "the unrecoverable years: the little, unhistorical, pretty good years when all the dead boys in the 12th Regiment had been living and cutting in on other dead boys on lost dance floors . . ." (18).

Helen enters, talking away, as she thinks the caller to be the curtain man. After she asks Babe what is wrong with his eyes, he identifies himself, his sister, and his hay fever and says that he "was in the Army with Vincent Caulfield"; the two sol-

diers "were very good friends" (77). Helen does not like her living room and suggests they all go into her bedroom to talk. She wonders aloud why Babe came and quickly says she is "glad" (77). Babe is stunned by her looks: "there was never a way . . . that a man could condition himself against the lethal size and shape and melody of beauty by chance" (77). Helen learns that Babe has gotten out of the army "on that new points thing" (77) the previous week. Mattie proudly speaks of his battle stars and says she has his uniform "in a box" (77).

Babe clumsily says, "You know Vincent's— you know he was killed, don't you?" (77). Helen explains that Mr. Caulfield had called her shortly after it happened; she guesses that he had (erroneously) thought Vincent and she were "still engaged" (77). Babe explains the reason he has dropped in: He has come to tell Helen how Vincent died. Helen says she wants to know.

Babe explains that a mortar shell exploded in the Hürtgen Forest, hitting Vincent; Babe was standing nearby. Vincent died several minutes later, with Babe at his side. Babe thinks Vincent knew him and heard him, but Vincent was silent.

Babe stops talking when he realizes Helen is crying. Mattie interjects that Vincent visited their house; "he was a witty guy" (77). After Helen quickly stops crying, Babe apologizes for coming. He knew from Vincent that Helen once loved him, and Babe thought she would want to know how it all happened. Babe tells Helen that he does not know "what's wrong" (77) with him since his return to America.

Helen asks what a mortar is. After Babe explains, he thinks to himself how terrible it was that he would want to tell her all this. He thinks "a soldier's mind wanted accuracy above all else . . . don't let any civilian leave you, when the story's over, with any comfortable lies" (77). Then Babe says aloud to Helen that Vincent loved her "something terrific" (77). He imagines it was not anyone's fault that they did not stay together, but Helen contradicts him. She explains that she loved Vincent, "loved his brothers" (77) and parents. But "from the time little Kenneth Caulfield died," the brother "he was so crazy about," Vincent "didn't believe [in] anything" (77).

Babe takes out an envelope that he had once borrowed from Vincent. He explains that he discovered a poem on the back about Helen. He says she can have the poem and hands it to her. She reads it through and shakes her head, "but not as though she were denying anything" (77). Helen folds up the envelope and puts it in her pocket. Babe concludes the visit, saying, "I had the best and worst motives . . . I'm acting very peculiarly. I don't know what's the matter" (77).

When Helen expresses her appreciation for his coming, Babe begins to cry. He quickly walks toward the front door and then asks if they can catch a cab at this hour. As almost an afterthought, Babe invites Helen to accompany them to lunch and the theater. She cannot. When Helen asks Babe what he plans to do now, he answers, "Is there something to do?" (77). He then catches himself and says he will probably go back to college and later teach. Helen tells him to call her sometime, but Babe thinks she feels sorry for him. He says, "Don't be that way. I'm just not used to things yet" (77).

Once Babe and Mattie are on the street, he sees a doorman walking a dog. He imagines the man walked the dog during the entire Battle of the Bulge. Mattie talks Babe's ear off, suggesting different shows they could see. She suddenly asks him if he is glad to be back home. He answers, yes, and she exclaims, "You're hurting my hand" (77). While they wait for a bus, Mattie announces that she can use chopsticks. Babe replies, "that's something I'll have to *see*" (77). Mattie assures him he will, and she makes a "little jump from the curb to the street surface, then back again" (77). Babe wonders to himself, "Why was it such a beautiful thing to see?" (77).

CRITICAL ANALYSIS

"The Stranger" is the third and final story that concerns Babe Gladwaller and members of his family. Although "A BOY IN FRANCE," the second Gladwaller story, contains no mention of Vincent Caulfield, Salinger evidently realized that the relationship between Babe and Vincent, as established in "LAST DAY OF THE LAST FURLOUGH," provided the basis for a final story. The seed for the premise

of "The Stranger" lies in "Last Day of the Last Furlough." Salinger includes an offhand reference to Vincent's former girlfriend, Helen, who is married and expecting a child. In "The Stranger," Salinger has Babe visit the married Helen (there is no evidence of a child) to convey the story of Vincent's death. "The Stranger" reveals that Vincent and Babe were in the same regiment; Vincent is killed in the Hürtgen Forest as he stood around a fire with Babe and several other soldiers. (The battle of Hürtgen Forest dates Vincent's death to the period of November–December 1944.) Thus, "The Stranger" symbolically reunites the two main characters of "Last Day of the Last Furlough" and, like the earlier story, is known also as a Caulfield story.

"The Stranger" illustrates the difficult readjustment of a war veteran to civilian life. Babe has been out of the army for one week. His fragile state (he nebulously calls it "what's wrong" [77]) is confirmed when he breaks into tears as Helen says she is glad he came and also when he unknowingly holds Mattie's hand too tightly.

Babe feels compelled to tell Helen the story of Vincent's death, acknowledging that a soldier's "mind wanted to tell civilians these things [and] wanted accuracy above all else" (77). This sense of testifying to the truth forces him to come on this "mission." Babe understands that his being alive—instead of Vincent—is pure luck. He thinks to himself, "Don't let anybody good down" (77).

The unadorned story also portrays the honoring of the dead by the living. But this honoring has none of the pomp and circumstance one associates with public memorials. Salinger signals the honoring as an intimate act of one-on-one. In a nondescript New York apartment, Babe tells Helen how Vincent died. He delivers Vincent's poem about her that he found by chance. Salinger celebrates the power of poetry here, as the poem is the vehicle that brings words back from beyond the grave. (The first allusion in Salinger's work to his perennial favorite poet, RAINER MARIA RILKE, occurs at the story's outset.)

Within the narrative of "The Stranger," Salinger embeds one of the most moving passages of all of his work. As Babe waits for Helen, he picks up a prewar jazz record; he hears, in his mind, "the old Bakewell Howard's rough, fine horn playing" (18). Salinger's genius reveals itself as he immediately follows the word "playing" with: "Then he began to hear the music of the unrecoverable years: the little, unhistorical, pretty good years when all the dead boys in the 12th Regiment had been living and cutting in on other dead boys on lost dance floors: the years when no one who could dance worth a damn had ever heard of Cherbourg or Saint-Lô or Hürtgen Forest or Luxembourg" (18). Salinger, himself, was with the 12th Regiment; the roll call of places is where the regiment fought.

In the Gladwaller trilogy—"Last Day of the Last Furlough," "A Boy in France," and "The Stranger"—Salinger depicts, for the only time in his work, the spectrum of one man's experience of the war: prior to overseas deployment, the experience of the European battlefield, the return to America, postwar. Additionally, the trilogy introduces a recurring Salingerian motif: the importance of a female child's innocence to a male character. In each of the stories, Babe's young sister, Mattie, plays an important part. In the initial story, "Last Day of the Last Furlough," the look on her face when she sees her older brother outside her school inspires him to bravely meet his duty. Mattie's presence in the middle story, "A Boy in France," is embodied by her letter, which Babe treats as a talisman. And, finally, in "The Stranger," Babe experiences the first vestiges of healing as he notices Mattie make a small dancelike jump, which he finds inexplicably beautiful.

"The Stranger" is also important for additional information about the dynamics of the Caulfield family. When Babe asks Helen why she and Vincent broke up, she explains that Vincent had become totally disillusioned "from the time little Kenneth Caulfield died. His brother . . . the little one, the younger one he was so crazy about" (18). Kenneth Caulfield prefigures Allie Caulfield in *The* CATCHER IN THE RYE. The depth of Vincent's feelings toward Kenneth are later transposed into Holden's for Allie in the novel. (Neither Holden nor Phoebe is mentioned by name in "The Stranger.") "The Stranger" "kills off" Vincent Caulfield, the last living brother in the original

Caulfield family. The story marks an ending and will, in time, allow Salinger a new beginning. At some unknown moment (to which readers aren't privy), the author will decide to resurrect Holden Caulfield into a postwar incarnation, recast the Caulfield family, and write his masterpiece, *The Catcher in the Rye*. (For more information regarding the seven extant Caulfield stories, *see* CAUL-FIELD STORIES.

Collier's illustrated the story with one drawing—Babe sitting in a chair, talking, as he faces Helen and Mattie, who sit on the side of Helen's bed. (This illustration was used on the cover of the second edition of the bootleg set *The* COMPLETE UNCOLLECTED SHORT STORIES OF J. D. SALINGER [1974].)

PUBLICATION HISTORY

"The Stranger" was published in the December 1, 1945, issue of *Collier's*. Salinger never reprinted the story in his three books of collected stories. "The Stranger" later appeared in the bootleg editions *The Complete Uncollected Short Stories of J. D. Salinger* (1974) and TWENTY-TWO STORIES (1998).

CHARACTERS

Caulfield, Kenneth Helen Polk refers to Kenneth Caulfield when she explains that Vincent Caulfield stopped believing in life once Kenneth, "the little one, the younger one" (77), died.

Kenneth appears in or is referenced in additional Caulfield stories: "THIS SANDWICH HAS NO MAYONNAISE" and the unpublished "The LAST AND BEST OF THE PETER PANS" and "The OCEAN FULL OF BOWLING BALLS."

Caulfield, Mr. Mr. Caulfield phones Helen Polk to inform her of his son Vincent's death. He cannot remember Helen's first name and mistakenly believes Vincent and Helen are still engaged.

The Caulfield parents, either singly or together, appear in or are referenced in additional Caulfield stories: "Last Day of the Last Furlough," "This Sandwich Has No Mayonnaise," "I'M CRAZY," "SLIGHT REBELLION OFF MADISON," and the unpublished "The Last and Best of the Peter Pans" and "The Ocean Full of Bowling Balls."

Caulfield, Vincent   Babe Gladwaller drops in on Helen Polk to tell her about Vincent Caulfield's death in the Hürtgen Forest and to deliver Vincent's poem.

Vincent appears in or is referenced in additional Caulfield stories: "Last Day of the Last Furlough," "This Sandwich Has No Mayonnaise," and the unpublished "The Last and Best of the Peter Pans" and "The Ocean Full of Bowling Balls."

Gladwaller, Babe   The story's protagonist, Babe Gladwaller, one week out of the army, visits Helen Polk to tell her how Vincent Caulfield died. Babe, having trouble readjusting to civilian life, is accompanied by his sister, Mattie.

Babe is the protagonist of "Last Day of the Last Furlough" and "A Boy in France."

Gladwaller, Mattie   Mattie Gladwaller has accompanied her older brother, Babe, to New York City to see Helen Polk and to have lunch and see a show. Her dancelike jump, at the story's end, provides a healing effect upon her brother.

Mattie appears in "Last Day of the Last Furlough," and Babe reads her letter in "A Boy in France."

Mamma (Mrs. Gladwaller)   Mattie Gladwaller tells her brother, Babe, that their mother suggests they see either the musical *Oklahoma!* or the play *Harvey*.

Mrs. Gladwaller appears in "Last Day of the Last Furlough" and is referenced in "A Boy in France."

Polk, Bob   Helen Polk refers to her husband, Bob, who has easy access to entertainment tickets.

Polk, Mrs. Helen (Helen Beebers)   The beautiful Helen Polk, née Beebers, receives an unexpected visit from Babe and Mattie Gladwaller. Helen, the former girlfriend of Vincent Caulfield, tells Babe that she wants to hear how Vincent died.

Helen is referenced in "Last Day of the Last Furlough" and "This Sandwich Has No Mayonnaise."

FURTHER READING

French, Warren. *J. D. Salinger.* New York: Twayne Publishers, 1963.

———. *J. D. Salinger, Revisited.* New York: Twayne Publishers, 1988.

Lundquist, James. *J. D. Salinger.* New York: Ungar, 1979.

Purcell, William F. "World War II and the Early Fiction of J. D. Salinger." *Studies in American Literature* 28 (1991): 77–93.

Wenke, John. *J. D. Salinger: A Study of the Short Fiction.* Boston: Twayne Publishers, 1991.

"Summer Accident, A"

"A Summer Accident" is one of Salinger's "lost" stories, neither published nor to be found in a library archive. According to Ben Yagoda, after the NEW YORKER rejected a story with this title in 1949, Salinger resumed working on The CATCHER IN THE RYE. Unless the manuscript can be located among Salinger's literary estate, the story's whereabouts are unknown.

"Survivors, The"

"The Survivors" is one of Salinger's "lost" stories, neither published nor to be found in a library archive. According to the bibliographer Jack R. Sublette, Salinger mentions a story with this title in a 1940 letter to WHIT BURNETT. Unless the manuscript can be located among Salinger's literary estate, the story's whereabouts are unknown.

"Teddy"

"Teddy" is the ninth and final story in Salinger's second book, NINE STORIES (1953). Originally published in the January 31, 1953, issue of the NEW YORKER, "Teddy" features the 10-year-old God-seeker Teddy McArdle. The story, with its controversial ending, shows Salinger's interest in the Hindu philosophy, VEDANTA, referenced for the first time in the author's work. "Teddy" is Salinger's 30th published story.

SYNOPSIS

Teddy McArdle, an underweight 10-year-old boy, is standing on his father's new, expensive piece of luggage in order to put his head through the open porthole of his parents' stateroom. Mr. McArdle, wearing only his pajama bottoms on his sunburned body, lies on one of two twin beds. His pillow is on the floor between the beds, along with his ashtray. With his head uncomfortably positioned against the headboard, Mr. McArdle orders Teddy to get off the bag. Teddy doesn't reply, and his father again demands that his son get down off the bag.

Teddy is wearing dirty sneakers with no socks, a pair of oversized shorts, an old T-shirt, and an elegant alligator belt. He is badly in need of a haircut. Mr. McArdle asks Teddy whether he had heard the instruction. Though Teddy's head is leaning out the porthole, he can hear his father's voice, which is loud and deep. Teddy turns and gives his father "a look of inquiry, whole and pure" (255). Though Teddy's brown eyes are slightly crossed, "his face . . . carried the impact, however oblique and slow-travelling, of real beauty" (256).

After Mr. McArdle again commands Teddy to get off the bag, Mrs. McArdle speaks up. She is in the other twin bed; "her second sheet was drawn tight over her very probably nude body" (256). Teddy's mother tells Teddy not to move. She adds that he should jump on his father's bag and crush it. Mr. and Mrs. McArdle have a verbal spat. He says that he would like to kick open his wife's head. She muses that he will eventually have a heart attack and that she will be flirting at the funeral.

Teddy again looks out the porthole and remarks that their ocean liner's path had crossed the *Queen Mary*'s that morning. He doubts his parents are interested in this fact. Mr. McArdle again demands that Teddy get off the bag and suggests that his son go get a haircut. Teddy answers that he has no money. He tells his mother about a brief encounter with a man in the ship's gym. The man, Bob Nicholson, mentioned in passing that he had heard an audiotape Teddy had made when the boy was interviewed by the Leidekker examining group in Boston. Mrs. McArdle distractedly takes in what Teddy is telling her. She asks Teddy if he and his sister, Booper, have a swimming lesson later that morning.

Teddy notices that someone has dumped a garbage can of orange peels overboard, and the peels are floating on the water. He muses aloud that if he had not seen the orange peels he would not know of their existence. Mrs. McArdle interrupts Teddy and tells him to go and find his sister. Teddy watches the orange peels disappear into the water and remarks that "the only place they'll still be floating will be inside [his] mind" (261). As Teddy thinks aloud about whether the orange peels would exist if he had not seen them—for instance, if someone had decapitated him when he first put his head outside of the porthole—his mother again interrupts him. She wants to know where her daughter is, and adds that she does not want Teddy's sister bothering people. Teddy tells his mother that he has given Booper the camera. This causes his father to erupt, demanding that Teddy retrieve the expensive camera immediately or, he threatens, "there's going to be one little genius among the missing" (262).

Teddy finally steps down off of the bag. Mrs. McArdle tells Teddy to find Booper and to tell her that she wants her. Teddy gives his mother an asked-for kiss, but nonchalantly. He picks up his father's pillow and wipes the cigarette ashes on the nightstand into the ashtray. Teddy believes that his father could not be comfortable with his head against the headboard, and he puts the pillow on the foot of his father's bed. What Mr. McArdle wants, emphatically, is his camera. Teddy lingers at the cabin door and remarks, "After I go out of this door, I may only exist in the minds of all my acquaintances. I may be an orange peel" (265). This remark causes his mother to ask her son what he had said and to request another kiss. Teddy refuses to kiss her, saying that he is tired, and leaves the cabin.

Teddy picks up the ship's listing of the day's events that he finds lying outside the door. As he is reading the page, a woman in uniform passes and grazes the top of his head, remarking that he needs a haircut. Teddy reaches the Main Deck and encounters another ship employee, Ensign Mathewson. He asks her when the word game takes place. The ensign thinks that the game would be too advanced for Teddy, but he denies her assumption.

After looking around for a while, Teddy finds Booper on the Sports Deck. His six-year-old sister has stacked the shuffleboard disks. A younger child, Myron, stands deferentially to the side watching her show off her accomplishment. Teddy asks his sister where she has put the camera. Ignoring Teddy, Booper criticizes Myron, calling him "the stupidest person in this ocean" (269). Teddy reassures Myron that he is not, and he again asks Booper the camera's whereabouts. After he locates the camera, Teddy asks Booper to do him a favor. He wants her take the camera back to their parents because it is 10:00 A.M. and time for Teddy to write in his diary. Booper at first resists, but then she relents. Teddy tells her he will meet her at the pool at 10:30 for their swimming lesson. She yells that she hates him and everybody else.

Teddy goes to the Sun Deck in search of his family's deck chairs, where he can sit and write in his diary. Before beginning to write, he rereads his previous day's entry of October 27, 1952. Teddy has written that he should find his father's army dog tags and wear them because that would please his father. He reminds himself that he should answer Professor Mandell's letter and also ask him not to send any more books of poetry. Teddy imagines a situation where a wife, walking along a beach, finds her husband's head cracked open by a falling coconut, whereupon the wife is heartbroken. Teddy remarks, "that is exactly where I am tired of poetry" (274). He muses that the wife should instead pick up the two halves of her husband's head and shout into them "very angrily 'Stop that!'" (274). He admonishes himself not to mention this in his letter to the professor, because the professor's wife is a poet. Teddy additionally reminds himself to get Sven's address (Sven runs the gym), because he would like to meet Sven's wife and his dog; not to "lose consciousness" (275) during meditation; and to look up five words in the ship's library, one of which is "gift horse."

Teddy then starts to write in his diary, beginning with the date October 28, 1952. He first notates the recipients of the nine letters he wrote after this morning's meditation. Teddy also notes that he could have asked his mother about his father's dog tags, but he admits that she would say he did not have to wear them. He then writes, "Life is a gift horse in my opinion" (276). Teddy writes that Professor Walton is wrong to criticize Teddy's parents. The last entry Teddy writes down is the enigmatic comment, "It will either happen today or February 14, 1958 when I am sixteen. It is ridiculous to mention even" (277). Teddy stares at the page with his pen suspended.

While Teddy has been writing in his diary, he has been watched by Bob Nicholson, who has been standing at the Sports Deck railing. Nicholson, a young man and a university teacher, descends to the lower deck and approaches Teddy's chair. "Teddy seemed oblivious of the fact that someone was standing at the foot of his chair—or, for that matter, casting a shadow over his notebook" (278). Nicholson says hello to the boy and sits down next to Teddy. (They had briefly encountered each other in the gym earlier in the day.) After some small talk about how the weather affects him, Nicholson formally introduces himself. Nicholson asks Teddy about where he has been in Europe and if he had been interviewed anywhere. Teddy replies that he has been questioned at the University of Oxford and the University of Edinburgh.

Teddy asks whether Nicholson is a poet. Nicholson responds in the negative and wonders why Teddy had asked. Teddy remarks that poets take the weather personally; that "they're always sticking their emotions in things that have no emotions" (282). Nicholson believes that poets must deal with emotions. Teddy then quotes two Japanese haikus: "Nothing in the voice of the cicada intimates how soon it will die" and "Along this road goes no one, this autumn eve" (282). He tells Nicholson that these poems are not laden with emotions. While doing so, Teddy gives "his right ear a light clap with his hand" (283), trying to extract some water from a swimming lesson the day before.

Nicholson informs Teddy that he has heard from Al Babcock, and that Teddy "left a pretty disturbed bunch of pedants up at Boston," in fact "the whole Leidekker examining group" (283). Ignoring this statement, Teddy wonders why people value emotions; he does not see their usefulness. Nicholson says he heard from Babcock that Teddy loves God. The child acknowledges that he does, but that he does not love God sentimentally. He loves his parents, but not in the way Nicholson wants the word to mean. Teddy prefers to use the word "affinity." Teddy thinks that his parents cannot love him and his sister as they are. He explains that parents usually want to change their children. His parents "love their reasons for loving us almost as much as they love us, and most of the time more" (285).

Asking Nicholson the time, Teddy says they can talk for 10 more minutes. Nicholson says he understands that Teddy believes in the "Vedantic theory of reincarnation" (286). This elicits Teddy's reply that reincarnation is not a theory. Not wanting to argue the point, Nicholson remarks having heard that Teddy believes himself to have been a holy man in India during his last incarnation, but one who "fell from Grace before final Illumination" (287). Though Teddy disputes having been a holy man, he does admit to having been spiritually advanced in the past life; however, he became involved with a woman and had consequently stopped meditating. Teddy explains that he would have been reincarnated anyway, but due to the romantic entanglement, he was required to be reborn in America. Teddy states that "it's very hard to meditate and live a spiritual life in America. People think you're a freak if you try to" (287).

Nicholson tells of having heard on an interview tape that Teddy had recorded that the boy had his first mystical experience when he was six. Teddy affirms the fact and explains that, while watching his sister drink her milk, he realized "everything was God . . . *she* was God and the *milk* was God . . . all she was doing was pouring God into God" (288). Teddy tells Nicholson that he was able to "get out of the finite dimensions" (288) when he was four years old. With a laugh, Nicholson asks him how. Teddy explains that "everybody just thinks things keep stopping off somewhere. They don't" (289). To demonstrate, Teddy asks Nicholson to hold his arm up. Teddy then asks Nicholson why he thinks it is his arm. Nicholson's reply is merely logical, Teddy continues, instructing Nicholson that logic is the first thing to avoid in trying to escape finite dimensions. Teddy reveals to Nicholson that the apple Adam ate in the Garden of Eden was filled with "logic and intellectual stuff" (291) and nothing else. If one wants to see things as they really are, one must vomit up the apple. Teddy believes that people "don't even want to stop getting born and dying all the time. They just want new bodies all the time, instead of stopping and staying with God, where it's really nice" (291). He concludes by remarking that he has "never seen such a bunch of apple-eaters" (292).

Nicholson changes the subject and asks if Teddy told the men in the Leidekker examining group "when and where and how they would eventually die" (292). The boy emphatically denies the rumor. He had told the professors of religion and philosophy in the group some places and times they should watch out for. One of the professors, Walton, had started the discussion, saying he wished he knew when he was going to die so that he would know on which projects he should concentrate. Teddy says that he could have told each of the men precisely when they would die, but he realized that the men did not really want to know, explaining that they are afraid to die. He describes the fear as "silly. . . . everybody's done it thousands and thousands of times" (294).

Teddy next explains to Nicholson that, when he goes to take his swimming lesson, the pool may have been drained. Teddy could go to the edge of the pool to look at its bottom, and while doing so his young sister, who does not like him, might come up and "sort of push [him] in. [He] could fracture [his] skull and die instantaneously" (295). Teddy remarks that the incident would not be tragic. Nicholson counters that the death would be tragic from the perspective of Teddy's parents. Teddy attempts to explain his perspective with the story of a hypothetical death of Sven's dog. If Sven dreamed that his dog had died, he would be relieved when he woke and realized the death to be only a dream. On the other hand, if the dog had indeed died, Teddy explains, the situation would be actually the same. But Sven would realize this only when he, himself, died.

Teddy stands up, saying that he must leave for his swimming lesson on E Deck. Nicholson detains him by asking why Teddy advised Professor Peet to stop teaching. Teddy explains that the professor is spiritual but that "it's time for him to take everything *out* of his head, instead of putting more stuff *in*" (297), and that the professor would make more spiritual progress in this way. Nicholson asks how Teddy would change the education system, as Nicholson is in education. Teddy replies that he would first teach the children "how to meditate. I'd try to show them how to find out who they *are,* not just what their names are . . . I'd get them to empty out everything their parents and everybody ever told them" (298). Nicholson wonders whether the children would then end up ignoramuses, and Teddy disputes the idea. Teddy believes the children could learn all sorts of things later on, but he wants them "to *begin* with all the real ways of looking at things, not just the way all the other apple-eaters look at things" (299).

Nicholson wonders if Teddy would want to do medical research in the future, but Teddy responds in the negative, as he believes that doctors place undue emphasis on cells. Teddy believes people control their cells, that they know how to grow their own bodies. With enough meditation, he feels one could consciously learn again how this is done. Teddy then quickly takes leave of Nicholson— "Goodbye. I have to go" (301).

Nicholson remains seated, motionless, in the deck chair and then finishes his cigarette. He rises and rapidly makes his way down the different deck levels. On D Deck, he loses his way and asks a stewardess for directions. He opens a metal door leading to the pool. Halfway down the staircase, Nicholson hears "an all-piercing, sustained scream—clearly coming from a small, female child" (302).

CRITICAL ANALYSIS

In "SEYMOUR: AN INTRODUCTION" (1959), Salinger assigned Buddy Glass authorship of his works. In the story, Buddy alludes to "Teddy" (1953) as ". . . an ex*cep*tionally Haunting, Memorable, unpleasantly controversial, and thoroughly unsuccessful short story about a 'gifted' little boy aboard a transatlantic liner. . ." (205). The critic Laurence Perrine suggests that if one deletes "the three adverbs from this comment, it makes a fairly accurate judg-

ment on the story" (Perrine 223). To follow Perrine's suggestion yields an assessment of "Teddy" as a hauntingly memorable, controversial story within Salinger's body of work; whether unsuccessful or, in fact, successful, depends on the individual reader.

"Teddy" has engendered highly divergent interpretations. Critics disagree about the personality of the 10-year-old Teddy McArdle; whether Teddy or his six-year-old sister, Booper, plunges into the empty pool; about the story's meaning and ultimate worth.

"Teddy," the final story in Salinger's second book, *Nine Stories,* along with the volume's opening story, "A PERFECT DAY FOR BANANAFISH," appropriately bookend the collection. The stories feature Salinger's two most advanced spiritual characters, Teddy McArdle and Seymour Glass, respectively. The connection between them includes ". . . the God-seeker Teddy McArdle [as] the prototype for the re-designed Seymour in the Glass Family Series" (Alsen 100). (Alsen refers to the resurrection of Seymour Glass in the 1955 story "RAISE HIGH THE ROOF BEAM, CARPENTERS.") "Teddy," a crucial steppingstone to the Glass family stories, also signals Salinger's interest in Vedanta, a philosophical branch of Hinduism. By the time Salinger came to write "Teddy," the author was immersed in the study of ADVAITA VEDANTA at the RAMAKRISHNA-VIVEKANANDA CENTER OF NEW YORK. Salinger was attending classes taught by the center's founder and spiritual leader, SWAMI NIKHILANANDA. Swami Nikhilananda sums up Vedanta's "four cardinal principles . . . :the non-duality of the Godhead, the divinity of the soul, the unity of existence, and the harmony of religions" (Nikhilananda 8). "Teddy" signals Salinger's interest in Vedanta, which would endure throughout the remainder of his published work. In "Raise High the Roof Beam, Carpenters" (1955), Salinger references Vedanta in Seymour's diary (106); in "ZOOEY" (1957), the author mentions SRI RAMAKRISHNA (65) and quotes from *The Gospel of Sri Ramakrishna* (177); in "Seymour: An Introduction" (1959), Buddy Glass alludes to the importance of Advaita Vedanta as one of his "roots in Eastern philosophy" (242); in "HAPWORTH 16, 1924" (1965), Seymour states his admiration and respect for SWAMI VIVEKANANDA (92).

The first reference to Vedanta in Salinger's work occurs when Nicholson, the education professor, says to Teddy, "You hold pretty firmly to the Vedantic theory of reincarnation" (286). Teddy rejoins, "It isn't a theory" (286). Vedanta teaches that "after death the soul assumes a new body and that this rebirth is governed by the law of karma" (Nikhilananda 47). Teddy refers to his previous incarnation as an Indian "making very nice spiritual advancement" (287) who, after meeting a woman, "stopped meditating" (287). Salinger "burdens" Teddy's next incarnation as an American. As the character comments, "it's very hard to meditate and live a spiritual life in America. People think you're a freak if you try to" (287). The reader suspects that Teddy is voicing the author's own thoughts in 1950s America. (Salinger reiterates his belief in reincarnation in "Seymour: An Introduction." Buddy Glass states, "Not [and first blushes here, if any, will be the reader's, not mine]—not in this incarnation, at any rate" [154]. In the same story, Seymour Glass also expresses a belief in reincarnation in his "Dear Old Tyger That Sleeps" letter-memo addressed to Buddy. In "Hapworth 16, 1924," Seymour repeatedly alludes to reincarnation.)

The other reference in "Teddy" to Hinduism concerns the fate for a very advanced spiritual person after death: ". . . and then gone straight to Brahma and never again have to come back to earth" (287). Brahma is the "creator god" of the universe in the Hindu trinity of gods. The other two gods are Vishnu, the "sustainer god," and Shiva, the "destroyer god." It is unclear whether Salinger actually intended to write "Brahman" instead of "Brahma." Brahman ("described as the first principle; from it all things are derived, by it all are supported, and into it all finally disappear" [Nikhilananda 12]) manifests itself as Brahma, Vishnu, and Shiva. "According to the non-dualistic Vedanta philosophy, Brahman is identical with the self of man, known as atman" (Nikhilananda 12). Salinger employs a Vedantic image when Teddy "saw everything was God" (288). As the boy watches his sister drink milk, he sees that "she was God and the milk was God . . . all she was doing was pouring God into God" (288). Nikhilan-

anda writes, "As milk poured into milk becomes one with milk . . . so the illumined soul absorbed in Brahman becomes one with Brahman" (Nikhilananda 56). Teddy's yogic powers—his ability to know past lives, to foresee the future, to calmly keep his appointment with death—suggest that this is Teddy's final incarnation. Teddy has achieved these powers through intense meditation. "By the disciplines of yoga the mind can be 'gathered' and made 'one-pointed.' Then alone does the yogi attain total absorption, or samadhi, and realize the true nature of his self" (Nikhilananda 131). Nikhilananda explains that "in samadhi all the cells in the brain begin to function; thus a perfected yogi claims omniscience" (Nikhilananda 141). Several times in the story Salinger refers to Teddy engaging in meditation and, given the quotation above, revealingly describes the character's "instantly one-pointed concentration" (273).

Teddy, like Seymour Glass, is a God-seeker. His single-mindedness foreshadows that of the seven-year-old Seymour in "Hapworth 16, 1924." Although Teddy is not, like Seymour, presented as a budding poet, he does quote two haikus. This perhaps anticipates Seymour's own development as a poet when he switched to a double-haiku form for his late poetry. Interestingly, Salinger compares the two characters' eyes in "Seymour: An Introduction." Buddy Glass states that his brother's eyes and Teddy's were different, although two Glass family members "remarked that [he] was trying to get at [Seymour's] eyes with that description, and even felt [he] hadn't brought it off too badly, in a peculiar way" (205). Given the importance of the eyes in Buddy's assessment of a seer, Teddy's and Seymour's similarity further links the two characters.

Teddy's rejection of Western education, evident in his conversation with Nicholson, is embodied in his statement that the "apple Adam ate in the Garden of Eden" (291) was filled with "logic and intellectual stuff" (291). Teddy instead advocates teaching young children the technique of meditation so they can "find out who they are" (298). Salinger's critique of logic and intellectualism reflects his interest in ZEN. This perspective regarding education is similarly voiced by Buddy Glass in his letter to his brother Zooey in "Zooey" (65).

"Teddy" has attracted a significant amount of conflicting critical commentary; a chronological review is the most expeditious. Frederick L. Gwynn and Joseph L. Blotner, in their trailblazing 1958 pamphlet about Salinger's then-work-to-date, allude to "the confusion at the end of the tale" (Gwynn 40). The critics note that Teddy's sister, the six-year-old Booper, whose scream in the story's last line (which Salinger describes as "highly acoustical, as though it were reverberating within four tiled walls" [302]), "seems to place Booper either simply in the room surrounding the pool, which is often tiled, or in the pool, emptied, itself" (Gwynn 41). Gwynn and Blotner concede that the succession of clues planted throughout the story would indicate that Booper "pushes Teddy in and then screams as he is killed by the fall" (Gwynn 41). These clues, apart from the most obvious—Teddy's scenario of his death by Booper's hand, as hypothesized to the education professor, Bob Nicholson—gain prominence in a backward glance at the text. These clues include: Teddy's comment to his parents as he exits the cabin ("I may only exist in the minds of all my acquaintances" [265]); imagery referring to Teddy's head (254, 262, 265); Booper's statement to Teddy, "I hate you!" (271); two notations in Teddy's diary ("his head unfortunately cracks open in two halves" [274], and "it will either happen today or February 14, 1958" [276]); the haiku, "Nothing in the voice of the cicada intimates how soon it will die" (282), which Teddy quotes to Nicholson. Nonetheless, Gwynn and Blotner criticize Salinger for "the temporary ambiguity" he creates in the story's final paragraph (Gwynn 41). Although "Teddy" was published in 1953, and the critics offered their assessment in 1958, Gwynn and Blotner are not "put off" by the story's presentation of Eastern religious concepts, nor do they find the central character unbelievable. In fact, Gwynn and Blotner call Teddy "memorable and even inspirational" (Gwynn 41), a prodigy-mystic "who receives his inevitable death with a spiritual equanimity that contrasts starkly with the logical and emotional egocentricity of everybody else in the story" (Gwynn 42). By virtue of being the first assessment of the story, Gwynn and Blotner's became the critical benchmark.

Warren French, in his 1963 monograph, opines about "Teddys"'s conclusion: "Presumably . . . Teddy has been pushed into an empty swimming pool by his six-year-old sister; but it is also possible that he has pushed her, or that either of them has jumped or fallen into the pool, or even that the thoroughly nasty little girl is just having a tantrum" (French 1963, 132). French views Teddy's character diametrically opposite to Gwynn and Blotner. He labels Teddy as "one of the most obnoxious puppets in the whole history of bratty children" (French 1963, 133). French does not "take Teddy's word that he is unemotional and nonlogical . . . he is simply trying to disguise his shrewdly calculating nature" (French 1963, 133). The critic goes so far as to suggest, "the ending remains controversial, however, because the reader feels that Teddy would not be above simply jumping into the pool and shifting suspicion to the sister who hates him" (French 1963, 133). Thus, the first two critical readings of "Teddy" evince a spectrum of response.

One year later, Thomas Kranidas counters French with his own reading. Kranidas, perhaps shocked by French's characterization of Teddy, begins by affirming Gwynn and Blotner's view of the boy's character by stating: "Nowhere in his work has Salinger presented a figure of such gifts with such immense tact. The effect is one of strength and sweetness at once" (Kranidas 90). Kranidas then offers his interpretation of the story's ending and asserts that "the ambiguity of the last paragraph is directly relevant" (Kranidas 90) to the meaning of "Teddy." Kranidas's nuanced insight requires substantial quotation:

> The ending of the story beautifully develops the double attitude of Nicholson. He is won by Teddy, he believes in his powers of prophecy to the point where he jumps up from his chair and goes down to the swimming pool to warn or save or check on the boy, who has in a way predicted his own death in the empty swimming pool. But Nicholson's concern is misplaced. In Teddy's terms, death, even the death of a genius, is no tragedy. In the same way, our concern for the ambiguity at the end of the story is misplaced. There ought not to be worry over

the death of Teddy, whose very message was transcendence. And if there were regret or pity for the death of a human being, it ought not to be less for Booper. . . . The ambiguity is a brilliantly contrived obstacle to the easy resolution of the story. It prolongs our concern for Teddy to that point where we see that that concern is wrong: like Nicholson, our ignorance and this-worldly misemphasis has caused the concern. (Kranidas 91)

It is possible (though not ascertainable) that Kranidas drew inspiration for his interpretation of the story's ending from an endnote that Gwynn and Blotner appended to their pamphlet. They quote a colleague of theirs, Charles Murrah, who had read through their manuscript and, no doubt, was impressed by Salinger's artistry in "Teddy." Murrah rejected Gwynn and Blotner's criticism, couched in their phrase "temporary ambiguity" (Gwynn 40), and rejoined: "The reader's *distance* from the final catastrophe is appropriate—even necessary—because of *his* distance from Teddy's mind. We know that Teddy is a genius and a clairvoyant mystic; we do not, however, really understand him. At the end of the story we know that his sister has killed him, but the details are not graphically rendered. The unattached, reverberating scream from a child out of sight strikes just the right note of mystery and horror, sounding from behind the barrier imposed by our limited cognizance" (Gwynn 56).

Although in 1953 an anonymous reviewer of *Nine Stories* stated that, at the story's conclusion, Booper dies, no subsequent critic pressed this case until 1967. Laurence Perrine's essay focuses solely on the question of who dies. Perrine's thesis is that one could read the story as either Teddy or Booper falling into the pool, thus making "the ambiguity of the ending . . . permanent" (Perrine 218). Perrine begins his argument for the possibility of Booper's death with her scream, as described by Salinger: "highly acoustical, as though it were reverberating within four tiled walls" (302). Perrine argues: She screams as she falls; pools are always tiled, whereas rooms containing pools are not. Perrine asserts that Salinger's use of "sustained" in "all-piercing, sustained scream" (302) remains valid for Booper's death ("the

scream would be sustained—during the course of the fall" [Perrine 218]). He acknowledges, however, that "one might expect the author to describe it as being suddenly interrupted" (Perrine 218). Perrine believes the clues, which are planted throughout the story and which suggest Teddy's death, are inconclusive, or "they might even have been included deliberately to lead up to a purposely ambiguous conclusion" (Perrine 219). He argues that "the crucial consideration in interpreting the ending, however, is not the accumulation of ambiguous details adducible to support one possibility or the other; it is what happens to the meaning of the story under each of the two possibilities" (Perrine 220). For Perrine, the scenario that Booper pushes Teddy causes "Teddy" to become "a supernatural story about a boy with a supernatural gift for foretelling the future" (Perrine 220). The critic states that if it was Salinger's intention to have Booper push Teddy, then the author "is seriously asking us to accept the possibility that a man, or a boy, can predict the exact time and manner of his own death" (Perrine 222). On the other hand, if Teddy pushes Booper to her death, "then the story is a psychological one about an intellectually gifted but psychologically disturbed child, and the meaning of the story is the consequences of the failure of parental love" (Perrine 220). (To Perrine's way of thinking, the latter interpretation creates a better story.) Perrine then includes a third possibility: "Teddy is *both* genuine mystic and disturbed child, and perhaps it *is* Teddy who gets pushed into the pool, but through his own will, not through his sister's. . . . Both the idea and the intention, then, may exist in Teddy's mind alone. He goes to the pool not so much with the foreknowledge as with the fore*intention* that he will be pushed into it, though the knowledge may be conscious and the intention subconscious. . . . He places himself precariously at the edge of the pool so that he will fall in, willfully, when Booper so much as brushes against him. The contact occurs, not through Booper's malice, but through Teddy's subconscious wishing . . ." (Perrine 222). Perrine concludes: "Teddy" is "a vivid and brilliantly written story, but its focus is uncertain and its conclusion mystifying" (Perrine 222).

James Bryan's 1968 essay views the story as the dramatization of "the difficulties of living by Eastern religious concepts in the West, and, more especially, of communicating them to conventionally Western minds" (Bryan 352). Bryan terms the story successful: "However bizarre or doctrinaire Teddy's exposition may seem, the story works on the action level because we see that Teddy exemplifies what he tells Nicholson and that Nicholson . . . is won over at the end" (Bryan 353). The critic contrasts "Teddy" with "A Perfect Day for Bananafish": "Whereas Seymour's suicide in 'Bananafish' seems shocking and tragic, 'Teddy' systematically prepares the reader for the ending" (Bryan 367). Salinger accomplishes this in his elucidation of Teddy's view of death as "All you do is get the heck out of your body when you die . . . everybody's done it thousands and thousands of times" (294) and the succession of clues placed throughout the story that Teddy will die.

William Bysshe Stein's 1973 essay interprets the story as an exposition of Vedanta's "sacred axiom: 'Tat Tvam Asi.' . . . 'That Thou Art' affirms the identity of the 'That' (the Supreme Spirit) and 'Thou' (the individual Spirit)" (Stein 254). Stein enumerates details within the story that show Salinger "skillfully exploiting the Eastern context of the action, convert[ing] every literality of dialogue, gesture, act, and ambient detail into an interior mirror of the state of individual spiritual awareness" (Stein 253). Yet the critic dismisses the story as "a perfectly controlled embodiment of Salinger's artful banalities (of course, the method of all of his fiction)" (Stein 253).

In 1988, Warren French reassessed "Teddy" and decided that "there do not really seem to be any problems about the interpretation of the story" (French 1988, 84). French reads "Teddy" as "unsparingly satirical of the American way of life" (French 1988, 86–87), indicting Teddy's parents, his sister, Nicholson, and the religion and philosophy professors in the Leidekker group. French concludes that "for one as unworldly as Teddy, the only way is out of this world" (French 1988, 87).

John Wenke's reading of "Teddy" in his 1991 monograph stresses that "Salinger suspends exact knowledge of what transpired. Characteristically, he refuses to close off meanings. He encourages open-ended engagements with multiple possibilities . . ." (Wenke 62). Wenke notes that the narrative "presents Teddy in distinctly sympathetic terms" (Wenke 60) and that "the spiritual concerns of 'Teddy' anticipate the Glass family stories" (Wenke 62).

The most recent full-scale reading of "Teddy" is Anthony Kaufman's 1998 essay, in which the author develops a unique viewpoint: "'Teddy' is the story not of a cool and detached mystical prodigy, but of an unloved, frightened 10-year-old" (Kaufman 129). The critic asserts that Teddy, "in defensive reaction to the egotism, lovelessness, and incessant hostility of his parents toward each other and toward their children, and reinforced by his sense of the vulgarity, selfishness, and materialism of grown-up life . . . has instinctively felt his way to creating his persona of the mystic savant. That is, based on his precocious acquaintance . . . in Eastern philosophy, he has convinced himself (and some of the grown-up world) of his mystic powers" (Kaufman 130). Kaufman views the character as suffering from repressed anger, anxiety and depression. He reads the story in tandem with "A Perfect Day for Bananafish" and sees similarities between Seymour Glass and Teddy. "Teddy . . . commits suicide as the ultimate gesture of hostility and withdrawal, carefully planning it in advance to inspire terror and guilt. He deliberately designs his death so that the hateful Booper should be witness and victim, and her horror will later, of course, be shared by his miserable parents" (Kaufman 131). In Kaufman's reading, "the deeply disturbed Teddy throws himself into the empty pool (untouched by Booper) to protest and escape a life he cannot abide" (Kaufman 132). Booper's scream "can be thought of as an echo of the scream of Muriel a microsecond after the death of Seymour" (Kaufman 132).

Despite these divergent critical interpretations, the importance of "Teddy" within Salinger's works remains incontrovertible. In retrospect, the story signals Salinger's commitment to a spiritual quest. This quest would continue in his next story, "FRANNY," and find further amplification in his final publications during his lifetime, the four Glass family novellas.

PUBLICATION HISTORY

"Teddy" was first published in the *New Yorker* magazine on January 31, 1953. The story appeared in a book publication in *Nine Stories* (LITTLE, BROWN AND COMPANY, 1953). *Nine Stories*, Salinger's second book, has never gone out of print.

Nine Stories is available in three editions from Little, Brown and Company: an exact reproduction of the hardback first edition from 1953; a trade paperback that mimics the production of the hardback; and a mass-market paperback, with its pagination differing from the above editions.

CHARACTERS

Babcock, Professor Al Professor Al Babcock is a friend of Bob Nicholson's and is also known to Teddy McArdle. Babcock informs Nicholson of the rumor that Teddy told the Leidekker group members, after recording the audiotape, when each of them would die. Babcock, though not a member of the group, probably borrowed the audiotape for the party at which Nicholson hears Teddy's remarks.

Blond woman The nameless, blond woman, an employee of the ocean liner, passes Teddy McArdle in the passageway. With her left hand, she grazes Teddy's head and remarks that he needs a haircut.

Deck steward The nameless deck steward asks Teddy McArdle and Bob Nicholson if they would like to have some morning broth. Nicholson ignores the man, who is simply performing his duty, while Teddy gives a civil reply.

Ensign Mathewson Ensign Mathewson is a member of the ship's crew. Teddy McArdle asks the ensign if she knows at what time the word game is to take place. She suggests that the game is beyond Teddy's capabilities. When she asks Teddy his name, he says "Theodore." After Teddy asks the ensign her name, he wonders why she doesn't tell him her first name, but refers to herself as "Ensign."

Graham, Mr. Mr. Graham is one of the nine people to whom Teddy McArdle writes a letter on the morning the story takes place.

Grandma Hake Grandma Hake, Mrs. McArdle's mother, is one of the nine people to whom Teddy McArdle writes a letter on the morning the story takes place.

Hake, Burgess, Jr. Burgess Hake, Jr., is one of the nine people to whom Teddy McArdle writes a letter on the morning the story takes place. He is a relative on Teddy's mother's side of the family.

Hake, Roberta Roberta Hake is one of the nine people to whom Teddy McArdle writes a letter on the morning the story takes place. She is a relative on Teddy's mother's side of the family.

Hake, Sanford Sanford Hake is one of the nine people to whom Teddy McArdle writes a letter on the morning the story takes place. He is a relative on Teddy's mother's side of the family.

Larsen (Professor) Larsen is a member of the Leidekker examining group in Boston.

Leidekker examining group The Leidekker examining group in Boston interviewed Teddy McArdle and taped his responses in May. The group consists of professors of religion and philosophy interested in Teddy's advanced religious development. The group includes, among unnamed others, Walton, Peet, Larsen, and Samuels.

Lindy Lindy is Sven's dog in Elizabeth, New Jersey. Teddy McArdle expresses the desire to meet the dog. Lindy plays a role in Teddy's parable on the illusion of death.

Mandell, Mrs. Mrs. Mandell, wife of Professor Mandell, is a poet whom Teddy McArdle mentions in his October 27, 1952, diary entry.

Mandell, Professor Professor Mandell, husband of Mrs. Mandell, is mentioned in both days of Teddy McArdle's diary. He has been sending Teddy too many books of poetry. Mandell is one of the nine people to whom Teddy writes a letter on the morning the story takes place.

McArdle, Booper Booper is Teddy McArdle's willful six-year-old sister. At the outset of the story,

Booper, unlike Teddy and his parents, is not in the ocean-liner cabin but on the ship's Sports Deck, with Mr. McArdle's expensive camera. There, she bullies another child, named Myron. After Teddy persuades Booper to return the camera to their parents, she declares, "I hate you! I hate everybody in this ocean!" (271). At the story's close, the reader hears Booper's scream.

McArdle, Mr. Mr. McArdle is Teddy's father and husband to Mrs. McArdle. He is a successful radio performer in love with his own voice. The story opens with Mr. McArdle saying to Teddy, "I'll exquisite day *you*, buddy, if you don't get off that bag this minute" (253). Lying on one of the twin beds in his pajama bottoms, he repeatedly demands that Teddy get off his new piece of luggage. Later, Teddy obeys Mr. McArdle's command to find his expensive camera. Mr. McArdle and his wife have a rancorous marriage.

McArdle, Mrs. Mrs. McArdle is Teddy's mother and wife to Mr. McArdle. She is lying on the other twin bed, tightly wrapped in a sheet covering her nude body. Teddy's mother tells him to jump on her husband's bag. She does not pay attention to her son. Mrs. McArdle and her husband have a rancorous marriage.

McArdle, Theodore ("Teddy") Teddy McArdle, a 10-year-old boy, is an advanced religious adept. At the age of six, he had his first mystical experience. During the story, Teddy is seen in his parents' ocean-liner cabin, then on deck with his sister Booper and later alone, when he reads and writes in his diary. Teddy cryptically notates, "It will either happen today or February 14, 1958 when I am sixteen. It is ridiculous to mention even" (276–277). Teddy then has a long conversation with Bob Nicholson, an educator, who has heard an audiotape Teddy recorded with the Leidekker examining group. When Nicholson presses Teddy about the rumor that he told the men in the group when and where and how each of them would die, he denies this. Teddy, who believes in reincarnation, suggests that the fear of dying is unjustified because all one does is go from one body

to another. He explains, though, that people "just want new bodies all the time, instead of stopping and staying with God, where it's really nice" (292). Teddy has distinct views on education, believing that children should first be taught how to meditate and to know who they are, before they begin to learn facts and use logic. At one point in their conversation, Teddy tells Nicholson there is the possibility that the swimming pool will be drained that morning and, when he goes to its edge to look at it, his sister, Booper, could push him in, and he will die. Salinger leaves this chain of events open to interpretation at the story's end.

Myron Myron, a young child, watches Booper McArdle stack shuffleboard discs. His father was killed in Korea. After Booper tells Myron that he is stupid, Teddy McArdle reassures Myron it is not true.

Nicholson, Bob Bob Nicholson is a young university professor who teaches education. At a party in Boston, he heard an audiotape recorded by Teddy McArdle with the Leidekker examining group. Returning from Europe, he finds himself on the same ocean liner as Teddy and makes his acquaintance. Nicholson talks with Teddy about poetry, reincarnation, education, medicine, and Teddy's spiritual growth, before Teddy leaves for his swimming lesson. But what Nicholson most wants to know is if it is true that Teddy told the professors in the Leidekker group when and where and how each would die. Teddy denies the rumor, though he claims he could have. He suggests that the fear of dying is unjustified because all one does is go from one body to another. Teddy hypothesizes that it would not be a tragedy if the swimming pool were drained that morning and, when he went to its edge to look at it, his sister Booper pushed him in, and he died. After Teddy leaves to go to the pool, Nicholson believes that Teddy was predicting his own death and rushes there in an attempt to intervene.

Peet, Professor Bob Professor Bob Peet is a member of the Leidekker examining group in Boston and is an acquaintance of Bob Nicholson's.

Teddy McArdle states that Peet should stop teaching, which is impeding the professor's spiritual growth. Peet is one of the nine people to whom Teddy writes a letter on the morning the story takes place.

Samuels (Professor)   Samuels is a member of the Leidekker examining group in Boston.

Stewardess   Bob Nicholson encounters a nameless stewardess who is smoking and reading a magazine. She directs him to the pool.

Sven   Sven runs the gym on the ship. Teddy McArdle likes the man and notes in his diary that it would be nice to meet Sven's wife and his dog, Lindy. Sven plays a role in Teddy's parable on the illusion of death.

Walton, Professor   Professor Walton is a member of the Leidekker examining group in Boston. He initiated the post-tape conversation with Teddy McArdle by wanting to know when he would die. Walton is one of the nine people to whom Teddy writes a letter on the morning the story takes place.

Wokawara, Dr.   Dr. Wokawara, who has nephritis, is mentioned in both days of Teddy McArdle's diary. He is one of the nine people to whom Teddy writes a letter on the morning the story takes place.

FURTHER READING

Alsen, Eberhard. *A Reader's Guide to J. D. Salinger.* Westport, Conn.: Greenwood Press, 2002.

Bryan, James. "A Reading of Salinger's 'Teddy.'" *American Literature* 40, no. 3 (November 1968): 352–369.

French, Warren. *J. D. Salinger.* New York: Twayne Publishers, 1963.

———. *J. D. Salinger, Revisited.* New York: Twayne Publishers, 1988.

Gwynn, Frederick L., and Joseph L. Blotner. *The Fiction of J. D. Salinger.* Pittsburgh: University of Pittsburgh Press, 1958.

Kaufman, Anthony. "'Along This Road Goes No One': Salinger's 'Teddy' and the Failure of Love." *Studies in Short Fiction* 35 (Spring 1998): 129–140.

Kranidas, Thomas. "Point of View in Salinger's 'Teddy.'" *Studies in Short Fiction* 2 (Fall 1964): 89–91.

Lundquist, James. *J. D. Salinger.* New York: Ungar, 1979.

Nikhilananda, Swami. *Hinduism: Its Meaning for the Liberation of the Spirit.* New York: Harper and Brothers, 1958.

Paniker, Sumitra. "The Influence of Eastern Thought on 'Teddy' and the Seymour Glass Stories of J. D. Salinger." Ph.D. diss., University of Texas at Austin, 1971.

Perrine, Laurence. "Teddy? Booper? Or Blopper?" *Studies in Short Fiction* 4 (Spring 1967): 217–224.

Stein, William Bysshe. "Salinger's 'Teddy': *Tat Tvam Asi* or That Thou Art." *Arizona Quarterly* 29 (Autumn 1973): 253–265.

Wenke, John. *J. D. Salinger: A Study of the Short Fiction.* Boston: Twayne Publishers, 1991.

telegram protesting Tom Wolfe's profile of William Shawn

In the spring of 1965, Tom Wolfe, then a young journalist, had the idea of doing a piece on the NEW YORKER (the magazine had celebrated its 40th anniversary in February), including a profile of its editor in chief, WILLIAM SHAWN, who was nearly unknown to the general reading public. Wolfe, with the intention of exposing Shawn and the moribund state of the magazine, wrote a two-part inflammatory essay in an effort to attract attention to the new Sunday supplement of the *New York Herald Tribune*, for which he worked. He succeeded beyond his wildest dreams. The first part, titled "Tiny Mummies! The True Story of the Ruler of 43rd Street's Land of the Walking Dead!" portrays Shawn as a highly neurotic but manipulative embalmer of Harold Ross's original magazine; the second part, "Lost in the Whichy Thickets: *The New Yorker*," reduces the *New Yorker* to a glossy magazine for the educated suburban woman to display on her coffee table. Wolfe's articles provoked outrage among *New Yorker* editors and contributors, who sent letters of protest to the *New York Herald Tribune.* Salinger's telegram, addressed to Jock Whitney, the blue-blood owner of the newspaper, read, "With the printing of that inaccurate and sub-collegiate and gleeful and unrelievedly poisonous article on William Shawn, the name of the *Herald Tribune* and certainly your own will very likely never again stand for anything either respect-worthy or honorable." The entire story of the incident, along with a reprint of Wolfe's two articles and Salinger's telegram, can be found in a collection of Tom Wolfe's essays titled *Hooking Up* (Wolfe 249–293).

"This Sandwich Has No Mayonnaise"

Appearing in the October 1945 issue of *Esquire,* "This Sandwich Has No Mayonnaise" features Vincent Caulfield overwhelmed with the knowledge that his brother, Holden, has been classified as missing in action in the war. "This Sandwich Has No Mayonnaise" is Salinger's 14th published story. The author, however, chose not to include the story in his three books of collected stories.

SYNOPSIS

Sergeant Vincent Caulfield, his mind racing with thoughts, sits inside an army truck along with 33 other soldiers in Georgia. Rain beats on the canvas roof as the men wait for the arrival of a "lieutenant from Special Services" (54), whose family lives nearby. The soldiers become increasingly restless; they are headed to a dance. Vincent, who's in charge, agitatedly thinks to himself that four men must be forced off the truck.

Vincent laments his loss of "letters from Red, from Phoebe, from Holden" (54); someone stole his raincoat in which he had them. He fixates on Holden, his 19-year-old, "missing-in-action brother" (54). Vincent thinks he could pen "an immortal poem about this truck . . . call it 'Trucks I Have Rode In,' or 'War and Peace,' or 'This Sandwich Has No Mayonnaise'" (55).

A soldier asks him where he is from: "Manhattan. Just a couple of blocks from the Museum of Art" (55). A half dozen soldiers trade comments about the best cities in America for fun. Vincent flits between the conversations and his own thoughts. His mind rejects the news that Holden is missing: "the United States Government is a liar" (55). Vincent recalls a summer when his brother Red told him to go see the World's Fair. He takes Phoebe and her friend; he could not find Holden. Vincent fools Phoebe that a telephone exhibit will allow her to talk with one of her favorite authors. Outside the exhibit, Vincent and the two girls run into Holden. When Holden asks Phoebe for her autograph, she punches him. He suggests they leave the exhibits—"this educational junk" (147)—and go on some rides. Vincent's mind snaps back to the present: Holden cannot be missing; his brother is "at the World's Fair" (147). He and Phoebe can find Holden there. "What is this missing, missing, missing stuff?" (147).

The lieutenant finally shows up. He asks Vincent for the number of men in the truck, as his instructions were that only 30 could go to the dance to match the number of girls. Vincent pretends to count and tells him the number he has known all along: 34. It is Vincent's responsibility to get four men to give up going to the dance, and three finally do. Vincent does not know why he himself wants to go to the dance, but he confronts himself, "You're aching to go, Caulfield" (148). Vincent arbitrarily chooses the fourth from the back of the truck, who turns out to be a boy of 18. Unmilitary-like, the boy pleads with the lieutenant to overrule Vincent. The lieutenant tells him to get back into the truck and then asks for a phone, and Vincent walks him through torrential rain to its location. The lieutenant phones his family home and speaks with his younger sister. When, due to the inclement weather, she resists going to the dance as the last needed partner, he orders her to attend.

As Vincent and the lieutenant silently walk back toward the truck, Vincent pleads with Holden to tell someone "you're Here—not Missing, not dead, not anything but Here" (149). The story trails off as Vincent's mind reverts to the past, still addressing Holden: "Stop wearing my robe on the beach. Stop taking shots on my side of the court. Stop whistling. Sit up to the table . . ." (149).

CRITICAL ANALYSIS

"This Sandwich Has No Mayonnaise," Salinger's second published story to include Vincent Caulfield, is poignant and powerful. Its premise, however, does not mesh with Vincent's debut in "LAST DAY OF THE LAST FURLOUGH." In the earlier story, Vincent is on furlough at home when the news arrives that his brother Holden has been classified as missing in action. Soon thereafter, Vincent visits his friend Babe Gladwaller. Vincent, like Babe, is imminently departing overseas for battle. Vincent relishes this posting; he tells Babe that he is dying to avenge Holden's disappearance.

Salinger must have realized that he could dramatically heighten Vincent's reaction to his younger brother's disappearance. The result, "This Sandwich Has No Mayonnaise," surrealistically renders Vincent's tortured thoughts, as the older brother unsuccessfully copes with a mundane army assignment in Georgia. Told in the first person, the narrative careens between conversations within the army truck and Vincent's obsessive thoughts and memories of Holden. Although Vincent's mental anguish about his brother is the story's central fact, "This Sandwich Has No Mayonnaise" also depicts the boredom, discomfort, and sense of alienation of men from diverse regions of the country being thrown together at army bases, often located near small towns. Additionally, the story subtly reflects their sense of guilt being safe stateside, while fellow soldiers are overseas fighting and dying. This sense of guilt no doubt feeds into Vincent's own anguish about his younger brother's fate. It should be noted that when a soldier was classified as missing in action, it basically amounted to a death certificate. The lack of absolute certainty, however, adds its own cruelty; those left behind lack closure.

The story sheds significant further light on Salinger's earlier vision of Holden Caulfield and his family. As in "Last Day of the Last Furlough," Holden is 19 years old at the time he goes missing. Unlike the earlier story, which did not locate where Holden disappeared, Holden is reported to have survived his duty in Europe and is lost somewhere in the Pacific. Salinger memorably describes Holden as someone who "can't do anything but listen hectically to the maladjusted little apparatus he wears for a heart" (149). "This Sandwich Has No Mayonnaise" provides the first published mention of Vincent's and Holden's brother, Red (Kenneth's nickname because of his hair color; Red is the prototype for Allie Caulfield in The CATCHER IN THE RYE). Additionally, the story reveals their sister's name is Phoebe.

The story's unquestionable high point is Vincent's memory of an afternoon at the World's Fair on Long Island, which would date the idyllic outing to either 1939 or 1940. The critic John Wenke assesses Vincent's recollection as "one of the more remarkable passages in Salinger's work" (Wenke 21). All three of Vincent's siblings are still alive; each speaks in his or her distinctive voice. (Unfortunately, Salinger does not make clear the fact that, in the present time of "This Sandwich Has No Mayonnaise," Red has already died, which understandably accentuates Vincent's near-hysteria concerning Holden's fate.) Vincent hears, in his mind, Red say to him, "It won't hurt you to see the Fair either. It's very pretty" (149). His beloved youngest brother's advice compels Vincent to drive Phoebe and her friend (he cannot find Holden) to the fair. Vincent fools the young Phoebe into believing that a phone in the exhibit for Bell Telephone will allow her to talk with one of her favorite authors. Phoebe, excitedly "shaking like Phoebe," says, "Hello, this is Phoebe Caulfield, a child at the World's Fair" (149). She mentions that her parents are performing in a play. After the call, they run into Holden outside the exhibit. He demands that they go on the rides because he detests "this educational junk" (149). Vincent's mind snaps back to the present, remembering that Holden has been declared missing, but then crazily leaps to the conclusion that Holden is not missing; he and Phoebe know where to find Holden at the World's Fair.

The story poignantly winds down as Vincent's mind pleadingly addresses Holden to be "not Missing, not dead, not anything but Here" (149). Salinger signifies Vincent's heartbreaking slippage into fragmentary past memories through the use of phrases addressed to Holden as the story trails off with its ending ellipsis. The ellipsis bodes ill for both Vincent's mind and Holden's fate. Salinger's realistic depiction of Vincent's thought processes constitutes a tour-de-force achievement.

With the publication of "This Sandwich Has No Mayonnaise," the soldier Holden Caulfield disappears from Salinger's work. Two stories depicting a prep-school-age Holden, "I'M CRAZY" and "SLIGHT REBELLION OFF MADISON," stories whose incidents would be lifted almost wholesale into *The Catcher in the Rye*—would appear shortly thereafter. "This Sandwich Has No Mayonnaise" is the last published story depicting Vincent Caulfield alive. Vincent's ultimate fate would be revealed in "THE STRANGER," published two months later.

"This Sandwich Has No Mayonnaise" provides today's reader with two jarring realizations concerning *The Catcher in the Rye*. First, Salinger's original plans for Holden Caulfield situated the character in a World War II time period and, apparently, the character would be a casualty of that war. Second, the Caulfield family existed in an earlier, albeit similar, incarnation. Given these discrepancies, Salinger's decision not to collect this story, along with other stories that feature Caulfield characters, in his books of stories becomes understandable. (For more information regarding the seven extant Caulfield stories, *see* CAULFIELD STORIES.)

Esquire illustrated the story with a small, impressionistic drawing that locates the reader inside the truck among the soldiers.

PUBLICATION HISTORY

"This Sandwich Has No Mayonnaise" was published in the October 1945 issue of *Esquire*. The story was chosen by Arnold Gingrich and L. Rust Hills for inclusion in the anthology *The Armchair Esquire*, published in 1958. Salinger never reprinted the story in his three books of stories. "This Sandwich Has No Mayonnaise" later appeared in the bootleg editions *The COMPLETE UNCOLLECTED SHORT STORIES OF J. D. SALINGER* (1974) and *TWENTY-TWO STORIES* (1998).

CHARACTERS

Caulfield, Holden Holden Caulfield, 19 years old, has been classified as missing in action by the army. In the story, Holden's former prep school is referred to as "Pentey" (55) (not Pencey, as in *The Catcher in the Rye*). Holden was stationed in Europe, visited home on his furlough, and shipped out to the Pacific Theatre of Operations, where he has disappeared.

Holden appears in or is referenced in additional Caulfield stories: "Last Day of the Last Furlough," "I'm Crazy," "Slight Rebellion Off Madison," and the unpublished "The LAST AND BEST OF THE PETER PANS" and "The OCEAN FULL OF BOWLING BALLS."

Caulfield, Mr. and Mrs. Mr. and Mrs. Caulfield, referred to by Phoebe Caulfield (in Vincent Caulfield's memory of the World's Fair), are acting in a play aptly titled *Death Takes a Holiday*.

The Caulfield parents, either singly or together, appear in or are referenced in additional Caulfield stories: "Last Day of the Last Furlough," "The Stranger," "I'm Crazy," "Slight Rebellion Off Madison," and the unpublished "The Last and Best of the Peter Pans" and "The Ocean Full of Bowling Balls."

Caulfield, Phoebe Vincent Caulfield recalls his sister, Phoebe, twice. He hopes she is remembering to take his dog, Joey, for his walks, and that she is careful with his chain. Phoebe is tricked by Vincent into believing an exhibit phone will allow her to talk with one of her favorite authors. She punches her brother Holden when he asks for her autograph.

Phoebe appears in or is referenced in additional Caulfield stories: "Last Day of the Last Furlough," "I'm Crazy," and the unpublished "The Last and Best of the Peter Pans" and "The Ocean Full of Bowling Balls."

Caulfield, Red (Kenneth) Vincent Caulfield remembers his brother Red telling him to attend the World's Fair. Red is not with the other Caulfield siblings that afternoon.

Red (Kenneth) appears in or is referenced in additional Caulfield stories: "The Stranger," and the unpublished "The Last and Best of the Peter Pans" and "The Ocean Full of Bowling Balls."

Caulfield, Vincent Vincent Caulfield, the protagonist of the story, is an army sergeant stationed in Georgia. He is in charge of the men destined for the dance. Obsessed with the thought of his brother Holden missing in action, Vincent fails to attend to his duty regarding the number of men on the truck.

Vincent appears in or is referenced in additional Caulfield stories: "Last Day of the Last Furlough," "The Stranger," and the unpublished "The Last and Best of the Peter Pans" and "The Ocean Full of Bowling Balls."

Fergie The married Fergie is one of the soldiers on the truck. He and the soldier from Valentine Avenue visited Miami; Fergie enthuses about the showers and the women there. He volunteers to not attend the dance.

Helen (Beebers) Vincent Caulfield refers to his former girlfriend, Helen, and intimates that the reason he did not ask her to marry him was that he did not want her waiting for a soldier to return from war.

Helen is referenced in "Last Day of the Last Furlough" and appears in "The Stranger."

Lieutenant, Special Services The lieutenant from Special Services lives near the base in Georgia. He phones his sister to be the last needed girl partner for the dance.

Valentine Avenue soldier The soldier, who lives on Valentine Avenue in NEW YORK CITY, asks Vincent Caulfield where he is from. He wants Vincent to know that Valentine Avenue is not in the Bronx, but in MANHATTAN, like Vincent's address. The impressionable soldier visited Miami with Fergie.

FURTHER READING

French, Warren. *J. D. Salinger.* New York: Twayne Publishers, 1963.

———. *J. D. Salinger, Revisited.* New York: Twayne Publishers, 1988.

Lundquist, James. *J. D. Salinger.* New York: Ungar, 1979.

Purcell, William F. "World War II and the Early Fiction of J. D. Salinger." *Studies in American Literature* 28 (1991): 77–93.

Wenke, John. *J. D. Salinger: A Study of the Short Fiction.* Boston: Twayne Publishers, 1991.

"Total War Diary"

"Total War Diary" is one of Salinger's "lost" stories, neither published nor to be found in a library archive. According to the bibliographer Jack R. Sublette, Salinger mentions a story with this title in a 1944 letter to WHIT BURNETT. However, "Total War Diary" probably was reworked and retitled "The CHILDREN'S ECHELON," which is held at Princeton University's FIRESTONE LIBRARY.

Twenty-two Stories

Twenty-two Stories is the title of an illegal, unauthorized pirated book that appeared in 1998. It prints 22 stories Salinger published in various magazines but never included in one of his own books.

The stories in the paperback bootleg are: "THE YOUNG FOLKS" (STORY, March–April 1940), "GO SEE EDDIE" (UNIVERSITY OF KANSAS CITY REVIEW, December 1940), "THE HANG OF IT" (COLLIER'S, July 12, 1941), "THE HEART OF A BROKEN STORY" (ESQUIRE, September 1941), "THE LONG DEBUT OF LOIS TAGGETT" (Story, September–October 1942), "PERSONAL NOTES ON AN INFANTRYMAN" (Collier's, December 12, 1942), "THE VARIONI BROTHERS" (SATURDAY EVENING POST, July 17, 1943), "WAKE ME WHEN IT THUNDERS" (this is Salinger's title for the story now known as "BOTH PARTIES CONCERNED," a title chosen by the editors) (*Saturday Evening Post*, February 26, 1944), "DEATH OF A DOGFACE" (this is Salinger's title for the story now known as "SOFT-BOILED SERGEANT," a title chosen by the editors) (*Saturday Evening Post*, April 15, 1944), "LAST DAY OF THE LAST FURLOUGH" (*Saturday Evening Post*, July 15, 1944), "ONCE A WEEK WON'T KILL YOU" (Story, November–December 1944), "ELAINE" (Story, March–April 1945), "A BOY

IN FRANCE" (*Saturday Evening Post*, March 31, 1945), "THIS SANDWICH HAS NO MAYONNAISE" (*Esquire*, October 1945), "THE STRANGER" (*Collier's*, December 1, 1945), "I'M CRAZY" (*Collier's*, December 22, 1945), "SLIGHT REBELLION OFF MADISON" (*NEW YORKER*, December 21, 1946), "A YOUNG GIRL IN 1941 WITH NO WAIST AT ALL" (*MADEMOISELLE*, May 1947), "THE INVERTED FOREST" (*COSMOPOLITAN*, December 1947), "WIEN, WIEN" (this is Salinger's title for the story now known as "A GIRL I KNEW," a title chosen by the editors) (*GOOD HOUSEKEEPING*, February 1948), "SCRATCHY NEEDLE ON A PHONOGRAPH RECORD" (this is Salinger's title for the story now known as "BLUE MELODY," a title chosen by the editors) (*Cosmopolitan*, September 1948), and "HAPWORTH 16, 1924" (*New Yorker*, June 19, 1965).

Contrary to the assertion on the back cover, "This book contains twenty short stories and two novellas that have never before been collected or published outside of their original magazine appearances," *all* of the contents appeared in a much earlier illegal, unauthorized publication: the two-volume paperback bootleg titled *The* COMPLETE UNCOLLECTED *Short Stories of J. D. Salinger*. That infamous 1974 publication precipitated Salinger's first interview in 21 years; in early November 1974, he denounced the theft of his literary property.

Twenty-two Stories was issued in an edition of 1,000 copies by the unknown Train Bridge Recluse as a blue paperback with a white band containing promotional material. The copies were sold in various venues throughout the country, including bookstores and flea markets. A second edition of 200 copies in green, issued with two translucent sheets and color photographs separating each story, subsequently appeared. Given the paucity of Salinger publications, these bootlegs are considered collectors' items, though of lesser value than the historically important *The Complete Uncollected Short Stories of J. D. Salinger*.

"Two Lonely Men"

"Two Lonely Men" is an unpublished story whose 27-page, undated (circa 1943) typescript can be found at Princeton University's FIRESTONE LIBRARY, as part of the WHIT BURNETT–STORY magazine archive. "Two Lonely Men" is available for onsite reading only. According to the bibliographer Jack R. Sublette, the story is set "at a United States Army base in the South [and] tells the story of a developing friendship between Master Sergeant Charles Maydee and Captain Huggins" (Sublette 22). The relationship falters as "Maydee apparently begins having an affair" (Sublette 22) with Huggins's wife. "Two Lonely Men" was included in the proposed table of contents for Salinger's unpublished book, *The* YOUNG FOLKS.

"Uncle Wiggily in Connecticut"

"Uncle Wiggily in Connecticut" is the second story in Salinger's second book, *NINE STORIES* (1953). Originally published in the March 20, 1948, issue of the *NEW YORKER*, the story features the depressed and alcoholic Eloise, who recalls her dead boyfriend, Walt, the third-eldest son of the Glass family. "Uncle Wiggily in Connecticut" is the only Salinger work to have been made into a film. "Uncle Wiggily in Connecticut" is Salinger's 22nd published story.

SYNOPSIS

On a slushy, winter afternoon, near 3:00 o'clock, Mary Jane arrives at Eloise Wengler's house in Connecticut. Mary Jane was to have arrived earlier for lunch and a visit, and then to have continued on her way to her boss's house to deliver some mail, but she had gotten lost on the way. Eloise tells her the lunch is burned, but Mary Jane admits she has already eaten. The two women had been college roommates; each had quit during her sophomore year, in 1942. Eloise left in disgrace after she was discovered in an unused elevator with a soldier. Mary Jane married an aviation cadet and shortly thereafter got a divorce when he was convicted of stabbing a military policeman.

The two young women are drinking highballs in the living room and talking about old classmates.

They dispute the color Thieringer died her hair the night before she married Frank Henke. Eloise notices Mary Jane's cameo brooch and asks her where she got it. Upon hearing that the brooch belonged to Mary Jane's mother, Eloise comments that she will never inherit anything from her mother-in-law, with whom she does not get along. When Mary Jane states that she has had her last drink, Eloise counters that it was Mary Jane who got lost and was late. While Eloise leaves the room to make another round of drinks, Mary Jane notices that the ground is getting icy outside. Eloise returns with the drinks and tells Mary Jane that her black maid is in the kitchen reading a book, *The Robe*. Mary Jane again asserts this is her last drink. She tells Eloise that she saw Marcia Louise Jackson in Lord & Taylor's last week. Marcia Louise had received a letter from another classmate, Barbara Hill, with the news that Dr. Whiting was dead from cancer and died weighing only 62 pounds. Mary Jane thinks that Dr. Whiting's death is terrible, but Eloise disagrees with her. Mary Jane comments, "Eloise, you're getting hard as nails" (33). Mary Jane tells Eloise that Marcia Louise also told her about having been almost raped by a black soldier while she and her husband were stationed in Germany. Eloise interrupts the story when she hears the front door open; she calls out, asking if it is Ramona, her daughter. While Ramona is in the foyer, Eloise tells the little girl to go into the kitchen and have Grace, the maid, take off her galoshes. Ramona goes to the kitchen, saying, "C'mon Jimmy" (34).

Mary Jane spills half her drink on the rug and apologizes. She asks Eloise who Ramona looks like. After deadpanning, "Akim Tamiroff," an actor, Eloise says Ramona looks like her husband, Lew. "When his mother comes over, the three of them look like triplets" (35). Mary Jane wants to know how Ramona's eyes are after her operation, and whether she can see without her glasses. Eloise does not know the answer as her daughter keeps her vision a secret.

Ramona comes into the living room and, after her mother asks her who the lady is, Ramona correctly identifies Mary Jane. The child will not kiss Mary Jane, explaining, "I don't like to kiss people" (36). Eloise asks her daughter where Jimmy, her boyfriend, is. Mary Jane is intrigued by the idea of a boyfriend and learns his name is Jimmy Jimmereeno. When Mary Jane asks where Jimmy is, Ramona, who is alone, responds that Jimmy is standing there with her. Mary Jane then realizes Jimmy is an imaginary boyfriend. Eloise makes her daughter describe Jimmy to Mary Jane. Mary Jane thinks he is marvelous, but Eloise explains that Jimmy always accompanies Ramona to the point that Ramona "sleeps way over to one side of the bed, so's not to roll over and hurt him" (39). Ramona wants to go back outside because Jimmy has left his sword there, and Eloise agrees to this. She reminds Ramona to put on her galoshes. Eloise wants Mary Jane to have another drink. Mary Jane says she has to leave to go to her boss's house, but Eloise convinces her to call him and say she cannot come because of the weather.

At 4:45, with both women very drunk, Eloise starts to talk about her old boyfriend, Walt, who, she contends, Mary Jane did not really know. Eloise explains that only Walt could make her laugh. Walt did not have to try to do this because he was naturally funny. Once, when Eloise twisted her ankle, Walt consoled her, naming the ankle, "poor old Uncle Wiggily" (42). Walt "was nice . . . funny . . . sweet" (43). Eloise tells Mary Jane about when she and Walt were on a train during the war and he had his hand on her stomach. Walt said that her "stomach was so beautiful he wished some officer would come up and order him to stick his other hand through the window . . . because he wanted to do what was fair" (43–44). Mary Jane asks whether Eloise has ever told her husband about Walt. Eloise explains that she started to once, but Lew asked what Walt's rank was in the army. Mary Jane also asks about Walt's rank and Eloise laughs. Eloise explains to Mary Jane that Walt had a theory that he would advance in the army in his own way: With each promotion, he would lose some of his clothing until, upon making general, "all he'd be wearing would be a little infantry button in his navel" (45). Mary Jane tells Eloise that she should tell Lew about Walt, but Eloise will not, because Lew is not intelligent. Eloise warns Mary Jane that if she should ever marry again, she should never tell her husband anything about her past relationships.

Mary Jane asks Eloise why she married Lew. Eloise does not know, but then tells Mary Jane that she married Lew because he professed to love Jane Austen. After they were married, she discovered Lew had never read Austen. His favorite author was L. Manning Vines, who wrote a book about men starving to death in an igloo. Mary Jane wonders if Eloise will ever tell Lew that Walt was killed in the war. Eloise will not because Lew would become a "ghoul" (47). All Lew knows is that Mary Jane went out with a GI named Walt who made wisecracks. Mary Jane asks Eloise how Walt died and promises not to tell anyone. After Eloise twice refuses to discuss the circumstances of Walt's death, she begins to tell Mary Jane that Walt and another soldier were boxing up a stove in Japan that an officer wanted sent home. The stove was full of gasoline and exploded. The other soldier lost an eye, but Walt was killed. Eloise begins to cry, and Mary Jane tries to console her.

The front door opens, and they hear Ramona enter. Eloise asks Mary Jane to go into the kitchen and tell the maid to fix Ramona's dinner. Mary Jane returns with Ramona and declares to Eloise that she cannot get Ramona to take off her galoshes. Eloise wants the maid to do it, but according to Ramona, the maid is in the bathroom. While Eloise is taking off Ramona's galoshes, Mary Jane tells Eloise that Jimmy got run over. Ramona goes upstairs to bed, as instructed. Mary Jane goes into the kitchen to get more drinks and bring back the bottle.

At 7:05, the phone rings. Mary Jane is fast asleep on the couch. Eloise, who is awake, gets up and answers it. Her husband needs a ride from the train station. Eloise tells him that she cannot come because Mary Jane is parked in front of her car. She also lies by saying that earlier they had unsuccessfully looked for Mary Jane's lost keys. Eloise suggests to Lew that he get a lift from Dick and Mildred. When told he cannot, she suggests that he march home, military style, which he thinks is meant to be funny. Grace turns on the dining room light and startles Eloise. She tells the maid to hold dinner until eight o'clock, since her husband will be late. Grace asks Eloise if her own husband, who is currently in the kitchen, can spend the night due

to the inclement weather. Eloise twice denies this request, adding, "I'm not running a hotel" (53).

As Eloise climbs the stairs, she comes across one of Ramona's galoshes. She hurls it over the banister. Entering her daughter's room, she turns on the light and discovers Ramona is sleeping on the edge of her bed. "Her glasses were on a little Donald Duck night table, folded neatly and laid stems down" (54). Eloise wakes Ramona and asks her why she is sleeping on the side of the bed since Jimmy is dead. When Ramona tells her mother that she is sleeping on the side of the bed because she does not want to hurt Mickey Mickeranno, Eloise shrieks at her to get in the middle of the bed. Ramona is too frightened to move. Eloise grabs Ramona's ankles and pulls her to the bed's center. She demands that Ramona close her eyes, and Ramona does. Eloise turns off the light and stays in the doorway. Abruptly, she goes to the night table, picks up Ramona's glasses, and puts them against her cheek. Eloise is crying, and her tears wet the glasses. "Poor Uncle Wiggily" (55), Eloise repeatedly laments. She then replaces the glasses on the nightstand, but now with the lenses down. Eloise tucks in Ramona's blankets, only to find her daughter is awake and crying. Eloise kisses Ramona on the mouth and leaves the room.

A very drunk Eloise returns downstairs and wakes up Mary Jane. Eloise, crying, tells Mary Jane to recall their freshman year in college. Eloise had brought a dress to New York that she had bought in her hometown of Boise. After a girl told her that no one wore such dresses in New York, she had cried all night. The story ends as Eloise pleadingly asks Mary Jane, "I was a nice girl . . . wasn't I?" (56).

CRITICAL ANALYSIS

"Uncle Wiggily in Connecticut," according to the critic Warren French, is "the only one of Salinger's works that offers in a few pages visions of both worlds with which he is concerned" (French 38). French designates these worlds by employing Salinger's often-used adjectives, "nice" and "phony." In "Uncle Wiggily in Connecticut," the reader experiences the "nice" world when "Eloise recalls her idyllic days with Walt" (French 38) during the early years of World War II; Eloise's present life in

Connecticut, in a loveless marriage to Lew Wengler, constitutes the "phony" world. "Nowhere in Salinger's writings is the contrast between these two worlds more tragically conjured up than in Eloise's final cry to her stone-drunk college chum, 'I was a nice girl, wasn't I?'" (French 38). "Uncle Wiggily in Connecticut" is significant for two other reasons. The story introduces Walt (the character lacks a surname), whom Salinger will later identify as the fourth-eldest child of the Glass family. Additionally, the story is the sole Salinger work that the author allowed to be re-created in another medium—a film titled *My Foolish Heart*.

Told in a third-person narrative, "Uncle Wiggily in Connecticut" takes place one winter's afternoon in Connecticut, several years after the end of World War II, at the well-appointed suburban home of Lew and Eloise Wengler. Eloise receives a visit from her college roommate of the early 1940s, Mary Jane, and as the two women reminisce, they become progressively drunk. "Uncle Wiggily in Connecticut" concludes with Eloise's sudden "recognition of what has happened to her" (French 41).

Mary Jane provides the first clue of Eloise's change in personality. When Eloise disagrees that the death of a former professor is "terrible" (33)—the woman had cancer and weighed 62 pounds when she died—Mary Jane exclaims, "Eloise, you're getting hard as nails" (33). Although Eloise's comments in the conversation portray her in an unflattering light, it is her interactions with her young daughter, Ramona, that reflect the mother's debased character. Eloise exhibits a complete lack of affection for her daughter; her continuous nagging extends to correcting the child's grammar. Ramona, an only child about five years old, must wear very thick glasses after an eye operation. She has created an imaginary boyfriend named Jimmy Jimmereeno, who accompanies her everywhere. Jimmy's "needs" exasperate Eloise. Ramona "sleeps way over to one side of the bed, so's not to roll over and hurt him" (39). The child exhibits more concern for her imaginary boyfriend than does the mother for her child. Jimmy "provides a compensatory world" for Ramona and prefigures Eloise's telling Mary Jane of her "lost idyll" (Wenke 39) with Walt.

Walt was Eloise's boyfriend at the beginning of the war. Eloise stresses his sense of humor: "He was the only boy I ever knew that could make me laugh. I mean *really* laugh" (41). Eloise tells Mary Jane that Walt was "nice" and "sweet" but "a special kind of sweet" (43). She then illustrates Walt's special quality with three anecdotes. These anecdotes not only define Walt within the story but also remain the defining moments of Walt Glass within the Glass saga. When Eloise sprained her ankle, Walt, to console her, called the ankle "Poor old Uncle Wiggily" (42). (Uncle Wiggily is a name "borrowed by Walt from Howard Garis' children's stories about a whimsical rabbit" [French 38].) Another time, Eloise and Walt (who had been drafted) were traveling together on a train. Walt had placed his hand on her stomach. Walt said that her "stomach was so beautiful he wished some officer would come up and order him to stick his other hand through the window ... because he wanted to do what was fair" (43–44). The critic John Wenke glosses Walt's statement as "a way of speaking about love, the words suggesting rather than denoting the nature of the feeling. . . . Conventional words cannot express certain notes on the emotional register" (Wenke 39–40). The final anecdote illustrates Walt's unique conception of how he would advance in the army. Instead of receiving insignias signifying a promotion, he would lose a piece of his clothing until, upon making the rank of general, "all he'd be wearing would be a little infantry button in his navel" (45).

Walt was killed in a freakish accident that Eloise initially refuses to divulge to Mary Jane but subsequently describes. (Eloise has steadfastly refused to tell her husband Lew that Walt died. She advises her friend, who is divorced, never to tell a future husband the truth about any past relationships. Salinger has Eloise quip to Mary Jane: "you'll go through hell if you ever give 'em any credit for intelligence" [46].) After Eloise tells Mary Jane how Walt died, she cries, and her friend comforts her. When Ramona comes into the house for the second time, Mary Jane learns that the child's imaginary boyfriend, Jimmy, has been killed, and Mary Jane informs Eloise of this. "Her loss of Jimmy emphasizes as it replicates her mother's loss of Walt" (Wenke 40).

Throughout the story, Salinger contrasts Mary Jane with Eloise. Mary Jane initiates the visit; she wants to keep her word and reach her employer's house as promised; she brings up Ramona's eye operation and inquires of its success; she wants to help and remove Ramona's galoshes. The child remembers Mary Jane's name, signifying awareness of authentic feelings toward her. Mary Jane's capacity for concern is repeatedly evident.

Eloise, on the other hand, has lost the ability to empathize; instead, she hurts everyone. She makes Mary Jane miss her appointment with her boss; she denies permission for her maid's husband to stay overnight, thus endangering him on the icy roads; she lies to her husband, in addition to making cutting remarks, and forces him to walk home in the snow; she disparages old college acquaintances and is unmoved by her former professor's painful death. Ironically, Eloise treats Ramona like a sergeant might treat a private (Walt's army rank most likely was a private).

The story's climactic scene commences after Mary Jane has fallen asleep on the sofa from the bout of drinking. The alcoholic Eloise is awake in the dark; her drinking does not afford a complete escape from her hell. The nadir of Eloise's actions occurs when she goes into Ramona's bedroom and finds the child still sleeping on the edge of the bed. She wakes her daughter to interrogate why she is not in the middle, now that Jimmy is dead. When Ramona explains that she does not want to hurt her new friend, Mickey Mickeranno, Eloise shrieks at her to move to the bed's center. When Ramona, "extremely frightened" (55), remains motionless, Eloise forcibly drags her to the center. Eloise "insists that the child destroy the illusion by moving to the center of the bed that she pretends to share" (French 40). After standing "for a long time in the doorway" (55), Eloise, "struck by the enormous cruelty of her behavior, . . . sees the contrast between the happy past and the defiled present . . . she picks up her daughter's thick glasses, presses them against her tear-stained cheek, and cries 'Poor Uncle Wiggily'" (French 40). The glasses, which Ramona had "folded neatly

and laid stems down" (54), are now returned to the nightstand by Eloise "lenses down" (55). By specifying "lenses down," Salinger suggests several things: Eloise's tears are (mostly) for herself and not for her daughter; Eloise, unlike Ramona, cannot really see her boyfriend; and Eloise is oblivious to Ramona's needs (in this case, unscratched glasses).

A different reading is offered by Eberhard Alsen. When Eloise shrieks at Ramona, she is "angry because Ramona can let go of her love for the dead Jimmy and transfer it to her new friend Mickey while she, Eloise, has not been able to let go of her dead lover Walt and is therefore not allowing herself to love her husband Lew and her daughter Ramona, who looks a lot like Lew" (Alsen 92). Alsen supports his reading by observing that Eloise subsequently picks up Ramona's glasses and invokes, "Poor Uncle Wiggily." The critic concludes that the story's symbolism suggests that "Ramona is unwittingly teaching her mother how to deal with the loss of her lover" (Alsen 92).

Rushing downstairs, Eloise now wakes up a second person, Mary Jane. She is desperate to ask her former roommate a question, "the answer to which she both cherishes and fears" (French 40). Eloise wants to know from Mary Jane what kind of person she (Eloise) was when she arrived in New York to attend college. The story's final line reads, "'I was a nice girl,' she pleaded, 'wasn't I?'" (56). Throughout his career, Salinger uses "nice" as his highest accolade for people and things. (The word finds its apotheosis in The CATCHER IN THE RYE where Holden Caulfield repeatedly invokes it. The most notable instances are: when Holden speaks of his beloved, dead brother Allie, "God, he was a nice kid" [50]; and Holden's happiness as his equally beloved sister, Phoebe, rides the carousel, and she "looked so damn *nice*" [275].) Eloise is thus pleading for redemption in the story's final scene. But, as Wenke comments, "Salinger offers no inkling as to what might come next . . . the ending of 'Uncle Wiggily' evokes meditation on the story's unresolved emotional matrix" (Wenke 41).

"Uncle Wiggily in Connecticut," published less than three years after the end of World War II, shows Eloise to be one of the war's casualties, for Walt's death denies Eloise of her true love. Eloise, who reads classic literature, tells Mary Jane that she married Lew because he said his favorite author was Jane Austen. After the marriage, she discovers that Lew's favorite author is the preposterous L. Manning Vines, a fictitious author whose one book depicts "four guys that starved to death in an igloo" (47). The ironic subtext in Eloise's preference of author lies in that, in Austen's novels, women end up with the right man for a husband; not so in this case. Salinger infers, however, that Eloise has married for economic reasons. She comes from a poor family in Idaho (her mother had nothing of value to bequeath her) unlike Mary Jane, who has received her mother's brooch. Eloise has a bad relationship with her mother-in-law and expects nothing (except "some old monogrammed ice-pick" [31]). Eloise is the outsider in the Connecticut milieu: She knows the neighborhood makes fun of her; more importantly, Ramona, Lew, and Lew's mother "look like triplets" (35).

A significant part of "Uncle Wiggily in Connecticuts"'s importance resides in its status as a Glass story. Though Walt's surname is never specified in the story, there is critical consensus that Salinger took the Walt character from this narrative and incorporated him into his creation of the Glass family. Details about Walt in "Uncle Wiggily in Connecticut" approximate what is known about Walt Glass, the fourth-born child of Les and Bessie Glass. In "ZOOEY," Salinger states that Walt "was killed in a freakish explosion while he was with the Army of Occupation in Japan" (53) (Army of Occupation denotes that the war is over). In "Uncle Wiggily in Connecticut," Walt died when a "little Japanese stove . . . exploded" as he and another soldier were packing it for a commanding officer; the only significant difference is that the incident occurs "between battles" (48). In "Zooey," Walt is termed the "only truly lighthearted son" (90) of the Glass family. In "Uncle Wiggily in Connecticut," Eloise attests to Walt's sense of humor when she states, "he was the only boy I ever knew that could make me laugh. I mean *really* laugh" (41). Salinger incorporates an additional aspect of the story into the Glass saga. Lew Wengler's favorite author is L. Manning Vines. Wengler was an officer in the war, alluded to in Eloise's nasty

remark to him to "form a platoon and march home . . . you can be the big shot" (52) as the snowstorm has stranded him at the station. Because the fictitious Vines is the favorite author of Buddy Glass's company commander in "RAISE HIGH THE ROOF BEAM, CARPENTERS," the reader may infer that it was Lew Wengler who gave Buddy the three-day pass to attend Seymour Glass's wedding. (For more information regarding the eight published Glass stories, *see* GLASS STORIES.)

Salinger sold the movie rights to "Uncle Wiggily in Connecticut," and the story was quickly made into a film, *My Foolish Heart,* released for general distribution in January 1950. The author had been hoping, since the early 1940s, to score a Hollywood sale of his work. Though Salinger's relationship to the movies can be termed "conflicted," references to the movies are generally benign in his work until *The Catcher in the Rye* (for example, in the earlier fiction, the movies offer a means of comfort to characters such as Aunt Rena in "ONCE A WEEK WON'T KILL YOU" and the family of Elaine Cooney in "ELAINE"; Salinger, however, chafed at the movies' false representation of war as early as the 1944 story "SOFT-BOILED SERGEANT"). *My Foolish Heart* garnered mixed reviews but proved a financial success and was nominated for two Oscars (leading actress; song). Salinger, however, was gravely embarrassed by the film, which barely resembles his story. French summarizes the differences in the movie's interpretation: "Ramona proves to be the issue of premarital intimacies between Eloise and Walt, who was killed in a plane crash during the war. After hearing the news, the distraught Eloise had lured away and married the fiancé [Lew] of the girl [Mary Jane] who is visiting her. When the picture begins, Eloise's marriage is on the rocks; when it ends, the husband is departing with the other girl, leaving Eloise with the souvenirs of her blighted romance" (French 44–45).

When *My Foolish Heart* was released, Salinger was still at work on *The Catcher in the Rye.* Critics attribute the portrayal of Holden Caulfield's brother, the short-story writer D. B., who now writes for the movies—"he's out in Hollywood, D. B., being a prostitute" (4)—as Salinger's exorcism of the "Uncle Wiggily in Connecticut"/*My*

Foolish Heart debacle. IAN HAMILTON suspects that Salinger, so affected by his mistake, set the time period of the novel's events to coincide with the imminent release of *My Foolish Heart*. Holden goes to Radio City Music Hall to see an unnamed film shortly before Christmas 1949. The next film to be shown at Radio City Music Hall, scheduled for January 1950, would have been advertised: *My Foolish Heart*, with the poster noting that the film was based on a story by J. D. Salinger. Recent scholarship by George Cheatham and Edwin Arnaudin reveals that Salinger, within the text of *The Catcher in the Rye*, embeds a reference to *My Foolish Heart*. In the film, as the character of Walt tries to seduce Eloise, he refers to her aristocratic ear. The "aristocratic" motif carries throughout the film to include other parts of Eloise's body, including her aristocratic fingers. In *The Catcher in the Rye*, Holden, after seeing a movie, goes to the Wicker Bar to meet Carl Luce. While waiting for Luce, Holden overhears a guy "snowing hell out of the babe he was with. He kept telling her she had aristocratic hands" (185). The novel shows Holden's own conflicted obsession with the movies.

"Uncle Wiggily in Connecticut," Salinger's next publication in the *New Yorker* after the stunning "A PERFECT DAY FOR BANANAFISH," reinforced the perception of Salinger as an author to watch for. In Salinger's collection, *Nine Stories*, "Uncle Wiggily in Connecticut" also follows its more famous chronological predecessor. Although of decidedly lesser importance than "A Perfect Day for Bananafish," the story retains its own power and provides a stark contrast to the depiction of a mother-child relationship in the 1949 story "DOWN AT THE DINGHY."

PUBLICATION HISTORY

"Uncle Wiggily in Connecticut" was first published in the *New Yorker* magazine on March 20, 1948. The story appeared in a book publication in *Nine Stories* (LITTLE, BROWN AND COMPANY, 1953). *Nine Stories*, Salinger's second book, has never gone out of print.

Nine Stories is available in three editions from Little, Brown and Company: an exact reproduction of the hardback first edition from 1953; a trade paperback that mimics the production of the hardback; and a mass-market paperback, with its pagination differing from the above editions.

CHARACTERS

Ball, Miriam Miriam Ball tells Eloise Wengler, her college classmate, that Eloise's dress from Boise, Idaho, is inappropriate for New York.

Dick and Mildred Dick and Mildred are neighbors of Eloise and Lew Wengler's in Connecticut. Eloise tells Lew to catch a ride home with them, since she can't come and pick him up at the station.

Grace Grace is the Wenglers' black maid. She asks if her husband can stay overnight because of the inclement weather, but Eloise Wengler refuses the request.

Grace's husband Grace's husband joins Grace in the kitchen later that afternoon. In spite of the inclement weather, Eloise Wengler won't allow him to stay overnight.

Henke, Frank Frank Henke is an army private who married Eloise Wengler and Mary Jane's former classmate, Thieringer.

Hermanson, Louise Louise Hermanson, while at college with Eloise Wengler and Mary Jane, once convulsed Eloise with laughter when she entered a room wearing a black bra.

Hill, Barbara Barbara Hill, a former classmate of Eloise Wengler and Mary Jane's, informs Marcia Louise Jackson, another former classmate, that Dr. Whiting, their college professor, has died of cancer.

Jackson, Marcia Louise Marcia Louise Jackson, a former classmate of Eloise Wengler and Mary Jane's, runs into Mary Jane at Lord & Taylor's. Jackson tells Mary Jane about the time she was almost raped by a black soldier while living in Germany after the war and conveys Barbara Hill's news about Dr. Whiting's death from cancer.

Jimmereeno, Jimmy Jimmy Jimmereeno is Ramona Wengler's make-believe boyfriend and constant companion. He will die and be replaced by Mickey Mickeranno.

Mary Jane Mary Jane (whose surname is never stated), an old college roommate of Eloise Wengler's, visits Eloise at her house in Connecticut. Mary Jane is divorced and works as a secretary to Mr. Weyinburg. Mary Jane's intention was to stop by for lunch, visit, and continue on her way to her boss's house. Mary Jane loses her way to Eloise's house and arrives quite late. During the afternoon she becomes progressively drunk. The icy road conditions, coupled with her inebriation, prevent her from leaving Eloise's house. Mary Jane believes that Eloise is "getting hard as nails" (33). She, on the other hand, shows genuine feeling and concern for Eloise's young daughter, Ramona Wengler. Eloise, at the story's close, needs Mary Jane to confirm that she was "a nice girl" (56) when the two met in college.

Mickeranno, Mickey When Jimmy Jimmereeno, Ramona Wengler's make-believe playmate, dies, Mickey Mickeranno becomes her new imaginary companion. Eloise Wengler finds Ramona asleep way over to one side of the bed in order not to hurt Mickey.

Morrow, Joyce When Eloise Wengler is on the train with Walt, she is wearing Joyce Morrow's blue cardigan sweater.

Thieringer Thieringer, a former classmate of Eloise Wengler and Mary Jane's, dyes her hair red the night before she marries Frank Henke.

Vines, L. Manning L. Manning Vines is Lew Wengler's favorite author. The fictitious Vines wrote a novel about four men freezing to death in an igloo.

Vines is also mentioned in "Raise High the Roof Beam, Carpenters" as the favorite author of Buddy Glass's company commander. One might infer from this fact that Lew Wengler was the company commander of Buddy Glass during World War II.

Walt [Glass] Walt is Eloise Wengler's boyfriend during World War II; he was killed between bat-tles when a Japanese stove exploded in his face as he was handling the stove for packing (or, possibly, for unpacking) at the behest of his commanding officer. Eloise describes him as "the only boy I ever knew that could make me laugh. I mean *really* laugh" (41). Once, when Eloise twisted her ankle, Walt consoled her, naming the ankle, "poor old Uncle Wiggily" (42). Eloise recounts to Mary Jane that, when she and Walt were on a train during the war, he had placed his hand on her stomach. Walt said that her "stomach was so beautiful he wished some officer would come up and order him to stick his other hand through the window . . . because he wanted to do what was fair" (43–44).

Though Walt's surname is not specified in the story, there is critical consensus that Salinger took the Walt character from "Uncle Wiggily in Connecticut" and incorporated him later into his creation of the Glass family. Walt has minor roles in the four Glass family stories: "Raise High the Roof Beam, Carpenters," "Zooey," "SEYMOUR: AN INTRODUCTION," and "HAPWORTH 16, 1924."

Wengler, Eloise Eloise Wengler is the protagonist of the story. She is Mary Jane's former college roommate, Lew Wengler's wife, and Ramona's mother. Eloise hosts Mary Jane's visit at her house in Connecticut. The two young women drink highballs in the living room and talk about old roommates. Eloise, in a loveless marriage, does not care for or show love toward her young daughter. Walt, her true love, died in World War II. Eloise has lost all feeling for everyone and everything in her life except the memory of Walt. Mary Jane's visit causes Eloise to make the recognition that she has become "hard as nails" (33). Eloise, at the story's close, needs Mary Jane to confirm that she was "a nice girl" (56) when they met in college.

Wengler, Lew Lew Wengler is married to Eloise. He phones to ask her to pick him up at the station, only to be told to march home army style. Eloise thinks Lew is neither intelligent nor funny. Lew's favorite author is L. Manning Vines and not, as he told Eloise during their courtship, Jane Austen (her favorite).

Because the fictitious Vines is the favorite author of Buddy Glass's company commander in "Raise High the Roof Beam, Carpenters," an assumption may be made that Lew Wengler gave Buddy the three-day pass to attend Seymour Glass's wedding.

Wengler, Mrs. Mrs. Wengler is Lew's mother and Eloise's mother-in-law. She and Eloise don't get along. Eloise jests to Mary Jane that Mrs. Wengler would probably bequeath her a monogrammed icepick, rather than anything "holy" (30), such as the cameo brooch Mary Jane is wearing, inherited from her mother.

Wengler, Ramona Ramona Wengler is the daughter of Lew and Eloise Wengler. Ramona's age is not specified; she is "a small child" (34), who looks like her father and his mother. She has had an eye operation and must wear thick glasses. Ramona has no siblings, and there are no children to play with in the neighborhood. By way of compensation, she shows an active imagination, creating Jimmy Jimmereeno and Mickey Mickeranno for her companions.

Weyinburg, Mr. Mr. Weyinburg, at home with a hernia, is Mary Jane's boss. After visiting Eloise Wengler, Mary Jane intended to go to his house in order to deliver his business mail.

Whiting, Dr. Dr. Whiting, a former professor of Eloise Wengler and Mary Jane's, has died of cancer. She weighed only 62 pounds when she died, a fact that Eloise callously dismisses.

FURTHER READING

Alsen, Eberhard. *A Reader's Guide to J. D. Salinger.* Westport, Conn.: Greenwood Press, 2002.

Cheatham, George and Edwin Arnaudin. "Salinger's Allusions to *My Foolish Heart*—the Salinger Movie." *ANQ: A Quarterly Journal of Short Articles, Notes, and Reviews* 20, no. 2 (Spring 2007): 39–43.

French, Warren. *J. D. Salinger* [includes final version of his essay, "The Phony World and the Nice World"]. New York: Twayne Publishers, 1963.

Gwynn, Frederick L., and Joseph L. Blotner. *The Fiction of J. D. Salinger.* Pittsburgh: University of Pittsburgh Press, 1958.

Hamilton, Ian. *In Search of J. D. Salinger.* New York: Random House, 1988.

Hassan, Ihab. "Rare Quixotic Gesture: The Fiction of J. D. Salinger." *Western Review* 21 (Summer 1957): 261–280.

Lundquist, James. *J. D. Salinger.* New York: Ungar, 1979.

Wenke, John. *J. D. Salinger: A Study of the Short Fiction.* Boston: Twayne Publishers, 1991.

"uncollected" stories

"Uncollected" stories are stories that Salinger published in magazines but chose not to collect in his three books of collected stories. When Salinger, for his first story collection (NINE STORIES, 1953), selected only nine of his 30 published stories, he consigned 21 stories, published from 1940 through 1948, to obscurity. These 21 stories are: "THE YOUNG FOLKS" (STORY, March–April 1940), "GO SEE EDDIE" (UNIVERSITY OF KANSAS CITY REVIEW, December 1940), "THE HANG OF IT" (COLLIER'S, July 12, 1941), "THE HEART OF A BROKEN STORY" (ESQUIRE, September 1941), "THE LONG DEBUT OF LOIS TAGGETT" (Story, September–October 1942), "PERSONAL NOTES ON AN INFANTRYMAN" (Collier's, December 12, 1942), "THE VARIONI BROTHERS" (SATURDAY EVENING POST, July 17, 1943), "BOTH PARTIES CONCERNED" (Saturday Evening Post, February 26, 1944), "SOFT-BOILED SERGEANT" (Saturday Evening Post, April 15, 1944), "LAST DAY OF THE LAST FURLOUGH" (Saturday Evening Post, July 15, 1944), "ONCE A WEEK WON'T KILL YOU" (Story, November–December 1944), "ELAINE" (Story, March–April 1945), "A BOY IN FRANCE" (Saturday Evening Post, March 31, 1945), "THIS SANDWICH HAS NO MAYONNAISE" (Esquire, October 1945), "THE STRANGER" (Collier's, December 1, 1945), "I'M CRAZY" (Collier's, December 22, 1945), "SLIGHT REBELLION OFF MADISON" (NEW YORKER, December 21, 1946), "A YOUNG GIRL IN 1941 WITH NO WAIST AT ALL" (MADEMOISELLE,

May 1947), "The Inverted Forest" (Cosmopolitan, December 1947), "A Girl I Knew" (Good Housekeeping, February 1948), "Blue Melody" (*Cosmopolitan*, September 1948).

After publication of his final book during his lifetime, Raise High the Roof Beam, Carpenters and Seymour: An Introduction (1963), Salinger published only one more story: "Hapworth 16, 1924" (The *New Yorker*, June 19, 1965). When the author chose not to reprint "Hapworth 16, 1924" in a book, the story became his 22nd uncollected story. The 22 uncollected stories were illegally reprinted in a two-volume paperback set titled *The Complete Uncollected Short Stories of J. D. Salinger*, in 1974. (In 1998, the same stories were reprinted in an unauthorized volume, Twenty-Two Stories.)

Ursinus Weekly writings

Salinger wrote nine columns and two theater reviews for Ursinus College's student newspaper, the *Ursinus Weekly*, during the fall semester of 1938. Each column consists of a variety of items commenting on college life, recent movies and plays, actors, and general observations. In a number of instances, Salinger includes rhyming poems and snatches of dialogue.

The first column is titled "Musings of a Social Soph: The Skipped Diploma." (Salinger indeed skipped his diploma; he left Ursinus after his only semester there.) In this first column, Salinger explains his return to college: "Once there was a young man [. . . who] did not want to go to work for his Daddykins—or any other unreasonable man. So the young man went back to college" (October 10, 1938, p. 2). The first entry of the column takes the narrative form of an imagined letter by a freshman named Phoebe who complains to her parents that they "have failed to raise [her] properly" (October 10, 1938, p. 2). Later in the column, a Holden Caulfield-like remark appears in a short poem, "Children floor me; / Society stinks" (October 10, 1938, p. 2). The remaining eight columns contributed by Salinger to *Ursinus Weekly*

are titled "J. D. S.'s The Skipped Diploma." Sprinkled within the total of nine columns that Salinger wrote for the newspaper are literary references to Ernest Hemingway, Margaret Mitchell, Shakespeare, and Oscar Wilde. The last column to appear is dated December 12, 1938. Donald M. Fiene reproduces the nine columns in the appendix of his thesis, "A Bibliographical Study of J. D. Salinger: Life, Work and Reputation." Some excerpts from the columns and reviews can be found in Ian Hamilton's *In Search of J. D. Salinger* (Ian Hamilton 1988, 45–49).

"Varioni Brothers, The"

Published in the July 17, 1943, issue of the Saturday Evening Post, "The Varioni Brothers," although an early work by Salinger, remains an important one in the author's canon. The story introduces several themes, in kernel form, that will grow to greater dimension in Salinger's later fiction—especially the philosophical question of the writer's true calling and the conflict that the artistic/spiritual path may create in adapting artistic talent to cultural demands and to the practical aspects of life in general. "The Varioni Brothers" is Salinger's seventh published story. The author, however, chose not to include the story in his three books of collected stories.

SYNOPSIS

"The Varioni Brothers" begins with a newspaper column titled "Around Old Chi," usually written by Gardenia Penny. An omniscient narrator explains that Penny is vacationing and that the column's stand-in writer will vary, with the current week's contribution guest-written by Vincent Westmoreland, a witty storyteller and producer. Westmoreland, who next takes up the narrative in the first-person voice, wants to know the answer to a single question: "Where is Sonny Varioni?" (12). Westmoreland believes himself to have been the only sober witness to a shooting at a decadent Roaring Twenties party given by the music publisher Teddy Barto at the Varioni mansion 17 years ago. At that event, Rocco, the hit man for the gambler Buster Hankey, shot the wrong Varioni brother. Westmoreland explains how Sonny, the piano player of the songwriting duo, had lost $40,000 to Buster in a card game but refused to pay because he suspected cheating. Arriving at the party, Rocco asks where he can find Sonny Varioni, but he is misdirected to Joe Varioni, the lyricist of the team, who happens to be playing the piano when the hit man arrives. Joe dies tragically when Rocco fires five shots into the wrong brother's back.

Westmoreland ends his column by asking for news of Sonny Varioni's whereabouts from "some little person somewhere [who] must have the inside dope" (13). In the following paragraph, Salinger switches from the text of the newspaper column to another first-person narrative voice: "My name is Sarah Daley Smith. I am one of the remotest little numbers I know. And I have the inside dope on Sonny Varioni" (13).

Sarah not only has information about Sonny, but she also assumes the narration of the rest of the story. Sarah claims that Sonny is at work in Waycross, Illinois, on a major manuscript that his brother, Joe, never finished putting together before he died. She then returns reluctantly to "the high, wide, and rotten Twenties" (13) to tell her tale.

Sarah Daley met Joe Varioni at Waycross College, where she was a sophomore and he was teaching English. The two took walks together, and he would read parts of his novel-in-progress to her. Also at the college, Professor Voorhees, most probably the head of the English department, is aware that Joe is writing a novel. Joe stops working on his novel when Sonny needs him to write the lyrics to his music compositions. Joe explains to Sarah that his songwriting stint is temporary and that he is only doing it until his musically talented brother gains success.

Sarah, an admiring student of Joe Varioni's, is also the niece of Teddy Barto's lawyer, and she accompanies the brothers when they attempt to sell their music to Barto. Barto buys all three songs that the brothers play for him, and he insists that they move to Chicago. Joe protests and Sarah also speaks up, declaring Joe to be a talented novelist who should not be wasting his time writing songs.

Later, on the train back to Waycross, Sarah pleads with Sonny to allow Joe to continue with his novel writing and says that, unlike Sonny, Joe has ideals. Sonny thinks only that she is smitten with Joe. Both Sonny and Sarah seem to share an understanding, however, that Joe is an artist who needs their guidance and control.

The Varioni Brothers enjoy an instant and overwhelmingly popular financial success. Joe, now living in Chicago, has continued to work as Sonny's lyricist, forsaking (for the time being) his novel writing. Sarah and Joe remain in touch, and she encourages him to leave the music business. Sarah tells Joe that she must accompany her father, who has fallen ill, to California. Before departing, she asks Joe to go with her and asks, as well, whether he has been working on his prose. Finally, she reveals her love for him and expresses her worry that he is burning out by working on songs with his brother. Joe reassures Sarah that he has informed Sonny that he will quit songwriting in two weeks. Lou Gangin will write song lyrics for Sonny in the future. While Joe sees Sarah off, Professor Voorhees visits Sonny (at Sarah's request) to persuade him to free Joe to write his novel. Sonny, however, has no intention of working with Gangin as a lyricist. When the professor explains that Joe is a poet and a genius, Sonny asks how the professor can be so certain of Joe's writing talent. Sonny has read only one short story by his brother and did not think it very good. The professor stands his ground, questioning Sonny about why he is trying to "burn out" (77) his brother's life. Sonny replies that he can only "hear the music" (77) when it is made with his brother.

Sarah now continues her story in the first-person voice to describe how she learned to let go of her love for Joe after his death, and how she subsequently married and gave birth to two children with Douglas Smith. Now, 17 years after Joe's murder, Sonny has appeared at Waycross College in search of her and Professor Voorhees. The musician, who seems ill, is in possession of his brother's manuscript. Sonny explains that Joe had finished the novel before his death but had not had time to put it together. Sonny asks for help and shelter so that he might reconstruct Joe's work. Sarah and

Voorhees wonder why Sonny would want to undertake such a "tremendous job" (77). Sonny explains, "Because I hear the music for the first time in my life when I read his book" (77).

CRITICAL ANALYSIS

Salinger experimented with text-within-text techniques throughout his career, and the beginning of "The Varioni Brothers" displays this artifice. The story is introduced within a fictional Chicago gossip column, an element extraneous to the events of the plot. Once readers get past Mr. Gardenia Penny's "Around Old Chi," however, Salinger's talent as a serious writer emerges. "The Varioni Brothers" is not only a story within a story but its theme is a recurring one throughout Salinger's work. Joe Varioni may be seen as a version of Raymond Ford in "The INVERTED FOREST," because Joe, like Ford, is talented but easily manipulated by others. Joe and Sonny Varioni, moreover, are prototypes of Buddy and Seymour Glass in that each brother is artistically talented. Salinger, in this story, also works with themes of sibling and family conflict, themes that he will continue to develop in later works. "The Varioni Brothers," however, represents the first story in which Salinger creates the figure of a very gifted writer who is such a good prose writer that he is considered a poet. Salinger seems to crown his most gifted characters with the title of "poet" although, in doing so, he is not stressing the idea that they write poetry so much as the idea that there is something very special and precious about every word written in their prose.

The central conflict of "The Varioni Brothers" turns on whether Joe Varioni will "sell out" to the demands of the music industry of the 1920s or whether he will write a great novel and be able to live happily with Sarah at Waycross College. This conflict creates narrative tension as Joe, who bends to his brother's influence and insistence that he write lyrics to Sonny's compositions, also feels the pull of Sarah and Professor Voorhees's belief in him and in his artistic calling as a novelist. The tragic circumstance of mistaken identity, where Joe receives five bullets intended for his brother, is due to Sonny's belief that only his brother can make him "hear the music" (77) like no one else can.

Sonny's control over his brother, his insistence that Joe remain in the music business at the expense of his artistic pursuit, has prevented Joe from realizing his true gift. When a broken Sonny appears at Waycross College 17 years after the shooting, he repeats the same refrain about "hearing the music." This time, however, the music is his dead brother's prose.

Again, the relationship and events in the lives of Joe and Sonny Varioni reflect elements in the story of Seymour and Buddy Glass in that, when one brother dies, the other must assume the lingering literary responsibilities. In this story, however, Sonny carries the onus of having been partially responsible for his brother's death. Warren French believes "The Varioni Brothers" contains some of Salinger's most interesting wartime writing. French also observes Salinger's early use of first-person narration as a technique the author will develop more powerfully in his major work.

"The Varioni Brothers" is Salinger's first, and most extensive, use of a female narrative voice. Through Sarah Daley Smith, Salinger captures the dilemma of a young woman in love with a man whom she later comes to realize could not have made her "happy" (77) in the sense that she has found happiness in a more "reasonably normal" (77) life as wife of Douglas Smith, as mother to her children, and as teacher. Sarah's voice describes simply and clearly her thought process as she accepts the tide of events and her relationship to Joe Varioni: "Joe was always too wretched, too thwarted, too claimed by his own *unsatisfied genius* [emphasis added], to have had either inclination or time to examine . . . my love" (77). In contrast to Joe, Sarah describes Douglas Smith, her husband, as possessing "a wonderful, *ungeniuslike* thing" (77) [emphasis added] about him. Within Sarah's emotional struggle and growth, Salinger signals the very real conflict presented by a love for artistic/poetic genius and the difficulty in marrying that love to a life of practical survival and "happiness."

The two talented Varioni brothers are situated by Sarah's vision of the 1920s. Sarah sees the circumstances of those times as having polluted Joe's true artistic talents. Only Joe's death and the passage of time will make Sonny see this corruption as well. Salinger understands that, for stories to work, characters must not only be made to come alive but also show dimensions of understanding that change with the cycle of events. Sarah's depth of memory and her emotional growth and Sonny's capacity to finally hear his brother's real music build meaning into the story's concluding message.

With "The Varioni Brothers," Salinger may also be seen to subtly explore the theme of the artist's conflict between his need to survive financially and thus to bend to the "establishment" demands to create a popular art, and the artist's pursuit of a truer calling that leads to spiritual fulfillment. The name of the college where Joe Varioni teaches "beautifully" (13) is "Waycross" (Salinger's hint, perhaps, at a place that embodies the religious/spiritual path or "Way of the Cross"). At Waycross, writing his novel, Joe remains true to his higher artistic calling. Sarah, moreover, underscores this dilemma in her description of Sonny Varioni arriving at Waycross to put together his brother's novel. In that goal, Sarah explains that Sonny "has a hope for a kind of salvation" (13). The conflict is also captured, from the opposite viewpoint, in Sonny's concern that Joe may not meet with success, even after having spent years pursuing his artistic goals. As the critic Warren French suggests, Salinger may have been questioning his own conflicted concerns about the direction of his writing.

From a biographical perspective, "The Varioni Brothers" provides an uncanny twist of hindsight into Salinger's personal journey. The story presages decisions that the author would take in his personal life, just as his career had established him as one of the more popular and successful writers of his period. At the time of the story's publication, however, the young Salinger struggled with his conflicting role as a writer of stories for the "slicks" (such as COLLIER'S and the *Saturday Evening Post*) and his growing need to write a fiction in pursuit of his truer calling. Just as Sonny Varioni would abandon the big city of Chicago "near the pulse of things" (13) to seek shelter in the "remote" college town of Waycross, Illinois, in order to find "salvation" in putting together his brother's manuscript, so would "Sonny" Salinger ("Sonny" was Salinger's family nickname) choose to abandon the influence of NEW YORK CITY for the sheltering town of CORNISH, NEW HAMPSHIRE, where, one hopes, he continued to put his own manuscripts together.

Salinger's ability to tell a sentimental story without overdoing the sentiment is evidenced in "The Varioni Brothers." Although one might argue that the author over-utilized the element of irony in Sonny's realization, Salinger's deft handling of technical experimentation (text-within-text) and his emerging interest in the theme of "writing as art" together with an emphasis on sibling love make this story a notable one and exemplary as an early attempt at themes the author will develop in more depth and detail in future work. As French suggests, "The Varioni Brothers" remains important as a kernel story for Salinger's "SEYMOUR: AN INTRODUCTION."

The story is accompanied by two illustrations: one of the Varioni brothers composing a song at the piano, the other of Sarah Daley Smith.

PUBLICATION HISTORY

"The Varioni Brothers" was published in the July 17, 1943, issue of the *Saturday Evening Post*. Salinger never reprinted the story in his three books of collected stories. "The Varioni Brothers" later appeared in the bootleg editions *The COMPLETE UNCOLLECTED SHORT STORIES OF J. D. SALINGER* (1974) and *TWENTY-TWO STORIES* (1998).

CHARACTERS

Barto, Teddy Teddy Barto, a music publisher and Sonny and Joe Varioni's agent, produced the brothers' first song releases. Although Joe held a teaching job at a college outside the city, Barto insisted that both brothers move to Chicago to "be near the pulse of things" (13). To celebrate their fifth year of commercial success, Barto threw an "ostentatious" (12) party for 200 guests at the Varioni mansion. While playing piano for the crowd of Roaring Twenties partygoers, Joe Varioni, mistaken for his brother, Sonny, was shot in the back and killed in the basement music studio.

Hankey, Buster A Chicago mobster, Buster Hankey hires a hit man, Rocco, to shoot and kill Sonny Varioni for refusing to make good on a gambling debt. Sonny had accused Buster of cheating in a poker game and thus would not make payment. The columnist Vincent Westmoreland, who initiates the story of the Varioni brothers, describes Hankey as the "late, little-lamented" (12) big shot, thus identifying the gangster as deceased.

Rocco   Rocco, the new "hit man" of Buster Hankey, a Chicago gangster, has been sent by his boss to shoot and kill Sonny Varioni in retribution for refusing to pay a gambling debt. On arriving at the Varioni mansion crowded with partygoers, Rocco is misdirected and mistakenly shoots and kills Sonny's brother, Joe Varioni, who is playing piano for guests in the basement music studio. Rocco's actions are described by the columnist Vincent Westmoreland as having taken place during the 1920s, 17 years prior to the writing of his column, in which he poses the question: "Where is Sonny Varioni?" (12).

Smith, Sarah Daley   Sarah Daley Smith answers the call put forward by the columnist Vincent Westmoreland for information on the whereabouts of Sonny Varioni. Describing herself as "one of the remotest little numbers I know" (13), she begins to recount, in a first-person narrative voice, the story of Joe and Sonny Varioni and her own relationship to Joe. Sarah, née Daley, was a sophomore at Waycross College when she met Joe, who was then teaching a survey course in English literature. Sarah describes herself falling in love with Joe, who reads excerpts to her from his novel-in-progress during walks they take together. When Sonny insists that Joe drop his novel writing to devote himself to being the lyricist of the songwriting duo, the Varioni Brothers, Sarah protests. She understands deeply that Joe's true talent, his poetic gift, lies in his novel writing and should not be wasted on writing song lyrics.

Sarah, who recounts her story from a vantage point of 17 years after Joe's death, views the 1920s and the demands of the music industry of that period as "rotten" (13). Sarah has found a way to fold the pain of loss into the pursuit of a "reasonably normal" (77) life and is happy in her present role as a mother of two children and wife to Douglas Smith, whom she met at teacher's college. When Sonny Varioni subsequently arrives at Waycross, Professor Voorhees (still at the college and in the post he most likely held as head of the English department during Sarah's student days) and Sarah (now teaching at Waycross) give shelter to Sonny, who wishes to "put . . . together" (77) his brother's novel for a book. Sarah thus answers the columnist's question "Where is Sonny Varioni?" (12) by giving the reader the "inside dope" (13) that Sonny is in Waycross, Illinois.

Varioni, Joseph ("Joe")   Joe Varioni, the lyricist of the songwriting duo, the Varioni Brothers, is the central character around which the lives and events of the story revolve. Joe, who teaches English "from Beowulf through Fielding" (13) at Waycross College, Illinois, is beloved by his female students. Sarah Daley, a sophomore in Joe's class, falls in love with him and encourages him to continue writing his novel-in-progress. She supports him when he protests Teddy Barto's request to leave Waycross for Chicago in order to promote the brothers' music career. Sarah also pleads with Sonny Varioni, Joe's brother, to release Joe from the commitment to write song lyrics, explaining that Joe has ideals (whereas Sonny does not). Both Sarah and her mentor, Professor Voorhees, recognize Joe's writing gift and his genius. The professor, moreover, considers Joe "a poet" (76). During the 1920s, Joe is taken for Sonny as he plays piano at a party at the Varioni mansion and is shot to death by a gangster's hit man. After the tragedy, Sonny disappears, only to turn up 17 years later at Waycross seeking shelter from Professor Voorhees and Sarah. Sonny wants to reconstruct Joe's novel, written in disarray on bits of paper and, as he says, "on the inside of a match folder" (77).

Sarah describes Joe in this way: "He was the tallest, thinnest, weariest boy I had ever seen in my life. He was brilliant. He had gorgeous brown eyes, and he had only two suits. He was completely unhappy, and I didn't know why" (13).

Joe Varioni is referenced in "BLUE MELODY."

Varioni, Sonny   Sonny Varioni, the music composer of the songwriting duo, the Varioni Brothers, wields great influence in the fate of his brother, Joe Varioni (the duo's lyricist). Although Joe wishes to leave the music business to continue writing his novel, Sonny will not give Joe his freedom. Sonny is bored and believes Joe to be bored as well. He views the duo's commercial success as a means to fend off the boredom both brothers experience. After Joe is mistaken for Sonny and is shot to death in retaliation for his brother's gambling debt, Sonny disappears from Chicago.

The story of the Varioni brothers is told as a recollection, 17 years after Joe's death, by Sarah Daley Smith. A Chicago gossip columnist has raised the question "Where is Sonny Varioni?" (12) to which Sarah responds, informing the reader that Sonny (now living with her and her husband in Waycross, Illinois) hopes to put together the pieces of his brother Joe's novel. Sonny, who throughout the story repeats the refrain, "I want to hear the music" (which also forms the title of one of the brothers' popular hit songs), has appeared at Waycross (where Sarah now teaches) because, as he confides to Sarah and to Professor Voorhees (Joe's former mentor at the college), ". . . I hear the music for the first time in my life when I read his [Joe's] book" (77). Sarah, who had described Sonny throughout her recollection as "handsome, charming, insincere, and bored" (13), a "brilliant creative technician at the piano" (13), and "conceited" (13), now describes him in current time: "He isn't at all well, and he looks much older than he is" (77). Sonny's strength, however, in undertaking to reconstruct Joe's novel, relies on his "hope for a kind of salvation" (13).

Sonny Varioni is referenced in "Blue Melody."

Voorhees, Professor A professor and most probably the head of the English department at Waycross College, Professor Voorhees recognizes and encourages Joe Varioni's talent as a serious writer. When the professor goes to see Sonny Varioni (at Sarah Daley's request) to persuade him to allow his brother, Joe, to be free from writing song lyrics, he tells Sonny flatly: "Your brother is a poet" (76). The professor moreover believes that Joe "has genius" (76). During the talk, Sonny confesses to having read only one of Joe's stories "about some kids coming out of a school," which he considered "lousy" because "nothing happened" (77). When Sonny refuses to consider the professor's plea for Joe, Voorhees concludes that Sonny wants to "burn out" (77) Joe's life. Salinger places Professor Voorhees in a mentor role to both Joe and Sarah. He is likewise seen as a protector of Sonny Varioni, who seeks shelter at Waycross in order to complete piecing together his brother's manuscript, 17 years after Joe's murder.

FURTHER READING

French, Warren. *J. D. Salinger.* New York: Twayne Publishers, 1963.

———. *J. D. Salinger, Revisited.* New York: Twayne Publishers, 1988.

Wenke, John. *J. D. Salinger: A Study of the Short Fiction.* Boston: Twayne Publishers, 1991.

"Wake Me When It Thunders"

"Wake Me When It Thunders" was retitled by the editors at the SATURDAY EVENING POST and published as "BOTH PARTIES CONCERNED."

"What Babe Saw, or Ooh-La-La!"

"What Babe Saw, or Ooh-La-La!" is one of Salinger's "lost" stories, neither published nor to be found in a library archive. According to the bibliographer Jack R. Sublette, Salinger mentions a story with this title in a September 9, 1944, letter to WHIT BURNETT. (It is possible that Salinger was indicating two alternate titles: "What Babe Saw" or "Ooh-La-La!") The story was revised (or was only retitled) and published as "A BOY IN FRANCE" in the March 31, 1945, issue of the SATURDAY EVENING POST. If the story was indeed revised, and if the original manuscript of "What Babe Saw, or Ooh-La-La!" is not located among

Salinger's literary estate, the story's whereabouts are unknown.

"What Got into Curtis in the Woodshed"

"What Got into Curtis in the Woodshed" is one of Salinger's "lost" stories, neither published nor to be found in a library archive. According to the premier Salinger Web site, www.deadcaulfields.com, a story with this title is included on a 1945 list of Salinger stories compiled by the author's literary agency. "What Got into Curtis in the Woodshed" was included in the proposed table of contents for Salinger's unpublished book, The YOUNG FOLKS. Unless the manuscript can be located among Salinger's literary estate, the story's whereabouts are unknown.

"Wien, Wien"

"Wien, Wien" was retitled by the editors at GOOD HOUSEKEEPING and published as "A GIRL I KNEW."

"Young Folks, The"

"The Young Folks" is Salinger's first published story. Originally written as an assignment for WHIT BURNETT's short-story class at Columbia University, "The Young Folks" sketches a group of college-age students at a party. Salinger was 21 years old when the story appeared in Burnett's STORY magazine in the March–April 1940 issue. The author, however, chose not to include "The Young Folks" in his three books of collected stories.

SYNOPSIS

Lucille Henderson, hosting a party at her parents' apartment for college-age "young folks," introduces William (Bill) Jameson, Junior, an unattractive, shy, fingernail-biting fellow, to Edna Phillips. The plain-looking Edna has been sitting in the same chair for three hours, smoking and "wearing a very bright eye which young men were not bothering to catch" (26). During the ensuing conversation between Edna and Bill, readers witness his resistance to the introduction. Edna is taller and smarter than Bill. Almost immediately, Bill tries to escape from Edna by saying he has to leave the party to write an essay for class. Bill has

E N D   PAGES

CONTRIBUTORS

J. D. SALINGER, who is twenty-one years old, was born in New York. He attended public grammar schools, one military academy, and three colleges, and has spent one year in Europe. He is particularly interested in playwriting.

Tower," is a graduate of the class of 1929 from Radcliffe, worked for a time on the New York World but is now married and the mother of two children. She is thirty years old.

EMMETT GOWEN, who has previously contributed to STORY, is the author of three novels, Mountain Born, Dark Moon of March and Old Hell, and of

Biographical note accompanying Salinger's first published story, "The Young Folks," in the March–April 1940 issue of Story (Courtesy of the Bruce F. Mueller Collection; photo by Laura Fairbanks)

had his eye on Doris Leggett, a small blond girl who is attracting the attention of several young men. Bill decides he wants a drink, and Edna invites herself to accompany him, suggesting there is "stuff" (27) on the terrace. The two go to the terrace whereupon Edna immediately becomes aware of "amorous voices" (28) emanating from a darker area, while Bill is ignorant of the voices' meaning.

Edna tries to interest Bill romantically by commenting on the beauty of the evening, but he is more concerned that there is no more alcohol available on the terrace. When Bill suggests that he look for some drinks inside, Edna persuades him to stay for a cigarette. She extracts two of her last three cigarettes from her rhinestone case. When Bill repeats that he has to go home to write a theme due Monday, Edna keeps him with her by talking about Doris. She tells Bill that Doris was rotten to her friend, Pete Ilesner, and proceeds to paint a less-than-favorable picture of the bleached blond. Edna then mentions Barry (whom she hasn't heard from since last summer), a boyfriend who wanted her to go too far sexually. Edna understands Barry's desires but explains to Bill that, for herself, it has to be true love first and that she has standards that she tries to live up to. Bill comments that the terrace railing is a little shaky. He tells Edna that he is going inside to get a drink and that he must then leave the party in order to write the essay.

Lucille joins Edna on the terrace and mentions seeing Bill inside. She asks whether Edna and Bill did not click. Edna evades the question by saying that Bill had to leave due to some homework. When Lucille reports that Bill is in fact sitting near Doris, Edna claims that he is "a trifle *warm*-blooded" (30). This information surprises Lucille, and Edna asks her hostess to keep Bill away from her. Lucille leaves Edna, who then smokes her last cigarette. After returning indoors, Edna goes upstairs to an area closed to party guests and remains there for 20 minutes. When she joins the party, Bill is still sitting near Doris on the living room floor. Edna sits down in the same chair she occupied before she was introduced to Bill. She takes out one of a dozen cigarettes from her rhine-

stone case and commands that someone change the radio channel to find better dancing music.

CRITICAL ANALYSIS

The rest of Salinger's published fiction obscures the fact that his first publication was originally written as an assignment for a short-story class taught by Whit Burnett at Columbia University. Salinger took the class during the spring and fall semesters of 1939, and "The Young Folks" appeared in his teacher's magazine, *Story*, in the March–April 1940 issue. The story takes place during a college party in an urban apartment, most likely in MANHATTAN. A fairly typical mix of "young folks," alcohol, smoking, and conversation is taking place at 11 P.M. The story is distinct in that it not only displays Salinger's fine-tuned ear for dialogue between young people but also produces conversations that adolescents have had and will always have as they learn to socialize among themselves.

The story's importance clusters around the phrase "amorous voices" (28). Young folks usually talk about love and dating in their social situations. The true "amorous voices" in the story are never really heard except as murmurs, and the speakers are not seen except as shadows when the mismatched protagonists, Edna Phillips and William Jameson, are on the terrace. Edna and Bill's conversation, during their brief encounter, reflects voices that are at cross-purposes and do not constitute "amorous voices." While "The Young Folks" exposes young people being phony and trying to behave like adults at parties, what stays distinctly below the surface of the story is the desire of young folks to seek their own, true "amorous voices." Bill is seeking the words to break into pretty blond Doris Leggett's world, and Edna is seeking attention. Though neither of the two young characters develops "amorous voices" in the story, Bill does end up sitting near Doris while Edna ends up alone wanting better music (or more "amorous voices") from the radio. When Edna commands that the radio station be changed to more danceable music, the reader recognizes the irony that no one will be asking her to dance.

Although most critics shy away from attributing much importance to "The Young Folks," the

THE YOUNG FOLKS

by

J. D. Salinger

ABOUT eleven o'clock, Lucille Henderson, observing that her party was soaring at the proper height, and just having been smiled at by Jack Delroy, forced herself to glance over in the direction of Edna Phillips, who since eight o'clock had been sitting in the big red chair, smoking cigarettes and yodeling hellos and wearing a very bright eye which young men were not bothering to catch. Edna's direction still the same, Lucille Henderson sighed as heavily as her dress would allow, and then, knitting what there was of her brows, gazed about the room at the noisy young people she had invited to drink up her father's Scotch. Then abruptly she swished to where William Jameson Junior sat, biting his fingernails and staring at a small blonde girl sitting on the floor with three young men from Rutgers.

"Hello, there," Lucille Henderson said, clutching William Jameson Junior's arm. "Come on," she said. "There's someone I'd like you to meet."

"Who?"

"This girl. She's swell." And Jameson followed her across the room, at the same time trying to make short work of a hangnail on his thumb.

"Edna baby," Lucille Henderson said, "I'd love you to really know Bill Jameson. Bill—Edna Phillips. Or have you two birds met already?"

26

"No," said Edna, taking in Jameson's large nose, flabby mouth, narrow shoulders. "I'm awfully glad to meet you," she told him.

"Gladda know ya," Jameson replied, mentally contrasting Edna's all with the all of the small blonde across the room.

"Bill's a very good friend of Jack Delroy's," Lucille reported.

"I don't know him so good," said Jameson.

"Well. I gotta beat it. See ya later, you two!"

"Take it easy!" Edna called after her. Then, "Won't you sit down?"

"Well, I don't know," Jameson said, sitting down. "I been sitting down all night, kinda."

"I didn't know you were a good friend of Jack Delroy's," Edna said. "He's a grand person, don't you think?"

"Yeah, he's all right, I guess. I don't know him so good. I never went around with his crowd much."

"Oh, really? I thought I heard Lu say you were a good friend of his."

"Yeah, she did. Only I don't know him so good. I really oughtta be gettin' home. I got this theme for Monday I'm supposed to do. I wasn't really gonna come home this week end."

"Oh, but the party's young!" Edna said. "The shank of the evening!"

"The what?"

First page of Salinger's first published story, "The Young Folks," in the March–April 1940 issue of *Story* (Courtesy of the Bruce F. Mueller Collection; photo by Laura Fairbanks)

reader may, in fact, see the story as the earliest published "seed" of Salinger's one novel, *The CATCHER IN THE RYE*. Aspects of Edna Phillips will morph into Holden Caulfield. Edna's repeated use of italics to stress things that young adults must stress, and her repeated use of the word "grand" to show how phony she can be, become part of Holden's awareness. Like Holden, Edna appears more mature than she is, and also like Holden, she seeks "real" love. When readers consider the dialogue and characterization in "The Young Folks," they are able to discern versions of some of the young folks that will show up in other early Salinger stories and in the later novel.

Despite the detached tone of the narrative, the possibility that Salinger had parts of Edna and Bill

in him should also not be overlooked. Young writers are encouraged to write about what they know. Although city-smart and prep-school-educated, Salinger shyly stayed on the outside of class discussion during his semesters with Whit Burnett. At the time he composed this story, Salinger, a neophyte writer, may possibly have felt some awkwardness around the opposite sex, around the academic environment at Columbia University, and around writers with more experience and success. However, the fact that Salinger's first publication is titled "The Young Folks" was nothing if not prophetic. Most of Salinger's best characters are young, and most writers today cannot write about young folks without reflecting something of Salinger's art.

PUBLICATION HISTORY

"The Young Folks" was published in the March–April 1940 issue of *Story* magazine. Salinger never reprinted the story in his three books of collected stories. "The Young Folks" later appeared in the bootleg editions *The COMPLETE UNCOLLECTED SHORT STORIES OF J. D. SALINGER* (1974) and *TWENTY-TWO STORIES* (1998).

CHARACTERS

Barry Edna Phillips refers to a previous older boyfriend, Barry, to pique William Jameson's jealousy. Barry, an artist who attended Princeton and once painted Edna, is not present at the party.

Delroy, Jack Jack Delroy, whom Edna Phillips terms "grand" (26), is the leader of the "in crowd." At the end of the party, he is seen putting peanuts down Doris Leggett's dress.

Frances and Eddie Frances and Eddie are the couple on the terrace whose "amorous voices" (28) are heard by Edna Phillips and William Jameson.

Henderson, Lucille ("Lu") Lucille Henderson, hostess of the party, introduces William Jameson and Edna Phillips. After Lucille tells her boyfriend, Harry, to get her a drink, she asks Edna whether she got along with Bill. Lucille is surprised by Edna's insinuation (which is a lie) that Bill was sexually forward with her.

Ilesner, Pete ("Petie") Edna Phillips refers to Pete Ilesner when she tells William Jameson that Doris Leggett treated Petie badly.

Jameson, Junior, William ("Bill") Bill Jameson, unattractive and socially inept, nonetheless is interested in Doris Leggett, but he is too shy to approach her. Instead, Bill is introduced by Lucille Henderson to Edna Phillips. He is not attracted to Edna and immediately says he was just about to leave the party because he has to write an essay. Much of the story shows him uncomfortably interacting with Edna. At story's close, he is sitting on the floor near Doris.

Leggett, Doris ("Dottie") Doris Leggett, an attractive bleached blond, is the object of Bill Jameson's attentions. At the outset of the story, she is seen surrounded by three young men from Rutgers. Although the reader never hears Doris speaking, her loud laughter punctuates the evening. By the story's close, Bill is sitting near her.

Phillips, Edna ("Ed") Edna Phillips is the story's main protagonist. At the outset of the narrative, she is seen sitting alone in a red chair while the party swirls around her. The party's hostess, Lucille Henderson, introduces the unattractive Edna to the equally unattractive Bill Jameson. Edna attempts to engage Bill's attention to no avail. Edna, a romantic, terms the sounds from the couple making out on the terrace as "amorous voices" (28). When Bill finally leaves her, she lies to Lucille that he was sexually forward. Edna, whose purse held three cigarettes during her conversation with Bill, now finds herself out of cigarettes. She disappears from the party and goes upstairs for 20 minutes. As the story ends, Edna is sitting in the same chair she occupied at the story's beginning. When she opens her rhinestone purse, her theft of cigarettes from the upstairs room is revealed (as her evening bag now displays "ten or twelve" [30] cigarettes).

FURTHER READING

French, Warren. *J. D. Salinger, Revisited.* New York: Twayne Publishers, 1988.

Lundquist, James. *J. D. Salinger.* New York: Ungar, 1979.

Wenke, John. *J. D. Salinger: A Study of the Short Fiction.* Boston: Twayne Publishers, 1991.

Young Folks, The

The Young Folks, which would have been Salinger's first book, was never published. In an April 14, 1944, letter, WHIT BURNETT proposed to Salinger that Story Press publish a volume of Salinger's short stories. Burnett suggested the title and explained, "All of the people in the book would be young, tough, soft, debutante, social, army, etc. Perhaps the first third of the book would be stories of young people on the eve of the war, the middle third in and around the army and then one or two stories at the close of the war" (Sublette 61). Salinger initially resisted the idea. Burnett convinced him, and the proposed table of contents would have been compiled from the following stories: "The DAUGHTER OF THE LATE, GREAT MAN,"* "ELAINE," "The LAST AND BEST OF THE PETER PANS,"* "BOTH PARTIES CONCERNED," "The LONG DEBUT OF LOIS TAGGETT," "BITSEY,"* "The YOUNG FOLKS," "I'M CRAZY," "BOY STANDING IN TENNESSEE,"* "ONCE A WEEK WON'T KILL YOU," "LAST DAY OF THE LAST FURLOUGH," "SOFT-BOILED SERGEANT," "The CHILDREN'S ECHELON,"* "TWO LONELY MEN,"* "A BOY IN FRANCE," "A YOUNG MAN IN A STUFFED SHIRT,"* "The MAGIC FOXHOLE,"* "SLIGHT REBELLION OFF MADISON," "WHAT GOT INTO CURTIS IN THE WOODSHED,"* and "The OCEAN FULL OF BOWLING BALLS."* (Salinger never collected any of these 20 stories in his books. Moreover, the stories followed by an asterisk were not even published by the author in a magazine.) Story Press's parent company, Lippincott, vetoed Burnett's publication of the book. In a July 27, 1945, letter to ERNEST HEMINGWAY, Salinger acknowledges that, although publication plans for a volume of short stories fell through, he was not disappointed, believing it to have been too soon in his career to have published a book. (Unless Salinger is referring to another publication plan, this letter would suggest that the *Story* publication faltered in 1945, instead of the generally accepted date of 1946.)

"Young Girl in 1941 with No Waist at All, A"

Appearing in the May 1947 issue of MADEMOI-SELLE, "A Young Girl in 1941 with No Waist at All" portrays a sensitive young woman's transition from girlhood to maturity through her decision to call off her engagement. "A Young Girl in 1941 with No Waist at All" is Salinger's 18th published story. The author, however, chose not to include the story in his three books of collected stories.

SYNOPSIS

The 18-year-old Barbara, vacationing on the *Kungsholm*, a cruise ship docked at Havana, Cuba, is noticed by the 22-year-old Ray Kinsella, a member of the staff's Junior Entertainment Committee. The year is 1941, and the impending American involvement in the war is much on the minds of the guests. Barbara, whose figure is "very young and sassy" (222), is also very young emotionally. Ray invites her to tour some of the nightlife on shore. On the tender boat there, they meet an older couple in their forties, Mr. and Mrs. Woodruff. Mrs. Woodruff becomes interested in Barbara and Ray. The party of four decides to enjoy some nightclubbing together. After exchanging introductions, Mrs. Woodruff asks Ray—addressing him twice by mistake as "Mr. Walters" (292, 295)—whether he thinks that the United States will soon enter the war. Ray explains that he has already enlisted in the army and, when the cruise is over, he will be given a commission in the artillery. The tender boat bumps gently, and Ray takes the opportunity to "put his arm around Barbara's waist" (292), whereupon Mrs. Woodruff remarks how "perfect" (292) it is for Ray to be out on such a night with Barbara, who "has absolutely no waist at all" (292).

At the nightclub, as the Woodruffs rumba, Barbara and Ray get to know each other. Barbara exclaims excitedly that she considers Mrs. Woodruff "nice" and "beautiful" (293). Ray concedes only that the older woman "certainly talks a lot" (293). Ray tells Barbara that he has only been on a cruise once before and that he has just dropped out of Yale. She confides that she used to work but no longer does. She did not go to college. Ray asks where Barbara's mother is, and she informs him that her mother is dead and that she is traveling with her "mother-in-law-to-be" (293). Barbara then begins to strike matches and to blow them out, telling Ray that her fiancé, concerned for her health (she had been sick recently), wanted her to get some rest. His mother, Mrs. Odenhearn, consequently volunteered to take Barbara on a cruise. Mrs. Odenhearn, Barbara explains, seems like Barbara's own age, as she was "a great athlete" (293) as a young woman.

Ray asks Barbara to dance (she proves to be inexperienced on the dance floor). As they dance, Ray questions her about her fiancé. Barbara responds that Carl is "very nice. He sounds lovely over the telephone. He's very—very considerate about stuff" (294). When Ray asks what Barbara means about "stuff," she responds: "Oh . . . stuff. I don't know. I don't understand boys. I never know what they're talking about" (294). Ray kisses Barbara impulsively on the forehead and asks her age; he also tells her his own age.

With the couples back at the table, Mrs. Woodruff goes to the powder room, and her husband tells Ray and Barbara that he is keeping information from his wife: the fact that their son will soon enlist in the army, hoping to become a flier. When Mr. Woodruff leaves the table, Barbara tells Ray that Carl will be going into the navy. She also seems nervous about hearing that, after this last cruise, the ship will not be used for holiday purposes until after the war.

With all four at the table again, Mrs. Woodruff exclaims abruptly, "Oh, how I hate 1941" (295), because, she explains, breaking into tears, 1941 is "full of armies waiting to fill up with boys, and girls and mothers waiting to live in mailboxes and smirking old headwaiters who don't have to go any-where" (295–296). Mr. Woodruff reminds her that boys have always been expected to go to war and that her own brothers had gone and he, himself, had gone (he is referring to his service during World War I). Mrs. Woodruff responds that things are "not rotten in the same way" (296) as before. Bobby (her son) will not even go on a date if he is short of money. She feels now that "it's entirely rotten" (296).

Barbara and Ray leave the Woodruffs. Back on the cruise ship, Ray kisses Barbara fervently for the next two hours and proposes marriage to her several times. He insists that they are "*right* for each other" (297). Barbara, hesitant, observes that they hardly know each other. Abruptly, she asks whether Ray thinks she is "dumb" (297). Although Ray replies emphatically to the contrary, Barbara tells him that the girls at school and the ones she chums with now consider her dumb. She wants to know why Ray has told her that she is "smart" (297). He can only respond with a kiss. Barbara begins to cry and decides to turn in for the night. Ray objects strongly that she seems to be treat-ing him as if she does not know him, and Barbara answers, "I told you I was dumb" (298).

Mr. and Mrs. Woodruff, returning to the ship in a very inebriated state, have trouble climbing the boarding ladder. As they struggle upward, Mrs. Woodruff declares her opinion that Barbara is "lovely" (299) but that Ray (whom she calls "Eddie") is "full of baloney" (299). She hopes Bar-bara will behave "sensibly" (299). She then recites a prayer from the Song of Solomon, asking that all the "children use their heads now" (299).

In her cabin, Barbara tries not to disturb Mrs. Odenhearn. Her companion, however, has not been asleep, kept awake by the noise of passing drunken guests. In their conversation, Mrs. Oden-hearn rehearses how she and Barbara must play to win the tennis match the next morning (she had been a "deadly serious tennis player in her day" [299]). With the lights out, Barbara, quiet for several minutes, suddenly but firmly tells Mrs. Odenhearn that she does not want to get mar-ried. Secretly pleased at Barbara's statement, Mrs. Odenhearn reassures Barbara that "It's always the best way to rectify a mistake *before* it's made" (301).

Barbara decides to take a stroll on deck. The reader learns that Mrs. Odenhearn is so happy about the turn of events that she can hardly con-tain herself. Mrs. Odenhearn looks at Barbara and feels she no longer bears any responsibility toward her. Barbara intuits the older woman's look "fault-lessly" (302). Mrs. Odenhearn's last words to Bar-bara are to warn her not to catch cold.

In the story's final paragraph, Barbara walks through the silent passages of the ship, through its concert lounge and onto the A Deck. "In less than four months' time . . . more than three hundred enlisted men would be arranged wakefully on their backs across the floor" (302). For the next hour, Barbara stands at the portside rail. In that "fragile hour" (302), she is not in danger of catching cold, but is "now exclusively susceptible to the difficult counterpoint sounding just past the last minutes of her girlhood" (302).

CRITICAL ANALYSIS

Although Salinger situates the story's events just before the month of December 1941, the qual-ity of the relationships among the characters and the concerns they express to one another lend a universal dimension to the narrative. From a third-person perspective, the author portrays the emotional anticipation of the impending war as felt by a number of diverse personalities as they meet and connect on a beautiful and balmy evening on a cruise ship off the coast of Havana.

The action concentrates at first on two couples: the young Barbara and her suitor, Ray Kinsella, and the older couple, Mr. and Mrs. Woodruff. The conversation among the four builds the tension surrounding the imminent American involvement in World War II. Mrs. Woodruff, a woman in her late forties—wealthy and kind—seems to represent the vatic voice of all women with her premonitions of the tragedy to come. She declaims 1941 as a "rotten year" (296) and the upcoming war as also rotten.

The scene shifts to the budding romance between Barbara and Ray. The young man, who will join the army just after the end of the cruise, falls in love with the innocent young woman and proposes marriage to her several times. Although naive and inexperienced with men, Barbara is, however, already engaged to be married. Obviously moved by Ray's proposal, Barbara nonetheless defers her answer. As a protagonist, Barbara is portrayed as a girl just on the threshold of her mature life. She has graduated from high school, has worked for a time, but now "doesn't do anything" (293). She is not attending college. No information is offered the reader about the reason Barbara has accepted a proposal of marriage to Carl Odenhearn, except that Carl "is very considerate about stuff" (294); that is, he does not press her in sexual matters. As Barbara wears a white dress and has a figure with "no waist at all" (292), Salinger represents in her character a symbol of unblemished and untried girlhood. Barbara believes herself to be "dumb" (297), but she displays a rational perspective in reacting to Ray's quick proposal of marriage. As she truthfully tells him: "I keep even forgetting your name" (297). She believes herself dumb because her female schoolmates have told her so. Perhaps, however, her schoolmates think her dumb because she "never knows what boys are talking about" (294). Hence, she may have accepted Carl's marriage proposal, believing there to be no alternative for her, such as furthering her education. The critic Eberhard Alsen sees Barbara as a nonconformist who, at the story's end, "rebels against the notion of marriage as a career goal" (Alsen 26). Considering Barbara's decision to break off her engagement with Carl, together with her deferral of an answer to Ray's marriage proposal, the text would seem to bear out Alsen's assessment. Likewise, Barbara's more general statement to Mrs. Odenhearn—"I just don't want to get married to anybody yet" (301)—would support this interpretation.

In Barbara's character, Salinger has drawn the vulnerability and sensitivity of youth, perhaps, as Mrs. Woodruff believes, as yet "unequipped" for what lies ahead. Barbara's foreboding or "funny" (295) feeling (as she expresses it to Ray) about the cruise ship on its last tour captures her real premonition and anticipatory fears of the imminent loss and grief of World War II. Although young, Barbara has already suffered losses in her life (the death of both parents) and understands disappoint-

ment (she tells Ray that her brother missed out on a college scholarship due to a football injury). Sensibly, she decides to forgo the almost giddy need for romance and hasty commitment that the impending war seems to be imposing on the young men and women around her. As a counterpoint to Ray's anxious plea for her to marry him right away, and his naive optimism of what lies in store for him in the artillery—"Oh, it won't be too bad . . . I'll have my own battery and all" (292)—Barbara seems to be seeking some perspective by pausing in her commitments.

The scene next shifts to Mr. and Mrs. Woodruff, who struggle drunkenly to climb to the ship's deck from the tender boat. Mrs. Woodruff utters, with an excerpt from the Bible's Song of Solomon, the prayer that love will not come until bidden; that is, until the time when young lovers' hearts will not surely be broken. The recitation lends poetic depth to the character of Mrs. Woodruff: "'I adjure you, O daughters of Jerusalem, By the roes, and by the hinds of the field, That ye stir not up, nor awaken love, Until it please'" (299).

The imagery at story's end, with Barbara alone on the empty upper deck gazing out to sea, casts her as a Nike figurehead. Salinger likewise casts the reader a ghostly vision of the 300 men who would, in the near future, lie wakefully on their backs as they are transported to their wartime destinies. Because the story is set just before the Pearl Harbor attack in December 1941, the reader, in hindsight and with more historical knowledge than the characters possess, feels the poignancy of the moment—almost as an elegy in suspension. Since the characters are not yet privy to that impending devastation and loss of life, the story provides a glance into a time that the reader realizes will soon come to an end, one yet innocent of the ravages of World War II. Barbara, along with the America she seems to symbolize in this scene, pauses on the cusp of that lost and "fragile" (302) hour.

Likewise, with this story, Salinger offers a backward glance at his younger self in a happier age. On February 15, 1941, the author sailed from New York on the cruise ship *Kungsholm* for a 19-day tour to the West Indies as a member of the ship's social staff. Donald M. Fiene (Salinger's first bibliographer), who confirmed the information about Salinger's employment on the *Kungsholm,* quotes Carl W. Hallengren, manager of public relations at the Swedish American Line, in his letter to Fiene of May 21, 1961. Hallengren's letter states that the cruise manager and social directress for whom Salinger worked in 1941 recorded: "this gentleman is very good" (Fiene 102). (Most critics mistakenly date Salinger's cruise year as 1937.) Among the ports of call on Salinger's trip in 1941 was Havana, Cuba, which is the setting of the story.

Mademoiselle illustrated the story with one drawing—Ray Kinsella, Barbara, and the Woodruffs standing in the tender boat, with the cruise ship behind them.

PUBLICATION HISTORY

"A Young Girl in 1941 with No Waist at All" was published in the May 1947 issue of *Mademoiselle.* Salinger never reprinted the story in his three books of collected stories. "A Young Girl in 1941 with No Waist at All" later appeared in the bootleg editions *The* COMPLETE UNCOLLECTED SHORT STORIES OF *J. D.* SALINGER (1974) and TWENTY-TWO STORIES (1998).

CHARACTERS

Barbara A very emotionally young 18-year-old from Coopersburg, Pennsylvania, Barbara (whose surname is never revealed) has a "sassy" figure (222) and, according to Mrs. Woodruff, "no waist at all" (292). Her hair is "blond . . . corn yellow" (294). Recently orphaned—her mother died at an undisclosed time, and her father has just died from a cerebral hemorrhage—she has one brother and also mentions one aunt. Barbara displays an innocent and sensitive openness to life and, at the same time, a practical and sound questioning of the opinions and attitudes of those around her. She considers herself "dumb" (297) because the girls from her school days have told her so. Yet, when Ray Kinsella proposes marriage to her, she reminds him that they hardly know each other. She does not, as Mrs. Woodruff fears she will, lose her head in the confusing emotional anticipation of the impending World War II. Although Ray's proposal causes her to cry, she refrains from giving

him an answer. Upon reflection in her cabin, Barbara makes the decision to break off her engagement to her fiancé, Carl Odenhearn. Barbara states to Ray, during their evening together, that she "used to work" (293), but that she doesn't "do anything now" (293). She adds that she did not attend college. Recovering from a recent illness, Barbara is traveling for her health, accompanied by her future mother-in-law, Mrs. Odenhearn. Although the anxiety of the American entry into the war seems to have affected those around her, Barbara, in her decision to break off her engagement, shows maturity and practical sense in determining her future.

Kinsella, Ray Twenty-two-year-old, good-looking, dark-haired Ray Kinsella is a staff member of the ship, the *Kungsholm,* working as part of the cruise's Junior Entertainment Committee. Ray, originally from Salt Lake City, has dropped out of Yale. He meets Barbara during the jai alai evening games on shore at Havana, Cuba, and is attracted by her pretty looks and figure. He invites her to see the nightlife of the city, and she accepts, as he reminds her of "a boy . . . in a lot of West Pointy pictures with Dick Powell and Ruby Keeler" (222). Ray is six-feet-four. Having already enlisted in the service, he has been promised a commission in the army artillery. He will enter the military immediately after the ship finishes this, its last, cruise. Ray falls in love with Barbara and "persuasively" (297) kisses her for two hours the evening they meet, proposing marriage to her several times. Despite Ray's urgent pleas that the two are "*right* for each other" (297), Barbara defers a definite commitment.

Odenhearn, Carl Fiancé to Barbara and son of Mrs. Odenhearn, Carl Odenhearn will go into the navy in the upcoming war. Worried about Barbara's health, Carl had suggested that Barbara travel for some rest. His mother has volunteered to accompany her future daughter-in-law on a cruise. According to Barbara, Carl is "very nice . . . very— very considerate about stuff" (294); that is, about what boys talk about, which, she confides to Ray Kinsella, she can never understand.

Odenhearn, Mrs. A possible future mother-in-law, Mrs. Odenhearn accompanies her son Carl Odenhearn's fiancé, Barbara, on the cruise to Havana. Carl has suggested that Barbara travel in order to get some rest. Mrs. Odenhearn, once a "deadly serious tennis player" (299), seems extremely youthful to Barbara. In instructing Barbara how the two will win the next day's doubles tennis tournament, Mrs. Odenhearn displays a take-no-prisoners attitude: "They're out for blood tomorrow" (300). Juxtaposed with the character of Mrs. Woodruff—a sensitive and caring mother figure who considers Barbara a "lovely" (299) and sensible girl—Mrs. Odenhearn secretly exalts in learning that Barbara no longer wishes to marry Carl. As Barbara leaves the cabin to walk on deck after telling Mrs. Odenhearn of her decision, the older woman feels only relief and no concern. She hopes only that Barbara will not "disgrace or embarrass" (302) her for the remainder of the cruise.

Woodruff, Mr. Fielding Mr. Woodruff, husband to Mrs. Woodruff, is a portly man in his late forties. He and his wife, wealthy San Franciscans, remain very much in love. Having fought in World War I, Mr. Woodruff reminds his wife—during her tearful declamation against the detestable year 1941—that all boys are expected to go to war (he himself had served and so had her brothers). Mr. Woodruff informs Ray Kinsella and Barbara that his son, Bobby, will enlist in the army, hoping to become a flier. However, he is keeping the information from Mrs. Woodruff, as the news would "kill" her (295). Mr. and Mrs. Woodruff drink heavily and dance the rumba energetically; they also play roulette. Very inebriated when returning to the cruise ship, Mr. Woodruff has a great deal of trouble climbing the ladder.

Woodruff, Mrs. Diane Mrs. Woodruff, thought "beautiful" (293) by Barbara—a definition that the third-person narrative voice confirms—is a woman in her late forties. She is traveling with her husband, with whom she is still very much in love. Mr. and Mrs. Woodruff, an extremely wealthy couple from San Francisco, have one son, Bobby, who will soon enlist in the army, where he wishes to be a

flier. Mrs. Woodruff, sensing the impending loss of life (with America's entry into World War II imminent), breaks into tears, exclaiming that she hates 1941. Later in the evening, and very inebriated, Mrs. Woodruff prays that all the "children" (299) will use their heads. She believes the young to be "unequipped" (299), presumably for the upcoming upheaval that the war will bring. Mrs. Woodruff's prayer, from the Bible's Song of Solomon, lends poetic depth to the narrative and makes of her a universal mother figure in her caring concern for all the youth who will suffer the devastations of war—both physical and emotional. When Ray Kinsella puts his arm around Barbara's waist, Mrs. Woodruff gently remarks to him that his night will be "perfect" (292), as he is with a young woman who has "absolutely no waist at all" (292). Mrs. Woodruff twice mistakenly addresses Ray as "Mr. Walters" and also mistakenly refers to him as "Eddie." Throughout the story's events, Mrs. Woodruff seems to be ever on the verge of tears, overwhelmed at the thought of the grief to come. She worries about her own son, Bobby, as well, and does not know that he will soon be enlisting.

FURTHER READING

Alsen, Eberhard. *A Reader's Guide to J. D. Salinger.* Westport, Conn.: Greenwood Press, 2002.
Fiene, Donald M. "A Bibliographical Study of J. D. Salinger: Life, Work and Reputation." Master's thesis, University of Louisville, 1961.
French, Warren. *J. D. Salinger, Revisited.* New York: Twayne Publishers, 1988.

"Young Man in a Stuffed Shirt, A"

"A Young Man in a Stuffed Shirt" is one of Salinger's "lost" stories, neither published nor to be found in a library archive. According to the bibliographer Jack R. Sublette, WHIT BURNETT, in a 1959 letter to Salinger, offered to buy the much-earlier-submitted story, which Burnett had found in the files of STORY magazine. (He was preparing to revive the magazine.) Salinger, however, refused to sell the story, and it was returned to the author. "A Young Man in a Stuffed Shirt" was included in the proposed table of contents for Salinger's unpublished book, *The YOUNG FOLKS*. Given that this "lost" story surfaced as late as 1959, "A Young Man in a Stuffed Shirt" probably can be located among Salinger's literary estate.

"Zooey"

"Zooey" provides the most extensive, central, and intimate experience of the Glass family. This novella-length story, a sequel to "FRANNY," concludes with the parable of the Fat Lady, which is the clearest extant expression of Salinger's philosophy. Originally published in the May 4, 1957, issue of the *NEW YORKER*, "Zooey" was later paired with the January 29, 1955, *New Yorker* story, "Franny," to form Salinger's third published book, the 1961 volume, *FRANNY AND ZOOEY*. "Zooey" is Salinger's 33rd published story.

SYNOPSIS

In a first-person prologue, Buddy Glass warns the reader that what is at hand is not a short story "but a sort of prose home movie" (47). He has been creating such "movies" since the age of 15. This one features his youngest sister, Franny, his youngest brother, Zooey, and his mother, Bessie. Buddy informs the reader that Zooey believes the publishing of this story will damage Buddy's literary reputation because the story's mystical properties will only reinforce the perception of his unhealthy interest in God. Buddy is not worried, though, because he defines this story as a love story, rather than a mystical one, calling it "a compound, or multiple, love story, pure and complicated" (49). He also warns the reader that his three relatives have not stinted in details when each separately informed him of the events occurring two years earlier. Buddy then adds that the family's last name is Glass, and that its members communicate in a "family language, a sort of semantic geometry in which the shortest distance between any two

points is a fullish circle" (49). With the prologue over, the story proper, consisting of five scenes, is told in a third-person narrative.

The first scene of the story opens with Zooey in the bathtub reading a letter Buddy had sent him four years earlier. Before reproducing the entire letter in the text of the story, Buddy gives a detailed description of Zooey. He is a small, thin, very successful young television actor. (At the time of receiving this letter, Zooey, however, had not yet fully committed to being an actor.) Buddy quotes his sister Boo Boo's description of Zooey: "the blue-eyed Jewish-Irish Mohican scout who died in your arms at the roulette table at Monte Carlo" (51). Buddy believes Zooey's face radiates with a special beauty, most particularly his eyes. Zooey, like all of the Glass children, appeared on a radio quiz program called *It's a Wise Child*. Many people remember the program, and they usually rank Zooey second only to Seymour as its best performer. In a footnote, Buddy lists the seven Glass children, and though only Franny and Zooey will be directly seen in "Zooey," the other five will be making their presences felt. At the time of the events of the story, two of the children—Seymour and Walt—are dead (Seymour by suicide, Walt in a post–World War II accident); Buddy is a writer-in-residence in Upstate New York; the elder daughter, Boo Boo, a wife and mother, is vacationing in Europe; and Waker, a Roman Catholic priest, happens to be at a conference in Ecuador.

Buddy's 14-page letter is dated March 18, 1951. In it, Buddy first mentions that he has received a letter from Bessie. She has harped on his lacking a phone at his own home, while he unfathomably keeps the phone in his and Seymour's old bedroom in the family apartment in MANHATTAN in working order. Buddy explains to Zooey that he lists the phone under Seymour's name; he likes "to browse through the G's confidently" (57). He admits that Bessie wants him to encourage Zooey to get his Ph.D. in case acting does not pan out (a doctorate in mathematics instead of Greek). Buddy has his doubts about concurring with Bessie but worries that Zooey will not be satisfied with acting due to the inherent limitations of the profession as an art form. Buddy admits he himself does not have even a B.A., in part out of snobbery and in part because Seymour completed his doctorate at such a young age that Buddy does not want to compete with him. Buddy mentions that he now realizes Zooey would have it easier as an actor if Buddy and Seymour had not bombarded him as a child with the religious texts that interested the eldest two boys. Buddy concedes that Zooey is a real actor (Bessie knows this) and that Zooey and Franny are the only two attractive-looking children in the family. Buddy then realizes and remarks that it is three years to the day of Seymour's suicide. Buddy tells Zooey about his flight down to Florida to retrieve Seymour's body after the suicide in a hotel room. He admits to having the "Wrong Expression" (62) on his face when deplaning and then meeting with Seymour's widow, Muriel. He also quotes the haiku Seymour wrote on the desk blotter the afternoon of his suicide: "The little girl on the plane / Who turned her doll's head around / To look at me" (64). Buddy relates an incident that happened to him this very day at the supermarket, when he had asked a little girl if she had any boyfriends, and she had replied, two: Bobby and Dorothy. This answer, plus his recalling Seymour's poem, provides Buddy with the impetus to write Zooey. Buddy attempts to explain to Zooey why he and Seymour "were regularly conducting home seminars, and the metaphysical sittings" (66). Seymour and Buddy were concerned that the relentless pursuit of academic knowledge by intellectually gifted children could lead to dire results, and they felt that an initial grounding in ZEN's "no-knowledge" would lessen the danger. Seymour believed "all legitimate religious study *must* lead to unlearning the differences, the illusory differences" (67) between things. Buddy acknowledges that the differences in age between members of the family added to their problems, particularly between the youngest siblings (Franny and Zooey) and the eldest (Seymour and Buddy). Buddy admits to being afraid, after Seymour's suicide, to visit NEW YORK CITY because of the possible questions Franny and Zooey might ask. He writes that Waker was right in saying that Zooey was the only member of the family "bitter about S.'s suicide and the only one who really forgave him for it" (68). The others acted exactly

opposite. Buddy acknowledges Zooey's desire to act and entreats him to "*act* . . . but do it *with all of your might*" (68). He points Zooey in the direction not of ordinary success but of true aesthetic achievement: to create something "beautiful . . . , nameless and joy-making" (68). If Zooey can achieve this, Buddy swears that he and Seymour will show up, dressed in formal attire and laden with bouquets of flowers, at Zooey's stage door.

After reading the letter, Zooey returns it to its envelope and begins to play a game of propelling it along the tub's edge, until he has to rescue it from falling into the water. He then inserts it into a script by the side of the tub. Zooey begins to read a script of a possible television play (a half-page of its turgid dialogue between two lovers is reproduced in the text). His reading is interrupted by his mother's desire to come into the bathroom; she has something for him. Exasperated, Zooey pulls the shower curtain, totally screening him from view. Bessie enters, attired in her old Japanese kimono, to which she has added pockets now bulging with a miscellany of things, including her cigarettes and assorted hardware items. She has brought Zooey some new toothpaste. Bessie opens the medicine cabinet and the contents within—several dozen items ranging from the expected (combs, razors, soaps) to the unexpected (ticket stubs and an azure marble)—are cataloged one by one. Mrs. Glass asks Zooey if he has spoken with his sister Franny today. Zooey answers no, telling Bessie he spoke with Franny for two hours the previous night. Thus begins an extended back-and-forth conversation in which Bessie attempts to gain Zooey's help regarding Franny, while Zooey banters and bullies her. Bessie sits down on the toilet seat. She castigates Buddy for not keeping a working phone in his Upstate New York home and for his hermitlike way of life. She worries about his safety, and Zooey protests. Bessie hands Zooey a washcloth; Zooey again tells her to leave, but she notices the script that Zooey's boss, Mr. LeSage, has sent: "The Heart Is an Autumn Wanderer." Bessie laments that her husband, Les, is no help regarding Franny's plight. According to Bessie, he is sentimentally lost in the past, as if he could turn on the radio and again, magically, hear all seven of his children on *It's a*

Wise Child. Les really is not aware of what is wrong with his younger daughter; one night he wanted to bring her a tangerine. Bessie describes Franny's emotional state, her crying at the slightest word and "mumbling heaven knows *what* to herself" (83). (During this scene, Franny is asleep in the living room with the family cat, Bloomberg, as her bedroom is being painted.) Mrs. Glass expresses deep concern about her daughter's well-being, and she realizes Buddy, Boo Boo, and Waker cannot help. Zooey deflects the seriousness of the subject. He warns his mother to leave the bathroom as he wants to get out of the tub. Bessie does not seem to notice his comment; she is staring at the bath mat, with eyes which once "could break the news . . . that two of her sons were dead, one by suicide (her favorite, her most intricately calibrated, her kindest son), and one killed in World War II (her only truly lighthearted son)" [89]. Abruptly, Mrs. Glass exits the bathroom.

The second scene opens with Zooey now dressed in slacks and engaged in his ritual of shaving. To Zooey's mirth, Mrs. Glass re-enters the bathroom and resumes her conversation. Bessie tells Zooey that she has asked Franny whether she wants to talk with Waker, but Franny answered that she did not want to talk with anybody. Bessie still wonders if she should try to get in touch with Waker, a priest, but she believes that her daughter actually needs a psychiatrist. That aside, she also doubts if the emotional Waker could deal with the situation: "If you tell Waker it looks like *rain*, his eyes all fill up" (94).

Bessie informs Zooey that she knows what lies behind Franny's breakdown. Questioned by Zooey as to how she knows, she answers that Lane, Franny's boyfriend, has phoned several times, concerned about Franny. Zooey doubts Lane's sincerity and labels Lane "a charm boy and a fake" (96). Zooey has met and spoken with Lane several times. On one occasion, Lane explained how he would listen, as a kid, to the radio program on which Franny and Zooey appeared weekly. Zooey believes that Lane attempted, with the anecdote, to ingratiate himself with Zooey (at the same time disparaging Franny's performance on the show). Zooey also believes that Lane's conversations are aimed at displaying his intellectual prowess and at calling attention to his Ivy League education. On the other hand, according to Bessie, Zooey has not given Lane a chance. She points out that Zooey and Buddy do not know how to talk to people they do not like or love. Zooey acknowledges Bessie's insight and looks at his mother, as have all of his brothers and sisters under similar circumstances, "with admiration, affection, and not least, gratitude" (98). Bessie tells Zooey that Lane explained the source of Franny's problem to be the book she has with her, which she had borrowed from her college's library. This information upsets Zooey, who tells Bessie that the book is *The Pilgrim Continues His Way,* a sequel to *The Way of a Pilgrim.* He knows that Franny actually got the two books from Seymour's desk in Buddy and Seymour's old bedroom in the family apartment. Bessie reminds Zooey that she herself no longer enters that room since Seymour's suicide. Zooey apologizes. However, when Bessie mentions Buddy's name, Zooey erupts, declaring that he can't stand hearing the names of Buddy and Seymour, as he believes both have made him and Franny into "freaks" (103). Zooey warns Bessie not to get in touch with Philly Byrnes's psychoanalyst and reminds her "of what analysis did for Seymour" (106). He predicts that if Franny were to undergo analysis, she would fare even worse than Seymour had. Only an extraordinary analyst—one grateful to God for his ability—might be able to help her, though Zooey doubts whether such a person could be found.

Changing the subject, Zooey asks Bessie if she wants to know what the two books Franny has with her are all about. Bessie is eager to understand, and Zooey proceeds to explain that both books concern themselves with an anonymous Russian peasant who wants to learn what it means to pray without ceasing. The peasant meets an old monk who teaches him the Jesus Prayer ("Lord Jesus Christ, have mercy on me") and how to say it. Zooey further explains that *The Way of a Pilgrim* is about the travels of the pilgrim, while the sequel, *The Pilgrim Continues His Way,* is an explication, in question-and-answer form, of the prayer. The method of the prayer is akin to that practiced in the East, where the repetition of any of God's names finally wakens the heart and in turn the third eye of the mystics. Bessie innocently asks how long one must repeat the prayer before it takes hold, and the question elicits a sarcastic response from her son. Zooey then states that he has to meet Mr. LeSage downtown. Bessie again asks Zooey whether he will talk with Franny, and he is unsure. Feeling defeated, Bessie leaves the bathroom, lamenting aloud about how the Glass kids used to be so loving toward one another when they were young. When she is out of earshot, Zooey again issues a sarcastic remark.

The third scene opens with a detailed description of the Glass's living room in a Manhattan apartment building in the East Seventies. The room is crowded with miscellaneous furniture, including a grand piano, a fish tank, multiple radios and phonographs, a collapsed ping-pong table, and bookcases overflowing with books. Initiated by Les Glass, the decor is defined by the three walls above the bookcases—surfaces crammed with memorabilia relating to the Glass children's appearances on *It's a Wise Child*. Additionally, Les has had seven scrapbooks, filled with related clippings, attached to one of the walls.

Zooey enters the living room with a lit cigar. The reader, for the first time in the story, physically encounters Franny; she is asleep on the couch with the family cat, Bloomberg. Zooey wakes her, calling her Franny, then Frances. She relates her dream to Zooey, a nightmare that includes the detested teacher of her religion seminar, Professor Tupper. Franny asks Zooey about the script delivered the previous night (the one from LeSage, which Zooey had been reading in the tub). Later that same night, Zooey had gone downtown to meet Dick Hess, a writer, who gave him his own script about a subway guard. Zooey notices Franny silently repeating the Jesus Prayer. She smiles at him, and he asks her not to, as he used to be bothered by Seymour's always smiling at him. Zooey says he might go to France to make a movie, but he is not happy about the idea. Though he believes he should not go, he is considering the trip because he is tired of being furious all the time. He is also upset that his exacting standards and judgments depress the people with whom he works. This reasoning strikes a responsive chord in Franny, and she relates how she, too, had

been judgmental that weekend regarding Lane and his paper on Flaubert. Zooey tells Franny that Seymour and Buddy have turned the two of them "into freaks with freakish standards" and likens them (Franny and Zooey) to "the Tattooed Lady" (139). Franny commiserates with Zooey and relates her disenchantment with college and how everything seems misguided there. Zooey replies, however, that the problem lies not with the world but with themselves. Franny talks about her life on campus and tells of one morning when she arrived early to her French literature class and covered the blackboard with recalled quotations from the Greek philosopher Epictetus. She confides to Zooey her belief that the accumulation of knowledge should lead to wisdom, but that the pursuit of wisdom is not a consideration in college classes.

Following Franny's long exposition, Zooey begins his confrontation with her about the reason why she is saying the Jesus Prayer. He believes her to be misguided if she feels that the pursuit of spiritual treasure is different from the pursuit of material wealth or intellectual accomplishment. Franny defends herself, telling Zooey his analogy is something she has already considered, and she begins to cry. Zooey asks if she wants to talk with Buddy, and Franny responds that she wants to talk with Seymour, their deceased eldest brother. In reaction, Zooey looks out the window and notices a young girl playing a game of hide-and-seek with her dog. He remarks, "There are nice things in the world," but people stupidly are "always referring every goddam thing that happens right back to [their] lousy little egos" (151). Zooey tells Franny something Buddy once said to him: that a man lying at the bottom of a hill and "slowing bleeding to death" should be able to raise himself "if a pretty girl or old woman should pass by with a beautiful jug balanced perfectly on top of her head . . . and see the jug safely over the top of the hill" (153). Zooey states that each of the Glass children has his or her own religion. He explains how Walt felt that they also had bad karma because "the religious life . . . is just something God sicks on people who have the gall to accuse Him of having created an ugly world" (153). He recalls Boo Boo thinking that a Mr. Ashe, not God, had made the world, because she had read a book in which a kid had given that reply to the question.

Assuming a prone position on the floor, where Franny can see only his shoes, Zooey asks that Franny just listen to him for a bit. He first qualifies what he is about to say because he himself once had the thought of saying the Jesus Prayer, and he admits he might be feeling a little jealous that she is now undertaking the practice. Zooey then launches into an extended critique of her behavior. He criticizes a number of her actions, saying that she is hurting their parents by coming home to have her breakdown; she is being sanctimonious; her attack on Professor Tupper is inappropriately personalized; and she does not understand the real nature of Jesus. Zooey calls Franny a sentimentalist in addressing her prayer to "Jesus and St. Francis and Seymour and Heidi's grandfather all [rolled] in one" (165). He believes her to be indulging in "tenth-rate thinking . . . tenth-rate religion [and] . . . a tenth-rate nervous breakdown" (165). Franny's sobbing interrupts the critique, but Zooey soon recommences and dissects her sloppy thinking regarding the definition of ego and its true nature. She continues to cry, but Zooey recapitulates his views on the correct approach to the Jesus Prayer. He explains his assessment of Jesus' character and why Jesus was chosen, of all the people in the Bible, to deliver God's word. Zooey arrives at the insight that "Jesus realized there is no separation from God" (169). He continues with his soliloquy but suddenly breaks off, realizing that Franny is sobbing in anguish. He apologizes to her and leaves the room.

In the fourth scene of the story, Zooey runs into his mother in the hallway. Bessie sees that Zooey is visibly sweating and asks him the reason. After replying, "I'm late now, Fatty" (173), he advises her to look in on Franny. Zooey does not change his shirt to go downtown (as his mother had suggested) but retrieves a cigar from his bedroom and, with a handkerchief over his head, enters Seymour and Buddy's old room. Closing the door, he begins reading "a sheet of what had once been snow-white beaverboard" (174) that his two eldest brothers had meticulously adorned with literary and religious quotations. Zooey starts reading from the top, where there appear sizable quotes from the *Bhagavad Gita*, Marcus Aurelius, a haiku by Issa, Epictetus, Ring Lardner, De Caussade, *Anna Karenina*, *The Gospel of Sri Ramakrishna*, two from FRANZ KAFKA, St. Francis de Sales, and *Mu-Mon-Kwan*. He then sits at Seymour's desk and meditates for 20 minutes. After meditating, he reaches into a desk drawer and pulls out a stack of shirt cardboards. He flips through the stack and pauses to read Seymour's notation on one of the cardboards—a joyous description of the Glass family's celebration of Seymour's 21st birthday in February 1938. Each family member had performed a vaudeville act in Seymour's honor. Seymour notes that the very young Zooey was furious at having slightly botched his performance. Zooey stops reading in midsentence and meditates for another 30 minutes. Abruptly, he moves to Buddy's desk and positions the handkerchief over the phone's mouthpiece to dial "a local number. A very local number indeed" (182).

The fifth and final scene backtracks a couple of minutes in time: Mrs. Glass is in the living room asking Franny if she would like a cup of chicken broth. The phone rings, and Mrs. Glass goes down the hallway to her and her husband's bedroom to answer. She returns saying that the caller is Buddy and that he wishes to speak with Franny. Stalling, Franny finally goes down the hallway to get to the phone.

Franny sits on her father's bed and, with some trepidation, picks up the phone and begins to converse. She says Buddy's voice sounds odd. When asked by Buddy if she feels like talking, she confesses she is tired of it, adding that she could murder Zooey. She is exasperated by his bitterness and his attack on the Jesus Prayer. Franny relates that Zooey, the previous night, even told her he once encountered Jesus in their kitchen when he was eight. She tells Buddy about Zooey's labeling the two of them as freaks, and she complains about the smell of his cigars pervading the apartment. At this point, Buddy tells her that Zooey needs the added weight of his cigars, otherwise he would float away. The remark triggers Franny's recognition that it is *Zooey*, and *not* Buddy, at the other end of the line. Admitting as much, Zooey apologizes for his earlier attack on her saying the prayer. He also regrets he has been "speaking up like a *seer*" (193). He wants to tell her a few more things and that is all. He points out that if Franny is intent upon a religious life, she is missing the fact that Bessie is offering "a cup of consecrated chicken soup" (194). If Franny does not even know that, he asks, how will she ever recognize the right person to teach her the intricacies of the prayer? He adds that he and Buddy saw Franny perform in *The Playboy of the Western World* last summer, and they could see she was a real actress. He explains that, to lead a strict religious life, a person must practice "detachment[,] desire-lessness" (196). Zooey believes that someone who wants to act has a yearning, a desire, to do so, and tells Franny it is obvious she has a yearning to act. "The only thing you can do now, the only religious thing you can do, is *act*. Act for God, if you want to" (197). He cautions her that, though time is always running out, he knows he wants "an honor-able goddam skull like Yorick's" (197). He admonishes her not to concern herself with the audience's reactions; that the "artist's only concern is to shoot for some kind of perfection, and *on his own terms, not anyone else's*" (198). As Zooey is telling all this to Franny, she remains in rapt attention and silent. He then relates to her an incident from the past. When he was young, he substituted for Walt one time on *It's a Wise Child*. Seymour told him to shine his shoes before going to the studio; Zooey thought it was a ridiculous thing to do. Seymour "said to shine them for the Fat Lady" (199), though he didn't tell Zooey who the Fat Lady was. Zooey pictured the Fat Lady on a porch, ill with cancer, the radio as her only solace, and realized that to shine his shoes for her somehow "made sense" (199). Franny interrupts to tell Zooey that Seymour once told her "to be funny for the Fat Lady" (199). She, too, had had a similar vision.

Zooey then explains to Franny the secret identity of the Fat Lady: Everyone, including even her detested Professor Tupper, is the Fat Lady. Zooey pauses and asks, "*don't you know who that Fat Lady really is?*" (200). He reveals the Fat Lady's true identity to be "Christ Himself" (200). The revelation transports Franny to a state of joy. She now possesses "what little or much wisdom there is in

the world" (201). Franny gets into her father's bed, and the story ends on the line: "For some minutes, before she fell into a deep, dreamless sleep, she just lay quiet, smiling at the ceiling" (201).

CRITICAL ANALYSIS

"Zooey," published on May 4, 1957, is the sequel to the story "Franny" that had been published two years earlier in the *New Yorker* magazine. Also published in the *New Yorker*, "Zooey" picks up Franny's situation two days later, after her return from Lane Coutell's college to the Glass family home in Manhattan, and likewise resolves her dilemmas as portrayed in "Franny." (In publication chronology, "Zooey" follows the Salinger story that introduced the entire Glass family, "RAISE HIGH THE ROOF BEAM, CARPENTERS" (*New Yorker*, November 19, 1955) and precedes "SEYMOUR: AN INTRODUCTION" (*New Yorker*, June 6, 1959). For more information regarding the eight published Glass stories, *see* GLASS STORIES.) "Zooey" centers on one family member's effort, that of the youngest brother, Zooey, to help his sister Franny overcome a spiritual dilemma that has brought her to the brink of a nervous breakdown. Franny has reached the point where she sees all of life's actions as driven by petty ego concerns and wants to escape this situation by retreating into an incessant repetition of the Jesus Prayer. She has withdrawn from acting in plays—her true passion—during her last year of college. In the story, Zooey attempts to find a way to free Franny from her delusion that the prayer offers the true answer to her predicament. He moreover leads her to the realization that acting is her spiritual pathway. Zooey's effort will culminate in his remembrance of Seymour's Fat Lady (she is the imagined audience for the radio quiz program *It's a Wise Child*, in which Franny and Zooey participated as children). In the epiphany of "Zooey," the Fat Lady seems to symbolize all of humanity; the reader is told by Zooey that the Fat Lady is, in fact, Jesus Christ.

Unlike "Franny," "Zooey," at its outset, is not written in a third-person narrative. Coming to "Zooey" directly after having read "Franny," the reader finds an intrusive "I" announcing itself in the first sentence. This first-person address creates a jarring disturbance when juxtaposed with the atmosphere of the third-person prose of "Franny." Because each story was initially published in a magazine, Salinger was not required, at the time of issue, to take into account the narrative problem of consistency of voice. However, with the publication of "Franny" and "Zooey" together as one book, Salinger allowed each story to stand as originally conceived. At the time of the book's publication, there had been speculation that Salinger might be in the process of refashioning from his already-published Glass stories a Glass novel or even a Glass trilogy, as he had done with some of his Caulfield stories to create The CATCHER IN THE RYE. (Salinger referred to "Franny" and "Zooey" as "stories" and as "entries in a narrative series" on the dust jacket of *Franny and Zooey*, a statement emphasizing the fact that the book did not constitute a novel.) The speculation proved to be groundless, moreover, as the book would reveal that the beginning of "Zooey" had not been altered to create a seamless third-person novel. Salinger surely chose not to alter the beginning of "Zooey" because he needed to portray Buddy Glass in a visible role of narrator. This decision would create the effect of continuing the Glass family stories, as begun in the previously published story, "Raise High the Roof Beam, Carpenters," with Buddy's authorship.

The "I" of "Zooey" soon identifies itself as none other than Buddy Glass, blood relative to the three protagonists of the story-to-come. Buddy's somewhat awkward introduction spans four pages (47–50) and reveals his identity; the manner of how he gained knowledge of the events to follow; that his three relatives have tried to dissuade him from publishing the story; and that he believes the story to be "a compound, or multiple, love story pure and complicated" (49) and not one in which "the plot hinges on mysticism, or religious mystification" (48) (and that hence will not damage his faltering writer's reputation). Buddy finally announces that he is withdrawing from the story and then proceeds, in a third-person narrative voice, with the description of Zooey in the bathtub (50). Though the first page of the story refers to a "leading lady . . . a languid, sophisticated type" (47–48), the reader does not yet know that this story will con-

tinue the plot of "Franny." No sooner does the bathroom scene begin than Buddy interrupts and asserts his own opinions and even a footnote in the first person. But once he writes "To resume:" on the ninth page of the story (55), the remainder of the text will be told in the third person, excepting his reproduction of his 14-page letter to Zooey, which appears in full (56–69). The first 23 pages of the story are therefore framed and dominated by Buddy's personality and presence.

Zooey, in reading Buddy's four-year-old letter (received before he [Zooey] fully committed himself to the profession of acting), hopes to glean some help in his efforts to rescue Franny from her breakdown. The main import of the letter consists in Buddy's encouragement of Zooey to act, if indeed acting is what he wants to do. The letter also explains Seymour and Buddy's philosophy of education. The older brothers' concern was not to acquire knowledge for knowledge's sake but to know the source of knowledge, which is God. The approach is centered in Seymour's belief that one must unlearn the arbitrary differences the mind constructs between things: "the illusory differences, between boys and girls, animals and stones, day and night, heat and cold" (67). The wish on Seymour and Buddy's part to know God thus led to their providing religious instruction to the other children in the family.

Buddy's letter is likewise of import because, within its contents, he will mention each member of the Glass family by name (except Walt, included only in a reference to the twins). This naming of family members, in effect, mirrors the roll call of the family at the outset of Salinger's previously published story, "Raise High the Roof Beam, Carpenters."

The letter is being composed on the third anniversary of Seymour's suicide. Buddy acknowledges that he avoided coming back to the family home because he did not know how to answer the question of why Seymour killed himself. (It is not until "Seymour: An Introduction" that Buddy will laboriously, and provisionally, attempt to provide an answer.) Buddy quotes a poem Seymour wrote in the hotel room shortly before he died. In the poem, the girl who turns her doll's head to look at Seymour instinctively knows *not* to make a distinction between the doll's ability to see and her own ability to perceive. The child has not yet lost her innate state of consciousness. Seymour believes this kind of consciousness—and not the consciousness created by formal education—allows one to know God. Buddy's letter also introduces the working phone kept in Seymour and Buddy's old room in the Glass apartment in New York, the phone that will prove essential at the story's close. Buddy tells Zooey, "*Act . . .* but do it *with all your might*" (68). He challenges Zooey to "do anything at all beautiful on a stage, anything nameless and joy-making" (68). If Zooey will do so, Buddy promises that he and Seymour (who is dead at the time of the writing of the letter) will appear together outside the stage door to pay homage to Zooey. This promised summoning of Seymour to life indicates Buddy's own triumph over the division between the living and the dead. The onslaught of dates at the beginning of the story—in the first 10 pages, Buddy alludes to 1955, 1927, 1943, 1957, 1942, 1951 and infers 1945 and 1948—draws the reader backward and forward until time itself is obliterated, thus allowing Salinger, as well, to triumph over time in his narrative, in accordance with Seymour's educational dictates. In order to "see more," one must break through the divisions of places and things, and, ultimately, between past and future, to be able to see or know God. Salinger's underlying intent is to instill this consciousness in the reader and to lift the Glass stories into an eternal present.

With Buddy in focus at the story's beginning, Salinger then turns the first scene over to a detailed interaction between Zooey and his mother, Bessie, in the bathroom. The scene allows the reader to come to know Zooey and Bessie in depth. (Until now, each had appeared only in "Raise High the Roof Beam, Carpenters" in very minor roles.) The repartee dialogue creates a comical/serious interaction between the 25-year-old Zooey—who, somewhat inexplicably, is still living at home, even though he is a successful television actor—and his mother, Bessie, an Irish Catholic and former song-and-dance vaudevillian. Zooey's father, Les, who performed with his wife on the Pantages Circuit, is Jewish and is never seen during the story, though

he is referenced several times. Les's absence from the apartment during the several hours in which the story takes place allows for a more prominent showcasing of Bessie's dominance within the family circle. In this first conversation of the story, Salinger underlines the situation of the second working phone number in Seymour and Buddy's room in the Glass apartment. Bessie laments Buddy's lack of a phone in his Upstate New York cabin, even as he continues to pay for the phone listed in Seymour's name. (Salinger succeeds in firmly establishing the existence of this phone in the reader's mind so when he brings its use into play as a crucial element at the story's close, the action does not feel contrived.) After some initial verbal sparring between Zooey and Bessie, the narrative makes apparent nearly 40 pages into the story that "Zooey" will be focusing on Franny's life two days after her luncheon at Sickler's in "Franny." The reader now realizes that Salinger has written a sequel to "Franny," the story the reader will more than likely have just finished reading.

The seriousness of Franny's situation is conveyed by Bessie Glass's comments, while Zooey, in this first conversation, seems to take the problem as a joke. (Bessie, however, is unaware that Zooey has already reread Buddy's old letter in an effort to extract some wisdom that he might use to help Franny.) By the second conversation between mother and son—composing the second scene, in which Zooey has gotten out of the tub and has partially dressed (91)—Zooey's concern becomes apparent to Bessie. This scene of the story contains several other important happenings. Lane Coutell and *The Way of a Pilgrim* are referenced, thereby giving concrete continuance of the earlier story, "Franny." The reference to Franny's book allows Zooey to mention its sequel, *The Pilgrim Continues His Way*, a parallel that mimics the sequel relationship between "Franny" and "Zooey." Zooey gives an overview to Bessie of the pilgrim books and the religious use of the repetition of God's name in much the same way as Franny did for Lane. In this scene, the reader learns about Zooey's anger at Seymour and Buddy for turning him and Franny into "freaks" (103). (This anger produces the conflict within Zooey; he must work through his anger to achieve the wisdom necessary to help Franny.) Bessie's suggestion of having a psychoanalyst help Franny precipitates Zooey's statement regarding Seymour's suicide: "Just think of what analysis did for Seymour" (106). Zooey allows that a remarkable analyst, grateful to God for his abilities, might be able to help Franny, but such a one would be difficult to find. Zooey categorically states that Franny would "come out of analysis in even worse shape than Seymour did" (109). (The statement implicates the experience of undergoing analysis as a catalyst of Seymour's suicide.) The goal of Bessie's conversation is to re-enlist Zooey's help regarding Franny. (Zooey had spoken with Franny the previous night.) By the end of this scene, though, Zooey says he isn't sure if he will try again but adds that he will only do so if he has something of worth to say to her.

After a total of 69 pages in the Glass family's bathroom, the reader is brought into the living room (118). In this third scene of the story, Salinger, as he did with the medicine cabinet in the bathroom scene, reproduces a detailed list of the room's contents. Salinger's technique of cataloging the settings of the action with such precision serves to immerse the reader into the surroundings, thereby encouraging an intimate relationship with the Glass family members. No doubt this technique is utilized, in some measure as well, to offset the extraordinariness of the characters. The fashionable apartment house in the East Seventies in Manhattan becomes a character in and of itself as Salinger asserts the physical reality around the Glasses. Moreover, the third scene, comprising 55 pages, brings the reader into direct contact with Franny Glass. Franny was last physically seen on the final page of "Franny" (43) in a supine position, repeating the Jesus Prayer. On page 123 of "Zooey," she is encountered by the reader as she sleeps on a couch in the living room. (Salinger immediately introduces one detail that allows the reader to gauge the extent of Franny's breakdown: He notes that she has washed her hair each day for the past three days, something that would not occur in a fully incapacitating illness. Zooey likewise will tell Franny that she is not having a full-fledged breakdown [165], though he does not doubt she is falling apart.)

With the conversation in the living room, Zooey attempts for the second time to help his sister. (An earlier talk between them the previous evening is alluded to but not shown in the story. Zooey's comment to Bessie that he does not think Franny wants to speak with anyone today indicates that the first conversation was highly unsuccessful.) When Zooey wakes Franny, she mentions a bad dream. The narrative thus places Zooey in the role of analyst (123–125). The imagery of Franny on the couch and Zooey's cigar gives a nod to Sigmund Freud and further symbolizes the analysis Zooey will undertake of Franny in the upcoming scene. The conversation between these two Glass children will also allow Salinger to provide insight into Zooey's character and to reveal Zooey's unhappiness with his own professional and personal life. Fanny will repeat some of the happenings that took place in "Franny" (143–144) and will also reiterate her disgruntlement with the world and her feeling of confinement in living for the needs of the ego.

Zooey points out to Franny that she does not have a clear picture of Jesus's character and nature. Thus, her saying the Jesus Prayer makes no sense (163–171). The lengthy disquisition by Zooey continues the Jesus theme, as Salinger needs to create a palpable sense of Jesus in preparation for the story's end and epiphany. Zooey's involvement with his soliloquy on Jesus—delivered from a position of lying on the floor—shields him from Franny's reaction to what he has been saying. He finally sits up and realizes she is crying. He apologizes and leaves the room, thus ending the third scene (172). With only 30 pages left in the book, the reader fears that no resolution will be found for Franny's predicament.

"Zooeys"'s buildup of dramatic tension through 126 pages will converge in the fourth and fifth scenes of the story. In the fourth scene, Zooey, running into Bessie in the hallway, feels unsure of what to do next. (Salinger signals Zooey's uncertainty with the comment, "Zooey's first step—an indecisive, almost dazed one..." [172].) Purportedly headed for lunch and a meeting with his boss, Zooey alerts Bessie to Franny's condition but then disappears into his own bedroom. The narrative neither follows Zooey into the bedroom nor specifies what occurs inside the room during the two minutes Zooey remains there. But a decision has obviously been made, as Zooey emerges with a lit cigar and a handkerchief draped over his head. He enters Seymour and Buddy's old bedroom. The room has been left exactly as it was at the time of Seymour's suicide and thus symbolically serves as a shrine to his memory. Zooey's belief that the room is a holy place is conveyed by his covering his head before entering. Additionally, the working phone is still listed in Seymour's name and represents a symbolic link to his consciousness. Zooey already knows he will make a call to Franny from there, pretending to be Buddy. (He has brought the handkerchief to conceal his voice, and he regrets there is no key to lock the door behind him.) The reader realizes that the phone call is to Franny when the number Zooey dials is described as "a very local number indeed" (182).

Before proceeding to the culminating phone-call scene, it should be noted that, although Franny's dilemma seemingly forms the crux of the story, what drives the narrative forward is, in actuality, the spiritual developments that are taking place within Zooey. Before Zooey is able to impart to Franny the secret of the Fat Lady, he must accomplish his own growth processes. First, he recognizes the truth of Bessie's insight that he does not know how to talk with people he does not love (98–99) (Bessie admonishes him for his lambasting of Lane Coutell). Later, when Zooey sees the little girl playing with her dachshund, he comments that people make the error of being ego-centered and cannot get beyond themselves to see the "nice things in the world" (151). In Zooey's exposition of Jesus's true character to Franny, he experiences his own religious epiphany when he says, "Jesus realized there *is* no separation from God" (169). Salinger underscores this realization with the authorial comment, "Zooey here clapped his hands together—only once, and not loud, and very probably in spite of himself" (169). Zooey's growth as a character culminates when he is in Seymour and Buddy's old room. After entering and reading the various religious and literature quotations on their beaverboard (attached to the back of the door), he meditates on their significance for 20 minutes

at Seymour's desk, then flips through a substantial number of shirt cardboards that Seymour utilized for diarylike notes. Zooey pauses at only one cardboard, on which Seymour recorded the family events of his 21st birthday celebration. Though the critic John Wenke terms Seymour's written note about his birthday in February 1938 on a loose shirt cardboard "a seemingly inconsequential entry from Seymour's diary" (Wenke 87), it is of paramount importance to the character Zooey, the story "Zooey," and the Glass canon. The entry conveys Seymour's delight in the vaudeville performances done in honor of his birthday. He meticulously records each act as performed by each family member. The entry represents the *only* time in the Glass stories that *all nine* members of the family are gathered together in one scene. (Death has stalked the family to a great degree and, given the spread in ages of the children—with Franny born as late as 1935, and the first death in the family [Walt's in the autumn of 1945] but 10 years after that—all nine Glasses were simultaneously alive only from 1935 to 1945. In addition, the four war years— 1942 through 1945—geographically separated the family members.) The birthday performance from 1938 is as intimate and as auspicious a scene as Salinger has portrayed of the Glass family.

Still seated at Seymour's desk, Zooey meditates for 30 minutes more, this time upon the notation he has just read. A close examination of Seymour's note will reveal how certain key words and ideas in it converge at the end of "Zooey." First, the motif of performing is uppermost in the entry. Two strands of the Fat Lady parable are being prepared: acting, and for whom. (Recall that, earlier in the story, the conversation between Zooey and Franny associated Seymour with Jesus Christ.) The word "shoe" in Seymour's sentence, "Les and Bessie did a lovely soft-shoe" (180), and the observation by Seymour that the very young Zooey "was *furious*" (181) when he muffed up his performance ("furious" is the only italicized word in the note) will help trigger Zooey's recollection of shining his shoes for the Fat Lady. For when Zooey tells Franny about Seymour's request to him to shine his shoes for the Fat Lady, he describes his initial reaction as, "I was furious" (198). (This aspect of

Zooey's nature forms a continuing motif throughout the story, most notably when Zooey admits to
an ulcer [140] and his explanation of possibly going
to France to make a movie because he is ". . . tired
as hell of getting up furious in the morning and
going to bed furious at night" [136].) The reading
by Zooey of Seymour's 17-year-old insight into his
(Zooey's) own nature precipitates a change in Zooey's bearing. (He will be much gentler with Franny
in his upcoming phone conversation with her than
he had been earlier, face-to-face, and he moreover
seems almost a different person when he tells her
about Yorick and Seymour's Fat Lady.)

The fifth and final scene of the story backtracks
in time a couple of minutes to allow the reader to
return to Bessie and Franny together as the phone
begins to ring. The technique thus heightens the
dramatic tension. Though Franny will see through
Zooey's impersonation fairly quickly, she does not
hang up on the call. Zooey's name (he is addressed
as "Zooey" by Franny on page 192) will not be
mentioned again. (Franny's name, however, is
repeated a number of times in the final 10 pages
of the narrative.) Salinger thus succeeds in giving more weight to what is being said, rather than
by whom. Zooey becomes Salinger's mouthpiece in
the closing pages of the story as the character will
articulate the author's artistic credo and overarch-
ing religious philosophy. Franny becomes a stand-
in for the reader, for through her, the reader will
hear Salinger's wisdom being transmitted via a
disembodied voice over the phone. Franny/reader
hears, through this voice, the combined wisdom of
Salinger/Seymour/Buddy/Zooey.

After Franny recognizes that she is speaking to
Zooey, and not Buddy, on the phone, Zooey apolo-
getically tells her to continue with the Jesus Prayer
if she cares to. He admits he should not be "speaking up like a *seer*" (193), though he asks, since she
is failing to recognize the religious act of Bessie's
offering her chicken soup, how she will be able to
discern someone qualified to teach her the true
method of saying the prayer. Zooey next remarks
that he has "just one or two very small things more
[to tell her] . . ." (195). The first thing Zooey wants
to convey to Franny is that she is a good actress;
he and Buddy had seen her perform in *The Playboy*

of the Western World. He explains that her nature
isn't detached or without desire, and thus she is
not suited for the monastic, religious life. He points
out that Franny's desire to be an actress (which
she is loath to acknowledge) rules out the benefits
of the prayer for her. But he makes the connection that solves Franny's problem: For her, a religious life would be to act, and she could "be *God's*
actress" (197). (The statement pre-echoes the idea
in the Fat Lady parable of performing for Jesus.)
To achieve this—to earn "an honorable goddam
skull like Yorick's" (197)—takes hard work, Zooey
explains, and he advises her that there is little time
to waste if she really wants to become such an
actress. Zooey's "one other thing. And that's all, I
promise you" (198) concerns the audience.

Zooey points out to Franny that some of the
audience will fail to understand what they are
watching, but he cautions that an "artist's only
concern is to shoot for some kind of perfection,
and *on his own terms,* not anyone else's" (198). This
is Salinger's artistic credo, his explanation of what
he was attempting to do with his own life of writing, regardless of what the critics might say about
him and his works. One might suggest that Zooey's
remark to Franny about being God's actress can
be transposed onto Salinger's desire to have been
God's writer. Remarking that Franny "bitched"
(198) about the audience, Zooey is prompted to
segue into telling Franny about his own "bitching
one night" (198) before performing on *It's a Wise
Child,* and Seymour's admonition that Zooey shine
his shoes for the Fat Lady. Zooey then conveys to
Franny the double identity of Seymour's Fat Lady.
Zooey has already attained the knowledge that the
Fat Lady is everyone (made evident by his remark,
"Don't you know that goddam secret *yet* [empha-
sis added]?" [200]). He quickly follows by asking
Franny if she knows "*who that Fat Lady really is?*"
(200). Since Salinger does not make explicit the
exact instant in which Zooey finally identifies the
Fat Lady with Christ, critics generally assume this
connection to occur in Zooey's mind at the very
moment he is speaking to Franny on the phone.
However, even before Zooey brings up Seymour's
Fat Lady, he has already suggested to Franny that
she perform for God (197). Additionally, Zooey's

"one other thing" (198) is all about the audience, and the audience speech ends with the identity of the Fat Lady. Thus, once Zooey starts to tell Franny about shining his shoes for the Fat Lady, he already knows the Fat Lady is everyone. Moreover, since everyone "carr[ies] the Kingdom of Heaven around with [him], *inside* . . ." (170), Zooey knows that each person is divine and, by extension, that the audience is holy. Therefore, a close reading of the narrative sequence strongly suggests that Zooey has crystallized the heart of his realizations during his meditations in Seymour and Buddy's room.

Nearly all critics believe, on the other hand, that Zooey comes to his realizations during the phone call itself. Salinger's use of italics has led to this conclusion. For example, Eberhard Alsen asserts, "to indicate his characters' agitated state of mind, [Salinger] italicizes words that they are speaking more loudly than the rest" (Alsen 2002, 151). Alsen concludes that "Zooey gets very excited because he finally comprehends what Seymour's Fat Lady stands for. He shouts with excitement . . ." (Alsen 2002, 150). Actually, Salinger utilizes italics not to convey agitation or louder speech but to indicate *emphasized* words. Salinger, himself, indicates how to read his italics. Note when Franny remarks to Zooey: ". . . 'please hurry up and say it and leave me *alone*.' This last, *emphasized* [emphasis added] word was oddly veered away from, as if the *stress* [emphasis added] on it hadn't been fully intended" (192). That italics do *not* indicate volume, note this italicized sentence spoken by Bessie: "'*Just stop that, now*,' Mrs. Glass broke in, her voice *quiet* [emphasis added] but dangerous" (86). Salinger's italics, when read properly, reveal speech one character wants another character to take special heed of (or, in the case of single syllables of a word, an inflected speech pattern). Thus, when Zooey tells Franny, "*There isn't anyone out there who isn't Seymour's Fat Lady*" (200) and "*listen to me now— don't you know who that Fat Lady really is?*" (200), he is not agitated or excited; he is underscoring what he wants Franny to heed, to really hear. The fact that Salinger does not then include "Christ Himself" (200) in italics might be thought contradictory to this, but it can possibly be explained as Salinger pulling back from a "grand statement." Yet, with or without italics, Salinger's equation of the Fat Lady with Jesus Christ (in other words, Salinger's belief in the sacred nature of each and every person) is clearly shown through Zooey's conversation.

Upon hearing Zooey's final words, Franny experiences a joyful epiphany. The wisdom she so missed in college has been given to her in the parable of the Fat Lady: "what little or much wisdom there is in the world were suddenly hers" (201). Franny (who at the end of "Franny" had fainted and was lying on a couch, looking at a ceiling while repeating the Jesus Prayer) now gets into bed and smiles at the ceiling, before falling "into a deep, dreamless sleep" (201). This use of symbolic, healing sleep is akin to the end of Salinger's earlier story, "FOR ESMÉ—WITH LOVE AND SQUALOR" (1950). At "Zooey's" close, the reader must infer that Franny's transformation is not a temporary one. This is confirmed in Salinger's next published story, "Seymour: An Introduction," which lets the reader know that in 1959 (four years after the events of "Zooey," in November 1955) Franny has become a professional actress.

Though "Zooey" has been popular with Salinger's general readers (*Franny and Zooey* is, by far, his second most-read book, after *The Catcher in the Rye*), a number of critics have not liked the story, which initially ran into resistance as well from the editors at the *New Yorker*. As was customary, the story was submitted to the fiction editors, only to be unanimously rejected. This decision, however, did not sit well with WILLIAM SHAWN, the magazine's editor in chief, who decided to edit the story himself, and who eventually devoted nearly an entire super-sized issue to its publication. In gratitude, Salinger dedicated *Franny and Zooey* (in which the story "Zooey" appeared in book publication) to Shawn. (*See* DEDICATIONS.) The most damning review of "Zooey" appeared when *Franny and Zooey* was released in 1961. (Most assessments of the story didn't see print until "Zooey" appeared in book format.) A young but confident John Updike reviewed the volume, noting "Zooey" to be "just too long; there are too many cigarettes, too many goddams, too much verbal ado about not quite enough" (Updike 52). Updike also stated "that a lecturer has usurped the writing stand" (Updike 52). But even more stinging was his assertion that Salinger "loves the Glasses more than God loves them. He loves them too exclusively. . . . He loves them to the detriment of artistic moderation" (Updike 52). Joan Didion termed the book "spurious" because of "Salinger's tendency to flatter the essential triviality within each of his readers, his predilection for giving instructions for living . . . it is self-help copy" (Didion 79). Mary McCarthy reacted by declaring the Glass family "a closed corporation" (McCarthy 131): "these wonder kids [are] but Salinger himself, splitting and multiplying like the original amoeba" (McCarthy 131). Norman Mailer found "nothing in *Franny and Zooey* which would hinder it from becoming first-rate television" (Mailer 68). The review that Flannery O'Connor endorsed, that of Richard Gilman, accused *Franny and Zooey* of being "a pseudo-mystical pronouncement to the effect that the world stinks to heaven, together with directions for applying a spiritual deodorant" (Gilman 39). The amplitude of these harsh critical reactions could possibly be viewed as a backlash to Salinger's notoriety and celebrity at the time of the book's publication. The author had been riding a crest of mostly positive critical commentary on his work, and the month of the book's publication saw Salinger adorning the cover of *Time* magazine (during the 1960s, considered a certified sign of mass-media anointment) as well as his being featured in *Life* magazine.

It is not known exactly why Salinger decided to write a sequel to "Franny" two years later. When he announced the entire Glass family in "Raise High the Roof Beam, Carpenters"—published just 10 months after "Franny"—there was a Franny Glass, though at that time it was not absolutely certain that the Franny included in the family was the same Franny who had dined at Sickler's. (It is imperative to remember that this Franny had no surname in the story that bears her name.) Be that as it may, the second Glass family story, "Zooey," reclaims "Franny" as a Glass story.

Salinger goes to painstaking efforts to knit "Zooey" together with "Franny," apart from the obvious continuation of the basic story line. He also indulges in some revisionist readings of "Franny." In "Franny," the heroine borrows *The Way of a Pil-*grim from her college library after the book is mentioned by the teacher of her religion survey class ("Franny" 32). Her access to the book is repeated to Mrs. Glass by Lane Coutell in the story that follows ("Zooey" 100). However, in "Zooey," the author reveals that Franny has taken the book, along with its sequel, from her brother Seymour's desk ("Zooey" 101). (It is somewhat plausible she did not want to tell Lane the truth about the origin of the book in "Franny," but this is unlikely for two reasons: one, why suppress the information of how she came upon the book; two, Lane would have seen that the book lacked the usual library ownership markings and her lie would have been easily discovered.) In "Zooey," Salinger has Franny more appropriately and convincingly enrolled in a religion seminar, taught by a visiting Oxford professor, Tupper ("Zooey" 127), instead of attending a basic religion survey taught by the nameless teacher referred to in "Franny" ("Franny" 32).

To further build up the continuity between the stories, and to join them seamlessly together, Salinger does the following: Franny recounts her travails of two days earlier, down to the detail of Lane's Flaubert paper ("Zooey" 137–138). Lane is woven into the later story; he phones the family residence several times and speaks with Mrs. Glass, and a reference to Lane's meeting Zooey is also included ("Zooey" 96–100). Even the relative duration of the Franny-Lane relationship is referenced in both stories: "eleven months" by Franny ("Franny" 5), and "a whole year" by Mrs. Glass ("Zooey" 96). Zooey discourses on *The Way of a Pilgrim* and the repetition of God's name ("Zooey" 110–113) in the same manner that Franny does in the first story ("Franny" 32–39). Zooey informs Franny that he and Buddy saw her act in *The Playboy of the Western World* ("Zooey" 195), thus repeating the name of the play Franny mentions in the earlier story ("Franny" 28). This link makes Franny's statement about not wanting people she respected to see her in some of her amateur productions—for example, her unnamed brothers ("Franny" 28)—identify those brothers retroactively as being Buddy and Zooey. Salinger even makes use of subtle word repetitions between the two stories: the same unusual word, "caviling," is used to describe Franny's voice

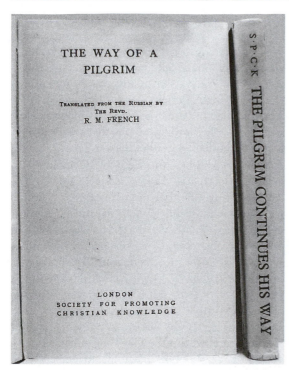

The Way of a Pilgrim and *The Pilgrim Continues His Way,* the two books that Franny Glass borrows from her brother Seymour's desk *(Courtesy of the Bruce F. Mueller Collection; photo by Laura Fairbanks)*

in both stories ("Franny" 24 and "Zooey" 143); the word "reticent," which is highlighted in Franny's letter ("Franny" 5), is now used by Zooey on the very page where it becomes apparent to the reader that Franny's story is being continued ("Zooey" 83); Franny stares at a spot of sunlight in each story ("Franny" 15 and "Zooey" 143); Franny touches her forehead with her fingertips ("Franny" 41) and strikes her forehead with her hand ("Zooey" 190); there is a reference to Christian Science at the outset of "Franny" ("Franny" 4) and, early in "Zooey," the founder of Christian Science—Mary Baker Eddy—is mentioned ("Zooey" 55); characters warn another character that they are about to burn their fingers with unattended cigarettes—Lane to Franny ("Franny" 38), Zooey to Bessie ("Zooey" 105); characters have the flat of their hand pressed against their face (Lane, "Franny" 14; Franny, "Zooey" 198); Zooey calls his sister both "Franny" and

"Frances" ("Zooey" 124), echoing her two names appearing in her letter to Lane ("Franny" 5–6); and Zooey refers to Franny's teachers Manlius and the other "goon" ("Zooey" 160), who are invoked by Lane in the earlier story ("Franny" 18). In the most obvious parallel between the stories, Salinger ends each with Franny in a supine position, looking at the ceiling. The imagery, while mirroring the visual likeness, represents, however, starkly contrasting meanings ("Franny" 43; "Zooey" 201).

Though "Zooey" follows the publication of the first Glass family story, "Raise High the Roof Beam, Carpenters," by only two years, certain inconsistencies in dates and ages concerning Glass family members occur between the two stories. Given Salinger's decidedly perfectionist tendencies and his various efforts to create realistic verisimilitude in the Glass stories, these lapses are unfortunate but surely not intentional. The inconsistencies, however (together with ambiguous aspects of other Glass stories), preclude the possibility of creating an incontrovertible chronology for the Glass saga. Because Buddy Glass gives the exact time for the occurrences of events within the two stories—late May and June 4, 1942, for "Raise High the Roof Beam, Carpenters," and November 1955 for "Zooey"—the chronological discrepancies are discernable.

In "Raise High the Roof Beam, Carpenters," the reader is told by Buddy that Franny is eight and Zooey is 13 ("Raise High the Roof Beam, Carpenters" 13). Yet, in "Zooey," whose events take place thirteen and one-half years after those in "Raise High the Roof Beam, Carpenters," Zooey remarks that Franny is 20 and he is 25 ("Zooey" 103). (Thus, if Salinger had adhered to the ages of Franny and Zooey in the earlier story, "Raise High the Roof Beam, Carpenters," Franny would have been 21 and Zooey 26 at the time of the events in "Zooey.") Salinger specifically states the birth years for Franny and Zooey in "Seymour: An Introduction"—"Zooey and Franny were not born till 1930 and 1935, respectively" (169)—which confirm that their ages are correctly given in "Zooey."

In "Raise High the Roof Beam, Carpenters," the story opens with a ten-month-old Franny being read to by a 17-year-old Seymour. This age difference between the oldest child, Seymour, and the youngest, Franny, isn't, however, carried over to "Zooey." In the latter story, Salinger states the gap in ages between Franny and Seymour to be "almost 18 years" ("Zooey" 53) (not 16 years). As Buddy will identify Franny's birth year (1935) in "Seymour: An Introduction," and Seymour's birth year is 1917, the gap mentioned in "Zooey" is accurate.

Another inconsistency concerns Zooey's appearances on *It's a Wise Child.* In "Zooey," he starts at age seven ("Zooey" 52) and remains on the program for five years ("Zooey" 152). In "Raise High the Roof Beam, Carpenters," Zooey is said to be still on the radio show at age 13 ("Raise High the Roof Beam, Carpenters" 7).

Within "Zooey" itself, Salinger creates an internal error. Buddy refers to the date of Seymour's suicide as March 18, 1948 ("Zooey" 56), yet in his footnote about the family members, he says that Seymour "had been dead *almost* [emphasis added] seven years" ("Zooey" 52). Since the events during "Zooey" take place during November 1955, and Seymour's suicide occurred in March 1948, Seymour would have been dead for seven years, eight months; in other words, almost eight years, not almost seven years as stated in "Zooey." (Another seeming inconsistency is that Seymour's birthday in "Zooey" is given as February [180], which contradicts Seymour's statement to Sybil in "A PERFECT DAY FOR BANANAFISH" that he is a Capricorn and thus has a birthday between December 21 and January 20.)

In each of the four Glass family stories, Salinger maintains a correlation between the time that Buddy Glass says he is writing the story and when the story was published in real time. Specifically: In "Raise High the Roof Beam, Carpenters," Buddy writes, ". . . now, in 1955 . . ." (6); the story was published November 19, 1955. In "Zooey," Buddy writes, ". . . at this writing (1957) . . ." (54); the story was published May 4, 1957. In "Seymour: An Introduction," Buddy writes, ". . . topical in 1959 . . ." (136); the story was published June 6, 1959. In "HAPWORTH 16, 1924," Buddy dates his introductory note "May 28, 1965" (32); the story was published June 19, 1965. With these corre-

lations, Salinger hopes to buttress the reader's belief in the "realness" of the Glass family. However, in piecing together the chronology of the Glass family, one should note that Salinger makes choices in "Zooey" that inadvertently undermine this belief. In "A Perfect Day for Bananafish" (the story of Seymour's suicide), no calendar month is specified (only the year, 1948); the story was published on January 31, 1948. However, in "Zooey," Salinger establishes the date of Seymour's suicide as March 18, 1948 ("Zooey" 56). In the story "Franny," neither month nor year is stated (only that the events took place on a Saturday, in autumnal weather); the story was published on January 29, 1955. However, in "Zooey," Salinger establishes the time of Franny's breakdown as November 1955 ("Zooey" 50). Although in "A Perfect Day for Bananafish" and "Franny" nothing internally contradicts the temporal events of each story, Salinger could have maintained a greater verisimilitude within the Glass saga by having the events of "Zooey" take place in November 1954, instead of November 1955, and in dating Seymour's suicide within the month of January 1948, instead of March 1948.

PUBLICATION HISTORY

"Zooey" was first published in the *New Yorker* magazine on May 4, 1957. The story appeared in a book publication in *Franny and Zooey* (LITTLE, BROWN AND COMPANY, 1961). *Franny and Zooey*, Salinger's third book, has never gone out of print.

Franny and Zooey is available in three editions from Little, Brown and Company: an exact reproduction of the hardback first edition from 1961, that includes the dust-jacket comments written by Salinger; a trade paperback that mimics the production of the hardback, though Salinger's dust-jacket comments are not retained; and a mass-market paperback, also lacking Salinger's dust-jacket comments, with its pagination differing from the above editions.

CHARACTERS

Bev Bev is Franny Glass's roommate at college. Franny feels guilty that her rude behavior has been upsetting Bev.

Bloomberg Bloomberg is the family cat, sleeping with Franny Glass on the couch. The cat is an impassive witness to the conversation between Zooey Glass and Franny.

Boston research group Zooey Glass, as a preadolescent, was tested by a research group in Boston. The purpose was to discover "the source of Zooey's precocious wit and fancy" (55).

Byrnes, Philly Philly Byrnes is the son of Bessie Glass's acquaintances and fellow vaudevillians. Philly has undergone psychoanalysis, which Bessie feels has helped him immeasurably; Zooey Glass emphatically disagrees. Bessie wonders if Philly's Catholic psychoanalyst could help Franny Glass. In this exchange between Bessie and Zooey, Zooey remarks that Franny would come out of analysis in even worse shape than Seymour Glass had. The statement confirms that Seymour has indeed undergone analysis, as he had promised to, after he failed to show up for his wedding in "Raise High the Roof Beam, Carpenters."

Coutell, Lane Lane Coutell, Franny Glass's boyfriend in the story "Franny," is, in "Zooey," referred to by name, but he does not physically appear. Lane has been repeatedly phoning Franny's mother, Bessie, to ask about Franny's condition. Lane tells Bessie Glass that the source of Franny's problem is the book *The Way of a Pilgrim*. Zooey Glass suspects Lane's motives. Bessie tells Zooey that Franny thinks Lane is brilliant. This statement leads the reader to understand that the relationship with Lane, also in Franny's mind, is still intact. One does not learn if Lane was able to sneak up to Franny's room later that Saturday in "Franny." However, the possibility seems unlikely, as it is revealed that Franny did not stay for the entire weekend but instead left Lane's college sometime that Saturday and arrived back at the Glass apartment Saturday night. In "Zooey," the reader learns that Lane is the editor of his college's literary magazine.

For a complete account of Lane's involvement in the events leading up to "Zooey," *see* "FRANNY." In the story that follows "Zooey" and portrays events four years later in time—"Seymour: An Introduction"—there is no mention of Lane; the reader may probably infer that by this time the relationship has ended.

Fallon, Professor Fallon is Franny Glass's professor of French literature. Early before class, Franny, from memory, covers Fallon's classroom's blackboard with quotations from the Greek philosopher Epictetus. (An Epictetus quotation appears on Seymour and Buddy Glass's beaverboard.) Franny's enrollment in a French literature class underscores her capacity to understand, in "Franny," Lane Coutell's luncheon lecture to her on the French novelist Gustave Flaubert.

Glass, Bessie Bessie (née Gallagher) Glass is the Catholic wife of Les Glass and the mother of the seven Glass children. She is also a former vaudevillian who sang and danced with her husband. Bessie is one of three protagonists in "Zooey," where she is seen interacting with her two youngest children, Zooey and Franny. Bessie appears in two long scenes with Zooey in the bathroom (72–90, 92–118). At the beginning of the fourth scene (172–174), she runs into Zooey in the hallway. (She notices he is perspiring profusely and wonders why. Unless they are typographical errors in both the original magazine publication and the Little, Brown and Company editions, Bessie says, "What is that? Prespiration? . . . It *is* prespiration" [173]. This pronunciation of the word, sounding the beginning as "pre" instead of "per," may be a private bow, possibly to the way Salinger's own mother pronounced the word *perspiration*.) Bessie appears with Franny in the beginning of the fifth scene of the story. The reader hears her offer Franny a cup of chicken broth, which Franny declines. This will become the "consecrated" (194) cup Zooey later refers to, "which is the only kind of chicken soup Bessie ever brings to anybody around this madhouse" (194–195). Bessie's focus throughout the story is on getting help for Franny; she will do whatever it takes to see her daughter well again. To this end, Bessie thinks of first turning to Buddy but laments his lack of a phone; her eldest daughter, Boo Boo, is vacationing in Europe and will not return until the 10th of the month; her son Waker is too emotional, and she memorably sketches him, "If you tell Waker it looks like *rain*, his eyes all fill up" (94); her husband Les "doesn't even like to *talk* about anything like this" (82); she toys with the idea of a psychoanalyst, but abandons that possibility after Zooey's vehement opposition; this leaves Zooey, himself, as her last hope. Bessie is portrayed as a loving, if somewhat slightly eccentric, mother. She is described throughout the story as smoking, wearing a hairnet, and attired in a kimono, its added pockets filled with miscellaneous items. Salinger does not pinpoint Bessie's age, but he notes that she was "a once quite widely acknowledged public beauty" (88). Bessie still retains remarkable "legs, which were comely by any criterion" and "an elegant tremor" (88) to her holding of her cigarettes. Bessie is not an intellectual, but she exhibits commonsense insight into her children. Her importance to her children is portrayed in the bathroom scene with Zooey. While Zooey is shaving, Bessie comments that he does not know how to talk to people he does not love. He stops and turns around to acknowledge "in precisely the same way that, at one time or another, in one year or another, all his brothers and sisters . . . had turned around and looked at her. Not just with objective wonder at the rising of a truth, fragmentary or not, . . . but with admiration, affection, and, not least, gratitude" (98).

Bessie appears in all of the Glass family stories, but it is in "Zooey" that she is given by far her most substantial role. She was introduced in "Raise High the Roof Beam, Carpenters" as the mother of the clan and a retired vaudevillian. In that story, she is living in Los Angeles with Les, her husband, and with Zooey and Franny, but is not seen in it. "Seymour: An Introduction" contains several references to Bessie. The reader learns that she had a twin sister who died young, backstage. Thus, she comes from a family of entertainers. It was Bessie who decided when Les and she would retire from vaudeville. While a young mother, Bessie would consult with Irish traffic cops about sundry family matters. In "Hapworth 16, 1924," it is Bessie who mails Seymour's letter, written 41 years previously, to Buddy, who has not yet seen it. Bessie is the first of five addressees of the letter, in which Seymour writes many passages specifically to her.

Glass, Boo Boo Boo Boo (Beatrice) is the older of the two Glass daughters and the third-eldest child in the family. At the time of the action in "Zooey," she is vacationing in Europe with her husband and three children. Though Boo Boo does not make an appearance in the apartment, she is mentioned several times in the dialogue. Boo Boo, along with her sister, Franny, actively dislikes Bessie's kimono; she thinks that Mr. Ashe of Kilvert's *Diary* (Robert Francis Kilvert, 1840–1879, an English curate and later vicar), rather than God, created the world; she has a quirky sense of humor as evidenced when describing a look on her mother's face as meaning either that Mrs. Glass has just talked with one of her sons on the phone or that everyone's bowels in the world will be flawlessly working for a week. Her sense of humor is revealed again in her description of her brother Zooey as quoted by Buddy Glass, ". . . the blue-eyed Jewish-Irish Mohican scout who died in your arms at the roulette table at Monte Carlo" (51).

Boo Boo first appears in the story "DOWN AT THE DINGHY" (1949), in which she is the protagonist and mother of Lionel Tannenbaum. In that story (collected in NINE STORIES), she is summarily described, "her joke of a name aside, her general unprettiness aside, she was—in terms of permanently memorable, immoderately perceptive, small-area faces—a stunning and final girl" (115). With astute child psychology, Boo Boo solves her son's emotional crisis. Boo Boo figures in all of the other Glass family stories. In "Raise High the Roof Beam, Carpenters," her saucy, opinionated letter to Buddy imploring him to get to the wedding is reproduced (as a secretary in the Waves, she, on the other hand, must accompany her boss, an admiral, on an out-of-state trip and is therefore unable to attend); her message to her brother Seymour—quoting the Sappho poem that supplies the title of the story—is written with a sliver of soap on the bathroom mirror. In "Seymour: An Introduction," Boo Boo chooses Seymour's John Keats poem, written when he was eight, for inclusion by Buddy in that story. Boo Boo is one of the five addressees of Seymour's letter, "Hapworth 16, 1924." Seymour tells Boo Boo to work on her manners; he also devises a non-offensive prayer specifically for her.

Glass, Buddy Buddy, the second eldest of the Glass children, is the author of the story "Zooey." In his author's introduction, he tells the reader that his three relatives have conveyed to him the events that transpired two years prior to the writing. Buddy is a professional fiction writer whose reputation has been suffering because of his interest in God and mysticism. Buddy believes, however, that his current story is not in that vein but "a compound, or multiple, love story, pure and complicated" (49). At the time of the story, he is the eldest living Glass sibling and teaches part time at a girls' junior college in Upstate New York, where he was when the action of "Zooey" took place. Nonetheless, he figures prominently in the story via his first-person author's introduction, in addition to his 14-page letter that Zooey Glass reads in the bathtub. (Thereafter, the story will be told in the third person, though several references to Buddy occur throughout.) Buddy's habit of keeping the phone in his and his brother Seymour's old room in the family apartment in working order facilitates a plot turn and resolution at the story's end. He keeps the phone active because he likes to see Seymour's name in the phone book, a name that, he states, is "essential to [his] inner harmony" (57). Buddy, along with Seymour, devised the religious training for the other children.

Buddy appears in all of the other Glass family stories. He narrates the story "Raise High the Roof Beam, Carpenters," in which his 13-year-younger self is the protagonist trying to attend Seymour's wedding. He writes "Seymour: An Introduction," in which he and Seymour are the main characters. In that story, the reader is offered a most intense experience of the middle-aged Buddy as chronicler of the Glass family saga. Many anecdotes from Buddy's youth are, in addition, related in that story. In "Hapworth 16, 1924," Buddy receives from his mother, Bessie, Seymour's 41-year-old letter and types a copy for publication. In Seymour's letter, the five-year-old Buddy is at summer camp with Seymour and is referenced often.

Glass, Franny Franny is the youngest of the Glass children and one of the three protagonists in "Zooey." Though she is not physically seen until the 76th page of the story, her return home from a disastrous visit to her boyfriend Lane Coutell's college and her subsequent breakdown in New York City provide the dramatic situation. In "Zooey," Franny is in her senior year of college and is 20 years old. She is described as having black hair and blue eyes, and though she has "half circles under her eyes, and other, subtler signs that mark an acutely troubled young girl . . . no one could have missed seeing that she was a first-class beauty" (125). Experiencing a breakdown due to a religious crisis, she has returned to her parents' apartment in New York City. Franny's retreat from what she perceives as the ego-driven world has taken the form of repeating the Jesus Prayer. Seeking refuge in the prayer, she has dropped out of her college theater productions. Her brother, Zooey, realizes she has mistaken the prayer as her salvation; he sees that she is a real actress, and he tells her that "the only thing you can do now, the only religious thing you can do, is act. Act for God, if you want to—be God's actress" (197). When Zooey relates to her the story of their brother Seymour having once told him to shine his shoes for the Fat Lady, Franny chimes in that Seymour had told her to be funny for the Fat Lady. When Zooey reveals to Franny that the Fat Lady is everyone in the world, and in fact, the Fat Lady is Jesus Christ, Franny experiences a joyous illumination. At the end of "Franny," she is seen, after fainting, lying down, repeating the Jesus Prayer. At the end of "Zooey," on the other hand, she gets into bed and falls "into a deep, dreamless sleep" (201). This healing sleep contrasts with how the reader first perceives her in "Zooey," when she is woken by her brother from a bad dream.

Franny first appears in the story "Franny" (1955), though without her surname. (For a complete account of Franny and the events leading up to "Zooey," see "FRANNY.") Franny is introduced as a member of the Glass family in the prologue of "Raise High the Roof Beam, Carpenters." Later in the story, her performance on *It's a Wise Child* is praised in Boo Boo Glass's letter to Buddy Glass.

On that radio program, Franny will memorably reply to the announcer that she knows she flew around the Glass apartment because, afterward, she would always find dust on her hands from the light bulbs. At the time of the story (1942), she is living in Los Angeles with her parents. In "Seymour: An Introduction," Franny makes several cameo appearances, the most important reference being that, in 1959 (four years after the events of "Zooey"), she has become a "budding young actress" (135). The psychological-spiritual transformation she experiences at the end of "Zooey" has indeed taken permanent effect. At the time of "Hapworth 16, 1924," Franny has not yet been born.

Glass, Les Les, the Jewish father of the Glass family and husband to Bessie, lives in the apartment along with his wife and his two youngest children, Zooey and Franny (when Franny is not at college). However, Les is never seen during the story, and his whereabouts are unspecified (though one deduces he is out of the apartment during the several-hour time span of "Zooey's" action). A sentimentalist, according to Bessie, Les does not face reality and lives in the past. He is unaware of the seriousness of Franny's condition (he thinks she has a stomachache). One night, Les entertains Franny by reminiscing about old songs from vaudeville and, most likely, playing them on the piano for Franny's benefit; on another, he wonders if she might want a tangerine. Les has decorated the living room walls with mementos and scrapbooks of his seven children's appearances on the radio quiz program *It's a Wise Child.*

Les appears in all of the other Glass family stories but never to the extent of his wife, Bessie. In "Raise High the Roof Beam, Carpenters," he is referred to as a "retired Pantages Circuit vaudevillian" (6) and currently employed by a motion-picture studio as a talent scout. In "Seymour: An Introduction," Les asks his eldest son, Seymour, the important question of whether Seymour remembers riding on Joe Jackson's bicycle in Australia in 1922. Les is one of the five addressees of Seymour's "Hapworth 16, 1924" letter. A few passages of the letter are directly addressed to Les, though

Seymour, more than once, excuses his father from reading the entire letter due to its length. In that story, the reader finally learns that Les was born in Australia.

Glass, Muriel Fedder Muriel is Seymour Glass's wife and, at the time of "Zooey," his widow. Though she is not directly named in the story, Buddy Glass refers to her in his letter to Zooey Glass as the "Bereaved Widow" (62). Buddy is recounting the time he went to Florida to collect Seymour's body after the suicide. Muriel meets him at the airport decked out in "Bergdorf Goodman black" (62), a remark that indicates that Buddy suspected Muriel of enjoying the role of widow. (Buddy has never held a high opinion of Muriel; Seymour surmised that Buddy would not respect her and notes as much in his diary in "Raise High the Roof Beam, Carpenters.")

Muriel takes part in other Glass stories. She is one of the three major characters (along with Seymour Glass and Sybil Carpenter) in "A Perfect Day for Bananafish." She is seen talking with her mother on the phone about Seymour, and she becomes a widow in the story's final paragraph. Her wedding day is the subject matter of "Raise High the Roof Beam, Carpenters." She is briefly seen being led dejectedly to a car after Seymour fails to show up for the ceremony. However, she appears in many of Seymour's diary entries reflecting their courtship period. In these, the reader is given the clearest sense of her pre–"A Perfect Day for Bananafish" character. In "Seymour: An Introduction" she will not allow Buddy to quote any of Seymour's final 184 poems in the story (though he has been given power to seek a publisher for them). This prohibition by Muriel allows Salinger an out; he does not have to create the text of the poems, poems that would be required to support the fact that they were written by one of the greatest American poets (as per Buddy's assertion). Buddy does, however, paraphrase several poems from Seymour's collection.

Glass, Seymour Seymour is the eldest Glass child and has been dead for more than seven and a half years at the time that the events in "Zooey"

take place. Nonetheless, Seymour plays a significant role in a number of ways throughout the story, which also provides important information about him. Seymour's perspective on education moved him and his brother Buddy to teach their younger siblings about the great holy men and spiritual practices, and this religious instruction infused their childhood (and, moreover, caused Franny and Zooey adjustment problems later in life). In "Zooey," Buddy quotes Seymour's haiku written shortly before his suicide. This is, to date, the only significant detail concerning Seymour's suicide that Salinger has added to the events of "A Perfect Day for Bananafish." The reader learns that Seymour did undergo psychoanalysis as he promised at the end of "Raise High the Roof Beam, Carpenters" and that the experience greatly harmed him. Zooey relates that Seymour was always smiling at him during his childhood, but in "Raise High the Roof Beam, Carpenters," Seymour, in his diary, writes that Muriel Fedder "was trying to teach me to smile, spreading the muscles around my mouth with her fingers" (83). The reader thus surmises that the advent of World War II seriously affected Seymour's nature. Zooey reads Seymour's important account of his 21st birthday, which represents the only time in Salinger's fiction that the entire Glass family is witnessed together. The telephone that Zooey uses at the story's close is listed in Seymour's name. Most importantly, Seymour's parable of the Fat Lady will bring Franny to joy and understanding of her life's purpose.

Seymour was initially introduced in the 1948 story "A Perfect Day for Bananafish," where he is seen on a beach, meets a very young girl, goes for a swim, tells her a parable about bananafish, and later shoots himself on the hotel bed next to his sleeping wife. (A minor reference to Seymour appears in the 1949 story "Down at the Dinghy.") The character is resurrected in the first Glass family story, the 1955 "Raise High the Roof Beam, Carpenters." This story is a description of Seymour's wedding day, although Seymour fails to show up for the ceremony. However, Seymour's physical absence informs the action and dialogue of the story. Seymour's revealing diary entries, moreover, serve as a stand-in for him, dominate the story's

close, and afford the reader an opportunity to assess this remarkably complex character. The story that follows "Zooey"—"Seymour: An Introduction"—is Buddy's most extensive effort to convey the life and identity of his brother. "Hapworth 16, 1924" contains the most extended example of Seymour's own words, albeit written at the age of seven.

Glass, Waker Waker, along with his twin brother, Walt, is born after Boo Boo Glass and before Zooey Glass. (Technically, he is 12 minutes younger than Walt.) During "Zooey," Waker is a Roman Catholic priest attending a conference in Ecuador. Bessie Glass wonders whether she should try to get in touch with him, but she concludes that Waker is too emotional to help with Franny's crisis. Waker is quoted in Buddy Glass's letter to Zooey regarding Zooey's attitude towards their eldest brother Seymour's suicide. Waker felt that Zooey was the only family member "who was bitter about S.'s suicide and the only one who really forgave him for it. The rest of us . . . were outwardly unbitter and inwardly unforgiving" (68).

Of the seven Glass children, Waker is the least known. He appears in the other Glass family stories but without much attention being paid him. During the time of "Raise High the Roof Beam, Carpenters," Waker is interned in a conscientious objectors' camp. In "Seymour: An Introduction," in one of the most important scenes of the story, he gives away his ninth-birthday present—a Davega bicycle—to a stranger who asks for it; the memory of this action triggers Buddy's illuminated realization that Seymour is *his* (Buddy's) Davega bicycle. Waker is one of the five addressees of Seymour's "Hapworth 16, 1924" letter; Seymour admonishes him to practice his juggling. In "Seymour: An Introduction" it is revealed that an older Waker canonized W. C. Fields and juggled cigar boxes.

Glass, Walt Walt, along with his twin brother, Waker, is born after Boo Boo Glass and before Zooey Glass. At the time of the story, he has been dead 10 years, killed in a senseless noncombat accident in Japan shortly after the end of World War II. Walt is described as Bessie Glass's "only truly lighthearted son" (90). Zooey describes the time when Walt told Waker that he suspected the Glass children had incurred bad karma because "the religious life, and all the agony that goes with it, is just something God sicks on people who have the gall to accuse Him of having created an ugly world" (153). In 1937, because Walt was in a cast, Zooey substituted for him on the radio program *It's a Wise Child*; during that occasion, Seymour Glass told Zooey to shine his shoes for the Fat Lady.

Walt is better known to readers than is his twin, Waker, because Walt appears in the 1948 story "UNCLE WIGGILY IN CONNECTICUT," though without his surname. In that story, Walt is the former boyfriend, with a unique sense of humor, of the protagonist, Eloise Wengler. Walt once called Eloise's twisted ankle "Uncle Wiggily." Walt is mentioned in all of the other Glass family stories. In "Raise High the Roof Beam, Carpenters," he is in the Pacific or en route, a member of a field-artillery unit. In "Seymour: An Introduction," Walt receives a poem by Seymour about a boy who catches a fish; he terms Seymour's facial expression of excited discovery as "his Eureka Look" (158). Walt is one of the five addressees of Seymour's "Hapworth 16, 1924" letter; Seymour admonishes him to practice his tap dancing. In "Seymour: An Introduction," the narrative reveals that the mature Walt was a dancer in civilian life.

Glass, Zooey Zooey (Zachary Martin) Glass is the second-youngest child in the family, its youngest male, and one of the three protagonists in the story bearing his name. Of the three Glasses—Bessie, Franny, and Zooey—he is the most important character. It is through Zooey's efforts that his sister Franny is rescued from her religious crisis and nervous breakdown. In "Zooey," he is a 25-year-old successful actor and a leading man in television plays. He is single; there is no mention of a girlfriend. (When his mother suggests that he get married, he replies that he does not want to because you then no longer get the window seat on trains.) Before becoming an actor, Zooey earned an M.A. in mathematics, and he is proficient in ancient languages. (He translated the Sanskrit "Mundaka Upanishad" into classical Greek.) He is a short, thin, handsome young man, with a ferocious wit

and analytical intelligence. As did his four brothers and two sisters, Zooey appeared on the radio program *It's a Wise Child*. In the opinion of the show's listeners, his performances were considered, among the Glass children, second only to Seymour's. Zooey happens to still live in his parents' apartment in the East Seventies in Manhattan.

The story proper opens with Zooey soaking in the bathtub while he reads a four-year-old letter from his eldest living brother, Buddy. Zooey is hoping to discover in the letter some wisdom that might assist him in dealing with Franny's dilemma. The previous evening, he had talked with Franny, but to no avail. Though his mother will invade the bathroom to pressure him to again speak with Franny that morning, it is evident by his rereading the letter that he is already preparing to do so. Yet, at least in his reply to his mother, Bessie, Zooey is noncommittal about attempting to once again help his sister. In the two long bathroom scenes, various aspects of Zooey's personality are revealed. He is combative and verbally abusive toward his mother, calling her "stupid" and "Fatty" (173). At one point, Zooey says to Franny, "We're the Tattooed Lady" (139). Taken together, the two instances oddly combine into a pre-echo of the Fat Lady. He is furious and angry with his brothers, Seymour and Buddy, for having indoctrinated him and Franny with a religious education, which he feels has turned them into freaks. He lets his mother know of these feelings in no uncertain terms. Zooey also possesses a cruel streak, evidenced by a particular comment to Bessie. With her eldest son already a suicide, Zooey comments to her, regarding Buddy, "I don't mind so much being haunted by a dead ghost, but I resent like *hell* being haunted by a half-dead one. I wish to God Buddy'd make up his mind. He does everything else Seymour ever did—or tries to. Why the hell doesn't he kill himself and be done with it?" (102–103). Zooey's furious nature forms a motif throughout the story and is also symbolized by an ulcer caused from sitting "in judgment on every poor, ulcerous bastard" (137) he knows. But Zooey is depressed by the way he affects the morale of his coworkers. Caring aspects of Zooey's character are also shown, as when Bessie provides him with an insight into his own nature; Zooey will regard her "with admiration, affection and, not least, gratitude" (98). Zooey sees Bessie's true loving intentions toward Franny and will describe the chicken soup Bessie continually offers Franny as "consecrated" (194). Zooey shows concern that Franny's breakdown will have an adverse effect on their parents; he calls her behavior unfair and hard on both Bessie and Les.

Zooey exhibits a great deal of erudition regarding Jesus, the Jesus Prayer, and the use of the repetition of God's name by the world's religions (as only befits a student of the Seymour-Buddy "home seminars, and the metaphysical sittings" [66]). He uses his analytical skills to attempt to show Franny how she misunderstands the personality and intent of Jesus. But Zooey becomes too wrapped up in the vehemence of his argument, thus failing to see how he has lost her to her continued repetition of the prayer.

Only after Zooey enters Seymour and Buddy's old room does he find a way to save Franny. After closing the door, he reads the various quotations on the beaverboard and falls into meditation after reading them. He next reads Seymour's note written upon the occasion of the latter's 21st birthday. The full importance of this note is manifold, as explained in the "Critical Analysis" above. But the central dual import is that Zooey comes to fully recognize the abiding dark side of his psyche—his furious, unloving aspect—and this recognition will change his manner of interacting with Franny in the final phone call. Most importantly, the note lays the foundation for Zooey's recounting of the Fat Lady parable. After reading Seymour's note, Zooey once again falls into meditation at Seymour's desk. When he finally phones Franny, he explains to her the importance for an artist to disregard the critical perceptions of the audience so as "to shoot for some kind of perfection, and *on his own terms,* not anyone else's" (198). This perfection is no easy matter to achieve, for time is always running out. The reader feels a calmness and assuredness in Zooey as he tells Franny about Seymour's Fat Lady. In transmitting to Franny the joy and wisdom she then experiences, Zooey enacts a gurulike role.

Zooey is referenced in "Raise High the Roof Beam, Carpenters," and also in "Seymour: An Introduction." In "Raise High the Roof Beam, Carpenters," Seymour, in his diary, notes Zooey's appearance on *It's a Wise Child* and records his youngest brother's comments from the show. In the latter story, Seymour remarks that Zooey, Buddy, and he "have been brothers for no fewer than four incarnations, maybe more" (183). (Of the five brothers, these three brothers interest Salinger the most; the other two brothers, Walt and Waker, are given exponentially fewer words and descriptions in Salinger's work.) At the time of "Hapworth 16, 1924," Zooey has not yet been born.

Hess, Dick   Dick Hess is the author of one of the two television play scripts that Zooey Glass has received. Originally from Des Moines, Iowa, Hess now lives in New York and regularly supplies Zooey with scripts to perform on television. Sunday night, after Zooey's first talk with Franny Glass, Hess telephones and begs to meet Zooey for a drink. Zooey unwillingly obliges, and Hess gives him his newest script.

LeSage   LeSage is Zooey Glass's television producer and employer. He has sent the television script that Zooey is seen reading in the bathtub. Everything LeSage owns, according to Zooey, is the very best.

Little girl and mother at meat counter   Referred to in Buddy Glass's letter to Zooey Glass, the little girl answers Buddy's question of whether she has any boyfriends. She responds with two names: Bobby and Dorothy. This interaction, which supports Seymour Glass's ideal of education—to unlearn the differences one has been taught—is one of the two real reasons Buddy wrote Zooey the 1951 letter that the reader observes Zooey rereading.

Little girl with dachshund   From the window, Zooey Glass sees the little girl across the street. She is playing a game of hide-and-seek with her young dog. The incident causes Zooey to question why people are ego-centered; he then comments that there are "nice things in the world" (151).

Logan, Stephanie Stephanie Logan, a girl in Franny Glass's dorm, appears in the nightmare that Franny relates to her brother Zooey.

Manlius Franny Glass's professor-poet, Manlius, is referred to by Zooey Glass as an example of someone who ruins education. This reference to Manlius helps tie "Zooey" to "Franny." In the latter story, Manlius plays an important role in exemplifying sham poets.

Painters, the Though never actually seen in the story, the unspecified number of painters are the only other people in the Glass family apartment besides Bessie, Franny, and Zooey. Because they are painting Franny's room, she must bed down in the living room. The painters' invisible presence is akin to the reader's.

Philippe Philippe is the person with whom Zooey Glass has recorded an album. The record album was heard by an unnamed Frenchman who subsequently invited Zooey to lunch. This meeting may cause Zooey to go to France to make a movie.

Pinchot, Bishop Bishop Pinchot is Waker Glass's superior; Bessie Glass considers phoning him to ask where she might wire Waker (who is at a conference in Ecuador) about his sister Franny.

Pomeroy Pomeroy is one of the people at Zooey Glass's workplace; he is probably the director of the television shows.

Seligman, Mr. Mr. Seligman is the Glasses' downstairs neighbor (at least in 1938, when he complains about the noise during Seymour Glass's 21st birthday).

Sheeter, Dean Sheeter is a dean at Buddy Glass's college. He has requested Buddy to lecture on Zen and Mahayana Buddhism. Sheeter's name delights Franny Glass.

Sherman, Sharmon Sharmon Sherman, a girl in Franny Glass's dorm, appears in the nightmare Franny relates to her brother Zooey.

Tupper, Professor Professor Tupper is an egotistical Oxford professor who teaches Franny Glass's religion seminar. Franny considers Tupper a fake. Along with Sharmon Sherman and Stephanie Logan, he appears in the nightmare Franny relates to her brother Zooey.

Woman seated behind Buddy Glass In his letter to Zooey, Buddy refers to a woman seated behind him on the airplane flight to Florida to pick up their brother Seymour's body after the suicide. The weeping Buddy is convulsed with laughter when he overhears the woman remark, ". . . and the *next morning*, mind you, they took a pint of pus out of that lovely young body of hers" (62).

FURTHER READING

Alsen, Eberhard. *A Reader's Guide to J. D. Salinger.* Westport, Conn.: *Greenwood Press,* 2002.

———. *Salinger's Glass Stories as a Composite Novel.* Troy, N.Y.: Whitston Publishing Company, 1983.

[Anonymous]. *The Pilgrim Continues His Way.* London: Society for Promoting Christian Knowledge, 1943.

———. *The Way of a Pilgrim.* London: Society for Promoting Christian Knowledge, 1941.

Antico, John. "The Parody of J. D. Salinger: Esmé and the Fat Lady Exposed." *Modern Fiction Studies* 12, no. 3 (Autumn 1966): 325–340.

Baskett, Sam S. "The Splendid/Squalid World of J. D. Salinger." *Wisconsin Studies in Contemporary Literature* 4, no. 1 (Winter 1963): 48–61.

Brinkley, Thomas Edwin. "J. D. Salinger: A Study of His Eclecticism—Zooey as Existential Zen Therapist." Ph.D. diss., Ohio State University, 1976.

Bryan, James. "J. D. Salinger: The Fat Lady and the Chicken Sandwich." *College English* 23, no. 3 (December 1961): 226–229.

Chester, Alfred. "Salinger: How to Love Without Love." *Commentary* 35 (June 1963): 467–474.

Cotter, James Finn. "Religious Symbols in Salinger's Short Fiction." *Studies in Short Fiction* 15 (Spring 1978): 121–132.

Dev, Jai. "Strategies of Self-Defence: Self-Reflexivity in *Franny and Zooey.*" *Panjab University Research Bulletin* 21, no. 1 (April 1990): 17–41.

Didion, Joan. "Finally (Fashionably) Spurious" [originally published in *National Review,* November 18,

1961]. In *Salinger: A Critical and Personal Portrait*, edited by Henry Anatole Grunwald, 77–79. New York: Harper & Row, 1962.

French, Warren. *J. D. Salinger*. New York: Twayne Publishers, 1963.

Gilman, Richard. "Salinger Considered." *Jubilee* 9 (October 1961): 38–41.

Hassan, Ihab. "Almost the Voice of Silence: The Later Novelettes of J. D. Salinger." *Wisconsin Studies in Contemporary Literature* 4, no. 1 (Winter 1963): 5–20.

Kurian, Elizabeth N. *A Religious Response to the Existential Dilemma in the Fiction of J. D. Salinger*. New Delhi: Intellectual Publishing House, 1992.

Mailer, Norman. "Some Children of the Goddess." *Esquire*, July 1963, 64–69, 105.

McCarthy, Mary. "J. D. Salinger's Closed Circuit" [originally published in *Harper's*, October 1962]. In *If You Really Want to Hear about It: Writers on J. D. Salinger and His Work*, edited by Catherine Crawford, 127–133. New York: Thunder's Mouth Press, 2006.

Mizener, Arthur. "The Love Song of J. D. Salinger." *Harper's*, February 1959, 83–90.

Purcell, William F. "Waker Glass: Salinger's Carthusian Doppelganger." *Literature and Belief* 20 (2000): 153–168.

Ranchan, Som P. *An Adventure in Vedanta: J. D. Salinger's The Glass Family*. Delhi: Ajanta Publications, 1989.

Razdan, Brig M. "From Unreality to Reality: *Franny and Zooey*—A Reinterpretation." *Panjab University Research Bulletin* 9, nos. 1–2 (April–October 1978): 3–15.

Seitzman, Daniel. "Therapy and Antitherapy in Salinger's 'Zooey.'" *American Imago* 25 (Summer 1968): 140–162.

Updike, John. "Anxious Days for the Glass Family." *New York Times Book Review*, 17 September 1961, pp. 1, 52.

Wenke, John. *J. D. Salinger: A Study of the Short Fiction*. Boston: Twayne Publishers, 1991.

Wiegand, William. "Salinger and Kierkegaard." *Minnesota Review* 5 (May–July 1965): 137–156.

PART III

Related People, Places, and Topics

Advaita Vedanta   *See* VEDANTA.

Burnett, Whit (1899–1973) Whit Burnett is inextricably connected with Salinger's early years as a writer. In 1939, Salinger enrolled in Burnett's short-story class in Columbia University's Extension Division for the spring and fall semesters. Burnett, a short-story writer, was the editor of the esteemed STORY magazine. He published four of Salinger's early stories, including his very first, "The YOUNG FOLKS," in the March–April 1940 issue. After Salinger did not return to Columbia, he corresponded with Burnett from 1940 to 1944. In 1944, Burnett suggested to Salinger that Story Press publish a volume of his short stories. Through no fault of Burnett's, the project collapsed the following year when the copublisher, Lippincott, vetoed the volume. This ruptured Salinger's relationship with Burnett. Nonetheless, at Burnett's request, Salinger wrote a foreword for the 1965 anthology *Story Jubilee: Thirty-three Years of Story.* However, Burnett did not use Salinger's foreword because it focused on Burnett instead of the magazine. In 1975, Salinger's two-page foreword was published as an epilogue in Hallie Burnett's *Fiction Writer's Handbook* (although deceased, Whit Burnett was credited as coauthor).

Whit Burnett was born in Utah in 1899. He attended several universities but kept leaving to work in the newspaper business. In 1922, Burnett met his future wife and coeditor of *Story*, Martha Foley, in San Francisco. They went their separate ways but became reacquainted in 1925 in New York. Soon the couple moved to Europe, both continuing to work as reporters for newspapers while writing short stories. They ended up in Vienna, Austria. Foley had the idea of starting a magazine devoted to the short story. Burnett initially wasn't interested but finally agreed. *Story*'s first issue was dated April–May 1931 and included stories by Burnett, Foley, Kay Boyle, and several other writers. The magazine's second issue had a story by the great Austrian writer Robert Musil. Burnett and Foley married in 1931 and soon had a child. They moved to Majorca, Spain, the next year and returned to New York in 1933. The magazine continued to grow, with its circulation and prestige increasing until the late 1930s. At some point in the mid-

to-late 1930s, Burnett began teaching short-story courses in Columbia University's Extension Division. In 1941, Burnett's marriage to Foley ended, and she left *Story*. He married a student, Hallie Abbett, in 1942, and she assisted him in editing *Story* and numerous anthologies. Burnett published a volume of his own short stories in 1934, *The Maker of Signs: A Variety.* The November–December 1942 issue of *Story* was devoted to a novella coauthored by Whit Burnett about the life of Robert Burns. The first page quotes from a Burns poem, "[if] a body meet a body . . . coming through the rye." In 1965, Burnett sold his archives to Princeton University's FIRESTONE LIBRARY. Copies of 21 letters Burnett wrote to Salinger were included.

Central Park In *The* CATCHER IN THE RYE, Holden Caulfield tells the reader: "I know Central Park like the back of my hand" (200). Several sites within the park play significant roles in the book. The carousel featured in the novel's climactic scene (272–275) predates the one in existence today. Holden and Phoebe Caulfield's carousel burned down on November 8, 1950. (Although by this time Salinger had finished writing the novel, it is possible that the fire influenced the book's dust-jacket design. A red wash spreads from the top of the cover and engulfs a carousel horse, while the book's title is in yellow.) The carousel (which Salinger spells in the French manner, "carrousel") replaced a carousel from the early 1920s (the first carousel in Central Park dates from 1870). The *Catcher* carousel was located in an octagonal building opposite 65th Street on the west side of the park. It had walls of Victorian gingerbread and a red roof with a cupola, topped by a horse weather vane. The carousel featured 44 wooden horses, hand-carved in North Tonawanda, New York, by the famous Herschell-Spillman/Spillman Engineering factory. Phoebe rides a "big, brown, beat-up-looking old horse" (273). The lagoon with the ducks, which Holden talks about thrice (18, 78, 106–108) and which he visits once (200–202), is located in the southeast corner of the park, near the street Central Park South. (The lagoon is also known and marked on maps as "The Pond.") The first instance of Holden's concern about where the ducks go during winter occurs in the 1945 short story "I'M CRAZY," events of which were incorporated into *The Catcher in the Rye.* Holden and Phoebe visit the zoo (270–271) on their way to the carousel. The Mall, where people roller-skate in front of the bandstand, is referenced in both the novel (153–155) and in "DOWN AT THE DINGHY." Other stories that mention Central Park include "The LAUGHING MAN," "The INVERTED FOREST," "ZOOEY," and "SEYMOUR: AN INTRODUCTION."

Central Park, located in New York City's borough of MANHATTAN, is rectangular in shape, two-and-one-half miles long, a half-mile wide. The park is bounded by Central Park South (West 59th Street), Central Park North (West 110th Street), Central Park West (Eighth Avenue), and, on the east, Fifth Avenue. The park, designed by Frederick Law Olmsted and Calvert Vaux, opened in 1859 and was finished in 1873. Central Park, one of the most famous parks in the world, has more than 25 million visitors a year.

Collier's *Collier's* published four of Salinger's stories: "The HANG OF IT" (July 12, 1941), "PER-

SONAL NOTES ON AN INFANTRYMAN" (December 12, 1942), "The STRANGER" (December 1, 1945), and "I'M CRAZY" (December 22, 1945). Salinger scored his first financial success with a mainstream magazine when *Collier's* bought "The Hang of It." At the time, *Collier's* circulation was more than 2 million readers. "The Hang of It" and "Personal Notes on an Infantryman" were both published in *Collier's* "A Short Short Story Complete on This Page" format. Each of Salinger's four stories was illustrated. The illustration for "I'm Crazy" depicts Holden Caulfield, the story's narrator, and constitutes the first artist's rendering of the character. The illustration is most readily found in John C. Unrue's *The Catcher in the Rye* (Unrue 2001, 32). Founded in 1888, *Collier's* remained in print until December 16, 1956.

Cornish, New Hampshire Salinger, wanting to escape the notoriety of being a best-selling author, moved to Cornish, New Hamsphire, in 1953. He lived there until his death in 2010. Cornish is 260 miles north of NEW YORK CITY, five hours by car,

J. D. Salinger's first home in Cornish, New Hampshire (as photographed in 1978) *(Courtesy of Greg Herriges, from his book,* JD: A Memoir of a Time and a Journey)

and 130 miles northwest of Boston, Massachusetts. Salinger purchased a modest cottage on 90 wooded acres. In the early 1960s, he built a second house for himself, with a splendid view of Mount Ascutney. MARGARET ANN SALINGER, the author's daughter, gives detailed descriptions of the two Salinger homes and life in Cornish in her memoir, *Dream Catcher*.

Cornish, a rural town of 1,660 people, with a total of 645 households (2000 census), is spread over 42 square miles. The Salinger scholar Warren French lived there for nearly a decade in between writing his two monographs on the author. French, in 1988, called Cornish "almost out of this world" (French 1988, 118). Only five roads lead into Cornish, one of which is the famous Cornish, New Hampshire–Windsor, Vermont wooden covered bridge (built 1866), the longest two-span covered bridge in the world and the longest wooden covered bridge in America. French remarks that it takes "a hardy soul to survive the Cornish year, especially where Salinger live[d] high in the hills" off a dirt road (French 1988, 120). The critic speaks of the "long, hard winter of four months when the ground is frozen too hard even to bury the dead" (French 1988, 120) and the temperature "may often drop to twenty-five below zero" (French 1988, 121).

In the late 19th century, a small art colony began to form around Cornish, and it would eventually include Augustus Saint-Gaudens and Maxfield Parrish. Augustus Saint-Gaudens's house, studio, and grounds are now the Saint-Gaudens National Historical Site and provide a pleasant visit. Cornish became a summer retreat for select New Yorkers, including Judge Learned Hand, who was a close friend of Salinger's. The film crew for the unauthorized documentary *J. D. Salinger Doesn't Want to Talk* visited Cornish and shot footage there.

Cosmopolitan   *Cosmopolitan* published two of Salinger's stories: "The INVERTED FOREST" (December 1947) and "BLUE MELODY" (September 1948). "The Inverted Forest" was run as a "Cosmopolitan Complete Short Novel" and was introduced with, "To say that this short novel is unusual magazine fare is, we think, a wild understatement . . . you will find it the most original story you've read in a long time—and the most fascinating" (73). "Blue Melody," the magazine's title instead of Salinger's "SCRATCHY NEEDLE ON A PHONOGRAPH RECORD," was advertised as "The Blue Ribbon Story." "The Inverted Forest" and "Blue Melody" were both illustrated. Despite Salinger's objections, *Cosmopolitan* reprinted "The Inverted Forest" in its Diamond Jubilee issue (March 1961). The author, however, was successful in blocking the story's appearance in an anthology, *The Best from Cosmopolitan*, published later that year. The anthology's editor, Richard Gehman, recounts his exasperation dealing with Salinger in the preface to the book. Initially established in 1886 as a family magazine, *Cosmopolitan*, during the period of Salinger's two publications, focused on fiction. In the late 1960s, *Cosmopolitan*, under the editorship of Helen Gurley Brown, was transformed into its present, successful incarnation.

Douglas, Claire   *See* SALINGER, CLAIRE.

Eliot, T. S. (1888–1965)   T. S. (Thomas Stearns) Eliot is referenced in two Salinger stories ("The INVERTED FOREST" and "FRANNY") and quoted, without attribution, in "A PERFECT DAY FOR BANANAFISH." During the period of these three stories (1947–1955), Eliot was the reigning poet and critic in the English language. In "The Inverted Forest," he is referred to three times (80, 86, 88). Salinger's most important use of Eliot, however, is an unstated one. The only quoted lines of poetry written by the poet of the story, Raymond Ford, are considered to be a rebuttal to T. S. Eliot's 1922 poem, "The Waste Land": "Not wasteland, but a great inverted forest / with all foliage underground" (80). In "A Perfect Day for Bananafish," the opening story of NINE STORIES, Seymour Glass quotes from the second and third lines of "The Waste Land" ("mixing memory and desire" [19]). In "Franny," Franny alludes to a passage in Lane Coutell's letter about Eliot (5). She later rails against two poet-professors at her college who write sterile academic poetry. Eliot was the preferred poet of the universities in the 1950s, and Lane and the two poet-professors pay allegiance to an academic approach to poetry. Thus, linking the

T. S. Eliot, influential American-born poet and critic. In "The Inverted Forest," Salinger rebuts Eliot's poetics. *(Courtesy of Library of Congress, NYWT&S Collection)*

rebuttal of Eliot in "The Inverted Forest" with the allusion in "Franny," Eliot seems, for Salinger, to represent false poetry. However, one critic, John M. Howell, suggests that "The Waste Land" provides a template for *The Catcher in the Rye*, in a provocative essay, "Salinger in the Waste Land."

Eliot was born in Missouri to an influential family, originally of New England. Although his father was a businessman, his grandfather was a famous Unitarian minister and founder of a university. Eliot nearly completed his Ph.D. in philosophy from Harvard University. Relocated to London, Eliot was discovered by Ezra Pound, who eventually edited "The Waste Land." The poem made Eliot famous and continues to this day to define his career. After a disastrous marriage, he became a British subject and joined the Anglican Church in 1927. During the 1930s and 1950s, he wrote a number of plays. In 1939, he published a volume of poems for children, *Old Possum's Book of Practical*

Cats, the basis for the musical *Cats* (1981). Eliot's important late poetry consists of *Four Quartets* (1943). In 1948, he was awarded the Nobel Prize in literature.

Esquire *Esquire* published two of Salinger's stories: "The Heart of a Broken Story" (September 1941) and "This Sandwich Has No Mayonnaise" (October 1945). The latter story was selected for an anthology, *The Armchair Esquire,* published in 1958. For the young Salinger, *Esquire* and the *New Yorker* were his two magazines of choice. After *Esquire* had rejected "Go See Eddie," its acceptance of "The Heart of a Broken Story," only his fourth published story, must have been gratifying. "This Sandwich Has No Mayonnaise" was illustrated with an impressionistic line drawing.

In February 1977, *Esquire* published an unsigned story, "For Rupert—with No Promises." The story initially sparked a debate over whether the author might be Salinger. Gordon Lish, fiction editor at the time, soon thereafter admitted authorship. He explained, "The story was not a parody of Salinger at all. It was an effort to guess at certain circumstances in his life, in respect to silence, the kind of stories he used to write, and of relating them to other stories that mattered to me and to my own life" ("Controversial" 18). In the same article, Lish is quoted that he learned through third parties that Salinger "was 'furious' and thought the story 'despicable and absurd'" ("Controversial" 18). Founded in 1932 as a men's magazine, *Esquire* continues publication to this day.

Faulkner, William (1897–1962) In 1939, Whit Burnett read aloud Faulkner's story "That Evening Sun Go Down" to his class of aspiring writers; 25 years later, Salinger recalled that reading. In his tribute to Burnett, Salinger writes, "Regretfully, I never got to meet Faulkner, but I often had it in my head to shoot him a letter telling him about that unique reading of Mr. Burnett's" (Burnett 188). Faulkner, in an April 1958 lecture to young writers, rated *The Catcher in the Rye* as the "best" (Faulkner 244) novel of the new generation. He memorably said of Holden Caulfield, "his tragedy was that when he attempted to enter the human race, there was no human race there" (Faulkner 244). Salinger does not mention Faulkner or any of his works by name in his own fiction; nonetheless, the influence is there. Faulkner's technique of using characters of families beyond the confines of one novel or story anticipates Salinger's own approach to the Caulfield and Glass families.

Faulkner was born in Mississippi. His first book, *The Marble Faun* (1924), was a volume of poems. His acquaintanceship with Sherwood Anderson helped him focus on writing prose. Of his first great work, *The Sound and the Fury* (1929), Faulkner said he wrote it for himself, without an eye to publication. Important novels that followed include *As I Lay Dying* (1930), *Light in August* (1932), and *Absalom, Absalom!* (1936). But Faulkner's readership declined, and his books went out of print. In difficult financial straits, he worked in Hollywood as a scriptwriter. Malcolm Cowley's *The Portable*

William Faulkner, American Nobel Prize winner, considered *The Catcher in the Rye* to be the best novel of Salinger's generation. *(Courtesy of Library of Congress, Carl Van Vechten Collection)*

Faulkner (1946), a selection of stories and excerpts from the novels, resurrected Faulkner's reputation. He was awarded the Nobel Prize in literature in 1949.

Firestone Library   Firestone Library of Princeton University, located in Princeton, New Jersey, is considered the premier Salinger research destination in the world. In 1965, Firestone Library acquired the archives of WHIT BURNETT and STORY magazine and press. Included within this voluminous acquisition are five unpublished Salinger stories written between 1942 to 1945 ("The LAST AND BEST OF THE PETER PANS," "The OCEAN FULL OF BOWLING BALLS," "The MAGIC FOXHOLE," "TWO LONELY MEN," and "The CHILDREN'S ECHELON"), 36 Salinger letters addressed to Burnett or the magazine (mostly from 1939 to 1944), copies of 21 Burnett letters to Salinger, and Salinger's original "Foreword" written at Burnett's request for *Story Jubilee: 33 Years of Story* (1965). Additionally, the library acquired all of the working papers of IAN HAMILTON and miscellaneous items regarding his suppressed book, *J. D. Salinger: A Writing Life* (1986). The archive contains the drafts, notes, and manuscript drafts of the book; the legal papers concerning the case *J. D. Salinger v. Random House*; Hamilton's letters to and responses from people who knew Salinger at VALLEY FORGE MILITARY ACADEMY and URSINUS COLLEGE; photocopies of Salinger letters dating from 1934 to 1973; a photocopy of the 1936 Valley Forge Military Academy yearbook; and two copies of *J. D. Salinger: A Writing Life*, the uncorrected bound galleys of Hamilton's suppressed book. The Department of Rare Books and Special Collections has an extensive Web site at www.princeton.edu/~rbsc that delineates holdings, access, restrictions, and services.

Fitzgerald, F. Scott (1896–1940)   In *The CATCHER IN THE RYE*, Holden Caulfield tells the reader, "I was crazy about *The Great Gatsby*" (183). Buddy Glass, at the age of 12, identified with the novel as other boys did with *The Adventures of Tom Sawyer* ("ZOOEY" 49). Salinger read Fitzgerald works closely; he admired the author's intelligence, sensibility, and brilliance. The first allusion to Fitzgerald's work in Salinger's own occurs in "LAST DAY OF THE LAST FURLOUGH" (1944). Babe Gladwaller rereads passages from *The Great Gatsby* (1925) before embarking for war. In "The STRANGER" (1945), Babe notices "some fine books" (18), one of which is Fitzgerald's *The Beautiful and Damned* (1922). As Paul Kirschner notes, "the endings of 'A Perfect Day for Bananafish' (1948) and [Fitzgerald's] 'May Day' (1920) bear a striking family resemblance" (Kirschner 59). In Fitzgerald's story's final words, the protagonist, realizing he is trapped in a bad marriage, "fired a cartridge into his head just behind the temple" (Fitzgerald 2000, 902). Salinger's story, which opens *NINE STORIES*, ends, "fired a bullet through his right temple" (26). "May Day" appears in the 1922 collection, *Tales of*

F. Scott Fitzgerald, author of the American masterpiece *The Great Gatsby*. Salinger invokes the novel in several works. *(Courtesy of Library of Congress, Carl Van Vechten Collection)*

the Jazz Age, which bore a dedication to "those who read as they run and run as they read" (Fitzgerald 2000, 802). Salinger partially dedicates RAISE HIGH THE ROOF BEAM, CARPENTERS AND SEYMOUR: AN INTRODUCTION to "anybody who just reads and runs." Salinger's most important borrowing from Fitzgerald concerns Holden Caulfield's attempt to eradicate the written instances of "Fuck you" (260, 262) that he encounters near the end of *The Catcher in the Rye*. On the last page of *The Great Gatsby*, the narrator, Nick Carraway, notices that on Gatsby's "white steps an obscene word, scrawled by some boy with a piece of brick, stood out clearly in the moonlight, and [he] erased it, drawing [his] shoe raspingly along the stone" (Fitzgerald 2004, 180).

Fitzgerald was born in Minnesota. With the publication of his novel *This Side of Paradise* (1920), he became famous. Fitzgerald wrote numerous short stories for well-paying magazines of the time that made him rich. He and his wife, Zelda, became emblematic of the Roaring Twenties. Fitzgerald published his masterpiece, *The Great Gatsby*, in 1925, but the book was a financial flop. The author published one more novel during his lifetime, *Tender Is the Night* (1934). Personal tragedy haunted Fitzgerald; his wife suffered a mental breakdown, and his heavy drinking led to alcoholism. The author was eventually reduced to hack screenwriting for Hollywood. In 1940, the first year Salinger published a short story, Fitzgerald died at age 44 from a heart attack, his reputation in tatters. The American critic Edmund Wilson edited a collection of Fitzgerald essays, notes, and letters, *The Crack-Up* (1945), which slowly began the restoration of the writer's name. By the 1960s, Fitzgerald joined ERNEST HEMINGWAY and WILLIAM FAULKNER to form the trinity of great American prose writers between the two World Wars.

Good Housekeeping *Good Housekeeping* published one of Salinger's stories: "A GIRL I KNEW" (February 1948). Salinger's original title, "WIEN, WIEN," was overruled by the editor, Herbert Mayes. IAN HAMILTON quotes the editor's lack of comprehension: "'I don't know what upset Salinger but he protested vehemently and ordered his agent,

Dorothy Olding, never again to show me any of his manuscripts.' Mayes's complacent manner here . . . gives some idea of what the author in those days, and in those places, was up against" (Hamilton 1988, 104). The story was illustrated. *Good Housekeeping* had a tradition of publishing notable fiction by writers of stature. Founded in 1885, the women's magazine continues publication to this day.

Hamilton, Ian (1938–2001)   Ian Hamilton wrote two biographies of Salinger. The first, *J. D. Salinger: A Writing Life*, was blocked from publication by Salinger's legal action initiated in October 1986. Random House had originally intended to publish 20,000 copies of the biography, a straightforward but slim account of Salinger's life, augmented by numerous quotations from the author's unpublished letters. Even after Hamilton paraphrased the quotations (albeit closely), the court did not allow the book to be published. The second biography, *In Search of J. D. Salinger* (1988), excises both the quotations and the paraphrases. The book utilizes sections of *J. D. Salinger: A Writing Life* and introduces Hamilton and a companion, his "biographizing alter ego" (Hamilton 1988, 9), as characters. The book presents their discovery of materials about Salinger's life and the effort to construct a biography of the author. *In Search of J. D. Salinger* climaxes with an inside account of the court cases that resulted in the suppression of *J. D. Salinger: A Writing Life*. Hamilton thought the second biography had "a stronger plot and certainly a more riveting denouement, and at the same time it raise[d] key questions about the whole business of 'biography'—what is it for, why do we write it, why do people want to read it" (Douglas Martin B-6). *In Search of J. D. Salinger* generally received poor to tepid reviews. *J. D. Salinger: A Writing Life* exists as an edition of 150 copies of bound galleys, highly sought-after due to the quotations from Salinger's letters. These bound galleys have become very expensive collectors' items.

Hamilton was a respected English critic, poet, editor, and author of a well-received biography of Robert Lowell before he undertook to write his Salinger biography. But as Hamilton notes in *In Search of J. D. Salinger*, "my name and J. D.

Salinger's will be linked in perpetuity as those of litigants or foes" (Hamilton 1988, 212). This linkage has, to a certain degree, overshadowed Hamilton's career. Hamilton published seven volumes of poetry from 1964 to 1999. He edited a dozen books, ranging from *The Faber Book of Soccer* to the standard anthology, *The Oxford Companion to Twentieth-Century Poetry in English*. In addition to the Lowell biography (1982), Hamilton wrote *Writers in Hollywood, 1915–1951* (1990), *Keepers of the Flame: Literary Estates and the Rise of Biography* (1992), and an essay that sheds further light on his Salinger experience, "A Biographer's Misgivings," collected in *Walking Possession: Essays and Reviews, 1962–1993* (1996).

Harper's   *Harper's* published one of Salinger's stories: "DOWN AT THE DINGHY" (April 1949). To accompany the story's publication, Salinger submitted an expansive contributor's note and (presumably) a photograph, both of which *Harper's* chose not to use. Nearly a decade later, in their February 1959 issue, *Harper's* printed Salinger's contributor's note (which it titled "J. D. Salinger—Biographical") and a photograph, dated 1945, alongside Arthur Mizener's article, "The Love Song of J. D. Salinger." Salinger's note is most readily found in Henry Anatole Grunwald's *Salinger: A Critical and Personal Portrait* (Grunwald 21). The photograph is most readily found in MARGARET ANN SALINGER's *Dream Catcher: A Memoir* (see first insert of plates) and in John C. Unrue's *The Catcher in the Rye* (Unrue 2001, 12), albeit in each case the caption misstates Salinger's age as 31. Salinger, dressed in army garb, is clearly younger than in the LOTTE JACOBI photographs taken in October 1950. The publication of "Down at the Dinghy" in *Harper's* marked the final time that a Salinger story was published in an American magazine other than the NEW YORKER. Founded in 1850, *Harper's* continues publication to this day.

Harry Ransom Center   The Harry Ransom Center at the University of Texas at Austin, located in Austin, Texas, has a sizable Salinger collection. The majority derives from the purchase of Elizabeth Murray's Salinger materials: 38 letters from 1940 to

1963; the unpublished story "BIRTHDAY BOY" (circa 1946); the draft of an untitled story, circa 1941 ("MRS. HINCHER," later known as "PAULA"); multiple versions of sections of the Holden Caulfield story, "I'M CRAZY"; and other miscellaneous material. Additionally, the center has acquired uncorrected advance page proofs of *The CATCHER IN THE RYE*; bound galley proofs of *FRANNY AND ZOOEY* and *RAISE HIGH THE ROOF BEAM, CARPENTERS AND SEYMOUR: AN INTRODUCTION*; and nine Salinger letters addressed to various people.

The center was established in 1957 by Harry Ransom, vice president and provost of the University of Texas at Austin, and remains one of the world's most richly endowed collections of literary and artistic artifacts. The Harry Ransom Center maintains an extensive Web site, which includes online exhibits, at www.hrc.utexas.edu.

Hemingway, Ernest (1899–1961) During Salinger's first decade of writing, Hemingway was America's most famous author. Salinger, in his 1938 *Ursinus Weekly* column, thought Hemingway's work had declined after *The Sun Also Rises* (1926), *A Farewell to Arms* (1929), and a short story about Nick Adams, "The Killers." In *The CATCHER IN THE RYE* (1951), Holden Caulfield terms *A Farewell to Arms* "a phony book" (182) and, in contrast, likes the work of Ring Lardner and F. SCOTT FITZGERALD. Salinger met Hemingway in Paris in August 1944. Hemingway praised Salinger's story "LAST DAY OF THE LAST FURLOUGH." In a September 1944 letter to WHIT BURNETT, Salinger speaks highly of Hemingway. Salinger wrote Hemingway an adulatory letter in July 1945.

The catalog of Hemingway's personal library includes copies of *The Catcher in the Rye* and *NINE STORIES*. The critic Sandra Whipple Spanier detects the influence of Salinger's novel on the final Nick Adams story Hemingway wrote, "The Last Good Country." "The characters in these two works are surprisingly alike, even in their idiosyncrasies, and their similarities extend beyond the family resemblances to be expected among characters of a type" (Spanier 36). Hemingway's flat style of prose resides on the other end of the spectrum from Salinger's. Nonetheless, Hemingway's cycle of stories about

Ernest Hemingway, the most famous American writer of the 1940s, met Salinger in Paris in August 1944. *(Courtesy of Library of Congress)*

Nick Adams may be seen as an influence on Salinger's own series of stories about Holden Caulfield.

Hemingway was born in Illinois. Originally a reporter, he moved to Paris. He soon became acquainted with F. Scott Fitzgerald, James Joyce, Ezra Pound, and Gertrude Stein, among others. In 1923, Hemingway's first book, *Three Stories and Ten Poems,* was published in Paris. With the publication of *In Our Time* (1925), a collection of stories, he moved to the front rank of American writers. Hemingway's *The Sun Also Rises* (1926), which defined the Lost Generation, is considered an American masterpiece. Hemingway's persona as a man of action soon overshadowed his literary work. *For Whom the Bell Tolls* (1940) and *The Old Man and the Sea* (1952) are notable later works; in 1954, Hemingway was awarded the Nobel Prize in literature. He committed suicide with a shotgun in 1961. Numerous posthumous publications ensued, including a fascinating memoir of his early days in Paris, *A Moveable Feast* (1964).

Jacobi, Lotte (1896–1990)   Lotte Jacobi took the photograph of Salinger that appeared on the dust jacket of his first book, *The CATCHER IN THE RYE*. Taken when Salinger was a youthful 31-year-old, this photograph has become the iconic representation of the writer.

In October 1950, LITTLE, BROWN AND COMPANY sent Salinger to Jacobi's MANHATTAN studio to have an author's photo taken for their upcoming publication, *The Catcher in the Rye*. (Salinger initially resisted the need for a photo on the book's jacket and had to be convinced by the editor in chief, Angus Cameron.) At least 17 photographs were composed during two sittings. Jacobi later informed Salinger's first bibliographer, Donald M. Fiene, "Mr. Salinger doesn't enjoy being photographed. I find him an exceptionally interesting person" (Fiene 1961a, 99). The photo chosen for the dust jacket was substantially cropped. It appears in reverse so that the left side of Salinger's face in

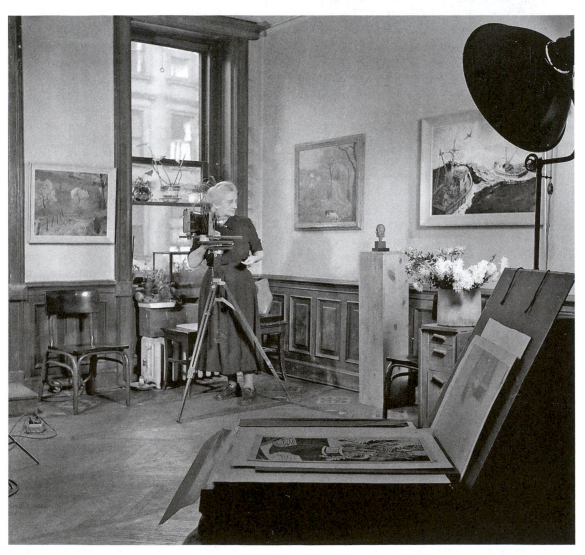

Lotte Jacobi in her Manhattan studio, 1953. Photographed by Frank H. Bauer. *(© The Lotte Jacobi Collection, University of New Hampshire)*

the dust-jacket photo is actually the right side of his face. His picture filled the entire back panel of the dust jacket. The photo (sometimes reversed, sometimes not) was subsequently reproduced in many reviews of the book and in contemporary articles. At Salinger's insistence, the photograph was removed for the book's third printing. Salinger said, "I'm getting good and sick of bumping into that blown-up photograph of my face on the back of the dust-jacket. I look forward to the day when I see it flapping against a lamp-post in a cold, wet Lexington Ave. wind" (Hazard 16). (The image that Salinger employs here derives from the ending of his 1949 story "The LAUGHING MAN.")

Prior to the publication of the Jacobi photograph on Salinger's first book, only two photos of Salinger had ever seen print: a very young Salinger in the September 1941 issue of ESQUIRE (to accompany the publication of "The HEART OF A BROKEN STORY") and an army photo of Salinger in the October 1945 issue of *Esquire* (to accompany the publication of "THIS SANDWICH HAS NO MAYONNAISE"). (The latter photo was reused in the May 1947 issue of MADEMOISELLE to accompany the publication of "A YOUNG GIRL IN 1941 WITH NO WAIST AT ALL.") Thus, the photograph used on *The Catcher in the Rye,* with its subsequent reproduction at the time, defined Salinger's "look" to his reading public. Since Salinger forbade author photos for his later books, and due to his retreat from the limelight, the Jacobi photo became the standby representation of Salinger worldwide.

It should be noted that three of the other Jacobi photos of Salinger saw very limited publication; they were used to accompany articles about him. *Glamour,* in September 1951, and *Mademoiselle,* in October 1961, published two severely cropped photos; *People,* in its February 25, 1980, issue, published a third intact. Many years after Jacobi's death, *OP Magazine* published a revealing article about the photographer, Scott Brown's excellent "Literary Lotte," in its March–April 2004 issue. Included in the article are eight of the Salinger photos, all uncropped. Seven had never appeared in any form until that time.

Jacobi was born in West Prussia into a Jewish family steeped in professional photography. She took up the trade in her mid-twenties, just in time to move to Berlin and document its theater and dance worlds of the late 1920s and early 1930s. Among in her subjects were Emil Jannings Lotte Lenya, Peter Lorre, and Kurt Weill. With Hitler's rise to power, Jacobi was forced to flee and eventually settled New York in 1936. She continued to earn her living through taking photographs. Some notable subjects included Albert Einstein, Robert Frost, Thomas Mann, Paul Robeson, and Eleanor Roosevelt. In 1956, Jacobi left Manhattan and moved to Deering, New Hampshire. During her later years she became a political activist. Jacobi bequeathed her 47,000 negatives, in addition to her letters and documents, to the University of New Hampshire, which now holds the Lotte Jacobi Collection.

Kafka, Franz (1883–1924) In 1951, Salinger listed in the Book-of-the-Month Club newsletter that accompanied *The CATCHER IN THE RYE* the 17 writers he loved. The very first name was that of a Jewish writer, born and buried in Prague. This preeminent place was not mere chance. "The great Kafka" (152) is how Salinger refers to him in "SEYMOUR: AN INTRODUCTION."

The Kafka that mattered to Salinger is Kafka, the man and writer, and not his fictive universe. Kafka's role as a guide to Salinger's later writing life is essential to note. Kafka is not mentioned in Salinger's fiction up through 1955. Then, in the 1957 "ZOOEY" and the 1959 "Seymour: An Introduction," Kafka is directly quoted four times, and his name appears eight times. This exceeds any other writer invoked in the Glass stories. Seymour and Buddy Glass's beaverboard in "Zooey" hold the first direct quotations from Kafka. Of the quotes from the beaverboard reproduced in the story, only one author is represented more than once: Kafka. The two quotes are juxtaposed, and it is that juxtaposition that gives them resonance: "'Don't you want to join us?' I was recently asked by an acquaintance when he ran across me alone after midnight in a coffeehouse that was already deserted. 'No, I don't,' I said" (177); "The happiness of being with people" (178). Though both quotes come from the second volume of Kafka's diaries as originally published in America, the first quote is from 1914 (Brod 1949, 44), the latter from 1922 (Brod 1949, 218). Salinger's reclusion would embrace the first; the follow-up might speak to his ability to enjoy people, but on a very select basis.

The most prominent quotation from Kafka reproduced in Salinger's work leads off "Seymour: An Introduction." The 89-word quote begins, "The actors by their presence always convince me, to my horror, that most of what I've written about them until now is false" (111). This quote, from Kafka's 1911 diaries (Brod 1948, 108), along with a companion quote from Søren Kierkegaard, lays the theoretical groundwork for the story and also emphasizes Salinger's focus on "the life" of his characters. The Kafka quotation sums up the dilemma of wanting to render into words those whom you love, yet realizing that the ability to fully express those who are loved can fall short and thus leave a flawed portrait. It is this very dilemma that Buddy Glass experienced time and again as he tried to write about his beloved brother Seymour.

Salinger, through Buddy Glass in "Seymour: An Introduction," again expresses his feeling for Kafka when he acknowledges "quoting from works of [a] writer [he] loves" (117). Kafka is one of but four people Buddy turns to for "perfectly credible information about modern artistic processes" (118). (The others are Kierkegaard, Vincent van Gogh, and Seymour.) Kafka seems to repay this trust by virtue of his repeatedly commenting in his diaries, notebooks, and letters on the act and nature of writing. Two, among many additional examples, that would speak to Salinger are: "My attitude to my writing and my attitude to people is unchangeable; it is part of my nature, and not due to temporary circumstances. What I need for my writing is seclusion, not 'like a hermit,' that would not be enough, but like the dead" (Kafka 1973, 279); "Writing as a form of prayer" (Kafka 1954, 312). Salinger's 57-year residence in his CORNISH, NEW HAMPSHIRE, hermitage would echo the first quote; the second quote succinctly expresses the essence of his life.

Salinger's fascination with Kafka's diaries is evidenced by the realization that all four direct Kafka quotes come from the remarkable diaries.

(The fourth quotation—"The young girl who only because she was walking arm in arm with her sweetheart looked quietly around"—is found in "Seymour: An Introduction" [142] [Brod 1948, 140].) This perhaps contributed to the idea of Seymour keeping a diary. Max Brod, Kafka's close friend, literary executor, and first biographer, spoke about Kafka in a tone of near-adoration. After Kafka died at age 40, no superlative was high enough for the man whose every word and scrap of paper Brod tried to rescue from oblivion. Brod's relationship to Kafka mirrors that of Buddy's to Seymour. Brod's own adulatory tone infuses Buddy's prose in "Seymour: An Introduction." Additionally, Kafka's problematic, mismatched relationship with Felice Bauer (twice engaged, they never married) might have influenced Salinger's depiction of the mismatched Seymour and Muriel.

Kafka's words and example permeated Salinger's life. To Peter de Vries, Salinger quoted Kafka's "Writers speak a stench" (Brod 1948, 11), which no doubt reinforced Salinger's attitude toward giving interviews. (In "Zooey," Salinger has Buddy remark, ". . . a professional writer, and the usual stench of words that goes with it . . ." [64].) Both Kafka and Salinger were drawn to solitude, and the realms of their imagination at times seem to almost supplant human relationships. Both writers spent their lives burrowing into silence and returning with words embodying their own spiritual worlds.

Kafka's publishing history eerily anticipated Salinger's. Kafka was a perfectionist and, like Salinger, an admirer of Flaubert. Kafka published a total of 40 stories, 16 of which are but *one*-page long. The whole of Kafka's works published during his lifetime fits into a single volume of 250 pages. Salinger's four published books consist of only one novel and 13 stories, three of which could be termed novellas. His total pagination barely crests 1,000 not-closely-printed pages. Yet Kafka wrote a tremendous amount of work. Only after his death did this become apparent as Brod found publishers for the three novels, scores of stories, diaries, notebooks, and copious letters. Only time will tell if Salinger, too, had substantially more unpublished than published work. It is possible that all the writing known to date is but the iceberg's tip of Salinger's art.

The final linkage of these two writers waits to be seen in another respect. In one of the most famous incidents in literary history, Kafka requested Brod to destroy all of his unpublished work. Brod refused, and though Kafka himself destroyed a portion, much of it was in other hands and was rescued by Brod. It waits to be seen if Salinger has emulated Kafka's desire to erase his unpublished writings, or if he has intended to be his own "Brod" and authorized publication. There is evidence in MARGARET ANN SALINGER's *Dream Catcher* that Salinger had plans to publish posthumously. She reports that he had devised a color-coded system to denote stories, as is, ready for publication; those, after editing, that should be published; and those not to be published. Additionally, Salinger had his lawyers create the J. D. Salinger Literary Trust in 2008. As of June 2010, the trust has not divulged any publication plans.

Kafka's place in the pantheon of 20th-century literature is beyond dispute. Kafka's stories "The Judgment," "The Metamorphosis," "In the Penal Colony," and "A Hunger Artist," and his novels *The Trial* and *The Castle,* are generally the works singled out by critics. Yet the nonfiction writings that so attracted Salinger should not be overlooked. These writings helped to indelibly create the portrait of Kafka. They would include *The Diaries; Letter to His Father; Letters to Milena; Letters to Felice; Letters to Friends, Family and Editors;* and *The Blue Octavo Notebooks,* among others. Brod's *Franz Kafka: A Biography* has been augmented by Ernst Pawel's *The Nightmare of Reason* and Ronald Hayman's *K: A Biography of Franz Kafka.* In 1983, the year of Kafka's centenary, John Updike spoke of Kafka as "the last holy writer" (Updike, "Foreword" xxi).

Little, Brown and Company   Little, Brown and Company published each of Salinger's four books and continues, to this day, to keep them in print in hardback, trade paperback, and mass-market editions. Little, Brown and Company published *The CATCHER IN THE RYE* in 1951; *NINE STORIES* in 1953; *FRANNY AND ZOOEY* in 1961; and *RAISE*

HIGH THE ROOF BEAM, CARPENTERS AND SEYMOUR: AN INTRODUCTION in 1963. After paperback rights sold to New American Library and, later, Bantam Books, expired, Little, Brown and Company issued its own mass-market edition in 1991. The books were published as an austere matching set, each volume bound in white covers, with Salinger's name and the book's title in black. In 2001, Little, Brown published the four books in trade paperback editions with covers that mimicked the original dust jackets and matched the original typeface and pagination. The mass-market edition soon adopted the same covers.

In 1950, the (now legendary) editor Robert Giroux failed to persuade his boss, Eugene Reynal of Harcourt Brace, to publish *The Catcher in the Rye.* Salinger was recruited to Little, Brown and Company by John Woodburn, the editor in charge of the New York office of the Boston-based firm. Relations between publisher and writer were strained from the outset. Salinger did not want his photograph included on the dust jacket of *The Catcher in the Rye.* Angus Cameron, editor in chief, had to convince the author of its importance and the necessity of a biographical blurb. Nonetheless, after the first two printings of the book quickly sold out, at Salinger's request the photograph was removed for the third printing. Henceforth, no author photograph appeared on subsequent books nor were any biographical blurbs utilized. In 1970, Salinger repaid Little, Brown and Company a $75,000 advance and no longer was under contract for a new book. To the publishing world's shock, in late 1996 a new Salinger book (HAPWORTH 16, 1924) was announced as forthcoming from a small press, Orchises. (The book, however, never was released.) It is not known why Salinger chose to bypass Little, Brown and Company. Salinger's four books, especially *The Catcher in the Rye* and *Franny and Zooey,* have sold substantial numbers of copies, although Little, Brown and Company does not divulge exact figures.

Little, Brown and Company, founded in 1837 in Boston, Massachusetts, is one of America's oldest publishing houses. Its original emphasis was on law books. In 1859, John Bartlett joined the firm, bringing with him his recent book, *Bartlett's Famil-*

iar Quotations. In 1925, Little, Brown and Company partnered with the *Atlantic Monthly* and expanded into trade titles. Salinger was one of the company's best-selling fiction authors of the 1950s and 1960s. To Salinger's disgust, Little, Brown and Company was purchased by Time Inc. in 1968. (*Time* magazine had put Salinger on its cover and conducted extensive research into his life in 1961; the author greatly resented this intrusion on his privacy.) In 1989, a merger took place that created the Time Warner Book Group. In 2006, Time Warner Book Group was bought by a French publisher, Hachette Livre. The Little, Brown and Company imprint is now part of the Hachette Book Group USA.

Lobrano, Gus (1902– or 1903–1956) Gus Lobrano was Salinger's second editor at the NEW YORKER, working with the author from circa late 1947 until his sudden death by cancer at the age of 53. Lobrano became a close friend of the author; Salinger dedicated NINE STORIES to Lobrano and DOROTHY OLDING.

Lobrano, a college friend of E. B. White, joined the *New Yorker* in 1937 as a fiction editor. When Katharine Angell White, head of the fiction department, moved to Maine in 1938, Lobrano replaced her. The outgoing, convivial editor formed close friendships with many of his writers, including John Cheever, S. J. Perelman, and Irwin Shaw. Lobrano was responsible for creating the magazine's "first reading agreement," which allowed the magazine first option on all of a writer's work. Salinger was offered the agreement after publication of "A PERFECT DAY FOR BANANAFISH" in January 1948; nonetheless, three stories were rejected that year, along with seven in 1949. A photocopy of a Lobrano rejection letter to Salinger's agent, Dorothy Olding, may be found in Ben Yagoda's *About Town: The New Yorker and the World It Made* (Yagoda 236). Lobrano had high hopes of succeeding Harold Ross as editor in chief, only to be deeply disappointed when the job was offered to WILLIAM SHAWN in January 1952.

Mademoiselle *Mademoiselle* published one of Salinger's stories: "A YOUNG GIRL IN 1941 WITH NO WAIST AT ALL" (May 1947). The story was illustrated. *Mademoiselle* had a tradition of publishing notable fiction by writers of stature. Founded in 1935, the women's magazine ceased publication in 2001.

Manhattan Although Salinger's work is generally identified with NEW YORK CITY, nearly all New York references are to places and institutions located in the borough of Manhattan. The last three-quarters of *The* CATCHER IN THE RYE take place in Manhattan, as do the stories "RAISE HIGH THE ROOF BEAM, CARPENTERS," "ZOOEY," "JUST BEFORE THE WAR WITH THE ESKIMOS," "The LONG DEBUT OF LOIS TAGGETT," "The HEART OF A BROKEN STORY," "The STRANGER," "SLIGHT REBELLION OFF MADISON," and segments of additional stories. Landmark sites frequently appear in Salinger's works (see CENTRAL PARK). Holden Caulfield (in *The Catcher in the Rye*) and Buddy Glass (in "Raise High the Roof Beam, Carpenters") arrive at Penn Station. Holden later stores his bags in Grand Central Station. Holden meets Sally Hayes at the Biltmore Hotel, which is also referenced in "SEYMOUR: AN INTRODUCTION," "Raise High the Roof Beam, Carpenters," and "BLUE MELODY." The Waldorf-Astoria Hotel is referenced in "The Long Debut of Lois Taggett," "ONCE A WEEK WON'T KILL YOU," "A BOY IN FRANCE," and "The INVERTED FOREST." In "DE DAUMIER-SMITH'S BLUE PERIOD," the narrator and his stepfather live at the Ritz Hotel. The Hotel Pierre is referenced in "The Long Debut of Lois Taggett," as is the Stork Club. Holden Caulfield mentions both the Stork Club and El Morocco. Greenwich Village is the location for Ernie's in *The Catcher in the Rye*. The Village is referenced in "ZOOEY" and "PRETTY MOUTH AND GREEN MY EYES." Columbia University is where Ray Ford ("The Inverted Forest") and Seymour Glass (the Glass stories) both teach, Carl Luce (*The Catcher in the Rye*) is a student, and Lois Taggett ("The Long Debut of Lois Taggett") takes a few courses; and Joanie ("Pretty Mouth and Green My Eyes") attends a class at Columbia's Extension. Holden Caulfield and the three women from Seattle separately attend Radio City Music Hall, also alluded to in "THIS SANDWICH HAS NO MAYONNAISE." Salinger always refers to Rockefeller

Center as Radio City; Holden and Sally go skating there in both the novel and in the story "Slight Rebellion Off Madison." The Museum of Natural History provides Holden with a pleasant memory in *The Catcher in the Rye* and is also referenced in "The LAUGHING MAN." The Metropolitan Museum of Art is where Holden tells two kids about mummies; Vincent Caulfield lives two blocks from the museum ("This Sandwich Has No Mayonnaise"); the museum is also referenced in "The Laughing Man" and "Seymour: An Introduction." The Glass family originally live on the Upper West Side of Manhattan; they move to the East 70s. Seymour and Buddy's apartment is also on the Upper East Side. The Caulfield family in *The Catcher in the Rye* live on East 71st. The apartments of Helen and Bob Polk ("The Stranger") and Corinne von Nordhoffen ("The Inverted Forest") are on the Upper East Side, as is Muriel Fedder's grandmother's brownstone, located down the block from Carl and Amy's on 63rd ("Raise High the Roof Beam, Carpenters"). Throughout numerous stories, there are repeated references to major streets: Fifth Avenue, Madison Avenue, Park Avenue, Lexington Avenue, Riverside Drive, Broadway, 42nd Street. Manhattan of the 1920s through the mid-1950s provides its quintessential backdrop to many of Salinger's works.

Manhattan, one of New York City's five boroughs, occupies Manhattan Island and several small islands. It covers 23 square miles, with a population of 1.6 million. When Salinger first lived on the Upper West Side of Manhattan in the 1920s, population had peaked at 2.3 million. Additional censuses for the borough reflected 1.9 million in 1930 and 1940, and 2.0 million in 1950. By 1960, Salinger had been ensconced in CORNISH, NEW HAMPSHIRE, for seven years. Manhattan hosts major financial, cultural, and corporate institutions. It is second only to Washington D.C., in terms of political power. Divided into different neighborhoods, the borough is most frequently represented in Salinger's works by the Upper East Side and the Upper West Side.

Maxwell, William (1908–2000)   William Maxwell was the first of three NEW YORKER editors who worked with Salinger. Maxwell also wrote the first extended essay about Salinger; it accompanied the Book-of-the-Month Club's 1951 edition of *The* CATCHER IN THE RYE.

Maxwell's initial reaction to Salinger's stories is reflected in a 1943 letter to the author's agent: "We think Mr. Salinger is a very talented young man and wish to God you could get him to write simply and naturally" (Yagoda 233). In 1947, he writes: "If Mr. Salinger is around town, perhaps he'd like to come in and talk with me about New Yorker stories" (Yagoda 234). Salinger met with Maxwell. Between 1948 and 1950, Salinger published five classic *New Yorker* stories: "A PERFECT DAY FOR BANANAFISH," "UNCLE WIGGILY IN CONNECTICUT,"

William Maxwell, *New Yorker* fiction editor and distinguished American novelist and short-story writer, was Salinger's first editor at the magazine. *(Courtesy of Library of Congress, NYWT&S Collection)*

"JUST BEFORE THE WAR WITH THE ESKIMOS," "The LAUGHING MAN," and "FOR ESMÉ—WITH LOVE AND SQUALOR."

The Book-of-the-Month Club essay is a historically important document because it reveals Salinger's unusual cooperation with his book's publicity. Less than a thousand words in length, Maxwell's essay contains early information about Salinger's life and work. His NEW YORK CITY childhood is invoked, and his beginnings as a writer at VALLEY FORGE MILITARY ACADEMY are described: "At night in bed, under the covers, with the aid of a flashlight, he began writing stories" (Maxwell 6). Salinger's description of his first and only time addressing a college class is also included. He spoke to a short-story class at Sarah Lawrence College, but regretted that he "got very oracular and literary . . . labeling all the writers" (Maxwell 6) he held in respect. Maxwell quoted what Salinger considered was the proper response to any discussion of the literary craft: "A writer . . . ought to get up and call out in a loud voice just the *names* of the writers he *loves*. I love Kafka, Flaubert, Tolstoy, Chekhov, Dostoyevsky, Proust, O'Casey, Rilke, Lorca, Keats, Rimbaud, Burns, E. Bronte, Jane Austen, Henry James, Blake, Coleridge. I won't name any living writers. I don't think it's right" (Maxwell 6). This list gives the reader a firsthand roll call of the writers Salinger considered to be his masters. Unless an oversight, the omission of Emily Dickinson, F. SCOTT FITZGERALD, and Ring Lardner is odd. (Salinger erred by including Sean O'Casey, who didn't die until 1964.)

Maxwell tantalizingly speaks of the existence of an earlier version of *The Catcher in the Rye*. It was originally a novella, approximately 90 pages long, finished in 1946. But instead of accepting a publisher's offer, Salinger decided to rewrite the work. Maxwell's essay also includes the best description of Salinger's devotion to the writer's craft: ". . . it means a great deal to say that a novelist *works* like Flaubert (which Salinger does), with infinite labor, infinite patience and infinite thought for the technical aspects of what he is writing, none of which must show in the final draft. Such writers go straight to heaven when they die, and their books are not forgotten" (Maxwell 6). This Flaubertian

care is evident throughout Salinger's four published books. Yet it was not until his stories started to consistently appear in the *New Yorker* that this craftsmanship became fully evident.

Salinger, on his part, valued Maxwell. Alec Wilkinson reports in his memoir about Maxwell that "when J. D. Salinger finished *The Catcher in the Rye*, he drove to the Maxwells' house and over the course of an afternoon read it to them on their porch" (Wilkinson 93). In 1956, Salinger was approached to be one of four *New Yorker* writers whose stories would be gathered in a group book; he declined, but recommended that Maxwell take his place.

Maxwell was on the *New Yorker* editorial staff from 1936 to 1976. He worked with such luminaries as Harold Brodkey, John Cheever, Mary McCarthy, Vladimir Nabokov, John O'Hara, John Updike, and Eudora Welty. Maxwell was a notable American fiction writer, born in Illinois, whose work captured a vanished Midwest. His novels and short stories are collected in two volumes in the prestigious Library of America series; a selection of his essays and reviews appears in *The Outermost Dream*. The essay on Salinger, however, is not in this volume; it can be most readily found in Al Silverman's *The Book of the Month: Sixty Years of Books in American Life* (Silverman 1986, 128–130).

Maynard, Joyce (1953–) Joyce Maynard's 10-month-long affair with Salinger during 1972 and 1973 is recounted in her memoir, *At Home in the World* (1998). The memoir covers her life up to age 44, with a substantial portion of text devoted to Salinger. Although Maynard vowed never to write about the relationship, rumors quickly started when she moved to CORNISH, NEW HAMPSHIRE (after dropping out of Yale before her sophomore year). The publication of *At Home in the World* provoked a heated discussion in the literary and media worlds; the question centered on whether Maynard should have waited until Salinger was deceased. When Maynard, during the next year, auctioned the letters Salinger had sent her, the controversy continued.

Maynard has been a published writer since her teenage years. She has always openly used her personal life as a source for her writing. Her break-through article in the *New York Times Magazine* was the one Salinger read, "An Eighteen-Year-Old Looks Back on Life." This article was expanded into a book titled *Looking Back: A Chronicle of Growing Up Old in the Sixties* (1973), finished while living with Salinger in Cornish. After she and Salinger broke up, Maynard continued to live in rural New Hampshire as a freelance journalist. She published her first novel, *Baby Love*, in 1981. Two volumes of children's fiction, both illustrated by her husband, Steve Bethel, were released in the mid-1980s. The couple married in the late 1970s, had three children, and underwent an acrimonious divorce in the early 1990s. Maynard collected her syndicated *New York Times* column, "Hers," about being a wife, motherhood, and life in New Hampshire, in the book *Domestic Affairs: Enduring the Pleasures of Motherhood and Family Life* (1987). Her novel *To Die For* (1991) was made into a 1995 film directed by Gus Van Sant and starring Nicole Kidman. Maynard had a small part in the film as the lawyer of Kidman's character. In 2005, Maynard published a young-adult novel, *The Cloud Chamber*, which won the California Book Award for best young-adult novel. In 2009, her newest novel, *Labor Day*, was published and was optioned by the film director Jason Reitman.

New York City See MANHATTAN.

New Yorker, The The *New Yorker* published 13 of Salinger's stories: "SLIGHT REBELLION OFF MADISON" (December 21, 1946), "A PERFECT DAY FOR BANANAFISH" (January 31, 1948), "UNCLE WIGGILY IN CONNECTICUT" (March 20, 1948), "JUST BEFORE THE WAR WITH THE ESKIMOS" (June 5, 1948), "The LAUGHING MAN" (March 19, 1949), "FOR ESMÉ—WITH LOVE AND SQUALOR" (April 8, 1950), "PRETTY MOUTH AND GREEN MY EYES" (July 14, 1951), "TEDDY" (January 31, 1953), "FRANNY" (January 29, 1955), "RAISE HIGH THE ROOF BEAM, CARPENTERS" (November 19, 1955), "ZOOEY" (May 4, 1957), "SEYMOUR: AN INTRODUCTION" (June 6, 1959), and "HAPWORTH 16, 1924" (June 19, 1965). (The 13 publications exceed, by far, Salinger's second-highest number of acceptances, five by

the *SATURDAY EVENING POST*.) Salinger is indelibly linked with the *New Yorker*. Of his 35 stories published in magazines, Salinger chose to reprint only 13 of them in his books, and of these 13 stories, all but two had appeared in the *New Yorker*.

"A Perfect Day for Bananafish" and "Raise High the Roof Beam, Carpenters" were selected for inclusion in *New Yorker* anthologies representing the best stories published in the magazine during the 1940s and 1950s, respectively. Distinguished contributors of fiction during these two decades include Maeve Brennan, Harold Brodkey, John Cheever, Mavis Gallant, Nadine Gordimer, Shirley Jackson, WILLIAM MAXWELL, Mary McCarthy, Carson McCullers, Vladimir Nabokov, Frank O'Connor, John O'Hara, V. S. Pritchett, Irwin Shaw, James Thurber, John Updike, Eudora Welty, and E. B. White. Salinger's sole appearance in the magazine during the 1960s was his final story published during his lifetime, "Hapworth 16, 1924," in the June 19, 1965, issue. Following that publication, Salinger readers would unfailingly look in the *New Yorker* for another story, only to be disappointed as months, years, and decades elapsed.

The *New Yorker* was founded by Harold Ross and his wife, Jane Grant, as a weekly magazine of sophisticated humor. The inaugural issue was dated February 21, 1925. The legendary Ross, as editor, led the magazine until his death in December 1951. (Salinger wrote a complimentary letter to E. B. White after reading White's obituary for Ross that appeared in the magazine. Salinger attended the memorial service for Ross.) After Ross's death, WILLIAM SHAWN was appointed editor. Shawn's equally legendary tenure lasted from 1952 to 1987. The editor, age 79, was forced out by S. I. Newhouse, who had purchased the magazine in 1985. Subsequent editors have been Robert Gottlieb (1987–1992), Tina Brown (1992–1998) and, since 1998, David Remnick. Writers, artists, cartoonists, and staff whose names are part of the *New Yorker* constellation include Charles Addams, Roger Angell, Peter Arno, Donald Barthelme, Ann Beattie, Robert Benchley, Louise Bogan, John Cheever, Janet Flanner, James Geraghty, Wolcott Gibbs, Brendan Gill, Rea Irvin, Pauline Kael, A. J. Liebling, John McPhee, William Maxwell, Joseph

Mitchell, John O'Hara, Eleanor Gould Packard, Carmine Peppe, S. J. Perelman, George Price, Lillian Ross, Irwin Shaw, William Steig, Saul Steinberg, James Thurber, Calvin Trillin, John Updike, E. B. White, and Katharine Angell White.

The *New Yorker* became known for its cover art, single-panel cartoons, "The Talk of the Town," short comic pieces, extended nonfiction articles, profiles, a genre of fiction known as the *New Yorker* short story, fact checking, and highly extensive copyediting of all text. The magazine eschewed a masthead (to this day) and did not introduce a full table of contents until 1969. During the period of Salinger's publications, the magazine's circulation grew from approximately 300,000 to 465,000. Although the circulation has continued to grow, it has never reached one million subscribers. Nonetheless, the magazine's influence and prestige vastly exceed its relatively modest circulation figures. The *New Yorker* holds a distinctive place in the history of American magazines and culture. The definitive history of the *New Yorker* during the Ross and Shawn eras may be found in Ben Yagoda's *About Town: The New Yorker and the World It Made.* Insider accounts include James Thurber's *The Years with Ross,* Brendan Gill's *Here at The New Yorker,* and Renata Adler's *Gone: The Last Days of The New Yorker.*

Nikhilananda, Swami (1895–1973) Swami Nikhilananda founded the RAMAKRISHNA-VIVEKANANDA CENTER OF NEW YORK, frequented by Salinger. The author took classes and attended lectures on VEDANTA given by Nikhilananda. Nikhilananda was a direct disciple of SRI SARADA DEVI, the wife and spiritual companion of SRI RAMAKRISHNA. He arrived in America in 1931, founded the center in 1933, and was its spiritual leader until his death in 1973. Nikhilananda translated *The Gospel of Sri Ramakrishna* into English, prefaced with a substantial biographical introduction. A quotation from the book appears on Seymour and Buddy Glass's beaverboard in "ZOOEY" (177).

Sumitra Paniker's dissertation, "The Influence of Eastern Thought on 'Teddy' and the Seymour Glass Stories of J. D. Salinger" (1971), reveals that Salinger had a friendship with Nikhilananda. In a June 21, 1969, letter to Paniker, Nikhilananda

Swami Nikhilananda founded the Ramakrishna-Vivekananda Center of New York in 1933. Salinger attended Nikhilananda's classes and lectures on Vedanta. *(Courtesy of the Ramakrishna-Vivekananda Center of New York)*

conveyed that "Salinger was a personal friend of his and that he used to attend his classes and lectures on Hindu philosophy" (Paniker 2). When Paniker attempted to elicit further information, a novice monk informed her that the swami was too ill to continue corresponding. The monk added: "He, Salinger, presented the Swami with a copy of *Franny and Zooey* when it was first published, and I saw the inscription by the author, but the exact wording escapes me now. Something about Salinger's being able to circulate the ideas of Vedanta only through the medium of such stories as these, and expressing appreciation for his contacts with the Swami" (Paniker 2). The full extent of Salinger's relationship with Nikhilananda remains intriguing. Whether the relationship included initiation by the swami cannot be confirmed by the Ramakrishna-Vivekananda Center of New York.

Nikhilananda was also a talented translator and writer. In addition to translating *The Gospel of Sri Ramakrishna*, he translated the *Upanishads* and the *Bhagavad Gita*; wrote biographies of Ramakrishna, Sarada Devi, and SWAMI VIVEKANANDA; compiled works by Vivekananda; and wrote *Hinduism: Its Meaning for the Liberation of the Spirit* for the influential 1950s series World Perspectives.

Olding, Dorothy (1909– or 1910–1997)   Dorothy Olding was Salinger's literary agent from 1941 to 1990, when she was forced to retire due to a stroke. In 1953, Salinger dedicated NINE STORIES to Olding and his editor, GUS LOBRANO. Earlier that year, Salinger had moved to CORNISH, NEW HAMP-SHIRE, signaling his withdrawal from the Greater New York Area literary scene. As the decades elapsed, Olding was Salinger's "chief guardian of the reclusive author's privacy" (Lyman D-23). At the author's request, she destroyed more than 500 of his letters before the Harold Ober Agency files were donated to Princeton University's FIRESTONE LIBRARY.

Dorothy Olding joined the Harold Ober Agency in 1938. (Ober was famous for being F. SCOTT FITZGERALD's agent.) Salinger signed with the agency in 1941 and was assigned to Olding. Her specialty at the time was authors selling stories to magazines. Olding's stable of writers grew to include the Nobel Prize winner Pearl S. Buck and a number of mystery writers, including Agatha Christie and Ngaio Marsh. Olding became the president of the agency in 1973. Olding's obituary in the *New York Times* quoted one of her clients who described her as "the Unsinkable Molly Brown, but with class. She was always just clear-spoken, forthright, the kind of person you could never imagine going back on her word" (Lyman D-23).

Ramakrishna, Sri (1836–1886)   Sri Ramakrishna, "saint of modern India" (Nikhilananda 182), was born in Bengal. Ramakrishna's talks were transcribed by a disciple as *The Gospel of Sri Ramakrishna*. A quotation from the book appears on Seymour and Buddy Glass's beaverboard in "ZOOEY" (177). In the same story, Salinger references Ramakrishna in "Jesus and Gautama and

Sri Ramakrishna preached the harmony of religions. Salinger quotes from *The Gospel of Sri Ramakrishna* in "Zooey." *(Courtesy of the Ramakrishna-Vivekananda Center of New York)*

Lao-tse and Shankaracharya and Hui-neng and Sri Ramakrishna, etc." (65).

Ramakrishna experienced "the harmony of religions" (Nikhilananda 185), the essence of his message to the modern world. He "practiced all the dualistic and non-dualistic disciplines of Hinduism and always arrived at the same state of God-consciousness. He pursued the teachings of Christ and Mohammed, and attained the same spiritual goal. . . . he taught from actual experience, and not from mere book knowledge, that all religions are but different paths to reach the same goal" (Nikhilananda 182–183). Ramakrishna's wife and spiritual companion was SRI SARADA DEVI, and his greatest disciple was SWAMI VIVEKANANDA.

Ramakrishna-Vivekananda Center of New York   The Ramakrishna-Vivekananda Center of New York was founded in 1933 by SWAMI NIKHILANANDA. Since 1939, the center has been located at 17 East 94th Street on the Upper East

Side of MANHATTAN. The Salinger family residence at 1133 Park Avenue, where Salinger lived from 1932 to January 1947, was a few blocks away. It is not known exactly when Salinger first visited the Ramakrishna-Vivekananda Center of New York. In the early 1950s, he took courses and attended lectures by Nikhilananda. Salinger also took part in retreat classes conducted by Nikhilananda at the Vivekananda Cottage in Thousand Island Park in Upstate New York. Salinger

maintained contact with Nikhilananda and later, to some extent, with his successor, Swami Adiswarananda.

The Ramakrishna-Vivekananda Center of New York bases its teachings on VEDANTA, a philosophy that evolved from the world's oldest religious writings, the *Vedas* of ancient India. The center promulgates Vedanta as explained by SRI RAMAKRISHNA, SRI SARADA DEVI (Ramakrishna's wife and spiritual companion), and SWAMI VIVEKANANDA (Ramakrishna's disciple), and as demonstrated in the lives of these three Indians.

In addition to the temple on the Upper East Side, the center maintains a summer cottage at Thousand Island Park. The Vivekananda Cottage is considered a historically important place of pilgrimage because Swami Vivekananda lived and taught there for seven weeks in the summer of 1895. The center has published a number of seminal religious and philosophical books, including *The Gospel of Sri Ramakrishna* and *Vivekananda: The Yogas and Other Works.*

The minister, or swami, of the center is a monk of the Ramakrishna Order. Swami Nikhilananda led the center from 1933 to 1973; he was followed by Swami Adiswarananda (1973–2007); the current minister and spiritual leader is Swami Yuktatmananda. The Ramakrishna-Vivekananda Center of New York "seeks to stimulate the growth of the individual's innate spirituality through lectures, discourses, publications, and individual guidance," as stated on the extensive Web site at www.ramakrishna.org.

The Ramakrishna-Vivekananda Center of New York, located on the Upper East Side of Manhattan, where Salinger studied Vedanta *(Courtesy of the Ramakrishna-Vivekananda Center of New York)*

Rilke, Rainer Maria (1875–1926) In 1951, Salinger listed in the Book-of-the-Month Club newsletter that accompanied *The CATCHER IN THE RYE* the 17 writers he loved most. The first poet on the list was Rilke. Rilke is referred to, or his poetry is utilized, in Salinger's works from 1945 to 1955.

The first reference to Rilke in Salinger's work occurs in "The STRANGER" (1945), when Babe Gladwaller notices "some fine books . . . [by] Rainer Maria Rilke . . ." (18). In "The INVERTED FOREST" (1947), Rilke is referred to twice (80, 88). Raymond Ford, the story's poet, is described as "Coleridge and Blake and Rilke all in one" (80). Ford seems especially interested in Rilke. He improvises an essay on Rilke for his wife-to-be; the only time he comes to her apartment before they marry is to see her Rodin that formerly belonged to Rilke's wife, Clara. Salinger does not allude to Rilke by name in "A PERFECT DAY FOR BANANA-FISH" (1948); nonetheless, all critics agree that the author of the German book of poems is Rilke. (As Warren French notes in his 1963 monograph, "Even if Rilke were not praised elsewhere in Salinger's work, his imagination and sensitivity make it obvious that to Seymour he would be the 'only great poet of the century,' whom he wishes Muriel to read in German" [French 1963, 80].) The last reference to Rilke and his work occurs in "FRANNY" (1955). Lane Coutell has been assigned the "Fourth Duino Elegy" written by "this bastard Rilke" (6). In the story, Rilke and Sappho represent authentic poets, those who "*leave* something beautiful" (19) on the page.

The influence of Rilke's works on Salinger's fiction has been discerned by critics. Edward Stone, in "Salinger's Carrousel," was the first to indicate that the ending of *The Catcher in the Rye* was indebted to Rilke. A Rilke poem, "The Carousel," includes "a little blue girl buckled up," along with "girls . . . who almost have outgrown/this leap of horses" (Rilke 1938, 173). Combined, these become Phoebe Caulfield thinking she's "too big" (272) but nonetheless riding her carousel horse in "her blue coat" (275). In the same volume of translations published in America in 1938, Christiane Faris notes that the poem "Autumn" laments "we are all falling" (Rilke 1938, 75). The motif of falling is woven throughout Salinger's novel (Faris 25–26). Faris observes that in "DE DAUMIER-SMITH'S BLUE PERIOD" the reproduction of a Picasso painting, "Les Saltimbanques," which Picasso himself looks at, is the very painting that inspired Rilke's "Fifth Duino Elegy." (Rilke lived with the original painting during 1915.) A reproduction of "Les Saltimbanques" is the frontispiece for the first American edition (1939) of the *Duino Elegies* (Faris 2). Frederick L. Gwynn and Joseph L. Blotner suggest a connection between Rilke's *saltimbanques* (acrobats) of the "Fifth Duino Elegy" and the performing Glass family (Gwynn

55). Edward Stone detects the influence of Rilke's poem "Archaic Torso of Apollo" in the description of de Daumier-Smith's mystical experience before the shop window (Stone 1969, 124–125). This poem also appears in the same 1938 volume of translations as above (Rilke 1938, 181).

J. B. Leishman, in his introduction to his translation of Rilke's uncollected poems of 1906 to 1926, remarks about the poet: "One of the most remarkable facts about the last twenty years or so of Rilke's life is that publication seems to have become more and more indifferent, or even irrelevant, to him, as though all that mattered was that he should continue to be and to remain a poet" (Rilke 1957, 1). This eerily parallels Salinger's refraining from publication; in fact, a number of biographical aspects of Rilke fore-echo Salinger's life. The critic Kenneth Hamilton suggests about Rilke's influence on Salinger: "Rilke's dedicated efforts to protect his artistic sensitivities may have influenced [Salinger's] own pattern of withdrawal" (Kenneth Hamilton 1967, 7). Although Salinger does not directly allude to Rilke's one novel, *The Notebooks of Malte Laurids Brigge*, undoubtedly he must have read the work. There, Rilke warns about fame: "Fame, that public destruction of one in process of becoming, into whose building-ground the mob breaks, displacing his stones" (Rilke 1949, 74). Rilke also admonishes, "profit by the fact that no one knows you" (Rilke 1949, 74), which informs Salinger's statement on the dust jacket of FRANNY AND ZOOEY: "It is my rather subversive opinion that a writer's feelings of anonymity-obscurity are the second-most valuable property on loan to him during his working years."

Rilke was born in Prague when it was still part of the Austro-Hungarian Empire. Although he identified with the aristocracy, he came from a middle-class family. Over his mother's objections, Rilke was sent to military school to become an officer. After five years, he left at age 15 due to poor health and his desire to write poetry. Unlike most of the great European writers of his day, Rilke's education was very sporadic; he never earned a university degree. Rilke depended on support from relatives until he was 27. Rilke's spotty education and financial dependence into his maturity mirror Salinger's own experience. In 1900, Rilke met Tolstoy, one of Salinger's artistic heroes. The poet married a young sculptress, Clara, who had studied with Rodin. Rilke would soon be commissioned to write a monograph on Rodin, and he later became Rodin's secretary for a while. This ended his home life in Germany with Clara and their newborn daughter. By 1902, Paris was his base until the outbreak of World War I. Rilke was exceedingly poor until 1906. Thereafter, the peripatetic poet depended on the support of his new publisher, Anton Kippenberg, plus gifts from patrons, to maintain his cherished solitude.

The Parisian years, as they are generally called, yielded Rilke's first enduring works: *The Book of Hours* (1905), the enlarged edition of *The Book of Pictures* (1906), the two volumes of *New Poems* (1907, 1908), and *The Notebooks of Malte Laurids Brigge* (1910). The attempt to complete *The Notebooks* (over a six-year period) tortured the poet, and he finished them devastated. After two sterile years, Rilke, befriended by the patron of the arts Princess Marie von Thurn und Taxi-Hohenlohe, stayed at her seaside castle, Duino, some 50 miles from Venice. There, in the roaring wind, he heard a voice call to him, "Who, if I cried, would hear me among the angelic orders?" (Rilke 1939, 21). Rilke quickly wrote his first two "Duino Elegies." Realizing these poems were his life's task, he spent another 10 years trying to complete the last eight elegies. The "Fourth Duino Elegy," mentioned in "Franny," was written in Munich, Germany, in late 1915, as the poet waited to be called up for infantry duty for World War I. When the war was over, Rilke fled Germany (which he detested) for Switzerland. A patron eventually allowed him to live in a small, old, towerlike chateau, named Muzot. Rilke completed the cycle of poems there by writing five elegies in the space of three weeks during February 1922 (he also wrote 55 sonnets). These two cycles of poems, *Duino Elegies* (1923) and *Sonnets to Orpheus* (1923), were Rilke's last major works and are generally ranked with the greatest volumes of Western lyric poetry. Rilke died of leukemia (the same illness as did Allie Caulfield) in 1926, at the age of 51.

Salinger, Claire (1933–)   Claire Salinger, née Douglas, was Salinger's second wife and mother of his two children, MARGARET ANN SALINGER and MATTHEW ROBERT SALINGER. Born in England to the noted art scholar Robert Langton Douglas, Claire, along with her brother, Gavin, was relocated to America to escape the bombing of London during World War II. The children lived with various host families. Claire initially met Salinger in 1950. In 1953, the author asked her to drop out of Radcliffe and join him in CORNISH, NEW HAMPSHIRE. Claire refused, which caused the relationship to falter. Shortly thereafter, she married a man from Harvard, but the marriage was quickly annulled. In January 1955, Claire dropped out of Radcliffe one semester shy of graduation. She and Salinger married on February 17, 1955. The marriage license states that it was a first marriage for both. Claire, along with her children, is co-dedicatee of Salinger's 1963 book, *RAISE HIGH THE ROOF BEAM, CARPENTERS AND SEYMOUR: AN INTRODUCTION*. In 1966, Claire filed for divorce, which was granted on October 3, 1967.

Claire eventually returned to college and earned a Ph.D., training at the C. G. Jung Institute of New York. Along with DORIS SALINGER, she was a major source for Margaret Ann Salinger's memoir, *Dream Catcher*. Six photographs of Claire may be found in the memoir. Dr. Claire Douglas is a clinical psychologist and Jungian analyst in private practice. She has published a number of articles and several books, including, *The Woman in the Mirror* (1990), *Translate This Darkness: The Biography of Christiana Morgan* (1997), and *The Old Woman's Daughter: Transformative Wisdom for Men and Women* (2006).

Salinger, Colleen (1959–)   Colleen Salinger, née O'Neill, Salinger's widow, was the wife of the author's third marriage. The marriage became public knowledge when Colleen, in October 1992, phoned in a fire at the Salinger home, as reported by the *New York Times*. The date of the wedding is undocumented but is believed to have been in the late 1980s.

Colleen is mentioned in two memoirs about Salinger: JOYCE MAYNARD's *At Home in the World* and MARGARET ANN SALINGER's *Dream Catcher*.

Maynard states that Colleen came from Maryland and was a nursing student. She met Salinger on a bus, worked as an au pair, and married a young man, who had a son, in the early 1980s. According to Maynard, Colleen left the marriage after engaging in a correspondence with Salinger and joined him in CORNISH, NEW HAMPSHIRE. According to Margaret Ann Salinger (who does not explain how her father met his wife), Colleen, an upbeat, pretty, former cheerleader from a Southern college, has no literary interests; her passion is quilt making, and she usually wins the contests at the Cornish Fair. After Salinger's death, Colleen thanked the townspeople of Cornish for protecting the author's privacy. Colleen Salinger is now cotrustee of the J. D. Salinger Literary Trust.

Salinger, Doris (1912–2001) Doris Salinger is the author's older sister by six years and two weeks; the siblings were close until late in life. Doris accompanied Salinger when he looked for a house outside of the Greater New York Area. Along with CLAIRE SALINGER, Doris was a major source for MARGARET ANN SALINGER's memoir, *Dream Catcher.*

Doris married and divorced twice; she worked for Bloomingdale's as a buyer of women's fashions. Six photographs of Doris Salinger may be found in *Dream Catcher.*

Salinger, Margaret Ann (1955–) Margaret Ann Salinger, better known as Peggy, is the author's first child and only daughter. Margaret Ann, along with her mother, CLAIRE SALINGER, and brother, MATTHEW ROBERT SALINGER, shares the dedication of Salinger's 1963 book, RAISE HIGH THE ROOF BEAM, CARPENTERS AND SEYMOUR: AN INTRODUCTION.

Margaret Ann Salinger published *Dream Catcher,* a 435-page memoir of the Salinger family, in 2000. She had sought assistance from her mother, Claire, and her aunt, DORIS SALINGER, in piecing together the past that predated her own memories. The first 25 percent of the book tells the story of the Salingers up to 1955 and interprets Salinger's writings utilizing biographical information. The next 60 percent takes the reader through

Margaret Ann's senior year of high school. The final 15 percent covers her life from the summer of 1973 up to writing the book.

Margaret Ann Salinger's memoir provides biographical information about Salinger unavailable elsewhere, in addition to the largest amount of information about Claire Salinger, Doris Salinger, SOLOMON SALINGER, and MIRIAM SALINGER. The memoir also delineates her numerous trials and tribulations, both physical and mental, but ends on a positive note. During her late thirties, Margaret Ann graduates from Harvard Divinity School, enters into a successful marriage, has a child, and begins work as a hospital chaplain. Although her brother, Matthew, has disputed her characterizations of their parents, the memoir nonetheless remains essential reading. *Dream Catcher* contains numerous family photographs, including 17 of Salinger and 26 of Margaret Ann.

Salinger, Matthew Robert (1960–) Matthew Robert Salinger, better known as Matt, is the son of the author and his second wife, CLAIRE SALINGER, and the younger brother of MARGARET ANN SALINGER. The dedication of FRANNY AND ZOOEY to WILLIAM SHAWN begins with an allusion to the one-year-old Matt. Matt, along with his mother and sister, shares the dedication of Salinger's 1963 book, RAISE HIGH THE ROOF BEAM, CARPENTERS AND SEYMOUR: AN INTRODUCTION.

Matt Salinger graduated from Columbia University with a B.A. in art history and drama and became an actor. He has acted in films and television and on the stage; he has also been a producer and executive producer. Matt had the lead role in the 1990 film *Captain America.* He is now cotrustee of the J. D. Salinger Literary Trust.

In a 1984 interview with David Remnick, Matt comments about his father: "He wants to write for the page and he wants his characters to be on the page and in the readers' minds. He doesn't want people to make him into something he's not. He thinks it's bad for him and his work to have a public life" (Remnick C-2). After his sister, Margaret Ann, published her memoir about the Salingers, Matt wrote a letter to the *New York Observer* stating, "I can't say with any authority that she is consciously making anything up. I just know that I grew up in a very different house, with two very different parents from those my sister describes" (Malcolm 22). Three photographs of Matt Salinger may be found in Margaret Ann Salinger's memoir, *Dream Catcher*.

Salinger, Miriam (1893–1971) Miriam Salinger, born Marie Jillich in Atlantic, Iowa, and Catholic, is the mother of the author and his one sibling, DORIS SALINGER. Salinger dedicated his first book, *The CATCHER IN THE RYE*, to his mother. She doted on her only son and believed he would become a successful writer just as he said he would.

Marie secretly married SOLOMON SALINGER in a civil ceremony at the age of 17. Two years later Marie converted to Judaism and changed her name to Miriam for the formal Jewish wedding ceremony. Three photographs of Miriam Salinger may be found in MARGARET ANN SALINGER's memoir, *Dream Catcher*.

Salinger, Solomon (1887–1970) Solomon Salinger, better known as Sol, is the author's father. Father and son had a discordant relationship. Sol Salinger wanted Salinger to learn the food importing business at the J. S. Hoffman and Company, where he was the head executive. To that end, Salinger was sent to Europe to improve his German and French. The author had no intention of following in his father's footsteps.

Sol Salinger's father, Simon, a rabbi and later a noted medical doctor, immigrated to America in 1876. Sol was born in Cleveland. The author's father dropped out of school at 13 and began working. He secretly married Marie Jillich, a gentile, in a civil ceremony. Sol lived apart from Marie for two years before admitting the marriage to his father. The couple ran a movie theater in Chicago until Sol became successfully employed at Hoffman and Company. He was later sent to NEW YORK CITY to head the company's office. According to extended Salinger family members, Sol was an unpretentious, extroverted millionaire with a sense of humor, although after World War II he was uncomfortable when questioned about his son. One photograph

of Sol Salinger may be found in MARGARET ANN SALINGER's memoir, *Dream Catcher*.

Salinger, Sylvia (1919–2007) Sylvia Salinger, née Welter, the author's first wife, remains a mysterious figure in Salinger's biography. According to IAN HAMILTON, Sylvia was French, a psychologist or an osteopath; the couple married in September 1945. On May 10, 1946, the Salingers returned to America and lived with his parents. In July, Sylvia returned to Europe and would file for a divorce. According to MARGARET ANN SALINGER (whose sources would have been her mother, CLAIRE SALINGER, and her aunt, DORIS SALINGER), Salinger arrested Sylvia, a low-level German Nazi; the couple entered into a conflicted marriage, which faltered after a short time back in America.

The premier Salinger Web site, www.deadcaulfields.com, ran an obituary for Sylvia, which suggests that the Web site gained access to either her or one of her relatives. In the obituary, the following facts were related: Sylvia was born in Frankfurt am Main, Germany, on April 19, 1919. She and her parents moved to Paris, and she was granted French citizenship. She is described as very beautiful and fluent in German, French, and Italian, but with little English. When and how Sylvia and Salinger met is unclear; their marriage took place in November 1945, in Switzerland. The couple lived in Germany. In May 1946, they returned to New York and lived with Salinger's parents. Two months later, Sylvia returned to Europe and filed for divorce. In 1956, she came to America and soon married an automotive engineer. They lived in Michigan. Sylvia was an ophthalmologist and researched glaucoma. Her second husband died in 1988; she passed away on July 16, 2007.

Sarada Devi, Sri (1853–1920) Sri Sarada Devi, also known as Holy Mother, was SRI RAMAKRISHNA's wife and spiritual companion. Her photograph adorns the altar of the RAMAKRISHNA-VIVEKANANDA CENTER OF NEW YORK along with those of Ramakrishna and SWAMI VIVEKANANDA. SWAMI NIKHILANANDA was a direct disciple of Sarada Devi. Thus, through Nikhilananda and Sarada Devi it may be said that Salinger experienced a direct

Sri Sarada Devi, wife and spiritual companion of Sri Ramakrishna. *(Courtesy of the Ramakrishna-Vivekananda Center of New York)*

linkage with Ramakrishna. Salinger, in July 1952, wrote Hamish Hamilton, his English publisher, in an effort to persuade him to publish a British edition of *The Gospel of Sri Ramakrishna.*

Saturday Evening Post, The   The *Saturday Evening Post* published five of Salinger's stories: "The Varioni Brothers" (July 17, 1943), "Both Parties Concerned" (February 26, 1944), "Soft-Boiled Sergeant" (April 15, 1944), "Last Day of the Last Furlough" (July 15, 1944), and "A Boy in France" (March 31, 1945). (The last story was included in an anthology, *The Saturday Evening Post Stories, 1942–1945,* published in 1945.) Salinger's total number of publications in the *Saturday Evening Post* is second only to the 13 stories published by the New Yorker. When Dorothy Olding sold three stories to the *Saturday Evening Post* in January 1944, Salinger was pleased. He marveled at the size of the magazine's readership (more than 3 million) and generously contributed some of

his remuneration to Whit Burnett's short-story contest for college students. Salinger's pleasure was short lived. The *Saturday Evening Post* changed two of his titles: "Wake Me When It Thunders" became "Both Parties Concerned"; "Death of a Dogface" became "Soft-Boiled Sergeant." As was the custom of the "slicks," each of Salinger's stories contained illustrations. In an April 22, 1944, letter to Burnett, Salinger satirizes the illustrations and expresses deep frustration in writing to the specifications of mainstream magazines.

Founded in 1821, the *Saturday Evening Post* was the quintessential "American" magazine of the 1940s with its numerous Norman Rockwell covers. The magazine ceased publication in 1969.

Shawn, William (1907–1992)   William Shawn, editor in chief of the New Yorker (1952–1987), became Salinger's editor after the death of Gus Lobrano in 1956. In the author's dedication of *Franny and Zooey* (1961) to Shawn, Salinger speaks of him as "mentor and . . . closest friend . . . most unreasonably modest of born great artist-editors." Salinger dedicated the book to Shawn in part for Shawn's overruling the fiction editors' rejection of "Zooey." Shawn worked with Salinger on the manuscript and on the author's final two published stories. In 1965, when Tom Wolfe attacked Shawn and the *New Yorker* in two articles, Salinger protested with a telegram (Wolfe 247– 293). In 1987, Salinger was one of the signatories to the letter of protest against Shawn's dismissal as editor. Whether Salinger shared any of his writings with Shawn after his final *New Yorker* publication in 1965 remains unknown.

Shawn was born in Chicago to a successful Jewish merchant named Benjamin Chon. He attended college but dropped out when he turned 21 to marry. Shawn changed his name, worked as a newspaperman in New Mexico, lived briefly in Europe, and, having aspirations to be a songwriter, moved to New York in 1932. Through his wife, Cecille, Shawn got his start at the *New Yorker* as a freelance reporter for "The Talk of the Town" in 1933. He became the managing editor for nonfiction in 1939. The depletion of the staff during World War II allowed Shawn to become indispensable to Harold Ross. Ross said that Shawn was doing the work of two and a half jobs; others have testified that he worked 18 hours a day, seven days a week, getting the weekly magazine out. Ross and Shawn's greatest triumph occurred in 1946. Shawn suggested to John Hersey that he write about the dropping of the atomic bomb on Hiroshima from the perspective of the victims. Ross, Shawn, and Hersey labored over the 30,000-word text. Originally planned as a four-part article, Shawn persuaded Ross to devote an entire issue, devoid of all other matter except ads, to the article alone. The issue made history and sold out in one day. After Ross's death in December 1951, Shawn was appointed editor by the magazine's owner in January 1952. He would eclipse Ross's length of editorship; Shawn remained editor until February 1987.

Shawn was renowned for his editorial skills: "a poet with a pencil, capable of eliminating extraneous, repetitive, or discordant material with deft and vigorous strokes, and inserting just the word, phrase, or sentence to gracefully make matters clear . . . his changes were always in the spirit of the piece as written" (Yagoda 248). Shawn was a perfectionist, known for "his quiet, considerate, infinitely courteous way" (Pace A-1), in addition to certain eccentricities, such as a fear of automatic elevators. Shawn's managerial style became increasingly questioned over the years. He did not delegate responsibilities, retained increasing power, and was perceived as secretive. He was beloved by his writers; Ben Yagoda estimates that between 60 and 80 books were dedicated to Shawn. In Shawn's 55 years at the *New Yorker*, he never signed one piece. The closest was the use of his initials for a short creative work, "The Catastrophe," in 1936. Shawn wrote the obituaries of 21 staff members and contributors. Shawn's essay on Harold Ross may be found in Brendan Gill's *Here at The New Yorker* (Gill 388–395). Shawn's last decade with the magazine was overshadowed by the question of a successor to his position. At the age of 79, he was finally forced out by the new owner. (This is the subject of Gigi Mahon's *The Last Days of The New Yorker*.) To date, no biography of Shawn has been published. Ben Yagoda's *About Town: The New Yorker and the World It Made* contains substan-

tial information. Two relevant memoirs have also been published: *Here but Not Here: A Love Story*, by Lillian Ross (no relation to Harold Ross), about her 40-year affair with Shawn, and Ved Mehta's *Remembering Mr. Shawn's New Yorker: The Invisible Art of Editing*.

Story *Story* published four of Salinger's stories: "The Young Folks" (March–April 1940), "The Long Debut of Lois Taggett" (September–October 1942), "Once a Week Won't Kill You" (November–December 1944), and "Elaine" (March–April 1945). *Story* had the distinction of publishing Salinger's first work of fiction, "The Young Folks," in addition to first stories by Truman Capote, John Cheever, Joseph Heller, Tennessee Williams, and Richard Wright. "The Long Debut of Lois Taggett" was selected for inclusion in an anthology, *Story: The Fiction of the Forties*, published in 1949. At Whit Burnett's request, Salinger wrote a foreword for the 1965 *Story* anthology, *Story Jubilee: Thirty-three Years of Story*. Salinger's foreword wasn't used because it focused on Burnett instead of the magazine.

Story was founded by Whit Burnett and his wife, Martha Foley, in Vienna, Austria, in 1931, to publish and promote the short-story genre. In 1933, the coeditors moved to New York and became increasingly successful. By 1936, circulation had reached 23,000. That year, *Story* joined with Harper and Brothers to publish a limited number of books under the imprint Story Press. (In 1944, Burnett suggested to Salinger that Story Press print a volume of his stories and title it *The Young Folks*.) In 1937, the magazine opened its pages to the novella. (The November–December 1942 issue was devoted to a novella coauthored by Whit Burnett about the life of Robert Burns. The first page quotes from a Burns poem, "[if] a body meet a body . . . coming through the rye.") The magazine's success began to falter, and by the time Salinger's first story appeared in 1940, circulation had fallen to 8,000. After Burnett and Foley divorced in 1941, Burnett, who also taught, married a former student, Hallie Abbett, in 1942. The couple continued to publish *Story* six times a year until 1948, whereupon they cut back to two issues.

By 1951, the magazine had folded. Burnett revived the magazine with several other editors in 1960; it lasted until 1967.

Taoism Salinger, in "SEYMOUR: AN INTRODUCTION," includes classical Taoism as one of Buddy and Seymour Glass's acknowledged sources of Eastern philosophy (242). Salinger was drawn to the ancient Chinese philosophy as manifested in the writings of Lao-Tzu, Chuang-Tzu, and Lieh-Tzu. In "HAPWORTH 16, 1924," Seymour requests books by Lao-Tzu and Chuang-Tzu (104). Chuang-Tzu is quoted in "ZOOEY" ("Beware when the so-called sagely men come limping into sight" [143]) and in "Seymour: An Introduction" ("The sage is full of anxiety and indecision in undertaking anything, and so he is always successful" [240]). Lieh-Tzu's parable story about the superlative horse is quoted in full at the beginning of "RAISE HIGH THE ROOF BEAM, CARPENTERS" (4–5) (though Salinger does not name the author, referring to it simply as a Taoist tale). Within the Glass stories, Lao-Tzu is not directly quoted. In "Raise High the Roof Beam, Carpenters," Seymour refers to the Tao in his diary in relation to the concept of indiscrimination: "*Followed purely* it's the way of the Tao, and undoubtedly the highest way" (86). Eberhard Alsen and Dennis O'Connor have written essays on Taoism's influence on Salinger ("'Raise High the Roof Beam, Carpenters' and the Amateur Reader" and "J. D. Salinger's Religious Pluralism: The Example of 'Raise High the Roof Beam, Carpenters,'" respectively). Eugene Dale Antonio's dissertation, "The Fiction of J. D. Salinger: A Search through Taoism," is the most extensive treatment of the subject. Antonio finds Salinger's "dependence on anecdotes and the use of self-deprecation to elicit humor" (Antonio 5) characteristic of Taoist tales. Taoist tales also "tend to be didactic, building to a climax in which a message or moral is presented" (Antonio 5); Antonio sees their structural influence on the ending of "Zooey."

Lao-Tzu (sixth century B.C.E.) is credited with the authorship of the founding document of Taoism, the *Tao Te Ching*. Less than 6,000 lines of poetic prose, the text elevates the Tao ("the path" or "the way") to a mystical level of meaning.

Another main concept is *wu wei*, to act without acting. Scholars disagree whether Lao-Tzu, Lieh-Tzu (fifth century B.C.E.) or Chuang-Tzu (fourth century B.C.E.) were actual persons. The three "authors" of classical Taoism may be thought to embody idealized Chinese sages.

Twain, Mark (1835–1910) In 1958, the critics Joseph L. Blotner and Frederick L. Gwynn foretellingly commented, "It is not inconceivable that some day Holden Caulfield may be as well known an American boy as Huck Finn" (Gwynn 29). Mark Twain (pseudonym of Samuel Langhorne Clemens), possibly the most famous author in American literature, created the immortal Huck Finn. Salinger never names Twain or Huck Finn in his works. He refers to *The Adventures of Tom Sawyer* in "ZOOEY" (49), and Tom himself, Huck Finn's equally immortal friend, in "SEYMOUR: AN INTRODUCTION" (161). In 1951, Salinger listed the (deceased) writers he loved. The only American on the list was Henry James. Nonetheless, since the 1950s, critics have noted the link between The CATCHER IN THE RYE (1951) and *Adventures of Huckleberry Finn* (1884). The classic essay is Edgar Branch's 1957 "Mark Twain and J. D. Salinger: A Study in Literary Continuity." Branch explores the use of a first-person vernacular narrative and the similarity between the authors' characterization of the two boys, and con-

Mark Twain wrote *Adventures of Huckleberry Finn*, which critics view as a source for *The Catcher in the Rye*. *(Courtesy of Library of Congress)*

cludes that "each book is a devastating criticism of American society and voices a morality of love and humanity" (Branch 153).

Twain was born in Missouri. At one time a licensed steamboat pilot on the Mississippi River, after the Civil War he was a journalist who wrote humorous sketches about frontier life. Twain became a very successful author but would experience personal tragedy with the death of his wife and two daughters. The humorist ended his life with a pessimistic vision of mankind. Twain's best known works include *The Celebrated Jumping Frog of Calaveras County, and Other Sketches* (1867), *The Innocents Abroad* (1869), *The Adventures of Tom Sawyer* (1876), and *A Connecticut Yankee in King Arthur's Court* (1889). *Adventures of Huckleberry Finn* ranks as one of America's most important 19th-century novels.

University of Kansas City Review *University of Kansas City Review* published one of Salinger's stories: "Go See Eddie" (December 1940). Earlier that year, Salinger had informed the editor, Professor Alexander P. Cappon, that he wrote verse and may submit some later. The subject matter of "Go See Eddie" required the editor to defend his decision to the college administration.

The review was founded by the University of Kansas City, a small, private college in 1934. Rechristened *New Letters* in 1971, the review reprinted "Go See Eddie" in the Fall 1978 issue. The editor, David Ray, had the idea of reprinting the story and, over a five-year period, wrote Salinger three times, without receiving a response. After a copyright search failed to indicate the story had passed to Salinger, Ray went ahead and reprinted "Go See Eddie," doubling the journal's usual print run to 5,000 copies.

Ursinus College Salinger attended small, insular Ursinus College in Collegeville, Pennsylvania, for the fall semester of 1938. He wrote a column and two drama reviews for the student newspaper, *Ursinus Weekly*. Salinger possibly had enough units from his year at New York University's Washington Square College to be classified as a sophomore (his first column for the newspaper was titled, "Mus-

ings of a Social Soph: The Skipped Diploma"). An article, however, appearing in *Ursinus Weekly* during 1961 refers to Salinger as a "retread" freshman whose "record in the Dean's office is tantalizingly blank" (Swinton 2). Salinger's second through ninth weekly columns were titled "J. D. S.'s THE SKIPPED DIPLOMA." This prophetically foretells Salinger's abrupt exit from Ursinus in December 1938. In the documentary *J. D. Salinger Doesn't Want to Talk*, a former classmate, Frances Glassmoyer, says that no one at Ursinus had ever seen or met anyone like Jerry Salinger. He arrived on campus dressed in an elegant chesterfield coat and hat, a former resident of MANHATTAN and seasoned traveler of Europe. Salinger had gone back to college to avoid entering his father's business. Perhaps Ursinus was chosen due to its proximity to VALLEY FORGE MILITARY ACADEMY, 17 miles away.

Ursinus College, founded in 1869, was named after Zacharias Ursinus, a 16th-century German theologian. The 168-acre campus is located 25 miles from Philadelphia. Salinger undoubtedly is the most famous person to attend Ursinus. A framed Salinger letter, which speaks fondly of his time at Ursinus, hangs in the lobby of the school's admissions office. In 2006, the college created a four-year scholarship totaling $100,000 for a creative-writing student and named it after Salinger. The winner would also get to live in Salinger's former room on the third floor of Curtis Hall. The college, however, had failed to get the author's permission to use his name. Salinger's agent requested that his name be removed from the scholarship. Ursinus College today has 1,700 students; they come from 28 states and seven foreign countries.

Valley Forge Military Academy Salinger graduated in the class of 1936 from Valley Forge Military Academy, an all-male college preparatory boarding school, located in Wayne, Pennsylvania. He attended Valley Forge for his junior and senior years only. During his senior year, he was the literary editor of the class yearbook, *Crossed Sabres*, and composed a substantial though unsigned portion of it. Salinger's first "publication" of his writing career is the signed "CLASS POEM," which closes the yearbook. The poem describes the cadets' graduation day; it has since become established as the school's graduation song. Salinger graduated with final scores of English 88, German 84, French 83, Modern European History 79. He acted in several plays as a member of the Mask and Spur, a drama club. Valley Forge Military Academy served as a model for Holden Caulfield's Pencey Prep in *The CATCHER IN THE RYE*.

Valley Forge Military Academy was founded in 1928 by Colonel Milton G. Baker. His original vision of a military ethos based on the American Revolutionary War evolved into one influenced by the British army and West Point. The campus is located 15 miles west of Philadelphia and 105 miles from NEW YORK CITY. Salinger's parents most likely saw ads for the school. In *The Catcher in the Rye*, Holden Caulfield says of Pencey Prep, "they advertise in about a thousand magazines, always showing some hot-shot guy on a horse jumping over a fence" (4). Sean McDaniel's *A Catcher's Companion: The World of Holden Caulfield* reproduces an ad for Valley Forge Military Academy that ran in *National Geographic* magazine in 1949. The ad shows a boy in military uniform on a horse jumping over a fence. The ad mentions "30 fireproof buildings, Motorized Field Artillery, Cavalry (75 horses), Infantry, Band, Sr. R.O.T.C." (McDaniel 26). After his induction into the army, Salinger wrote Colonel Baker asking for a letter of recommendation so the author could apply for Office Candidate School. In 1952, Salinger was chosen to receive a distinguished alumnus award. Other notable Valley Forge alumni include the American playwright Edward Albee, U.S. senator Warren B. Rudman, and General Norman Schwarzkopf.

Vedanta Vedanta is a philosophy that evolved from the world's oldest religious writings, the *Vedas* of ancient India. The essential principles of Vedanta are "the non-duality of the Godhead, the divinity of the soul, the unity of existence, and the harmony of religions" (Nikhilananda 8). Salinger references Vedanta in three of his stories: "TEDDY" (286), "RAISE HIGH THE ROOF BEAM, CARPENTERS" (106), and "SEYMOUR: AN INTRODUCTION" (242).

Vedanta "does not repudiate the various deities of the different faiths, but includes them as the manifestations of the One" (Nikhilananda 8). It stresses that "no prophet is unique in the sense that he is the greatest of all. . . . Christ, Buddha, Mohammed, Krishna, and Moses . . . all experienced the same goodness, beauty, and truth" (Nikhilananda 182). Vedanta can be likened to the universal religion. It "is not a creed or a doctrine; it is an experience. It is God-consciousness" (Nikhilananda 193). Salinger's Glass stories fully exhibit the importance of Vedanta for the author's works. The spectrum of references to Christianity, ZEN, Mahayana Buddhism, TAOISM, the Old Testament, and Vedanta attest to Salinger's embracing the idea of the harmony of religions. His references to Christ, Saint Francis, Buddha, SRI RAMAKRISHNA, SWAMI VIVEKANANDA, Shankaracharya, Lao-tzu, Chuang-tzu, and Hui-neng attest to Salinger's belief in nonhierarchical religious prophets.

Sumitra Paniker was the first scholar to stress the importance of Vedanta to Salinger and his works. Paniker's dissertation, "The Influence of Eastern Thought on 'Teddy' and the Seymour Glass Stories of J. D. Salinger" (1971), represents a historically important advance in Salinger scholarship. Until that time, Zen was perceived as the dominant influence on Salinger's later works. Paniker's dissertation predates, by a dozen years, Eberhard Alsen's exploration of Vedanta in *Salinger's Glass Stories as a Composite Novel*. Som P. Ranchan's *An Adventure in Vedanta: J. D. Salinger's The Glass Family*, an explication written in the late 1960s by an Indian steeped in his country's religions and philosophies, was not published until 1989.

Vivekananda, Swami (1863–1902) Swami Vivekananda, SRI RAMAKRISHNA's most important disciple, came to America in 1893 to represent Hinduism at the Parliament of Religions held in Chicago. In 1895, he founded the first Vedanta Society in America "to serve Western men and women by bringing to them the message of Vedanta in order to deepen their spiritual consciousness and their religious outlook" (Nikhilananda 144). Salinger has Buddy Glass approvingly quote from "the great" Vivekananda in "SEYMOUR: AN INTRODUCTION" (127). Seymour Glass writes memorably about

Swami Vivekananda, who founded the first Vedanta Society in America in 1895, is praised by Salinger in the Glass stories. *(Courtesy of the Ramakrishna-Vivekananda Center of New York)*

one. A writer, a poet, a dreamer, and a dynamic speaker, he was also the founder of the Ramakrishna Order of monks, which is dedicated to religious, educational, and philanthropic activities" (Vivekananda viii).

World Review   *World Review,* a literary monthly based in London, England, published one of Salinger's stories: "DE DAUMIER-SMITH'S BLUE PERIOD" (May 1952). This publication marked the only time a Salinger story was first published abroad. (To the author's dismay, the NEW YORKER had rejected the story.) *World Review* had previously reprinted "FOR ESMÉ—WITH LOVE AND SQUALOR" in its August 1950 issue, four months after the story's publication in the *New Yorker*. Founded in 1936, *World Review* ceased publication in 1953.

Zen   Zen Buddhism, better known as Zen, is first referenced in Salinger's work in the epigraph of NINE STORIES (1953): "We know the sound of two hands clapping. But what is the sound of one hand clapping?–a Zen koan." This reference to the most famous of Zen koans, in addition to later references to Zen, led critics to initially overvalue Zen's importance to Salinger. (Salinger has Buddy Glass, the author's alter ego, state, in the 1959 story, "SEYMOUR: AN INTRODUCTION," that he is "neither a Zen archer nor a Zen Buddhist, much less a Zen adept" [242].) Although Salinger had referenced VEDANTA in the last story of *Nine Stories* (the 1953 "TEDDY"), and would reference both Vedanta and TAOISM in the 1955 "RAISE HIGH THE ROOF BEAM, CARPENTERS," critics seemed to notice only the allusions to Zen in the latter story (53, 82). The 1957 story, "ZOOEY," contains the most Zen allusions in his work. Salinger refers to D. T. Suzuki, the Japanese professor and writer who single-handedly introduced Zen to the Western world. Suzuki also taught at Columbia University in NEW YORK CITY (1952–1957), and Salinger reportedly attended lectures and became acquainted with him. Additionally in "Zooey," there are two references to Hui-neng (637–713), the sixth and last patriarch of Chinese Zen (65, 190), and Salinger quotes from *Mu-Mon-Kwan (The Gateless Gate),* a collection of Zen stories (178).

Vivekananda in "HAPWORTH 16, 1924" as "one of the most exciting, original, and best equipped giants of this century . . . my personal sympathy for him will never be outgrown or exhausted as long as I live" (92), and he mentions two of Vivekananda's books on yoga.

Vivekananda lived and taught for seven weeks in 1895 at what is now called the Vivekananda Cottage in Thousand Island Park, in Upstate New York. The cottage is a historically important place of pilgrimage. Salinger took part in retreat classes taught there by SWAMI NIKHILANANDA. Vivekananda is honored as one of the great men of modern India. Nikhilananda, in his introductory biography to Vivekananda's compendium of works, calls him "a philosopher, a man of action, a devotee of God, and an introspective yogi, all in

The critics Bernice and Sanford Goldstein elucidate their interpretation of Zen's influence on Salinger in four main essays: "Zen and Salinger," "Some Zen References in Salinger," "Bunnies and Cobras: Zen Enlightenment in Salinger," and "Zen and *Nine Stories*." A pamphlet, *Zen in the Art of J. D. Salinger*, by Gerald Rosen, despite the title, focuses on the critic's perception of the influence of Buddha and Buddhism on *The Catcher in the Rye*.

Zen (the word means "meditation") is a form of Mahayana Buddhism that emphasizes meditating on nonrational, paradoxical koans to, as it were, trick or trigger the mind into sudden illumination, known as *satori*. Zen was brought from India into China in the year 520 by Bodhidharma, the first patriarch of Chinese Zen. In the 12th century, Zen was introduced into Japan. Its impact on that country's culture and arts was profound. In the 1940s, Zen started to become known in America and, as Salinger suggests in "Seymour: An Introduction," by the late 1950s it was widely misunderstood (242).

In relation to Salinger, of special significance is Zen's infusing the poetic form, the haiku. R. H. Blyth's translations of haikus, and his interpretation of Zen and haiku, greatly influenced Salinger. Of particular note is Salinger's decision to make Seymour Glass a haiku poet or, one better, a "double-haiku" poet. Blyth defines haiku as "the expression of a temporary enlightenment, in which we see into the life of things" (Blyth 1949, 241). The poet's task is "to convey something of what he has seen, to convey rather, *the power of seeing*" (Blyth 1949, 249). Blyth's most telling statement is that he understands "Zen and poetry to be practically synonyms, [but] if there is ever imagined to be any conflict between Zen and the poetry of haiku, the Zen goes overboard; poetry is the ultimate standard" (Blyth 1949, 7). Throughout Salinger's works, poetry's eminence is upheld.

PART IV

Appendices

A Salinger Chronology

1919

January 1: Jerome David Salinger is born in New York City. He is the second child of Solomon ("Sol") Salinger (born in Cleveland, Ohio, and of the Jewish faith) and Marie Jillich (born in Atlantic, Iowa, and of the Catholic faith). Marie converted to Judaism and changed her name to Miriam for the formal Jewish wedding ceremony. Salinger's only sibling, Doris, was born on December 17, 1912.

1930

Summer: Salinger attends a summer camp, Camp Wigwam, in Harrison, Maine. Performing in at least four plays, he is voted the most popular actor.

1931

Fall: Salinger begins his last year at a public school.

1932

January: Salinger is bar mitzvahed; shortly thereafter, he and his sister are shocked when told that their mother is not Jewish by birth. (In her memoir, Margaret Ann Salinger, the author's daughter, infers that the bar mitzvah may have been delayed until 1933.)

Fall: The Salingers move from the Upper West Side of Manhattan to 1133 Park Avenue on the Upper East Side. Sol has become progressively successful as an executive at Hoffman and Company, an importer of cheeses and meats.

For his first year of high school, Salinger is enrolled in McBurney School, a private school in Manhattan. He performs in one school play. Academically, he does poorly.

1933

Fall: In his second year of high school, Salinger performs in two school plays and is manager of the fencing team. His grades worsen, and he will be forced to attend summer school.

1934

September: Salinger is enrolled in Valley Forge Military Academy, an all-male college-preparatory boarding school in Wayne, Pennsylvania. During his two years at Valley Forge, he will perform in a number of school plays. His grades markedly improve. He scores 115 on an IQ test.

Fall: Salinger begins to write creatively at Valley Forge.

1935

September: Salinger begins his senior year at Valley Forge. He is the literary editor of the Class of '36's yearbook, *Crossed Sabres.*

1936

June: Salinger's first signed publication, a poem titled "Class Poem," appears in the Valley Forge yearbook, *Crossed Sabres.* Salinger graduates from Valley Forge Military Academy.

Fall: Salinger attends New York University's Washington Square College during the academic year 1936–37. He will not return the following year.

Events in Literature—1936: [Note: In this section, books of poetry and staged plays will be included for 1936 through 1945, the last known year that Salinger is writing in those two genres. The Pulitzer Prizes for fiction, poetry, and drama will be listed through 1945. From 1946 through 1965, the final year of a new Salinger work, only the publication of books of fiction will be listed. The Pulitzer Prize for fiction will be noted up to the present. The National Book Award for fiction will be noted from its year of inception, 1950, up to the present. The Nobel Prize in literature will be noted when awarded to an American author.]

The following books are published during the year of Salinger's first signed publication: *Kit Brandon*, by Sherwood Anderson; *My Ten Years in a Quandary, and How They Grew*, by Robert Benchley; *The Big Money*, by John Dos Passos; *Collected Poems, 1909–1935*, by T. S. Eliot; *Absalom, Absalom!* by William Faulkner; *A Further Range*, by Robert Frost; *Gone with the Wind*, by Margaret Mitchell; *The Pangolin and Other Verse*, by Marianne Moore; *Not So Deep as a Well*, by Dorothy Parker; *Inhale and Exhale*, by William Saroyan; *In Dubious Battle*, by John Steinbeck. The following theatrical productions are staged: *End of Summer*, by S. N. Behrman; *Stage Door*, by George S. Kaufman and Edna Ferber; *You Can't Take It with You*, by George S. Kaufman and Moss Hart; *The Women*, by Clare Boothe Luce.

The Pulitzer Prize for fiction is awarded to H. L. Davis's *Honey in the Horn*; for poetry to Robert Coffin's *Strange Holiness*; for drama to Robert Sherwood's *Idiot's Delight*.

The Nobel Prize in literature is awarded to Eugene O'Neill.

1937

Mid-August: Salinger sails for Europe, where he will travel for about eight months, mostly in Vienna, Paris, London, and Poland. In Vienna, he writes English advertising copy and improves his German. In Poland, he experiences pig-slaughtering. He mails stories to American magazines only to have them rejected.

Events in Literature—1937: The following books are published: *The Sleeping Fury*, by Louise Bogan; *To Have and Have Not*, by Ernest Hemingway; *They Came Like Swallows*, by William Maxwell; *Conversation at Midnight*, by Edna St. Vincent Millay; *Strictly from Hunger*, by S. J. Perelman; *Of Mice and Men*, by John Steinbeck; *Selected Poems*, by Allen Tate; *Let Your Mind Alone! and Other More or Less Inspirational Pieces*, by James Thurber. The following theatri-

cal productions are staged: *The Headless Horseman*, by Stephen Vincent Benet; *The Fall of the City*, by Archibald MacLeish; *Golden Boy*, by Clifford Odets.

The Pulitzer Prize for fiction is awarded to Margaret Mitchell's *Gone with the Wind*; for poetry to Robert Frost's *A Further Range*; for drama to George S. Kaufman and Moss Hart's *You Can't Take It with You*.

1938

Early: Salinger returns to New York City from Europe.

Summer: Salinger meets Elizabeth Murray, the older sister of a school friend. Murray encourages his writing.

September: Salinger enrolls in Ursinus College, in Collegeville, Pennsylvania. He will not return for the spring semester.

October 10: Salinger publishes the first of nine weekly columns, and two reviews of college plays, in the student newspaper, *Ursinus Weekly*. Apparently, he doesn't perform in any plays.

Events in Literature—1938: The following books are published: *Collected Poems*, by e. e. cummings; *U.S.A.*, by John Dos Passos; *The Unvanquished*, by William Faulkner; *The Fifth Column and the First Forty-nine Stories*, by Ernest Hemingway; *The Prodigal Parents*, by Sinclair Lewis; *I'm a Stranger Here Myself*, by Ogden Nash; *Hope of Heaven*, by John O'Hara; *The Happy Island*, by Dawn Powell; *Love, Here Is My Hat, and Other Short Romances*, by William Saroyan; *Complete Collected Poems, 1906–1938*, by William Carlos Williams. The following theatrical productions are staged: *Kiss the Boys Goodbye*, by Clare Boothe Luce; *Our Town*, by Thorton Wilder.

The Pulitzer Prize for fiction is awarded to J. P. Marquand's *The Late George Apley*; for poetry to Marya Zaturenska's *Cold Morning Sky*; for drama to Thorton Wilder's *Our Town*.

The Nobel Prize in literature is awarded to Pearl S. Buck.

1939

Spring: Salinger enrolls in Whit Burnett's short-story class and Charles Hanson Towne's poetry-writing class in the Columbia University Extension Division.

May 24: Charles Hanson Towne inscribes a copy of his book, *An April Song,* to "Jerome Salinger, for his unfailing attention in the Spring Course, 1939, at Columbia University."

September 1: World War II begins.

Fall: Salinger enrolls in Whit Burnett's short-story class in the Columbia University Extension Division for a second semester.

Events in Literature—1939: The following books are published: *The Big Sleep,* by Raymond Chandler; *Old Possum's Book of Practical Cats,* by T. S. Eliot; *Pale Horse, Pale Rider,* by Katherine Anne Porter; *The Grapes of Wrath,* by John Steinbeck; *Johnny Got His Gun,* by Dalton Trumbo; *The Day of the Locust,* by Nathanael West. The following theatrical productions are staged: *The Philadelphia Story,* by Philip Barry; *No Time for Comedy,* by S. N. Behrman; *The Family Reunion,* by T. S. Eliot; *The Little Foxes,* by Lillian Hellman; *My Heart's in the Highlands,* by William Saroyan.

The Pulitzer Prize for fiction is awarded to Marjorie K. Rawlings's *The Yearling;* for poetry to John Gould Fletcher's *Selected Poems;* for drama to Robert Sherwood's *Abe Lincoln in Illinois.*

1940

January: Whit Burnett decides to publish one of Salinger's class assignments, the story "The Young Folks," in an issue of his magazine, *Story.*

January 13: Salinger informs the editor of the *University of Kansas City Review* that he writes verse and may submit some later.

January 15: Salinger learns of *Story's* acceptance of "The Young Folks." He tells Whit Burnett that, since the age of 17, writing has been important to him.

January 28: Salinger informs Whit Burnett that he will not be returning to Columbia.

Mid-late February: The March–April issue of *Story* is published. Pages 26 to 30 are devoted to Salinger's first published story, "The Young Folks." (Salinger shares the table of contents with Vivian Connell, Frank Brookhouser, V. G. Calderon, Jeanne Singer, Emmett Gowen, Alphabelle Daily, Edward Havill, and Lionel Wiggam.) Salinger will publish 35 stories in his career (four of them in Burnett's magazine) and one novel before his decision to forgo future publication of his work.

May 3: Salinger continues to work on plays and tells Whit Burnett that he wants to act in them. He asks whether Burnett knows of an agent who specializes in plays.

May 15: Salinger attends the Writers Club dinner with Whit Burnett.

September 4: Salinger informs Whit Burnett that he is thinking about an autobiographical novel.

September 5: Following Salinger's reminder, *Story* finally sends him the $25 payment for "The Young Folks."

December: "Go See Eddie," Salinger's second published story, appears in the *University of Kansas City Review.*

December 21: F. Scott Fitzgerald dies.

Events in Literature—1940: The *New Yorker* publishes its first anthology of short stories. The 68 selections are taken from the magazine's first 15 years. Some of the chosen authors include Sherwood Anderson, Sally Benson, Louise Bogan, Kay Boyle, Erskine Caldwell, John Cheever, Christopher Isherwood, William Maxwell, John O'Hara, Dorothy Parker, Dawn Powell, Marjorie Kinnan Rawlings, Irwin Shaw, James Thurber, E. B. White, and Thomas Wolfe.

The following books are published: *Another Time,* by W. H. Auden; *Against the Cold,* by Witter Bynner; *Sapphira and the Slave Girl,* by Willa Cather; *But Who Wakes the Bugler?* by Peter de Vries; *The Hamlet,* by William Faulkner; *For Whom the Bells Toll,* by Ernest Hemingway; *The Heart Is a Lonely Hunter,* by Carson McCullers; *Cantos LII-LXXI,* by Ezra Pound; *My Wife Ethel,* by Damon Runyon; *World's End,* by Upton Sinclair; *You Can't Go Home Again,* by Thomas Wolfe; *Native Son,* by Richard Wright. The following theatrical productions are staged: *Pal Joey,* by Lorenz Hart and Richard Rodgers; *Long Day's Journey into Night,* by Eugene O'Neill.

The Pulitzer Prize for fiction is awarded to John Steinbeck's *The Grapes of Wrath;* for poetry to Mark Van Doren's *Collected Poems;* for drama to William Saroyan's *The Time of Your Life.*

1941

February 15: Salinger sails from New York on the *Kungsholm* for a 19-day cruise to the West Indies as a member of the social staff.

Summer: Elizabeth Murray introduces the 16-year-old Oona O'Neill, daughter of the playwright Eugene O'Neill, to Salinger. Oona and Salinger begin to date and correspond.

July 12: "The Hang of It," Salinger's third published story, appears in *Collier's*. Salinger will publish three more stories in this magazine.

September: "The Heart of a Broken Story," Salinger's fourth published story, appears in *Esquire*. Salinger will publish one more story in this magazine.

October 31: Salinger informs Elizabeth Murray that he has sold the story "Slight Rebellion Off Madison" to the *New Yorker* and that the magazine wants him to write more stories about its protagonist, Holden Caulfield.

December 7: Japan bombs Pearl Harbor; the United States enters World War II.

After December 7: To Salinger's great dismay, the *New Yorker* decides to delay the imminent publication of "Slight Rebellion Off Madison" because the story clashes with recent war developments.

December 12: Salinger informs Colonel Milton Baker of Valley Forge Military Academy that he was classified 1-B, unfit to be drafted, due to a slight cardiac condition. He tells Baker, however, that he wants to do defense work.

During 1941: Salinger signs with the Harold Ober Agency; Dorothy Olding becomes his agent.

The *New Yorker* rejects seven Salinger stories.

Events in Literature—1941: The following books are published: *The Last Tycoon*, by F. Scott Fitzgerald; *Be Angry at the Sun*, by Robinson Jeffers; *Reflections in a Golden Eye*, by Carson McCullers; *Open House*, by Theodore Roethke; *What Makes Sammy Run*, by Bud Schulberg; *A Curtain of Green, and Other Stories*, by Eudora Welty. The following theatrical productions are staged: *Arsenic and Old Lace*, by Joseph Kesselring; *The Beautiful People*, by William Saroyan.

The Pulitzer Prize for poetry is awarded to Leonard Bacon's *Sunderland Capture*; for drama to Robert Sherwood's *There Shall Be No Night*; no fiction award.

1942

April: Salinger is reclassified as fit to serve and is drafted into the army.

April 27: Salinger reports to Fort Dix, New Jersey, and is then transferred to Fort Monmouth, New Jersey, for an instructor's course with the Signal Corps.

Summer: Salinger wants to attend Officer Candidate School but is not accepted. He is assigned an instructor's job with the Army Aviation Cadets in Bainbridge, Georgia.

September–October: "The Long Debut of Lois Taggett," Salinger's fifth published story, appears in *Story*.

November–December: *Story* devotes an entire issue to a novella about Robert Burns, coauthored by Whit Burnett. The first page quotes from a Burns poem, "[if] a body meet a body . . . coming through the rye."

December 12: "Personal Notes on an Infantryman," Salinger's sixth published story, appears in *Collier's*.

During 1942: Salinger's first publication in a book appears when the story "The Hang of It" is reprinted in *The Kitbook for Soldiers, Sailors, and Marines*, edited by R. M. Barrows.

Events in Literature—1942: The following books are published: *Never Come Morning*, by Nelson Algren; *The Robe*, by Lloyd C. Douglas; *Go Down, Moses and Other Stories*, by William Faulkner; *A Witness Tree*, by Robert Frost; *The Company She Keeps*, by Mary McCarthy; *The Moon Is Down*, by John Steinbeck; *My World—and Welcome to It*, by James Thurber. The following theatrical productions are staged: *This Is the Army*, by Irving Berlin; *The Doughgirls*, by Joseph Fields.

The Pulitzer Prize for fiction is awarded to Ellen Glasgow's *In This Our Life*; for poetry to William Rose Benet's *The Dust Which Is God*; no award for drama.

1943

June 16: Oona O'Neill weds Charlie Chaplin.

Summer: Salinger is transferred from Nashville, Tennessee, to Patterson Field in Fairfield, Ohio.

July 17: "The Varioni Brothers," Salinger's seventh published story, appears in the *Saturday Evening Post*. Salinger will publish four more stories in this magazine.

October: Salinger is transferred to Fort Holabird, Maryland, to train for the Counter Intelligence Corps.

Events in Literature—1943: The following books are published: *Two Serious Ladies,* by Jane Bowles; *The Way Some People Live,* by John Cheever; *Four Quartets,* by T. S. Eliot; *The Fountainhead,* by Ayn Rand; *The Human Comedy,* by William Saroyan; *The Big Rock Candy Mountain,* by Wallace Stegner. The following theatrical productions are staged: *One Touch of Venus,* by S. J. Perelman and Ogden Nash; *Oklahoma!* by Richard Rodgers and Oscar Hammerstein.

The Pulitzer Prize for fiction is awarded to Upton Sinclair's *Dragon's Teeth;* for poetry to Robert Frost's *A Witness Tree;* for drama to Thornton Wilder's *The Skin of Our Teeth.*

1944

January 14: Salinger informs Whit Burnett that he has sold three stories to the *Saturday Evening Post* and that he is awaiting military orders to ship overseas.

January 18: Attached to the 12th Infantry Regiment, 4th Division, Salinger begins an 11-day voyage to England.

February 26: "Both Parties Concerned," Salinger's eighth published story, appears in the *Saturday Evening Post.* The magazine supplies the title, instead of Salinger's "Wake Me When It Thunders."

February–May: Salinger is in Devon, England, for more training with the Counter Intelligence Corps.

April 14: Whit Burnett suggests Salinger publish a volume of short stories, titled *The Young Folks,* with Story Press.

April 15: "Soft-Boiled Sergeant," Salinger's ninth published story, appears in the *Saturday Evening Post.* The magazine supplies the title, instead of Salinger's "Death of a Dogface."

May 2: Salinger informs Whit Burnett of his ambivalence about publishing a book of his stories at this time, but he lists what he considers his best stories to date: "The Young Folks," "The Long Debut of Lois Taggett," "Elaine," "Last Day of the Last Furlough," "Death of a Dogface," "Wake Me When It Thunders," "Once a Week Won't Kill You," and "Bitsey." Salinger has also completed six stories about Holden Caulfield that are slated for the novel. He decides, however, that the novel needs to be written in the first person and put off until after the war. Salinger contributes $200 to *Story's* short-story contest for college students.

June 6: D-day. Salinger, with the 12th Infantry Regiment, 4th Division, lands on Utah Beach, Normandy. The event begins his 11-month experience of the inferno of World War II, until victory is declared on May 7, 1945.

July 15: "Last Day of the Last Furlough," Salinger's 10th published story, appears in the *Saturday Evening Post.* This story is the first published Salinger work to contain a character named Caulfield (Vincent) and a reference to his brother Holden.

August 25: Salinger's regiment arrives in Paris on Liberation Day.

After August 25: Salinger meets Ernest Hemingway in Paris. Hemingway praises Salinger's work.

November–December: "Once a Week Won't Kill You," Salinger's 11th published story, appears in *Story.*

Salinger's regiment takes part in the bloody battle of Hürtgen Forest.

During 1944: The *New Yorker* rejects all of Salinger's submissions.

Events in Literature—1944: The following books are published: *Dangling Man,* by Saul Bellow; *The Walls Do Not Fall,* by H. D.; *A Bell for Adano,* by John Hersey; *Land of Unlikeness,* by Robert Lowell; *The Leaning Tower and Other Stories,* by Katherine Anne Porter; *Boston Adventure,* by Jean Stafford. The following theatrical productions are staged: *The Man Who Had All the Luck,* by Arthur Miller; *The Glass Menagerie,* by Tennessee Williams.

The Pulitzer Prize for fiction is awarded to Martin Flavin's *Journey in the Dark;* for poetry to Stephen Vincent Benet's *Western Star;* no award for drama.

1945

March–April: "Elaine," Salinger's 12th published story, appears in *Story.*

March 31: "A Boy in France," Salinger's 13th published story, appears in the *Saturday Evening Post.*

ca. April–May: Salinger is among the first to arrive at an unidentified concentration camp. Margaret Ann Salinger quotes her father as saying,

"You never really get the smell of burning flesh out of your nose entirely, no matter how long you live."

May 7: V-E Day: The Allies achieve victory in Europe.

July 27: Salinger, who has admitted himself to an army hospital in Germany because of depression and battle fatigue, writes to Ernest Hemingway. Since last seeing Hemingway, Salinger has written a couple of stories, several poems, and part of a play about Holden Caulfield. He tells Hemingway that he does not mind that the publication of his volume of stories has fallen through. (If, indeed, this refers to the Story Press publication, it possibly alters the usual assignation of 1946.) In the letter, Salinger expresses his desire to leave the army, but not on a psychiatric discharge. The honorable discharge is important to him, as he plans to publish an emotional novel circa 1950 and does not want to provide future reviewers with a basis of attack.

August 6: The United States drops the atomic bomb on Hiroshima, Japan.

October: "This Sandwich Has No Mayonnaise," Salinger's 14th published story, appears in *Esquire*.

November: Salinger is honorably discharged from the army. In Switzerland, he weds Sylvia, a German-born, naturalized French citizen. She is an ophthalmologist. According to Salinger's daughter, Margaret Ann, Sylvia was a low-level Nazi who had previously been arrested by Salinger.

December: Salinger signs a six-month contract with the U.S. Department of Defense for undisclosed civilian work.

December 1: "The Stranger," Salinger's 15th published story, appears in *Collier's*.

December 22: "I'm Crazy," Salinger's 16th published story, appears in *Collier's*. This story is the first Salinger work narrated by Holden Caulfield to see publication.

During 1945: "A Boy in France" is included in a book collection, *The Saturday Evening Post Stories, 1942–1945*, edited by Ben Hibbs.

The *New Yorker* rejects all of Salinger's submissions, including 15 poems.

The parent publisher of Story Press, Lippincott, nixes the publication of *The Young Folks* (as per July 27, 1945, letter to Hemingway).

Angered, Salinger severs relations with Whit Burnett. The table of contents would have been chosen from "The Daughter of the Late, Great Man," "Elaine,"* "The Last and Best of the Peter Pans," "Both Parties Concerned,"* "The Long Debut of Lois Taggett,"* "Bitsey," "The Young Folks,"* "I'm Crazy,"* "Boy Standing in Tennessee," "Once a Week Won't Kill You,"* "Last Day of the Last Furlough,"* "Soft-Boiled Sergeant,"* "The Children's Echelon," "Two Lonely Men," "A Boy in France,"* "A Young Man in a Stuffed Shirt," "The Magic Foxhole," "Slight Rebellion Off Madison,"* "What Got into Curtis in the Woodshed," and "The Ocean Full of Bowling Balls." Salinger never collected any of these 20 stories in one of his own books. The stories followed by an asterisk were published in magazines.

Events in Literature—1945: The following books are published: *Bolts of Melody*, by Emily Dickinson (previously unpublished poems); *The Crack-Up*, by F. Scott Fitzgerald; *The Forest of the South*, by Caroline Gordon; *The Ghostly Lover*, by Elizabeth Hardwick; *The Folded Leaf*, by William Maxwell; *Cannery Row*, by John Steinbeck; *The Thurber Carnival*, by James Thurber. The following theatrical productions are staged: *State of the Union*, by Russel Crouse and Howard Lindsay; *Home of the Brave*, by Arthur Laurents.

The Pulitzer Prize for fiction is awarded to John Hersey's *A Bell for Adano*; for poetry to Karl Shapiro's *V-Letter and Other Poems*; for drama to Mary Chase's *Harvey*.

1946

May 10: Salinger and his wife, Sylvia, arrive in New York; they live with his parents.

July: Salinger's wife returns to Europe and will file for a divorce.

December 21: "Slight Rebellion Off Madison," Salinger's 17th published story, finally appears in the *New Yorker* five years after its initial acceptance. Salinger will publish a total of 13 stories in this magazine.

During 1946: Salinger finishes a 90-page version of *The Catcher in the Rye*. Instead of accepting a publisher's offer, he decides to rewrite the work.

Salinger reads two stories by A. E. Hotchner and tells him that there is "no hidden emotion in these stories . . . no fire between the words."

The *New Yorker* rejects all of Salinger's submissions.

Don Congdon of Simon and Schuster fails to persuade Salinger to publish a volume of short stories with the firm.

Events in Literature—1946: The following books are published: *Thirty Stories,* by Kay Boyle; *The Member of the Wedding,* by Carson McCullers; *The Adventures of Wesley Jackson,* by William Saroyan; *All the King's Men,* by Robert Penn Warren; *Delta Wedding,* by Eudora Welty; *Memoirs of Hecate County,* by Edmund Wilson.

The Pulitzer Prize for fiction is not awarded.

1947

January: Salinger moves out of his parents' apartment for good and rents an apartment over a garage in Tarrytown, New York.

May: "A Young Girl in 1941 with No Waist at All," Salinger's 18th published story, appears in *Mademoiselle.*

December: "The Inverted Forest," Salinger's 19th published story, appears in *Cosmopolitan.* Salinger will publish one more story in this magazine.

Late: Salinger moves from Tarrytown to a barn studio in Stamford, Connecticut.

During 1947: A previous arrangement falls through between Salinger and Harcourt, Brace to publish "The Inverted Forest" as a separate book.

Events in Literature—1947: The following books are published: *The Victim,* by Saul Bellow; *Kingsblood Royal,* by Sinclair Lewis; *Tales of the South Pacific,* by James Michener; *Bend Sinister,* by Vladimir Nabokov; *The Harder They Fall,* by Bud Schulberg; *In a Yellow Wood,* by Gore Vidal; *Aurora Dawn,* by Herman Wouk.

The Pulitzer Prize for fiction is awarded to Robert Penn Warren's *All the King's Men.*

1948

January 31: "A Perfect Day for Bananafish," Salinger's 20th published story, appears in the *New Yorker.* This story inaugurates the Seymour Glass saga and represents the first published magazine story Salinger will eventually collect into one of his own books. The week the story appears, John Cheever writes, "I thought the Salinger piece was one hell of a story."

February: "A Girl I Knew," Salinger's 21st published story, appears in *Good Housekeeping.* The magazine supplies the title, instead of Salinger's "Wien, Wien."

March 20: "Uncle Wiggily in Connecticut," Salinger's 22nd published story, appears in the *New Yorker.*

June 5: "Just Before the War with the Eskimos," Salinger's 23rd published story, appears in the *New Yorker.*

September: "Blue Melody," Salinger's 24th published story, appears in *Cosmopolitan.* The magazine supplies the title, instead of Salinger's "Scratchy Needle on a Phonograph Record."

During 1948: The *New Yorker* offers Salinger a "first reading agreement" after publishing "A Perfect Day for Bananafish." The magazine will pass on three Salinger stories.

Events in Literature—1948: Stories by other notable authors published the same year as Salinger's "A Perfect Day for Bananafish," "A Girl I Knew," "Uncle Wiggily in Connecticut," "Just Before the War with the Eskimos," and "Blue Melody" include James Baldwin's "Previous Conditions," Paul Bowles's "Under the Sky," Kay Boyle's "Evening at Home," John Cheever's "O City of Broken Dreams," Peter de Vries's "Fagin's Pants," Ralph Ellison's "Battle Royal," Elizabeth Hardwick's "Evenings at Home," Joseph Heller's "Castle of Snow," Shirley Jackson's "Charles," James Jones's "Temper of Steel," Mary McCarthy's "The Cicerone," Flannery O'Connor's "The Train," John O'Hara's "Requiescat," and Jean Stafford's "Children Are Bored on Sunday."

The following books are published: *Peony,* by Pearl S. Buck; *Other Voices, Other Rooms,* by Truman Capote; *Guard of Honor,* by John Gould Cozzens; *Intruder in the Dust,* by William Faulkner; *The Naked and the Dead,* by Norman Mailer; *Time Will Darken It,* by William Maxwell; *The Young Lions,* by Irwin Shaw; *The Pearl,* by John Steinbeck; *The City and the Pillar,* by Gore Vidal.

The Pulitzer Prize for fiction is awarded to James Michener's *Tales of the South Pacific.*

The Nobel Prize in literature is awarded to T. S. Eliot.

1949

March 19: "The Laughing Man," Salinger's 25th published story, appears in the *New Yorker.*

April: "Down at the Dinghy," Salinger's 26th published story, appears in *Harper's.*

Fall: Salinger moves from Stamford, Connecticut, to a rented house in Westport, Connecticut.

November: Salinger speaks to a writing class at Sarah Lawrence College, at the invitation of Mrs. Hortense Flexner King, a faculty member.

During 1949: "A Perfect Day for Bananafish" is included in a book, the *New Yorker* anthology *55 Short Stories from The New Yorker.* Salinger is one of 55 authors selected for the publication and is joined by S. N. Behrman, Sally Benson, Kay Boyle, John Cheever, Shirley Jackson, William Maxwell, Mary McCarthy, Carson McCullers, Vladimir Nabokov, Frank O'Connor, John O'Hara, Marjorie Kinnan Rawlings, Irwin Shaw, Jean Stafford, James Thurber, and E. B. White.

"Just Before the War with the Eskimos" is included in a book, *Prize Stories of 1949,* edited by Herschel Brickell.

"The Long Debut of Lois Taggett" is included in a book, *Story: The Fiction of the Forties,* edited by Whit and Hallie Burnett.

"A Girl I Knew" is included in a book, *The Best American Short Stories of 1949,* edited by Martha J. Foley.

The *New Yorker* rejects seven Salinger stories.

Robert Giroux, an editor at Harcourt, Brace, contacts Salinger, asking him if he would be interested in publishing a volume of his short stories. Salinger tells him not yet; that the novel he is working on should come out first. Giroux agrees.

Events in Literature—1949: Stories by other notable authors published the same year as Salinger's "The Laughing Man" and "Down at the Dinghy" include Saul Bellow's "A Sermon by Dr. Pep," John Cheever's "The Temptations of Emma Boynton," Evan S. Connell's "I'll Take You to Tennessee," William Goyen's "A Bridge of Breath," Patricia Highsmith's "The Envious One," Wright Morris's "The Lover," Flannery O'Connor's "Woman on the Stairs," John O'Hara's "The Kids," William Saroyan's "The Parsley Garden," Gore Vidal's "The Robin," and Eudora Welty's "Moon Lake."

The following books are published: *The Man with the Golden Arm,* by Nelson Algren; *The Sheltering Sky,* by Paul Bowles; *Tree of Life and Other Stories,* by Truman Capote; *The Grand Design,* by John Dos Passos; *The Cannibal,* by John Hawkes; *A Rage to Live,* by John O'Hara; *The Golden Apples,* by Eudora Welty.

The Pulitzer Prize for fiction is awarded to James Gould Cozzens's *Guard of Honor.*

The Nobel Prize in literature is awarded to William Faulkner.

1950

January 21: *My Foolish Heart,* a movie based on "Uncle Wiggily in Connecticut," goes into general release. Embarrassed by the result, Salinger will not allow any of his other works to be made into films.

April 8: "For Esmé—with Love and Squalor," Salinger's 27th published story, appears in the *New Yorker.*

Early fall: After completing *The Catcher in the Rye,* Salinger, as he had promised, shows the work to Robert Giroux. Giroux wants to publish the novel but is overruled by Eugene Reynal of Harcourt, Brace, who wonders if Holden Caulfield is crazy. Later that fall, Salinger will sign a contract with Little, Brown and Company.

Salinger meets Claire Douglas, a 16-old schoolgirl, at a party given in the New York City apartment of the Flaubert scholar and translator Francis Steegmuller. Salinger and Claire begin a correspondence.

October: Salinger is photographed by Lotte Jacobi in her New York City studio on two occasions. At least 17 photos are taken; one will be used on the dust jacket of *The Catcher in the Rye.*

November 8: The carousel in New York City's Central Park, featured in the climactic scene of *The Catcher in the Rye,* is destroyed by fire.

During 1950: "For Esmé—with Love and Squalor" is included in a book, *Prize Stories of 1950: The O. Henry Awards,* edited by Herschel Brickell.

Events in Literature—1950: Stories by other notable authors published in the same year as Salinger's "For Esmé—with Love and Squalor," include Roger Angell's "Flight through the Dark," Saul Bellow's "The Trip to Galena," Whit Burnett's "The Everlasting Quartet," Truman Capote's "A Diamond Guitar," William Faulkner's "A Name for the City," Mavis Gallant's "The Flowers of Spring," Carson McCullers's "The Sojourner," Bernard Malamud's "The Cost of Living," Katherine Anne Porter's "The Prisoner," Dawn Powell's "Lemon, Please," William Saroyan's "The Poet Ashamed," James Thurber's "The Figgerin' of Aunt Wilma," and Tennessee Williams's "The Resemblance Between a Violin Case and a Coffin."

The following books are published: *The Delicate Prey and Other Stories*, by Paul Bowles; *Collected Stories*, by William Faulkner; *The House of Breath*, by William Goyen; *Across the River and into the Trees*, by Ernest Hemingway; *The Wall*, by John Hersey; *Strangers on a Train*, by Patricia Highsmith; *The Town and the City*, by Jack Kerouac; *Cast a Cold Eye*, by Mary McCarthy; *The Family Moskat*, by Isaac Bashevis Singer; *World Enough and Time*, by Robert Penn Warren; *The Roman Spring of Mrs. Stone*, by Tennessee Williams.

The Pulitzer Prize for fiction is awarded to A. B. Guthrie's *The Way West*.

The National Book Awards, in its first year, gives the prize for fiction to Nelson Algren's *The Man with the Golden Arm*.

1951

January: To Salinger's deep dismay, the *New Yorker* declines to publish any excerpts from the forthcoming *The Catcher in the Rye*.

Early: Salinger writes a four-paragraph autobiographical statement to be used in the promotion of the upcoming publication of *The Catcher in the Rye*. A portion of the text is incorporated into the author's biography on the dust jacket (designed by E. Michael Mitchell). The most interesting paragraph is not included on the dust jacket: "I'm aware that a number of my friends will be saddened, or shocked, or shocked-saddened, over some of the chapters of *The Catcher in the Rye*. Some of my best friends are children. In fact, all of my best friends are children. It's almost unbearable to me to realize that my book will be kept on a shelf out of their reach."

April: To generate orders, Little, Brown and Company sends 861 booksellers a prepublication publicity broadside consisting of the first three pages of *The Catcher in the Rye* and the dust-jacket author photo.

Mid-May: Salinger sails to England and will be out of the country when *The Catcher in the Rye* is released.

July 14: "Pretty Mouth and Green My Eyes," Salinger's 28th published story, appears in the *New Yorker*.

The cover of *Saturday Review* carries an artist sketch of Salinger. *The Catcher in the Rye* is a featured review.

July 16: Salinger's first book, and only novel, *The Catcher in the Rye*, is published by Little, Brown and Company. Salinger dedicates the book to his mother. A photograph of Salinger fills the back cover of the dust jacket. The novel is extensively reviewed; critical opinion runs the gamut from laudatory to damning.

Summer: *The Catcher in the Rye* is a Book-of-the-Month Club selection. To accompany the book, William Maxwell writes the first extended biographical article on Salinger. Salinger is quoted as saying, "I think writing is a hard life. . . . The compensations are few, but when they come, if they come, they're very beautiful."

Late July: At Salinger's insistence, his photograph is removed from the third printing of *The Catcher in the Rye*. Henceforth, books by Salinger will not carry author photos.

Upon his return from his trip, Salinger rents an apartment at 300 East 57th Street in Manhattan.

Fall: Flannery O'Connor writes, "I certainly enjoyed *The Catcher in the Rye*. Read it up the same day it arrived."

December 2: Salinger tells the *New York Times*, "I may give it [*The Catcher in the Rye*] away this Christmas, but not till I'm sure that boys really talk that way."

December 6: Harold Ross, founder and editor in chief of the *New Yorker*, dies.

December 10: Salinger attends the memorial service for Harold Ross.

December 30: Elizabeth Bowen calls *The Catcher in the Rye* "the novel about adolescence to end all: here the potential of tragedy is given an enchantingly comic sheath."

During 1951: *The Catcher in the Rye* is reprinted 11 times. The novel remains on the *Publishers*

Weekly best-seller list for five months but fails to make the list of the year's 10 top-selling fiction.

Spanning much of the second half of 1951, and into the early months of 1952, *The Catcher in the Rye* remains on the *New York Times* best-seller list for 29 weeks, reaching a high of number four.

The British edition of *The Catcher in the Rye* is published but is not a best seller.

Events in Literature—1951: The 10 top-selling volumes of fiction are, in descending order of sales: *From Here to Eternity*, by James Jones; *The Caine Mutiny*, by Herman Wouk; *Moses*, by Sholem Asch; *The Cardinal*, by Henry Morton Robinson; *A Woman Called Fancy*, by Frank Yerby; *The Cruel Sea*, by Nicholas Monsarrat; *Melville Goodwin, U.S.A.*, by J. P. Marquand; *Return to Paradise*, by James Michener; *The Foundling*, by Cardinal Spellman; *The Wanderer*, by Mike Waltari.

Stories by other notable authors published the same year as Salinger's "Pretty Mouth and Green My Eyes" include James Baldwin's "The Outing," Paul Bowles's "A Gift for Rinza," Truman Capote's "The House of Flowers," John Cheever's "Goodbye, My Brother," Bernard Malamud's "The Bill," Mary McCarthy's "The Groves of Academe," Jean Stafford's "The Healthiest Girl in Town," and Wallace Stegner's "The Traveler."

Books by other notable authors published the same year as Salinger's *The Catcher in the Rye* include *The Morning Watch*, by James Agee; *In the Absence of Angels*, by Hortense Calisher; *The Grass Harp*, by Truman Capote; *Requiem for a Nun*, by William Faulkner; *Birth of a Hero*, by Herbert Gold; *The Beetle Leg*, by John Hawkes; *Barbary Shore*, by Norman Mailer; *The Ballad of the Sad Café*, by Carson McCullers; *Man and Boy*, by Wright Morris; *Rock Wagram*, by William Saroyan; *Lie Down in Darkness*, by William Styron.

The Pulitzer Prize for fiction is awarded to Conrad Richter's *The Town*; the National Book Award for fiction to William Faulkner's *The Collected Stories of William Faulkner*.

1952

January: William Shawn becomes the editor in chief of the *New Yorker*.

February 16: Salinger is quoted in *Saturday Review* as saying, "I feel tremendously relieved that the season for success for 'The Catcher in the Rye' is nearly over. I enjoyed a small part of it, but most of it I found hectic and professionally and personally demoralizing. . . . Many of the letters from readers have been very nice."

May: Salinger's 29th published story, "De Daumier-Smith's Blue Period," appears in *World Review*, a magazine based in London. Due to the *New Yorker's* rejection, it is the only time a Salinger story is first published abroad.

June: Salinger returns to New York from a trip to Florida and Mexico. He learns that while he was away, he was selected for a distinguished alumnus award at Valley Forge Military Academy.

July: Salinger suggests to his English publisher, Hamish Hamilton, that he should publish a British edition of *The Gospel of Sri Ramakrishna*. Salinger's interest in religion began in the mid-to-late 1940s and included Zen and Mahayana Buddhism, Vedanta, Taoism, and Christian mysticism.

Fall: Salinger, searching to buy a home outside of the Greater New York Area, discovers Cornish, New Hampshire, a five-hour drive from New York City. In the tiny, remote township, he will purchase a modest house with 90 acres. Salinger moves in as early as January 1, 1953, his 34th birthday.

November 20: Antony di Gesu takes 48 photographs of Salinger. None were published during Salinger's lifetime. Twenty-nine images are now viewable on the Web site, www.gettyimages.com.

During 1952: Italy, Japan, and Norway publish translations of *The Catcher in the Rye*.

Events in Literature—1952: Stories by other notable authors published the same year as Salinger's "De Daumier-Smith's Blue Period" include James Agee's "A Mother's Tale," John Cheever's "The Chaste Clarissa," William Gaddis's "Le Chemin des Anes," Mavis Gallant's "One Morning in June," Shirley Jackson's "Journey with a Lady," Vladimir Nabokov's "Lance," Sylvia Plath's "Sunday at the Mintons'," Clay Putman's "Our Vegetable Love," Irwin Shaw's "Peter Two," Jean Stafford's "The Violet Rack," and Eudora Welty's "No Place for You, My Love."

The following books are published: *Invisible Man,* by Ralph Ellison; *Giant,* by Edna Ferber; *The Old Man and the Sea,* by Ernest Hemingway; *Go,* by John Clellon Holmes; *The Natural,* by Bernard Malamud; *The Groves of Academe,* by Mary McCarthy; *Wise Blood,* by Flannery O'Connor; *The Catherine Wheel,* by Jean Stafford; *East of Eden,* by John Steinbeck; *Player Piano,* by Kurt Vonnegut.

The Pulitzer Prize for fiction is awarded to Herman Wouk's *The Caine Mutiny;* the National Book Award for fiction to James Jones's *From Here to Eternity.*

1953

January 31: "Teddy," Salinger's 30th published story, appears in the *New Yorker.*

February 16: The deed to the Cornish, New Hampshire, property passes to Salinger.

February 26: The first paperback edition of *The Catcher in the Rye* is published in America by New American Library. After requesting there be no illustration, Salinger is very unhappy with the cover depicting Holden Caulfield. He is quoted as saying, "This is not my book, and if it were up to me, I would have my works mimeographed and distributed in that form." The first printing of the paperback edition consists of 350,000 copies, priced at 25 cents.

March 13: Maurey Garber takes a minimum of seven photos of Salinger. The cover portrait of Salinger on *Time* magazine in September 1961 will be based on one of them.

April 5: Eudora Welty's review of *Nine Stories* appears in the *New York Times:* "J. D. Salinger's writing is original, first rate, serious and beautiful."

April 6: Salinger's second book, *Nine Stories,* is published by Little, Brown and Company. Of his 30 stories already published in magazines, Salinger chooses to include only "A Perfect Day for Bananafish," "Uncle Wiggily in Connecticut," "Just Before the War with the Eskimos," "The Laughing Man," "Down at the Dinghy," "For Esmé—with Love and Squalor," "Pretty Mouth and Green My Eyes," "De Daumier-Smith's Blue Period," and "Teddy." (This is the first book publication for "Uncle Wiggily in Connecticut," "The Laughing Man," "Down

at the Dinghy," "Pretty Mouth and Green My Eyes," "De Daumier-Smith's Blue Period," and "Teddy.") Salinger dedicates the book to Dorothy Olding, his agent, and to Gus Lobrano, his *New Yorker* editor.

April 12: A sketch of Salinger, by E. Michael Mitchell, accompanies Gene Baro's review of *Nine Stories* in the *New York Herald Tribune Book Review.*

November 13: The first formal interview with Salinger is published. Conducted by a high-school girl, Shirlie Blaney, the interview, though slated for the high-school page of a local New Hampshire newspaper, appears, instead, on the editorial page. (Upon moving to Cornish, New Hampshire, Salinger had befriended some teenagers in Windsor, Vermont, just across the river. After this publication, he will stop socializing with them.) When asked in the interview whether *The Catcher in the Rye* is autobiographical, Salinger is quoted as saying, "Sort of. I was much relieved when I finished it. My boyhood was very much the same as that of the boy in the book, and it was a great relief telling people about it."

November 20: Samuel Beckett writes, "Have you read *The Catcher in the Rye?* Bowles lent it to me and I liked it very much indeed, more than anything for a long time."

During 1953: *Nine Stories* remains on the *New York Times* best-seller list for 15 weeks but fails to make the *Publishers Weekly* list of the year's 10 top-selling fiction volumes.

The British edition of *Nine Stories* is published as *For Esmé—with Love and Squalor, and Other Stories.*

Nearly simultaneously with its inclusion in *Nine Stories,* "Pretty Mouth and Green My Eyes" appears in Modern Library's *Anthology of Famous American Short Stories,* edited by J. A. Burrell and B. A. Cerf.

Salinger asks Claire Douglas to drop out of college and move in with him in Cornish, New Hampshire. When she refuses, the relationship falters. Claire will shortly thereafter marry on the rebound. The marriage will be annulled.

Events in Literature—1953: The 10 top-selling volumes of fiction are, in descending order of sales: *The Robe,* by Lloyd C. Douglas; *The*

Silver Chalice, by Thomas B. Costain; *Desiree,* by Annemarie Selinko; *Battle Cry,* by Leon Uris; *From Here to Eternity,* by James Jones; *The High and the Mighty,* by Ernest K. Gann; *Beyond This Place,* by A. J. Cronin; *Time and Time Again,* by James Hilton; *Lord Vanity,* by Samuel Shellabarger; *The Unconquered,* by Ben Ames Williams.

Stories by other notable authors published the same year as Salinger's "Teddy" include Elizabeth Bishop's "In the Village," John Cheever's "The National Pastime," Bruce Jay Friedman's "Wonderful Golden Rule Days," Shirley Ann Grau's "The Sound of Silver," Randall Jarrell's "Pictures from an Institution," Mary McCarthy's "The Figures in the Clock," Carson McCullers's "The Pestle," Katherine Anne Porter's "The Seducers," B. Traven's "The Third Guest," and Jessamyn West's "Breach of Promise."

Books by other notable authors published the same year as Salinger's *Nine Stories* include *Go Tell It on the Mountain,* by James Baldwin; *The Adventures of Augie March,* by Saul Bellow; *Junkie,* by William Burroughs; *The Enormous Radio, and Other Stories,* by John Cheever; *The Deep Sleep,* by Wright Morris; *Children Are Bored on Sunday,* by Jean Stafford; *The Outsider,* by Richard Wright.

The Pulitzer Prize for fiction is awarded to Ernest Hemingway's *The Old Man and the Sea;* the National Book Award for fiction to Ralph Ellison's *Invisible Man.*

1954

Summer: Salinger and Claire Douglas resume their relationship.

July 12: The first paperback edition of *Nine Stories* is published in America.

Fall: Salinger and Claire read *The Autobiography of a Yogi* by Paramahansa Yogananda. They will be initiated into Yogananda's Self-Realization Fellowship shortly after their February 1955 wedding.

During 1954: The first cases of *The Catcher in the Rye* censored by schools as objectionable reading are recorded in Los Angeles and Marin Counties, California.

Events in Literature—1954: The following books are published: *The Long Goodbye,* by Raymond Chandler; *Tunnel of Love,* by Peter de Vries; *A*

Fable, by William Faulkner; *The Bird's Nest,* by Shirley Jackson; *Pictures from an Institution,* by Randall Jarrell; *Sweet Thursday,* by John Steinbeck; *Messiah,* by Gore Vidal; *The Ponder Heart,* by Eudora Welty.

The Pulitzer Prize for fiction is not awarded; the National Book Award for fiction is awarded to Saul Bellow's *The Adventures of Augie March.*

The Nobel Prize in literature is awarded to Ernest Hemingway.

1955

January: Claire Douglas, one semester short of graduation, drops out of Radcliffe College at Salinger's insistence.

January 29: "Franny," Salinger's 31st published story, appears in the *New Yorker.*

February 17: Salinger weds Claire Douglas in Barnard, Vermont. His best man is E. Michael Mitchell, designer of the first-edition dust jacket for *The Catcher in the Rye.*

November 19: "Raise High the Roof Beam, Carpenters," Salinger's 32nd published story, appears in the *New Yorker.* This story introduces the entire Glass family.

December 10: Salinger's first child, Margaret Ann (known as Peggy), is born.

During 1955: Salinger is included in a standard reference work, *Twentieth Century Authors.* Reproduced in the entry in full is Salinger's 1951 autobiographical statement written for Little, Brown and Company.

Events in Literature—1955: Stories by other notable authors published the same year as Salinger's "Franny" and "Raise High the Roof Beam, Carpenters" include Roger Angell's "In an Early Winter," Gina Berriault's "Something in His Nature," Harold Brodkey's "Cassie Dressing," John Cheever's "Just Tell Me Who It Was," William Faulkner's "By the People," Shirley Jackson's "One Ordinary Day, with Peanuts," Jack Kerouac's "The Mexican Girl," Mary McCarthy's "September Morn," Carson McCullers's "The Haunted Boy," Philip Roth's "The Contest for Aaron Gold," William Saroyan's "The Inventor and the Actress," Terry Southern's "The Sun and the Still-born Stars," and Marguerite Young's "Strange Death of Mr. Spitzer."

The following books are published: *The Ginger Man,* by J. P. Donleavy; *The Recognitions,* by William Gaddis; *The Talented Mr. Ripley,* by Patricia Highsmith; *The Deer Park,* by Normal Mailer; *A Good Man Is Hard to Find, and Other Stories,* by Flannery O'Connor; *Ten North Frederick,* by John O'Hara; *The Bride of Innisfallen, and Other Stories,* by Eudora Welty; *The Man in the Gray Flannel Suit,* by Sloan Wilson.

The Pulitzer Prize for fiction and the National Book Award for fiction are both awarded to William Faulkner's *A Fable.*

1956

March: Gus Lobrano, Salinger's *New Yorker* editor, friend, and a co-dedicatee of *Nine Stories,* dies. William Shawn will become Salinger's next editor.

Spring: The first article on Salinger's work is published in a scholarly journal: Arthur Heiserman and James E. Miller, Jr.'s "J. D. Salinger: Some Crazy Cliff." Most of the article focuses on *The Catcher in the Rye,* which "belongs to an ancient and honorable narrative tradition, perhaps the most profound in Western fiction . . . the tradition of the Quest."

During 1956: Salinger is included in the newest edition of the definitive reference work on American literature, the *Oxford Companion to American Literature.* The entry reads in its entirety, "New York writer, author of *The Catcher in the Rye* (1951), about an unhappy teenager who runs away from his boarding school, and *Nine Stories* (1953)."

Salinger builds a one-room cabin as his writing studio.

Events in Literature—1956: The following books are published: *A Walk on the Wild Side,* by Nelson Algren; *Giovanni's Room,* by James Baldwin; *The Floating Opera,* by John Barth; *Seize the Day,* by Saul Bellow; *The Field of Vision,* by Wright Morris; *The City of the Living and Other Stories,* by Wallace Stegner; *A Thirsty Evil,* by Gore Vidal.

The Pulitzer Prize for fiction is awarded to MacKinlay Kantor's *Andersonville;* the National Book Award for fiction to John O'Hara's *Ten North Frederick.*

1957

Early: While in New York City on a short trip, Claire Salinger plans to kill her daughter and herself. Instead, she leaves Salinger, takes an apartment, and undergoes therapy.

May 4: "Zooey," Salinger's 33rd published story, appears in the *New Yorker.*

May 10: Edmund Wilson writes, "I think they [Salinger's Glass stories] are very remarkable, quite unlike anything else."

Summer: Claire Salinger and her daughter return to Salinger in Cornish, New Hampshire.

Ihab Hassan's "Rare Quixotic Gesture: The Fiction of J. D. Salinger" is the first article devoted to Salinger's entire career-to-date to appear in a scholarly journal. "We like to think that in the talent which he undoubtedly possesses we have found something winning and unexpected, a quality as refreshing as it is unique, though, to be sure, rather acute and eccentric."

November 18: In an article on America's college students, *Time* magazine states, "The one new American author who has something approaching universal appeal is J. D. Salinger, with his picture of the tortured process of growing up."

December: Truman Capote is quoted as saying, "I'll tell you a young writer who has what I mean; let's don't say personality, it is such a cheapened word. That's J. D. Salinger. He makes an immediate electrical contact. I like his stories very much."

Events in Literature—1957: Stories by other notable authors published the same year as Salinger's "Zooey" include James Agee's "The Waiting," James Baldwin's "Sonny's Blues," Paul Bowles's "The Frozen Fields," Harold Brodkey's "Sentimental Education," Herbert Gold's "Paris and Cleveland Are Voyages," Arthur Miller's "The Misfits," Flannery O'Connor's "A View of the Woods," Dorothy Parker's "The Banquet of Crow," Terry Southern's "South's Summer," Jean Stafford's "A Reasonable Facsimile," E. B. White's "The Seven Steps to Heaven," and William Carlos Williams's "The Farmer's Daughter."

The following books are published: *A Death in the Family,* by James Agee; *First Love and Other Stories,* by Harold Brodkey; *The Wapshot Chronicle,* by John Cheever; *Some Came Running,* by

James Jones; *On the Road,* by Jack Kerouac; *Pnin,* by Vladimir Nabokov; *Atlas Shrugged,* by Ayn Rand; *The Hunters,* by James Salter.

The Pulitzer Prize for fiction is not awarded; the National Book Award for fiction is awarded to Wright Morris's *The Field of Vision.*

1958
April 24: William Faulkner, in regard to novels written by the new generation, comments, ". . . I rate the best one: Salinger's *Catcher in the Rye.*"

During 1958: "This Sandwich Has No Mayonnaise" is included in a book, *The Armchair Esquire,* edited by Arnold Gingrich and L. Rust Hills.

The first monograph devoted to Salinger's work, Frederick L. Gwynn's and Joseph L. Blotner's *The Fiction of J. D. Salinger,* is published. ". . . the only Post-War fiction unanimously approved by contemporary literate American youth consists of about five hundred pages by Jerome David Salinger. Just why he is the one writer to whom so many young men and women, high-brow and middle-brow, in college and out, are devoted is not yet clear, although there is no lack of critical guesses as to the magnetic core of his work."

Events in Literature—1958: The following books are published: *Crazy in Berlin,* by Thomas Berger; *Breakfast at Tiffany's,* by Truman Capote; *The Housebreaker of Shady Hills,* by John Cheever; *The Dharma Bums,* by Jack Kerouac; *The Magic Barrel,* by Bernard Malamud; *Lolita,* by Vladimir Nabokov (American publication); *The Long Dream,* by Richard Wright.

The Pulitzer Prize for fiction is awarded to James Agee's *A Death in the Family;* the National Book Award for fiction to John Cheever's *The Wapshot Chronicle.*

1959
June 6: "Seymour: An Introduction," Salinger's 34th published story, appears in the *New Yorker.*

June: Sylvia Plath writes in her journal, "Read J. D. Salinger's 'Seymour: An Introduction' last night and today, put off at first by the rant at the beginning about Kafka, Kierkegaard, etc., but increasingly enchanted."

September 9: Elizabeth Bishop, after reading "Seymour: An Introduction," writes, "I HATED the Salinger story. . . . It took me days to go through it, gingerly, a page at a time, blushing with embarrassment for him every ridiculous sentence of the way."

November 14: George Steiner's "The Salinger Industry" appears in the *Nation.* Steiner questions the quantity of articles devoted to Salinger's work, which he calls "a new, probably rather minor achievement." The apex of scholarly articles on Salinger will not occur until four years later.

November 18: Whit Burnett returns two Salinger stories found in the *Story* archives, "A Young Man in a Stuffed Shirt" and "The Daughter of the Late, Great Man," after Salinger refuses to sell them for publication.

December 9: In the *New York Post Magazine,* Salinger publishes a letter to the editor under the headline "Man-Forsaken Men," about men sentenced to life imprisonment.

During 1959: Norman Mailer writes, "Salinger is everyone's favorite. I seem to be alone in finding him no more than the greatest mind ever to stay in prep school."

Events in Literature—1959: Stories by other notable authors published the same year as Salinger's "Seymour: An Introduction" include John Cheever's "The Scarlet Moving Van," Stanley Elkin's "Among the Witnesses," Mavis Gallant's "August," Elizabeth Hardwick's "The Purchase," Bernard Malamud's "The Maid's Shoes," Vladimir Nabokov's "The Vane Sisters," James Purdy's "Everything under the Sun," and Philip Roth's "Defender of the Faith."

The following books are published: *Henderson the Rain King,* by Saul Bellow; *The Naked Lunch,* by William Burroughs; *Mrs. Bridge,* by Evan Connell; *The Tents of Wickedness,* by Peter de Vries; *The Mansion,* by William Faulkner; *The Little Disturbances of Man: Stories of Men and Women at Love,* by Grace Paley; *Malcolm,* by James Purdy; *Goodbye, Columbus and Five Short Stories,* by Philip Roth; *The Poorhouse Fair,* by John Updike.

The Pulitzer Prize for fiction is awarded to Robert Lewis Taylor's *The Travels of Jamie McPheeters;* the National Book Award for fiction to Bernard Malamud's *The Magic Barrel.*

1960

February 13: Salinger's second and last child, Matthew Robert (known as Matt), is born.

May: Salinger tells a photographer, hired by *Newsweek*, "My method of work is such that any interruption throws me off. I can't have my picture taken or have an interview until I've completed what I've set out to do."

May 30: The first article in the popular press about Salinger's life is published by *Newsweek*, "The Mysterious J. D. Salinger . . . His Woodsy, Secluded Life." It does not include a photograph of Salinger.

During 1960: "Raise High the Roof Beam, Carpenters" is reprinted in the *New Yorker* anthology *Stories from The New Yorker, 1950–1960.* Salinger is one of 47 authors selected; he is joined by Roger Angell, Saul Bellow, Maeve Brennan, Harold Brodkey, John Cheever, Mavis Gallant, Nadine Gordimer, Elizabeth Hardwick, R. Prawer Jhabvala, William Maxwell, Mary McCarthy, Vladimir Nabokov, Dorothy Parker, V. S. Pritchett, Philip Roth, Jean Stafford, John Updike, and Eudora Welty.

Salinger's open-letter essay about Harold Ross, William Shawn, and the *New Yorker* is rejected for publication by *Saturday Review.*

Philip Roth gives a lecture at Stanford University and calls Salinger "the man who, by reputation at least, is *the* writer of the age."

Events in Literature—1960: The following books are published: *The Sot-Weed Factor,* by John Barth; *Welcome to Hard Times,* by E. L. Doctorow; *A Separate Peace,* by John Knowles; *To Kill a Mockingbird,* by Harper Lee; *The Violent Bear It Away,* by Flannery O'Connor; *Set This House on Fire,* by William Styron; *Rabbit, Run,* by John Updike.

The Pulitzer Prize for fiction is awarded to Allen Drury's *Advise and Consent*; the National Book Award for fiction to Philip Roth's *Goodbye, Columbus and Five Short Stories.*

1961

March: Despite Salinger's objections, *Cosmopolitan* reprints his 1947 story "The Inverted Forest" in its Diamond Jubilee issue.

May 2: The 17th printing of the American paperback edition of *The Catcher in the Rye* brings the total number of paperback copies printed since February 1953 to 1,675,716.

May: Salinger informs Little, Brown and Company that he doesn't want *Franny and Zooey* sold to any book clubs.

July 2: Ernest Hemingway commits suicide.

August: Alfred Kazin's review of the forthcoming *Franny and Zooey* is published in the *Atlantic.* "I am sorry to have to use the word 'cute' in respect to Salinger, but there is absolutely no other word that for me so accurately typifies the self-conscious charm and prankishness of his own writing and his extraordinary cherishing of his favorite Glass characters."

Donald M. Fiene submits his thesis devoted to Salinger's work, the groundbreaking "A Bibliographical Study of J. D. Salinger: Life, Work and Reputation." The unpublished thesis reflects Fiene's effort to gather and document all then-known materials relating to Salinger's life and work. In an appendix, Fiene includes rare photographs of Salinger, the *Ursinus Weekly* columns, birth and marriage certificates, magazine contributors' notes, and three Salinger letters, among other items.

September 14: Salinger's third book, *Franny and Zooey,* is published by Little, Brown and Company. On the dust jacket, Salinger says that "new material [Glass stories] is scheduled to appear there [in the *New Yorker*] soon" and that he has "a great deal of thoroughly unscheduled material on paper, too." He dedicates the book to William Shawn.

September 15: *Time* magazine puts Salinger on its cover and includes an extensive article on his life and work. This positive assessment represents the culmination of *Time's* exhaustive research into Salinger's life, an effort that causes Salinger much discomfort. The article includes three photos of Salinger, one of his wife, Claire, one of their house, and artist's renderings of Holden, Franny, Zooey, and Bessie.

September 17: John Updike's review of *Franny and Zooey* appears in the *New York Times*: "Salinger loves the Glasses more than God loves them. . . . He loves them to the detriment of artistic moderation."

October 29: *Franny and Zooey* tops the *New York Times* best-seller list for the first of 26 consecutive weeks. The work will remain on the list for a total of 54 weeks.

November 3: A long, illustrated article on Salinger and his work appears in *Life* magazine.

December: The *New Yorker* gives away 6,000 copies of *Franny and Zooey* at William Shawn's behest.

During 1961: *Franny and Zooey*, though published as late as September, achieves the status in *Publishers Weekly* of the second best-selling fiction of the year.

Events in Literature—1961: The 10 top-selling volumes of fiction are, in descending order of sales: *The Agony and the Ecstasy*, by Irving Stone; *Franny and Zooey*, by J. D. Salinger; *To Kill a Mockingbird*, by Harper Lee; *Mila 18*, by Leon Uris; *The Carpetbaggers*, by Harold Robbins; *Tropic of Cancer*, by Henry Miller; *Winnie Ille Pu* (a translation of Milne's classic into Latin by Alexander Lenard); *Daughter of Silence*, by Morris West; *The Edge of Sadness*, by Edwin O'Connor; *The Winter of Our Discontent*, by John Steinbeck.

Books by other notable authors published the same year as Salinger's *Franny and Zooey* include *The Soft Machine*, by William Burroughs; *Some People, Places and Things That Will Not Appear in My Next Novel*, by John Cheever; *Midcentury*, by John Dos Passos; *The Lime Twig*, by John Hawkes; *Catch-22*, by Joseph Heller; *A New Life*, by Bernard Malamud; *Horseman Pass By*, by Larry McMurtry; *The Moviegoer*, by Walker Percy; *The Spinoza of Market Street and Other Stories*, by Isaac Bashevis Singer; *The Winter of Our Discontent*, by John Steinbeck; *Mother Night*, by Kurt Vonnegut; *Revolutionary Road*, by Richard Yates.

The Pulitzer Prize for fiction is awarded to Harper Lee's *To Kill a Mockingbird*; the National Book Award for fiction to Conrad Richter's *The Waters of Kronos*.

1962

October: Mary McCarthy's scathing review of *Franny and Zooey*, originally published in England, is reprinted in *Harper's*. "And who are these wonder kids [the Glasses] but Salinger himself, splitting and multiplying like the original amoeba? . . . To be confronted with these

seven faces of Salinger, all wise and lovable and simple, is to gaze into a terrifying narcissus pool."

During 1962: *Franny and Zooey* remains continuously on best-seller lists and achieves the status in *Publishers Weekly* of the fifth best-selling fiction of 1962.

The British edition of *Franny and Zooey* is published.

The first casebooks on Salinger's work are published: *Salinger: A Critical and Personal Portrait*, edited by Henry Anatole Grunwald, and *J. D. Salinger and the Critics*, edited by William F. Belcher and James W. Lee.

Events in Literature—1962: The 10 top-selling volumes of fiction are, in descending order of sales: *Ship of Fools*, by Katherine Anne Porter; *Dearly Beloved*, by Anne Morrow Lindbergh; *A Shade of Difference*, by Allen Drury; *Youngblood Hawke*, by Herman Wouk; *Franny and Zooey*, by J. D. Salinger; *Fail-Safe*, by Eugene Burdick and Harvey Wheeler; *Seven Days in May*, by Fletcher Knebel and Charles W. Bailey; *The Prize*, by Irving Wallace; *The Agony and the Ecstasy*, by Irving Stone; *The Reivers*, by William Faulkner.

The following books are published: *Portrait in Brownstone*, by Louis Auchincloss; *One Flew Over the Cuckoo's Nest*, by Ken Kesey; *Pale Fire*, by Vladimir Nabokov; *Tell Me a Riddle*, by Tillie Olsen; *Letting Go*, by Philip Roth; *The Slave*, by Isaac Bashevis Singer; *Pigeon Feathers and Other Stories*, by John Updike.

The Pulitzer Prize for fiction is awarded to Edwin O'Connor's *The Edge of Sadness*; the National Book Award for fiction to Walker Percy's *The Moviegoer*. *The Moviegoer* is selected over J. D. Salinger's *Franny and Zooey*, Joseph Heller's *Catch-22*, William Maxwell's *The Chateau*, Richard Yates's *Revolutionary Road*, and five other finalists.

The Nobel Prize in Literature is awarded to John Steinbeck.

1963

January 28: Salinger's fourth book, *Raise High the Roof Beam, Carpenters and Seymour: An Introduction*, is published by Little, Brown and Company. Salinger dedicates the book to his wife and two children, and to the "amateur reader." On the dust jacket, Salinger mentions unpublished "new material in the series . . . several new Glass stories coming along." *Raise High the Roof Beam, Carpenters and Seymour: An Introduction* is Salinger's last authorized book published during his lifetime. (Salinger will publish only one more new story, "Hapworth 16, 1924," on June 19, 1965.)

March 10: *Raise High the Roof Beam, Carpenters and Seymour: An Introduction* tops the *New York Times* best-seller list for the first of 10 consecutive weeks. The work will remain on the list for a total of 21 weeks.

Spring: Salinger and Claire are invited to a White House function; Salinger refuses the invitation even after a personal phone call from Jacqueline Kennedy.

July: Norman Mailer, in an article in *Esquire*, slams Salinger's two Glass books. "There is a taste of something self-absorptive, narcissistic, even putrefactive in his long contemplation of a lintless navel."

November 22: President John F. Kennedy is assassinated.

December 5: Whit Burnett unsuccessfully pleads with Salinger to allow the inclusion of "The Long Debut of Lois Taggett" in a *Story* anthology. Burnett offers to insert a disclaimer about the early story; he notes that Salinger's inclusion would help *Story* magazine continue publication.

During 1963: *Raise High the Roof Beam, Carpenters and Seymour: An Introduction* achieves the status in *Publishers Weekly* of the third best-selling fiction of the year.

The British edition of *Raise High the Roof Beam, Carpenters and Seymour: An Introduction* is published.

The first book-length volume on Salinger and his work, written by one author, is published: Warren French's *J. D. Salinger*, in Twayne's United States Authors series. "This book is not written for Salinger's fans, who don't need to be told why they admire him and who, indeed, would be affronted by any effort to tell them. It is rather for those parents, teachers, and other representatives of a beleaguered older generation who are puzzled by the enthusiasm aroused by [Salinger's fiction]."

Studies in J. D. Salinger: Reviews, Essays, Critiques of "The Catcher in the Rye" and Other Fiction, edited by Marvin Laser and Norman Fruman, is published.

If You Really Want to Know: A "Catcher" Casebook, edited by Malcolm Marsden, is published.

Salinger's "Catcher in the Rye": Clamor vs. Criticism, edited by Harold P. Simonson and Philip E. Hagar, is published.

An issue of *Wisconsin Studies in Contemporary Literature* is devoted to critical essays on Salinger's work. Included is a revised (and condensed) bibliography by Donald M. Fiene.

Saul Bellow is quoted as saying, "[Salinger] is an excellent craftsman, and I never underestimate the value of craftsmanship, but I do think he has made up a Rousseauian critique of society which comes from the vatic judgment of the immature. . . ."

Events in Literature—1963: The 10 top-selling volumes of fiction are, in descending order of sales: *The Shoes of the Fisherman*, by Morris L. West; *The Group*, by Mary McCarthy; *Raise High the Roof Beam, Carpenters and Seymour: An Introduction*, by J. D. Salinger; *Caravans*, by James Michener; *Elizabeth Appleton*, by John O'Hara; *Grandmother and the Priests*, by Taylor Caldwell; *City of Night*, by John Rechy; *The Glass-Blowers*, by Daphne du Maurier; *The Sand Pebbles*, by Richard McKenna; *The Battle of the Villa Fiorita*, by Rumer Godden.

Books by other notable authors published the same year as Salinger's *Raise High the Roof Beam, Carpenters and Seymour: An Introduction* include *Run River*, by Joan Didion; *Visions of Gerard*, by Jack Kerouac; *By the North Gate*, by Joyce Carol Oates; *The Bell Jar*, by Sylvia Plath; *V.*, by Thomas Pynchon; *The Benefactor*, by Susan Sontag; *The Centaur*, by John Updike; *Cat's Cradle*, by Kurt Vonnegut.

The Pulitzer Prize for fiction is awarded to William Faulkner's *The Reivers*; the National Book Award for fiction to J. F. Powers's *Morte D'Urban*.

1964

During 1964: The first American paperback edition of *Franny and Zooey* is published and sells 938,000 copies this year.

The paperback rights to *The Catcher in the Rye* are acquired by Bantam Books after the publisher agrees to Salinger's stipulation that he design the book's cover.

Events in Literature—1964: The following books are published: *Come Back, Dr. Caligari*, by Donald Barthelme; *Herzog*, by Saul Bellow; *Little Big Man*, by Thomas Berger; *A Confederate General from Big Sur*, by Richard Brautigan; *The Wapshot Scandal*, by John Cheever; *Boswell: A Modern Comedy*, by Stanley Elkin; *The Keepers of the House*, by Shirley Ann Grau; *Second Skin*, by John Hawkes; *Sometimes a Great Notion*, by Ken Kesey; *Last Exit to Brooklyn*, by Hubert Selby; *Candy*, by Terry Southern; *Julian*, by Gore Vidal.

The Pulitzer Prize for fiction is not awarded; the National Book Award for fiction is awarded to John Updike's *The Centaur*.

1965

February: Warren French's article, "An Unnoticed Salinger Story," is published. French reveals that J. C. Cederstrom has discovered an unknown-to-date Salinger story, "Go See Eddie," in a 1940 issue of the *University of Kansas City Review*. No other undocumented Salinger stories have since been discovered.

April: Tom Wolfe publishes two long articles in the new Sunday supplement of the *New York Herald Tribune* skewering the *New Yorker* and William Shawn: "Tiny Mummies! The True Story of the Ruler of 43rd Street's Land of the Walking Dead!" and "Lost in the Whichy Thickets: The New Yorker." Salinger sends a telegram of protest to Jock Whitney, the owner of the *Herald Tribune*: "With the printing of that inaccurate and sub-collegiate and gleeful and unrelievedly poisonous article on William Shawn, the name of the *Herald Tribune* and certainly your own will very likely never again stand for anything either respect-worthy or honorable."

June 19: "Hapworth 16, 1924," Salinger's 35th published story, appears in the *New Yorker*. "Hapworth 16, 1924" is Salinger's final story published during his lifetime.

June 26: Louise Bogan writes, "The Salinger ["Hapworth 16, 1924"] is a disaster. [William] Maxwell came to call, and rather deplored its total cessation of talent."

During 1965: The first American paperback edition of *Raise High the Roof Beam, Carpenters*

and Seymour: An Introduction is published, thus making all of Salinger's four books available in paperback in America.

Salinger is included in the fourth edition of the *Oxford Companion to American Literature* (issued nine years after the third edition). His alphabetical entry has been enlarged to half a page, and a second entry devoted exclusively to *The Catcher in the Rye* appears.

James E. Miller, Jr.'s *J. D. Salinger* is published in the University of Minnesota's Pamphlets on American Writers series. "Although Salinger's total creative production, to date, has been relatively small, his impact and influence—and his artistic achievement—have been enormous. No serious history of post-World War II American fiction can be written without awarding him a place in the first rank, and even, perhaps, the pre-eminent position."

Princeton University's Firestone Library acquires the archives of Whit Burnett and *Story* magazine. Included are five unpublished Salinger stories written from 1942 to 1945 ("The Last and Best of the Peter Pans," "The Ocean Full of Bowling Balls," "The Magic Foxhole," "Two Lonely Men," and "The Children's Echelon"), 36 Salinger letters addressed to Burnett or the magazine, and copies of 21 Burnett letters to Salinger.

Events in Literature—1965: Stories by other notable authors published the same year as Salinger's "Hapworth 16, 1924," his last published story during his lifetime, include Thomas Berger's "A Monkey of His Own," Stanley Elkin's "A Poetics for Bullies," Mavis Gallant's "The Statues Taken Down," Herbert Gold's "A Haitian Gentleman," Shirley Jackson's "The Bus," William Maxwell's "Further Tales about Men and Women," Joyce Carol Oates's "The Stone House," John O'Hara's "The Gambler," William Saroyan's "The Accident at the Country Fair," and Richard Yates's "A Good and Gallant Woman."

The following books are also published: *The Mistress, and Other Stories*, by Gina Berriault; *The Painted Bird*, by Jerzy Kosinski; *An American Dream*, by Norman Mailer; *The Orchard Keeper*, by Cormac McCarthy; *Everything That Rises Must Converge*, by Flannery O'Connor;

Collected Stories, by Katherine Anne Porter; *Mrs. Stevens Hears the Mermaids Singing*, by May Sarton; *If Morning Ever Comes*, by Anne Tyler; *Of the Farm*, by John Updike; *God Bless You, Mr. Rosewater*, by Kurt Vonnegut; *Miss MacIntosh, My Darling*, by Marguerite Young.

The Pulitzer Prize for fiction is awarded to Shirley Ann Grau's *The Keepers of the House*; the National Book Award for fiction to Saul Bellow's *Herzog*.

1966

September 9: Salinger's wife, Claire, files for divorce.

During 1966: An issue of *Modern Fiction Studies* is devoted to critical essays on Salinger's work.

Salinger helps Lillian Ross adopt a baby; along with William Shawn, he becomes a godfather of the boy.

Events in Literature—1966: The Pulitzer Prize for fiction and the National Book Award for fiction are both awarded to Katherine Anne Porter's *Collected Stories*.

1967

October 3: Salinger and Claire are divorced. Claire gets the original house and custody of the children; Salinger retains an adjacent property and a house he built in the early 1960s (the same house in which he resided until his death).

During 1967: Kenneth Hamilton's *Jerome David Salinger: A Critical Essay* is published in Eerdmans's Contemporary Writers in Christian Perspective series.

Events in Literature—1967: The Pulitzer Prize for fiction and the National Book Award for fiction are both awarded to Bernard Malamud's *The Fixer*.

1968

During 1968: James Bryan's dissertation, "Salinger and His Short Fiction," is the first scholarly work to utilize Salinger's letters to Whit Burnett. Bryan also unearths important biographical information unavailable in Warren French's 1963 *J. D. Salinger*.

Events in Literature—1968: The Pulitzer Prize for fiction is awarded to William Styron's *The Con-*fessions of Nat Turner*; the National Book Award for fiction to Thornton Wilder's *The Eighth Day*.

1969

During 1969: Elizabeth Murray's collection of nearly 40 Salinger letters and two unpublished stories, "Birthday Boy" and a draft of an untitled story ("Mrs. Hincher," reworked and retitled as "Paula"), is purchased by the Harry Ransom Center at the University of Texas at Austin.

"Go See Eddie" is included (without Salinger's permission) in a book, *Fiction: Form and Experience*, edited by William M. Jones.

Events in Literature—1969: The Pulitzer Prize for fiction is awarded to N. Scott Momaday's *House Made of Dawn*; the National Book Award for fiction to Jerzy Kosinski's *Steps*.

1970

During 1970: Salinger repays Little, Brown and Company's $75,000 advance for a future book publication. He is now under contract to no one for another book.

Salinger's father, Sol, dies.

S. J. Perelman dedicates his book, *Baby, It's Cold Inside*, to Salinger.

Events in Literature—1970: The Pulitzer Prize for fiction is awarded to Jean Stafford's *Collected Stories*; the National Book Award for fiction to Joyce Carol Oates's *Them*.

1971

September 29: Vladimir Nabokov regrets he doesn't have time to write an article about Salinger for the *New York Times Book Review*, as he tells the editor in a letter, "I do admire him very much."

During 1971: Salinger's mother, Miriam, dies.

Kenneth Starosciak's *J. D. Salinger: A Thirty-Year Bibliography 1938–1968* is published.

Sumitra Paniker's dissertation, "The Influence of Eastern Thought on 'Teddy' and the Seymour Glass Stories of J. D. Salinger," spotlights Salinger's interest in Vedanta.

David Lodge observes that Salinger's works "have been received with increasing disfavor because they have been taken too much at their face value as disingenuous gospels of a new religion, to the neglect of their literary experimentation."

Events in Literature—1971: The Pulitzer Prize for fiction is not awarded; the National Book Award for fiction is awarded to Saul Bellow's *Mr. Sammler's Planet.*

1972

April 25: Salinger, after reading Joyce Maynard's illustrated article, "An 18-Year-Old Looks Back on Her Life," in the *New York Times Magazine,* writes his first letter to her.

May: In response to Joyce Maynard's question as to why he doesn't publish, Salinger is quoted as saying, "Publication is a messy business. . . . It's just more of a damned interruption than I can tolerate anymore."

September: Joyce Maynard drops out of Yale University to move in with Salinger in Cornish, New Hampshire.

Fall–winter: Though unable to consummate the relationship due to Joyce Maynard's vaginismus, Salinger and Maynard talk of having a baby.

November 20: Vladimir Nabokov includes "A Perfect Day for Bananafish" as one of his choices for American short stories that deserve to be graded A plus.

Events in Literature—1972: The Pulitzer Prize for fiction is awarded to Wallace Stegner's *Angle of Repose;* the National Book Award for fiction to Flannery O'Connor's *The Complete Stories.*

1973

Spring: Salinger and Joyce Maynard travel to Daytona Beach, Florida, with Salinger's children for a vacation and to consult a naturopathic practitioner for Maynard's vaginismus. Later on the beach, Salinger is quoted as saying, "I can never have any more children. I'm finished with all this." He tells Maynard abruptly that he wishes her to return to Cornish and clear her belongings out of the house before he and his children return.

During 1973: Alfred Kazin reassesses the Glass stories and now believes, "Salinger's Holy Family stand out from the great mass of unvalued, unregarded and undescribed individuals in contemporary fiction. His people will last."

Events in Literature—1973: The Pulitzer Prize for fiction is awarded to Eudora Welty's *The Opti-*

mist's Daughter; the National Book Award for fiction is shared by John Barth's *Chimera* and John Williams's *Augustus.*

1974

September–October: *The Complete Uncollected Short Stories of J. D. Salinger* appears in a two-volume pirated edition, purportedly the work of a John Greenberg. The collection contains 21 stories from 1940 to 1948 and one 1965 story, none of which Salinger included in any of his own story collections. The edition represents the first book publication for "The Young Folks," "The Heart of a Broken Story," "Personal Notes on an Infantryman," "The Varioni Brothers," "Both Parties Concerned," "Soft-Boiled Sergeant," "Last Day of the Last Furlough," "Once a Week Won't Kill You," "Elaine," "The Stranger," "I'm Crazy," "Slight Rebellion Off Madison," "A Young Girl in 1941 with No Waist at All," "The Inverted Forest," "Blue Melody," and "Hapworth 16, 1924." (Additionally, the bootleg edition includes "Go See Eddie," "The Hang of It," "The Long Debut of Lois Taggett," "A Boy in France," "This Sandwich Has No Mayonnaise," and "A Girl I Knew.") A number of bookstores in the San Francisco Bay Area, Chicago, and New York City illegally sell circa 25,000 copies. Salinger will file a lawsuit against certain bookstores.

November 3: Salinger grants his first interview in 21 years, protesting the pirated publication of his uncollected stories. Making the front page of the *New York Times,* Salinger is quoted as saying, "I'm not trying to hide the gaucheries of my youth. I just don't think they're worth publishing." As for new work: "Publishing is a terrible invasion of my privacy. I like to write. I love to write. But I write just for myself and my own pleasure."

November 18: *Newsweek,* following up on the *New York Times* interview, sends a reporter to Cornish. The journalist quotes Salinger as saying, "I like to hang onto my privacy—my undocumented privacy. . . . Is there anything more boring than a talking writer?"

November: The FBI joins two detectives hired by Salinger's lawyers in search of the elusive John Greenberg, who is never apprehended.

Events in Literature—1974: The Pulitzer judges for fiction select Thomas Pynchon's *Gravity's Rainbow* only to be overruled by the advisory board; no Pulitzer Prize is awarded this year. The National Book Award for fiction is shared by Thomas Pynchon's *Gravity's Rainbow* and Isaac Bashevis Singer's *A Crown of Feathers and Other Stories.*

1975

During 1975: Salinger's "A Salute to Whit Burnett 1899–1972" is published as an epilogue to *Fiction Writer's Handbook* by Hallie and Whit Burnett. There is no acknowledgment of Salinger's permission to print the piece, which one may conclude was published without his knowledge, and which therefore does not represent an instance of Salinger publishing after 10 years of silence. Written in 1964, the piece was an intended foreword solicited (and rejected) by Whit Burnett for *Story Jubilee: 33 Years of Story.*

The total sales figure for *The Catcher in the Rye* in America, from 1951 to 1975, is 5,985,626. Of these, 421,726 are hardback editions.

For the period of 1966 through 1975, *The Catcher in the Rye* is banned in schools more often than any other book.

Events in Literature—1975: The Pulitzer Prize for fiction is awarded to Michael Shaara's *The Killer Angels*; the National Book Award for fiction is shared by Robert Stone's *Dog Soldiers* and Thomas Williams's *The Hair of Harold Roux.*

1976

April 22: John Calvin Batchelor, in an article in the *Soho Weekly News*, asserts that Salinger, no longer wanting to publish under his own name, has been publishing under the name of Thomas Pynchon (no doubt, to the surprise of Thomas Pynchon).

Events in Literature—1976: The Pulitzer Prize for fiction is awarded to Saul Bellow's *Humboldt's Gift*; the National Book Award for fiction to William Gaddis's *JR.*

The Nobel Prize in literature is awarded to Saul Bellow.

1977

February: Esquire publishes an unsigned story, "For Rupert—with No Promises," which sparks a debate over whether the story had been written by Salinger. Soon afterward, Gordon Lish is revealed as the author.

December 4: In response to a *New York Times* survey, Richard Yates chooses Salinger as the living writer he most admires. Yates writes, "Here was a man who used language as if it were pure energy beautifully controlled, and who knew exactly what he was doing in every silence as well as in every word."

During 1977: Gerald Rosen's pamphlet, *Zen in the Art of J. D. Salinger,* is published.

Events in Literature—1977: The Pulitzer Prize for fiction is not awarded; the National Book Award for fiction is awarded to Wallace Stegner's *The Spectator Bird.*

1978

February: Salinger's lawsuit against 17 bookstores for selling *The Complete Uncollected Short Stories of J. D. Salinger* is settled, with Salinger receiving a nominal sum.

June 29: Salinger attends a testimonial dinner for John L. Keenan, a friend from World War II. He gives a short speech, praising Keenan, "He was a great comfort in the foxholes. . . . In Normandy, he led us in song."

November: Exasperated by the disruption to his life by winning the Nobel Prize, Isaac Bashevis Singer is quoted as saying, "Sometimes I think of Mr. J. D. Salinger, who in his wisdom has gone somewhere and does his work."

Events in Literature—1978: The Pulitzer Prize for fiction is awarded to James Alan McPherson's *Elbow Room*; the National Book Award for fiction to Mary Lee Settle's *Blood Tie.*

The Nobel Prize in literature is awarded to Isaac Bashevis Singer.

1979

January 1: The *New York Times* notes that Salinger turns 60 today. Dorothy Olding is quoted as saying that Salinger is "working right ahead. He just writes and keeps it there."

January: Greg Herriges's article, "Ten Minutes with J. D. Salinger," is published in *Oui* magazine. Salinger is quoted as saying, "Contact with the public hinders my work. . . . Everything I have to say is in my fiction."

July 30: *Newsweek* quotes a college-age couple who spoke with Salinger: "He told us not to take anybody's advice, including his, and that it's very important to read."

November: Michael Clarkson publishes an article about seeking out Salinger. He quotes Salinger as saying, "I've made my stand clear. I'm a private person. Why can't my life be my own?"

During 1979: *J. D. Salinger*, by James Lundquist, is published in Ungar's Modern Literature Monographs series.

Events in Literature—1979: The Pulitzer Prize for fiction is awarded to John Cheever's *The Stories of John Cheever*; the National Book Award for fiction to Tim O'Brien's *Going after Cacciato*.

1980

February 25: *People* magazine features an article on Michael Clarkson's visit with Salinger, titled, "A Young Writer Brings the World a Message from J. D. Salinger: 'Go Away.'"

June 29: Betty Eppes publishes a newspaper article about her meeting with Salinger. Salinger is quoted as saying, "There's no more to Holden Caulfield. Read the book again, it's all there. Holden Caulfield is only a frozen moment in time."

December 8: Mark David Chapman murders John Lennon in New York City. After firing the shots, he calmly sits down and starts to read *The Catcher in the Rye*.

Events in Literature—1980: The Pulitzer Prize for fiction is awarded to Norman Mailer's *The Executioner's Song*; the National Book Award for fiction to William Styron's *Sophie's Choice*.

1981

February 15: The *New York Times* reports a rumor that Salinger is publishing under the name of William Wharton. The rumor is denied by the two writers' agents.

February: Mark David Chapman claims *The Catcher in the Rye* explains why he killed John Lennon.

Summer: An expanded version of Betty Eppes's June 29, 1980, article is published in the *Paris Review* and gains widespread notice.

During 1981: Thirty years after the publication of *The Catcher in the Rye*, translations of the novel are available in 27 countries. Eleven countries have all four of Salinger's books available in translation.

Events in Literature—1981: The Pulitzer Prize for fiction is awarded to John Kennedy Toole's *A Confederacy of Dunces*; the National Book Award for fiction to Wright Morris's *Plains Song*.

1982

May: Salinger, age 63, travels to Jacksonville, Florida, to see his new girlfriend, the 37-year-old actress Elaine Joyce, perform in a dinner theater production.

June 6: A full-page ad appears in the *New York Times* hyping a manuscript by an S. K. Barnett. The ad is signed by Buddy Glass.

September 30: Salinger files an impersonation lawsuit against a young freelance journalist and writer, Steven Kunes. Kunes attempted to sell a faked interview with Salinger to *People* magazine, forged some Salinger letters, and undoubtedly placed the Buddy Glass ad.

October: The *Washington Post* quotes Elaine Joyce as saying, "Salinger has accumulated enough manuscripts to fill two safes and will permit at least one to be published in 1983."

During 1982: W. P. Kinsella publishes *Shoeless Joe*, a novel that features a character named J. D. Salinger.

Events in Literature—1982: The Pulitzer Prize for fiction and the National Book Award for fiction are both awarded to John Updike's *Rabbit Is Rich*.

1983

Summer: Gordon Lish publishes in the *Antioch Review* a story titled "For Jerome—with Love and Kisses" (a fictional long letter from Sol Salinger to his son).

During 1983: The first critical monograph devoted solely to the Glass family, Eberhard Alsen's *Salinger's Glass Stories as a Composite Novel*, is published.

Ian Hamilton begins to work on a biography of Salinger.

Events in Literature—1983: The Pulitzer Prize for fiction and the National Book Award for fiction are both awarded to Alice Walker's *The Color Purple*.

1984

During 1984: Jack R. Sublette's definitive Salinger bibliography, *J. D. Salinger: An Annotated Bibliography, 1938–1981*, is published.

Events in Literature—1984: The Pulitzer Prize for fiction is awarded to William Kennedy's *Ironweed*; the National Book Award for fiction to Ellen Gilchrist's *Victory over Japan: A Book of Stories.*

1985

January 3: Matt Salinger, an aspiring actor, makes his Broadway debut as the lead in the play "Dancing in the End Zone."

November–December: An article in *Saturday Review* suggests that Salinger published two long autobiographical pieces in 1970 and 1971 in a small literary journal, the *Phoenix,* under the name of Giles Weaver. (Discerning readers are unconvinced.)

Events in Literature—1985: The Pulitzer Prize for fiction is awarded to Alison Lurie's *Foreign Affairs*; the National Book Award for fiction to Don DeLillo's *White Noise.*

1986

May 7: One hundred and fifty bound galleys of Ian Hamilton's biography, *J. D. Salinger: A Writing Life*—due to be published in August—are sent to reviewers. The short biography incorporates many direct quotations from Salinger's unpublished letters. One of the bound galleys is sold to a book dealer and, in turn, quickly reaches Salinger.

May 25: Ian Hamilton and Random House are informed that Salinger wants the quotations from his letters excised from the biography or he will sue to stop publication.

Summer: Ian Hamilton attempts to comply with Salinger's request by closely paraphrasing nearly all of the quotations. Salinger copyrights all of his letters on deposit with institutions.

September 18: Hamilton's revised book is delivered to Salinger's lawyers. Ian Hamilton and Random House believe Salinger will be placated by the changes.

October 3: Salinger sues to stop the publication of the biography, citing copyright infringement.

October 10: Salinger travels to New York City to be deposed for the lawsuit. In answer to a question about the nature of his writing over the past 20 years, Salinger says, "Just a work of fiction. That's all. That's the only description I can really give it. . . . It's almost impossible to define. I work with characters, and as they develop, I go from there."

November 5: Judge Pierre N. Leval, of the Federal District Court in Manhattan, rules against Salinger and will not block the publication of the biography. A day-and-a-half later, he reverses himself and blocks publication for one week to allow for an appeal. Salinger's lawyers file an appeal.

December 12: The *New York Times* reports that depositions in the lawsuit reveal that approximately 500 Salinger letters to Dorothy Olding (Salinger's longtime agent) were destroyed before the Harold Ober Agency files were placed at Princeton University.

Events in Literature—1986: The Pulitzer Prize for fiction is awarded to Larry McMurtry's *Lonesome Dove*; the National Book Award for fiction to E. L. Doctorow's *World's Fair.*

1987

January: Salinger is informed that William Shawn has been fired. He assents to having his name added as a signer to the letter of protest.

January 29: The Federal Appeals Court in Manhattan rules in Salinger's favor and blocks publication of Ian Hamilton's book. The ruling shocks many biographers and publishers. Random House appeals to the U.S. Supreme Court as a last resort.

October 5: The U.S. Supreme Court declines to hear the case, and the decision stands: Ian Hamilton's book cannot be published. The 150 extant review copies of *J. D. Salinger: A Writing Life* become very expensive collectors' items.

During 1987: *J. D. Salinger*, a collection of critical essays, edited and with an introduction by Harold Bloom, is published in Chelsea House's Modern Critical Views series.

Events in Literature—1987: The Pulitzer Prize for fiction is awarded to Peter Taylor's *A Summons to Memphis*; the National Book Award for fiction to Larry Heinemann's *Paco's Story.*

1988

April: Salinger is accosted and provoked by two paparazzi in the parking lot of a grocery store near his home. Several unflattering photos are published in the *New York Post.*

June: Ian Hamilton's extensively rewritten and revamped biography of Salinger, now titled, *In Search of J. D. Salinger,* is published and represents the first biography of J. D. Salinger.

During 1988: Gigi Mahon's *The Last Days of The New Yorker* is published. Mahon notes that William Shawn, trying to hold onto his editorship in December 1978, invoked "J. D. Salinger, 'who is a genius and who admires almost nothing about our contemporary culture,' had spoken of his pleasure at reading *The New Yorker,* and his hopes that it would not change."

Warren French's second book on Salinger, *J. D. Salinger, Revisited,* is published in Twayne's United States Authors series.

Events in Literature—1988: The Pulitzer Prize for fiction is awarded to Toni Morrison's *Beloved;* the National Book Award for fiction to Pete Dexter's *Paris Trout.*

1989

During 1989: Som P. Ranchan's *An Adventure in Vedanta: J. D. Salinger's The Glass Family* is published in India.

Events in Literature—1989: The Pulitzer Prize for fiction is awarded to Anne Tyler's *Breathing Lessons;* the National Book Award for fiction to John Casey's *Spartina.*

1990

During 1990: *Holden Caulfield,* a collection of critical essays, edited and with an introduction by Harold Bloom, is published in Chelsea House's Major Literary Characters series.

Critical Essays on Salinger's The Catcher in the Rye, edited by Joel Salzberg, is published.

After Dorothy Olding's stroke, Phyllis Westberg becomes Salinger's agent.

Events in Literature—1990: The Pulitzer Prize for fiction is awarded to Oscar Hijuelos's *The Mambo Kings Play Songs of Love;* the National Book Award for fiction to Charles Johnson's *Middle Passage.*

1991

April: Brandeis University withdraws an award to Salinger at his request. One of the judges, the author Harold Brodkey, comments, "His [Salinger's] is the most influential body of work in English prose by anyone since Hemingway."

May: Little, Brown and Company assumes from Bantam the mass-market paperback editions of Salinger's works. Subsequently, editions appear as an austere matching set, each volume bound in white covers, with Salinger's name and the book's title in black.

During 1991: John Wenke's *J. D. Salinger: A Study of the Short Fiction* is published in Twayne's Studies in Short Fiction series.

New Essays on The Catcher in the Rye, edited by Jack Salzman, is published.

Don DeLillo publishes *Mao II,* partially inspired by the 1988 *New York Post* photos of Salinger.

Events in Literature—1991: The Pulitzer Prize for fiction is awarded to John Updike's *Rabbit at Rest;* the National Book Award for fiction to Norman Rush's *Mating.*

1992

October 23: The *New York Times* reports that a fire damages half of Salinger's house. The fire was phoned in by Salinger's third wife, Colleen O'Neill. (The date of the wedding is undocumented.) The fate of Salinger's manuscripts is not publicly addressed.

December 8: William Shawn, *New Yorker* editor in chief and dedicatee of *Franny and Zooey,* dies.

During 1992: Elizabeth N. Kurian's *A Religious Response to the Existential Dilemma in the Fiction of J. D. Salinger* is published in India.

Events in Literature—1992: The Pulitzer Prize for fiction is awarded to Jane Smiley's *A Thousand Acres;* the National Book Award for fiction to Cormac McCarthy's *All the Pretty Horses.*

1993

During 1993: Sanford Pinsker's *The Catcher in the Rye: Innocence under Pressure* is published in Twayne's Masterwork Studies series.

Events in Literature—1993: The Pulitzer Prize for fiction is awarded to Robert Olen Butler's *A Good Scent from a Strange Mountain;* the National Book Award for fiction to E. Annie Proulx's *The Shipping News.*

The Nobel Prize in literature is awarded to Toni Morrison.

1994

January 1: Salinger turns 75.

Events in Literature—1994: The Pulitzer Prize for fiction is awarded to E. Annie Proulx's *The Shipping News*; the National Book Award for fiction to William Gaddis's *A Frolic of His Own*.

1995

November: "The Holden Server" appears on the World Wide Web. Created by Luke Seemann, the Web site offers random quotes from *The Catcher in the Rye* after the user clicks on a red hunting hat.

During 1995: An online listserv, named banana-fish and dedicated to discussing Salinger and his work, is created by Stephen Foskett. Several years later, bananafish will be hosted by Tim O'Connor and will remain the premier online discussion group about Salinger and his work until O'Connor's tragic death in June 2004.

Events in Literature—1995: The Pulitzer Prize for fiction is awarded to Carol Shields's *Stone Diaries*; the National Book Award for fiction to Philip Roth's *Sabbath's Theater*.

1996

June 27: Luke Seemann, creator of the popular "Holden Server," receives notification from Harold Ober and Associates that he is in violation of Salinger's copyright. In July, Seemann eliminates the direct quotes from Salinger's work and posts his e-mail exchanges with Ober.

Fall: Amazon.com lists the availability of *Hapworth 16, 1924* (simply a reprint of the 1965 *New Yorker* story, "Hapworth 16, 1924") for advance orders. The book, to be published by the small Orchises Press with an unspecified print run, is to be released in a blue buckram hardcover with no dust jacket, priced at $15.95.

November 15: The first article in the print media about the release of *Hapworth 16, 1924* appears in the *Washington Business Journal*. Articles proliferate; orders steadily increase at Amazon.com.

During 1996: J. D. Salinger's *The Catcher in the Rye*, a collection of critical essays, edited and with an introduction by Harold Bloom, is published in Chelsea House's Bloom's Notes series.

Events in Literature—1996: The Pulitzer Prize for fiction is awarded to Richard Ford's *Independence Day*; the National Book Award for fiction to Andrea Barrett's *Ship Fever and Other Stories*.

1997

Late January–early February: Prepublication orders for *Hapworth 16, 1924* make this forthcoming title the fourth-biggest seller on Amazon.com, and soon the third biggest.

February 20: In expectation of the imminent publication of "Hapworth 16, 1924" as a book, Michiko Kakutani's critical review of the story is published in the *New York Times*. "The infinitely engaging author of *The Catcher in the Rye . . .* has produced, with 'Hapworth,' a sour, implausible and, sad to say, completely charmless story."

April: The March publication date for *Hapworth 16, 1924* passes without its release. The book's publication date is reset, passes, and, without explanation from the publisher, lapses into limbo. In 2002, Amazon.com rescinds all prepublication orders. *Hapworth 16, 1924* was not published during Salinger's lifetime.

May: Dorothy Olding, Salinger's former agent and co-dedicatee of *Nine Stories*, dies.

June: Ron Rosenbaum's essay, "The Man in the Glass House," is published in *Esquire*. Rosenbaum suggests that "the Wall of Silence [Salinger had] built around himself, around his work—was in a way his most powerful, most eloquent, perhaps his most lasting work of art."

Events in Literature—1997: The Pulitzer Prize for fiction is awarded to Steven Millhauser's *Martin Dressler: The Tale of an American Dreamer*; the National Book Award for fiction to Charles Frazier's *Cold Mountain*.

1998

January 31: Fifty years ago today "A Perfect Day for Bananafish" was published in the *New Yorker*.

March: The Morgan Library announces the receipt of 11 letters written by Salinger to his artist friend, E. Michael Mitchell, designer of the original dust jacket of *The Catcher in the Rye*. In consideration of Salinger's privacy, the Morgan Library decides that the letters will not be made available to scholars until after Salinger's death.

November: An unauthorized Iranian film, *Pari*, loosely based on *Franny and Zooey*, is withdrawn from screening in New York City under threat of lawsuit.

During 1998: Joyce Maynard writes about her 1972–73 affair with Salinger in her highly publicized book, *At Home in the World: A Memoir.* The question of whether her publication during Salinger's lifetime constitutes an invasion of Salinger's privacy roils the literary world.

   Readings on The Catcher in the Rye, edited by Steven Engel, is published.

   Lillian Ross's memoir about her 40-year affair with William Shawn, *Here but Not Here: A Love Story*, is published. Ross asserts that only Salinger, of Shawn's writer-friends, "would go out of his way to be helpful to [Shawn] without asking for anything in return." She quotes Salinger as saying the letter protesting Shawn's firing wasn't "strong enough."

   Twenty-two Stories, a pirated edition of Salinger's uncollected stories in one paperback volume, is published by Train Bridge Recluse. All of the included stories originally appeared in magazines and were reprinted in 1974 in the unauthorized two-volume set *The Complete Uncollected Short Stories of J. D. Salinger.*

Events in Literature—1998: The Pulitzer Prize for fiction is awarded to Philip Roth's *American Pastoral*; the National Book Award for fiction to Alice McDermott's *Charming Billy.*

1999

January 1: Salinger turns 80.

March: BBC2's *Close Up* program broadcasts an unauthorized documentary film on Salinger titled *J. D. Salinger Doesn't Want to Talk.*

   Jerry Burt, a neighbor of Salinger's, is quoted in the film as saying that Salinger has "a huge bank safe" in his house. "He told me [in 1978] there were about 15 or 16 books finished but that he didn't know if they would be published."

May: Joyce Maynard announces her plans to auction love letters written to her by Salinger. Her decision further fuels the 1998 controversy regarding invasion of Salinger's privacy.

June: The second Salinger biography is published: Paul Alexander's *Salinger: A Biography*, issued by a small press. No advanced bound galleys are sent to reviewers.

June 22: Sotheby's auctions off the 14 letters written to Joyce Maynard by Salinger. The letters are purchased for $156,500 by Peter Norton, a software entrepreneur, who then offers to return the letters to Salinger or to destroy them. The fate of the letters is not publicly known.

During 1999: *Understanding The Catcher in the Rye: A Student Casebook to Issues, Sources and Historical Documents*, by Sanford and Ann Pinsker, is published.

   J. D. Salinger, edited and with an introduction by Harold Bloom, is published in Chelsea House's Bloom's Major Short Story Writers series.

   Renata Adler publishes her memoir, *Gone*, about the *New Yorker*. Adler asserts that Salinger once told her "the reason he chose not to publish the material he had been working on was to spare Mr. Shawn the burden of having to read, and to decide whether to publish, Salinger writing on sex."

Events in Literature—1999: The Pulitzer Prize for fiction is awarded to Michael Cunningham's *The Hours*; the National Book Award for fiction to Ha Jin's *Waiting.*

2000

April 8: Fifty years ago today "For Esmé—with Love and Squalor" was published in the *New Yorker.*

Fall: Salinger's daughter, Margaret Ann, publishes a book about the Salinger family, *Dream Catcher: A Memoir.* In the memoir, she reveals that Salinger has labeled his unpublished stories for future publication after his death: "a red mark [means], if I die before I finish my work, publish this 'as is,' blue [means] publish but edit first."

During 2000: "Slight Rebellion Off Madison" is reprinted in a book, *Wonderful Town: New York Stories from The New Yorker.* (The story originally appeared in the December 21, 1946, issue of the *New Yorker.*)

   In Cold Fear: The Catcher in the Rye Censorship Controversies and Postwar American Character, by Pamela Hunt Steinle, is published.

   J. D. Salinger's The Catcher in the Rye, a collection of critical essays, edited and with an introduction by Harold Bloom, is published in Chelsea House's Modern Critical Interpretations series.

The Fiction of J. D. Salinger: A Study in the Concept of Man, by Subhash Chandra, is published in India.

The American Library Association's tabulation for the 100 most frequently challenged books taught in schools for 1990–99 ranks *The Catcher in the Rye* 10th.

Events in Literature—2000: The Pulitzer Prize for fiction is awarded to Jhumpa Lahiri's *Interpreter of Maladies*; the National Book Award for fiction to Susan Sontag's *In America*.

2001

January: Little, Brown and Company publishes Salinger's four books in trade paperbacks with covers that mimic the original dust jackets and with text that matches the original typeface and pagination.

July 16: The 50th anniversary of the publication of *The Catcher in the Rye* passes unmarked by its publisher, Little, Brown and Company, at the author's request.

August 21: Doris Salinger, Salinger's sister and sole sibling, dies.

December 12: Margaret Ann Salinger puts up for auction 32 letters she received from her father. The minimum bid is not met, and the letters are returned to her.

December 27: Ian Hamilton, Salinger's ill-fated biographer, dies.

During 2001: *The Catcher in the Rye*, by John C. Unrue, is published in the Gale Group's Literary Masterpieces series.

With Love and Squalor: 14 Writers Respond to the Work of J. D. Salinger, edited by Kip Kotzen and Thomas Beller, is published.

Events in Literature—2001: The Pulitzer Prize for fiction is awarded to Michael Chabon's *The Amazing Adventures of Kavalier & Clay*; the National Book Award for fiction to Jonathan Franzen's *The Corrections*.

2002

During 2002: *J. D. Salinger*, by John C. Unrue, is published in the Gale Group's Literary Masters series.

Eberhard Alsen's second book of literary criticism on Salinger, *A Reader's Guide to J. D. Salinger*, is published.

The Catcher in the Rye: New Essays, edited by J. P. Steed, is published.

An Annotated Bibliography, 1982–2002, of J. D. Salinger, by Brett E. Weaver, is published.

J. D. Salinger, a collection of essays, edited and with an introduction by Harold Bloom, is published in Chelsea House's Bloom's BioCritiques series.

Letters to J. D. Salinger, edited by Chris Kubica and Will Hochman, is published.

Events in Literature—2002: The Pulitzer Prize for fiction is awarded to Richard Russo's *Empire Falls*; the National Book Award for fiction to Julia Glass's *Three Junes*.

2003

April 6: Fifty years ago today, *Nine Stories* was published.

Fall: Dominic Smith's "Salinger's *Nine Stories*: Fifty Years Later" appears in the *Antioch Review*: "Not since Hemingway's *In Our Time* had a collection of stories so raised the bar on the form, creating characters and scenes that were hypnotic, mysterious, and unusually powerful."

Events in Literature—2003: The Pulitzer Prize for fiction is awarded to Jeffrey Eugenides's *Middlesex*; the National Book Award for fiction to Shirley Hazzard's *The Great Fire*.

2004

January 1: Salinger turns 85.

Events in Literature—2004: The Pulitzer Prize for fiction is awarded to Edward P. Jones's *The Known World*; the National Book Award for fiction to Lily Tuck's *The News from Paraguay*.

2005

January 29: Fifty years ago today, "Franny" was published in the *New Yorker*.

June 19: Salinger's publishing silence reaches 40 years. His last authorized publication was "Hapworth 16, 1924" in the June 19, 1965, issue of the *New Yorker*.

September: The *New Yorker* releases *The Complete New Yorker* on DVD. The eight-disc set contains every issue of the magazine to date. All 13 of Salinger's stories, including the noncollected stories, "Hapworth 16, 1924" and "Slight Rebellion Off Madison," are now readily available in their original publication format.

November 19: Fifty years ago today, "Raise High the Roof Beam, Carpenters," the story that introduced the entire Glass family, was published in the *New Yorker*.

During 2005: *Consuming Silences: How We Read Authors Who Don't Publish*, by Myles Weber, is published and includes a long chapter on Salinger.

The second edition of *Holden Caulfield*, a new selection of critical essays, edited and with an introduction by Harold Bloom, is published in Chelsea House's Bloom's Major Literary Characters series.

Events in Literature—2005: The Pulitzer Prize for fiction is awarded to Marilynne Robinson's *Gilead*; the National Book Award for fiction to William T. Vollmann's *Europe Central*.

2006

January: Ursinus College announces a writing scholarship named in honor of J. D. Salinger.

March: Having failed to seek Salinger's permission to use his name on the scholarship, Ursinus College removes the dedication upon notice from Salinger's agent.

April: A multimedia installation, ostensibly depicting the Glass family's bathroom, appears in a New York City storefront display.

November 19: Seventeen Salinger letters to Janet Eagleson, a close friend in the early 1980s, are sold at auction.

During 2006: *If You Really Want to Hear about It: Writers on J. D. Salinger and His Work*, edited by Catherine Crawford, is published.

JD: A Memoir of a Time and a Journey, by Greg Herriges, is published.

Events in Literature—2006: The Pulitzer Prize for fiction is awarded to Geraldine Brooks's *March*; the National Book Award for fiction to Richard Powers's *The Echo Maker*.

2007

May 4: Fifty years ago today, "Zooey" was published in the *New Yorker*.

July 16: Salinger's first wife, Sylvia, dies. An obituary appears on the premier Salinger Web site, www.deadcaulfields.com.

During 2007: *J. D. Salinger: The Catcher in the Rye and Other Works*, by Raychel Haugrud Reiff, is published in Marshall Cavendish Benchmark's Writers and Their Works series.

J. D. Salinger's The Catcher in the Rye, edited and with an introduction by Harold Bloom, is published in Chelsea House's Bloom's Guides series.

Sarah Graham publishes two books on *The Catcher in the Rye*: *Salinger's The Catcher in the Rye*, in Continuum's Reader's Guides series, and a more scholarly text (which includes several commissioned critical essays), *J. D. Salinger's The Catcher in the Rye*, in Routledge's Guides to Literature series.

Brother Dumb, by Sky Gilbert, is published in Canada (but not in America). The novel employs the conceit of being Salinger's memoir—his true confessions—published after his death. To avoid litigation, the author names neither Salinger nor any of his works' specific titles.

Events in Literature—2007: The Pulitzer Prize for fiction is awarded to Cormac McCarthy's *The Road*; the National Book Award for fiction to Denis Johnson's *Tree of Smoke*.

2008

January 28: Forty-five years ago today Salinger's last authorized book during his lifetime—*Raise High the Roof Beam, Carpenters and Seymour: An Introduction*—was published.

March: The Harris Poll surveys 2,500 American adults and finds that *The Catcher in the Rye* ranks 10th as the most favorite book of all time.

July: Salinger's lawyers create the J. D. Salinger Literary Trust. Salinger is the sole trustee during his lifetime.

October 15: In Hanover, New Hampshire, Salinger signs a legal document that "sets over and assigns to The Trustee of the J. D. Salinger Literary Trust his entire right, title and interest in and to the copyrights" of his work.

December: The 2008 Nobel Laureate in Literature, Jean-Marie Le Clézio, cites Salinger as his greatest literary influence, singling out *The Catcher in the Rye*.

During 2008: For the second edition of *J. D. Salinger,* a new selection of essays is chosen by Harold Bloom; the volume is published in Chelsea House's Bloom's Modern Critical Views series.

The American Library Association's tabulation for the 100 most frequently challenged books taught in schools for 2000–07 ranks *The Catcher in the Rye* 19th.

The movie *Chapter 27,* portraying Mark David Chapman's murder of John Lennon in 1980, is released. Chapman's twisted obsession with *The Catcher in the Rye* is once again brought to the public's attention.

Events in Literature—2008: The Pulitzer Prize for fiction is awarded to Junot Diaz's *The Brief Wondrous Life of Oscar Wao*; the National Book Award for fiction to Peter Matthiessen's *Shadow Country.*

2009

January 1: Salinger turns 90. His birthday is noted in the press worldwide. The *New York Times* discounts Salinger's ideas and spiritual aspirations but lauds his powers of observation and comedy: "He remains an original and influential stylist."

February 9: Amazon.com releases *J. D.: The Plot to Steal J. D. Salinger's Manuscripts,* by the mystery writer Sierra Philpin, as a Kindle book.

Spring: *60 Years Later: Coming through the Rye,* by "John David California," is published by a small London-based press. The book calls itself a "sequel to one of our most beloved classics" and is dedicated to J. D. Salinger. The pseudonymous author, according to his publisher's Web site, is a Swedish-American freelance travel writer; *60 Years Later: Coming through the Rye* is his first novel.

Mid-May: Salinger's lawyers learn of *60 Years Later: Coming through the Rye.* A spokesperson for the publisher eschews the basis for legal action in America, noting that the novel's first-person narrator, the 76-year-old "Mr. C," never reveals his name. "Mr. C" has left a nursing home in Upstate New York to return to New York City to revisit people and places from his past.

May 30: With word of a lawsuit imminent, "John David California" states that, because *60 Years Later* and *The Catcher in the Rye* are so different in nature, his book should not be considered a sequel to Salinger's novel.

June 1: Salinger's lawyers file a complaint in the U.S. District Court in New York City, seeking an injunction against the sale and distribution of *60 Years Later: Coming through the Rye* in America. Salinger's complaint publicly reveals that the author, in 2008, created the J. D. Salinger Literary Trust, of which he is sole trustee during his lifetime. Phyllis Westberg, Salinger's agent, reveals in an affidavit that Salinger, though in ill health, is aware of the legal action. Westberg estimates that were Salinger to write a sequel to *The Catcher in the Rye,* that novel would command a $5 million advance. The lawsuit generates worldwide attention.

June 6: Fifty years ago today, "Seymour: An Introduction" was published in the *New Yorker.*

June 10: "John David California" identifies himself as Fredrik Colting, a 33-year-old Swede. Cofounder of a small Swedish publishing house, Nicotext (which founded Windupbird, publisher of *60 Years Later*), Colting has written several books of humor.

Mid-June: Colting's lawyers defend *60 Years Later,* describing the book as parody and denying it is a sequel to *The Catcher in the Rye.* The lawyers assert that Colting's book critiques Salinger's relationship with Holden Caulfield—noting Colting's use of a character named Salinger—and they seek protection to publish in America under the doctrine of fair use.

July 1: Judge Deborah Batts rules in Salinger's favor, rejecting the defendant's claim of fair use. Batts issues a temporary order against the publication and distribution of *60 Years Later: Coming through the Rye* in America. Colting's lawyers will appeal and seek an expedited hearing. Salinger's lawyers offer no further comment.

July 10: Colting expresses disappointment in Batts's decision but states that the judge's order affects only American distribution.

August: Briefs in support of Colting's appeal are filed by major media corporations and library associations.

September: The U.S. Second Circuit Court of Appeals in Manhattan hears Colting's appeal.

During 2009: Depression in J. D. Salinger's The Catcher in the Rye, a collection of critical essays, plus supplementary material on teenage depression, edited and with an introduction by Dedria Bryfonski, is published in Greenhaven Press's Social Issues in Literature series.

For the second edition of *J. D. Salinger's The Catcher in the Rye,* a new selection of essays is chosen by Harold Bloom; the volume is published in Chelsea House's Bloom's Modern Critical Interpretations series.

A Reader's Companion to J. D. Salinger's The Catcher in the Rye, by Peter G. Beidler, is published.

A Catcher's Companion: The World of Holden Caulfield, by Sean McDaniel, is published.

Events in Literature—2009: The Pulitzer Prize for fiction is awarded to Elizabeth Strout's *Olive Kitteridge;* the National Book Award for fiction to Colum McCann's *Let the Great World Spin.*

2010

January 27: Jerome David Salinger, age 91, dies of natural causes at his home in Cornish, New Hampshire.

January 28: The announcement of Salinger's death commands worldwide notice. His representatives refuse comment about unpublished works. (As of June 2010, no publication plans have been announced.)

Phyllis Westberg, Salinger's agent, tells the *Hollywood Reporter* that the trustees of the J. D. Salinger Literary Trust (whose identities she would not reveal) will honor his desire that there be no film made of *The Catcher in the Rye.*

January 29: An article, "Why J. D. Salinger Never Wanted a 'Catcher in the Rye' Movie," by Dave Itzkoff, appears on the Web site of the *New York Times* (www.nytimes.com). Itzkoff quotes from a July 19, 1957, letter in which Salinger explains his hesitancy in selling the movie and stage rights to his novel. A link to the entire letter reveals that M.I.T. Memorabilia Inc. has priced the two-page letter at $54,000.

Late January: The *New Yorker* magazine creates a tribute to Salinger on its Web site (www.newyorker.com). The tribute includes an appreciation by Adam Gopnik, reminiscences by Lillian Ross and John Seabrook, a gallery of photographs from Ross's personal collection, links to Salinger's 13 stories as they appeared in the original *New Yorker* issues, and a reader forum. Gopnik cites *The Catcher in the Rye* as one of "three perfect books" in American literature. He heretically (though correctly) assesses the Glass family saga, when compared with the novel, as "the larger accomplishment." Ross, drawing on her decades-long correspondence with Salinger, reveals that Salinger, at one point, considered writing an autobiography, and that Ralph Waldo Emerson was perhaps his favorite American author. Seabrook recalls the beginning of his friendship with Salinger, sketching an evening in Cornish, New Hampshire, with Salinger as movie projectionist. The articles create a memorable, and moving, triptych of the author.

More previously unknown Salinger correspondence begins to surface, promising future additional information about the author's life and work.

The existence of a recently completed, two-hour documentary, *Salinger,* by Shane Salerno, becomes public knowledge.

February 1: The Smithsonian's National Portrait Gallery displays Robert Vickrey's portrait of Salinger. The painting originally appeared as the September 15, 1961, cover of *Time* magazine.

February 8: The *New Yorker,* in its print issue, includes the contributions by Gopnik, Ross, and Seabrook that earlier appeared on its Web site tribute to Salinger, two color photographs of Salinger with his young children and his godson (from Ross's collection), and a portrait sketch in "The Talk of the Town."

February 11: Salinger's lawyers file a motion to continue his lawsuit against Fredrik Colting. The motion reveals that the new trustees of the J. D. Salinger Literary Trust are Salinger's widow, Colleen, and his son, Matthew.

February 26: The Harry Ransom Center at the University of Texas at Austin opens an exhibition of its rare Salinger holdings.

March 15: The third unauthorized biography of Salinger is published: *J. D. Salinger: A Life Raised High.* Authored by Kenneth Slawenski, creator of the premier Salinger Web site, www.deadcaulfields.com, the book is released in Britain by a small press, Pomona Books.

March 16: The Morgan Library in New York City opens the first half of its two-part exhibit of Salinger's letters to E. Michael Mitchell, designer of the first edition dust jacket of *The Catcher in the Rye* and Salinger's best man at his 1955 wedding to Claire Douglas. The correspondence, composed of 11 letters dating from 1951 to 1993, indicates that Salinger, by 1966, had amassed a number of unpublished manuscripts, including two completed books. The letters likewise show that the author maintained a strict writing schedule into at least the 1980s, and that his manuscripts survived the 1992 fire that destroyed half of his house.

March 28: The John F. Kennedy Library in Boston displays Salinger's important July 27, 1945, letter addressed to Ernest Hemingway, on the occasion of the PEN/Hemingway Award.

April 4: The Web site of *New York* magazine (www.nymag.com) runs a feature article, "Betraying Salinger," by publisher Roger Lathbury. Lathbury gives the fullest account of the story surrounding *Hapworth 16, 1924,* which would have been Salinger's fifth published book.

April 30: The U.S. Second Court of Appeals, in general agreement with Judge Deborah Batts's original ruling in Salinger's favor, returns the case to her for additional consideration. (As of June 2010, no decision has been announced.)

BIBLIOGRAPHY OF SALINGER'S PUBLISHED WORKS

Books

The Catcher in the Rye. Boston: Little, Brown and Company, 1951.

Nine Stories. Boston: Little, Brown and Company, 1953.

Franny and Zooey. Boston: Little, Brown and Company, 1961.

Raise High the Roof Beam, Carpenters and Seymour: An Introduction. Boston: Little, Brown and Company, 1963.

Salinger's four books have never gone out of print and are currently available in multiple editions. Three of the books—*Nine Stories*; *Franny and Zooey*; *Raise High the Roof Beam, Carpenters and Seymour: An Introduction*—collect 13 of Salinger's 35 stories originally published in magazines. *Nine Stories* collects "A Perfect Day for Bananafish," "Uncle Wiggily in Connecticut," "Just Before the War with the Eskimos," "The Laughing Man," "Down at the Dinghy," "For Esmé—with Love and Squalor," "Pretty Mouth and Green My Eyes," "De Daumier-Smith's Blue Period," and "Teddy." *Franny and Zooey* collects the stories "Franny" and "Zooey." *Raise High the Roof Beam, Carpenters and Seymour: An Introduction* collects the stories "Raise High the Roof Beam, Carpenters" and "Seymour: An Introduction." For detailed information concerning Salinger's 35 published stories, see below.

FICTION IN CHRONOLOGICAL ORDER OF PUBLICATION

1940

"The Young Folks." *Story,* March–April 1940, 26–30. [uncollected by JDS]

"Go See Eddie." *University of Kansas City Review* 7 (December 1940): 121–124. [uncollected by JDS]

1941

"The Hang of It." *Collier's,* 12 July 1941, 22. [uncollected by JDS]

"The Heart of a Broken Story." *Esquire,* September 1941, 32, 131–133. [uncollected by JDS]

1942

"The Long Debut of Lois Taggett." *Story,* September–October 1942, 28–34. [uncollected by JDS]

"Personal Notes on an Infantryman." *Collier's,* 12 December 1942, 96. [uncollected by JDS]

1943

"The Varioni Brothers." *Saturday Evening Post,* 17 July 1943, 12–13, 76–77. [uncollected by JDS]

1944

"Both Parties Concerned." *Saturday Evening Post,* 26 February 1944, 14, 47–48. [uncollected by JDS]

"Soft-Boiled Sergeant." *Saturday Evening Post,* 15 April 1944, 18, 82, 84–85. [uncollected by JDS]

"Last Day of the Last Furlough." *Saturday Evening Post,* 15 July 1944, 26–27, 61–62, 64. [uncollected by JDS]

"Once a Week Won't Kill You." *Story,* November–December 1944, 23–27. [uncollected by JDS]

1945

"Elaine." *Story,* March–April 1945, 38–47. [uncollected by JDS]

"A Boy in France." *Saturday Evening Post,* 31 March 1945, 21, 92. [uncollected by JDS]

"This Sandwich Has No Mayonnaise." *Esquire,* October 1945, 54–56, 147–149. [uncollected by JDS]

"The Stranger." *Collier's*, 1 December 1945, 18, 77. [uncollected by JDS]

"I'm Crazy." *Collier's*, 22 December 1945, 36, 48, 51. [uncollected by JDS, but incorporated into *The Catcher in the Rye*]

1946

"Slight Rebellion Off Madison." *New Yorker*, 21 December 1946, 82–86. [uncollected by JDS, but incorporated into *The Catcher in the Rye*]

1947

"A Young Girl in 1941 with No Waist at All." *Mademoiselle*, May 1947, 222–223, 292–302. [uncollected by JDS]

"The Inverted Forest." *Cosmopolitan*, December 1947, 73–80, 85–86, 88, 90, 92, 95–96, 98, 100, 102, 107, 109. [uncollected by JDS]

1948

"A Perfect Day for Bananafish." *New Yorker*, 31 January 1948, 21–25. [collected by JDS in *Nine Stories*]

"A Girl I Knew." *Good Housekeeping*, February 1948, 36–37, 186, 188, 191–196. [uncollected by JDS]

"Uncle Wiggily in Connecticut." *New Yorker*, 20 March 1948, 30–36. [collected by JDS in *Nine Stories*]

"Just Before the War with the Eskimos." *New Yorker*, 5 June 1948, 37–40, 42, 44, 46. [collected by JDS in *Nine Stories*]

"Blue Melody." *Cosmopolitan*, September 1948, 50–51, 112–119. [uncollected by JDS]

1949

"The Laughing Man." *New Yorker*, 19 March 1949, 27–32. [collected by JDS in *Nine Stories*]

"Down at the Dinghy." *Harper's*, April 1949, 87–91. [collected by JDS in *Nine Stories*]

1950

"For Esmé—with Love and Squalor." *New Yorker*, 8 April 1950, 28–36. [collected by JDS in *Nine Stories*]

1951

"Pretty Mouth and Green My Eyes." *New Yorker*, 14 July 1951, 20–24. [collected by JDS in *Nine Stories*]

The Catcher in the Rye. Boston: Little, Brown and Company, 16 July 1951.

1952

"De Daumier-Smith's Blue Period." *World Review*, No. 39, n.s. (May 1952): 33–48. [collected by JDS in *Nine Stories*]

1953

"Teddy." *New Yorker*, 31 January 1953, 26–34, 36, 38, 40–41, 44–45. [collected by JDS in *Nine Stories*]

Nine Stories. Boston: Little, Brown and Company, 6 April 1953.

1955

"Franny." *New Yorker*, 29 January 1955, 24–32, 35–43. [collected by JDS in *Franny and Zooey*]

"Raise High the Roof Beam, Carpenters." *New Yorker*, 19 November 1955, 51–116 [of which 20 pages are full-page ads]. [collected by JDS in *Raise High the Roof Beam, Carpenters and Seymour: An Introduction*]

1957

"Zooey." *New Yorker*, 4 May 1957, 32–139 [of which 31 pages are full-page ads]. [collected by JDS in *Franny and Zooey*]

1959

"Seymour: An Introduction." *New Yorker*, 6 June 1959, 42–119 [of which 24 pages are full-page ads]. [collected by JDS in *Raise High the Roof Beam, Carpenters and Seymour: An Introduction*]

1961

Franny and Zooey. Boston: Little, Brown and Company, 14 September 1961.

1963

Raise High the Roof Beam, Carpenters and Seymour: An Introduction. Boston: Little, Brown and Company, 28 January 1963.

1965

"Hapworth 16, 1924." *New Yorker*, 19 June 1965, 32–113 [of which 32 pages are full-page ads]. [uncollected by JDS]

[Note: The 22 stories uncollected by Salinger in any of his books were illegally and anonymously collected in a two-volume, paperback edition, *The Complete Uncollected Short Stories of J. D. Salinger,* which appeared in 1974.]

MISCELLANEOUS PUBLICATIONS IN CHRONOLOGICAL ORDER

1936

"Class Poem." *Crossed Sabres,* Valley Forge Military Academy Yearbook, 1936: 138.

1938

"Musings of a Social Soph: The Skipped Diploma." *Ursinus Weekly,* October 10, 1938: 2.

"J. D. S.'s The Skipped Diploma." *Ursinus Weekly,* October 17, 1938: 2.

"J. D. S.'s The Skipped Diploma." *Ursinus Weekly,* October 24, 1938: 2.

"J. D. S.'s The Skipped Diploma." *Ursinus Weekly,* October 31, 1938: 2.

"J. D. S.'s The Skipped Diploma." *Ursinus Weekly,* November 7, 1938: 2.

"J. D. S.'s The Skipped Diploma." *Ursinus Weekly,* November 14, 1938: 2.

"Strong Cast Scores in Priestley's Sombre Post-War Drama." *Ursinus Weekly,* November 14, 1938.

"J. D. S.'s The Skipped Diploma." *Ursinus Weekly,* November 21, 1938: 2.

"J. D. S.'s The Skipped Diploma." *Ursinus Weekly,* December 5, 1938: 2.

"J. D. S.'s The Skipped Diploma." *Ursinus Weekly,* December 12, 1938: 2.

"Seniors Present Comedy, Ball as Final Social Contributions." *Ursinus Weekly,* December 12, 1938.

1942

[Autobiographical statement in "Contributors"] *Story,* September–October 1942, 2.

1944

[Autobiographical statement in "Contributors"] *Story,* November–December 1944, 1.

1945

[Autobiographical statement in "Backstage with Esquire"] *Esquire,* October 1945, 34.

1951

[Autobiographical statement on dust jacket] *The Catcher in the Rye.* Boston: Little, Brown and Company, 1951.

1955

[Letter to the editor] *Twentieth Century Authors,* edited by Stanley J. Kunitz and Vincent Colby, 859. New York: H. W. Wilson, 1955.

1959

"J. D. Salinger—Biographical." *Harper's,* February 1959, 87.

"Man-Forsaken Men." *New York Post Magazine,* 9 December 1959, p. 49.

1961

[Autobiographical statement on dust jacket] *Franny and Zooey.* Boston: Little, Brown and Company, 1961.

1963

[Autobiographical statement on dust jacket] *Raise High the Roof Beam, Carpenters and Seymour: An Introduction.* Boston: Little, Brown and Company, 1963.

1965

[Telegram protesting articles on William Shawn and the *New Yorker*] *New York Herald Tribune* [in April 1965]. Reprinted in *Hooking Up,* by Tom Wolfe, 288–289. New York: Farrar, Straus and Giroux, 2000.

1975

"A Salute to Whit Burnett 1899–1972." In *Fiction Writer's Handbook,* by Hallie and Whit Burnett, 187–188. New York: Harper & Row, 1975.

FICTION IN ALPHABETICAL ORDER BY TITLE

"Blue Melody." *Cosmopolitan,* September 1948.

"Both Parties Concerned." *Saturday Evening Post,* February 26, 1944.

"A Boy in France." *Saturday Evening Post,* March 31, 1945.

The Catcher in the Rye. Little, Brown and Company, July 16, 1951.

"De Daumier-Smith's Blue Period." *World Review,* May 1952.

"Down at the Dinghy." *Harper's,* April 1949.

"Elaine." *Story,* March–April 1945.

"For Esmé—with Love and Squalor." *New Yorker,* April 8, 1950.

"Franny." *New Yorker*, January 29, 1955.

Franny and Zooey. Little, Brown and Company, September 14, 1961.

"A Girl I Knew." *Good Housekeeping*, February 1948.

"Go See Eddie." *University of Kansas City Review*, December 1940.

"The Hang of It." *Collier's*, July 12, 1941.

"Hapworth 16, 1924." *New Yorker*, June 19, 1965.

"The Heart of a Broken Story." *Esquire*, September 1941.

"I'm Crazy." *Collier's*, December 22, 1945.

"The Inverted Forest." *Cosmopolitan*, December 1947.

"Just Before the War with the Eskimos." *New Yorker*, June 5, 1948.

"Last Day of the Last Furlough." *Saturday Evening Post*, July 15, 1944.

"The Laughing Man." *New Yorker*, March 19, 1949.

"The Long Debut of Lois Taggett." *Story*, September–October 1942.

Nine Stories. Little, Brown and Company, April 6, 1953.

"Once a Week Won't Kill You." *Story*, November–December 1944.

"A Perfect Day for Bananafish." *New Yorker*, January 31, 1948.

"Personal Notes on an Infantryman." *Collier's*, December 12, 1942.

"Pretty Mouth and Green My Eyes." *New Yorker*, July 14, 1951.

"Raise High the Roof Beam, Carpenters." *New Yorker*, November 19, 1955.

Raise High the Roof Beam, Carpenters and Seymour: An Introduction. Little, Brown and Company, January 28, 1963.

"Seymour: An Introduction." *New Yorker*, June 6, 1959.

"Slight Rebellion Off Madison." *New Yorker*, December 21, 1946.

"Soft-Boiled Sergeant." *Saturday Evening Post*, April 15, 1944.

"The Stranger." *Collier's*, December 1, 1945.

"Teddy." *New Yorker*, January 31, 1953.

"This Sandwich Has No Mayonnaise." *Esquire*, October 1945.

"Uncle Wiggily in Connecticut." *New Yorker*, March 20, 1948.

"The Varioni Brothers." *Saturday Evening Post*, July 17, 1943.

"The Young Folks." *Story*, March–April 1940.

"A Young Girl in 1941 with No Waist at All." *Mademoiselle*, May 1947.

"Zooey." *New Yorker*, May 4, 1957.

FIRST BOOK PUBLICATION OF STORIES

"Blue Melody." In *The Complete Uncollected Short Stories of J. D. Salinger* [unauthorized publication], 1974.

"Both Parties Concerned." In *The Complete Uncollected Short Stories of J. D. Salinger* [unauthorized publication], 1974.

"A Boy in France." In *The Saturday Evening Post Stories, 1942–1945*, edited by Ben Hibbs. New York: Random House, 1945.

"De Daumier-Smith's Blue Period." In *Nine Stories*. Boston: Little, Brown and Company, 1953.

"Down at the Dinghy." In *Nine Stories*. Boston: Little, Brown and Company, 1953.

"Elaine." In *The Complete Uncollected Short Stories of J. D. Salinger* [unauthorized publication], 1974.

"For Esmé—with Love and Squalor." In *Prize Stories of 1950: The O. Henry Awards*, edited by Herschel Brickell. Garden City, N.Y.: Doubleday, 1950.

"Franny." In *Franny and Zooey*. Boston: Little, Brown and Company, 1961.

"A Girl I Knew." In *The Best American Short Stories of 1949; and the Yearbook of the American Short Story*, edited by Martha J. Foley. Boston: Houghton Mifflin, 1949.

"Go See Eddie." In *Fiction: Form and Experience*, edited by William M. Jones. Lexington, Mass.: D. C. Heath [unauthorized publication], 1969.

"The Hang of It." In *The Kitbook for Soldiers, Sailors, and Marines*, edited by R. M. Barrows. Chicago: Consolidated Book Publishers, 1942.

"Hapworth 16, 1924." In *The Complete Uncollected Short Stories of J. D. Salinger* [unauthorized publication], 1974.

"The Heart of a Broken Story." In *The Complete Uncollected Short Stories of J. D. Salinger* [unauthorized publication], 1974.

"I'm Crazy." In *The Complete Uncollected Short Stories of J. D. Salinger* [unauthorized publication], 1974.

"The Inverted Forest." In *The Complete Uncollected Short Stories of J. D. Salinger* [unauthorized publication], 1974.

"Just Before the War with the Eskimos." In *Prize Stories of 1949*, edited by Herschel Brickell. Garden City, N.Y.: Doubleday, 1949.

"Last Day of the Last Furlough." In *The Complete Uncollected Short Stories of J. D. Salinger* [unauthorized publication], 1974.

"The Laughing Man." In *Nine Stories*. Boston: Little, Brown and Company, 1953.

"The Long Debut of Lois Taggett." In *Story: The Fiction of the Forties*, edited by Whit and Hallie Burnett. New York: E. P. Dutton, 1949.

"Once a Week Won't Kill You." In *The Complete Uncollected Short Stories of J. D. Salinger* [unauthorized publication], 1974.

"A Perfect Day for Bananafish." In *55 Short Stories from The New Yorker: 1940–1950*, edited by the *New Yorker* Editors. New York: Simon and Schuster, 1949.

"Personal Notes on an Infantryman." In *The Complete Uncollected Short Stories of J. D. Salinger* [unauthorized publication], 1974.

"Pretty Mouth and Green My Eyes." In *Nine Stories*. Boston: Little, Brown and Company, 1953.

"Raise High the Roof Beam, Carpenters." In *Stories from The New Yorker, 1950–1960*, edited by the *New Yorker* Editors. New York: Simon and Schuster, 1960.

"Seymour: An Introduction." *Raise High the Roof Beam, Carpenters and Seymour: An Introduction.* Boston: Little, Brown and Company, 1963.

"Slight Rebellion Off Madison." In *The Complete Uncollected Short Stories of J. D. Salinger* [unauthorized publication], 1974.

"Soft-Boiled Sergeant." In *The Complete Uncollected Short Stories of J. D. Salinger* [unauthorized publication], 1974.

"The Stranger." In *The Complete Uncollected Short Stories of J. D. Salinger* [unauthorized publication], 1974.

"Teddy." In *Nine Stories*. Boston: Little, Brown and Company, 1953.

"This Sandwich Has No Mayonnaise." In *The Armchair Esquire*, edited by Arnold Gingrich and L. Rust Hills. New York: G. P. Putnam's Sons, 1958.

"Uncle Wiggily in Connecticut." In *Nine Stories*. Boston: Little, Brown and Company, 1953.

"The Varioni Brothers." In *The Complete Uncollected Short Stories of J. D. Salinger* [unauthorized publication], 1974.

"The Young Folks." In *The Complete Uncollected Short Stories of J. D. Salinger* [unauthorized publication], 1974.

"A Young Girl in 1941 with No Waist at All." In *The Complete Uncollected Short Stories of J. D. Salinger* [unauthorized publication], 1974.

"Zooey." In *Franny and Zooey*. Boston: Little, Brown and Company, 1961.

ANTHOLOGIZED STORIES

"A Boy in France." In *The Saturday Evening Post Stories, 1942–1945*, edited by Ben Hibbs. New York: Random House, 1945.

"For Esmé—with Love and Squalor." In *Prize Stories of 1950: The O. Henry Awards*, edited by Herschel Brickell. Garden City, N.Y.: Doubleday, 1950.

In *50 Great Short Stories*, edited by Milton Crane. New York: Bantam, 1952.

In *Better Reading Two: Literature*, edited by Walter Blair and John C. Gerber. Chicago: Scott, Foresman, 1954.

In *Interpreting Literature*, edited by K. L. Knickerbocker and H. Willard Reninger. New York: Henry Holt, 1955.

In *Reportory*, edited by Walter Blair and John C. Gerber. Chicago: Scott, Foresman, 1960.

"A Girl I Knew." In *The Best American Short Stories of 1949; and the Yearbook of the American Short Story*, edited by Martha J. Foley. Boston: Houghton Mifflin, 1949.

"Go See Eddie." In *Fiction: Form and Experience*, edited by William M. Jones. Lexington, Mass.: D. C. Heath, 1969.

"The Hang of It." In *The Kitbook for Soldiers, Sailors, and Marines*, edited by R. M. Barrows. Chicago: Consolidated Book Publishers, 1942.

"Just Before the War with the Eskimos." In *Prize Stories of 1949: The O. Henry Awards*, edited by Herschel Brickell. Garden City, N.Y.: Doubleday, 1949.

In *Manhattan: Stories from the Heart of a Great City*, edited by Seymour Krim. New York: Bantam, 1954.

"The Long Debut of Lois Taggett." In *Story: The Fiction of the Forties*, edited by Whit and Hallie Burnett. New York: E. P. Dutton, 1949.

"A Perfect Day for Bananafish." In *55 Short Stories from The New Yorker: 1940–1950*, edited by the *New Yorker* Editors. New York: Simon and Schuster, 1949.

"Pretty Mouth and Green My Eyes." In *Anthology of Famous American Short Stories*, edited by J. A. Burrell and B. A. Cerf. New York: Modern Library, 1953.

"Raise High the Roof Beam, Carpenters." In *Stories from The New Yorker, 1950–1960*, edited by the *New Yorker* Editors. New York: Simon and Schuster, 1960.

"Slight Rebellion Off Madison." In *Wonderful Town: New York Stories from The New Yorker,* edited by David Remnick. New York: Random House, 2000.

"This Sandwich Has No Mayonnaise." In *The Armchair Esquire,* edited by Arnold Gingrich and L. Rust Hills. New York: G. P. Putnam's Sons, 1958.

"Uncle Wiggily in Connecticut." In *Short Story Masterpieces,* edited by Robert Penn Warren and Albert Erskine. New York: Dell Books, 1954.

Year-by-Year Time Line of Salinger Publications

1936

"Class Poem," a poem published in *Crossed Sabres*, a high-school yearbook.

1938

"J. D. S.'s The Skipped Diploma," a column published nine times in *Ursinus Weekly*, a college student newspaper.

Two reviews of student plays published in *Ursinus Weekly*, a college student newspaper.

1940

"The Young Folks" published in *Story* magazine.

"Go See Eddie" published in the *University of Kansas City Review* journal.

1941

"The Hang of It" published in *Collier's* magazine.

"The Heart of a Broken Story" published in *Esquire* magazine.

1942

"The Long Debut of Lois Taggett" published in *Story* magazine.

Autobiographical statement published in *Story* magazine.

"Personal Notes on an Infantryman" published in *Collier's* magazine.

"The Hang of It" reprinted in an anthology, *The Kitbook for Soldiers, Sailors, and Marines*.

1943

"The Varioni Brothers" published in the *Saturday Evening Post* magazine.

1944

"Both Parties Concerned" published in the *Saturday Evening Post* magazine.

"Soft-Boiled Sergeant" published in the *Saturday Evening Post* magazine.

"Last Day of the Last Furlough" published in the *Saturday Evening Post* magazine.

"Once a Week Won't Kill You" published in *Story* magazine.

Autobiographical statement published in *Story* magazine.

1945

"Elaine" published in *Story* magazine.

"A Boy in France" published in the *Saturday Evening Post* magazine.

"This Sandwich Has No Mayonnaise" published in *Esquire* magazine.

Autobiographical statement published in *Esquire* magazine.

"The Stranger" published in *Collier's* magazine.

"I'm Crazy" published in *Collier's* magazine.

"A Boy in France" reprinted in an anthology, *The Saturday Evening Post Stories, 1942–1945*.

1946

"Slight Rebellion Off Madison" published in the *New Yorker* magazine.

1947

"A Young Girl in 1941 with No Waist at All" published in *Mademoiselle* magazine.

"The Inverted Forest" published in *Cosmopolitan* magazine.

1948

"A Perfect Day for Bananafish" published in the *New Yorker* magazine.

"A Girl I Knew" published in *Good Housekeeping* magazine.

"Uncle Wiggily in Connecticut" published in the *New Yorker* magazine.

"Just Before the War with the Eskimos" published in the *New Yorker* magazine.

"Blue Melody" published in *Cosmopolitan* magazine.

1949

"The Laughing Man" published in the *New Yorker* magazine.

"Down at the Dinghy" published in *Harper's* magazine.

"The Long Debut of Lois Taggett" reprinted in an anthology, *Story: The Fiction of Forties*.

"A Girl I Knew" reprinted in an anthology, *The Best American Short Stories of 1949; and the Yearbook of the American Short Story*.

"A Perfect Day for Bananafish" reprinted in an anthology, *55 Short Stories from The New Yorker: 1940–1950*.

"Just Before the War with the Eskimos" reprinted in an anthology, *Prize Stories of 1949: The O. Henry Awards*.

1950

"For Esmé—with Love and Squalor" published in the *New Yorker* magazine.

"For Esmé—with Love and Squalor" reprinted in an anthology, *Prize Stories of 1950: The O. Henry Awards*.

1951

"Pretty Mouth and Green My Eyes" published in the *New Yorker* magazine.

The Catcher in the Rye published by Little, Brown and Company.

Autobiographical statement included on dust jacket of *The Catcher in the Rye*.

1952

"De Daumier-Smith's Blue Period" published in *World Review* journal.

"For Esmé—with Love and Squalor" reprinted in an anthology, *50 Great Short Stories*.

The Catcher in the Rye reprinted in library edition (Grosset and Dunlap).

1953

"Teddy" published in the *New Yorker* magazine.

Nine Stories published by Little, Brown and Company.

The Catcher in the Rye reprinted in paperback edition (New American Library).

"Pretty Mouth and Green My Eyes" reprinted in an anthology, *Anthology of Famous American Short Stories*.

1954

Nine Stories reprinted in paperback edition (New American Library).

"Uncle Wiggily in Connecticut" reprinted in an anthology, *Short Story Masterpieces*.

"Just Before the War with the Eskimos" reprinted in an anthology, *Manhattan: Stories from the Heart of a Great City*.

"For Esmé—with Love and Squalor" reprinted in an anthology, *Better Reading Two: Literature*.

1955

"Franny" published in the *New Yorker* magazine.

"Raise High the Roof Beam, Carpenters" published in the *New Yorker* magazine.

Letter to the editor published in *Twentieth Century Authors*.

"For Esmé—with Love and Squalor" reprinted in *Interpreting Literature*.

1957

"Zooey" published in the *New Yorker* magazine.

1958

The Catcher in the Rye reprinted in a Modern Library edition.

"This Sandwich Has No Mayonnaise" reprinted in an anthology, *The Armchair Esquire*.

1959

"Seymour: An Introduction" published in the *New Yorker* magazine.

Autobiographical statement published in *Harper's* magazine.

Letter to the editor published in *New York Post Magazine*.

Nine Stories reprinted in a Modern Library edition.

1960

"Raise High the Roof Beam, Carpenters" reprinted in an anthology, *Stories from The New Yorker, 1950–1960*.

"For Esmé—with Love and Squalor" reprinted in an anthology, *Reportory*.

1961

Franny and Zooey published by Little, Brown and Company.

Autobiographical statement included on dust jacket of *Franny and Zooey*.

"The Inverted Forest" reprinted in *Cosmopolitan* magazine.

1963

Raise High the Roof Beam, Carpenters and Seymour: An Introduction published by Little, Brown and Company.

Autobiographical statement included on dust jacket of *Raise High the Roof Beam, Carpenters and Seymour: An Introduction*.

1964

Franny and Zooey reprinted in paperback edition (Bantam Books).

The Catcher in the Rye reprinted in paperback edition (Bantam Books).

Nine Stories reprinted in paperback edition (Bantam Books).

1965

"Hapworth 16, 1924" published in the *New Yorker* magazine.

Telegram published in *New York Herald Tribune* protesting Tom Wolfe's articles.

Raise High the Roof Beam, Carpenters and Seymour: An Introduction reprinted in paperback edition (Bantam Books).

1967

The Catcher in the Rye reprinted in large-type edition (Franklin Watts).

1969

"Go See Eddie" reprinted, without Salinger's consent, in *Fiction: Form and Experience*.

1974

The Complete Uncollected Short Stories of J. D. Salinger illegally published.

1975

"A Salute to Whit Burnett 1899–1972" published, without Salinger's consent, in *Fiction Writer's Handbook*.

1978

"Go See Eddie" reprinted, without Salinger's consent, in *New Letters* journal.

1991

The Catcher in the Rye, Nine Stories, Franny and Zooey, and *Raise High the Roof Beam, Carpenters and Seymour: An Introduction* reprinted in a matching paperback set (Little, Brown and Company).

1998

Twenty-two Stories illegally published (same stories as in *The Complete Uncollected Short Stories of J. D. Salinger*).

2000

"Slight Rebellion Off Madison" reprinted in an anthology, *Wonderful Town: New York Stories from The New Yorker*.

2001

The Catcher in the Rye, Nine Stories, Franny and Zooey, and *Raise High the Roof Beam, Carpenters and Seymour: An Introduction* reprinted in a trade paperback edition (Little, Brown and Company).

BIBLIOGRAPHY OF SECONDARY SOURCES

BOOKS ON SALINGER AND HIS WORKS

Alexander, Paul. *Salinger: A Biography*. Los Angeles: Renaissance Books, 1999.

Alsen, Eberhard. *A Reader's Guide to J. D. Salinger*. Westport, Conn.: Greenwood Press, 2002.

———. *Salinger's Glass Stories as a Composite Novel*. Troy, N.Y.: Whitston Publishing Company, 1983.

Beidler, Peter G. *A Reader's Companion to J. D. Salinger's The Catcher in the Rye*. Seattle: Coffeetown Press, 2009.

Belcher, William F., and James W. Lee, eds. *J. D. Salinger and the Critics*. Belmont, Calif.: Wadsworth Publishing Company, 1962.

Bloom, Harold, ed. and intro. *Holden Caulfield*. Major Literary Characters. New York: Chelsea House, 1990.

———. *Holden Caulfield*. New ed. Bloom's Major Literary Characters. Philadelphia: Chelsea House, 2005.

———. *J. D. Salinger*. Modern Critical Views. New York: Chelsea House, 1987.

———. *J. D. Salinger*. New ed. Bloom's Modern Critical Views. New York: Chelsea House, 2008.

———. *J. D. Salinger*. Bloom's Major Short Story Writers. Broomall, Pa.: Chelsea House, 1999.

———. *J. D. Salinger*. Bloom's BioCritiques. Philadelphia: Chelsea House, 2002.

———. *J. D. Salinger's The Catcher in the Rye*. Modern Critical Interpretations. Philadelphia: Chelsea House, 2000.

———. *J. D. Salinger's The Catcher in the Rye*. New ed. Bloom's Modern Critical Interpretations. New York: Chelsea House, 2009.

———. *J. D. Salinger's The Catcher in the Rye*. Bloom's Notes. New York: Chelsea House, 1996.

———. *J. D. Salinger's The Catcher in the Rye*. Bloom's Guides. New York: Chelsea House, 2007.

Bryfonski, Dedria, ed. *Depression in J. D. Salinger's The Catcher in the Rye*. Detroit: Greenhaven Press, 2009.

Chandra, Subhash. *The Fiction of J. D. Salinger: A Study in the Concept of Man*. New Delhi: Prestige, 2000.

Crawford, Catherine, ed. *If You Really Want to Hear about It: Writers on J. D. Salinger and His Work*. New York: Thunder's Mouth Press, 2006.

Creeger, George R. *'Treacherous Desertion': Salinger's The Catcher in the Rye*. Middletown, Conn.: Wesleyan University, 1961.

Engel, Steven, ed. *Readings on The Catcher in the Rye*. San Diego, Calif.: Greenhaven Press, 1998.

French, Warren. *J. D. Salinger*. New York: Twayne Publishers, 1963.

———. *J. D. Salinger*. Rev. ed. Boston: G. K. Hall, 1976.

———. *J. D. Salinger, Revisited*. New York: Twayne Publishers, 1988.

Graham, Sarah. *J. D. Salinger's The Catcher in the Rye*. London: Routledge, 2007.

———. *Salinger's The Catcher in the Rye*. London: Continuum, 2007.

Grunwald, Henry Anatole, ed. *Salinger: A Critical and Personal Portrait*. New York: Harper & Row, 1962.

Gwynn, Frederick L., and Joseph L. Blotner. *The Fiction of J. D. Salinger*. Pittsburgh: University of Pittsburgh Press, 1958.

Hamilton, Ian. *In Search of J. D. Salinger*. New York: Random House, 1988.

———. *J. D. Salinger: A Writing Life*. New York: Random House, 1986 [bound galleys; book publication blocked by Salinger].

Hamilton, Kenneth. *Jerome David Salinger: A Critical Essay*. Grand Rapids, Mich.: Eerdmans, 1967.

Herriges, Greg. *JD: A Memoir of a Time and a Journey*. La Grande, Ore.: Wordcraft of Oregon, 2006.

Kotzen, Kip, and Thomas Beller, eds. *With Love and Squalor: 14 Writers Respond to the Work of J. D. Salinger*. New York: Broadway Books, 2001.

Kubica, Chris, and Will Hochman, eds. *Letters to J. D. Salinger*. Madison, Wis.: University of Wisconsin Press, 2002.

Kurian, Elizabeth N. *A Religious Response to the Existential Dilemma in the Fiction of J. D. Salinger*. New Delhi: Intellectual Publishing House, 1992.

Laser, Marvin, and Norman Fruman, eds. *Studies in J. D. Salinger: Reviews, Essays, Critiques of "The Catcher in the Rye" and Other Fiction*. New York: Odyssey Press, 1963.

Lundquist, James. *J. D. Salinger*. New York: Ungar, 1979.

Marsden, Malcolm, ed. *If You Really Want to Know: A "Catcher" Casebook*. Chicago: Scott, Foresman, 1963.

Maynard, Joyce. *At Home in the World: A Memoir*. New York: Picador, 1998.

McDaniel, Sean. *A Catcher's Companion: The World of Holden Caulfield*. Santa Monica, Calif.: Lit. Happens Publishing, 2009.

Miller, James E., Jr. *J. D. Salinger*. Minneapolis: University of Minnesota Press, 1965.

Pinsker, Sanford. *The Catcher in the Rye: Innocence under Pressure*. New York: Twayne Publishers, 1993.

Pinsker, Sanford, and Ann Pinsker. *Understanding The Catcher in the Rye: A Student Casebook to Issues, Sources, and Historical Documents*. Westport, Conn.: Greenwood Press, 1999.

Ranchan, Som P. *An Adventure in Vedanta: J. D. Salinger's The Glass Family*. Delhi: Ajanta Publications, 1989.

Reiff, Raychel Haugrud. *J. D. Salinger: The Catcher in the Rye and Other Works*. Tarrytown, N.Y.: Marshall Cavendish Benchmark, 2008.

Rosen, Gerald. *Zen in the Art of J. D. Salinger*. Berkeley, Calif.: Creative Arts Book Company, 1977.

Salinger, Margaret A. *Dream Catcher: A Memoir*. New York: Washington Square Press, 2000.

Salzberg, Joel, ed. *Critical Essays on Salinger's The Catcher in the Rye*. Boston: G. K. Hall, 1990.

Salzman, Jack, ed. *New Essays on The Catcher in the Rye*. Cambridge: Cambridge University Press, 1991.

Simonson, Harold P., and Philip E. Hager, eds. *Salinger's "Catcher in the Rye": Clamor vs. Criticism*. Lexington, Mass.: D. C. Heath, 1963.

Slawenski, Kenneth. *J. D. Salinger: A Life Raised High*. Hebden Bridge, England: Pomona Books, 2010.

Starosciak, Kenneth. *J. D. Salinger: A Thirty-Year Bibliography 1938–1968*. St. Paul, Minn.: Croixide Press, 1971.

Steed, J. P., ed. *The Catcher in the Rye: New Essays*. New York: Peter Lang, 2002.

Steinle, Pamela Hunt. *In Cold Fear: The Catcher in the Rye Censorship Controversies and Postwar American Character*. Columbus: Ohio State University Press, 2002.

Sublette, Jack R. *J. D. Salinger: An Annotated Bibliography, 1938–1981*. New York: Garland Publishing, 1984.

Unrue, John C. *The Catcher in the Rye*. Detroit: Gale Group, 2001.

———. *J. D. Salinger*. Detroit: Gale Group, 2002.

Weaver, Brett E. *An Annotated Bibliography (1982–2002) of J. D. Salinger*. Lewiston, N.Y.: Edwin Mellen Press, 2002.

Wenke, John. *J. D. Salinger: A Study of the Short Fiction*. Boston: Twayne Publishers, 1991.

ARTICLES ON SALINGER AND HIS WORKS IN BOOKS, JOURNALS, MAGAZINES, AND NEWSPAPERS; BACKGROUND MATERIALS

Adler, Renata. *Gone: The Last Days of The New Yorker*. New York: Simon and Schuster, 1999.

Alighieri, Dante. *The Inferno*. Translated by John Ciardi. New York: New American Library, 1954.

Alsen, Eberhard. "New Light on the Nervous Breakdowns of Salinger's Sergeant X and Seymour Glass." *C.L.A. Journal* 45, no. 3 (March 2002): 379–387.

———. "'Raise High the Roof Beam, Carpenters' and the Amateur Reader." *Studies in Short Fiction* 17 (Winter 1980): 39–47.

———. "The Role of Vedanta Hinduism in Salinger's Seymour Novel." *Renascence* 33, no. 2 (Winter 1981): 99–116.

———. "Seymour: A Chronology." *English Record* 29, no. 4 (Fall 1978): 28–30.

Amur, G. S. "Theme, Structure, and Symbol in *The Catcher in the Rye*." *Indian Journal of American Studies* 1 (1969): 11–24.

[Anonymous]. *The Pilgrim Continues His Way.* London: Society for Promoting Christian Knowledge, 1943.

———. *The Way of a Pilgrim.* London: Society for Promoting Christian Knowledge, 1941.

Antico, John. "The Parody of J. D. Salinger: Esmé and the Fat Lady Exposed." *Modern Fiction Studies* 12, no. 3 (Autumn 1966): 325–340.

Antonio, Eugene Dale. "The Fiction of J. D. Salinger: A Search through Taoism." Ph.D. diss., Florida State University, 1991.

"Backstage with Esquire." *Esquire,* September 1941, 24.

Baro, Gene. "Some Suave and Impressive Slices of Life." *New York Herald Tribune Book Review,* 12 April 1953, p. 6.

Barr, Donald. "Ah, Buddy: Salinger." In *The Creative Present,* edited by Nona Balakian and Charles Simmons, 27–62. New York: Gordian Press, 1973.

———. "Saints, Pilgrims and Artists." *Commonweal,* 25 October 1957, 88–90.

———. "The Talent of J. D. Salinger." *Commonweal,* 30 October 1959, 165, 167.

Barron, Cynthia M. "The Catcher and the Soldier: Hemingway's 'Soldier's Home' and Salinger's *The Catcher in the Rye.*" *Hemingway Review* 2, no. 1 (Fall 1982): 70–73.

Baskett, Sam S. "The Splendid/Squalid World of J. D. Salinger." *Wisconsin Studies in Contemporary Literature* 4, no. 1 (Winter 1963): 48–61.

Baumbach, Jonathan, Jr. "The Saint as a Young Man: A Reappraisal of *The Catcher in the Rye.*" *Modern Language Quarterly* 25 (December 1964): 461–472.

Bawer, Bruce. "Salinger Redux." *New Criterion* 6, no. 10 (June 1988): 92–96.

———. "Salinger's Arrested Development." *New Criterion* 5, no. 1 (September 1986): 34–47.

Beckers, Marion, and Elisabeth Moortgat. *Atelier Lotte Jacobi: Berlin, New York.* Berlin: Nicolai, 1998.

Beckett, Samuel. "Letters to Barney Rosset." *Review of Contemporary Fiction* 10, no. 3 (Fall 1990): 64–71.

Beebe, Maurice, and Jennifer Sperry. "Criticism of J. D. Salinger: A Selected Checklist." *Modern Fiction Studies* 12, no. 3 (Autumn 1966): 377–390.

Behrman, S. N. "The Vision of the Innocent." *New Yorker,* 11 August 1951, 71–76.

Beidler, Peter G. "What Holden Looks Like and Who 'Whosis' Is: A Newly Identified Movie Allusion in *The Catcher in the Rye.*" *ANQ: A Quarterly Journal of Short Articles, Notes, and Reviews* 20, no. 1 (Winter 2007): 52–57.

Bellman, Samuel Irving. "New Light on Seymour's Suicide: Salinger's 'Hapworth 16, 1924.'" *Studies in Short Fiction* 3 (Spring 1966): 348–351.

Berry, David W. "Salinger Slept Here." *Philadelphia Magazine* 82, no. 10, October 1991, 53–56.

Bhaerman, Robert D. "Rebuttal: Holden in the Rye." *College English* 23, no. 6 (March 1962): 508.

Bidney, Martin. "The Aestheticist Epiphanies of J. D. Salinger: Bright-Hued Circles, Spheres, and Patches: 'Elemental' Joy and Pain." *Style* 34, no. 1 (Spring 2000): 117–131.

Bishop, Elizabeth. *One Art: Letters.* New York: Farrar, Straus & Giroux, 1994.

Bishop, John. "A Study of the Religious Dimensions in the Fiction of J. D. Salinger." Master's thesis, McMaster University, 1976.

Bixby, George. "J. D. Salinger: A Bibliographical Checklist." *American Book Collector* NS 2 (May–June 1981): 29–32.

Blaney, Shirlie. "Twin State Telescope: Interview with an Author." *Daily Eagle,* 13 November 1953, editorial page.

Blotner, Joseph L. "Salinger Now: An Appraisal." *Wisconsin Studies in Contemporary Literature* 4, no. 1 (Winter 1963): 100–108.

Blyth, R. H. *Haiku.* [4 volumes] Tokyo: Hokuseido Press, 1949–1952.

———. *Zen in English Literature and Oriental Classics.* Tokyo: Hokuseido Press, 1942.

Blythe, Hal, and Charlie Sweet. "The Caulfield Family of Writers in The Catcher in the Rye." *Notes on Contemporary Literature* 32, no. 5 (November 2002): 6–7.

———. "Falling in Salinger's Catcher in the Rye." *Notes on Contemporary Literature* 32, no. 4 (September 2002): 5–7.

———. "Holden, the Bomb, and Dr. Strangelove." *Notes on Contemporary Literature* 34, no. 3 (May 2004): 11–12.

———. "Holden's Mysterious Hat." *Notes on Contemporary Literature* 32, no. 4 (September 2002): 7–8.

Boe, Alfred F. "Salinger and Sport." *Arete* 2, no. 2 (1985): 17–22.

Bonetti, Kay. "An Interview with William Maxwell." *Missouri Review* 19 (1996): 83–95.

Booth, Wayne C. "Censorship and the Values of Fiction." *English Journal* 53 (March 1964): 155–164.

———. *The Rhetoric of Fiction.* Chicago: University of Chicago Press, 1961.

Bostwick, Sally. "Reality, Compassion, and Mysticism in the World of J. D. Salinger." *Midwest Review* 5 (1963): 30–43.

Bowen, Elizabeth. "Books of 1951: Some Personal Choices." *Observer*, 30 December 1951, 71.

Bowen, Robert O. "The Salinger Syndrome: Charity Against Whom?" *Ramparts*, May 1962, 52–60.

Boyle, Robert S. "Teaching 'Dirty Books' in College." *America*, 13 December 1958, 337–339.

Bradbury, Malcolm. "Other New Novels: Franny and Zooey." *Punch*, 27 June 1962, 989–990.

Branch, Edgar. "Mark Twain and J. D. Salinger: A Study in Literary Continuity." *American Quarterly* 9 (Summer 1958): 144–158.

Brandon, Henry. "A Conversation with Edmund Wilson: 'We Don't Know Where We Are.'" *New Republic*, 30 March 1959, 13–15.

Bratman, Fred. "Holden, 50, Still Catches." *New York Times*, 21 December 1979, p. A-35.

Breit, Harvey. "Reader's Choice." *Atlantic*, August 1951, 82–85.

Brenna, Duff. "Secondary Educations: An Interview with Greg Herriges." *South Carolina Review* 38, no. 2 (Spring 2006): 33–45.

Brinkley, Thomas Edwin. "J. D. Salinger: A Study of His Eclecticism—Zooey as Existential Zen Therapist." Ph.D. diss., Ohio State University, 1976.

Brod, Max, ed. *The Diaries of Franz Kafka 1910–1913*. New York: Schocken Books, 1948.

———. *The Diaries of Franz Kafka 1914–1923*. New York: Schocken Books, 1949.

Brookeman, Christopher. "Pencey Preppy: Cultural Codes in *The Catcher in the Rye*." In *New Essays on The Catcher in the Rye*, edited by Jack Salzman, 57–76. Cambridge: Cambridge University Press, 1991.

Brooks, Richard. "J. D. Salinger 'Has 15 New Books in Safe.'" *Sunday Times*, 21 March 1999, p. 3.

Brown, Scott. "Literary Lotte." *OP Magazine* 2, 2004, 4–7.

Browne, Robert M. "In Defense of Esmé." *College English* 22, no. 8 (May 1961): 584–585.

Brozan, Nadine. "J. D. Salinger Receives an Apology for an Award." *New York Times*, 27 April 1991, p. 26.

Bruccoli, Matthew. "States of Salinger Book." *American Notes & Queries* 2 (October 1963): 21–22.

Bryan, James. "The Admiral and Her Sailor in Salinger's 'Down at the Dinghy.'" *Studies in Short Fiction* 17 (Spring 1980): 174–178.

———. "J. D. Salinger: The Fat Lady and the Chicken Sandwich." *College English* 23, no. 3 (December 1961): 226–229.

———. "The Psychological Structure of *The Catcher in the Rye*." *PMLA* 89, no. 5 (October 1974): 1,065–1,074.

———. "A Reading of Salinger's 'For Esmé—with Love and Squalor.'" *Criticism* 9 (Summer 1967): 275–288.

———. "A Reading of Salinger's 'Teddy.'" *American Literature* 40, no. 3 (November 1968): 352–369.

———. "Salinger and His Short Fiction." Ph.D. diss., University of Virginia, 1968.

———. "Salinger's Seymour's Suicide." *College English* 24, no. 3 (December 1962): 226–229.

———. "Sherwood Anderson and *The Catcher in the Rye*: A Possible Influence." *Notes on Contemporary Literature* 1, no. 5 (November 1971): 2–6.

Bryden, Ronald. "Living Dolls." *Spectator*, 8 June 1962, 755–756.

Buchan, John. "Skule Skerry." In *The Far Islands and Other Tales of Fantasy*, 75–92. West Kingston, R.I.: Donald M. Grant, Publisher, 1984.

Bufithis, Philip. "J. D. Salinger and the Psychiatrist." *West Virginia University Bulletin: Philological Papers* 21 (December 1974): 67–77.

Burger, Nash K. "Books of The Times." *New York Times*, 16 July 1951, p. 19.

Burke, Brother Fidelian. "Salinger's 'Esmé': Some Matters of Balance." *Modern Fiction Studies* 12, no. 3 (Autumn 1966): 341–347.

Burnett, Hallie, and Whit Burnett. *Fiction Writer's Handbook*. New York: Harper & Row, 1975.

Burnett, Whit, and John Pen. "Immortal Bachelor: The Love Story of Robert Burns." *Story*, November–December 1942, entire issue.

Burrows, David J. "Allie and Phoebe: Death and Love in J. D. Salinger's 'The Catcher in the Rye.'" In *Private Dealings: Modern American Writers in Search of Integrity*, edited by David J. Burrows et al., 106–114. Rockville, Md.: New Perspectives, 1974.

Burt, Daniel S., ed. *The Chronology of American Literature: America's Literary Achievements from the Colonial Era to Modern Times*. Boston: Houghton Mifflin, 2004.

Cagle, Charles. "*The Catcher in the Rye* Revisited." *Midwest Quarterly* 4 (Summer 1963): 343–351.

Cahill, Robert. "J. D. Salinger's Tin Bell." *Cadence* 14 (Autumn 1959): 20–22.

California, John David [Fredrik Colting]. *60 Years Later: Coming through the Rye*. London: Windupbird Publishing, 2009.

Carpenter, Frederic I. "The Adolescent in American Fiction." *English Journal* 46 (September 1957): 313–319.

Carvajal, Doreen. "Salinger's Daughter Plans to Publish a Memoir." *New York Times*, 24 June 1999, p. E-10.

Castronovo, David. "Holden Caulfield's Legacy." *New England Review* 22, no. 2 (Spring 2001): 180–186.

"The Catcher on the Hill." *Newsweek*, 18 November 1974, 17.

Cawelti, John G. "The Writer as a Celebrity: Some Aspects of American Literature as Popular Culture." *Studies in American Fiction* 5 (1977): 161–174.

Cecile, Sister Marie. "J. D. Salinger's Circle of Privacy." *Catholic World* 194 (February 1962): 296–301.

Chambers, Andrea. "In Search of J. D. Salinger, Biographer Ian Hamilton Discovers a Subject Who Didn't Want to Be Found." *People*, 6 June 1988, 51–53.

Cheatham, George, and Edwin Arnaudin. "Salinger's Allusions to *My Foolish Heart*—the Salinger Movie." *ANQ: A Quarterly Journal of Short Articles, Notes, and Reviews* 20, no. 2 (Spring 2007): 39–43.

Chester, Alfred. "Salinger: How to Love without Love." *Commentary* 35 (June 1963): 467–474.

Clarkson, Michael. "Catching the 'Catcher in the Rye,' J. D. Salinger" [originally published in *Niagara Falls Review*, November 1979]. In *If You Really Want to Hear about It: Writers on J. D. Salinger and His Work*, edited by Catherine Crawford, 49–62. New York: Thunder's Mouth Press, 2006.

Cohen, Hubert I. "'A Woeful Agony Which Forced Me to Begin My Tale': *The Catcher in the Rye*." *Modern Fiction Studies* 12, no. 3 (Autumn 1966): 355–366.

Coles, Robert. "Anna Freud and J. D. Salinger's Holden Caulfield." *Virginia Quarterly Review* 76, no. 2 (Spring 2000): 214–224.

———. "Reconsideration: J. D. Salinger." *New Republic*, 28 April 1973, 30–32.

"Contributors." *Story* 16 (March–April 1940): 2.

"Controversial Story Not by J. D. Salinger." *New Orleans Times Picayune*, 27 February 1977, p. 18.

Corbett, Edward P. "Raise High the Barriers, Censors." *America*, 7 January 1961, 441–443.

Costello, Donald P. "The Language of 'The Catcher in the Rye.'" *American Speech* 34, no. 3 (October 1959): 172–181.

———. "Salinger and His Critics." *Commonweal*, 25 October 1963, 132–135.

Cotter, James Finn. "Religious Symbols in Salinger's Shorter Fiction." *Studies in Short Fiction* 15 (Spring 1978): 121–132.

———. "A Source for Seymour's Suicide: Rilke's 'Voices' and Salinger's *Nine Stories*." *Papers on Language and Literature* 25, no. 1 (Winter 1989): 83–98.

Cowan, Alison Leigh. "To a Dear Buddyroo: Salinger Letters Unsealed." *New York Times*, 12 February 2010, pp. C-23, C-28.

Cowan, Michael. "Holden's Museum Pieces: Narrator and Nominal Audience in *The Catcher in the Rye*." In *New Essays on The Catcher in the Rye*, edited by Jack Salzman, 35–55. Cambridge: Cambridge University Press, 1991.

Cox, James M. "Toward Vernacular Humor." *Virginia Quarterly Review* 46 (Spring 1970): 311–330.

Cronin, Gloria, and Ben Siegel, eds. *Conversations with Saul Bellow*. Jackson: University of Mississippi Press, 1994.

Cullen, Frank. *Vaudeville, Old and New*. New York: Routledge, 2007.

Curry, Renee R. "Holden Caulfield Is Not a Person of Colour." In *J. D. Salinger's The Catcher in the Rye*, by Sarah Graham, 78–88. London: Routledge, 2007.

Cutchins, Dennis. "*Catcher* in the Corn: J. D. Salinger and *Shoeless Joe*." In *The Catcher in the Rye: New Essays*, edited by J. P. Steed, 53–77. New York: Peter Lang, 2002.

Dahl, James. "What *about* Antolini?" *Notes on Contemporary Literature* 13, no. 2 (March 1983): 9–10.

"A Dark Horse." *Virginia Kirkus' Bookshop Service*, 15 May 1951, 247.

Daughtry, Vivian F. "A Novel Worth Teaching: Salinger's The Catcher in the Rye." *Virginia English Bulletin* 36, no. 2 (Winter 1986): 88–94.

Davis, Kenneth C. *Two-Bit Culture: The Paperbacking of America*. Boston: Houghton Mifflin, 1984.

Davis, Tom. "J. D. Salinger: A Checklist." *Papers of the Bibliographical Society of America* 53 (January–March 1959): 69–71.

———. "J. D. Salinger: The Identity of Sergeant X." *Western Humanities Review* 16 (Spring 1962): 181–183.

———. "J. D. Salinger: 'Some Crazy Cliff' Indeed." *Western Humanities Review* 14 (Winter 1960): 97–99.

———. "J. D. Salinger: 'The Sound of One Hand Clapping.'" *Wisconsin Studies in Contemporary Literature* 4, no. 1 (Winter 1963): 41–47.

Davison, Richard Allan. "Salinger Criticism and 'The Laughing Man': A Case of Arrested Development." *Studies in Short Fiction* 18 (Winter 1981): 1–15.

Deer, Irving, and John H. Randall III. "J. D. Salinger and the Reality beyond Words." *Lock Haven Review* 6 (1964): 14–29.

Dempsey, David. "Ten Best-Selling Authors Make Their Holiday Choices." *New York Times Book Review*, 2 December 1951, p. 244.

"Depositions Yield J. D. Salinger Details." *New York Times*, 12 December 1986, p. C-27.

Dev, Jai. "Franny and Flaubert." *Journal of American Studies* 25, no. 1 (April 1991): 81–85.

———. "Strategies of Self-Defence: Self-Reflexivity in *Franny and Zooey*." *Panjab University Research Bulletin* 21, no. 1 (April 1990): 17–41.

Dickstein, Morris. *Leopards in the Temple: The Transformation of American Fiction 1945–1970.* Cambridge: Harvard University Press, 2002.

Didion, Joan. "Finally (Fashionably) Spurious" [originally published in *National Review*, 18 November 1961]. In *Salinger: A Critical and Personal Portrait*, edited by Henry Anatole Grunwald, 77–79. New York: Harper & Row, 1962.

Dodge, Stewart. "The Theme of Quest: In Search of 'The Fat Lady.'" *English Record* 8 (Winter 1957): 10–13.

Dolbier, Maurice. "Franny and Zooey." *New York Herald Tribune*, 14 September 1961, p. 19.

Drake, Robert Y. "Two Old Juveniles." *Georgia Review* 13 (Winter 1959): 10–13.

Ducharme, Edward R. "J. D., D. B., Sonny, Sunny, and Holden." *English Record* 19, no. 2 (December 1968): 54–58.

Dudar, Helen. "In Search of J. D. Salinger, Publishing's Invisible Man." *Chicago Tribune*, 19 June 1979, sec. 2, pp. 1, 6.

Dudley, Robin. "J. D. Salinger's Uncollected Stories and the Development of Aesthetic and Moral Themes in *The Catcher in the Rye*." Master's thesis, Idaho State University, 2004.

Dugan, Lawrence. "Holden and the Lunts." *Notes and Queries* 52, no. 4 (2005): 510–511.

Edwards, Duane. "Holden Caulfield: 'Don't Ever Tell Anybody Anything.'" *Journal of English Literary History* 44, no. 3 (Fall 1977): 554–565.

Eisman, Gregory Dwight. "The Importance of Being Seymour: The Dramatic Function of Seymour Glass in the Works of J. D. Salinger." Master's thesis, Florida Atlantic University, 1974.

Elfin, Mel. "The Mysterious J. D. Salinger . . . His Woodsy, Secluded Life." *Newsweek*, 30 May 1960, 92–94.

Eliason, Marcus. "Conspiracy of Silence Guards Private World of J. D. Salinger." *New Orleans Times Picayune*, 21 December 1975, sec. 3, p. 15.

Eliot, T. S. *Collected Poems 1909–1962*. New York: Harcourt Brace & Company, 1963.

Elmen, Paul. "Twice-Blessed Enamel Flowers: Reality in Contemporary Fiction." In *The Climate of Faith in Modern Literature*, edited by Nathan A. Scott, Jr., 84–101. New York: Seabury Press, 1964.

Engle, Paul. "Brilliantly Detailed Glimpses of the Glass Family." *Chicago Tribune*, 24 September 1961, p. 3.

Eppes, Betty. "What I Did Last Summer." *Paris Review* 23 (Summer 1981): 221–239.

Erwin, Kenneth J. "An Analysis of the Dramatic and Semantic Use of Altruism in the Writings of J. D. Salinger." Ph.D. diss., University of Texas at Austin, 1968.

Evertson, Matt. "Love, Loss, and Growing Up in J. D. Salinger and Cormac McCarthy." In *The Catcher in the Rye: New Essays*, edited by J. P. Steed, 101–142. New York: Peter Lang, 2002.

Fadiman, Clifton. *Book-of-the-Month Club News*, July 1951: 1–4.

Faris, Christiane Brandt. "The Pattern of Withdrawal in J. D. Salinger and R. M. Rilke." Master's thesis, Bucknell University, 1969.

Faulkner, William. "A Word to Young Writers." In *Faulkner in the University: Class Conferences at the University of Virginia 1957–1958*, edited by Frederick L. Gwynn and Joseph L. Blotner, 244–248. Charlottesville: University of Virginia Press, 1959.

Fiedler, Leslie. "The Eye of Innocence." In *Salinger: A Critical and Personal Portrait*, edited by Henry Anatole Grunwald, 218–245. New York: Harper & Row, 1962.

———. "Up from Adolescence." *Partisan Review* 29 (Winter 1962): 127–131.

Field, Michele. "In Pursuit of J. D. Salinger." *Publishers Weekly*, 27 June 1986, 63–64.

Fiene, Donald M. "A Bibliographical Study of J. D. Salinger: Life, Work and Reputation." Master's thesis, University of Louisville, 1961a.

———. "From a Study of Salinger: Controversy in *The Catcher*." *The Realist* 1 (December 1961b): 23–25.

———. "J. D. Salinger: A Bibliography." *Wisconsin Studies in Contemporary Literature* 4, no. 1 (Winter 1963): 109–149.

———. "Rye on the Rocks." *Time*, 30 May 1960, 2.

Fitzgerald, F. Scott. *The Great Gatsby*. New York: Scribner, 2004.

———. *Tales of the Jazz Age*. In *Novels and Stories 1920–1922*. n.p.: Library of America, 2000.

Fleissner, Robert F. "Salinger's Caulfield: A Refraction of Copperfield and His Caul." *Notes on Contemporary Literature* 3, no. 3 (May 1973): 5–7.

Fogel, Amy. "Where the Ducks Go: *The Catcher in the Rye*." *Ball State Teacher's College Forum* 3 (Spring 1962): 75–79.

Foley, Martha J., ed. *The Best American Short Stories; and The Yearbook of the American Short Story* [vol. 1948–1966]. Boston: Houghton Mifflin, 1948–1966.

Foran, Donald J. "A Doubletake on Holden Caulfield." *English Journal* 57 (October 1968): 977–979.

Fosburgh, Lacey. "J. D. Salinger Speaks about His Silence." *New York Times*, 3 November 1974, pp. 1, 69.

———. "Salinger Books Stir F.B.I. Search." *New York Times*, 10 November 1974, p. 75.

Fowler, Albert. "Alien in the Rye." *Modern Age* 1 (Fall 1957): 193–197.

Frank, Jeffrey. "Riches of Embarrassment." *New Yorker*, 24 May 2004, 46–55.

Freedman, Carl. "Memories of Holden Caulfield and of Miss Greenwood." *Southern Review* 39, no. 2 (Spring 2003): 401–417.

Freedman, Ralph. *Life of a Poet: Rainer Maria Rilke*. New York: Farrar, Straus & Giroux, 1996.

Freeman, Fred B., Jr. "Who Was Salinger's Sergeant X?" *American Notes and Queries* 11 (September 1972): 6.

Fremont-Smith, Eliot. "Franny and Zooey." *Village Voice*, 8 March 1962, pp. 5–6.

French, Warren. "The Age of Salinger." In *The Fifties: Fiction, Poetry, Drama*, edited by Warren French, 1–39. Deland, Fla.: Everett/Edwards, 1970.

———. "Holden's Fall." *Modern Fiction Studies* 10 (Winter 1964–1965): 389.

———. "J. D. Salinger." In *American Novelists since World War II*, edited by Jeffrey Helterman and Richard Layman, 434–444. Detroit: Gale, 1978.

———. "The Phony World and the Nice World." *Wisconsin Studies in Contemporary Literature* 4, no. 1 (Winter 1963): 21–30.

———. "An Unnoticed Salinger Story." *College English* 26, no. 5 (February 1965): 394–395.

Fry, John R. "Skill Is the Word." *Christian Century*, 6 February 1963, 175–176.

Frye, Northrop. *The Critical Path*. Bloomington: Indiana University Press, 1971.

Fulford, Robert. "Newsstand: Seymour Glass at 7." *Toronto Star*, 21 June 1965, p. 16.

Furst, Lilian R. "Dostoyevsky's *Notes from the Underground* and Salinger's *The Catcher in the Rye*." *Canadian Review of Comparative Literature* 5 (Winter 1978): 72–85.

Galloway, David D. *The Absurd Hero in American Fiction*. Austin: University of Texas Press, 1966.

Gehman, Richard. "Introduction." In *The Best from Cosmopolitan*, edited by Richard Gehman, xiii–xxvii. New York: Avon Books, 1961.

Geismar, Maxwell. "J. D. Salinger: The Wise Child and *The New Yorker* School of Fiction." In *American Moderns: From Rebellion to Conformity*, edited by Maxwell Geismar, 195–209. New York: Hill and Wang, 1958.

Genthe, Charles V. "Six, Sex, Sick: Seymour, Some Comments." *Twentieth Century Literature* 10, no. 4 (January 1965): 170–171.

Giles, Barbara. "The Lonely War of J. D. Salinger." *Mainstream* 12, no. 2 (February 1959): 2–13.

Giles, Lionel, trans. *Taoist Teachings from the Book of Lieh Tzu*. London: John Murray, 1925.

Gill, Brendan. *Here at The New Yorker*. New York: Random House, 1975.

Gilman, Richard. "Salinger Considered." *Jubilee* 9 (October 1961): 38–41.

Glasser, William. "The Catcher in the Rye." *Michigan Quarterly Review* 15 (Fall 1976): 432–457.

"The Glass House Gang." *Time*, 8 February 1963, 86.

Glazier, Lyle. "The Glass Family Saga: Argument and Epiphany." *College English* 27, no. 3 (December 1965): 248–251.

Gold, Arthur R. "J. D. Salinger: Through a Glass Darkly." *New York Herald Tribune Books*, 7 April 1963, p. 8.

Goldhurst, William. "The Hyphenated Ham Sandwich of Ernest Hemingway and J. D. Salinger." In *Fitzgerald/Hemingway Annual 1970*, edited by Matthew J. Bruccoli and C. E. Frazer Clark, Jr., 136–150. Washington, D.C.: NCR, 1970.

Goldstein, Bernice, and Sanford Goldstein. "Bunnies and Cobras: Zen Enlightenment in Salinger." *Discourse* 13 (Winter 1970): 98–106.

———. "Ego and 'Hapworth 16, 1924.'" *Renascence* 24 (Spring 1972): 159–167.

———. "'Seymour: An Introduction'—Writing as Discovery." *Studies in Short Fiction* 7 (Spring 1970): 248–256.

———. "Seymour's Poems." *Literature East and West* 17 (June–December 1973): 335–348.

———. "Some Zen References in Salinger." *Literature East and West* 15 (1971): 83–95.

———. "Zen and *Nine Stories*." *Renascence* 22 (Summer 1970): 171–182.

———. "Zen and Salinger." *Modern Fiction Studies* 12, no. 3 (Autumn 1966): 313–324.

Goodman, Anne L. "Mad about Children." *New Republic*, 16 July 1951, 20–21.

Gopnik, Adam. "J. D. Salinger." *New Yorker*, 8 February 2010, pp. 20–21.

Gospel of Sri Ramakrishna. Transcribed by Mahendranath Gupta; translated and introductory biography by Swami Nikhilananda. New York: Ramakrishna-Vivekananda Center, 1942.

Graustark, Barbara. "Newsmakers." *Newsweek*, 17 July 1978, 57.

Green, Martin Burgess. "American Rococo: Salinger and Nabokov." In *Re-Appraisals: Some Common-Sense Readings in American Literature*, 211–219. New York: Norton, 1965.

———. "Amis and Salinger: The Latitude of Private Conscience." *Chicago Review* 11 (Winter 1958): 20–25.

———. "Cultural Images in England and America." In *A Mirror for Anglo-Saxons: A Discovery of America, A Rediscovery of England*, 69–88. New York: Harper & Brothers, 1960.

———. "Franny and Zooey." In *Re-Appraisals: Some Common-Sense Readings in American Literature*, 197–210. New York: Norton, 1965.

Greiner, Donald J. "Updike and Salinger: A Literary Incident." *Critique: Studies in Contemporary Fiction* 47, no. 2 (Winter 2006): 115–130.

Gross, Theodore L. "J. D. Salinger: Suicide and Survival in the Modern World." *South Atlantic Quarterly* 68 (Autumn 1969): 454–462.

Grunwald, Henry Anatole. "He Touches Something Deep in Us." *Horizon* 4 (May 1962): 100–107.

Gutwillig, Robert. "Everybody's Caught 'The Catcher in the Rye.'" *New York Times Book Review*, 15 January 1961, pp. 38–39.

Haberman, Clyde. "Notes on People: A Muted Singer." *New York Times*, 29 November 1978, p. C-18.

———. "A Recluse Meets His Match." *New York Times*, 18 June 1999, p. B-1.

Hackett, Alice Payne, and James Henry Burke. *80 Years of Best Sellers, 1895–1975*. New York: R. K. Bowker Company, 1977.

Hagopian, John V. "'Pretty Mouth and Green My Eyes': Salinger's Paolo and Francesca in New York." *Modern Fiction Studies* 12, no. 3 (Autumn 1966): 349–354.

Hainsworth, J. D. "Maturity in J. D. Salinger's 'The Catcher in the Rye.'" *English Studies* 48 (October 1967): 426–431.

Haitch, Richard. "Follow-up in the News: J. D. Salinger." *New York Times*, 12 February 1978, p. 41.

Hale, John K. "Salinger's The Catcher in the Rye." *Explicator* 60, no. 4 (Summer 2002): 220–221.

Hamilton, Ian. "A Biographer's Misgivings." In *Walking Possession: Essays and Reviews, 1968–1993*, 5–21. New York: Addison-Wesley, 1996.

Hamilton, Kenneth. "Hell in New York: J. D. Salinger's 'Pretty Mouth and Green My Eyes.'" *Dalhousie Review* 47 (Autumn 1967): 394–399.

———. "J. D. Salinger's Happy Family." *Queen's Quarterly* 71 (Summer 1964): 176–187.

———. "One Way to Use the Bible: The Example of J. D. Salinger." *Christian Scholar* 47 (Fall 1964): 243–251.

Harper, Howard M., Jr. "J. D. Salinger—Through the Glasses Darkly." In *Desperate Faith: A Study of Bellow, Salinger, Mailer, Baldwin, and Updike*, 65–95. Chapel Hill: University of North Carolina Press, 1967.

Hart, James D. *The Oxford Companion to American Literature*. 3rd ed. New York: Oxford University Press, 1956.

———. *The Oxford Companion to American Literature*. 4th ed. New York: Oxford University Press, 1965.

Hassan, Ihab. "Almost the Voice of Silence: The Later Novelettes of J. D. Salinger." *Wisconsin Studies in Contemporary Literature* 4, no. 1 (Winter 1963): 5–20.

———. "The Casino of Silence." *Saturday Review*, 26 January 1963, 38.

———. "The Character of Post-War Fiction in America." *English Journal* 51 (January 1962): 1–8.

———. *The Dismemberment of Orpheus: Toward a Postmodern Literature*. New York: Oxford University Press, 1971.

———. "The Idea of Adolescence in American Fiction." *American Quarterly* 10 (Fall 1958): 312–324.

———. *Radical Innocence: Studies in the Contemporary American Novel*. Princeton: Princeton University Press, 1961.

———. "Rare Quixotic Gesture: The Fiction of J. D. Salinger." *Western Review* 21 (Summer 1957): 261–280.

Havemann, Ernest. "The Search for the Mysterious J. D. Salinger." *Life*, 3 November 1961, 129–130, 132, 135, 137–138, 141–142, 144.

Hazard, Eloise P. "Eight Fiction Finds." *Saturday Review*, 16 February 1952, 16–18.

Heiserman, Arthur, and James E. Miller, Jr. "J. D. Salinger: Some Crazy Cliff." *Western Humanities Review* 10 (Spring 1956): 129–137.

Hekanaho, Pia Livia. "Queering *Catcher*: Flits, Straights, and Other Morons." In *J. D. Salinger's The Catcher in the Rye*, by Sarah Graham, 90–97. London: Routledge, 2007.

Hermann, John. "J. D. Salinger: Hello Hello Hello." *College English* 22, no. 4 (January 1961): 262–264.

Herriges, Greg. "Ten Minutes with J. D. Salinger." *Oui*, January 1979, 86–88, 126–130.

Hicks, Granville. "Another Look at the Deserving." *Saturday Review*, 23 December 1961, 18.

———. "A Glass Menagerie." *Saturday Review*, 26 January 1963, 37–38.

———. "J. D. Salinger: Search for Wisdom." *Saturday Review*, 25 July 1959, 13, 30.

———. "Sisters, Sons, and Lovers." *Saturday Review*, 16 September 1961, 26.

Highet, Gilbert. "New Books: Always Roaming with a Hungry Heart." *Harper's*, June 1953, 100–109.

Hoban, Phoebe. "The Salinger File." *New York*, 15 June 1987, 36–42.

Hochman, Will. "Strategies of Critical Response to the Fiction of J. D. Salinger." Ph.D. diss., New York University, 1994.

———. "Swimming with Bananafish: The Literary Suicides of Seymour Glass and J. D. Salinger." In *The Image of Violence in Literature, the Media, and Society*, edited by Will Wright and Steven Kaplan, 458–462. Pueblo, Colo.: Society for the Interdisciplinary Study of Society Imagery, University of Southern Colorado, 1995.

Honan, William H. "Fire Fails to Shake Salinger's Seclusion." *New York Times*, 24 October 1992, p. 13.

Hotchner, A. E. *Choice People*. New York: William Morrow & Company, 1984.

Howe, Irving. "More Reflections in the Glass Mirror." *New York Times Book Review*, 7 April 1963, pp. 4–5, 34.

Howell, John M. "Salinger in the Waste Land." *Modern Fiction Studies* 12, no. 3 (Autumn 1966): 367–375.

Hughes, Riley. "New Novels: The Catcher in the Rye." *Catholic World* 174 (November 1951): 154.

———. *Catholic World* 178 (June 1953): 233.

Hugh-Jones, Siriol. "The Salinger Puzzle." *The Tatler and Bystander*, 20 June 1962, 748.

Hutchens, John K. "On an Author." *New York Herald Tribune Book Review*, 19 August 1951, p. 2.

Hyman, Stanley Edgar. "J. D. Salinger's House of Glass." In *Standards: A Chronicle of Books of Our Time*, 123–127. New York: Horizon Press, 1966.

"In Place of the New, A Reissue of the Old." *Newsweek*, 28 January 1963, 90, 92.

Jacobs, Robert G. "J. D. Salinger's The Catcher in the Rye: Holden Caulfield's 'Goddam Autobiography.'" *Iowa English Yearbook* 4 (Fall 1959): 9–14.

Jacobsen, Josephine. "The Felicity of J. D. Salinger." *Commonweal*, 26 February 1960, 589–591.

J. D. Salinger Doesn't Want to Talk. VHS and DVD. Directed by Sarah Aspinall. London: BBC, 1999.

"J. D. Salinger Files Impersonation Lawsuit." *New York Times*, 14 October 1982, p. C-13.

"J. D. Salinger Sues to Bar a Biography." *New York Times*, 4 October 1986, p. 8.

Johannson, Ernest J. "Salinger's Seymour." *Carolina Quarterly* 12 (Winter 1959): 51–54.

Johnson, James W. "The Adolescent Hero: A Trend in Modern Fiction." *Twentieth Century Literature* 5 (April 1959): 3–11.

Johnston, Laurie. "Carrousel Burns in Central Park." *New York Times*, 8 November 1950, p. 35.

Jones, Ernest. "Case History of All of Us." *Nation*, 1 September 1951, 176.

Jonnes, Denis. "Trauma, Mourning and Self-(Re)fashioning in *The Catcher in the Rye*." In *J. D. Salinger's The Catcher in the Rye*, by Sarah Graham, 98–108. London: Routledge, 2007.

Jordan, Joseph William. "J. D. Salinger as a Writer of Fiction for Students in Senior High School." Ph.D. diss., Ohio State University, 1962.

Kafka, Franz. *Dearest Father: Stories and Other Writings*. New York: Schocken Books, 1954.

———. *Letters to Felice*. New York: Schocken Books, 1973.

Kakutani, Michiko. "From Salinger, A New Dash of Mystery." *New York Times*, 20 February 1997, pp. C-15, C-19.

Kaplan, Charles. "Holden and Huck: The Odysseys of Youth." *College English* 18, no. 2 (November 1956): 76–80.

Kapp, Isa. "Salinger's Easy Victory." *New Leader*, 8 January 1962, 27–28.

Karlstetter, Klaus. "J. D. Salinger, R. W. Emerson and the Perennial Philosophy." *Moderna Sprak* 63, no. 3 (1969): 224–236.

Kaufman, Anthony. "'Along This Road Goes No One': Salinger's 'Teddy' and the Failure of Love." *Studies in Short Fiction* 35 (Spring 1998): 129–140.

Kazin, Alfred. *Bright Book of Life: American Novelists and Storytellers from Hemingway to Mailer.* Boston: Little, Brown and Company, 1973.

———. *Contemporaries.* Boston: Little, Brown and Company, 1962.

———. "J. D. Salinger: 'Everybody's Favorite'" [originally published in *Atlantic*, August 1961]. In *If You Really Want to Hear about It: Writers on J. D. Salinger and His Work*, edited by Catherine Crawford, 109–119. New York: Thunder's Mouth Press, 2006.

Kearns, Francis E. "Salinger and Golding: Conflict on Campus." *America*, 26 January 1963, 136–139.

Keating, Edward M. "Salinger: The Murky Mirror." *Ramparts* 1, May 1962, 61–66.

Keerdoja, E., and P. E. Simons. "The Dodger in the Rye." *Newsweek*, 30 July 1979, 11, 13.

Kegel, Charles H. "Incommunicability in Salinger's *The Catcher in the Rye*." *Western Humanities Review* 11 (Spring 1957): 188–190.

Kennedy, Sighle. "New Books: Franny and Zooey." *Catholic World* 194 (February 1962): 312–313.

Kermode, Frank. "The Glass Menagerie." *New Statesman*, 15 March 1963, 388.

———. "J. D. Salinger: One Hand Clapping." *New Statesman*, 8 June 1962, 831.

Kilicci, Esra. "J. D. Salinger's Characters as Existential Heroes: Encountering 1950s America." Ph.D. diss., Indiana University of Pennsylvania, 2008.

Kingston, Anne. "Lolita Writes Back." *Saturday Night*, October 1998, 64–72, 111.

Kinney, Arthur F. "J. D. Salinger and the Search for Love." *Texas Studies in Literature and Language* 5 (Spring 1963): 111–126.

———. "The Theme of Charity in *The Catcher in the Rye*." *Papers of the Michigan Academy of Science, Arts, and Letters* 48 (1963): 691–702.

Kinnick, Bernard C. "Holden Caulfield: Adolescents' Enduring Model." *High School Journal* 53 (May 1970): 440–443.

Kinsella, W. P. *Shoeless Joe.* Boston: Houghton Mifflin, 1982.

Kirschner, Paul. "Salinger and His Society: The Pattern of *Nine Stories*." *London Review* 6 (Winter 1969–1970): 34–54.

———. "Salinger and Scott Fitzgerald: Complementary American Voices." *Dutch Quarterly Review of Anglo-American Letters* 17 (1987): 53–73.

Kleban, Barbara. "Young Writer Brings the World a Message from J. D. Salinger: 'Go Away.'" *People*, 25 February 1980, 43–44.

Kosner, Edward. "The Private World of J. D. Salinger." *New York Post Week-End Magazine*, 30 April 1961, p. 5.

Kranidas, Thomas. "Point of View in Salinger's 'Teddy.'" *Studies in Short Fiction* 2 (Fall 1964): 89–91.

Krassner, Paul. "An Impolite Interview with Alan Watts." *Realist* 14 (December 1960): 1, 8–11.

Krim, Seymour. "Surface and Substance in a Major Talent." *Commonweal*, 24 April 1953, 78.

Kukil, Karen V., ed. *The Unabridged Journals of Sylvia Plath.* New York: Anchor Books, 2000.

Kunitz, Stanley J., and Vineta Colby, eds. *Twentieth Century Authors.* New York: H. W. Wilson, 1955.

Lacy, Robert. "Sing a Song of Sonny." *Sewanee Review* 113 (2005): 309–316.

Lane, Gary. "Seymour's Suicide Again: A New Reading of J. D. Salinger's 'A Perfect Day for Bananafish.'" *Studies in Short Fiction* 10 (Winter 1973): 27–33.

Larner, Jeremy. "Salinger's Audience: An Explanation." *Partisan Review* 29 (Fall 1962): 594–598.

Larrabee, C. X. "Nine Short Stories by a Writer with an Extraordinary Talent." *San Francisco Chronicle*, 3 May 1953, p. 13.

Laser, Marvin. "Character Names in *The Catcher in the Rye*." *California English Journal* 1 (Winter 1965): 29–40.

Lee, Robert A. "'Flunking Everything Else Except English Anyway': Holden Caulfield, Author." In *Critical Essays on Salinger's The Catcher in the Rye*, edited by Joel Salzberg, 185–197. Boston: G. K. Hall, 1990.

Leitch, David. "The Salinger Myth." *Twentieth Century* 168 (November 1960): 428–435.

Lerman, Leo. "It Takes 4." *Mademoiselle*, October 1961, 108–111.

Lettis, Richard. "Holden Caulfield: Salinger's 'Ironic Amalgam.'" *American Notes & Queries* 15 (November 1976): 43–45.

Levin, Beatrice. "J. D. Salinger in Oklahoma." *Chicago Jewish Forum* 19 (Spring 1961): 231–233.

Levine, Paul. "J. D. Salinger: The Development of the Misfit Hero." *Twentieth Century Literature* 4, no. 3 (October 1958): 92–99.

Lewis, Jonathan P. "'All That David Copperfield Kind of Crap': Holden Caulfield's Rejection of Grand Narratives." *Notes on Contemporary Literature* 32, no. 4 (September 2002): 3–5.

Lewis, Roger. "Textual Variants in J. D. Salinger's *Nine Stories*." *Resources for American Literary Study* 10 (Spring 1980): 79–83.

Light, James F. "Salinger's *The Catcher in the Rye*." *Explicator* 18 (June 1960): item 59.

Limmer, Ruth, ed. *What the Woman Lived: Selected Letters of Louise Bogan, 1920–1970*. New York: Harcourt, Brace, Jovanovich, 1973.

Lish, Gordon. "A Fool for Salinger." *Antioch Review* 44, no. 4 (Fall 1986): 408–415.

———. "For Jerome—with Love and Kisses." In *What I Know So Far*, 153–225. New York: Four Walls Eight Windows, 1996.

———. "For Rupert—with No Promises" [originally published anonymously in *Esquire*, February 1977]. In *What I Know So Far*, 85–104. New York: Four Walls Eight Windows, 1996.

Livingston, James T. "J. D. Salinger: The Artist's Struggle to Stand on Holy Ground." In *Adversity and Grace*, edited by Nathan A. Scott, Jr., 113–132. Chicago: University of Chicago Press, 1968.

Lodge, David. "Family Romances." *Times Literary Supplement*, 13 June 1975, p. 642.

———. *The Modes of Modern Writing*. Ithaca, N.Y.: Cornell University Press, 1979.

———. *The Novelist at the Crossroads and Other Essays on Fiction and Criticism*. Ithaca, N.Y.: Cornell University Press, 1971.

Longstreth, T. Morris. "New Novels in the News." *Christian Science Monitor*, 19 July 1951, p. 11.

Lorch, Thomas M. "J. D. Salinger: The Artist, the Audience, and the Popular Arts." *South Dakota Review* 5, no. 4 (Winter 1967–1968): 3–13.

Lowrey, Burling. "Salinger and the House of Glass." *New Republic*, 26 October 1959, 23–24.

Lubasch, Arnold H. "Salinger Biography Is Blocked." *New York Times*, 30 January 1987, pp. A-1, C-26.

Luedtke, Luther S. "J. D. Salinger and Robert Burns: *The Catcher in the Rye*." *Modern Fiction Studies* 16, no. 2 (Summer 1970): 198–201.

Luscher, Robert M. "Textual Variants in J. D. Salinger's 'De Daumier-Smith's Blue Period.'" *Resources for American Literary Study* 18 (1992): 53–57.

Lyman, Rick. "Dorothy Olding, Loyal Literary Agent, Dies at 87." *New York Times*, 20 May 1997, p. D-23.

Lyons, John O. "The Romantic Style of Salinger's 'Seymour: An Introduction.'" *Wisconsin Studies in Contemporary Literature* 4, no. 1 (Winter 1963): 62–69.

Mahon, Gigi. *The Last Days of The New Yorker*. New York: McGraw Hill, 1988.

Mailer, Norman. *Advertisements for Myself*. New York: G. P. Putnam's Sons, 1959.

———. "Some Children of the Goddess." *Esquire*, July 1963, 64–69, 105.

Malcolm, Janet. "Justice to J. D. Salinger." *New York Review of Books*, 21 June 2001, pp. 16, 18–22.

Mandel, Siegfried. "Salinger in Continental Jeans: The Liberation of Boll and Other Germans." In *Critical Essays on Salinger's The Catcher in the Rye*, edited by Joel Salzberg, 214–226. Boston: G. K. Hall, 1990.

Maple, Anne. "Salinger's Oasis of Innocence." *New Republic*, 18 September 1961, 22–23.

Marcus, Fred H. "*The Catcher in the Rye*: A Live Circuit." *English Journal* 52 (January 1963): 1–8.

Margolis, John D. "Salinger's *The Catcher in the Rye*." *Explicator* 22 (November 1963): item 23.

Martin, Augustine. "A Note on J. D. Salinger." *Studies: An Irish Quarterly Review* 48 (Fall 1959): 336–345.

Martin, Douglas. "Ian Hamilton, 63, Whose Salinger Book Caused a Stir, Dies." *New York Times*, 7 January 2002, p. B-6.

Martin, Hansford. "The American Problem of Direct Address." *Western Review* 16 (Winter 1952): 101–114.

———. "Four Volumes of Short Stories: An Irreverent Review." *Western Review* 18 (Winter 1954): 172–174.

Martin, John S. "Copperfield and Caulfield: Dickens in the Rye." *Notes on Modern American Literature* 4 (1980): item 29.

Martin, Robert A. "Remembering Jane in *The Catcher in the Rye*." *Notes on Contemporary Literature* 28, no. 4 (September 1998): 2–3.

Matis, Jim. "'The Catcher in the Rye': Controversy on Novel in Texas Is Just One in Long List of Episodes." *Houston Post*, 4 May 1961, sec. 7, p. 6.

Matthews, James F. "J. D. Salinger: An Appraisal." *University of Virginia Magazine* 1 (Spring 1956): 52–60.

Matthews, Marsha Caddell. "Death and Humor in the Fifties: The Ignition of Barth, Heller, Nabokov, O'Connor, Salinger, and Vonnegut." Ph. D. diss., Florida State University, 1987.

Maxwell, William. "J. D. Salinger." *Book-of-the-Month Club News* (July 1951): 5–6.

Mayhew, Alice Ellen. "Salinger's Fabulous Glass Family." *Commonweal*, 6 October 1961, 48–50.

Maynard, Joyce. "Afterword." In *At Home in the World: A Memoir*, 349–354 [paperback edition only]. New York: Picador, 1999.

McCarthy, Mary. "J. D. Salinger's Closed Circuit" [originally published in *Harper's*, October 1962]. In *If You Really Want to Hear about It: Writers on J. D. Salinger and His Work*, edited by Catherine Crawford, 127–133. New York: Thunder's Mouth Press, 2006.

McCort, Dennis. "Hyakujo's Geese, Amban's Doughnuts, and Rilke's Carrousel: Sources East and West for Salinger's Catcher." *Comparative Literature Studies* 34 (1997): 260–278.

McDowell, Edwin. "154 at The New Yorker Protest Choice of Editor." *New York Times*, 15 January 1987, p. C-22.

McGrath, Charles. "J. D Salinger, Author Who Fled Fame, Dies at 91." *New York Times*, 29 January 2010, pp. A-1, A-16, A-17.

———. "Still Paging Mr. Salinger." *New York Times*, 31 December 2008, p. C-1.

McIntyre, John P. "A Preface for 'Franny and Zooey.'" *Critic* 20 (February–March 1962): 25–28.

McKinley, Jesse. "Iranian Film Is Canceled after Protest by Salinger." *New York Times*, 21 November 1998, p. B-9.

McNamara, Eugene. "Holden as Novelist." *English Journal* 54, no. 3 (March 1965): 166–170.

McSweeney, Kerry. "Salinger Revisited." *Critical Survey* 20, no. 1 (Spring 1978): 61–68.

Mehta, Ved. *Remembering Mr. Shawn's New Yorker: The Invisible Art of Editing*. New York: Overlook Press, 1998.

Mellard, James M. "The Disappearing Subject: A Lacanian Reading of The Catcher in the Rye." In *Critical Essays on Salinger's The Catcher in the Rye*, edited by Joel Salzberg, 197–214. Boston: G. K. Hall, 1990.

Menand, Louis. "Holden at Fifty: 'The Catcher in the Rye' and What It Spawned." *New Yorker*, 1 October 2001, 82–87.

Meral, Jean. "The Ambiguous Mr. Antolini in Salinger's *The Catcher in the Rye*." *Caliban* 7 (1970): 55–58.

Metcalf, Frank. "The Suicide of Salinger's Seymour Glass." *Studies in Short Fiction* 9 (Summer 1972): 243–246.

Miller, Edwin Haviland. "In Memoriam: Allie Caulfield in *The Catcher in the Rye*." *Mosaic: A Journal for the Interdisciplinary Study of Literature* 15, no. 1 (Winter 1982): 129–140.

Miller, James E., Jr. "*Catcher* In and Out of History." *Critical Inquiry* 3, no. 3 (Spring 1977): 599–603.

Miltner, Robert. "Mentor Mori; or, Sibling Society and the Catcher in the Bly." In *The Catcher in the Rye: New Essays*, edited by J. P. Steed, 33–52. New York: Peter Lang, 2002.

Mirza, Humayun A. "The Influence of Hindu-Buddhist Psychology and Philosophy on J. D. Salinger's Fiction." Ph.D. diss., SUNY at Binghamton, 1976.

Mizener, Arthur. "The American Hero as Poet: Seymour Glass." In *The Sense of Life in the Modern Novel*, 227–246. Boston: Houghton Mifflin, 1964.

———. "In Genteel Traditions." *New Republic*, 25 May 1953, 19–20.

———. "The Love Song of J. D. Salinger." *Harper's*, February 1959, 83–90.

"Mlle Passports." *Mademoiselle*, May 1947, 34.

Monas, Sidney. "Fiction Chronicle: 'No Mommy and No Daddy.'" *Hudson Review* 6 (Autumn 1953): 466–470.

Montgomery, Paul L. "Lennon Murder Suspect Preparing Insanity Defense." *New York Times*, 9 February 1981, p. B-12.

Moore, Robert P. "The World of Holden." *English Journal* 54 (March 1965): 159–165.

Moss, Adam. "Catcher Comes of Age." *Esquire*, December 1981, 56–58, 60.

Murray, James G. "Franny and Zooey." *Critic* 20 (October–November 1961): 72–73.

Nabokov, Dmitri, and Matthew Bruccoli, eds. *Vladimir Nabokov: Selected Letters*. New York: Harcourt, Brace and Jovanovich, 1989.

Nabokov, Vladimir. *Strong Opinions*. New York: McGraw-Hill Book Company, 1973.

Nadel, Alan. "Rhetoric, Sanity, and the Cold War: The Significance of Holden Caulfield's Testimony." *Centennial Review* 32, no. 4 (Fall 1988): 351–371.

Naparsteck, Martin. "Collecting J. D. Salinger." *Firsts: The Book Collector's Magazine* 19, no. 1 (January 2009): 28–37.

Newlove, Donald. "'Hapworth 16, 1924.'" *Village Voice*, 22 August 1974, p. 27.

Nikhilananda, Swami. *Hinduism: Its Meaning for the Liberation of the Spirit*. New York: Harper and Brothers, 1958.

Noland, Richard W. "The Novel of Personal Formula: J. D. Salinger." *University Review* 33 (Autumn 1966): 19–24.

"The No-Nonsense Kids." *Time*, 18 November 1957, 51–52, 54.

Nordell, Rod. "The Salinger Phenomenon." *Christian Science Monitor*, 14 September 1961, p. 7.

"Notes on People: J. D. Salinger Privately Passes a Milestone." *New York Times*, 1 January 1979, p. 22.

Oates, Joyce Carol. "Words of Love, Priced to Sell." *New York Times*, 18 May 1999, p. A-23.

O'Connor, Dennis L. "J. D. Salinger: Writing as Religion." *Wilson Quarterly* 4 (Spring 1980): 182–190.

———. "J. D. Salinger's Religious Pluralism: The Example of 'Raise High the Roof Beam, Carpenters.'" *Southern Review* 20, no. 2 (Spring 1984): 316–332.

O'Connor, Flannery. *Collected Works*. n.p.: Library of America, 1988.

O'Hara, J. D. "No Catcher in the Rye." *Modern Fiction Studies* 9 (Winter 1963–1964): 370–376.

O'Hearn, Sheila. "The Development of Seymour Glass as a Figure of Hope in the Fiction of J. D. Salinger." Master's thesis, McMaster University, 1982.

Ohmann, Carol, and Richard Ohmann. "Reviewers, Critics, and *The Catcher in the Rye*." *Critical Inquiry* 3, no. 1 (Autumn 1976): 15–37.

———. "Universals and the Historically Particular." *Critical Inquiry* 3, no. 4 (Summer 1977): 773–777.

Olan, Levi A. "The Voice of the Lonesome: Alienation from Huck Finn to Holden Caulfield." *Southwest Review* 48 (Spring 1963): 143–150.

Oldsey, Bernard S. "The Movies in the Rye." *College English* 23, no. 3 (December 1961): 209–215.

———. "Salinger and Golding: Resurrection or Repose." *College Literature* 6 (Spring 1979): 136–144.

Pace, Eric. "William Shawn, 85, Is Dead: New Yorker's Gentle Despot." *New York Times*, 9 December 1992, pp. A-1, B-15.

Panichas, George A. "J. D. Salinger and the Russian Pilgrim." In *The Reverent Discipline: Essays in Literary Criticism and Culture*, 292–305. Knoxville: University of Tennessee Press, 1974.

Paniker, Sumitra. "The Influence of Eastern Thought on 'Teddy' and the Seymour Glass Stories of J. D. Salinger." Ph.D. diss., University of Texas at Austin, 1971.

Panova, Vera. "On J. D. Salinger's Novel." In *Soviet Criticism of American Literature in the Sixties*, edited and translated by Carl R. Proffer, 4–10. Ann Arbor, Mich.: Ardis, 1972.

Parker, Christopher. "'Why the Hell *Not* Smash All the Windows?'" In *Salinger: A Critical and Personal Portrait*, edited by Henry Anatole Grunwald, 254–258. New York: Harper & Row, 1962.

Pattanaik, Dipti R. "'The Holy Refusal': A Vedantic Interpretation of J. D. Salinger's Silence." *MELUS* 23, no. 2 (Summer 1998): 113–127.

Paul, Marcia B., and Kevan Choset. "Complaint: J. D. Salinger, individually and as Trustee of the J. D. Salinger Literary Trust, Plaintiff, v. John Doe, writing under the name John David California, [et al.]." Filed in United States District Court, Southern District of New York, June 1, 2009.

Pawel, Ernst. *The Nightmare of Reason: A Life of Franz Kafka*. New York: Farrar, Straus & Giroux, 1984.

Peavy, Charles D. "'Did You Ever Have a Sister?' Holden, Quentin and Sexual Innocence." *Florida Quarterly* 1, no. 3 (Winter 1968): 82–95.

Peden, William. "Esthetics of the Story." *Saturday Review*, 11 April 1953, 43–44.

"People." *Time*, 25 June 1965, 52.

Perrine, Laurence. "Teddy? Booper? Or Blopper?" *Studies in Short Fiction* 4 (Spring 1967): 217–224.

"Personal and Otherwise." *Harper's*, April 1949, 9–10.

Phelps, Robert. "The Difference Is Qualitative." *Freeman*, 24 August 1953, 857.

———. "Salinger: A Man of Fierce Privacy." *New York Herald Tribune Books*, 17 September 1961, p. 3.

———. "A Writer Who Talks to and of the Young." *New York Herald Tribune Books*, 17 September 1961, pp. 3, 14.

Phillips, Mark. "J. D. Salinger: A Hidden Hand?" *Saturday Review*, November–December 1985, 39–45.

Phillips, Paul. "Salinger's *Franny and Zooey*." *Mainstream* 15 (January 1962): 32–39.

Pickering, John Kenneth. "J. D. Salinger: Portraits of Alienation." Ph.D. diss., Case Western Reserve University, 1968.

Pickrel, Paul. "Outstanding Novels." *Yale Review* 42 (Summer 1953): vi–xvi.

Pilkington, John. "About This Madman Stuff." *University of Mississippi Studies in English* 7 (1966): 67–75.

Pillsbury, Frederick. "Mysterious J. D. Salinger: The Untold Chapter of the Famous Writer's Years as a

Valley Forge Cadet." *Sunday Bulletin Magazine*, 29 October 1961, pp. 23–24.

Pinsker, Sanford. "*The Catcher in the Rye* and All: Is the Age of Formative Books Over?" *Georgia Review* 40, no. 4 (Winter 1986): 953–967.

Piwinski, David J. "Salinger's 'De Daumier-Smith's Blue Period': Pseudonym as Cryptogram." *Notes on Contemporary Literature* 15, no. 5 (November 1985): 3–4.

Poore, Charles. "Books of The Times." *New York Times*, 9 April 1953, p. 25.

———. "Books of The Times." *New York Times*, 14 September 1961, p. 29.

Poster, William. "Tomorrow's Child." *Commentary* 13 (January 1952): 90–92.

Prescott, Orville. "Books of The Times." *New York Times*, 28 January 1963, p. 9.

Prigozy, Ruth. "*Nine Stories*: J. D. Salinger's Linked Mysteries." In *Modern American Short Story Sequences: Composite Fictions and Fictive Communities*, edited by J. Gerald Kennedy, 114–132. Cambridge: Cambridge University Press, 1995.

Pugsley, Alexander Hunt. "'The Secret Goldfish': A Study of J. D. Salinger's Short Fiction." Master's thesis, University of Toronto, 1990.

Purcell, William F. "From Half-Shot to Half-Assed: J. D. Salinger and the Evolution of a *Skaz*." *Studies in American Literature* 35 (February 1999): 109–123.

———. "Narrative Voice in J. D. Salinger's 'Both Parties Concerned' and 'I'm Crazy.'" *Studies in Short Fiction* 33 (Spring 1996): 278–280.

———. "Waker Glass: Salinger's Carthusian Doppelganger." *Literature and Belief* 20 (2000): 153–168.

———. "World War II and the Early Fiction of J. D. Salinger." *Studies in American Literature* 28 (1991): 77–93.

Quagliano, Anthony. "Hapworth 16, 1924: A Problem in Hagiography." *University of Dayton Review* 8, no. 2 (Fall 1971): 35–43.

Quinn, Judy. "Is It Possible? A J. D. Salinger for Spring." *Publishers Weekly*, 27 January 1997, 10.

———. "A Spotlight on Salinger." *Publishers Weekly*, 12 July 1999, 26–27.

Rachels, David. "Holden Caulfield: A Hero for All the Ages." *Chronicle of Higher Education*, 30 March 2001, p. B-5.

Ralston, Nancy C. "Holden Caulfield: Super-Adolescent." *Adolescence* 6 (Winter 1971): 429–432.

Ranchan, Som P. "Echoes of the Gita in Salinger's 'Franny and Zooey.'" In *The Gita in World Literature*, edited by C. D. Verma, 214–219. New Delhi: Sterling, 1990.

Ranly, Ernest W. "Journey to the East." *Commonweal*, 23 February 1973, 465–469.

Raymond, John. "The Salinger Situation." *Sunday Times*, 3 June 1962, p. 33.

Razdan, Brij M. "From Unreality to Reality: *Franny and Zooey*—A Reinterpretation." *Panjab University Research Bulletin* 9, nos. 1–2 (April–October 1978): 3–15.

Rees, Richard. "The Salinger Situation." In *Contemporary American Novelists*, edited by Henry T. Moore, 95–105. Carbondale: Southern Illinois University Press, 1964.

Reiman, Donald H. "Salinger's The Catcher in the Rye, Chapters 22–26." *Explicator* 21 (March 1963): item 58.

Remnick, David. "Matt Salinger, into the Spotlight." *Washington Post*, 28 December 1984, pp. C-1, C-2.

Rilke, Rainer Maria. *Duino Elegies*. New York: W. W. Norton & Company, 1939.

———. *The Notebooks of Malte Laurids Brigge*. New York: W. W. Norton & Company, 1949.

———. *Poems 1906 to 1926*. Intro. by J. B. Leishman. New York: New Directions, 1957.

———. *Translations from the Poetry of Rainer Maria Rilke*. New York: W. W. Norton & Company, 1938.

Roberts, Preston Thomas, Jr. "*The Catcher in the Rye* Revisited." *Cresset* 40 (November–December 1976): 6–10.

Robinson, Sally. "Masculine Protest in *The Catcher in the Rye*." In *J. D. Salinger's The Catcher in the Rye*, by Sarah Graham, 70–76. London: Routledge, 2007.

Roemer, Danielle M. "The Personal Narrative and Salinger's The Catcher in the Rye." *Western Folklore* 51, no. 1 (January 1992): 5–10.

Rogers, Lydia. "The Psychoanalyst and the Fetishist: Wilhelm Stekel and Mr. Antolini in *The Catcher in the Rye*." *Notes on Contemporary Literature* 32, no. 4 (September 2002): 2–3.

Romano, John. "Salinger Was Playing Our Song." *New York Times Book Review*, 3 June 1979, pp. 11, 48–49.

Roper, Pamela E. "Holden's Hat." *Notes on Contemporary Literature* 7, no. 3 (May 1977): 8–9.

Rosen, Gerald. "A Retrospective Look at The Catcher in the Rye." *American Quarterly* 29 (Winter 1977): 547–562.

Rosenbaum, Ron. "The Catcher in the Driveway" [originally published as "The Man in the Glass House" in *Esquire*, June 1997]. In *If You Really Want to Hear about It: Writers on J. D. Salinger and His Work*, edited by Catherine Crawford, 63–87. New York: Thunder's Mouth Press, 2006.

Rosenthal, Edward H., et al. "Brief for Defendants-Appellants Fredrik Colting, writing under the name John David California, [et al.] v. J. D. Salinger, individually and as Trustee of the J. D. Salinger Literary Trust." Filed in the United States Court of Appeals for the Second Circuit, July 23, 2009.

Ross, Lillian. "Bearable." *New Yorker*, 8 February 2010, pp. 22–23.

———. *Here but Not Here: A Love Story*. New York: Random House, 1998.

Ross, Theodore J. "Notes on J. D. Salinger." *Chicago Jewish Forum* 22 (Winter 1963–1964): 149–153.

Rot, Sandor. "J. D. Salinger's Oeuvre in the Light of Decoding Stylistics and Information-Theory." *Studies in English and American* 4 (1978): 85–129.

Roth, Philip. *My Life as a Man*. In *Novels 1973–1977*. n.p.: Library of America, 2006.

———. "Writing American Fiction." In *Reading Myself and Others*, 117–135. New York: Farrar, Straus & Giroux, 1975.

Rowe, Joyce. "Holden Caulfield and American Protest." In *New Essays on The Catcher in the Rye*, edited by Jack Salzman, 77–95. Cambridge: Cambridge University Press, 1991.

Rowland, Stanley J., Jr. "Love Parable." *Christian Century*, 6 December 1961, 1,464–1,465.

Rupp, Richard H. "J. D. Salinger: A Solitary Liturgy." In *Celebration of Postwar American Fiction, 1945–1967*, 113–131. Coral Gables, Fla.: University of Miami Press, 1970.

Russell, John. "Salinger, From Daumier to Smith." *Wisconsin Studies in Contemporary Literature* 4, no. 1 (Winter 1963): 70–87.

———. "Salinger's Feat." *Modern Fiction Studies* 12, no. 3 (Autumn 1966): 299–311.

Saha, Winifred M. "J. D. Salinger: The Younger Writer and Society." Ph.D. diss., University of Chicago, 1957.

"Saint or Slob?" *Times Literary Supplement*, 8 March 1963, p. 165.

Salinger, Margaret A. "Afterword." In *Dream Catcher: A Memoir*, 435–447 [paperback edition only]. New York: Pocket Books, 2001.

Schiff, Stacy. *Vera: Mrs. Vladimir Nabokov*. New York: Random House, 1999.

Schrader, Allen. "Emerson to Salinger to Parker." *Saturday Review*, 11 April 1959, 52, 58.

Schriber, Mary Suzanne. "Holden Caulfield, C'est Moi." In *Critical Essays on Salinger's The Catcher in the Rye*, edited by Joel Salzberg, 226–238. Boston: G. K. Hall, 1990.

Schulz, Max F. "Epilogue to 'Seymour: An Introduction': Salinger and the Crisis of Consciousness." *Studies in Short Fiction* 5 (Winter 1968): 128–138.

Schwartz, Arthur. "For Seymour—with Love and Judgment." *Wisconsin Studies in Contemporary Literature* 4, no. 1 (Winter 1963): 88–99.

Scott, Walter. "Personality Parade." *St. Louis Post-Dispatch Parade*, 23 May 1971, p. 4.

Seabrook, John. "A Night at the Movies." *New Yorker*, 8 February 2010, p. 23.

Searles, George J. "Salinger Redux via Roth: An Echo of *Franny and Zooey* in *My Life as a Man*." *Notes on Contemporary Literature* 16, no. 2 (March 1986): 7.

———, ed. *Conversations with Philip Roth*. Jackson: University Press of Mississippi, 1992.

Seed, David. "Keeping It in the Family: The Novellas of J. D. Salinger." In *The Modern American Novella*, edited by A. Robert Lee, 139–161. New York: St. Martin's Press, 1989.

Seelye, John. "Holden in the Museum." In *New Essays on The Catcher in the Rye*, edited by Jack Salzman, 23–33. Cambridge: Cambridge University Press, 1991.

Seitzman, Daniel. "Salinger's 'Franny': Homoerotic Imagery." *American Imago* 22 (Spring–Summer 1965): 57–76.

———. "Therapy and Antitherapy in Salinger's 'Zooey.'" *American Imago* 25 (Summer 1968): 140–162.

Seng, Peter J. "The Fallen Idol: The Immature World of Holden Caulfield." *College English* 23, no. 3 (December 1961): 203–209.

Senzaki, Nyogen, and Paul Reps. *101 Zen Stories*. Philadelphia: David McKay Company, 1940.

Shapira, Ian. "For a Very Brief While, J. D. Salinger Returned His Calls." *Washington Post*, 29 January 2010, p. C-1.

Shaw, Peter. "Love and Death in *The Catcher in the Rye*." In *New Essays on The Catcher in the Rye*, edited by Jack Salzman, 97–114. Cambridge: Cambridge University Press, 1991.

Sheed, Wilfred. "J. D. Salinger, Humorist" [originally published in *New York Review of Books*, 27 October 1988]. In *Essays in Disguise*, 3–25. New York: Knopf, 1990.

———. "Raise High the Roof Beam, Carpenters and Seymour: An Introduction." *Jubilee* 10 (April 1963): 51, 53–54.

Sherr, Paul C. "'The Catcher in the Rye' and the Boarding School." *Independent School Bulletin* 26 (December 1966): 42–44.

Silverberg, Mark. "A Bouquet of Empty Brackets: Author-Function and the Search for J. D. Salinger." *Dalhousie Review* 75, no. 2 (Summer–Fall 1995): 222–246.

———. "'You Must Change Your Life': Formative Responses to *The Catcher in the Rye*." In *The Catcher in the Rye: New Essays*, edited by J. P. Steed, 7–32. New York: Peter Lang, 2002.

Silverman, Al. *The Time of Their Lives: The Golden Age of Great American Book Publishers, Their Editors and Authors*. New York: St. Martin's Press, 2008.

———, ed. *The Book of the Month: Sixty Years of Books in American Life*. Boston: Little, Brown and Company, 1986.

Simms, L. Moody, Jr. "Seymour Glass: The Salingerian Hero as Vulgarian." *Notes on Contemporary Literature* 5, no. 5 (November 1975): 6–8.

Skow, Jack. "Sonny: An Introduction." *Time*, 15 September 1961, 84–90.

Slabey, Robert M. "*The Catcher in the Rye*: Christian Theme and Symbol." *College Language Association Journal* 6 (March 1963): 170–183.

———. "Salinger's 'Casino': Wayfarers and Spiritual Acrobats." *English Record* 14 (February 1964): 16–20.

———. "Sergeant X and Seymour Glass." *Western Humanities Review* 16 (Autumn 1962): 376–377.

Slethaug, G. E. "Form in Salinger's Short Fiction." *Canadian Review of American Studies* 3, no. 1 (Spring 1972): 50–59.

———. "Seymour: A Clarification." *Renascence* 23 (Spring 1971): 115–128.

Slide, Anthony. *The Encyclopedia of Vaudeville*. Westport, Conn.: Greenwood Press, 1994.

Sloan, Robin Adams. "The Gossip Column." *Washington Post*, 17 October 1982, p. A-1.

Smith, Dinitia. "Salinger Letters Are Sold and May Return to Sender." *New York Times*, 23 June 1999, p. B-1.

Smith, Dominic. "Salinger's *Nine Stories*: Fifty Years Later." *Antioch Review* 61, no. 4 (Fall 2003): 639–649.

Smith, Harrison. "Manhattan Ulysses, Junior." *Saturday Review*, 14 July 1951, 12–13.

Spanier, Sandra Wipple. "Hemingway's 'The Last Good Country' and *The Catcher in the Rye*: More Than a Family Resemblance." *Studies in Short Fiction* 19 (1982): 35–43.

Stein, William Bysshe. "Salinger's 'Teddy': *Tat Tvam Asi* or That Thou Art." *Arizona Quarterly* 29 (Autumn 1973): 253–265.

Steiner, George. "The Salinger Industry." *Nation*, 14 November 1959, 360–363.

Stern, James. "Aw, the World's a Crumby Place." *New York Times Book Review*, 15 July 1951, p. 5.

Stevenson, David L. "J. D. Salinger: The Mirror of Crisis." *Nation*, 9 March 1957, 215–217.

Stoltz, Craig. "J. D. Salinger's Tribute to Whit Burnett." *Twentieth Century Literature* 27, no. 4 (Winter 1981): 325–330.

Stone, Edward. "De Daumier-Smith's Blue Period." In *A Certain Morbidness: A View of American Literature*, 121–139. Carbondale: Southern Illinois University Press, 1969.

———. "Naming in Salinger." *Notes on Contemporary Literature* 1 (March 1971): 2–3.

———. "Salinger's Carrousel." *Modern Fiction Studies* 13, no. 4 (Winter 1967–1968): 520–523.

Strauch, Carl F. "Kings in the Back Row: Meaning through Structure—A Reading of Salinger's *The Catcher in the Rye*." *Wisconsin Studies in Contemporary Literature* 2, no. 1 (Winter 1961): 5–30.

———. "Salinger: The Romantic Background." *Wisconsin Studies in Contemporary Literature* 4, no. 1 (Winter 1963): 31–40.

Streitfeld, David. "Salinger Book to Break Long Silence." *Washington Post*, 17 January 1997, p. D-1.

Strong, Paul. "Black Wing, Black Heart—Betrayal in J. D. Salinger's 'The Laughing Man.'" *West Virginia University Philological Papers* 31 (1986): 91–96.

Surace, Peter Carl. "Round Trips in the Fiction of Salinger, Bellow and Barth during the Nineteen Fifties." Ph.D. diss., Case Western Reserve University, 1996.

Suzuki, D. T. *Manual of Zen Buddhism*. London: Rider, 1950.

Swados, Harvey. "Must Writers Be Characters?" *Saturday Review*, 1 October 1960, 12–14, 50.

Swinton, John. "A Case Study of an 'Academic Bum': Salinger Once Stayed at Ursinus." *Ursinus Weekly*, 12 December 1960, pp. 2, 4.

Symula, James Francis. "Censorship of High School Literature: A Study of the Incidents of Censorship

Involving J. D. Salinger's 'The Catcher in the Rye.'" Ph.D. diss., State University of New York at Buffalo, 1969.

Tae, Yasuhiro. "Between Suicide and Enlightenment." *Kyushu American Literature* 26 (1985): 21–27.

Takeuchi, Yasuhiro. "The Burning Carousel and the Carnivalesque: Subversion and Transcendence at the Close of *The Catcher in the Rye*." *Studies in the Novel* 34, no. 3 (Fall 2002): 320–336.

———. "Salinger's *The Catcher in the Rye*." *Explicator* 60, no. 3 (Spring 2002): 164–166.

———. "The Zen Archery of Holden Caulfield." *English Language Notes* 42, no. 1 (September 2004): 55–63.

Teachout, Terry. "Salinger Then and Now." *Commentary* 84, no. 3 (September 1987): 61–64.

Thorp, Willard. "Whit Burnett and Story Magazine." *Princeton University Library Chronicle* 27 (Autumn 1965): 107–112.

Thurber, James. *The Years with Ross*. Boston: Little, Brown and Company, 1959.

Tierce, Mike. "Salinger's 'De Daumier-Smith's Blue Period.'" *Explicator* 42, no. 1 (Fall 1983): 56–58.

———. "Salinger's 'For Esmé—with Love and Squalor.'" *Explicator* 42, no. 3 (Spring 1984): 56–57.

Tosta, Michael R. "'Will the Real Sergeant X Please Stand Up?'" *Western Humanities Review* 16 (Autumn 1962): 376.

Toynbee, Philip. "Voice of America." *Observer*, 14 June 1953, p. 9.

Travis, Mildred K. "Salinger's *The Catcher in the Rye*." *Explicator* 21 (December 1962): item 36.

Trombetta, Jim. "On the Untimely Demise of J. D. Salinger." *Crawdaddy*, March 1975: 34–38.

Trowbridge, Clinton W. "Hamlet and Holden." *English Journal* 57 (January 1968): 26–29.

———. "Salinger's Symbolic Use of Character and Detail in *The Catcher in the Rye*." *Cimarron Review* 4 (June 1968): 5–11.

———. "The Symbolic Structure of *The Catcher in the Rye*." *Sewanee Review* 74 (July–September 1966): 681–693.

Turner, Decherd, Jr. "The Salinger Pilgrim." In *Seventeenth Annual Conference: American Theological Library Association*, 59–69. Austin, Tex.: Episcopal Theological Seminary of the Southwest, 1963.

Updike, John. "Anxious Days for the Glass Family." *New York Times Book Review*, 17 September 1961, pp. 1, 52.

———. "Foreword." In *Franz Kafka: The Complete Stories*, edited by Nahum N. Glatzer, ix–xxi. New York: Schocken Books, 1983.

Vail, Dennis. "Holden and Psychoanalysis." *PMLA* 91, no. 1 (January 1976): 120–121.

Vanderbilt, Kermit. "Symbolic Resolution in *The Catcher in the Rye*: The Cap, the Carrousel, and the American West." *Western Humanities Review* 17 (Summer 1963): 271–277.

Vivekananda, Swami. *Vivekananda: The Yogas and Other Works*, compiled and biography by Swami Nikhilananda. New York: Ramakrishna-Vivekananda Center, 1953.

Vogel, Albert W. "J. D. Salinger on Education." *School and Society* 91 (Summer 1963): 240–242.

Wain, John. "Go Home, Buddy Glass." *New Republic*, 16 February 1963, 21–22.

Wakefield, Dan. "Salinger and the Search for Love" [originally published in *New World Writing*, No. 14, 1958]. In *Salinger: A Critical and Personal Portrait*, edited by Henry Anatole Grunwald, 176–191. New York: Harper & Row, 1962.

Walker, Gerald. "Salinger and the Purity of Spirit." *Cosmopolitan*, September 1961, 36.

Walker, Joseph S. "The Catcher Takes the Field: Holden, Hollywood, and the Making of a Mann." In *The Catcher in the Rye: New Essays*, edited by J. P. Steed, 79–99. New York: Peter Lang, 2002.

Walter, Eugene. "A Rainy Afternoon with Truman Capote." *Intro Bulletin* 2 (December 1957): 1–2.

Way, Brian. "'Franny and Zooey' and J. D. Salinger." *New Left Review* 15 (May–June 1962): 72–82.

Weatherby, W. J. "J. D." *Guardian*, 15 January 1960, p. 8.

Weber, Myles. "Augmenting the Salinger Oeuvre by Any Means." In *Consuming Silences: How We Read Authors Who Don't Publish*, 88–116. Athens: University of Georgia Press, 2005.

Weinberg, Helen. "J. D. Salinger's Holden and Seymour and the Spiritual Activist Hero." In *The New Novel in America: The Kafkan Mode in Contemporary Fiction*, 141–164. Ithaca, N.Y.: Cornell University Press, 1970.

Wells, Arvin R. "Huck Finn and Holden Caulfield: The Situation of the Hero." *Ohio University Review* 2 (1960): 31–42.

Welty, Eudora. "Threads of Innocence." *New York Times Book Review*, 5 April 1953, p. 4.

Wenke, John. "Sergeant X, Esmé, and the Meaning of Words." *Studies in Short Fiction* 18 (Summer 1981): 251–259.

Wexelblatt, Robert. "Chekhov, Salinger, and Epictetus." *Midwest Quarterly* 28 (Autumn 1986): 50–76.

Whitfield, Stephen J. "Cherished and Cursed: Toward a Social History of *The Catcher in the Rye*." *New England Quarterly* 70, no. 4 (December 1997): 567–600.

Wiebe, Dallas E. "Salinger's 'A Perfect Day for Bananafish.'" *Explicator* 23 (September 1964): item 3.

Wiegand, William. "J. D. Salinger's Seventy-eight Bananas." *Chicago Review* 11, no. 4 (Winter 1958): 3–19.

———. "The Knighthood of J. D. Salinger." *New Republic*, 19 October 1959, 19–21.

———. "Salinger and Kierkegaard." *Minnesota Review* 5 (May–July 1965): 137–156.

Wilkinson, Alec. *My Mentor: A Young Man's Friendship with William Maxwell*. Boston: Houghton Mifflin, 2002.

Wilson, Edmund. *Letters on Literature and Politics*. New York: Farrar, Straus & Giroux, 1977.

Wiseman, Mary B. "Identifying with Characters in Literature." *Journal of Comparative Literature and Aesthetics* 4, nos. 1–2 (1981): 47–57.

"With Love & 20–20 Vision." *Time*, 16 July 1951, 97.

Wolfe, Tom. "The *New Yorker* Affair." In *Hooking Up*, 247–293. New York: Farrar, Straus & Giroux, 2000.

"Writers' Writers." *New York Times Book Review*, 4 December 1977, pp. 3, 58, 62, 68, 74.

Yagoda, Ben. *About Town: The New Yorker and the World It Made*. n.p.: Da Capo Press, 2001.

"Young Authors: Twelve Whose First Novels Make Their Appearance This Fall." *Glamour*, September 1951, 202–205.

"Youthful Horrors." *Nation*, 18 April 1953, 332.

INDEX